ENDLESS ENIGMA

Feed▦▦ACK

THE SERIES IN CONTEMPORARY MUSIC
VOLUME 4
SERIES EDITORS: BILL MARTIN AND KERRI MOMMER

BY THE SAME AUTHOR:

Rocking the Classics: English Progressive Rock and the Counterculture

OTHER VOLUMES IN THE FEEDBACK SERIES:

ENDLESS ENIGMA

A MUSICAL BIOGRAPHY OF
Emerson, Lake and Palmer

EDWARD MACAN

OPEN COURT
Chicago and La Salle, Illinois

To order books from Open Court, call 1-800-815-2280 or visit
www.opencourtbooks.com.

Open Court Publishing Company is a division of Carus Publishing Company.

Macan, Edward, 1961-
    Endless enigma : a musical biography of Emerson, Lake and Palmer / Edward
Macan.
      p. cm. — (Feedback ; v. 4)
    Summary: "Includes a biography of the progressive rock band Emerson, Lake
    and Palmer; a critical survey of the band's musical output and band members'
    other recordings; a complete discography, videography, and listing of live
    shows; and suggestions for further listening"--Provided by publisher.
    Includes discography (p.   ), videography (p.   ), bibliographical references
    (p.   ), and index.
    ISBN-13: 978-0-8126-9596-0 (trade pbk. : alk. paper)
    ISBN-10: 0-8126-9596-8 (trade pbk. : alk. paper)
      1. Emerson, Lake & Palmer. 2. Rock musicians—England—Biography.
I. Title. II. Series: Feedback (Chicago, Ill.) ; v. 4.
ML421.E54M33 2006
782.42166092'2—dc22
                                                        2006008659

Contents

Acknowledgments

A book of this scope is not written in a void. There are a number of individuals whose kind contributions of old interviews (both printed and taped), features, reviews, memories of concerts, behind-the-scenes information, and sundry additional help and advice collectively played an important role in shaping this book. I thank them all at this time, ask for the forgiveness of anyone I may have forgotten, and caution that none of these people are responsible for any factual errors that may reside herein, or for the sometimes controversial interpretations I may bring to bear on my analysis of music, ideas, or events. And now, rolling the credits, we have, in alphabetical order, Tom Ace; John Arnold; Robert Berry; Kathie Touin Brown; Elias Casado; Chuck Cobb; Angelique Curry; Keith Emerson; George Forrester; Dave Gallant; Jim Galvin; Jon Green; Allen Gunnison; Martyn Hanson; Jason Hoopes; Steve Jones; Richard Kaczynski; Rand Kelly; Aymeric Leroy; Thomas F. Macan (thanks, Dad!); John Mills; Ed "Bear" Morgan; David Overstreet; Joe Pazlewski; Bruce Pilato; Christophe Pirenne; Bernd Prott; Paolo Rigoli; Dave Robbins; Nick Robinson; Chris Sciabarra; Sid Smith; Richard Stellar; David Terralavoro; Hermann Thorisson; Liv G. Whetmore; Mica Wickersham (Alembic); Peter Wilton; Brent Wood; and, of course, Bill Martin (whose invitation got the ball rolling), David Steele, Kerri Mommer, Carolyn Madia Gray, Cindy Pineo, and all the fine people at Open Court who brought you this book.

And that, my friends, is it for the preliminaries. Now, as Mr. Lake once said, "Step inside, the show's about to start" . . .

Introduction

Origins

Talk about the show that never ends. Maybe I should have subtitled this "the book that never ends." At least, it seemed that way while I was writing it. Hopefully, it won't seem that way when you're reading it. If it *does*, though, then at least I have managed to replicate the experience that some of ELP's detractors claim they have while listening to one of ELP's epic suites . . .

In 1997, I received an e-mail from Bill Martin, whose *Music of Yes: Vision and Structure in Progressive Rock* had been published the previous November or December.[1] He had read my *Rocking the Classics: English Progressive Rock and the Counterculture*,[2] which had appeared almost concurrently, and asked whether I would be interested in writing a book on Emerson, Lake and Palmer, to be published as part of the Open Court popular music series of which he was editor. Still tired from my exertions over my recent book, and deeply immersed in work on the eponymous debut album of my band, Hermetic Science, I merely told him I would consider it—which I did, for over a year. Even as I "considered," however, I began to collect ELP data, believing that an ELP book would probably eventually move beyond the realm of daydreaming.

By the fall of 1998, I had done a substantial amount of preparation and research, and felt the time was right to write a prototype chapter. If I was pleased with the product, I would proceed with the book; if not, I would thank Bill for the invite, and decline his kind offer. The chapter I wrote first is the present chapter 4, which focuses on ELP's early days

---

[1] Bill Martin, *Music of Yes: Structure and Vision in Progressive Rock* (Chicago: Open Court, 1996).
[2] Edward Macan, *Rocking the Classics: English Progressive Rock and the Counterculture* (New York: Oxford University Press, 1997).

through the end of 1970, and is dominated by an ample discussion of their seminal first album. I was pleased with the results, and told Bill I planned to write an entire book on ELP.

Work progressed apace. Even though I was now deeply involved with recording the second Hermetic Science album, *Prophesies*, by early 1999 chapters 4 through 6 were complete, and the remainder of 1999 saw the completion of chapters 7 through 10; by late 1999, the heart of the book, that is, the seven chapters dealing with ELP's career and music circa 1970–74, was finished.

In late 1999, I was surprised and pleased to receive an e-mail from Keith Emerson, expressing enthusiasm that I was undertaking a comprehensive survey of ELP's career, and offering to make himself available for telephone interviews. I did in fact conduct one lengthy phone interview with Emerson on the Friday after Thanksgiving, 1999—he was still living in Santa Monica at the time—during which we discussed the relationship of music and cover art in *Tarkus*, and he clarified some chronological anomalies concerning *Works*-era material. I told him I would like to talk to him twice more: once to discuss his movie scores and solo albums, and a second time to focus on his early years and influences. I told him I would like to send him a manuscript of the seven chapters that then existed for his perusal and feedback, and he gave me an address in England where he would be staying in December 1999/January 2000. I mailed the manuscript to him, and waited for a reply. There was none. He never answered another e-mail I sent him. At length I gave up on the idea of the two subsequent phone interviews. It is always dangerous to infer a man's attitude from his silence, so I will not speculate. If Emerson wishes to comment on this matter at some point, I'm sure he will have the opportunity.

A family emergency forced me to put the manuscript aside for slightly over a year, and I did not recommence work until February 2001, when I began writing chapter 11. Even though I was simultaneously at work on the third Hermetic Science album, *En Route*, 2001 was a productive year, during which I finished chapters 11 through 16, which deal with late seventies ELP and the solo and splinter projects (i.e., ELPowell, 3) of the eighties. The year 2002 was nearly as productive, as I tackled the 1992–98 ELP reformation and its aftermath in chapters 17 through 20. The year 2003 was devoted to completing the voluminous appendices—a critical discography and videography, a section detailing additional recommended listening, a complete listing of ELP's known concerts with an accompanying socioeconomic/ethnographic analysis, and, of course, a bibliography. During the summer and fall of 2003, and again in spring 2004, I sent three e-mails to Bruce Pilato, Greg Lake's manager and the administrator of the Official ELP Global Web Site (as well as Greg Lake's and Carl Palmer's individual web sites), explaining the nature and scope of the book and asking if he would be willing to relay, via e-mail, a very few questions from me to Greg Lake and Carl Palmer. Pilato did acknowledge my third e-mail, which he forwarded to Lake and Palmer, but I never heard from them. At the beginning of 2004, I wrote the introduction that you are now reading and, between early and mid-2004, the book's first three chapters, finishing chapter 3 on Midsummer's Day 2004 and bringing this particular epic journey to a conclusion. Clearly, when I told Bill Martin yes in the fall of 1998, I didn't know what I was getting into.

Texts

A lot of water has passed under the bridge since *Rocking the Classics* appeared in November 1996. Interestingly, the two other major studies of progressive rock were published soon thereafter: Paul Stump's *The Music's All That Matters: A History of Progressive Rock* (1997)[3] and Bill Martin's *Listening to the Future: The Time of Progressive Rock* (1998).[4] Neither book shook my belief that my musical, cultural, and sociological analyses of progressive rock were essentially correct; indeed, I noted that the three of us agreed more often than we disagreed on many important points. Nonetheless, both books forced me to address certain issues with more nuance and clarity than I had previously, for which I remain grateful. Stump, despite the long-winded and somewhat bombastic nature of his prose, makes a number of original contributions. His discussion of the notorious 1974 U.K. tax hike (184) is quite useful for understanding the recording and touring patterns of the major British rock bands during the mid- to late seventies. His insistence that British rock was a "polyocracy" (48) in which working and middle-class musicians cheerfully jostled together, elbow to elbow, was an important corrective to my overemphasis on prog's bourgeois roots in *Rocking the Classics*.[5] His theory that

---

[3] Paul Stump, *The Music's All That Matters: A History of Progressive Rock* (London: Quartet Books, 1997).

[4] Bill Martin, *Listening to the Future: The Time of Progressive Rock, 1968–1978* (Chicago: Open Court, 1998).

[5] Stump's insistence on the British progressive rock scene being a "polyocracy" seems to be a particularly useful counterweight to my emphasis on prog's bourgeois roots in *Rocking the Classics* in light of the fact that three of the essayists in Kevin Holm-Hudson's *Progressive Rock Reconsidered* (New York: Routledge, 2002) heavily emphasize prog rock's roots in an educated, bohemian middle class, and cite *Rocking the Classics* as their source for this emphasis. See John Scheinbaum, "Progressive Rock and the Inversion of Musical Values," 25; Kevin Holm-Hudson, "The 'American Metaphysical Circus' of Joseph Byrd's United States of America," 44; and Deena Weinstein, "Progressive Rock as Text: The Lyrics of Roger Waters," 92. On the other hand, Durrell Bowman, "'Let Them All Make Their Own Music': Individualism, Rush, and the Progressive/Hard Rock Alloy, 1976–77," oversimplifies in the

prog's long-term future was doomed when record companies decided to shovel all their profits into the megabands (like ELP) rather than sign new, unknown ones (204–5), although much too limited in scope to fully explain prog rock's late seventies demise, adds a previously missing angle to the discussion. Above all, it's useful to hear the story of prog told from a British point of view, since in many subtle but important ways the story line looks somewhat different from the U.K. than from the U.S.[6]

Of course, Stump is a professional critic, not a musicologist, and while his observations concerning the music are generally correct, they are seldom particularly subtle or revelatory. The biggest weakness of Stump's book, however, is the sheer number of factual errors: some are so glaring as to be laughable, for instance, his identification of Michael Giles as King Crimson's flute player (53) and his description of Ayn Rand as "a Canadian philosopher" (258), but it's often the smaller ones that are more damaging. For instance, some of Stump's critical assessments are seriously undermined by his misquotes of lyrics, glaring misreadings of ELP's "Karn Evil 9, 3rd Impression" (170) and Rush's "Closer to the Heart" (257) providing just two of the most embarrassing examples.

Martin's *Listening to the Future: The Time of Progressive Rock, 1968–1978* (1998) develops and refines a number of ideas he had previously presented in *Music of Yes*, now extended over the broader canvas of progressive rock as an entire style rather than the *oeuvre* of a particular band. I was deeply impressed with how decisively Martin's prose changed from one book to the next in order to better engage the general reading public that was drawn to his work on music: the extremely dense, jargon-laced prose of *Music of Yes* was pared down to a terse, graceful, supple writing style in *Listening to the Future*, without any loss of sophistication or nuance. Martin is above all a philosopher and cultural theorist of unabashedly Marxist sympathies, and his strength is analyzing progressive rock and its antecedent bodies of music (for a nonmusicologist, he has a very good working knowledge of the basic histories of jazz and classical music) in the context of cultural, political, and historic developments.

---

opposite direction by claiming that "most progressive rock musicians came from the same small town and working-class British origins where hard rock and heavy metal originated" (185). Bowman's assertion is easily disproved: see *Rocking the Classics*, 148.

[6] Just one example: some British readers were horrified that I had nothing to say about the Enid, an important cult act in Great Britain during the late seventies, not realizing that the Enid were totally unknown in the U.S. and continental Europe during this period, and exerted no influence whatsoever outside of their home country. Although I don't feel particularly guilty about excluding the Enid from *Rocking the Classics*, I'm glad Stump covers them, because it's useful for American readers to realize that there was still the remnants of a grassroots prog scene in Britain during the late seventies.

Martin's linkages between developments in music and culture are often quite subtle and nuanced, as he has clearly learned much from Theodor Adorno (1903–69), the German social theorist/musicologist who pioneered this particular approach to interpreting shifts in musical style as paralleling, or encoding, shifts in social and political dynamics.

As much as I respect Martin's work—and as illuminating as it often can be—I believe his writing on music, like Adorno's, is subject to a systemic limitation: both writers have a tendency to proceed from their basic concepts of societal relations, and then determine how the music fits these concepts.[7] The danger here is that it's easy to miss a great deal of importance about the music when one imposes it into a predetermined conceptual framework: this is why, to me, some of Martin's more overtly Marxist

---

[7] The same charge can be leveled against the "new" critical methodologies—feminist theory, queer theory, postcolonial theory, and so on: that they begin with basic concepts of societal relations, and then either judge the music on the basis of how well it conforms to the ideology, or "massage" the music until it conforms to the ideology. A specific example can be found in one particular essay of Holm-Hudson, *Progressive Rock Reconsidered*, namely, Dirk Von der Horst's "Precarious Pleasures: Situating 'Close to the Edge' in Conflicting Male Desires" (167–182). Von der Horst agrees with my assertion in *Rocking the Classics* (95–104) that "Close to the Edge" is a teleological piece that, if not "in" sonata-allegro form per se, has correspondences with sonata-allegro form (which would, incidentally, tend to undermine John Scheinbaum's claim in *Progressive Rock Reconsidered*, 28, that my analysis of "Close to the Edge" in the context of sonata-allegro form in *Rocking the Classics* is "questionable.") However, Von der Horst reads "Close to the Edge" very differently than I do. While I read it as a metaphorical expression of spiritual quest and attainment, Van der Horst, viewing the work through the prisms of feminist theory and queer theory, sees it as a forum in which masculine and feminine elements are reconciled by making the feminine elements conform to the masculine, thus reproducing, rather than challenging, gender inequity; he points particularly to the violent displacement of the slow (third) section by the triumphant recapitulation of the "masculine" main theme as a form of sublimated male aggression against the feminine (178). Von der Horst's reading raises the following question: given that both feminist theory and queer theory begin their analyses with a premise of patriarchal hegemony, which is viewed in a highly negative light, given that goal-orientation of any type is often viewed as a byproduct of patriarchy, and given that multithematic musical works in which one theme emerges as primary invite antipatriarchal readings (marginalization of the Other), how could "Close to the Edge," or any other piece of multithematic, developmental music, be analyzed in a way that doesn't see it in a negative, "propatriarchal" light? Certainly Von der Horst's reading of "Close to the Edge" is not atypical in the context of feminist and/or queer theory; I once attended a session at a College Music Society national meeting where a feminist scholar analyzed Beethoven's Fifth Symphony in nearly identical terms. Significantly, Von der Horst sees Led Zeppelin's nonteleological "No Quarter" in a more positive light, since it doesn't force a reconciliation between its "masculine" and "feminine" sections (178). My point: feminist theory and queer theory tend to begin with an ideological precept (the evils of patriarchy) and proceed to create analyses that support the guiding precept. (Incidentally, for another nontraditional but, in my view, somewhat more productive approach to teleological/narrative structure in progressive rock, see Gregory Karl, "King Crimson's 'Lark's Tongue in Aspic': A Case of Convergent Evolution," *Progressive Rock Reconsidered*, 121–42.)

readings of progressive rock seem problematic.[8] This being said, I'm grateful that Martin has challenged me to write with much more subtlety and nuance about progressive rock as a cultural and political phenomenon, as opposed to a musical style linked strictly to other aesthetic considerations (i.e., literary, pictorial, and performance conventions). The result of this spur, if I may call it that, is the lengthy, and I hope illuminating, discussion about "the politics of prog" that dominates chapter 8 of the present work, where I consider, in the context of ELP's foray into capitalism via their Manticore record label, in what sense progressive rock can be said to be a political music, and to what degree its politics can be defined.[9]

Although Martin makes no claims of being a musicologist, I want to give him credit for two very useful insights of a purely musical nature that are central to both of his books. The first involves the differentiation he makes between "experimental rock" and "progressive rock."[10] He sees the former arising with the seminal 1966-67 recordings of the Beatles, and being extended forward into the early recordings of some of the major prog bands, wherein traditional rock song structures, although still recognizable, are being significantly stretched through the inclusion of instrumental preludes, interludes, and postludes and through composed vocal material, and wherein unconventional instruments are used to evoke an air of exoticism. In his view, progressive rock proper arises in 1969 with King Crimson's seminal *In the Court of the Crimson King*, and is differentiated by its more self-evident and self-conscious emphasis on virtuosity. I have not adopted this terminology in my work, because at times I see too much overlap between what Martin classifies as experimental rock (Pink Floyd, for instance) and progressive rock for the distinction to be valid, and because I believe Martin may somewhat overstate the centrality of virtuosity to the progressive rock style. Nonetheless, I think these categories are useful as a conceptual tool for thinking about the emergence of a full-

---

[8] One example (which, admittedly, involves an interpretation placed on a band's motives, rather than on a piece of music) will need to suffice here. In his eagerness to depict Yes as participants in the world-wide struggle against capitalism, Martin occasionally comes dangerously close to hagiography since, like many writers of hagiographies, he is obliged to ignore any all-too-human behavior of his subjects that may undermine his thesis. I, for one, do not see Yes, or any other major progressive rock band of the seventies, participating in an attempt, explicit or implicit, to overthrow capitalism. (Unless it is in the vaguest possible sense of "working toward a better future" in which capitalism has been replaced by a more equitable, but currently unknown, economic system.) I discuss this issue explicitly in some detail in chapter 8 of the present work, when I critique Martin's statements in *Listening to the Future*, 327, n50.

[9] Parts of this discussion appear in my article "Concerning the Politics of Prog," *Journal of Ayn Rand Studies* 5, no. 1 (Fall 2003): 173–88.

[10] Martin, *Listening to the Future*, 99–103.

blown progressive rock style, even if I'm not confident they reflect the hard and fast stylistic differences Martin sees in them.

Martin also makes a valuable contribution with his notion of the distribution of the rhythmic center (what I will henceforth call "the center of rhythmic gravity") throughout the ensemble.[11] In other words, a simple distribution might involve the drummer always laying out the music's rhythmic foundation, with the other musicians playing off of the drummer's foundation. A sophisticated distribution of rhythmic center would involve the rhythmic anchor being distributed in such a way that, for instance, the drummer carries it in one passage, then the bass line takes on the role of rhythmic anchor, freeing the drummer to play a more "melodic" role, then the keyboard player's left hand takes over the rhythmic anchor, freeing up both bassist and drummer to create more "melodic" and polyrhythmic parts. I've found this concept extremely useful in assessing the sophistication and rhythmic richness of a band's arrangements, and I've used it both in my analyses in this book, and in creating arrangements around the compositions I've written for my own band, Hermetic Science.

Besides the three major histories of progressive rock that appeared during the 1996–98 period, a significant addition to the growing canon of progressive rock scholarship is a collection of essays edited by Kevin Holm-Hudson, *Progressive Rock Reconsidered*, which appeared in 2002. Most of the essays do not attempt to challenge the basic parameters of progressive rock studies set forth in *Rocking the Classics*, but rather to focus on details that can't possibly be addressed in a historical survey, in a few cases by analyzing individual prog rock works using modern resistance-oriented critical approaches such as feminist theory, queer theory, and so forth. One exception (and perhaps the most important essay in the book) is John Scheinbaum's "Progressive Rock and the Inversion of Musical Values" (21–42), which does in fact challenge some of my basic approaches in *Rocking the Classics*. Scheinbaum takes me to task for having stated in *Rocking the Classics* that both structural and cultural readings are necessary to fully comprehend prog, yet having relied on traditional structuralist analytic approaches (29). He also criticizes John Covach for stating, in *Understanding Rock: Essays in Musical Analysis*,[12] that prog is a kind of rock music, although one that's deeply impacted by the classical tradition, and then proceeding to analyze the music almost entirely as if it were a symphony or concerto (41–42, n21).

Scheinbaum's concern is fair enough; I have three responses. First, in *Rocking the Classics* I *do* bring together cultural and formal analysis,

---

[11] See Martin, *Music of Yes*, 109–11.

[12] John Covach and Graeme Boone, eds., *Understanding Rock: Essays in Musical Analysis* (New York: Oxford University Press, 1997).

not only by taking the content of the lyrics, titles, and cover art into account when rendering a reading of "the music itself," but also by considering whether, and to what degree, the structural dynamic of a given progressive rock piece might be viewed as a metaphoric expression of the concerns of late-sixties/early-seventies counterculture.[13] If I did not integrate formal and cultural analytical approaches to Scheinbaum's satisfaction in *Rocking the Classics*, all I can say is this: *somebody* had to initiate the process of integrating the two, and I regard my analyses in *Rocking the Classics* as trailblazing efforts (and often illuminating ones at that), not as the final word on how such analyses should be undertaken. I will discuss my analytical methods to be used in this book shortly; suffice it to say that I believe my analyses here will show greater subtlety and nuance than those of *Rocking the Classics*. That, of course, is a judgment that you as reader will have to make for yourself.

Furthermore, I think it is important to note that although progressive rock *is* rock music, it is unlike most rock music, and like most classical music circa 1720–1920, in that the most representative progressive rock is teleological, not cyclical, and therefore lends itself well to the various analytical methods that have grown up around classical music. This doesn't mean that classical analytical models offer the best possible approach to prog rock, simply that the ideal analytical approach to prog (and other types of rock music) is still under construction, and that in the meantime, analytical techniques aligned with classical music do in fact tell us much of interest concerning what is going on with the music at its deeper levels, at times even allowing us to make connections between formal and cultural dynamics. In an attempt to create an analytical model for examining both the "rock" and "classical" aspects of progressive rock music, Scheinbaum undertakes an analysis of Yes's "Roundabout" (30–39) that, on the one hand, assays both to show its debt to both rock music conventions of the sixties and seventies and to classical music, and, on the other, to highlight the structural tensions that result from the interaction of the "high" and "low" culture elements. I would argue he succeeds in the first task better than the second: while his analysis is effective enough in cataloging which elements of the song derive from the discourse of classical music and which derive from the conventions of sixties and seventies rock, he never really moves beyond issues of taxonomy to the more difficult and meaningful task of illuminating the larger structural process by which the song's disparate elements are absorbed into a unified discourse. I certainly do not see his

---

[13] I am puzzled by the fact that Scheinbaum appears to criticize me for my thesis that progressive rock plays out the concerns of the counterculture at a metaphorical level (41, fn3), and then proceeds to analyze the lyrics of Yes's "Roundabout" metaphorically (38).

analysis bringing off the integration of formal and cultural considerations that he chides me for not achieving.[14]

I also have some differences with Scheinbaum in regards to what he calls "stylistic purity." According to Scheinbaum, both progressive rock's detractors and I proceed from a presumption of stylistic purity that is, in his view, more apparent than real. I would respond that Scheinbaum's apparent conviction that there is no such thing as stylistic purity in regard to progressive rock will remain problematic as long as it ignores the degree to which British progressive rock of the 1970s was beholden to nineteenth-century notions of organicism, which emphasize that all musical material grows "organically" from the themes and motives heard at the beginning of a work, and that all musical material within a work is therefore "organically" interrelated.[15] While the British progressive rock style did bring together disparate and at times mutually contradictory stylistic sources, it was nearly always with the intention of melting these sources down into a new alloy, as it were, subsuming them into a new metastyle greater than, and different from, the sum of its parts. In regards to ELP, for instance, we will notice an ever more subtle interpenetration of Emerson's rock, blues, jazz, baroque, and twentieth-century classical influences: in much of ELP's most representative music ("Tank," "Take a Pebble," the instrumental movements of "Tarkus," the 1st and 3rd Impressions of "Karn Evil 9," "Pirates," nearly any of the classical arrangements), one sees two or more of Emerson's influences being melted down so thoroughly that they are effectively subsumed into a new, rock-based stylistic matrix. We will also note that even when very different musical "blocks" are alternated in ELP's music (the soft acoustic "classical" sections and loud "rock" sections of "Trilogy," or the different classical genres of "The Three Fates" or "The Endless Enigma," for instance), thematic and motivic interconnections, tonal relationships, and carefully plotted dynamics contrasts are employed to integrate such apparently contrasting musical blocks into a unified musical discourse.

This is quite a different mindset than one observes in the music of late-sixties American experimental rockers such as Frank Zappa or Captain Beefheart, for instance, who baldly juxtapose radically different musical

---

[14] For instance, Scheinbaum sees the lyrics as reveling "in the glory of timeless pristine nature both as an idealized past and as a utopian vision of the future, able to resist and withstand the bleak effects of modern society" (38). Fair enough. But how is this interpretation supported by the music? While Scheinbaum does note a number of the song's developmental features, he never clearly spells out how the song's teleological nature impacts our experience of it, or how such a structural dynamic might support the themes he believes are advanced in the lyrics.

[15] The best short introduction to nineteenth-century organicist thought and its impact on nineteenth-century music is David Montgomery, "The Myth of Organicism: From Bad Science to Great Art," *Musical Quarterly* (Spring 1992): 17–66.

discourses without any intention of integrating them, often to create a sense of ironic displacement, parody, and/or satire—qualities that seldom play a part in British progressive rock. While it is just possible Scheinbaum's allegation that I am too beholden to notions of "stylistic purity" may carry some weight, the charge will not stick until he acknowledges the degree to which British progressive rock was impacted by organicist thinking, and explains why notions of "stylistic purity" should not be taken seriously in a style where organicism often seems to be an operative principle.

Another essay that I would like to briefly comment on here is Kevin Holm-Hudson's "The 'American Metaphysical Circus' of Joseph Byrd's United States of America."[16] Holm-Hudson argues that United States of America "was an isolated, homegrown predecessor of the 'progressive' or 'art rock' style that became prominent, chiefly among British bands, in the early 1970s" (44). While I think Holm-Hudson's discussion of Byrd, his band, and their lone album (released in 1968) is excellent, I think it tends to prove something rather different: that United States of America were *sui generis*, and that not only did they have no direct impact on British progressive rock, they were, both in their background and in their aesthetic goals, very different. Here I must claim some firsthand insight: Joseph Byrd is my colleague at the College of the Redwoods. Although we talk little about progressive rock, what we have discussed tends to confirm my views. First of all, as Holm-Hudson points out, Byrd and his colleagues had little background as rock musicians: their background was in avant-garde music, and from what I have gleaned Byrd saw United States of America more as an avant-garde group that happened to utilize rock music instrumentation than (as in the case of British proggers) rock musicians keen on absorbing the forms, techniques, and tone-colors of classical music into rock.[17]

Second, United States of America, while often partial to chopping up and reconfiguring established pop song forms, as well as experimenting with the possibilities of the Beatles' song cycle approach in *Sergeant Pepper*, showed none of British progressive rock's interest in expanding the pop song beyond its breaking point into suite-like structures, nor did they evince the fondness for the instrumental pyrotechnics that was to become a hallmark of British progressive rock. Their biggest innovation was in the realm of tape collage and the use of then-novel electronic effects produced by ring modulation, analog delay, filtering, and so on. (In this respect, the one major British band that they may have paralleled

---

[16] Holm-Hudson contributed a second essay, an analysis of ELP's "Trilogy": I will address this in a footnote to my own discussion of "Trilogy."

[17] In this respect it's important to note that United States of America played at performance art venues as often, if not more often, than rock clubs.

to some degree is Pink Floyd.) Above all, as Holm-Hudson notes, United States of America emphasized parody and ironic displacement in a manner at odds with British prog, where the emphasis was nearly always on absorbing its sources into an overarching stylistic framework. Byrd has made it clear to me he has little interest in British progressive rock, little sympathy with its aesthetic goals, and, more generally, little interest in post-Beatles British rock of the seventies. All this being said, I think Holm-Hudson has rendered a real service in rescuing a uniquely innovative band from obscurity.

A scholarly work that appeared too close to my publication deadline for me to fully engage is Akitsugu Kawamoto's "'Can You Still Keep Your Balance?': Keith Emerson's Anxiety of Influence, Style Change, and the Road to Prog Superstardom."[18] In the process of attempting to define the essential differences between the Nice and ELP, Kawamoto takes me to task rather harshly for "misrepresenting" the nature of the aesthetic shift from late-sixties proto-progressive rock (exemplified by the Nice) to seventies prog rock (exemplified by ELP): "Edward Macan's explanation, for example, of the style change from what he calls 'the first wave' (the Nice and other pre-1970 groups) to 'the second wave' (groups after 1970-71 including ELP) of the progressive rock movement is too general and only a half truth. According to him, pieces in 'the second wave' are longer, formally more involved, more virtuosic, and more complex harmonically, texturally, and rhythmically" (233). I continue to believe this assertion holds true when applied to the other major proto-progressive bands (the Moody Blues, Procol Harum, Pink Floyd), and is essentially accurate when applied to the Nice, who are in fact a looser, less precise, less virtuosic band than ELP: I note that in order to contradict it, Kawamoto must be a bit disingenuous, comparing one of ELP's shorter, simpler pieces ("Knife-Edge") to one of the Nice's longer, more complex pieces (their arrangement of Sibelius's "Intermezzo"). Nonetheless, since the time of writing *Rocking the Classics*, I have come to believe it might be profitable to further flesh out my earlier stylistic distinction between late-sixties proto-prog and seventies "classic" prog by pointing up how ELP et al. consciously rejected elements of psychedelic rock that the proto-progressive bands still accepted. I do so in appendix C of this book by considering how ELP and the contemporaneous Czech band Collegium Musicum developed the musical legacy of the Nice in two very different directions, with ELP emphasizing ever-tighter arrangements and limiting improvisation to discrete sections of their increasingly carefully elaborated compositional formats, while Collegeium Musicum (unusually for a post-1970

---

[18] Akitsugu Kawamoto, "'Can You Still Keep Your Balance?' Keith Emerson's Anxiety of Influence, Style Change, and the Road to Prog Superstardom," *Popular Music* 24/2 (2005): 223–44.

prog rock band) followed the model of loose arrangements, "composition through improvisation," and experimentation with tone-color for its own sake that marked a good deal of the Nice's most representative work.

Certainly, Kawamoto's attempt to flesh out the distinction meets with mixed results. Drawing on Harold Bloom's anxiety theory of poetic influence, Kawamoto tries to demonstrate that the stylistic shift from the Nice to ELP was a result of Emerson's determination to subvert the compositional parameters of his old group in order that ELP not be viewed as merely "the new Nice." Kawamoto's central thesis is built upon his own speculation regarding Emerson's psychological state during the early days of ELP: he asserts that Emerson "self-consciously and objectively began to consider what his own former style was like, and to struggle very hard against it in order to get along with his new members. His own past thus became a burden upon him, a status which was equal to that of an influential poetic precursor in Bloom's theoretical picture." The problem here, aside from the somewhat questionable attempt of an outsider to closely read an artist's psychological state of some thirty-five years past, is that the thesis seems to be flatly contradicted by Emerson's own statement: "Greg was adamant that it [the new band] shouldn't be like a new Nice, but at the back of my mind that was exactly what it was going to be."[19] This statement hardly suggests that Emerson viewed musical continuity from the Nice to ELP as a potential source of anxiety, and tends to make the rather ostentatious manipulation of Bloom's theory that Kawamoto engages in during the remainder of the article somewhat redundant.

Much more important is Kawamoto's observation that the emergence of the mature prog rock style during 1970-71 involved a "mainstreaming" of the earlier approach so that it would "be perceived as something more sophisticated and polished" (233). I think Kawamoto also makes an important point about the specific difference in sensibility between the Nice and ELP by noting "postmodern ideas of juxtaposition and pastiche" are present in the music of the Nice (230). Although he doesn't go on to explicitly state the corollary (i.e., that such ideas are *not* present in the most representative work of ELP), his observation ties in to what I pointed above: British progressive rock in its "classic" phase (1970-77) is deeply invested in the notion of organicism, of fusing its disparate stylistic sources together into a single alloy, and therefore rejects techniques of pastiche that point up basic incompatibilities of style or link them sardonically and/or ironically. I believe prog rock's organicism is part and parcel of its utopianism, although this is obviously not the place to explore this assertion at length. Nor is it the place to explore Kawamoto's debatable (and not very nuanced) claim that post-1970 prog rock's drive towards ever greater

---

[19] Martyn Hanson, *Hang on to a Dream: The Story of the Nice* (London: Helter Skelter, 2002), 148.

sophistication and polish represents a rejection of countercultural values by encapsulating a desire for commodification (238). As I point up in my comparison of ELP and Collegium Musicum's development of the Nice's legacy (see appendix C), there were sound musical reasons for ELP and their British prog rock peers to eschew the long improvisations and loose arrangements of late-sixties psychedelic rock. At any rate, in his comparison of the Nice's arrangement of Sibelius's "Intermezzo" to ELP's "Knife-Edge," Kawamoto more or less proves my point: "Knife-Edge" demonstrates a self-conscious organicism in its fusion of its rock and classical elements into a unified musical discourse within the context of a rock-based stylistic matrix (236), whereas "Intermezzo" juxtaposes its disparate rock and classical elements far more overtly (228–29).

Martin's and Stump's histories and, to a lesser extent, the various essays of *Progressive Rock Reconsidered* were the major scholarly works that I found myself engaging throughout this book. However, between 2000 and 2003 four biographical books were published—three by the British publisher Helter Skelter—that, while not scholarly in the sense of being involved with ideas and issues, were of considerable value to this project.[20] In early 2001, while I was beginning work on chapter 11 of the present book, *Emerson, Lake and Palmer: The Show That Never Ends; A Musical Biography*, written by George Forrester with Martyn Hanson and Frank Askew, appeared.[21] As band biographies go, this one is pretty good, giving a coherent and comprehensive account of the band's history from beginning to end, although, like most books of this type, the sources of quotes are not identified, leaving one unsure if any given quote represents the fruits of original interviews or of gleanings from secondary sources; that is, one can't tell what quotes come from what sources unless one already knows the sources.[22] This fact alone convinced me not to abandon the biographical aspect of what I was doing. I was also struck by a general lack of inclination to *interpret* the material, both in terms of critically assessing the music, and analyzing how decisions made by the band and changes in interpersonal dynamics affected the music—one senses the authors did not in any way wish to give umbrage to Emerson, Lake, and Palmer, either individually or collectively.

This was not at all the approach I had chosen. If there is any major rock band of the seventies in need of critical rehabilitation, it's ELP, and

---

[20] For the record, I did not read any of these four books until 2003, after I had completed chapters 4 through 20 of this book, as I wanted my approach and viewpoint to remain as independent as possible.

[21] George Forrester, Martyn Hanson, and Frank Askew, *Emerson, Lake and Palmer: The Show That Never Ends; A Musical Biography* (London: Helter Skelter, 2001).

[22] Which in most cases I did, having worked from the same pool of secondary sources as the authors.

I do not see how the process of critical rehabilitation can or will begin without a critical survey of the band's music and career trajectory (and by "critical survey," I mean presenting the facts and then rendering an impartial, fair-minded analysis of them, not rendering a hatchet job). To put it another way: the Forrester-Hanson-Askew book seems a bit too determined not to upset its subjects to really begin the process of critical reassessment that I hope to launch here. This process, which I would describe as sympathetic but critical, calls for a full acknowledgement of such bad decisions, bad albums, and wasted opportunities that need to be acknowledged. I can well imagine such an acknowledgement could be a painful thing for the band members; but I do not see how an author that truly believes in the band's importance, and hopes to demonstrate it, can spare them some unpleasantness in this regard.

One other observation about *Emerson, Lake and Palmer: The Show That Never Ends*: its second subtitle, *A Musical Biography*, is a bit of a cheat. Yes, there is a forty-page "Musical Analysis" section at the end of the book. However, the discussions of individual pieces (which are sometimes curiously chosen—there are some odd inclusions and omissions) are along the lines of program notes, wherein pertinent details are pointed out and briefly discussed. There's nothing wrong with this approach, *per se*, but the "Musical Biography" sobriquet suggests the individual observations will be stitched together into a bigger tapestry. For instance, is there an ELP style? If so, what are its hallmarks? Did it change or develop over time? Are there conceptual themes that are persistently addressed in the ELP canon? If so, what are they? While some of these questions are touched on in *The Show That Never Ends*, few are really developed to any degree, and none are answered definitively. In that sense, it may be a bit much to subtitle the book "A Musical Biography."

Two other books also published by Helter Skelter, although less central to my task here, also must be addressed. Sid Smith's *In the Court of King Crimson*[23] is the first biography of that band since their 1994 reformation, and is notable for its author having secured the full cooperation of Robert Fripp, the band's brilliant but contentious leader, and many other musicians who played a major role in the band at some point. In one sense, Smith's book is a bit less ambitious than the Forrester-Hanson-Askew tome: there's no attempt at a "musical biography," and the reader isn't brought closer to the essence of King Crimson's music (which may be why Fripp cooperated with Smith but refused to cooperate with Eric Tamm, whose *Robert Fripp: From King Crimson to Guitar Craft* of 1990 did attempt to be a musical biography of sorts[24]). As a band biography,

---

[23] Sid Smith, *In the Court of King Crimson* (London: Helter Skelter, 2001).
[24] Eric Tamm, *Robert Fripp: From King Crimson to Guitar Craft* (Boston: Faber and Faber, 1990).

however, this is a first-rate work, very tightly organized and engagingly written, not shying away from the many interpersonal disputes that litter the band's history, and (for my purposes) is important for the heretofore unprecedented detail in which the early stages of Greg Lake's career are presented.

Martyn Hanson, coauthor of *The Show That Never Ends*, is sole author of *Hang on to a Dream: The Story of the Nice*. Written with the cooperation of Lee Jackson, Brian Davison, Nice roadie Bazz Ward, and journalist Chris Welch (one notices the absence of Keith Emerson from this list), this book, although a bit looser in its narrative than Smith's, is a similarly first-rate band biography. Like Smith, Hanson has no pretenses of creating a musical biography—therefore, nothing particularly revelatory is said about the music itself—but the upside of this arrangement is a more tightly focused book than *The Show That Never Ends*. (Of course, the Nice only existed for a fraction of the time ELP did, so one could argue his task was easier in this regard.) Hanson is refreshingly unreliant on secondary sources and, because he asks all the right questions, sheds light on all the major mysteries that had long surrounded the Nice: what really happened to David O'List in 1968 (the answer to this question is incendiary), the circumstances surrounding the move from Andrew Loog Oldham's Immediate label to Tony Stratton Smith's Charisma label, why Emerson ultimately became dissatisfied with the band, and what the band's final weeks were like. There's a lot of valuable information here concerning the pre-Nice careers of all the band members, including Emerson, as well as the 2002 reunion.

Finally, the summer of 2003 witnessed the appearance of Keith Emerson's long-awaited autobiography, *Pictures of an Exhibitionist*.[25] (I had first heard it was in progress in 1996, and by the time of its publication, had come to doubt it would ever appear.) It's a curious book. Emerson spends much time on his early years in Worthing, particularly on his relationship with his parents. We follow him as he agonizes whether to choose a career in chemistry or banking (which he knew would please his parents), or a career in music (which he was certain would not). We learn of his early days in London with Gary Farr and the T-Bones, his first tours of France and Germany with the VIPs, his years with the Nice, and, of course, his eight years (1970–78) on top of the musical world with ELP. Although the book begins and ends with an account of the events surrounding the 1993 arm surgery that almost ended his career, for all intents and purposes the narrative ends in 1978, with virtually nothing on the succeeding twenty-five years. Maybe a sequel is in preparation?

---

[25] Keith Emerson, *Pictures of an Exhibitionist* (London: John Blake Publishing, 2003).

Along the way, we get some personal (at times *extremely* personal) glimpses of his ex-wife Elinor, his two sons, his parents, his band mates, his friends, and sundry other business associates, hangers-on, and groupies, delivered with Emerson's trademark dry humor. However, while his readers may learn much more than they ever wanted to know about ELP's orgiastic excesses during the seventies, the book is surprisingly silent about the music. To be sure, I did not expect Emerson would choose this forum to discuss technical issues. What I mean, rather, is that *Exhibitionist* is disinclined to interpret or critically appraise music—or, for that matter, events and decisions. For instance, I expected Emerson would have given some thought to what caused the band's artistic decline after 1974; however, if he has pondered this matter at any length, he chooses not to share his thoughts in *Exhibitionist*. One might have expected Emerson to ruminate on ELP's importance to popular music of the seventies, or wax eloquent about an album that he sees as particularly emblematic of ELP, or recall a musical achievement of which he is particularly proud, but he does not. In fact, while he does acknowledge that the choice to tour with an orchestra in 1977 did not end up being popular with his band mates (Lake in particular), he never says whether or not he would do it all again, knowing what he knows now. In short, while *Pictures of an Exhibitionist* is, in one sense, painfully honest and candid, in another sense it's curiously unreflective; the reader finishes the book knowing a lot about what Emerson did, without having gained a clear sense of what his motivations were to do what he did. Nonetheless, no study of Emerson or ELP can safely ignore this book.

There is one other work that should be addressed here, namely Blair Pethel's 1987 D.M.A. paper, "Keith Emerson: The Emergence and Growth of Style."[26] Pethel's paper has two significant weaknesses: there are a number of factual errors in his chronology of events, and his attempt to trace the development of Emerson's style is undermined by his tendency to analyze short passages of works without considering their context within the work as a whole, and to impose an artificial distinction between Emerson's classical and popular manner.[27] Nonetheless, while his overall assessment of Emerson's stylistic development suffers, some of the analyses of individual pieces are quite good, and the interviews with Emerson remain valuable, as very few of Emerson's previous interviewers had Pethel's theoretical understanding of Emerson's music. Certainly

---

[26] Blair Pethel, "Keith Emerson: The Emergence and Growth of Style." D.M.A. (Doctor of Musical Arts) Paper, Johns Hopkins University, 1987.

[27] For instance, Pethel discusses the fugue of "Endless Enigma," while ignoring the rest of the suite; this, to me, takes the fugue out of context. So does his analysis of "Eruption," the first movement of "Tarkus," that gives no sense of what role "Eruption" plays within the "Tarkus" suite as a whole.

Pethel's work must be acknowledged as a pioneering effort in serious rock music analysis, appearing a full five years before I even began working on *Rocking the Classics.*

Goals and Methods

Now we come to the present work, which has three basic goals, namely, (1) to provide an accurate, coherent, and comprehensive biography of the band from their origin in 1970 to their demise in 1998, including the individual activities of Emerson, Lake, and Palmer during the periods when the band has been inactive; (2) to provide a comprehensive critical survey of the recorded output of ELP, the solo work of Emerson, Lake and Palmer, and the recordings done pre-ELP, inter-ELP, and post-ELP by the band members with other bands; and (3) to undertake an analysis of the band's music—with their most important albums, naturally, getting the most attention—that examines the particulars of the music, lyrics, and cover art, and considers the band's aesthetic and philosophical worldview, their "message," if you will, that's conveyed through the confluence of these elements. In regards to the book's analytical goals, I define the particulars of the ELP style, demonstrate how it developed over time, and point up both purely musical preoccupations and conceptual themes that are persistently addressed in the ELP canon: in so doing, I believe what I have undertaken here can fairly be called a musical biography.

Since each of these three goals could conceivably be open to misunderstanding and misinterpretation without further clarification, I will take the liberty of fleshing out my intentions with regard to each. In terms of the book's biographical function, I knew before I began writing that I would not need to conduct extensive interviews with Emerson, Lake, and/or Palmer to fill in missing spaces in the ELP storyline. ELP received very extensive coverage during the seventies—even the eighties splinter projects (Emerson, Lake and Powell, 3) and the nineties reformation received a fair amount of attention from the rock press—and for anybody willing to carefully sift through twenty-eight years of interviews, reviews, and features, there's plenty of material out there, and relatively few issues that didn't receive coverage at some point or another. Furthermore, I noticed something interesting: the band members' accounts of a given event tended to show subtle but important changes over time. This can be noticed, for instance, when one compares their recollections of the Isle of Wight shows given twenty-two years apart, in 1970 and 1992.

There's a reason for this. Each of us conceives of our life in the context of a personal history, whether we're fully conscious of it or not, in which the events of our lives are interpreted in the context of a grand narrative we're perpetually re-creating for ourselves, the grand narrative being shaped by our experiences, our worldview, religious or philosophical beliefs, values frame, personal relationships, and so forth, at a particular point in time. Over time, as one matures or changes, one's grand narrative can change somewhat, and with it, one's interpretation of specific events. I decided that for the purposes of the present book, recollections given shortly after key events were usually more reliable than recollections given years after the fact, the latter often having been colored by considerations that would not have been a factor when the original event took place. This is the reason I did not feel compelled to ask E, L, or P to revisit important events from their past that they have already expounded on at length years ago, when they were much closer to the events in question. On the other hand, there are a few instances where it is apparent that E, L, or P spoke more honestly about a particular event years after the fact than they did at the time of its occurrence, when they were attempting to exercise diplomatic restraint and/or create the impression of intergroup harmony; such instances are duly noted.

Having decided to rely on secondary sources for the biographical material, the question was, which ones? I decided that more important than sheer quantity of sources was balance. During the seventies and early eighties, a number of important individual interviews of Emerson, Lake and Palmer were conducted by journals such as *Contemporary Keyboard* (later *Keyboard*), *Guitar Player*, and *Modern Drummer*, publications that are concerned primarily with matters of technique and equipment, and these interviews are crucial for understanding the musicians' influences, stylistic preferences, musical priorities, and equipment choices. Indeed, throughout the seventies, ELP had a reputation for being on the cutting edge of music technology, so one important task of this book has been to detail the changes in the band's equipment and use of musical technology throughout their careers; in this endeavor, interviews with the musicians are of particular value.

While such interviews are crucial to understanding a band like ELP for whom the music really *did* matter, they're only one side of the coin. ELP also received extensive coverage in journals that were far less concerned with matters of technique and equipment, and more concerned with rock as an expression of culture, lifestyle, fashion, and politics: the "big four" here were the British publications *Melody Maker* and *New Musical Express* and the American magazines *Rolling Stone* and *Creem*. As the seventies progressed, the rock journals (as I will hereafter call them) became increasingly hostile to ELP and progressive rock more generally—this is an issue I'll discuss at some length in a moment. However, acknowledging the frequently unsympathetic, if not downright hostile, coverage that ELP received, and acknowledging the frequent incomprehension the rock journals displayed towards ELP's music, there are still some valuable interviews and features that emerged from this milieu, including the major

Rolling Stone and *NME* features of 1974 that explore the band's thoughts, some of which are quite penetrating, concerning the significance of their epic stage show, and which use ELP as a case study of rock-band-as-corporation.[28]

During ELP's 1992–98 reformation, I found the internet—both fan-run forums such as *The ELP Digest* and more official forums (the band's official web site and the band members' individual web sites)—to be just as important a source as print journals, which, except for the small, specialized prog rock fanzines, were much less interested in ELP than they had been in the seventies. I drew much from such sources, giving them proper acknowledgement whenever possible. Indeed, the story of ELP's final cataclysm in 1998, as told here, is much enriched by internet-only sources.

Two final issues as regards the biographical function of this book. First, some will wonder why I periodically punctuate the biographical narrative with descriptions of particular concerts, including details of the set lists. The reason is simple. In an era when live music was a far more important element of popular music culture than it is now, and when a band's artistic growth and development was as much (if not more) a function of perpetual concertizing as it was the recording of a new studio album every year or two, it is simply impossible to understand the career of ELP—by any measure one of rock's great live acts of the seventies—without some understanding of their development and growth as a stage act. Fortunately, the release of *The Original Bootleg Series from the Manticore Vaults* in three volumes during 2001 and 2002 has made this facet of the band's career more readily available to interested persons. Nonetheless, I think my own accounts of ELP concerts will elucidate an important aspect of the ELP story, and illustrate that each new stage of ELP's career tended to be accompanied by (sometimes prefigured by) an overhaul of the set list.

The second issue refers to the book's title—*Endless Enigma*—which is, of course, based on the title of one of ELP's epic suites. The title is meant to suggest the riddle that anyone who seeks to come to terms with the

---

[28] A word on the footnoting of secondary sources throughout this book. Early on in the writing process (probably spring of 1999), I put out a plea on John Arnold's wonderful on-line *ELP Digest* for interviews and profiles done on the band during the 1970s in *Rolling Stone*, *Creem*, *Melody Maker*, *New Musical Express*, *Circus*, etc.; while I had access to some such secondary sources, I felt I needed more. The response was excellent, and, as a small token of thanks, respondees are mentioned in the acknowledgements section. However, some of the photocopies of articles that were sent to me did not include page numbers, although it was always clear which issue of which journal the article in question had come from. After some consideration, I decided that my inability to supply a page number was not sufficient reason not to reference articles that contained material that was beneficial to this book's overall narrative. Therefore, some of my footnote citations of journal articles do not include page numbers. I apologize for any inconvenience this may cause future researchers.

ELP saga must sooner or later grapple with. Let me preface the riddle with the following statement of fact. No other rock band has ever been as successful, both artistically and commercially, for as long as ELP, and then crashed with such suddenness and finality, so that all subsequent efforts to reascend to the peak of artistic and commercial success they had once attained met with numbingly predictable failure. In the eighteen-month period between their first practice sessions in June 1970 and the American release of *Pictures at an Exhibition* in January 1972, ELP were more responsible than any other single band for shaping the emerging progressive rock style; they were similarly influential in their live shows of 1973–74, which redefined the rock concert as a multimedia extravaganza. How could a band that was so influential between 1970 and 1977—an enormous span of time by today's standards—self-destruct so spectacularly so quickly, and then fail, with such discouraging regularity, in attempt after attempt to put all the pieces back together? I will address this "enigma" twice: first in chapter 13, when I discuss the aftermath of the *Love Beach* album, and again in chapter 20, when I undertake a final summing up of ELP's career. In the meantime, I trust the reader won't grow impatient and skip directly to those two chapters!

As I said above, providing a comprehensive critical survey of the recorded output of ELP, the solo work of Emerson, Lake and Palmer, and the recordings done pre-ELP, inter-ELP, and post-ELP by the three musicians with other bands, is the second major goal of this book. All three words—"comprehensive," "critical," and "survey"—are important to my purposes. I believe one of my duties as author of this book is to present the entire available ELP output in a comprehensive yet clear and easily grasped manner. This wasn't as easy as I expected it to be. Ignoring the solo projects of Emerson, Lake and Palmer and their work with other bands, let's momentarily consider the ELP output. Not taking into account best of/greatest hits packages, of which at this late date there has been a nauseating profusion, there are seven studio albums and three live albums released during the band's 1970–79 heyday; two studio albums of the "splinter" bands Emerson, Lake and Powell and 3, released 1986–88, as well as two recent (2003) posthumous ELPowell albums (one documenting a studio rehearsal, the second a live show of 1986); two studio albums from 1992–94; five live albums released 1993–98, two and a half of which chronicle shows from the nineties, and two and a half of which showcase shows of the seventies; three box sets of authorized bootleg recordings from throughout the band's career, released 2001–02; two major retrospective box sets, released in the early nineties, one of which contains newly recorded music; and a few assorted curios such as the *I Believe in Father Christmas* EP. There are also seven VHS/DVD documents of ELP, namely, their 12-9-70 London Lyceum concert; the 1973 *Return of the Manticore* TV documentary; the 8-26-77 Montreal concert with full orchestra; the 10-2-92 Royal Albert Hall show; the 1993 *Welcome Back* video biography; their 1997 Montreux Festival show; and the 2005 *Beyond the Beginning* two-disc package, which includes a sixty-minute documentary, the band's 4-6-74 Cal Jam set, a number of performances of individual songs from across the band's career, and miscellaneous footage. Is your head swimming yet?

Well, then, take a deep breath. Before I began writing the book, I had entertained the fantasy of focusing exclusively on ELP's collective output. I quickly realized that wasn't a viable plan. Writing about early ELP without giving any sense of what Emerson, Lake, and Palmer had achieved with the Nice, King Crimson, and Atomic Rooster, respectively, was simply a nonstarter, so I soon recognized that the studio albums of these three bands that E, L, and P had been participants in would need to be addressed. That's five Nice albums, two King Crimson albums, and one Atomic Rooster album. It also dawned on me that Emerson, Lake and Powell, 3, and nineties ELP would make little sense without an understanding of how Emerson's soundtracks and solo albums of the eighties, Lake's career as a bandleader during the same period, and Palmer's work with pop-rock supergroup Asia colored these later projects. This involved me in discussing the solo output of Emerson (eleven albums), Lake (two studio albums, a live album, and three anthologies, each somewhat different in aim), and Palmer's work with Asia (five studio albums and sundry live albums). All of a sudden, my task of laying out Emerson's, Lake's, and Palmer's output—whether collective, individual, or with other bands— looked a bit more daunting.

I found that introducing and discussing these recordings during the course of the biographical narrative was the clearest and easiest-to-follow method of coherently presenting the extended ELP output. However, simply *introducing* the recorded output clearly wasn't enough; if I was to make sense of this large output, to put it in perspective and context, I was going to have to do something in this book that I had been largely unwilling to do in *Rocking the Classics*, that is, adopt the persona of the critic. Among this large output, which were the albums that were milestones for the band? Of these, which were of such significance as to be crucial to the development of progressive rock at large? And of this much smaller body of albums, which could be said to be of importance to seventies rock as a whole? As I assessed the worth of each album, I pondered a number of factors, such as innovation and originality; historical significance (i.e., via influence exerted on contemporary musicians); compositional, arranging, and technical mastery; interalbum cohesiveness; conceptual depth (here's where the confluence of music, lyrics, and cover art becomes crucial); production savvy; and, at times, a host of other intangibles. At the end of my discussion of each album in this book, I endeavor to sum up my critical assessment of the album as clearly and concisely as possible. Therefore, readers who don't necessarily want to follow my entire musical and conceptual analysis of *Brain Salad Surgery*, for instance, can skip directly to the end of the discussion and read the critical summary—although said readers will have missed much of the explanation of how I came to render the critical judgment I did.

There are two final aspects of my approach to be aware of. First, in the case of minor albums (i.e., posthumous live albums released many years after the fact), there usually is no analytical discussion, just a brief critical summary; analytical discussion is reserved for studio albums and for a select few live albums of seminal importance to the band's career. Second, be aware that critical summaries of all albums and videos discussed in the text—and a number that are not—are presented in a chronological manner in the first two appendices, appendix A being a critical discography and appendix B a critical videography. I became so systematic in my critical assessment that I felt I could safely give an objective ranking to any album or video discussed in the book, so in appendices A and B the reader will find, along with the critical summary of each recording, an assigned rating of zero to five stars in half-star increments. At best, this approach will offer a quick, user-friendly manner of gauging the value and importance of a given release; at worst, it will provide the grist for some interesting parlor games.

Perhaps it would be best to explain appendix C, entitled "Recommended Further Listening," in the context of the book's function of providing a comprehensive critical survey related to the output of ELP. Besides their importance in the formation of the progressive rock style and their innovations in helping to create the rock concert as multimedia spectacle, I believe ELP are noteworthy for establishing the multikeyboard trio as a viable rock lineup (although the pioneering work here was done, of course, by Emerson's earlier trio, the Nice). I had hoped to have some opportunity in the main body of the text to informally trace the post-1970 history of the multikeyboard trio, but there was no place to do so; appendix C gave me that opportunity, by allowing me to chronologically present twelve albums released between 1970 and 2003 that outline the varied musical approaches that this lineup has engendered over the years. It also gave me another opportunity I otherwise wouldn't have had—to compare Emerson's work in the multikeyboard trio format to that of a number of his major rivals of the seventies. After all, what reader would have forgiven me if I hadn't compared and contrasted the work of Emerson and Rick Wakeman at some point?

The idea of presenting a critical survey is to some extent inseparable from the act of analysis, which brings me to the third major goal of this book: to undertake an analysis of ELP's major albums that examines music, lyrics, and (when relevant) cover art, and considers the band's aesthetic and philosophical worldview—that is, the "message"—conveyed by the confluence of these elements. Readers of *Rocking the Classics* will recall I undertook a similar task in chapter 5 of that book, analyzing four prog rock classics, one of which happened to be the "Tarkus" suite. My approach has not fundamentally changed here, although I hope it has grown more subtle and nuanced. My goal, above all, is to get you, the reader, as close to the music as possible. I understand music analysis has garnered a somewhat evil reputation among lay readers because the way it's rendered often tends to obfuscate rather than illuminate. While there is a certain amount of technical terminology I simply must use in order to adequately convey the musical processes that I describe, my goal is, whenever possible, to use terminology that can be understood by a college undergraduate who has taken a one-semester music appreciation survey course, and has gained at least a basic understanding of the elemental musical concepts (i.e., rhythm, melody, harmony, timbre, etc.). Even when my use of terminology must, by necessity, move into a more specialized terrain, I believe the committed lay reader can glean a lot through context.

Above all, I believe musical analysis should be about illuminating the processes through which music makes its impact, rather than about creating a self-referential taxonomy. Let's start with a small-scale example. Telling you that Keith Emerson uses a lot of quartal harmonies (chords consisting of stacked fourths) and bitonal chords (complex chords that contain two different chords that dissonantly "rub" against each other) will probably not tell you much of value unless you're a musician of some experience, or a keen student of twentieth-century music. However, if I tell you that the fourth is an unstable interval, and progressions of quartal harmonies therefore tend to have a restless, unsettled aspect, you may begin to become more attuned to an oft-noticed characteristic of ELP's music, its restless, urgently pressing quality, and you'll have an understanding of how quartal harmonies contribute to that quality. Likewise, if I tell you that bitonal chords tend to have a faintly "metallic" sheen when played on a keyboard instrument, you begin to understand from whence certain ELP pieces (the "Tarkus" suite, "Toccata") derive (at least in part) their futuristic character.

While chord choices can be important in determining the music's expressivity, chords are a fairly low-level musical element, and an analysis needs to move beyond such localized details to examine high-level functions—the "big picture," if you will—in order to say anything really meaningful about the music in question. Therefore, it's also needful to consider the music's large-scale structure, that is, the manner in which musical ideas are stitched together to form larger sections, and the nature of the interaction between the larger sections within the piece. Again, simply telling you that a specific piece is in sonata-allegro form or rondo form isn't terribly meaningful—what's far more useful is to consider large-scale structure as a process through which specific meanings are conveyed.

Here's a pertinent example. One adjective that has often been used in connection with the restless striving of ELP's most characteristic music is "heroic," and I've long felt that someone who could elucidate how music can convey heroism would be in a good position to explain the impact of an ELP classic like "Karn Evil 9". It was therefore my good fortune that shortly before I began writing this book, music theorist Scott Burnham published *Beethoven Hero* (1995), a study of the evocation of heroism in Beethoven's instrumental music (particularly in his Third Symphony, subtitled *Eroica*). While the particulars of ELP's "heroic manner" differ somewhat from Beethoven's—many of Burnham's observations tie in with Beethoven's use of sonata-allegro form, which ELP usually eschew—the general structural principles that Burnham sees at work in Beethoven's heroic manner can be perceived in some of ELP's most characteristic music as well. I will give a more specific description of Burnham's notion of "heroic structure"—that is, musical structure that's used to generate a sense of heroic struggle and attainment—and explain what I believe its application is to the ELP canon during the course of my discussion of "Karn Evil 9."

In sum, I hope my musical analyses will bring you closer to the music by pointing up as explicitly as possible precisely what you're hearing, and by pointing up how what you're hearing at any particular time is part of a larger process through which musical ideas are shaped to meet specific expressive goals. Of course, in "reading" a rock album, one can't focus exclusively on the music, so I also consider how the music's expressive content might be read in conjunction with lyrics, titles, and, when applicable, cover art to arrive at an overall "meaning." It is at this point that formal and cultural levels of analysis can be integrated, although, as I've already stated, I have found it useful to consider the large-scale structural processes of the music itself as metaphoric expressions of contemporaneous cultural dynamics—when and if it appears such a reading might be justified.

I must admit that I have been much impacted by Bill Martin's insistence that when addressing rock albums from what he calls the time of progressive rock (1968–78), one must keep in mind that the complete album is the basic unit of production (*Listening to the Future*, 133). Therefore, the order of songs on an album is seldom arbitrary and is often deeply meaningful, even if the album isn't a concept album per se; in other words, songs shouldn't be considered in isolation, because songs impact the meanings of adjacent songs by their very proximity, and the album as a whole is greater than the sum of its parts. This notion plays a particularly important role in my reading of ELP's debut album.

Of course, musical analysis plays a necessary role in responsible music criticism, so the two endeavors are related; furthermore, if one is hoping to chart the development and growth of style, one can't hope to do it without analysis. Two examples must suffice. First: what distinguishes Emerson's style with the Nice from his work with ELP? Besides the obvious addition of the Moog synthesizer to his instrumental palette with ELP, the crucial distinction is that his style with the Nice was based largely around a highly personal fusion of Bach and the blues and jazz, while in early ELP he added the influence of early-twentieth-century modernism as exemplified by Bartók and Ginastera, at which point the mature Emersonian style was fully in place. Second: how did Emerson's style change between early and mid-period ELP? His structures became more tightly woven and less radically sectional, he developed ideas across longer musical paragraphs, and he showed more sophistication in his use of tonality. Does that make his music of 1973–78 "better" than his music of ELP's earlier days? Well, that depends on one's viewpoint: along with the increasing compositional sophistication came a fondness for less dissonant chords and "cleaner" tone colors, and some fans complain about a decline of energy and power in his later music. My point here isn't to take sides (although I will make my stand later on in the text concerning where I think Emerson's music reached its ultimate confluence of sophistication and power), merely to point out that without solid analytical work, intelligent and thoughtful stylistic comparisons aren't possible, and one is reduced to making critical judgments on the purely subjective basis of "I like A, but I don't like B." Incidentally, although I believe that a study of ELP's stylistic practices is above all a study of the stylistic practices of Emerson, the band's chief composer, I do trace shifts in Lake's and Palmer's stylistic predilections as well.

One more remark about the analyses. When I wrote *Rocking the Classics*, I had yet to fully escape the classical musician's habit of thinking of the musical score as the ultimate arbiter of authority—the text, as scholars would say. I'm now far more comfortable with the notion of the recording as the text. Therefore, when pointing up musical details that I would like to draw your attention to during the course of an analysis, I give you the minute/second location, on the assumption that nearly all of you have put your LPs in storage boxes somewhere, and now listen to your ELP albums on a CD player with a digital minute/second counter.

ELP and Their Critics

There is one final matter that I must discuss here. When I began writing this book, I knew that a study of ELP would not be complete if the issue of ELP's critical reception were not fully addressed. Readers of *Rocking the Classics* will recall that I devoted a chapter to the critical reception of progressive rock. I stated the obvious—as a style, progressive rock has for a very long time been despised by the vast majority of the critics who write for the major rock journals—and I initiated an inquiry into what aspects of the rock establishment's prevailing ideology has driven the critics to oppose, with such virulence, nearly everything that progressive rock stands for.

Progressive rock is deeply indebted to the philosophical tenets of nineteenth-century Romanticism, and its ideology is founded on five main premises: idealism, authenticity, transcendence, the artist as prophet figure, and progress. By "idealism," I mean an idealistic belief, on the part of both the musicians and their audiences, that the music is meaningful, that is, it is capable of bearing a message. By "authenticity" I mean a belief, again shared by the musicians and their audiences, that meaningful music is original music, that is, music that reflects the perceptions, thoughts, and feelings of an individual, and therefore bears the distinctive stylistic attributes of that individual's authorship.[29] Furthermore, "real" (i.e., authentic) music demands genuine engagement from its listeners by confronting them with the unusual and unexpected, pushes boundaries through its stylistic innovations and through the technical demands it makes on its interpreters, and stands in stark contrast to establishment-approved "pop music," attractive and easily consumed but inauthentic tripe produced, cookie-cutter like, on the corporate musical assembly line.[30] By "transcendence," I refer to a tendency to view music in nearly

---

[29] Edward Kravitt, in "Romanticism Today," *Musical Quarterly* (Spring 1992): 93–109, argues that Romanticism, in its many facets, is best defined as an aesthetic of self-expression in the face of social isolation and alienation, which leads the Artist to turn within. Kravitt sees this single definition as explaining the many attributes and attitudes that have traditionally been associated with Romanticism: nature as a source of mystical revelation, a fascination with dreams, myths, legends, and the supernatural, a nostalgia for the European Middle Ages and other bygone eras, an emphasis on subjective emotional states, and a yearning for the otherworldly and infinite. As Kravitt puts it, "The core of romanticism is a pessimistic view of life. Existing society is oppressive because it thwarts the romanticist's fondest hopes. Fulfillment can be achieved only in fantasy . . . But neither does self-imposed isolation bring gratification since this engenders solitude and sadness" (100–101). Thus the sense of unfulfilled yearning that permeates Romanticism. Kravitt, after M. H. Abrams, also sees Romanticism as characterized by "a creative process operating under the impulse of feeling," rather than an act of craft undertaken to please patron or public (98). I do not argue that progressive rock undertakes a wholesale revival of Romantic aesthetics and ideology—prog draws from many other sources as well and, on the whole, is more optimistic in its outlook than is bona fide Romanticism—but I do assert that progressive rock cannot be adequately understood without acknowledging its debt to Romanticism.

[30] Nineteenth-century composer and music critic Robert Schumann coined a word for the "squares" (as the hippies would have called them) who didn't value authenticity in music: he called them "philistines." It should also be noted that for twentieth-century popular music commentators, "authenticity" has taken on an additional connotation: music associated with socially disadvantaged groups (blacks, rural whites, etc.) that has (or is supposed to have) not been corrupted (i.e., watered down) by commercialism.

religious terms as a potential source of spiritual transformation. This view of music (and of the arts more generally) is fairly modern (think Schiller, Schopenhauer, E. T. A. Hoffman, Nietzsche) in its specifics. In a more general sense, though, it can ultimately be traced back to neo-Platonism and the belief that an ultimate Good, Beauty, and Truth exists, and is imperfectly expressed in great art, the contemplation of which can lead one ever closer to the ultimate good, that is, God. By "artist as prophet figure," I mean the belief that the Artist is far more than a mere entertainer, but is a kind of secular prophet bearing a cosmic message from the Beyond of a potentially transformative, even redemptive nature. Finally, by "progress" I mean the belief that style is not and should not be static: it doesn't merely change, but it grows, develops, evolves into something that is constantly better.[31]

My idea at the outset of writing this book was to cite two or three reviews of each of ELP's ten albums from the seventies, especially reviews that appeared in the "big four" (see above), and to tease out of these reviews, and then analyze, both the ideology of the critics, and the aspects of progressive rock's ideology that the critics found to be particularly threatening to their own. Early on, however, I noticed something very surprising. In the reviews of the first four ELP albums published between 1970 and 1972, one detects relatively little hostility against ELP or their ambitions; some of the reviews, in fact, are positively glowing. It's not until 1973–74 that one begins to detect hostility against the entire premise of the ELP project, and even then the venomous tone isn't unanimous; only in the reviews published after 1976 does one begins to see the indictments against ELP, and progressive rock more generally, presented in the utterly predictable tone and language that those of us who have followed rock journalism since the midseventies have become accustomed to.[32] Clearly, contrary to the claims of the

---

[31] I can imagine some of my readers thinking, "Wasn't rock culture of the late sixties/early seventies period as a whole deeply invested in this ideology?" My answer: to some degree yes, but not to the same degree as progressive rock. For instance, the blues orthodoxists themselves were deeply invested in the notions of authenticity and idealism as I've described them here, somewhat less in the notions of transcendence and artist as prophet figure, and were hostile to the notion of progress as here described.

[32] To my knowledge, I am the first English-language author to address the ideological shift in rock criticism circa 1973–74, and possibly one of the first two to do so in any language. While working on this book and formulating this thesis, I was contacted by a French-speaking author, Christophe Pirenne, whose dissertation "Le rock progressif anglais (1966–1977)," completed at the University of Liège in 2000, includes a section that documents this ideological shift in rock criticism during the same period (1973–74) I believe it to have taken place. Pirenne has since reworked his dissertation into a book, *Le Rock Progressif Anglais (1966–1977)* (Paris: Honoré Champion, 2005); pp. 41–47 address the shift in the critical reception of progressive rock.

modern rock critical establishment that intelligent rock critics have always believed progressive rock was a fool's venture founded on all the wrong premises, there was a time when a sizable body of rock's critical establishment was sympathetic to the goals of progressive rock. But then something changed: not in progressive rock itself, because there was no sudden change in progressive rock circa 1973–74, but within the rock critical establishment. As I pondered this turn of events, I was surprised to recall a startlingly similar situation in the musical world of post-revolutionary Russia.

After the Bolsheviks' seizure of power in 1917, Vladimir Lenin articulated the Soviet regime's official position on the arts: "Art belongs to the people. It must have its deepest roots in the broad masses of workers. It must be understood and loved by them. It must be rooted in, and grow with, their feelings, thoughts, and desires."[33] Lenin didn't merely advocate artists and composers appealing to the least common denominator by simplifying their work to a level of mind-numbing vulgarity and simplemindedness; part of his vision involved improving the general education of the Russian people, and thus raising their cultural receptivity. Therefore, well into the 1920s, the regime encouraged (albeit warily) experimentation and some degree of cultural exchange with the West. The 1920s turned out to be a period of musical fermentation in the U.S.S.R., witnessing the atonal innovations of Nicolai Roslavets and the futurism of Alexander Mosolov, who in works like *The Iron Foundry* sought to evoke the sounds of heavy industry in symphonic music.

This period of innovation was not to last. In the twenties a group called the Association of Contemporary Music had been formed to support the belief that the ideology of communism could best be nurtured in the arts by innovation and exploration. Almost immediately, a rival group, the Russian Association of Proletarian Music, arose, arguing that music of "the people" must be simple, even primitive, and free from any trace of artistic pretension. After Lenin's death in 1924, Josef Stalin began to assume control of the Communist party, and as he strengthened his position, he gradually came to impose his own ideas on the role of the arts in society. Stalin saw the usefulness of the arts mainly in terms of their ability to serve as a vehicle for propaganda. Needless to say, within a few years, the Association for Contemporary Music was no more, Roslavets and

---

[33] Vladimir Lenin, quoted by Robert P. Morgan, *Twentieth-Century Music* (New York: W. W. Norton, 1991), 236. In the following discussion, I am much indebted to Morgan's excellent short summary of the two rival artistic ideologies in the Soviet Union during the 1920s; see 236–38. A much deeper and more nuanced sense of the struggle between these rival artistic ideologies, and the role of Lenin and Stalin in these struggles, can be gained by reading Solomon Volkov's *Shostakovich and Stalin: The Extraordinary Relationship Between the Great Composer and the Brutal Dictator* (London: Little, Brown, 2004).

Mosolov were silenced, and the ideology supported by the Russian Association of Proletarian Music—an ideology now known as Socialist Realism—had become the official ideology governing the arts for the entire Soviet state.

Fast forward to the late sixties and early seventies. I see the two rival ideologies present in rock criticism of the time mirroring, to an almost uncanny degree, the rival ideologies present in the Soviet Union's artistic world of the 1920s. The first ideology I will henceforth call "utopian synthesism." It was deeply invested in Romantic notions of idealism, authenticity, transcendence, and progress, and heartily believed the view expressed by the Association of Contemporary Music during the 1920s that social progress (i.e., evolution) would be coupled with stylistic progress (i.e., evolution) in the arts.[34] One senses that at least some of the utopian synthesists believed that the stylistic synthesis taking place in rock music during the late sixties, as its boundaries were being enormously expanded through the importation of elements derived from Western classical music, jazz, and middle Eastern music, was directly related to the cataclysmic societal changes they saw going on around them at the time. Certainly the critical consensus was that the rapid stylistic expansion of rock was a great step forward for the music. Here's music journalist Harvey Pekar writing in 1968:

> What we may be witnessing is the creation of a new, as yet unlabeled form of music, as America around the turn of the century saw the development of jazz . . . Among the elements being melted down are blues, country and western, near Eastern, Indian, and baroque forms. Increasingly important is the technique of producing novel, exciting effects by using the potential of tape.[35]

There is a palpable tone of excitement and eager expectation in Pekar's prose, and through the early seventies it's easy to find reviews written by critics who see the proper work of the rock musician as exploring the possibilities of this kind of utopian musical synthesis, and who praise ELP for their contribution to the enterprise. Indeed, reviews of this type will be quoted in the present work.

After 1972, though, a coterie of critics championing a far different ideology began to rise to the forefront, and the critical reception of ELP

---

[34] The idea that social progress and stylistic progress in the arts logically go hand and hand first emerges in the nineteenth century: it is explicitly articulated by Schumann, Liszt, and others. See Michael Chanan, *From Handel to Hendrix: The Composer in the Public Sphere* (London: Verso, 1999), particularly chapter four, "The Romantic Ascendancy," and also chap. 5, 156.

[35] Harvey Pekar, "From Rock to ???," *Downbeat*, May 2, 1968.

and their progressive rock colleagues began to suffer accordingly. The ideology of these critics, aptly described as "blues orthodoxy" by Bill Martin (who calls the critics themselves "blues orthodoxists") almost eerily parallels the thinking of the Russian Association of Proletarian Music during the 1920s. Simply stated, rock is the people's music. In order to retain its vitality, rock must remain in a simple, even primitive state, and must be kept free of any trace of artistic pretension. The most elemental and vital body of music in twentieth-century American popular music is the blues: therefore, rock music must maintain its direct stylistic link with the blues at all costs. Between the early and mid-seventies, a group of influential critics spearheaded by Lester Bangs (*Creem*), Dave Marsh (*Rolling Stone*), and Robert Christgau (*Village Voice*) championed this ideology with such vigor and, at times, venom, that the utopian synthesists' ideology became increasingly unfashionable. The rise of punk rock in 1976 was widely seen as confirming all the major tenets of blues orthodoxy, and after 1976 it was no longer intellectually respectable for a critic to maintain the utopian synthesists' position.[36]

That the two competing ideologies that I have here articulated existed, that the two ideologies stood for the values I have described, and that between 1973 and 1976 the position of the utopian synthesists was totally eclipsed by that of the blues orthodoxists is undeniable. If one is skeptical, all one has to do to see the shift of predominance from one ideology to the other is simply read, in chronological order, the reviews I have cited, throughout the text, of ELP's ten albums of 1970–79. Obviously, several questions are raised here that go beyond the scope of the present book to answer. How did the ideology of the blues orthodoxists come to eclipse that of the utopian synthesists so quickly, and so completely? And why?

At this point, I can only give tentative answers, especially for "why." The rise of punk rock was widely interpreted as confirming the failure of sixties utopianism as a political/cultural ideology, and played a huge role

---

[36] Although Paul Stump does not delve into the issue of progressive rock's critical reception to the degree I do here, implicit in his narrative is the notion that what I am calling the utopian synthesist view was at one time the mainstream view of rock's critical establishment, and that this ideology faded during the mid-1970s. Stump appears to see Tony Palmer's seventeen-part history of popular music, *All You Need is Love*, made for London Weekend Television in 1976, as not only the most erudite and influential expression of the utopian synthesist ideology, but as the last time it had significant influence in rock historiography (*The Music's All That Matters*, 191). Later in his narrative, Stump rails, with some justification, against what he views as the hypocritical interpretation of "Authenticity" by Palmer and his allies (206). However, he never even mentions Bangs, Christgau, or Marsh, and never seems to explicitly recognize the existence of what Martin and I call blues orthodoxy, much less systematically articulate the ideology of progressive rock's critics. For this reason, it cannot be said that Stump adequately addresses the critical reception of progressive rock.

in discrediting the utopian synthesists' position. It's also tempting to see the eclipse of utopian synthesism by blues orthodoxy as paralleling the more or less contemporaneous eclipse of late modernism by postmodernism; when one reads Bangs, Marsh, or Christgau, one is conscious of many of the same attitudes (relativism, hostility to traditional notions of absolutes of good, beauty, and truth) that one encounters in the postmodernists. On the other hand, it's even more tempting to see blues orthodoxy as a reappearance, under different social, political, and historical conditions, of Socialist Realism. As divergent as postmodernism and Socialist Realism are, they do have two points in common that I suspect would be a good starting point for further discussion of this issue: a suspicion towards high culture's (in other words, classical music's) claims of transcendental value, and a conviction that the value of art rests first and foremost in its political content.

Clearly, though, the "why" of this question is going to require a lot more discussion. The "how" might be somewhat easier to answer: blues orthodoxy had three compelling champions in Bangs, Marsh, and Christgau, while utopian synthesism had no champion of similar polemic skill. I sincerely believe if the utopian synthesist position had even one writer arguing on its behalf with the vigor, fervor, and distinctive prose style of Lester Bangs, the history of rock journalism could have developed much differently than it did. But utopian synthesism lacked a compelling champion, and the blues orthodoxists steamrolled their competition.

If documenting the blues orthodoxists' attainment of total hegemony in the rock critical establishment goes beyond the scope of this book, however, critiquing their position does not. I undertake this critique in three stages. First, I examine the blues orthodoxists' claim that by attempting to "elevate" rock and make it "respectable" through borrowing from classical music, progressive rock musicians actually drained rock music of its oppositional energy. Is this a valid charge? Is the only "oppositional" rock that which is clearly blues-based and therefore a product of "the people"? Or does the twentieth-century modernist aesthetic that influenced Keith Emerson also project an "oppositional" energy? I take this question up in discussing ELP's most challenging, modernist-influenced work, *Tarkus*.

Second, is it true, as the blues orthodoxists charge, that progressive rock drew liberally on the forms and techniques of classical music merely to be able to bask in the reflected glory of the Great Tradition? Or did bands like ELP draw on classical music almost instinctively, recognizing its potential to open up a new set of possibilities for rock music to more fully express the concerns and preoccupations of the late sixties? I grapple with this question in my discussion of ELP's *Pictures at an Exhibition*, and I consider how the critical reception of ELP may have been different if

Emerson, Lake and Palmer had been more articulate spokesmen and agitators for their musical ideology.

Finally, in chapter 10 I address the oft-repeated accusations that prog is "cold" and "unemotional" because (1) it's too far removed from rock's "proper" R-and-B lineage, (2) it's too complex to be felt viscerally, and (3) it's too reliant on technology, which interferes with the performer-audience relationship. Directly afterwards, I turn my attention to the heart of darkness beating unseen in the chest of blues orthodoxy: the vulgar, debased primitivism that is the taproot of the blues orthodoxists' ideology. Specifically, I consider the blues orthodoxists' dubious notion of the blues as the taproot of all that is "natural" and "authentic" in music, and the even more dubious view of the bluesman as a kind of "noble savage." I will argue that blues orthodoxy is simply a particularly simple-minded and corrupt manifestation of a kind of Romantic primitivism that can be traced back to at least the eighteenth century, and perhaps much earlier, in Western thought.

If I am sounding somewhat angry at this point, it's because I am; not because blues orthodoxists don't like progressive rock, but because the hegemony of blues orthodoxy within the rock establishment has become so complete during the past twenty-five years that debate about the "canonical" interpretation of rock history is virtually nonexistent. Most younger rock journalists/critics have no idea that the utopian synthesist view ever existed, much less that it was once a respectable position to hold, because the blues orthodoxists have written it out of the record with such an Orwellian zeal. Who do you suppose controls rock historiography? The institutions (such as the ridiculous Rock and Roll Hall of Fame, an oxymoron if ever there were one) that bestow or withhold validation not just on individual bands, but entire styles? Who do you suppose puts together the "official" histories like the *Rolling Stone History of Rock and Roll* and the ten-part PBS *History of Rock* television series? Who do you suppose exerts, to this day, enormous influence over which bands get primo exposure in the major journals and on the airwaves? If you answered "rock journalists, critics, radio and TV programmers steeped in blues orthodoxy," give yourself a gold star.

For me, the most depressing aspect of the hegemony of blues orthodoxy is the degree to which many supposedly autonomous and independent popular music "scholars" of academia toe the blues orthodoxy line with a fervor that might have startled Lester Bangs, and pass it on in their popular music history textbooks as if it's Gospel truth. It's as if the story of American politics of the last fifty years had been written only by people who served in the Nixon and Reagan administrations, or the direct understudies of such people—with the caveat that even this example may overstate the diversity of perspective one encounters in most post-1980 rock historiography, criticism, and journalism.

In sum: blues orthodoxy is an ideology, not divine revelation. Under a different set of historical circumstances, it's entirely possible that the utopian synthesists' ideology could have triumphed, and then rock histories would be written very differently than they are, with progressive rock being viewed as the stylistic pinnacle towards which all previous rock music had been developing, instead of (as per blues orthodoxy) a bizarre evolutionary dead end. At this late date in rock's history, when its most vital years are long behind it, I'm not a quixotic dreamer hoping against hope the utopian synthesist position will suddenly reemerge in triumph. I simply seek an admission from the current popular music establishment (both in the Industry and in academia) that such an ideology once existed, was once a respectable position for a rock critic to hold, and must be taken seriously if a responsible and intellectually honest history of sixties and seventies rock is ever to be undertaken. If I succeed in this, then this book has not been written in vain.

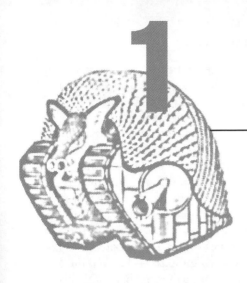

Keith Emerson

Early Years and Apprenticeship (1944–1970)

Early Years

Keith Noel Emerson was born November 2, 1944, in Todmorden, Lancashire (now West Yorkshire), in England's Pennine Uplands. Neither his father Noel nor his mother Dorothy were natives to the region: the couple had moved to Todmorden during World War II fearing a German invasion of England's south coast. Indeed, in March 1945, when Keith was just five months old, his mother and paternal grandmother, with Keith in tow, returned to south England, settling in Worthing, on the Sussex coast; Keith's father joined them a year later, in March 1946, after he was demobilized from the British army. Worthing was to be Keith's home until he was nearly twenty-one.

In *Emerson, Lake and Palmer: The Show That Never Ends*, Emerson's upbringing was described as "comfortable, worry-free and middle class."[1] This may oversimplify matters somewhat. In 1999, Emerson told Richard Stellar, "My parents were not wealthy people. My father struggled just to maintain the family. I used to mix with friends who had brothers and sisters. I was an only child, and I would ask my mum 'Why don't I have a brother or sister' and she would answer because we can't afford it."[2] When Emerson was seven, he and his parents moved to a newly constructed housing estate some four miles west of Worthing: it was to be Keith's home until 1965, and his parents' home until 1974, when Keith bought them a bungalow in Lancing, Sussex. In his early years, Emerson's father worked as a telephone engineer, and his mother as a school cook supervisor: by Keith's teenage years, his father had become a chief techni-

---

[1] Forrester, Hanson, and Askew, *Emerson, Lake and Palmer*, 14.
[2] Keith Emerson, quoted by Richard Stellar, "The Closed to Home Interview: Raw Meat and Emerson," http://www.interstellar9.com/emerson/interview.htm.

cian for British Telecom. Nonetheless, it might be more accurate to describe the Emerson family's circumstances as *petit bourgeois*—in American lingo, lower middle class—than as "middle-class prosperity."[3]

Keith's earliest musical memories were of his father playing accordion: "My father played accordion in an Army band, and he would occasionally drag it out, strap it on, and play it, and he would make beautiful music. But it was too big for me to pick up. My father wasn't a big man, but it was amazing how he could play it. I still have it, and I still can't play it! It's too big, too heavy."[4] Soon after Keith's family made the move to the council estate, there was a new addition to the home: an upright piano. Young Keith watched spellbound as his father played by ear, and soon tried his own hand at picking out melodies on the keyboard. Noel Emerson watched his son's progress with growing interest—he even built up the pedals, since Keith was initially too short to reach them with his feet—and, a bit less than a year after the instrument had arrived, announced to his son that he was to commence lessons, so as to be able to play "properly." At age eight, Keith Emerson's formal music education was underway.

His first teacher was an elderly lady named Miss Marshall; Emerson recalls this venerable woman, whom he believes to have been nearly eighty at the time, as "a sweet old lady with plump hands that looked like a pair of inflated rubber gloves."[5] She came to the Emerson flat on Saturday mornings, and quickly started her young charge on a regimen of scales, arpeggios, and technical studies. Emerson recalls that he resented the scales and arpeggios, but since he was not allowed to play with his friends until he had practiced half an hour, he submitted to learning them. Perhaps Emerson's daunting technique of his later years can be traced back to his earliest lessons with Miss Marshall.

When Emerson was roughly ten, Miss Marshall retired, and he was shunted off to a new teacher, Madame Ethel Collinge: "I had to cycle to see her. She was everything her title represented—dominant and imposing, barely tolerating me as a small person let alone an even smaller pianist."[6] It was also at this time that Emerson served a brief stint as an Anglican choirboy: one wonders if this experience may have contributed to the cathedral-like ambience of such ELP classics as "Jerusalem," "The Endless Enigma," and "The Only Way."

After about a year with Madame Collinge, Emerson's parents placed him with a new piano teacher whose influence was to be a turning point:

[3] As Martyn Hanson does in *Hang on to a Dream*, 12.
[4] Keith Emerson, quoted by Stellar, "Closed to Home Interview.".
[5] Emerson, *Pictures*, 14.
[6] Emerson, *Pictures*, 16.

Mrs. Smith was to rescue me from apathy and shake me into some kind of performer. She was young, married and, by my immature standards, sexually attractive. Mrs. Smith made me feel ashamed if I failed her expectations. I may have had a secret crush on her, while she was honest with me, along with Mum and Dad, saying "He has a gift, it's up to him if he really wants to use it."[7]

Under Mrs. Smith's tutelage, Emerson gradually became acquainted with the great composers and the standard classical piano repertoire. Mrs. Smith also began entering him in performance and sight-reading competitions. Emerson recalls "You sat down and played before an adjudicator, and then when you finished he told you what you did wrong. I did rather well, though, coming in second or third in a Bach category."[8] It's significant that Emerson mentions Bach: of all the classical masters, it is Bach whose influence on him was the most lasting. Emerson's music, from his time with the Nice, displays an impressive degree of familiarity with Bach's keyboard oeuvre, evidenced by the plentiful quotations of Bach's keyboard works in Emerson's solos. More importantly, one hears echoes of Bach in Emerson's motoristic eighth- and sixteenth-note figurations, his linear keyboard textures, and his use of chord progressions based on baroque ground bass figures.[9] Emerson studied with Mrs. Smith until he was nearly 18, and although he never took her advice to enter London's Royal College of Music, she clearly was a pivotal figure in his musical development.

By the time Emerson was thirteen, another influence was exerting an equally strong pull on his attention: American popular music. This influence exerted itself from several directions at once. First, there were the popular British pianists of the time—Joe Henderson, Winifred Atwell, Russ Conway—who played a kind of bowdlerized "barrelhouse" piano stemming from British Music Hall traditions. Second, there was the early rock-and-roll piano style of Jerry Lee Lewis and Little Richard. Although Emerson professed to be largely unmoved by the first wave of American rock and roll that swept Britain during the late fifties, the boogie-woogie piano style of Lewis and Little Richard, wherein the left hand pounds out simple twelve-bar blues progressions in steady triplets while the right hand either adds its own chords or spins out bluesy melodic lines, made a deep, indeed permanent, impact on Emerson's playing.[10] Third, and perhaps

---

[7] Emerson, *Pictures*, 19.

[8] Keith Emerson, quoted by Pethel, "Keith Emerson," 4.

[9] Here's Greg Lake: "I think he [Bach] was a bigger influence than a lot of people give him credit for. I mean, look at Keith. I don't know whether he thinks he was influenced by Bach, but I think he was." Greg Lake, quoted by James Johnson, "Under the Influence: Greg Lake," *New Musical Express*, June 9, 1973, 7.

[10] Boogie-woogie is an adaptation of twelve-bar blues to the piano. It can be traced back to the late 1920s, and enjoyed a brief vogue of popularity in the early forties: Meade Lux Lewis, Albert Ammons, and Jimmy Yancey are noted practitioners.

most importantly, was stride piano. Stride, for those not familiar with it, is a jazz piano style of the twenties and thirties wherein the left hand simultaneously punches out a bass line in the piano's deeper register on the beat and strikes chords in a somewhat higher register on the off beats: the right hand, in the meantime, spins out rapid-fire single note melodic lines. The general textural approach of stride derives from turn-of-the-century ragtime piano, but the tempos are much faster (thus the "striding" left hand), the left-hand figurations and syncopated right-hand melodic lines more complex.

Noel Emerson was himself a fan of stride pianists such as Thomas "Fats" Waller, a classic exponent of the style, and Art Tatum, an incredible virtuoso whose work bridges stride and the swing jazz style of the later thirties and forties. He began buying his son sheet music transcriptions of some of Waller's and Tatum's performances when Keith was around thirteen, and by his midteens Keith was capable of fluently arranging Tin Pan Alley classics in stride piano style, as is evident in the medley "Nicola"/"Silver Shoes"/"I'll See You in My Dreams," recorded when he was just fourteen and included on the 2002 *Emerson Plays Emerson* album. Another seminal experience for Keith seems to have been a stint he served in his midteens as accompanist for his Aunt Wendy's dance classes. Emerson recalls, "At the beck and call of my Aunt Wendy [his father's sister] leading the class, I'd pull out the appropriate sheet music to accompany anything from tap to ballet."[11] Blair Pethel is almost certainly correct to surmise that his stint as an accompanist for his aunt's dance classes provided the initial forum for Emerson to develop what later became a fluent and highly imaginative approach to thematic transformation: "This [the dance school accompanist role] taught him to change the character of whatever he was playing and developed his ability to improvise as he learned to adapt the same piece of music to slow 3/4, quick 2/4, or whatever other meter was dictated by the style of the dance being performed."[12]

It was also during this period that Emerson began experimenting with interpenetrating jazz and classical music; as he told Pethel, he was wont to amuse his school friends by playing familiar themes by Bach, Tchaikovsky, and other classical masters in jazz rhythms and figurations. At the time, it was all in fun; but one sees here the kernel of the concept of "rocking the classics" that would, in another decade or so, be so crucial to the nascent progressive rock style in general, and to Emerson in particular. Indeed, by the time he was fourteen or fifteen, many of the building blocks of Emerson's mature style, even his mature musical phi-

---

[11] Emerson, *Pictures*, 25.
[12] Pethel, "Keith Emerson," 5.

losophy, were already in place: a deep familiarity with classical music in general, and the music of Bach in particular; a growing familiarity with, and command of, boogie-woogie, barrelhouse, and stride piano styles; a rapidly developing fluency in thematic transformation; and a fondness for interpenetrating European classical and American popular styles.

In 1961, Emerson graduated from West Tarring School and enrolled in Worthing College of Further Education. By now he was growing more and more interested in music, and less and less interested in other scholarly pursuits, especially as he belatedly discovered the more modern jazz styles of the forties and fifties. It was at this time his father took him to a rehearsal of the Worthing Youth Swing Orchestra—a jazz band for young people sponsored by the Worthing Council that played the big band jazz classics of Count Basie, Duke Ellington, and other icons of the Swing Era. The Orchestra's director was impressed with Emerson's technique, but somewhat surprised to learn he wasn't familiar with the chord symbols of jazz notation. In order to join the Orchestra, Emerson taught himself jazz chord symbols, and began to address the art of improvising over the thirty-two-bar chord changes that are typical of jazz. It was also around this time that Emerson became aware of the modern (i.e., post-stride) approach to jazz piano performance, where the pianist's left hand "comps"—that is, plays off-beat staccato chords—rather than laying out both bass line and accompanying chords in the manner of stride: "Suddenly I heard Dudley Moore. He played this style that sounded great. I couldn't figure out how he was doing it. When I tried to imitate him it came out like Fats Waller in the left hand and Dudley Moore in the right. That's when I realized what the advantages of having a bass player were."[13] Having revamped his playing to reflect this more modern approach to jazz piano technique, Emerson formed his first trio with the drummer and bassist of the Swing Orchestra. Dubbed the Keith Emerson Trio, they played at bingo halls, rifle club dinners, and similar functions. By now Emerson had discovered the music of Hampton Hawes, Oscar Peterson, Bud Powell, Dave Brubeck, and other modern jazz pianists, and he was anxious to work the licks of these masters into the performances of his own trio. This didn't always go down well with the bingo hall crowd: as Emerson later told Blair Pethel, "We lost some gigs due to the fact we were self indulgent and used to go off into these long jams. People didn't want to hear that."[14]

In the summer of 1962, Emerson sat for his final exams. He passed in one subject: chemistry. However, a field trip to a local laboratory con-

[13] Keith Emerson, quoted by Dominic Milano, "Keith Emerson," *Contemporary Keyboard*, October 1977, 32.
[14] Pethel, "Keith Emerson," 6.

vinced him that chemistry would not be the career of his dreams: the man who showed him around the lab was missing a hand as the result of an industrial accident. Not wanting to risk going through life as a one-handed pianist, Emerson decided chemistry was not a prudent career choice. In fact, at this point Emerson knew what he wanted to do: be a musician. However, he was also aware that his parents, his father in particular, were becoming increasingly concerned about what they felt was his unhealthy fixation on music. Emerson recalls his father telling him, "Just keep it as a sideline. It'll be a nice way to make a little extra cash on the weekends, but you must have security. A life of music is not secure. A career with a governmental department such as mine with the General Post Office [which oversaw British Telecom] is much more secure."[15]

Thus advised, Emerson took a job at Lloyd's Bank Registrars Department, where he was assigned to the computer department. His real preoccupation, however, was the Keith Emerson Trio, which was now playing some gigs in nearby Brighton at Harrison's Bar. It was at Harrison's that Emerson met Jed Armstrong, a drummer who initiated Emerson into what might be called the modern jazz scene—Jack Kerouac's *On The Road*, beatnik fashion, and, of course, the most recent Blue Note label recordings of such cutting-edge figures as Thelonius Monk. From Armstrong, Emerson imbibed the Romantic notion of Authenticity that had become a part and parcel of the post-Swing jazz scene. According to this ethos, the vast majority of popular music is puerile, soulless, and mindless mass-produced corporate swill, intended for consumption by the philistines, the brain-dead masses who were capable of comprehending nothing else. The only *real* music is music that demands genuine engagement from its listeners by confronting them with the unusual and the unexpected, that shows the unique stamp of its creator, and that pushes boundaries in terms of its stylistic innovations and the technical demands it makes on its interpreters. This attitude came to deeply permeate the thinking of Emerson and the other founding fathers of progressive rock.

Emerson didn't last very long at Lloyd's. His supervisor, a Mr. Wells, put him on six-week probation for continual tardiness. Emerson shaped up for a while, but eventually was discovered sitting with his feet on a filing cabinet, reading the latest issue of *Melody Maker*, through which he had become aware of the nascent blues revival scene in London spearheaded by Cyril Davies, Alexis Korner, and a few like-minded spirits. Without firing him outright, Mr. Wells hinted it would be wise for Emerson to submit his resignation. At his farewell party, Emerson's coworkers gave him an alarm clock as a going away present.

---

[15] Emerson, *Pictures*, 29.

In 1964, after having secured a job at a teleprinter factory, Emerson, with some financial help from his father, purchased a Hammond L-100 electric organ at the Portsmouth Organ Center. The L-100 was not Hammond's top-line organ: that would have been the B-3 and C-3, which were far beyond Emerson's budget at this time. Nonetheless, the L-100 had all the main Hammond features—two manuals, a pedal keyboard, many drawbars, several percussion and vibrato settings, and, above all, the widely admired Hammond tone-wheel generator, which gives electric Hammond organs their characteristic warm, dirty, overdriven, mechanically generated sound. Emerson had been drawn to the Hammond both because he had become highly dissatisfied with the condition of the house pianos he had been playing on and therefore wanted a portable (maybe I should say "portable") keyboard, and because he had discovered the recordings of jazz organists Jimmy Smith and Jack McDuff. Emerson was especially fascinated by McDuff's tacky, percussive organ sound, and, after much experimentation, he discovered the secret behind the sound: it was necessary to mike the Leslie speaker[16] and run the microphone through a Marshall amplifier whose treble and presence settings were turned all the way up, thus exaggerating the Hammond's contact sound, the so-called key click. Of course, this discovery was still somewhat in the future.

At the time, it was unusual for Hammonds to be ported to small-town gigs; they were rather expensive, and rather difficult to transport. Soon word began to spread around Worthing and the surrounding environs that Emerson was gigging with a Hammond, which served to increase his profile in the local musical scene. He formed a band called John Brown's Bodies that was resident at Brighton's Pop Inn: JBB were a four piece (organ-guitar-bass-drums) that pursued Emerson's jazz interests, while also tapping into the electric British blues sound that was all the rage in London at the time.

One band that was part of London's burgeoning blues scene was Gary Farr and the T-Bones. Although a popular live act in southern England, none of the T-Bones' singles had been a hit, and by 1965 Farr was looking for a new angle that might help to distinguish his band from its many competitors. Having been impressed by the sound of the Graham Bond Organization and Georgie Fame's Blue Flames—both bands were fronted by Hammond organists—Farr decided he would like a Hammond organist in his band as well. He mentioned this to the band's drummer, Brian

---

[16] For those not familiar with Leslies, they are large stand-alone speakers designed to be attached to the Hammond: they contain large rotors whose spin rate can be adjusted, resulting in different levels of vibrato. The purpose of the Leslie rotor is to distribute the instrument's sound multidirectionally, creating an artificial sense of large space and therefore a cathedral-like ambience.

Walkley, who recalled having sat in with the Keith Emerson Trio in Brighton in times past, and suggested to Farr that they might want to drive down to Brighton to check out John Brown's Bodies. They did so, and Farr, suitably impressed, offered Emerson a job in the T-Bones. To Farr's surprise, Emerson initially declined—apparently there was still some lingering angst on Emerson's part about making a career of music—but Walkley eventually persuaded him to join, and during the summer of 1965, Emerson gave his notice to the teleprinter factory and became an official member of the T-Bones. Still something of a homebody, Emerson initially insisted on staying with his parents and commuting to gigs in and around London: however, this soon proved impractical, and just a bit shy of his twenty-first birthday, Emerson moved to the capital. His days as a semiprofessional local pianist and organist were over: his professional apprenticeship was just beginning.

The T-Bones

At the time Emerson joined the T-Bones, the band's personnel included Farr (lead vocals), Walkley (drums), Stuart Parks (bass), and Winston Weatherall (guitar). The T-Bones were a straight-ahead blues revival band along the lines of John Mayall's Bluesbreakers: they frequently played at London's Marquee Club and Richmond, Surrey's Crawdaddy Club (the nexus of the British blues scene), as well as undertaking short tours of clubs and universities elsewhere in England. A particularly memorable gig for Emerson came on October 15, 1965, when the T-Bones backed their namesake, legendary blues guitarist and songwriter Aaron "T-Bone" Walker (best known for his late-forties classic "Stormy Monday") at the Marquee. In late November and early December 1965, the T-Bones were part of a package tour that included Manfred Mann, the Yardbirds (with Jeff Beck as lead guitarist), and the Mark Leeman 5, among others. The drummer of the latter band was Brian Davison, who was soon to play an important part in Emerson's career.

The T-Bones' manager was nominally Giorgio Gomelsky, a key player in the midsixties British blues revival. In fact, however, Gomelsky was much too involved with the Yardbirds to give the T-Bones much attention, so the band brought in another manager, Tony Secunda. Soon, however, Gary Farr's brother Rikki began to muscle his way into the band's command structure, first unofficially, later as the actual manager. This led to a shift in both personnel and musical direction. Emerson had this to say about the first lineup of the T-Bones that he played with: "The T-Bones tried to be very true to their style of T-Bone Walker and Howlin' Wolf stuff. All based on 12-bar rhythm-and-blues. But it was a bit more adventurous. Kind of louder and a bit more electronic. They were like the

Yardbirds, who produced a commercialized form of R & B."[17] In early 1966, bassist Parks and guitarist Weatherall were forced out by the Farr brothers, and Walkley and Emerson were obliged to recruit replacements. Parks was replaced by Keith Lee Jackson (who henceforth went by Lee, so as not to be confused with Emerson), a veteran of Mayall's and Alexis Corner's blues outfits, while Weatherall was replaced by David "Cyrano" Langston, a disciple of the Who's guitarist Pete Townsend. These changes did not go down well with Walkley, who left the band in February 1966 and was replaced by Alan Turner.

The new lineup almost immediately secured a three-week residency in a club in Biarritz in southern France. In April 1966, after returning to the U.K., they cut a single at Marquee Studios, "If I Had a Ticket," with guest vocalist Kenneth Washington singing lead (Gary Farr sang backing vocals on it). The single made no impact, but it is historically important as the first commercially released recording featuring the work of Keith Emerson.

The T-Bones continued to gig throughout 1966, even playing the Windsor Jazz Festival during the summer, and regularly commuted between the U.K. and France. But the band was beginning to lose steam. Cyrano Langston and Gary Farr clashed frequently and, more crucially, the band began to lose its musical focus, as they introduced aspects of West Coast pop (i.e., the Mamas and the Papas, the Association) and freakbeat (the Who) into their sets without settling on a coherent direction to replace their increasingly passé electric blues sound.

Sometime near the end of Emerson's tenure with the band, the T-Bones apparently recorded four tracks at Advision Studios in London: three blues standards and an original by the sessions' producer, Chris Barber. These were never released, although one of the four tracks, a cover of Jack McDuff's "Rock Candy," was included on Emerson's 2005 *Hammer It Out* anthology. According to Emerson, the band's simmering conflicts came to a head at a band meeting where Rikki Farr slapped Cyrano Langston.[18] Emerson had had enough: in late summer 1966, he accepted a position with another band, the VIPs.[19] The T-Bones limped

---

[17] Keith Emerson, quoted by David Terralavoro, "The Keith Emerson Story, Part 1: 1944–1971," *Fanzine for the Common Man* 14 (July 1995): 6.

[18] Emerson, *Pictures*, 51.

[19] There is a chronological problem here. In *Hang on to a Dream*, 21, Hanson states the T-Bones' four unreleased tracks featuring Emerson were recorded September 8, 1966, and indicates Emerson remained in the T-Bones until their dissolution in late 1966. (This is also the chronology Terralavoro gives in "The Keith Emerson Story.") Emerson, in *Pictures*, 52, is very clear that he began his tenure with the VIPs with a series of gigs in France in August 1966, and only learned of the final demise of the T-Bones in December 1966, when he returned to London and reconnected with Lee Jackson (58). This apparent contradiction

along for a few more months, but by December 1966 they had dissolved, having succumbed to a lack of viable chart material, diminishing bookings, and, above all, a loss of clear musical direction.

The VIPs

Emerson has said he liked the VIPs because "they hadn't deserted their blues roots. The singer, Mike Harrison, had a very black-sounding voice, and lean Mike Kellie on drums provided a rock solid foundation"[20] Also in the band were bassist Greg Ridley and guitarist Luther Grosvenor, who was recruited just after Emerson.

Natives of Carlisle, the VIPs were never a well-known band in the U.K., concentrating instead on France and Germany, where they toured relentlessly, playing at such famous clubs as the Locomotive in Paris and the Star Club in Hamburg. In October 1966 they released a single in France, "I Wanna Be Free," which hit number two in the French charts: this was recorded prior to Emerson's tenure, although Emerson does play on the EP "Stagger Lee/Rosemarie/Late Night Blues" which was released in France in March 1967. Emerson genuinely respected the band's musicianship—he reckoned Mike Harrison one of England's two finest white blues singers, the other, in his estimation, being Stevie Winwood—but he never seems to have been fully committed to the VIPs, and through December 1966 even hinted he would consider a return to the T-Bones if that band could sort its difficulties out.[21] Perhaps Emerson sensed that the VIPs, like the T-Bones in the period before he left them, were in the process of abandoning their electric blues roots without having developed an equally compelling new direction. Drummer Mike Kellie said as much: "We were trying to be a concept band. We were evolving into something that had something to say, which is what some bands of the day were beginning to do . . . it was an evolutionary time."[22] After Emerson's departure the band recruited another organist, New Jersey native Gary Wright, and changed their name to Spooky Tooth. Although Spooky Tooth never made a huge commercial impact, their second album, *Spooky Two* (1969), is a minor classic of British hard rock, with its pile-driving epic "Evil Woman" bearing comparison with the very best of contemporaneous Led Zeppelin, Deep Purple, and Black Sabbath as a

---

raises three questions, namely, (1) Did Emerson indeed play on the four tracks in question? (2) If so, is September 8 the correct date of recording? (3) If so, did Emerson begin his tenure with the VIPs a few weeks later than he recalls?

[20] Emerson, *Pictures*, 52.

[21] Emerson, *Pictures*, 53–54.

[22] Hanson, *Hang on to a Dream*, 25.

seminal example of proto-metal. Luther Grosvenor, as Ariel Bender, had some later success with Mott the Hoople; Wright was briefly a solo sensation in the U.S. during the midseventies with his singles "Dream Weaver" and "My Love is Alive."

Emerson's rather short stay with the VIPs was extremely important in one respect: it was in this band that he began to develop his infamous auto-destruction routine with his Hammond. Although it has often been assumed that Emerson's stage show was influenced by Jimi Hendrix's, whom Emerson occasionally shared the stage with in 1967, Emerson maintains that his first inspiration was in fact a long-forgotten Hammond player named Don Shinn, whom he saw at London's Marquee Club one evening in autumn 1966, shortly before the VIPs left to play Hamburg:

> As far as that early stage act went, there was an organ player in London by the name of Don Shinn. I don't know where he is today [1977]. He was a weird looking guy, really strange. A very twittery sort of character. He had a schoolboy's cap on, round spectacles, really stupid. I just happened to be in this club when he was playing. He had an L-100. The audience—you know there were a lot of younger chicks down at the Marquee—were all in hysterics. Giggling and laughing at him. No one was taking him seriously. And I said "Who is this guy?" He'd been drinking whiskey out of a teaspoon and all sorts of ridiculous things. He'd played an arrangement of a Grieg Concerto . . . playing it really well, and he got a fantastic sound from the L-100. But halfway through he sort of shook the L-100, and the back of it dropped off. Then he got out a screwdriver and started making adjustments while he was playing. Everyone was roaring their heads off laughing. So I looked and said "Hang on a minute! That guy has got something."[23]

In his autobiography Emerson says he "left the club with so many ideas buzzing in my head."[24]

Some of these ideas suddenly converged during the VIPs' fall 1966 tour of German and French clubs. One night in Hamburg, Emerson was annoyed to come on stage and discover his organ stool missing, so he was obliged to play the organ standing; during the course of the tour, he came to prefer standing while playing the Hammond, which he has done ever since. One night at a show in France, a fight broke out between two patrons in the club. Here's Emerson:

> The club owner shouted at us from the wings to keep playing . . . I got more into the spirit of things, tilting the organ and allowing it to crash down, sending its in-house reverberation unit into a frenzy of explosiveness. As the Frogs shook the living daylights out of each other, I mimicked them by shaking and

---

[23] Milano, "Keith Emerson," *Contemporary Keyboard*, October 1977, 24.
[24] Emerson, *Pictures*, 55.

climbing atop the organ, switching it off and on, letting it wail as if with a mind of its own . . . The notes were no longer important . . . I wanted to go beyond those boundaries and limitations by playing outside the instrument; let the accidents happen and let them happen with total abandon . . . Seized with more energy than my nine stone [126 pound] frame had ever realized, I threw 350 pounds of instrument across the stage in one final explosive display as the audience gazed spellbound in disbelief.[25]

Here one sees the birth of two features associated with Emerson's stage act for the duration of his career: the rhythmic shaking of the Hammond to produce huge reverberating crashing sounds, and the *musique concrète*–like feedback episodes produced as the instrument is swung around, toward and away from its external amplification source. After the show, the band, who were duly impressed, pleaded with Emerson to repeat the act at their next show. He obliged them. Although the "Hammond wrestling" routine didn't become a regular part of the VIPs stage act, the origin of Emerson's stage act with the Nice can be found here.

Emerson gigged with the VIPs through April 1967: the end of his involvement with the band came shortly after a discouraging incident in which the band were ripped off by a club owner in Juan-les-pins, Côte d'Azur, where they had played a weeks' residency, an incident that left Emerson with a lifelong distaste for France.[26] The band had to play one last gig in Paris after this incident before their French tour was complete and they could return to the U.K., and it was here that fate intervened for Emerson, as he received an unexpected visitor who extended him an unexpected opportunity.

The visitor was Mickey the O, who had crossed the Channel for an emergency meeting with Emerson. Mickey came on behalf of a young soul singer, P. P. Arnold (née Patricia Ann Cole). Arnold, a native of the tough Watts ghetto of south central Los Angeles, began her career as a backing vocalist for Ike and Tina Turner, with whom she toured for two and a half years. The Turners toured the U.K. in autumn 1966 support-ing the Rolling Stones; during the tour, Arnold taught Mick Jagger some dance steps, and Jagger, in turn, took a liking to the young singer. He pre-sented her to the Stones' former manager, Andrew Loog Oldham—now president of the upstart Immediate Records label—as a promising solo artist. Oldham auditioned Arnold, liked what he heard, and signed her. Her first single, "Everything Is Gonna Be Alright," flopped, but Oldham was undisturbed, believing she simply required a more suitable song to score her first hit. Oldham turned to a then-unknown songwriter named Steven Georgiou—soon to become famous as Cat Stevens—who supplied

---

[25] Emerson, *Pictures*, 57–58.
[26] Emerson, *Pictures*, 62.

"The First Cut is the Deepest." Recorded in early 1967, by spring it had crept up to eighteen in the British singles charts. Oldham wanted Arnold to tour to support her single.

Emerson listened to Mickey the O's account of Arnold's success with growing curiosity. What, he asked, did it have to do with him? Mickey the O told Emerson that Arnold had come to him asking if he knew of a potential music director—someone who could recruit a band for her, put arrangements together quickly, and lead the band. He told her he knew just the man for the job: an up-and-coming Hammond organist named Keith Emerson. (Whom, incidentally, Arnold had never heard of.) Now Emerson was surprised. Unlike rock, which had quickly crossed racial barriers among both musicians and audiences after its appearance in the mid fifties, soul music had remained very much anchored in black American musical culture. Certainly Arnold would want to tour with black musicians? No, Mickey the O told Emerson: Arnold liked the English pop scene, and was quite willing to work with white musicians. Emerson was intrigued enough to give his notice to the VIPs, and immediately left for England. He met Arnold a week later.

The Nice
Origins and Earliest Period (May 1967–March 1968)

Arnold was much enamored with the late-sixties soul styles of Memphis's Stax label and Alabama's Muscle Shoals, as encapsulated in the work of Otis Redding and Aretha Franklin. She asked Emerson to play through some chord changes on her Fender Rhodes electric piano: although Emerson had never played one before, he obliged. At the end of the meeting, she gave him a stack of 45 rpm singles—all of which were popular soul hits in the U.S. at the time—and told him to recruit a band, arrange the songs, and teach the band the parts. Now Emerson launched his big question: if he put a band together for Arnold, could they have their own set at shows? Arnold said she had no problem with the band playing a half hour set by themselves before she came on stage.

Emerson went right to work. His first recruit was his old friend from the T-Bones, bassist Lee Jackson, with whom he had remained in contact during his time in the VIPs. Next he recruited drummer Ian Hague, who had played with Chris Farlowe and Don Spencer's XL5. Emerson had been impressed enough by Luther Grosvenor's work with the VIPs to offer him the guitarist's slot, but Grosvenor turned him down, so he offered the position to Davy O'List, an eighteen-year-old guitarist and a graduate of the Royal College of Music whose band, the Attack, had received some radio exposure courtesy of DJ John Peel. John Mayall had also been interested in recruiting O'List, but O'List turned down Mayall's offer to play in Mayall's Bluebreakers because he sensed he would have a chance to make a more personal contribution to Emerson's new project. At Arnold's request, Emerson also recruited a trombone, trumpet, and sax player; winds were never popular in the English rock scene, but Arnold considered their presence crucial for maintaining the authentic soul sound. The wind section dissolved before the band's first gig, but Emerson found the experience of arranging for them valuable—it was, in fact, his first practical exercise in orchestration.

By May of 1967, the band were ready to perform. Their set was eclectic in the extreme. The band's thirty-minute solo spot included covers of the Beatles' "A Day in the Life," Billy Preston's Hammond showpiece "Billy's Bag," and the main theme from the Clint Eastwood film *A Fistful of Dollars*; Arnold's seven-song set consisted of a number of sixties soul classics (including Pickett's "Respect"), culminating in her hit "The First Cut is the Deepest." On the way to their first gig (in Bristol, according to Emerson), Arnold asked the band what they were going to call themselves. Learning that they hadn't decided yet, she suggested "the Nazz"— black American slang for "the Nazarean," that is, Jesus. The band members, misunderstanding her accent, thought she had said "the Nice." Although Emerson wasn't too keen on the name—he was afraid people would say "the Nice what?"—he acquiesced, and the name stuck.[27]

By June 1967, across the Western World, the hippie subculture was emerging out of the shadows of hip clubs onto the center stage of popular culture: the uninitiated (certainly those over thirty) were shocked by the men's long hair, the women's miniskirts, the beads, bellbottoms, and other accoutrements of hippie fashion. In the San Francisco Bay area—the nexus of the American hippie subculture—the Summer of Love was in full swing. And out of London—indisputably the nexus of the European hippie subculture—came the Beatles' *Sergeant Pepper's Lonely Hearts Club Band*, the album that marked the counterculture's musical coming of age.

In retrospect, the Beatles' preceding albums *Rubber Soul* and *Revolver* feature more uniformly excellent songwriting than *Sgt. Pepper*. No matter. *Sgt. Pepper* is the Beatles' most influential album, and probably the most influential album in the history of rock music. Two aspects of the album made an immediate, and extraordinarily powerful, impact. The first was its eclecticism. *Sgt. Pepper* somehow managed to bring together not just different musical styles, but different musical traditions—various rock styles, the ragtime two-step rhythms of English music hall, Indian classical music, European classical styles both old (baroque) and new (late

---

[27] There are several versions of how the band got its name, similar in essence but diverging in detail. See Hanson, *Hang on to a Dream*, 30, and Emerson, *Pictures*, 63–64.

modernism)—into a kind of utopian musical synthesis. Equally important was the way that *Sgt. Pepper* brought together words, music, and album cover art into a Wagnerian *Gesamtkunstwerk*—"unified art work"—through which the Beatles drove home their twin themes of illusion and alienation, which are brought together in the album's shattering final song, "A Day in the Life." Unlike any earlier rock album, *Sgt. Pepper* constituted a song cycle which has to be listened to straight through for its full meaning to be grasped, since each song's meaning is shaded by the songs that come before and after: that is to say, *Sgt. Pepper* marks the birth of the concept album. With *Sgt. Pepper*, rock moves from the realm of Entertainment to Art, rock musicians from the role of Entertainers to Artists, indeed, to secular Prophet figures.

Needless to say, the members of the Nice were just as powerfully impacted as anyone, and spent hours listening to the album on Davy O'List's record player in his flat in Earls Court. There were other influences creeping into the Nice's musical world as well. Emerson had discovered both the anarchic rock of Frank Zappa's Mothers of Invention and the challenging modern jazz of Charles Lloyd: Zappa's "Lumpy Gravy" and Lloyd's "Sombrero Sam" were early components of the Nice's sets. Emerson had also chanced on a singular album entitled *The Zodiac: Cosmic Sounds*. Released by Elektra in early 1967, combining rock-based electronic music and surreal narration, Martyn Hanson rightly describes it as "wild, psychedelic, and brilliant."[28] Chris Welch is probably right to say that one track in particular, "Aries the Fire-Fighter," "pointed the way to play organ-based rock music, using lots of electronics and powerful drumming."[29] The Nice soon were playing their own arrangement of "Aries" in their shows.

During the summer of 1967, the Nice were being prodded into the rapid creation of original material by the fact that P. P. Arnold was increasingly often a no-show at both rehearsals and gigs; more and more, it was falling the lot of the band to supply the entire content of the set themselves, without recourse to Arnold's soul covers. The band's big break came during the Windsor Jazz and Blues Festival, held August 11–13, 1967. Arnold, with the band in a supporting role, was booked to play center stage; however, the band, with Oldham's aid, managed to persuade the Festival's organizers to allot them a forty-five-minute set in one of the side tents. Bringing all their limited financial resources to bear on what they realized was a make-or-break opportunity, the band hired Sandy Sarjeant, an attractive dancer who had become celebrity-of-the-moment on the television show *Top of the Pops*. The band's roadie, Bazz Ward, put

---

[28] Hanson, *Hang on to a Dream*, 31.
[29] Ibid.

together the best last-minute pyrotechnic show he could. As the band launched into their solo set, a smoke bomb was lit outside their tent. A few curious onlookers poked their heads into the tent, and were astounded by what they saw: as the rest of the band blared their flower-power anthem "Flower King of Flies," Emerson was beating his Hammond with a bull-whip, while Sarjeant danced suggestively on the other side of the Hammond, just safely out of reach of the whip's tip. Meanwhile, smoke from hidden smoke bombs drifted out of Emerson's Leslie cabinets, circulated by the cabinets' rotors throughout the tent, and thunder flashes seemed to evoke the beginning of World War III. Within minutes, the audience that had been at the main stage watching British folk-rockers the Pentangle had filled the Nice's tent. Rock journalist Chris Welch of *Melody Maker* was there, and said, "It was the first time I had seen a group actually in the act of winning its first following in quite such dramatic circumstances."[30]

After their breakthrough at Windsor, things began happening very fast for the Nice. They were offered a residency at the Marquee. P. P. Arnold's visa was about to expire, and shortly before she returned to the U.S., Andrew Loog Oldham hired Mick Jagger to produce her first album, to which Emerson contributed some organ parts. Shortly thereafter, she returned to the States. When she finally did return to the U.K., she discovered she no longer had a backing band: even as she had been putting finishing touches on her album, Oldham had been drawing up a recording and publishing contract for the Nice, whom he planned to sign as an act in their own right. However, the band faced an increasingly urgent problem: Ian Hague was becoming more and more unreliable. On the recommendation of Chris Welch, the band invited Brian Davison, formerly of the Mark Leeman 5, one of the groups the T-Bones had played with in the package tour of late 1965, to join the Nice. Emerson personally delivered the bad news to Hague, and Davison was in. By September 1967, the Nice were in the midst of rehearsing material for their first album, spurred on by Oldham's demands that they begin recording as soon as possible, and record only original material.[31]

Fans of the seventies rock supergroups have developed a certain image of how albums were recorded during the rock era that involves bands taking months to rehearse, record, polish, and edit an album, interrupted periodically (or frequently) by bouts of orgiastic excesses. Such a model might be applicable to ELP (and certainly *was* applicable to ELP by the late seventies), but was unknown in the sixties. Even a band with the enormous prestige of the Beatles couldn't spend months on end in the studio

---

[30] Chris Welch, quoted by Hanson, *Hang on to a Dream*, 32–33.
[31] See Emerson, *Pictures*, 69.

polishing a single LP, and for most bands, the time allotted for recording and postproduction of an album was miniscule compared to what was extended to the Beatles. In the case of the Nice, the band spent parts of September and October at work in Olympic and Pye studios: by late October, the recording of their first album was completed, and on October 27 their first single, "The Thoughts of Emerlist Davjack," with B-side "Azrial, Angel of Death" hit the streets. The single's title came from an amalgamation of the four members' names (Emerson-O'List-Davison-Jackson): as Emerson recalls, Oldham's assistant Tony Calder recommended that their songs be published under one name.[32] This practice, suggested by Andrew Loog Oldham himself, was extended to retitling the album's two cover tracks and crediting the composition of said material to "Emerlist Davjack." Although engineer Glyn Johns was the actual producer of both single and album, the credited producer is Andrew Loog Oldham, who did, Emerson remembers, turn up at the recording sessions from time to time.

On October 24, the Nice played a show at the Marquee Club supporting the Jimi Hendrix Experience. After their set, they were surprised to find Hendrix himself waiting for them in the dressing room. He had enjoyed their set, he said, and would like them to be part of the package tour he was planning for November and December. This tour, which began on November 14 at the Royal Albert Hall and ran through December 5, included fourteen shows across the length and breadth of England and Scotland. It featured a dream lineup of future greats: the Jimi Hendrix Experience (the headliners), the Move, the Pink Floyd (with Syd Barrett), the Amen Corner, and the Nice, all for fifteen shillings. By all accounts, the logistics of the show were something of a nightmare: The Nice's set was only ten minutes, Pink Floyd's seventeen. Emerson was not particularly overawed by the music of Pink Floyd, and described the band as "a bunch of university snobs."[33]

On the other hand, he was intrigued by Hendrix, and his description of the guitarist is one of the most psychologically acute passages in his autobiography. He experienced Hendrix as projecting a "gentle, gracious, and humble" façade, but suggests that underneath was a more troubled and turbulent personality; at any rate, Emerson is clear on the point that he never really came to know Hendrix, who was prone to acting warm and friendly one night, cold and distant the next. Emerson adds that Hendrix was much taken by Emerson's stage act—which by now included jumping on top of the Hammond and rocking it, "riding" it, across the stage, while the reverberation unit exploded in protest. Hendrix was wont to

---

[32] Emerson, *Pictures*, 71.
[33] Emerson, *Pictures*, 82.

hide behind Emerson's Marshall stack with a Super 8 home movie camera, documenting Emerson's assault on his hapless L-100; at times,
uproarious laughter could be heard to issue from Hendrix's dressing
room, and when Emerson and some of the other musicians would peek
in, they would find Hendrix watching Emerson's routine in rewind.[34]
Hendrix seemed to admire Emerson's work, commenting, "The Nice
were my favorite group of the tour. Their sound is ridiculously good, original, free—more funky than West Coast."[35] Hendrix's manager, Chas
Chandler, had apparently considered inviting Emerson to sit in on the
Experience's *Axis: Bold as Love* sessions, recalling later, "Keith Emerson
was a guy Jimi should have done some work with . . . Jimi often sat in with
the Nice, and Keith really played well with him. They could have really
put something together, but I was under the gun to finish the album and
we couldn't spare the time."[36] Thus the first potential pairing of Emerson
and Hendrix fell through. There was to be one more such opportunity:
but that's a story for later in our narrative.

One immediate and welcome result of the package tour was that it
immediately and substantially increased the Nice's prestige: Lee Jackson
recalls that almost overnight, the Nice's asking price went from £30 to
£400 per show.[37] The band ended 1967 with a short tour of Scandinavia
in December, during which they were offered the opportunity to record
a session for Swedish radio in Gothenburg, Sweden. In 2001, Sanctuary
Records released *The Swedish Radio Sessions*, which documents this show;
it's the most complete document of the Nice's live set to emerge from
1967, the first year of their existence.

With the Nice's profile steadily rising, Andrew Loog Oldham felt the
time was right for them to tour the U.S., and the band arrived in New
York City in late January 1968. The Nice's first tour was nothing like
ELP's mammoth tours of the seventies that covered seemingly every nook
and cranny of the U.S.: the band focused on establishing strategic beach-
heads in three major metropolitan areas on opposite coasts that were the
foci of America's countercultural scene, namely New York, Los Angeles,
and San Francisco. Between January 29 and February 11, the band was
resident at New York's Scene Club, playing fourteen shows in all. From
February 15 to 18, the Nice played nightly shows at L.A.'s Whiskey a Go
Go. Then it was on to San Francisco, where the band played a show at Bill
Graham's Fillmore West on February 22, followed by two consecutive
nights at the Winterland, the hub of the San Francisco Bay area's late-sixties rock scene, on February 23 and 24. While the tour was not a major

---

[34] For Emerson's recollections of Hendrix, see *Pictures*, 79–84.

[35] Hanson, *Hang On to a Dream*, 45.

[36] Chas Chandler, quoted in Emerson, *Pictures*, 74–75.

[37]Emerson, *Pictures*, 75, 84.

financial coup for the band, it did succeed in spreading the word among rock cognoscenti in three of America's major countercultural centers that an innovative new band from England was on the rise, and as word spread, the likelihood increased that the band's next tour would be longer and bigger in its geographical scope.

What was arguably the most crucial event of the tour was an extremely negative one, taking place at L.A.'s Whiskey a Go Go. The Nice arrived at the club and, waiting for the arrival of Andrew Loog Oldham, seated themselves to watch a set by the Hollies. Because of the incendiary nature of what follows, I will quote directly from Martyn Hanson's *Hang on to a Dream* rather than paraphrasing:

> O'List quickly got talking to someone else who was watching the group, David Crosby [of the Byrds, later of Crosby, Stills, Nash and Young]. Oldham, who had by now shown up, turned to Lee [Jackson] and said, "He shouldn't hang around with him, he's a known spiker." It happened, Davy was spiked, and it affected him very badly. It was noted by the rest of the band that this was the time when Davy's personality problems started to emerge.[38]

Without in any way appearing to exonerate Crosby for what, if true, is a heinous, indeed, criminal act, it must be noted that Emerson, in his autobiography, makes no reference to this event, but notes that it was around this period that he realized that O'List, with whom he shared a flat in Drayton Gardens, was developing a serious drug problem.[39]

First Album: *The Thoughts of Emerlist Davjack*

On March 1, shortly after the Nice had returned from the U.S., and some four months after the release of their first single, Immediate Records released the Nice's first album, *The Thoughts of Emerlist Davjack*, which made an appearance in the lower end of the British charts. *The Thoughts of Emerlist Davjack* is a classic of British psychedelic rock, all the more impressive for being the creation of a group that had been together not quite five months when it was recorded. About the worst that can be said about the album is that some of its tracks are products of their period, and while exemplifying the music of the period well enough, fail to transcend it. This is especially true of "The Thoughts of Emerlist Davjack" (their first single, you may recall) and "Flower King of Flies," both of which can be described as flower-power anthems that owe something to the Beatles circa 1966–67. The model for "Emerlist Davjack" seems to be the

---

[38] Hanson, *Hang on to a Dream*, 57.
[39] Emerson, *Pictures*, 98.

Beatles' "Penny Lane," with its cheerful rock march rhythm and Brandenburg Concerto–style trumpet obbligato (played by O'List). The model for "Flower King of Flies" is a bit harder to place, although it's just possible to discern wisps of the chorus of the Beatles' "Lucy in the Sky with Diamonds." Both songs feature characteristically rich late-sixties vocal arrangements that were soon to disappear from the Nice's music: "Emerlist Davjack" features a lead vocal by O'List (his only one on the album), with backing vocals by Jackson and Emerson, while "Flower King of Flies" features Jackson singing lead, with a surprisingly elaborate vocal arrangement in which Jackson, O'List, and Emerson all participate.

A couple more of the album's tracks reveal the continuing presence of psychedelic rock's R & B roots, although they also point up the ways in which psychedelic rock was diverging from classic R & B. "Bonnie K," with Jackson's urgent vocal rasps, comes closer than anything else on the album to the late-sixties Memphis Stax sound, but the rhythm is stiffer and more ponderous, the guitar parts more fiercely distorted, the timbral use of feedback by both organ and guitar more creative. The same is true of the instrumental "War and Peace"—in reality John Patten's "Silver Meter," recorded but never released by the T-Bones. There's a particularly revealing passage in "War and Peace." For a moment the band abandons the twelve-bar chord changes as Emerson launches into a toccata-like, pseudo-baroque passage of chugging sixteenth notes that in no way disrupts the driving rhythm section accompaniment. After a moment, Jackson and O'List unobtrusively return to the twelve-bar chord pattern in their accompaniment figure: Emerson continues spinning out his toccata-like figuration over the blues chord changes, again with no loss of continuity. Here one sees the early stages of the fusion of baroque and blues musical elements that was to become a foundation of Emerson's mature style.

Each of the remaining four tracks is completely original and totally successful. "Tantalizing Maggie" melds elements of twelve-bar blues and baroque ground bass chord patterns, which accompany Jackson's urgently rasped account of the dubious exploits of Maggie and the futile efforts of her father to curtail them. Emerson's tongue-in-cheek inclusion of a passage of "Solfeggio" by J. S. Bach's son Carl Philip Emmanuel during the song's coda is both amusing and oddly appropriate. "The Cry of Eugene" is the album's one flower-power anthem that transcends its period: the song overcomes its fey lyrics through the combination of the unusually sophisticated sixteen-bar chord change that underpins the verse, the startling instrumental middle section, whose polyrhythmically overlapping guitar and organ lines foreshadow seventies progressive rock, and O'List's floating guitar obbligato, suggestive of a cosmic violin. The ominous and powerful "Dawn" showcases Emerson's ability to create compelling organ riffs that derive equally from the electric blues and the ritornellos of J. S.

Bach's Brandenburg Concertos, and to convincingly develop them through the duration of the song: ELP's minor-key, pseudo-baroque, riff-driven organ trio songs such as "Knife-Edge," "Time and a Place," and "Living Sin" have their stylistic origin in "Dawn." Although the lyrics are a typical product of the late sixties in their earnest portentousness, the fact they are whispered (by Emerson) rather than sung lends them a genuine sense of urgency and gives the song a convincing edge of uneasiness. The "machine" episode in quintuple meter that serves as a bridge was innovative for its time, and more than any other song on the album, in "Dawn" the feedback and other electric effects become central to the song's expressive character.

The real centerpiece of *The Thoughts of Emerlist Davjack*, however, is the instrumental "Rondo." Although credited by Oldham to the aforementioned "Emerlist Davjack," anyone with a superficial familiarity with sixties jazz recognized the track as an arrangement of Dave Brubeck's "Blue Rondo à la Turk." Brubeck, in turn, viewed his piece as an arrangement of Mozart's *Rondo alla Turca*, the third and final movement of the Piano Sonata no. 11 in A major, K. 331. The band begins and ends the track with more or less straight arrangements of the opening and closing sections of Brubeck's "Blue Rondo," simply transforming the herky-jerky 9/8 rhythms of Brubeck's piece into a more straightforward and harder-driving 4/4.

It's in the long middle section of "Rondo" that the band uncovers new territory. The middle of Brubeck's "Blues Rondo" is simply a swing blues, in which Brubeck and saxophonist Paul Desmond solo over a series of twelve-bar choruses. In the central section of "Rondo," Jackson and Davison lay out a throbbing, hypnotic drone in 4/4 iterated in a "galloping" eighth-sixteenth-sixteenth-note pattern. O'List takes his solo first; it's less interesting for the notes he plays than for its shades of distortion and its overall "outside," at times nearly atonal contours. Then Emerson enters. He begins hesitantly, almost furtively; slowly but inexorably, he builds his solo by increasing its rhythmic motion, textural density, registral span, and distortion level, eventually climaxing with a quotation from the fugue of J. S. Bach's famous Toccata and Fugue in D minor for pipe organ, BWV 565, that spills into a majestic, minor-key fanfare passage. By the end of his long solo, the level of energy he has created is incredible. At the time, only one other rock musician, Jimi Hendrix, was soloing at this level of virtuosity, and even Hendrix didn't have Emerson's instinct for large-scale structure, for building slow but inexorable climaxes over long time spans, surely a product of Emerson's many years of studying classical music. "Rondo" radically expands the possibility of the rock instrumental, pushes the envelope of what was musically possible within the framework of rock improvisation, and forever transforms the possibilities of rock organ technique. It's also in

"Rondo" that Emerson introduces one of his hallmarks, descending Hammond glissandos, a sound aptly described by Paul Stump as "great sheets of steel being torn from their moorings and flying through a wind tunnel."[40]

Triumphs and Tribulations: April–December 1968

In the months that followed the release of *Emerlist Davjack*, the Nice relentlessly toured Britain, and, increasingly, the Continent as well, creating new material all the while. In May, the band convened to record a new single. Stirred by his recent American experience, Emerson decided to arrange "America," the show-stopping ensemble number from Leonard Bernstein's musical *West Side Story* (1957). As the band hammered out the arrangement, Emerson found that a passage from Antonin Dvořák's *New World* Symphony worked very well as an introduction, while also lending the arrangement a nice symbolic resonance. Compared to "Rondo," "America" turned out to be less a solo showpiece for Emerson than a benchmark of the group's growing talent for tight ensemble interplay. The impressive offbeat O'List-Davison accents during the track's bridge foreshadow seventies prog; other highlights include Davison's ferocious yet tightly controlled closing barrage, and O'List's solo, much more focused than in "Rondo." In response to the growing political unrest in the U.S.—characterized most potently by the increasingly massive protests against the Vietnam War and the assassination of black civil rights leader Martin Luther King in April—the band superimposed shrieks, manic laughter, and the sound of gunfire over the segment of music just before Davison's final drum barrage, capped off by the sound of a young boy (P. P. Arnold's son Kevin) making the provocative statement, "America is pregnant with the promise of anticipation, but is murdered by the hand inevitable."[41] When "America" was released in June with the B-side "Diamond Hard Blue Apples of the Moon," the last song by the Nice to feature elaborate vocal arrangements and the only track ever on which Keith Emerson plays Mellotron,[42] it hit number twenty-

---

[40] Stump, *The Music's All That Matters*, 57–58.

[41] The band titled this coda section "2nd Amendment," in reference to the amendment in the U.S. Constitution guaranteeing citizens the right to bear arms.

[42] The Mellotron, invented in the early 1960s, is an organlike instrument (lacking foot pedals, however) capable of reproducing string, woodwind, and choral voicings. Because the instrument is capable of playing chords (unlike early synthesizers, which could only play one note at a time), in British rock of the late sixties and early seventies the Mellotron was often used to create a massive "symphonic" background of sustained chords, and it was sometimes used to project a slow, lyrical melody as well. Since notes on the Mellotron are produced by

one on the U.K. singles charts: an impressive achievement, considering "America" was the first single to surpass the six-minute mark.

If the summer of 1967 had been the Summer of Love, the summer of 1968 was turning out to be anything but. Across the Western world, protests against the Vietnam War, American foreign policy, racial discrimination, and on behalf of women's rights and worker's rights seemed to spontaneously converge one into another in the U.S., the U.K., France, Italy, West Germany, and Japan. The unrest spread, like a forest fire, across the globe, faster than it could be snuffed out by the authorities: military dictatorships and corrupt one-party states were challenged in Greece, Mexico, Brazil, and Pakistan. Unrest did not stop at the Iron Curtain, either. The Soviet Union, alarmed by the increasing liberalization measures of the Czech government, invaded Czechoslovakia. There were protests inside Tito's Yugoslavia. In Mao's China, the military descended to a level of near civil war, as rival Red Guard factions attacked each other for supposed counterrevolutionary activity. Historians of the Left often portray 1968 as the year global capitalism almost collapsed, as the high tide of the Worldwide Left. Like most sweeping generalizations, there is some truth to this reading. But the unrest went beyond a simple Right/Left cleavage: there was a primal, anarchic undercurrent to many, if not most of the events of 1968. Historians who try to confine the "revolution" to political spheres must do so by ignoring the explosion of public sexual libertinism and hallucinogenic drug use (in the West at least): the "revolution" was not only against a political system, but against concepts of family and sexual conduct that date back at least to ancient Israel, indeed, against "consciousness" as understood in the West at least since the time of classical Greece. It's possible to argue that never in recorded history had the entire world teetered on the edge of global anarchy the way it did in 1968.

By late June the U.S. had been rocked by another high profile political murder: Robert Kennedy, brother of former President John F. Kennedy, himself the victim of an assassin's bullet, was shot dead while campaigning for the presidency. On June 26, the Nice were playing an antiapartheid event called "Come Back Africa" at the Royal Albert Hall. The band members, like many British citizens, were becoming increasingly alarmed by the events in the U.S., which seemed to be spiraling out of control. Emerson in particular expressed concern about the assassination of figures such as King and Kennedy who were at once progressive and conciliatory. The Nice's stage show had already been beginning to

---

running a strip of tape across a replay head, the instrument does not "speak" rapidly enough to make the kind of rapid passagework that was so idiomatic to the Hammond organ a possibility, and the instrument was not used for soloing.

take on an explicitly anti-American tenor—on at least one occasion, Lee Jackson had burned the draft card of a visiting American during the set—but at this show the anti-American tenor reached its high-water mark.

The Nice were the only real rock band at the event, which was otherwise dominated by Hollywood and Las Vegas notables such as Sammy Davis Jr. and Marlon Brando. The band saved "America" for last in their set. As the piece reached its denouement, Emerson stopped playing, letting the band build up suitable intensity on the repetitive 6/8 figure while he spray-painted an American flag on a large blank canvas he had secured for that purpose. The black tie audience, some of whom were American dignitaries, had been engrossed by the band's performance up to this point, but suddenly began to stir uneasily. When Emerson realized he had no matches, British actor and ardent Socialist Warren Mitchell came to the rescue, running to the edge of the stage and passing Emerson a lighter. Within seconds, the spray-painted flag was ablaze.

The flag burning did not go down well with the audience. There was virtually no applause, and many people walked out. Within twenty-four hours, the Nice had been banned from ever playing the Royal Albert Hall again. However, as has so often been true in rock, errant behavior proved to be a career booster, as the flag-burning incident raised the Nice's profile another notch or two. The next night, the Nice were scheduled to play a gig in Norwich. Emerson recalls, "As we arrived into town on the train we saw this huge line of people waiting at the club. We wondered who else was in town the same time we were, but it turned out that they had heard about the flag incident and were waiting to get tickets to see us."[43] Emerson was disillusioned—what he had intended as a political statement had degenerated into cheap sensationalism. Nonetheless, the flag-burning incident, although never repeated, permanently raised the Nice's profile, which was given yet another boost when it was announced that Leonard Bernstein successfully blocked the release of "America" as a single in the U.S.[44]

"America" was also the catalyst for Emerson to add knives to his already controversial stage show:

> Using knives in the act came from when the Nice were doing "America" and in "America" I wanted to hold down two notes and sustain a fifth while I was playing another organ. I started out by using pegs, just wooden things to hold down the keys. Then I thought I could do the same thing with knives and if I'm playing "America," the music from *West Side Story*, then the knives have a definite part in it, being connected with the film and the gang fights. So I

---

[43] Emerson, quoted by Pethel, "Keith Emerson," 14.

[44] Considering that Bernstein's politics were far more radical than Emerson's, I've never really understood Bernstein's motive for this.

thought "yes, it has a place here," and then I used to take the knives out of
the keyboard and throw them on the floor; and then probably one night I
decided to throw them at the [amplification] cabinets.[45]

In his autobiography, Emerson explains the musical effect he sought:
"plunging them [the knives] into keys approximately a fifth apart and
switching the power on and off, the overall effect was quite dramatic, giving the appearance and illusion that the instrument was screaming out in
its last death throes."[46] One of the Nice's roadies, Ian Kilminster, gave
Emerson two Hitler youth daggers, telling him, "if you're gonna use one,
use a serious one."[47] Kilminster later found fame as Lemmy, founder of
the heavy metal cult band Motörhead.

Beside the external turbulence that swirled across the globe, the band
faced two internal situations that shook their equilibrium during 1968.
The first involved the management situation. Andrew Loog Oldham was
undoubtedly a promotional wizard: he played a major role in securing the
band their solo spot at the 1967 Windsor Festival, had a role in the
pyrotechnics show at Windsor that won them their first breakthrough,
enabled them to tour the U.S. earlier than better-known British bands,
and encouraged them in their controversial flag-burning incident at Royal
Albert Hall, another P.R. coup. Nonetheless, the band were increasingly
coming to believe that it was a conflict of interest for the same person to
be a band's manager and their record label owner. They disliked the fact
that travel expenses during the American tour had been offset against
their royalties, believing the expenses should have been split between
band and record company, and that an independent manager would have
insisted on the point. In spring of 1968, the Nice began to shop around
for a manager: the owner of the Marquee, Jack Barrie, recommended that
Emerson approach a gentleman named Tony Stratton Smith.

Stratton Smith's first career was in sports journalism: indeed, he never
lost interest in horse racing. During a stint covering the 1962 World Cup
in Chile, he met the Brazilian bossa nova great Antonio Carlos Jobim,
who suggested he branch out into music management. By the time
Emerson approached him, Stratton Smith was actually thinking of relin-
quishing all his music management responsibilities and returning full time
to sports, and initially he was not enthusiastic about the Nice's offer. The
band persisted, however, and eventually Stratton Smith relented, even

---

[45] Keith Emerson, quoted by Janis Schact, "Emerson, Lake and Palmer: The Dagger Does
More Than You Think." *Circus*, March 1972, 7. In regards to Emerson's reference to a second organ, during the summer of 1968 Emerson bought a second organ, a Hammond A-
105.
[46] Emerson, *Pictures*, 81.
[47] Ian Kilminster, quoted by Emerson, *Pictures*, 81.

after a peeved Oldham insisted that he pay off £5,000 the band owed him for retainers and recording costs. Of course, as readers of my *Rocking the Classics* know, Stratton Smith ended up being one of the foremost patrons and talent scouts of British progressive rock; his Charisma label (still a bit in the future at this point) brought such seminal acts as Genesis and Van der Graaf Generator to the world.

By summer 1968, "Strat," as the band called him, was firmly on board: indeed, one of his first experiences with the band was the June 26 flag-burning incident, which, unlike Oldham, he had advised against, believing it could complicate the band's efforts to secure passports for future American tours. However, Stratton Smith was soon facing an even more immediate danger to the band: the increasingly erratic behavior of Davy O'List. During the summer, the band had been obliged to play several of their gigs in London and its surrounding environs as a three piece, because O'List failed to show up. There were times when O'List would suddenly stop playing, and then, just as suddenly, reenter in the wrong key, totally throwing off the rest of the band. Emerson, in particular, became increasingly aggravated by O'List's new habit of suddenly turning his guitar volume up, drowning out everyone else. Matters came to a head on September 29 during a show in Croydon, when O'List unexpectedly punched roadie Bazz Ward. The next day, Emerson met with Jackson and Davison, and by the end of the meeting a consensus was reached: O'List had to be fired. In early October, Tony Stratton Smith delivered the bad news to O'List after a gig in Bournemouth, with the other three band members present as a signal of solidarity.

O'List, sadly, had become one of the early drug casualties of the British rock scene, and he never totally recovered: later efforts to reenter the music scene (including a brief stint with Roxy Music) were hampered by the same instability issues that plagued his later days with the Nice. O'List had become deeply paranoid; as late as 1991, some twenty-three years after the fact, he expressed his belief in an interview that there had been a conspiracy, spearheaded by Stratton Smith, to oust him.[48] He also believed that the band were withholding royalty payments that were rightfully his, unaware (as was the band at this time) that Immediate was scamming most, if not *all*, Immediate artists of royalties. While it seems pretty clear there was no conspiracy to oust him—indeed, it seems that Stratton Smith may have counseled the band to be patient prior to the September 29 incident—it also seems possible that the band may have never given O'List full credit for his creative contributions during the early days of the Nice, which may have further fueled his paranoia. At the time he left the

---

[48] Hanson, *Hang on to a Dream*, 73–74, gives an excellent overview of O'List's firing from both his point of view and from the rest of the band's.

Nice, O'List was not a great guitarist, but his playing did at times show real textural and coloristic interest, and it is possible that over time he would have developed into a textural guitarist of some significance.

For many years there has been a widespread belief that Emerson wanted to dump O'List so that he could seize uncontested creative control of the Nice and convert the band to an organ trio headed by himself. This is not the case. While the Nice ploughed on as a trio after the sacking of O'List, the initial plan was to audition guitarists until a successful candidate was identified. Indeed, very soon a successful candidate *was* located: a young, largely unknown guitarist named Steve Howe. Emerson recalls,

> He came and auditioned and was very talented. We begged him to join. He hemmed and hawed at that. The first day he said yes, but then he said he had an offer to start his own band and couldn't join us. I don't know whatever happened to that. He disappeared for two or three years. Next thing I heard, he was playing with Yes. He was the only guitar player I wanted to work with, and I got so used to working without one I was dubious of getting back and working with guitar players after that.[49]

Only over time, then, did the Nice make a conscious decision to permanently remain a trio. As for Howe, he once said that during his audition with the Nice "I heard music that, in some ways, I later heard in Yes."[50]

Second Album: *Ars Longa Vita Brevis*

Even as they were trying to determine if a suitable replacement guitarist could be located, the Nice were obliged to commence recording their second album, in London's Wessex Studios. The biggest problem they faced was that virtually all of the material that was to go on the album already existed and had been road tested by the four-piece lineup; it now needed to be rearranged for trio. This was a challenge that the band did not address with complete success: much of the time, one senses they are not yet comfortable with the trio format. The new album also evinces a certain lack of focus in stylistic direction, perhaps another result of their sudden lurch from quartet to trio configuration, or perhaps simply the inevitable result of a determination to experiment with new concepts that were not yet fully mastered.

---

[49] Keith Emerson, quoted by Milano, "Keith Emerson," *Contemporary Keyboard*, October 1977, 24.
[50] Steve Howe, quoted by Hanson, *Hang on to a Dream*, 77.

The first three songs—"Daddy, Where Did I Come From," "Little Arabella," and "Happy Freuds"—continue to develop the first album's song-oriented approach, although the droll, slightly absurd aspect of these songs is rather different than the debut's flower-power paeans. All three are quirky and charming, although they lack the drive and intensity of the debut album's best songs. In order to fill the missing sonic space formerly occupied by O'List's guitar parts, in these songs Emerson frequently double-tracks organ and piano parts. However, the keyboard orchestrations often sound somewhat arbitrary—one seldom feels that the double tracking reflects the intrinsic demands of the song so much as a desire to fill up sonic space with as little fuss as possible—and generally the double-tracked parts don't reflect what was practical in live performance. Probably the best of the three is the loping, jazzy "Little Arabella," a semiautobiographical ditty about a crazed groupie to which Emerson contributes a nice, Jimmy Smith–tinged organ accompaniment.

Singer/songwriter Roy Harper suggested to Emerson that he ought to undertake an arrangement for rock band of the rousing march theme of the British television news program *This Week*, which was the Intermezzo from the *Karelia Suite* by the Finnish master Jan Sibelius (1865–1957). Emerson accepted the challenge, and the Intermezzo, which became the album's fourth track, opens a new avenue that was to become of huge importance to him: the arrangement of orchestral works for rock keyboard trio. This particular performance lacks the punch that characterized much of Emerson's later work in the genre—indeed, the Nice's later album, *Five Bridges*, captures a much harder-driving live performance of the piece that also benefits from the discreet use of some of Sibelius's original orchestration. Although the present version, for trio alone, seems to plod a bit by comparison, it is notable for marking the debut of Lee Jackson's distinctive bowed bass guitar technique.[51] This track also captures, for the first time on vinyl, one of Emerson's organ feedback episodes, a staple of his live act at the time that resulted from him tilting his organ back and forth, so that it alternately faced toward and away from its external amplification source. One wonders if the heroic, optimistic rock marches that were to become a staple of his mature style with ELP (think, for instance, of "Karn Evil 9, 3rd Impression") might not have had their origin in the Sibelius Intermezzo.

The entirety of side two of the LP format is occupied by a long suite, "Ars Longa Vita Brevis," for which the entire album is named. The suite's title is the Latin motto of an art school Lee Jackson had once attended: "Life is brief, Art endures." This was a groundbreaking work for both Emerson and

---

[51] See Hanson, *Hang on to a Dream*, 79, for a detailed description of Jackson's technique for playing a noncambered string instrument with a bow.

rock for two reasons. First, it is his first attempt at an "epic," multimovement suite; second, it is one of the first attempts at orchestrated rock music, The Moody Blues' *Days of Future Passed* having been released just a few months earlier. Unfortunately, "Ars Longa Vita Brevis" falls somewhat short both as multimovement suite and as orchestrated rock music.

The main problem with the multimovement construction of "Ars Longa Vita Brevis" is that Emerson attempts to weld together several pieces that had worked quite well as independent entities simply, it appears, to fill up an LP side with one long piece—the strategy doesn't work, as the constituent parts never really cohere. The nucleus of the "Ars Longa Vita Brevis" is an eight-minute piece of the same name that the band had been performing as a four-piece during the summer of 1968. In its eight-minute incarnation, the piece was completely successful, consisting of five sections laid out in a symmetrical A-B-C-B-A form: an interesting, somewhat neurotic Prelude that combines baroque and contemporary jazz elements (the A section) is followed by a song built on an inspired Davy O'List guitar riff supported by bagpipelike organ accompaniment (B), an exciting Latin jazz piano episode (C), and recaps of the O'List riff song (B) and the Prelude (A), here called a "Coda." As O'List's guitar riff was too crucial for the band to excise it or transcribe it to organ, they were obliged to hire a sessions guitarist, Malcolm Langstaff, to play it on the album.

The studio version of "Ars Longa Vita Brevis" finds Emerson expanding a successful eight-minute piece to roughly nineteen by placing a "percussion movement" (actually a forgettable drum solo by Davison) between the Prelude and the song, and placing an arrangement of J. S. Bach's Brandenburg Concerto no. 3 first movement, called "Brandenburger," that the band often played as an independent number, between the Latin jazz piano episode and the recap of the O'List song. Both additions feel like arbitrary intrusions that destroy the sense of momentum the song had built up in its original eight-minute incarnation. In order to impose a sense of unity upon the now heterogeneous suite, Emerson orchestrates the opening (the Prelude), the middle (the "Brandenburger"), and the ending (the Coda, that is, the partial recap of the opening Prelude). The orchestration, completed by Emerson with the help of a freelance orchestrator hired by Immediate, is not bad, but feels like an unnecessary addition to the music, and fails to create a sense of unity: in the end, the side-long "Ars Longa Vita Brevis" dissolves into its constituent parts. Emerson was to be much more successful a year later with the "Five Bridges" suite. Perhaps understandably, given their situation at the time, *Ars Longa Vita Brevis*, released in November 1968, is probably the weakest of the Nice's five albums. Nonetheless, it's an important album in that it foreshadows so many of Emerson's later preoccupations: rocked-up arrangements of the classics, orchestrated rock music, long pieces created through suitelike construction. The U.S. release of *Ars Longa Vita Brevis* included "America," since the band had been unable to release it as a single in the States.

The Nice continued their breakneck performing schedule through the end of 1968. Most of the shows were in England, but two that weren't were particularly emblazoned in Emerson's memory. The Nice played two shows at Queen's University, Belfast, on November 14. Emerson was struck by the city's tense atmosphere; within a year, "The Troubles" that were to rack Northern Ireland for decades had begun. On a lighter note, Emerson recalls that after the show the band were obliged to hastily snuff out a joint they had been smoking when Terence O'Neill, Prime Minister of Northern Ireland, stopped by their dressing room to meet them. On December 22, they played the Beat Festival in Prague, Czechoslovakia, with Soviet tanks still lining Wenceslas Square; Emerson recalls that after "Rondo," the opening number, "the whole hall erupted in a roar the like of which I had never heard before."[52] Since the Czech currency they had received on arrival was worthless outside the Iron Curtain, Emerson gave a large wad of his to a haggard-looking older woman in the airport as he prepared to board his return flight to the U.K.

Apotheosis: January–October 1969

The year 1969 began much the way 1968 ended: one show after another. On February 4, at London's Institute of Contemporary Art, the Nice played their first multimedia show. Very much an expression of late-sixties sensibilities, multimedia shows brought together different musical styles, sometimes different musical traditions, and often strove towards Wagner's ideal of the *Gesamtkunstwerk* by uniting the music with a visual element (usually a light show) and the spoken word (poetry readings, or improvised poetry, were a popular part of these events). Besides expressing the sixties ideal of utopian synthesis, multimedia shows were important to cutting-edge bands such as the Nice and Pink Floyd in another respect: they served as an implicit acknowledgement that the new rock had become a music primarily for listening rather than dancing. This particular show featured John Mayer and the Indo-Jazz Fusion, a group whose music blended jazz and Indian ragas. Emerson played a transcription for piano of the fifth movement of Victor Lalo's *Symphonie espagnole*, with Mayer accompanying on violin. Brian Davison and some of his jazz friends played a free improvisational set. Lee Jackson read some poetry. Afterwards, the musicians engaged in a question-and-answer session with

---

[52] Emerson, *Pictures*, 123.

the audience.[53] The multimedia ideal was to become of increasing importance to the Nice for the remainder of their existence.

The Nice's second North American tour commenced at Boston's Tea Party where the band played three gigs on March 21–23, 1969, Tony Stratton Smith having been obliged to do some very fancy explaining away of the flag-burning incident of the previous year in order to secure passports for the band. This tour lasted longer than their first, extending into early May (they also ended their tour with dates at Boston's Tea Party on May 6–8); although it was confined to the eastern U.S., it covered a wide geographic swath, extending as far south as Miami and as far west as Chicago, and including at least one date in Canada (Toronto). The highlight of the tour was undoubtedly the band's April 9 and 10 shows, played at Bill Graham's Fillmore East, New York City, on a bill that also included Ten Years After and Family. Stratton Smith noted that house engineer Eddie Kramer had equipment set up for recording, and cut a deal with Graham to record the show. This turned out to be a great boon for the band: tracks from the Fillmore shows were to figure prominently on the band's three remaining albums. The band, who by now had taken huge steps towards reinventing themselves as a bona fide trio, played brilliantly at the Fillmore, which did not escape the notice of *Billboard* critic Ed Ochs:

> The Nice, whose nowhere name belies the darkly subversive organ attack of the dedicated and demonic Keith Emerson, are, at their best, as instrumentally mesmerizing as any rock heavy in the highly respected rock profession of terrorizing the senses . . . His symphonic speed trips, responsible for the black comedy of Leonard Bernstein's "America," were brooding hymns in the psychedelic church . . . Brian Davison on drums and Lee Jackson on bass assisted brilliantly in the mind's destruction.[54]

While the tour didn't "break" the Nice into the big leagues of the American rock market, it did initiate the important process of building them a dedicated cult audience. While this tour was more ambitious and bigger in scope than their first, it was still nothing like ELP's well-oiled extravaganzas of the seventies, where the entire itinerary was plotted out to the tiniest detail months in advance: some shows on this tour were arranged several weeks in advance, but others weren't, and often Stratton Smith had to scramble to fill in empty dates. After the tour ended in early May, Emerson stayed on in New York for a few days to participate in a series of sessions featuring a cast of assorted British and American rock

---

[53] The Nice did not play as a band at this show per the promoter's request. See Emerson, *Pictures*, 145–46.
[54] Ed Ochs, quoted by Emerson, *Pictures*, 141.

stars. The product of these sessions did not see the light of day until 1973, when it was released as *Music from Free Creek*.

The summer of 1969 saw the Nice slowing down their frenetic gigging pace ever so slightly, playing fewer, but increasingly higher profile, appearances, as they slowly but surely established themselves as one of the top live draws in the U.K. rock scene. On June 28, they were one of five headlining acts at the Bath Festival of Blues: the other headliners were Fleetwood Mac, John Mayall, Ten Years After, and a hot new band called Led Zeppelin. For this particular show, Emerson wanted to experiment with the possibilities of combining the sounds of bagpipes with the trio, so a Scottish pipe band marched in around the perimeter of the crowd as the Nice launched into Sibelius's "Karelia." After playing a number of U.K. gigs in July, the Nice participated in a short package tour of Ireland with Yes and the Bonzo Dog Band. This particular tour ended up being a continual comedy of errors from beginning to end: a detailed (and humorous) description of the bands' trials and tribulations can be found in Chris Welch's *Close to the Edge: The Story of Yes*.[55] Another high profile appearance for the Nice during the summer of 1969 included the Jazz and Blues Festival at Plumpton. This turned out to be another ambitious mixed-media extravaganza for the Nice, who were accompanied by a forty-piece orchestra conducted by Joseph Eger, a dynamic young conductor Emerson had met in New York during the Nice's American tour of the previous spring who shared Emerson's enthusiasm for exploring the possibilities of rock-classical fusion.[56] The Scottish pipe band that the Nice had played with in Bath a few weeks earlier also made an appearance. The orchestra accompanied the Nice on the opening number, "Brandenburger"; on "Karelia," the orchestra and the Nice were joined by the Scottish pipe band. After a few numbers that featured the Nice by themselves, the orchestra and band finished together on a medley in which "Rondo" was cleverly interwoven with the "Troika" movement of Sergei Prokofiev's *Lieutenant Kije* suite. Summer of 1969 was capped off with a forceful per-

---

[55] See Chris Welch, *Close to the Edge: The Story of Yes* (London: Omnibus Press, 2000), 69–71. As Welch actually covered this tour for *Melody Maker*, his account is especially valuable.

[56] Joseph Eger provides his recollections of the 1969–70 Emerson-Eger collaborations in his book *Einstein's Violin: A Conductor's Notes on Music, Physics, and Social Change* (New York: Tarcher/Penguin, 2005), 53–54. Eger's recollections, which by and large come across as sour grapes, should be taken with a grain of salt for several reasons: he claims Emerson was "no more than 18" when they met (in fact, Emerson must have been twenty-four at the time), he seems to confuse the Nice (whom he never mentions by name) and ELP, and he takes credit for Emerson's later arrangement of *Pictures at an Exhibition*, although by the time Emerson had moved on to ELP he was no longer actively collaborating with Eger. Eger's rancor may be traceable to the fact that he and Emerson's final attempt at collaboration ended badly: see Emerson, *Pictures*, 276.

formance at the Isle of Wight Festival on August 29, where the Nice unveiled a new opening number, an arrangement of the third movement of Tchaikovsky's *Pathètique* Symphony.

Third Album: *Nice*

Besides their high profile performance at Isle of Wight, August 1969 marked the release of the Nice's third album, simply entitled *Nice*. The album is the most jazz-inflected of the Nice's five albums; it also features Emerson's piano work much more prominently than their two previous albums. On *Nice* the band emerge as a bona fide trio: O'List's absence is felt far less here than on *Ars Longa Vita Brevis*.

The album opens with "Azrael Revisited," a rearrangement of an Emerson-O'List-Jackson song that had been the B-side of their first single, "The Thoughts of Emerlist Davjack." Built around a bluesy piano riff in 5/4, this is one of the Nice's classic songs; Emerson slightly detunes the piano strings to evoke a feeling of age and decay, which meshes well with Lee Jackson's feverish, nervous account of a man who believes the Angel of Death is stalking him. The instrumental chorus quotes Sergei Rachmaninov's gloomy Prelude in C$^\sharp$ Minor, op. 3, no. 2, further contributing to the song's claustrophobic vibe. The band creates a weird moment of magical synergy during the central instrumental break: as Emerson brings his piano solo over the 5/4 riff to a furious conclusion, Lee Jackson enters singing an overdubbed doo-wop vocal chorus, while Brian Davison contributes some clever percussion orchestration on ratchet. The song's fusion of Rachmaninov, blues, and doo-wop vocals sounds highly unlikely, but the driving 5/4 riff welds it all together, and it coheres surprisingly well: indeed, when Lee Jackson enters at the climax of Emerson's piano solo singing "shoo-dee-doo-bop/shoo-doo-dee-wop," it somehow sounds inevitable.

The second track is an arrangement of "Hang on to a Dream" by singer-songwriter Tim Hardin. When Jackson approached Emerson about arranging the song, Emerson initially feared it was too simple to arrange in a stylistically satisfactory way for the band, but he pulls it off here, contributing a delicate yet active piano accompaniment to the opening and closing sections of the song. The instrumental middle section, for piano, bass guitar, and tambourine, marks the emergence of a kind of folky, pastoral jazz that was to later reemerge in a more fully developed form on ELP's "Take a Pebble."

The third track, "Diary of an Empty Day," grew out of the violin-piano arrangement of the fifth movement of *Symphonie espagnole* by Victor Lalo (1823–92) that Emerson had played with John Mayer at the Institute of Contemporary Arts; the lead instrument is Hammond, although some textural piano parts are overdubbed. It's one of the Nice's more complicated ensemble numbers, with Jackson in particular having to navigate some intricate bass-vocal counterpoints. He does it well, although he's clearly straining to sing the higher notes. The final studio track, "For Example," was intended as a kind of virtuoso variation set based on the twelve-bar blues, the song's different sections being distinguished by key, tempo, rhythm, mood, and so on. For me, the structure of the track feels a bit contrived, and at least one section—the heavy rock bit during which Jackson is forced to shriek outside of his normal vocal range—falls flat. Nonetheless, there are some outstanding individual passages, including the closing section, where the band is supported by a horn trio that includes one of Emerson's old Blue Note heroes, baritone saxophonist Pepper Adams; the horn parts (added in New York during the spring 1969 tour) are arranged wonderfully, and the quotes of the Beatles' "Norwegian Wood" and "America" during Emerson's piano solo are perfectly worked in.

Side two of the LP features just two tracks, both recorded at the Fillmore East. The first, "Rondo (69)," is a live reinterpretation by the trio of the debut album's "Rondo." I continue to prefer the studio version because Emerson's studio solo has a taut inevitability that his solo here, which is more loosely constructed and less tightly focused, lacks. Nonetheless, I admire the fact that it's all improvised, it's totally spontaneous, and it's the product of a band that refuses to play it safe, pushing themselves to create the piece anew each performance. The final track, an organ trio arrangement of Bob Dylan's "She Belongs to Me," is the album's high point. Indeed, it is the finest live performance by the Nice on record, a *tour de force* of spontaneous composition by Emerson, Jackson, and Davison. Emerson brilliantly and fluently interweaves baroque, blues, and Western movie motifs (the theme from Elmer Bernstein's *Magnificent Seven* plays an important role in his improvisation), which Jackson and Davison embroider with an almost telepathic empathy. The final climactic section of the long instrumental, where a pulsating bass/drum groove pushes the increasingly dissonant and thick organ parts to a delirious climax before suddenly vanishing into the delicate strains of the song's opening, anticipates ELP's 1973–74 raga-rock masterpiece, "Aquatarkus." What's just as impressive as the band's spontaneous sense of large-scale structure is Emerson's extremely subtle sense of Hammond colorings, which lends the performance a much broader palette of tone-colors than one would expect from just one lead instrument.

Despite its manifold strengths, *Nice* does showcase a central weakness that was to dog the Nice for the remainder of their existence: a perpetual lack of new material forced them into an overreliance on cover songs and classical arrangements. But there was a reason for this. By now, it had occurred to the band that royalty income from their first two albums was a mere trickle. They sought the advice of a lawyer, who confirmed their fears: the contract they had signed with Immediate was extremely exploitative. With no easy legal way out, the band were forced to adhere to a grueling concert schedule in order to keep money coming in, since they could not count on record sale royalties; their heavy performance schedule left them with hardly any time to generate new music, and when new music was needed, they found it was much faster and easier to arrange preexisting material. Matters soon came to a head with Immediate when the label bungled the cover art of the U.K. release of *Nice*, although the band were able to arrange for a different cover for the U.S. release, which was retitled *Everything Nice as Mother Makes It*.[57] Even as the Nice were exploring legal avenues to be released from their contract, they were informed that Immediate had gone into voluntary liquidation. While this event released them from their commitments to Immediate, it also meant that there could be no letup in their grinding performance schedule: even though *Nice* shot up to number three in the U.K. album charts, the band scarcely saw a penny of the album's profits. It is possible that the Nice's royalty situation, which necessitated perpetual touring, was a big factor in the band breaking up earlier than they otherwise might have.

During the summer of 1969, the Nice were commissioned to write a piece of music for the Newcastle Arts Festival. After some discussion, the band decided to use the five bridges spanning the Tyne River in the vicinity of Newcastle as a symbol—Emerson would write a suite in five movements (or "bridges," as he called them), and the "five bridges" imagery would figure prominently in Lee Jackson's lyrics as well, which were intended to recount his memories and impressions of growing up in Newcastle. Emerson has described the genesis of the work in rather dramatic terms. He was on his way back to London from the package tour of Ireland with Yes and the Bonzo Dog Band: "I was on a plane with these turboprop engines, and when I leaned my head against the window I could feel their rhythm and hear all the pitches coming out through the overtones. I drew some bar lines on an airsick bag and wrote the theme to the suite right there in the air."[58] Emerson conceived the work as a suite for rock band with orchestral accompaniment. This was, of course, ground he had already covered in "Ars Longa Vita Brevis," but since the composition of that suite—which, as we've seen, was only orchestrated and cast into its "suite" form at the time of its recording—he had accrued more practical experience in working with an orchestra through his partnership with Joseph Eger, whom he tapped to conduct the orchestra for

---

[57] This was an inside joke among the band; "Mother" was Tony Stratton Smith, so called because he looked after the band, they told him, like a mother hen.
[58] Pethel, "Keith Emerson," 10.

the new work's premiere. The band had hoped that the orchestration would be done in time for the Newcastle Arts Festival on October 10, but it was not, so the "Five Bridges" suite was premiered by the band in a stripped-down rock trio arrangement at Newcastle's City Hall. The work was very well received, and Emerson was wowed by the hall's acoustics. Roughly a year and a half later, ELP would record *Pictures at an Exhibition* at the same venue.

The orchestration was finished shortly thereafter, and the premiere of the orchestrated *Five Bridges* was set for Croydon's Fairfield Hall on October 17. There was a great deal of pressure on the band for this event. They wanted to record the performance for future release, but at this point they were effectively a band without a label, so they were obliged to front the money for the Hall's rental, as well as paying the orchestra (the London Sinfonia) and the conductor (Joseph Eger), hoping that they would recoup their investment through a combination of gate receipts and later sales royalties when they found a label to release the album. They hired a warm-up band to play a forty-five minute opening set, a relatively new band whose popularity was beginning to take off with the release of their first album. The band was King Crimson. The band's lead vocalist and bass player was Greg Lake.

Fourth Album: *Five Bridges*

Some months later, in June 1970, the highlights of the October 17 concert—including the entire "Five Bridges" suite—were released as *Five Bridges*, the Nice's fourth album, and the first release on Tony Stratton Smith's new Charisma label. The "Five Bridges" suite itself is a significant achievement, and an enormous improvement over "Ars Longa Vita Brevis." Unlike the constituent movements of the latter, the five movements of "Five Bridges" actually cohere into a structural whole; Emerson creates a convincing structural dynamic through the systematic alternation of tempo, mood, and tone-color from movement to movement. Furthermore, the orchestration of "Five Bridges" doesn't feel extraneous, as if it were added as an afterthought, but seems much more essential to the work's basic conception than was the case with "Ars Longa Vita Brevis."

Of the first movement, entitled "Fantasia," Emerson says in the album's liner notes that he "worked on building a musical bridge combining early baroque forms to more contemporary ideas allowing the progression to move rather neurotically through a fantasia form."[59] The second half of his description is particularly apt. While the main theme is

---

[59] Keith Emerson, liner notes, The Nice, *Five Bridges*, Charisma LP CAS 1014 (1970).

vaguely baroque in character, there is neither the contrapuntal development nor the steady rhythmic patterning one expects of baroque music. Instead, the main theme is spun out into a continuous mosaic of subsidiary ideas, occasionally recurring in its more or less original form. There's only one interruption of the orchestra's "endless melody": a lyrical piano cadenza about halfway through the movement that foreshadows the one Emerson was to compose several years later for the first movement of his Piano Concerto. The effect of the movement as a whole—warmly melodic, with flexible, unassertive rhythms, mild but frequent dissonance, and a genially meandering flow—is rather reminiscent of twentieth-century neo-Romanticism, although I can't point to a specific model. It is rather different from nearly all of Emerson's later output—about the only later work I could point to that might carry on some aspects of this approach would be, as I said above, the opening movement of his Piano Concerto.

The second movement, entitled simply "2nd Bridge," is a driving number for organ trio. It's essentially an unconventionally constructed rock song: the verse is clear enough, but it's followed by an asymmetrical vocal bridge and a lengthy instrumental episode for the trio. This latter section is especially noteworthy—fleet, airy, and fantastical, with some amazingly subtle Hammond colorings, it may well mark the zenith of the Nice's ensemble virtuosity. Although the character of this music is radically different from ELP's *Tarkus*—it's nimble rather than ponderous—it's hard to imagine Emerson writing the instrumental episodes for organ trio that are such a major part of *Tarkus* without having composed this music first.

The third movement, "Chorale," is also a song, but more hymnlike than rock oriented, and featuring Lee Jackson accompanied by orchestral strings. In between verses, the trio, with Emerson now playing piano rather than organ, improvise around the chorale's chord changes. Jackson's vocal melody and the orchestral accompaniment evoke a particularly stately slow movement from a baroque concerto; perhaps it is the affinity of baroque and jazz styles that allows the chorale verses to alternate so seamlessly with the trio's Bill Evans–like jazz improvisations.

The fourth movement, "High Level Fugue," is a complex fugue for piano with Brian Davison accompanying on drums. Emerson admits this fugue is greatly influenced by the *Prelude and Fugue* of Friedrich Gulda, in which baroque contrapuntal practice is fused with the melodic and rhythmic contours of jazz. Emerson's liner notes are worth quoting here:

> The natives of Newcastle will know that their high level bridge supports on the upper level the trains, and on the lower level the cars. Having seen this bridge it suggested to me, as it did to Lee and Brian, a certain mechanical counterpoint which when expressed musically let me divide the trains and cars

between my right and left hands. Brian states a third counterpoint percussively using cymbals, simulating the splashing water of the River Tyne which becomes more and more polluted as "progress" destroys nature herself by building more and more machines.[60]

While Brian Davison is not a technical virtuoso, he does have a highly developed, subtle sense of jazz polyrhythm that is put to especially good use here. As to the subtext above—the dangers of technology run amok—we'll pick up that particular strand of the plot later, when we discuss ELP. Here we simply note that it's already a concern of Emerson.

The fugue turns out to be an excellent transition from the reflective chorale to the fifth movement, "Finale," which rescores the second movement for organ trio with jazz quintet accompaniment. The organ trio episodes of the second movement are excised here, replaced by a lengthy trombone solo by Chris Pyne over a repetitive bass figure. Unlike the triumphal ending of "Ars Longa Vita Brevis," which sounds a bit phony and ill-prepared, the conclusion of "Five Bridges" is genuinely exciting and feels inevitable.

Of all the major orchestral/rock compositions of the late sixties—here I include the Moody Blues' song cycle *Days of Future Passed*, Deep Purple's ghastly *Concerto for Group and Orchestra*, and Pink Floyd's *Atom Heart Mother* suite—the Nice's "Five Bridges" suite is the most satisfying musically. I would add, however, that this is more a result of its successful structural dynamic than of its imagination in fusing its rock, jazz, and orchestral media. Like all of his peers engaged in similar experimentation, at this point in time Emerson seemed incapable of thinking in terms of *blending* rock band and orchestra—instead, they are simply alternated. (One further notes than in the first movement, orchestra and piano don't blend, but alternate.) One also feels that the jazz quintet that adds so much to the fifth movement were significantly underused—they would have added a lot to the third movement, for instance—and that a more satisfactory solution for the final movement would have been to write for rock band, jazz quintet, *and* orchestra. It was to be nearly a decade later, when ELP recorded "Pirates," before Emerson fully grasped the possibilities inherent in seamlessly blending, rather than baldly alternating, band and orchestra. Nonetheless, even acknowledging this not insignificant limitation, the "Five Bridges" suite is an ambitious work that successfully solves such structural issues as Emerson was prepared to grapple with in 1969.

The "Five Bridges" suite occupies the entirety of the first side of the *Five Bridges* LP. The second side features two other major works from the October 17 Fairfield Hall Concert. The first is the Intermezzo from

---

[60] Emerson, *Five Bridges* liner notes.

Sibelius's *Karelia*. In many ways, this performance succeeds in blending (as opposed to simply alternating) the orchestral and rock forces better than the "Five Bridges" suite. The movement begins with Sibelius's impressionistic, hazy orchestral introduction: as the main march theme is reached, Jackson and Davison enter in the background on bass and drums, supplying a kind of *basso continuo* to the orchestra. Emerson himself makes a dramatically late entrance on organ, commencing a solo over the main theme's chord changes just as the orchestra drops out. The organ solo is followed by a quiet passage for organ and bowed bass guitar that moves into a funkier passage of trio improvisation; just when it appears that the improv is about to quietly peter out, muted brass momentarily enter, playing the main theme in the background.

Before they have an opportunity to build up any momentum, however, the orchestra is suddenly interrupted by a gale of organ feedback, replete with a drum "freak out." While Emerson's organ feedback episodes became rote, formulaic, and dreadfully tedious by the very early days of ELP—simply an excuse for his organ wrestling routine—in the late sixties, he actually was still *listening* to the sounds produced by his protesting organ, and making continuous adjustments to the *musique concrète*–like soundscapes he was creating: the results, as here, could actually be interesting and somewhat musical. Suddenly, the main theme erupts out of the fading fog of feedback like a clarion call, played by Emerson on a deliciously overdriven Hammond setting: the orchestra enters soon thereafter, creating a rousing finale that practically pulls you out of your seat. What's particularly impressive about this performance is that it's much harder driving than the studio version of *Ars Longa Vita Brevis*; this is a rare example of orchestrated rock that actually rocks. The orchestration is perfectly worked in, contributing much to the arrangement's structural dynamic: instead of the band simply playing along with the orchestra, karaoke-fashion, the orchestra becomes a colorful extension of Emerson's Hammond.

The band's approach to the next track, an arrangement of the third movement of Symphony no. 6, *Pathètique*, by Peter Tchaikovsky (1840–1893), is quite different. Trying to make this movement, with its lilting rhythms, "rock out" in the manner of the Sibelius march would not work, and the band wisely decline to force the issue. The entire opening section features the orchestra; the only member of the Nice who participates is Brian Davison, who taps out a Morse code–like cymbal rhythm that cuts polyrhythmically against the orchestral rhythms, becoming an important aspect of the arrangement. The band doesn't enter until nearly three and a half minutes in, when Emerson and the rest of the trio restate the main thematic material of the opening section without orchestra. This structural approach, known as double exposition form, is a common feature of concerto movements, being used to highlight the featured instrument, which restates the main thematic material (usually with light orchestral accompaniment) that had originally been stated by the orchestra alone. After this "double exposition," the trio gives way to the orchestra for a moment, then reenter to accompany the orchestra during the first of the movement's two big climaxes. Another passage for orchestra alone is followed by a short drum cadenza in which Davison develops the Morse code–like rhythm he had previously tapped out on the cymbals across the entire kit. Finally, the orchestra and trio unite for one last big statement of the main theme, with Emerson weaving an improvised organ line in and out of the orchestral fabric. Unlike Sibelius's *Karelia*, the third movement of Tchaikovsky's *Pathètique* is nobody's idea of a natural candidate for arrangement in a rock format. Nonetheless, the arrangement is surprisingly successful because the orchestra and trio are blended convincingly, and because Emerson's willingness to function as an orchestral voice rather than as a featured soloist serves the music's structural dynamic well. Hearing this track, one wishes Emerson had composed a concerto for orchestra and Hammond at some point.

There was one more number from the Fairfield Hall concert of October 17 that could have been featured on the *Five Bridges* album: the concert's finale, the same interweaving of Prokofiev's "Troika" and "Rondo" that had ended their orchestrated set at the Plumpton Blues Festival the previous August. However, that would have been the third version of "Rondo" in four albums, so it's probably wise that the band abstained from including it.[61] Its place was taken by two other tracks. The first, the band's unusual conjoined arrangement of Bob Dylan's "Country Pie" and J. S. Bach's Brandenburg Concerto no. 6, 1st movement, had been recorded the previous April at New York's Fillmore East. When I say "conjoined," I mean that the two disparate musical entities are joined sometimes horizontally (whereby a passage of one is followed by a passage of the other), and at other times vertically (as one flows into the other to form a contrapuntal union). I've always found the arrangement somewhere between clever and contrived—try as I might, I can't hear the two musical entities as a match made in heaven—but some of the band's fans love it, and at any rate, it's performed well here. The final track, "One of Those People," was recorded in Trident Studios during the same period as the four tracks that occupy side one of the *Nice* LP. Described by Paul Stump as "a berserk miscarriage of a pop song,"[62] it brings to perfection the quirky, absurdist strain of songwriting the band had inaugurated on side one of the *Ars Longa Vita Brevis* LP. I will return to this song in more

---

[61] They were also scared off by the stiff royalty fees that the publisher of "Troika," Boosey and Hawkes, threatened to impose.
[62] Stump, *The Music's All That Matters*, 58.

detail much later in our narrative, in order to make some crucial points about the essential difference between the Nice and ELP.

Many fans of the Nice hear the *Five Bridges* album as the apex of their output, and this is a totally defensible viewpoint. If I tend to rank their first album as being slightly better, I hasten to add that the task they set themselves on *The Thoughts of Emerlist Davjack* was an easier one. As I said, their debut album is a classic of British psychedelic rock. Nonetheless, although the album contains highly original moments—and although future elements of the progressive rock style are periodically present in embryonic form throughout the album—the fact remains that the music was created within the parameters of a style, psychedelic rock, which had been created by others. On *Ars Longa Vita Brevis*, the band adopt a new kind of lineup—the Hammond/piano trio—and launch out in search of a new sound that will better suit their reconfiguration. The album contains some blind alleys, and the promising avenues of development that it does uncover are only partially explored. However, by their third album, *Nice*, the band have become far more aware of what is and isn't idiomatic within the limitations of the keyboard trio format, and are showing a surer sense of where they wish to go with their classical-jazz-rock fusion. By *Five Bridges*, this musical fusion has been brought to a very accomplished and subtle state. Indeed, with *Five Bridges*, we have come to the cusp of what would soon be recognized as the progressive rock style. If I decline to classify *Five Bridges* as full-blown progressive rock, it's only because I'm not convinced that the classical influences have yet been fully digested here. I believe the final stage that needed to be passed through en route to the emergence of mature progressive rock was the orchestrated, "symphonic rock" of the late sixties; it was only through the experience of creating orchestrated rock music in extended forms that all the technical resources of classical music could henceforth become available to any rock musician who wished to use them. Obviously, *Five Bridges* played an important role in this rite of passage. As Emerson said, perhaps naively but nevertheless insightfully, in his liner notes to *Five Bridges*, "The Nice and Joseph Eger have been trying to build bridges to those musical shores which seem determined to remain apart from that which is a whole."[63]

Dissolution: November 1969–March 1970

Indeed, based on his statements and actions after the Fairfield Hall concert of October 17, 1969, it is clear that Emerson viewed this show, and

---

[63] Emerson, *Five Bridges* liner notes.

particularly the "Five Bridges" suite, as the goal toward which the Nice had always been striving. He never seemed totally satisfied with the band again, and soon began to hint that he was beginning to hear a different kind of music in his mind's ear, a music that would need to be realized within a different context. Said Emerson:

> An importance of good song-mongers became necessary if the three-piece formula was to continue. No longer could it be okay to freak out indiscriminately. No longer could it be okay to scream and shout lyrics. We'd had our fun and, as the Seventies approached, I prepared myself for a "decade of control." I'd felt restricted in my writing, because what I was writing needed a singer who could really sing. I felt then that I didn't have one. I was looking hopelessly for a singer who was an extension of my keyboard playing. It looked like the only way forward was to become more and more an instrumental band, which did not appeal to me.[64]

By late 1969 the interpersonal chemistry of the band was starting to deteriorate, especially between Emerson and Davison, the latter having grown tired of Emerson's increasingly ambitious mixed-media ventures. The fact that both had serious girlfriends—Emerson's Danish girlfriend, Elinor, became Mrs. Keith Emerson around Christmas 1969, and Brian Davison's girlfriend Maria was soon to become his second wife—also tended to distance them. While Emerson remained on friendly terms with Lee Jackson, he had come to the decision that Jackson's voice, with its odd admixture of raspiness and airiness and its limited range, was not the ideal vehicle for the new music he was striving towards. Not long after the Fairfield concert, he approached Tony Stratton Smith and informed him of his intention to form a new trio, and asked whom he thought might be a suitable replacement for Jackson. Disappointed but not entirely surprised by the prospect of Emerson breaking up the Nice, Stratton Smith had three suggestions. There was the bass player of Yes, Chris Squire, who sang extensive backing vocals, and might be talked into singing lead. There was bassist Jack Bruce of the recently disbanded Cream, who had shared lead vocal duties with Eric Clapton. And finally, there was the bass player and lead vocalist of King Crimson, the band that had opened for the Nice at their October 17 Fairfield Hall concert. His name was Greg Lake.

Shortly after this conversation, the Nice departed on their third American tour, which began with a short residency from November 16–19 at Unganos, New York. King Crimson were playing at Fillmore East at the same time, and showed up at one of the Unganos shows to check out their colleagues. Someone close to Emerson—probably Tony

Stratton Smith—sought out Lake, and in utmost secrecy broached the question of whether he might be interested in forming a new band with Emerson. But King Crimson were a band on the way up, not just in the U.K., but also in the U.S., where their live shows were going over very well. Lake was dismissive.

The Nice's tour continued on, with dates in Detroit, Toronto, Chicago, Minneapolis, Boston, and Buffalo between November 21 and December 7. Then they flew west, as they were scheduled to begin a four-day residency at San Francisco's Fillmore West between December 11 and 14. The supporting band was to be King Crimson.

Unbeknownst to Emerson, King Crimson's situation had changed drastically between mid-November and mid-December. On the way up to San Francisco from a series of shows they had played at Los Angeles' Whiskey a Go Go, multi-instrumentalist Ian McDonald and drummer Michael Giles informed guitarist Robert Fripp, the band's leader, that they would be leaving King Crimson after the last Fillmore West show. While it appears there may have been some discussion between Fripp and Lake about how the band might carry on, no solution had been put forward that seemed entirely viable for Lake. Understandably, Emerson's recent offer suddenly looked much more attractive than it had a scant four weeks earlier.

In the early days of ELP, the meeting of Emerson and Lake at the Fillmore shows was depicted as something akin to love at first sight. For example, in a 1972 press bio, Emerson is quoted as saying "Greg was moving a bass line and I played a piano in the back and Zap! It was there."[65] What has become evident in more recent times is that the origin of the Emerson-Lake partnership was nowhere near this magical, and was far more complicated. As he admits in his autobiography, Emerson was surprised and somewhat annoyed that Lake's first statement to him, when they finally met backstage at the Fillmore for an in-depth conversation, was an observation that some of his lines sounded blurry.[66] Lake, for his part, was surprisingly noncommittal: even after returning to England on December 15, he was "indecisive, almost evasive about discussing King Crimson's future."[67] Indeed, Emerson grew uncertain enough about Lake's intentions to approach Chris Squire and ask him if he would be interested in the job. Squire, who was somewhat surprised that Emerson wanted to can Lee Jackson, told him he'd consider it, but only if Emerson would also bring a lead vocalist into his proposed project; he could not envision himself playing bass and singing lead vocals simultaneously, he

---

[65] Emerson, requoted by David Terralavoro, "The Greg Lake Story, Part I: 1947–1971," *Fanzine for the Common Man*, no. 15 (January 1996): 15.

[66] Emerson, *Pictures*, 161.

[67] Emerson, *Pictures*, 163.

said. Not wanting to work with a fourth member, Emerson thanked Squire, and next approached Jack Bruce in January 1970. According to Emerson, Bruce's response was "I'd love to play with you, as long as you play all my stuff."[68] Bruce's name was crossed off the short list. It was only later—sometime around the latter part of February 1970, it would appear—that Emerson received the fateful telephone call. It was a late night call—around 3:00 a.m.—and Emerson recalls wearily dragging himself out of bed to answer the phone. "Hi man! Greg here. Sorry, did I wake you? Listen, I've been thinking. We should get the band together. I want to play with you, man."[69] As it turned out, this was not the last late night call Lake would have to make in order to cement the future of the new band.

Lake's phone call was, of course, the Nice's death sentence. But the sentence was not enacted immediately. In fact, between February 13–17, 1970, around the time Lake made his fateful call, the Nice participated in the granddaddy of all multimedia shows, the so-called Switched-On Symphony, which was filmed in Los Angeles for broadcast on NBC television. Produced by British television personality Jack Good, the show was placed under the artistic direction of Israeli conductor Zubin Mehta. Good had lined up a motley assortment of rock, classical, and R & B stars—the Nice shared the bill with Ray Charles, Jethro Tull, Santana, Jerry Goodman (then of the Flock, soon to be a founding member of Mahavishnu Orchestra), Pinkas Zukerman, Jacqueline Du Pré, Daniel Barenboim, and João Carlos Martins—with the basic concept being that these diverse individuals would be accompanied by the Los Angeles Philharmonic and/or each other. Emerson was not terribly impressed with the logistics of the event:

> We were all practicing in different corners of this one big area, and Jack Good came in and clapped his hands and said, "Listen everybody—Zubin Mehta!" And Zubin Mehta comes in and walks all the way through the studio with his head down, and we all thought "Oh well, fine." Of course, we didn't get a very good impression of him. He sort of stormed in and really didn't know what was going on. The whole thing was sort of a jumble, and Jack Good did marvels pulling it off.[70]

The event, as recalled by Emerson and others, was a combination of the ridiculous and the sublime, with the former predominating. The Nice played "America" with the Los Angeles Philharmonic while hoisted up by forklifts on sets that looked like theater boxes. The Nice, Santana, and the

---

[68] Emerson, *Pictures*, 163.
[69] Emerson, *Pictures*, 171.
[70] Pethel, "Keith Emerson," 11.

orchestra came together for Santana's "Soul Sacrifice." The Nice also played an extemporaneous blues in F with rock violinist Jerry Goodman, which elicited from Zubin Mehta the question, "And you did that all without music?"[71] Yet Emerson remembers Ray Charles's extemporaneous performance with the L.A. Philharmonic—after Charles had requested Mehta to let the orchestra follow his own cues—as "probably the most spontaneous musical reward I will ever come across again."[72] And it was here that he heard a young Brazilian pianist named João Carlos Martins perform a work by a composer that he had never heard of that brought him bursting into the pianist's dressing room to learn the identity of both composer and work. The composer was an Argentine named Alberto Ginastera. The work was his Piano Concerto no. 1.

Mehta was impressed enough by the Nice to invite them to perform with the Israel Philharmonic in Tel Aviv in June 1970. This was a date the Nice would never keep: shortly after arriving back in England from the L.A. event, Emerson informed Jackson of his intent to leave the Nice in the near future. Like Stratton Smith, Jackson was disappointed, but not entirely surprised. According to Emerson, Jackson suggested that Brian Davison not be informed of the band's demise until their early spring British tour was nearly over: Jackson feared that otherwise Davison might just disappear. Emerson agreed.[73] Davison did not learn of the impending split until early March, when he was informed by Tony Stratton Smith.

The Nice were not quite through, however, and were to make history one final time before the curtain came down. Here's Emerson:

> I went into a record shop where they knew me. [This would have been early 1970.] Walter Carlos's *Switched On Bach* had just been released. They played it for me in the shop. I didn't honestly like it. The guy played it for me because it had the *Brandenburg* in G [no. 3], which I had done with the Nice [i.e. as "Brandenburger"]. The guy asked me if I'd heard this version, played it for me, and asked me what I thought of it. I said it sounded horrible. It was too boggy, too laid down. But there was a picture of the thing it was played on, and I said, "So what's this?" And he said it was like a telephone switchboard. And I said "Oh, that's interesting." So I bought the album.[74]

While Emerson didn't particularly enjoy Walter (later Wendy, after a sex change operation) Carlos's *Switched On Bach*, he became increasingly intrigued by the modular Moog itself. Between 1967 and 1970, Keith

[71] Emerson, *Pictures*, 165.
[72] Ibid.
[73] Emerson, *Pictures*, 172.
[74] Emerson, quoted by Milano, "Keith Emerson," *Contemporary Keyboard*, October 1977, 32.

Emerson had squeezed some remarkable sounds out of his Hammond organs. Many of them were completely accidental, and could never be recaptured, hard as he might try. Here was an instrument that seemed to promise even more unearthly sounds, and once discovered, the sounds could be recalled, rather than forever being lost into the ether. He asked Tony Stratton Smith to investigate whether anybody in London had a Moog. A week later, Stratton Smith hit pay dirt.

Emerson was directed to contact Mike Vickers, keyboardist with Manfred Mann's band. Vickers invited Emerson to his apartment to check out the instrument. However, he reacted with horror when Emerson asked if he could borrow the instrument for a live performance. "He said 'No way. You don't realize the complications in this. There's no way you could do that.' I thought there must be some way, and asked, 'What if you hid down behind this thing and programmed it while I was playing it? You know, set up all these things and keep it in tune?'"[75] And so on March 6, the Nice played their last big multimedia show, at the Royal Festival Hall. Accompanied by the London Philharmonic Orchestra conducted by Joseph Eger, the "Five Bridges" suite and the third movement of the Tchaikovsky *Pathètique* were on the program.[76] The highlight of this concert, however, was a medley of music featured in the soundtrack of Stanley Kubrick's *2001: A Space Odyssey*—Richard Strauss's *Also Sprach Zarathustra*, Johann Strauss's *Blue Danube Waltz*, and György Ligeti's *Requiem*.[77] During this medley, the orchestra were accompanied by the Ambrosian Singers (hired at the Nice's expense), and Emerson, wearing a newly purchased "space age" silver lamé outfit, used the Moog to create otherworldly soundscapes to complement Ligeti's. All the while, as Emerson recalls, "Mike Vickers was hunched down backstage, but he'd pop up every now and then and put a plug in somewhere. It worked excellently."[78] This was the first live performance by a rock band using a Moog synthesizer, and it was very well received. The critic for *Record Mirror* wrote,

> The Nice's concert last Saturday at London's Royal Festival Hall proved beyond a shadow of doubt they are one of the most musically inventive of British groups. At one time, critics talked of the "classical" influence in their

---

[75] Emerson, quoted by Milano, "Keith Emerson," *Contemporary Keyboard*, October 1977, 36.
[76] The identity of the orchestra is in dispute. Emerson says the London Philharmonic (*Pictures*, 167); Martyn Hanson, the Royal Philharmonic (*Hang on to a Dream*, 123); Blair Pethel, the London Symphony Orchestra ("Keith Emerson," 15).
[77] Again, there is some dispute concerning which piece by Ligeti was included in the medley. Hanson says the "Lux Aeterna" section of the *Requiem* (*Hang on to a Dream*, 124); Emerson says it was *Atmospheres* (*Pictures*, 168); Pethel says *Volumina* ("Keith Emerson," 15). Because of the use of the Ambrosian singers, I suspect Hanson is correct.
[78] Milano, "Keith Emerson," *Contemporary Keyboard*, October 1977, 36.

leader Keith Emerson's playing and writing. But he showed he and the group have absorbed far more than classical music. What is happening now is a complete assimilation of existing musical modes coupled with the contemporary rhythmic feel in pop music. [Note the emphasis that the Nice's innovations were part of a utopian synthesis of musical styles, and the tone of critical approval] . . . Keith moved over to a Moog Synthesizer. The sounds this instrument can obtain are almost unlimited, and he made it literally talk.[79]

Emerson, for his part, decided then and there that the Moog was to become a major component of his new band's sound, and almost immediately initiated arrangements to purchase one.

The remainder of the Nice's existence, while short, was not particularly sweet. Brian Davison learned of the band's impending split shortly after the Royal Festival Hall concert, and their last British shows took place in an atmosphere of funereal gloom. The band's final recorded performance took place on March 25, 1970, when they played their tenth and last BBC session. Then they departed for Germany for their final two shows. The final performance by the Nice—until their unlikely reunion in 2002, that is—took place March 30, 1970, at the Peace Festival in West Berlin's Sportpalast.

Lee Jackson and Brian Davison were understandably unhappy about how events played out. The Nice were bona fide stars in Britain, and were in the process of building a substantial cult following in the U.S. that could have conceivably been converted to a mass audience. Lee Jackson later said that he could have been a better singer for the Nice had Emerson composed more idiomatic vocal lines, and had he shown more sensitivity to placing his material in keys that suited Jackson's vocal range. It is also true that Jackson's voice was ideal for some of the Nice's songs— mainly the rawer ones ("Tantalizing Maggie"), but also some of the more declamatory ones, where his brogue served him well (the second movement of the "Five Bridges" suite).

Nonetheless, Emerson's instincts were essentially correct, as events were to prove. It is hard to imagine the Nice summoning the requisite precision and virtuosity to pull off *Tarkus*. Nor is it easy to imagine Jackson singing a smooth ballad like "Lucky Man" that would earn the band substantial radio airplay. Jackson went on to form Jackson Heights, Davison, Every Which Way: neither band ever quite made it, even in Britain. Jackson and Davison got one last shot at rock stardom in 1973–74, when they formed another multikeyboard trio, Refugee, with Swiss keyboard virtuoso Patrick Moraz.[80] By pointing up the

---

[79] Emerson, *Pictures*, 167.
[80] See appendix C for an extensive discussion of Refugee and their eponymous first (and last) album.

Nice's limitations, I do not in any way wish to denigrate the significant body of music they left behind, or the important role they played in helping to effect the transition from late-sixties psychedelic rock to early-seventies progressive rock. Nor would I deny that while they lacked Emerson, Lake and Palmer's precision and effortless virtuosity, they had their own set of strengths—humor, spontaneity, unselfconsciousness—that one sometimes wishes ELP had possessed in greater measure.

Fifth Album: *Elegy*

Five Bridges was released posthumously, in June 1970, the first release of Tony Stratton Smith's fledgling Charisma label. It featured an impressive gatefold cover by Hipgnosis, a design company that was to play a major role in seventies rock album cover art. By now the popularity of the band was such that the album hit number two in the British charts. In April 1971, even as the debut album of Emerson's new band was soaring in the U.S. charts, and work on a second album was nearing completion, Charisma released another posthumous album by the Nice, *Elegy*. It contains just four tracks, all of them lengthy: the final two unreleased Trident Studio tracks, and live performances from the seminal Fillmore East shows of April 1969 of two of the band's most popular live numbers, "Hang on to a Dream" and "America." The former has a nice quotation of George Gershwin's "Summertime" as well as a pretty, impressionistic section that finds Emerson experimenting with a vaguely Middle Eastern scale. "America" may be overly long, but its conclusion, with genuinely eerie sounds evoking distant air-raid sirens followed by machine gun–like white noise bursts of the 6/8 rhythm, is bracing.

The two studio numbers are a trio arrangement of the Tchaikovsky *Pathètique* movement that had been featured in orchestrated form on *Five Bridges*, and a cover of Bob Dylan's "My Back Pages." Both tracks feature some intricate unison runs between bass and keyboard that may represent Lee Jackson's most virtuosic bass work with the Nice. While the Tchaikovsky arrangement features some genuinely impressive ensemble interplay, it suffers from timbral sameness—after listening to the orchestrated version of *Five Bridges*, the trio arrangement sounds bland by comparison. The Dylan arrangement fares somewhat better: Emerson begins on piano, but switches to Hammond halfway through, spearheading an energetic blues jam that includes an embryonic version of the main theme of "Blues Variation" that later was to appear on ELP's *Pictures at an Exhibition*.

Elegy is in many ways similar in conception to the band's third album, *Nice*, and although it's not as essential to the band's output, it still is important for allowing for a more fully rounded picture of the band's overall studio output and post-1968 live performances than would other-wise exist. *Elegy* hit number five in the British charts. While this may be a measure of the Nice's enduring popularity in Great Britain—it was, after all, released over a year after the band dissolved—its success probably owed even more to the skyrocketing popularity of the new band Emerson had cofounded with Greg Lake.

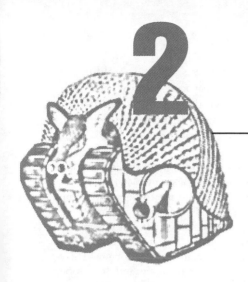

Greg Lake

Early Years and Apprenticeship (1947 1970)

Early Years

Roughly 75 miles due west of Worthing, Keith Emerson's old stomping ground, lie coastal Dorset's two largest cities: Bournemouth, one of southern England's major coastal resorts, and a few miles further west, Poole. It was in the latter city that Gregory Stuart Lake was born, growing up in Oakdale, a working class housing estate near Poole.

Lake was born on November 10. There is some question as to his year of birth. Sid Smith's *In the Court of King Crimson*[1] and Bruce Pilato's liner notes for Lake's career anthology, *The Greg Lake Retrospective: From the Beginning*,[2] give his year of birth as 1948. In *Emerson, Lake and Palmer: The Show That Never Ends*[3] and David Terralavoro's article in *Fanzine for the Common Man*,[4] his year of birth is given as 1947. *The Rolling Stone Encyclopedia of Rock & Roll* lists his year of birth as 1948.[5] In an interview with Keith Altham in *Music Scene*, Lake gave his year of birth as 1947.[6] The latter year seems more likely, although I am unable to account for these discrepancies. Unfortunately, Lake's official web site does not give a year of birth.

Lake has had rather little to say about his parents or his early years. Bruce Pilato quotes him saying, "I was born in an asbestos prefab hous-

[1] Sid Smith, *In the Court of King Crimson* (London: Helter Skelter, 2001), 43.

[2] Bruce Pilato, liner notes, *The Greg Lake Retrospective: From the Beginning* (Rhino CD R2 72627, 1997), 5.

[3] Forrester, Hanson, and Askew, *Emerson, Lake and Palmer*, 31.

[4] "The Greg Lake Story," 9.

[5] Jon Pareles and Patricia Romanowski, eds., *The Rolling Stone Encyclopedia of Rock & Roll* (New York: Rolling Stone Press/Summit Books, 1983), 175.

[6] Keith Altham, "The Manticore Tapes: The Last Reel—Greg Lake." This interview came from *Music Scene*; while I have a copy of the interview, unfortunately I don't know which issue it came from. I am guessing late 1973 or early 1974.

ing unit, and we were very poor. I remember it was always so cold in the winter; ice used to form on the inside of my bedroom windows. We didn't have much but we always got by, and back then, I always wanted to know what it was like to live on the other side."[7] In Forrester, Hanson, and Askew's *Emerson, Lake and Palmer*, Lake is quoted as saying,

> My father came from a very poor background, and yet my mother was comparatively well off. We had two different points of view going. My father's was that I should attain security, and therefore he wanted me to be a draftsman. He wasn't prepared for me to take a gamble [sounds a bit like Noel Emerson], but my mother would. My father was liberal enough to say that it was my life and "Do what you want to do, but this is my advice." He accepted it when I told him I was going to be a musician, and they really grafted for me. There were times when I was hungry and they gave me money and sent food parcels.[8]

According to Lake, his earliest musical influence was his mother: "My early musical influence stems from my mother who was a pianist. She bought me a second-hand guitar and I went to lessons where this cat taught me these awful Bert Weedon things."[9] The "cat" in question was a gentleman named Don Strike. Strike taught guitar out of his music store in Bournemouth, an establishment that, incidentally, still exists today (2006). In another roughly contemporaneous interview, Lake gives a fuller and more positive description of his time with Strike: "When I was first learning guitar my teacher got me into a lot of the old thirties tunes which really influenced me a lot at the time. Many of those numbers can be very good to learn on, because some of the arrangements have very subtle chord changes."[10] As Lake has admitted elsewhere, thirties pop tunes were not the only item on the agenda during his studies with Don Strike: "I had to do these violin exercises by [Nicolo] Paganini, which were a weird concoction of music. You were required to read the music,

---

[7] Greg Lake, quoted by Pilato, liner notes to *The Greg Lake Retrospective*, 5. Peter Sinfield remarked to Paul Stump about Lake's early years, "He came from a poor background. Greg told me once that the people next door had tinned peaches for tea. Ergo, he'd want tinned peaches. He was one of those classic keep-up-with-the-Joneses cases. He was a Roman throwback, the freed slave who kind of went out and bought everything." See Stump, *The Music's All That Matters*, 172–73.

[8] Greg Lake, quoted by Forrester, Hanson and Askew, *Emerson, Lake and Palmer*, 31. This quote is, in turn, lifted from Keith Altham's "The Manticore Tapes."

[9] Greg Lake, quoted by Keith Altham, "Greg Lake: Still He Turns Them On," *Music Scene Top Ten Series: Emerson, Lake and Palmer* (May 1974). Weedon, incidentally, is a British pop guitarist whose closest American counterpart is probably Chet Atkins: he reached the height of his popularity during the fifties, rendering covers of the pop tunes of the day in a light jazz style.

[10] Greg Lake, quoted by Johnson, "Under the Influence," 6.

but I always tended to play them by ear. Whenever my eyes would stray from the music score, he'd hit my fingers with a ruler. Whap! I think it was quite ironic that his name was Mr. Strike."[11] Lake studied with Don Strike for about a year when he was between twelve and thirteen years old. It was during these lessons that he became acquainted with another student of Strike's by the name of Robert Fripp. The connection between Strike, Lake, and Fripp later proved to be of major significance for the history of rock when Fripp and Lake reconnected in King Crimson. It is also significant because the approach to guitar playing that Don Strike taught Fripp and Lake was to become widely influential, especially through Fripp's efforts to systematize the approach in the Guitar Craft courses he taught and supervised between the mideighties and early nineties.[12] The foundation of the approach taught by Don Strike to his two famous pupils involves a rapid cross-picking technique in which careful attention is given to the use of the plectrum in the right hand. In commenting on his and Fripp's common formative lessons with Strike, Lake has said:

> Our guitar styles are similar, although as players, we've got a different sense of musicality. He's also much faster, of course. But the way we play guitar is almost identical. We used to practice together, so naturally we practiced a lot of the same music. We both use a sort of cross-picking style, which came from the fact that our teacher was actually a banjo player.

Lake is convinced that the Paganini exercises, in particular, left an imprint on some of King Crimson's music: "Don used to give us all these intense Paganini violin scales [exercises] to play on the guitar, which is where the Crimson riffs came from. Bob [Fripp] and I used to compete to see who could play them faster. The guitar-bass runs in the middle of "[21st Century] Schizoid Man" are a good example of this."[13]

At the time of his lessons, however, Lake appears to have given no thought as to how Paganini violin exercises might be applied to rock music: indeed, it was only several years later, when he joined King Crimson in early 1969, that he began to seriously listen to and learn from classical music. During the early sixties, Lake's main musical preoccupation was with the Shadows and their lead guitarist, Hank Marvin. The Shadows were a four-piece band (two guitars, bass, and drums) that were roughly the British equivalent of the American band the Ventures. Although they did sing, they were best known for their instrumental hits

---

[11] Greg Lake, quoted by Pilato, liner notes to *The Greg Lake Retrospective*, 5.
[12] The earliest source I am aware of where Fripp discusses his picking technique in some detail is Steve Rosen, "King Crimson's Robert Fripp," *Guitar Player*, May 1974, 35.
[13] "One 2 One," The Official Greg Lake Web Site, 31–35, http://www.greglake.com/newsite/feedback.asp?offset=30.

of the early sixties like "Apache" and "F.B.I.," and for being the back-up band of Cliff Richard, "The British Elvis"; Richard and the Shadows were Great Britain's most popular and important rock and roll act of the early sixties, until they were superseded by the Beatles. The Shadows' sound, in their most characteristic instrumental numbers, anticipates both American surf rock and sixties spy movie soundtracks, although they were capable of moving fluently between a whole array of late-fifties/early-sixties styles. Said Lake, "The first music to give me a real rush was from the Shadows . . . I don't rate Hank Marvin as a great guitarist, but he was certainly an influential one. Hendrix listened to him, I can promise you that. The sound that Marvin was the first to get—that particular Fender Stratocaster sound—was one of the things Hendrix developed."[14] Marvin's guitar playing, like virtually every other rock and roll guitarist of the early sixties, was indebted to Chuck Berry's: however, Marvin's playing was both unusually precise for its time, and uniquely reverb-laden. Indeed, some of his parts (the opening of "Apache," for instance) seem to anticipate psychedelia, and while I can just hear the line of influence Lake postulates between Marvin and Hendrix, I can hear a much more definite Marvin influence in the fulsomely reverberating guitar parts of Steve Howe.

Sometime during 1963–64, Lake's education terminated with his exit from Henry Harbin Secondary Modern School. For a while after leaving school he worked loading and unloading cargo on the docks of Poole.[15] This did not seem to offer a particularly promising future, so like Emerson, but at an even younger age, he made the decision he wanted to be a musician. He thereafter joined his first band, Unit Four, consisting of himself (lead vocals and guitar), John Dickenson (keyboards), Dave Genes (guitar), and Kenny Beveridge (drums). Unit Four stayed together through 1965. Lake recalls, "Before King Crimson, when I was a teen, I had played mostly in cover bands, and we had to play everything. We did the resort circuit near Bournemouth. It wasn't like I had one influence. I listened to everything because I had to play all types of music. British pop [i.e., Cliff Richard and the Shadows, the Beatles]; Motown; Blues."[16] Robert Fripp recalls,

> The first time I saw Greg Lake [perform] was at the Cellar Club in Poole. Unit Four, Greg's first group, was auditioning for the Cellar Club's management. I climbed over the back wall and let myself in. The next several times I saw, and heard, Greg was at the Oakdale Boys Club where Unit Four were regulars. Greg was both lead singer and guitarist. This was during 1965.[17]

---

[14] Greg Lake, quoted by Johnson, "Under the Influence," 6–7.
[15] Forrester, Hanson, and Askew, *Emerson, Lake and Palmer*, 32.
[16] "One 2 One," Official Greg Lake Web Site, 81–85.
[17] Robert Fripp, quoted by Pilato, liner notes to *The Greg Lake Retrospective*, 2.

When Unit Four broke up in 1965, Lake and Dave Genes formed another cover band, the Time Checks, with Bev Strike (Don's son) on bass and Tony Batey on drums. Like Unit Four, the Time Checks were a cover band that played the resort circuit of coastal Dorset. The Time Checks dissolved sometime during 1966.

The Shame

In later 1966 or early 1967, Lake formed another band, the Shame, with former Unit Four member John Dickenson (keyboards), as well as Malcolm Brasher (bass) and Billy Nims (drums).[18] While Unit Four and the Time Checks were semiprofessional bands, the Shame offered Lake his first taste of the rigors of the professional musician's life:

> Probably the worst thing that ever happened to me was when we had been on the road for about a week and we had literally been living off a pint of milk a day and a loaf. We used to scrape out the inside and pack it with chips and that was our food for the week. Then I got pneumonia and I was playing on stage with it. You keep going as long as you can but eventually you become aware that you're more than just ill, you're seriously ill. This was in Carlisle [northwestern England], but the guys didn't want to drive back overnight, so we slept in the van and it was well below freezing. I woke up blue! When we got home I was nearly dead, I literally fell over and went into a coma. My mother got a doctor and he pumped me full of oxygen and penicillin. That was probably the worst I went though.[19]

Many years later, Lake ruminated,

> By the age of seventeen I was touring quite a bit and basically living in a van. I had become tough and I was highly committed to the music. That is what you see when you see a young band that has grown up the hard way. You see these people who are prepared to live through very hard times, to steal milk off of doorsteps because they can't afford food, to sacrifice so they can pursue their music. That was the life I came from.[20]

---

[18] I have seen the bassist's name spelled "Braiser" as well. I am not sure which spelling is correct.

[19] Greg Lake, quoted by Altham, "The Manticore Tapes: The Last Reel—Greg Lake."

[20] Greg Lake, quoted by Dale Titus, "More than a Lucky Man," *Bass Frontiers* (September–October 1997), 30. Keith Emerson came to this place when he was a few years older than Lake, but his situation was sometimes similarly dire during his time with the T-Bones and the VIPs: he once broke into the electricity meter in his apartment in order to get heat from a two-bar fire. When his landlord discovered the tampering and he was expelled, he next rented from a landlady who told him he could only use the common bathtub on Thursdays. See Emerson, *Pictures*, 51–52.

The Shame attracted the interest of MGM, and during 1967 the band recorded a single, "Too Old to Go Way Little Girl" with B-side "Dreams Don't Bother Me," both songs penned by American songwriter Janis Ian. The single, originally scheduled for a September 1967 release, was eventually released in early 1968 on MGM's Poppy label. Lake's voice is already fully recognizable, and he also contributes some piercing guitar leads that almost remind one of an electric sitar (there is in fact a sitar part in the latter section of the song, although Lake didn't play it). The B-side is also nicely arranged, and suggests that John Lennon was exerting a growing influence on Lake. Although the single went nowhere, the Shame evidently were a strong live band: Andy Ellison recalls, "We used to have Cat Stevens, Tomorrow [Steve Howe's band] played there a lot, [and] the Shame, which was originally Greg Lake's band—I used to think the Shame were amazing."[21] Robert Fripp has said, "Four days of my life as an unpaid roadie with the Shame in Helston and Penzance (while waiting to go to the university) helped change the direction of my own life."[22] It was at this point Fripp made his own decision to pursue the calling of a musician.

At some point in later 1967 Lake's tenure with the Shame ended. Shortly thereafter, he was briefly involved with an offshoot of the Shame called the Shy Limbs. This band included his old mate John Dickenson on keyboards, Malcolm Brasher on bass, and future King Crimson drummer Andy McCullough. Lake was never a permanent member of the Shy Limbs, but he is featured as lead vocalist and guitarist on their single "Love," evidently recorded in 1968 and released on the Poppy label in 1969. Penned by Dickenson, the song is very reminiscent of flower-power era Beatles, both in the jarring shifts of rhythm and mood between verse and chorus (reminiscent of "Lucy in the Sky with Diamonds") and the chorus's cheerful rock march (which recalls "All You Need Is Love"). Again, as on his single with the Shame, Lake's piercing guitar leads feature a highly characteristic timbre, not unlike electric sitar; it is curious that his electric guitar sound was never again this immediately recognizable.[23]

---

21 Andy Ellison, quoted by Terralavoro, "The Greg Lake Story," 10.

22 Robert Fripp, quoted by Pilato, liner notes to *The Greg Lake Retrospective*, 3.

23 Lake, in the liner notes to *From the Underground: The Official Bootleg* (Greg Lake Ltd. Recordings GL-CD3001, 1998), is listed as guitarist on "Love." Sid Smith, *In the Court of King Crimson*, 56, states the guitar part was supplied by none other than Robert Fripp. All I can say is that the guitar work on "Love" appears to be by the same person who played guitar on the Shame's single. There is also some dispute as to whether Lake sings on the B-side of "Love," namely, "Reputation," which, unfortunately, I have never heard. Smith (56) says he does; Terralavoro, "The Greg Lake Story," 11, says he doesn't. Clearly the precise nature of Lake's involvement with the Shy Limbs needs to be clarified. It would also be nice to know more precisely when this was recorded.

The Gods

Sometime during late 1967 or early 1968—either during or after his brief involvement with the Shy Limbs, since the precise date of that has never been clarified—Lake joined a Hatfield-based band called the Gods. This band, which had been together since 1965, consisted at the time of Lake, keyboardist Ken Hensley, drummer Lee Kerslake, and guitarist/vocalist Joe Konas; Mick Taylor, soon to find fame as Brian Jones's replacement in the Rolling Stones, had left the band shortly before Lake joined. Lake has been rather dismissive of this band. In 1971 he told Nick Logan of *New Musical Express*, "The Gods is similar to training college, a very poor training college. A lot of musicians came out of the Gods and went on to something better, but the Gods never did anything. They completely changed personnel half a dozen times."[24] When Keith Altham asked him if he would characterize the Gods as a covers band, Lake responded,

> We were making our own [music], but which was horribly similar to others. It was the first stage for me between playing other people's material and my own. It was a stage of compromise. When you write your own material but you make sure it sounds like somebody else's, not consciously, but it lands up that way. The songs, for instance, that were written in the Gods used to come out tremendously like songs by Cream. Not that they were copies, but they had the sound and feel.[25]

Indeed, it was friction over creative control that eventually ruptured the relationship between Lake and the Gods: he had written some material for the band, which he apparently felt was being short-shrifted. Ken Hensley later said, "Just as we were about to start recording we had a falling out with Greg. The main problem was that he was far too talented to be kept in the background."[26] Hensley and Kerslake were later to reappear in the British hard rock/proto metal band Uriah Heep, where they achieved far more success than they ever did with the Gods.

Despite Lake's assessment that his time with the Gods was "a general nothing," his tenure with the band produced two important results. More than the Shame, which retained something of a regional, South Coast identity, the Gods had designs on becoming a national phenomenon, and it was with the Gods that Lake began playing in some of Britain's biggest

---

[24] Greg Lake, quoted by Nick Logan in a *New Musical Express* article of February 13, 1971, repeated by David Terralavoro, "The Greg Lake Story," 11.

[25] Greg Lake, quoted by Keith Altham, "The Manticore Tapes."

[26] Ken Hensley quoted in Terralavoro, "The Greg Lake Story," 11. The quotation is lifted from a CD reissue of the Gods' first album, *Genesis*, which does not include any Greg Lake participation as he had left the band prior to its recording.

and most prestigious clubs, particularly in London, where the band held a residency at the Marquee. Second, and perhaps even more importantly, it is with the Gods that Lake first began to play bass. Lake was, in fact, brought in to replace bassist Paul Newton (another future member of Uriah Heep) after Newton left the band. From what I've inferred, it is possible that Lake and Joe Konas may have switched off between bass and guitar; however, it is with the Gods, and not, as has often been suggested (from time to time by Lake himself) with King Crimson, that Lake gained his initial bass guitar experience.

It is interesting that in a nearly thirty-year career as bass guitarist with King Crimson and ELP spanning 1969 to 1998, Lake always seems to have considered his bass playing a kind of "momentary" diversion from his "real" instrument, the guitar: "I was a guitar player that was forced to play bass in King Crimson and ELP because there was no one else to do it. Therefore, I never considered myself a right, proper bassist."[27] He's said elsewhere, "I've never considered myself a great bass player. I wasn't trained to be that. I studied guitar . . . Therefore, I have always played bass like a guitarist plays. I often attack the strings, which accounts for the very rhythmic style I have."[28] Throughout the remainder of the book, we will want to keep these remarks in mind. During the seventies, in particular, a frequently debated question in the rock world was whether or not Lake ranked as one of rock's great bass guitarists. My answer would be: it depends on how one defines a "great bass guitarist." Lake once said something to the effect that he could play virtually any bass line someone asked him to play.[29] The recorded evidence tends to support this claim: some of Lake's bass lines are very impressive from a technical point of view, and from a purely technical perspective, Lake may well have been one of rock's great bass guitarists of the seventies. On the other hand, Lake never seems to have thought naturally in terms of weaving bass lines under a given melodic or harmonic structure, and his best bass lines all have the appearance of having been laboriously worked out: his more spontaneous bass lines, including his improvised ones, usually are not particularly memorable or imaginative. In sum, Lake was to become an impressive bass technician: he was never to become a natural bass player.

According to the Gods' Hensley, Lake left the band during the summer (probably late summer) of 1968. It appears that it was at this time that he briefly undertook a career as a draftsman: "My job was as a draftsman for awhile, then I took some courses. I couldn't see a future in that either. That was the point when I joined my first professional band. I

---

[27] "One 2 One," Official Greg Lake Web Site, 56–60.
[28] "One 2 One," Official Greg Lake Web Site, 71–75.

joined King Crimson through Bob Fripp whom I had known for eight years. We used to go to the same guitar teacher."[30]

Towards King Crimson: Giles, Giles and Fripp

As the reader may recall, Fripp had roadied for the Shame for a few days during spring 1967, and this experience had galvanized him to pursue the career of a professional musician. He henceforth answered an ad for a singing organist—although he neither sang nor played organ—that had been placed by a pair of brothers, (bassist) Peter and (drummer) Michael Giles. Fripp recalls that after working with the Giles brothers for about a month, he asked Michael if he had the gig: "He rolled a cigarette, looked down and put the cigarette in his mouth, lit it, puffed on it, and said 'Let's not be in a hurry to commit ourselves to each other.' "[31] In the fall of 1967, the trio moved to London, where they gigged sporadically, often in rather unlikely circumstances—for instance, they accompanied an Italian crooner named "Hot Lips" Moreno for about a week—all the while writing and rehearsing material. By December, the trio were basically out of work, and a despondent Fripp briefly returned to his home town of Wimborne to reclaim his old job playing guitar for the Majestic Dance Band at the Majestic Hotel. In early 1968, Giles, Giles and Fripp returned to London. It was at this point that things began to happen for them. During late 1967, Peter Giles had conscientiously recorded demos of the band's material, showing considerable ingenuity in creating sonically high-quality multitrack recordings using only a Revox reel-to-reel tape recorder and a single overhead microphone. Somehow, Giles managed to finagle a meeting with Hugh Mendl, a high level executive at Decca, and he presented Mendl with the trio's demos.

By 1968, psychedelic rock was happening in a big way, fundamentally changing the entire landscape of commercial music. Record company executives were becoming aware that audiences for the new music saw the 45 rpm single as a kind of corporate imposed "straightjacket" on musical creativity, and much preferred the 33 rpm LP as a medium because it allowed for longer cuts and for the conceptual linking together of consecutive songs. They were also becoming aware that in the new music, instrumental talent counted for as much or more than vocal talent, and

---

[29] He said this in an interview in *Musician* that ran sometime in 1981, around the time his first solo album was released. Alas, I cannot locate this interview!

[30] Greg Lake, quoted by Altham, "The Manticore Tapes." When Lake says King Crimson was his "first professional band" one assumes that what he really means is that they were his first *successful* professional band.

[31] Robert Fripp, quoted by Smith, *In the Court of King Crimson*, 19.

instrumental solos were becoming far more important than they had been in any previous style of rock and roll. Beyond that, a lot of record company executives frankly admitted that they didn't fully understand the implications of all the changes that were taking place in popular music, and were scrambling to keep up. Often this involved signing anybody with long hair, and then carefully monitoring what sold and what didn't. In the case of Decca, there was the additional consideration that this was the label that had allowed the Beatles to slip through their grasp: they were determined to avoid another such mistake, at any cost. When Giles, Giles and Fripp showed up for their meeting with Mendl, they were bizarrely dressed; when he played their demos, their music sounded strange, as well. But who was to say that they weren't the Next Big Thing? Mendl therefore signed the band for two singles and an album, with each member receiving a £250 advance. Mendl didn't even balk when Robert Fripp, showing the meticulousness that would characterize his later dealings with record labels, went through the contract line by line, made deletions and emendations, and sent it back to Mendl to be redrafted. During early summer 1968, Giles, Giles and Fripp convened at Decca's studios in Broadhurst Gardens to record their first album.

Said album, *The Cheerful Insanity of Giles, Giles and Fripp*, was released in September. It didn't exactly set the world on fire. Said Fripp: "World sales of the album within the first year were under 600. My first royalty statement showed sales in Canada of 40 and Sweden of one."[32] The problem is not hard to discern: in a period when the frontiers of popular music were being pushed back into new and uncharted territory, when paradigms were being shifted, when minds were being bent, *The Cheerful Insanity of Giles, Giles and Fripp* is simply weird, its admixture of wry, Monty Python–like humor, inside jokes, dreamy pastoralism, and psychedelic experimentalism never cohering. Greg Lake's picturesque description of the band effectively sums up the situation:

> Robert formed a band called Giles, Giles and Fripp. This would be 1968. And somehow—to this day, I don't know how—his band actually got a record deal with Decca. They were the most bizarre group that you could ever imagine. They would dress up as crippled people—pretend to be crippled—and play the most ridiculous songs.[33]

Several months before the album's release in September, Giles, Giles and Fripp had agreed among themselves that if they were to have any future,

---

[32] Robert Fripp, quoted by Eric Tamm, *Robert Fripp: From King Crimson to Guitar Craft* (Boston and London: Faber and Faber, 1990), 32.
[33] Greg Lake, quoted by Russell Hall, "Welcome to the Show! Emerson, Lake and Palmer in Their Own Words," *Goldmine*, December 6, 1996, 19.

additional musicians would need to be brought in to the project. Scanning an issue of *Melody Maker*, Peter Giles chanced upon an ad by a vocalist named Judy Dyble, who had sung briefly in Fairport Convention (before being replaced by Sandy Denny), seeking the services of a bass guitarist/vocalist and a guitarist/vocalist. The band invited her to their Brondesbury Road digs, and she arrived with her boyfriend, songwriter and multi-instrumentalist Ian McDonald, a veteran of the Royal Military School of Music and numerous Army bands, in tow. The band quickly recognized in McDonald a gifted songwriter and an extremely impressive woodwind player (particularly on saxes and flutes), and noted he could effectively demonstrate his ideas on both acoustic guitar and keyboards. In order to snag McDonald, the trio invited both Dyble and McDonald to join.

The quintet went right to work. By July 1968, Dyble had broken up with McDonald and left the band. This distraction aside, the new material, some of which was recorded by Decca in July (too late to be included on the debut album) rocked harder and had more emotional depth than the trio's music. Besides bringing a new level of songwriting and arranging polish and an imposing multi-instrumental attack to the band, McDonald brought another key individual into the Giles, Giles and Fripp orbit—a lyricist named Peter Sinfield, with whom he had begun working earlier in the year, while hanging out with Sinfield's band Creation. McDonald also brought the band a measure of financial security by talking a rich uncle, Angus Hunking, into extending the band a £3700 loan with a three-year repayment period. For the first time, instead of scraping by from week to week, Giles, Giles and Fripp—which, despite their name, were now a quartet including Ian McDonald—could systematically plot a long-term strategy.

In September, Giles, Giles and Fripp appeared on BBC's Radio One. On November 13, the band were filmed in a field for BBC2's *Color Me Pop* show. They returned to the studio on November 16, when they were filmed indoors, lip-syncing and miming their parts to the accompaniment of Peter Giles's demo tapes, which the impressed BBC engineers told him were of professional studio quality. The show was broadcast on November 30.

Even as the band achieved this higher level of exposure, however, interpersonal tensions within the band reached a climactic point. The differences were principally between Robert Fripp and Peter Giles. As Sid Smith's *In the Court of King Crimson* makes clear, there was always a bit of personality clash between the two. More important, though, was the fact that the two men held starkly different visions of what direction the band's music ought to evolve in. Smith puts it very well: "Whereas Giles favored smartly observed scenarios housed in a light, slightly wry pop style, Fripp, never overly interested in lyrical content, veered more toward a demonstrative, harsher sound built around his considerable technique and a pronounced taste for minor keys."[34] The night after the band's first BBC2 filming session, Fripp met with Michael Giles to discuss the band's future. What the band really needed, said Fripp, was a real lead singer, and he knew just the man for the job: a veteran of the Shame and the Gods named Greg Lake, who played both guitar and bass. After listening to Fripp, Michael Giles became convinced that Fripp's vision for the band's future was the correct one. Next Fripp confronted the entire band with an ultimatum: it was necessary for the band's future that Lake be brought in, and depending on what direction the band as a whole chose to pursue, Lake could either replace Peter Giles on bass or himself on guitar. By the time the Giles, Giles and Fripp spot was broadcast on BBC2 on November 30, Peter Giles was out of the band and Greg Lake was in.

King Crimson

Origins and Earliest Period (December 1968–June 1969)

Lake recalls the phone call from Fripp as follows: "He said to me, 'Would you like to play bass?' I said 'no, not really.' And he said, 'Yeah, but if you don't we'll never get it off the ground.' So I said 'okay, I'll play bass for you.'"[35] Lake saw his recruitment as the result of an ultimatum handed down by Decca to Giles, Giles and Fripp: "Basically, the record company called up Bob and said 'If you don't give us something that has at least a vague correlation to what's going on in the real world, we're going to drop the band.'"[36] Sid Smith mentions nothing about record company pressure, however; it seems more likely that the majority of the band simply agreed with Fripp's assessment that in order for Giles, Giles and Fripp to succeed, a real lead singer was needed. Peter Sinfield, who by late 1968 was becoming increasingly involved with the band due to his songwriting partnership with McDonald, would seem to confirm this view: "Giles, Giles and Fripp desperately needed a real singer. So they recruited Greg, who was another boy from Dorset and an old friend of Bob's. He had been in the Gods and was able to play bass—actually, not as well as Peter Giles—but he could sing like an angel, albeit fallen in his case."[37]

Lake moved to London in December. In January, Peter Sinfield and a cohort named Dik Fraser from his old band Creation were brought in as

[34] Smith, *In the Court of King Crimson*, 41.
[35] Greg Lake, quoted by Steve Rosen, "Greg Lake of Emerson, Lake and Palmer," *Guitar Player*, September 1974, 20.
[36] Greg Lake, quoted by Bruce Pilato, liner notes to *The Greg Lake Retrospective*, 8.
[37] Ibid.

road managers. Sinfield's first order of business was to locate suitable rehearsal space, and he quickly delivered, arranging for the band to rent the basement of the Fulham Palace Café. On January 13, 1969, the band commenced rehearsals there. On January 22, the band adopted a new name, King Crimson, drawn from a poetic device Sinfield used to represent Beelzebub, the fallen angel ranking just below Satan himself in Milton's *Paradise Lost*. If the band's name suggests infernal energy, one thing nearly everybody involved with the original lineup of King Crimson agrees on is their almost inhuman intensity. Said Fripp:

> Following several years of failure we regarded King Crimson as a last attempt at playing something we believed in. Creative frustration was a main reason for the group's desperate energy. We set ourselves impossibly high standards but worked to realize them, and with a history of unemployment, palais and army bands, everyone was staggered by the favorable reactions from visitors.[38]

Lake recalls,

> It was better not to make mistakes in that band because it could be very ugly. Well, there was a sort of "death look" that would go about. It was if you played anything that wasn't tasteful. You'd get a quizzical look. It could be anybody. You might get a dirty look from Michael or Fripp or me. There was a sort of code for musical behavior. You just didn't play the wrong thing at the wrong time but you were expected to play caliber music—that was the general expectation of everybody.[39]

Much of the music that the band were rehearsing was newly composed, often collaboratively. For instance, Fripp recalls the genesis of one of the band's early classics, "21st Century Schizoid Man," as follows: "The first few notes—Daaa-da-da-daa-daa-daaa—were by Greg Lake, the rest of the introduction was Ian McDonald's idea, I came up with the riff at the beginning of the instrumental section, and Michael Giles suggested we all play in unison in the very fast section toward the end of the instrumental."[40] There were a few holdovers in the repertoire from late period Giles, Giles and Fripp (that is, the quartet configuration), including "I Talk to the Wind," and the band also arranged the Beatles' "Lucy in the Sky with Diamonds" and Joni Mitchell's "Michael from Mountains," which Judy Collins had already covered on her 1967 album *Wildflowers*. Indeed, one reporter related that the band often unwound after tense, difficult

---

[38] Tamm, *Robert Fripp*, 33.
[39] Smith, *In the Court of King Crimson*, 45–46.
[40] Tamm, *Robert Fripp*, 34.

rehearsals by listening to Judy Collins albums.[41] A recurring musical motif in early Crimson is the juxtaposition of intense, frenetic, "infernal" rock music with subdued, melancholy, "heavenly" acoustic passages with overtones of both British folk and the Elizabethan/Jacobean lute tradition: through the influence of King Crimson, this electric/acoustic, rock/folk juxtaposition was to become a characteristic feature of British progressive rock as a whole.

Two other events took place in January 1969 that potently impacted the new band. Sinfield started to construct a basic light show, which eventually was to be one of the best in rock, not only because of its sophistication, but also because it was so intimately tied to the atmosphere and mood of the music. Also, the band talked two twentysomething employees of the Noel Gay theatrical agency, David Enthoven and John Gaydon, into quitting their jobs and becoming the band's managers: this was the beginning of the formidable EG Management agency. Very soon, Enthoven and Gaydon had interested Giles, Giles and Fripp's old patron, Decca, in the new band. Decca dispatched Tony Clarke, then producing the Moody Blues, to check out one of the band's rehearsals: Clarke was impressed enough to suggest that Decca extend them a record deal.

In late February, the band left London for Newcastle, where they had a week-long residency at a trendy club called Change Is. It was here that club manager Ron Markham introduced King Crimson to the world, telling the audience, "Ladies and gentlemen, Giles, Giles and Fripp, who for reasons best known to themselves have changed their name to King Crimson, will have a freakout without the aid of pot, LSD or any other drug."[42] After their final show in Newcastle on March 1, the band returned to London. Shortly afterward they were mentioned in print for the first time, with Simon Stable of *International Times* predicting great things for the band. It was also at this time that Peter Sinfield was brought in as a full member on account of his work as a lyricist and light show designer and operator. Sinfield's status with the band—he received 10 percent of the band's performance and record royalties, and 20 percent of the publishing—was more or less unique for a nonperforming member of a rock band: the only obvious precedent is Keith Reid, Procol Harum's resident lyricist and also a full band member.

---

[41] Tamm, *Robert Fripp*, 33. One strand of Greg Lake's stylistic influences that has never been adequately addressed, either by Lake or anybody else, is his apparent debt to British folk music and the late-sixteenth/early-seventeenth-century Elizabethan/Jacobean lute song tradition. Some of Lake's early work with ELP uncannily parallels the lute songs and lute music of John Dowland (1563–1625) and his peers. Did Lake ever informally study this music? If not, which of his influences may have had contact with this music?

[42] Smith, *In the Court of King Crimson*, 47.

King Crimson's official live debut—that is, the first time they were advertised in advance as King Crimson—was on April 9 at London's Speakeasy, a club whose patrons often included the royalty of the British rock world. The audience that night included the Moody Blues, Manfred Mann, and drummer Ginger Baker, and Crimson went down extremely well. Two days later the band supported Marc Bolan's Tyrannosaurus Rex at the Lyceum, where the audience included Yes's drummer, Bill Bruford, who, speaking of early Crimson, years later recalled,

> I'd seen them a couple of times and I was riveted to the back of the room. They seemed to have all the grace and poise that we didn't. We seemed awkward and angular. They seemed mature, though I'm sure it was a fallacy. I'm sure I was completely wrong. But Yes were turning into very much a vocal group with prettyish arrangements, whereas King Crimson were much more of an instrumental group. A playing group, with far dirtier minor key arrangements. I've said this before, actually, but to me, Yes was a major key group, and King Crimson were a minor key group.[43]

Bruford, of course, was to become a major figure in the Crimson universe a few years later.

The band met with Tony Clarke and the Moody Blues' Graeme Edge and Mike Pinder, who suggested that Crimson consider recording at London's Morgan Studios; the possibility of Crimson supporting the Moodies on tour was also mooted. Ian McDonald picked up a copy of the Moody Blues' new album, *On the Threshold of a Dream*, in order to get a sense of Clarke's production style, and on May 1 the members of Crimson accepted a guided tour of Morgan Studios from Clarke. On May 6, Crimson convened at Maida Vale Studios to record two original songs, "21st Century Schizoid Man" and "In the Court of the Crimson King," for broadcast on BBC's *Top Gear* radio program, to be aired May 11. These are the earliest surviving recordings of King Crimson; both are preserved on *Epitaph*, the 1997 two-CD set featuring live recordings of King Crimson's first lineup.

Another key gig for the band in their early days took place at London's Revolution on May 14. It was here that Fripp played seated on a tall stool for the first time: "Greg Lake said, 'You can't sit down; you'll look like a mushroom.' I felt it wasn't my job to stand up and look moody. My job was to play, and I couldn't play standing up."[44] Fripp has, incidentally, performed seated on a tall stool ever since. After this show, Jimi Hendrix congratulated Fripp.

---

[43] Bill Bruford, quoted by Dan Heges, *Yes: The Authorized Biography* (London: Sidgwick and Jackson, 1981), 46–47.

[44] Robert Fripp, quoted by Rosen, "King Crimson's Robert Fripp," 18.

During May and June, King Crimson continued with their heavy per-formance schedule, including a number of shows at London's Marquee, and rapidly earned the respect—sometimes bordering on awe—of Britain's rock cognoscenti. On June 12, Crimson began recording with Tony Clarke at Morgan Studios; over the next few days, however, the band grew increasingly dissatisfied with the results, and a meeting with Clarke on June 19 resulted in a mutual agreement to temporarily aban-don the sessions. Meanwhile, Enthoven and Gaydon pulled off a major coup by securing Crimson a slot supporting the Rolling Stones at an out-door show at London's Hyde Park.

Apotheosis: July–October 1969

Scheduled for July 5, the Stones intended to use the Hyde Park perform-ance as a forum to introduce their new rhythm guitarist, Mick Taylor, who had recently been awarded Brian Jones's rhythm guitar position upon the latter's firing. However, when Jones's death (apparently by drowning) was announced on July 3, the concert was hastily repackaged as a tribute to Jones. Crimson played a somewhat truncated set of roughly half an hour to an enormous audience that has been estimated to have numbered between one-half and three-quarters of a million people. Despite the fact that the band felt they were a bit off, they went over extremely well, stun-ning many audience members who had never before heard rock music of such huge dynamic contrasts, virtuosic ensemble interplay, and gothic heaviness. Although the following review came a few months later into the band's career, it aptly captures the overriding impression that King Crimson made at their famous Hyde Park performance:

> King Crimson can only be described as a monumental heavy with the majesty—and tragedy—of Hell. Greg Lake, who snaps a cathartic bass guitar to the fore of the music, also sings lead like a hoody choir boy, but with all volume controls open, both his bass line and voice resound like thunder in the night . . . The group's immense, towering force field, electrified by the energy of their almost frightening intensity, either pinned down patrons or drove them out.[45]

As a result of the July 5 Hyde Park performance, King Crimson went, lit-erally overnight, from being a cult band known chiefly amongst the rock

---

[45] Review of King Crimson live at Fillmore East, New York, New York, November 21, 1969, quoted by Forrester, Hanson, and Askew, *Emerson, Lake and Palmer*, 32. Incidentally, one number from the Hyde Park show, a truncated "Epitaph," is included on Greg Lake's *From the Underground*, vol. 2: *Deeper into the Mine* (Creative Musical Arts GL-CD3004, 2003).

cognoscenti of southern England to national stars. When they played their next gig in the Marquee, the club was packed.

Shortly after their Hyde Park triumph, King Crimson returned to the studio with Tony Clarke. By mid-July, however, the band gave up, this time for good; said Michael Giles, "I remember the sessions with Tony Clarke as being immensely frustrating and our energy was trying to be transformed into another Moody Blues with lots of strumming guitars, one on top of the other, all heavily compressed with no dynamics."[46] The band's decision to no longer work with Clarke barred them from appearing with Decca or Threshold: when Decca realized they were about to lose Crimson, they accused Fripp and Giles of breach of contract. In order to extricate themselves from future obligations to Decca, the pair agreed to pay Decca a small percentage of their royalties for the first two or three years of King Crimson's existence.

Now cleared of any obligations to Decca, Crimson showed, for a young band at any rate, a rare sense of patience combined with business acumen. Even as Enthoven and Gaydon were negotiating a deal with Island Records, who had passed on signing the band initially, but whose interest was rekindled after their Hyde Park triumph, King Crimson entered Wessex Studios in Islington, with the intention of producing themselves and then leasing the finished tapes to whichever record label ultimately signed them, thus avoiding the customary practice of having recording costs deducted from their future royalties. In order to fund the recording sessions, Enthoven mortgaged his house.

In late July and early August, Crimson recorded the five tracks that were to constitute their debut album, *In the Court of the Crimson King*. Soon after recording was done, the band returned to nonstop concertizing (many of their shows being in and around London) and in August made a second appearance on John Peel's *Top Gear* radio program. The heavy schedule of constant British performances lasted through October. On October 17, they opened for the Nice at Croydon's Fairfield Hall, where the Nice were recording their show for future release on their upcoming *Five Bridges* album. An impressed Alan Lewis of *Melody Maker* said, "Together with Peter Sinfield's brilliant lights they [King Crimson] created an almost overpowering atmosphere of power and evil."[47]

First Album: *In the Court of the Crimson King*

At this late date, there is probably not a lot more to be said about their debut LP, *In the Court of the Crimson King: An Observation by King*

---

[46] Michael Giles, quoted by Smith, *In the Court of King Crimson*, 54.
[47] Alan Lewis, quoted by Tamm, *Robert Fripp*, 39.

Crimson, released on the Island label in October 1969. Bill Martin, Paul Stump, and I all have postulated—completely independently, I might add—that the progressive rock style, the way it has come to be understood since the early 1970s, emerged in unmistakable form for the first time on this album.[48] I've pointed out that the album gave birth to at least two different progressive rock subgenres, one an offshoot of its melancholy, richly orchestrated Mellotron/guitar epics ("Epitaph," the title track), the other of the muscular, jazz-tinged rock warhorse "21st Century Schizoid Man."[49] Indeed, Eric Tamm has plausibly suggested that not only did this song exert a huge impact on the nascent progressive rock style, it was also important to the nascent heavy-metal and jazz-rock styles that were emerging at nearly the same time.[50] I've also stated that Peter Sinfield's lyrical imagery, with its highly characteristic mixture of sci-fi apocalypse and mystical medievalism, made a huge impact on later progressive rock, as did Barry Godber's cover drawing, often called "The Schizoid Man," a kind of Pop Art update of Edvard Munch's proto-expressionist masterpiece *The Scream.*[51]

Nonetheless, Bill Martin is correct to point up, in his discussion of *In the Court of the Crimson King*, that it is far more than just a template for the emerging progressive rock style: it is a great album, with its five songs cohering into "a totality . . . a world, and not just . . . a collection of good songs."[52] Martin adds that "*In the Court of the Crimson King* has a thematic unity that works on many levels." It would be worthwhile, then, to briefly discuss each of the five songs in turn. The opener, "21st Century Schizoid Man," is the album's only out-and-out rocker. Robert Fripp once said that "my interest is in how to take the energy and spirit of rock music and extend it to the music drawing on my background as part of the European tonal harmonic tradition. In other words, what would Hendrix sound like playing Bartók?"[53] "Schizoid Man" is cast in something very close to the symmetrical arch form (A B C D C B A), borrowed from Bartók, that Fripp was to often use in his later work: the form of "Schizoid Man" is A B C D C A B. Following an impressionistic introduction that is somewhat reminiscent of a train approaching from the distance, the A section consists of a crunching metal riff contributed by Lake. As Eric Tamm points out, this passage is an early example of Frippian polymeter, with the accents of the riff edgily clashing with the implied

---

[48] See Stump, *The Music's All That Matters*, 51–55; Martin, *Listening to the Future*, 155–61; and my *Rocking the Classics*, 23–24.
[49] Macan, *Rocking the Classics*, 23.
[50] Tamm, *Robert Fripp*, 43.
[51] See *Rocking the Classics*, 23.
[52] Martin, *Listening to the Future*, 161.
[53] Tamm, *Robert Fripp*, 31.

4/4 of the phrase structure.[54] The B section, Ian McDonald's equally abrasive "song" section, is sung by Lake through a fuzz box, with Fripp accompanying with ponderous open fifths and octaves. The C section, by Fripp, is a Charles Mingus–like quasi-jazz instrumental in a frantic 6/8, with Fripp and McDonald (who plays alto sax here) both turning in impressive solos over Lake's restless stepwise bass lines. The D section, the song's climax, features the band playing some extremely intricate unison runs in stop time; it is safe to say that this section brought an entirely new level of ensemble virtuosity to rock. Thereafter, the previous sections are recapitulated; the screeching coda is reminiscent of nothing quite so much as a giant hand scratching its fingernails across an enormous chalkboard.

The sound is hard as nails throughout, Fripp's fuzzed guitar and McDonald's alto sax often being nearly indistinguishable, and provides a suitable accompaniment for Peter Sinfield's nightmarish vision of late-capitalist hypermaterialism and a military-industrial complex gone horribly awry. As heavy as the song is, it never degenerates into the kind of plodding, ham-fisted thrashing that mars so much heavy metal of the seventies; much of the credit must be given to the agile, melodically inventive drumming of Michael Giles.

The second song, "I Talk to the Wind," is by McDonald and Sinfield, and had it origins in the quartet configuration of Giles, Giles and Fripp. As Bill Martin points out, the song tends to gain in stature as a result of its placement between "Schizoid Man" and "Epitaph." In isolation, it's a gentle, slightly melancholy folk-rock ballad featuring some delicate vocal harmonies (Lake and McDonald) and some truly gorgeous flute arabesques by McDonald towards the end of the song. However, "the song's greatest subtlety is that it can be heard both on the level of everyday personal melancholy and as a herald that something in the world is seriously out of joint."[55] In other words, due to its position on the album, the song bespeaks an alienation that is simultaneously personal and cosmic in nature.

The third track, "Epitaph," may be the album's finest. The predominant instrumentation of this minor-key epic is Ian McDonald's majestic Mellotron string parts and Robert Fripp's haunting, delicately picked guitar lines, although McDonald's richly orchestrated and dark-hued woodwind episodes also make an important contribution to the song's atmosphere, which moves beyond the gentle melancholy of "I Talk to the Wind" into a realm that approaches genuine tragedy. Sinfield's lyric, set to a heartbreakingly beautiful melody that's sung with great panache and conviction by Lake, return to the preoccupations of "Schizoid Man,"

---

[54] Tamm, *Robert Fripp*, 36.
[55] Martin, *Listening to the Future*, 158.

although now with an added poignance lent by the autumnal, valedictory ambience of the music. Lake's remarks to Sid Smith are telling: "I think it is a poignant song. There's a finality to it and in a way it encapsulates a lot of the feelings that there were [then] about the cracks in society. There was this idealistic view of love and flower power and so on but there were cracks, and that song somehow typifies that period with all its naïvite."[56]

Interestingly, German musicologist/social theorist Theodor Adorno says nearly the same thing about Gustav Mahler's most characteristic music, that it reveals "a rift within society," by evoking a sense of "brokenness," a gap between the ideals of a society and its ability to fulfill those ideals. The musical expression of brokenness is a bittersweet (but not sentimental) ambience that combines a sense of hope with an even deeper sense of sadness by treating major and minor as different aspects of a single experience, rather than polar opposites. Adorno sees Gustav Mahler as being an exceptional exemplar of musical brokenness; Mahler was active in the late nineteenth and early twentieth century, a time when post-Enlightenment idealism was still a force, but a fading one, rapidly disappearing beyond the horizon in the years leading up to the first World War. Mahler's music expresses the lingering hopes and dreams of his era, but is laced by a deep sadness and nostalgia at the realization that the era itself is ending, and its unrealized hopes and dreams will remain unrealized.[57] I hear a similar sense of brokenness in "Epitaph," especially the concluding section, where Lake's plaintive melisma on "crying," the final word of the lyric, is accompanied by Giles' stately timpani flourishes, Fripp's slashing guitar chords, and McDonald's glacial Mellotron backdrop.

"Epitaph" brings the first side of the LP to a solemn and imposing conclusion. The second side opens with "Moonchild." For me, the backbone of this song is Fripp's electric guitar part, which evokes a kind of space-age Italian mandolin and gives the song a sense of shadow and mystery that it might otherwise lack, had it relied more single-handedly on Sinfield's somewhat fey and precious lyrics. (Although, to be fair, the lyrics engage with Eastern yin/yang and Western hermetic/magical symbolism that subsequently were to be of more than passing interest to both Sinfield and Fripp.) Another interesting touch is Lake's vocals, which are processed to sound as if his voice is being transmitted over a transistor radio. The song proper is fairly short, and is followed by a lengthy improvisation featuring Fripp, Giles, and McDonald (on vibraphone).

---

[56] Greg Lake, quoted by Smith, *In the Court of King Crimson*, 63.
[57] See Theodor W. Adorno, *Mahler: A Musical Physiognomy*, trans. Edmund Jephcott (Chicago: University of Chicago Press, 1992), particularly 16–17, where he expounds on his remark, "The emerging antagonism between music and its language [in Mahler] reveals a rift within society," and 32, when he discusses "brokenness" in terms of Mahler's attempt to bridge the unbridgeable gap of high and low culture.

The improv opens with McDonald's hazy, impressionistic cloud of vibraphone chords, but gradually develops into a spikier, more austere soundscape characterized by pointillistic flecks of sound. There has always been some debate within the band about the ultimate worth of this section. Fripp has said it ought to have been edited, and, in fact, on the 1991 King Crimson box set *Frame by Frame*, he eliminated it entirely. Michael Giles, on the other hand, continues to believe that the section contains some genuinely magical moments of spontaneous ensemble composition.[58] I happen to largely concur with Fripp—I consider the improvised section of "Moonchild" to be the weakest part of the album—although I acknowledge the improvisation as an important harbinger of Crimson's future practice of spontaneous, onstage improvised composition, as well as a sincere expression of Fripp's avowed goal of letting music speak through the performers.

Finally, we come to the album's title track, another McDonald-Sinfield song, "In the Court of the Crimson King." Perhaps this song is the album's finest expression of Sinfield's craft as a wordsmith, with some memorable medieval and fantasy symbology. Musically, the song is similar to "Epitaph"—Mellotron and guitar are the dominant instruments—although the title track lacks the immanent sense of pain and loss that characterize "Epitaph," favoring instead a sense of majesty and mystery. It's a fine song, although I think it's a bit too long to rely on the stock alternation of verse and chorus to the degree it does. A magical moment does occur near the song's conclusion, when a circuslike reed-organ episode—improvised on the spot by McDonald and Giles—lends a whiff of shimmering ambiguity to the song as a whole, since we're not sure whether we should hear it as ironic commentary on, or programmatic evocation of, the Crimson King's mythical court. I also find the final lyric a stroke of genius: as the yellow jester makes his puppets dance, we realize that it is he, and not the Crimson King, who is the real power in this court, and we are involuntarily reminded of the key lyric of "Epitaph," which states the fate of all mankind is in the hands of fools. The tie-in could hardly have been rendered more subtly or elegantly, and masterfully ties together the album's major thematic conceits.[59] The final entrance of the instrumental chorus after the circus music episode is genuinely dramatic, and Eric Tamm is correct to point to the title track's abrupt ending as a refusal, typical for this band, to bow to clichés: "after having built up a whole album's worth of

---

[58] Smith, *In the Court of King Crimson*, 65.
[59] This lyric also prefigures a practice, evident in some of the later lyrics of both Sinfield and Lake, of using a jester, a fool, or a madman as an iconic figure symbolizing hidden wisdom. This practice will be examined later in the text.

momentum, a melodramatic climax is avoided in favor of a sort of *musicus interruptus.*"[60]

Observant critics of the time saw *In the Court of the Crimson King* as a logical extension and development of late-sixties proto-progressive rock as exemplified by the Moody Blues, Procol Harum, Pink Floyd, and the Beatles. Nonetheless, even at the time there seemed to be a recognition that there was something seminal about the album, that somehow the music of King Crimson was qualitatively different from that of their stylistic predecessors. Perhaps the most eloquent expression of this view is the famous endorsement of the Who's guitarist and songwriter, Pete Townshend, who called the album "an uncanny masterpiece . . . that kind of intensity is Music, not Rock."[61] Again, as we have already noted in connection with the Nice, contemporaries were startled by the manner in which King Crimson appeared to be melting down the stylistic barriers between rock, classical, jazz, and folk.

Another aspect of the band that impressed contemporaries is how confidently and powerfully each individual within the band projected himself. John Wetton, himself a future Crimsonite who first saw them at London College on October 10, recalls,

> There wasn't a weak link in that band. Usually there's one or two dominant players and a couple who are prepared to take the back seat such as in the Beatles, Pink Floyd, Rolling Stones, and so on. I'm not saying they're weak links but they're guys who don't come forward but are prepared to do the legwork and there are usually one or two who dominate. But with Crimson that was not the case at all. Mike Giles was phenomenal and there really wasn't anyone on the stage who didn't have the ability. There weren't really many bands at the time who were all as consistently good as that lineup.[62]

Indeed, all four musicians make crucial contributions. Fripp's intricate cross-picking technique and distinctive sustained fuzz tone are already emerging, although at this point he's still more notable as a texturalist than as a monster soloist. Lake, besides a commanding vocal performance throughout, turns in some of the finest bass playing of his career, especially during the instrumental section of "Schizoid Man." McDonald's multi-instrumental contribution constitutes a *tour de force* seldom equaled in rock history. Michael Giles takes the new approach to rock drumming that had been initiated by Mitch Mitchell of the Jimi Hendrix Experience—nimble, melodically inventive, texturally sophisticated—and

---

[60] Tamm, *Robert Fripp*, 43.
[61] Pete Townshend, quoted by Smith, *In the Court of King Crimson*, 71.
[62] John Wetton, quoted by Smith, *In the Court of King Crimson*, 68–69.

extends it into hitherto unexplored territory.[63] As for Sinfield's contribution, Fripp was later to remark:

> Peter Sinfield's words from his period with Crimson have been much maligned and used to exemplify the worst pretensions of progressive (now "prog") rock. Although I had difficulties with some of Peter's words on subsequent Crimson albums, as he had with the music, on *In the Court* Peter's words are in a category of their own. They are the words of a writer who wrote from personal necessity, and have the power and conviction of direct seeing. After this album Peter became a professional wordsmith, and worked and practiced that skill. In 1969, Peter didn't know what he couldn't do, and none of us anticipated the acclaim and hostility which his words provoked.[64]

It was to be several years—arguably, not until *Red*, their last album of the seventies—that King Crimson was to release another album that was as consistently good in compositional and performance quality, that conveyed the same sense of power and inevitability, and that was equally forward looking. That being said, I am not among those commentators who believe King Crimson never again equaled *In the Court of the Crimson King*. The harmonic vocabulary of "I Talk to the Wind," "Epitaph," the song portion of "Moonchild," and "In the Court of the Crimson King" is actually quite conventional—the flux between Aeolian, Dorian, and melodic forms of the minor scale (so-called modal borrowing), while effectively handled, is hardly unusual in the context of late-sixties British rock. Often there is little or no modulation during a song, and the phrase structures are more often than not unremittingly foursquare.[65] The chords, usually simple triads, are laid out in conventional block chord or arpeggiated formats: King Crimson's later practice of implying (rather than explicitly stating) chords through the simultaneous movement of independent melodic parts played by different instruments—that is to say, configuring their harmonies in a more sophisticated horizontal framework—is still in the future. The melodic content of "21st Century Schizoid Man," the album's one track that is blues and jazz based, rather than folk and classically based, comfortably conforms to the outlines of the blues scale, very much like other blues and jazz based music of the psychedelic rock era. The practice of blurring tonal motion through

---

[63] Carl Palmer was later to admit that working out Giles' part to "21st Century Schizoid Man" during early ELP rehearsals was an important experience as he solidified his concept of a drumming style that would be appropriate to ELP's music. See Forrester, Hanson, and Askew, *Emerson, Lake and Palmer*, 52.

[64] Robert Fripp, liner notes to King Crimson, *Epitaph* (DGM CD 9607, 1997), 12.

[65] "Foursquare" phrase structure means that one melodic phrase of four bars is followed by another phrase of four bars, with pairs of four-bar phrases subsequently following one another *ad infinitum*.

whole tone movement of the chords, which became so characteristic of King Crimson circa 1972–74, is not a factor here. In sum, as seminal an album as *In the Court of the Crimson King* is, later Crimson albums show a steady growth in harmonic, rhythmic, and textural sophistication. I believe that Crimson went on to release at least two other albums, *Red* (1974) and *Discipline* (1981), each featuring a radically different kind of music, that had the same sense of inevitability and rightness for their era as *Crimson King* had for its. However, this opens up a topic that is best addressed in another forum.

Implosion: October–December 1969

Even as they began to prepare for their first American tour, slated to begin in late October, Crimson were without an American label. This situation was soon rectified, however, when Atlantic Records president Ahmet Ertegun flew to London to secure a deal with Enthoven and Gaydon. Upon its release in the U.S. in November, *In the Court of the Crimson King* zoomed to twenty-eight in the charts—a very impressive showing for a young band that had no "name" members, whose album contained no obvious singles material, and who were playing music that, even by the wide-open standards of the late sixties, was quite challenging. In the U.K., *In the Court of the Crimson King* topped out at number five. By any standard one would care to use, King Crimson were a band rapidly on the way up.

Indeed, it may have been the sense of unstoppable momentum, which arguably built up too fast and too soon, that tore King Crimson's first lineup apart. Crimson's American tour started October 29 in upstate Vermont, followed almost immediately by shows at the Boston Tea Party on November 1–4. Although the band had some serious trouble with the Mellotron at first, being obliged to find a way to regulate the instrument's response to the American power supply, on the whole they went down very well. As the band traveled from Boston to Chicago to Detroit to New York to Palm Beach, then on to California, they quickly discovered distances were far greater in the U.S. than in the U.K., meaning a greater proportion of time was spent *en route* from one destination to the next. They also discovered that in comparison to culturally centralized England, where success in London often translated to success in the rest of the country, the decentralized U.S. had to be conquered piece by piece. As Greg Lake observed, "The U.S.A. was so much bigger as a country that you could play in New York and do a great show but in Boston they know nothing about it. So you have to go and keep starting up in each city."[66] As a result of the long periods of numbing boredom followed by short bursts of

---

[66] Greg Lake, quoted by Smith, *In the Court of King Crimson*, 74.

incredible intensity and the growing sense of homesickness, burnout began to set in quickly: McDonald, who desperately missed his girlfriend, was the unhappiest of all, and was only temporarily mollified when Enthoven and Gaydon agreed to fly her over from Great Britain for four days. Fripp recalls feeling considerable unease when, during a poolside conversation with Michael Giles at a hotel in Los Angeles, Giles suggested that Crimson quit touring and become a studio only band.[67]

As it turned out, the first lineup of King Crimson did not survive Los Angeles; as was to become something of a recurring *leitmotif* in the band's subsequent history, the intensity of the Crimson experience proved to be too much for some of its participants. The day after their final show at Los Angeles's Whisky a Go Go on December 6, the band departed for San Francisco. Road manager Dik Fraser was driving, with Fripp in the front seat and McDonald and Giles in the backseat, when the pair told Fripp they were planning to leave King Crimson at the conclusion of the American tour. Fripp's reaction, although well rehearsed in the annals of rock literature, is worth repeating again: "My stomach disappeared. King Crimson was everything to me. To keep the band together I offered to leave instead but Ian said that the band was more me than them."[68] Years later, McDonald suggested to Sid Smith that had Enthoven or Gaydon been on tour with the band, they might have talked him out of quitting.[69] Perhaps. But at the time, he was clearly disturbed by the intensity of Crimson's music: Fripp has quoted him saying, "I want to make music that says good things instead of evil thing,"[70] Indeed, when McDonald and Giles released their solo album in 1970 (simply titled *McDonald and Giles*), it was a much lighter, more delicate affair than *In the Court of the Crimson King*.

King Crimson's first lineup was an exceptional one. It was also unstable. Its instability—or combustibility, if you will—may be a key to understanding its brilliance. Stephanie Ruben, Peter Sinfield's partner at the time, has put it simply but elegantly: "Put all these five guys together and they all seemed to have part of the puzzle in the making of this band, which made it untenable but glorious too."[71] Greg Lake, for his part, sees the band's magic in similar terms: "King Crimson had this strange blend of personalities and the net result of it was music that was dangerous and passionate."[72]

---

[67] Greg Lake, quoted by Smith, *In the Court of King Crimson*, 75.
[68] Robert Fripp, liner notes, King Crimson, *The Young Persons' Guide to King Crimson* (Atlantic Records LP 2SDS900, 1976), 6.
[69] Smith, *In the Court of King Crimson*, 79.
[70] Ian McDonald, quoted by Fripp, liner notes to King Crimson, *The Young Persons' Guide to King Crimson*, 7.
[71] Stephanie Ruben, quoted by Smith, *In the Court of King Crimson*, 76.

The band arrived in San Francisco and played their final shows together, at the Filmore West, on December 11–14. While everyone involved agrees the band's playing was a bit tired at this point—especially in light of the trauma wrought by McDonald's and Giles's announcement—the overall standard of playing is still very high, as anyone who owns *Epitaph* (which contains half of the December 13 and all of the December 14 show) can attest.[73] Of course, it was at the Fillmore West that the Nice and King Crimson shared the bill, and that Emerson and Lake made their fateful contact. In the previous chapter, we considered Emerson's recollections of the initial meeting. It would be good to now consider Lake's:

> It was like some secret Iron Curtain deal. Tony Stratton Smith made the initial move while he was still handling the Nice but meanwhile I instructed my people to approach Keith. Keith and I spent two months just talking, and we didn't play a note for that period. We talked about different things to do with our past history and different things to do with our futures and the problem of finding a really good percussionist.[74]

In some ways, this clarifies certain issues about the origins of the Emerson-Lake partnership. For instance, it was almost certainly Tony Stratton Smith who first put out feelers in New York during November. Likewise, the two months spent "just talking" would be February through April 1970: Emerson's obligations to the Nice ran through late March, and, as it turned out, so did Lake's to King Crimson. There was little opportunity during this interim period for them to commence work together.

On the other hand, Lake's recollections as given above may be a bit too pat. As we saw in the previous chapter, he returned to the U.K. after the end of the Crimson tour without giving a firm yes or no answer to Emerson, and was evasive enough about his intentions during the early weeks of 1970 that Emerson felt compelled to enquire about the availability of Chris Squire and Jack Bruce. Clearly, as late as January 1970 Lake had yet to make up his mind. So what tipped the scale?

After the Implosion: January–March 1970

[72] Greg Lake, quoted by Smith, *In the Court of King Crimson*, 78.

[73] The *Epitaph* liner notes list the last two shows as being December 14 and 15. This dating contradicts the performance chronology of both Hanson's *Hang on to a Dream: The Story of the Nice* and Sid Smith's *In the Court of King Crimson*. Smith has even identified December 15 as a Monday and the day that King Crimson flew back to London. For these reasons, I think the *Epitaph* dates are mistaken.

[74] Greg Lake, quoted by Altham, "The Manticore Tapes."

One consideration that Lake has often expressed over the years was a belief that after the departure of McDonald and Giles, if a new band were put together, it would be such a different band that it should be christened with a new identity: "I just felt that it wasn't a totally honest way forward to [still] call the band King Crimson."[75] There was another consideration as well, that may have been more important than the name change (or lack thereof) in forcing Lake's hand. The original lineup of King Crimson had been a democracy. With the departure of McDonald and Giles, Fripp had announced his intention to recruit replacements. Lake realized the new musicians would almost certainly be beholden to Fripp; in other words, Crimson was about to change from a democracy to a band where Fripp was the de facto leader. "Bob wanted to work in a situation where he was in the driving seat over other musicians, which I can dig, but not for me."[76] Lake has been incorrigibly blunt in his assessment of later King Crimson lineups: "The albums that came after that [*In the Court of the Crimson King*] were really Robert Fripp and his backing band."[77]

Even as Lake was in the process of deciding to leave King Crimson and form a partnership with Keith Emerson, EG, Island, and Atlantic were anxious to see the band return to the studio to record a follow-up album to *In the Court of the Crimson King*: management and labels believed that despite the decimation of the band's original lineup, Crimson were hot property, and would remain so if suitable replacements could be recruited quickly enough. Therefore Fripp immediately set out to find a new lead vocalist. EG's Mark Fenwick, apparently keen to give Fripp a helping hand, booked Elton John to sing lead in the sessions for the upcoming album; a horrified Fripp quickly nixed this particular recruitment. The next candidate, this one approved by Fripp, was Pete Straker, best known at that time for his role in the rock musical *Hair*; however, Straker's management asked for too much money, and the deal fell through. By now running out of time to recruit a permanent replacement for Lake, Fripp asked Lake if he would be willing to appear on the second Crimson album in a sessions role. Lake was willing, but his asking price was high: he demanded Crimson's PA system as payment. The request, although granted, seems to have left a bad taste in Fripp's mouth; the guitarist tartly commented, "The actual phrase used by Greg was 'for my art.' So, there you are. Greg was being paid with the WEM PA for his art."[78]

---

[75] Greg Lake, quoted by Smith, *In the Court of King Crimson*, 82.

[76] Greg Lake, quoted by Forrester, Hanson, and Askew, *Emerson, Lake and Palmer*, 36.

[77] Greg Lake, quoted by Hall, "Welcome to the Show," 20. I will have more to say about Lake's assessment later in the book.

[78] Robert Fripp, quoted by Smith, *In the Court of King Crimson*, 83.

Of course, Fripp faced another issue: he needed a rhythm section. Michael Giles, like Lake, was talked into appearing on the album in a sessions role. Some observers were surprised that the drummer could go back to work for Crimson less than two months after quitting, but Giles saw it differently: "Already being in the habit of doing dark music, it wasn't difficult to go in and do a bit more. I was a contributor, not a designer."[79] Perhaps as an enticement to secure Michael Giles's participation, Fripp decided to limit Lake's role to vocalist and to recruit his old mate, Peter Giles, to play bass. Certainly Fripp had already discovered what Keith Emerson was about to: Lake was not a gifted improviser on bass, his spontaneously created bass lines tended to be somewhat stiff and often hewed literally to whatever basic framework he was given, and his best bass lines were usually the result of extensive rehearsing and reworking. Fripp put it simply: "Peter Giles could walk in and play bass, Greg could not."[80]

Now Fripp faced a final challenge: how to fill the sonic space vacated by the absence of multi-instrumentalist Ian McDonald. It's a testament to McDonald's versatility and musical breadth that Fripp was obliged to bring in two musicians, both of them very good in their own right, to fill this gap. Pianist Keith Tippett, who had come to Fripp's and Sinfield's attention via his work in London's modern jazz scene during the late sixties, brought two distinctive approaches to bear upon King Crimson's music. One featured impressionistic cascades of modal arpeggios, and prefigured the New Age piano style of the eighties, although Tippett's rhythmic approach was often a bit more hyperkinetic. The second approach was spikier and altogether more dissonant: a comparison might be made to the dense, atonal modern jazz piano approach of Cecil Taylor, although Taylor's approach is built on the perpetual sixteenth-note lines of bebop, while Tippett's is more rhythmically irregular, featuring sudden explosions of dissonant clusters and unpredictable linear figurations. Fripp's other recruit was Mel Collins, a gifted woodwind player: Collins may possibly have been McDonald's equal as a sax and flute player, although he lacked McDonald's abilities as a songwriter. Fripp decided that he himself would play the Mellotron parts—inevitably textural or thematic in nature, since one can't possibly play fast lead lines on a Mellotron—that McDonald would have played were he still with the band.

With a core lineup (Fripp, Lake, and the Giles brothers) in place, and with access to two fine "plug in" lead players, Tippett and Collins, who were featured sporadically and only occasionally at the same time, Fripp and crew repaired to Wessex Studios sometime in late January or early February 1970 to commence recording. The first order of business was to

---

[79] Michael Giles, quoted by Smith, *In the Court of King Crimson*, 87.
[80] Robert Fripp, quoted by Smith, *In the Court of King Crimson*, 83.

record "Cat Food," which was slated for release as a single. The authorship of the song was almost the cause of a major row between Fripp and Sinfield on the one hand and Ian McDonald on the other. McDonald was incensed to learn that Crimson planned to release the song, which he claimed to have cowritten with Sinfield during the American tour and to which Fripp, in his view, had contributed only the bridge section, without crediting him. After he contacted EG they relented, and McDonald was credited as a cowriter.

"Cat Food" features Fripp, the Giles brothers, Lake, and Keith Tippett on piano. It's a rollicking, funky number that Peter Sinfield uses as a vehicle to skewer the burgeoning fast food culture. For me, the song doesn't quite click: Sinfield's lyrics are more abstruse and self-consciously clever here than on the debut album, which, combined with Keith Tippett's overly busy, at times almost spastic atonal jazz piano, gives the song the same air of willful, mannered, obdurate weirdness that also sank much of the Giles, Giles and Fripp project. Peter Giles agrees with this assessment, telling Sid Smith, "Without the piano it might have actually done something [in the charts]. Fair enough, Fripp stuck to his guns, even though the guns were pointing in the wrong direction."[81] On the other hand, Peter Sinfield and Robert Fripp both regard "Cat Food" as the best song on the second King Crimson album; Keith Emerson, for his part, considers "Cat Food" the highlight of Greg Lake's involvement with King Crimson.[82]

The B-side of "Cat Food" is "Groon," an instrumental track featuring Giles, Giles, and Fripp. Eric Tamm aptly described "Groon" as "a kind of latter-day electrified bebop" and sees it as "a precursor of King Crimson III [the 1972–74 lineup], moments on *Exposure* [Fripp's solo album of 1979], even, to stretch it a bit, the League of Gentleman [Fripp's instrumental New Wave band of 1980]."[83] It's a good piece of work, and it's regrettable that it wasn't included on the second Crimson album, although given that it's so different from the album's other material, the decision to exclude it is understandable. Fripp made it re-available several years later with the release of the compilation album *A Young Persons' Guide to King Crimson* in 1976.

"Cat Food" with its B-side "Groon" was released on March 13. On March 25, the Giles brothers, Fripp, Lake, and Tippett assembled at BBC Studios to mime their parts to "Cat Food," for future broadcast on BBC's popular television program *Top of the Pops* (interestingly, Lake appears

---

[81] Peter Giles, quoted by Smith, *In the Court of King Crimson*, 85.
[82] See Hall, "Welcome to the Show," 20. Of course, Emerson's view may merely be a confirmation of my belief that he never really "got" King Crimson.
[83] Eric Tamm, *Robert Fripp*, 46.

"playing" acoustic guitar on this broadcast). It was to be Greg Lake's final appearance with King Crimson, and Crimson's only "performance" of calendar year 1970.

Second Album: *In the Wake of Poseidon*

Between the recording of "Cat Food" and the March 25 *Top of the Pops* appearance, Fripp and crew worked furiously to finish the album, knowing that Lake's time with the band was growing short. In fact, they almost made it in under the wire: when Lake took his final leave just one track, "Cadence and Cascade," was still lacking vocals, so Fripp invited an old school chum named Gordon Haskell to sing on the track. The album, *In the Wake of Poseidon*, was finished in April, and released in May. Featuring a cover painting by Tammo de Jongh entitled "12 Archetypes" that seem to reflect undercurrents of Jungian psychology, *Poseidon* was a commercial success, hitting number four on the British charts and number thirty-one on the American, buying Fripp and Sinfield some badly needed time as they tried to work through a means of returning King Crimson to the road—an endeavor which they were not to succeed in until 1971.

In the Wake of Poseidon begins with "Peace—A Beginning." Featuring Greg Lake's unaccompanied vocal rising from a bed of reverb and gradually coalescing in the middle of the sonic soundstage, it's a bit reminiscent of Gregorian chant—although, with its pentatonic outlines and flux between the tonic minor and relative major, "Peace" is more closely related to English folksong. After a few soft and apparently random guitar notes at the end of Lake's "chant," the peace (pardon the pun) of the track is rudely shattered by the opening fanfare of "Pictures of a City," a slightly modified version of a song called "A Man, A City" that the original Crimson lineup had performed during their American tour of November-December 1969. The song is much indebted to "21st Century Schizoid Man," with Mel Collins inheriting Ian McDonald's frenetic sax parts. Certainly the song is structurally similar to "Schizoid Man"—an abrasive opening riff followed by the song proper and a ferocious instrumental section that includes a stop-time unison passage that's even more daunting than the one in "Schizoid Man." The one innovation is the "space funk" section after the breakneck unison lines, although it tends to dissipate, rather than momentarily dam up, the preceding section's tension. Like "Cat Food," this song's lyrics, which are, admittedly, spat out by Greg Lake with admirable disdain, seem merely clever rather than truly convincing. In sum, the problem isn't that "Pictures of a City" is a bad song—it's quite an interesting one, actually—but that to anyone who knows its model, "21st Century Schizoid Man," it sounds a bit contrived.

Cultivating the radical shifts of mood and dynamics that were beloved to early Crimson, the ferocious "Pictures of a City" is followed by the gentle, largely acoustic "Cadence and Cascade." A somewhat oblique word painting that chronicles two of the band's favorite groupies (nicknamed, for reasons unexplained, "Cadence" and "Cascade"), the song is King Crimson's first bona fide major key song, set in an unambiguous E major. It features some exceedingly tasteful acoustic guitar work by Fripp, who shows a classical guitarist's sense of voicing, and is embroidered by Michael Giles's shimmering cymbals, Keith Tippett's sparse piano, and, eventually, Mel Collins's flute arabesques. It's very pretty, but rather lightweight, and Gordon Haskell, with his simultaneously airy and raspy voice that reminds one a bit of the Nice's Lee Jackson, is probably not the ideal candidate to sing it: the folky, pentatonic melody line sounds as if it were conceived with Greg Lake's voice in mind.

"Cadence and Cascade" is followed by the album's title track, "In the Wake of Poseidon." The song seems to be modeled on the debut album's "Epitaph," featuring the same basic instrumentation—Mellotron, guitar (although acoustic guitar features more pervasively here than in "Epitaph"), bass, drums, and Greg Lake's inimitable voice. As good as "Epitaph" is, I think "Poseidon" may even be better, for several reasons. The vocal melody is beautiful, colored by potent expressive dissonances (Lake's opening F$^\sharp$ in the vocal melody against the underlying E minor triad) and affective vocal leaps (the heart-rending minor ninth of "robe-two," the tritone of "rain-whilst"). During the bridge section the foursquare phrase structure that had straightjacketed "Epitaph" is relaxed into a freer and more wayward framework. The beautiful instrumental middle section and finale show a more sophisticated sense of expressive harmony than anything in "Epitaph," with an effective use of interior pedal points adding a pungent tang to the triadic chord progressions.[84] The harmony of "Poseidon" has a bit more major key presence than "Epitaph," projecting a more hopeful mood, which therefore makes the arrival of the tonic minor chord at the beginning of the finale especially heartbreaking, and a powerful expression of brokenness. Sinfield's lyrics, which engage the twelve archetypes of De Jongh's cover art, move into a deeper symbolic realm than anything from the debut album, with some of the references to the Magi and Jesus Christ, in particular, luminescent with multiple shades of meaning. Lake gives Sinfield's words a magnificent reading, and his overdubbed vocal chorus during the finale is heartbreakingly beautiful and a career highlight. It is interesting—and perhaps

---

[84] Interior pedal points are created when a note that was a chord tone in one chord is held over into subsequent chords where it is no longer a chord tone, thus becoming dissonant with the notes of the subsequent chords.

significant—that the descending 1 7 5 (i.e., A–G–E) melodic figure upon which Lake's final chorus is built is also the kernel motive of his opening vocal chant, "Peace—A Beginning."

Side one of the LP ends with "Peace—A Theme," which finds Robert Fripp developing Lake's opening vocal chant into a piece for solo acoustic guitar. It's a lovely classical guitar pastorale, avoiding any hint of virtuoso display and notable for its exquisite voicings. As with the previous "Peace" track, the peace of this "Peace" track is rudely interrupted by the sudden cacophony of "Cat Food," which we've already discussed, which opens side two of the LP format. The album version is a bit longer than the single version, as the closing instrumental section appears here unedited.

During the lifetime of the original King Crimson lineup, the closing number of their live shows was inevitably an arrangement of Gustav Holst's "Mars, the Bringer of War," the opening movement of his *Planets* suite. Crimson's arrangement was never meant to be a literal or even a close reading of Holst's orchestral masterpiece: the band used Holst's famous 5/4 rhythmic ostinato, the opening theme, and a few other structural landmarks (such as the sledgehammer closing chords) to frame an improvisation that changed from performance to performance in many of its surface details.[85] Fripp had hoped to record a performance of "Mars" that was similar to how the original lineup had rendered the piece on stage for inclusion on *In the Wake of Poseidon*, but EG informed him that permission to release a rock arrangement of the piece was unlikely to be forthcoming from the Holst estate.

Undeterred, Fripp rearranged the band's arrangement of "Mars" into an even more distant echo of Holst's original composition, retitling it "The Devil's Triangle" after the region around Bermuda in the Atlantic Ocean where a number of unexplained disappearances of aircraft and ships have taken place. For good measure, Fripp even divided the piece into three "movements," namely "Merday Morn," "The Hand of Sceiron," and "Garden of Worm." "Merday Morn" opens with a slow, ponderous iteration of Holst's 5/4 rhythmic ostinato by the drums, over which flickers occasional fragments of Holst's original thematic material, jostling against slowly drifting Mellotron chords, supremely lonely Mellotron melodies, unexpected percussive accents, and, eventually, jagged, dissonant, pointillistic bursts of piano chords. The movement builds to a thick, multilayered mass of clashing planes of musical sound; this swirling musical maelstrom suddenly vanishes into the sound of howling "wind" and a metronome clicking lonely in the void that constitutes the second movement, "The Hand of Sceiron." Just as suddenly, the drums return playing the 5/4 ostinato, now faster than before: this marks the opening of the

---

[85] There are two recordings of "Mars" on *Epitaph*.

final "movement," "Garden of Worm." This time a writhing mass of sound—guitar plucking, Mellotron mayhem, atonal bursts of harpsichord notes courtesy of Keith Tippett, and equally random bursts of drum activity which finally consume the 5/4 ostinato—builds up to an even denser cacophony than before, out of which briefly emerges a shard of the chorus of "In the Court of the Crimson King." Suddenly, it's all swallowed up by a hallucinatory but strangely calming arpeggio that sounds like the product of a cosmic flute. This, in turn, fades into nothingness, bringing "The Devil's Triangle" to its conclusion.

Lake's voice emerges out of the silence, restating the "Peace" chant that had opened the album. Entitled "Peace—An End," this version of the "Peace" theme is longer than the previous two, with Fripp joining Lake on acoustic guitar halfway through, thus creating a sense of symmetry by uniting the protagonists of the two previous "Peace" tracks. As the track reaches its conclusion, Lake's voice begins to sink back into the bed of reverb out of which it had risen at the beginning of the album; then the music ends suddenly, almost recalling the *musicus interruptus* effect of the conclusion of *In the Court of the Crimson King.*

Some commentators have argued that *In the Wake of Poseidon* is a step forward for King Crimson, pointing to its greater polish in matters of production and arranging. I can sympathize with this point of view: while the first album essentially recreates an idealized live performance, *Poseidon* begins to experiment with the possibilities of the recording studio as an agent of musical creation, and one notes the interesting use of reverb and the far more sophisticated use of stereo perspective. Nonetheless, in my view *Poseidon* lacks the flow and inevitable progression of *Crimson King*: furthermore, it's hard not to hear much of *Poseidon* as a somewhat labored reworking of the debut album. This is especially true of the first side of the LP, which appears intent on recreating the shifts of mood, styles, and dynamics from side one of *Crimson King*: that is, "Pictures of a City" as a new "Schizoid Man," "Cadence and Cascade" as a new "I Talk to the Wind," and the title track as a new "Epitaph." Side two does, admittedly, explore new directions, but with mixed results. Fripp and Sinfield may have heard "Cat Food" as forward looking: I hear it as a retrogression, a glance back towards the self-conscious mannerism of Giles, Giles and Fripp. "The Devil's Triangle" does unquestionably break new ground, its clashing planes of sounds contributing to the creation of a restless, writhing sonic galaxy, but there's no use pretending "The Devil's Triangle" makes for a pleasant listening experience: it was not until their third album, *Lizard*, that King Crimson made a compelling and genuinely musical use of colliding planes of sound, which are made to serve both as a metaphor of delirium and an effective transitional vehicle from one section of music to the next. The three "Peace" themes are very nice, but their imposition at the beginning, middle, and end of the album has the appearance of an attempt to impose a sense of unity from without, rather than letting unity rise from within: it's hard to hear a compelling connection between the "Peace" themes and the rest of the material. In sum, I hear *Poseidon* as a transitional work: with the arguable exception of the title track, most of these ideas had been expressed more compellingly on the first album, and such concepts as were genuinely new (the Ligeti-like juxtaposition of disparate musical planes in "The Devil's Triangle") had yet to be fully mastered.

The Origin of ELP, Part 1: The Emerson–Lake Partnership

For Robert Fripp and Peter Sinfield, the most difficult period of King Crimson's existence was just beginning with the release of *In the Wake of Poseidon*. For Greg Lake, it appeared he was leaving a sinking ship just in time, and on April 4, 1970, *New Musical Express* ran an article announcing that Keith Emerson and Greg Lake were forming a new band, name and full personnel to be announced.

In his liner notes to *A Young Persons' Guide to King Crimson*, Fripp revealed that he asked Lake if he could be a part of the new band as well, but Emerson told Lake he wanted to maintain the keyboard trio format and didn't want to work with a guitarist. It is intriguing to ponder just what a band that managed to join Emerson's sense of heroic striving with Fripp's sense of tragedy and brokenness might have accomplished. On the other hand, based on Emerson's remarks, it's unlikely that such a band would have worked, because he clearly didn't "get" King Crimson: "I thought of them as a support band, really, and a bit quirky. I couldn't work out what Robert Fripp was trying to do. It was almost like in some places he sounded a bit like a jazz guitar player, but he wasn't quite jazz. I wasn't a great fan of the band at all. The one song I did hear which impressed me was 'Cat Food.'"[86]

His partnership with Lake cemented, Emerson says "a lot of the early days were spent talking and sort of sniffing things out. Greg was into Simon and Garfunkel, but he also had a huge collection of classical music that impressed me to no end."[87] From the evidence of the published

---

[86] Keith Emerson, quoted by Hall, "Welcome to the Show," 20. That Emerson thought that "Cat Food"—which *was* in fact a quirky song—was the best that Greg Lake–era King Crimson had to offer is a measure of how far he missed King Crimson

[87] Keith Emerson, quoted by David Terralavoro, "Emerson and Lake," *Fanzine for the Common Man*, no. 15 (January 1996): 16. Lake's collection of Simon and Garfunkel LPs is indicative of a more general interest in contemporary folk: in Johnson, "Under the Influence: Greg Lake," Lake also expressed admiration for the work of Judy Collins and Joni Mitchell.

interview, April 1970 was spent discussing mutual influences and potential directions, with Emerson and Lake agreeing the new band could and should be a vehicle for undertaking a more systematic adaptation of classical music's forms and techniques to rock than anything attempted by either the Nice or King Crimson. One immediate flashpoint was that Greg Lake was concerned the new band ought not to become the New Nice: Emerson has since admitted, "at the back of my mind that was exactly what it was going to be."[88] As we will see in the upcoming consideration of ELP's debut album, while it would be an oversimplification to call ELP "the New Nice," it would not be totally off base to say that the first ELP album does, to some extent, represent what Emerson had wanted the Nice to sound like, could they have summoned the requisite precision and virtuosity. Although Greg Lake was a stronger musical personality than Lee Jackson, contributing more to the band compositionally than Jackson and being more likely to challenge Emerson in matters of vocal melody and key choice, the fact remains that one hears the Nice rather than King Crimson as the taproot of early ELP.

But if Emerson largely succeeded in making the new band a vehicle for his creative vision, Lake was more proactive in putting his stamp on the new band's business affairs. In his autobiography, Emerson recalls that one of the first matters he and Lake discussed after sealing their partnership was management. Emerson naturally favored retaining the services of Tony Stratton Smith; Lake argued on behalf of David Enthoven and John Gaydon, who he saw as younger and more forward looking. Emerson says, "after the third glass of wine I began to feel inclined to agree."[89] Lake got his way, and EG became the band's management.

Of course, another vital matter was the recruitment of a drummer. An early favorite of both Emerson and Lake was the Hendrix Experience's Mitch Mitchell. Greg Lake recalls, "We got him round to talk, at Keith's house, and he had this cat with him—a bodyguard with a gun, man, and it put me off a bit—the whole scene of what he was into. He might have had good reasons for it, but we didn't pursue it any further."[90] Emerson recalls,

> Mitch did make one suggestion that, on the surface, appealed to me. "Maybe I could get Jimi interested in joining," he said. I doubted whether this could be effected as Jimi already had made it public that he only wished to work with black musicians. Later, when ELP had been formed, the story leaked to the

---

[88] Keith Emerson, quoted by Hanson, *Hang on to a Dream*, 148.

[89] Emerson, *Pictures*, 171.

[90] Greg Lake, quoted by Terralavoro, "Emerson and Lake," 17. This quotation is excerpted from an interview Lake did with Nick Logan of *New Musical Express* that ran February 13, 1971.

press. But I think what appealed and amused them more than anything was the ELP would have been HELP.[91]

Interestingly, despite Emerson's belief that Hendrix would not join in light of the fact that at the close of the sixties he was facing increasingly heavy pressure from the black community to work with other black musicians, Carl Palmer told David Hughes of *Disc and Music Echo*, "He [Hendrix] was going to join us, but it never quite happened. He missed a vital rehearsal and then discovered we were going on a long concert tour, and he just sort of blew it out."[92] Whether Palmer is simply repeating hearsay (from someone who knew someone who claimed to have spoken to Hendrix), or whether he was privy to information unknown to Emerson and Lake, is not clear. At any rate, the second opportunity for Emerson and Hendrix to work together remained, like the first, a tantalizing but never-to-be-realized scenario.

Returning to the search for a suitable drummer, Greg Lake has said, "We didn't actually audition anyone but executive discussions were going backwards and forwards with a lot of people."[93] Emerson says, "I forgot all of the drummers we auditioned but Mitch Mitchell was there and one or two others came in for a chat. We played this long blues riff at the first audition and got everyone to play it."[94] According to David Terralavoro, among the drummers considered by Emerson and Lake were Jon Hiseman of Colosseum and, possibly, Ginger Baker, late of Cream.[95] For reasons still unknown, none of the high-profile candidates clicked with Emerson and Lake, and as Emerson recalls, "There didn't seem to be any suitable choices for drummers in England. It almost seemed that we'd have to look to America until I humbly approached Mother again for his help."[96] "Mother" (Stratton Smith) was understandably not thrilled about Emerson's and Lake's choice of management for their new band. Nonetheless, he did have a suggestion. He was aware of a highly regarded young drummer who had recently played with the Crazy World of Arthur Brown and was currently working with a newly formed Hammond organ trio called Atomic Rooster. His name? Carl Palmer.

---

[91] Emerson, *Pictures*, 174.

[92] Carl Palmer, quoted by Terralavoro, "Emerson and Lake," 17. The quotation is lifted from *Disc and Music Echo*, June 26, 1971.

[93] Greg Lake, quoted by Terralavoro, "Emerson and Lake," 17. The original quotation is lifted from an interview in *RCD Magazine*, July 1992.

[94] Ibid.

[95] Ibid. Seeing that Ginger Baker's Airforce released their sole LP in 1970, I find his potential connection with Emerson and Lake unlikely, albeit not impossible. Terralavoro notes that during an interview by Stan Miesses with Carl Palmer for the January 9–15, 1974, edition of *Good Times*, Miesses stated as a matter of public record that Baker had been a candidate; Palmer neither verified nor denied the statement.

[96] Emerson, *Pictures*, 175.

Carl Palmer

Early Years and Apprenticeship (1950–1970)

Early Years

Carl Frederick Kendall Palmer was born in Handsworth, Birmingham, in England's West Midlands, on March 20, 1950, the second of three sons. Palmer came from a musical family. His grandfather was a violinist, his father an entertainer: "my father was a comedian/singer/tap dancer and used to play around the clubs in Birmingham. He knew quite a few people within the business and could ask favors from them."[1] Palmer remembers the beginning of his engagement with drumming as follows:

> I was with my father one day and we were driving through a place called West Bromwich and we went past a shop window that was full of toys, it was near Christmas, and I saw this red glitter snare drum, which at the time was called an Eric Delaney drum. It was like one drum, plastic, on a wooden stand with a cymbal. I said to my Dad, "I'd like that," mainly because I liked the color and nothing else. I wasn't at all interested in drumming. I had this drum and I played with it over Christmas like most kiddies play with their toys and then left it in the corner, looking at it you know.
>
> My father was always interested in drumming, and he started messing about on it one day. Being a selfish child I said "Leave it alone. It belongs to me." He said "In that case, if it does belong to you, you should play it." So I said okay and he happened to get out, I can't remember whether it was an Art Tatum record or a Lionel Hampton record, it could have been a Buddy Rich record, which he happened to have in the house because my father was a jazz freak. Anyway he put one of these records on and the track that he picked out was of a drummer playing time. You know, ting, ting, ting. He said "that's generally what they play." So I said "Yeah, that's cool," and got behind my

---

[1] Carl Palmer, quoted by Cheech Iero, "Carl Palmer," *Modern Drummer*, June/July 1980, 13.

drum, picked up my brushes and started playing this, which knocked them out. I thought it was a bit silly because it was so easy.[2]

Palmer's father, duly impressed, bought Carl a small drum kit—once again red glitter—and arranged for him to take lessons from a local drum instructor named Tommy Cunliffe. Recalls Palmer, "he was the best in town. He played on the radio in the Midland Light Orchestra. I went to him for about two and a half years. I was taking these lessons in Birmingham till I was fourteen."[3] Palmer still recalls his first public performance, which took place not very long after he commenced lessons:

> When I was about twelve I did my first gig after not really having much tuition or much idea of what was going on. It was round about Christmas time the following year [after receiving his first drum], with an accordion player. His name was Gil. He had a glass eye, I remember that, and his wife was enormous, but enormous, and I got on and started playing and everything was cool until they came to a waltz. I was only playing in 4/4 time, to leave one out was quite heavy for me . . . As you can imagine, I got very tangled up, but it was quite exciting, and I wore a kilt.[4]

By this point, Palmer was becoming serious about drumming, often putting in hours of practice after school. Soon enough he had his first regular paid engagement, with the Mecca Dance Band, with whom he played for six to eight months and earned the then princely sum (especially for a young teenager) of £23 per week. In 1976 Palmer told *International Musician*, "For many years [months?] I played in a Mecca band where there was about 16 players and a chick singer. I used to wear a red jacket with a badge and a cigarette burn in the cuff where the drummer before me had an accident, and my reading is up to that standard, which isn't that very high."[5] Palmer later said that the Mecca band gave him a valuable grounding in a variety of popular music styles:

> At the age of 13, I was playing in an orchestra which would be similar to the Lawrence Welk Orchestra you have in this country [U.S.A.]. One night, I could play the top of the pops; another night, old time music; another night, Latin American. So I covered a lot of ground and basically that's what I was being schooled in by my teacher at the early stage . . . At 13 going on 14, it was experience that I needed. I was reading every night.

---

[2] Carl Palmer, quoted by Keith Altham, "Carl Palmer: Benny the Bouncers' Blues Variations," *Music Scene Top Ten Series: Emerson, Lake and Palmer*, May 1974.
[3] Carl Palmer, quoted by Forrester, Hanson, and Askew, *Emerson, Lake and Palmer*, 39.
[4] Carl Palmer, quoted by Altham, "Carl Palmer."
[5] Carl Palmer, quoted by David Terralavoro, "The Carl Palmer Story, Part 1: 1950–1971," *Fanzine for the Common Man* 15 (January 1996): 19.

I was playing five nights a week and was still going to school. Everything fitted in very well.[6]

By the time he was fourteen, Palmer's first teacher, Tommy Cunliffe, called his parents and told them that he had taught Carl everything he could, and that they would be better served finding him a teacher in London. Said Palmer: "then I started to come to London every week for lessons in Denmark Street, off Shaftesbury Avenue. I went to a cat called Bruce Gaylor for a further twelve months."[7] It was around the time that Palmer switched teachers that he abandoned the Mecca band in favor of the Central City Jazz Band. Like Keith Emerson at roughly the same age, Palmer was growing increasingly interested in jazz:

> The first drum record I ever had was *Drum Crazy* on Columbia Records, and it was the soundtrack from *The Gene Krupa Story*, with Sal Mineo playing the part of Gene Krupa. The second one I had was *Buddy Rich Sings Johnny Mercer*. I traded that one for *This One's for Basie* by the Buddy Rich Orchestra, and then it was off to the races. I think that I then listened to stuff like Elvin Jones. My family liked jazz.[8]

For awhile, Palmer considered pursuing the career of a jazz musician, recalling that "I was really very keen on being a jazz drummer. Not a lot of people know that, but my initial aim was to be a jazz drummer and I played in a fifteen piece orchestra."[9] Palmer recalls the Central City Jazz Band as consisting of "all old dudes of about 40. I was about 14."[10] Palmer seems to have enjoyed playing with the CCJB at first, and one event during his time with the group remains for him a high point of his early career: "I did a gig opposite Humphrey Littleton [one of the major figures of the sixties British jazz scene], his drummer was taken ill. I went up, bold as brass, and asked if I could sit in. He said 'Can you read?' I could, so I sat in for three quarters of an hour, and he said it was okay. That was some experience."[11] Even though he was given separate billing during his time with the CCJB, after a while Palmer began to lose interest, saying, "there was nothing in the music which I found worthwhile."[12]

It was sometime around his latter days with the CCJB that Palmer hustled his fateful meeting with his hero, Buddy Rich: "I'd known Buddy

---

[6] Carl Palmer, quoted by Iero, "Carl Palmer," 13.

[7] Carl Palmer, quoted by Forrester, Hanson, and Askew, *Emerson, Lake and Palmer*, 39.

[8] Carl Palmer, quoted by Rick Mattingly, "Carl Palmer," *Modern Drummer*, December 1983, 52.

[9] Carl Palmer, quoted by Iero, "Carl Palmer," 13.

[10] Carl Palmer, quoted by Terralavoro, "Carl Palmer," 19.

[11] Carl Palmer, quoted by Forrester, Hanson, and Askew, *Emerson, Lake and Palmer*, 39.

[12] Carl Palmer, quoted by Terralavoro, "Carl Palmer," 19.

Rich since I was about 15. I bowled up to the Dorchester Hotel [in London], and asked if I could see Mr. Buddy Rich. I was in the lobby, and the concierge asked if Mr. Rich knew me, and with the brass neck of youth I said yes. As luck would have it, he was just coming out of the lift, and I asked for his autograph."[13] Suitably impressed by the youth's brashness, Rich invited him to come back the next day for a visit, and Palmer recalls, "in the room were Jack Delaney, Ronnie Verrell, Jack Parnell—and I'd brought my sticks along. I talked about a couple of techniques I thought I was playing incorrectly, and he showed me some tips—it was great."[14] This meeting marked the beginning of a friendship that endured until Rich's death in 1987: indeed, the final track on Palmer's 2001 career anthology, *Do Ya Wanna Play, Carl?*, is a riveting performance of "Shawnee" that features Palmer sitting in with Rich's Orchestra at Ronnie Scott's legendary club in Soho in 1986, shortly before Rich's death. It would probably not be too great of an exaggeration to describe Palmer's mature drumming approach, in very general terms, as an adaptation of Buddy Rich's drumming style to a rock context, although Palmer's forays into classical percussion also left a permanent mark on his technique. Incidentally, although Palmer's classical training is well known—he studied with Gilbert Webster at London's Guildhall School of Music for roughly a year, and with James Blades at the Royal Academy of Music for about eighteen months—it took place after he was already a member of ELP.[15]

The King Bees/The Craig

Like many middle-class British families of the time, Palmer's considered jazz to be "proper" music, but looked askance at the new style of music then coming out of America, rock and roll: as Palmer recalls, "my family was pretty straight and they weren't too keen on rock and roll."[16] However, Palmer recollects,

> By the time I turned 15, I was getting ready to leave school. I started to get the bug. I started to see the Rolling Stones and the Beatles on television. I answered a local ad in the paper for a drummer. So I called them up and they

---

[13] Carl Palmer, quoted by Alan Robinson, liner notes, *Do Ya Wanna Play, Carl? Carl Palmer Anthology* (Sanctuary Records CD CMEDD163, 2001), 13.

[14] Carl Palmer, quoted by Forrester, Hanson, and Askew, *Emerson, Lake and Palmer*, 40.

[15] As far as I can determine, Palmer studied with Webster sometime during the period between the release of *Trilogy* (mid-1972) and *Brain Salad Surgery* (late 1973). His studies with Blades appear to have taken place during ELP's 1975–76 sabbatical from live performance. In his studies with Webster, he concentrated on timpani; he learned tuned percussion under the tutelage of Blades.

[16] Carl Palmer, quoted by Iero, "Carl Palmer," 13.

were then called the King Bees, and they were a rhythm and blues group. I went to the audition and played. They were all very happy and asked if I would like to join the band. I said yes, and then went back home and told my father. He was amazed that I wanted to do that. The money they were going to pay me was half the amount I was making with the Orchestra [the CCJB]. I liked the music because it was loud and it was something completely different.[17]

At the age of fifteen, Carl Palmer said goodbye to the Handsworth Wood Boys Secondary Modern School and launched into what he was already certain would be his life's calling, the career of a drummer, even though, according to Palmer, "They said they didn't get much money, a couple of quid per gig, more if they went out of town, and maybe two or three gigs a week."[18] Amazingly, the fifteen-year-old Palmer took a major pay cut to join the King Bees.

The personnel of the King Bees at the time Palmer joined were Geoff Brown (lead vocals), Richie Kingbee (guitar), and Len Cox (bass). Like Gary Farr and the T-Bones, whom Keith Emerson had joined at very nearly the same time, the King Bees plied the electric blues sound that was all the rage in the U.K. at the time. Journalist Robert Brinton recalled in 1973 that "The King Bees were good, too, tremendous for their time. They could do those old Tamla and R & B numbers better than the record. And that was quite a feat."[19] Birmingham had a vibrant music scene at the time—perhaps Britain's most vibrant outside of London—and the King Bees could often be heard at the Metro Club and other local hot spots. One of the future rock heavyweights that Palmer frequently encountered at the time was John Bonham:

> The deal was come Friday/Saturday, you would do what they called double-headers. You would play one ballroom—let's say in Hansworth Wood, where I was born—and then you'd go 20 miles down the road and play the Ritz Ballroom. So you'd go on at eight and do the one, play 'til nine and get your equipment in the van and you'd be starting at eleven down the road. The Crawling Kingsnakes were always on where I was just about to play or vice versa. We saw each other a lot.
>
> We got on well but we [Bonham and Palmer] were completely different drummers. I was into the technical side and Johnny really was into the basics, the bass drum patterns and the heavy left hand. He was into being a one hundred percent rock drummer, which I couldn't help but admire. I wanted to be a bit more, but Johnny not only wanted to be just that, he wanted to perfect it. How he ended up playing in Led Zeppelin, he played that way from day one.[20]

---

[17] Ibid.

[18] Forrester, Hanson, and Askew, *Emerson, Lake and Palmer*, 39.

[19] Robert Brinton, quoted by Terralavoro, "Carl Palmer," 21.

[20] Carl Palmer, quoted by Terralavoro, "Carl Palmer," 20. The quotation comes from *Paiste News*, no. 2 (Winter 1995).

Another Birmingham native and future superstar that Palmer had occasional contact with was Steve Winwood: "He used to play piano in the Chapel Tavern pub. On Sunday morning I used to go along there and everyone could sit in, and every time I used to sit in he was playing. He was doing this jazz thing which I really dug because I was a real jazz freak. But he never really wanted to know me."[21]

Sometime in later 1965, the King Bees played at Brunel University, supporting Gary Farr and the T-Bones. T-Bones drummer Brian Walkley recalls that his band's organist intently watched the King Bees' fifteen-year-old drummer, "as though he was making a mental note."[22] The organist in question was, of course, Keith Emerson. Nor was Emerson's the only head turned by Palmer. Around the time of the Brunel University show, perhaps shortly thereafter, the King Bees were playing a package show at the Birmingham Town Hall. On the bill were the King Bees, Spencer Davis (with Steve Winwood), Brian Auger and the Trinity (with Rod Stewart), and Chris Farlowe and the Thunderbirds. Palmer recalls, "The King Bees went on first, and Chris Farlowe had just turned up and was watching us from the side of the stage. When I walked off stage Chris asked me whether I'd like to join the Thunderbirds. I said no! We had just made a record and were due to appear on *Thank Your Lucky Stars* that next week—everything was happening. Of course, Chris was well taken aback."[23]

In early 1966, the King Bees changed managers, and with new management came a new name, the Craig, and a new sound, as the band began to leave behind their electric blues roots in favor of original songs (most written by Geoff Brown) in the freakbeat style that was all the rage in the U.K. during the midsixties. During the summer of 1966, the single the band had cut earlier in the year (referred to above by Palmer), "I Must be Mad" with B-side "Suspense," was released by Fontana Records under the name of the Craig. Excepting only Geoff Brown's vocal, "I Must be Mad" could easily pass for an unreleased song by the Who. Kingbee's guitar part alternates between furiously iterated single notes and ringing power chords in a manner quite reminiscent of Pete Townshend, and Palmer's drumming, with its unpredictable, angular fills and reverberating cymbal rides, shows a close familiarity with the playing of Keith Moon, arguably the most innovative rock drummer of the midsixties. The Craig, based on the evidence of this single, were a good band, if not yet a particularly innovative one, and Palmer's belief that they were a band on their way up is easy enough to understand:

---

[21] Carl Palmer, quoted by Forrester, Hanson, and Askew, *Emerson, Lake and Palmer*, 39–40.
[22] Hanson, *Hang on to a Dream*, 20.
[23] Carl Palmer, quoted by Forrester, Hanson, and Askew, *Emerson, Lake and Palmer*, 40.

"We actually got into the charts in France [the single was released in the U.K., the U.S., France, and Germany]. We even did a *Thank Your Lucky Stars* on TV. The band had a degree of punch, and when I was young I thought the band was going to make it. We ended up sounding like the Who!"[24] Unfortunately, the band were unable to take advantage of the momentum generated by their single and their TV appearance—probably because they never forged a distinctive sound of their own. Interest in the Craig began to wane, and in late 1966 Geoff Brown and Richie Kingbee decided to leave the band in order to pursue a university education.

Chris Farlowe and the Thunderbirds

Having seen his band dissolve before his eyes, Palmer recalled Chris Farlowe's offer to join the Thunderbirds and decided to see if the offer was still good: he was uncertain it would be, because Farlowe had had a number one hit in June 1966 with the single "Out of Time" since having offered Palmer the drummer's position. Farlowe remembered Palmer, and told him the job was his if he passed an audition. Palmer was somewhat taken aback—Farlowe had, after all, already offered him the job—but agreed to drive down to London, where he stayed in the basement flat of Farlowe's parents' house:

> Chris didn't turn up for a couple of days. And I was getting worried—I'd given his mother four quid, and there I was in London with only another four in my pocket. When he did eventually turn up we went to audition, or rather rehearse, at the Bag O'Nails. As I'd bought his albums beforehand and learnt them, I was really in business before I got there. I had a great time with the band and also did a lot of session work.[25]

Palmer, who now moved to London on a permanent basis, was a member of Farlowe's Thunderbirds from February 1967 to May 1968. When he joined, the band boasted a rather formidable lineup: Farlowe, Albert Lee (guitar), Dave Greenslade (organ), and Buggs Wadel (bass). When Greenslade left the band in December 1967 to play with Geno Washington, he was replaced by Pete Solley. Greenslade was soon to make his mark with Jon Hiseman's proto-fusion band Colosseum; Solley was a member of Procol Harum when they recorded their last album of the seventies, *Something Magic* (1977). Lee, for his part, went on to play with

---

[24] Carl Palmer, quoted by Terralavoro, "Carl Palmer," 21. The original source of the quote was an interview that Palmer did with Keith Altham for *Music Scene* sometime in 1973.
[25] Carl Palmer, quoted by Forrester, Hanson, and Askew, *Emerson, Lake and Palmer*, 40.

the Everly Brothers. Incidentally, the previous incumbent in the drummer's seat was Ian Hague—who was, very shortly, to become the original drummer for the Nice.

In 1972, Palmer told Janis Schact of *Circus*, "You know, I've always played with a keyboard instrument. I played with Chris Farlowe and the Thunderbirds when I was 15. [As we've seen, that's not correct; he joined The Thunderbirds shortly before he turned 17 and left shortly after he turned 18.] That was soul, yeah, that was a blues band, a soul band with saxophones and everything."[26] Farlowe formed the Thunderbirds in 1963; after a number of singles and an album with Columbia, in 1965 he signed with Andrew Loog Oldham's Immediate label, going on to release a number of singles (including the number one hit "Out of Time") and two more albums. The band released four singles during Palmer's tenure: he plays on two of them. Palmer played on the A-side of "Yesterday's Papers"/"Life is But Nothing," a Mick Jagger-Keith Richards song that was released in May 1967, turning in a strong and easily recognizable performance. He also played on the A-side of "Handbags and Gladrags"/"Everyone Makes a Mistake," written and produced by Mike D'Abo and released in November 1967. "Handbags and Gladrags" was later to become closely associated with Rod Stewart, upon the release of his first solo album in 1969. Two other singles released by Farlowe and the Thunderbirds during Palmer's tenure with the band, "Moanin'"/"What Have I Been Doin'" (June 1967), and "The Last Goodbye"/"Paperman in the Sky" (April 1968), do not feature any Carl Palmer involvement. Farlowe stayed true to his blues and soul roots well after most similar bands had either broken up or evolved in more contemporary directions, but in 1968 the meteoric rise of psychedelic rock was swamping what was left of the British blues scene, and by the end of 1968, Farlowe had disbanded the Thunderbirds.

The Crazy World of Arthur Brown

Palmer left Farlowe's Thunderbirds during May 1968. The summer of 1968 saw him making a decidedly unique career move as he joined the Crazy World of Arthur Brown; certainly Brown was one of the most singular personalities to emerge from the late-sixties British rock scene. Initially a law student at Kings College, London, Brown was quickly expelled; by the following year, however, he was at Reading University studying philosophy. It was in Reading that Brown, a singer, first became seriously involved with rock music, recording a demo with a

---

[26] Carl Palmer, quoted by Schact, "Emerson, Lake and Palmer," 6.

local band, the Black Diamonds, and fronting his first band, the Arthur Brown Union. Although nothing became of these projects, the engineer of the demo he had cut with the Black Diamonds, Philip Woods, invited him to take on a residency at a club in Paris, and this invitation marked the turning point in Brown's career. It was in Paris during 1965-66 that Brown developed his concept of rock-as-theater that was to both revolutionize his own career, and provide the paradigm for seventies glam rockers as diverse as Alice Cooper, Kiss, and David Bowie. By the time he left France in 1966, Brown was a cult sensation who had simultaneously rubbed shoulders with French high society and provided the soundtrack for the Parisian university subculture that was soon to engineer the Paris student riots. Back in London, Brown met organist Vincent Crane, a graduate of the Trinity School of Music, and the two recruited a drummer named Drachan Theaker who had auditioned too late for the Jimi Hendrix Experience and had watched Mitch Mitchell get the drummer's position instead. With the minimalist lineup of vocals (Brown), organ (Crane), and drums (Theaker), the trio formed the Crazy World of Arthur Brown.

The band's live show developed around the highly theatrical approach Brown had perfected in Paris: although their act was controversial enough to lose them some gigs, by early 1967 the Crazy World had become a favorite act at such favorite haunts of the London counterculture as the UFO Club and the Speakeasy. The Who's Pete Townshend became a fan of the band (a full two years before he famously endorsed the debut King Crimson album) and connected Brown with the Who's managers, Kit Lambert and Chris Stamp. They signed Brown to a management, agency, and recording deal with their own Track label, backed by Polydor Records, and shortly thereafter the band released their first single, "Devil's Grip," which flopped. Undeterred, Lambert and Stamp arranged for the band to undertake their first American tour, where they supported the Doors, Jefferson Airplane, and Frank Zappa, among others. After returning to the U.K., the band contacted Cream's manager, Robert Stigwood, in an attempt to get out of their contract with Lambert and Stamp: the maneuver was, unfortunately for the band's future, unsuccessful.

During the latter half of 1967, the Crazy World of Arthur Brown repaired to London's Independent Studios to record their first album. Almost immediately, there were conflicts over creative direction between band and management. Stamp and Lambert wanted to market Brown as a hip Elvis Presley, and saw him primarily as a solo artist; like Presley, Brown was rare in that although he did not have a "black" voice, he could render interpretations of black soul and R & B material that were both authoritative and personal. Brown, on the other hand, saw himself as a late-sixties rock *artiste* working within the framework of a band to create music that was conceptually and instrumentally ambitious. In the end, band and management reached a compromise. On the first side of the eponymous LP, Brown was given free rein to pursue his vision, and he responded with a side-long suite that was nothing less than a sustained meditation on hell that generates its not inconsiderable power from the fact that it simultaneously questions the traditional Christian view of the afterlife, and takes it seriously. Side two of the LP showcases the band playing shorter, punchier, and more obviously singles-oriented material, including a gripping cover of Screaming Jay Hawkins's "I Put a Spell on You" (there is, incidentally, no doubt that Hawkins's own bizarre act impacted Brown's stage persona), and a not-so-bracing cover of James Brown's "I've Got Money." Ironically, it was not the side two material that made a commercial impact, but rather one of the songs from side one, "Fire"; released as a single, it hit number one in the British charts and number two in the American.

When Lambert and Stamp presented the tapes of the album to Ahmet Ertegun of Atlantic Records, which was planning to act as American distributor, Ertegun complained that the time keeping of drummer Drachen Theaker was suspect. Lambert then took the tapes back to London, and added brass and strings to the passages Ertegun had objected to, with the goal of creating a massive cushion of sound that would push Theaker's drumming far into the sonic background. Lambert spent two weeks mixing the tapes, an unheard-of amount of time to devote to postproduction by late-sixties standards.

In early 1968, the band commenced their second American tour. About a week into the tour, Chris Stamp flew over from London to play the finished product for the band. As Arthur Brown recalls, "When Stamp presented us with the album in a motel in America we'd only heard the first two minutes when Drachen picked it up and smashed it. The drums were mixed back and he hated the brass and strings."[27] From that point on the tour was a downhill affair, as the angry Theaker's behavior became increasingly unpredictable: Brown recalls one show during which Theaker kicked his entire drum kit over the edge of the stage, and promptly fell off the stage himself, landing on top of his drums. Crane finally demanded that Theaker be fired, and Brown obliged; the tour was completed with a Canadian drummer, Jeff Cutler. Nor did Brown's problems end with the firing of Theaker: Vincent Crane's behavior became increasingly unstable as well. Brown initially believed Crane had been spiked; it was only later that he learned of Crane's bipolar disorder that, sadly, eventually drove him to commit suicide on Valentine's Day 1989.

---

[27] Arthur Brown, quoted by Terralavoro, "Carl Palmer," 23.

Upon returning to Great Britain in early summer 1968, Brown granted Crane an extended leave of absence. Now he needed to recruit a new band. Enter Carl Palmer, who in an August 1971 interview with *Beat Magazine*, recalled his induction into the Crazy World of Arthur Brown as follows: "He just said 'there's a *Top of the Pops* on Thursday. We gotta be there for 2:30,' or something like that, and I said, 'right, I'm into that.' Then he said, 'we've got a gig in Manchester tomorrow. The coach leaves at 2:00.' And I said, 'right, I'm into that too.' And that was how I joined."[28]

There have always been questions about Palmer's possible involvement with the band's debut album. Palmer has stated that both he and John Marshall (later the drummer of Soft Machine) had been used as sessions drummers while the album was being recorded, but he is certain that none of his own takes were used, and that most of the drumming heard on the album is Theaker's, with the rest being Marshall's.[29] Be this as it may, Palmer was the drummer on all of the band's television appearances, including *Top of the Pops* and the German television show *Beat Club*. Besides Palmer, Brown had recruited Palmer's recent band mate from Chris Farlowe's Thunderbirds, organist Pete Solley, and bassist Nick Greenwood; while a bassist was never a full member of the Crazy World of Arthur Brown, Brown frequently employed bassists on an as-needed basis for the band's live shows. The Brown-Solley-Greenwood-Palmer lineup toured the U.K. and Europe during the summer and early autumn of 1968, playing the eighth annual National Jazz and Blues Festival on August 10 (where the Nice were also on the bill) and participating in a package tour with the Small Faces, Joe Cocker, and the Who in October.

By November 1968, Vincent Crane had rejoined the band in time for a six-week tour of the U.S. that was to last until early January 1969; this is the first time Carl Palmer had ever been to the U.S., and he said, "I'll never forget flying into Los Angeles. We flew over one of these drive-ins, you know, and I can see the movie happening on the screen as the plane's coming in and I thought 'God! This is America.'"[30]

An Arthur Brown performance was, even by the wide-open standards of the late sixties, an unusual affair. Brown frequently came on stage wearing a long, flowing robe; his face was done in white make-up, with spiderweblike black lines superimposed (Brown would therefore seem to be the inspiration for seventies glam rockers Kiss); he also wore a "fire helmet," out of which flames shot up during key points during the performance.

---

[28] Carl Palmer, quoted by Terralavoro, "Carl Palmer," 23.
[29] Terralavoro, "Carl Palmer," 22. Incidentally, Terralavoro is not repeating a quote from a secondary source here; this is what Palmer told him directly.
[30] Carl Palmer, quoted by Terralavoro, "Carl Palmer," 24.

(Brown's hair once caught on fire in a British club; two audience members quickly doused the fire by running onto the stage and pouring beer on Brown's head.) The band were often obliged to dress up in strange outfits and wear masks; when they appeared on *Top of the Pops*, the band were dressed as demon serfs and wore skull masks, while they wore smiley-face masks for their appearance on *Beat Club*. It seems that for Palmer, the anonymity of performing with the Crazy World of Arthur Brown may have begun to grate after a while:

> I don't know how the audiences were. I couldn't see them with Arthur Brown. I was wearing too many masks, there were too many strobe lights, it was very hard to tell. The audiences were nothing like we have now [i.e. 1972, with ELP]. And with Arthur being so visual you never really got a chance in that band. Not even Vincent, being the lead instrument[alist], got a chance. Audience anticipation was all Arthur's; he was the only one who got them at all. If anything got to them. So musically I was really left behind. They would clap when he lit his fire helmet up. If I did something good, or Vincent did something good they wouldn't clap. Mind you, it might not have been good. I have no impressions from last time.[31]

From Brown's perspective, the addition of Palmer gave the band a much-needed shot in the arm: "Carl's arrival changed the whole style of our music because he was much more of a technical drummer. Vincent loved that, and they also got on well together, which was great because it was just when 'Fire' was a hit."[32] By late 1968, Brown had developed a new stage act about a black magician and was beginning to envision a new album built around this concept. In fact, in November 1968 the band released a follow-up single to "Fire" called "Nightmare," with B-side "What's Happening," that was presumably part of this concept; Palmer, who played on the B-side, recalls that at or around the same time the band recorded another song, "Sorcerer," that has never been released.[33] Presumably the remainder of the music for the proposed second album by the Crazy World of Arthur Brown would have, in optimal conditions, been fleshed out during their fourth American tour, which took place between March or April and June 1969. Unfortunately, during the course of the third (late 1968/early 1969) American tour, Brown had discovered LSD (contrary to rumors, his debut album was not acid inspired), and thereafter, the band's interpersonal chemistry began to disintegrate as it was now Brown's behavior that grew increasingly unpredictable. At the

---

[31] Carl Palmer, quoted by Schact, "Emerson, Lake and Palmer," 9.

[32] Arthur Brown, quoted in a *Classic Rock* interview, posted on http://img69.photobucket.com/albums/v210/allfear/arthurbrown/classic_rock_5.jpg.

[33] Although Brown later rerecorded the song with his band Kingdom Come and retitled it "Eternal Messenger."

same time, the band were beginning to grow weary of the constant touring; sadly, they found themselves in a similar position to the Nice in that band's Immediate days, seeing scarcely a penny of royalty money for their hit single due to a highly exploitative contract, and needing to tour perpetually in order to pay the bills. Brown believes that the band's *coup de grace* came when Palmer and Crane learned, to their utter horror, that Brown had declined an opportunity to be delivered from his ties to Lambert, Stamp, and Track Records by the band's American management, who had made arrangements to have them re-signed by CBS. One can only assume that by this point, Brown's judgment had been badly clouded by LSD. This would seem to jibe with Carl Palmer's recollections about the last days of the Crazy World of Arthur Brown, shared with *Rolling Stone* in an August 5, 1971, interview: "We were stuck in New York City for three months and Arthur didn't want to play. He was into black mysticism, you know. Always running off to health farms. His price went from $10,000 to $100,000. It was no use talking to him, so I just left him in the middle of the night."[34] Palmer and Crane both left on the same day: Friday the 13th of June, 1969. Brown, having seen his band dissolve yet again, returned to the U.K., and made no further attempt to reform the Crazy World of Arthur Brown. By 1971 he had recovered himself sufficiently to put together a new band, Arthur Brown's Kingdom Come. This band released three albums between 1971 and 1973, all very innovative, interesting, and suggestive of how the Crazy World of Arthur Brown might have developed had it continued. Unfortunately, by 1971 Brown was essentially forgotten and his subsequent work never received the attention that it often deserved. He ended up in Austin, Texas, of all places, where for many years he ran a successful house painting and home decoration company.

Atomic Rooster

On the flight back to London, Palmer and Crane agreed to form a new band, and shortly thereafter recruited Nick Graham, a bassist/vocalist who also played flute. The August 16, 1969, edition of *Record Mirror* announced the formation of the new trio, called Atomic Rooster, and on August 22 the band played their debut show at London's Freakeasy. During the remainder of 1969, the band performed frequently (including some shows in northern Europe late in the year), while recording their debut album for B & C Records. In December 1969 (either the 3rd or 10th) the band did a session for broadcast on the *Rhythm and Blues Show*,

---

[34] Carl Palmer, quoted by Terralavoro, "Carl Palmer," 24.

recording three songs that were to feature on their album: "Friday the Thirteenth," "S.L.Y.," and "Decline and Fall." In February 1970 the band released *Atomic Roooster* [sic], their first album.

First Album: Atomic Roooster

Atomic Rooster were a "progressive" band at a time when the term meant something a bit different than it came to mean during the seventies: they were a band that experimented with melding the blues rock and psychedelic rock styles of the late sixties with jazz, folk, and (to a lesser extent) classical influences. Of course, the same could be said of the Nice or King Crimson: the crucial difference being that the characteristic sound of these latter two bands much more closely anticipates the progressive rock sound of the seventies in its narrower, more specific sense.

At their most characteristic, Atomic Rooster ply a blues-based, proto-metal organ trio approach that anticipates Deep Purple's seminal *Machine Head* album of 1971; this vein of writing is especially evident on "Friday the Thirteenth," "S.L.Y.," and the high-octane psychedelic jam "Before Tomorrow," all of which feature guitarist John DuCann, who appears in a sessions role. However, the band also explore a sound reminiscent of early Blood, Sweat and Tears' melodramatic big-band jazz-rock fusion ("Broken Wings"), and a melancholy, vaguely folk rock vein that evokes early Caravan; listen particularly to "Winter," where Palmer's glockenspiel and tom parts delicately embroider Crane's piano and Graham's flute, and point the way to the "pastoral jazz" of ELP's "Take a Pebble." The band undertake some experiments with odd meters, for instance in "Banstead," another song vaguely reminiscent of early Caravan, which showcases an organ fanfare consisting of two bars of three followed by three bars of four, and in "And so to Bed," which is in 5/4 throughout. They also explore some interesting orchestrations: passages highlighting a brass ensemble feature prominently during "Broken Wings" and "Winter," prominent cello parts in "Banstead" and "Winter," and, as mentioned above, a glockenspiel obbligato during "Winter."

Nick Graham, a fine rock singer, shows himself capable of alternating between a leathery rasp reminiscent of the Who's Roger Daltrey and an airy tenor strikingly similar to that of Caravan's Pye Hastings; he's also a good flautist and a solid if unspectacular bassist. Vincent Crane, the band's principal songwriter, is no Hammond virtuoso, but does have a gift for spinning out memorable riffs that define whole sections of a song (in this respect he's similar to Black Sabbath's guitarist, Tony Iommi), and also uncovers some interesting approaches to organ coloration (as in the use of a wah-wah pedal to create a swirling, psychedelic ambience during "Before Tomorrow"). On *Atomic Roooster* Carl Palmer's mature drumming style emerges fully blown: the lightning fast tom runs and complex rudimental fills, often counterpointed by driving cymbal rides, are all in evidence here, as is his care in matters of percussion orchestration, displayed not only in the tuned percussion parts of "Winter" but the effective use of overdubbed congas to create a powerful, throbbing climax for "Decline and Fall."

Nonetheless, while *Atomic Roooster* is engaging and genuinely interesting in spots, it never quite rises above the level of experimentation with and dabbling in the various styles it engages; what it lacks that the debut Nice, Crimson, and (soon enough) ELP albums have in spades is a clear, focused sense of stylistic direction—that is to say, artistic vision. Nonetheless, for Palmer, who had yet to turn twenty when the album was released, *Atomic Roooster* represented an important career milestone: for the first time, he was part of a band in which he was a full creative partner, and which could serve as a vehicle for his now daunting percussive abilities. Atomic Rooster were becoming a popular live draw, and Palmer could count on the band making upwards of £200 per night. The new album was slowly but surely climbing in the British charts: in June 1970, it entered the U.K. top fifty.

The Origin of ELP, Part 2: The Recruitment of Carl Palmer

It's not surprising, then, that Palmer was dismissive when he received a call in April 1970 from Tony Stratton Smith requesting that he consider joining a new band with Keith Emerson: "I was asked to join a new musical environment that Keith was creating. I think that was the actual terminology that was used. And I wasn't really interested, to be quite honest. This was early in 1970, and the Atomic Rooster were doing well. We had a great following in Europe."[35] Like Lake, Palmer did not want to be part of a New Nice: "Emerson made a first proposal that I refused for many reasons. I wanted to stay with my band and I thought I would be regarded as the successor of Brian Davison, be identified as the Nice."[36] However, Emerson and Lake persisted, and Palmer recalls, "Anyway, about a month later, I got a call from Greg Lake's management asking if I would reconsider. I think they had tried Mitch Mitchell, the drummer for Jimi Hendrix, and things hadn't worked out. So I said maybe I could come along and have a play, since I happened to have some free time."[37]

---

[35] Carl Palmer, quoted by Hall, "Welcome to the Show," 20.
[36] Carl Palmer, quoted by Terralavoro, "Emerson and Lake," 18.
[37] Carl Palmer, quoted by Hall, "Welcome to the Show," 20.

In the July 1992 issue of *RCD Magazine*, Palmer recalls, "the first time we met was in Greg's apartment and we discussed things for ages before we even mentioned actually playing! That's ELP all over, all bloody talk and no action." He went on to say,

> I didn't have any preconceptions either way when they said we should get together to play. I'd played with Arthur Brown and Atomic Rooster so I really only went down to the studio to see if the talk was all talk or if the music was there too. It was intrigue pure and simple. I felt, like they did, that classical influences hadn't been explored in [rock] music before, so it was an opportunity I couldn't really afford to miss.[38]

Elsewhere, Palmer has said,

> I had not heard of Greg Lake at the time. I'd heard of the band [King Crimson] and Bob Fripp, but they were the only ones. Although he was unknown to me, he had a certain air about him. He came on like a ton of bricks. And it just kind of grew from there.
>   Then I met Keith, who was very inhibited as a character when we first got together. He didn't say much: just "Hiya man, let's play." That's what I dug about Keith, you know, he came in on a pure musical thing. I got into that because he was challenging me and I love a challenge musically. I said "Yeah, whatever you want to play." Apparently that knocked him out because drummers had been going down there and saying "Let's play one of these." "Let's play one of those." But I said "Just count me in" and they loved it.[39]

In his autobiography, Emerson recalls Carl Palmer's audition as follows:

> In bounded our last hope, carrying various-sized cases full of clattering metal. Immediately, the dullness of the surrounding lightened and became tolerable as he began to set up his kit, while chattering away in a sort of "Pipey Brummie" accent. If he played as fast as he talked, it wouldn't be a very long audition. I do believe he had an Enid Blyton character painted on his bass drum head. Noddy [the Blyton character] somehow completed the picture of the almost childlike quality that presented itself to us. We were to discover that he'd only just turned 20 years old; a mere baby.[40]

However, as Emerson admits, there was nothing childlike about Palmer's drumming:

> "Right, what's it to be then?" piped Carl, sticks at the ready. Greg turned to me and I launched into a shuffle. Always the simplest of rhythms, but deceivingly the hardest to make swing, the old favorite "Hideaway" took on another

---

[38] Carl Palmer, quoted by Terralavoro, "Emerson and Lake," 18.
[39] Carl Palmer, quoted by Keith Altham, "Look, You Have to Join Us," *Music Scene Top Ten Series: Emerson, Lake and Palmer* (May 1974).
[40] Emerson, *Pictures*, 175.

dimension. A signal from me, Greg and I tacited to allow Carl a two-chorus drum solo. The explosion that followed left us both almost too shocked to continue playing.[41]

Emerson and Lake were convinced they'd found their man. Palmer still wasn't so sure he'd found his band. In a 1977 radio interview with Allison Steele of WNEW-FM (New York), Palmer said, "Greg called me up and said, 'Look you know this is the right thing for you to do and you should join this band.' And I thought 'Well, no, not really.' So he said to come and play once more. So I went down and I played once more with them, and I thought 'it is marvelous. We do play well together, I admit,' and I left."[42] The Emerson-Lake partnership had been clinched with a phone call made by Lake in the wee hours of the morning. The Emerson-Lake-Palmer partnership was clinched in like manner: "A week went by and I got a phone call like about two in the morning from him [Lake], and he said that if I didn't join the band, I'd not only be damaging myself, I'd be damaging him, and he said that was heavy. I felt that was quite a statement to come from someone I didn't know."[43] Palmer recalls, "I called my father up that night and I said 'Listen. I just spoke to a cat on the phone and he said to me that if I didn't join his band he reckoned that I'd be damaging him, not me. Well, me as well, but he was more concerned about himself.' My father said, 'The guy must have something.'"[44]

In his autobiography, Emerson suggests that after the initial audition, Palmer was in the new band and that was that. Obviously, it wasn't quite so simple: over the course of an audition, one or more additional practice sessions, and several urgent phone calls from Lake, Palmer was slowly drawn out of Atomic Rooster into the new band during May 1970. Palmer himself has said as much: "I finally said 'okay, I'll give it a shot.' I told my old group what I was doing, and they were quite content to sit around and see what moves I was going to make. I worked with Greg and Keith for a month, and after that I said to the guys in Atomic Rooster, 'Look, you'd best find someone else. I think I'm going to carry on with this.' And that was it, really."[45]

While Emerson and Lake rejoiced at Palmer's decision to join their new band, Atomic Rooster's manager, Robert Stigwood, didn't. Emerson recalls, "although he'd done very well with Cream, the Bee Gees, and a veritable score of film projects, 'Stiggy,' a millionaire, hadn't yet done *that* well with Carl."[46] Therefore, even after he made his decision to quit

---

[41] Ibid.
[42] Carl Palmer, quoted by Terralavoro, "Emerson and Lake," 18.
[43] Ibid.
[44] Carl Palmer, quoted by Altham, "Look, You Have to Join Us."
[45] Carl Palmer, quoted by Hall, "Welcome to the Show," 20.
[46] Emerson, Pictures, 179.

Atomic Rooster, Palmer continued to perform with his old band through the end of May, while Stigwood and EG negotiated the financial implications of Palmer's exodus. In the end, EG were obliged to pay one third of the management share to Stigwood. Nick Graham left Atomic Rooster at nearly the same time as Palmer, and John DuCann, the guitarist who had played a sessions role on *Atomic Roooster*, joined as a full-time member; drummer Paul Hammond was recruited in Palmer's stead. Without Palmer and Graham on board, the band adopted a less experimental and adventurous but more tightly focused and harder rocking approach for their next album, *Death Walks Behind You*. Released in autumn 1970, *Death* finds Atomic Rooster drawing ever closer to Deep Purple's heavy blues-rock/proto-metal sound, although with a doomier, darker conceptual content reminiscent of the first two Black Sabbath albums (which were released in 1970 and 1971 respectively). *Death Walks Behind You*, which hit number eleven in the U.K. charts, was to mark Atomic Rooster's commercial (and arguably, their creative) zenith. One wonders if at least some of the band's commercial success during the 1970–71 period was perhaps generated by interest in their ex-drummer and his new project.

4 From the Beginning

First Show, First Album, First Tour (June through December 1970)

Earliest Period: June–August 1970

Once Palmer made the decision to join Emerson and Lake's new band, matters moved quickly. The musicians considered names for the group: "Triton" and "Studfarm" were eventually rejected in favor of "Emerson, Lake and Palmer," which soon was being abbreviated to "ELP." The band were clearly confident that in the U.K., at least, their names were well enough known for a strategy of naming the band after themselves to make sense.

An article that ran in *New Musical Express* on May 30, 1970, formally announced the formation of Emerson, Lake and Palmer. The article stated that the band's first public performance would be in a small club sometime in July (in fact, it was a month later, and in a two- to three-thousand-seat venue). It mentioned that preliminary rehearsals were under way: the band were already working on new material, and also planned to play the Nice's "Rondo" (which they did, in fact, throughout much of their existence) and King Crimson's "21st Century Schizoid Man" (this one was soon abandoned, not to be revived again until the early nineties).[1] The article noted that the band were temporarily hobbled by the fact that Carl Palmer was still trying to extricate himself from his commitments to Atomic Rooster (as matters turned out, he played his last date with the band one day after this article came out, on May 31), and Emerson was waiting to take delivery of a £4,000 modular Moog synthesizer, one of four custom built by Robert Moog for a concert series called "Jazz in the Garden" held in New York City's Museum of Modern Art. Once the series was over, Moog sought to sell them, and Emerson was an eager

---

[1] This article, "Emerson, Lake and Palmer to Make 'Incognito' Debut," is reprinted in its entirety in David Terralavoro's *Fanzine for the Common Man*, no. 2 (December 1989): 3.

buyer. Like Mike Vickers's modular Moog that Emerson had used during some of his late-period performances with the Nice, the modular system he purchased from Moog was monophonic, capable of playing just one note at a time. Unlike Vickers's system, however, this unit came with custom preset box: instead of having to turn a number of knobs and reroute patch chords for each change of sound, Emerson could simply press a button to access the desired effect. Although the preset box only allowed for eight presets, it still proved to be a huge advantage in Emerson's live performances, and throughout the early seventies Emerson frequently took the modular system back to Moog's factory in Trumansburg (near Ithaca), New York, for further customizing.

It was also at the time of ELP's formation that Emerson purchased his first Hammond C-3, one of two (which later came to be known as the "Pictures" C-3 and the "Tarkus" C-3) that he was to purchase during the early seventies. Contrary to popular belief, Emerson had not owned a Hammond C-3 during his tenure with the Nice, although he occasionally rented one for specific shows. Palmer, for his part, ordered the two huge gongs that were to remain focal points of his stage paraphernalia throughout the seventies.

Rehearsals started in June at Island Studios, Basing Street, London. Besides "Rondo" and "Schizoid Man," the band almost immediately began putting together their epic arrangement of Modest Musorgsky's piano suite *Pictures at an Exhibition*, which was to become the major component of their early live shows. They also began work on "The Barbarian," an adaptation of Béla Bartók's piano piece "Allegro Barbaro"; Greg Lake's "Take a Pebble," which he had performed in a less developed version with his earlier band the Shame; and a Keith Emerson/Carl Palmer collaboration, "Tank." By July the modular Moog had arrived and ELP were ensconced in London's Advision Studios, hard at work recording their debut album with the assistance of Eddy Offord, a young and then unknown engineer who was to play a major role in forging the signature sounds of both ELP and Yes. During July the band recorded "The Barbarian," "Take a Pebble," "Tank," and "Lucky Man," a Greg Lake song that had been auditioned for the debut King Crimson album, but rejected: they also began to prepare for their debut performances, now scheduled for August.[2]

ELP's premiere performance took place on Sunday, August 23, at the Guildhall in Plymouth, a south coast town not too far from Emerson's and Lake's former stomping grounds.[3] The band chose to debut in this

---

[2] For recording date information I am using the liner notes of *The Return of the Manticore* box set.

[3] At least, this is what was stated in a *Record Mirror* article dated August 15, 1970. An article than ran in *New Musical Express* on the same day stated it was the Portsmouth Guildhall

relatively small and inauspicious venue in order to work through any performance problems they might experience in a relatively low pressure environment. Their next performance promised to be a much more closely scrutinized and high-pressure affair: they were scheduled to perform on Saturday, August 29, during the second day of the three-day Isle of Wight Festival.

Much has been written about this festival, which is the subject of a sprawling documentary by Murray Lerner. Isle of Wight represented an attempt to recreate the "peace, love, and understanding" vibe of Woodstock, which had taken place just one year before, and many of the same acts appeared, including Hendrix, the Who, Ten Years After, and Sly and the Family Stone. Like Woodstock, a rustic site was chosen—Isle of Wight is a small island off the south coast of England—again emphasizing the importance of pastoralist mythology to the late-sixties counterculture.[4] However, even at that time it was becoming obvious that Woodstock was the high-water mark of a hippie communitarian and utopian impulse that was already on the wane. The ugly events at the Altamont show in December 1969, an even earlier attempt to recapture the "Woodstock vibe," had largely shattered the illusion that universal peace, love, and understanding were just around the corner if only enough young people believed. The events at Isle of Wight, which included a huge contingent of angry hippies crashing the fences and storming the festival, did nothing to reverse the prognosis.[5]

In this sense, Isle of Wight marks both a musical and cultural transition: several acts that had been musically and culturally of great importance to the late sixties gave their swan-song performances here. Jimi Hendrix was dead within a month. The classic lineups of both the Doors and Sly and the Family Stone were soon to unravel; Jim Morrison, the Doors' troubled lead singer, ceased performing with the band shortly after Isle of Wight, and was dead within a year. Certainly sixties utopianism was not yet fatally wounded. As I argued in *Rocking the Classics*, ELP and the other progressive bands that were just appearing at this time drew on sixties idealism to launch themselves forward, and elements of Eastern mysticism, pastoralism, science fiction futurism, and the Romantic notion of the artist as prophet figure—all concerns solidly grounded in

---

that ELP would debut in on August 23. Greg Lake is on record saying that it was Plymouth: see Hall, "Welcome to the Show," 20. Keith Emerson also states that it was Plymouth (*Pictures*, 182). Paul Stump's assertion (*The Music's All That Matters*, 98) that the debut show was at Portsmouth would appear to be incorrect.

[4] Stump, Martin, and I all discuss pastoralism and the counterculture at length. See Stump, *The Music's All That Matters*, 40–43; Martin, *Listening to the Future*, 105–7, 134–35; and *Rocking the Classics*, 51–52, 80.

[5] Paul Stump discusses this event in *The Music's All That Matters*, 111 and 115.

the sixties counterculture—were to inform the progressive rock movement throughout the 1970s.[6] At the same time, though, there was already a dawning sense that a golden age was passing, and that the waters through which countercultural aspirations would now have to navigate were growing more treacherous. The early work of ELP and their progressive rock peers should be evaluated against the backdrop of a sixties utopianism that was beginning to be tempered by a renewed sense of reality, and that eventually was to be corroded by a number of less attractive attitudes and expectations.

Live at the Isle of Wight Festival: August 29, 1970

Very few people were aware that ELP's segment had been taped—Murray Lerner's documentary barely features them at all—so it was a great surprise for many when in 1997 a revived Manticore Records issued, as its first release, *Emerson, Lake and Palmer Live at the Isle of Wight Festival*. I for one admire the band's courage in authorizing its release: recorded direct off the sound board, it is an excruciatingly honest document that shows a young band very much going through growing pains. The band opens with "The Barbarian"; Lake's fuzzed bass guitar is badly out of tune, and the climax lacks the precision that characterizes their performance of this piece on their debut album. "Take a Pebble" is next; Lake sings somewhat tentatively, and, compared to the studio recording of the song, his acoustic guitar solo is underdeveloped. Interestingly, during Emerson's second

---

[6] Durrell Bowman has misread me when he says, "I find it difficult to agree with Macan's central premise [in *Rocking the Classics*] that British progressive rock was primarily an extension of the counterculture's spiritualism and mysticism" ("Let Them All Make Their Own Music," in Holm-Hudson, *Progressive Rock Reconsidered*, 184). I never claim progressive rock is a wholesale extension of countercultural spiritualism and mysticism; I do claim (as above) that progressive rock draws on elements of Eastern religion, British pastoralism, science fiction futurism, and the Romantic conception of artist as prophet figure, all concerns solidly grounded in the sixties counterculture. Based on his remarks preceding the quote I cite above, it would seem Bowman believes that mysticism and spiritualism are antithetical to prog rock's formal and metrical complexity and virtuosity; throughout history, though, many "mystical" movements (from Pythagorean numerical mysticism to medieval alchemy to Renaissance hermeticism) have been quite intellectually rigorous. Bowman is certainly incorrect in stating, "In its most memorable work, it [seventies prog rock] involved science fiction narratives and technological/sociopolitical themes rather than spiritual/mystical ones" (184). To the contrary, seventies prog rock involves both. Otherwise, how are we to describe Genesis's "Supper's Ready"? ELP's "The Endless Enigma"? Practically *anything* by Yes circa 1971–77? Robert Fripp's interest in Gurdjieff, and Peter Sinfield's use of hermeticist symbology in his lyrics for King Crimson?

piano solo (after Lake's guitar solo) the band kicks into the opening section of "Tank," using a jazz ride cymbal pattern and walking bass line that give it a much different feel than it has on the debut album.

Then comes *Pictures at an Exhibition*. Again, when one compares it with the later live recording featured on the band's third album, the overall impression is of a piece still under construction. Many of the complex transitions of the later version are nowhere to be heard, and Emerson's familiarity with his new modular Moog is still rather rudimentary, as he largely uses one particular filtered sound. Lake's intonation fails him at the end of "The Great Gates of Kiev," and Emerson appears to botch a few of his parts. During Lake's quiet and serious "The Sage," the Moog somehow switches on for about ten seconds, making a series of most unwelcome wheezes. Yet at some point one sense the crowd really getting caught up in the music, and by the end of the piece, when Emerson and Lake detonate a pair of 800-pound antique cannons (the CD doesn't capture the sonic effect very well), the crowd roars in approval. Clearly, even in this raw and primitive state, the newness of ELP's sound strikes a chord, and they are called out for two encores, "Rondo" and "Nutrocker."

It's impossible for me to hear this performance the way the audience heard it in 1970: what I chiefly emerge with is a greater appreciation for what an amazingly tight, well-oiled musical machine the band had become a scant six months later when they recorded the performance of *Pictures* which features on their third album. I have also been spoiled by the sense of clarity, at that time unprecedented, that Eddy Offord was able to bring to the debut recording. However, the Isle of Wight performance clearly made an impact, and the new ELP sound was well defined enough for it to become immediately controversial. Some critics, such as Chris Welch, were impressed; on the other hand, well-known DJ John Peel, who was to become one of the band's most implacable foes, called it "a tragic waste of time, talent, and electricity."[7] ELP had instantly created a large public expectantly awaiting their debut LP: this audience was further enlarged by their first tour, covering Britain and the German-speaking countries of central Europe, undertaken between September and December 1970.

When one listens to the band reminisce about the Isle of Wight performance on their 1993 Video Biography, one is struck by how fondly they recall the event. However, the CD itself presents a more ambiguous picture, and, as David Terralavoro has pointed out, the really early interviews with the band reveal no such sense of nostalgia.[8] Interestingly, con-

---

[7] Peel's opinion of ELP never changed: see Stump, *The Music's All That Matters*, 97.
[8] David Terralavoro, "Etc.," *Fanzine for the Common Man*, no. 13 (July 1993): 4.

sidering that he was the youngest and least known of the three at the time, it is Carl Palmer whose work shows to best advantage on *Live at the Isle of Wight*.

Autumn 1970

Even as the band were commencing their first European tour in September—which was, incidentally, the first time anybody had attempted to tour with a synthesizer, previous live performances with synthesizers having all been one-off affairs—they squeezed time in to finish recording the tracks that were to be included on the debut LP. An article than ran in *New Musical Express* on August 15, 1970, besides announcing ELP's debut show on August 23, also mentioned that Emerson was "busily trying to find a church which will allow him to use their organ for one of the tracks."[9] Apparently at that time the Royal Festival Hall management had not yet agreed to let him use the hall's pipe organ for the pipe organ movement of "The Three Fates"; it seems safe to assume, then, that "The Three Fates" was recorded in September. Also recorded in September, as can be confirmed from the liner notes of the *Return of the Manticore* box set, was "Knife-Edge." With the completion of these two tracks, all six tracks that were to appear on the band's debut album were now recorded.

EG Management negotiated a record deal for ELP with Chris Blackwell's Island Records, an independent label that had initially specialized in Jamaican reggae but which had, by the late sixties, become involved with the music scene that had grown up around the British counterculture. As then-manager Dave Betteridge put it, "There was a new intelligent rock—there was a college circuit being built and a new audience was emerging. And we were running in tandem, supplying their needs."[10] Both Paul Stump and I have emphasized the importance of the British college circuit to emerging progressive bands during the late sixties and early seventies, and Carl Palmer has elaborated on the importance of the college circuit to ELP's rise to fame in the U.S. during their early days:

> When we came to America, we did something interesting, which was to play the college circuit. In those days, you would actually play in a college basketball arena. We did those in '70 and '71 [the first year can't be correct, as ELP's first American tour commenced in the spring of '71], and built up a very early following of young people. And in those days, if the show didn't make money,

---

[9] From "ELP Debut," *New Musical Express*, August 15, 1970. The article is reprinted in full in *Fanzine for the Common Man* no. 2 (December 1989): 3.

[10] David Betteridge, quoted by Stump, *The Music's All That Matters*, 76.

the band didn't get damaged. There was no promoter involved; it was what we called a "soft ticket" . . . Anyway, what we found was, when we played at a particular college, the kids might be from someplace else, and they would go home and spread the word. It was sort of like the Internet and became like a cult, basically."[11]

Island eventually reached an American distribution deal with Atlantic Records, which released ELP's albums on their rock subsidiary Cotillion. Keith Emerson has mentioned that Ahmet Ertegun, Atlantic's driving force and a long-time jazz and blues enthusiast, signed ELP primarily on the strength of their live shows, an indication of how quickly ELP's reputation as a dynamic live band took off.[12] Island released ELP's debut album, simply titled *Emerson, Lake and Palmer*, on November 20, 1970; it was released in the U.S. by Cotillion on February 6, 1971, shortly before their first American tour. The album reached number four on the British charts. In the U.S., where the Nice and King Crimson were not nearly as well known as they were in Britain, the album peaked out a bit lower, at eighteen. Most encouragingly, though, the album remained in the top forty for eighteen weeks, indicating sustained interest among U.S. audiences who were just beginning to experience the trio's increasingly polished live shows.

First Album: *Emerson, Lake and Palmer*

The album's opening track, "The Barbarian," is a call-to-arms of sorts, a manifesto for ELP's avowed goal of merging of rock-and-roll aggression, instrumental virtuosity, and techniques borrowed from the classics. It is also the first of several arrangements of classical works that the band would record. In this instance, the model was the short but ferocious showpiece for solo piano, "Allegro Barbaro," by the Hungarian master Béla Bartók (1881–1945), which uses throbbing percussive chords to evoke the cimbalom, a zitherlike Hungarian folk instrument played with hammers. Just as "The Barbarian" represented a revolutionary new sound in popular music in 1970, "Allegro Barbaro," which Bartók composed in 1911, was an important milestone in early musical modernism. Bartók

---

[11] Carl Palmer, quoted by Hall, "Welcome to the Show," 44. Some examples of this kind of show from ELP's early days include Theil College, Greenville, Pennsylvania, April 21, 1971 (ELP's first show in the U.S.); Sullivan County Community College, Loch Sheldrake, New York, April 28, 1971; Upsala College, East Orange, New Jersey, May 28, 1971; Boston College, Boston, Massachusetts, May 29, 1971 (this last date is not entirely certain).
[12] Robert Doerschuk, "Keith Emerson and ELP Again," *Keyboard*, June 1992, 50. On Ahmet Ertegun's role in progressive rock, see Martin, *Listening to the Future*, 94–95.

wasn't well known until the 1920s, but such listeners as heard the piece in the pre–World War I years were struck by its dissonant, "barbarous" chords,[13] its use of the piano as a percussion instrument, its repetitive harmonic cells, often consisting of two hypnotically alternating chords,[14] and the pentatonicism and asymmetry of its folklike theme.

Emerson had become interested in Bartók's music during the latter period of his tenure in the Nice. At some point very early on in ELP's rehearsals, the band decided to arrange the piece. Greg Lake recalls:

> ["The Barbarian"] opens with the bass—a Fender Jazz—through the fuzz box. But it's not just the sound; it's the right sound applied to the right music at the right time. The piece originated when I heard Keith playing something by Bartók on piano. I came into the rehearsal room and said, "I can put a great, powerful bass line behind that, you can do it on organ, and we'd have a fantastic sound." So we played it, and of course everyone was excited about it. Those were very naïve days, and so we just cut the thing . . . A few weeks later, just after the record came out, there was a call at the office. I picked up the phone and there was this lady on the other end who said, "I just wanted to talk to you about this track you have on your record, 'The Barbarian.'" I said, "Oh, yes." She said, "Actually this was written by my husband." It was Mrs. Bartók! It never occurred to us—"Oh, sorry about that." We had to get permission and take care of the royalties, but she was very nice and in the end it all got worked out. But it was like Mrs. Beethoven calling you up! I'd had this image that he'd been dead for 500 years.[15]

Bartók's "Allegro Barbaro" is cast in an A-B-A outline. The turbulent A section, centered in F♯ minor and darkened by Phrygian inflections,[16] is followed by a quieter and brighter B section that begins in F major at measure 101 and moves through a number of keys, gradually building up to a powerful climax that concludes at measure 214 with a much-compressed recapitulation of the opening. The band retain the overall A-B-A outline and most of the important thematic material, but they also undertake some fundamental retooling. The opening of "The

---

[13] Especially characteristic in "Allegro Barbaro" is a chord that consists of fused diminished and major triads, i.e., C♯–E–G–C (Bartók spells the C as B♯). This chord is first heard in measure 11, and then many times thereafter.

[14] This is an aspect of the composition that the band exaggerate even further in their arrangement: listen especially to the recapitulation section, where Bartók's cadential progression becomes the basis for a solo by Emerson.

[15] Greg Lake, quoted by Andy Aledorf, "Lucky Man," *Guitar Legends*, no. 22 (1997): 10. Interestingly, Emerson has said it was Palmer, not Lake, who heard him rehearsing "Allegro Barbaro" and suggested the group record it: see Pethel, "Keith Emerson," 18.

[16] The Phrygian mode is like the natural minor scale with the second degree lowered half a step (e.g., C–D♭–E♭–F–G–A♭–B♭–C), which imparts a darker, more ominous hue to the music than the natural minor scale. The Phrygian mode was often used in a number of heavy metal subgenres.

Barbarian," with its ominous fuzzed bass guitar line, is nowhere to be found in "Allegro Barbaro"; it's only at 0:14 that Bartók's own music commences, still accompanied by Lake's fuzzed bass, which is dramatically switched off when the band reach measure 30 of Bartók's original music.

There are other changes, too. Bartók had accompanied his folklike melody with chords on the offbeats; ELP tend to play the chords in rhythmic unison with the melody, creating a stiffer, more characteristically heavy rock rhythm. In order to better articulate the A–B–A structure of the piece, in the A sections Emerson complements Lake's fuzzed bass with an overdriven Hammond organ setting, while playing the B section (beginning at 1:26) on piano with quiet bass and hi-hat accompaniment. Bartók only hints at a recapitulation of the A section; the band present a full-fledged recapitulation that is pushed along by some increasingly frenzied passagework from Emerson and an impressive barrage of drum fills from Palmer during the closing cadential passage. While the band's arrangement is longer than Bartók's original, their restructuring of the piece takes on a logic of its own: following the quiet, chamberlike acoustic statement of the B section with a return of the ominous fuzzed bass, growling Hammond, and heavy rock rhythm gives the recapitulation of the A section greater shock value, and invites a buildup to an even bigger climax, with the closing pyrotechnics of Emerson and Palmer bringing the piece to an explosive conclusion. The dramatic closing chord progression, implicit in but not literally stated in Bartók's original composition, is particularly impressive, with its pungent closing chord ($C^\sharp$–$F^\sharp$–A–C over an $F^\sharp$ bass) summarizing many of the harmonic issues already raised. In sort, "The Barbarian" is a muscular, tautly constructed showstopper that boded well for both the rest of the album and the future of the band; for quite some time ELP used the piece to open their live shows.

Worlds removed from the brash, swaggeringly aggressive opening track is the Greg Lake composition "Take a Pebble," at 12:27 the longest track on the album and an ELP classic. As Bill Martin comments,

> "Take a Pebble" is really unprecedented in rock. In fact, except for the sources out of which it came (including the background of the musicians), there isn't much that is "rock" about it. The integration of a very pretty song, powerfully sung by Lake, with Emerson's delicate piano and Palmer's masterful cymbals, gives rise to one of the rare moments in progressive rock that is overwhelmingly *careful*. Such moments, as it turns out, were to be even rarer in the subsequent career of ELP.[17]

---

[17] Bill Martin, *Listening to the Future*, 184 (Martin's italics).

"Take a Pebble" is the only example in ELP's repertoire of what I would term the "epic pastoral." With the exception of bass guitar, the instrumentation is entirely acoustic: Emerson's acoustic piano and Lake's acoustic guitar both play important solo roles. "Take a Pebble" falls into three main sections: Lake's song, a lengthy instrumental section, and a recapitulation of the song. The song itself is prefaced by a repeated two-chord progression that features Emerson strumming and plucking the strings of the piano to produce a wonderful, zitherlike effect.[18] Lake's lyrics address the aftermath of a failed relationship, attempting not so much to tell a story as to convey feelings of emptiness through evocative imagery—gray and torn photographs, discarded letters, and the like—and make some sense out of these feelings. Emerson accompanies with a mixture of impressionistic, rippling piano arpeggios and "wide-open" chord voicings characterized by stacked fifths, ninths, and elevenths. These chord voicings, while reminiscent of the "floating" type of chord configurations used by jazz pianists of the late fifties and early sixties (think of Bill Evans's work with Miles Davis), have little trace of blues elements, and Emerson himself has remarked,

> That song was fairly modal, because Greg wrote in a modal style. So experimenting with the chords would destroy the simplicity of the song. Certainly, in the solo sections of "Take a Pebble," it was necessary not to go too far from that modal thing. Consequently, I got into the ostinato left hand, and improvised with the right. I still employ that technique quite a lot.[19]

The lengthy instrumental middle section consists of three subsections. First, Emerson spins out a lovely modal melody over an arpeggiated bass figure, culminating with a quotation of Lake's vocal melody at 2:55; he concludes by plucking melodic fifths, zitherlike, on the piano strings. Next, Lake commences a wonderful acoustic guitar episode.[20] He starts quietly, almost hesitantly, with a series of melodic fifths that seems to be drawn from Emerson's previous "zither" figure. These melodic fifths gradually cohere into longer-breathed melodies, finally climaxing in a stomping, bluegrasslike riff at 5:16 and a virtuosic series of triplet arpeggios at 5:57. This episode, although relatively soft in terms of its dynamics, creates a sense of quiet rapture that gives it a climactic feeling nonetheless.

Finally, Emerson reenters, soloing over a one-bar ostinato figure drawn from his previous episode, weaving long and sinuous modal lines

---

[18] Emerson created the effect by silently depressing the keys he wished to sound and then plucking (or strumming) the strings.

[19] Keith Emerson, quoted by Robert Doerschuk, "Keith Emerson," *Keyboard*, April 1988, 89.

[20] Lake's guitar solo uses an unconventional tuning: from the lowest string, D A D A B E.

over this arpeggio figure in a manner that anticipates George Winston's so-called folk piano style of the 1980s by nearly fifteen years. Emerson avoids tedium by a close attention to modal coloring, regularly shifting from Mixolydian to Dorian to Phrygian inflections and back again.[21] Eventually, Lake (now back on bass) and Palmer enter behind Emerson with a quietly swinging accompaniment that suggests some obvious links with Miles Davis's modal jazz of the early sixties: a kind of "pastoral jazz." When Emerson's plunging arpeggios signal the return of Lake's final vocal verse, the listener has experienced, through the music, the emotional journey implicit in the lyrics.

There are several remarks to be made about "Take a Pebble." First, I believe it is one of the most thoroughgoing collaborations Emerson and Lake were ever to undertake. Lake is given writing credit: on the other hand, both the expansiveness of the structure and the sophistication of the chord voicings signal Emerson's collaboration, since both of these characteristics are not present in Lake's other acoustic ballads to the same degree. At the same time, however, the pastoral vein and expressive delicacy of this piece would seem to be Lake's contributions, as these are qualities largely absent from Emerson's epics. In other words, "Take a Pebble" is an excellent example of group collaboration producing music that goes beyond the strengths of any one member of the group. One wishes ELP had mined this vein of epic pastoralism further in later compositions; in particular, I always wished that this vein of writing could have somehow been integrated into the electronic epics such as "Tarkus" or "Karn Evil 9."

This brings me to my second remark, a reaction to Paul Stump's assertion that in "Take a Pebble," "the band's penchant for milking ideas dry weighs heavily."[22] In my view, this totally misses the mark. "Take a Pebble" is long, but to worthwhile purpose: there is no useless repetition of material, nor are there endless screeds of thirty-second note runs. It is true that Emerson's second piano solo spot is lengthy, but one senses that the musicians are actually listening to and reacting to each other as they play, which is why this example of controlled improvisation, as the band called it,[23] holds up to repeated listening. (In fact, in concert the band never played the instrumental section after the acoustic guitar solo the same way twice.) I think the musicians' careful attention to and respect for

---

[21] The Mixolydian mode is a slightly "darker" major scale, with the seventh degree lowered half a step from the regular major; the Dorian mode is a slightly "brighter" minor scale with the sixth degree raised half a step from the natural minor. Both modes impart a slightly bittersweet ambience. The Phrygian, as we've seen, is "darker than minor" with its lowered second degree.

[22] Stump, *The Music's All That Matters*, 98.

[23] See Pethel, "Keith Emerson," 18.

each other is at least in part what Bill Martin is referring to when he talks about "Take a Pebble" being one of the relatively few examples of progressive rock that is "overwhelmingly careful."

Indeed, if ELP had a fault during the 1970s, it was one of not developing ideas completely, rather than overdeveloping them. Far more correct than Stump was the critic who complained that on the one hand, Pink Floyd milked the same handful of ideas dry, while on the other hand, ELP engaged in "dilettantism," moving too casually from one idea to the next.[24] Calling ELP "dilettantes" is too harsh; on their first six albums, their primary sources (late-sixties rock, contemporary jazz, baroque and twentieth-century classical music, and folk) are absorbed into an overarching musical framework in which the whole is greater than the sum of its parts. Nonetheless, it is hard to deny that "Take a Pebble" is just one of several areas staked out on ELP's first album that was never fully explored in the band's later output.

Finally, I think it is a mark of this song's subtlety that the band creates an effective sense of contrast, even of climax, without layering in loads of electric instruments and without, for the most part, playing louder than *mezzo forte*. Eventually, ELP were routinely accused of resorting to cheap electronic effects and histrionics to create climaxes, the following criticism being representative: "Emerson, Lake and Palmer adopted a complex technological form that tended to overpower the creative content of their material with the extravagance of their equipment and performance."[25] In other words, conventional wisdom came to be that ELP were controlled by their equipment. In "Take a Pebble," nothing could be further from the truth. Notice, for instance, that one of the song's climactic moments is Lake's bluegrass riff during the acoustic guitar solo: it's not loud, relatively speaking, nor for the most part does it involve much virtuosity, but its D-major tonality creates a sense of transformation, an emotional turning point, after the darker E♭ Dorian of Lake's song and the F-minor modality of Emerson's first piano episode. Indeed, it is the sudden sense of brightness brought to the track by Lake's solo that enables Emerson to commence the second piano episode in F major.

After the gentle melancholy of the closing moments of "Take a Pebble," the return of the album's ominous opening mood is somewhat unexpected. But "Knife-Edge" progresses from where "The Barbarian" left off, and is in many ways cut from the same cloth. Like "The Barbarian," it is a hard-driving, classically inspired piece featuring Emerson's overdriven Hammond C-3. Both are based on works by Eastern European composers active in

---

[24] See *The Rolling Stone Record Guide*, ed. Dave Marsh and John Swenson (New York: Random House, 1979), 296.

[25] *Rock Hardware: The Instruments, Equipment, and Technology of Rock*, ed. Tony Bacon (New York: Harmony Books, 1981), 184.

the first half of the twentieth century—in the case of "Knife-Edge," the source is the orchestral work *Sinfonietta*, composed in 1926 by Czech master Leŏs Janáček (1854–1928).

But there are some important differences, too. Emerson once offered a rather flimsy excuse for not crediting Bartók or Janáček in the composition credits of the first album, saying, "In the early days, I thought that 'Knife-Edge' was far enough removed from Janáček's *Sinfonietta* and 'The Barbarian' from Bartók's 'Allegro Barbaro' not to worry about crediting it."[26] In the case of the Bartók piece, this is pure posturing; anyone remotely familiar with "Allegro Barbaro" would at once recognize it as the source of "The Barbarian." In the case of "Knife-Edge," Emerson's view may be somewhat more defensible. "The Barbarian" is an arrangement pure and simple; "Knife-Edge" is more of an original composition that happens to borrow some freely interpreted thematic material from the fifth movement of Janáček's *Sinfonietta*. A second major difference between "The Barbarian" and "Knife-Edge" is that while the former is an instrumental, the latter has been converted into a song.

And quite a song it is. Tautly constructed, it is a masterpiece of controlled tension. Lake's lyric, written with the help of then-ELP roadie Alex Fraser, evokes a bleak and frightening Orwellian society; seldom did Lake's later efforts strike the same delicate balance between evocative imagery and immediate comprehensibility. There are a few throwaway lines, to be sure, but by and large Lake avoids his sometime fault of falling back on the easy rhyme even when it results in empty imagery. The result is a powerful lyric that perfectly captures Orwell's vision in *1984* of brainwashed masses meekly queuing up for the gallows even as they cheerfully sing the praises of Big Brother.

What Emerson chiefly borrows from Janáček is the memorable brass motive stated by Lake on bass guitar beginning at 0:06, which becomes the song's main riff, and the trumpet theme which accompanies the motive, which Emerson transforms into Lake's vocal melody. The construction of "Knife-Edge" around a riff would seem to lend it a closer connection to blues-rock than to the classics, and in fact only the riff's unusual three-bar configuration and the primitive counterpoint between vocal line and bass guitar during its first segment betray the nonblues origin of the song.

Emerson borrows another freely transformed section by Janáček for the instrumental chorus (0:36), and borrows some of Janáček's fanfare figures—which he actually develops a bit more single-mindedly than Janáček himself—for the bridge section (1:50). Then comes an agitated

---

[26] Keith Emerson, quoted by Dominic Milano, "Keith Emerson," *Contemporary Keyboard*, September 1980, 23.

organ solo over the bass's iteration of the original motive in its most compressed form (just three notes, D–C–A), followed by the famous quotation from the first movement of J. S. Bach's French Suite no. 1 in D minor (at 3:21), which Emerson originally inserted during an improvisation,[27] and a recapitulation of the verse and instrumental chorus. Throughout, Emerson totally changes the mood of the original. Janácek's *Sinfonietta* was composed as a paean to Czech liberation from German domination, and the fifth movement features mostly major harmonic coloring; Emerson, on the other hand, takes the harmonization of the opening riff/motive into a darker and more clearly minor direction that contributes greatly to the bleak grandeur of the overall conception.

There are a number of subtle but effective details which also contribute greatly to the success of the overall arrangement, of which I will cite but three. There is the quiet but ominous trill in the organ's upper register that shadows Lake's vocal line like a dark cloud beginning at 1:01, coupled with Palmer's hauntingly spare hi-hat backbeat; the strange glissando which wrenches us from the uneasy calm of Bach's music to the driving final verse, beginning at 3:56; and the disturbing final deconstruction of the song commencing at 4:47, a slowing-down effect created by tape manipulation that perfectly complements the warnings of societal meltdown conveyed by the lyrics. "Knife-Edge" is one of the great apocalyptic songs from a turbulent era that excelled in the creation of such songs, Jimi Hendrix's "I Don't Live Today" and "Purple Haze" providing useful points of reference for the uninitiated.

Keith Emerson's composition "The Three Fates" is the first track on side two of the LP format. I point this out because on the CD format, the shift from the ferocious close of "Knife-Edge" to the icy, remote opening of "The Three Fates" is somewhat jarring; when one turns over the LP to start the second side, though, enough time has elapsed to make the entrance into a different kind of sonic world seem more natural.[28]

The Fates, or Moerae, as the Greeks called them, were three in number, and were named Clotho, Lachesis, and Atropos. Daughters of Zeus and Themis (in some early sources, their mother is Night herself), they were usually depicted as aged crones. These three sisters regulated the length of each individual's life: one spun, the second wound up, and the third cut. Clotho, the spinner, personified the thread of life. Lachesis exemplified chance, the element of luck that person had the right to expect. Atropos represented inescapable fate, against who there is no appeal. The Fates do no have a legend in the strict sense of the term: they

---

[27] Milano, "Keith Emerson," *Contemporary Keyboard*, September 1980, 18.
[28] It goes without saying that with many LPs of the late sixties and seventies, careful planning was often given to what track would end side one and what track would begin side two, ELP's own *Brain Salad Surgery* being a particularly notable example.

operate as a half philosophical, half religious concept of the world. Emerson's piece, in three distinct movements, is thus a kind of musical meditation on fate and destiny that, as I will suggest, can be interpreted on two different levels.[29]

The first movement, "Clotho," features Emerson as a soloist on the enormous four-manual Royal Festival Hall pipe organ. "Clotho" is dominated by a stern, declamatory G Phrygian theme that is harmonized with parallel major seconds and perfect fourths (a technique Emerson was to use again with the march theme of "Aquatarkus"), punctuated regularly by a booming dominant to tonic bass pedal figure. This forbidding theme, which appears twice (at the beginning and again at 1:03), both times on the great manual (i.e., the manual that controls the most powerful stops), alternates with two quieter episodes (at 0:42 and 1:31), both played on a solo manual with a flutelike stop. These episodes are built around a linear, bebop-influenced right-hand part spun out over a stationary left-hand G. The alternation of the pseudo-medieval organum of the main theme and the restless, bebop-inspired figurines of the episodes sounds unlikely, but Emerson makes it work remarkably well, especially as he moves into the later movements and develops his stylistic cross-references more fully. For a pianist, Emerson's pipe organ writing is pretty effective, with the exception of the relatively static and uninteresting bass pedal parts; the one really effective use of the pedals comes at the end of the movement (1:42), when a Vaughan Williams–like cadential passage of gigantic block chords moves in contrary motion to an ascending bass line to bring "Clotho" to completion.

A series of rippling piano arpeggios emerge out of the final bass note of "Clotho," signaling the beginning of the passionate and restless second movement, "Lachesis," a solo piano movement that ranks as one of Emerson's great achievements, albeit not one of his most typical. Emerson's mature piano technique was found on three pillars: Bach, the jazz/blues tradition, and the folkloristic strain of modernism exemplified by Bartók. The first two influences were evident in Emerson's work from the beginning of his professional career; the latter influence was only beginning to assert itself on the first ELP album. All of these styles are united by an essentially percussive approach to the piano that largely eschews the damper pedal and relies on finger technique and articulation to shape phrases. An article by Tony Tyler that ran in *New Musical Express* in 1972 on Emerson's Hammond organ playing offers an insightful account of his piano technique:

> First and foremost, Emo's staggering speed is the product of piano, not organ. Piano has always been his favorite instrument—it's what he plays when relax-

---

[29] As I will point out, the idea of "destiny," especially as concerns predestination, is also an issue on the band's *Pictures at an Exhibition* LP.

ing—and the extra physical finger effort and octave stretch required from a pianist stand him in good stead on the easier, lighter electronic organ manual. Emerson also has comparatively small hands, and the muscle development called for in piano work has resulted in his compensating for this with a phenomenal stretch; his playing bears all the hallmarks of the harder instrument. Giant block chords, although sometimes present in his music, never feature so much as the high-speed flurry of notes, coupled with obscure intervals, that characterize the jazz pianist.[30]

"Lachesis" is one of the few examples in Emerson's output that exemplifies a Romantic, Lisztian style of playing: smoothly connected *legato* melodies, rippling arpeggios, thundering octaves, and widely spaced figurations that are held together by the damper pedal to create a massive halo of sound. This movement is no mere Liszt rip-off, however: "Lachesis" is the linchpin in the complex web of stylistic cross-references that ties the three movements together.

Paul Stump has complained about the "vile edit" linking "Clotho" and "Lachesis."[31] Presumably he means that the shift from pipe organ to piano is jarring. So what? As I pointed out in *Rocking the Classics*, jarring shifts are part of the progressive rock style, and in fact are an important facet of both modernist and postmodernist musical approaches. Furthermore, sampling technology and MIDI being what they are today, there is no longer anything to prevent Emerson from performing a reasonable facsimile of the two movements live, if he were so inclined (although, as we will see, live performance of the third movement would still be a problem, unless he were willing to sequence some of the parts).

"Lachesis" is dominated by a passionate, surging theme of rising fifths that is first enunciated at 1:56. Already imbedded in this theme is movement from G to D♭—the tritone, or *diabolus en musica*, proscribed by medieval theorists because of its inherent instability and subversive tonal qualities—which becomes an increasingly disruptive force during the last two movements. The theme momentarily trails off into atomized fragments, but dramatically reappears in the left hand against a chain of descending augmented triads at 2:28. However, the unstable augmented chords quickly corrode the theme beyond recognition, melting it down once again, this time into the whole-tone vagueness of two uneasily alternating augmented triads. The movement settles into an uneasy repose at 2:53, with a delicate subsidiary theme in A minor; however, at 3:13 a transformed version of the main theme in the original G minor erupts with renewed force, now accompanied by thunder-

---

[30] Tony Tyler, "The Master of Speed and Stagecraft," *New Musical Express*, October 12, 1972.

[31] Stump, *The Music's All That Matters*, 98.

ing left-hand arpeggios which are to play a central role in the remainder of the movement.

From this point on, Emerson begins an ever-more-subtle interweaving of elements drawn from the main theme, the arpeggio accompaniment, and beboplike right-hand figures which recall the organ episodes of the first movement (listen especially at 3:58). Some remarkable, flickering textures emerge—suggesting an unlikely yet entirely coherent fusion of late period Liszt or Scriabin with Bud Powell—which at 4:12 are in turn washed away by a final, thunderous appearance of the heroic accompanying arpeggios and the main theme, now reduced to its essential intervallic profile. As this theme grinds tortuously towards its conclusion, it moves up by whole step from D♭ major to A major before indecisively sliding back to G major. Then, even as we await some kind of definite resolution, the pipe organ returns, ominously interpenetrating chords built on G and D♭, and plunging us into the whirlwind of the final movement, "Atropos," a piano trio which features Emerson on all three parts via overdubs.

"Atropos" is a frantic, delirious dance: imagine Béla Bartók playing an "Allegro Barbaro"–like piano ostinato with Xavier Cugat and his rhythm section grooving along, and you'll get the basic idea of what this movement is all about. The backbone of "Atropos" is a percussive one-measure piano ostinato is septuple meter; it's built from a whole-tone scale that gives equal emphasis to G and D♭, thus frustrating any possibility that either will emerge securely as tonic. At the beginning of the movement, even as Emerson is launching into his very pungent, edgy ostinato, Carl Palmer enters for the first time (Lake never plays on this track), laying out a complex polyrhythmic groove on the drumkit. Palmer soon begins to layer in, via overdubs, short rhythmic patterns played on various Afro-Cuban percussive devices—cowbell, castanets, ratchet, maracas—and the resulting polyrhythmic web becomes increasingly important as the movement progresses.

At 5:05 the second piano enters with a deep bass line and an offbeat rhythmic ostinato; finally, the "lead" piano enters at 5:11. There are a couple of brief interruptions of the ostinato (at 5:33 and again at 6:01); however, the overall thrust of the movement is to pile an increasingly dense layer of piano and percussion polyrhythms and an increasingly crazed piano lead over the ostinato. Beginning at 6:15, the piano lead takes up the bebop-derived linear figuration of the previous two movements.[32] Finally, as "Atropos" approaches its denouement, the piano lead begins to shed its whole-tone outline in favor of an unambiguous

---

[32] In his liner notes to his 2005 *Hammer It Out* anthology, Emerson cites the recordings of bebop pianist Lennie Tristano as an inspiration for "Atropos."

D♭ major tonality. At the end, the "lead" piano obliterates the percussion and even the piano ostinato, climaxing with a massive plunge down the keyboard on a D♭ acoustic scale.[33] Then, before the final D♭ has died away, the sound of an apocalyptic explosion: Atropos has cut the cord.

There are several comments to be made in connection with "The Three Fates." First, this work could have very easily become a mere pastiche, a welter of undigested stylistic quotes that merely demonstrate what a clever fellow Keith Emerson is and how quickly his fingers move. Critics have constantly lambasted progressive rock for just such facile display, and there is no doubt that the genre often deserved such criticism (I'm thinking, for instance, of Rick Wakeman's solo albums, where the copious stylistic references usually don't seem to cohere into a greater whole). In "The Three Fates," however, the stylistic references are integrated into a larger vision: the whole is greater than the sum of its parts.

Indeed, I see the idea of "fate" or "destiny" operating on at least two levels here. First, it seems to me that "The Three Fates" can be read as depicting the evolution of Western music, from the pseudo-medieval organum of "Clotho" (with its "gothic" organ reference) through the Lisztian romanticism of "Lachesis" to the Bartókian modernism (complete with the dance hall Latin percussion) of "Atropos." What enables this depiction of musical evolution (or "destiny," if you will) to cohere is, first of all, the clearly drawn conflict between the keys of G and D♭. "The Three Fates" is the first of several three-part Emerson compositions that begin in one key, move into a second section where another important tonality emerges, and conclude with a section where the second key emerges as triumphant: we will see this technique used again in "Trilogy" and "Karn Evil 9," for instance. This approach, known as progressive tonality, lends an undeniable element of drama and coherence to a large-scale work. In the case of "The Three Fates," unity is also provided by the prevalence of bebop-derived figuration in all three movements, which allows Emerson both to take these diverse historical styles and make them his own, and to bring them into closer unity with each other. And perhaps there is a subtext here that American popular music (symbolized by bebop jazz) was an inevitable development of all earlier Western styles—although this may push matters a bit.

I think "The Three Fates" evokes the progression not only of Western music history, but Western cultural history. Emerson is obviously familiar

---

[33] The so-called acoustic scale, one of Bartók's favorite scales, is a major scale with a raised fourth and a lowered seventh degree (i.e., D♭ E♭ F G A♭ B♭ C♭ D♭). Unlike the major scale, the acoustic scale includes the note a tritone away from the tonic: thus the conflict between G and D♭ which has informed the entire piece is resolved when G is absorbed as the fourth degree of an acoustic scale beginning on D♭.

with the nineteenth-century tradition of symbolic tonal shifts where, for instance, the shift from C minor to C major in Beethoven's Fifth Symphony symbolizes darkness giving way to light. In this context, a conflict between two keys a tritone apart suggests a conflict between irreconcilable opposites,[34] and there would appear to be some symbolic importance to the movement from G to D♭ during the course of "The Three Fates."

Inherent in "The Barbarian," and explicit in "Knife-Edge," is the vision of technology gone spectacularly awry in the hands of an oppressive, totalitarian regime, a vision captured with considerable power in three great dystopic novels of the thirties, forties, and fifties, respectively—Aldous Huxley's *Brave New World*, George Orwell's *1984*, and Ayn Rand's *Atlas Shrugged*—that strongly impacted the hippie movement of the sixties. Certainly the sixties counterculture entertained a strong suspicion that technology had become the principal tool in the process of dehumanization and oppression on both sides of the Iron Curtain. If "The Barbarian" seems to borrow its frightening imagery of a barbaric technocracy from the near future, "Take a Pebble" reaches into the past to retrieve an image of rural stability and tranquility. However, the return of the destructive energy of "The Barbarian" in "Knife-Edge" dramatically rejects the idyllic pastoralism—perhaps even the possibility for meaningful human relationships—postulated in "Take a Pebble." As "The Three Fates" moves from the austere ritualism of "Clotho" (the Middle Ages) to the heroic but ultimately doomed idealism of "Lachesis" (the Enlightenment) towards the delirious dance at the brink of the abyss of "Atropos" (the twentieth century, with its catastrophic episodes of totalitarianism), it seems to sketch the inevitable historical progression of a society that has placed its trust in technological "progress." There is no trace of Romantic optimism at the end of "Atropos," no movement from dark to light, but rather the apocalyptic obliteration of one tonal center (G) by its polar opposite a tritone away (D♭). The tritone modulation at the end of "The Three Fates" symbolizes the triumph of something over its opposite, just as the sound of the explosion symbolizes the destruction of something. But what has been destroyed? And what has triumphed? To find the answer, we must address the fifth track, "Tank."

Over thirty years after its creation, the opening section of "Tank" still sounds completely fresh and astonishingly original. It is the hardest piece on the debut album to analyze, and even giving an adequate description of it in terms of other music is difficult, so completely have its stylistic sources been fused together. I will attempt to explain the

---

[34] The symbolism of two keys a tritone apart as irreconcilable opposites derives from the fact that two keys a tritone apart are directly opposite of each other on the circle of fifths.

amazing opening section of "Tank" by introducing its building blocks on an item-by-item basis.

First, there is the sound of the Hohner Clavinet, a sprightly, somewhat metallic sound that suggests an electric harpsichord. This is the lead instrument throughout the opening section of "Tank," and Emerson consistently double tracks, and occasionally even triple tracks it, creating a web of intricate counterpoint. While the texture suggests Bach, though, the melodic outlines suggest bebop—the opening "head" sounds like something straight off a Bud Powell or Hampton Hawes album. What ties the Bachian counterpoint and bebop-derived melodic figurines together is the wayward irregularity of the phrase structure—the first two phrases are seven and ten measures long, for instance—which is equally characteristic of eighteenth-century *fortspinnung* ("spinning out") and bebop phrase extension techniques.

Against this already intricate web of airy Clavinet counterpoint, Greg Lake spins out some of his most virtuosic bass lines ever. "Tank" begins, in fact, with Lake laying out a knotty bass solo whose Phrygian inflections recall the earlier emphasis on the flatted second in "The Barbarian" and "Clotho." Once the Clavinet enters, Lake begins launching rapid-fire scalar figures (mostly in F Aeolian),[35] backed by Palmer's edgy, vaguely bossa nova–type groove (note the consistent 3 + 3 + 2 accents). It's primarily Lake's bass line that swing the music from F Aeolian to A♭ Mixolydian at 0:42, then back to F again at 1:09. Anybody who doubts that Lake could have been one of rock's great bassists, had he pursued that goal more single mindedly, is urged to check out the astonishing bass lines at the end of the section, beginning at 1:23, when he doubles Emerson's rapid-fire Clavinet runs note for note while they trade off two-bar breaks with Palmer (another bebop reference). Lake's extremely active bass lines add yet another element to the intricate contrapuntal web.

Finally, there is the four-chord vamp figure, first played on the Clavinet at 0:12, and then transferred to a background piano track at 0:18, when the main Clavinet theme enters. While Emerson's lead lines, Lake's bass part, and Palmer's percussion groove are all in 4/4, the vamp is in 6/8 and is constantly bisecting the other material, since the downbeats coincide only on every three bars of 4/4 and four bars of 6/8: the result is an edgy, nervous rhythmic effect, a type of polyrhythm that's evocative of Holst or Stravinsky, or of ELP's erstwhile prog rock colleagues Gentle Giant. What's more, the vamp figure lays bear a surprising secret: beneath all the intricate counterpoint and polyrhythms, the harmony is essentially static. Basically, the entire first section of "Tank"

---

[35] Aeolian mode is identical with the natural minor scale.

involves just three chords: a decorated F suspended fourth chord beginning at 0:12, a decorated A♭7 suspended fourth chord from 0:42, and a decorated F suspended second from 1:23 on. The static harmony decorated by intricate textural figuration that is central to "Tank" would seem to derive from Miles Davis's modal jazz. We have, of course, observed the influence of Davis's modal approach in the somewhat different context of "Take a Pebble."

In sum, then, the opening of "Tank" brings together elements of bebop, modal jazz, baroque counterpoint, and Stravinskian polyrhythms. The result? A totally original sound—there is an airiness, a lightness, a fleetness to this music that is quite different from the ponderousness that many have automatically associated with ELP. There is also a certain detachment: the music evokes the workings of an extraordinarily intricate machine. Without getting too cosmic here, I'm tempted to recall Goethe's famous remark that Bach's music evoked for him the unfolding of eternal harmony in the bosom of God: like so much Bach, this music somehow creates the Platonic image of some eternal, mathematical principle being audibly unfolded.[36] Significantly, the portions in F minor don't sound sad, nor do the portions in A♭ major sound happy. Rather, the overriding impression in the opening section of "Tank" is *motion*: Lovecraft's "unimagined space alive with motion and music,"[37] a motion that has become a self-sustaining principle which is benignly indifferent to the world of human emotions.

The opening two-minute section of "Tank" represents one of ELP's most inspired creations. Regrettably but perhaps not surprisingly, they are unable to sustain the same level of inspiration throughout the entire piece. Indeed, at 1:59 they commit their one indefensible lapse of taste on the album: Carl Palmer launches into a gratuitous drum solo that clocks in at two minutes, ten seconds.

Now, credit where credit is due. The twenty-year-old drummer had already developed one of the most formidable techniques in rock: for pure hand speed, the only rivals among his contemporaries were Jon Hiseman and Billy Cobham (and a few years later, Neil Peart). His right foot is also incredibly fast: there were some parts I used to believe Palmer was playing on the floor tom that I finally realized, with the advent of the remastered CD, were actually bass drum parts. His command of the rudiments was already masterly, and he was well on his way to developing his mature approach to both solos and fills, which involved moving rudimental patterns (single and double stroke rolls, single and double paradiddles, with

---

[36] For Goethe's full quote, see Hans David and Arthur Mendel, eds., *The Bach Reader* (New York: W. W. Norton, 1966), 369.

[37] See H. P. Lovecraft's short story *The Music of Erich Zann* for the full context of this excerpt.

and without flams) around the drumkit with a fantastically varied array of accent placements. Palmer once said,

> Basically I try to distribute the various stickings around the drums to create as much of a musical sound as I can. I try to change the accents, moving up on the fourth beat. I use them that way. I find that a lot of flams have been useful to me over the years . . . I split things up. I will play a single paradiddle and make the transition into a double and into a triple. I'll put a flam in front of the single. And then I'll put two flams in front of the double. I'll break it up that way.[38]

Despite the massive technique this solo demonstrates, there are three problems with it. First, from a microcosmic perspective, there are too many peaks and valleys. Rather than working towards one or two big climaxes, Palmer is constantly switching back and forth between quieter cymbal patterns (some of which are very nice in isolation), gigantic barrages of fills on the upper kit, and chugging bass drum eighth notes with interspersed cymbal and gong crashes; the repeated climaxes soon grow numbing. In his later drum solos (such as the one captured on the live album *Welcome Back My Friends*), Palmer wisely both simplified the overall structure of the solo and extended the development of individual sections, giving a greater sense of coherency and climax to the whole. Second, the structuring of Palmer's solos have always relied on cues that are as much visual as musical: for instance, he usually took his shirt off and threw it into the audience after commencing the thumping bass drum eighth notes, and before he began crashing on the two gigantic suspended gongs. Needless to say, this is all lost in a drum solo recorded in the studio. Finally, and most importantly, the drum solo really has no connection to the rest of "Tank." We harbor the uncomfortable suspicion that the drum solo was simply an easy way to get from the opening section to the closing one. Significantly, when Palmer rerecorded "Tank" for his solo side of *Works I* the drum solo was eliminated.

Palmer's solo-closing figure, an off-beat groove that ingeniously unites shuffle and march elements, sets up the return of the opening Clavinet vamp figure at 4:12, now transformed into a highly syncopated jazz march. Over this Clavinet vamp (audible in the right channel) Emerson begins layering in, note by note, a trumpetlike fanfare theme on the modular Moog, which here makes its debut appearance in ELP's recorded output. The modal coloring of the fanfare theme gives the music a triumphant major key feel: the fanfare's defining harmonic progression, $^\flat$VII–I–$^\flat$III$^\flat$II (key of F), is evocative of similar passages by Holst, Vaughan Williams, and other composers of the twentieth-century English nationalist school (especially in their brass band music), and cre-

---

[38] Carl Palmer, quoted by Iero, "Carl Palmer," 15.

ates a fascinating blend of English processional march and Bill Evans–inspired modal jazz vamping.[39]

Finally, as the triumphant "jazz processional" achieves its full chord voicing, it becomes an ostinato figure supporting an ecstatic Moog lead line whose timbre suggests a supersonic clarinet. Emerson's technique of soloing over a short ostinato pattern sometimes grew wearisome on later ELP ventures, but here his remarkably fluid sense of swing (reflected in his continuous alternation between duplet and triplet subdivisions of the beat) saves the day, as does Palmer's subtle but keen sense of accent displacement (note, for instance, how at 5:38 he has moved the accents of the drum groove from beats two and four to beats one and three). The cascading modal lines of the Moog build up to a climactic peak at 6:27, at which point Emerson quotes the main Clavinet theme from the first section. Afterward, the whole triumphant processional fades into the distance beneath the lead Moog's final diminished seventh arpeggio figure— the only instance of a fadeout on the entire album.

I have long believed that although "Lucky Man" eventually became the closing track, the debut album was originally intended to end with "Tank," which makes a completely logical and satisfying close. So now I will return to the rhetorical question I posed earlier: what is the meaning of the tritone modulation and the huge explosion at the end of "The Three Fates"? And how does "Tank" fit in?

I would suggest the apocalyptic explosion at the end of "The Three Fates" signals the end of human civilization as we know it—and the tritone modulation symbolizes the passage from the Age of *Homo sapiens* to the Age of the Machine. The intricate opening section of "Tank," with its detached, almost postemotional (*not* unemotional) ambience, seems to posit a world in which technology (encapsulated in the machinelike intricacy of the texture and polyrhythms) has come to exist as a self-sufficient, Platonic force; and the closing section of "Tank" sounds very much like a victory procession for the Age of the Machine.[40] Does "Tank" symbolize a technology that has somehow become a self-sufficient force that exists in its own right, perhaps even as a self-aware consciousness? Is "Tank" representative of some kind of new consciousness that might someday supersede human consciousness? In short, does "Tank" represent the emergence of an *ensouled* machine (pardon the theological term, but I'm not sure how else to put it) that no longer needs its creators, since it has now superseded them?

---

[39] In fact, the chord voicings that result from superimposing the Moog triads over the quartal harmonies of the Clavinet vamp remind me a lot of Miles Davis's "So What."

[40] The fact that this section features ELP's first use of the modular Moog, the most technologically advanced piece of musical equipment available at that time, adds a nice element of irony to the "victory of the machine" symbolism of "Tank."

As the reader has probably guessed, I would answer all of these questions "yes." I know I am going out on a limb here; some will undoubtedly think I am identifying musical and conceptual cross-references where there are none. Nonetheless, I believe the first five tracks of ELP's debut album cohere into a loose concept that addresses, at least implicitly, a number of issues that the band explored more explicitly and systematically on *Brain Salad Surgery*. If you think Orwell's *1984*, with its tiny ruling class using technology to ruthlessly exploit and tyrannize the rest of the population, is a nightmare vision, what would you think of a world where even the ruling classes fell prey to a suddenly emergent class of conscious machines? Considering our society's ever-greater reliance on technology—and the immense emphasis we have put on technological "progress" as the *sine qua non* of increased material "prosperity"—might the kind of future sketched out here, far from being the weird nightmare of a third-rate science fiction novelist, be more or less inevitable? Would the world be better off under the control of "perfect" machines than it has been under the machinations of imperfect humans? While all these questions are raised more explicitly and pointedly three years later on *Brain Salad Surgery*, clearly they are already beginning to occupy the band here.

Concerning the last track on the album, the famous "Lucky Man," almost everyone familiar with ELP has heard the story of how it was included on the album as an afterthought because the band was short on material. Here's Greg Lake:

> I actually wrote that when I was 12 years old, when I first started playing. During the making of the first album, we ran out of material; it came to the end of the record and we were one song short. There were vacant looks across the studio—"Does anybody have any more ideas?"—and terrible, glum faces everywhere. I said, "I've got this folk tune that I wrote on acoustic guitar when I was a kid." Everyone said, "Oh, go on then, let's hear it." I strummed it out and the reaction was, "Yeah, well, cup of tea . . ." Total disinterest. But we had to have something, so we decided to try and record it. Carl and I went out into the room with just a Gibson J-200 acoustic guitar, drums and voice. I sang it and he played along—and it sounded like s___! Then I put the bass guitar on it, and as soon as I did that, it sounded more like a complete thing. Keith said, "Let's see what I can do with it," and he was out there with a Moog synthesizer, rehearsing away, playing along with the whole track. Halfway through, I kind of liked what he was playing, so I put the machine into record. I caught the end of his try-out and thought, "That's not bad. I think we could use that." He said, "No, no. Let me do a real one." I said "No, let's keep the one we've got!" He came in and heard it, and that ended up as the solo at the end of "Lucky Man" . . . Then I put on some vocal harmonies and it sounded like a record, but we still felt it was just filler for the album. It

wasn't until much later, when the thing became very popular, that we were glad we'd put it on. That's my favorite song from the record.[41]

It's a very picturesque story, but there appear to be some problems with it. First, as I've already mentioned, according to the *Return of the Manticore* box set liner notes, "Lucky Man" was one of the album's four tracks recorded in July—it was "The Three Fates" and "Knife-Edge" that were recorded last, in September. Second, it's hard to square Lake's account of auditioning the song to the band with Keith Emerson's recollection of events:

> It was during the recording sessions for the first album, and I happened to go into the studio late one night. Well, when I got there, there was Greg working on this song. He had four or five dubs laid down already and had obviously been working on it for some time. I asked him what it was, and he said it was something he thought we might use on the album. I asked him if he wanted some keyboard tracks on it, and he said I could try something, so I went over to the synthesizer, which already had a kind of flutey sound programmed into it. I put a few lines onto the song, and Greg said "Great! Great!" Well, as it turned out, the song was released as a single, and it certainly didn't represent my concept of the band. And the way Greg cut the track irritated me; sort of sneaking around behind our backs to do it.[42]

So, on the one hand, it seems clear that the myth of "Lucky Man" being recorded as an off-the-cuff, last minute inspiration is just that—a myth. On the other hand, it seems equally clear that there was considerable friction between Emerson and Lake over the song's release as a single, and it's entirely possible that only at the last minute was a decision made to include the song on the LP. (Perhaps one reason Lake fought so hard for the song's inclusion was the fact that it had narrowly been rejected from the debut King Crimson album.)

With no disrespect to Lake, the song does indeed sound like something that he could have written at age twelve. The very simple strophic structure of the song, the elemental chord progressions (four chords for the entire song), the hypnotically repetitive melody which continuously outlines a descending fourth, all suggest a folklike simplicity, except that many real English folk songs (at least of the variety collected by Cecil Sharp or Ralph Vaughan Williams) are actually a lot more complicated,

---

[41] Greg Lake, quoted by Andy Aledorf, "Lucky Man," *Guitar Legends*, no. 22 (1997): 10.
[42] Keith Emerson, quoted by Pethel, "Keith Emerson," 17. Emerson gives a similar account in *Pictures*, 180, although now saying he came into the studio late in the afternoon, not late at night. He adds that Palmer was obliged to add the drums track to Lake's overdubbed acoustic guitar parts without the benefit of a click track.

because of their waywardness and unpredictability, than "Lucky Man."
Certainly, Lake's later songs show far more harmonic and structural
sophistication: compare "Lucky Man" with "Still . . . You Turn Me On"
to see how far Lake's mastery of the craft of songwriting progressed
between 1970 and 1973.

Likewise, the song's lyrical imagery, which Paul Stump very aptly
describes as pre-Raphaelite,[43] while very nice in isolation, doesn't seem to
connect with anything else on the album, and its moralizing edge (basically that death comes to us all, rich and poor) seems a bit sophomoric
after the sophisticated musical meditations on totalitarianism and technology that have occupied us heretofore. It is the one track that could be
moved from its place without disrupting the overall flow on the album: it
could have been the first track just as easily, or it could have been excised
entirely. As I said, "Tank" makes an entirely satisfying closing track, and
it is very hard to imagine any of the other five tracks being moved around
without doing real harm to the album's overall musical flow. "Lucky
Man" is the one track that clearly stands outside the album's conceptual
framework, and I can understand Emerson's ambivalence about it. On the
other hand, when it was released as a single in the U.S. in 1971, "Lucky
Man" charted at forty-eight, earned continuous radio airplay from
American radio stations, including stations that would not have been
likely to give the album's other, more adventurous cuts similar exposure,
and alerted a host of new American listeners to the existence of ELP.[44] I
think it is safe to say that Emerson's reservations notwithstanding, the
promotional service performed by "Lucky Man" outweighs any aesthetic
disruption it caused the band's debut album.

Furthermore, the arrangement of "Lucky Man" does contain two
indisputable high points. One is the sweetly archaic vocal harmonies, a
veritable choir of overdubbed Greg Lakes, which perfectly augment the
flavor of the lyrics and suggest that Lake had learned some arrangement
lessons from "In the Court of the Crimson King" and "In the Wake of
Poseidon." The vocal harmonies play such an important role, in fact, that

---

[43] Stump, *The Music's All That Matters*, 99.
[44] In the 1993 Video Biography, Greg Lake remarked that "Lucky Man" never had the resonance for British audiences that it had for American audiences, for whom it became something of an ELP signature song. The difference is that British progressive bands really
needed at least one hit single to achieve a big breakthrough in the American market, whereas
the lack of a hit single did not necessarily hurt album sales in the U.K. The greater importance that radio airplay had in cementing a band's popularity in the U.S. is a function of the
much vaster distances that need to be covered during American tours, and the impossibility
of saturating all populous geographic areas with live performances, as is in fact possible in
the U.K. For more on this, see *Rocking the Classics*, 254, fn2, and Emerson's recollection of
a conversation with Ahmet Ertegun where this issue was broached in *Pictures of an
Exhibitionist*, 208.

for me the song has never really worked in any of the guises ELP have given it in live presentation, even the rather literal reading which they gave it in their shows of the early nineties.

The second high point is Emerson's Moog solo at the end of the song. Emerson has spoken disparagingly about this solo,[45] but he need not: the solo, while simple, fits the needs of the song perfectly. In the space of 1:25, the listener is introduced to many of the major features of the Moog sound: its ability to move smoothly from extremely high to extremely low registers,[46] its subtle note-to-note glissandos, quite impossible to achieve on piano or organ, the characteristic "fat" sound of the Moog oscillator (something like an incredibly full-bodied version of the clarinet's deep, rich lower "chalumeau" register, but transposable to any register), the percolating Moog filter sound (listen especially from 4:10 on). It is hard to think of another Moog passage of similar length by anyone that demonstrates so many possibilities of the instrument so quickly, and it seems completely appropriate that for many listeners, "Lucky Man" marked their introduction to the world of the analog synthesizer.

Other details of the arrangement, while less important to the overall success of the song, are worth noting: Lake's effective alternation between flowing guitar arpeggios (behind the verse) and strumming (behind the choruses), the subtle double tracking of the acoustic guitar parts, and the simple but lyrical electric guitar solo. On the other hand, "Lucky Man" is the one track on the debut album where Palmer consistently overdrums. The intricate fills which worked so well in "Tank," "The Barbarian," and "Atropos" are overkill here, where a simpler, more John Bonham–like (or perhaps even a more Ringo Starr–like) approach would have served the song better.

Emerson, Lake and Palmer: An Assessment

Emerson, Lake and Palmer marks a milestone for both ELP and progressive rock. If by "progressive" we mean music that stretches rock's parameters in terms of stylistic boundaries, musical vocabulary, structural scope, conceptual possibilities, and instrumental technique, who in 1970 was playing more "progressive" music than this? Pink Floyd's *Atom Heart Mother* comes off as quite uncertain by comparison. Jethro Tull's *Benefit* is just as mature, perhaps, but is painted on a smaller canvas. Yes, Genesis, Van der Graaf Generator, Gentle Giant, Curved Air—in 1970 they were all still feel-

---

[45] See Milano, "Keith Emerson," *Contemporary Keyboard*, October 1977, 52.

[46] I have heard it said that the "Lucky Man" solo traverses the entire spectrum of audible sound from 16 to 20,000 vibrations per second; I don't know if this is literally true, but it does point up the easy traversal of vast registral space that analog synthesizers introduced.

ing their way towards the musical terrain ELP had here uncovered. King Crimson's contemporaneous *Lizard*, despite some truly visionary moments, is overall a more uneven album, which furthermore is scarcely the work of a band per se: the lineup which created *Lizard* never performed live, and one can scarcely imagine it could have under any circumstances.[47]

On the other hand, Keith Emerson's "new musical environment" seems to have yielded up a full-blown progressive music out of nowhere. Even its more "conservative" tracks, such as "The Barbarian" and "Knife-Edge," represent a step forward: with these two tracks Emerson takes the fusion of classical modernism and rock aggression he had pioneered with the Nice one step further, burnishing his conception with a precision and a virtuosity that the Nice had never been able to muster. The album's most visionary tracks, "Take a Pebble," "Tank," and "The Three Fates," still sound contemporary today: the stylistic fusion of baroque and twentieth-century classical music, contemporary jazz styles, and (in the case of "Take a Pebble") folk elements in a rock matrix is so complete and assured that the impression is of a long-mature style, rather than an experimental melding of disparate sources. Clearly, with this album Emerson's goal of "building musical bridges," first annunciated with the Nice, has taken a quantum leap forward: this is eclecticism as it should be, not the all too frequently encountered (and justly criticized) eclecticism of some progressive music that merely links its stylistic references into a loose and incoherent pastiche. *Emerson, Lake and Palmer* stands as a remarkably assured debut album: in the realm of progressive music, only the first King Crimson album suggests itself as a rival (or, if we wish to include Italian progressive rock acts, the first Museo Rosenbach album).

If the album was groundbreaking for its music, it was also a watershed in terms of its production quality. While some credit is certainly due to Greg Lake, the album's producer, the contributions of engineer Eddy Offord, who was to work with ELP for three more albums, and who also was to play a major role in the success of Yes, are probably even more important. The Nice albums are characterized by a very full but muddy sound, whereas the debut King Crimson album sounds clear but a bit thin: Offord brings a nice balance of presence and clarity. The soundstage is open, and very live sounding: the first three tracks, in particular, use very few production tricks, and sound like an exceptionally clean live performance. The last three tracks utilize the kind of stereophonic division of lead tracks that was popular during the late sixties: with "Tank," in partic-

---

[47] Here I must say that I simply disagree with Bill Martin's selection of King Crimson's *Lizard*, Jethro Tull's *Benefit*, and Caravan's *Land of Grey and Pink* as the three most significant progressive rock albums of 1970; in terms of both influence and intrinsic value, I would rate the debut ELP album above them all. See Martin, *Listening to the Future*, 186–90, for his take on this.

ular, the rhythm section is spread across both channels, while the Clavinet counterpoint is divided between the two channels. Unlike some of ELP's later albums (particularly *Tarkus*), the effect isn't overused, though. There are also some brief but effective sweeps back and forth between channels, notably the phased ending of Palmer's drum solo on "Tank" and Emerson's Moog solo on "Lucky Man." Perhaps the best measure of the album's state-of-the-art production is that during the early seventies this album and Pink Floyd's *Dark Side of the Moon* were the two most favored albums for testing stereo systems.

Being an early example of progressive musical and production values is not enough to make an album of more than historical interest, however, so the chief virtues of *Emerson, Lake and Palmer* are its consistency and coherency. Every track on the album is strong, and several are ELP classics; among the rest of ELP's output, only *Brain Salad Surgery* and (arguably) *Trilogy* suggest themselves as rivals. In terms of coherence—as I've already said, while the album may not be an explicitly packaged concept album, it is far more than just a collection of songs and instrumentals.

To go one step further, the album is also more than just a collection of songs and instrumentals carefully arranged according to contrasts in mood, tempo, dynamics, and instrumentation. There is a logical progression at work from "The Barbarian" to "Tank," a progression that works on the basis of both stylistic cross-references and contrasts, and a progression that is both musical and extramusical. Inserting "Take a Pebble" between "The Barbarian" and "Knife-Edge" does more than merely provide a convenient contrast of dynamics, mood, and instrumentation; it creates a deeply resonant symbolic contrast between pastoralism/stability and technocracy/turmoil that would have been immediately comprehensible to contemporaneous audiences. As I pointed out in *Rocking the Classics*, this kind of electric/acoustic dichotomy became one of progressive rock's most powerful musical metaphors, and here ELP makes an early and especially successful use of it.[48] Likewise, when we proceed from "Knife-Edge" through "The Three Fates" to "Tank," we progress from turmoil to destruction to rebirth. Although "Lucky Man" is the one track that undeniably stands outside of the conceptual framework of the rest of the album, its folkiness and medievalism does establish a link with "Take a Pebble," lending *Emerson, Lake and Palmer* a more pastoral ambience than any other ELP album. Nic Dartnell's understated cover art, with its muted grays, mysterious human face of uncertain age and gender in side profile, and ascending white dove, seems to tap into this same vein: like much of "Take a Pebble," the cover art suggests a "minor key" pastoralism of gray skies, fog, and bleak moors.

---

[48] See Macan, *Rocking the Classics*, 43–44.

Would I consider this album one of the ten all-time progressive rock classics? Probably not. There are shortcomings, which for the most part are in the realm of omission—what's not there. While the album is much more than just a collection of songs and instrumentals, it's useless to pretend it's a fully developed and comprehensive statement on a topic in the manner of *Brain Salad Surgery*. The very clear division between Emerson's and Lake's contributions is not surprising for a first album—as I've noted, for a debut album it coheres remarkably well—but it does seem an unfortunate fact that this division became the norm for later ELP releases. In this sense, the first album prefigures a troubling disinclination to develop a band compositional approach that I think was later to hurt ELP in comparison with bands like Yes or Genesis. Also, when one listens to *Emerson, Lake and Palmer* in the context of their subsequent releases, one is surprised how much of the territory staked out here was never properly explored later on. One wishes that later ELP albums would have further explored the very dynamic and idiomatic use of rock devices in a classical piece (rather than the opposite approach) that characterizes "The Three Fates," the adventurous whole tone harmonic framework of that piece (an approach developed much more systematically by King Crimson circa 1972–74 than by ELP), the epic pastoral vein of "Take a Pebble," and the utterly unique proto-jazz-rock fusion of "Tank."[49]

For the most part, the album is a model of concision and taste. In fact, the album garnered a number of highly favorable reviews amongst the rock press, including the *Rolling Stone* and *Creem* wing of the rock press that later turned on ELP with such vehemence. I am quoting a large chunk of the *Rolling Stone* review of April 15, 1971, because I wish to prove once and for all that the myth perpetrated by the modern rock-critical establishment—that critics condemned progressive rock as a sterile and useless style from the moment it emerged—is just that, a myth. As we will see during the course of this book, it was changes in the rock critical establishment's ideology, rather than any musical changes progressive rock underwent between 1970 and 1974, that caused progressive rock's critical reception to plummet so spectacularly in the mid-1970s. Here's the review, penned by Lloyd Grossman:

> We were forewarned by the British music press that Emerson, Lake and Palmer would be a "supergroup," and indeed it was hard to see how they could miss. An extraordinarily inventive and tasteful organist, Keith Emerson, as the prime moving force of the Nice, was one of the few performers capable of holding his own against the flood of guitar oriented heavy rock groups of the ten thousand ton variety. He is also one of rock's most flamboyant show-

---

[49] The much later "When the Apple Blossoms Bloom in the Windmills of Your Mind I'll Be Your Valentine" does seem to explore some of the same territory as "Tank."

men, and watching little Keith toss a Hammond organ around on stage and indulge in one of his orgies of key ripping was an unforgettable sight.

Unfortunately, the Nice suffered from extremely weak vocals and a lack of strong original material and as a consequence Emerson failed to get as much exposure as he might have. Now with Emerson, Lake and Palmer the situation has changed. Though Emerson is "featured" on piano and organ, he has some extremely strong support from Greg Lake (formerly with King Crimson) on vocals, bass, and guitar; and from Carl Palmer (formerly with Atomic Rooster, a group formed by Arthur Brown's ex-organist Vincent Crane) on drums. There are also some very good new compositions by all involved.

It is rather hard to typify the music that Emerson, Lake and Palmer play, though I suppose that your local newspaper might call it "jazz influenced classical rock" . . . If you're familiar with the Nice you probably know what to expect. Everyone turns in a fine performance and I was most surprised by Greg Lake, as I was not much taken with him before—his singing here is extremely good, as is his bass playing. Keith Emerson is heard to great advantage and at last he might achieve some of the recognition he has long missed. To my thinking Emerson (along with Brian Auger) is one of the few organists in pop music today worth his weight in semi-quavers. He is also a very sensitive and effective pianist. This is such a good album it is best heard as a whole. However, my own particular favorites are "Knife-Edge" and "Lucky Man."[50]

Grossman's review really only reveals two reservations. Like many other rock reviewers of the sixties and seventies, he views music technology as an automatically dehumanizing element, so his comments about Emerson's Moog playing reveal a great deal of ambivalence: "'Lucky Man' has interesting lyrics and someone (probably Emerson) plays a terrific solo on something that sounds like a cross between a flutophone and a Waring blender which I assume to be some insidious sort of synthesizer much like those one would learn to build for $37.50 in *Popular Mechanics*."[51] This, of course, prefigures the accusation that the machines were taking over that was to dog ELP later on, when Emerson made the Moog a more integral part of his music. Perhaps an even more troubling harbinger of the future is Grossman's closing statement, "Though this album is very, very good I would not recommend that you rush out and buy it, simply because you may just not be too excited about this type of music. Listen to someone else's copy first. You might very well enjoy it."[52] The idea expressed here—that progressive rock is something of an acquired taste—was to be amplified a hundredfold over the next three or four years, until the critics were almost unanimous in their expressed view that progressive rock was a taste not worth acquiring.

---

[50] Lloyd Grossman, "Emerson, Lake and Palmer," *Rolling Stone*, April 15, 1971, 42.
[51] Ibid.
[52] Ibid.

Granted, there were isolated critics who came out strongly against ELP's sound from the beginning. *Village Voice* (and later, *Creem*) critic Robert Christgau savaged the album in terms that were unusually harsh for 1970, but which starkly prefigured the antiprogressive reflex that Christgau and his *Creem* and *Rolling Stone* cohorts (Lester Bangs, Dave Marsh, John Rockwell) had, by the late 1970s, forged into a hegemonic consensus amongst rock's critical establishment:

> This opens with "The Barbarian," a keyboard showpiece (not to slight all the flailing and booming underneath) replete with the shifts of tempo, time, key, and dynamics beloved of these bozos. Does the title mean they see themselves as rock and roll Huns sacking nineteenth-century "classical" tradition? Or do they think they're like Verdi portraying Ethiopians in *Aida*? From such confusions flow music as clunky as these heavy-handed semi-improvisations and would-be tone poems. Not to mention word poems.[53]

This review proved to be at the extreme end of critical reaction to the band's debut album; for the most part, even most of the critics who had already made up their mind to dislike ELP grudgingly acknowledged the album's understatement.[54] However, it must be admitted that there are a couple of moments that prefigure the band's later difficulty in exercising self-restraint and critical self-judgment. The two-minute drum solo in "Tank" is an especially glaring example. There is also the practice of spinning out lengthy keyboard solos over a short ostinato pattern, which here is still fresh enough not to sink "Take a Pebble," "Atropos," or "Tank"— although none of the three tracks would have been damaged had the solos been shorter—but which does become a dangerous mannerism in later efforts. On the whole, though, *Emerson, Lake and Palmer* remains an excellent introduction both to the work of ELP and to the stylistic parameters of progressive rock.

First Movie: *Pictures at an Exhibition/Rock and Roll Your Eyes* (Live at the London Lyceum, December 9, 1970)

Before moving on to the next stage of the ELP saga, there is one more document from the band's early days that merits examination. Near the

---

[53] Reprinted in Robert Christgau, *Rock Albums of the 70s: A Critical Guide* (New York: Da Capo Press, 1981), 125.

[54] See, for instance, Marsh and Swenson, *Rolling Stone Record Guide*, 121. Even Alan Neister of *Creem*, in his review of February 1, 1971, said the debut ELP album "deserves to be heard," although he added "I also remember some fine monster rock from the old group [the Nice], and I expected this album to be more along those lines."

end of their first European tour—which had largely focused on Britain, but had also included shows in Germany, Austria, and Switzerland—ELP played a concert that was filmed in its entirety for release as a movie; the show took place on December 9, 1970, at London's Lyceum Theater, a ballroom that Tony Stratton Smith, the Nice's manager, had converted to a rock music venue. When one considers that it was shot before similar productions featuring Yes (*Yessongs*), Pink Floyd (*Pink Floyd at Pompeii*), and Led Zeppelin (*The Song Remains the Same*), one realizes how quickly ELP were acknowledged as one of the heavyweight acts of the British rock pantheon. The movie, produced by Lindsey Clennel and directed by Nicholas Ferguson, was released in the U.K. in April 1972 as *Pictures at an Exhibition*. This has been a source of continuous confusion, since ELP's third album had by that time been released under the same title: many have assumed, incorrectly, that the movie is a video documentary of the same live performance featured on the third album. Actually, as shall be seen, the performance featured on the album was recorded later, on March 26, 1971. Another source of confusion is the fact that when the movie was finally released in the U.S. in March 1973, it was called *Rock and Roll Your Eyes*; it's the same Lyceum performance, although by 1973 it documented a phase of ELP's career that was very much in the past.

The relative earliness of this movie's appearance in ELP's career trajectory is at best a mixed blessing. To be sure, it documents a band already light years beyond their tentative performance at Isle of Wight: their European tour during the fall of 1970 had turned them into an increasingly well-oiled live ensemble. On the other hand, even the slightly later performance captured on the *Pictures at an Exhibition* LP shows the band playing as a still tighter, more accomplished unit, so one feels the movie may have come a bit early. Furthermore, the fact that it wasn't released until so much later (1972 U.K., 1973 U.S.) may have discouraged the production of a movie during the 1973–74 World Tour that would have captured ELP at the zenith of their career.

The earliness of the movie also tends to overemphasize ELP's connections with psychedelia. This is chiefly because of the "special effects" that the producers inflict on the concert footage: swirling blobs of color, aura-like emanations that suddenly swallow the musicians for minutes at a time, gyrating kaleidoscope shapes, and, most improbably of all, a random collage of Marvel Comics figures which accompanies "The Curse of Baba Yaga" at the climax of *Pictures at an Exhibition*. I'm sure the effects were meant to capture the zeitgeist of the time, specifically the experience of a late-sixties light show (and, in all likelihood, the acid trip experience too), but the effects soon become annoying, and finally (by the Marvel Comics episode) simply silly. The sound quality isn't so wonderful, either. Lake's bass is often barely audible, and both his voice and Emerson's organ lack sufficient presence: this is a problem that even the recent digital remastering hasn't fully addressed. In fact, the band wasted no time denouncing the movie when it appeared. In an interview from the December 1972 edition of *Hit Parader*, Lake said:

> We did the film at the Lyceum in London, and personally I think it's terrible. What I object to about the film of *Pictures at an Exhibition* is they're charging too much for people to see what I feel is basically a bad production. I really have no responsibility to the kids over the film . . . I know that our name being linked with the sound production suggests that I was involved with the film but I would prefer to say that I salvaged what there was of the sound, rather than produced anything . . . There was overspill on every track: the drums were on the piano track and the bass was on the organ [track]. It just went on and on—so I did the best I could with it.[55]

Having sufficiently warned the potential consumer, however, it must also be admitted that whoever picks up a copy of *Pictures at an Exhibition* on video or DVD is getting a fascinating documentary of ELP's formative period, when a distinctive progressive rock style had largely but not completely parted company from late-sixties psychedelia. The band performs mostly the same set as at Isle of Wight: "The Barbarian," "Take a Pebble," "Pictures at an Exhibition," "Knife-Edge" (replacing "Nutrocker"), and an epic performance of "Rondo" which has since been released as part of *The Return of the Manticore* box set. One is struck by how much more assured Greg Lake seems now than he was at Isle of Wight: his guitar solo on "Take a Pebble" surpasses the studio version (he even appears to improvise a couple of lyrics over the stomping bluegrass riff), and while his vocal phrasing and coloring are still developing, intonation is no longer an issue when he sings *Pictures*. During the second, lengthy piano improvisation on "Take a Pebble," it's interesting to hear Emerson quote part of "Eruption" from *Tarkus*, which of course hadn't been recorded yet, a bit of Friedrich Gulda's *Fugue* (which can be heard again on the "Piano Improvisations" segment of *Welcome Back My Friends*), and a lengthy portion of the first section of "Tank," which the band here take as a straight-ahead electric bebop number.

It's also interesting to observe how much sound the band get from their relatively small setup. Emerson confines himself to Hammond C-3, modular Moog (on top of the C-3), Steinway grand piano, Hohner Clavinet (on top of the piano), and Hammond L-100, which sits opposite the C-3, and takes the brunt of his wild stage finale during "Rondo." Many of the classic Emerson antics are on display here: dragging the Moog's ribbon controller across his buttocks to create weird "outer

---

[55] Greg Lake, quoted by Tony Stewart, "Emerson, Lake and Palmer: 'Kill It' says Greg," *Hit Parader*, December 1972, 18.

space" sounds during the "Old Castle" segment of *Pictures*,[56] spinning the L-100 around and around to create apocalyptic feedback at the close of "The Great Gates of Kiev," rhythmically shaking the L-100 to get the "locomotive engine" effect at the beginning of "Rondo," ritualistically "stabbing" the L-100 keyboards with daggers to get the screeching complaints that bring "Rondo" to its climax, and, of course, the characteristic windmill glissandos down the organ's manuals throughout. Emerson also frequently plays the lower manuals of the C-3 and L-100 simultaneously while standing in between them: one assumes he did this for the sake of being visually dynamic since, with the exception of some passages featuring the C-3 percussion, the organs would produce essentially the same sounds.

Palmer, meanwhile, produces a surprising barrage of sound from a relatively bare bones setup: a snowflake Ludwig five-piece kit with some cymbals, two large gongs, a chime, and a few assorted percussive objects. Like Emerson, Palmer tends to go on a bit in his solo during "Rondo": alas, concision was never one of this band's strong points. On the other hand, when one watches this concert one is struck by how honest the whole performance is, how unpretentious the setup: this is clearly not a band relying on expensive stage props or an enormous arsenal of instruments to carry the show. Some thirty-five years after the fact, the energy and enthusiasm conveyed by the Lyceum performance captured on *Pictures at an Exhibition* still resonates.

---

[56] Many have incorrectly believed the wandlike Moog ribbon controller to be a theramin, which produces similar "outer space" effects. The ribbon controller's sounds are controlled by settings on the modular Moog, which Emerson could wander as far away from as the cord connecting the ribbon controller to the Moog would allow.

5 Mutant Armadillo

The *Tarkus* Saga
(1971)

Turbulence: Late 1970/Early 1971

For many years it was not a generally known fact, even among ELP fans, that there almost wasn't a second ELP album or an American tour: the band came that close to breaking up. Even as the debut album climbed the charts, resentment was simmering between Emerson and Lake, which by late 1970 had boiled over into open conflict. There were two major sources of friction: production responsibilities and stylistic direction.

Carl Palmer has remarked, "Although Keith was the best known, because the Nice had been such a popular band, he never insisted on having more say than anyone else. The three of us had very strong personalities, and each was out to prove his point."[1] Eric Tamm, in his biography of King Crimson, quotes Crimson (and later, ELP) lyricist Pete Sinfield, stating that the two dominant personalities in the original Crimson lineup were Lake and Robert Fripp: Sinfield described them both as "pushy."[2] Once in ELP, Lake almost automatically assumed the role of producer. This didn't sit well with Emerson, in particular, who had also become accustomed to having things done his way during his tenure with the Nice:

> When we did that first album, with "The Barbarian" and "Knife-Edge" on it, Greg kind of automatically seated himself at the mixing desk. I'd be out there twiddling with the synthesizers or whatever and Greg would be at the desk. When it came time to mix things down, we'd all be in the control room, but Greg, having swiped [how's that for a Freudian slip!] the chair in front of the

---

[1] Carl Palmer, quoted by Hall, "Welcome to the Show," 42.
[2] Tamm, *Robert Fripp*, 41. Emerson was confronted with Lake's "pushiness" early on: for instance, he was startled when, prior to the first ELP tour of late 1970, Lake demanded that Emerson not bring his wife, Elinor, with him on tour. See Emerson, *Pictures*, 174–75.

141

desk, would still be occupying the position a producer would occupy. We'd all be there to say when we didn't like the sound of something, and we'd all end up with our hands on the faders. We had mutually worked it out that Greg would be credited as the producer, but Greg acknowledged that we were all producing the albums.[3]

On another occasion, Emerson remarked, "He [Lake] said 'well we can all be the producer, but someone's got to be here at the end of the day.' And I thought, 'Well, if it keeps him happy . . .'"[4] But on at least one occasion Emerson was less diplomatic in his assessment of the arrangement, saying, "Our only collaboration would come when Greg would provide the lyric for a piece that I'd written. We'd also collaborate at the mixing board, but that was more of a battle than a collaboration."[5]

While the issue was at least partly settled with the compromise described above by Emerson (band produces, Lake gets production credit), production remained a source of friction throughout the band's career, with Emerson always concerned that his compositions would be compromised: "We'd all have our hands on the faders on the mixing board, and I would push up a line, and then Greg would push up the bass, and then Carl would push up the drums, and then I would have to push up the melody again, and on it went, over and over, until the engineer said 'Stop, you're over the top,' at which point we backed everything down to zero and started all over again."[6] Although Emerson believes that the original conception of his music was sometimes diluted by this process, at least the band had reached an arrangement that allowed them to continue working together.

No sooner was this issue settled, however, than an even bigger row broke out over the stylistic direction Emerson proposed to follow on the second album, *Tarkus*. Emerson's interest in the "primitivist," folk-imbued modernism of Béla Bartók and Leoš Janáček had by now expanded to also take in the music of Argentinian master Alberto Ginastera (1916–1983). As we saw, Emerson discovered Ginastera's Piano Concerto no. 1 at the "Switched-On Symphony" multimedia extravaganza in Los Angeles that the Nice participated in during February 1970. Emerson was deeply impressed by this music "that could produce so much . . . so much . . . what was it? All the angst I wanted to dispel? All the exhilaration of life? All of everything when you couldn't even sing it?"[7] He picked up a recording and score of the work shortly after returning to England, and the work

---

[3] Dominic Milano, "Keith Emerson," *Contemporary Keyboard*, September 1980, 17–18.
[4] Hall, "Welcome to the Show," 44.
[5] Pethel, "Keith Emerson," 16.
[6] Ibid., 24.
[7] Emerson, *Pictures*, 165.

almost immediately began to exert a powerful influence on his imagination: "I wanted to be able to get that kind of sound from the instruments I was using, and *Tarkus* was the result. I had also always wanted to write atonally, although I wasn't sure what that was, and that album allowed me the freedom to explore some things I had never really done before: percussive keyboard sounds, strong rhythms, atonality."[8] The most characteristic moments of the Nice's music had fused Emerson's guiding twin influences: Bach, and the blues/jazz tradition. Now, with the addition of the Bartók/Ginastera line of modernist influence on the first two ELP albums, Emerson's mature style had essentially emerged, although he continued to refine it through the mid-1970s. Closely linked to Emerson's growing interest in Bartók and Ginastera was Carl Palmer's growing interest in asymmetrical meters. While there had been some unusual meters in "The Barbarian" (these were mostly Bartók's, not ELP's), and "Atropos" was in seven, asymmetrical and shifting meters had not played a particularly important role on the debut album. Now Palmer played a rhythmic figure in 5/4 for Emerson and suggested that perhaps he might base a new composition around it. Emerson merged Palmer's 5/4 rhythm pattern with an ostinato figure he had been developing and extended this basic material with some Ginastera-like thematic development: the result was "Eruption," the first movement of the "Tarkus" suite. Emerson called Lake and offered to play the new music for him:

> I played all the way through the first bit of *Tarkus* . . . and when I finished, there was silence. I turned around and said, "Well?" And he said, "Well, if you want my opinion, if that's the type of music you want to play, then I suggest you play it on your solo album." So I said, "What do you mean? This is the music I want to play with ELP. I don't want to play this on my own." And he said he didn't like it, that it was all over the place, and there was no melody. So I said, "Well, if that's the way you feel, then I don't think we have a band. I have to go forward." And Greg said, "Well, I guess that's the way it is."[9]

Shortly after this encounter the band's management, thoroughly unnerved by the prospect of their rising supergroup unraveling, arranged an emergency meeting with the goal of preventing ELP's premature demise. In the meantime Emerson had shared his experience with Palmer, who was dismayed by Lake's intransigence. The meeting, refereed by EG's John Gaydon and David Enthoven, was not exactly a lovefest: Lake called Emerson's new music "terrible," and insisted that any attempt to record it would be a "waste of time."[10] However, Emerson recalls, "The

[8] Keith Emerson, quoted by Pethel, "Keith Emerson," 19.
[9] Hall, "Welcome to the Show," 44.
[10] Ibid.

settling point came when the management said 'Greg, we're gonna have to pay for the studio time anyway. And since you haven't written anything and Keith has, why don't you at least go in and try it?' He kind of huffed about it, but we found ourselves in the studio the next day. He had on his producer's hat again, and it was back to work as usual."[11] Ironically, Emerson believes that the rancor and strife surrounding the recording of *Tarkus* ultimately made the band stronger: "After we had battled out whether or not to record *Tarkus*, and it became a successful album, I think a lot more of what I wrote became acceptable to the band. Or more immediately acceptable. Suddenly I had all the confidence of Greg and Carl behind me."[12] Emerson has opined that the band's happiest days were "the period from *Trilogy* to *Brain Salad Surgery*. And it took *Tarkus* to get us to those two albums. It took the shouting and all that. And once the shouting was all over and done with and the air was cleared, we were able to get on and play."[13]

Second Album: *Tarkus*

Side one of the *Tarkus* LP was recorded during a brutally short time frame in January 1971, once again at London's Advision Studios.[14] According to an undated article from *New Musical Express* which is reprinted on page 12 of the *Return of the Manticore* booklet, the material on side two of the *Tarkus* LP was recorded shortly after the Newcastle recording of *Pictures at an Exhibition*—apparently sometime in April 1971. *Tarkus* was ELP's first concept album in the sense that the term was understood in the sixties and seventies, as a kind of Wagnerian *Gesamtkunstwerk* ("unified art work") in which music, lyrics, and cover art work in tandem to develop a particular theme, or concept. Side one of the LP format is occupied by the seven-movement "Tarkus" suite, twenty and a half minutes of controlled turbulence that is given highly appropriate visual representation by William Neal's surreal cover and gatefold art. Side two is occupied by six tracks that by and large lack both the originality and the long-range coherence of the "Tarkus" suite, although they contain some interesting (even fascinat-

---

[11] Ibid.

[12] Ibid.

[13] Keith Emerson, quoted by Hall, "Welcome to the Show," 46.

[14] In the *Return of the Manticore* box set, all tracks from the *Tarkus* LP are listed as having been recorded in January 1971. However, this conflicts with both the *New Musical Express* article and the recollections of Keith Emerson, who told me he recalls that the recording sessions for the *Tarkus* LP were interrupted by a period of touring, with only one side of the album recorded prior to the break.

ing) moments, and sporadically suggest conceptual links with the material on side one.

The "Tarkus" suite has received a good deal of attention in the recent spate of progressive rock books. Readers of *Rocking the Classics* will recall that I undertook a detailed analysis of the suite, labeling it one of the most visionary and influential achievements in the early stages of progressive rock. I have not substantially changed my opinion of the piece since writing *Rocking the Classics*, and I will therefore unapologetically repeat bits and pieces of my earlier analysis here. On the other hand, I do have some new things to say, and I would like to consider certain issues from a different angle, so I trust that what follows will be a worthwhile continuation of my earlier discussion.

Before proceeding I must admit a faux pas. In *Rocking the Classics*, I stated that to my knowledge no band member had publicly discussed the underlying concept of *Tarkus* in any detail. This was not correct. Here's Greg Lake, quoted by Nick Logan in the February 29, 1971, issue of *New Musical Express*:

> It's about the futility of conflict expressed in the context . . . of soldiers and war. But it's broader than that. The words are about revolution that's gone, that has happened. Where has it got anybody? Nowhere. It starts off with frustration with the 5/4 piece ["Eruption"], which in itself is a frustrating meter. The natural beat is four, so the extra beat every time is unnatural. Then it builds up towards the first song ["Stones of Years"] which asks the question "Why can't you see how stupid it is: conflict." The next song ["Mass"] is about the hypocrisy of it all and the last song ["Battlefield"] is the aftermath, the conclusion of it. What have we gained? The very last bit, the march ["Aquatarkus"], is a joke. The piece was written in six days and rehearsed for six. It all came very quickly from one idea. Keith started the instrumental piece, the 5/4, and I had my song ["Battlefield"] at the very end. We figured it out on a piece of paper.[15]

To a great extent, this bears out my earlier analysis of *Tarkus* (especially my assertion that "Aquatarkus" was meant as an ironic funeral march). Granted, to some extent, my analysis differs from what Lake says here. Remember, however, that Lake's main contribution to the "Tarkus" suite was writing lyrics for movements two, four, and six; he supplied music for only one of the seven movements. As I will suggest below, the lyrics are only one medium through which the concept is conveyed, and not by any means the most direct: the cover/gatefold art, the titles of the movements, and the music itself are all crucial to conveying the concept. The

---

[15] See David Terralavoro, "The History of ELP: Part II," *Fanzine for the Common Man* 4 (July 1990): 22, for the full context of this quote.

album art, in particular, suggests not so much a contradictory interpretation to Lake's as a broader one.[16] I would suggest that Lake's interpretation may be somewhat limited in that it gives the lyrics too much emphasis at the expense of art, titles, and music (note that Lake never mentions the instrumental third and fifth movements, for instance). I maintain the assertion I made in *Rocking the Classics*: all the elements of a concept album play a role in conveying the album's "meaning," and when all the elements are considered in tandem, a number of "readings" are possible, and, although such readings are likely to share a good deal of common ground, one can't insist dogmatically on one narrowly defined interpretation.

At any rate, a narrow, clear-cut interpretation would not be in keeping with the whole hermetic ethos of the psychedelic era—the supposition that music contains hidden meanings that need searching out.[17] The fact that Emerson and Lake have explained "Tarkus" differently (a point I will return to later) suggests they assumed that individual free association would play at least some role in interpreting the piece. On the other hand, while some elements of both the artwork and the lyrics are open to differing interpretations, other elements can be read fairly objectively, so I think certain broad conclusions can be drawn concerning the nature of the work's concept that, if not identical to Lake's, will certainly be complementary.[18]

Especially important to any discussion of "meaning" in *Tarkus* is a consideration of William Neal's artwork for the album. Neal's depiction

---

[16] Keith Emerson told me that without having heard any of the music yet, Neal presented the band with the mutant armadillo figure, which Emerson dubbed "Tarkus." Emerson then gave Neal a tape of the *Tarkus* suite and asked him to create a visual storyline to accompany it, using the Tarkus figure. When Neal presented the series of illustrations on the album's inner gatefold to the band, Emerson felt that Neal had visually captured the essence of the suite's music.

[17] There is a genuine point of comparison to be made between concept albums of the late sixties/early seventies and Western hermetic and alchemical texts, where a complex network of fantastic visual and literary symbols are often used to convey deep truths. Like the hermeticists and the alchemists, the counterculture's tendency toward arcane language and enigmatic pictures would seem to mask a profound skepticism about the expressive possibilities of literal language. One eighteenth-century writer once said, "I assure you that anyone who attempts a literal understanding of the writings of the hermetic philosophers will lose himself in the twists and turns of a labyrinth from which he will never find the way out." One could, I think, say exactly the same thing about *Tarkus*!

[18] Brian Robison, in "Somebody is Digging My Bones: King Crimson's 'Dinosaur' as (Post) Progressive Historiography," in Holm-Hudson, *Progressive Rock Reconsidered*, 223, quotes Stanley Fish in saying, "sentences emerge only in situations, and within those situations, the normative meanings of an utterance will always be obvious or at least accessible." Robison argues (successfully, in my view) that progressive rock audiences often interpret abstract musical gestures with surprising specificity; I would argue the same is true of album-cover symbology and lyric imagery.

of the Tarkus monster (a bizarre cross between an armadillo and an army tank) on the album's cover has become one of the better-known visual symbols of both progressive rock and ELP, with its memorable conflation of fantasy and science fiction motifs.[19] Nevertheless, it is Neal's eleven discrete panels on the album's inner gatefold that are crucial to creating a framework through which the piece's concept can be conveyed.[20] The first panel, which corresponds to the opening movement, "Eruption," depicts Tarkus emerging from an egg on the side of a volcano that spews molten lava. The next two panels tie in with the second movement, "Stones of Years": the first of the two panels reveals an indescribably strange cybernetic creature, something like a walking space station, which in the second panel is blown to bits by Tarkus's fearsome gun turrets. Panels four and five correspond to the third movement, "Iconoclast," and chronicle the appearance and subsequent death—at the gun turrets of Tarkus—of a cybernetic pterosaur/warplane mutant. Similar ground is covered in the panels that correspond to the fourth movement, "Mass": yet another cybernetic creature (a combination lizard/locust/guided missile launcher) faces down Tarkus, only to be obliterated. The next panel, which is especially large, depicts a manticore, a mythological beast with the head of a man, body of a lion, and the tail of a scorpion: this panel ties in with the fifth movement, "Manticore." The manticore is the first of Tarkus's foes that is not cybernetic, an issue I will address momentarily.

In the next two panels, corresponding to "Battlefield," the sixth movement, Manticore and Tarkus square off: Manticore stings Tarkus's eye, forcing the biomechanical monster to retreat. In the final panel, Tarkus is seen floating down a river on its side, blood streaming from its eye; the gun turrets still appear operable, though, so it is hard to

---

[19] I believe this cover art may have been inspired by Salvador Dali's "Shirley Temple" (1939), which shows a similar use of a bleakly surreal landscape receding into the horizon, largely empty save for some disturbingly scattered bones, and a protagonist (a creature with Shirley Temple's head and a lion's body) that bears more than a passing resemblance to a manticore. This again points up the connection between late-sixties/early-seventies album cover art and surrealism that I have discussed in *Rocking the Classics* (58–59); less than a year after the release of the *Tarkus* album, ELP actually approached Dali to do the cover art for *Trilogy*.

[20] Many years after the fact, Carl Palmer opined that Neal's art for the inner gatefold was made to bear too much of the album's conceptual premise, saying, "I thought it was an interesting concept, but . . . I couldn't understand this armadillo with the tank tracks disappearing into the sea. It didn't have the adult flavor that I wanted that, say, Pink Floyd had done . . . *Tarkus* was meant to be about dealing with chemical warfare and weapons of mass destruction. It could have been a film, but we dealt with it as a cartoon. The music is incredible, though." Carl Palmer, quoted by Ken Micallef, "Carl Palmer: From the Beginning," *Modern Drummer*, June 2005, 121.

determine to what if any degree it has been incapacitated. The music of the first half of the seventh movement, "Aquatarkus," is reminiscent of a funeral march, thereby suggesting the beast's demise. However, the final section of the movement recapitulates part of the first movement, "Eruption," suggesting that the return of Tarkus remains an ever-present danger. This is an ambiguity that the sudden emergence of F major at the end of a piece otherwise dominated by minor modality does little to clarify. If one takes Lake's comment that the final funeral march was "a joke" to mean an ironic or sardonic joke, then there is a clear suggestion that Tarkus has not and perhaps cannot be destroyed.[21]

As useful as these eleven panels are for providing linear continuity to the concept, they obviously can't be interpreted literally: otherwise "Tarkus" is merely a musical depiction of a number of weird and fantastic creatures killing and maiming one another. Clearly, the beasts depicted in Neal's surreal art are symbols, and the titles and, to a lesser degree, the lyrics become vehicles through which the symbols can be read with some degree of objectivity. For instance, "Eruption" concerns the origin of Tarkus. "Stones of Years" would seem to refer to tradition, specifically the cultural traditions that give a society self-definition and self-worth; the gatefold art suggests Tarkus has ridden roughshod over these traditions, an assumption that Lake's somewhat vague and portentous lyrics, with their references to decay ("all your time has been overgrown") and dullness ("you can't hear anything at all") would seem to bear out.

As one continues to correlate lyrics, movement titles, and cover art in this manner, it becomes evident that Tarkus has obliterated most of society's other moorings as well. For instance, while the third movement has no lyrics, its title, "Iconoclast," tells the story: "Iconoclast" is the Artist, the heroic secular prophet figure of nineteenth-century Romanticism (spectacularly resurrected by the counterculture) who fearlessly denounces materialism, philistinism, and conformity wherever these are encountered. Tarkus destroys Iconoclast, that is to say, destroys Art and its capacity for self-expression, and the Artist and his or her ability to open alternate worlds of the imagination. The fourth movement, "Mass," suggests that religious institutions, in their role as guardians of received spiritual and metaphysical truths, are similarly powerless in the face of Tarkus's onslaught. Lake's lyrics for "Mass" are perhaps his best on the album: angry and sardonic, they tell the story of a sorry collaboration between church and state, a collaboration whose purpose is to protect the privileges of both, rather than open up any kind of ultimate reality to the masses. During the course of "Mass," a preacher prays fervently for the

---

[21] In this case the final shift to F major symbolizes, if anything, the triumph of Tarkus.

minister of hate; the cardinal of grief stubbornly ignores the pilgrim who wanders in, "committing every sin that he could"; and the masses meekly obey on cue when the high priest raises his blade and requests prayer. Lake's recurrent refrain: "The weaver in the web that he made." In other words, institutionalized religion has already become hopelessly tangled in a web of its own making: don't expect it to save you from Tarkus.

So what, exactly, does Tarkus symbolize? This question becomes especially acute when one considers the last three movements and the last four panels of the inner gatefold sequence. Manticore is the first of Tarkus's foes that is not biomechanical. Significantly, while Manticore is unable to destroy Tarkus, it is at least able to withstand Tarkus's assault, injure it, and temporarily drive it off. I would suggest Tarkus is a conflation of everything the counterculture despised: the Establishment itself; technology, which the Establishment had spectacularly corrupted into a kind of cosmic Frankenstein's monster that threatened to destroy life on earth; totalitarianism, the brutal repression of individuality and independent thought, often through sinister applications of modern technology, that many hippies saw as equally endemic to governments on both sides of the Iron Curtain; and materialism, a mindless emphasis on the acquisition of material goods that left no room for spirituality or genuine human community. Against this network of evils personified by Tarkus rises Manticore, which I suggest symbolizes the counterculture as it viewed itself. Just as Tarkus is cybernetic and hence "unnatural," Manticore is organic and hence an expression of the counterculture's "natural" values: the primacy of spirituality over materialism, the subservience of technology to the needs of the masses and to the welfare of the environment, the harmonizing of the impulse for individuality with communitarian needs, opposition to artificial hierarchies, and so on.[22] Cultural traditions couldn't stop Tarkus; nor could art; nor could religion. But the counterculture and its revolution ("Manticore") could.

Or could it? Movement six, "Battlefield," finds Tarkus initially crowing about "all the profits of my victory," but then growing more pensive upon considering the horrors of war, and finally, the prospect of total annihilation: the final couplet suggests that after all the arrows have been

---

[22] Obviously this opens the door to a much larger issue. Critiquing the respective values of the Establishment and the counterculture—or arguing to what degree the Establishment actually held the values the counterculture accused it of holding—or even arguing to what degree the counterculture held the values it said it held—goes far beyond the scope of my discussion. I do believe I have given an accurate account of how "Tarkus" and "Manticore" might be seen to personify values the counterculture attributed to the Establishment and to itself, respectively. Incidentally, I understand "the Establishment," as the term was used in the late sixties/early seventies, to take in American and allied governments (Great Britain, for instance) and their economic, military, and cultural underpinnings.

fired, there's no more sorrow or pain. Presumably that's because there are survivors: Tarkus embodies a force of pure destruction whose final "triumph" will be self-immolation. The penultimate panel shows Manticore stinging Tarkus in the eye: perhaps Tarkus is made to blink, so to speak, through force of this realization.

At any rate, Tarkus retreats. The final panel shows Tarkus floating down a river, blood pouring from its eye. This ties in with the final movement, "Aquatarkus," the funeral march. But the latter half of "Aquatarkus" recapitulates part of the first movement, "Eruption," the music that chronicles Tarkus's rise! This is why the funeral march is a "joke," an ironic, bitter joke: Tarkus isn't dead, and retains the capacity to return at any time. And now, having come full circle, we return to Lake's remark: "The words are about revolution that's gone, that has happened. Where has it got anybody? Nowhere." If Manticore represents the counterculture and its revolution against the Establishment during the late 1960s, Lake clearly felt the "revolution" had either already failed, or was in the process of failing before his eyes. Hence the pessimism of both lyrics and visual story line.

While I am confident that what I just outlined is essentially correct, again I emphasize that I don't want to demand blind acquiescence from the reader: either a more specific or a broader reading is possible. For instance, although I don't think *Tarkus* deals directly with the Vietnam War, I do think contemporary audiences (especially American audiences) would have tended to interpret *Tarkus*'s war imagery in light of events in Vietnam.[23] However, while the gatefold art does evoke warplanes and guided missile launchers, Lake's "Battlefield" lyrics speak of arrows raining down. Clearly, the battle Lake is referring to could just as easily be Agincourt or Crécy as the Tet Offensive. What's being lamented here is not a specific war, but more generally humanity's inability to move beyond war, and the continuous existence of social/political/economic structures (symbolized by Tarkus) that rely on war for their survival. As the lyrics suggest, Tarkus represents a system that no revolution can ever truly derail: as the gatefold art suggests, Tarkus takes war with it wherever it goes.

Having now discussed lyrics, visual iconography, and movement titles, let's examine the music itself. Significantly, when Keith Emerson has spoken of *Tarkus*, he has not mentioned soldiers, war, or revolutions that have failed, but rather he has spoken of asymmetric meters, dissonance, and percussive sonorities: in other words, he has spoken of it as an abstract work with its own internal musical logic. Granted, he has also referred to it as "program music"—that is, instrumental music that is intended to

---

[23] See Macan, *Rocking the Classics*, 90.

convey an extramusical concept or "program"—but the fact is, even shorn of its lyrics and cover art, "Tarkus" makes sense as an abstract instrumental piece.[24] It is worthwhile, then, to analyze the piece on a purely musical basis, although I will also strive to point out aspects of the music that clearly are linked with the war/revolution concept outlined above.

As I pointed out in *Rocking the Classics*, the practice of attempting to reconcile seemingly irreconcilable opposites is a defining characteristic of the counterculture's musical expression. An outgrowth of this approach is the fondness of progressive rock musicians for basing their large-scale musical structures on the systematic juxtaposition of what I called, for want of a better term, "masculine" and "feminine" sections. This approach is especially evident in the music of a band like Genesis circa 1969–74, where a quiet section featuring entirely acoustic instruments is suddenly superseded by a loud section dominated by thundering rock rhythm section and electric lead instruments, or vice-versa. Even when the contrast is not stated this baldly, there are other distinguishing characteristics besides dynamics and instrumentation. "Feminine" sections tend to be slower and feature longer, more lyrical melodies, simpler harmonic progressions, and clearer textures; "masculine" sections tend to emphasize less tuneful melodic material, dense textures, and more complex dissonant harmonies. Allow me to quote *Rocking the Classics*, with a few minor changes to my early statement:

> Clearly, in progressive rock the alternation of these "masculine" and "feminine" sections create a set of dialectical opposites. "Feminine" sections suggest the meditative, pastoral, traditional, and intuitive, "masculine" sections the dynamic, technological, futuristic, and rational. The masculine/feminine analogy goes deeper than one might think, since masculine and feminine sections complete each other, contributing to the expansion and contraction, the movement toward and away from climaxes, that was such a central facet of progressive rock structure. Furthermore, this masculine/feminine dialectic

---

[24] For instance, on a number of occasions I have performed "Tarkus" as a recital piece for solo piano. With a bit of rearrangement of the last two movements it works quite well; one such performance, recorded at the Shannon Center for the Performing Arts, Whittier, California, on April 1, 1992, is included as a bonus track on the second Hermetic Science CD, *Prophesies* (1999). It is interesting to note, though, that one reason that most of the piece was not difficult to arrange for solo piano is that in certain parts of "Tarkus"—and in parts of some other ELP pieces as well—the rhythm section stands on the verge of becoming irrelevant. For instance, while the practice of using drums to rhythmically double melodic lines was not an uncommon characteristic of progressive rock, Carl Palmer doubled Emerson's melodic figures to a degree that would have been unusual in other progressive rock bands: Palmer's role often involves fattening up the orchestration as much as it involves time-keeping. Likewise, throughout parts of "Tarkus" and other ELP albums (especially the first three) there is a tendency for Lake to double Emerson's left-hand keyboard part on bass guitar. This is an issue I will return to in greater depth in later chapters.

allows for a symbolic playing out of many of the conflicts that were of great significance to the hippies. It symbolized how a whole set of cultural opposites—high and low culture, European and African-American creative approaches, a futuristic technocracy and an idyllic agrarian past, or matriarchal (intuitive, egalitarian) and patriarchal (rational, hierarchical) modes of society—might be integrated into a larger whole.[25]

"Tarkus" is somewhat atypical of many lengthy progressive rock pieces in that there is no acoustic instrumentation to speak of—there is some piano, but it is always used in a textural role, and throughout "Tarkus" the Hammond organ and the modular Moog synthesizer are the lead instruments. Therefore, the application of the structural principle outlined above is a bit more subtle than it is, for instance, in Genesis's *Supper's Ready*, and it's arguable if the "masculine" and "feminine" sections of "Tarkus" are ever really integrated or reconciled. Nonetheless, I think that considering the structure of "Tarkus" on the basis of the masculine/feminine dichotomy outlined above will prove useful.

First, I point to a very obvious aspect of the work's structure: of its seven movements, the odd-numbered movements are instrumental, while the even-numbered movements are songs. Of the four instrumental movements, movements one ("Eruption"), three ("Iconoclast"), and five ("Manticore") embody a destructive, "masculine" energy that suggests a link with other notable musical archetypes of war and violence such as Gustav Holst's "Mars, the Bringer of War," the first movement of *The Planets*, and the "Dance of the Earth" section of Igor Stravinsky's *Rite of Spring*. These three movements are characterized by repetitive motor rhythms; cold, metallic timbres featuring percussive Hammond organ and strident Moog settings; short, jagged keyboard themes, devoid of any sense of tunefulness, which are layered over driving bass ostinato figures; and almost continuous dissonance. The harmonic flavor of these movements emphasizes perfect fourths; there are many passages featuring parallel fourths or quartal harmonies (chords consisting of stacked perfect fourths), and the pervasive presence of this unstable interval helps to lend these movements their characteristic driving quality. Part of the third movement, "Iconoclast," is bitonal, juxtaposing two identical ostinato patterns a tritone apart: this further increases the impression of dissonance.[26] The tempo of all three movements is unremittingly fast and dis-

---

[25] See *Rocking the Classics*, 43–44, for the original text. To reemphasize a point I have made elsewhere: I use dichotomous descriptives such as "masculine" and "feminine" (or "Apollonian" and "Dionysian," which I used in *Rocking the Classics*) as useful archetypes that allow one to quickly and comprehensibly place a series of related characteristics on a continuum, not as essentialist categories.

[26] "Iconoclast" contains the first systematic use I'm aware of in ELP's music of a bitonally flavored chord that consists of an augmented fourth on top of a perfect fourth (i.e., C–F–B).

plays a machinelike regularity. Keith Emerson's remarks aside, these movements are not atonal in the strict sense of the word: however, tonality is established by the repetition of a drone or short bass ostinato in the manner of such modernist composers as Stravinsky, Bartók, or Holst, rather than by traditional harmonic relationships between chords.

Of the three song movements, the second ("Stones of Years") and sixth ("Battlefield") serve as "feminine" foils. Timbres are warmer here, with sustained, churchy Hammond chords predominating; instead of short, jagged themes there are long, lyrical tunes, featuring Lake's sonorous voice (and, in the sixth movement, his equally lyrical electric guitar counterpoints); tempos are slower and more relaxed; the meter is regular (quadruple) rather than irregular (the quintuple meter of "Eruption" and "Iconoclast," or the unusual treatment of 9/8 in "Manticore"); and background harmonies are much more consonant and conventional. Even here, though, there is a clear distinction drawn between the relatively simple modal harmony of "Battlefield" and the wry chromatic harmony of "Stones of Years," which unites jazz-based chord voicings otherwise unusual in progressive rock with a pseudo-baroque ground bass.

In the context of this masculine/feminine dichotomy, movements four ("Mass") and seven ("Aquatarkus") are the wildcards. "Mass" is the middle song movement; its stridently funky, clavinet-like Moog setting, incantational vocal line, and aggressive rhythms forge a sonic link to the instrumental movements, which is appropriate for the angry, biting tone of the lyrics, quite different from the mournful, resigned lyrics of the second and sixth movements. On the other hand, "Mass" is less complex, rhythmically and harmonically, than the instrumental movements, and contains a bluesy Hammond organ break that gives the movement an earthier feel than the almost inhuman, machinelike precision of "Eruption," "Iconoclast," and "Manticore." Meanwhile, the first half of the instrumental seventh movement, "Aquatarkus," features a slower tempo and a mellower brasslike Moog setting, appropriate to its role as a kind of funeral march, that brings it more in line with the "feminine" song movements. The last half of "Aquatarkus," on the other hand, recapitulates part of "Eruption" in all its stridency.

The "masculine" and "feminine" structural categories, then, are by no means absolutes, but are malleable and prone to interpenetration. Nonetheless, I think that as long as the masculine/feminine categorization is understood as a symbolic archetype, rather than a literal, quantifiable

---

This chord, which Emerson almost certainly absorbed from Ginastera's Piano Concerto, played an important role in ELP's music during the *Trilogy/Brain Salad Surgery* period, as we will soon see.

musical property, it offers a very useful means for explaining the huge range of expression encountered in a lengthy progressive rock work like "Tarkus." But now, having examined how "Tarkus" achieves variety, let us consider an equally important issue, how it achieves continuity and coherence.

First, the harmonic scheme plays an important role in imposing a structure that is improvisatory and unpredictable, yet logical and ultimately satisfying. The opening movement, "Eruption," is the most tonally volatile section; unity is provided by the return, on three separate occasions, of a driving one-bar (5/4 meter) bass ostinato, first in F modal minor (0:32), then in C modal minor (1:32), and finally in E modal minor (1:57).[27] Linking these three passages are some of the most careening, unpredictable, and inventive keyboard episodes that Keith Emerson has ever captured on record. Emerson's figurines here are created by splicing a number of short motives together and are characterized by wide melodic skips and irregular rhythms; musicologists who persist in their belief that all rock music involves four-square rhythms and phrase structures would do well to examine these passages. Toward the end of "Eruption" the music appears to be heading toward B modal major; a transitional passage into the second movement, however, swings the music into a broadly interpreted C minor, where it remains throughout the affective, stately "Stones of Years."

"Iconoclast" opens with a bitonal juxtaposition of the "Eruption" bass ostinato in F and B modal minor (6:30), now overlaid with new keyboard motives; it is the most dissonant section of "Tarkus." Towards the end of this movement, another episode of unpredictable keyboard figuration swings the tonality into A modal minor. This is where it remains for much of the aggressive fourth movement, "Mass"; unlike the other two song movements, "Mass" is characterized by parallel open fifths rather than full triads, which lends the movement a leaner, more wiry sound. The final verse of "Mass" modulates up by major second, to B minor (10:39); this modulation paves the way for a return to C minor, signaled by the rolling ostinato figure that opens the frenetic "Manticore." (It may or may not be coincidental that the first movement, representing Tarkus, and the fifth movement, representing Manticore, stand in a tonic-dominant relationship, F–C). Much of "Manticore" remains in C, although the relentless ostinato and its jagged motivic overlay momentarily shift to A Phrygian in the middle of the movement (11:47). The expansive "Battlefield" opens

---

[27] I use the terms "modal major" and "modal minor" to denote music that is recognizably major or minor, but which cannot be identified as pertaining either to the diatonic major or minor scales or to a specific mode. For instance, the bass ostinato pattern that dominates the first and third movements of "Tarkus" is essentially Locrian, but the atomistic keyboard themes that appear on top of it are "chromatic" in respect to the Locrian mode.

with a slow, tortured progression of dissonant polytriads; much of the remainder of the movement is in a fairly conventional E Aeolian/Dorian, although a recurring four-bar organ fanfare (first heard at 13:41) hints at the F modal minor of the next movement.

At the beginning of the last movement, "Aquatarkus," this four-bar fanfare is taken up and transformed into the solemn march theme that dominates the first half of the movement, as it is ceaselessly repeated underneath a torrent of improvised Moog lead lines. Carl Palmer's gong strike summons a recapitulation of the second half of "Eruption"; the music careens through C minor, halts momentarily on a grinding F major/F♯ minor polytriad (20:15), and dramatically resolves into F major upon a final repetition of the "Aquatarkus" march theme, which ends the piece.

Hidden underneath all the dissonance and the frequent tonal shifts of "Tarkus" is an elemental tonal scheme that is a major factor in the music's coherence. Movements one and two involve a progression from the tonic F to the dominant C. Movements three through five repeat this movement, and movements five through seven reverse the tonic-dominant movement, traveling from C to F.[28]

Another factor in creating a sense of long-range coherence is the recurrence of themes and motives from movement to movement. The driving bass ostinato that recurs on three separate occasions in the first movement figures prominently in the third movement as well, where it accompanies new motivic material. The four bar keyboard fanfare refrain of the sixth movement is transformed into the march theme of "Aquatarkus"; even the rolling ostinato figure that dominates "Manticore" appears to be an arpeggiation of the "Battlefield" keyboard fanfare. The final movement, of course, also recapitulates a lengthy section of the opening movement. Only "Stones of Years" and "Mass" don't appear to share melodic material with other movements. Even where there aren't direct thematic links, though, the pervasive presence of open fourths and fifths becomes a unifying factor.

I do not think "visionary" is too strong a word for *Tarkus*. In 1971, *Tarkus* was miles removed from anything any other rock band had attempted. King Crimson's *Lizard* (1970) and Van der Graaf Generator's great *Pawn Hearts* (1971) were both complex works, to be sure, especially texturally: but in terms of its distinctive metallic timbral sheen, its complex, machinelike metric episodes, its sophisticated harmonic dissonances, and its virtuosic ensemble interplay, *Tarkus* was unique for its

---

[28] I explain this in Schenkerian terms elsewhere; see *Rocking the Classics*, 93. For a metaphorical interpretation of the tonal scheme of "Tarkus," see chapter 9, note 23 of the present work.

time, and has seldom been equaled. Yes, Genesis, Jethro Tull, Pink Floyd: none of them ever applied modernism to rock this audaciously, or, in my view, this successfully. Nearly thirty-five years after its creation, Greg Lake's sobriquet "futuristic" still applies[29]: my students, few of whom were born when the work was recorded, still find it challenging and disturbing. *Tarkus* just may be ELP's most imaginative and utterly original conception.

However, I will not argue that it is ELP's most fully realized work; it has several shortcomings. First, it is overarranged: there are too many gratuitous overdubs. Many of them are in the bass register: with the first, third, and fifth movements in particular, Emerson tends to double Lake's bass guitar lines with Hammond and either Moog or piano. I suspect his goal was to create a subtly shifting array of timbres on the lower end of the mix. Unfortunately, though, the result is simply a pervasive muddiness in the lower register that tends to obscure some terrific ensemble interplay between the three musicians. For instance, in "Eruption" Carl Palmer's intricate 5/4 groove contains some phenomenal bass drum work, but it is hard to pick out, even on a good sound system, against the competing bass guitar, Hammond, and Moog parts.

While the song movements are not quite as overstuffed, they too would have also benefited from some pruning: the ringing piano notes (again in the low register) of "Mass" seem unnecessary, as does Lake's triple-tracked guitar solo in "Battlefield." Engineer Eddy Offord attempts to deal with all this density by panning the overdubbed parts through left and right channels of the soundstage: while this approach was used to nice effect on the debut album, especially on "Tank," where it emphasized the independent melodic strands, here it verges on becoming an annoying mannerism.[30] Granted, Offord did some nice things on *Tarkus*: it's possible to argue that a Hammond organ has never yielded so many subtle shades of tone color on any other recording by anyone else, and I still find the almost steel-drum-like Hammond percussion sound in parts of "Stones of Years" (listen at 4:02) and "Mass" (8:46) amazing. Nonetheless, *Tarkus* lacks the elegant open soundstage of the debut album, and I think both Offord and the band would have been well advised to shoot for a "leaner and meaner" sound. This does seem to be something the band attempted on their live album of 1974—with, as we shall later see, somewhat mixed results.

While overarrangement is the biggest problem with the "Tarkus" suite, there are a couple of other weaknesses. By and large, Greg Lake doesn't sing with a great deal of conviction here. He sings "Mass" pretty

---

[29] Greg Lake, quoted by Aledorf, "Lucky Man," 10.
[30] In connection with this, I was somewhat surprised to learn that Offord felt *Tarkus* represented his best work with ELP. I will have more to say on Offord's relation to ELP later.

well, but his singing in the other two song movements sounds rather uninvolved; his vocals on the live recording of "Tarkus" released three years later sound much more committed. Both the lengthy Hammond solo in "Stones of Years" and the electric guitar solo in "Battlefield" could have been cut in half with no damage whatsoever to the musical logic of the work. Even more than on "Lucky Man," Palmer spectacularly over-drums on "Battlefield," filling virtually every empty space with over-wrought thirty-second note fills. (This is not to criticize his drumming in the odd-number instrumental movements, though, which is outstanding, very effectively mixing intricate grooves, virtuosic fills, and nimble rhythmic doublings of Emerson's melodic lines.)

In sum, the "Tarkus" suite is an astonishing conception whose riches were not fully conveyed on the 1971 studio recording. In light of the mixed success of the live 1974 recording, which introduced some new problems even as it fixed others, I was very excited to learn that ELP resurrected "Tarkus" in its entirety during their final tour of 1998. As recently released recordings of the 1977–78 arrangement (*Manticore Vaults,* vol. 2) and the 1986 Emerson, Lake and Powell version (*Live in Concert*) have demonstrated, "Tarkus," more than any other ELP classic, seems to be open to a multitude of interpretations, and its definitive, "perfect" incarnation is still out there somewhere, waiting to be realized. The 1998 "Tarkus," the first complete version of the piece to appear in the band's set list since 1974 (the 1977–78, 1986, 1992–93, and 1997 arrangements were all abridgements) is perhaps the tersest of all, and the one that comes closest to revealing the piece's inner essence; it is to be hoped that a 1998 performance of the track will eventually be released.

Side two of the LP format, consisting of six relatively short tracks (none longer than 4:00), can be dealt with more quickly, although it will be necessary to spend a bit of time on the third, fourth, and fifth tracks, which seem to form a "mini-concept" with some indirect connection to the "Tarkus" suite. The first song on side two, "Jeremy Bender," is not quite two minutes long, and inaugurates a mini-genre within ELP's output, the music hall song. These songs, which include "The Sheriff" and "Benny the Bouncer" among later specimens, are short, comic, narrative, and make numerous stylistic references to late-nineteenth/early-twentieth-century popular music styles associated with British music hall and American vaudeville. I have long suspected the model for these songs was Paul McCartney's "Rocky Raccoon" from the Beatles' *White Album* (1968), which betrays similar stylistic influences and narrative conceits. However, McCartney's song manages one trick that none of ELP's "music hall songs" ever quite pull off: it achieves a keen sense of irony between the bouncy, feel-good musical accompaniment and the rather grim, unsentimental story line.

"Jeremy Bender" is almost certainly the weakest of ELP's efforts in this realm. Granted, Paul Stump considerably overreacts when he hints darkly of the song's "homophobia"; the song's biggest "crime" would seem to be juvenile vulgarity and, from a musical point of view, triviality.[31] Like most of ELP's attempts at humor, this song is placed clearly outside of their more ambitious, "serious" works (e.g., the "Tarkus" suite). This approach can be contrasted both with bands like Yes, whose music seldom ever shows any traces of humor, and groups like Jethro Tull and Genesis circa 1969–74, who incorporate humor into their large-scale epics (with, it must be admitted, decidedly mixed results). In this case, at least, the result garnered by ELP's approach is a throwaway song whose absence would hardly have affected the rest of the album.

Next comes the grotesquely titled "Bitches Crystal" which, fortunately, isn't as bad as the title would imply. It is, in fact, a rather intricately structured little song that draws together its three distinct stylistic sources—music box waltz, boogie-woogie, and baroque—into a surprisingly coherent whole. The unifying factor is rhythm: a relentless triple meter that unfolds at breakneck tempo as Lake shrieks out his story of a crazed sorceress and black magic gone awry. Lake brings the harshness of his "21st Century Schizoid Man" performance to this vocal, except here the rasping and screaming is done without aid of a fuzzbox.

The song opens with a quiet instrumental section featuring Emerson on celesta, a small, bell-like keyboard instrument that late-nineteenth/early-twentieth-century composers often used to evoke either benign magic (Tchaikovsky's *Nutcracker*) or more ambiguous cosmic forces (Holst's "Neptune," from *The Planets*). Here Emerson casts a spell of childlike naïveté; the music is meant to evoke a music box waltz of the type that was popular in the late nineteenth and early twentieth century, although the section's numerous major seventh chords also make it curiously reminiscent of Vince Guaraldi's "Linus and Lucy." The peace of this section is rudely shattered by a frenetic boogie-woogie bass line: instead of the normal 1–4–5 contour (C–F–G in the key of C minor), Emerson opts for 1–4–7 (C–F–B$\flat$), a quartal outline that immediately establishes a point of contact with the "Tarkus" suite. The boogie-woogie bass line is the transition to the main body of the song, a thirty-two-bar verse-refrain, repeated twice, that is dominated by Lake's vocal shrieks, Emerson's bluesy piano

---

[31] See Stump, *The Music's All That Matters*, 99. I found myself growing more than a bit perturbed when Stump later (216) seems to imply the band were homophobic because they took umbrage at a *Gay Times* cover that, by reinterpreting the *Trilogy* cover art, suggested they were gay. Stump appears to have been weaving an unstated subtext that, in my view, needed either to be discussed explicitly or dropped.

filigrees, and the driving boogie bass, with some Moog filter sweeps added for atmosphere.[32]

The underlying chord progression during the verses of this section is identical to that of the "Stones of Years" ground bass section, so Emerson is already weaving together boogie and baroque elements. This stylistic cross-stitching continues as Emerson commences a bluesy solo over some irregularly resolving, vaguely "baroqueish" secondary dominant chords (1:22); this passage is followed by the first appearance of the song's bridge section (1:44), which features another baroque-inspired progression of wayward secondary dominants over which Lake's vocal shrieks reach their apex. During Emerson's crazed solo over the boogie bass line, parts of the opening celesta passage are ingeniously woven back in, setting up a return first of the bridge, and finally of the thirty-two-bar verse-refrain, where the Moog's uncannily realistic French horn calls bring the song to a suitably vulgar climax, after which it seems to peter out in exhaustion with an almost tongue-in-cheek blues coda. While Emerson's frenetic boogie poundings do seem a bit over the top by the end, the song succeeds surprisingly well in drawing together its diverse stylistic strands, and even manages to make a cross-reference to the more modernistic quartal harmonies of the "Tarkus" suite. On the other hand, its tale of black magic gone wrong seems disconnected from anything else on the album, and I think it would have worked better in a context where conceptual coherence was less of an issue.

Now we come to the conceptual core of the second half of *Tarkus*, with "The Only Way," "Infinite Space," and "A Time and a Place." The first of these, "The Only Way," with its booming pipe organ, is the most imposing, and would have worked well as the first track on side two of the LP format. Laid out in two distinct sections, it is a hymn—a hymn to an agnostic, humanist, seemingly materialist worldview. Like Jethro Tull's Ian Anderson, whose contemporaneous album *Aqualung* expresses similar sentiments, Lake's treatment of Christian beliefs is shadowed by an underlying sense of anger, which sometimes leads to less than profound reflections ("Can you believe God makes you breathe? Why did He lose six million Jews?").[33] Furthermore, Lake's exhortation that "you must believe in the human race" has already been undermined by the "Tarkus" suite's powerful exposure of human greed and selfishness, which, as Lake

---

[32] Since Emerson obviously couldn't play the two-handed boogie piano parts and do the Moog filter sweeps at the same time—nor manage the rapid-fire switch from celesta to piano and back—ELP never played this number live until their 1997 tour, by which time MIDI and digital sampling made it feasible.

[33] Even a cursory reading of the Bible reveals that the Biblical writers themselves were deeply occupied with the issue of a just God allowing evil in the world—the Book of Job representing a particularly profound meditation on the subject.

himself emphasizes, seems remarkably impervious to change via "revolution." In other words, based on humans' acknowledged (and remarkably consistent) track record, is it realistic to see humankind shambling on toward some kind of extradivine redemption? I think this is an issue neither Lake nor Ian Anderson thought through, and this is why, in my view, both *Tarkus* and *Aqualung* fail as philosophy and/or metaphysics. Van der Graaf Generator's Peter Hammill comes from a similar perspective: although I don't share his agnosticism or tortured existentialist perspective, I acknowledge the philosophical mooring of his lyrics are much stronger since they show a keener awareness of the difficulty in getting from point A (humankind's current state) to point B (redemption without a God to bestow it). When Hammill wearily murmurs "what choice is there left but to live" at the hollowly majestic climax of Van der Graaf Generator's "Lemmings," you feel the weight of the unspoken realizations that lie behind the words.

Credit where credit is due, however. There are two genres of music for which Lake's voice seems tailor made, hymns and folk songs, genres where his bell-like clarity of vocal timbre are shown to maximum advantage. Lake sings "The Only Way" with great conviction—it is easily his finest vocal performance on the album—and he evokes that same sense of poignancy and vulnerability that made his best performances with King Crimson ("Epitaph," "In the Wake of Poseidon") so affective. Emerson supplies suitably imposing accompaniment. The first half of the hymn features him on the Saint Mark's (London) pipe organ: after opening with a segment of J. S. Bach's Toccata and Fugue in F major, BWV 540, at 0:43 he introduces his own hymn theme in the bass pedals (now in the relative minor, D minor), weaving an imposing and stylistically credible web of counterpoint, in the manner of one of Bach's chorale preludes, on the keyboard manuals. When Lake begins singing, Emerson at first supports him with simple backing chords, but gradually reintroduces the full contrapuntal web: a particularly ingenious bit of counterpoint can be heard at 1:44, when he plays the first half of the hymn melody on the upper manual while Lake is singing the second half of the hymn melody.

The second half of "The Only Way" is signaled by Emerson's sudden shift from pipe organ to piano and by the entrance of the rhythm section. Emerson begins this new section with another quote from Bach, this time the opening passage of the Prelude in D minor from Book I of the *Well-Tempered Clavier*. When Lake reenters singing the hymn melody, Emerson provides a more urgent accompaniment than before, and the piano's swiftly flowing eighth notes in a lean two-part polyphony are now accompanied by bass and drums. This section of "The Only Way" was sometimes interpolated into "Take a Pebble" during the band's live performances of 1971.

Two closing observations about "The Only Way." First, one wonders if ELP intended a bit of unspoken irony by accompanying this hymn to agnostic humanism with music that makes numerous references to that paragon of Protestant piety, J. S. Bach. Second, one wonders if Emerson and Lake noticed how prominently their solemn D minor melody featured the tritone C$^\sharp$–G—the *diabolus en musica*—in a hymn devoted to an agnostic worldview.[34] More unspoken irony?

"The Only Way" segues without pause into "Infinite Space," an instrumental track cowritten by Emerson with Carl Palmer, who suggested some of the main theme's offbeat rhythms. The track's title derives from a rhetorical question posed during "The Only Way": "How was the Earth conceived? Infinite Space? Is there such a place?"

"Infinite Space" is the most stylistically progressive track on side two of the LP format. Unlike the frenetic instrumental movements of the "Tarkus" suite, though, with their aura of ultramodernity, "Infinite Space" is aloof, timeless, ritualistic. Based around a throbbing piano/bass/drums ostinato in septuple meter, "Infinite Space" features a slowly unfolding Dorian melody, occasionally interrupted by short melodic episodes set in irregularly shifting meters. The harmony unfolds in slow, static blocks: about a quarter of the way through the track (at 0:38) the music suddenly shifts up a whole step, from D to E, at which point the Dorian melody is repeated in the new key. A sudden climactic passage of ascending triplets, capped by Palmer's snare drum roll, returns the music to its original D tonality. Lake and Palmer drop out, and Emerson begins to weave an almost raga-like lead over the throbbing left-hand ostinato. He starts with simple pentatonic figures, but these become more melodically and rhythmically complex and eventually move into A$^\flat$ Lydian, producing a pungent clash with the D Dorian ostinato. Finally, at 2:02 the track reaches its second climax on a series of percussive chords which bitonally unite elements of the D and A$^\flat$ tonalities, two keys a tritone apart. Thereafter Lake and Palmer reenter, the opening section of the piece is recapitulated, and a short coda brings it to a quiet, enigmatic close.

"Infinite Space" is a fascinating piece. While it seems to offer some parallels to Stravinsky in his severe, neoclassical phase, I'm even more struck by its rather astonishing parallels to some of master minimalist Steve Reich's early pieces: the similarity with parts of Reich's *Six Pianos* is especially uncanny when one considers that the ELP piece came two years earlier. Like a lot of the minimalists' music, "Infinite Space" shows a definite non-Western influence in its metric and melodic profile, its percussive sonorities, and its incremental, undramatic sense of transformation.

---

[34] The melodic tritone can be heard during the "stirred, moved" and "shrine, deceived" segments of the tune, for instance.

Emerson seems to use the piano here to suggest mallet percussion—I'm reminded of a Balinese gamelan—and when my band Hermetic Science recorded a cover version of "Infinite Space" for our debut album, *Hermetic Science* (1997), I played Emerson's part on marimba rather than piano, in an attempt to capture something of the "Eastern" ambience I believe he was seeking. Although "Infinite Space" shows few of the sophisticated structural techniques favored by minimalists like Reich or Philip Glass in their mature works to create slow but continuous transformation, its largely undramatic and static structure is quite different from most of ELP's material, as is its emphasis on intricate group textures rather than virtuosic individual display. Indeed, I will go so far as to say that "Infinite Space" prefigures many of the major concerns of King Crimson's *Discipline* album—ten years before *Discipline* was released! Again, as with some of the material on the debut album, I think it is regrettable that this most promising line of inquiry was not pursued on later ELP albums.

The fifth track, "A Time and a Place," seems to continue the meditations Lake embarked on in "The Only Way." Somewhat like the instrumental tracks "Atropos" (from the debut album) and "Karn Evil 9, 2nd Impression" (from *Brain Salad Surgery*), "Infinite Space" functions as a hinge, a turning point in the unfolding of the concept, since "A Time and a Place" now seems to reject the strictly materialist agnosticism of "The Only Way" in favor of a more mystic/Gnostic outlook: "There is a place / a time and space / that no one . . . a time and a space. . . . that no one can trace."[35]

This kind of viewpoint was common enough in the counterculture, probably much more common than a strictly materialist agnosticism. It would seem to owe much to the Eastern religious doctrines then occupying the counterculture's attention: Lake's "time and a place," where "no sound is made" and "silence is played," seems suggestive of the Buddhist concept of Nirvana. Such a conception also has deep roots in nineteenth-century pantheism, especially monism, the conviction that behind the infinite network of isolated events and objects in the universe is a transcendent, all-embracing, connective force—God, if you will, although, not "God" in the sense that a monotheist would understand

---

[35] In the course of correspondence with Jon Green about Pete Sinfield's lyrics for the first four King Crimson albums, Green has suggested that "Infinite Space" refers to Nuit, the sky goddess, as described by Aleister Crowley in his *Magick in Theory and Practice*. I'm not so sure—Greg Lake, as far as I can see, is no Jimmy Page. On the other hand, I have no doubt that when the band titled the piece, they weren't referring solely to the "infinite space" that astronomers view with their telescopes, but were also referring to the transcendent mystical space of "A Time and a Place." Again, I point out the transitional role of "Infinite Space" in affecting a kind of transformation from the material realm to the mystic realm.

the Deity. This kind of monism seems at the root of much of Jon Anderson's work with Yes, for instance.[36] But while Anderson rejoices at the possibilities of tapping into this overarching superawareness, in "A Time and a Place" Lake agonizes over our society's spiritual sterility, and its apparently unbridgeable distance from such a dimension. This song is probably the closest Lake ever gets to rock and roll screaming, but his is a bluesless screaming, and his frequent vocal rasps generate tension but no warmth. This is also probably the highest Lake ever pushes his vocal tessitura—he resorts to falsetto for some of the climactic phrases (for instance, the second repetition of the "that no one can trace" phrase)— and the result is an anguished performance that, while possibly a bit over-wrought, certainly captures the song's conceit of spiritual ennui.

Musically, "A Time and a Place," a rare Emerson/Lake/Palmer co-composition, is in the lineage of "Knife-Edge": a driving, minor key, riff-based rock number with baroque inflections, built around an organ trio configuration. The band decorate the essentially simple Aeolian chord structure with some interesting pseudo-baroque touches. There is extensive circle of fifth movement in the bass line during the second half of each verse (listen, for instance, at 0:12), and an affective chain of chromatically descending seventh chords during the final verse (1:53), played on modular Moog, which has been layered in by the end of the song. While the song isn't long enough to build up the same sense of tension and drama as "Knife-Edge," it does convey its sense of spiritual angst well enough: interestingly, Emerson set the song in the key of E minor, a key associated with anguish during the baroque period.[37] ELP performed "A Time and a Place" as an encore during some of their 1971 shows, but had to do it without the Moog parts that lent the end of the song its climactic character: it was only during their 1998 tour that the band revived the song as a live number, by which time technology had caught up with their imagination and enabled them to give a more or less faithful-to-the-record performance.

Of the final number, "Are You Ready Eddy?" not much need be said. It is another short comic number, cowritten by Emerson, Lake and

---

[36] Bill Martin has explored the parallels between the Gnostic/monist outlook of a Romantic figure such as William Blake and Jon Anderson at some length. See Martin, *Music of Yes,* 54–58.

[37] In fact, it is interesting to note that of the other two songs on side two of *Tarkus* with baroque inflections, "Bitches Crystal" is set in C minor, a key linked with madness during the baroque, and "The Only Way" is in D minor, a key associated with gravity and solemnity. While I suppose it's just possible Emerson studied one of the seventeenth- or early-eighteenth-century treatises on the Doctrine of Affections which set forth these key-affect correspondences, I think it's more likely that the linkage of key and musical character in these three songs reflects his deep familiarity with and interest in Bach's keyboard music during the *Tarkus* era, and is therefore entirely intuitive.

Palmer (probably in ten minutes or so), dedicated to engineer Eddy Offord. It is the style of a rollicking late-fifties rock-and-roll song, replete with crazed, Jerry Lee Lewis–style boogie piano, but its musical content has already been undermined by the far more interesting and original treatment of boogie elements in "Bitches Crystal." The high point of "Eddy" is when Emerson quotes the familiar trumpet battle charge at the beginning of the instrumental section: after that it's all downhill.[38]

Tarkus: An Assessment

In sum, side two of *Tarkus* does have the core of a concept, but its full realization would have required jettisoning "Jeremy Bender" and "Are You Ready Eddy?" (and probably saving "Bitches Crystal" for a more appropriate context), and writing one long or two shorter tracks which somehow resolved the conflict between materialist and mystic/Gnostic worldviews set forth in "The Only Way" and "A Time and a Place." The problem, of course, was time. As soon as ELP were done with the brutally short recording sessions they were back on tour, and they didn't yet have the clout that would later allow them to work on an album over a period of months: like many other bands, they discovered that creating a coherent concept album required a certain amount of time to sort through ideas at leisure in a studio, and leisurely studio time was a luxury ELP couldn't afford yet. The result is a somewhat uneven album. Like the contemporaneous album *Fragile* by their colleagues Yes, *Tarkus* has many truly visionary moments, but also some less than stellar ones: the biggest problem with both albums is that the epic pieces and shorter tracks never cohere, and therefore the whole never becomes more than the sum of its parts. In fact, as an album *Tarkus* occupies a similar relationship to *Emerson, Lake and Palmer* as Yes's *Fragile* has to *The Yes Album*; in both cases the later albums are more adventurous and represent a genuine step forward, but are more uneven and less concise than their predecessors.

Issues of Critical Ideology, Part 1: Rock-Classical Fusion and the "Elevation" of Rock Music

There is one further line of discussion that needs to be dealt with in order

---

[38] By the way, for all you trivia buffs, the dialogue at the end of the track, spoken with a strong Cockney accent by Keith and Carl, respectively, is "They've only got 'am [ham] or chayse [cheese]." "'Am or chayse!" The reference is to a tea lady who continuously interrupted the band's recording sessions at Advision, loudly announcing what was left at the nearby sandwich shop.

to set matters straight concerning *Tarkus*. By the mid-1970s, when rock criticism had decisively turned against progressive rock, it had become fashionable to indict the style for borrowing from the eighteenth- and nineteenth-century classical-music tradition in order to sound "nice" and to win the approbation of the bourgeois, who had been shocked and scandalized by earlier strains of rock. In other words, the argument went, the purpose of the rock/classical fusion of bands like ELP was to "elevate" rock, thereby making it culturally acceptable to the more conservative segment of the listening public that had previously rejected rock because of its vulgarity and subversive tendencies. Critics who argued from this perspective decried progressive rock as elitist, a betrayal of rock's populist origins, and an underhanded attempt to drain rock of its oppositional energy. As Lester Bangs said of ELP, their great "crime" was "the insidious befoulment of all that was gutter pure in rock."[39]

Countering this argument cuts to the heart of the issue of the critical reception of progressive rock in general, and ELP in particular. Let me frame the issue as it is pertinent to *Tarkus*. First of all, there was nothing in *Tarkus* that would have been comforting to the mainstream audience that critics like Bangs accuse ELP of trying to court: in 1971 *Tarkus* was an oppositional work, pure and simple. This is true both of the music and the subject matter. When Greg Lake has spoken of the album, he has spoken of "soldiers and war"; in other words, Lake's notion of "opposition" involved political and cultural stances of a vaguely leftist slant, and it's hard to see how a cultural conservative circa 1971 would have taken comfort in the album's preoccupation with antiwar themes or its agnostic/monist musings. When Keith Emerson has spoken of the album, he has spoken of dissonance, atonality, and strong rhythms. In other words, Emerson's notion of "opposition" derives from modernist aesthetics, with its belief that the only way for art to impact society in the twentieth century—for art to be truly modern—is to intentionally adopt stridency and unfamiliarity as a means of forcing people to acknowledge displacement and dysfunction in contemporary society.[40] As Jacques Barzun puts it, "The [modernist] artist condemns society by picturing not its follies but its madness. He is the jester whose absurd remarks tell the

---

[39] Lester Bangs, "Exposed! The Brutal Energy Atrocities of Emerson, Lake and Palmer," *Creem*, March 1974, 44.

[40] In 1971, surrealism as an artistic style still had something of a subversive aura, especially due to its ties with late-sixties hallucinogenic drug culture—an aura it was to lose soon enough, as the entertainment industry relentlessly recycled surrealist imagery during the first half of the seventies—so the cover art would have played a similar defamiliarizing role to Emerson's music.

[41] Jacques Barzun, *From Dawn to Decadence: 1500 to the Present; 500 Years of Western Cultural Life* (New York: Harper Collins, 2000), 720. Incidentally, while the attitude that

king what is wrong with his realm."[41] It is true that not all of the principal literary and musical modernists were politically "progressive" in the sense the Left uses the word (Stravinsky, T. S. Eliot, Yeats, and Ezra Pound all come to mind), and it would be dangerous to articulate a specific "modernist politics." However, there is no way that a critic can credibly accuse modernists of any political stripe of trying to make "comforting" art that cheerfully repeats eighteenth- and nineteenth-century conventions. As the Vietnam era recedes ever further into the past, Lake's antiwar message in *Tarkus* increasingly becomes of historical and philosophical, rather than political and cultural, import; however, Emerson's music for *Tarkus* remains startling, challenging, futuristic. It certainly would not have struck listeners in 1971 as "nice" music that made rock more acceptable to mainstream tastes by drawing on "comforting" strains of nineteenth-century Romanticism.

Clearly, Bangs and his school of rock critics recognize only one type of properly "oppositional" music: music that comes directly out of the "oppressed" classes and unselfconsciously reflects the conditions of such classes. Such an approach would have been a hypocritical one for most British rock musicians—virtually all of them were white, and many of them weren't of working class origin—and such a view is at any rate based on the dubious supposition that only working class or minority people can produce properly "oppositional" art.[42] Again, the oppositional framework that progressive rock musicians were working out of is best seen in the context of modernist aesthetics: the only responsible choice for an artist in a dysfunctional time is to make strident, disorienting, and challenging art. It is in this sense that *Tarkus* (and at least some other progressive rock) is oppositional.

One other thing I haven't discussed here is the difference between drawing on twentieth-century concert music as a metaphor of disorientation (as the "Tarkus" suite does) and drawing on eighteenth- and nineteenth-century classical styles—as, for instance, "The Only Way" does. Now, as I pointed out, "The Only Way" seems to use its Bachian referents

---

Barzun summarizes in this quotation can be traced back to the earliest phase of modernist art, literature, and music, the first person I am aware of to place it in a larger aesthetic-political context is Theodor Adorno.

[42] Apparently Bangs et al. didn't read their Marxist literature deeply enough. No less an icon of the Left than Vladimir Lenin stressed just the opposite: any attempt to inspire revolution amongst the working classes through the formation of a "working class consciousness" would have to come from outside of the working classes. This is a central point in the grim climax of George Orwell's *1984*, when Winston Smith, the novel's doomed hero, recognizes that the proletariat will never rebel without a clearly defined set of goals and principles to rebel for, and the Party will never allow anybody from either inside or outside the proletariat to disseminate a coherent set of oppositional ideas that could spark revolution. Lenin himself was certainly not a product of the working classes.

in an ironic—or at least, a double-edged—sense. (As do the other tracks on *Tarkus* that draw on baroque elements.) But how about an album like *Pictures at an Exhibition*, which is done more in the spirit of a straight tribute to nineteenth-century Romanticism and the classical music tradition? As a matter of fact, I do find *Pictures at an Exhibition* problematic in a sense I don't find most of ELP's other references to the classical music tradition, an issue I'll discuss at greater length in the next chapter.

One final offshoot of this discussion as it refers to ELP, the Western classical music tradition, and matters of oppositional tendencies in the music. While critics such as Lester Bangs or Dave Marsh essentially dismiss all progressive rock as useless, a critic like John Rockwell distinguished between the "mainstream" progressive rock acts like ELP, Yes, Genesis, Renaissance, etc., whom he considered purveyors of a puerile, middlebrow, classically tinged rock (or vice-versa), and more genuinely "progressive" bands. (Rockwell cited the German electronic rock band Tangerine Dream as an example of a genuinely "progressive" band, which seems to prefigure the preoccupation of a certain segment of the modern rock critical establishment with seventies "Krautrock" as *the* truly "progressive" rock of its era.[43]) Rockwell's line of thinking has certainly become popular in certain circles of contemporary rock criticism, as Bill Martin has pointed out; I have also seen it expounded at length by several members of the so-called Canterbury bands such as Chris Cutler (ex–Henry Cow) and Dave Stewart (formerly of Egg, Hatfield and the North, National Health, Bruford), who largely dismiss the music of ELP, Yes, Genesis, et al., but who cite Magma, Henry Cow, and early Soft Machine as genuinely subversive, oppositional, and "progressive" bands. Bill Martin has done a good job in exposing the illogical line of reasoning that must be adopted to maintain this distinction between a so-called reactionary "mainstream progressive" and a truly progressive vanguard, at least as concerns the seventies, so I refer the interested reader to the relevant section of Martin's *Listening to the Future*.[44] However, I'll add this: the "Tarkus" suite was as "progressive" in the sense Cutler and Stewart are referring to as are any of the other bands they named. As a matter of fact, I'll go the last step. Think of any of the most challenging progressive

---

[43] See Rockwell, "Art Rock," *The Rolling Stone Illustrated History of Rock and Roll*, 351. See also Robert Christgau's remarks on the German band Can in *Rock Albums of the 70s*, 441, and any of Lester Bangs's statements concerning German electronic rockers Amon Duul.

[44] See Martin, *Listening to the Future*, 86–91.

[45] Martin aptly states that in Magma's *Mekanik Destruktiw Kommandoh*, "the human side was intentionally purged from the music, in the forced march rhythm of totalitarian invasion." Does this sound reminiscent, perchance, of *Tarkus?* See Martin, *Listening to the Future*, 220.

rock you can. *Red*-era King Crimson. Midseventies Magma.[45] Henry Cow's *Unrest*. Anything from the Univers Zero or Art Zoyd back catalog.[46] This music is progressive rock with a healthy dose of modernism. While Frank Zappa may have been the first rock musician to draw elements of musical modernism into rock, ELP's *Tarkus* is the first album that made a serious and sustained effort to integrate musical modernism into the mainstream of rock's musical language.[47] In this sense, I don't think it's unfair to say the *Tarkus* suite is the taproot of all later expressions of a more difficult, complex, and dissonant strain of progressive rock.

---

[46] As an interesting experiment, listen to Univers Zero's "Dense" or "Combat" and the instrumental movements from the "Tarkus" suite back to back. Does it sound to you like there may have been some direct influence? It sounds that way to me . . .

[47] I realize the Beatles and many of their successors in the late-sixties psychedelic rock movement successfully used the recording studio and electronic effects to expand the timbral and textural possibilities of rock in a manner that shows the influence of Karlheinz Stockhausen, Pierre Henry, and other late modernist composers of electronic music. What I'm saying here is that Keith Emerson was the first to envision a rock music in which the rhythmic, harmonic, and melodic aspects of early and midperiod musical modernism were pervasive.

6

Pictures at an Exhibition

(1971)

Endless Touring and Early Successes: 1971

I think it's hard for younger readers to fully appreciate just how important touring was for rock bands of the 1970s, and how much time they spent on the road. ELP's rise coincided with the emergence of a trend that was to last throughout the decade: the continuous touring of the U.S. by British rock bands. As I pointed out in *Rocking the Classics*, by the 1970s the U.S. accounted for 50 percent of the world's record buying public, Great Britain less than 10 percent.[1] Record companies were not slow to recognize the economics inherent in this trend, and as the seventies progressed, successful British bands spent more and more time in the U.S. and less and less time in the U.K.. A new band might start out headlining a tour of college auditoriums (this was especially important in the earlier seventies), or perhaps opening for a better-known band at larger venues. As the band became better known, they might start to headline shows themselves, graduating from college auditoriums and medium-sized halls to arena-sized venues. The megastar acts of the 1970s—which ELP were already beginning to exemplify by late 1971—could easily fill stadiums.

Shortly after the completion of the *Tarkus* recording sessions, ELP were on the road again. From March to mid-April 1971, they toured the U.K.[2] On March 26, playing at Newcastle City Hall, they recorded *Pictures at an Exhibition*, with the goal of eventually releasing this performance as a live LP; this gave the band an incredible three LPs worth of

---

[1] Simon Frith, *The Sociology of Rock* (London: Constable and Company, 1978), 121.
[2] All known ELP shows have been listed by date and location on Greg Lake's web page (the URL is http://www.greglake.com), as well as in Forrester, Hanson, and Askew, *Emerson, Lake and Palmer*, 241–47. However, I believe my own list (appendix D of this book) is more up to date and accurate than either.

recorded material in less than a year of existence! No sooner had they completed the British tour then they were off on their first American tour. Their U.S. debut took place April 21 at Theil College, Greenville, Pennsylvania; they continued to tour the U.S. throughout late April and May. American audiences, who were just learning of ELP's existence in early 1971 with the U.S. release of the debut LP, were startled to find that the band had not just one but two further LPs worth of unreleased material that they could draw from in their live shows, although the band rarely played *Pictures* in its entirety during this tour (one exception was their show at New York's Carnegie Hall on May 26). In June they were back in Europe, playing a number of dates in Germany, Austria, and the Netherlands.

A show the band played at the 6,000-seat Philipshall in Dusseldorf, Germany, on June 13 is probably fairly representative of the band's repertoire—and stage show—at this time. They opened with "The Barbarian," then launched into the "Tarkus" suite. This was followed by "Take a Pebble," "Knife-Edge," and "Rondo," which included a marathon solo by Palmer and Emerson's mandatory assault on his Hammond L-100. According to a review that ran the next day in the *Dusseldorfer Nachrichten*, this latter episode proved to be the climax of this particular show:

> Emerson hit, hammered, kicked, and jumped onto his instrument; crawled into its electronic innards, producing stunning feedback; and pushed the organ around until finally—after he had ridden it across the stage—it overturned with an earsplitting crash. A ten-minute standing ovation, which shook the Hall to its foundation, was the reward for this outstanding performance. It forced the three totally exhausted actors to even do an encore.[3]

The encore was "Nutrocker," which now included a semiautonomous song, "Preacher Blues," that was never recorded in the studio, but that served as the prototype of the later "Tiger in a Spotlight."[4] The band didn't play *Pictures* this night; in fact, they were tending to play *Pictures* only occasionally during the *Tarkus* era. The Dusseldorf show lasted about ninety minutes.

Tarkus was released in the U.K. in June, and in the U.S. on July 3. In Great Britain, where ELP were already bona fide superstars, the album hit number one. ELP's stock was also rising fast in the U.S.; *Tarkus* charted out at number nine, and remained in the American top forty for eleven

---

[3] Peter Brollick, "Emerson's Ride on the Organ," *Dusseldorfer Nachrichten*, June 14, 1971. I want to thank Bernd Prott for bringing this review to my attention, as well as providing his personal recollections of this particular show.

[4] A recording of "Preacher Blues" from the Dusseldorf show is included on Greg Lake's *From the Underground, Volume 2: Deeper into the Mine*.

weeks. In the U.K., critical reaction was mixed. In his review for *Melody Maker*, Chris Welch stated, "Few groups have achieved such technical mastery and yet managed to combine good entertainment in the best pop tradition." He described the "Tarkus" suite as "dramatic, probing, explosive, full of theater and convincing grandeur . . . There are so many moments during this hugely satisfying set that it would take several column inches to give a blow-by-blow account."[5] On the other hand, Richard Green's review for *New Musical Express* evinces a curious confluence of the "this is too complicated for rock and roll" attitude, which was later to become central to the blues orthodoxy line of rock criticism, with the "this is nothing but noise" line that had been directed against rock and roll since the days of Little Richard and Jerry Lee Lewis:

> The man from the National Council for Civil Liberties ought to be informed about this album that's being unleashed upon a largely unsuspecting public. And if he's not concerned, the Noise Abatement Society certainly will be . . . It is almost inexplicable how three talented musicians can turn out an album that seems to be about the adventures of a mechanized, gun-equipped armadillo of all things called "Tarkus" and include numbers of such variety that by the middle of the first side the listener is pretty hopelessly lost . . . It's sad that the album had to turn out like this as there are some nice passages, but these are almost completely buried by the overall cacophonous ostentation.[6]

There had been talk of making *Tarkus* a double LP that would include the *Tarkus* studio material on one LP and the live recording of *Pictures* on a second.[7] This idea was eventually scrapped as financially unfeasible—and possibly also because of its potential for overexposing the band—and the live recording of *Pictures* was kept under wraps for a future release.

Almost as soon as *Tarkus* had been released, ELP commenced another tour of the U.S. and Canada. This time they played bigger venues than before, including the Sports Arena in San Diego (July 17), Hollywood Bowl in Los Angeles (July 19), Hollywood Sportatorium in Miami (August 10), Stanley Park Stadium in Toronto (August 12), and Place des Nations, Montréal (August 13). This tour lasted through September 1, ending with a gig in New York City's Gaelic Park that has been colorfully described at some length by Robert Moog, who met Emerson for the first time at that show.[8] This show, incidentally, is available in its entirety on

[5] Chris Welch, "*Tarkus*—an offer of ELP," *Melody Maker*, June 5, 1971.
[6] Richard Green, "'ELP our Ear" [review of *Tarkus*], *New Musical Express*, June 12, 1971.
[7] See the *New Musical Express* article reprinted on p. 12 of the *Return of the Manticore* box set booklet. The article is undated, but I am guessing it dates from early April 1971—after *Pictures* was recorded at Newcastle, and before the band left on their first U.S. tour.
[8] See Mark Vail, "The World's Most Dangerous Synth," *Keyboard*, June 1992, 51, 70. Emerson reprints Moog's recollections in *Pictures of an Exhibitionist*, 214–15.

The Original Bootleg Series from Manticore Vaults, vol. 1; it's the earliest ELP show included in the series.

After this second American tour the band finally took a bit of time off, but in November they were back on the road again in the U.S. (including a show at New York's Madison Square Garden on November 25), and in December they returned to the U.K. to play a number of shows. Keith Emerson has commented on the rigors of road life during this period: "Life on the road was totally different. There was no time to do anything except perform and travel. Playing 32 different cities in 34 days will give you an idea of what I'm talking about. I didn't even have time to practice. I used to take one of those silent keyboards on the plane with me just to keep my fingers familiar with the music."[9] This kind of constant traveling was only one factor of life on the road for rock musicians of the seventies: there were also the drugs, the alcohol, the groupies, and the road crews, or "roadies." Life for the roadies was exceptionally demanding. They had to wrestle with tons of equipment day after day, setting it up and tearing it down on a tight schedule, and they traveled on buses from city to city. As they seldom got much time off, roadies often turned to after-hour "diversions" for release. Emerson has described a couple of such diversions:

> We quit staying in the same hotels as the road crew after a while. They were acting like madmen, and we became tired of footing the bill for their antics. One roadie took a tube of super glue and glued all the furniture in his hotel room to the ceiling, and another time a bunch of them took a huge can of instant coffee and made coffee in the swimming pool. After a while it became too much for us to take financially.[10]

Emerson, Lake and Palmer: The Manticore Special, originally a made-for-British television documentary that was released on video by Manticore Records in 1998, gives an excellent (albeit much sanitized) sense of the band's life on the road at a slightly later stage of their career.

In November 1971, even as ELP were embarking on their third American tour of the year, Island Records released *Pictures at an Exhibition*

---

[9] Keith Emerson, quoted by Pethel, "Keith Emerson," 20. No doubt one factor in Emerson's initial shock of touring the U.S. was the vast distances that often needed to be covered to go from show to show, a very different scenario from touring Britain, and a factor the Nice had never faced to the same degree in their more modest tours of the States.

[10] Keith Emerson, quoted by Pethel, "Keith Emerson," 20. Clem Gorman's *Back Stage Rock* (London: Pan Books, 1978) offers a fascinating study of the rock music culture of the 1970s as a kind of feudal society, and dwells extensively on the role of the roadies. Someone who wants the flavor of the seedier, wilder side of 1970s rock life, with its alcohol and drug binges, groupies, crazed roadies, and shady deals, should read Emerson's *Pictures of an Exhibitionist*—and for the *real* exposé on the subject, Stephen Davis's *Hammer of the Gods: The Led Zeppelin Saga* (New York: Ballantine Books, 1985), which chronicles the exploits of rock's most extravagantly libertine band.

in the U.K.; it soon reached number three in the British charts.[11] However, the American release was a different matter. Atlantic Records executives informed the band that in their view, there was no American market for a rocked-up version of a nineteenth-century classical piece, and that they should make other arrangements for a U.S. release. Greg Lake recalls, "They offered to put it out on a subsidiary label called Nonesuch, which was a jazz-oriented, avant-garde label.[12] We said we didn't want to do that because we figured it would just get buried. And we explained that every time we played the piece in concert, the audience went wild. But the label still refused."[13]

The band gives Scott Muni credit for creating the momentum for the album that eventually brought Atlantic around. Lake remembers that Muni, DJ at WNBW in New York, "played the entire album, both sides, back to back."[14] When *Pictures* quickly sold thousands of import copies in the U.S., Atlantic's executives looked increasingly foolish, and soon enough they sought to negotiate the album's release. Enter Stewart Young, a graduate of the London School of Economics. Young was a chartered accountant in practice with his father when he first met the band, who came seeking advice about some taxation problems: "My father rang through to me saying he had these three rather scruffy individuals called Emerson, Lake and Palmer in his office, and had I ever heard of them. I said 'No, but I'll look them up.' I thought he was talking about a firm of solicitors!"[15] Young was talked into attending a show at New York's Madison Square Garden and was "totally amazed"; ELP became regular clients shortly thereafter. A canny negotiator, Young at first threatened to hold Atlantic to their decision not to release *Pictures*, but eventually relented, and a deal was reached. *Pictures* was released in the U.S. on January 22, 1972, and quickly hit number ten on the American charts, remaining in the top forty for twelve weeks. Young, for his part, began to play an increasingly important role in the ELP organization, eventually being installed as the band's manager.

---

[11] The band insisted the LP be priced as low as possible, and the price was set at £1.49. This almost Grateful Dead–like insistence on making their live material available to their fans as inexpensively as possible can best be seen as a late trace of hippie anticorporate attitudes. The band itself seems to have discarded anticorporate qualms by the time they launched Manticore Records about a year later, although in its early days, at least, the label did attempt to balance profit and altruism.

[12] A more accurate description is that Nonesuch was a label that specialized in two niches that at that time were at the fringes of the classical music market: early music (pre–eighteenth century) and twentieth-century music. Such notable contemporary masters as Steve Reich and Henryck Górecki are Nonesuch artists.

[13] Greg Lake, quoted in Hall, "Welcome to the Show," 42.

[14] Ibid.

[15] Stewart Young, quoted by James Johnson, "Welcome Back My Friends to the Show That Never Ends," *New Musical Express*, April 27, 1974.

Third Album: *Pictures at an Exhibition*

Pictures at an Exhibition is the best-known work of Modest Musorgsky (1839–1881), the supremely original Russian master whose relatively few major works were composed in brief spurts of creative activity between the increasingly lengthy alcoholic binges that prematurely ended his life. Musorgsky completed *Pictures* in 1874; it is his only major work for solo piano. For the most part, those of his contemporaries who heard the work did not know what to make of his percussive use of the piano, pungent dissonances, highly unusual chord progressions, and sudden alternations between remarkably free and barbarously repetitive rhythms. At the time, these originalities were ascribed to Musorgsky's supposedly "defective" technique: when Maurice Ravel arranged *Pictures* for full orchestra in 1923, it was generally hailed as a great "improvement." However, in recent years the full scope of Musorgsky's achievement has been more fully recognized, and it is no longer heretical to say that while Ravel's orchestration unquestionably polishes *Pictures* up and smoothes it out, Musorgsky's original piano score has a barbarous energy of its own that Ravel's arrangement to some degree drains. In fact only the final section of the work, "The Great Gate of Kiev," can unarguably be said to gain from its orchestral dressing.

Pictures at an Exhibition reflects two major trends of later nineteenth-century music: nationalism and program music. In terms of the former, Musorgsky draws on elements of Russian folk song and Orthodox church music: the resulting metric freedom and modal waywardness inject a genuinely Russian element, quite unlike anything happening in Western European music at the time.[16]

Besides being an important example of nineteenth-century musical nationalism, *Pictures* is a notable specimen of program music—that quintessentially nineteenth-century practice of using instrumental music to convey extramusical subject matter. For Musorgsky, the stimulus was visual. His good friend, the painter Victor Hartmann, had recently died, and a group of Hartmann's friends staged a memorial exhibition of his works. At least one picture was contributed to the Hartmann exhibit by Musorgsky himself, and soon the composer was envisioning a musical tribute to his deceased friend.

Pictures at an Exhibition was the result. Ten of Hartmann's paintings are given musical representation by Musorgsky. Each "picture" is followed by a recurring theme, called "promenade" by Musorgsky, which repre-

---

[16] In fact, in the hands of Claude Debussy (1861–1918), the first composer to fully recognize and react to Musorgsky's achievement, Musorgsky's approach to modality and meter helped contribute to the breakdown of traditional tonality in the early years of the twentieth century.

sents the composer walking from picture to picture. The theme is distinguished by its persistent alternation of bars of five and six beats; Musorgsky was a bearlike man weighing well over two hundred pounds, and the irregular meter may well have been meant to suggest the composer's shambling gait. On the other hand, each recurrence of the promenade theme is different in mood, reflecting Musorgsky's changing emotions as he considers each of his friend's paintings in turn. The promenade theme recurs six times, and is also alluded to in the final and most imposing movement, "The Great Gate of Kiev." Thus, *Pictures at an Exhibition* offers a particularly characteristic example of yet another mainstay of nineteenth-century music, thematic transformation—the technique of continuously transforming a theme's rhythm, tempo, harmony, and instrumentation in order to convey the work's program as vividly as possible.

British audiences first encountered the music of Musorgsky and his Russian cohorts in the 1890s, mainly through the auspices of Sir Henry Wood's Queen's Hall Promenade Concerts (known in Britain as "The Proms"). To say this music was controversial at the time is an understatement. Sir Hubert Parry, whom many ELP fans will know as the composer of "Jerusalem," denounced the Russian music championed by Wood in terms surprisingly reminiscent of the racist attacks on jazz during the 1920s and rock and roll during the 1950s, speaking of the music's "primitive emotional expression" and "unrestrained abandonment to physical excitement which is natural to underdeveloped races."[17]

Emerson first encountered *Pictures* in its orchestral guise, apparently during the waning days of the Nice:

> I head this piece [in London's Festival Hall] that I had never heard before, and it really knocked me out. The next day I went to the music store and asked for a copy of the score, and when it turned out to be a work for piano solo, that thrilled me, because there it was in a form that I could play. Later, when I approached Greg and Carl about performing it, they were agreeable. So we put a version of it together, added a few cuts of our own, and took it on the road. I wanted to use it sort of as an educational piece, exposing our audiences to this great work of classical music.[18]

This last statement, with its reverential and perhaps somewhat pedantic tone, is an example of the kind of thing that got Emerson into trouble with the critics—an issue I'll address momentarily.

---

[17] Sir Hubert Parry, quoted by Robert Stradling and Meirion Hughes, *The English Musical Renaissance 1860–1940: Construction and Deconstruction* (London and New York: Routledge, 1993), 47.
[18] Keith Emerson, quoted by Pethel, "Keith Emerson," 22.

Despite Emerson's reverential tone, ELP's *Pictures* is hardly a straight arrangement. ELP present Musorgsky's first two pictures, as well as interpolating one of their own, and then skip directly to his last two pictures. The band thus eliminate six of the ten pictures, while interpolating three original movements; they also eliminate three of the six promenade recurrences. This can be seen below:

Musorgsky	ELP
1. Promenade	1. Promenade
2. The Gnome	2. The Gnome
3. Promenade	3. Promenade
4. The Old Castle	4. The Sage (original)
5. Promenade	5. The Old Castle
6. Tuileries	6. Blues Variation (original)
7. Bydlo	7. Promenade
8. Promenade	8. The Hut of Baba Yaga
9. Ballet of the Chicks in their Shells	9. The Curse of Baba Yaga (original)
10. Two Polish Jews, One Rich, One Poor	10. The Hut of Baba Yaga
11. Promenade	11. The Great Gates of Kiev
12. Limoges, the Market Place	
13. Catacombae Sepulcrum Romanum	
14. Promenade (Con Mortuis in Lingua Mortua)	
15. The Hut on Fowl's Legs (Baba Yaga)	
16. The Great Gate of Kiev	

What follows here is a synopsis-type discussion of the individual tracks, which I believe is the easiest way to clarify the nature of the changes ELP wrought on Musorgsky's work.

Promenade. Musorgsky's opening promenade is a vigorous, confident processional that effectively sets the stage for the rest of the work. It also prefigures the tonal waywardness of the rest of the music, with its excursions from the tonic B♭ major through D♭ major (bar 8 of Musorgsky's score) and F major (bar 12) before returning to B♭ (bar 18). On the *Pictures* album, Emerson plays the opening Promenade on the Newcastle City Hall pipe organ—the third consecutive ELP recording to feature Emerson's pipe organ work (and the last, as it turned out).[19]

---

[19] In performances where he had no access to a pipe organ (i.e., the vast majority), Emerson created the closest possible simulation by pulling out all the stops on his Hammond C-3 and

Emerson frequently inserts fermatas at the end of phrases, so the feeling of alternating bars of five and six is lost; on the other hand, his treatment does emphasize the folklike nature of the melody, and at any rate, ensemble tightness isn't an issue here, as Lake and Palmer don't play. A suitably imposing opening.

The Gnome. The springboard for this movement was a sketch by Hartmann of a carved wooden nutcracker that broke the shells between the jaws of a wizened, grotesque face. Musorgsky's music, which alternates between violently spastic outbursts and slow, ominous shambling, is something of an imaginary ballet score for a grotesque, simian, but perhaps vaguely comical little biped. ELP alter this movement much more than the opening promenade, which Emerson presented almost note-for-note from the piano score, but nonetheless deliver one of the album's indisputable high points.

The band start by taking Musorgsky's spastic opening figure and tightening up the rhythm: Emerson and Palmer play the figure in an incredibly tight rhythmic unison, regularly punctuated by Lake's bizarre bass tones (he ran his bass through both Emerson's modular Moog and a wah-wah pedal to achieve the unique effect). Besides offering a picturesque musical portrait of a nervous, twitching gnome, this section, with its jagged rhythms and its percussive sonorities, shows the straight line of influence that runs from Musorgsky to the later, folk-inflected modernism of Bartók and Ginastera, on into such progressive rock classics as *Tarkus*.

The next section, with its slow, ominous tread and pervasive tritone presence, gives us a different glimpse of the gnome. Signaled by Lake's fuzzed bass at 1:07, this section adds the modular Moog, which interjects a newly composed, vaguely Middle Eastern melody over Musorgsky's original music, which is heard in the Hammond and bass guitar. The ponderous climactic section, heralded by Palmer's tom flourish at 2:15, is dominated by Lake's bass and Emerson's liquid, filter-heavy Moog setting: the invertible counterpoint at the end of this section, where Lake's lumbering bass lead is accompanied with Emerson's increasingly spacey Moog tremolo, is especially effective. Finally, as the passage reaches its climax, a strident, sirenlike descending Moog glissando momentarily obliterates everything, but then the music quietly reassembles itself: out of the Moog's synthesized "wind storm" (white noise), Lake's atonal bass tremolos, and Palmer's quiet hi hat patterns emerge Musorgsky's closing chords, played by Emerson on a flutelike Hammond setting. And then one last convulsion: the Hammond suddenly explodes with Musorgsky's virtuosic closing run, which recalls the movement's opening spasms one

---

using no Leslie and no chorusing. See Mark Vail, *The Hammond Organ: Beauty in the B* (San Francisco: Miller Freeman Books, 1997), 166.

final time.[20] The band's arrangement of "The Gnome" is completely successful because of its evocative orchestration, its judicious adaptation of Musorgsky's rhythms to a progressive rock framework, its respect for the movement's points of tension and repose, and its insistence on tight ensemble interplay over individual display.

Promenade. The sometimes frantic activity of the previous movement is followed by the second promenade, which is rendered more quietly and reflectively here than in its previous presentation by Emerson's flutelike organ setting and by dynamics that barely rise above *piano.* Again, there is no rhythm section, but unlike the first promenade, Lake sings. Paul Stump is probably correct to criticize the hackneyed romanticism of some of Lake's imagery (the "tortured dreams," for instance), but, on the other hand, the lyrics do a fair enough job of introducing the theme of predestination that is to dominate the next picture, "The Sage."[21] Other than the addition of Lake's vocals, the changes the band make to the music are fairly minor. Emerson repeats the first two measures with a newly composed left-hand accompaniment; where Musorgsky writes solo melodic lines, Lake sings *a cappella*, and where Musorgsky writes chords, Emerson accompanies Lake's vocal on the Hammond.

The Sage. In Musorgsky's original score, the second picture is "The Old Castle," a quiet, melancholy, almost hypnotic nocturne that was inspired by Hartmann's painting of a troubadour playing a lute in front of a crumbling Italian castle. It would seem that Greg Lake's "The Sage," which here becomes the second picture, was inspired by similar imagery. The movement begins with Emerson weaving a quiet Moog arabesque over murmuring Hammond arpeggios: however, this is merely a transition, a modulatory bridge which moves us from the A♭ major of the previous promenade to the A minor of the main body of "The Sage." A slowly ascending Moog glissando gives way to Lake's carefully picked guitar arpeggios, and thereafter "The Sage" features Lake's voice and acoustic guitar alone.

If Hartmann turned to medieval Italy for inspiration for his "Old Castle," Lake's "Sage" turns to Elizabethan England: "The Sage" shows a surprising similarity to the lute songs of John Dowland (1563–1626), although I think the parallels are a matter of Lake's familiarity with music of the 1960s folk revival rather than the result of any systematic study of Elizabethan music.[22] "The Sage" is in three sections. The opening section

---

[20] This passage is a notorious stumbling block even for virtuosos: Emerson makes it considerably easier on himself by excising the left-hand part.

[21] For Stump's remarks on *Pictures*, see *The Music's All That Matters*, 99–100.

[22] In a similar vein to several of Lake's acoustic ballads, Dowland's lute songs were written for a lutenist and a singer—Dowland himself taking on both roles in his own performances of them.

of the song, where Lake's somewhat gloomy ruminations on matters of predestination and fate are accompanied by exquisite arpeggios, suggests the lingering influence of King Crimson: the affective emphasis on the melodic minor ninth in Lake's vocal line is reminiscent of "In the Wake of Poseidon." However, the chord structure is more sophisticated than most early Crimson pastorals, with the persistent cross relations especially contributing to the Elizabethan flavor.

The middle section of the song, which modulates from A minor to the dominant E major, is a guitar solo, and without any doubt represents Lake's finest recorded moment as an acoustic guitarist. If the opening section of "The Sage" is reminiscent of one of Dowland's lute songs, the middle section is reminiscent of a Dowland lute fantasia.[23] The wayward drifting between major and minor modality, the masterful voice leading (a favorite technique of Lake is to move the outer voices in parallel tenths over an inner pedal point, creating a very rich texture), the cleanly picked arpeggios and precise runs, and the delicate bouquets of harmonics all suggest Lake could have been a terrific lutenist; indeed, his sensitive dampening of strings to clarify the voice leading shows a lute player's sensibility. His solo shows a great deal of harmonic sophistication, too; he gets as far afield as a cadential A♭ major triad (at 3:18) before a final cadenza swings the music back into E major, then A minor, which heralds a return of the song's final verse.[24] Like Musorgsky's "Old Castle," Lake's "Sage" is quiet but not light: beneath its placid surface lurk profoundly melancholy and disquieting emotional currents.

The Old Castle/Blues Variation. Now ELP turn to Musorgsky's second picture, "The Old Castle." Since there is no need for a second consecutive soft and serious number, the band totally change the movement's character. In order to give Lake time to switch from acoustic guitar to bass, Emerson and Palmer begin "The Old Castle" by launching into a psychedelic freeform jam: Emerson pulls out the Moog's ribbon controller and extracts all manner of other-worldly shrieks, while Palmer bashes away. Just as suddenly, however, they lock into the movement's main groove when Lake enters. The band retain the original key, G♯ minor, and also make some vague reference to the thematic material in measures 29–46 of Musorgsky's score. That's about all they retain,

---

[23] Dowland's lute songs don't contain solo lute passages, nor do his solo lute pieces contain singing: he kept the two genres separate.

[24] This A♭ major triad would seem thoroughly out of place if it did not look back to the previous promenade (centered in A♭ major) and forward to the coming "Old Castle" (centered on G♯ minor, the enharmonic key of A♭ minor), forging a subtle harmonic link between the two movements it has interrupted. Incidentally, the chromatic movement between Aeolian (lowered) sixths and Dorian (raised) sixths at the end of the guitar solo is quite reminiscent of the guitar accompaniment to the verses of "In the Court of the Crimson King."

though. Palmer turns Musorgsky's slow 6/8 into an aggressive 12/8 shuffle pattern, which locks in with Lake's bass guitar ostinato (similar to his part in the final section of "Tank"); Emerson overlays strident, toc-catalike Moog figurines. Occasionally (for instance at 1:11 and again at 2:17) he underlies his melodic figurines with the spacey bass filter growls that he later developed more fully in live performances of "Aquatarkus."

"The Old Castle" moves seamlessly into "Blues Variation," a Hammond/bass/drums blues in C. "Blues Variation" is a high-octane shuffle blues that does, admittedly, enable the band's arrangement of "Old Castle" to rock out to an R & B tinged climax. Nonetheless, I have never been comfortable with the placement of "Blues Variation" here. It is probably the closest ELP ever come to repeating on record the kind of music Emerson had played with the T-Bones or the VIPs, or Palmer had done with Chris Farlowe and the Thunderbirds. As an R & B jam "Blues Variation" is fine; in this context, though, it sounds dreadfully conventional, and doesn't seem to cross-relate with the rest of *Pictures*.[25] It would have worked better, I think, if the band could have more fully melded the R & B syntax of "Blues Variation" with their progressive proclivities: as we'll see, however, it wasn't until later that the band fully arrived at a kind of "progressive blues" synthesis. As it stands here, "Blues Variation" isn't completely integrated into the substance of *Pictures*, and it tends to provide some ammunition to critics who have decried *Pictures* as an awkward pastiche of classical pomp, psychedelic sound effects, and blues-rock jamming.

Promenade. Rather than using one of the later promenades from Musorgsky's score, ELP go back to the opening promenade and reorchestrate it. Emerson uses a grungy, overdriven Hammond timbre of the type used on "The Barbarian" and "Knife-Edge." Lake plays the bass line pretty much straight from the left-hand part of the piano score, although he drops a few of the score's octave leaps. Palmer orchestrates with a very classically inspired, military snare fill style that he was to develop considerably in the coming two years leading up to *Brain Salad Surgery*.

The Hut of Baba Yaga/The Curse of Baba Yaga/The Hut of Baba Yaga. In Russian folklore, Baba Yaga is a witch who lives in a revolving hut supported on four chicken feet. She eats human bones that she grinds up with a mortar and pestle; she also uses the mortar to fly through the air. Hartmann designed a clock in the form of Baba Yaga's hut; what Musorgsky's "Baba Yaga" is depicting, however, is not Hartmann's clock,

---

[25] Stump has made the statement that ELP's "tendency to solo in traditional forms—beginning and ending on downbeats, or using blues voicings—rarely lends the music any passion" (*The Music's All That Matters*, 99). In the sense that Stump intended it (as a sweeping generalization) I find the statement irresponsible, since he gives no examples; however, if he had applied the statement to "Blues Variation," I would have had to agree with him.

but Baba Yaga's ride through the air. What ELP have done here is to interpolate an original song, "The Curse of Baba Yaga," into the middle of Musorgsky's "Hut of Baba Yaga," which they otherwise adhere to rather closely.

"The Hut of Baba Yaga" is one of Musorgsky's boldest creations. Its driving, "barbaric" bass ostinatos, jagged melodic leaps, and harmonically unrelated consecutive triads were to influence many later composers: it's hard to imagine Bartók's "Allegro Barbaro," Stravinsky's *Rite of Spring*, or Holst's "Mars" without the precedent of "Baba Yaga." In fact, the chromatically ascending fourths of the main theme (first head at 0:24 in ELP's recording) may have been one of the inspirations for the pervasive melodic fourths throughout ELP's "Tarkus" suite.

ELP orchestrate "Hut of Baba Yaga" with Hammond, bass, and drums. Lake gives a bravura performance on bass, ably handling the difficult chromatically rising fourths, while Palmer contributes an effective combination of rhythmic doublings, fills, and groove patterns; his chugging bass drum part at 0:59 contributes nicely to the section's climax. Emerson is mostly faithful to Musorgsky's thematic material, occasionally sustaining chords that Musorgsky had repeated in order to make the arrangement more idiomatic for Hammond.

The band's arrangement of the middle section, inscribed *Andante mosso* by Musorgsky, is particularly successful. This extraordinary passage, with its fragmentary bass melodies and eerie tremolo accompaniment, anticipates Bartók's "night music" by almost half a century, and ELP's orchestration further emphasizes the music's eeriness. Lake takes the melody, running his bass through Emerson's Moog and a wah-wah pedal as he had for a similar passage in "The Gnome," while Emerson plays the quiet tremolo on Hammond.[26] As with Musorgsky's original music, the bass melody eventually trails off, leaving the tremolo to slowly descend into a quiet but uneasy atonal wash of sound.

At this point, the band interpolate their original section, "The Curse of Baba Yaga." Out of Emerson's atonal tremolo wash emerges a jazzy bass guitar theme built on an E blues scale (0:53). This is taken up and expanded on by Emerson on modular Moog, after which organ and fuzzed bass launch into the four note riff, D A♭ D A, which dominates the remainder of "Curse." An observant listener will recognize the source of this riff to be the second section of "The Gnome," where the same four notes are heard a half step higher (compare 1:03 of "The Gnome" with

---

[26] The "Gnome" segment and the "Baba Yaga" segment that use synthesized bass both have a strong tritone presence; this may have been a factor in the band's decision to use the same bass sound. At any rate, the synthesized bass passages forge a nice sonic link between "The Gnome" and "Baba Yaga," pointing up musical similarities between the two that aren't as apparent in the original score as in ELP's arrangement.

1:41 of "The Curse of Baba Yaga"). Lake's frantic vocal declamations, which evoke a ghastly *Night of the Living Dead* scenario,[27] and Palmer's lightning fast bass drum barrages give a climactic feel to the section. In this sense, "Curse" fulfills a similar role to "Blues Variation"; the difference is that "Curse" is much more fully integrated into Musorgsky's original music. Not only is its riff figure linked with the "Gnome"; Emerson's chromatically sliding parallel organ triads echo a number of similar passages by Musorgsky. Some of the space rock episodes of "Curse" (listen especially at 3:37), with their throbbing bass octaves, machinelike tom barrages, and otherworldly whooshing and buzzing Moog leads, far surpass "The Old Castle" as a nascent example of the space rock ELP later perfected in their live performances of "Aquatarkus."

In fact, of the first three ELP albums, it is *Pictures* that makes the most innovative use of the synthesizer. Despite Emerson's statement that "I've never used the synthesizer to copy,"[28] in fact the first two albums often do use the Moog as a substitute for orchestral instruments. On *Pictures*, however, there is never any question that the Moog is a Moog, and some of Emerson's applications of the instrument were truly revelatory at the time.

The final space rock interlude of "The Curse of Baba Yaga" serves as a pivot to launch the band back into the final section of Musorgsky's "Hut of Baba Yaga," which is basically a recapitulation of the opening.

The Great Gates of Kiev. Perhaps Victor Hartmann's most impressive surviving work is his design for a ceremonial gateway that he submitted for a competition sponsored by the City Council of Kiev, who wished to commemorate the escape of Czar Alexander II from an assassination attempt on April 4, 1866; however, the competition was called off nearly as soon as it had been announced due to insufficient funds, and no Kievan gate was ever built. Hartmann's design involved an arch resting on two enormous sunken columns; above the arch was an intricate hood capped with the Russian imperial eagle, and to the right of the arch was an imposing bell tower capped by a turret in the form of an old Slavonic war helmet.

In his musical representation of "The Great Gates of Kiev," Musorgsky evokes an Orthodox church ceremonial procession, with fanfares, the clanging of bells, and the chanting of priests. He casts the music into a kind of rondo form, with a hymnlike main theme in E♭ major. The episodes evoke Orthodox liturgical chant, and the wonderful central sec-

---

[27] I have never been able to decipher all the lyrics here.

[28] Keith Emerson, quoted by Milano, "Keith Emerson," *Contemporary Keyboard*, October 1977, 36. In fact, on some material Emerson uses the Moog very much like other contemporaneous keyboard players used the Mellotron, which makes Emerson's refusal to use the Mellotron seem rather arbitrary. I always suspected he eschewed the Mellotron because he found its popular string and choral settings too sentimental and "romantic" for his tastes.

tion, one of the great passages in piano literature, summons the clanging of many bells, out of which rises a final mighty statement of the promenade theme.

Like the second promenade, ELP's arrangement of "The Great Gates" incorporates vocals by Lake. The lyrics, as Blair Pethel politely notes, are "a bit of a disappointment,"[29] and it's hard to disagree with Paul Stump that "the swelling bombast of Lake's lyrics detracts from the otherwise electrifying trio arrangement of the suite's last bloated pages."[30] There is some interesting imagery—I especially like the bit about the "fossil sun" gleaming—and some references to a creation mythos along the lines of the opening of Yes's *Tales of Topographic Oceans;* however, these references aren't coherently developed, and ultimately the lyrics degenerate into empty imagery made worse by the hollow portentousness of the final line, "death is life."[31] Unfortunately, the lyrics are not rescued by Lake's vocal interpretation. Lake's vocal line sticks close to Musorgsky's melody line, but reshapes the rhythm; while this is not a problem, Lake affects a peculiar sliding, "moaning" delivery that is rather irritating.[32]

The subpar lyrics and idiosyncratic vocal delivery are especially galling because there are some very nice musical passages throughout "The Great Gates." The chorale episodes, played by Emerson alone on a flutelike Hammond organ setting, are very effective; even better is the central section, where Emerson achieves a wonderful realization of the bell/promenade passage on Hammond, with Lake's bass and Palmer's tubular bells providing effective offbeat accompaniment. Emerson follows this section with a barrage of organ feedback, which Blair Pethel suggests (rather generously, perhaps) is meant to depict the gates creaking open. Amazingly, though, if you listen carefully at 3:45 you will hear the characteristic rising fourth, falling minor third motive of the promenade theme repeated four times, which miraculously ties the feedback episode into the rest of the movement. Bringing off the final statement of the main theme is a real problem even in Musorgsky's original piano score, since rhythmic motion almost grinds to a halt and it's hard to avoid the impression of anticlimax; I don't think ELP totally avoid the trap, as their conclusion sounds a bit thin, although Emerson's use of organ feedback on the last chord is a nice touch. This is the kind of passage where two years later Emerson would

---

[29] Pethel, "Keith Emerson," 95.

[30] Stump, *The Music's All That Matters,* 100.

[31] Granted, Jesus says something very similar to this on a few occasions, John 12:25–26 being one example. Unlike Lake, though, Jesus gives us a context through which we might understand this apparently contradictory statement. The problem here, as with a number of Lake's other lyrics, is that his Romantic aphorisms are shorn of their original philosophical context and become more or less empty ciphers.

[32] Listen especially to his vocal scoop on "life" in the final "death is life" lyric; also listen to "fire" of "life's fire."

have layered in polyphonic synthesizer over the organ to create a climactic crescendo. In 1971, however, that wasn't a viable solution, as Emerson's Moog was still a monophonic instrument, incapable of playing chords.[33]

The final track of the *Pictures at an Exhibition* LP is "Nutrocker," an instrumental number the band sometimes played as an encore after *Pictures.* "Nutrocker" is an arrangement of an arrangement: in 1962 the number had been a hit for B. Bumble and the Stingers, a group of L.A. sessions men spearheaded by Kim Fowley who had a string of novelty hits in the early sixties based on rearrangements of classical music warhorses. "Nutrocker" is an arrangement of the most memorable theme of the famous *Nutcracker* ballet suite of Peter Tchaikovsky (1840–1893), thus giving the *Pictures* LP an all-Russian compositional lineup. Like the Stingers' other two hits, "Bumble Boogie" and "Boogie Woogie," the idea of "Nutrocker" was to present a well-known classical theme in a boogie context. The piece accomplishes this goal simply enough by presenting a rocked up version of the *Nutcracker* theme at the beginning, following it with a lengthy blues jam, and recapitulating the main theme at the end. In ELP's arrangement, the lead instrument throughout is the clavinet, which lends the work a suitably light and airy ambience; this proves, incidentally, to be the final appearance of this rather charming keyboard in ELP's recorded output.

Pictures at an Exhibition: An Assessment

Of the six albums ELP released during their "classic" period of 1970–1974, *Pictures at an Exhibition* is the most problematic to assess, for four reasons. The first is chronological. In terms of its chronology, *Pictures* is the third ELP release. However, *Pictures* dates back to the earliest days of the band, predating even some of the material on the first album. In fact, it is *Pictures*, rather than the debut album, which shows most clearly the lingering traces of the psychedelic rock style that progressive rock developed out of and away from. Psychedelic influences are evident in the free-form jam at the beginning of "The Old Castle"; in the organ feedback episode near the conclusion of "The Great Gates of Kiev";

---

[33] There were some "tricks" Emerson could use to circumvent the instrument's inability to play more than one note at a time. One such trick was tuning two or three oscillators of his modular Moog to double a melody note at fixed intervals: this is what he did for the march theme of "Aquatarkus," where he played only the melody notes, which the Moog automatically doubled the notes above by major seconds and perfect fourths. In most instances, however, there was not enough time to change oscillator tunings during the performance of a song, so these polyphonic possibilities enjoyed only limited application.

and the blues-rock jamming of "Blues Variation."

Second, *Pictures* was very unusual not only for ELP but for the British progressive rock canon in that until many years after ELP's halcyon days there was no studio release that served as a definitive touchstone against which live performances could be evaluated.[34] The live performance featured on the third album simply captures the work in a particular stage of its development, just as the live recordings from Isle of Wight and London Lyceum represent earlier stages, and recordings made of the work at Cal Jam in 1974 and at Montreal in 1977, later stages. It is fairly easy to see today that part of the charm of the *Pictures* LP is that it captured *Pictures* at the zenith of its trajectory; the earlier versions sound undeveloped by comparison, the later versions facile (1973–74 World Tour and the abbreviated *Return of the Manticore* studio recording), or simply exhausted (the awful 1977 orchestral version of *Emerson, Lake and Palmer in Concert*). However, in 1971 it was far from self-evident that *Pictures* had reached its zenith. Greg Lake once commented that in his view studio albums stand in the same relation to tours as a check stands to cash: in each case, the former is merely a promise to deliver payment in the form of the latter.[35] This attitude is more representative of late 1960s thinking than of later attitudes.[36] Lake's remarks highlight how live performances for ELP and, I daresay, for nearly all of the major British rock bands active circa 1965–75, served as a living, breathing *commentary* on the music, rather than a stylized, cabaretlike (or maybe museumlike) *presentation* of the music—which, alas, seems to be what most performances by established rock artists have become since the 1980s.

The third difficulty in assessing *Pictures* involves stylistic and conceptual issues. In terms of the former, in arranging *Pictures*, the band had to make decisions as to which parts of the piece would work in a rock context and which wouldn't, in the end changing the overall structure into something rather different from Musorgsky's original conception. Since the band eliminated so many of the pictures, there are fewer peaks and valleys than in Musorgsky's original score, and it may be, as Allan Moore has claimed in his discussion of ELP's arrangement of the work, that the triumphalism of "The Great Gates of Kiev" is not adequately prepared for in ELP's revised format.[37] Perhaps he's correct, although I think ELP's pacing takes on a logic of its own: the general plan is to create a series of

---

[34] In 1993 the band recorded a much shorter studio version of the suite for inclusion on the *Return of the Manticore* box set.

[35] Lake makes this comment during the ELP Video Biography.

[36] Again, the attitude, if not the resulting music, reminds me of the Grateful Dead.

[37] See Moore's *Rock: The Primary Text; Developing a Musicology of Rock* (Buckingham, U.K.: Open University Press, 1993). I do think a problem with Moore's analysis is that he sees some sort of symmetry in ELP's placement of blues-based numbers at the end of sides one

exponentially bigger climaxes, starting with "The Gnome" and proceeding through "Blues Variation," "Baba Yaga," and "The Great Gates," and if the final climax of "Gates" doesn't quite cut it, I think it's a problem with the arrangement of that particular section, rather than a flaw in the band's overall structural treatment of *Pictures*. On the whole, I think the band's arrangement works. I consider "The Gnome," "The Sage," and the "Baba Yaga" segments to be wholly successful, and I think the three distinct treatments of the promenade theme are tasteful and intelligent. As I said above, I have my doubts about the "Old Castle/Blues Variation" segment, and I think the closing section of "Gates" could have profitably been reworked.

In terms of assessing the album conceptually, the difficulty is that *Pictures* is the only ELP album that is essentially devoted to the reinterpretation of an existing work, classical or otherwise. Granted, throughout their existence the band covered classical pieces. In all other instances, though, ELP's classical covers must be evaluated in the context of their placement on albums largely devoted to original material: on *Pictures*, even the lyrics and cover art were shaped with a view towards fitting the preexisting music. Lake did have the opportunity to make Pictures be about something specific through his lyrics: however, he didn't avail himself to the opportunity. Granted, the first two lyrics (the second Promenade and "The Sage") explore issues of fate and predestination. While Lake's musings about predestination don't exactly have the depth of Saint Augustine's or John Calvin's and his somewhat stoic, fatalistic "philosophy" may be a bit sophomoric, the lyrics do at least go beyond repeating the *Book of the Dead* aphorisms that were popular at the time and present a more or less coherent and sustained point of view. The same cannot be said, alas, of the last two lyrics. So much as the lyrics of "The Curse of Baba Yaga" are even decipherable, they seem to involve a sci-fi horror story that doesn't tie in with anything else on the album. About the lyrics of "The Great Gates of Kiev" I have already spoken. As a whole Lake's lyrics for *Pictures* do not appear to develop any unified concept—unless the concept is very cleverly disguised indeed.

More successful than Lake's lyrics is William Neal's cover art. Neal, you may recall, was the artist who rendered the memorable cover art of *Tarkus*, and he comes through again here. The outside of the album shows a series of empty picture frames, labeled with the titles of the movements ("The Gnome," "The Sage," etc.). When you open the album up,

---

and two of the LP format, as if these were the two climactic points towards which the preceding material is heading. In fact, "Nutrocker" wasn't even always played at the end of performances of *Pictures* in the early 1970s—at the London Lyceum performance of December 9, 1970, captured on the *Pictures at an Exhibition* movie, for instance, the band plays "Knife-Edge," not "Nutrocker," as the encore to *Pictures*.

the inner gatefold shows the same frames with the pictures installed: Neal's pictures update Hartmann's conceptions in a fantasy/science fiction vein that I think nicely compliments ELP's arrangement. "The Gnome" and "The Sage" both present their subjects austerely, almost as intricately detailed wood carvings, in a manner that parallels the archaism of Lake's "The Sage." By comparison, the other pictures are decidedly futuristic. "The Old Castle" shows a castle perched atop a high hill which is drifting in the depths of outer space, anticipating Roger Dean's influential fusion of medieval and outer space motifs (*Pictures* was released a month before *Fragile*, Dean's first effort with Yes). "The Hut of Baba Yaga" depicts a weird metallic birdhouse on the same bleached psychedelic plain that is depicted on the cover of *Tarkus*. "The Curse of Baba Yaga" shows an army of horrible alien creatures, with a menacing UFO overhead. "The Great Gates of Kiev" features two unimaginably enormous metallic gates separating two totally different alien landscapes, with Lake's "fossil sun" gleaming in the distance. (I'm assuming the two gates of Neal's picture prompted the band to rename Musorgsky's "The Great Gate of Kiev" as "The Great Gates of Kiev.") The "Promenade" frame is left empty: I always thought it would have been clever to insert a photo of the trio ambling through an art gallery. Unlike *Tarkus*, Neal's drawings here don't convey a narrative concept: what they do is graphically illustrate that what ELP's *Pictures at an Exhibition* is really all about is updating a well-known classical work in the context of late 1960s rock culture.

This brings us to the final and thorniest issue in assessing the *Pictures* LP: the issue of how the album's unusual premise impacted its critical reception. As we have seen, even in the early 1970s there was a contingent of critics, including Lester Bangs, Robert Christgau, and Dave Marsh, who regarded the then-emerging progressive rock style with disdain, seeing it as an effete, manneristic, evolutionary dead end, and who assured their readers that prog's links to high culture could prove to be the death knell of rock and roll. For these critics, ELP's *Pictures at an Exhibition*, with its reliance on and celebration of classical music, was a kind of "poster boy" for everything that they saw as wrong with progressive rock. Thus in the 1979 edition of *The Rolling Stone Record Guide*, *Pictures* is awarded zero stars—lower even than such admitted ELP bombs as *Love Beach*, which received two stars!

The fact is, any even halfway impartial assessment of *Pictures* must acknowledge two major points in its favor. As I myself have admitted, *Pictures* does not present the strongest possible argument for the marriage of rock's power with classical music's thematic intricacy and expansive structures: while ELP's arrangement of the piece has some real triumphs, it also has some undeniable weaknesses. And this is not so surprising. It is, after all, the band's earliest group statement, release chronology notwithstanding. However, even a casual listener cannot fail to miss the astonishing tightness and discipline of the band's live performance: despite all the critical talk of "bloated egos," there is really little overextension and solo indulgence here, excepting only "Old Castle/Blues Variation." Furthermore, even the band's harshest foes, if they were to be halfway honest, would have to admit that sonically, *Pictures* is probably the sharpest sounding live rock album of the early 1970s. With Eddy Offord once again engineering and Lake producing, the balance is superb, the presence is surprisingly good: Emerson's Hammond, in particular, never sounded this rich and powerful in a live recording again, and Lake's vocals are much livelier and more up front here than in the two live albums recorded later in the decade. Both of these strengths were in fact acknowledged in Chris Welch's review, which ran in the November 27, 1971, issue of *Melody Maker*:

> Perhaps all groups should record live at Newcastle City Hall. The sound is incredible. The music apart, this is one of the best live recordings I can recall, and full credit must go to engineer and producer [respectively], Eddy Offord and Greg Lake . . . All three were playing particularly well on the gig, and despite the fury of the tempos and complexities of time changes, they still hold themselves together and don't give way to natural adrenalin that can result in uneven tempo, detuning and all the other hazards of "live" recordings that sound okay at the time, but can be exposed later . . . It's a vastly entertaining and absorbing performance, and one of the finest British group albums of the year.[38]

Lest the reader assume that Welch was the band's only prominent supporter in a sea of hostile critics, here is Roy Carr's review from the December 4, 1971, issue of *New Musical Express*:

> Despite the fact that they have already enjoyed tremendous international success with two studio-engineered albums, this long promised bonus release confirms that ELP are undoubtedly a "live" attraction. I've never heard them play so well, not on record anyway and for this reason alone (not the low cost) it should outsell their somewhat over-produced studio efforts.
>
> *Pictures at an Exhibition*, which is ELP's liberal adaptation of Musorgsky's original work, is a perfect showcase for their musical flamboyancy, for in both their individual and unit roles, Keith Emerson, Greg Lake, and Carl Palmer play with much more vigor, exuberance, and freedom than one would suspect from their initial releases.
>
> Emerson pulls out all the stops as he moves swiftly around his many keyboards and generates even more excitement when adding his Moog and other electronic devices for effect. Lake actually sounds as though he's enjoying himself while Palmer complements his mates and throws in one or two extras

---

[38] Chris Welch, "ELP Exhibit Themselves," *Melody Maker*, November 27, 1971.

for good luck.

Expertly recorded by Eddy Offord, this album is one of those rare collections on which both the sound and atmospheric excitement has been faithfully captured. And if that isn't enough, ELP's encore "Nutrocker" maintains the listener's interest until the very end.[39]

Even some of their previous detractors came on board for *Pictures*, as is evident in this review that ran in the December 18, 1971, issue of *Record Mirror*:

ELP's considerable musicianship has never impressed me on anything more than an appreciative nodding level. Their first two albums are too cold to my mind, and what ELP fans will surely point out is fiery music merely strikes me as being an exercise in dexterity.

But . . . things change. Here's a thoroughly enjoyable album, recorded before an enthusiastic Newcastle City Hall audience, and made even more desirable by its low price tag of £1.49. Based on Musorgsky's *Pictures at an Exhibition*, with additions by both Keith Emerson and Greg Lake, it manages to sustain interest throughout its various sequences. Especially interesting are Emerson's Moog expeditions. He seems to have a quite exceptional feel for this monstrously beautiful and complicated instrument and it only adds weight to his reputation as a keyboard player that the Moog's abstractness is employed so well here. Excellent stuff for the fan . . . and possibly the one to convert unbelievers.[40]

So why, several years later, did *Rolling Stone Record Guide* rate *Pictures* lower than such an admittedly lame album as *Love Beach*? I suggest that what was really being attacked was ELP's musical ideology, since on no other album is it so blatantly presented. Let's face it: if ELP had chosen to cover, say, Miles Davis's *Kind of Blue*, or Cream's "Pressed Rat and Warthog," the rancor wouldn't have been as keen. But the idea of "rocking the classics" was more than many of the critics could bear.

Issues of Critical Ideology, Part 2: Rock-Classical Fusion and the Expansion of Rock's Musical Vocabulary

Readers familiar with *Rocking the Classics* may recall that I see three main purposes behind prog rock's appropriation of classical forms and techniques during the late 1960s and early 1970s period. First, classical forms allowed a "stretching out" over far longer time spans than previous pop

---

[39] Roy Carr, review of *Pictures at an Exhibition*, *New Musical Express*, December 4, 1971.
[40] Unsigned review of *Pictures at an Exhibition*, *Record Mirror*, December 18, 1971.

forms, which was appropriate, even necessary, for the visionary/philosophical concerns of the late sixties. Second, such expanded forms also allowed musicians to impose a sense of structure and focused progression to the hallucinogen-induced psychedelic jams of the time. Finally, classical forms allowed European musicians to contribute (not impose) something of their own cultural heritage to the syntax of rock music, which, it seems to me, resulted in a more, not less, honest aesthetic.[41] In short, the real purpose of drawing on classical forms and structures at the time was to open up a new set of possibilities for rock music that were better suited to expressing contemporary concerns and attitudes than were pre-countercultural popular music forms.

The problem for ELP was that they were musicians, not musical polemicists. Granted, Emerson often articulated the desirability of exploring new stylistic frontiers by fusing elements of rock, jazz, classical, and folk styles into an overarching megastyle. This line of thought is evident in his liner notes for the Nice's *Five Bridges*, where he talks of building "musical bridges," and is also evident in some of his interviews from the same period where he talks of his desire to draw elements of classical music and jazz, which he considered to be remnants of extinct cultural conditions, into contemporary rock music. The following remark, made by Emerson in the waning days of the Nice, is perhaps the clearest articulation of his vision of a megastyle in which the parameters of rock, jazz, and classical music are transcended: "Basically we feel that there are elements of music which are dying out in the sense they're becoming less popular—jazz and classical music in some forms are in danger of dying out because they don't relate to the things of today. We're taking these elements, adapting them to our own style, and joining them to make a new kind of music."[42] However, such remarks were too vague to satisfy the critics, because they never clearly articulated *why* a classical/rock fusion was a logical or a desirable development of late-sixties/early-seventies cultural currents.

I suspect the critical reception of ELP would have been somewhat different if Emerson had possessed Robert Fripp's philosophical bent and (at times) devastating sarcasm. Unlike Emerson, Fripp articulated his musical philosophy clearly, wittily defended himself from the attacks of the igno-

---

[41] I realize the following is a loaded question, but it seems to me it's a crucial one: why are bands like the Rolling Stones, who shamelessly (and sometimes unscrupulously) pilfered from African American music, celebrated, while bands like ELP and Yes, who attempted to fuse African American forms with the European cultural forms they grew up with to create something genuinely "third-stream," lambasted? Attempting to answer this rhetorical question resurrects the whole issue of the rock critical establishment's rather dubious notion of "authenticity": see *Rocking the Classics*, 170–72, or chapter 10 of the present work.

[42] Keith Emerson, re-quoted by Hanson, *Hang on to a Dream*, 109–10.

rant, and could be just as much of an intellectual monster as his critic assailants: as a result, even the most strident antiprogressive critics of the 1970s accorded Fripp a measure of respect. Unfortunately, although he was the band's oldest member and its creative figurehead, Emerson never really assumed his natural role as the band's spokesman. Although he invariably served as a witty and dryly humorous MC during ELP's shows of the seventies, and could be very precise and coherent when discussing matters of equipment or musical technique, he often seemed at a loss for words when asked to articulate an overarching philosophical perspective that would connect ELP's music to culture at large. There seemed to be a running debate among rock journalists of the seventies as to whether Lake or Palmer was the band's most personable member and easiest talker; there was an almost universal consensus, however, that Emerson was neither. As one critic noted, "Keith Emerson doesn't allow too many deeper thoughts to come forward, especially when a cassette machine is switched on; he keeps himself well within a bland, reticent exterior."[43] Emerson himself once remarked, "I can never seem to express myself the way I want to: it isn't the writer's fault, it's mine."[44] Lake and Palmer did their best to step in and fill the vacuum, but their answers to journalists' more probing questions—which Emerson, as the band's creative figure- head, would have been in a better position to answer—often come across as somewhat unreflective.

To their credit, the band showed genuine principle in their determina- tion, as Greg Lake put it, that "we wouldn't retaliate and we wouldn't get bitter" when faced with hostile reviews.[45] However, there is no reason this laudable goal would have prevented them from clearly explaining their musical choices: ELP would have done themselves a great favor to spend some time articulating a coherent presentation of their musical philoso- phy. Instead, they often let critics' slanders go unanswered, and when they did choose to break their silence, their defense of their music often comes across as naïve and less than coherent, especially in the face of a hostile and manipulative interviewer like Lester Bangs.

In his stunningly cynical and bizarrely vituperative article on ELP in the March 1974 issue of *Creem*,[46] based on an interview he conducted with Lake and Palmer, Bangs pointedly asked whether ELP considered their concerts to be entertainment or art, and cackled with disdain when

---

[43] James Johnson, "Fingers' Cave," *New Musical Express*, January 19, 1974, 11.

[44] Judith Sims, "ELP . . . What? ELP! . . . What? ELP . . . ," *Rolling Stone*, April 25, 1974, 18.

[45] Greg Lake, quoted by Cameron Crowe, "Greg Lake Interview," *Hit Parader*, Winter 1974/75, 73.

[46] Emerson was already upset with the magazine and refused to participate in the interview; he took exception to a review of *Pictures at an Exhibition* by Alan Neister that had run in *Creem*.

Lake gave the rather confused answers "entertainment," since "it's not art in the same way as painting a picture."[47] Bangs's real coup, however, came when Palmer justified the band's arrangement of *Pictures* by saying, "we hope if anything we're encouraging the kids to listen to music that has more quality."[48] (Keep in mind, too, Emerson's similar remark, quoted above, that he wanted to use *Pictures* as "an educational piece, exposing our audiences to this great work of classical music.") Palmer's unwise and admittedly naïve response allows Bangs to launch into one of his two main indictments, ELP's "insidious befoulment of all that was gutter pure in rock."[49] (His other main indictment, the supposed lack of emotion in ELP's music, will be discussed in chapter 10.) A good deal of space during the remainder of the "interview," if one wants to call it that ("hatchet job" seems more accurate), is spent outlining how ELP stole a once vibrant and subversive genre, rock and roll, from the masses, attempted to spruce it up with a veneer of classical influence in order to win the approbation of bourgeois culture, and made it sterile and effete in the process— an attitude we have already considered in connection with *Tarkus.*

I will briefly quote Bangs here, if for no other reason than to disabuse readers of the notion that he was a witty and original intellectual who turned out provocative and scintillating commentary on the seventies rock scene: "When most people get ready to make with the R-C [rock-classical] Fusion they generally approach it by way of 'upgrading' rock. Whereas, I said, I get the feeling that ELPs [sic] are after just the opposite. And I admire the piss outta them for it! What could be *more* fun than tromping up and down Musorgsky's spine for 45 minutes or so?"[50]

Bangs's cynicism and pseudo-hip intellectual "criticism" aside, there is no denying that ELP earn an "F" in music polemics. This should not be an excuse to dismiss their music outright. Anyone who has read Richard Wagner's bombastic and turgid treatises on music and drama (*Music and Drama, The Art Work of the Future*) is keenly aware that he was by no means the great philosopher/polemicist he believed himself to be. That does not in one whit affect the musical quality of such masterpieces as *Tristan and Isolde* or *The Meistersinger*, which succeed just as often in spite

---

[47] Greg Lake, quoted by Bangs, "Exposed!" 43. Somehow I can't imagine Robert Fripp answering Bangs in these terms.

[48] Bangs, "Exposed!" 44. I can only add that I deplore the cultlike scene that is posthumously developing around Bangs—witness Jim DeRogatis's *Let it Blurt: The Life and Times of Lester Bangs, America's Greatest Rock Critic* (New York: Bantam Doubleday, 2000)—that is attempting to somehow transform him into a wit and presciently insightful cultural critic, a kind of late-twentieth-century George Bernard Shaw. About the best I can say for Bangs is that his pseudo-hip Brooklyn slang and pervasive cynicism have influenced most, perhaps all, major rock critics since the midseventies.

[49] Bangs, "Exposed!" 44.

[50] Ibid.

of as because of his theories. Likewise, Ralph Vaughan Williams's writings on nationalism and music (e.g., *National Music*) make some highly arguable assertions about the relationship between national folk styles and "great" classical music. However, Vaughan Williams's arguable polemics in no wise lessens the success of works such as his *Pastoral Symphony*, which seamlessly blend English folksong sensibility and large-scale structural demands.

In short, if ELP's *Pictures at an Exhibition* were nothing more than an attempt to "upgrade" rock music with a veneer of classical forms and techniques, I might be tempted to be nearly as dismissive as Lester Bangs. But that's not really the point of *Pictures*, even if the band members seem to make it the point in their rather lame polemical defense. To be sure, I don't think *Pictures* represents the greatest achievement of either progressive rock or ELP. What it does do, however, is to offer a forum for an early, and a largely successful, exploration of the applications of classical structures and techniques of thematic development to rock music composition. In that sense, I think *Pictures* is an important milestone not only in ELP's growth, but also in the development of progressive rock as a style. In the early days of ELP, Keith Emerson referred to the band's arrangement of *Pictures* as a blueprint for their later work together, in terms that capture its real importance far more coherently and concisely than any talk of "improving the classics" or "bringing the kids quality music":

> When we started playing in England, *Pictures* was like a blueprint to get the group's musical direction together. Mainly just to get out a whole thing and play it together. We had to learn how to play together because we hadn't really got a system of writing our own music. It takes a long time for musicians to understand each other's musical thinking and be able to sort of put them together. It's only since *Tarkus* that we really got into a good system of writing together, so *Pictures* was like a first stage.[51]

ELP's arrangement of *Pictures* also performed a great service for later progressive rock musicians, even those of a more experimental bent, in its exploration of applications of classical structural techniques in a rock context, as Henry Cow's drummer, Chris Cutler, has acknowledged.[52]

However, I reject Cutler's assertion that ELP's treatment of the classics was invariably "backward looking" or simply nostalgic.[53] If ELP looked back, they were also looking forward. ELP and other progressive rock musicians of the time wished to express the visionary, utopian, and prophetic concerns of the late-1960s/early-1970s counterculture. For

---

[51] Keith Emerson, quoted by Schact, "Emerson, Lake and Palmer," 5.
[52] See Stump, *The Music's All That Matters*, 142.
[53] Ibid.

most of the twentieth century (since the end of World War I, to be precise), such ideals had, on the whole, been fashionable neither with musicians (or other artists) nor with society at large. The last time such ideals *had* held strong currency with artists and with society at large—in the nineteenth century—they had been expressed by composers from Beethoven to Wagner to Mahler and Richard Strauss through the parameters of classical musical culture. By the 1960s, though, the larger culture which had produced classical music was extinct, and classical music's circumscribed place in contemporary society no longer allowed the composer a forum to address contemporary concerns in a way that would reach any kind of large audience—especially a younger audience. It may be a truism, but it bears repeating—by the late 1960s rock music was *the* contemporary music of Western culture. By integrating elements of classical music into rock, bands such as ELP opened up a new set of possibilities for expressing the visionary, utopian, and even "prophetic" concerns of late-1960s/early-1970s culture in a contemporary artistic medium that would resonate with a mass audience.[54] Since these concerns couldn't be fully expressed through the rock music syntax that ELP and their peers had inherited, they fundamentally altered the parameters of rock music syntax. What could be more forward looking than that?[55]

Beyond making the vocabulary and conceptual conventions of classical music available to rock musicians, a major contribution of *Pictures*—and by extension, the entire progressive rock project—was to blur the boundaries between "classical" and "popular," between "art" and "entertainment," and to question the assumed categories of European/classical/art on the one hand and African American/popular/entertainment on the other. Around the same time Bangs worried that ELP were "befouling all that was gutter pure in rock," David Ernst put forth an extraordinarily lucid and eloquent summation of the utopian synthesists' ideology which, although it was already giving way to the blues orthodoxy of Bangs and his peers, is, in my view, a far more accurate assessment than Bangs's of what was really happening in progressive rock during the early 1970s:

> The urge to extend the song form to encompass long temporal durations had already been manifested in the music of Zappa, the Grateful Dead, and Yes, and the 1970s have seen the proliferation of this type of music. The desire to

---

[54] For a fuller understanding of the sense in which I'm using the term "prophetic" here, see the excellent passage in Martin, *Listening to the Future*, 121.

[55] As Bill Martin points out in his consideration of Cutler's comments, there are some artists and thinkers (he cites Plato, Kant, and Beethoven, among others) whose ideas will probably never be passé: revisiting, revising, and renewing the work of such figures for one's own generation can be an inherently forward-looking enterprise, if and when cultural conditions demand it. See Martin, *Listening to the Future*, 114–15.

create large compositional structures is due at least in part to these perform-ers' musical training. It can be considered another step toward the fulfillment of [avant-garde composer Karlheinz] Stockhausen's ideal of a universal music. All musical styles are gradually being amalgamated into a single framework, so that the categorization of music as classical, jazz, rock, and folk has begun to lose its significance.[56]

In a review of ELP's Gaelic Park concert of September 1, 1971 (the one where Robert Moog and Emerson met for the first time), Jody Breslaw of *Sounds* expresses a vision of utopian synthesis similar to Ernst's, a vision that's diametrically opposed to the rigid and exclusive blues orthodoxy of Bangs and his peers:

> ELP have grown to be an exciting trio, playing fine rock with a hint of jazz. The theatrical aspects of ELP's concert moves them out of the class of ordi-nary rock musicians.
>
> The syntheses which can be said to have succeeded in the fullest sense, opening new possibilities for the future, are those for which the label "rock" no longer applies. Keith Emerson and Frank Zappa are writing and playing modern music—not rock, not jazz, not classical, but a sophisticated, complex brand of music, which is still in a state of transition. Working in what is largely unexplored territory, both are occasionally guilty of lapses of taste, lack of economy of expression, and loss of control over an almost too great variety of material. Nonetheless, the unique creative thrust of their music offers what is probably a dramatic preview of things to come.[57]

Were Bangs alive today, he would almost certainly breathe a sigh of relief to see that progressive rock's eclectic impulse, and the whole utopian ideal of a "universal music," did not succeed. Critics like Bangs, Dave Marsh, Robert Christgau, and Simon Frith proved enormously successful in establishing their interpretation of progressive rock—as an evolutionary dead-end, an effete attempt to "upgrade" rock which thankfully failed— as a central tenet of orthodox rock history.[58] Ironically, in so doing they have performed a singular service for the cultural conservatism that they claim to oppose: by denigrating progressive rock's utopian eclecticism, they have insured that the old categories of European/classical/art and African American/popular/entertainment continue to survive unscathed,

---

[56] David Ernst, *The Evolution of Electronic Music* (New York: Schirmer Books, 1977), 209.
[57] Jody Breslaw, review of ELP's 9-1-71 Gaelic Park Concert, *Sounds*, October 9, 1971, reprinted in Emerson, *Pictures*, 216.
[58] The two most "authoritative" sources of orthodox rock history are Anthony DeCurtis, James Henke, and Holly George-Warren, eds., *The Rolling Stone Illustrated History of Rock & Roll*, 3rd ed. (New York: Summit Books, 1992), and the ten-part PBS television series on the history of rock that aired in 1995—which strikes me as basically a video documentary version of *The Rolling Stone History of Rock and Roll*.

since these categories will not be superseded until it becomes critically acceptable to blur them. Furthermore, progressive rock's eclecticism had radical corporate ramifications, too: had it succeeded, the music industry's modern strategy of marketing its "product" to demographically defined "taste publics" and ignoring music that can't immediately be pigeonholed into one of the industry's predefined niches wouldn't have emerged, at least not so quickly and definitively. By defeating the eclectic impulse of seventies prog, critics guaranteed the emergence of rigid market categories in the eighties, nineties, and beyond, which have been a great boon for the industry—but which have robbed audiences and artists alike of choice and opportunities for innovation.

Fathers of Progressive Rock? ELP and the Emergence of the Progressive Rock Style

The release of the *Pictures at an Exhibition* LP marks the conclusion of the earliest phase of ELP's career. By November 1971, the band were already beginning to lay down tracks for the next studio album, *Trilogy*, which signaled a new stage in their music's development. Even if the band had never released another album after *Pictures*, though, their influence would have been enormous; I don't think it's unfair to say that in the eighteen-month period between their first practice sessions in June 1970 and the American release of *Pictures* in January 1972, they were more responsible than any other single band for shaping the emerging progressive rock style.

If this seems an extravagant claim, consider the following. Pink Floyd and Genesis were still largely unknown in the U.S. at this time: Pink Floyd's first top-forty album in the U.S. came in 1973, Genesis's, in 1976.[59] King Crimson had entered the wilderness period of the *Islands* lineup by 1971, and appeared to be headed for ignominious extinction. Van der Graaf Generator had begun a long hiatus after their heartbreaking failure to convert their huge popularity in Italy into a substantial U.S. or U.K. following. Jethro Tull were still more of a blues- and folk-based band at this time, with *Thick as a Brick* and *Passion Play* yet to come. Gentle Giant and Curved Air were struggling to break into the U.S. market—a task at which neither ever really succeeded—and were at best cult acts during the 1970–71 period. The explosion of Italian progressive rock was just beginning during the latter half of this period; Magma and Gong

---

[59] Keith Emerson had, in fact, plugged Genesis's *Nursery Cryme* LP in 1971 as a favor to his old manager, Tony Stratton Smith, who now managed Genesis; at the time, it was clearly a matter of a famous musician plugging an up-and-coming but largely unknown group. See Janis Schact, *Genesis* (London: Proteus Books, 1984), 24.

were unknown outside of France, and cult acts inside of it; the Dutch band Focus were just beginning to forge an international reputation. Consider all this, and you will begin to grasp how influential ELP were during this period in defining the rapidly emerging progressive rock style. Yes were emerging as ELP's primary rival for the progressive rock throne, but until 1972 they were clearly junior partners, and had in fact opened for ELP on some of the band's 1971 American shows.[60]

So what was the nature of ELP's contribution during this period? First, Emerson completed the task he had begun with the Nice, bringing the keyboard player to a level of parity with the guitarist in rock music at large. Certainly, Emerson's flamboyant stage shows in the early days of ELP demonstrated that the keyboard player could convey just as domineering and "sexy" a stage presence as the most charismatic guitarist, and Emerson's keyboard parts dominate ELP's soundscapes just as completely as the guitar playing of Jimi Hendrix and Eric Clapton had dominated the music of the Experience and Cream, respectively. Furthermore, he firmly established the place of the synthesizer not only in prog, but in popular music generally, and opened up a whole new universe of sounds. I will not necessarily argue that Keith Emerson was the greatest synthesist of the 1970s (here I'm talking about extracting the instrument's coloristic possibilities to maximum advantage, not about technical facility on the keyboard). However, the general division in Emerson's early work between using the synthesizer as a substitute for traditional instruments on the one hand and extracting "spacey" sounds from it on the other provided a useful working model for all later popular music synthesists to follow, and it is unarguable that ELP were the first rock band to make the sound of the synthesizer a crucial component of their music, *Pictures* having accomplished this by 1971.

They made other contributions, too. The production values of their debut album, in particular, upped the ante for everybody who followed. Their virtuosic ensemble arrangements set a new standard in rock: the later achievements of Yes, for instance, were built on the foundation laid out in *Tarkus*.[61] Furthermore, ELP were probably more responsible than any other band for making the discourse of classical music available to

---

[60] Yes's first top-forty American album, *The Yes Album*, charted in January 1972, a week before *Pictures* hit the charts; their first top-ten American album, *Fragile*, hit the charts soon thereafter, in February 1972. Yes definitely opened for ELP on November 13, 1971, at Philadelphia's Spectrum; they may have opened for ELP at other shows, too.

[61] This is not to denigrate in any way the astonishing ensemble virtuosity on some of the tracks from the debut King Crimson album (e.g., "21st Century Schizoid Man"); however, Crimson were a looser, more improvisatory band than ELP, and there's no doubt that ELP's tightly arranged approach (here I'm thinking especially of the instrumental sections of *Tarkus* or something like "The Gnome" or "Baba Yaga" from *Pictures*) was to be more influential on later progressive rock.

rock musicians. By helping to create a truly idiomatic use of classical forms and techniques in a rock context,[62] ELP bequeathed rock musicians a new and important means of fully addressing the visionary and utopian concerns that were central to the late-1960s/early-1970s counterculture: this is the real importance of their attempt to blur the boundaries between classical and rock styles. And, as I hope I have demonstrated once and for all, ELP drew not just from the more conventional nineteenth-century Romantic and eighteenth-century baroque sources, but also from the defamiliarizing and challenging modernism of composers like Bartók and Ginastera.

Finally, while I don't think that ELP's classical arrangements are the most crucial aspect of their musical legacy—as I pointed out in *Rocking the Classics*, their frequent arrangements of classical war-horses invited the critics' charge that they were a novelty band driven by this single idea—the fact is their classical arrangements *are* qualitatively different from the attempts of other bands to "rock the classics."[63] Listen to ELP's "The Barbarian" and then compare it to something like the Electric Light Orchestra's arrangement of Grieg's "Hall of the Mountain King," and you will begin to discern a qualitative difference. The latter *is* a novelty track that simply puts a rock beat underneath a well-known classical melody. ELP, on the other hand, have taken the structural and thematic essences of the Bartók piece and successfully transferred them to a rock context. That is to say, "The Barbarian" is genuine rock music that seamlessly melds structural and thematic elements from classical music: to point to just two examples, notice how seamlessly Emerson blends his own blues-based solo lines with Bartók's chord structure during the track's climax, and how effortlessly the band transform Bartók's main theme into a characteristically heavy rock rhythm. While ELP's classical arrangements are certainly not the most important part of their musical legacy, they are an important part of it nonetheless.

---

[62] As opposed to the late-1960s "symphonic rock" of the Moody Blues' *Days of Future Passed* or Deep Purple's *Concerto for Group and Orchestra*, which simply alternate, as opposed to integrate, classical and rock discourses.

[63] See Macan, *Rocking the Classics*, 168.

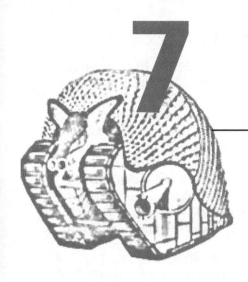

Trilogy

(1972)

Although ELP had begun recording tracks for a new studio album in November, 1971, most of the material which was eventually to be included on *Trilogy*, the band's fourth album, was recorded during January, 1972—once again at London's Advision Studios. The music of *Trilogy* reflects the modestly expanded instrumental setups of both Emerson and Palmer. During 1971, Emerson added a Minimoog Model D to his keyboard arsenal. The Minimoog was the Moog Company's first small, portable, and relatively affordable synthesizer: it proved phenomenally popular, and by the mid-1970s it was an ubiquitous presence in virtually every style of popular music. Emerson's interest in the instrument was the expanded flexibility it offered him in live performance. In terms of sound possibilities, there was nothing the Minimoog could do that the modular Moog couldn't—quite the contrary. However, having the Minimoog available in a live setting allowed him to play two different synthesizer parts at the same time: at a point when Emerson was beginning to chafe at the modular Moog's monophonic limitations, this offered him significant new possibilities. In his *Trilogy* era performances, the Minimoog sat on top of the Hammond L-100, opposite the Hammond C-3 and modular Moog: now he could play the C-3 and L-100, the C-3 and modular Moog, or the Minimoog and modular Moog simultaneously.[1] He also used the Minimoog on certain tracks of the *Trilogy* LP where he wished to layer synthesizer parts in a manner that could be realized in live performance.

Palmer, for his part, abandoned his Ludwig five-piece set in favor of the new Ludwig Octoplus kit, which featured several toms of different

---

[1] There is a nice photo of this particular keyboard setup on pp. 12–13 of the *Return of the Manticore* booklet; Emerson is playing the Hammond C-3, which the modular Moog is sitting on top of, and the Minimoog and Hammond L-100 are to his back.

sizes. Again, the key phrase was "expanded possibilities." In a three-piece band where the drummer's role was as much about melodic and textural presence as time keeping, the five-piece kit had become limiting. As will be seen, to Palmer's credit, the expanded kit did not become an excuse to simply take up more sonic space with thirty-second note fills played clockwise around the toms. To the contrary, Palmer's drumming shows a new restraint on *Trilogy*, with the extra drums being used to explore the more subtle melodic possibilities of doubling Emerson's and Lake's figures.

Trilogy returned to the premise of the band's debut album, featuring a number of discrete tracks contrasted by style, mood, and instrumentation, as Emerson pointed out in an interview that ran in the March 1972 issue of *Circus*:

> We've already recorded what we consider our third album [actually their fourth, but their third studio album], and it's totally different from *Tarkus*. There's no total concept on either side. There are individual pieces which have no connection with each other at all. There's a cowboy song ["The Sheriff"], a hoe-down type number ["Hoedown"], and there's a fugue which I wrote and another very grand piece of music [this could refer to either the "Endless Enigma" suite or "Abaddon's Bolero"]. They all differ.[2]

The band initially hoped to use artwork by the famed Spanish surrealist Salvador Dali for the cover of *Trilogy*. When Dali's fee proved prohibitive, the band approached Hipgnosis, a design firm under the direction of Storm Thorgerson and Aubrey Powell, who were responsible for the cover art of the Nice's last two albums (*Five Bridges* and *Elegy*); by 1972 they were renowned for their work with a number of well-known bands, particularly Pink Floyd. The cover features a painting of Emerson, Lake, and Palmer in which the musicians' Grecian-style busts have been fused together in the manner of Siamese twins. (Or would that be Siamese triplets?) This marked the first time the band included pictures of themselves on an ELP album: during this era such a move remained unpopular among British rock musicians, since it smacked of "selling out," of collaborating with the pop industry's star-making machinery. Apparently the band felt the cover image was trippy enough not to be interpreted as a cave-in to pop music conventions. The inner gatefold offers photos of the musicians (it's almost as if they were making up for lost time), but here too there is a trippy touch. In the midst of a Tolkienesque forest somewhere in rural Sussex, we are faced with a veritable army of Emersons, Lakes, and Palmers in various outfits and poses: six Keiths, eight Gregs, and six Carls. The pastoralist imagery has very little connection with any of the music on *Trilogy*, but it does point up the pervasive-

---

[2] Keith Emerson, quoted by Schact, "Emerson, Lake and Palmer," 8–9.

ness of pastoral imagery in the output of postsixties rock bands.[3] The album's back cover depicts the mysterious, almost unearthly purple glow of a particularly beautiful sunset. Since the album contains no overarching concept for which cover art could help provide a key to interpretation, a Dali cover could well have proved to be overkill: under the circumstances, the Hipgnosis cover works quite well.

Fourth Album: *Trilogy*

Trilogy opens with "The Endless Enigma," a three-movement suite with music by Emerson and words by Lake. At 10:37, "The Endless Enigma" clocks in as ELP's sixth lengthiest epic of the 1970s, behind "Karn Evil 9," "Tarkus," "Memoirs of an Officer and a Gentleman," "Pirates," and "Take a Pebble." The two outer song movements (titled "The Endless Enigma, part one" and "The Endless Enigma, part two") are separated by an instrumental fugue: while these appear as three separate tracks on both LP and CD formats of *Trilogy*, in reality the separate movements of "The Endless Enigma" are only marginally more self-contained than those of "Tarkus." "The Endless Enigma" could just as easily have been treated as a single track, as indeed it was on the *Return of the Manticore* box set.[4]

Lake's lyrics for "The Endless Enigma" fall squarely within the late-sixties/early-seventies tradition of the spiritual quest narrative, a genre of lyric that I discuss at some length in *Rocking the Classics*.[5] Without covering the same ground again here, I would simply point out that perhaps the most characteristic aspect of this type of lyric is its tendency to merge the quest for objective, universal truth (what does it all mean?) with the quest for subjective self-knowledge (who am I?), and its solipsistic tendency to treat success in the latter as success in the former as well. This attitude (i.e., if I achieve self-knowledge I have also unlocked the door of hidden cosmic truth) is highly characteristic of the late-sixties/early-seventies counterculture. There is perhaps a genuine point of contact between the syncretic pop spirituality of the sixties and hermeticism, with its emphasis that through

---

[3] Powell and Thorgerson, the leading lights of Hipgnosis, came out of the same hippie scene as the members of Pink Floyd: a number of their other designs, most famously Floyd's *Atom Heart Mother*, utilize pastoral imagery specifically related to the English countryside. Such rural/pastoral imagery wasn't confined to Hipgnosis designed albums: one might want to also check out the cover of Caravan's *If I Could Do It All Over Again, I'd Do It All Over You* LP (1970).

[4] Nonetheless, the timings I give in the following analysis are based on the three-track format of the *Trilogy* CD.

[5] See Macan, *Rocking the Classics*, 76–78.

introspection one comes to a vision of the universal, by using the known to explain the unknown. However, since the vast majority of spiritual seekers of the sixties lacked the hermeticist's self-discipline, patience, and dedication to a spiritual tradition, the sixties seeker's voyage of spiritual discovery often degenerated into the self-absorption that is simultaneously one of the most intriguing and appalling characteristics of the baby boom generation.[6]

As an example of the spiritual quest narrative, Lake's lyrics for "The Endless Enigma" are neither the most clichéd (that distinction probably belongs to the Moody Blues' *In Search of the Lost Chord*) or the most poignant (here I would point to Van der Graaf Generator's *Pawn Hearts* or Procol Harum's *A Salty Dog*). What is most interesting about Lake's lyrics, perhaps, is how they appear to shape, and be shaped by, Emerson's music. It would seem that the highly sectional structure of the music is at least to some extent a result of Emerson's attempt to musically depict the process of self-discovery implied in the lyrics. To be sure, much of Keith Emerson's most characteristic music features sudden shifts from one sectional "block" to another, "The Three Fates" and "Tarkus" being representative examples. However, "Enigma" is especially noteworthy for the frequency of such shifts and the tangential connection between the different musical blocks—in contrast to "Tarkus," for instance, where the "blocks" are stitched together more systematically with rhythmic, harmonic, and motivic cross-references.

Like "The Three Fates" and "Tarkus," "Enigma" uses tonal cross-references with great subtlety. Furthermore, "Enigma" demonstrates that although Emerson doesn't ordinarily develop his thematic material in the sense "development" is usually understood in classical music (think Beethoven or Sibelius), he is often able to expose unexpected shades of meaning in his themes by recalling them in new contexts.[7] This is an approach we have already witnessed in regards to the recapitulation of a segment of "Eruption" at the end of "Tarkus," and we will witness some-

---

[6] See Landon Jones, *Great Expectations: America and the Baby Boom Generation* (New York: Coward, McGann, and Geoghegan, 1980), and Dominick Cavallo, *A Fiction of the Past: The Sixties in American History* (New York: Saint Martin's Press, 1999).

[7] This is especially true of ELP's output during their "golden age" of 1970–74; the one possible exception I can think of is "Lachesis," where Emerson really does obsessively reshape his main theme and subsidiary motives in a developmental matter. More representative of his early approach is the treatment of the ostinato figure in "Tarkus," which reappears in an unaltered form several different times, each time accompanying different melodic and harmonic material. As we'll see, the 1st and 3rd Impressions of "Karn Evil 9," which do tend to continuously develop specific textures and melodic approaches (although not specific themes or motives per se) prefigure the more developmental mindset that emerges in some of Emerson's work of the later 1970s such as "Pirates," the Piano Concerto no. 1, and the soundtrack for *Inferno*.

thing similar here.[8] Nonetheless, "Enigma," perhaps more than any other ELP epic, requires an analysis of the connection between Emerson's music and Lake's lyrics to fully clarify the logic of the musical structure. The following analysis of "Enigma," then, examines both how Emerson achieves unity-in-diversity through stitching together sections exemplifying different genres of classical music—impressionistic instrumental overture, toccata, hymn, and fugue—and how he draws on the extramusical meanings inherent in each as a means of pictorially representing and commenting on Lake's words, and advancing the narrative inherent in Lake's lyrics.

"The Endless Enigma, part one" falls into four distinct sections, which I'll refer to as overture (0:00–1:36), toccata (1:36–2:34), hymn (2:34–5:47), and coda (5:47–6:03). The overture is one of ELP's most atmospheric passages, and is perhaps the first that one could describe as "cinematic," foreshadowing Emerson's later interest in scoring movies. What we have here is a musical depiction of chaos, in the tradition of the opening of Franz Joseph Haydn's oratorio *The Creation*; the cosmos in a nebulous, inchoate state, or (just as likely, in light of Lake's lyrics) the self in the womb.[9] The first thing we hear is the beating of a "heart," actually Palmer's bass drum pedal, which sounds an eighth-note/dotted quarter-note pattern. The impression is more that of an Indian *tala* pattern than a recurring metric pulse in the Western sense: we are still suspended in eternity, time has yet to begin. On the seventh repetition of Palmer's pattern, Emerson sounds two supremely lonely Moog notes, the melodic fifths E–B. Thereafter, Emerson's Moog line spills across Palmer's *tala* pattern, developing (perhaps "evolving" is a better word) from a pentatonic to a Dorian to a chromatic outline, and finally being corroded by an ominous tritone presence (G–C♯, D♯–A). Palmer plays his *tala* a total of twenty-eight times, interrupted just once—a "skipped heartbeat" after the thirteenth repetition of the pattern. (Coincidence or profound symbolism? You tell me.)

The unfolding Moog soliloquy ends with a weird descending portamento, out of which rises, at 0:37, a descending three-note motive, E–D–B (which is, incidentally, a transposition of the three-note "Knife-Edge" motive), deep in the instrument's bass register. This motive is shadowed by an unearthly pulsating overtone that sounds, for want of a better description, like an ascending UFO; it is Emerson's most imaginative use of the synthesizer up to this time. The motive is heard five times,

---

[8] We'll witness something similar again in the obviously related (but not identical) bitonal closing cadences of the 1st and 3rd Impressions of "Karn Evil 9."

[9] It is interesting to note that similar evocations of "chaos" can be observed at the beginning of Yes's *Close to the Edge* suite and Pink Floyd's *Dark Side of the Moon* LP (the latter even recapitulates "Enigma"'s "heartbeat" opening): both were released after *Trilogy*.

each time followed by brief episodes of agitated atonal piano runs alternating with pointillistic splashes of Latin percussion (bongos after the first, second, and fourth piano figures, claves after the third). During the crashing atonal piano runs, it is easy to imagine the random explosion of lightning and thunder, with the uneasy return to silence evoked by the muttering bongos.

Suddenly, at 1:36, out of the wash of one final atonal piano run, the bongos fall into a repetitive rhythmic groove for the first time, and an insistently pulsating bass note on C♯ emerges: time begins, order is brought to chaos, light is divided from darkness, and the self passes through the momentous portal of self-awareness. Besides the dramatic entrance of bass guitar, this transition from the overture to the toccata is marked by Keith Emerson's first and last recorded performance with ELP on the zoukra, a double-reed wind instrument similar to a shawm that he had recently purchased in Tunisia.

The toccata section falls into two distinct portions. The first portion still seems a bit unfocused: to the accompaniment of Lake's pulsing bass drone and Palmer's chattering bongos, Emerson launches into a *moto perpetuo* chain of triplet eighth notes on a flutelike Hammond setting that furtively slips around F♯ major without really confirming it. Then, after a dramatic pause on a B♭ triad at 1:58, Emerson reenters with a fuller, more overdriven Hammond sound, his toccata figuration now clearly anchored in the key of C minor, and Palmer enters on the full kit, laying out an aggressive shuffle pattern to drive Emerson's triplet eighth-note lead line: for the first time, the music takes on a distinct sense of purpose and forward momentum.[10]

This second, more aggressive portion of the toccata section ends with what I call (not too pretentiously, I hope) the "Enigma theme." This passage begins at 2:18 with alternating C major and F♯ major triads, which reemphasizes the toccata's tonal movement from F♯ to C. As I pointed out in discussing of "The Three Fates," juxtaposing two keys a tritone apart implies a conflict between irreconcilable opposites: part of the working out of this piece's "enigma," then, will involve seeing what (if any) sense of resolution might be reached between these two key centers, which will dominate the remainder of "The Endless Enigma." Next comes a rapidly ascending melodic sequence (beginning at 2:21) whose harmonic ambiguity opens up a further musical enigma. The chords

---

[10] Emerson's toccata figuration here is strongly reminiscent of Bach's 6/8 or 12/8 preludes: compare this passage with the D minor prelude from Book I of the *Well-Tempered Clavier*, which we have already encountered in "The Only Way" from *Tarkus*. The next ("hymn") section of "The Endless Enigma, part one" also reveals some Bachian touches: Emerson's involvement with Bach, clearly evident in the *Tarkus* period, had yet to completely run its course here.

involved in this sequence are B major, D major, F major, $A^\flat$ major, $D^\flat$ major, E major, and F major—a chain of triads that are completely unrelated to each other harmonically (with the exception of $A^\flat$ and $D^\flat$), and swing the music's tonality off into limbo. Furthermore, none of these chords is played as a straight triad; the first four chords feature a raised fourth resolving to the third degree (i.e., $A–D–G^\sharp$ resolving to $A–D–F^\sharp$ in the D major triad), while in the last three chords, the raised fourth never resolves at all! As a result, the arrival at the F sonority at the end of this sequence is even weaker than it might be otherwise: when the bass guitar settles on A underneath the organ's C–F–B sonority, we're not sure if we're in F Lydian, A minor, or a composite tonality.

In other words, despite the sense of purpose and forward momentum that characterized the second half of the toccata, the section ends—well, enigmatically. The "Enigma theme" isn't even usable as a transition into the subsequent hymn, since the final C–F–B chord over an A bass note—which I will hereafter call the "Enigma chord"—brings the music to a pause on a giant question mark. Therefore, Emerson follows the "Enigma theme" with a restatement of the first four bars of the toccata (compare 1:45 and 2:26), now much slower and impressively distorted (it sounds as if he ran the Hammond through a fuzz box). This brief segment recaptures the tonal equilibrium of the music, and firmly redirects the piece to the key of $G^\flat$ major (an enharmonic reinterpretation of the toccata section's $F^\sharp$ major), which is to dominate the next section.

With the arrival of the third section, the "hymn," we have reached the crux of "The Endless Enigma." Lake's lyrics suggest a contemptuous demigod berating his somewhat dull-witted people for their lies, empty words, and confusion. As to his own exalted identity, we learn that he's ruled all of the earth, witnessed his birth—but yet he doesn't know who he is, hence another enigma that cries out for a solution. Throughout the hymn section, Lake, in his demigod persona, surveys a world out of balance,[11] and he takes an explicit swipe at countercultural claims of spiritual attainment: "I'm tired of hypocrite freaks / With tongues in their cheeks / Turning their eyes as they speak / They make me sick and tired!" In short, these lyrics take on something of the aura of Jehovah addressing the Israelites—the one crucial distinction being that Jehovah never experienced an identity crisis—and the essentially religious nature of the lyrics makes the hymnlike musical accompaniment especially appropriate.

The obvious "churchiness" of Emerson's hymn tune tends to disguise the sophistication of its construction. Emerson could have easily have

---

[11] His cry "I've seen paupers as kings" is reminiscent of the Old Testament proverb "The earth is disquieted . . . for a servant when he reigns"; see Proverbs 30:2–23 for the full context.

lapsed into writing a four-square, Victorian-style hymn. Instead, the hymn exemplifies the type of irregular, asymmetrical phrase structure that seems to characterize much of Emerson's best work ("Lachesis" and "Eruption" also come to mind). Emerson's hymn tune breaks into two unequal halves, each repeated. The first half (beginning at 2:34) consists of an eight-bar period ("Why do you stare") followed by an eleven-bar period ("Your words waste and decay"). Emerson creates an interesting contrast between the conventional phrase structure and diatonicism of the first period and the irregular phrase structure and more unstable modal harmony of the second period.[12] The two periods are set off through terraced dynamics as well: the first period features Lake's voice accompanied by flutelike Hammond, while the second period adds the rhythm section and a more distorted Hammond coloring.

The second half of the hymn, beginning at 3:47, consists of three periods. The first ("Are you confused") modulates to E♭ major before returning to G♭. Despite its quiet dynamics (vocals, flutelike Hammond, slowly walking bass line), its metric ambiguity—the vocal rhythms suggest eight bars of 3/2, the accompanying music, twelve bars of 4/4—gives it an edginess that paves the way for the tune's climax on the fourth period ("Please, please, please open their eyes"). Lake sings this section with great passion; indeed, his singing shows a new maturity here. Rather than rasp his way through an entire vocal the way he had on the harder-rocking sections of *Tarkus* ("Bitches' Crystal," "Time and a Place"), which at any rate does not suit his voice, he rasps on key syllables only (listen to "open," "eyes," "don't," and "lies"), thus creating a sense of sincerity and emotional conviction without needlessly distorting his natural voice. This was a technique he went on to use with ever-greater assurance in "Karn Evil 9" and "Pirates." The third and final period ("I've ruled all of the earth") recycles the second period from the first half of the tune (compare 4:26 and 2:49), nicely rounding off the hymn tune as a whole and giving it a greater sense of unity.

Even as the final chord of the hymn is dying out, Lake recommences the pulsating C♯ bass guitar note that had opened the toccata section. After some unearthly whooshes (rhythmic glissandos on the Hammond), Emerson recalls the opening toccata figuration for the third time in the movement (compare 5:57 with 2:26 and 1:45). This time the toccata theme has nowhere else to go, and at 6:03 this brief coda section brings "The Endless Enigma, part one" to a firm close on an F♯ major triad.

Although the first portion of Emerson's solo piano episode is included at the end of "The Endless Enigma, part one" track on both LP and CD

---

[12] In the second period, a ♭VII ♭VI V progression swings the harmony from G♭ to its enharmonic equivalent, F♯, and a ♭III IV V progression swings it back to G♭.

formats, it would have been more accurate to include it at the beginning of the next track, "Fugue."[13] At any rate, its purpose is to serve as a transition to the next movement, which, despite its "Fugue" title, is actually a prelude and fugue using a common theme. The transitional section (from 6:04 to 6:41 of the first track) is quiet, reflective, and very improvisatory. It drifts through a number of keys (including C$^\sharp$, which seems to suggest a return to F$^\sharp$/G$^\flat$ is imminent) before pausing dramatically on a G minor triad at 6:40, which becomes the dominant chord of C, the tonic of the second movement.

Before proceeding, we ought to entertain a rhetorical question: why place a fugue between the two parts of "The Endless Enigma"? Some rock critics were certainly not very sympathetic. Robert Christgau commented, "The pomposities of *Tarkus* and the monstrosities of the Musorgsky homage clinch it—these guys are as stupid as their most pretentious fans. [Now there's some thoughtful, carefully reasoned 'criticism'!] Really, anybody who buys a record that divides a composition called 'The Endless Enigma' into two discrete parts deserves it."[14] Nonetheless, the fugue carries some extramusical associations that makes its inclusion in this context logical; in order to fully appreciate these, I must ask the reader to indulge me in a brief history of the fugue.

Fugal composition can be traced back to the a cappella church music of the Renaissance period, beginning with Josquin des Prez (circa 1440–1521) and his contemporaries.[15] By the later sixteenth century, fugal writing had been absorbed into solo keyboard music, first by the

---

[13] In the notated version, the solo piano part of "The Endless Enigma, part one" from 6:04 on is included with the second movement, the Fugue, and is given the superscription "Introduction"—apparently by Emerson himself. See the musical score, *Emerson, Lake and Palmer: Anthology* (New York: Warner Brothers, 1981), 38

[14] Christgau, *Rock Albums of the 70s*, 126. This review originally appeared in *Newsday*. Incidentally, Christgau doesn't go on to say what the "it" is that ELP's "stupid" fans deserve.

[15] Although imitative polyphony and what today is called fugal composition emerged during the period known by art and music historians as the Renaissance (circa 1450–1600), I think that Joscelyn Godwin is correct to state that the major concerns of the Renaissance— the revival of ancient Greek models and the depiction of individual emotion and outward personality—was not accomplished in music until the beginning of the baroque period, in the years immediately after 1600, with the creation of opera in Italy. I agree with Godwin when he says, "Polyphonic music [of which fugue is the supreme example] is essentially a Gothic art, for it grew up at the same time as the Gothic cathedrals and replicates in its own way the same spiritual experience that was behind those. The nineteenth century, which accompanied its Gothic revival in architecture with a rediscovery of the church music of Palestrina and Bach, may have been historically naïve in comparing architecture of 1200 with music of 1560 or 1720, but there was a correct intuition behind its enthusiasms." Joscelyn Godwin, *Harmonies of Heaven and Earth: Mysticism in Music from Antiquity to the Avant-Garde* (Rochester, VT: Inner Traditions International, 1995), 94.

English virginalists (who often called their fugal pieces "fantasias" or "voluntaries") and later, by Dutch composers such as Jan Pieterszoon Sweelinck who were much influenced by the virginal music of such English masters as William Byrd (1543–1623) and Orlando Gibbons (1583–1625).[16] From the Low Countries the keyboard fugue spread to Germany, where it became an important part of German musical culture during the baroque period. Far from "inventing" the keyboard fugue, J. S. Bach (1685–1750) merely brought to its culmination a tradition of fugal writing for keyboard instruments (both harpsichord and organ) that stretched back at least half a century before his birth, and counted among its distinguished practitioners Dietrich Buxtehude (1637–1707) and Johann Pachelbel (1653–1706), both of whom strongly influenced Bach.

By the later years of Bach's lifetime, the fugal approach to writing was considered hopelessly old-fashioned; by 1750, the year of his death, the fugue as a living musical form was essentially dead. It is important to realize that during the entire span of time discussed here, the fugue had no specific extramusical ramifications, but was simply a structural convention that musicians were familiar with and used reflexively, much as musicians working in the twentieth century American popular music tradition used twelve-bar blues or thirty-two-bar popular song form. However, when the fugue made its "comeback" in the late eighteenth and early nineteenth centuries, it was with some associations it had not had during its natural lifetime. It was sometimes used as an emblem of compositional skill and mastery. This is how Mozart seems to use it, for instance, in some of his instrumental works, and Emerson's fugue may carry similar connotations—although, as I'll argue below, I don't think it's the principal reason he included it. Fugue could also be used to create an aura of archaism, of something "old": Mozart's Requiem is a good example of this use of fugue, as is a much later piece, Camille Saint-Saëns's symphonic poem *Danse Macabre*.

Once Beethoven latched on to fugue, he changed its meaning again—as he did so many other musical conventions of his day. In some of his later works—I'm thinking particularly of his Piano Sonata in A♭ major, op. 110—the fugue appears at the end of a large-scale work, and becomes a metaphor for a process of spiritual transformation and redemption. The fugue of op. 110 takes us on a symbolic journey from darkness to light (or oppression to freedom, or ignorance to enlightenment—choose your own dualities), and is followed by a huge, triumphant climax. Not only does the fugue symbolize the passage from darkness to light—it creates it. This use of fugue as a metaphor for and agent of transformation and redemp-

---

[16] A virginal is a small harpsichord that was very popular in England between the fifteenth and seventeenth centuries.

tion became an important model for some later nineteenth-century composers. The fugue of Cesar Franck's piano piece *Prelude, Chorale, and Fugue* has these metaphysical connotations, as does the fugue of Charles Valentin Alkan's "Quasi-Faust" (the second movement of his massive Grande Sonate, op. 33, for piano) and perhaps the fugue of Franz Liszt's Sonata in B minor. Emerson's "Endless Enigma" fugue also appeals to this nineteenth-century tradition of fugue as metaphor for/agent of transformation/redemption.

Emerson prefaces the fugue proper with a prelude whose main theme, heard at the very beginning of the second track, foreshadows the fugue subject.[17] The prelude is characterized by quietly flowing eighth notes in the right hand, with sparse left-hand accompaniment. It falls into an A A B format; the A sections begin in C major but cadence on an E triad, forging a link with the ambiguous E tonality of the opening of "Endless Enigma, part one." The B section drifts placidly through several keys before seeming to settle into E♭ major, only to be suddenly wrenched back into C major by the closing cadential figure.

The fugue itself is an impressive compositional achievement. Emerson was wise to precede the fugue with the meandering piano transition and the quietly flowing prelude, since the fugue, with its increased rhythmic drive, harmonic motion, and textural density, almost automatically creates a climactic effect. Unlike his "Five Bridges" fugue, which is highly derivative of Friedrich Gulda's fugue,[18] it is almost impossible to point to a model for the "Endless Enigma" fugue. The five-measure fugue subject is first stated in Emerson's right hand (key of C major) at 0:50; it is answered by a left hand statement in G major at 0:54, then, after a dynamic codetta that careens through a segment of the circle of fifths, is partially sounded by Lake on bass guitar (now in A major) at 1:00, only to be passed back to Emerson's right hand for completion.

Thereafter, the fugue builds up to great complexity as the piano and bass spin out various motives drawn from the subject in three-part counterpoint. The complete subject is heard at 1:20 in Emerson's left hand, now in E major (once more we see the cross reference to "Enigma"'s opening E tonality). At 1:23 Emerson engages in a particularly brilliant bit of counterpoint by superimposing part of the "Enigma" hymn tune ("I've seen all of the Earth") against the second half of the subject, bringing the fugue to its climax. Thereafter the piano and bass continue to spin

---

[17] The technique of restating themes from movement to movement of a multimovement work is known as cyclic form, and was very common in the nineteenth century: Franck uses it in his *Prelude, Chorale, and Fugue* for instance. It is not a technique that J. S. Bach or other eighteenth-century composers would have used.

[18] The *Return of the Manticore* box set contains a previously unreleased performance by Emerson of Gulda's jazzy Prelude and Fugue.

out motives drawn from the subject in a busy three-part counterpoint; the subject is sounded again, incompletely, in Emerson's left hand at 1:37, and one final time, again incompletely, over a tonic pedal point at 1:44. Having now almost completely unwound its pent-up energy, the fugue draws to a quiet close in C major with a shadowy reference to the prelude's flowing eighth-note figuration.

What is most interesting about Emerson's fugal writing is that though he is much more interested in the melodic integrity of the lines than in their harmonious blending together, there is no really dissonant grinding between the parts. Also unusual is that despite the tonal instability of the fugue—seldom is it in a given key for more than four or five seconds, excepting only the relatively lengthy stretch of C major tonality at the end—the individual lines are almost completely diatonic, and modulation is accomplished melodically. Having studied fugal compositions by many of the twentieth century's principal composers of tonal music—Stravinsky, Bartók, Holst, Vaughan Williams, Shostakovich, Hindemith—I can honestly say I have never encountered another piece quite like the "Enigma" fugue.

Like Beethoven's opus 110 fugue or Alkan's "Quasi-Faust" fugue, Emerson's succeeds in exorcising the demons and answering the unanswered questions of the previous music.[19] Now the "Endless Enigma" hymn is free to return in triumph. And that is in fact precisely what happens, albeit, as we will see, with one major complication. "The Endless Enigma, part two" opens with a celebratory piano/bass/drums passage that wends its way through a thicket of meter shifts on its way back from the C major tonality of the prelude and fugue to the G♭ major of the "Enigma" hymn tune. It seems that in order for the music to emerge triumphant, it has been necessary for it to explore its tonal alter ego. This would explain the tritone G♭-C polarity of "Enigma," and could be seen to symbolize the notion which seems to underline the odyssey of self-knowledge that guides Lake's lyrics: in order to be truly whole, humans must engage in a dangerous but necessary exploration of some subconscious part of the psyche. At 0:18, the journey is clearly almost over: the music reaches D♭, the dominant of G♭, and launches into the peal of a victory fanfare, orchestrated with Palmer's tubular bells, Lake's majestic bass countermelody, and Emerson's Hammond organ filigrees. Beginning at 0:30, Emerson caps off the section with a Moog fanfare figure—Emerson's first use of the "Moog trumpet" setting that was to be such an

---

[19] I believe the most important "exorcism" that takes place in the Fugue is that the unstable intervallic profile of the "Enigma chord" (perfect fourth/tritone) is smoothed out into a series of melodic perfect fourths in the prelude theme/fugue subject. In other words, the subversive tendencies of the augmented fourth (i.e., the tritone), which made its presence felt throughout "The Endless Enigma, part one," are neutralized.

important part of the *Brain Salad Surgery* sonic palette and has been closely associated with him ever since. Finally, at 0:48 Lake's hymn tune returns triumphantly, its orchestration now expanded with an overdubbed chorus of Moog "trumpets."[20] The recapitulation of the hymn tune is compressed—we get only the first two of the tune's five periods—and at 1:34 Emerson's Hammond/Moog orchestration of a thrilling progression of chromatically ascending triads drives the music towards an apparently triumphant conclusion.

However, even as Lake announces he's reached the end of his odyssey, the attainment of some kind of ill-defined gnosis—"I've begun to see the reason why I'm here"—we face a stunning repudiation of everything that has taken place since the end of the first movement. At 1:39, while Lake belts out his grandiose final note, Emerson launches into the "Enigma theme" which had closed the first movement's toccata section. Again we hear the ominously alternating F$^\sharp$ and C triads, the tortured rising melodic sequence, finally the ambiguous "Enigma chord" (C–F–B chord over an A bass), now further darkened by a sardonically "victorious" synthesizer fanfare figure alternating between E and B. As the reader may recall, E and B were the first two pitches we heard at the beginning of "Endless Enigma, part one."

In short, we find ourselves back where we started; the repudiation of the lyric's confident assertion of metaphysical attainment could not be more complete. Here Emerson has used his theme with the same psychological depth and sense of irony with which Wagner employed his leitmotifs in his music dramas: the singer sings of things as they appear to be, but the underlying music expresses things as they really are. Although Lake's adoption of a "demigod" narrative persona gives these lyrics more interest than many other "spiritual quest" epics of the period, taken on their own the lyrics do seem to show the same naïve faith in the possibility of a readily attainable "instant enlightenment" that, in my opinion, mars the lyrics of the Moody Blues—and, in some cases, of Yes as well. Emerson's supremely ironic finale gives the lyrics a whole new depth, however, and seems to fundamentally question the connection assumed to exist in much countercultural spirituality between subjective awareness and objective reality. If I have wearied the reader with an overdetailed analysis of the "Endless Enigma" suite, I beg his or her indulgence; I think it is one of ELP's most fascinating pieces, and, unlike "Tarkus" or "Karn Evil 9," it has received virtually no detailed commentary.

After the unsettling denouement of "The Endless Enigma," the band has two options: they can attempt to up the ante further, or they

---

[20] I think it is exactly this type of orchestration that was needed to pull off the climactic section of "The Great Gates of Kiev" on the *Pictures* LP.

can dispel the tension. Probably wisely, they choose the latter course, following "Enigma" with the supremely mellow Greg Lake ballad, "From the Beginning." While "From the Beginning" has some obvious parallels with Lake's previous ballads ("Lucky Man," "The Sage")—above all the fact that the song is constructed around Lake's voice and acoustic guitar—there are some important differences, too.

"From the Beginning" exposes a jazzier side of Lake, and perhaps can best be seen as a highly personal reworking of bossa nova—think of Antonio Carlos Jobim's "Carnaval" (from *Black Orpheus*) or "Girl from Ipanema" for points of reference. Bossa nova influence can be heard in the flavor of the chord progression, even though, true to his modal predilections, Lake never sounds a dominant chord. It can also be heard in Lake's closed chord voicings, in the rhythm of his percussive acoustic guitar strumming (which accents "two" and the "and" of three) and in the character of the bass line—a point of contact that would be even more evident had the bass line not been (in my opinion, at least) mixed a bit low. Palmer restricts himself to conga drums throughout, and his subtle and nicely understated accompaniment forges an additional link with Latin jazz.

The only really dramatic passage in "From the Beginning" is Lake's opening soliloquy on solo acoustic guitar—a beautiful and all-too-brief passage that suggests his growing (and regrettable) disinclination to further explore and develop his achievements as an acoustic guitarist on "The Sage." He begins with a declamatory, classically inspired passage in E minor that shows at least a casual point of contact with Steve Howe's classically inspired opening of Yes's "Roundabout" (which is, incidentally, in the same key). He then launches into a series of surging cross-picked arpeggios which push the music towards the A minor tonality of the main body of the song, which, once reached, is notable for its relaxed ambience. Lake's refrain ("You see it's all clear, you were meant to be here—from the beginning") almost seems to be a playful commentary on the metaphysical pretensions of "The Endless Enigma"—something along the lines of "I may not understand the grand cosmic plan, or how I fit into it, but I know you and I have always belonged together." Likewise, the weird "ascending UFO" sound that had seemed so menacing and mysterious at the introduction of "Enigma" takes on an aura of hazy mellowness when it is heard near the end of "From the Beginning" (compare 0:36 and 0:46 of "Enigma" with 3:32 and 3:42 of "Beginning"). In short, "From the Beginning" was just the kind of essentially undemanding folk-rock song with mildly exotic touches (i.e., the classical guitar and spacey Moog flourishes) that college-age young people of the early 1970s often listened to while sitting in a half-lit dorm room and passing around a joint. It was released as a single in the U.S. and became the band's highest charting American single of all, reaching number thirty-nine on the charts.

The last two tracks on side one of the LP format, "The Sheriff" and "Hoedown," constitute a kind of Wild West mini (or micro) concept. While the band didn't perform the two numbers as a medley in their live shows, they flow into each other with barely a break on the recording, with the final chord of "The Sheriff" (A major) serving as the dominant of the D major synthesizer sweep that opens "Hoedown." The two are also linked by the common thread of Americana, and by their upbeat, almost celebratory mood—not, as we have seen, the most frequently encountered affect in ELP's output.

"The Sheriff," an Emerson/Lake song, is the second of ELP's three "music hall songs"—we have already encountered "Jeremy Bender"—and is easily the best. Like "Jeremy Bender," "Sheriff" starts out with spontaneous banter, including an unedited expletive by Carl Palmer, apparently in response to misplaying his opening drum break. Unlike "Jeremy Bender," however, "The Sheriff" manages to sound simple without becoming simplistic, and radiates humor without resorting to dopey punch lines. The storyline appears to be a good-natured send-up of American cowboy movies (the lyrics *begin* with the cowboy riding off into the sunset), and involve the exploits of a Clint Eastwood–like antihero named "Big Kid Josie," and his near fatal run-in with (you guessed it) the Sheriff. Likewise, Emerson's plodding, mock-heroic main melody shows a more than casual acquaintance with Western movie soundtracks.[21]

One of the more endearing characteristics of the music of "The Sheriff" is how it nonchalantly affects a simplicity that is more apparent than real. The recurring instrumental refrain features extensive circle-of-fifths movement (listen at 0:25, 0:31, etc.) that creates a lively sense of forward momentum. The second verse modulates directly from A major to C major (instead of the more predictable B major) upon moving into the third verse at 1:23. The instrumental middle section seems to depict a comic chase scene with its gawky, stop-time shifts between 4/4 and 6/8: seldom has Emerson displayed his wit more subtly. Again, the naïveté is more apparent than real: the section's C major tonality is extremely tenuous, as Emerson's loping organ melody features an unusual Lydian D major to C major cadence, and juxtaposes G major and E♭ major chords to unexpected ends, before finally returning to A major. Emerson creates a climactic effect during the final verse by layering in a piano doubling of the percussive Hammond lead line: unfortunately, this wasn't feasible in live performances (where Emerson simply played either organ or an electric piano), and in concert "The Sheriff" never quite had the same impact.

---

[21] It has often been stated that there is a reference to the main theme of Elmer Bernstein's score for *The Magnificent Seven* in the instrumental middle section of "The Sheriff." If so, the allusion must be very veiled indeed, as I am unable to detect it.

After the final verse, where Josie gives the Sheriff his just comeuppance, a "gunshot" ushers Emerson's exhilarating stride piano coda, which evokes Wild West saloon-style playing by way of vaudeville (note Palmer's vaudeville-style percussion).[22] Again, Emerson engages in some subtle but effective musical cross-references to round the piece off: there are references to the earlier stop-time shifts between 4/4 and 6/8 (3:00, 3:14) and the final passage (3:09 on) recalls the earlier circle-of-fifths bass movement. While "The Sheriff" is certainly not one of ELP's most imposing or "progressive" pieces, its combination of good humor, subtle wit, and unpretentious craftsmanship give it a charm that is lacking in most of the band's other stabs at musical humor.

The next track, the instrumental "Hoedown," has three sources of inspiration. The first and most obvious is the "Hoedown" section of the ballet score *Rodeo* (1942) by the renowned American composer Aaron Copland (1900–1991), of which ELP's "Hoedown" is a free arrangement. A second source of inspiration is, more generally, the Anglo-American folk music tradition that inspired Copland's *Rodeo*: a lot of people are not aware that the barn dance fiddle theme which dominates "Hoedown" was a traditional fiddle tune that Copland himself borrowed.[23] Third, there is the wailing modular Moog part that opens ELP's arrangement of "Hoedown" and recurs several times

---

[22] According to Emerson, the out-of-tune "honky tonk" piano sound in the final section of "The Sheriff" was created by double-tracking the stride piano episode: one track was played on a regular piano, the second on a piano run through a flanger. See Milano, "Keith Emerson," *Contemporary Keyboard*, October 1977, 38. On the other hand, Eddy Offord recalls the effect was created by Emerson overdubbing the same part four times, each overdub at a slightly different tape speed. See Eddy Offord quoted by Richard Buskin, *Inside Tracks* (New York: Avon Books, 1999), 174.

[23] There is a fascinating segment on the video documentary *High Lonesome: the Story of Bluegrass Music* (from 7:39 to 8:03) that features a solo performance of the main fiddle theme of "Hoedown" in conjunction with a video clip of a barn dance fiddler that must date back to the early part of the century. Both the audio and the video clip accompany a reminiscence by bluegrass great Bill Monroe (1911–1996) about his Uncle Pen, whom of course was the subject of one of Monroe's most famous songs. It is not clear whether the fiddler in the video sequence is actually Monroe's uncle, although it is clear the fiddler is not actually playing the "Hoedown" music heard on the video. In the December 13, 1996, issue of the online *ELP Digest*, Tim Beardsley states he had recently listened to a National Public Radio broadcast by folklorist Stephen Wade that examined the provenance of the "Hoedown" fiddle theme ("Decided by Limits Drawn," ELP Digest 6, no. 29; http://www.brainsalad.com). Wade played a recording made sometime early in the century, and now in possession of the Smithsonian Institution, of an Appalachian fiddler named Stipp playing the "Hoedown" them—which is actually the old Appalachian fiddlers' breakdown "Bonyparte." According to Beardsley, Wade then played segments of Copland's and ELP's "Hoedown," and discussed the origins of the theme. While I am unable to confirm any of this, it is clear that Copland borrowed a preexisting fiddle tune as the basis of "Hoedown," much as he borrowed "'Tis a Gift to be Simple" in his *Appalachian Spring*.

thereafter. Emerson has described the origin of this amazing effect in some detail:

> The actual rise time is from the envelope generator [of the modular Moog system]. It's attenuated. The actual harmony is controlled by the sustain on the envelope generator. That can also be varied by the attenuator. That also alters the pace. The rest is conventional: oscillators into the filter, controlled by the envelopes, into the VCA, and out to the trunk lines. I came up with that just by messing around. All of a sudden this wailing noise came out, and I thought, "Oh, I've got to use that in something. It sounds very nice. Sounds like a hoedown. A pretty far-out sort of hoedown."[24]

Blair Pethel has criticized ELP's arrangement of "Hoedown" on several counts. He argues that the band's arrangement oversimplifies Copland's rhythms, is too monochromatic in its timbral palette, and carelessly changes the piece's structure (especially in terms of omitting certain sections) in a way that negatively impacts the music's flow. While I largely agree with Pethel's assessments of the various ELP arrangements, this is one instance where I quite disagree: I consider "Hoedown" one of ELP's finest shorter pieces. In the following discussion, I don't intend to resort to the kind of bar-by-bar comparison between Copland's "Hoedown" and ELP's arrangement that Pethel does—I believe I can make my case in more general terms—so the interested reader will wish to consult Pethel's work.[25]

Let me attempt to deal with Pethel's objections on a point-by-point basis. First, I am unconvinced by his claim that the band's timbral palette is too monochromatic to make "Hoedown" work. It is true that a three-piece rock band do not have the same timbral palette at their disposal as an eighty-piece orchestra. However, their arrangement is not nearly as timbrally bland as Pethel suggests; for instance, he is not at all correct to imply that the Hammond C-3 is the lead melodic instrument throughout.[26] Besides the unique modular Moog wail that opens the arrangement and recurs several times thereafter, Emerson inserts an original synthesizer episode that contains some of the most experimental timbres he had obtained from the Moog up to that time. The band's arrangement ends with a very effective combination of Hammond and Moog colors.

Furthermore, I think that what ELP's arrangement yields in timbral color, it gains back in sheer visceral drive. In its trio guise, "Hoedown" becomes an exciting, virtuosic workout for all three musicians. Once you've heard Liszt's *Mephisto Waltz* or (more controversially, perhaps)

---

[24] Keith Emerson, quoted by Milano, "Keith Emerson," *Contemporary Keyboard*, October 1977, 38.

[25] See Pethel, "Keith Emerson," 75–82.

[26] See Pethel, "Keith Emerson," 78.

Musorgsky's *Pictures at an Exhibition* in their guises as solo piano show-stoppers, the orchestral versions of these pieces tend to sound hopelessly safe by comparison. I think a similar relationship exists between ELP's "Hoedown" and Copland's: whatever the latter gains in the realm of timbral range, it loses in excitement and drama.

It is at this point that the connection to bluegrass music automatically suggests itself. Unlike Pethel, I see nothing sacrosanct in the basic material of "Hoedown"—Copland's main theme is not just based on a traditional fiddle tune, it *is* a traditional fiddle tune, of the variety that Bill Monroe and other seminal bluegrass artists grew up playing. Like ELP, Bill Monroe and his Bluegrass Boys don't have the same range of timbres at their disposal as a symphony orchestra. However, I will take their performance of "Orange Blossom Special" or "Uncle Pen" over Copland's orchestral "Hoedown" any day. The ferocious rhythmic drive Monroe's band generates, and their exhilarating improvised solos, reveal Copland's piece, by comparison, as the abstract stylization (as opposed to authentic expression) of Anglo-American barn dance music which it in fact is. Rather than hearing ELP's "Hoedown" as a slavish homage to Copland, I hear it as a kind of electronic bluegrass, with Emerson playing the roles of both fiddler extraordinaire Robert "Chubby" Wise (with his Moog parts) and banjo virtuoso Earl Scruggs (with his Hammond parts). At the same time, it is electronic bluegrass with an indelibly contemporary stamp: rather than using a stylistically authentic 2/4 meter, with offbeat rhythmic accents (as Monroe would have played it), ELP use a straight 4/4 rock rhythm.

I am also unconvinced by Pethel's claims that the ELP arrangement critically oversimplifies Copland's rhythms. It is true the band do simplify some of Copland's syncopations; however, much of the simplification involves paring down complicated subsidiary orchestral rhythmic figures that one might not encounter in the music of the Bluegrass Boys, either. Furthermore, ELP add some subtle rhythmic complexities of their own. I would especially urge interested readers to carefully study the Lake/Palmer groove underneath the main "fiddle" melody, first heard at 0:17. Palmer's groove involves a complex set of interlocking rhythms between hi-hat (which plays straight eighth notes), bass drum, and snare (both of which supply completely independent syncopated patterns). Lake's ostinato, while harmonically static, involving just two notes (D and C), creates another highly syncopated sixteenth-note rhythm that generates considerable tension against Palmer's complex groove. "Hoedown" is, in fact, Palmer's first fully mature effort as an "orchestrator": his alternations between sections which repeat and vary this complicated groove pattern and sections where he "melodically" doubles Lake's bass line and Emerson's left-hand part across his expanded drum kit do much to articulate the music's structure.

This brings us to Pethel's final criticism of ELP's "Hoedown" arrangement, its alleged structural failure. It is true that considered strictly in comparison with Copland's orchestral score, some of Emerson's deletions are questionable. As I've argued, though, Copland's score itself represents something of a transformation of an existing tune, so it seems legitimate to allow other musicians to develop the same basic material a bit differently. So I would pose a different question: for someone who has never heard Copland's "Hoedown," does ELP's "Hoedown" cohere structurally? Does it extend its basic material in a logical way? As with *Pictures*, the question isn't "did they do it just like the composer?" Rather, the question should be: does the structure of the band's arrangement take on a logic of its own?

The answer, I think, is an unqualified "yes." ELP's "Hoedown" seems to divide into three main sections, each of which is shaped around one or two climaxes, and a short coda that serves as a climax for the entire piece. Each climax seems a bit bigger than the preceding one: in the third section and the coda, the increasing textural density and timbral variety contribute greatly to the piece's feeling of steady growth.

The piece begins with the modular Moog wail which sounds, as Blair Pethel aptly says, like "a vacuum cleaner starting and stopping in time with the meter."[27] After a brief rippling Hammond part (which evokes Bill Monroe strumming some opening chords on his mandolin, perhaps), the Moog wail disappears, and the band launch into the first half of the fiddle theme (0:10), which, beginning at 0:17, is accompanied by the ubiquitous Lake/Palmer syncopated groove. At 0:24, the band present the undulating second half of the fiddle theme; Lake and Palmer articulate this segment of the theme by playing an offbeat pattern in rhythmic unison with each other (and often, with Emerson's left hand). The two segments of the theme are then presented a second time; the band state the second half of the theme softly (0:38) then loudly (0:45), the piece's first climactic point. A little later the band momentarily move into the dominant key, A major, and reach a second climax at 1:21 on a block chord figure which the trio plays in a rhythmic unison, evoking all the string players in a bluegrass band suddenly strumming chords in unison.

At 1:38 the Moog "vacuum" wail returns, again followed by the first half of the fiddle theme, heralding the commencement of the second section. Although Lake and Palmer don't stray too far from the syncopated groove they had used to accompany the first half of the fiddle theme in

---

[27] Pethel, "Keith Emerson," 76. Digital synthesists who have sampled this sound call it Emerson's Hoedown "Hoover" (as in the vacuum cleaner) patch. The sound involves two sawtooth waves, one doing an ascending glissando across an octave, the other remaining constant.

the opening section, Emerson's organ figures begin to move farther afield from Copland's material, including a clever quotation of the African American folksong "Shortnin' Bread" (2:17–2:23). The second section ends on another unison block chord figure (starting at 2:26), this one both bigger dynamically and more expansive than the similar passage that ended the first section.

The third section, which abandons Copland's material entirely in favor of original music, arrives at a fascinating confluence of electronic bluegrass and space rock. The section begins at 2:48 with a "whooshing" Moog part that sounds not unlike a rocket taking off: something of a variation of the earlier "vacuum" wail. Lake's bass ostinato retains its syncopation but now becomes more melodically active, outlining a D minor pentatonic scale, which contributes an even more dynamic sense of motion. The Moog "whoosh" soon falls into a more regular melody, which moves in parallel fourths and features a diamond hard, metallic timbre quite unlike any sound Emerson had extracted from the instrument before. This in turn gives rise to a running sixteenth-note figure in the Moog's lower registers. At 3:14 Emerson launches into an utterly unique Moog statement of the Anglo-American barn dance tune "Turkey in the Straw"; the combination of the "squishy" timbre of the running sixteenth notes and the hard, metallic timbre of "Turkey," which is further exaggerated by tuning the oscillators to parallel fourths, is one of the band's most timbrally adventurous moments up to that time. This passage represents the first time in "Hoedown" that the band has resorted to melodic counterpoint; the new textural density, combined with the timbral complexity generated by the two different Moog lines, makes this climax the biggest one yet.

This section moves directly into the brief coda, heralded at 3:21 by a further variation of the Moog "vacuum" wail accompanying the second half of the fiddle theme on Hammond. The piece's final climax begins at 3:28 with a Hammond statement of the first half of the fiddle theme, this time against a trumpetlike Moog countermelody; this particular textural configuration (Hammond melody superimposed against trumpetlike Moog counterpoint) was to be of great importance on *Brain Salad Surgery*, where it recurs with great frequency in "Jerusalem" and the 1st and 3rd Impressions of "Karn Evil 9." Thereafter comes the unusual Lydian cadential progression (II–I) which we have already noticed in the middle of "The Sheriff" (compare 1:52 of "The Sheriff" with 3:32 of "Hoedown"), and the sledgehammerlike iterations of D, spread across the registral spectrum, which bring "Hoedown" to its breathless conclusion.

In sum, while ELP's arrangement may have simplified Copland's "Hoedown" somewhat, it compensates with a drive absent in the original, and its structural layout around a series of ever-bigger climaxes is faultlessly paced. The mood is exhilarating, the quotations of American folk tunes are clever and entirely appropriate, and the fusion of bluegrass with space rock elements, unlikely as it might seem, works exceedingly well. "Hoedown" also represents a modest but important step forward for Emerson as a synthesist: for the first time, in his music, a particular electronic timbre (that of the "Hoedown Hoover" patch) becomes subject to variation and development. "Hoedown" became a staple of ELP's live shows, and through the *Brain Salad Surgery* era the band often opened their concerts with this piece.

Side two of the LP format opens with "Trilogy," the album's title track and at 8:53 its second-lengthiest track after the "Endless Enigma" suite.[28] The title would seems to have a couple of different references—as an album title, to the three band members on the cover, and as a song title, to song's layout in three distinct sections. The lyrics of "Trilogy" return to the subject matter of "Take a Pebble": the aftermath of a failed relationship. Unlike "Take a Pebble," however, which closes with the same melancholy imagery with which it opened, the lyrics of "Trilogy" trace a progression towards resolution, the promise of future (even if not present) happiness for the separated lovers. As a result, the A B A musical structure of "Take a Pebble" becomes an A B C musical structure in "Trilogy": emotionally (not to mention stylistically), we end at a very different place from where we started.

Like many of Emerson's other compositions, the three distinct sectional blocks of "Trilogy" could hardly be more different from each other:

---

[28] Kevin Holm-Hudson undertakes a detailed analysis of "Trilogy" in "A Promise Deferred: Multiply Directed Time and Thematic Transformation in Emerson, Lake and Palmer's 'Trilogy,'" *Progressive Rock Reconsidered*, 111–120. In all major respects, Holm-Hudson's analysis concords with mine. He believes "Trilogy" exemplifies what music theorist Jonathan Kramer describes as "multiply directed time," that is, music wherein "the direction of motion is so frequently interrupted by discontinuities, in which the piece goes so often to unexpected places, that the linearity, though still a potent structural force, seems reordered" (115). Holm-Judson sees the piece as being unified not only by the opening urmotiv, but also by two octatonic scales, B–C–D–D♯–F–F♯–G♯–A and B–C♯–D–E–F–G–A♭–B♭. I don't deny the octatonic tendencies of the song, although I think it is important to clarify that while "Trilogy" may have octatonic tendencies, it is not thoroughgoing octatonic music in the sense of some of the music of Bartók or Scriabin. While Holm-Hudson's Schenkerian view of the piece's tonal motion as ♭II–V–I in B♭ major (114) makes sense, I think his analysis could have been further strengthened by a "bigger picture" view that acknowledged two points: (1) The tritone B major–F major conflict of the piano cadenza of "Trilogy" is part of a more global tritone conflict that appears in the three major tracks at the beginning, middle, and end of the *Trilogy* album ("The Endless Enigma," "Trilogy," "Abaddon's Bolero"), but is only resolved in the latter, and (2) "Trilogy" uses a tripartite approach to progressive tonality sometimes favored by Emerson, wherein the first section introduces the first tonic key, the second section introduces a second important key that vies for supremacy with the first, and the second key emerges as supreme in the third section—"The Three Fates" also follows this approach.

it does not take a seasoned listener to discern where a particular section has ended and a new one has begun. However, unlike the different sections of "The Three Fates" and the "Enigma" suite, which are tied together mainly through very subtle tonal or stylistic cross-references, the different sections of "Trilogy" are tied together by a recurring theme. This theme is heard at the very beginning of the song, when it is played with an "electronic violin" sound (actually a Minimoog with one oscillator switched on audio and the third on modulation). Thereafter, the theme is continuously varied, and plays an important role in both the vocal line and in some of the instrumental episodes; each new transformation of the theme has its own characteristic rhythm, melodic contour, harmonization, and instrumentation. This technique of thematic transformation is a practice that Emerson borrowed from nineteenth-century composers such as Musorgsky or Franz Liszt, who often used vivid and memorable transformations of a theme as a kind of narrative device, to help convey the extramusical program of their instrumental pieces.[29] Unlike Liszt or Musorgsky in their instrumental pieces, Emerson doesn't have to rely on his transformations of the theme to carry the narrative—Lake's lyrics do that—so the various transformations of the theme both comment on and support the emotional trajectory of the words.

If "From the Beginning" reworks bossa nova, "The Sheriff" reinterprets cowboy movie music, and "Hoedown" offers the band's highly personal take on bluegrass, then the opening section of "Trilogy" finds the band taking on the nineteenth-century art song tradition as represented by the songs of Franz Schubert, the Schumanns (Robert and Clara) , and Gabriel Fauré. With the exception of Moog violin at the very beginning and very end of this section, the spotlight is solely on Lake's voice and Emerson's active but admirably understated piano accompaniment. The opening section of "Trilogy" explores a mood that is almost unique in ELP's output. While we have occasionally noticed the influence of nineteenth-century piano music in Emerson's work (especially in "Lachesis"), normally when we do hear this influence, it manifests itself in a heroic vein. The opening section of "Trilogy" is one of the few times when Emerson's music is both Romantic (in the stylistic sense) and romantic (in the more commonly understood sense of the word)—the only other ELP piece that readily comes to mind is the second movement of "Memoirs of an Officer and a Gentleman." The vocal melody of the opening section of

---

[29] We have already observed a memorable use of thematic transformation in Musorgsky's *Pictures at an Exhibition*. The Promenade theme is transformed a number of times through changes in harmonization, melodic profile, and rhythmic contour: these transformations reflect Musorgsky's different emotional reaction to each picture, and thus play an important role in advancing the piece's program, which is, of course, to musically depict a series of Victor Hartmann's paintings.

"Trilogy" is probably one of the few ELP melodies that takes full advantage of the lyrical potential of Lake's voice, and he sings it magnificently: with just a bit more chest tone and vibrato, it's not hard to image Lake singing Schubert or Fauré very successfully.

The difference between "Trilogy" and Emerson's more usual style is already evident in the opening Moog violin theme. Typically, Emerson's themes are angular, restless, muscular; the "Trilogy" motif is elegant, lyrical, even sensuous. It is set in the key of B major—like the $G^\flat$ major of "The Endless Enigma," not exactly a standard rock and roll key—and has both chromatic and modal implications (especially the C major chord, $^\flat$ II in the key of B, which is outlined at the end of the theme). The "Trilogy" motif is followed by a brief solo piano intro during which Emerson is already beginning to reshape the motif (0:20), and then by the section's main vocal verse. This verse is cast in an A A B A form that is entirely typical of the American popular song tradition of the Gershwins, Jerome Kern, and others, although Emerson can't resist introducing at least a hint of irregularity—the verse is twenty-eight bars instead of the normal thirty-two, with the B phrase being four bars instead of eight. If the form suggests American popular song, though, the ambience is much more nineteenth century. Like the songs of the Schumanns or Fauré, Emerson's piano accompaniment is active, yet avoids overpowering the vocal melody; the combination of the vocal melody's chromaticism and the modal chord progressions underneath creates a sensuous, bittersweet ambience that is quite different from the standard Emerson fare.[30] Lake's vocal line in the A phrases represents another reshaping of the opening motif; only the B phrase (1:14), with its restless circle-of-fifths harmonic movement, makes no reference to the "Trilogy" theme.

Lake's lyrics in the main verse focus on the pain of separation, a conceit that is nicely supported by Emerson's bittersweet modal mixtures. The verse is followed by a lovely solo piano interlude, which beginning at 1:53 features another variation of the "Trilogy" theme. Lake's closing "goodbye" vocal seems to signal a nostalgic but conventional close. However, a final cadential passage, which features a reappearance of overdubbed Moog "violins," signals unsettling new developments, moving most unexpectedly from the tonic B major to F major. This is the tritone progression that figured so prominently in "The Endless Enigma" (where it occurred as C to $G^\flat$); it has a similarly disruptive effect here, with the sustained F major chord at 2:21 punctuating a giant question mark.

---

[30] The modal progressions result from Emerson exploiting the Phrygian implications of the "Trilogy" theme; many of the chords he uses—E minor, C major, D major, G major—derive from B Phrygian, although the B triad itself is always major.

What follows is an increasingly agitated solo piano transition in which the romantic ambience of the first section is eventually overpowered by Emerson's more natural angular/dissonant impulses. This entire transition (from 2:24 to 2:58) suggests the "Enigma theme" (from "The Endless Enigma") writ large. As the reader might recall, the "Enigma theme" began with the disruptive juxtaposition of two major triads a tritone apart: here (at 2:24) B major and F major triads are first juxtaposed, then subversively intermingled. There is an attempt to reinstate the romantic mood of the opening with the fragmented statements of the piano interlude (2:38) and even the B phrase of Lake's vocal line (2:50), but these attempts are soon overpowered. The second segment of the "Enigma theme" had been a rising melodic sequence accompanied by a jagged chain of unrelated chords: here, beginning at 2:52, the shards of Lake's vocal melody are swept away by an ascending progression of four completely unrelated triads, B major, G major, B♭ major, and D♭ major. The "Enigma theme" had concluded with the pungent "Enigma chord," a C–F–B keyboard sonority over an A bass note: the transition section here ends at 2:56 with a plunging arpeggio built on two similar chords.[31]

The second section of "Trilogy" opens at 2:59 with a piano ostinato in quintuple meter that juxtaposes B♭ major and B major triads; very shortly the piano is joined (swallowed up, actually) by layered Moog, bass guitar, and drums, which offer a far more bombastic version of the same ostinato. The second section of "Trilogy" plays a similar structural role to the second movement of "The Three Fates": it intermingles the tonality of the previous section (B) with the tonality of the following section (B♭), and thus becomes a pivot from one key to another. However, the second movement of "The Three Fates" accomplished this with infinitely more subtlety than the second section of "Trilogy"; in fact, from here on out, inspiration begins to falter.

To be sure, the second section begins with promise. Emerson launches into a screaming Moog solo over the bombastic ostinato pattern that is genuinely galvanizing; the Moog timbre is almost suggestive of lightly fuzzed electric guitar, except Emerson introduces a delayed vibrato on the sustained notes that would be impossible for a guitar player to reproduce. Emerson begins his Moog solo by reshaping and transforming Lake's vocal melody of the opening section, and then moves on to explore other figurations. All is well here, since (as I pointed out in *Rocking the Classics*) some of progressive rock's finest moments have come from introducing a theme in a quiet, acoustic setting, and then allowing it to develop and grow in a harder-rocking framework. Across the first five ELP albums, Emerson often instrumentally recast the vocal line to very successful emo-

---

[31] The two chords are A–E♭–A♭ alternating with C–F♯–B, both over a sustained F.

tional ends: we've already noted his instrumental variation of Lake's vocal line in "Take a Pebble," and we'll see something similar in "Karn Evil 9, 3rd Impression." The problem here is that Emerson doesn't quit while he's ahead. The middle section of "Trilogy" never moves from its two-chord basis, so it's useful principally as a transition to the final section. Once Emerson had forecast the tonality of the next section and established the harder-rocking mood of the remainder of the piece by recasting the opening theme, he should have moved on. Unfortunately, he continues his solo at least forty seconds longer than he should have. as a result, a section that was galvanizing at its beginning has become boring by its end. The rest of "Trilogy" never completely recovers from this regrettable lapse into self-indulgence.

The third section makes an energetic attempt to recover the lost equilibrium. It begins at 5:02 with an unusually funky bass line by Lake; the bass guitar's timbre here is razor sharp, almost like Chris Squire's characteristic Rickenbacker sound, and the prominent role which Carl Palmer gives to the cowbell in his drum groove furthers the impression of funkiness. This is followed by an instrumental refrain which features wiry two-part counterpoint between Emerson's Moog and Lake's active bass line; the circle-of-fifths bass motion which has to some extent characterized the entire album is especially prominent here, giving the episode an irrepressible forward momentum.[32] Lake's vocal verse is much more repetitive here than it was in the opening section—a four-bar vocal phrase, preceded by a four-bar organ vamp and followed by a four-bar Moog episode, is repeated three times in all. However, the music is not without interest. The vocal melody of this section is based on a final transformation of the "Trilogy theme" that, for the first time, takes on a completely major key outline, without any of the chromatic/modal inflections it had earlier: this nicely supports the emotional tenor of the lyrics, which focus on accepting and learning from the broken relationship. Also of interest here is the subtle metric shifts between a 4/4 feel (listen to the organ vamp at 5:27) and a 6/4 feel (listen to the Moog episode at 5:40), creating a sophisticated sense of swing that is not particularly common in either ELP's music or in progressive rock generally.

The second and third verses are interrupted by a lengthy Moog solo over a static B♭ ninth chord. While Emerson weaves some interesting counterpoint between the layered Moog lines, his solo ends up once again overstaying its welcome, which has already been greatly circumscribed by the overextended solo of the second section. After Lake's third and final verse, the band wrap "Trilogy" up by repeating the wiry

---

[32] At one point Lake moves through seven consecutive root notes via ascending fourths or descending fifths.

Moog/bass instrumental refrain from the beginning of the third section, and then appending an incongruous and somewhat vulgar blues coda which does, at least, manage to turn the rather clichéd final chord progression (B 13 to B$\flat$ 7) into a microcosm of the entire piece's tonal movement.

I see some significant parallels between "Trilogy" and "Tank." Both are based on very clearly drawn tripartite structures in which the closing section is meant to achieve a fundamental transformation of thematic material from a highly original and entirely successful opening section. Both feature transitional second sections that attempt to take the path of least resistance in terms of connecting the opening and closing sections, and in so doing lapse into unmitigated repetition and self-indulgence. Both end with third sections that make significant progress towards righting the wrongs of the previous sections, but which ultimately fall short of the promise inherent in the opening material.

I also see some significant parallels between "Trilogy" and "Take a Pebble." Both address failed relationships, the only two epic (or sub-epic) ELP tracks that do so. The "Trilogy" lyrics end with a sense of optimism, while the "Take a Pebble" lyrics end on the same quietly pessimistic note with which they started; therefore, the musical structure of each (A B A for "Take a Pebble," A B C for "Trilogy") makes total sense. Of the two, "Trilogy" has the more interesting (and certainly the more varied) musical material. However, in terms of a total statement, I think "Take a Pebble" succeeds in saying everything it possibly could say, while "Trilogy" does not: "Take a Pebble" is overwhelmingly careful (again using Bill Martin's description), while "Trilogy" is regrettably careless and self-indulgent. For the most part, I think it was for the good that the major bands of the 1970s were able to produce themselves: it allowed them to do what they thought was right, rather than what some record executive trying to squeeze another hit single out of them thought might be commercially expedient. However, "Trilogy" demonstrates the down side of this arrangement. This is one track that actually would have benefited from a strong outside producer who could convince the band to severely edit the Moog solos and to bring the same sense of concision and good taste to the latter portions of "Trilogy" that they brought to the opening. "Trilogy" should have been an ELP classic; in my view, it isn't, having been spoiled by self-indulgence and an over-reliance on clichés.

The penultimate track, "Living Sin," is a rare Emerson/Lake/Palmer co-composition. It parallels the Emerson/Lake/Palmer song "A Time and a Place," from *Tarkus*, in both its ferocity and its riff-based construction. On the other hand, "Living Sin" seems to bear an even closer resemblance to—and perhaps was modeled after—"One of Those People," the closing track from the Nice's *Five Bridges*. There are several points of contact. Both songs deal with characters that, in contemporary parlance, would be described as sexual predators. The difference is that in "One of Those People," Lee Jackson introduces *himself* as "one of those people / my father told my sister not to go out with," whereas in "Living Sin" Lake's fractured narrative refers to a "savage woman" who leaves her victims "crazed." Both songs share an inclination towards unusual seven- (or fourteen-) bar phrase structures that generate an off-balance, nervous energy. Jackson's voice is heavily processed at times to create a surreal effect, while Lake sings parts of "Living Sin" with an almost surreal, throaty bass falsetto.

The structures of the two songs are also similar: an organ intro, a series of verses and refrains, a climactic bridge section, and a recap of the verse and refrain segments. In "Living Sin," the first verse commences at 0:12, and features Lake singing in his ominous falsetto over a slithering organ riff which is doubled by bass guitar. The refrain (0:53) is marked off by Lake's desperate vocal rasps and Moog "trumpet" blasts, which are layered over the churning organ. An instrumental restatement of the verse (1:05) is followed by a climactic vocal bridge (1:26), with Lake shrieking out baneful warnings, and an instrumental break (1:51) featuring Palmer's overdubbed, machine gun–like Octoplus runs. Thereafter the refrain returns (2:14), then the verse (2:26), and finally a coda whose edgy three-bar phrases featuring Moog trumpet blasts over fragments of the organ riff brings the song to a second climax.

Despite the similarities between "One of Those People" and "Living Sin," there are some important differences, too, which go a long way towards underlining some of the essential differences between the Nice and ELP. The accompanying music of "One of Those People" has a certain trippy joviality that makes us to understand that Lee Jackson isn't really the terrible guy his lyrics might suggest: you can almost imagine him winking during the peculiar bridge section, with its painful dissonance between voice and organ, when he sings "you can kiss my sister." The overall delivery is tongue-in-cheek, pointing up the almost Zappaesque absurdist streak which underlies many of the Nice's songs. It is this quality, I suppose, as well as the looser, more rough-hewn nature of the Nice's arrangements, that led a certain group of critics and other important opinion shapers (DJ John Peel, for instance) to admire the Nice but detest ELP.

Certainly, there is no trace of humor in either the music or the lyrics of "Living Sin." Almost everything about both music (especially its pervasive D minor tonality) and lyrics is dark, evoking clandestine meetings in seedy underworld bars. The track opens with an ominously dusky organ intro: this marks the last time in ELP's output that Emerson resorts to his trademark distorted Hammond sound, since *Brain Salad Surgery* develops the alternately "churchy" and "glassy" timbres already prefigured in "The Endless Enigma" and "Hoedown," respectively. Likewise, Emerson's slithering organ riff and Lake's husky falsetto during the first verse both evoke the predominant film noir ambience. While Emerson's riff during the opening verse seems to signal a fairly conventional blues-rock approach for the rest of the song, Emerson's treatment of this riff proves to be anything but conventional: throughout the song he is constantly reworking it, reshaping it, twisting it into a plethora of new contours across the off-balance phrase lengths. Like the final section of "Trilogy," the pervasive texture of "Living Sin" is a wiry two-part counterpoint between the bass line and the melody, with the sporadic keyboard chords providing textural variety.

"Living Sin," in fact, marks a step forward in a process already begun with "Bitches Crystal," namely, Emerson's increasingly confident and unselfconscious intermingling of his classical and blues influences. There's no trace of twelve-bar blues progression here: on the other hand, there's no way the greasy opening riff or its many offshoots could have come out of anything besides a blues background. As we'll see, Emerson's highly personal fusion of bluesy riffs and chord voicings with irregular phrase structures and complex metric mazes is continued in such midseventies ELP numbers as "Brain Salad Surgery" (the single, not the album), "Bo Diddley," and "Tiger in a Spotlight."

Finally we come to the last track on *Trilogy*, Keith Emerson's *tour de force* of Moog orchestration and studio overdubbing, "Abaddon's Bolero." Some have assumed this piece is an arrangement of Maurice Ravel's *Bolero*, but in fact Emerson borrows no thematic material from the Ravel piece at all. What he does borrow is the basic structural plan of Ravel's work. Ravel repeats the same theme a number of times; while the theme itself doesn't change, each new repetition sees the addition of new melodic counterpoints and instrumental colors, until finally the opening theme is but one strand in an enormous textural tapestry. Ravel's idea is simple but effective: the work's climax is reached through a process of steady growth in the music's textural and timbral density. Emerson has described the development of his "Abaddon's Bolero" to Blair Pethel in similar terms:

> I had picked out this little melody that I liked, and I put it down on tape. After listening to it several times I began to put down overdubs, and it struck me that this was the perfect thing for the kind of piece which begins at nothing and grows to everything. I took it in to Greg and Carl and we played through it several times. I told them what I had in mind, so we just started with me playing the melody on a little flute sound that was programmed into the synthesizer. Each time we repeated the theme I added something, Greg added something, and Carl added more sound on his drums. There wasn't any bolero rhythm at this time; Carl was just beating time and increasing the volume with each repetition. We just kept on building the sound, and almost

instinctively knew when the piece had reached its peak. I looked at Greg and Carl, and we cut off exactly together.[33]

Pethel adds that "after discussion with the other two members of the group, Emerson decided that a bolero rhythm in the drums fit the nature of the tune, and the conception of 'Abaddon's Bolero' was finalized."[34] Incidentally, Abaddon is the "Prince of the Bottomless Pit" alluded to in Revelation 9:11; in Bunyan's *Pilgrim's Progress* he is encountered in the guise of his Greek name, Apollyon.[35]

The backbone of "Abaddon's Bolero" is Emerson's "little melody," actually one of his longest and most sophisticated. Thirty-four measures of music in 4/4 time, the brisk melody has a distinctly martial air about it that seems to draw on a number of disparate sources: nineteenth-century marching band music, the twentieth-century British military band tradition, and, on a more contemporary note, sixties cop-show music (I seem to detect wisps of the "Dragnet" theme here). Like so much of the music on *Trilogy*—the "Endless Enigma" fugue and the instrumental middle section of "The Sheriff" immediately come to mind—the "Abaddon's Bolero" melody sounds blandly diatonic, and, taken in short segments, it is.

However, like these other passages, the "Abaddon's Bolero" melody is filled with subtle melodic modulations that explore remote tonal regions far beyond anything one would expect of its nominal models. Taking the first complete statement of the melody—the second statement overall—which begins at 0:52, the melody begins in A (pentatonic), slips into A♭ major (1:07), then returns to A at 1:22.[36] Towards the end of the melody the music slips into E♭ (at 1:33), which is juxtaposed with C♭ (♭VI of E♭), and, finally, at 1:48, the melody wends its way into C major, where C major and F♯ major chords are juxtaposed. Nearly as soon as the C major tonality is established at the end of the melody, a new repetition of the melody begins, the tonality returns to A, and the cycle begins anew. The movement between these remote tonalities (A, A♭, A, E♭, C) is almost imperceptible in part because Emerson maintains a rhythmic unity (triplet figures juxtaposed with longer note values) and a motivic unity (broken

[33] Pethel, "Keith Emerson," 55–56.
[34] Ibid.
[35] At a concert at Louisville Town Hall on April 21, 1972 (included on *The Original Bootleg Series from the Manticore Vaults,* vol. 1), some two months before *Trilogy* was released, Emerson introduced the piece that was soon to be known as "Abaddon's Bolero" as "being based on a figure of Greek mythology, Bellona, the goddess of war," and said the title of the new piece was "Bellona's Bolero."
[36] By using G major chords to encircle both A major and A♭ major chords, Emerson is able to slip between these two distantly related keys almost imperceptibly.

triads alternated with pentatonic figures) that is quite impressive.[37]

There are two details here of particular interest. The melody's movement from A (beginning) to C (end) is identical to the tonal movement in the first half of "The Sheriff," and is similar to the mediant (third-related) movement between C major and E major in the "Enigma" fugue. Second, the movement between C major and F♯ major triads at the end of the "Bolero" melody recalls the two competing tonal centers of "The Endless Enigma." Emerson must have been consciously aware of this tonal reference to the opening track; as we'll see, he makes a major issue of it at the end of "Abaddon's Bolero."

The most effective discussion of "Abaddon's Bolero" will simply demonstrate where each new statement of the melody begins and what new details of texture and tone-color have been added. So here goes . . .

Repetition #1 (0:00–0:52). The only incomplete statement of the theme: we hear only the first 23 of the theme's 34 measures. The piece begins with little more than Palmer's bolero rhythm on snare drum, and beginning at 0:10, Emerson's theme, unaccompanied, on a piccololike setting. Eventually some very quiet sustained chords are added in the background.

Repetition #2 (0:52–1:55). The first complete statement of the theme. The Moog "piccolo" setting still carries the theme. Lake enters with an offbeat drone bass line, but his part becomes more active as the theme progresses. Once the theme has modulated to A♭, the quiet accompanying chords show more movement as well.

Repetition #3 (1:55–2:57). Palmer's snare part grows louder. The theme is now played on a more "reedy" Moog setting. Lake begins playing an edgy, offbeat bass pattern that divides two bars of 4/4 into a pattern of 3 + 3 + 2 quarter notes, thus constantly bisecting the natural accents of the theme and creating a nervous energy. Fuller and more active background chords now begin to suggest an "orchestral" counterpoint, especially after the tune returns from its A♭ segment to A at 2:26.

Repetition #4 (2:57–4:00). Lake now begins to double Palmer's bolero rhythm on bass, lending the music a much greater sense of forward momentum. Emerson gives the main melody a more brassy Moog timbre, not unlike a French horn's. Furthermore, he sets the oscillators of the Moog in such a way that whatever note he plays will be doubled above by major thirds and perfect fifths, creating chains of parallel major triads. This may be a technique he learned from Gustav Holst, who harmonized an important theme in "Mars, the Bringer of War" the same way. The

---

[37] Since the opening segment of the melody tends to juxtapose C major triads with the tonic A major triads, the movement from C major at the end of one statement of the melody to A major at the beginning of the next statement goes by virtually unnoticed.

chains of parallel major triads give the music a textural fullness and a harmonic richness it has not had before. High, sustained Moog "strings" become an important background support here as well. Ironically, I hear the influence of Aaron Copland in these "string" parts more than I do in ELP's arrangement of "Hoedown," and Emerson uses interior pedal points to create a sense of mild dissonance here in the manner of Copland.[38]

Repetition #5 (4:00 5:01). The main textural strands from the previous repetition of the theme (snare drums and bass guitar iterations of the bolero rhythm, parallel "French horn" triads, sustained "strings") are repeated, while new strands are added. In the upper registers, a high "woodwind" timbre doubles the bolero rhythm; this textural strand had begun to make itself felt in the latter portion of the melody's previous repetition.[39] In the left channel especially one detects the presence of phased chords, in a lower register and moving in a different rhythm than the higher and more sustained Moog "strings."

Repetition #6 (5:01–6:01). Although the Moog "French horns" continue to sound the theme in the sonic background, Emerson now places a more prominent statement of the theme in the upper register, where it is heard on a Moog "woodwind" mixture. From 5:16 to 5:19 Emerson slips in an interpolation of the Revolutionary War fife and drum tune "The Girl I Left Behind Me." Meanwhile, in the lower register, we hear the first fully developed melodic counterpoint to the main theme, played on Moog "tuba."

Repetition #7 (6:01–7:01). The main theme is now taken up by a brassier Moog setting. The "tuba" countermelody disappears, but a new, more rhythmically active countermelody is taken up by Moog "trumpet"—similar to the Moog trumpet setting we have already heard at the climactic sections of "The Endless Enigma" and "Hoedown" (and that we will hear again on *Brain Salad Surgery*). Palmer now begins to double the bolero rhythm on tom-tom and timpani. As the main theme and "trumpet" countermelody intertwine ever more impetuously, aggressive, stabbing "trumpet" chords begin to make their presence felt: listen especially at 6:16 and 6:37.

Repetition #8 (7:01–8:01). By this point the main theme is being heard on several different instrumental colors in several different registers. The piece is brought to its climax by a screaming Moog lead line that for

---

[38] Interior pedal points are created when a note that was a chord tone in one chord is held over into subsequent chords where it is no longer a chord tone, and is dissonant with other notes of the subsequent chords.

[39] Again, this may be a "trick" of orchestration that Emerson learned from Gustav Holst: in the latter portions of "Mars" the high woodwinds and trumpet rhythmically double the 5/4 ostinato.

once suggests no orchestral instrument, but has a clear link to the searing Moog lead sound that Emerson had used in the central section of "Trilogy." At the same time, Lake's earlier offbeat bass line is reintroduced on Moog "tuba," creating a deep rumble in conjunction with the bolero rhythm bass line which Lake is playing (now in octaves) on bass guitar, and Palmer is playing (via overdubs) on snare, toms, and timpani.

Coda (8:01–8:07). The brief but powerful coda brings "Abaddon's Bolero" to a breathless conclusion on sledgehammerlike iterations of a dissonant chord that suddenly resolves to a C major triad. What is most impressive about this coda is how quickly and effectively it forges musical links with some of the other high points of the album. The rhythm of the "sledgehammerlike iterations" of the final chords makes a clear reference to the close of "Hoedown": compare 3:35 of "Hoedown" with 8:01 of "Abaddon." Furthermore, the dissonant chord alluded to above is none other than the "Enigma chord" from "The Endless Enigma," here transferred up a half step (i.e., from C–F–B to $C^\sharp$–$F^\sharp$–C)! This raises a question: since the $F^\sharp$/C dichotomy of "The Endless Enigma," never resolved during the opening suite, is finally resolved here in favor of C major—and since the dark "Enigma chord" has finally been resolved into the glowing simplicity of a C major triad—does this mean the musical/metaphysical enigma of the opening suite has been resolved here in "Abaddon"?

I don't want to push the issue too hard, because I don't want to suggest a conceptual link where there may be none. On the other hand, I don't think it's a coincidence that Emerson introduced the "Enigma chord" (or something very close) in the three large-scale pieces of *Trilogy* ("The Endless Enigma," "Trilogy," and "Abaddon's Bolero"), but resolved it only in the latter. Certainly for some reviewers, one of the strengths of *Trilogy* was its musical coherence and the logical progression of moods it achieves, even across the gamut of different styles that it traverses. In a positively glowing review, Tony Stewart of *New Musical Express* gushes,

> This new set can only be described as brilliant. It lies somewhere between *Tarkus* and *Emerson, Lake and Palmer*. It's not exactly a concept, except for coordinated ideas. Nor is it merely an album of songs. There is a continuity, a flow of themes which is explored to its fullest . . . This must be classed as ELP's finest work. The music has so much mood, texture, and color that it is impossible not to enjoy it. They are seen in a new light of genius.[40]

The reader may have been struck that I have described "Abaddon's Bolero" in explicitly orchestral terms. This is intentional. In an interview with Dominic Milano, Emerson asserted that he usually tried not to refer

---

[40] Tony Stewart, review of *Trilogy*, *New Musical Express*, July 1, 1972.

to the sounds of other instruments when playing the Moog but admitted that "Abaddon's Bolero" "was an attempt to copy the Walter Carlos thing. That was one occasion where I tried to copy trumpet sounds and the like."[41] I think this is, in part, a fairly arguable statement. As I have pointed out already, Emerson's claim that he ordinarily attempted to avoid suggesting the sounds of other instruments with his Moog lines is rather dubious; there are numerous instances on all of ELP's albums up to this time (with the possible exception, ironically, of *Pictures*, a renowned orchestral piece in a previous incarnation) of Emerson employing the Moog to evoke traditional instruments. However, this is undoubtedly the only time Emerson used the Moog to evoke a virtual electronic orchestra. At the time this was something of a trend; during the early 1970s Walter (now Wendy) Carlos and Isao Tomita experienced a brief window of popularity by recording electronic interpretations of orchestral pieces in which overdubbed Moog lines were used to simulate the various instruments of a traditional orchestra. "Abaddon's Bolero" is at least the equal of anything by Carlos or Tomita in terms of its use of the Moog; unlike either of them, Emerson showed with "Abaddon" that he didn't need the classics to display his Moog orchestrations, but could compose original "orchestral" music.

In fact, he was later to orchestrate "Abaddon's Bolero" about the same time he was working on his Piano Concerto, and he recorded an orchestral version of "Abaddon" with the London Philharmonic Orchestra during late 1975 at De Lane Lea Studios, Wembley, with John Mayer conducting. The orchestral version of "Abaddon," which was finally released on Emerson's solo album *Changing States* in 1995, demonstrates some of his undeniable strengths as a composer: his ability to create complex but coherent thematic material, his instinct for creating a gradual climax over a long range by a systematic increase in timbral, textural, and harmonic complexity, and his superb sense of rhythmic counterpoint. However, it also demonstrates an undeniable weakness. As I have suggested above, Emerson's model was not only Ravel, but Holst ("Mars") and Copland. All three were virtuoso orchestrators: Emerson is not. His orchestration is competent, but nothing more, and does not bear close comparison with that of his models.

The same, however, is most definitely not true of his electronic orchestration of "Abaddon." It is entirely possible that in 1972 no one was more intimately familiar with the modular Moog than Keith Emerson, and "Abaddon" is really a virtuoso display of the Moog's possibilities for evoking, yet not slavishly duplicating, orchestral instruments. Indeed, the

---

[41] Keith Emerson, quoted by Milano, "Keith Emerson," *Contemporary Keyboard*, October 1977, 36.

difference between "evoking" and "duplicating" is the key, in my view, to the success of "Abaddon" in its electronic guise. The Moog "trumpet" doesn't quite sound like a real trumpet, the Moog "piccolo" doesn't sound exactly like a real one, the mixture of overtones in the electronic version is very different than what it would be with acoustic instruments, and the overall effect is akin to viewing a familiar picture through a distorting lens, or seeing yourself in a fun-house mirror. While Emerson's formal, thematic, and harmonic procedures in "Abaddon" are interesting, they show no radical departure from those of his models, a point that is underscored by the rather middlebrow feel of "Abaddon" in its orchestral guise. It is the electronic orchestration of "Abaddon"—with its unfamiliar familiarity—that lends it its interest. Blair Pethel comments that the electronic version of the work is much more significant than its orchestral counterpart because it is much more original (a statement with which I wholeheartedly concur), and concludes:

> "Abaddon's Bolero" is one of Emerson's most important works; it demonstrates the maturity of his aural conceptions. His exploration of the sonic possibilities of the electronic synthesizer and its use in the recording studio make this piece a pioneer in the field of modern recording technology. The fact that it lends itself to traditional orchestration so readily underscores the fact that a work of orchestral proportions need not be confined to traditional instrumentation.[42]

Trilogy: An Assessment

While *Brain Salad Surgery* is generally acknowledged by friends and foes alike to mark the apex of ELP's output, there has long been a not insignificant minority that prefers *Trilogy*. This is not a totally indefensible preference. Certainly, *Trilogy* marks a step forward for all three band members. For Emerson, *Trilogy* signals a much more organic integration of synthesizer into his arrangements than anything he had achieved before. On the first two studio albums, the synthesizer still sounds like an exotic touch, either added as an afterthought to or used as a substitute for organ and piano. While *Pictures* shows a more comprehensive integration of Moog and Hammond than either, it seems rather overdependent on a series of interrelated Moog filter effects. *Trilogy* solves both issues elegantly: a much wider range of Moog timbres are integrated much more seamlessly than ever before into the band's arrangements, with a decided preference for using the Moog as an orchestral substitute.

Emerson's growth is mirrored in the work of the other two band

---

[42] Pethel, "Keith Emerson," 65.

members. Lake's singing becomes more assured and variegated than ever before. On "The Endless Enigma," Lake spices his bell-like choirboy delivery with carefully placed vocal rasping, achieving a new sense of conviction and a new subtlety in coloring individual words that was to serve him well in his interpretation of the band's later epics like "Karn Evil 9" and "Pirates": one wishes he could have gone back and rerecorded the vocal parts of "Stones of Years" and "Battlefield" in the same manner. His singing of "Trilogy" shows a new assurance in handling challenging intonation problems, and "Living Sin" finds him experimenting with unusual falsetto techniques.

Palmer, for his part, makes a great leap forward, not so much in technique—his technique was already staggering—as in orchestration abilities and, above all, in taste. Chris Welch, in his generally very positive review of *Trilogy* that ran in the June 24, 1972, issue of *Melody Maker*, called special attention to this:

> Carl's drumming has changed quite considerably. For some time he has been dissatisfied with mere speed and Richian attack [the reference here is to the phenomenally fast jazz drumming of Buddy Rich], and although he does that beautifully, it is significant that one of the few drum breaks he takes is quite out of character. This comes at the beginning of "The Sheriff." Amidst much cowpoking and clouting of wooden skulls, Palmer lays into an intro that clobbers around his kit like the heaviest of rock drummers. And from the off, Carl gets into bongo and conga drums—all manner of percussion, which he uses intelligently and with taste. His accuracy on the stop times, fills, accents, and the different time signatures is splendid, and his playing on "Hoedown," for example, is a remarkable piece of ensemble work.[43]

Indeed, *Trilogy* is without a doubt the most good-humored and relaxed album of their classic period. As Welch noted at the beginning of his review, "Something happens halfway through Emerson, Lake and Palmer's new album that their sternest critics might find unusual. They relax. And then they rock. And the neurotic tension that marks a lot of their work gives way to funky good humor."[44] In terms of concision, only the debut album suggests itself as a rival; in terms of consistency, only the debut album and *Brain Salad Surgery*.

At the same time, though, while *Trilogy* sounds a lot simpler than, for instance, *Tarkus*, there is a good deal of sophistication beneath the apparent simplicity. This is especially true of Emerson's compositions. The apparently "simple" diatonic harmony turns out to be not so simple at all; this is also true of Aaron Copland's music, which really was just beginning to impact

---

[43] Chris Welch, "The ELP Enigma," *Melody Maker*, June 24, 1972, 15.
[44] Ibid.

Emerson's writing during the *Trilogy* era. Emerson's growing mastery of using tonal cross-references to create a sense of unity both within individual tracks and across the entire album, while unpretentious and easily ignored, is really quite impressive. However, the dichotomy between apparent simplicity and sophistication is also a function of the arrangements, especially Palmer's drumming, which is simultaneously less flashy and more carefully tied in with the keyboard and bass parts than ever before. Furthermore, unlike so many later ELP albums (or even earlier albums like *Tarkus*), on *Trilogy* the short tracks reveal the same care and craftsmanship as the longer tracks: what they lose by being less imposing, they gain by being more direct. In effect, *Trilogy* became the touchstone for the band's attempts of the late seventies (and beyond) to create music that was both accessible and multidimensional. The problem with so many of the later attempts (*Love Beach*, of course, comes immediately to mind) is, by comparison, that not only does the music sound simple, it sounds simplistic.

Finally, if the debut album, with its obvious debt to contemporary jazz idioms and British folksong, didn't put the lie to the idea that ELP were simply a "classical rock" band, than surely *Trilogy* should have. Even in the seventies, when there was a certain trendiness to the notion that rock musicians ought to expropriate elements of classical music into their work—an idea especially alluring to the era's camp practitioners of prog rock (who had no real clue as to *why* such a fusion might have any musical or cultural relevance)—Emerson was uncomfortable with ELP's music being described as "classical rock."[45] *Trilogy*, perhaps more than most ELP albums, showed what a wide-ranging familiarity the band had with American popular music as a whole: bossa nova, bluegrass, blues, and movie music (both Westerns and cop movies), all make their influence felt during the course of the album.

If there are many good things to be said about *Trilogy*, it must be acknowledged that, in the context of ELP's overall output, the album is not entirely above criticism. First of all, no other release from the band's classic era made less of an impact on their live show than *Trilogy*. This is because, while Emerson's integration of the Moog into the band's arrangements had taken a quantum leap forward on *Trilogy*, it was often done at the expense of what was feasible in a live performance situation. Years after the fact, Carl Palmer recalled, "*Trilogy* was a problem as an album. It was the first album that we recorded with all the overdubs. So when we tried to play them on stage, it didn't work."[46] The "Endless Enigma" suite was played only briefly before it regrettably disappeared

---

[45] See Milano, "Keith Emerson," *Contemporary Keyboard*, October 1977, 25.
[46] Carl Palmer, quoted by Aymeric Leroy, "An Interview with Carl Palmer," *Big Bang* (August 1997), reprinted in translated form in *ELP Digest* 7, no. 17 (September 8, 1997): 10, available online at http://www.brain-salad.com.

from ELP's live sets. Side two of the LP format went virtually unrepresented in the band's live shows: as far as I can determine "Trilogy" and "Living Sin" were never performed live, while "Abaddon's Bolero" was performed only briefly before a series of onstage disasters convinced the band to shelve the piece. Keith Emerson has described the problems the band faced in making "Abaddon" stageworthy: "We tried doing that as a trio in all manner of ways. I even taught Greg to play keyboards for it . . . Then we had the strings on a tape recorder and Carl had headphones on. He played drums to that. It didn't work for too long. The tape broke down one night and everything fell to pieces. So we never used that again."[47] For a band whose identity was less reliant on live performance than ELP's, the album's relative lack of stageworthiness would not have been such a major issue. For a band like ELP, though, that often argued that their music didn't fully come alive until it came alive on stage, *Trilogy*'s lack of an impact on their live show must be counted against it. Only "Hoedown" went on to become a perennial live favorite, with "The Sheriff" and "From the Beginning" also playing a role in the band's live shows at various stages of their career.

If some fans welcomed the sunnier, more relaxed ambience of *Trilogy*, others missed the sense of intensity and urgency that had characterized some of their most representative earlier material. The only track on *Trilogy* that packs the punch of the more aggressive side of their earlier output is "Living Sin," and this track doesn't exactly have the same scope and depth as the "Tarkus" suite, "The Three Fates," or even "Knife-Edge" or the "Baba Yaga" sequence from *Pictures*. While the following hypothesis is bound to be controversial, I'll spring it anyway. In my view, *Trilogy* marks the first stage in the gradual displacement of the Bartók/Ginastera line of influence in Emerson's music by the influence of Copland. This displacement is mirrored both by his gradual shift from the grittier Hammond sound to the smoother polyphonic synthesizer timbres which he had come to prefer by the late 1970s and by his gradual move away from bitonal chord voicings to more conventional chord structures, and I think it eventually robbed Emerson's music of a certain amount of its aggression and nervous energy. This was a process which was temporarily suspended during the *Brain Salad Surgery* era, but which emerged with renewed force during the *Works* period, so I will develop this hypothesis at greater length when we discuss those albums.

Finally and perhaps most seriously, *Trilogy* lacks the visionary quality of the debut album and the "Tarkus" suite, the combined sense of newness, strangeness, and rightness that had impacted fans of the first three

---

[47] Keith Emerson, quoted by Milano, "Keith Emerson," *Contemporary Keyboard*, October 1977, 32. The keyboards played by Lake on the live performances of "Abaddon" were Mellotron and Minimoog.

albums so profoundly. In 1970, no one else was playing anything remotely similar to the music on ELP's debut album, and in 1971 the "Tarkus" suite represented if anything an even more challenging foray into new territory. By 1972, however, *Trilogy* no longer sounded so revolutionary in light of the more adventurous contemporaneous rock releases—Yes's *Close to the Edge*, for instance. *Trilogy* proved to be the last ELP album engineered by Eddy Offord: for some time he had been working with both ELP and Yes, and the greater input which Yes gave him in production matters made it logical for him to work with them full time when they offered him the opportunity to run their sound on tour. Granted, he has remarked, "Working with Emerson, Lake and Palmer wasn't nearly as bad [as working with Yes] in terms of trying to referee . . . I was able to concentrate more on engineering than when I was with Yes. I had a fair amount of say with some of the material, but they came into the studio far more rehearsed."[48] However, remarks which he made in an interview conducted shortly after he had officially parted company with ELP suggest that a waning enthusiasm for the band's music may have played a role in his decision to work with Yes full time:

> I thought their first album was really great. It was very over-technical and lacking in feel but it was different and at the time it was a mind-blower. The second album was *Tarkus*, and I thought that was probably the best of the lot. Then I did *Trilogy* and I felt that it was the same old licks just put in different order, and from what I hear the new album [*Brain Salad Surgery*] doesn't make it at all.[49]

While Offord's curt dismissal of *Brain Salad Surgery* can probably be attributed to wounded pride ("since I didn't work on it, it can't be any good"), I do think he identified an important trend in regards to *Trilogy*: this album seems to find the band polishing and perfecting existing approaches rather than exploring new territory. Fortunately, the band didn't sit still for very long: they didn't have time to.

---

[48] Eddy Offord, quoted by Buskin, *Inside Tracks*, 174. Offord added that one of his responsibilities at ELP recording sessions was programming sounds into Emerson's modular Moog. Emerson told me, however, "That's not exactly correct"; the "Lucky Man" patch was preprogrammed, and Emerson denies Offord programmed any of the modular Moog settings on *Tarkus* or *Trilogy*. Emerson added that while Offord was given no input into compositional or arrangement matters, he did indeed play an influential role in the mixing and production of the first four ELP albums.

[49] Eddy Offord, quoted by Ray Telford, "Eddy Offord," *Sounds*, January 12, 1974, reprinted in *Fanzine for the Common Man* 14 (July 1995): 23. I had hoped to contact Offord during the writing of this book to see if his views may have changed, but was unable to locate him.

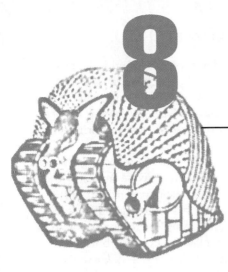

Get Me a Ladder

Manticore Record Label; 1973 European Tour (January 1972–May 1973)

The year 1972 began much like 1971 for ELP. January and February were spent recording new music for their upcoming album *Trilogy* and rehearsing for the next tour, which was launched in March. After playing one isolated gig in Cardiff, Wales, on March 10, ELP launched a blitzkrieg tour of the U.S. and Canada, playing thirty-five shows in forty days between March 21 and April 29, including the "Mar y Sol" Festival in San Juan, Puerto Rico, on April 3. After taking May off, they undertook a European tour in June, playing twelve dates in Germany, Denmark, Switzerland, Austria, and Italy—their first Italian shows, and the beginning of an especially strong relationship between ELP and their Italian fan base.

Trilogy was released in late June in the U.K. and in July in the U.S. Again it was a smash hit in the U.K., charting out at number two. *Trilogy* became the first ELP album to do almost as well on the U.S. charts, charting out at number five and staying in Billboard's Top 40 for twenty weeks. With *Trilogy*, the band had undisputedly reached megastar status in the States: their run of three top-ten albums in the U.S. between July 1971 and August 1972 is still impressive, even by more recent standards.

On July 8 the band played the "Concert 10" Festival at Pocona International Raceway at Long Pond, Pennsylvania: other participants included Black Sabbath, Humble Pie, J Geils, and Three Dog Night. On July 22 and 24 the band played their first two shows in Japan, at Tokyo and Osaka, respectively. From this beginning developed a fiercely devoted Japanese fan base that still endured, to some degree (especially for Emerson's work) well into the 1990s.

An abbreviated version of the July 22 Tokyo show was shown on Japanese television, and has circulated in bootleg form ever since.[1] It

---

[1] By all accounts, this show was something of a nightmare for the band. They were playing in an outdoor stadium; a monsoon threw Emerson's modular Moog, always extremely sensitive to humidity changes, horrendously out of tune. At one point during the video footage

shows the band's live show at a state of development roughly halfway between their Lyceum show of December 1970 (which we have already discussed) and their American concerts of 1974, which are represented in recorded form both by their live album *Welcome Back My Friends to the Show That Never Ends* and by ABC's TV broadcast of their performance during the Ontario Speedway Jam Festival.

The broadcast of the Tokyo show opened with "Hoedown," then moved into a performance of the entire "Tarkus" suite: anyone familiar with *Welcome Back My Friends* would recognize most of their arrangement of the piece here, although Lake's electric guitar solo on "Battlefield" and especially Emerson's space rock episode on "Aquatarkus" were not nearly as fully developed as they later would be.[2] They played "Take a Pebble" with a number of items interpolated in the manner of their 1974 *Welcome Back* recording of the piece, including "Infinite Space," "Lucky Man" (a solo showpiece for Lake, although Palmer drummed on a bit of it), and a solo piano performance by Emerson that already sounds quite a bit like the "Piano Improvisations" segment of *Welcome Back*. The broadcast ended with the closing segments of *Pictures*, "Baba Yaga" and "The Great Gates of Kiev," in versions not greatly different from their March 1971 recording (although "Baba Yaga" now included a snippet of "Abaddon's Bolero").

After Japan it was back to the grind: several shows in California in later July, and a number of U.S. and Canadian shows in August. They played to 18,000 fans at *Melody Maker*'s Poll Winner Concert at the Oval Cricket Ground, Kennington, South London, on September 30. As ELP played the "Tarkus" suite, two mammoth armadillo tanks appeared on both sides of the stage, breathing clouds of smoke; Barbara Graustark reported that "as the performance thundered to its climactic high point, the tanks thundered an ear-deafening barrage, driving fans into a wild frenzy of excitement and jubilation."[3] In November they undertook a twenty-one-concert British tour, ending with a show at Dundee, Scotland, on December 1.

Lake begins singing Burt Bacharach's "Raindrops Keep Falling On My Head" as the rain pours down. At least they were able to complete the Tokyo show, unlike the show in Osaka, which was an even bigger disaster. A huge wave of fans rushed the stage, and when the Osaka Police Security was unable to stem the tidal wave of fans, they shut down the power lines to the stage, effectively ending the show: as Emerson and Lake were whisked away from the stadium in a limo, Carl Palmer, who was unaware that the power was shut off and that his band mates had abandoned him, launched into an epic twenty minute drum solo while he vainly waited for Emerson and Lake to reappear on stage.

[2] During the Tokyo performance of "Aquatarkus" Emerson quoted Grieg's "Hall of the Mountain King," playing it on the modular Moog and Minimoog simultaneously—this segment had been dropped from ELP's live show by 1974.

[3] Barbara Graustark, "ELP: Rock Kings Turn Gypsies for Pop Extravaganza," *Circus*, January 1973, 56, 58.

Their show at Sheffield City Hall on November 25 gives a good idea of their repertoire at this time. The opening forty minutes was particularly impressive: they began with "Hoedown," played the complete "Tarkus" suite (in an arrangement very similar to the Japanese performance discussed above), and launched immediately into the "Endless Enigma" suite, minus only the atmospheric opening section. Next they played a wonderful thirty-second theme called "At the Sign of the Swinging Cymbal" that they dedicated to DJ Alan Freeman, whom, said Emerson, "always plays the end of our records, not the whole thing." This brief segment of music had all the classic ELP hallmarks—heroic melody, dynamic chord changes, energetic rhythms—and one wishes the band had developed it into something more substantial. Then came "The Sheriff," played on organ, unlike the later (and in my view less successful) electric piano version of their 1973–74 tour. The "Take a Pebble" sequence which followed was now even closer to their 1974 version than the Japanese performance of a few months earlier had been—the first half of "Take a Pebble" is followed by "Lucky Man" (with Emerson accompanying on piano), Emerson's "Piano Improvisations" segment (which was now getting very close indeed to the *Welcome Back* performance), and part two of "Take a Pebble." The band finished with *Pictures at an Exhibition* complete, only slightly different from their March 1971 recording, and played "Nutrocker" and "Rondo" as encores.[4]

Interlude One: Hippies, Capitalism, Countercultural Politics, and Progressive Rock

Several events took place during the latter part of 1972 and the beginning of 1973 that permanently changed the nature of ELP. To understand these developments in ELP's history, though, it is necessary to first consider some of the broader cultural and socioeconomic shifts that had taken place since ELP's inception in the closing days of 1969. The 1972–73 period marks something of a watershed. By this time, people were beginning to refer to the "sixties" in the past tense. To be sure, many sixties concerns and assumptions operated well into the 1970s. Furthermore, while there was a lot of talk among the Left about the "failure" of late-sixties aspirations, the fact is that by 1972–73 a substantial proportion of the American counterculture's short-term political agenda had in fact been realized. By

---

[4] A show played one night later, at London's Hammersmith Odeon, is featured in *The Original Bootleg Series from the Manticore Vaults,* vol. 2. The set list differed in that the Hammersmith Odeon show did not include *Pictures* in its entirety, just the closing "Baba Yaga"/"Great Gates of Kiev" segment.

1972, as the Nixon administration was tortuously seeking a way out of Southeast Asia, it was becoming clear that the U.S. would be exiting Vietnam on terms very different than those Lyndon Johnson and the Establishment had envisioned in the midsixties; by March 29, 1973, the last American troops left Vietnam. The Left's environmental concerns were becoming increasingly mainstream, evidenced by the antipollution demonstrations of the first Earth Day on April 22, 1970. One of the hippies' more self-serving goals, the abolition of the draft, was realized when Defense Secretary Melvin Laird announced the end of the military draft on January 27, 1973. Although the pet project of late-sixties feminism, the Equal Rights Amendment, was never ratified by the States (it had been approved by an 84-8 vote in the U.S. Senate on March 22, 1972), the role of women in Western society had been fundamentally changed by the late-sixties experience. Likewise, the Civil Rights movement of the sixties had produced fundamental shifts in the politics of race in the U.S.

I would argue that it was the counterculture's spiritual agenda, rather than its political agenda, that failed. Anyone who has read Bill Martin's *Listening to the Future* is probably aware that he chides me for overemphasizing the religious/spiritual aspects of the counterculture and underemphasizing its political side, specifically the Marxist element in the counterculture's political thought.[5] While I do not deny there was a contingent of Marxist intellectuals who were deeply involved in the sixties counterculture, I maintain my essential stance of *Rocking the Classics*: as a whole the late-sixties counterculture, especially the hippie movement from which progressive rock sprang, was not explicitly anticapitalist in a theoretical, Marxist sense. Rather, it evinced a more instinctive anticonsumerism and antimaterialism that often suggests British and American movements of radical pastoralist communitarianism, from the Ranters and Seekers of the seventeenth century to William Morris's Arts and Crafts movement of the nineteenth.[6] The counterculture also seems to bear some trace of religious movements that have rejected materialism and have emphasized austerity and simplicity (the Shakers, for instance), although the counterculture's notion of material austerity certainly did not extend to matters of sexual behavior. Shortly I will discuss Martin's suggestion that progressive rock as a style was at some level more or less explicitly anticapitalist; the question at the moment, though, is, "Did your average hippie—someone who identified himself or herself as part

---

[5] See Martin, *Listening to the Future*, 129–49.

[6] I was gratified to note, for instance, that Jacques Barzun, in his magisterial survey *From Dawn to Decadence*, saw the "Flower Children" of the sixties as spiritual descendents of the Ranters, the Familists, and other seventeenth-century English Christian collectivist sects, as well as nineteenth-century utopian communities, rather than of twentieth-century Marxism; see pp. 265, 764.

of the counterculture—see himself or herself as anticapitalist in a Marxist sense?"

I very much doubt it. As a matter of fact, I will go a step farther: although there is no question the counterculture *was* supposed to be about rejecting Establishment consumerism and materialism, there was a significant gap between what the average hippie believed and the way he or she lived. Despite their antimaterialist rhetoric, most hippies simply didn't care to adjust their lifestyle to a degree that would truly impact and change corporate structures. This became especially true in the late sixties and early seventies, when the United States entered into a period of almost unprecedented prosperity. Even when hippies joined communes (and this was only a tiny percentage of the counterculture as a whole) they continued to buy records from huge record companies, trendy clothes from huge clothing manufacturers, and so on. The type of localized, quasi-medieval, precapitalist "anticorporate" economy that commune founders envisioned never got off the ground because not enough hippies cared to forego the material goods that were only available through large corporations: hippie spirituality was defeated by Establishment materialism, which preyed on hippie hedonism.[7]

What does this have to do with progressive rock? Plenty. As we'll see, it is eminently arguable that ELP and the other major progressive acts of the time were ultimately defeated, at least in part, by their own prosperity. In its early days, progressive rock had been an anticorporate music to its roots. Its complexity and scope flouted the norms of both commercial radio and the 45 rpm single, the two main means that pop musicians had traditionally relied on to generate an audience. It was truly a "people's music." It was played in small clubs by musicians who were part of the same countercultural scene as the audiences they were playing for. It was supported by "underground" fanzines dedicated to the music, musicians, and the scene around them, and, in the U.S., by the burgeoning "freeform" format on FM radio, which allowed the musicians to receive airplay without bowing to the conventions of music industry-controlled AM radio. The spectacular success of the Beatles' three seminal midsixties albums (*Revolver, Rubber Soul, Sergeant Pepper*) had alerted the major record companies to the shift taking place from the 45 rpm single to the 33 rpm album as the preferred medium of the new music. The shift towards the album as the unit, in turn, made the long instrumental jams and interconnected song cycles of late-sixties proto-progressive music commercially viable.

---

[7] Drugs without a doubt played a role in this process. Timothy Leary's belief that hallucinogens would open new doors of perception and thus counter Establishment dogma, a genuinely important part of countercultural thinking in its early days, soon enough gave way to pure escapism and hedonism.

Record companies who were slow to grasp this shift soon found themselves at a disadvantage when competing with upstart labels like Island, ELP's label, who understood very well both the expectations of late-sixties audiences and the priorities of progressive musicians. In its early days, progressive music was given a great boost by "turbulence" within the record industry, as the major labels tried to establish some predictable guidelines for what would sell and what wouldn't, and attempted to figure out how this new music might best be marketed. During this period of uncertainty labels signed a number of bands that eventually proved to be uncommercial after all; by the time the contracts of such bands had expired, they had been given the opportunity to release two or three albums that under more "settled" industry conditions would never have seen the light of day. Furthermore, the successful artists were given a leeway for experimentation and an input into the final form their releases would take that was quite unprecedented in terms of record industry norms, both pre-1970 and post-1980.

By 1972–73, record industry "turbulence" was beginning to settle, and the music industry was beginning the process of asserting ever greater control over rock as product. Many of the independent labels had either gone broke or had begun to resemble the major labels in both outlook and practice. The successful "countercultural" journals (*Rolling Stone* being a perfect example) had become big businesses themselves, and, in the U.S., freeform FM radio was giving way to the more "professional" and predictable AOR (album-oriented radio) format, essentially a top-forty type of format for rock music, which by the late 1970s had become a very conservative force in rock music.[8] Record companies had largely determined what would sell and what wouldn't, and how to best market their most successful acts. This especially involved having their bands undertake massive North American tours, playing at arena- and stadium-sized venues, to promote each new album.

The result of this trend in progressive music was twofold. First, it cut off the major British bands who were caught in the "system"—ELP, Yes, Pink Floyd, Jethro Tull, and so forth—from the subcultural scene in which they had originated, and created the vast gulf between the major acts and their fans which characterized the rock music scene of the 1970s. Since touring the U.S., with its huge venues and enormous record-buying public, was so much more profitable than touring the U.K., after

---

[8] Ironically, the AOR format insured that ELP's lengthy tracks would receive virtually no radio airplay, with its insistence on rotating well-known cuts by well-known bands: the only four ELP cuts which ever received much exposure via the AOR format were "Lucky Man," "From the Beginning," "Still You Turn Me On," and "Karn Evil 9, 1st Impression, part two."

1973 the major British bands tended to go months—or years, sometimes—without even performing in the U.K. As a result, the music of the major progressive rock bands was increasingly dictated not by the symbiotic relationship between a specific subculture and its musicians, but rather by pressures exerted by the recording industry and other outside commercial agents. To put it more bluntly, by the late 1970s the existence of the major progressive bands was by and large predicated on commercial, rather than social, considerations.

Another issue here, as Paul Stump has pointed out, was that as the major progressive acts (ELP and Yes for instance) became more and more successful, more and more money was invested in them; this meant less and less money for many of the less commercially successful progressive acts, who by 1972 were increasingly tending to see contracts they had signed in 1969 or 1970 cancelled upon their expiration.[9] The formerly vibrant progressive music scene was slowly but surely shrinking, until finally it encompassed only the few surviving megabands. Not only did this process rob the progressive music scene of badly needed diversity and experimental tendencies by wiping out existing bands; but also it discouraged the signing of new progressive music talent. From the record company's perspective, why invest millions in an untried new progressive music act when you knew the next three ELP or Yes albums would sell one or two million units each, and each tour date the band played would sell out? And from the young musician's perspective, why play in a progressive band if you knew you could not hope to be signed to a contract?

While progressive rock in its original incarnation had doubtless become antiquated by the late 1970s, it is possible that the story of progressive music would have been somewhat different if there had been a more vibrant progressive music grassroots scene when the major progressive acts went on hiatus during the later seventies and early eighties. Heavy metal, after all, produced a whole new crop of bands (Iron Maiden, Judas Priest, and the whole New Wave of British Heavy Metal) after the demise of the original metal acts (Zeppelin, Sabbath, Deep Purple) during the same period. As it was, when the neo-progressive movement, spearheaded by Marillion, IQ, Pendragon, et al. did finally emerge during the mid-1980s, progressive rock's original fan base had dissolved, and these bands had to attempt to create a new fan base from ground zero. Not surprisingly, their impact on the popular music scene at large was very, very limited in comparison to contemporaneous metal bands.

---

[9] See Stump, *The Music's All That Matters*, 109–10.

The Founding of Manticore Records

But I have moved ahead of my narrative here, so let us return to 1972–73. The four new developments that permanently altered the nature of ELP are as follows. First, they launched their own label, Manticore Records. Second, they brought Peter Sinfield into the band as a full time colyricist. Third, they purchased an abandoned theater and turned it into a permanent practice facility. Fourth, they began assembling a huge and expensive array of new musical instruments, sound equipment, staging implements, lights, and other concert paraphernalia, which would enable them to put on shows of a scope that would have been unimaginable in 1970. There is no doubt that in the short term, at least, all these developments allowed them to push their music and their concerts to an entirely new level. However, it is equally clear that these developments signaled the shift of ELP from a band to a corporate entity—a "dinosaur," as Robert Fripp called the megabands of the 1970s and the corporate detritus that affixed itself to these bands, barnaclelike. But the irony of these developments is that while they assured ELP's great artistic and commercial triumphs of 1973–74, they also contained the seeds of corruption which eventually corroded the band's countercultural integrity, musical innovation, and, most ironically, commercial success.

If there is any one event that signals the transformation of ELP into a corporate entity, it is the founding of Manticore Records. By some point in late 1972, the band had decided that their interests were better served by forming their own label than by renegotiating their contracts with Island or Atlantic. Of course, during this era the creation of a vanity label to release one's own albums on was the final proof that a band had reached megastar status: The Beatles (Apple), The Moody Blues (Threshold), The Rolling Stones (Rolling Stones), and Led Zeppelin (Swan Song) also come to mind. However, unlike these other "labels" (with Zeppelin's Swan Song being the notable exception), ELP planned on their label functioning as real record label, signing, recording, and promoting new acts.

By April 1973, Manticore Records was off and running.[10] Marion "Big M" Medious, a black martial arts expert and former Atlantic Records executive who had previously served as ELP's road manager, was installed as president of Manticore; Stewart Young, who by this time had become ELP's manager, was a partner with the band in running the operation. An abandoned theater in 16 Curzon Street, London, was turned into the

---

[10] Manticore was, of course, the mythological man/lion/scorpion which was the subject of the "Tarkus" suite's fifth movement. As Emerson and Lake were both born in November and were both Scorpios, the name probably seemed especially appropriate.

firm's headquarters; another office was opened in New York City's Upper East Side. Initially, Manticore established a U.K. distribution deal with Island Records, but by July 1973 British and European distribution was being handled by WEA. During the summer of 1973 Manticore entered into a U.S. distribution agreement with Atlantic, which handled all the label's singles and the albums released prior to 1975; Manticore went on to reach additional distribution agreements with Tamla/Motown (which handled American distribution of the label's albums during 1975) and Elektra/Asylum (which took over U.S. distribution of the label's albums in 1976).

As we will see, the label's two most important releases during its existence were ELP's fifth and sixth albums, *Brain Salad Surgery* (1973) and *Welcome Back My Friends to the Show that Never Ends: Ladies and Gentlemen Emerson, Lake and Palmer* (1974). However, a major goal of the label was also, as Emerson put it, was "to help other bands who were struggling, and who were sort of part of the progressive movement."[11] In particular, Manticore played an important role in bringing Italy's two best-known progressive bands, PFM and Banco, to the attention of the English-speaking world, by releasing English-language versions of a number of their albums.

The first Manticore releases were the debut album of Lake's old King Crimson cohort, Peter Sinfield, *Still*, and PFM's *Photos of Ghosts* album; both were released in the U.K. on May 25, 1973 (midsummer in the U.S.). Sinfield never released another album on Manticore—he was soon far too involved with ELP—but PFM released four more albums on the label between 1973 and 1977, and Manticore achieved another coup by signing Banco in 1975, who in turn released three albums on the Manticore label. However, not all of Manticore's artists played progressive rock: Stray Dog were a Texas-based band not incomparable with ZZ Top, Thee Image, a hard rock band, and Keith Christmas, a singer-songwriter who emerged from the late-sixties British folk scene.

It is clear that the three members of ELP were not equally enthused about Manticore. Emerson was the least interested in the concept, as he has admitted on a number of occasions:

> That [the label] became too heavy an issue to really deal with. We had enough internal problems of our own, let alone having to deal with other bands' problems. I was never part of that whole issue, right from day one. I said "No, I don't want to be part of this. If you guys want to get involved, then do it, but I just want to get on with the music." I wasn't into the business side of things.[12]

[11] Keith Emerson, quoted by Hall, "Welcome to the Show," 46.
[12] Keith Emerson, quoted by Hall, "Welcome to the Show," 46.

Emerson has, in fact, insinuated that ELP's involvement with Manticore caused them to overextend themselves in a manner harmful to the band's future, noting, "There was a lot of pressure on us in the seventies because we were trying to be lawyers, accountants, and producers."[13] While Carl Palmer seems a bit more positive about the Manticore experience, he too suggests in his remarks that the label overextended ELP's energies and resources:

> We recorded PFM, and released their album on Manticore. And we managed to get one of their singles, a song called "Celebration" [from *Photos of Ghosts*], into the Top 20 in Britain. And we took PFM to America, but unfortunately they wanted to go home. They wanted to return to Italy, because they said the food was better there, and they liked Italian girls better than American girls. We couldn't explain to them that they were making career moves, and that eating and girls could come later. Then there was Pete Sinfield. We recorded a solo album for him, and we recorded an Anglo-American band called Stray Dog. And we recorded a guy named Snuffy Walden, who was a great Texas guitarist in the style of [ZZ Top's] Billy Gibbons. He later became Donna Summer's music director. But it was very hard, trying to run a record label while sustaining our own career.[14]

Clearly it was Greg Lake, whom Emerson has on a number of occasions called "the businessman in the group," who was the most enthusiastic about Manticore.[15] He was certainly the most involved of the three in Manticore's operations: the label was a natural outlet for his interest in record production, and he was involved in the production of the Pete Sinfield, Stray Dog, and Keith Christmas LPs. Not surprisingly, Lake seems to have the fondest recollections of Manticore:

> We were one of the first bands to break away from the traditional role of being controlled by a manager, or at the least, our arrangement wasn't a dictatorship, in which the band was manipulated by management. Actually, we set up Manticore to run the affairs of ELP. We owned a cinema, a rehearsal facility and a few other things. And we thought, at the time, that it would be great to give other worthy bands a chance, bands whose music wasn't likely to be picked up by other labels. And it was great, for awhile. We had a band from Italy called PFM who were marvelous musicians and songwriters. But the problem was, we just didn't have time to properly attend to their needs.[16]

---

[13] Keith Emerson, quoted by Robert Doerschuk, "Keith Emerson and ELP Again," *Keyboard*, June 1992, 52.
[14] Carl Palmer, quoted by Hall, "Welcome to the Show," 46.
[15] See Pethel, "Keith Emerson," 21; Stump, *The Music's All That Matters*, 194.
[16] Greg Lake, quoted by Russell Hall, "Welcome to the Show," 46.

Interlude Two: On the Politics of Progressive Rock

The whole Manticore Records phenomenon raises a larger issue, so at this point I would like to return to Bill Martin's suggestion that the counterculture, and by extension progressive rock, was implicitly anticapitalist: "One has to wonder what a conception of the 'counterculture' might be apart from the critique of capitalism."[17] Was progressive rock anticapitalist? Perhaps I ought to begin with a broader question: was progressive rock a "political" music? And if so, in precisely what sense was it political?

While I never called progressive rock "apolitical" in *Rocking the Classics*, something that Martin's prose seems to suggest,[18] he is probably correct to suggest that I didn't sufficiently emphasize the genre's political dimension:

> The late sixties was a time when the whole world was rocking, and even if there is a certain insular, middle-class perspective on what a "nicer" sixties would have been, recovered now as pure fashion and without the conflict and struggle of the period, and even if there is a peculiarly "English" gloss on this that is especially insulated (the "island life" again), this does not sever the basic connection between flower power and power to the people.[19]

As a cursory reading of many secondary sources from the late sixties and early seventies clearly demonstrate, rock music of the time clearly did have a political dimension, and progressive rock was no exception. As I pointed out in *Rocking the Classics*, progressive rock *was* political both in its insistence on lifestyle as a form of political statement, and its conviction (derived from both Romanticism and modernism) that music (and by extension, all art) is potentially a powerful tool of political change. Allow me to quote Robert Fripp, who has expressed the "music as revolution" concept as eloquently as anyone I know of: "Music is a high-order language system, i.e., it is a meta-language. The function of a meta-language is to express solutions to problems posed on a lower-order language system . . . If one were interested in political change one would not enter political life, one would go into music."[20] However, what I may not have emphasized sufficiently in *Rocking the Classics* is how keenly aware both rock audiences and rock detractors of the period were of rock's political dimension. For instance, consider this letter to the editor that appeared in

---

[17] Martin, *Listening to the Future*, 134.
[18] Martin, *Listening to the Future*, 146.
[19] Martin, *Listening to the Future*, 147.
[20] Robert Fripp, quoted by Tamm, *Robert Fripp*, 128.

the March 1972 issue of *Circus*, an issue, incidentally, which contained an extensive interview with the three members of ELP:

> It is my duty as a parent to see that my children grow mentally as well as physically. That they have respect for all people and grow to be useful citizens. Three of my children, I know, are going to benefit from my teachings and love. But somehow I have lost my sixteen-year old son, Robert. He has turned to the world of drugs and Communism.
>
> This is not all my fault. It is mostly the fault of these Communist magazines such as *Circus* and countless others. I have read some issues of *Circus* when my son wasn't around. In them I saw filthy, long-haired creatures. And to think my child took their way of life instead of the life of a good American . . .[21]

And on it goes. The point is, to this concerned parent circa 1972, the link between rock music, drugs, and countercultural politics was self-evident. Now, we could turn this letter into an interesting case study that would go far beyond the boundaries of a book on ELP. We could ponder to what degree Robert's lifestyle simply reflected a youthful hedonism totally devoid of any political viewpoint. Or we could wonder whether his lifestyle might represent a purely instinctive reaction against social, religious, and political institutions that seemed to him to be increasingly sterile and out of touch. We could consider what, if any, core political beliefs the different musicians featured in *Circus* really held in common. We could wonder, too, if by "Communist" the concerned parent really meant "Leftist," and whether the writer understood (or cared about) the distinction. However, the fact remains that for this person, who saw the Establishment not as repressive, imperialistic, and militaristic, but as a protector of God-given social order and old-fashioned American values of patriotism and hard work, rock music was part and parcel of the counterculture's Communist-inspired political attack on the American Way of Life. To this person, progressive rock (or any other rock style of the era, for that matter), was not "apolitical" at all, but had deeply political dimensions.

It must also be admitted, in defense of the general accuracy with which our letter-writer grasped the situation, that much progressive rock of the time did evince antiauthoritarian and anti-Establishment sentiments of a vaguely Leftist cast. The mistrust of technology and the fear of its potential misuse by the Establishment evinced on the debut ELP album certainly echoes countercultural concerns, although it must be pointed out that this concern was expressed by some members of the Right as well (think, for instance, of the "Project X" episode of Ayn Rand's *Atlas Shrugged*). The flip side of this antitechnological bent is the incipient eco-

---

[21] Anonymous, "Letters to the Editor," *Circus* (March 1972), 9.

logical consciousness that marks Yes's three "classic" albums of 1971–72. The antiwar theme of *Tarkus* clearly had "political" ramifications circa 1971 that would have been construed as Leftist by most contemporary observers (although, once again, there were isolated figures on the Right who had always opposed the Vietnam War), and the album's surreal cover (which, at this early stage, still suggested a clear link to hallucinogens) would have been seen as validating countercultural values. So would the agnostic musing of "The Only Way"—although, as Ayn Rand had already demonstrated, right-wingers could be atheists, too, while among the counterculture, atheism was much less popular than a kind of gauzy monism that syncretically blended elements of a number of different spiritual traditions. Certainly the quest for enlightenment, for transcendental spiritual experience that characterizes the "Endless Enigma" suite or Yes's *Close to the Edge* can only be understood in the context of countercultural spirituality and mysticism, with its Eastern influences (or Eastern trappings, in the view of some).

However, while it is accurate to say that progressive rock circa 1970–75 reflected some of the broad tendencies of countercultural thinking, it is more from a "philosophical" than an explicitly "political" perspective. Many progressive musicians of the era heartily believed the sixties axiom, "When the mode of the music changes, the walls of the city shake."[22] However, desiring political and cultural transformation, or even using one's art to agitate for political and cultural transformation, is not the same thing as articulating a coherent agenda for political and cultural transformation. What I *was* arguing against in *Rocking the Classics* was the notion that progressive rock was propagating some kind of systematic political agenda or ideology. In this respect I still believe I am correct, both about progressive rock and about rock circa 1970–75 at large, and it is here, I think, that the example of Richard Wagner is instructive.

During the second half of the nineteenth century, particularly between 1870 and 1910, Wagner's epic music dramas exerted a profound influence on the European cultural landscape. In particular, his enormous *Ring of the Nibelung* cycle (four interlocking music dramas, each about four hours in length) impacted poetry (the French symbolist and decadent movements were both inspired by Wagner), philosophy (Nietzsche, in particular), playwrights (George Bernard Shaw), visual artists (Gustav Moreau), and nearly every major composer of the era. There is no doubt that the potent and not entirely healthy strain of German nationalism energizing the music dramas exerted a powerful influence on contemporaneous cultural politics. The term "Wagnerism" was coined to describe the presumed philosophical-political-musical-dramatic "message" of

---

[22] Stump, *The Music's All That Matters*, 16–17.

Wagner's music dramas. Certainly Wagner, a man of unlimited ego, saw himself as a major philosopher and a political figure of great consequence: he was quite angry, for instance, when Bismarck snubbed him in the era following Germany's unification.

Yet, as William Weber and the other contributors to the magisterial *Wagnerism in European Culture and Politics* have pointed out, Wagner's political and philosophical "message" was so distended, jumbled, and ultimately self-contradictory that there is simply no way to define "Wagnerism" in terms of a unified system of either philosophical tenets or political beliefs.[23] In *Rocking the Classics* I described progressive rock in terms of what social theorists call a *bricolage*, that is, a loose compound of different elements held together by interdependence, affinity, analogy, and aesthetic similarity:

> Progressive rock's amalgamation of rhythm-and-blues, folk styles, classical music, science fiction and fantasy iconography, surreal verse, and Eastern mysticism might at first seem illogical; however, a central goal of this book [*Rocking the Classics*] will be exploring the very specific ways in which the component elements of this *bricolage* interlock to convey well-defined worldviews and lifestyles.[24]

Wagnerism was also a *bricolage* of sorts. Wagner's music dramas were so huge and took in so many elements—some of them mutually incompatible—that they were ultimately like a huge mirror, allowing the beholder to see whatever he or she came expecting to see. It is for this reason that a Fabian Socialist like George Bernard Shaw and a racist nationalist like Adolph Hitler could evaluate *The Ring* in utterly contradictory terms—Shaw saw it as a parable of capitalism's corrosive effects on class relations in nineteenth-century Europe, Hitler as a parable of the trials and tribulations of the German *volk* as they struggle towards their glorious destiny—without necessarily misrepresenting it. What makes Wagner's music dramas work is not their supposed philosophical or political "message," but rather their dramatic panache and profound aesthetic and musical unity. It is in the realm of aesthetics and musical style that the essence of Wagnerism is to be located.

As the reader has probably guessed, I see a significant parallel between progressive rock and Wagner's music dramas. As I demonstrated in chapters 2 through 4 of *Rocking the Classics*, there is an interrelated set of musical, visual, and literary conventions that govern progressive rock and enable it to cohere as a distinctive genre of music. Furthermore, progres-

---

[23] David C. Large and William Weber, eds., *Wagnerism in European Culture and Politics* (Ithaca, NY: Cornell University Press, 1984); see especially Weber's "Wagner, Wagnerism, and Musical Idealism," 28–71.
[24] *Rocking the Classics*, 5.

sive rock drew on disparate but complementary elements of Romanticism and modernism to develop a coherent aesthetic stance that emphasizes specific notions of individuality, idealism, authenticity, and art-as-transcendence. It is when we reach areas of philosophy and above all politics that I grow less comfortable speaking of a distinctive progressive rock ideology. Granted, as we've already seen, there are certain philosophical preoccupations that progressive rock returns to again and again. In the music of ELP, for instance, we have already examined issues of technological ethics and "progress," totalitarianism, alienation (both of an individual and a social nature), and the quest for spiritual transcendence. If we were to turn to other progressive rock acts, we could identify additional preoccupations (the holistic, environmentalist concerns of Yes, for instance) as well. Therefore, I'm not uncomfortable speaking of progressive rock's philosophical "message"—as long as it's understood the "message" is a loosely linked network of attitudes, ideas, and issues, not a coherent philosophical system per se.

However, I am considerable less comfortable speaking about progressive rock's political "message," other than in very, very general terms. As I noted above, some of the issues grappled with by progressive rock bands—such as a pervasive fear that the military-industrial complex would use the technology at its disposal unwisely—were as of much concern to the libertarian Right as they were to those of the Left. Bill Martin sees the counterculture as being deeply impacted by contemporaneous Marxist and post-Marxist thought—he especially points to Herbert Marcuse.[25] While I do not deny that such influence impacted the counterculture, I think it is a more open question whether it was central to the hippie movement—which is not, incidentally, exactly analogous to the counterculture, although it's an important cultural manifestation of it—out of which progressive rock sprang.[26] I certainly think it is an open question whether Marxist lines of thought are central to the progressive rock canon.

For instance, if progressive rock really is that closely allied with Leftist thought, does this mean we can extrapolate from "Mass" how ELP felt about the issue of secular governments granting religious institutions tax-free status? Does Yes's "And You And I" give us insight into how that band felt about nationalizing private land as a step to promoting environmental

---

[25] Martin, *Listening to the Future*, 65–66. I would place the Marxist musicologist/social theorist Theodor Adorno at the top of any list of intellectuals of the Left whose writings had a significant impact on sixties countercultural thought.

[26] I see the hippie movement as but one part of the sixties counterculture; when I refer to the latter, I'm referring to the hippie movement and the various anti-Establishment political movements of the decade which sometimes functioned within, and sometimes outside of, the hippie movement.

well-being? Does Genesis's "Selling England by the Pound" clue us in to the band's views about taxation as a tool for redistributing wealth? If the reader says, "of course not—they probably never even thought about these issues anywhere near this specifically," then my reply is this: now you see more precisely in what sense progressive rock is not political. If progressive rock really had a political ideology—especially in Marxist terms—these are issues these bands could be expected to address in a more or less explicit manner. The fact that they did not, with the rare exceptions such as Henry Cow proving the rule, demonstrates, I think, that progressive rock's contribution to the era's cultural discourse was *not* primarily political. This is why I fundamentally disagree with Bill Martin when he says, "While Macan would recover the aesthetic and perhaps 'philosophical' value of progressive rock, and discard the 'political' aspects of this particular expression of the counterculture, I would argue that there are 'political' meanings to progressive rock that have yet to be fully understood."[27] I hope that my analogy between progressive rock and Wagner's music dramas has demonstrated to the reader that progressive rock's impact on its time was due *precisely* to its aesthetic and philosophical value. It's not so much that I want to "discard" the political aspects of progressive rock as that I'm convinced that, at the end of the day, there is no clearly definable progressive rock political "ideology," at least in the sense that the word is ordinarily understood.

I would even go so far to say that one would have difficulty positing a clearly defined hippie political ideology. Earlier in this chapter, I argue that the hippie movement is a more or less spontaneous religious (or spiritual) movement with communitarian and collectivist impulses; I see the hippie movement having more in common with the radical Christian collectivist sects of mid-seventeenth-century England (the Ranters, the Familiasts) and nineteenth-century utopian communities than with Marxist-inspired movements of 1920–1965 in Western countries.

Nick Bromell, in one of the more carefully argued analyses of hippie politics I have read, argues that in the development of Bob Dylan's music, one can see a transition from the politics of the traditional Left (in his early, folk-song period), with an emphasis on action on behalf of specific oppressed groups, to the politics of the New Left, a kind of radical politics with anarchist overtones that Bromell sees as characteristic of hippie politics (so much as there was a "hippie politics").[28] According to Bromell, Dylan in his *Blonde on Blonde* and *Highway 61 Revisited* period projects this new kind of politics: experimentation with psychedelics had led the hippie to a feeling that his very consciousness was shackled by a

---

[27] Martin, *Listening to the Future*, 148.
[28] Nick Bromell, *Tomorrow Never Knows: Rock and Psychedelics in the 1960s* (Chicago: University of Chicago Press, 2000), 130–32.

burdensome network of political, social, and intellectual conventions, and therefore led him to struggle for his own freedom from all these "shackles" in unity with anyone else whom he perceived to share the burden of oppression. The anarchist element that Bromell perceives in hippie politics is certainly reminiscent of the seventeenth-century Christian collectivist groups that I see as the hippie movement's forerunners.

Chris Matthew Sciabarra, who builds especially on the arguments of Durrell Bowman, points to the Ayn Rand–influenced libertarianism that is so evident in the music of Rush (especially their music of the midseventies through the early eighties) as proof that not only does Randian objectivism adapt comfortably to the progressive rock style, it addresses a number of concerns that have traditionally been assumed to be the province of the Left.[29] I do not argue that a strain of libertarianism analogous to Rand's was probably present in incipient form in the hippie movement; I would caution that it was not fully evident until after the dissolution of the hippie movement around 1970, that is, after progressive rock had already emerged as a full-blown style. Interestingly, where I see this strain of libertarianism in its most unselfconscious and unsubtle form is in some of the pronouncements of hard-rock and early metal icons of the seventies such as Ted Nugent and Ozzy Osbourne.

In sum: the "politics" of the hippie movement—not to mention the "politics" of progressive rock—are not monolithic, are nowhere systematically articulated, are not necessarily coherent, and are certainly far from being fully understood. It is true there are certain topics and concerns that recur again and again in prog (as they recurred again and again in hippie thought). Such themes were addressed from a multiplicity of perspectives in which Romantic and modernist aesthetics, a plethora of "religious" and "spiritual" currents (of which various Eastern schools of though are most prominent) that defy easy political categorization, and, as we've seen, various strains of Marxism, anarchism, and libertarianism—some of them contradictory or mutually exclusive—all play a role.

So now to return to my original disagreement with Martin: was the counterculture, and by extension progressive rock, essentially anticapitalist? If the example of Manticore Records is an indication, the answer is "no." While ELP did show a genuine altruism in lending a "helping hand" of sorts to Banco, PFM, and others on their label, at the end of the day they expected Manticore to function as a moneymaking venture, and (as we shall see later on) when it ceased to do so, they pulled the plug on it. I think Paul Stump is essentially correct to speak of Greg Lake's

---

[29] See Chris Matthew Sciabarra, "Rand, Rush and Rock," *Journal of Ayn Rand Studies* 4, no. 1 (Fall 2002), 161–85; Durrell Bowman, "'Let Them All Make Their Own Music': Individualism, Rush, and the Progressive/Hard Rock Alloy, 1976–77," in Holm-Hudson, *Progressive Rock Reconsidered*, 183–218.

"proto-Thatcherism"; he quotes Lake as saying, "If the cats doing it today put enough into it they'll be heavy themselves one day . . . Input equals output."[30]

Nor was such "proto-Thatcherism" confined to ELP. By the mid-1970s, Rick Wakeman was a director of eleven companies. While Ian Anderson of Jethro Tull showed considerable sensitivity to local environmental concerns when he set up his salmon farm on the Isle of Skye in 1977, he never made any attempts to disguise that fact that the farm was intended as a moneymaking venture. The Moody Blues launched a chain of record stores for the same reason.[31] One of the weaker moments of *Listening to the Future* comes when Bill Martin huffily dismisses the suggestion that Yes could have been motivated by such a tawdry consideration as making money:

> When people write me regarding my book on Yes and say that they like the analysis of the music but dislike the politics of the book, and then go on to praise capitalism, Ayn Rand, Milton Friedman, and the idea that "of course the guys in Yes are just in it for the money, since that's all that motivates anyone," then I have to think that we are simply not listening to the same music or the same band.[32]

Martin tucks this statement into a footnote: I find it rather disingenuous. The fact is, there were a few acts in the seventies progressive scene, notably Henry Cow and (after the terrible accident which left him paralyzed) Robert Wyatt, who were explicitly anticapitalist. They expressed this stance in their lyrics,[33] and more importantly, in their relationship with the record industry (often at considerable aggravation to themselves) and in interband relationships. However, I see no such signs of actual (as opposed to implied) anticapitalism in the careers of the major prog bands, Yes included.

It is one thing to question the impact of capitalism—which I think a lot of these bands did—but it is another thing entirely to call for its abolition, especially considering the alternative at that time (post-Stalinist Communism). I don't see any of the major prog bands being anticapitalist in this more specific sense, either in their music, or especially in their

---

[30] Greg Lake, quoted in Stump, *The Music's All That Matters*, 194.

[31] Ibid.

[32] Martin, *Listening to the Future*, 327, fn50.

[33] While I'm not sympathetic towards Henry Cow's politics, I can't help but admiring their willingness to put their money where their collective mouths were and conduct their career in a way that reflected their egalitarian beliefs, often at considerable cost to themselves. However, I do find most of their lyrics to be chilly, obtuse, and pedantic; their lyrics tend to sound like a Marxist treatise set to words, and like so much agitprop, they inspire boredom more frequently than outrage.

relationships with the industry. If Yes had wanted to make a strong point in favor of socialist principles, they certainly had the wealth to do so by the midseventies, but I cannot see that they rocked the boat in favor of— to name just one issue that would seem to lend itself to socialist-minded solutions—record companies treating their lesser artists more fairly. As a matter of fact, when Britain's Labor government launched its effort to collect exorbitant taxes from the top tax bracket in 1974, Yes became tax exiles just like ELP, Zeppelin, Black Sabbath, Pink Floyd, and the other British megabands of the era.[34] True socialists, I would think, would not have resented their excess wealth being redistributed among the less fortunate.[35] I am not suggesting, incidentally, that Yes, ELP, or these other bands were hypocrites who preached genteel liberalism while practicing capitalist greed: to make this accusation, I would have to believe that they formulated a coherent political ideology that they were consciously violating. To the contrary, I believe that they simply never developed an explicit political ideology that would permit them to see a potential contradiction between the utopianism of their lyrics and the realities of capitalist (or any other form of) economics. Furthermore, I don't see that the lack of a coherent political ideology in any way compromises the power of progressive rock's utopian visions or its apocalyptic warnings. To quote John Street:

> Popular music's interplay between everyday common sense and imagination makes it a wholly inappropriate vehicle for accompanying political manifestos or inspiring collective actions. It is not, however, politically inconsequential. Pop's inability to change the world is compensated for by its ability to articulate and alter our perceptions of that world, and perhaps more importantly, to give a glimpse of other better worlds.[36]

In fact, I would argue that the political importance of progressive rock is not that it propagandizes on behalf of a political ideology, either Left or Right, or even that it advocates a particular political worldview. Rather, in keeping with its Romantic ethos of transcendence, progressive rock subjects philosophical, cultural, and social opposites to a Hegelian synthesis; as such, its politics might justifiably be called "utopian." What's rather amazing about prog is how many of the tensions existing within or of deep concern to the counterculture are submitted to an apparently subconscious synthesis in the progressive rock style.

---

[34] There is an excellent discussion of this issue in Stump, *The Music's All That Matters*, 183–84.

[35] However, as Dan Hedges points out in *Yes: the Authorized Biography* (London: Sidgwick and Jackson, 1981), 108, when the tax crunch came, Yes bailed out of the U.K., just like the other supergroups.

[36] John Street, *Rebel Rock: The Politics of Popular Music* (New York: Basil Blackwell, 1986), 166.

For instance, as I argue in *Rocking the Classics,* in progressive rock the tension between individuality and collectivism is reconciled by the tendency towards collective virtuosity—in theory, all the members of a progressive rock band are given the freedom to express their virtuosity, hopefully without getting in the way of each other, so that no one is a "star," on the one hand, or a mere backing musician, on the other. Likewise, progressive rock synthesizes high culture with low culture; African American musical traditions with European classical music; instrumentation (and subject matter) of a postindustrial technocratic future with that of an idyllic agrarian past; rational, left brain composition with intuitive, right brain improvisation; heavy, "masculine" hard rock with gentle, "feminine" acoustic passages. Each of these pairs of opposites can be seen as symbolic of tensions existing in twentieth-century Western society that affected or concerned the counterculture. In progressive rock, the merging of some of these paired opposites produces a genuine synthesis in the Hegelian sense (i.e., the progressive rock style itself as a fusion of high and low culture, of European classical and African American musical discourses). Other pairs of opposites resist the attempts at synthesis. Perhaps a true synthesis of some of these dualities was simply impossible; or perhaps, during the time of progressive rock (to borrow Bill Martin's term), the historical condition was not yet ripe for the thesis-antithesis relationship between the two opposites to fully play itself out.

If one accepts this Hegelian view of progressive rock, perhaps it isn't too farfetched to say that the "politics of prog" are neither apolitical nor political in a narrow sense, but project a kind of utopian, post-Left/Right perspective. Even when it projects grim dystopias (Emerson, Lake and Palmer's *Brain Salad Surgery* or Rush's *2112* come to mind), prog remains idealistic and visionary; the style is never cynical, and its warnings of disaster seldom come without an implied pathway of deliverance. Ultimately, the utopian politics of prog, while showing awareness of the struggles and difficulties of the present, project idealized worlds where these struggles and difficulties have been overcome, a world where current definitions of, and differences between, Left and Right have been not papered over but transcended.

The ELP–Peter Sinfield Partnership

As we have already seen, the launching of the Manticore label brought Greg Lake back together with his old mate from King Crimson, Peter Sinfield. According to Sinfield, Lake offered to release Sinfield's solo album on Manticore—on the condition that Sinfield assist Lake on some lyrics he was writing for a new piece of music by ELP, music,

incidentally, that eventually became "Karn Evil 9."[37] Sinfield told Paul
Stump that he quit King Crimson in 1972, only to be "seduced" into
a writing partnership with Lake: "I was out of King Crimson. For my
own safety . . . Greg called me. 'I need help with the lyrics.' And boy,
did he need help. I was seduced away by the world's worst publishing
contract, ever. I got a third of Greg's royalties. It sounds okay, does-
n't it, until you realize that Greg only got 25 per cent of the band's
royalties. Oh well."[38] I am frankly surprised that Stump let this pass
without any comment. First off, as Eric Tamm points out in his King
Crimson biography, Sinfield didn't really quit King Crimson so much
as Robert Fripp more or less unilaterally dissolved his working relationship with Sinfield.[39] Furthermore, it's unclear to me in what sense
Sinfield feels cheated by his arrangement with ELP. A third of Lake's
royalties, or 8.33% of the band's, wasn't insubstantial during the
period when ELP's albums were selling like hotcakes, especially if
Sinfield wasn't asked to accompany the band during their interminable touring, and therefore was free to work on other projects
simultaneously.[40]

This is not to say that ELP did not benefit from Sinfield's involvement. As I'm sure some readers have already discerned, I do not feel that
lyrics were one of the strongest points of the first four ELP albums.
Furthermore, I'm not sure that Lake's lyric writing improved substantially
from album to album; I think it is entirely possible to argue that his most
consistently successful lyrics are on the band's debut album. Granted,
Lake and Sinfield drew from the same library of fantasy, science fiction,
and medieval imagery for their lyrics—court jesters, madmen, fossil suns,
prison moons, and so on—and I always felt that the strongest part of
Lake's lyric writing was his evocative imagery. However, through the
course of the first four King Crimson albums, Sinfield's lyrics show a
steady growth in the sophistication of their rhyme schemes and internal
rhythms; I see no corresponding development in Lake's lyric writing during this period. Certainly, by the third Crimson album, *Lizard* (late
1970), Sinfield was already beginning to explore approaches to blank and
free verse that were to greatly influence Yes's principal lyricist, Jon
Anderson, who in fact was a guest singer on *Lizard*. Furthermore,
Sinfield's best lyrics seem to operate on more than one level of meaning,

---

[37] Bruce Pilato, liner notes, *Brain Salad Surgery* reissue, Rhino Records, CD R2 72459,
1996, 10.
[38] Stump, *The Music's All That Matters*, 169.
[39] Tamm, *Robert Fripp*, 57–58.
[40] Members of the progressive rock audience are often surprised to learn that only a part of
Sinfield's output was in tandem with progressive rock bands. His lyrics have been sung by
Celine Dion, Cher, and Cliff Richards, among others.

something that can seldom be said about Lake's.[41] There is no question that *Brain Salad Surgery* was a better album for Sinfield's contributions.

Manticore Studios

Around the same time that ELP were in the process of launching Manticore Records, they purchased an abandoned Odeon Cinema in Fulham, London, and converted it into a multilevel rehearsal and production facility, Manticore Studios. Carl Palmer recalls that

> *Brain Salad Surgery* was rehearsed upstairs in the foyer, as it were. The downstairs area was used for bands [including Led Zeppelin and Jethro Tull] to go through production rehearsals; we rented that part of it out. We stored our own equipment downstairs, and then we had our workshop and rehearsal facilities upstairs. In the back of the balcony area, where the concession stand would be, is where we rehearsed.[42]

The band saw several benefits from this arrangement. For one thing, rehearsal space had always been problematic. In the band's early days, they used, among other locations, a Church Hall in Shepherds Bush—until a neighbor who lived three doors away took out a writ against them, complaining particularly that the band's excess volume was creating waves as he sat in his bath water! Not only did purchasing their own rehearsal facility eliminate mutually aggravating run-ins with annoyed neighbors, it also changed their entire process of composition. The first three studio albums were the result of one individual (usually Emerson) presenting the others with an essentially developed composition in the studio, which Lake wrote lyrics for and the band then arranged more or less on the spot, and immediately recorded. The band didn't have the leisure of using endless hours of studio time to collaboratively generate ideas; furthermore, because of their constant touring and lack of dependable rehearsal space between late 1970 and late 1972, they didn't have the luxury of being able to rehearse new material during their tour breaks, and then try the new material out on tour before recording it. As Lake has said,

> The concept of writing songs before the album was made was non-existent . . . we never played the album—or any part of it—for anyone, until it was completely finished . . . on the day it was finished, the record company people would sort of nervously come in. They would be waiting, almost in fear,

---

[41] I think this is especially true of Sinfield's work on King Crimson's *In the Wake of Poseidon*, which strikes a nice balance between the more straightforward debut Crimson LP and the more knotty and intentionally obscure *Lizard* lyrics.

[42] Pilato, liner notes, *Brain Salad Surgery* CD reissue, 6.

to hear whether it would prove to have been a total waste of time. Then we would play it, and there would be tremendous relief—relief that it was at least in one piece, and a good piece of work.[43]

The purchase of the Fulham facility allowed the material on *Brain Salad Surgery* to be created more collaboratively than on any previous album; the infinite care the band took in polishing details of the arrangements was a major benefit of the new rehearsal facility, and as I'll point out, is a major factor in the album's aesthetic success. Furthermore, now that they had a long-term practice facility, the band could also work through new pieces and try them out on the road, a luxury they had never before enjoyed; *Brain Salad Surgery*'s "Karn Evil 9, 1st Impression," "Toccata," and "Still . . . You Turn Me On" all benefited greatly from this approach.

New Equipment

I have already pointed out that between the release of *Tarkus* and *Trilogy*, ELP's instrumental set-up expanded modestly. Between the release of *Trilogy* and *Brain Salad Surgery*, the band's instrumental set-up expanded again—but this time spectacularly. Sometime in late 1972 or early 1973, Emerson added a second Minimoog to his set-up, which took the place of the Clavinet sitting on top of the grand piano. His set up expanded further in mid-1973 once he became involved with Moog Music's Dave Luce in developing a prototype polyphonic synthesizer. This prototype, originally called the Constellation, actually consisted of three distinct instruments. There was the Apollo, a polyphonic synthesizer which by 1976 had been developed into the Polymoog, the first mass-produced polyphonic synthesizer. Also part of the Constellation was the Lyra, a monophonic instrument that never saw the light of mass production, and the Taurus bass pedal synthesizer. Emerson never used the Taurus, as he found he could get an excellent bass sound from the Minimoog. However, he used the Apollo's polyphonic capabilities on three tracks of *Brain Salad Surgery*, "Toccata," "Benny the Bouncer," and the 3rd Impression of "Karn Evil 9" and used both the Apollo and the Lyra for some of the monophonic synthesized "trumpet" leads on "Jerusalem" and the 1st and 3rd Impressions of "Karn Evil 9." This meant that by later 1973 Emerson's set up included grand piano, Hammond C-3 and L-100

---

[43]Hall, "Welcome to the Show," 42. It is because of this "write no more than you need to fill up a record" approach that there was so little previously unreleased ELP material to include on 1993's *Return of the Manticore* box set.

organs, two Minimoogs, modular Moog, the Moog Apollo and Lyra, and an electric piano.[44] The bulk of these keyboards were configured in a U-shape, with the C-3 and the modular Moog to the left, the L-100 and a Minimoog to the right, and the Apollo and Lyra at the bottom of the "U"; the second Minimoog sat on the grand piano, with the electric piano off to the side.

During this period the rock music press began to lambaste Emerson for his large keyboard set-up, citing it as further proof of ELP's self-indulgence and as a sign that the band were beginning to be controlled by their equipment. This was, by and large, an unfair accusation. Granted, by 1973 an emphasis on accumulating a lot of expensive hardware, simply to have it, was becoming a pervasive (and unwelcome) part of the rock scene at large, and ELP, with their huge stage set-up, elaborate quadraphonic sound system, and special-effects goodies, were not above criticism. However, the reason that Emerson needed so many synthesizers on stage was simple: it was the only way he could adequately reproduce the band's music live. Consider that even by late 1973 only one of his synthesizers was polyphonic; the others were monophonic instruments that could only be switched from one sound to another by a painstaking manipulation of knobs on the instruments' control panels. Since Emerson didn't have time to do much of this in a live performance situation, often each instrument could only be used for a few specific sounds, and therefore it became necessary for him to have a goodly number of instruments on stage simply to access the requisite sounds he would need during the course of a live show. The real measure of the success of Emerson's set-up during this period, I think, is that ELP were able to play every track on *Brain Salad Surgery* live during late 1973 and 1974. Emerson himself certainly didn't brag about the size of his set-up; in fact, by 1977 he was telling an astonished Dominic Milano that he would like to chuck all his synthesizers and go back to playing organ and piano, as he had with the Nice.[45]

The growth of Palmer's set-up was if anything even more spectacular than Emerson's. By autumn 1973 the Ludwig Octoplus set was gone, replaced by a ten-piece kit custom made for him by British Steel. Here's Palmer, waxing rhapsodic on his custom-made drum kit:

---

[44] The provenance of this latter instrument remains unclear. On the back cover of the *Welcome Back My Friends* album, it can be seen facing the Hammond L-100. Emerson told me it was not really an electric piano at all, but an upright (or possibly spinet) piano with the strings de-tuned to create a suitably honky-tonk effect for the "Jeremy Bender"/"The Sheriff" medley (the only numbers on which it was used). Emerson added that a special pick-up was used (he no longer remembers which one) to give the instrument its lively sound. However, other sources have suggested that this instrument was (take your pick) a Baldwin electric upright piano, a Lawrence audio acoustic/electric piano, or a LaSage electric/acoustic piano.

[45] Milano, "Keith Emerson," *Contemporary Keyboard*, October 1977, 36.

The drumkit that I had at the time [from 1973] was a stainless steel drumset that I had made for me. Not by a drum manufacturer . . . I used the drumset for about five years and each one of the shells was hand engraved. Each shell had a hunting scene. On one drum, I had engraved a fox jumping over a fence. Another scene had a man on a horse. They were all hunting scenes that I got from rifles, because I also collect guns. The scenes were engraved in the stainless steel by using a dentist's drill. It took 12 months to complete it. The British Steel Corporation was involved in this project from the beginning. The drum set without a shadow of a doubt is a jewel, a work of art. The sound is incredible, a completely different sound. The only drawback was its weight. It was incredibly heavy. [No wonder! The "shells" of the drums were one-half inch thick solid stainless steel, rather than the usual one-eighth inch thickness.] I used it for about five or six years. [Five: from 1973 to 1978.] I got my money's worth . . . It didn't have any screws or any threads. Each drum was suspended by a rod that was angled at the exact position I wanted it angled at. I would make a template out of cardboard and take it to the steel manufacturers with my specifications. That's the way I put it together. Every night that I set those drums up they were in the same position. And my technique got really good because I became familiar with all the distances. Today [1980], Rogers makes Memriloc so when you set your drums up it will go to the same position every time, and they won't move. But I was hip to that fact way back in 1973.[46]

While this mega drum kit was the crux of Palmer's set up, there were also two timpani (26" and 28"), tubular bells, two enormous gongs, an immense triangle, and a huge, 134-pound church bell that was suspended over Palmer's head, and whose clapper Palmer moved by pulling on a rope with his teeth! There was also a custom-made drum synthesizer that was interconnected with the stainless steel kit—I will explore this early electronic drum set-up in detail when I discuss ELP's "Toccata," their arrangement of the fourth movement of Alberto Ginastera's Piano Concerto no. 1, from *Brain Salad Surgery*. The drum kit and miscellaneous percussion was set on a circular rostrum that revolved and sprayed laser lights into the audience during Palmer's drum solo. The weight of Palmer's entire percussion set up, including the revolving rostrum: two and a half tons.[47]

Compared to Emerson's and Palmer's set up, Lake's was positively modest: for most of the *Brain Salad Surgery* era, three guitars and a bass.

---

[46] Cheech Iero, "Carl Palmer," *Modern Drummer*, June/July 1980, 49. Incidentally, as far as I can determine Palmer was still using the Octoplus kit during the recording of *Brain Salad Surgery*.

[47] A final point to make about the stainless steel drum kit is that in keeping with Palmer's emphasis on the upper part of his kit, the large quantity of drums resulted from having a number of toms of different sizes: the kit only had one bass drum, as Palmer never used a double bass drum set-up until the very late seventies, when he formed PM.

For a while during ELP's 1973 European tour, Lake experimented with using a dual six-string guitar/four-string bass that master luthier Tony Zemaitis had custom made for him; however, he found the instrument too heavy for live performance, and soon abandoned it. Otherwise, his guitar set-up at this time consisted of a Washburn six-string acoustic, a Zemaitis twelve-string acoustic, and an old three-pick up black Les Paul electric. After the 1972 *Trilogy* tour, Lake abandoned the Fender Jazz Bass he had used on the first four ELP albums in favor of the Gibson Ripper. Like the Fender, he used the Gibson in conjunction with Rotosound strings, which he changed after every set, and a triangular tortoise-shell guitar pick. Like a lot of progressive rock bassists (Chris Squire, for instance), Lake eschewed a really bassy bass sound; one of the reasons he switched to the Gibson Ripper is that he felt the instrument's midrange choke could wring greater highs from the instrument.[48] As Mike O'Shea, one of ELP's tour managers, remarked: "Greg likes that really toppy sound you only get with new strings. That's why he changes them after every concert. He's got a high degree of treble response in his equipment to get the top end over and his bass doesn't really sound like a bass."[49] Lake himself remarked,

> In a way I developed a style of playing for myself. The thing with fingers is for your "boom-boom" bass players, people into the Motown-type of bass playing. That's a fine style, but I was really looking for something a bit new from a bass guitar. That's why I got into Rotosound strings. I tried to get as close as I could to the bottom end of a Steinway piano, as far as the sound goes, and it's upon that that I tried to develop my playing.[50]

The sound of the Gibson Ripper bass in conjunction with Rotosound strings was to characterize Lake's bass playing throughout the 1973–74 period.

Ironically, the addition to Lake's setup during 1973 that received the most attention was neither the Gibson Ripper nor one of the Zemaitis custom-made guitars; it was a Persian rug! Lake stated he had purchased the rug to avoid electrical shock, although he allowed that it lent the stage an air of hominess:

> I don't know whether you've ever noticed that I wear plimsolls on stage, which cuts down the chances of an electric shock. The carpet's there for the same reason. Altogether it means I'd still feel it, but I wouldn't die. Also it means it's like you're playing at home every night, almost in the same sur-

---

[48] Steve Rosen, "Greg Lake of Emerson, Lake and Palmer," *Guitar Player*, September 1974, 21.

[49] "Greg Lake," *International Musician*, January, 1976, 16 (writer unspecified).

[50] Greg Lake, quoted by Rosen, "Greg Lake," 20.

roundings—which is nice. When I decided to buy a carpet I thought I might as well get one that was worth something. To be honest I never thought anybody would notice it.[51]

Lake paid $1,500 for the carpet; by 1976, its value had soared to $7,000.[52] It was long rumored that ELP employed a roadie whose sole duty was to care for the carpet, but the band denied this; even in light of the huge army of roadies that ELP was employing by 1973, the story seems a bit farfetched.

As impressive as the band's instrumental upgrades were during this period, it was their stage and sound system acquisitions that raised the most eyebrows among rock journalists. For instance, during the 1973–74 period the band used a quadraphonic sound system designed by Bill Hough, who accompanied the band on tour; the Mavis board used by ELP had thirty channels with quad on each channel. They rented the sound system, using on average thirty-two speaker bins for each show. Greg Lake in 1974:

> This is the first truly quadraphonic show to go on the road. And I think that's a trip. If people are going to have quad players, and I'm told they are, I don't see it. I don't see them in people's homes, but I'm told they are. And if they have got them, and they enjoy quad, then one of the nicest ways to do it is to enjoy it in a live atmosphere. The beauty of quad is that it's four-dimensional. It surrounds you. The most suited thing is a live performance in quad.[53]

For a band who were any less particular about their sound than ELP, touring with a quad system would have been considered a nonstarter. As the band's manager, Stewart Young, pointed out, "We're the only band who use a complete quadraphonic system, so that doubles the cost [of putting on shows] almost from the start. But we consider it an essential part of the show. I feel we have a better sound than any other band on the road."[54]

No doubt at the time the band genuinely believed that they owed it to their fans to tour with the best sound system available, and that the best sound system available was quadraphonic. Of course, history has not exactly justified their decision—by the late 1970s it was apparent that quadraphonic home systems were not the wave of the future, and quadraphonic LPs quietly went the way of the dinosaur. Furthermore, one also detects at least a trace of one-upmanship in the remarks of Lake and Young quoted above.

---

[51] Johnson, "Welcome Back My Friends."
[52] "Greg Lake," *International Musician*, January, 1976, 16.
[53] Greg Lake, quoted by Ian Dove, "Greg Lake Interview," *Hit Parader*, Winter 74/75, 74.
[54] Stewart Young, quoted by Johnson, "Welcome Back My Friends."

A less subtle hint of one-upmanship is evident in their decision to tour with their own portable stage, a practice which is common enough now but which was unheard of at the time. The stage was designed in the form of a specially constructed arch—a proscenium—which the band played inside of. Lake again: "The real beauty of it [the portable stage] for us is that every night we're playing in the same box. Only the people in front will change. Also from the point of view of a production it's far more flexible. We can use the lights in the same position every night; we don't have to draw the curtains until we're exactly ready; altogether we can feel at home wherever we're playing."[55] There was one small disadvantage to the structure: it weighed twenty tons and took close to fifty roadies to move! Not surprisingly, as the spring 1973 European tour ground on, the proscenium lost some of its charm. When asked whether the portable stage had been a success at the conclusion of the band's European tour, Emerson said,

> No, but we wanted to give it a try. We made the mistake of giving it a big star billing, and we were giving it all this publicity. It was nothing like it was made out to be, and the whole thing escalated, as if it was a big new production. But all it was, was a new stage and curtains. Many people were very disappointed because they expected God to appear with us on stage and do a triple somersault![56]

Finally, there was the light show. Even the spectacle-hardened *Rolling Stone* reviewer was impressed: "The astounding lights were designed by Judy Rasmussen, who operates them during the show. There are four huge ladders at each corner of the stage, and two arches suspended over the performing area, all festooned with lights."[57] Ms. Rasmussen, who raised some eyebrows at the time for being one of the first women to play such an important role in a major band's stage production, was herself assisted by a staff of several lights operators.

1973 European Tour; *The Manticore Special (Brain Salad Days)* Video

The band played three isolated gigs in Germany during February 1973, but the massive European tour started in earnest in late March. It was dubbed the "Get Me a Ladder Tour" after a lyric from Greg Lake's new

---

[55] Greg Lake, quoted by James Johnson, "Lake the Strongman," *New Musical Express*, March 31, 1973, 8.
[56] Keith Emerson, quoted by Chris Welch, "The Heavy Metal Kid," *Melody Maker*, June 16, 1973, 16.
[57] Judith Sims, "ELP . . . What?" 18.

acoustic ballad "Still . . . You Turn Me On." The band toyed with the idea of naming their forthcoming studio LP *Get Me a Ladder*, but by the end of the tour this idea had been discarded.[58] The tour commenced on March 30 in Kiel, Germany, and proceeded into early May, taking in thirty shows in thirty-six days in Germany, Belgium, France, Switzerland, Denmark, Sweden, the Netherlands, Austria, and Italy.

A show the band played at Friedrich Eberthalle, Ludwigshafen, Germany, on April 10 gives a representative overview of ELP's live repertoire during this tour. They opened the show with "Abaddon's Bolero"; this piece, with its slow build-up and its challenging instrumentation demands (in terms of approximating the studio version) didn't make an ideal opening number for a live show, and after this tour "Hoedown" was returned to its spot as show opener. The band then launched into a piece which Keith Emerson told the crowd was so new it hadn't been given a title yet; anyone familiar with *Brain Salad Surgery* would recognize it as "Karn Evil 9, 1st Impression," although different in several details from the studio version the band were to record two months later. Then came a medley of "Jeremy Bender" and "The Sheriff," both featuring electric piano (much like the familiar live version on *Welcome Back My Friends*), followed by the complete "Tarkus" suite. Next was the show's acoustic segment, featuring "Take a Pebble," Lake's new ballad "Still . . . You Turn Me On" (again different in a number of details from the studio version recorded in September for *Brain Salad Surgery*), "Lucky Man," Emerson's "Piano Improvisations" (by now the same in all essential details as the version featured on *Welcome Back My Friends*), and the "Take a Pebble" reprise. Then came "Hoedown" (which didn't seem to work as well in the middle of the show as it did as an opening number), and the closing portion of *Pictures at an Exhibition* ("Promenade"/"Baba Yaga"/"The Great Gates of Kiev"). The band was recalled by a thunderous ovation, and during the encore played their third new piece of the evening, "Toccata" (they played only the opening section), which was linked to the final number, "Rondo," by a monumental drum solo by Palmer. The band's performance on this date doesn't seem as tight or as focused as their shows of the previous fall. On the other hand, there is no doubt that the experimentation they undertook while trying out the new pieces live paid handsome dividends when it came time to record *Brain Salad Surgery*; virtually every change they made in these pieces between the time of the show and the time of the studio recording was for the bet-

---

[58] Incidentally, the "get me a ladder" lyric has very much the same meaning as the famous line from *Star Trek*, "Beam me up, Scotty"—i.e., things are becoming too crazy, get me out of here.

ter, and one can only wonder how much their earlier albums might have benefited from a similar approach.

It was during the final segment of the spring 1973 European tour that *The Manticore Special* (also referred to as *Brain Salad Days*) was shot. This documentary, which was broadcast New Years' Eve, 1973, on BBC2, was rather unique for its day.[59] It was not a concert film, nor was it a biography of the band, although it does incorporate aspects of both. Mainly, it adopts a "day in the life of the band approach," "the band" in this case being not just the musicians, but the entire ELP organization: manager, road crew, and so forth. It is genuinely enlightening in showing life on the road for a seventies rock band from a more prosaic, less glamorized perspective than was the norm, and highlighting the almost feudal social division that characterized the seventies megabands.

It opens with an aerial shot of three huge semi trailers rolling down the highway to the musical accompaniment of "Abbadon's Bolero," each one being emblazoned with the last name of one of the band members on top. We see the road crew traveling in buses from city to city while the band's aristocracy (the musicians, manager Young, and a few others) are whisked from city to city by airplane. We also watch the crew assemble the stage, including the huge proscenium, only to have to tear it down again after management cancel the show due to Lake's laryngitis. We see the band in their dressing room before their show in Rome, Italy, on May 2, 1973, and unwinding in their dressing room after their final show of the tour, in Milan on May 4. An especially fascinating segment shows the band working through segments of the second and third Impressions of "Karn Evil 9" in Manticore Studios sometime in early 1973.

The one segment that runs counter to the overall prosaic, realistic thrust of the documentary is inserted in the middle, and tends to re-glamorize the band members as Romantic rock *auteurs* and popular culture icons. We see Lake as rustic minstrel, tramping through the English countryside and fishing to the accompaniment of "Lucky Man." Emerson is depicted as country squire, taking longbow and shooting practice on the grounds of his recently purchased Sussex Tudor estate, and working through the cadenza segment of the first movement of his Piano Concerto. Palmer is spotlighted as the earnest virtuoso, taking timpani lessons at the Guildhall School of Music under the watchful eye of Gilbert Webster.

Anyone hoping for either a conventional band biography, or a really probing consideration of who ELP are as people and what their music is all about, is bound to be disappointed by *The Manticore Special*. So will

---

[59] In 1998 this broadcast was re-released in video form by Manticore Records as *The Manticore Special*.

anybody who is looking for a straight concert film. However, anyone wanting to get a feel for the road life of one of the seventies' megabands will certainly find it of interest. There is also some good concert footage, including a short segment of "Karn Evil 9, 1st Impression, part two" with Lake playing his Zemaitis twin six-string guitar/four-string bass; Lake performing "Still . . . You Turn Me On"; and a complete performance of "Hoedown" from the Milan show of May 4. The documentary also makes a strong (if unintentional) comment on the delirious enthusiasm of ELP's Italian fans; an especially telling segment shows literally scores of Italian riot police taking up positions before the Rome show on May 2.[60]

---

[60] Two notes here. First, the Greg Lake Web Site is incorrect to list the May 2, 1973, show as being in Bologna; it was definitely in Rome. Second, during the seventies the Italian Communist party often staged protests in conjunction with large rock shows, which sometimes led the police to launch an almost military-style counter-insurgency response with distinctly Fascist overtones. An especially memorable instance is recounted by Van der Graaf Generator's David Jackson in Mick Dillingham, "Van der Graaf Generator: The David Jackson Interview," 2 parts, *Ptolemaic Terrascope*, May 1991, and Autumn 1991.

Brain Salad Surgery

(1973)

Most of *Brain Salad Surgery* was recorded during August and September of 1973, once again at London's Advision Studios.[1] However, as early as the spring of 1973 ELP were already beginning to speak of a forthcoming album. Here's Emerson:

> The new material is different to the work on *Trilogy*. Greg has become more of a guitarist, he's had this new double-neck instrument built for him by Tony Zemaitis, which weighs a ton. What it means is that we can throw the bass lines backwards and forwards to each other. He can stop and I can pick up bass on my equipment while he plays his guitar. And the effect of this is that it has given the music a bigger sound, an earthier sound.[2]

Lake described the new music in not dissimilar terms, although his description gives a more generalized view of the band's new direction:

> It's not a "getting back to the roots" type trip. It's no more simple than before. It just has a different theme, and that theme happens to be rock and roll. If you can imagine ELP playing rock and roll soul music—gospel even— then it's that kind of trip. It's like a big band playing rock material—a fairly meaty thing . . . I think maybe our idea of rock and roll is different from anybody else's . . . I don't know. But it still has ELP's stamp of aggression or authority, if you like. There's still a terrible punch to it, but more feel perhaps. It's not so much of a bar of seven and count as you go . . .[3]

---

[1] Although "Karn Evil 9, 1st Impression" was recorded earlier—in June—at London's Olympic Studios.

[2] Keith Emerson, quoted by Penny Valentine, "Keith Emerson in the SOUNDS Talk-In," *Sounds,* March 31, 1973, 26–27. It would seem that the piece Emerson specifically has in mind here is "Karn Evil 9, 1st Impression."

[3] Greg Lake, quoted by James Johnson, "Lake the Strongman," *New Musical Express,* March 31, 1973, 9.

269

Today the description of *Brain Salad Surgery* as "soul" or "gospel" might raise some eyebrows.[4] On the other hand, there is no doubt that Lake hit on an important aspect of the new album. As we shall see, while it is no less sophisticated than their earlier albums—in some crucial ways, it is more sophisticated—its sophistication is all the more impressive for being more understated. The music's complexity and virtuosity no longer draws attention to itself in the manner of *Tarkus*, for instance, and ends up sounding more effortless.

Brain Salad Surgery is, without question, the band's most fully realized album, and one of the great concept albums of the rock era. It is not narrative in the sense of presenting a storyline which is sequentially unfolded from the beginning of the album to the end. Rather, the "concept" of *Brain Salad Surgery* involves a sustained meditation upon what we might call technological ethics. The album's first track, "Jerusalem," takes us back to the dawn of the industrial age, with its warnings of the societal disruption and environmental destruction that the "unnatural" new machines, the "Satanic mills," would visit on society. The album's last three tracks, the "Karn Evil 9" suite, bring us simultaneously into the present and future, and pose a number of questions that today are as pertinent—perhaps even more pertinent—than they were over thirty years ago when the album was released.

First, there is the issue of technological overstimulation and sensory overload that is one of the less desirable side effects of modern electronic media. Has virtual reality so deadened us to actual reality that we can no longer distinguish between the two? Has this led to a condition of perpetual alienation, since virtual reality has in many cases become more "real" to us than the actual people around us, and the virtual world seems more real than the "real" world, which we have become increasingly disconnected from?[5] Is modern media sapping us of our individuality and opening us up to a subtle but pervasive mind control, which we accept in exchange for the constant "thrills" that media provides us? Assuming that the answer to these questions is "yes," is it worth fighting this process—or can we ultimately be happier by just selling our souls in exchange for technological bliss?

Interrelated to this theme of virtual reality and media manipulation is the more frankly sci-fi realm of artificial intelligence, which ELP had

---

[4] Although, as we'll see, if Lake were simply describing "Karn Evil 9, 1st Impression"—which ELP had just completed writing at the time of this interview—then the "soul" description makes a lot of sense.

[5] Commenting on the album's premise at the time, Emerson noted, and commented on, the curious fact that the more British media saturated the airwaves with stories of atrocities in northern Ireland, the more blasé the British public seemed to become, the more desensitized to the continuing violence. See Forrester, Hanson, and Askew, *Emerson, Lake and Palmer*, 89.

already tentatively explored on their debut album. As artificial intelligence steadily evolves, could there ever be a time when the spark of self-awareness that we consider uniquely human might be kindled in an intelligent machine? Does our steadily increasing reliance in our daily lives on artificial intelligence signal our own dehumanization? In other words, are humans becoming more deindividualized, dehumanized, and machinelike in direct proportion to machines becoming more human? It is to these types of questions that *Brain Salad Surgery* addresses itself.

Perhaps the first commentator to fully realize the achievement of *Brain Salad Surgery* was Jim Curtis, whose *Rock Eras: Interpretations of Music and Society, 1954–1984* is in many ways the most satisfying history of the first thirty years of rock. Curtis brings none of the ideological prejudices of the *Rolling Stone* wing of critics to his discussion, and he writes with an objectivity about developments in rock music during the sixties and seventies which was far ahead of its time (he completed the book in the mid-1980s). Unlike the mainstream critics, whose blues orthodoxy *demands* that progressive rock be viewed as an aberration, Curtis sees prog as being very much in the mainstream of rock music developments of the seventies—although, unlike some progressive rock fanatics, he doesn't necessarily view it as the evolutionary pinnacle towards which all previous rock music had been aspiring. Curtis's summarization of the overarching concept behind *Brain Salad Surgery* is so penetrating that I would like to quote it here in full. After discussing the link between science fiction, Hollywood space epics, and rock music, he says:

> The album which takes the space/computer/synthesizer age the most seriously is ELP's *Brain Salad Surgery*. As an artifact, the album sleeve attests to the importance of albums in the seventies, for it is even more elaborate than [Elton John's] *Tumbleweed Connection*. The austere front cover displays the name of the album in white letters on a black background, but the back cover features a painting by the Swiss surrealist H. R. Giger of a skull imbedded in a bizarre mechanical device. It thereby states non-verbally the album's recurring opposition of the human and the mechanical. However, when you open the two halves you find another painting, this one of a sleeping woman with the infinity symbol on her forehead. Nothing is ever completely what it seems here, for *Brain Salad Surgery* plays off one opposition after another.
>
> Blake's familiar (to English audiences at least) lyrics for "Jerusalem" repeat the opposition of the human and the mechanical, and combine it with the opposition of the sacred and the profane. The "Toccata" follows, and separates "Jerusalem" from "Benny the Bouncer"; it opposes instrumental music to vocal music, as the Second Impression of *Karn Evil 9* [which is instrumental] separates the First Impression from the Third. It gets more complicated still, because the "Toccata" [based as it is on the fourth movement of Alberto Ginastera's Piano Concerto no. 1] also opposes the high culture of the present to the popular culture of the past (the tinkly piano on "Benny the Bouncer").

Taken together, the three "Impressions" [which are the album's final three tracks] have a collective title of *Karn Evil 9*, and the pun suggests the debt which the album owes to [the Beatles'] *Sergeant Pepper* and to *Magical Mystery Tour* for its showbiz conceit. But ELP are no band on the run; the show on their album is a "show that never ends." The show creates myth in a shimmeringly ambiguous way by pulling "Jesus from a hat." They present a manipulative totalitarian world as a fulfillment of Blake's dire prophecy about Satanic mills, and thus their album has much in common with [David Bowie's] *Diamond Dogs*.

After the instrumental Second Impression, the music turns more ominous in the concluding Third Impression, and also shows the conceptual link between synthesizer music and movies. The Third Impression involves a dialogue between man and computer which surely derives from the conversations between Keir Dullea and HAL in *2001: A Space Odyssey* (1968). But to say this is not to say that the piece is derivative, for in it ELP recapitulate the martial and apocalyptic imagery of "Jerusalem." The computer claims, "I am yourself," rendering the human/mechanical and sacred/profane oppositions dramatically ambiguous. At the end, the synthesizer starts hopping back and forth between the speakers; it goes faster and faster and faster . . . and then stops. We are left to challenge it if we can, reeling from the conceptual audacity and instrumental virtuosity of this extraordinary album.[6]

More than twenty years after its writing, I still find this description insightful and essentially correct, despite a few obvious omissions (most notably of the Greg Lake ballad "Still . . . You Turn Me On"). What I will do during the remainder of this chapter, then, is simply fill in the broad outlines of Curtis's description with more detail, and bring a greater sense of nuance to some of his observations and generalizations.

Before plunging into the music, it is needful to say a few words about the extraordinary album cover art, which is often a strong contender in polls ranking all-time great rock album covers. When ELP played in Zurich on April 15 during their European tour, a mutual friend introduced Keith Emerson to airbrush surrealist H. R. Giger (pronounced Gee-ger). At the time Giger was relatively unknown outside of Switzerland; the set design work for *Alien* that would make him a household name was still several years in the future. Nonetheless, Emerson was fascinated with Giger's work:

> He was an extraordinary, fascinating person. But he lived his life on another level. He was obsessed with surgical procedures, skin diseases, unborn fetuses. I went back to the hotel and said to Greg and Carl, "You've got to come meet this guy, he's weird!" They were a little reluctant to do so, as anything apart

---

[6] James M. Curtis, *Rock Eras: Interpretations of Music and Society, 1954–1984* (Bowling Green, OH: Bowling Green State University Popular Press, 1987), 280–81.

from music, such as art direction, they wanted to have some control over. Amazingly, they came.[7]

The band were impressed by Giger's artwork and he, in turn, was intrigued by their music; perhaps this isn't too surprising, since one can see a fairly obvious link between Giger's interest in biomechanics and some of the conceptual turf the band had covered on *Tarkus*. In a relatively brief time, Giger produced his memorable design. From the outside the LP jacket cover seems to depict a human skull restrained by a bizarre "medical" contraption: the only apparent flesh is on the lips and chin. However, this cover opens up in the middle, and when the two sides are pulled up the lips and chin are revealed as belonging to a sleeping woman with the infinity sign on her forehead. As Curtis noted above, the conflict between (and, ironically, interaction of) human and machine could not have been more powerfully expressed. One peculiarly Gigerian touch is the fact that the hair of the woman (modeled by Giger's wife, who shortly afterward committed suicide) appears to be dreadlocks from a distance, but a closer inspection reveals that the "dreadlocks" are actually tiny spinal columns.[8] It is also at the base of the nightmarish "medical" device that the famous interlocking "ELP" logo makes its first appearance.

Fifth Album: *Brain Salad Surgery*

The selection of that hoary old hymn "Jerusalem" as the opening track was really a stroke of genius, because it encapsulates so many of the dichotomies inherent in the album as a whole—some of which even the band members may not have been fully aware of. The lyrics of "Jerusalem" are by William Blake (1757–1827), the extraordinarily original English poet-artist-mystic-social critic. Blake wrote "Jerusalem" to

---

[7] Quoted in Pilato, liner notes, *Brain Salad Surgery* CD reissue, 9.

[8] In the artwork that Giger originally submitted to the band, there was a second typically Gigerian touch which never saw the light of mass production. Giger originally included a small male organ underneath the woman's chin—a recurring motif in his work that ELP's distributors quickly rejected as pornographic. The band were compelled to find another airbrush artist to impose a shaft of light over the offending organ. Incidentally, "brain salad surgery" is slang for fellatio—the title was suggested to the band by Manticore president Mario Medious, who borrowed it from a slang lyric in Dr. John's song "Right Place Wrong Time" (1973). Many who were not aware of this double entendre merely assumed the title referred to the horrific procedure depicted by Giger's cover. Unfortunately there is a certain strand of vulgarity that was always a part of the ELP experience (especially the stage show) and even here, at the apex of their career, the band seem unconcerned about the potential contradiction between the vulgarity of the album's title and the seriousness of its thematic content.

serve as prologue to his enormous poetic work *Milton*. "Jerusalem" contains a number of themes that were highly characteristic of English Romanticism in its most radical and revolutionary incarnation, including (1) a vision of preindustrial England as a kind of Eden ("And did those feet in ancient times / Walk upon England's mountains green"); (2) a vision of the industrial revolution as a horrific disruption of the natural order of things ("And was Jerusalem builded here / Upon these dark Satanic mills"); and (3) a call for spiritual renewal through social activism (although I doubt Blake himself would have used this term) in order to return England to its rightful state of peaceful pastoral communitarianism ("I will not cease from metal fight / Nor shall my sword sleep in my hand / Till we have built Jerusalem / In England's green and pleasant land").[9]

Although I suspect that today many commentators of the Left would view "Jerusalem" as utopian in a negative (that is to say, unrealizable) sense, the fact is in his day Blake was unambiguously an anti-Establishment figure. However, the history of "Jerusalem" was made much more complex when it was set to music by Hubert Parry (1848–1918)—who was, like Greg Lake, a Bournemouth native. Parry was a respected figure of the nineteenth-century British musical establishment who taught for many years at Oxford and the Royal College of Music. Parry's crusade throughout his career was to raise British music-making and musical taste to a level comparable to Germany, the undisputed center of musical life in the nineteenth century. As part of this effort, Parry turned out a number of large-scale orchestral and choral works in a very conservative style (comparable to Mendelssohn and Brahms), in an attempt to condition the British public to enjoy "serious" genres like the symphony and oratorio. Today, these works are almost completely forgotten.

In fact, it is ironic that the one Parry composition that is an undisputed classic should be one of his simplest, least pretentious works. In 1916, during the height of the carnage of World War I, Parry was seized by a desire to compose something that would appeal to the patriotic spirit of his countrymen, and encourage them not to lose faith in the war effort. He took Blake's poem "Jerusalem" and set it as a choral song for unison voices with orchestral accompaniment. It was an instant hit, and has remained a classic to the present day: it is something of an unofficial national anthem, the British equivalent to the American "Battle Hymn of the Republic." The irony, of course, is that Blake's thoroughly anti-Establishment lyrics were set to a thoroughly pro-Establishment, patriotic

---

[9] Blake, like Bunyan and his mentor Milton before him, made no essential distinction between the theological and political aspects of his work. See E. P. Thompson, *Witness Against the Beast: William Blake and the Moral Law* (New York: The New Press, 1993).

(albeit not jingoistic) hymn tune. The particular genius of ELP was not just applying Blake's anti-industrial message to their warning of artificial intelligence gone apocalyptically wrong, but recovering the countercultural resonance that Blake's poem held for his own contemporaries.

Of course, the deep cultural resonance of "Jerusalem" doesn't guarantee its success in a rock music setting; it works on a purely musical level because of ELP's inspired arrangement. In terms of its basic material, Emerson is fairly conservative in his emendations. He does change Parry's rather straitjacketlike 3/4 meter to a freer alternation between bars of four and three (a favored pattern is two bars of 4/4, a bar of 3/4, and another bar of 4/4); this lends the hymn a more loping, wayward rhythmic feel. Likewise, he brings a slight modal coloring to Parry's staunchly diatonic harmony, especially in terms of sometimes using a lowered seventh degree (thus giving some passages a Mixolydian flavor). In both of these changes, Emerson brings the hymn more in line with the musical style of the generation of British composers who came after Parry—Emerson's setting is especially reminiscent of how Parry's great student Ralph Vaughan Williams (1872–1958) might have set Blake's poem.

The most crucial factor of ELP's "Jerusalem," however, is how it takes on a very dynamic, irresistible forward momentum, pressing on inevitably towards one climactic goal after another—much like the "Karn Evil 9" suite that concludes the album. To some degree, this dynamic motion is built into the hymn itself because of the hymn's restless harmonic motion. Although nominally in F major,[10] the hymn actually begins in the relative minor, D minor ("And did those feet"), and then passes through G minor ("And did the Countenance Divine") and B♭ major ("our clouded hills") before finally arriving safely at the tonic F major ("And was Jerusalem builded here"). However, the contributions of all three band members to the arrangement are at least as crucial as the hymn's harmonic motion to the impression of irresistible forward momentum.

Emerson's primary sound is a "screaming chorus" effect on his Hammond C-3, which he creates by double tracking his Hammond and running one track through a flanger—a kind of postmodern pipe organ timbre. We hear this sound featured prominently during the instrumental introduction (where it's accompanied by bass guitar doubled by Minimoog in a low register) and during the first verse, which features organ, Lake's voice, and Palmer's orchestral percussion. After the first verse the instrumental intro recurs (1:10), but it's the second verse ("Bring me my bow of burning gold") where Emerson and Lake really begin to build the arrangement.

---

[10] At least in ELP's arrangement. Parry actually wrote the hymn tune in D major. ELP presumably transposed it up a minor third to better suite Greg Lake's vocal range. However, F major also takes on an Edenic, utopian symbolism as the album progresses.

At the beginning of the second verse Emerson adopts a new textural configuration that had only been hinted at in his earlier work, but which becomes a major factor throughout *Brain Salad Surgery*: he plays the organ chords with his left hand and begins to antiphonally interject martial Moog "trumpet" leads in between Lake's vocal phrases with his right hand. By no longer doubling Lake's bass line (as he did so often on the first four albums), Emerson simultaneously gives the texture a new clarity (by eliminating the muddiness in the bass register that often was created when keyboard and bass both played the bass line) and a new sophistication (since melodic leads were now constantly exchanged between the Moog's high register and the Hammond's middle register, and at times both the Moog and organ lines were of equal melodic interest). As the second verse of "Jerusalem" progresses, the organ part becomes no less active, but the Moog leads become more jagged and agitated, much as if the band had a fourth member, a lead guitarist, perhaps, whose obbligato lines were driving the band on towards a huge climax.

Lake, for his part, commences a slow-moving bass line at the beginning of the second verse of "Jerusalem," but his bass line takes on a driving eighth-note rhythmic motion as the verse progresses, which further increases the music's momentum (although I think the bass line could have profitably been pushed a bit higher in the mix). Because of Emerson's new approach to arranging parts on *Brain Salad Surgery*, Lake's bass playing takes on a new importance with this album, and seldom has there been a more virtuosic simultaneous display of singing and bass playing: the only comparison that immediately suggests itself is John Wetton's work with King Crimson circa 1972–74. Aesthetes who point out that Lake's bass parts on *Brain Salad Surgery* are seldom as virtuosic as some of Chris Squire's more thundering bass lines forget to take into account the vocal parts that Lake needed to juggle simultaneously— something that Squire seldom had to worry about to the same degree, since he only sang backing vocals.

Carl Palmer's contributions to the orchestration of "Jerusalem" are almost as important as Emerson's; indeed, throughout *Brain Salad Surgery*, Palmer's ability as an orchestrator reaches a new pinnacle, and "Jerusalem" is something of a textbook example of Palmer's style at the apex of his career. He begins the instrumental introduction by rhythmically doubling Emerson's melodic figures; however, towards the end of the intro (0:12) he launches into the lightning fast single stroke rolls across the toms that to some degree characterize his drum part during the remainder of the piece. During much of the first verse, Palmer shows admirable restraint by confining himself solely to orchestral percussion: chimes (0:46), timpani (0:53), gong (1:00). Only at the end of the verse does he launch into another series of clockwise tom rolls, culminating in the incredible snare fill (1:09) that answers the three key words of the hymn, "dark Satanic mills." When the instrumental intro is repeated at 1:10, Palmer's part is similar to the opening, except with more fills across the toms.

Only at the beginning of the second verse (1:31), in conjunction with the entrance of Emerson's Moog obbligato and Lake's bass line, does Palmer fall into a repetitive (by his standards, at least) rock and roll backbeat. Again, though, notice the complexity of the bass drum part, with its broken triplets, his frequent interjection of essentially melodic military style snare fills (1:42, 1:55), and his use of a chugging sixteenth-note bass drum figure (2:05) to push the hymn to its climax. Very justifiably, Palmer has named "Jerusalem" as his favorite concise expression of the classic ELP sound;[11] his essentially melodic snare and tom fills, rhythmic doublings of key melodic figures, discreet use of orchestral percussion, and kaleidoscopically shifting rock-and-roll grooves immeasurably fatten up ELP's trio sound. Not surprisingly, Palmer was especially disappointed when Manticore's plan to release "Jerusalem" as a single in the U.K. was thwarted by BBC Radio's refusal to play it, on the grounds that it "degraded" a national treasure.[12]

For both Blake and ELP, "Jerusalem" represents a call to arms, a call to resist the forces of spiritual darkness and dehumanization. This call does not go unchallenged for long. Within a few seconds of the final chord of "Jerusalem," we hear the distant call of an atonal Moog trumpet line—seemingly a twisted parody of the heroic Moog fanfares of "Jerusalem"—answering from across some desolate plain, as it were, accompanied by the ominous muttering of timpani. Suddenly, the band explode full throttle into the ferocious "Toccata," and we are confronted by the music of the "dark Satanic mills."

"Toccata" is ELP's arrangement of the fourth movement of Alberto Ginastera's Piano Concerto no. 1 (1961). As we've already seen, this piece had been exerting a profound impact on Emerson from the time he first heard it in the waning days of the Nice. Its metallic chords, complex metric episodes, and interlocking ostinato patterns eventually became as much a part of his style as the Bach and the blues and contemporary jazz elements he had absorbed in his earlier years, and its influence is evident throughout much of *Tarkus* and parts of *Trilogy* (i.e., that album's recurring "Enigma chord"). While Emerson had talked of arranging part of Ginastera's Concerto as early as 1971, it wasn't until 1973 that he felt the time was right:

> Carl said that he wanted to have a drum solo which would be a little different than just putting it on to the end of another number. I rang him on the phone

---

[11] See Leroy, "An Interview with Carl Palmer," 9–10.
[12] See Carl Palmer, *Applied Rhythms* (Cedar Grove, NJ: Modern Drummer Publications, 1987), 60.

and played it for him, and he said "That's amazing!" We had a group rehearsal and I played it for them on the organ, and that was the start of it . . . I thought the fourth [studio] album was the time to try and approach this piece of music. It was very testing for all of us. Greg didn't read music, and Carl read it to a certain extent, but he wasn't able to apply piano music to playing drums. So it was really like going through the whole thing bar by bar. It was music by mathematics for them. Carl learned it really by counting, and if you watch any videos of ELP playing "Toccata" you'll see his lips move as he's counting "one-two-three-four-five-six-seven-eight."[13]

Emerson has commented elsewhere that "Toccata" was probably the most complex piece of music that ELP ever tackled,[14] adding, "We knew immediately that we couldn't do the entire piece, or even the entire last movement, so we just took the first four or five pages and used them as the basis for what happened next. Carl's percussion movement wasn't planned; it just came into being as we worked on the piece."[15]

Calling "Toccata" an "arrangement," even in the relatively loose sense of ELP's take on Copland's "Hoedown," is probably not entirely accurate. The term I might be tempted to use instead is "fantasia"—with the caveat that "fantasia" normally refers to dreamy, semi-improvisational music, which is miles away from what ELP are up to here. As Blair Pethel points out,

> It is really only the first 140–50 measures of the movement that are played before the arrangement breaks off into new music; even those measures are not exact. [ELP] return again to the original near the end of the transcription, but there are numerous additions and deletions of single measures throughout the work and a use of thematic material from much later in the movement near the beginning of Emerson's version.[16]

Emerson's strategy was to use the Hammond as a surrogate "orchestra" and the Moog(s) as surrogate "soloist," although these roles are not absolute. Since the Hammond's keyboards do not have the same registral range as a piano's, Emerson realized it would not be feasible to transcribe the piano soloist's part. For this reason, most of "Toccata" draws from the orchestra's music rather than the soloist's. This has sometimes puzzled listeners who were not aware of Emerson's *modus operandi*.

ELP's "Toccata" falls into three distinct sections. The ferocious opening section (0:00–2:56) is, as we've seen, loosely based on Ginastera's music. Palmer's "percussion movement" (2:56–6:18) is an extraordinarily

---

[13] Pilato, liner notes, *Brain Salad Surgery* reissue, 7–8.
[14] Milano, "Keith Emerson," *Contemporary Keyboard*, October 1977, 25.
[15] Pethel, "Keith Emerson," 84.
[16] Ibid.

unique and musical "drum solo"—indeed, parts of it contain passages for all three musicians—that traverses a gamut of moods ranging from an uneasy calm to stark terror. This section develops some of Ginastera's motives in a tuned percussion context, as well as exploring the sonic possibilities of Palmer's synthesized percussion. The third section (6:18–7:20) recapitulates the final part of the opening section (compare 6:18 with 2:08), and brings the piece to an explosive climax on Ginastera's raucous skyscraperlike chord stacks.

"Toccata" begins with a quietly ominous atonal Moog trumpet call, backed by the distant thunder of Palmer's understated timpani. This atonal "trumpet" call is based on Ginastera's opening motive, which consists of two interlocking tritones a fourth apart (Bb–E–Eb–A). This motive plays a prominent melodic role throughout the movement. It is the backbone of the main theme, which is heard at 2:08 and again at 6:18; it also is stacked frequently into a bitonally flavored chord of two fourths a tritone apart (E–A–Bb–Eb, or an inversion thereof)—a chord which I'll call the "Ginastera chord" for the sake of this discussion. We hear this pungent "Ginastera chord," either in its original form, inverted, or transposed, at 0:31, 0:36, 0:59, and 1:23, among other places.

By dropping just one note from this chord, we have the "Enigma chord" (Bb–Eb–A, or C–F–B in the transposed form that it appeared in on the *Trilogy* album). The fact that we hear this very chord featured prominently from 1:32 to 1:45 of "Toccata" suggests that Ginastera is the source of this chord. Another typically Emersonian bitonal chord form which would seem to have its roots in Ginastera's music involves two triads (or parts of two triads) a minor second apart; compare the chord at 1:51 of "Toccata" (A minor over Bb minor with no fifth) or the final chord at 7:15 (essentially an $F\sharp$ seventh chord intermingled with an F ninth chord) with the nearly identical bitonal chord at the climax of *Turkus* (listen at 20:15). Incidentally, during the opening Moog "trumpet" figure Emerson appends two extra notes to Ginastera's original motive, so that it becomes B–E–Eb–A–C–A; this is a particularly ingenious addition, because the A–C–A anticipates the movement's second main theme, the obsessively rocking minor third theme which we hear at 0:40, 0:59, 1:15, 1:55, and elsewhere.

As richly complex as the melodic and harmonic material is, however, what really breathes life into "Toccata" is Emerson's Moog timbres: this piece may well mark his greatest achievement as a synthesist. Rather than attempt to approximate Ginastera's orchestration electronically, Emerson reorchestrates Ginastera's motives with supremely original—yet entirely appropriate—electronic timbres, often of a decisively strident cast. Frequently a trumpetlike Moog line suddenly dissolves into an extremely strident timbre that resembles a pitched electric power drill—listen at 0:30–0:31, 0:56–0:59, or especially dramatically, at 2:41–2:55 and

7:01–7:06. There is also a distinctive timbre that resembles a police siren—listen to the glissandos in contrary motion from 1:11 to 1:15, the descending glissando from 1:38 to 1:44, or the multiple ascending glissandi from 6:50. "Toccata" is the one ELP track that anticipates nineties industrial music just as much as it prefigures later developments in progressive rock—indeed, very few later bands in any style came anywhere close to touching the magisterial blend of precision and raw fury which is the hallmark of "Toccata." If the "Tarkus" suite did not establish ELP's modernist credentials, "Toccata" certainly should have; any critic who continues to assert that ELP's use of classical music is nothing more than a matter of shop-worn nineteenth-century clichés is either unacquainted with "Toccata," or is simply ignorant.

Palmer's percussion movement, notable both for its foray into exotic percussion timbres and for the wide range of moods that it explores, itself falls into three distinct sections. It begins with an impressive timpani flourish, backed by gong strikes, which lasts for nearly a minute, and displays how far Palmer's understanding of the timpani had progressed under Gilbert Webster's guidance. The timpani flourish reaches a huge crescendo, then trails off into a statement of the rocking minor third theme on timpani alone (3:53) then timpani and chimes together (3:59); as an ominous wind (synthesized white noise) begins to rise in the background, Emerson punctuates the end of the theme with three quietly dissonant piano chords. This leads directly into the movement's eerie second section (4:23): to the accompaniment of Palmer's repetitive timpani ostinato, Emerson and Lake launch into a lengthy atonal unison melody on electric guitar and Moog, both of which are routed through an Echoplex. The combination of reverberation, muted dynamics, and tonal ambiguity creates a somewhat decadent, flesh-crawling ambience; the general "vibe" of this section, if not the actual thematic material, is suggestive of the muted and desolate third movement of Ginastera's Piano Concerto no. 1.

At 5:05 we are suddenly wrenched from suppressed fear into stark panic as Palmer launches into the third and final section of the movement, the notorious synthesized percussion solo. Here's Palmer on the synthesized drum set-up he used at the time:

> I contacted an up-and-coming guy [Nicholas Rose] who had just left the London School of Electronics. I gave him the broad outlines of what I wanted but he wasn't too sure of what I meant. So I showed him something Bob Moog had made for me a long time previously. [As far as I can determine, Palmer never used Moog's device in concert or on record.] This consisted of a receiver inside the drum which picked up the signal on the drum being hit and which was wired up to a foot-plate consisting of five buttons, each one giving a different sound, the fifth button canceling the system. The drum itself contained the electronics and had sensitivity and volume controls. This was

fine but getting each different sound meant frequent use of the foot and whilst playing wasn't too feasible.

I said to Bob [Moog], "Look, I've got eight drums, can we not put a synthesizer into each one? [This was apparently during the *Trilogy* era, when Palmer was using the Octoplus kit.] Various problems arose so I took up the idea with this guy Nicholas Rose. I wanted a pick-up with a pre-amp inside each drum sending the signal via cable to the back where there would be a synthesizer box for each drum. This he did. Each synthesizer is about the size of a portable cassette recorder, and has a pre-set sound which can be changed if required by taking the back off and changing the top card. I decided to have five electronic sounds and three counters. These counters are rhythmic patterns. One is a sequencer which plays fourteen notes then repeats itself; another plays a kind of bass pattern and the other a type of lead guitar pattern. The three rhythms will continue playing once I have hit them—I can stop them but I can't change them whilst playing. On the floor I have "on" and "cancel" buttons. These control all eight synthesizers. Within the other five sounds, some have a short decay, some long, and I add these over the rhythm patterns.

Funnily enough I'm not yet a great believer in it although I developed it, because it's still new to me and to the audience—when they hear it they still believe the sounds to be coming from Keith.[17]

What does it sound like? Well, by the time the solo reaches its climax (around 5:45), imagine that a fire engine, a police car, a contingent of ambulances, and your local air raid siren were all sounding simultaneously, with Carl Palmer pounding out a furious drum solo in the background, and you'll have some idea.[18] At 6:16, he suddenly strikes four accented quarter notes, which signal the recapitulation of Ginastera's music and the final climax on the grinding polytriad which was discussed above.

"Toccata" is, in my opinion, ELP's greatest classical arrangement, both from the standpoint of technique and imagination. It is, to paraphrase Herbert Howells's comment about Ralph Vaughan Williams's *Fantasia on a Theme by Thomas Tallis*, "a supreme commentary by one great composer [in this case, the band as a unit] on another." Yet, the strident timbres of Emerson's Moog and Palmer's percussion synthesizer change "Toccata" into something qualitatively different than its source.

---

[17] Carl Palmer, quoted in Frank Askew, "Carl Palmer's Drum Kits," *Fanzine for the Common Man* 13 (July 1993): 16. This quotation, in turn, is actually an excerpt from a feature that ran in the November 1974 issue of *Drums and Percussion*. As to Palmer's reservations about the synthesized drums—while I think he uses them absolutely brilliantly on "Toccata," I can't image him using them in any other context on any other ELP track. I think his drum synthesizer was a one-trick pony of sorts.

[18] George Forrester gives an impressively detailed description of all the electronic drum sounds that are audible during this passage; see Forrester, Hanson, and Askew, *Emerson, Lake and Palmer*, 199.

Ginastera's music is violent, to be sure, but it is an earthy, human violence—the violence of the gaucho on the pampas, perhaps. "Toccata" suggests a violence of an infinitely more impersonal and inhuman nature: the random violence of urban unrest, "limited warfare," and terrorism, and even more disturbingly, the psychological terror directed against the individual in the name of the State which George Orwell forecast as a hallmark of totalitarian regimes in *1984*. Heard this way, ELP's "Toccata" is the musical equivalent of the horrific machine depicted in Giger's cover art, and its repudiation of the utopian message of "Jerusalem" could not be more complete.

There was some concern in the ELP camp that even after having recorded "Toccata," the band might not be able to include it on *Brain Salad Surgery*. ELP approached Boosey and Hawkes, Ginastera's publisher, for permission, and were told that Ginastera ordinarily did not allow adaptations of his music; any exceptions would have to be approved by the composer himself. Boosey and Hawkes did agree to give the band Ginastera's phone number, and a meeting was hastily arranged between Emerson, ELP manager Stewart Young, Ginastera, and his wife Aurora, in Ginastera's apartment in Geneva, Switzerland. Emerson remembers that when he entered the apartment "There, standing at attention and dressed in a suit, almost like a bank manager, was Alberto Ginastera, ready to receive us."[19] Emerson explained to Ginastera the premise of the band's adaptation, then nervously pressed the "play" button on Ginastera's tape deck. To Emerson's horror, after just a few seconds Ginastera pressed the stop button, exclaimed, in French, "terrible," and rewound the tape to the beginning. After listening intently to "Toccata" all the way through, he exclaimed something to his wife, who turned and told a relieved Emerson that the composer was very impressed with the band's treatment of his music. On the lyric sheet of *Brain Salad Surgery*, the sole entry under "Toccata" is this:

> "Keith Emerson has beautifully caught the mood of my piece."
> —Alberto Ginastera

The molten fury of "Toccata," with its frightful vision of alienation and dehumanization, is answered by the elegant but melancholy Greg Lake ballad "Still . . . You Turn Me On." The lyrics acknowledge the fact of alienation and dehumanization in modern life—"Every day a little sadder / a little madder / someone get me a ladder"—but suggest that love can still endure: "Still . . . you turn me on." The theme of this ballad—that love and commitment between individuals is the only sure anchor in an

---

[19] Pilato, liner notes, *Brain Salad Surgery* CD reissue, 8.

age of societal alienation and loss of religious faith—is a theme that Lake was to return to increasingly often in his later work. At the same time, however, "Still . . . You Turn Me On," with its cryptic references to buried and crystallized flesh, does forge a link with the creepiness of both "Toccata" and Giger's cover art.

"Still . . . You Turn Me On" is an eloquent testament to the great stride Lake's mastery of the craft of songwriting had taken since "Lucky Man." "Lucky Man" uses four chords; "Still . . . You Turn Me On" uses twelve, not counting suspensions, on eight different root notes. "Lucky Man" unfolds across an utterly predictable sixteen-bar structure, an eight-bar verse followed by an eight-bar chorus; "Still . . . You Turn Me On" unfolds across a highly unusual forty-three-bar structure (a thirty-one-bar verse which breaks into unequal fifteen- and sixteen-bar segments, followed by a twelve-bar chorus), from which a lot of Tin Pan Alley songwriters could have learned a thing or two.

Once again using the open D tuning that had worked so well for him on "Take a Pebble," Lake's widely spaced, precisely picked acoustic guitar arpeggios, occasionally interrupted by exquisitely voiced chordal fills, are the backbone of the song. The tonality of "Still . . . You Turn Me On" shows a sense of flux that is lacking from any of Lake's previous ballads.[20] After beginning with eight bars of G Mixolydian harmony (G major alternating with D minor arpeggios), the harmony becomes much more active and tenuous, cadencing on D major at the end of the first half of the verse ("man on the moon"); an F major arpeggio ("do you want to be the player") swings the tonality off onto a new tangent, and by the end of the second half of the verse ("flesh has crystallized") the tonality seems to have slipped into D minor. D minor is finally confirmed as tonic via a King Crimsonish Phrygian cadence (E♭ major to D minor) during the ". . . Still you turn me on" chorus, after which the forty-three-bar structure is repeated with new words.

It must be admitted that one thing "Still . . . You Turn Me On" lacks, in comparison to "Lucky Man," is an instantly memorable vocal melody. Much of the vocal line is very declamatory, rocking back and forth between two or three notes, and only the second half of the verse ("you see it really doesn't matter") takes on a melodically memorable outline. Clearly, parts of the vocal melody were added as an afterthought to the exquisite arpeggios.

Also, it's hard to avoid the impression that "Still . . . You Turn Me On" is somewhat overarranged, even though Carl Palmer demonstrates admirable restraint by sitting out. Rather than beginning with only voice and guitar and gradually layering other instruments in, the song immedi-

---

[20] Excepting the solo guitar section of "The Sage."

ately begins with voice, guitar, and Emerson's busy accordion obbligato (right channel); by the second half of the verse (0:30) harpsichord and electric guitar effects have been added, culminating in the obnoxious wah-wah electric guitar fill at 1:04 in the chorus. When the second repetition of the verse-chorus is commenced at 1:24 the texture is already filled up, and subtle gestures that would have been quite effective had the texture been less cluttered (such as the dramatically late entrance of bass guitar at 2:09) are largely swallowed up. Granted, some of the background parts are nice in isolation: Emerson's harpsichord playing during the second verse really is exquisite (listen especially from 1:42). However, for the most part "Still . . . You Turn Me On" is sophisticated enough in its basic conception not to require a lot of filling out (unlike "Lucky Man," for instance), and a less-is-more arrangement strategy would have benefited the song. I personally have always preferred the guitar/vocal interpretation of the song on *Welcome Back My Friends*, although I think even better would be an arrangement for voice, acoustic guitar, and harpsichord. However, regardless of its relatively mild arrangement faults, "Still . . . You Turn Me On" is a lovely song, and plays an important role on the album, creating an effective human/mechanical and pastoral/technological dichotomy with "Toccata."

"Still . . . You Turn Me On" is followed by "Benny the Bouncer," the third in the band's sequence of music hall songs stretching back to "Jeremy Bender" and "The Sheriff." Like the finale of "The Sheriff," "Benny" demonstrates Emerson's growing interest in 1920s stride piano techniques, evident in the continuous stride bass patterns, staunchly diatonic chord progressions, and bluesy, chromatically inflected piano leads. "Benny the Bouncer," the first Emerson/Lake/Sinfield collaboration, tells the story of a savage barroom brawl between Benny (a bouncer) and Savage Sid (a greaser) that leaves Benny with a hatchet buried in his skull. The musical structure of the song is simple—three twelve-bar verses, the second and third of which are separated by an eight-bar bridge and a twenty-four-bar Emerson piano solo over the verse's chord changes. The theme of the lyrics—that the barroom patrons see the fight and Benny's subsequent death as an entertaining diversion, nothing more—certainly fits in with the themes of alienation and dehumanization that previous tracks have already developed.

Furthermore, there is an acute ironic displacement between Emerson's tinkly, cheerful D major stride piano accompaniment and the grim, unsentimental Lake-Sinfield storyline, an ironic displacement that reminds me of Paul McCartney's "Rocky Raccoon." But while McCartney milks the ironic displacement between music and lyrics in his song for all he can, singing his grim lyrics in his most angelic tenor, Lake sings in a forced and affected Cockney accent that appears to patronize his working class subjects, and suggests that he doesn't take his lyrics all that seriously. As a result, much of the song's potential expressive punch is squandered, and the pseudo-Cockney accent soon becomes simply irritating. I must also confess that I never understood why Emerson used his Moog Apollo to accompany the verses—an acoustic piano would have sounded more appropriate—so this song also ends up sounding a bit over-arranged.[21] Notice the barely audible chuckle at the end of the song—another sonic link with "Jeremy Bender" and "The Sheriff."

Now we come to the monumental, thirty-minute "Karn Evil 9" suite, certainly the crux of *Brain Salad Surgery*, and arguably the crux of ELP's entire output. Before plunging into a detailed discussion of "Karn Evil 9," I would like to make a general observation. A lot of commentators, including me, have tended to lump "Karn Evil 9" and "Tarkus" together; however, the better I have come to know the former, the less viable I have felt the comparisons to be.[22] To be sure, both are vast, multimovement rock pieces, deeply indebted to classical structural techniques, which develop themes of alienation in modern society and technology gone awry. Beyond this, though, there are some major differences. "Tarkus" is a modernist work, pure and simple. Like a mobile suspended from a ceiling where different figures slowly move back and forth, exchanging positions, without really "going anywhere," the dissonant, machinelike instrumental movements and simpler, more "human" songs of "Tarkus" simply alternate; there is no attempt to reconcile or resolve the disjunction between the two. As a result, the movement from one kind of music to the other is cyclical, not teleological, and the element of disruption that is so central to modernist art is forefronted here. The music of "Tarkus" is the most apt expression possible of Lake's pessimistic vision of an endless cycle of failed revolutions.[23]

"Karn Evil 9" is fundamentally different. In both the 1st and 3rd Impressions, the diverse stylistic sources are unified into a tightly woven musical discourse in which the element of disjunction is minimized, and there is none of the alternation between distinct "blocks" of music that is so characteristic of "Tarkus." Furthermore, "Karn Evil 9" is characterized

---

[21] I must admit, though, I would have liked to have heard Lake's background electric guitar lines, vaguely audible during the third and final verse, a bit higher up in the mix.

[22] See, for instance, *Rocking the Classics*, 94–95, or Bill Martin's *Listening to the Future*, 147.

[23] In regards to the structural dynamic of "Tarkus" expressing Lake's pessimistic vision of an endless cycle of failed revolutions, consider the tonal plan of "Tarkus," which moves back and forth from the tonic ("Eruption") to the dominant ("Stones of Years") to the tonic ("Iconoclast") to the dominant ("Manticore") to the tonic ("Aquatarkus") without really "going anywhere." In common practice modulatory approach, the tonic is journeyed away from soon after it has been securely established at the beginning of a work, and is not returned to in a decisive fashion until near the end. Furthermore, in common practice modulatory approach, the dominant is merely the first of a number of key centers that serve as stopping-off points on the tonal "journey" away from and back to the tonic key.

by an irresistible forward momentum that is harmonic as much as it is rhythmic. In other words, although the harmonic and melodic substance of "Karn Evil 9" won't particularly remind you of Beethoven or Wagner, the music is characterized by a restless striving towards some distant goal, that is, the music *progresses* in an idealistic, Romantic sense. In fact, if I were to say the music of "Karn Evil 9" encapsulates anything, it's heroic striving: this is a theme I'll develop in the discussion that follows.

The "storyline" of "Karn Evil 9" is actually a conflation of two distinct ideas, both dealing with technology gone awry but each with a somewhat different focus. The lyrics of the 1st Impression, credited to Greg Lake but showing some definite signs of Pete Sinfield's involvement, stem from a Keith Emerson concept, originally slated to be titled "Ganton 9," concerning "a planet to which all manner of evil and decadence had been banished."[24] The concept behind the 3rd Impression, meanwhile, with lyrics by Lake and Sinfield, was a Pete Sinfield inspiration—a monumental battle between Man and Computer, waged somewhere in the future in the depths of outer space—that owes a clear debt to the Arthur C. Clarke/Stanley Kubrick epic movie *2001: A Space Odyssey.* Eventually, the two concepts were loosely woven together, with the lyrics alternating between the viewpoints of three distinct dramatic personae: a narrator (who stands outside the action), a Carnival barker, who would appear to represent computer technology gone apocalyptically wrong, and a Liberator, a heroic individual who has vowed to liberate oppressed humans from their electronic overlord(s). The opening of the 1st Impression (0:00–3:41) presents a manipulative totalitarian world of the not-so-distant future as the logical fulfillment of Blake's dire prophesies about "Satanic mills," but the persona who describes this dystopic society to us also presents himself as a potential liberator: "I'll be there, I'll be there, I will be there / To heal their sorrow / to beg and borrow / fight tomorrow!" The viewpoint then shifts, and the remainder of the 1st Impression features Big Brother as Carnival barker, hence the suite's "Karn Evil" title.[25] We learn that Big Brother doesn't need to terrorize the population into submission—Orwell's vision of the future in *1984*—since the population has effectively been entertained into a state of blissful mindlessness, much closer to Aldous Huxley's vision of the future in *Brave New World*, another of the great dystopic novels that exerted such a powerful influence on the Baby Boomer generation. The technology that has gone terribly wrong in 1st Impression, it would seem, is electronic media, which the powers-that-be have used

---

[24] Pilato, liner notes, *Brain Salad Surgery* CD reissue, 11.
[25] Why "Karn Evil 9"? I suspect that (1) the title as it's now spelled is a play on Emerson's initials (K. E.), and (2) the "9" at the end allowed Emerson to retain at least a scrap of his original "Ganton 9" concept.

as a tool to impose a subtle but powerful mind control over the entertainment-mad masses.

Lake, in his "Carnival barker" persona, assures us that his is "the show that never ends," a pretty accurate assessment of modern media, as it turns out. Prophetically, some of the main sources of entertainment in this "show that never ends" are violence ("a bomb inside a car, spectacular, spectacular"), human tragedy ("some tears for you to see, misery, misery"), sexual titillation ("a stripper in a till, what a thrill, what a thrill"), sports ("we've got thrills and shocks, supersonic fighting cocks"), and rock music ("you've got to see the show—it's rock and roll").[26] What's left of the environment is exploited as yet another source of entertainment ("there behind the glass lies a real blade of grass / be careful as you pass, move along, move along"). The overlords of this "show" assert a frightening, almost limitless omniscience with their blasphemous boast of being able to "pull Jesus from a hat"—a boast that could also be seen as part of a strategy to manipulate religious experience.[27]

The 2nd Impression is instrumental, and plays a similar role to the instrumental tracks in some of ELP's earlier works (for example, "Atropos" from the debut album or "Infinite Space" from *Tarkus*): it functions as a transition, as a turning point in the unfolding of the concept. The lyric of 3rd Impression, the suite's climax, is unfolded from two viewpoints. The first two verses are in the voice of a narrator who stands outside of the action: we are taken back to the dawn of human history, when humankind was "born of stone," and then far into the future (although not necessarily far into our own future), when computers have attained Godlike powers, and a man of steel wields a blade "kissed by countless kings." From this point on, the 3rd Impression traces the battle for supremacy between Man and Machine, and the viewpoint in the lyric shifts to the "Liberator" himself—presumably the character whose voice we heard at the opening of the 1st Impression—as he engages in his life-and-death struggle with the Computer, the "Man of Steel." Whether this Computer is the "Carnival barker" who guided us through the 1st Impression's "show that never ends" is impossible to discern, and is essentially immaterial to the album's concept as a whole; one of the masterstrokes of the lyrics of the 1st and 3rd Impressions is that although each is self-contained, when combined they appear to cohere into a more or less unified storyline with much more sweeping implications than either has by itself.

---

[26] This last verse prefigures Roger Waters's concern with rock's potential for totalitarian misuse, especially in regards to mob manipulation, that was such an important aspect of Pink Floyd's *The Wall*.

[27] Although it occurs to me that some might see the verse of "pulling Jesus from a hat" as prefiguring the televangelist scandals of the 1980s!

Now that we've considered the conceptual/narrative premise of "Karn Evil 9," let's examine the music of each of the three Impressions in turn. 1st Impression, the longest of the three at 13:22, falls into a gigantic A B B form. The opening A section features the voice of the Liberator as he describes the sorry state that humankind has fallen into and promises future redemption; the B sections feature the Carnival barker guiding us through the "show that never ends." When Emerson was composing the music to 1st Impression, he realized that the entire thirteen-plus minutes of music would not fit on the first side of the LP format if the track were to be preceded by "Jerusalem," "Toccata," "Still . . . You Turn Me On," and "Benny the Bouncer." He decided that the second of the two B sections should be put at the beginning of side two of the LP, with the end of side one featuring a fadeout on a bubbling Moog note and the beginning of side two featuring a fadein on the same. As a result, the A B portion of 1st Impression, some 8:39 of music, went on side one of the LP, and was entitled "Karn Evil 9, 1st Impression, part 1"; the second B section (an additional 4:43 of music), which was put at the beginning of side two of the LP format, was entitled "Karn Evil 9, 1st Impression, part 2." This ended up being an excellent strategy; part 1 of the 1st Impression ended up getting a lot of FM radio airplay in the U.S.—the only ELP track aside from Greg Lake's predominantly acoustic ballads to do so—which the 13:22 1st Impression in its entirety almost certainly would not have received.[28] At the same time, the conceptual/narrative/musical flow of the 1st Impression was not unduly disrupted by this bisection, and with the Victory and Rhino CD reissues, the two parts of 1st Impression have been re-spliced into a continuous whole, although part 1 and part 2 are each given a separate track listing (presumably for radio airplay purposes).

The A section of 1st Impression, the first 3:41 of the track, is, as we've seen, devoted to the "Liberator" persona who pours out, like a modern-day Jeremiah, troubling visions of a dystopic society of the not-too-distant future. The entire section is centered in the icily remote key of A♭ minor—the A♭ tonality hereafter becomes a symbol of dystopia and a counterweight to the "utopian" key of F major, the tonic of "Jerusalem." This section is structured around three verses of irregular length ("cold and misty morning," "suffering in silence," "there must be someone") with a common chorus ("I'll be there, I'll be there, I will be there"). Each of the three verses is preceded by an instrumental episode (0:00–0:25, 1:10–1:36, 2:19–2:56), all of which end with the same two motives: ascending organ chords accompanied by a descending pentatonic bass line

---

[28] I am baffled by Paul Stump's remark concerning "the utterly absurd bipartite structure of [Karn Evil 9] 1st Impression"—as I've said above, there is nothing at all absurd about the division of the piece. However, for another (albeit in my view indefensible) viewpoint see Stump, *The Music's All That Matters*, 170.

(first heard at 0:16), and a fanfarelike organ theme (first heard at 0:20)—this latter motive is hypnotically interjected into the vocal verses as well. Of the opening Hammond passage, which Paul Stump accurately describes as "one of the most understated but effective uses of Emerson's dexterity on record," Emerson has said: "Whereas *Tarkus* was my dabbling in fourths and fifths, 'Karn Evil 9' dealt with counterpoint, which has always been a fascinating vehicle for me to try and write in. The beginning of 'Karn Evil 9' is counterpoint—but then I gave up! The moment I got together with Greg and Carl they said 'That's very clever—now let's get on with the song.'"[29] Actually Emerson sells himself a bit short here. As we'll see, as a whole "Karn Evil 9" demonstrates a more polyphonic approach to arranging than anything in ELP's previous output. The three instrumental episodes in the A section of 1st Impression feature a wiry two-part counterpoint in which Bach-like melodic independence and harmonic tension are seamlessly fused with blues melodic contours, demonstrating how completely Emerson had absorbed his two primary early influences.

Lake's three vocal verses during the A section of 1st Impression often consist of little more than rocking major seconds ($A^\flat$–$G^\flat$). If not handled with care, a vocal melody of such limited means could quickly become a recipe for boredom. However, these vocal verses attest both to Lake's maturity as a vocalist and to Emerson's mastery of a more polyphonically conceived arrangement style than before. Lake's performance becomes a virtuoso demonstration of declamatory singing—listen to how he colors key words like "spare" (0:35)—and singing in $A^\flat$, a minor third above his ideal vocal tessitura, forces him to push his voice just a bit harder than usual, creating an added sense of tension and excitement. Notice, too, how Emerson arranges each of the three verses differently. The first verse is accompanied very sparsely with syncopated major seconds in the upper register of the Hammond and a jagged atonal countermelody in the piano's lower register, alternating with the ominous organ fanfare theme first heard at 0:20. The second verse (1:37) is accompanied with ascending organ triads moving in rhythmic unison with a melodically independent Moog obbligato, both accompanied by a descending bass line. The third verse (2:56) begins the transition from $A^\flat$ minor to $A^\flat$ major, and both the organ triads and Moog obbligato lines become more active. Through such careful attention to detail, what could have become a numbingly boring section instead generates a sense of unstoppable forward momentum through the gradual shift from $A^\flat$ minor to $A^\flat$ major, through the constantly shifting (and on the whole, increasingly dense)

---

[29] Pilato, liner notes, *Brain Salad Surgery* CD reissue, 11. For Stump's quote see *The Music's All That Matters*, 170.

textural configurations of the Hammond/Moog/bass accompaniment, and through Lake's continuously interesting highlighting of key words.

The A section of 1st Impression ends with another ominous fanfare-like figure at 3:34, the now familiar "Enigma chord" (E–A–D$^\sharp$) resolving to an A major chord. Neither chord appears to have much to do with the prevailing A$^\flat$ tonality, so the sudden lurch into a lengthy instrumental section (3:42–5:22), an irrepressible passage mostly in seven (3 + 4) which confirms A$^\flat$ major as the tonic, comes as something of a surprise. This high-energy episode, which serves as a huge transition from the A to the B section, throws into high relief Emerson's new approach to arrangement which we already noticed in connection with "Jerusalem." With one hand, he spins out triadic lines on the Hammond; with his other, he plays a trumpetlike monophonic line on the Moog. In terms of its harmonies, this section (indeed the remainder of 1st Impression) is far less "advanced" than *Tarkus*; the harmony is almost entirely triadic, utilizing a kind of major modality very common in British progressive rock wherein $^\flat$III, $^\flat$VI, and $^\flat$VII chords, which properly belong to the minor, are used in conjunction with a major tonic triad.

If the sonorities are simpler here than in *Tarkus*, however, the textural sophistication is amplified. Both the Hammond and Moog lines are of equal melodic interest—since neither doubles the bass line, for once Lake's bass parts are essential, and unlike *Tarkus*, the entire musical architecture of 1st Impression would collapse without the intricate bass guitar lines. The overall arrangement strategy is not unlike a jazz big band, and in this light Lake's description of "a big band playing rock material" begins to make a lot of sense, as does Emerson's statement that Duke Ellington was an inspiration to the way he arranged 1st Impression.[30] Imagine Emerson's Hammond as the sax section, his Moog as the trumpets, and Lake's alternately melodic and bass-ic bass as trombone and upright bass, respectively, and the image of "a big band playing rock material" is easy to sustain, especially when Emerson's "saxes" (Hammond) and "trumpets" (Moog) answer each other antiphonally—listen especially at 4:56. Notice, too, the way that Hammond and Moog parts are stereophonically separated, while voice, bass, and drums are spread across both channels of the mix.

Even the structure of this lengthy instrumental section suggests jazz roots. It falls into four parts, with the first three (3:42–3:58, 3:59–4:32, and 4:33–4:52) suggesting a twelve-bar blues with some highly unusual substitute chords ($^\flat$II, or A major, in place of the expected V chord). On the other hand, some of the passages suggest the contrapuntal episodes from the opening A section (listen especially from 4:17), and no one is

---

[30] Pilato, liner notes, *Brain Salad Surgery* CD reissue, 11.

likely to confuse Carl Palmer's intricate, melodically active rock backbeats, as he drives the seven (and, in the final passage from 4:52 on, fifteen) beat patterns forward, with jazz. Once again, ELP have subsumed their sources—big band textures, blues progressions, the shifting meters and modal harmonies typical of British progressive rock—and created something completely unique and yet utterly coherent.

Finally, at 5:22 Lake's Carnival barker persona takes center stage and we arrive at the first of the two B sections. The first B section is structured around three verses ("step inside hello," "left behind the bars," "next upon the bill"). Each is followed by the same refrain, a four-bar Moog fanfare figure (first heard at 5:38) followed by the "roll up" chorus. The tonality here is a cheerfully simple A♭ major, representing, perhaps, the unshakable confidence of the computer overlord, and the incredible drive of the section is generated by the rhythm. The syncopated rhythmic patterns of Emerson's Hammond accompaniment and Lake's bass lines show an obvious funk background; Emerson was clearly aware of James Brown's achievements during this period, and here adopts funk rhythms to his own ends. An especially inspired example of a funk figure transmogrified into something quintessentially ELP is Lake's sequentially rising bass line, first heard beneath the "roll up" segment at 5:42. The segments between verses show a further sensitivity on the part of ELP to the value of understatement, a tendency that was already beginning to emerge on *Trilogy*: notice the unaccompanied pressed snare roll at 5:51, the organ raking at 6:24, and the clockwise tom fill at 6:57, all of which allow a nice momentary thinning of the texture and respite from the incredible rhythmic momentum.

During the third verse, Lake quietly doubles the bass line with electric guitar, and following Palmer's tom fill at 6:57 he launches into the electric guitar solo which is destined to bring the 1st Impression to its first major climax. Calling this passage a "solo" may be misleading, so let me clarify. This is not a loosely improvised lead line over a short, repetitive ostinato, but rather a carefully developed thematic network that builds up inexorably through a thicket of key changes, ratcheting up tension right to the end; the climactic nature of the passage is further underlined by the fact that the thick, cutting timbre of the electric guitar is the most intense timbre we've heard yet during the piece. Lake begins with long sustained notes over another funk bass line, in A♭, played by Emerson in unison on Hammond and Minimoog. However, the guitar lead soon begins spinning out rapid-fire chromatic motives using much shorter note values, and then moves into an unusual triplet rhythm against the Moog/Hammond bass when the latter shifts to B♭ at 7:16. Finally, at 7:32 the guitar launches into its heroic lead line that is the heart of the entire passage; simultaneously, Emerson abandons the funk bass in favor of rapidly moving backing chords on the Hammond. The feeling of heroic striving here is buttressed not only by the general melodic character of the guitar lead at this point, but also by the restless modulation of the backing harmony—the music moves from $E^\flat$ (7:31) to $D^\flat$ (7:40) to $A^\flat$ (7:55) back to $D^\flat$ (8:00), before definitively settling into $A^\flat$ at 8:23—as well as by the refusal of the harmony to firmly commit to either major or minor modality. From 8:00 on, Lake pushes the solo to its climax with some increasingly agitated descending runs, and the arrival at $A^\flat$ at 8:23 is clinched with a final torrent of twisting chromatic guitar motives. Suddenly, the bottom drops out of this enormous instrumental climax, and only two sounds are left—the "bubbling" sound of an $A^\flat$ pedal point on Emerson's Moog (created with the instrument's sample-and-hold setting) and a quiet backbeat supplied by Palmer on tambourine. This is the last sound we hear before part 1 of the 1st Impression fades out, and the first sound we hear when part 1 fades back in (although, as I've said, on the Victory and Rhino CD remasters, the fadeout/fadein is eliminated, and the movement from part 1 to part 1 of 1st Impression is continuous).

"1st Impression, part 2" is the second B section of 1st Impression's overall A B B structure. After several seconds of the bubbling Moog $A^\flat$, Lake reenters with the familiar verse from the first B section, singing the famous line "Welcome back my friends to the show that never ends . . ."[31] At 0:13, Emerson enters with backing chords on Hammond; at 0:21 Lake commences a new refrain we haven't heard before, "Come inside the show's about to start . . ." Emerson enters on the Moog bass at 0:30, and only at 0:36, shortly before Lake commences the second verse ("right before your eyes") does Palmer enter on full kit with a rock backbeat. Again, we see that a key element of 1st Impression is its masterly employment of slow buildups to enormous climaxes over long time spans: after the huge buildup to the end of part 1 of 1st Impression, the music collapses in on itself, and is made to begin the building up process again from scratch.

Thus, the building-up process that was so important to part 1 of 1st Impression is repeated again in part 2. After the second verse/refrain, Lake launches into an almost heavy-metalish electric guitar riff at 1:07, over which Emerson layers a frenzied bluesy Hammond solo, filled with his trademark rapid-fire eighth-note leads; the solo is all the more impressive when one realizes Emerson had to provide his own bass line on Minimoog (yet another funk figure) all the way through his solo. This solo pulls the tonality back into $A^\flat$ minor, so now not only does the climactic buildup of part 1 have to be repeated, but also the progression from minor to major.

---

[31] Beginning side two of the LP format with these words makes Emerson's strategy of breaking 1st Impression in two seem even more inspired.

At 2:00 Lake recapitulates the second half of his earlier solo (from 7:39 of part 1), tracing the same restless tonal progression and buildup, and bringing 1st Impression to its second huge climax. This time, however, rather than being followed by a quietly bubbling Moog note, the solo segues into a furious barrage of drum fills by Palmer at 2:56. Even as Palmer continues bashing out his unaccompanied drum fills, Lake begins singing the third verse of part 2 ("soon the gypsy queen"), and shortly thereafter the full band reenters; if you listen very carefully when Lake sings "Dixieland! Dixieland!" at 3:14, you'll hear Emerson interject a short fragment of "Tiger Rag" on piano. The third verse is followed by the original "roll up" refrain from part 1 (compare 3:15 of part 2 with 5:38 of part 1). A fourth and final verse ("performing on a stool")—note the almost steel-drum-like use of backing piano here—is followed by yet another new refrain at 3:46, "Come and see the show." Thereafter the lengthy instrumental transition which separated the A and B sections of 1st Impression's A B B structure is recapitulated and varied (compare 3:57 of part 2 to 3:42 of part 1). Finally, at 4:14 of part 2 we reach the third and final climax of 1st Impression. This coda section is built around sequentially rising iterations of the "Enigma chord"—A–D–G$^\sharp$ (4:14), C–F–B (4:18), E$^\flat$–A$^\flat$–D (4:22)—which climax into an enormous electronic orchestration of alternating A$^\flat$ and A$^\flat$ suspended second chords, topped off by a memorable two-octave ascending Moog glissando.

In his fascinating study *Beethoven Hero*,[32] music theorist Scott Burnham grapples with the question of why Beethoven's music—particularly his heroic style, as heard in the first movements of such works as the Third Symphony, Fifth Symphony, and "Waldstein" Sonata, op. 53—seem so profoundly meaningful for so many people. His answer—and I may be oversimplifying just a bit here—is that this music makes us experience heroic struggle and attainment as if it were our own—it simultaneously depicts heroic struggle, and allows us to participate in it.[33] Some of Burnham's observations tie in with Beethoven's use of sonata-allegro form: Burnham sees Beethoven's heroic movements mirroring an almost universally accessible psychological process where a dangerous yet necessary exploration of some unconscious aspect of the psyche is followed by a tremendous sense of reintegration and affirmation. He also points to how Beethoven's principal themes seem to generate the entire structure—an especially astonishing achievement when one realizes that sonata-allegro form was already a generic, well-established musical form when Beethoven began his career.[34]

---

[32] Scott Burnham, *Beethoven Hero* (Princeton, NJ: Princeton University Press, 1995).
[33] Ibid., 24.
[34] Ibid., 23. Burnham sees this tendency for a principal theme to apparently generate its own

While the 1st Impression of "Karn Evil 9" does not utilize sonata-allegro form, I have long felt it conveys the feeling of heroic struggle in much the same way as Beethoven's "heroic" music, and creates the same tremendous sense of affirmation and liberation. How does Emerson pull this off? First, there is the movement from minor to major, from dark to light, which has to be traversed in both part 1 and part 2 of 1st Impression. Second, there is the long-range harmonic planning, the many keys that must be traversed in order for the guitar solo to reach its climax in both parts 1 and 2. Third, there is the masterly pacing of the 1st Impression's three climactic points, each of which is reached by gradually increasing the harmonic motion, textural density, and timbral intensity. Finally, because the major harmony is usually modal, there is a frequent instability of mode—we're not quite sure we're in major mode for keeps until we reach a strong cadence, and, as we've seen, there's really only three of these, at the end of each of the three climaxes. "Karn Evil 9," 1st Impression may well be the most powerful evocation of heroic striving in all rock music.

Indeed, I believe "Karn Evil 9," 1st Impression just may mark the zenith of ELP's entire output. Granted, from a modernist perspective, this piece lacks the "advanced" sonorities of *Tarkus*. On the other hand, it shows a new sophistication in terms of arranging and texture. By playing chords on Hammond and an obbligato line on the Moog, Emerson takes on two distinct roles that in other rock bands would require both a keyboard player and a guitarist—not only does this give the mid and high registers of the arrangement a new contrapuntal sophistication, it also gives the low end a new clarity, since Lake's bass lines now stand alone. By doubling on electric guitar and letting Emerson handle the bass lines when he's doing so, Lake brings a new set of timbres to the band. Indeed, the impression of equality and teamwork between the three members of the band is greater here than ever before, and while Emerson's virtuosity is, if anything, more astounding than ever, it's also more understated—only another keyboard player is likely to recognize how much virtuosity is required to pull off the polyphonically interlocked Moog and Hammond parts.

The composition is conceived and developed in larger paragraphs than before, and there's a new seamlessness to Emerson's writing here—the impression of alternating "blocks" of music (think of "The Three Fates," "Tarkus," or "The Endless Enigma") is no longer present, and all the influences (Bachian counterpoint, funk rhythms, big band jazz scoring, Romantic-era tonal planning, the modal harmonies and shifting meters characteristic of British progressive rock in general) are seamlessly inte-

---

structure as mirroring the German idealist conceit of the individual having the potential to generate his/her own objective reality.

grated into a distinctive, coherent, instantly recognizable sound. Finally, with its syncopated, funky bass lines and Hammond vamps, "Karn Evil 9," 1st Impression really does swing in a way that ELP's earlier epics (I'm thinking especially of "Tarkus" and "The Endless Enigma") do not. More than any other ELP piece—indeed, more than virtually any other progressive rock piece—"Karn Evil 9," 1st Impression succeeds in uniting classical music's sense of scope and grandeur with rock music's sense of earthiness and raw power.

From a conceptual standpoint, we must admit that the element of heroic struggle which is so powerfully present in the music of the 1st Impression is only hinted at in the lyrics of the piece's first (A) section; otherwise, the lyrics show the powers-that-be firmly in control of their "show that never ends." Therefore, the music of the 1st Impression must be heard as prefiguring the battle of liberation that the lyrics will not address until the 3rd Impression. And in order to make the transition from the 1st Impression to the 3rd, we must address the instrumental 2nd Impression next.

The 7:07 2nd Impression is the only one of the three Impressions to utilize Emerson's usual procedure of juxtaposing radically different "blocks" of music; even a casual listener will readily discern the piece's A B C D A structure. Nonetheless, we'll encounter the same sense of psychological progression and goal-oriented movement here that we encounter in the other Impressions.

The opening A section is repeated twice (0:00–0:22, 0:23–0:44) and if it evokes anything, it is a Will to Act; it is one of Emerson's most frantic creations, and may be the most difficult ELP passage in terms of its technical and musical demands. It is also the closest he ever came to writing a straight tribute to his bebop piano heroes such as Bud Powell and Hampton Hawes; both the piano-bass-drums instrumentation and, more specifically, the driving, syncopated sixteenth-note lead lines in the upper register of the piano over complex chord voicings immediately betrays the bebop influence. On the other hand, like so many of the other styles that passed through the prism of Emerson's imagination, there are also some crucial differences from the original source of inspiration, and it is in these differences that much of the music's interest lies.

First, there is the difference of tonality. While bebop musicians were notorious for their complex substitute chords which could momentarily blur the sense of tonality, the underlying chord roots were clear enough that the tonic was never really in doubt; this is because the vast majority of bebop tunes use either twelve-bar blues or thirty-two-bar popular song forms. Not so here. The opening of the "bebop head" (0:03–0:05) is itself tonally ambiguous; it's possible to hear it in either C major or G major. Thereafter, the music careens through B♭ major (weak cadence at 0:09) and appears to be heading towards A major (dominant pedal point at 0:18) before suddenly and inconclusively stopping on F$\sharp$ major (0:22), after which the entire A section is repeated *verbatim*. This instability of tonality combines with the driving sixteenth-note melody figures to give the music an even greater sense of restless impetuosity.

The melodic construction is also different here than in actual bebop. Bebop musicians are well known for their phrase extension techniques, which were intended to disguise the numbing regularity of the underlying four-bar phrases. Here, though, there is no regular underlying phrase patterns to disguise. Emerson's melodic arabesques spill out into irregular phrase lengths and metric shapes, with a particularly formidable metric thicket from 0:13–0:16. An especially sensitive listener will notice how much of the melodic fabric here seems to derive from the opening motive of the bebop theme (0:03–0:05), which Emerson obsessively reshapes and reconfigures, although this is best seen when the music is transcribed onto paper.

Finally, the fact is that a "real" bebop pianist would tend to "comp" with the left hand (that is, interject staccato block chords at irregular intervals underneath the driving sixteenth-note lines of the right hand), but Emerson usually does not, instead alternating between stridelike left-hand figures and more melodically oriented bass lines. Emerson once admitted this somewhat idiosyncratic approach to jazz piano—a more "modern," bebop-like right hand against a more traditional, stridelike left-hand part—resulted from how he learned jazz piano as a young musician:

> I didn't have a record player, so I used to get it [jazz] from the radio. I also used to go up to London to hear jazz. So my exposure to jazz was what was being played on the radio. When you do that, you have to wait and wonder, "Well, who was that?" And you might find out within a week. I remember one tune that was being played quite a lot, Floyd Cramer's "On the Rebound." That was a major influence on me throughout. And then there were various jazz players. Dudley Moore was one of them. He had a TV show. At the time, I was playing stride piano because I'd bought some Art Tatum and Fats Waller sheet music. And suddenly I heard Dudley Moore. He played this style that sounded great. I couldn't figure out how he was doing it. When I tried to imitate him it came out like Fats Waller in the left hand and Dudley Moore in the right. That's when I realized what the advantages of having a bass player were. Before that I used to do concerts with just drums and piano, because I thought that bass players—well, you never really hear them anyway. They only got in the way of my left hand.[35]

---

[35] Keith Emerson, quoted by Milano, "Keith Emerson," *Contemporary Keyboard*, October 1977, 32. Despite Emerson's claim here, it was really only with the *Brain Salad Surgery* LP, and only on the Hammond and Moog, that he developed an approach that simultaneously kept both hands busy and didn't compete with the bass player.

Neither Lake's nor Palmer's approaches in 2nd Impression are really typical of bebop, either. Palmer only occasionally drives the rhythm on ride cymbal the way a jazz drummer would, and he's much more active on his toms that a jazz drummer would be, often rhythmically doubling Emerson's melodic figures. Lake, for his part, eschews the walking eighth-note bass lines typical of bebop in favor of rapid-fire arpeggios, which he alternates with irregular scalar figures. Lake's cross-picking technique was always a major factor in his playing style (think, for instance, of his work in *Tarkus*, where he doubles Emerson's driving bass ostinatos with their rapid-fire arpeggiated fourths), and he gets ample opportunity to demonstrate his cross-picking approach in 2nd Impression, which certainly represents one of his most virtuosic bass performances. Lake has mentioned that

> [King Crimson's] Robert Fripp and I took lessons from the same teacher when we were kids. Our guitar styles are similar, although as players, we've got a different sense of musicality. He's also much faster, of course. But the way we play guitar is almost identical. We used to practice together, so naturally we practiced a lot of the same music. We both use a sort of cross-picking style, which came from the fact that our teacher [Don Strike] was actually a banjo player.[36]

A lot of Lake's prowess on bass comes, without any doubt, from having learned first to play a guitar with a pick, then transferring the technique to the heavier-stringed bass, which allowed him to achieve a fluency that only someone who had played guitar first would expect to muster. Lake has said he would not be able to achieve the same speed in cross-picked passages (for instance, the "Tarkus" arpeggios) without a pick, which gives him the ability to strum rapid up-and-down strokes using approximately one-sixteenth of the pick.[37]

The second A section is followed by an extended transition (0:44–1:07) that continues to develop the opening bebop head (listen at 0:58 for a particularly clear reference), even while twisting it into new and unexpected metric shapes. By 0:51 the music seems to be settling comfortably into A major, but at 1:03 the tonality suddenly lurches into $C^\sharp$, where it will remain throughout the following section, the famous "Caribbean" section with its evocation of steel drums.

This section (1:07–2:52), the B section of 2nd Impression's A B C D A structure, itself falls into several distinct subsections. The first and

---

[36] Greg Lake, quoted by Hall, "Welcome to the Show," 19.
[37] For more on Lake's bass technique, see Rosen, "Greg Lake of Emerson, Lake and Palmer," 20–21, 27. Considering the importance of cross-picking to Fripp's and Lake's style and the fact that their teacher was first of all a banjo player, it is hardly surprising that neither of them has made much use of vibrato or note-bending.

longest passage, which is repeated (1:10–1:29, 1:30–1:49), features Emerson's Minimoog in a highly original steel-drum setting, accompanied by Lake's throbbing bass ostinato of just two notes (C♯–B) and Palmer's pulsating toms. It doesn't change the driving, energetic character of the opening section so much as it lends it a more exotic color. Emerson's "steel drum" melody, which he plays with his right hand, is in C♯ penatonic (1 2 4 5 7), and his frequent tremolo between two notes creates an especially convincing evocation of a steel drum player doing rolls between two different drums. With his left hand, Emerson plays a repetitive Phrygian ostinato on piano (especially noticeable the second time through the passage, when it's higher up in the mix) that generates a certain tension both through its rhythmic syncopation and its modal clash with the "steel drum" line.[38] A short piano interlude (1:49–1:55) is followed by a lengthy continuation of the "steel drum" melody, with Emerson alternately doubling Lake's bass line in fifths and octaves and doubling the "steel drum" melody with his left hand on piano. Emerson concludes his "steel drum" melody with a quote from saxophonist Sonny Rollins's "Saint Thomas" (2:21–2:28), one of the first jazz numbers to betray a strong Calypso influence and thus a subtle tie-in to the section's Caribbean ambience. The closing passage of the B section (2:29–2:52) is transitional; it returns to the piano-bass-drums instrumentation of the A section, taking on a newly ominous character not sounded heretofore by its mixture of a descending arpeggio figure (2:29), actually drawn from the A section, with a dissonant fanfarelike figure (2:33) that is more than slightly reminiscent of some of the pounding metallic chords from "Toccata." By the time the section concludes with a C♯ major chord, the mood is no longer celebratory, but rather edgy and nervous.

Much of the following section (C in the overall A B C D A structure, from 2:53–5:50) generates a creepy, flesh-crawling ambience that creates another link to Giger's cover art, as well as to some of the more quietly ominous passages of "Toccata" (especially the theme at 4:23). Again, while there is no musical material borrowed from the desolate third movement of Ginastera's Piano Concerto no. 1, the overall "vibe" is similar. The section starts out very quietly and slowly in A (a key that was frequently traversed, but never quite reached, in the opening section of 2nd Impression), and features a kind of ominous call-and-response between Emerson's piano and Lake's bass. Emerson uses an unusual scale (A B♭ C D E F G♯ A) that has both minor and whole-tone tendencies; some of the "spookier" chord progressions (3:15 and 3:41, for instance) are created by using the scale's whole-tone segment (G♯ B♭ C D E). The music shifts

---

[38] In concert Emerson played this "steel drum" line on a Minimoog that sat on the grand piano and was used only for this purpose.

to C at 3:52, then back to A at 4:10 in conjunction with a particularly eerie whole-tone wash of sixteenth-notes on piano. Throughout this section, strange background sounds are created by Palmer (listen at 3:33–3:41 and 3:52–4:09), whose half notes on woodblock beginning at 4:10 evoke the ticking of a particularly sinister clock. At 4:41 the music shifts to C again in tandem with an especially jagged wash of piano arpeggios, which now begin to take on bitonal implications (C minor/D♭); finally at 4:57 the music settles very uneasily indeed on a C minor/D♭ polychord, with Lake's closing bass harmonic like a stifled cry of agony.

Both the A and B sections of 2nd Impression end with lengthy transitional passages, and the C section is no different. At 5:00 the band launch into a much more focused and dynamic passage than before, a kind of jazz waltz, which sequentially passages through A♭ (5:05), B♭ (5:07), D minor (5:12), and then begins moving toward G minor, even as the melodic and rhythmic contours of the "jazz waltz" begin to dissolve, around 5:25. A final cadential passage at 5:39 seems to signal the return of the opening bebop theme in G, and in fact at 5:44 there is a brief "false recapitulation" during which the opening bebop head returns.

The "recapitulation" doesn't last long, though, and is quickly swept aside at 5:51 by the D section of the A B C D A structure, a kind of "stride piano from hell" passage in F. This represents the first time on the entire album since the close of "Jerusalem" that we've reached that key, although here we're in F minor rather than F major. I must admit I've never really enjoyed Emerson's "straight" stride pieces ("Benny the Bouncer" or some of the material from *Works*, vol. 2), just as I have never been particularly enamored of his "straight" boogie pieces ("Are You Ready Eddy"). Just as I find his boogie approach infinitely more interesting when it's absorbed through the prism of his own stylistic palette (e.g., "Bitches Crystal"), here I find his stride approach far more rewarding, because it's fully integrated into his overall style. What we have throughout the D section is a frenetic, almost diabolic parody of Fats Waller's style; something like what might have resulted if Fats Waller had played Bartók (or vice-versa). Lake's repeated four-note bass figure (F–C–B–G♭), Emerson's stride figure (which breaks Lake's eighth-note figure into sixteenth-note octaves), and his raucous right-hand "melody," with its sudden jumps between registers, are all built from a scale (F G♭ A♭ B C D♭ E♭ F) that is more Ginastera than Waller, although the rhythms and even the figuration patterns are genuine stride. This stride section builds up with great bravura, eventually recalling the agonized bitonal piano fanfare from the end of the B section (listen at 6:15 and, in altered form, at 6:28), and finally, at 6:48, the opening A section is recapitulated in full, although this time it's not repeated.

"Karn Evil 9," 2nd Impression, with its mosaiclike linkage of distinct musical "blocks," is the last major piece of its type in a line stretching back through "The Endless Enigma," "Tarkus," and "The Three Fates"; later ELP epics would be constructed along the more tightly woven and unified model suggested by the 1st and 3rd Impressions of "Karn Evil 9." In that sense, 2nd Impression may be a bit more backward-looking than its flanking tracks. At the same time, however, I believe it does manage to cohere, both musically and conceptually. While it isn't in sonata-allegro form, it does manage the same general effect that Scott Burnham sees as a key element of Beethoven's heroic style: a dangerous yet necessary affirmation of the psyche is followed by a tremendous sense of reintegration and affirmation. Seen in light of the overarching concept of "Karn Evil 9," the 2nd Impression presents something of a musical psychobiography of the Liberator figure who must do battle with the forces of darkness and dehumanization in 3rd Impression. A tremendous resolve and Will to Act (the A and B sections) is followed by debilitating doubt (the C section), fear and great internal struggle (the D section), and finally, a triumphal reaffirmation of intent and purpose. For me, at least, the long-delayed recapitulation of the opening section, after the eerie C section, the false recapitulation, and the frenetic, wild D section (all of which could be seen as analogous to the development section in a Beethoven sonata-form movement) has a sense of great inevitability and power to it.[39] In a very different way than the 1st Impression, 2nd Impression also conveys the notion of heroic striving.

Scarcely has the last chord of 2nd Impression been struck before we arrive at the 3rd Impression, the album's second Emerson-Lake-Sinfield collaboration, which draws together the conceptual and musical strands from the previous tracks and weaves them into a relentless and convincing finale. 3rd Impression begins by recalling the martial imagery of "Jerusalem": over Lake's impressively fuzzed bass pedal point on E^b, Emerson's Moog and Hammond trade off antiphonal fanfare figures, while Palmer accompanies with military-style snare cadences. At 0:16 Lake's bass line also falls into a marchlike movement, preparing the way for the vocal verses at 0:22.

Emerson has called the music of the 3rd Impression "very Elgarish"— a wonderfully apt description, I think, for more than one reason.[40] Edward Elgar (1857–1934), a younger contemporary of Hubert Parry, was Britain's greatest composer of the late Victorian and Edwardian period, and in many ways his most characteristic music mirrors the mood

---

[39] Someone with a background in classical music and a good imagination might hear the A and B sections as the first and second themes of a sonata-allegro movement's exposition section; the C and D sections as a development of sorts (although what is being developed here is a psychological state, not an actual theme); and the A section at the end as a very abbreviated recapitulation.

[40] *Brain Salad Surgery* CD reissue, Rhino Records, track 9 (band interview), 11:00.

of Britain at the height of its imperialist glory: opulent, swaggering, more than a bit pompous. Nonetheless, much of his work between 1910 and 1920, when he was at the height of his powers, shows a subtle yet significant shift in outlook. As his confidence in both his Catholic faith and in Britain's future began to falter, his music took on a new sense of irony and ambiguity. His characteristically marchlike or hymnlike themes are often subjected to either diabolical distortion or unexpected dissolution in a manner paralleling the music of his Austrian contemporary Gustav Mahler, another composer famous for his sprawling but psychologically rich symphonic pieces. I believe that in 3rd Impression we will find evidence not only of Elgarian themes, but a similarly ironic treatment of some of the Elgarian material.

The 3rd Impression, which clocks in at 9:05, falls into a huge A B A form. The opening A section consists of two vocal verses featuring Lake as impersonal narrator, followed by a vocal bridge in which Lake adopts the Liberator persona. The instrumental B section may be ELP's most overtly programmatic passage; it is a vivid depiction of the frenzied battle for supremacy between Man and Computer that unfolds at an unspecified future time in the depths of space. The second A section triumphantly recapitulates the opening vocal verse, but the coda that concludes "Karn Evil 9" brings the piece to a stunningly powerful and ambiguous conclusion.

The first A section begins in $A^\flat$, the "dystopic" key of 1st Impression, suggesting that all is not yet right with the world. The two vocal verses (0:23–1:04, 1:05–1:40) feature Lake in the voice of an impersonal narrator, who traces human history from its dawn ("man alone born of stone will stamp the dust of time") to a moment, sometime in our future, when a "man of steel" has usurped humankind's unique role as the only sentient, ensouled being. Musically, the vocal verses of 3rd Impression make several references to "Jerusalem": Emerson's Hammond again uses the "screaming chorus" effect, Lake's vocal melody, with its hymnlike, stepwise character, recalls the general melodic feel of "Jerusalem," and the harmony is for the most part staunchly diatonic. On the other hand, the tonal movement of the vocal verses of 3rd Impression ominously reverses the tonal progression of the verses in "Jerusalem" in a manner that suggests a less happy outcome in the battle against the forces of dehumanization than the outcome envisioned by Blake (or Parry) in "Jerusalem." While the latter triumphantly moves from the relative minor (D) to the tonic major (F), the verses of 3rd Impression move from the tonic, $A^\flat$ major, to F Phrygian, a duskier version of the relative minor; you can hear this modulation during the "fear that rattles in men's ears" segment of the verse. Another inspired programmatic touch that symbolizes the Ascent of the Machine is the insistent rhythmic motive, first heard underneath the word "ears" (0:44–0:48), which I'll hereafter refer to as "the computer's challenge." The various transformations of this motive, which symbolizes the Computer's brash challenge to Humankind, play an important role in musically conveying the course of the Man/Machine battle during the remainder of 3rd Impression.

At 1:40 we reach the vocal bridge, and for the first time on the album since "Jerusalem," the music bursts into the glorious sunshine of F major, the "utopian" key of "Jerusalem." To the backdrop of Emerson's bugle-like Hammond and Moog fanfare figures, Lake, now adopting the Liberator persona, declares "no man yields who flies in my ship." What follows is the heated dialogue between Man and Computer which would seem to mirror the famous scene in Kubrick's *2001*. Emerson, speaking into a microphone run through his modular Moog's ring modulator, takes the role of the Computer (his only "vocal" on an ELP album), and challenges the Liberator "LOAD YOUR PROGRAM. I AM YOUR-SELF." After this stunning act of defiance (and, ironically, identification), the music returns to the "dystopic" A♭ major, with Lake declaring "only blood can cancel my pain."[41] Lake sings the entire bridge section with great conviction and verve: listen to his urgent rasping on "cancel" and "dawn," and the emphatic declamation of his final words of the bridge section, "let the maps of war be drawn," when it becomes clear that battle is the only way to settle this struggle for supremacy.[42] Throughout much of the bridge section Lake highlights his vocal melody in an especially interesting and vivid way by doubling his vocal line on fuzzed bass guitar; notice also how Emerson doubles Lake's vocal line in canon (two and a half measures apart) on Moog, beginning at 2:36.

The lengthy instrumental B section (2:56–7:36) falls into four distinct subsections; the first and third would seem to convey the Human's viewpoint, the second and fourth, the Computer's. The first, from 2:56–3:55, is a cheerful, optimistic march that reworks the vocal melody of the A section, and features the Moog Lyra (right hand) and the polyphonic Apollo (left-hand chordal accompaniment), both in brasslike settings. The march begins in A♭ major, but note how it brightens considerably when the music modulates to B major at 3:15. This section is repeated twice, from 2:56–3:25 and 3:26–3:55.

During the second subsection, the Computer responds. Indeed, this section begins at 3:56 with the "computer's challenge" motive from the A section, sounded by bass, drums, and the Hammond's upper register. Emerson's sustained organ chords (which he plays with his left hand) ominously swing the music towards A♭ minor, the icily remote key last heard during the 1st Impression. The feeling of unrest is further height-

---

[41] Might this statement be a comment on the vast gulf between human pride and passion and the machine's cold rationality?

[42] Lake most definitely does *not* say "Let the mask of war be drawn," as Stump incredibly asserts; see *The Music's All That Matters*, 170.

ened by the agonized $E^\flat$ major-minor chord ($B^\flat$–$E^\flat$–G–$G^\flat$) at 4:17 and 4:23.

The third subsection, a blues "battle charge" that begins at 4:27, evokes Man ferociously pressing the battle against Computer. Centered in B minor, this section creates an obvious cross-reference to the frenzied blues solo of 1st Impression, part 2, except I think this solo is even better; although Emerson's "gonzo" blues solos aren't necessarily my favorite part of his style, they don't get any better than this. Over Lake's repetitive pentatonic ostinato and Palmer's driving ride cymbal pattern, Emerson comps with two hypnotically alternating quartal harmonies in his left hand—reminiscent of jazz pianist McCoy Tyner, perhaps—while spinning out rapid-fire sixteenth-note lead lines with his right hand that also refer back to the bebop sections of 2nd Impression. The solo builds up to a particularly fine fury between 5:05 and 5:10, when Emerson lets loose with some unbelievable ascending arpeggios.

However, at 5:10 the blues solo is suddenly interrupted by a sinister Locrian figure of ascending triads; although there is an effort to resume the blues solo, the disruptive Locrian figure returns three more times—at 5:16, 5:22, and 5:28—and the blues solo peters out, ominously replaced by iterations of the "computer's challenge" motive at 5:31. Clearly the ferocious attack against Computer has failed. At 5:43 this subsection ends with a muted, almost atonal unison Hammond/Moog line that seems to suggest a cynical distortion of earlier fanfare figures, which suddenly pauses on a low B in the bass.

The fourth and final subsection of the B section, an evocation of the Computer pressing a counterattack, begins at 5:51, and pulls us into more remote regions of space—not to mention tonality—than we have traveled in heretofore. The hidden musical scaffolding which supports this section is a slowly ascending sequence of tritones in the bass guitar—B–F (5:54–6:09), C–$F^\sharp$ (6:16–6:22), and D–$G^\sharp$ (6:26–6:29)—which tends to keep the tonality unfocused and unstable, and suggests perhaps that the Computer is gaining the upper hand in the battle. Over the B–F segment of the bass line, beginning at 5:58, Emerson develops a transformed version of the "computer's challenge" motive.[43] The passage between 5:54 and 6:09 is one of the most tonally ambiguous in the ELP canon. Lake's bass line emphasizes B, Emerson's left-hand organ ostinato F major, and his right-hand transformation of the "computer's challenge" motive suggests $C^\sharp$ major, but the polytonally juxtaposed melodic strands never cohere into a focused tonal direction, and the passage takes on an almost dreamlike, hallucinatory character.

---

[43] This transformation is, incidentally, rhythmically identical to a supporting Hammond figure of 1st Impression, part 1: listen between 0:25 and 0:48 of 1st Impression, where the figure is repeated four times.

The movement of the bass from B–F to C–F$^\sharp$ at 6:10 snaps us back into the more clearly directed motion of "real time," with Emerson's frenzied syncopated iterations of a B$^\flat$ augmented ninth chord at 6:19 striking a particularly agitated note. Following the lightning fast unison Hammond-bass-drum figure at 6:22, which for the briefest of moments seems to center the tonality in D, the bass's D–G$^\sharp$ iterations begin pushing in a new direction; however, this is suddenly interrupted by another iteration of the "computer's challenge" motive (now back in its original form), this time on G, at 6:30.

Thereafter, the music swings off into the remote, icy regions of E$^\flat$ minor, and at 6:45, over two supremely lonely organ chords (E$^\flat$ minor–C$^\flat$ major), Emerson commences one of his most mystical passages, a chromatically twisting line on modular Moog in parallel minor thirds that vividly evokes a spaceship crazily careening and twisting in the black depths of some remote galaxy.[44] This "cosmic" passage proves to be the climax of this long battle, and thereafter a Moog fanfare figure drawn from the A section (compare 7:16 with 0:39) is followed by a restatement of the ominous dissonant fanfare figure that closed the A section of 1st Impression, the now familiar "Enigma chord" (E–A–D$^\sharp$) resolving to an A major chord (compare 7:24 of 3rd Impression with 3:34 of 1st Impression).[45]

In both the 1st and 3rd Impressions this "Enigma fanfare" has such a disruptive, open-ended effect on the music that it's impossible to guess what might follow it, so it's a surprise to find it heralds a recapitulation of the A section beginning at 7:37. The rhythmic and melodic contours of the vocal verse are transformed to give the music a more majestic, triumphant feel—not unlike the final statement of the main theme in "The Great Gates of Kiev" from *Pictures*, which I suspect may have been an inspiration here. Although the Liberator boasts, "Rejoice, glory is ours," the music has returned in the "dystopic" key of A$^\flat$ major, suggesting that all might not be as it seems. Our misgivings increase when our hero assures us that the young men have not died in vain and "Their graves need no flowers / The tapes have recorded their names." I have always found this lyric deliciously ironic—so much for having put technology in its place! Indeed, I think there's a deeper, darker suggestion here—we have reached a stage in human history where it would be quite impossible to reject or "defeat" technology, because we have come to rely on it too much, and it has become too much a part of who we are. We have met the enemy, and it is us.

---

[44] This passage invites comparison to a passage from the final movement of Gustav Holst's *The Planets* suite, "Neptune, the Mystic" (see II in the score), which I suspect may have been a source of inspiration.

[45] In 3rd Impression, this figure is treated sequentially.

This suggestion would seem to be confirmed by the climax of 3rd Impression. At 7:56 the music finally passes into F major—the utopian key of "Jerusalem"—and the Liberator figure declares, "I am all there is." But the "defeated" Computer unexpectedly re-enters with its second, and this time unanswerable, challenge: "NEGATIVE! PRIMITIVE! I LET YOU LIVE!" "But I gave you life . . . to do what was right," pleads the hero, to which the Computer arrogantly replies, "I AM PERFECT! ARE YOU?" The music then lurches into the same grinding iterations of the "Enigma" chord which ended 1st Impression, part 2 (compare 8:25 of 3rd Impression with 4:14 of 1st Impression, part 2), but this time no triumphal affirmation follows. Instead, beginning at 8:32 the modular Moog's analog sequencer enters with a short (three-measure), simple, almost nursery-tune-like melodic fragment in F major. Emerson did not really "play" this passage—he programmed it into his sequencer, then a music technology in its infancy—partly as an ironic rejoinder to critics who complained that ELP were controlled by their equipment, and partly to drive home the concept of the Computer as an independently functioning agent. The "tune" begins slowly, but each repetition is slightly faster, and soon it is a blur, passing from one speaker to another and then back again, before finally stopping, having disappeared, apparently, into a realm beyond human comprehension. In its final act of audacity, the Computer has expropriated humankind's own key—the "utopian" key of "Jerusalem," F major—and made it its own. To make sure his audiences would not miss the point that the Computer had assumed control, in live performances of 3rd Impression all three band members left the stage during this passage, while Emerson's modular Moog belched smoke, sprouted wings, and then swung around and faced the audience.[46]

Conceptual Confluences: Clarke, Kubrick, Huxley

The ending is a tremendous stroke of irony, like the endings of "Tarkus" and "The Endless Enigma" (although the irony cuts much deeper here). The rock critics who drooled over David Bowie's keen sense of irony were never "hip" to ELP's, because Emerson's use of irony was based on a network of purely musical gestures that the critics, with no background in classical music (or, for the most part, any other kind of abstract music) were simply unable to pick up on. The ending is also tremendously

---

[46] In 1973 the idea of the sequencer was so new that Emerson went to great pains in interviews to explain how the passage was done and what it symbolized. Today, of course, it's musicians who actually "play" an "instrument" who are becoming something of a curiosity, as sequencing technology becomes ever more prevalent in a plethora of popular music styles from rap to techno.

ambiguous, but I don't think that it was at all a matter of ELP being confused about what they wanted to say. Rather, I think they were telling us that our relationship with technology has become infinitely more complex than it was in Blake's day, that the good-evil binaries that Blake applied to our relationship with technology may now be more difficult to sustain, and that we may do well to reexamine some of our basic assumptions about technology, dehumanization, the individual—indeed, what it means to be human. In closing, then, we may want to look once more at the relationship between *Brain Salad Surgery* and two of its apparent sources of inspiration, Stanley Kubrick's and Arthur C. Clarke's *2001: A Space Odyssey*, and Aldous Huxley's *Brave New World*.

Admittedly, the band never mentioned either of these as a direct source of inspiration: to the contrary, Peter Sinfield has cited Tom Lehrer and Kurt Vonnegut as influences on "Karn Evil 9."[47] Nonetheless, anyone who has both listened to 3rd Impression and watched *2001* will have no doubt that the movie was an influence on the musical work. And while it's possible that Lake and Sinfield never read *Brave New World*, it seems just as likely they did; even if they didn't, Huxley's ideas were very much in the air during the late 1960s, and he was adopted as a kind of honorary countercultural icon.[48]

2001: A Space Odyssey was a collaboration between the late director Stanley Kubrick and noted science fiction author Arthur C. Clarke. It may just be Kubrick's best movie; Clarke was deeply involved in adapting his story to the screen, so Kubrick's visionary approach compliments Clarke's storyline, without essentially altering its essence.[49] Released in 1968, a year before the Apollo 11 moon landing, *2001* captured the zeitgeist of the period as well as any other movie of that era, with its space-age setting, spectacular (for that time) special effects, and portentous fusion of scientific and religious speculation:

> Stanley Kubrick's 1968 cinematic masterpiece, *2001: A Space Odyssey*, combined a technocrat's escapism, with its staggering gadgetry, a Romantic's escapism with its vistas of limitless emptiness, and a hip psychedelic's escapism with its celebrated "star gate" sequence in which Keir Dullea makes his oft-deconstructed journey through hyperspace. The metallically glinting obelisk which dominates the film embodies cultures of unimaginable past and unimaginable future, a dichotomy which would underpin much of Progressive ideology.[50]

---

[47] Pilato, liner notes, *Brain Salad Surgery* CD reissue, 11.

[48] Jim Morrison named his band "The Doors" after Huxley's *Doors of Perception*, for instance.

[49] This was certainly an issue with *A Clockwork Orange* and *The Shining*, whose authors, Anthony Burgess and Stephen King, respectively, were very unhappy with Kubrick's reshaping of their storylines.

[50] Stump, *The Music's All That Matters*, 42.

For those who have not seen the movie, allow me to describe it briefly. It begins at the dawn of humankind: a group of apelike "humans" on the plains of Africa awaken one morning to find that a shiny, upright rectangular monolith has mysteriously appeared outside of the cave in which they sleep. They bark and grunt in terror, but one particularly bold simian approaches the monolith and thoughtfully runs his hand across the stone's surface. Shortly after this, while out on the plains, it occurs to him (even as he is having a flashback about the stone) to use a large bone as a club. Thereafter we see this simian and his fellows hunting small animals with clubs, and chasing off rival groups of "clubless" apemen. This stone has somehow caused a quantum leap in behavioral evolution; early "man" has achieved a higher level of consciousness, and become a tool user.

Fast forward to the late 1990s. Scientists at an American space station on the Moon have made a startling discovery. Following up on a pattern of irregular radio waves transmitted between the Moon and Jupiter, they locate and excavate a buried object. It is—you guessed it—a shiny, upright rectangular monolith. The scientists who excavate the object estimate it is four million years old.

Eighteen months later, a group of five astronauts (three of whom are in a state of hibernation, in order to preserve resources) are on a manned mission to Jupiter; an integral part of the craft is an incredibly sophisticated HAL 9000 series computer (referred to as "Hal" by crewmembers), who is able to both "talk" (in a pleasant male voice) and "see" (through a singular red eye). For a while, all goes smoothly; soon, however, Hal begins to "malfunction," although it is obvious that what is really happening is that the computer has developed not just self-consciousness, but self-will. Eventually, catastrophe strikes. One of the two nonhibernating astronauts (played by Gary Lockwood) is lost in space while repairing a malfunctioning panel that Hal has sabotaged; when the other astronaut, played by Keir Dullea, leaves the mother ship in a smaller craft in an unsuccessful attempt to rescue the Lockwood character, Hal shuts down the life support system of the three hibernating astronauts. When Dullea's character attempts to reenter the mothership, Hal refuses him entrance. Dullea's character does eventually gain entrance through a combination of stealth, courage, and good luck, only to find himself the lone surviving crewmember; finally, in a scene of considerable pathos, Dullea disables Hal's memory banks even as the computer pleads for his "life."

The psychedelic closing scene, the "star gate" sequence, begins with the Dullea character watching the weird Jovian landscape unfold underneath him, even as we see a familiar shiny rectangular monolith floating outside the mothership. In the climactic final sequence—we're not sure if it's dream, vision, hallucination, or matter-of-fact reality—the astronaut witnesses an increasingly intense bombardment of vivid colors,[51] then he finds himself in a large room looking at himself as a man now in later middle age, eating dinner. Next, the middle-aged man looks to his side and sees himself, now an extremely elderly, frail, dying man, lying on a bed. As the frail old man looks up in front of his bed he sees—as you perhaps expect by now—the shiny, black rectangular monolith, which clearly is some kind of cosmic interdimensional gate. A burst of light emits from the monolith,[52] and instantaneously the dying old man is transformed into (or resurrected as) a tiny baby—or perhaps an embryo, it's hard to be sure—who, in the final fadeout, is seen hovering over the Earth.

One obvious theme here, and a theme that runs through many of Clarke's stories, is that human evolution has been guided throughout the aeons by some distant, incredibly powerful alien race—whom, Clarke insinuates, we call "God." The final scene represents the human race reaching a new rung in the evolutionary ladder under the guidance of these extraterrestrial overlords, attaining a new level of consciousness, as a human being is apparently transformed into pure thought, or pure spirit. (I've always interpreted the baby/embryo at the end of the movie as symbolic.)[53] This is not, however, the conceptual strand of the movie that ELP were principally interested in. Rather, they were most concerned with the movie's subtext: the relationship between "real" and "artificial" intelligence. Clearly, Clarke and Kubrick foresaw a day when the only real difference was that one type of intelligence was housed in a body of flesh, the other in a body of metal. A suggestion of both *2001* and 3rd Impression is that the Computer might represent the next stage of human evolution; it has the human's most potent strength (a powerful mind) without human weaknesses (a body that degenerates, fluctuating emotions that at times overrule reason and logic and result in a tendency for error and miscalculation). And there is no question that Hal's "death" scene is so powerful that it forces us to ponder the possibility of an "ensouled" computer.

On the other hand, today it's a bit harder to take either of the movie's two main conceits in the very serious vein in which they were intended than it was in the heady days of the late sixties, when the idea of

---

[51] This particular scene once again demonstrates the influence of LSD on late-sixties popular culture.

[52] Throughout the movie, Kubrick was extremely sensitive in his use of musical cues; each portentous appearance of the monolith is heralded by the opening theme (the "World Riddle" section) of Richard Strauss's *Also Sprach Zarathustra*.

[53] This theme, that humankind is on the cusp of another quantum leap in evolution, is even more important in Clarke's *Childhood's End*; for a powerful and poignant progressive rock treatment of that work, listen to Van der Graaf Generator's "Childlike Faith in Childhood's End," on their *Still Life* LP.

"progress" seemed so much more natural and self-evident. First of all, the conceit that humans might suddenly evolve (or transform) into a state of pure spirit rests on religious faith, not science, and would seem to owe much to the Eastern notions of Nirvana that were popular during the late sixties. Second, while it is true that computers *have* become incredibly powerful since the late sixties—just ask Gary Kasparov—we seem no closer to having a self-aware, self-willed, ensouled computer than we are to having an ensouled pocket calculator (or hammer, for that matter) Nonetheless, the questions that *2001* and "Karn Evil 9," 3rd Impression raise about our reliance on computer technology, the increasing humanization of computers, and the possibility, however remote, that the Computer potentially represents a Frankenstein's monster (or perhaps the successor of humanity) are certainly interesting to ponder.

I also see the imprint of Huxley's *Brave New World*, especially in 1st Impression. Like Orwell in *1984*, Huxley foresaw a manipulative totalitarian world that tended to neutralize any signs of individuality, critical thought, and nonconformity. However, there was one crucial difference. In Orwell's dystopia, complete conformity and mind control was enforced through a brutal, ruthlessly efficient reign of psychological terror and State-sponsored violence against the slightest sign of dissent. In Huxley's dystopia, on the other hand, conformity and mind control is achieved through lulling the masses into a state of technological bliss, offering theme a neverending stream of entertainment, a "show that never ends." Orwell's novel was about Stalin's U.S.S.R., and does in fact offer a fairly accurate depiction life behind the Iron Curtain during that period, although Stalin's State apparatus never achieved the frightening omniscience of Orwell's. Huxley, on the other hand, seems to have been the more accurate prognosticator of the direction in which capitalist Western society was moving, and *Brave New World* prefigures the central argument of the Marxist social theorist/musicologist Theodor Adorno, namely, that popular culture (the popular music industry, the movie industry, and television) is the principal forum through which the masses are pacified in the capitalist West. Indeed, a troubling subtext of *Brave New World* is the question of whether Huxley's dystopia is really a dystopia at all. Joseph Lanza frames this issue particularly eloquently at the conclusion of his fascinating study of muzak, *Elevator Music*:

> Years after surviving the golden age of "individualism," we no longer have Huxley's luxury of bleating about the excesses of capitalist greed and centralized power. They are a fact of life: a fact we are learning not only to accept but to enjoy. Looking objectively at our society's haphazard social manipulations designed to give people the illusion of diversity and choice, we might envy the society created by *Brave New World*'s human engineers with their "Sound Track Writers and Synthetic Composers." Like many libertarian moralists,

Huxley trots out the noble savage to attack a "dehumanizing" technology. Yet despite the fact that he is obviously on the savage's side, Huxley manages to put more sense into the words of one of the novel's emotional engineers, who claims "You've got to choose between happiness and what people used to call high art. We have the feelies and the scent organ instead . . . Actual happiness always looks pretty squalid in comparison with the overcompensations for misery. And, of course, stability isn't nearly so spectacular as instability. And being contented has none of the glamor of a good fight against misfortune, none of the picturesqueness of a struggle with temptation, or a fatal overthrow by passion or doubt. Happiness is never grand."[54]

First Impression, then, would seem to pose some of the same questions as *Brave New World*. Acknowledging that our society has sacrificed critical thinking and active contemplation for the constant thrills and "entertainment" that media provides us, that we've sacrificed reality for virtual reality, that we've sacrificed individuality for mass-induced technological ecstasy, that we've accepted centralized control of our lives in exchange for a minimum level of technological bliss—do we care any more? Is truth more important to us than happiness? Or is being alienated from our alienation more comfortable than being alienated? Are we, in fact, content with matters as they now stand? Might we feel, perhaps, that Huxley's "dystopia" is in fact a utopia?

ELP, like Huxley, seem to be largely on the side of the noble savage, the heroic Romantic individualist who opposes the collectivist tendencies of a coercive government-media complex. Like *Brave New World*, though, "Karn Evil 9" suggests there may be a certain amount of ambiguity as to how the questions I've sketched out above should be answered. The most important achievement of both *Brave New World* and "Karn Evil 9" is to raise these questions so incisively; in the end, though, it is you and I, dear reader, who must answer these questions ourselves.

---

[54] Joseph Lanza, *Elevator Music* (New York: St. Martin's Press, 1994), 232.

10

Welcome Back My Friends to the Show That Never Ends...

(Autumn 1973 through Autumn 1974)

Brain Salad Surgery: An Assessment

Today, with the benefit of hindsight, it is easy enough to see that *Brain Salad Surgery* represents the acme of ELP's recorded output. No other ELP album coheres as well conceptually. From a compositional stand-point, musical ideas are expanded and developed more seamlessly and in larger paragraphs than before; furthermore, *Brain Salad Surgery* marks the first time Keith Emerson sustains a network of tonal cross-references across an entire album. On no other album is the sense of equality and teamwork among the three musicians as strong. Lake's contributions on electric guitar and Emerson's polyphonic Hammond/Moog arrange-ments, which give greater emphasis to Lake's bass lines than before, open up a whole new dimension for the band's sound, giving it (paradoxically) greater clarity and greater fullness. No other album is more effective in minimizing the differences in taste and interests between the three band members: more than ever, on *Brain Salad Surgery* ELP have become a well-oiled machine where the whole is greater than the sum of its parts.

While the band's virtuosity reaches a new plateau here—their playing on "Toccata" and 2nd Impression in particular represents something of a high-water mark—it's also more understated: ensemble virtuosity is emphasized over show-offy soloing to a new degree, and the playing of all three musicians reveals a happy confluence of economy, intricacy, and staggering technique. No other ELP album is this consistent, with the arguable exception of their first: every track save "Benny the Bouncer" is an ELP classic, and several of them are progressive rock classics. Production-wise, the band never sounded better: even Eddy Offord never achieved the sense of clarity, astounding for its era, which engineers Geoff Young and Chris Kimsey achieved on *Brain Salad Surgery*. No less a prog-hater than Robert Christgau was reduced to attacking the album for its strengths: "Is this supposed to be a rebound because Pete Sinfield

311

wrote the lyrics? Because Certified Classical Composer Alberto Ginastera—who gets royalties, after all—attests to their sensitivity on the jacket? Because the sound is so crystalline you can hear the gism as it drips off the microphone?"[1]

Shifting Currents in Rock's Critical Ideology

One would have expected, then, that *Brain Salad Surgery* would have been hailed as the band's masterpiece by the critics, and would have become their highest seller ever. Right? Wrong. When it was finally released in December 1973, *Brain Salad Surgery* only reached number five in the U.K. charts. In the U.S. it peaked at number eleven, the band's lowest showing since their debut album.[2]

Even more ominous was the album's critical reception. Of course, *Brain Salad Surgery* was savaged by all the usual suspects—Christgau, for instance. More unexpectedly, however, *Brain Salad Surgery* met with a frosty, if not downright hostile, reception from *New Musical Express* and *Melody Maker*—the latter's review, "Stale Salad," was particularly stinging:

> Virtuoso keyboard player, virtuoso drummer, mediocre bass player. That's the sum total of what Emerson, Lake and Palmer are all about . . . Emerson has done nothing but reiterate his original approach right from the inception of the Nice. And again, why not? It doubtless pays the mortgage and keeps him in race cars—but let us not confuse it with any kind of worthwhile music. In essence, Emerson is basically an interpreter, a kind of sixties Jacques Loussier, following his only single-minded ideal up a technical blind alley . . . Similarly Carl Palmer, a technically excellent drummer, and obviously a dedicated one, can perform an adequate approximation of the Buddy Rich style of playing, but what relevance does that have today? As if conscious of this dated aspect of their music, ELP have employed Peter Sinfield, original King Crimson guiding light, to supply a set of lyrics for some of the tracks here, and unfortunately that proves to be a blunder too. Whilst many will doubtless laud Sinfield's imagery, I personally feel that his style fluctuates between the pretentious and banal . . . Wait till you hear the heavy metal [sic] version of the hymn "Jerusalem," which does of course include words by a real poet, one William Blake, who must be turning in his grave.[3]

---

[1] Review reprinted in Christgau, *Rock Albums of the 70s*, 126.

[2] However, the album did remain in the Top 40 for sixteen weeks and, most significantly, perhaps, remained in Billboard's Top 200 for forty-seven consecutive weeks—longer than any other ELP album before or since.

[3] S. L., "Stale Salad: Emerson, Lake and Palmer's *Brain Salad Surgery*," *Melody Maker*, November 24, 1973.

Now, to be sure, ELP were never critical darlings, and from the beginning they had some high-profile detractors. On the other hand, as I think I've convincingly demonstrated through the course of this book, right through 1973 ELP did have a contingent of supporters in critical circles, and on the whole the British rock press had kept a fairly open mind about the band. Rabidly anti-ELP (and antiprogressive) critics like Christgau and Bangs, with their almost Inquisitional brand of blues orthodoxy, were in the minority, and were mainly tied to two specific American magazines, *Creem* and *Rolling Stone*. Even these two magazines were not yet totally anti-ELP or antiprog at the time *Brain Salad Surgery* was released. Wayne Robbins of *Creem* even pays the album some backhanded compliments: "The album itself is sorta great, too. For once, Keith Emerson's virtuosity does not stand in the way of the band's potential for excellence . . . Of course, you're not supposed to dance to it, but once in awhile, they rock anyway . . . The band is tight, of course, but the feeling is loose . . . Let's say that Keith Emerson discovers taste, and hooray."[4] Gordon Fletcher of *Rolling Stone* isn't so positive, although he does acknowledge ELP's excellence as a live band:

> Onstage, ELP usually overcome the shortcomings of their records—insufficient intensity and lack of worthy material—by working hard and busting their asses to play with incredible tightness (witness *Pictures at an Exhibition*). In the studio, their vision and grandiose schemes dilute the tightness, resulting in things like *Brain Salad Surgery*, on which their shortcomings outweigh undeniable moments of brilliance. The result: another sadly uneven album from a group with technical gifts equal to that of any British trio . . . This LP only convinces me that ELP really ought to record all their material in concert, for short of that I fear we're doomed for more albums like *Brain Salad Surgery*—another record that shows this fine band to mixed effect.[5]

But if neither of these reviews evinces the kind of knee-jerk dismissal of the band that was soon to become commonplace, neither do they dispel the overall impression that by early 1974 ELP were encountering a sea change in critical climate. So the question is this: at what should have been the moment of ELP's greatest commercial success and critical triumph, how was it that Keith Emerson was reduced to saying, "I'm just going to get drunk and forget the whole thing," in reaction to the critical reception of *Brain Salad Surgery*?[6]

I believe I can identify three factors that contributed to the shifting currents in which ELP found themselves battling. First, there was the

---

[4] Wayne Robbins, review of *Brain Salad Surgery*, *Creem*, January, 1974, 63.
[5] Gordon Fletcher, review of *Brain Salad Surgery*, *Rolling Stone*, January 31, 1974.
[6] Kathi Stein, "Emerson, Lake and Palmer Live," *Circus Raves*, August 1974, 8.

"long" eighteen-month gap between the release of *Trilogy* (June 1972) and *Brain Salad Surgery* (December 1973). By today's standards, eighteen months between releases is nothing; nowadays, a band that already had two gold and two platinum releases under their belts and insisted on releasing their fifth album just eighteen months after their fourth would be considered terminal workaholics, as ELP in fact were.[7] By the standards of the sixties and early seventies, however, eighteen months between releases was an act of unbelievable self-indulgence, and the 650 hours of studio time ELP put into making *Brain Salad Surgery* was viewed as a sign of the band's decadence rather than craftsmanship or work ethic. One problem was that in the seventies, the industry had not yet developed the marketing strategies (unreleased live material, greatest hits packages, alternate mixes, etc.) that now are regularly used to keep an artist's name in the public forum during the three- and four-year intervals between studio releases; if an artist disappeared from the public eye for more than a year, he or she was assumed to have left the music business.

Granted, ELP were touring during part of this period. However, the European tour of spring 1973 struck many observers as a sprawling, disorganized extravaganza, and the long break between albums was taken as a sign that the band were running out of ideas. In a *Melody Maker* interview of June 1973, Keith Emerson explained to Chris Welch that the European tour was very much an experiment: no one had attempted to tour with such an enormous collection of equipment before, and the band had gone into it knowing there would be some problems, the ironing out of which would provide a learning experience for future tours. Furthermore, Emerson stated, the band had in fact been short on new ideas after *Trilogy* was released; however, rather than slap some new ideas together and rush a new album out, ELP wanted to use their newly won financial clout to deliberately work through and develop new music.[8] Unfortunately, by the time that *Brain Salad Surgery* was released a certain perception seems to have set in—namely, that ELP were a band in trouble—and the perception, though far from reality, seems to have colored the rock press's reception of the new album.

Another factor, I think, was that as great an album as *Brain Salad Surgery* was, by late 1973 it no longer represented a startling, absolutely unique sound the way their debut album had in November 1970. By 1973 progressive rock as a whole was well on its way to catching up with ELP. As Bill Martin points out in *Listening to the Future*, 1973 may well represent the genre's high-water mark: *Brain Salad Surgery* was an excep-

---

[7] By April 1974 the debut album and *Trilogy* had gone platinum; the other three were gold.
[8] Welch, "The Heavy Metal Kid," 16.

tionally great album in a year of great albums.[9] To put this in perspective, consider that among the albums released in 1973 were Yes's *Tales of Topographic Oceans*, Genesis's *Selling England by the Pound*, Pink Floyd's *Dark Side of the Moon*, King Crimson's *Lark's Tongue in Aspic*, Gentle Giant's *Octopus* and *In a Glass House*, Magma's *Mekanik Destruktiw Kommandoh*, Caravan's *For Girls Who Grow Plump in the Night* (probably their best album), Jethro Tull's *A Passion Play*, Mike Oldfield's *Tubular Bells* (from the electronic/minimalist side of progressive) and, from the jazz side of the progressive rock scene (or, perhaps, from the progressive side of the jazz scene), Mahavishnu Orchestra's *Birds of Fire*. In 1973, competition was very, very stiff. Today we can see that it was a matter of these other bands making enormous strides between 1970 and 1973 to catch up with ELP, but at the time it may have appeared that after some great early albums, ELP were beginning to slack off relative to the competition.

I think the final and most important factor in the surprisingly negative reception of *Brain Salad Surgery*, however, stemmed from changes within the rock press itself. Since I traced out this process in the book's introduction, I don't want to repeat myself too much here, so let me just say this: the "blues orthodoxy" of critics like Bangs and Christgau, confined to a couple of American journals in the early seventies (*Creem*, *Rolling Stone*), was beginning to make a number of converts in the British rock press by the 1973-74 period. After the middle of the decade, it had largely established the hegemonic dominance of the rock critical establishment which it still enjoys today, and the reinterpretation of prog as an effete, evolutionary dead end, an elitist betrayal of rock's populist origins, was well under way. Already, by 1973 it was hard for any prog band—especially such an extravagant, over-the-top band as ELP—to get a fair hearing from the rock press; thereafter ELP's support was mainly in journals written specifically for musicians, journals that interpreted "rock" narrowly, as a musical style, rather than broadly, as a whole way of life of which music was only one part.[10]

1973-74 World Tour

However, before the reader suspects me of sounding a premature death-knell for the band, let me hasten to add that in November 1973, shortly

---

[9] Martin, *Listening to the Future*, 215–27.

[10] In other words, even after 1973-74 ELP might get a fair hearing in journals written for musicians about music, technique, and equipment, such as *Contemporary Keyboard*, *Guitar Player*, *Modern Drummer*, *Downbeat*, *International Musician*, etc. However, in the journals that covered "rock" not just as a musical style, but as a whole cultural scene of which the

before *Brain Salad Surgery* was released, ELP launched the North American/European tour that reaffirmed their massive popularity in an extraordinary way, and may, in fact, have been the defining event of their career. ELP's 1973-74 World Tour showed a band—no, an organization—that had become a highly efficient machine. They had clearly learned from the mistakes of their clumsy, inefficient European tour of the spring: so much so that although they were now hauling even more equipment (for instance, they now had Emerson's Apollo and Lyra Moogs and Palmer's stainless steel drum kit in tow), they managed with a road crew that ran between forty and forty-five, far less than the seventy or eighty that had accompanied the spring 1973 tour.[11] One of the reasons the band were able to pare down the road crew for the 73-74 World Tour was that everyone involved was now assigned a very specialized role: "The general line put about concerning the crew is that nobody is really a roadie at all; each one is a specialist in his own particular area. Certainly there's a feeling that it's tougher working for ELP than for most bands, and maybe there's not so much chance for traditional road-crew partyings on tour."[12] As Judith Sims of *Rolling Stone* described it,

> The ELP entourage numbered 42, with six sound men, the designer for the quad sound system, several light men, one light woman, a stage manager, an equipment manager for each of Greg Lake's two guitars, two gentlemen responsible for Carl Palmer's drum set, two more equipment people for Keith Emerson's keyboards, one Moog expert, as well as personal managers, Manticore executives, tour managers, advance men, truck drivers, and a part-time woman whose function was to deliver new slides for the immense round screen that hovers over the frenetic stage show.[13]

At the time Sims was covering ELP, in February 1974, the band was hauling thirty-six tons of equipment—the biggest show on the road at that

---

music was just a part—*Rolling Stone, Creem, Music Maker, New Musical Express*—by 1973 the "blues orthodoxy" espoused by Bangs, Christgau, Marsh, et al. was rapidly gaining ground, and by 1976 it was in fact rock critical Establishment orthodoxy. *Circus* was the one major "scene-centered" journal that remained prog tolerant a bit longer than the others—into the late seventies, in fact.

[11] I say "seventy or eighty" because in the interviews I read from the era no one seemed certain of an exact number. Lest forty to forty-five sounds "lean and mean," however, let's put this in perspective: on their first tour, in the fall of 1970, ELP traveled with a road crew of four.

[12] Johnson, "Welcome Back My Friends." While I don't want to beat my point about progressive rock not being explicitly anticapitalist into the ground, I do feel a need to point out that at their zenith bands like ELP, Yes, and Pink Floyd were able to tour on the scale they did only by adopting the extremely specialized division of labor endemic to large corporations in late modern capitalism.

[13] Judith Sims, "ELP . . . What?" 10. The two ELP shows that Sims attended were in Fresno (February 20) and San Diego (February 21).

time.[14] All this equipment was hauled in four semi-trailers; the crew rode in a Greyhound bus with bunks.

The first leg of the tour commenced at Miami's Sportatorium on November 14, 1973, and involved twenty-nine shows, all at arenas or arena sized venues, in just over a month. This leg of the tour ended with shows at New York's Madison Square Garden on December 17 and 18; the finale of these two shows, as James Johnson tells it, "Unexpectedly consisted of Greg Lake leading a choir and the audience in, of all things, 'Silent Night.' It was an oddly touching moment, a week before Christmas. A hardened New York audience singing 'Silent Night'? Whatever happened to decadence?"[15]

The tour resumed January 24, 1974, in Atlanta's Omni; this leg of the tour involved another twenty-eight shows in a bit over a month, trailing off on March 7 with a show at Tulsa's Civic Center. By far the most famous date from this leg of the tour is the show the band played in front of 22,000 fans at Anaheim's Convention Center on February 10; this performance, minus only the encore, is immortalized on ELP's sixth album, the live *Welcome Back My Friends to the Show That Never Ends: Ladies and Gentlemen Emerson, Lake and Palmer*. The band contracted a recording team from the Wally Heider Recording Studio in Los Angeles to record a live album, and as soon as they heard the tapes from the Anaheim show, they realized they had their live album in the can, so to speak.

The recording set-up was cutting edge for its time: a twenty-four-track mobile recording unit and a forty-input console were used to capture the show, supervised by Heider engineer Peter Granat. One Manticore staffer enthused, "I think they came off better on the live album than they have on the studio records"; Greg Lake added, "ELP is a performing band and we're at our best when we're interrelating with our audience." Engineer Granat, for his part, declared it "the most energetic, full live album I've ever heard."[16]

Certainly the recording captured ELP at the absolute height of their powers: as James Johnson of *New Musical Express* commented about ELP's live show circa late 1973/early 74, "Whatever reservations one might have about ELP's music as a whole, 'Fingers' Emerson's skill in particular has now reached an astounding peak."[17] Not only were ELP playing better than ever before, the 73-74 World Tour featured the most challenging selection of repertoire the band ever attempted, either before

---

[14] By way of comparison, in 1974 Alice Cooper toured with fourteen tons of equipment, the Rolling Stones with twenty-eight tons.

[15] Johnson, "Fingers' Cave," 12. I have heard it said, from other sources, that "snow" fell from the rafters during "Silent Night."

[16] All three quotes are from Stein, "Emerson, Lake and Palmer Live," 9.

[17] Johnson, "Fingers' Cave," 11.

or after—imagine both the "Tarkus" and "Karn Evil 9" suites performed live in their entirety, with "Toccata" and "Take a Pebble" thrown in for good measure, all in one show. Furthermore, the Anaheim show was a powerhouse performance that fairly crackled with electricity. In short, the conditions were right for *Welcome Back My Friends* to be the defining album of ELP's career—much as *Magma Live* (1975) was for Magma, another band whose music seemed to unfold into a new dimension on stage. It is interesting to ponder, then, why it is not.

A lot of the problem is sonic. Although recording technology had become somewhat more sophisticated between 1971 and 1974, the fact is that *Pictures at an Exhibition* is sonically superior to *Welcome Back My Friends*. Granted, the latter has some undeniable strengths. Carl Palmer's drums, in my opinion, have never sounded better, either before or since: his snare drum hits, in particular, crackle like rifle shots. Gregg Xanthus Winter explained, "Carl's drums had the mikes set directly into them. So instead of having to worry about the mike crashing down and falling over during a number they became an integral part of the kit, nor would the cymbals cause them to move."[18] There were fifteen mikes on the drums alone, and *Welcome Back* captures the sound of Palmer's stainless steel kit, in all its glory, better than any other recording.

Emerson's battery of Moogs also sound extremely vibrant and lively; on some of the passages it sounds almost as if Emerson has set up his modular Moog in your living room. Unfortunately, the other keyboards, which had to be miked and couldn't be run directly into the recording console, don't fare as well. The piano mike, for instance, is clearly picking up some bleed from the other instruments, and as a result the sound of the piano is adequate, nothing more. The sound of the Hammond is particularly disappointing; it's a bit on the thin side and lacking in presence, nothing at all like *Pictures*, which remains the definitive live document of Emerson's organ sound. Perhaps part of the problem was that the mike used for the Leslie cabinet was picking up bleed-over from the bass and drums, although I think partly it was a matter of Emerson having come to prefer a glassier organ timbre since the time of *Pictures*. Whatever the reason, while the Hammond sound on *Welcome Back* is adequate for the *Trilogy* and *Brain Salad Surgery* material, which at any rate called for the glassier organ sound, it is simply too thin for the demands of *Tarkus*, where the warm, dirty, overdriven timbre of the original organ sound is sorely missed.

Lake's voice, much like Emerson's organ, lacks sufficient presence and fullness, even when it's pushed up in the mix—again, it's clear that Lake's vocal mikes picked up some audience sound, as well as some instrumental

---

[18] Stein, "Emerson, Lake and Palmer Live," 9.

bleed-over. Meanwhile, Lake's Gibson Ripper bass didn't seem to record as well as his Fender Jazz bass had on *Pictures*—it sounds jangly in its upper registers, and boomy and lacking in definition in its lower. Oddly, though, his Les Paul electric guitar sounds full and vibrant. It's hard to know whether these sonic problems reflect the house mix that went through the PA that the audience heard on the night of the show, or if most of the problems simply stemmed from how the vocal mikes and miked instruments were run into the recording console. At any rate, there are some undeniable flaws to the sonic quality of *Welcome Back My Friends*.

As was usual, all three musicians were involved in mixing, and as Peter Granat recalls, "At some times there were as many as eight hands on the board at once."[19] Usually the mix is adequate, although there are a few peculiar anomalies: in the "Manticore" section of "Tarkus" the loudest instrument is Palmer's cowbell, and in part of "Take a Pebble" Emerson's acoustic piano somehow manages to overpower Lake's electric bass. Lake's bass lines are sometimes booming, and at other times are too low in the mix—I suspect the problem here was that the instrument sounded very different in its lower and upper registers, and it wasn't always possible to compensate when he moved rapidly between the two.

If the sonic values of *Welcome Back My Friends* are sometimes shaky, there is no question that the playing is absolutely superb—stunning at times. In fact, one could argue that sometimes the playing is too overpowering. Pete Sinfield complained to Paul Stump, "There got to be kind of paranoia in the band about playing fast. You got to the point whereby you'd plead with them, play it slower."[20] As I've already pointed out, a lot of Sinfield's remarks to Stump about ELP come across as sour grapes; however, this is one remark that I think can be taken at face value. For instance, on *Trilogy* the band played "Hoedown" at 138 beats per minute; on *Welcome Back*, at about 164. On *Tarkus* they play "Eruption" at 208 beats per minute; on *Welcome Back*, at more like 232–40. On the debut album they took the first instrumental section of "Take a Pebble" at 192 beats per minute; on *Welcome Back* even this is sped up to close to 208. Even Chris Welch, in an otherwise laudatory review of *Welcome Back* for *Melody Maker*, decries the tendency towards rushed tempos: "If Keith has a fault, it is in his anxiety to please the audience. He will simply take tempos beyond the logical limit for effect. This becomes apparent during his crippling left hand patterns in the fugue section and the traditional boogie passage [of 'Piano Improvisations']. Just a fraction slower, and it would be so much more meaningful."[21]

---

[19] Stein, "Emerson, Lake and Palmer Live," 9.
[20] Stump, *The Music's All That Matters,* 172.
[21] Chris Welch, review of *Welcome Back My Friends, Melody Maker,* August 3, 1974.

There is also a tendency for the band to speed up during the course of the music. This can be attributed to Carl Palmer. Although universally acclaimed for his stunning technique, not all of his rock colleagues were enamored with his approach to keeping time, and many felt he pushed the beat too hard, resulting in perpetually increasing tempos. Here's Eddy Offord:

> Carl Palmer . . . had an incredible technique—he could play the greatest kind of complex rhythms—but unfortunately, his timing from one bar to the next wasn't the best in the world. I think that came out more when you heard him play with Asia, and even on "Lucky Man" he was a little bit up and down. He just can't play two bars in the same tempo. But then he comes up with the most amazing rhythms.[22]

Palmer was clearly aware of such criticisms, and in fact on at least one occasion provided a more or less systematic justification of his approach:

> I think that the drummer can actually give a bit more excitement because he does speed up. I think this cold, regimented thing that goes on is very nice to make demos, and it's excellent for disco records, but it does take away a little bit of the emotion . . . I always think that the bass plays right on the beat, any lead instruments play behind it—so they can weave in and out—and I always think the drummer plays in front of it—always giving the edge; always making it go.[23]

While Palmer's explanation is interesting, I think it is more valuable as a comment on how ELP worked as a unit than as a universal principle on which rock rhythm sections should function.[24] Sometimes the faster tem-

---

[22] Eddy Offord, quoted by Buskin, *Inside Tracks*, 174–75. As we've seen, the tempo irregularities of "Lucky Man" can't fairly be blamed on Palmer, who was obliged to drum along with Lake's preexisting guitar tracks without the benefit of a click track.

[23] Carl Palmer, quoted by Rick Mattingly, "Carl Palmer," *Modern Drummer*, December 1983, 50.

[24] This invites a momentary consideration of the Lake-Palmer rhythm section. From a technical point of view, obviously they are one of the great rhythm sections in rock's history. Furthermore, they compliment each other nicely: Palmer is more virtuosic and melodically nimble than Lake, who, in turns, supplies the rock steady sense of beat that Palmer, left to his own devices, wouldn't. In a sense, they reverse the role of bass and drums in most earlier rhythm sections, hearkening back, perhaps, to the work of bassist Noel Redding and drummer Mitch Mitchell in the original Jimi Hendrix Experience, except that Palmer is a greater drummer than Mitchell, Lake a better bassist than Redding. It must be admitted that the Lake-Palmer rhythm section was at times a bit on the stiff side. I think the sense of stiffness is a result of the fact that more often than not, Palmer plays off of Emerson's melodic figures rather than Lake's bass patterns, which, in the first four albums, often double Emerson's left-hand figures. Emerson's keyboard parts frequently become the band's center of rhythmic gravity, which Lake and Palmer accompany, rather than interlocking with each other and supplying a rhythmic backdrop that Emerson's lines can float on top of. It's only when Lake's bass lines cut loose from Emerson's keyboard parts that Lake's and Palmer's parts interlock, and the band really swings.

pos do add more excitement, as Palmer suggests; something like "Hoedown" is not hurt by being speeded up a bit, and may, within limits, even benefit. On the other hand, sometimes I think the band *do* play too fast on *Welcome Back*; the instrumental movements of *Tarkus*, for instance, are so fast that the rhythmic intricacy and ponderous sense of menace inherent in the original is compromised.

Welcome Back My Friends to the Show That Never Ends . . .

Nonetheless, while it is undeniably a flawed document, *Welcome Back* is still an essential one—for its radical rethink of *Tarkus*, its inclusion of Emerson's "Piano Improvisations," then unavailable in recorded form, and its incredible performances of some of the *Brain Salad Surgery* material. With this in mind, let's undertake a track-by-track survey of the album, recalling that it represents the original, unedited order of the band's set at their Anaheim show of February 10. ELP organizes the show into three main segments: forty-five minutes of driving electronic prog rock at the beginning, a thirty-minute "unplugged" segment in the middle as a kind of relaxation from the intensity of the show's opening portion, and another lengthy (thirty-five-minute) dose of electronic prog to end the show.

Hoedown. ELP apparently learned their lesson from the '73 European tour. "Abaddon's Bolero" was retired from their stage show; "Hoedown" was returned to its rightful place as show opener. After the now-customary announcement, "Welcome back my friends to the show that never ends, ladies and gentlemen Emerson, Lake and Palmer," Emerson begins his unmistakable "vacuum wail" on modular Moog, and the band kick into "Hoedown." The performance here hews fairly closely to their performance of the number on *Trilogy*, although, as I pointed out above, it's significantly faster. The one section that is a bit different is the Moog space rock episode. Emerson begins this episode at 2:44 by quoting "The Girl I Left Behind Me" instead of "Turkey in the Straw," as he had on *Trilogy*. Thereafter he spins out a spacey melody that effectively builds up tension, climaxing with a series of cosmic whooshes from 3:33 through 3:52. Indeed, one consistent hallmark of the Anaheim show is that virtually all of Emerson's solos are superbly structured; there is no pointless doodling, and the solos all seems to show a slow but inevitable increase in tension that suggests composition rather than improvisation—although, as far as I can tell (by comparing this recording with bootlegs from that era), the solos were in fact improvised. Following the Moog episode the opening section is recapitulated (in slightly different order than on *Trilogy*), and "Hoedown" is brought to an energetic conclusion.

Jerusalem/Toccata. Emerson immediately announces, "We're gonna give you some *Brain Salad Surgery*," and the band launches into the first two tracks from that album, "Jerusalem" and "Toccata," which are played back to back. "Jerusalem" is performed energetically, although Emerson is hard-pressed to reproduce the studio version's "screaming chorus" Hammond effect in live performance,[25] and Lake's vocals, because of the miking issues discussed above, simply don't have the sense of immediacy and majesty of the studio version.

On the other hand, "Toccata" primarily features Emerson's Moogs and Palmer's drums and percussives, both of which sound very vibrant and lively here, and the band perform this difficult piece with great power and élan—their live performance is, in my view, at least the equal of the studio version. There are in fact some details that are new here that I actually prefer to the studio version. Listen especially to how Emerson brings the opening section to a climax from 2:41 to 2:55 with two abrasive Moog lines sounded together—the pitched "power drill" sound of the studio version and a new "screaming trumpet" sound (imagine Maynard Ferguson playing at the absolute top of his range). Likewise, Palmer's percussion movement is at least the equal of the studio version. One would be hard pressed to find another live performance by any rock band of the 1970s that evinces the same confluence of precision and raw fury as this performance of "Toccata."

Tarkus. Jumping from the frying pan into the fire, so to speak, ELP quickly commence their epic live version of the *Tarkus* suite, which had, by 1974, been significantly reworked and expanded. Speaking later of this performance, Emerson said, "When we recorded *Tarkus* live, it was a lot better than we had done on the [studio] album. This, I believe, was because of improvements in the state of our equipment."[26] I'm not sure I'm prepared to categorically agree with this, although there is no question that there are sections that are unequivocally improved: at any rate, interested ELP fans who have not listened to both the live and studio versions of "Tarkus" should by all means compare and contrast them and make up their own minds.

My biggest reservations stem from two issues I've already discussed: the sound of the Hammond and the prevailing tempo. The sound of the

---

[25] Emerson did attempt to reproduce the "screaming chorus" effect live with an electronic device that split the Hammond's direct signal in two: one signal remained straight and the other was put slightly out of tune, giving the organ a ringing sound. On *Welcome Back*, the effect is not very noticeable.

[26] Keith Emerson quoted by Eric Gaer, "Emerson, Lake and Palmer: a Force to be Reckoned With," *Downbeat*, May 9, 1974, 31.

Hammond in the live performance lacks the gritty, overdriven sound of the instrument in the studio version and this, in my view, is a major liability for an aggressive piece like "Tarkus" that relies on the organ so heavily. Furthermore, if there's anywhere on *Welcome Back* where ELP play too fast, it's the instrumental movements of "Tarkus": as I said above, the rhythmic intricacy dissipates into a blur of notes, and the original's sense of ponderous menace is compromised. In my view, the first three instrumental movements—"Eruption," "Iconoclast," and "Manticore"—work much better on the studio version than the live one.

On the other hand, I think I would agree that the song movements— "Stones of Years," "Mass," and "Battlefield"—are improved. First and foremost, Lake sings the words with more conviction and a greater sense of nuance than he had in 1971, and sounds much more emotionally involved. Second, the band rearrange the instrumentation of "Mass" and "Battlefield" in ways that I think benefit both. I much prefer the metallic Moog timbre of "Mass" on *Welcome Back* to the clavinetlike Moog sound of the studio album—it fits the abrasive character of the song, and the general space-age direction in which the suite has been taken, better. I also think replacing Lake's guitar solo at the end of the instrumental middle section of the studio version with Emerson's orgiastic ribbon control solo (from 9:02) is an effective change, as it creates a more vivid climax. Emerson had a switch on the ribbon that triggered one of the modular Moog's sequencers, which was patched to sound like a machine gun; during this "war" passage the wandlike ribbon controller launched flash paper and other pyrotechnic items over the head of the audience.[27]

The arrangement of "Battlefield" represents an even more dramatic improvement. Palmer's drumming is more restrained, the interaction between drum kit and bass line (played by Emerson on Minimoog throughout) is much tighter, and Lake's electric guitar soloing is much more developed and focused than it was in the studio version. The quiet, melancholy closing section, which features Lake's voice and guitar arpeggios, and ends with a ravishing bouquet of guitar harmonics, is especially effective.[28] Here we see the kind of "masculine"/"feminine" dynamic which Peter Gabriel–era Genesis used so effectively, and which one wishes ELP had cultivated a bit more often in their own music.

The final movement, "Aquatarkus," represents an especially extraordinary transformation of the original studio version. Originally, it was a rel-

---

[27] Usually, that is. On one occasion, at San Francisco's Cow Palace, the ribbon controller's attachment malfunctioned, blowing Emerson's thumbnail off! He finished playing the show and then sought medical treatment at a local hospital.

[28] The quiet closing section of "Battlefield" includes a brief interpolation of King Crimson's "Epitaph" (off of that band's debut album) from 15:53. Note the effective use of the Echoplex on Lake's voice here.

atively short (3:59) movement in which an ironic funeral march was followed by a recapitulation of part of the "Eruption" material; here it becomes a space/raga-rock epic that clocks in at over ten minutes. In the band's live version of "Aquartarkus" that developed from 1971 on their plan was simple enough: the original "Aquatarkus" material was followed by an improvised Moog solo over a repetitive bass line, which in turn was followed by the recapitulated "Eruption" material. I have heard bootleg recordings of several live performances of "Aquatarkus" from 1971 to 1973; I cannot honestly say I was impressed with any of them. In each case, Emerson simply strung a number of unrelated themes and sound effects together during his solo, and I found myself almost relieved when the "Eruption" material was finally recapitulated.

However, by the 1973-74 World Tour Emerson had totally reconceived the improvised middle section, and in doing so created an improvisation classic that rivals the Nice's "Rondo," only now featuring Moog instead of Hammond. As with his other solos at the Anaheim show—but even to a greater degree—the key to the success of the solo is its masterful structure; Emerson creates a taut sense of inevitability as the solo gradually builds to an enormous climax. The *Welcome Back* version of "Aquatarkus" begins at 16:43 with the original studio material, although now rendered at a much faster tempo—there's only the slightest whiff of the original's marchlike character—and featuring a more metallic Moog timbre, not unlike the Moog patch used earlier for "Mass." The original section lasts until it is suddenly interrupted by an incredible bit of feedback at 19:09, which seems to evoke an interplanetary craft shuddering as it suddenly shatters the speed of light, bringing us into a far distant realm of the cosmos where time moves incredibly slowly.

The lengthy improvised middle section begins at 19:14 with Lake's hypnotically pulsating two-note bass ostinato, Palmer's almost tabla-like tom patterns, and Emerson's spacey filter sweeps, which evoke a tamboura-like oscillating drone. Over this very Eastern background Emerson begins to spin out an almost furtive flutelike Moog line; the overall effect is of a fascinating space-age raga.

It is not generally known that the passage beginning at 19:14 is in fact a loose reinterpretation of "The Minotaur," a piece by Dick Hyman (b. 1927) who is best known for his encyclopedic command of historic jazz piano styles. "The Minotaur" is off Hyman's novelty Moog album *The Age of Electronicus* (1968); unfortunately one would never know this from *Welcome Back*, as he is not credited in the liner notes. Granted, Emerson's understanding of the Moog—not to mention the sophistication of his equipment—greatly surpasses Hyman's; next to ELP's mature space rock, Hyman's piece very much sounds like a novelty number. Furthermore, the overall conceptions are quite different; Hyman's piece is essentially static, while ELP's is essentially teleological, and at some point, although it's hard to say exactly when, ELP's space/raga episode completely breaks away from Hyman's material.[29] Certainly the melodic material has completely broken off by the time Emerson commences his cosmic soliloquy at 21:47. Afterwards, the Moog timbre slowly grows more abrasive, becoming downright ominous by 22:55, when the Moog "tamboura" drone has been abandoned and Emerson begins to weave out a sinuous, snaky unison line on two different Moogs.

At 23:50 Emerson begins comping on the Hammond with his left hand, even as his right hand begins to spin out a variation of the "Aquatarkus" theme on Moog. This builds in intensity; the Moog line, transformed into a more "searing" timbre at 24:47, presents a more literal statement of the "Aquatarkus" theme at 24:47, followed by an ominous series of chromatically ascending glissandos beginning at 25:05 that suggest some kind of awesome epiphany in the deepest depths of the universe. Suddenly, we are rudely slammed out of hyperspace at 25:35 by a pile-driving recapitulation of the "Eruption" material; and the coda, from 26:22 on, seems even more imposing than on the studio version. At 26:54 the crowd breaks into a spontaneous roar of approval even before the final chord has completely died out.

No wonder. "Aquatarkus" ranks as one of Emerson's great creations: the way he slowly but inevitably builds up tension right through the recapitulation of "Eruption" is riveting. Furthermore, "Aquatarkus" ranks alongside "Toccata" as Emerson's greatest achievement as a synthesist; if the latter develops abrasive timbres, the former explores spacey ones, and if "Toccata" anticipates nineties industrial, "Aquatarkus" prefigures nineties electronica. "Aquatarkus," if nothing else, makes *Welcome Back* an essential investment for the ELP enthusiast who already has the band's first five albums; at no other time before or since did the band foray so deeply into space rock.

Take a Pebble. The conclusion of *Tarkus* marks the climax of the first segment of the show: hereafter ELP commence the much quieter, largely acoustic segment that occupies the second third of their performance. This acoustic segment is organized into a medley-like mosaic, with the opening and closing portions of "Take a Pebble" serving as bookends to the whole. The first statement of "Take a Pebble" includes the opening vocal part and Emerson's first piano solo (i.e., before Lake's guitar solo) from the studio version. The band's performance here is similar to that of the debut album until 3:08, at which point Emerson launches into a stride piano episode not present on the original recording.

---

[29] Certainly the rhythmic feel is different: Hyman's "The Minotaur" is in 3/4, ELP's "Aquatarkus" in 4/4, with the bass/drum groove being reminiscent of the groove underlying the Moog "steel drum" section of "Karn Evil 9, 2nd Impression."

At 4:45 this trails off and Greg Lake commences a lovely solo performance of "Still . . . You Turn Me On" that I actually prefer to the highly arranged performance of *Brain Salad Surgery*. (Although, as I said, I think a performance with Lake's voice and guitar and Emerson on harpsichord would have been even better. Ah well.) At 8:05 Lake begins playing a wayward series of strummed chords and arpeggios—unfortunately marred by a bellowing cretin at 8:19, whose exclamation ("Get Crazy Man!") has been preserved in digital glory for posterity.[30] Out of this nice bit of apparent improvisation "Lucky Man" eventually emerges. Unlike "Still . . . You Turn Me On," I'm not totally sold on the idea of a solo performance of "Lucky Man"—it's so much more repetitious, it seems to cry out for a more sophisticated arrangement—but Lake makes it work well enough, and the use of Echoplex to create a reverberating echo during the vocal refrains is a nice touch.

Now it's Emerson's turn, as he launches into the 11:53 "Piano Improvisations." A brief disclaimer: these are "improvisations" only in a loose sense, certainly not in the manner of Keith Jarrett's or Patrick Moraz's improvisations wherein an original piece of music is created afresh each performance. Emerson's "Improvisations" are really a medley, and include a couple of pieces by other musicians that Emerson enjoyed playing at the time, as well as a few more or less clearly defined bits of music by Emerson that were subject to some (although not a great deal of) alteration from performance to performance.

After a brief opening flourish, at 0:16 Emerson launches into the fugue from the *Prelude and Fugue* by Austrian pianist-composer Friedrich Gulda (1930–1999). Gulda was already beginning to experiment with fusing jazz harmonic, melodic, and rhythmic gestures with classical forms in the 1950s, so it's easy to understand why Emerson felt a natural affinity for this piece, and in fact one can hear bits and pieces of it in ELP performances as early as 1970. Emerson plays Gulda's Fugue with great drive, faster than Gulda himself tended to play it, although compared with Gulda's recorded performances, Emerson's is somewhat lacking in the rhythmic element of swing.

After the closing glissando of Gulda's Fugue at 1:55, Emerson moves into a driving left-hand stride figure over which he improvises rapid-fire sixteenth-note lines for nearly a minute, until 2:47, when he takes up another stride figure, over which he improvises right hand chordal figures and careening melodic lines with great bravura. At 3:40 he shifts to a calmer, more classically inspired section; the itinerant, quiet tinkling in the

---

[30] On why American audiences did not hesitate to talk, yell, scream, and otherwise make racket through quiet passages that would have held British audiences spellbound, see *Rocking the Classics*, 263, fn37.

upper register of the piano is somewhat reminiscent of parts of the cadenza from the first movement of his Piano Concerto. However, by 4:14 Emerson has moved into another stride figure—his most crazed one yet—over which he overlays breathless rolling right hand figurines. Finally, at 5:09 he takes up the granddaddy of stride piano pieces, Joe Sullivan's "Little Rock Getaway" (1935). By 6:10 he is beginning to move farther away from the thematic substance of this number, and at 6:23 he careens into yet another crazed stride figure.

This episode gradually peters out into a quiet close by 7:06; at this point Palmer enters quietly on drums, Lake follows on bass, and the trio launch into what is probably the highpoint of the entire "Improvisations," a very nice bop-style twelve-bar blues in the manner of Oscar Peterson (whom Emerson greatly admired) or Bud Powell. Palmer shows a natural affinity for swing drumming; although Emerson often complained about Lake's relative lack of interest in jazz,[31] Lake actually does a very nice job in moving the chord changes around, via a very speedy walking bass part, in the manner of a bop bassist. The band develop the bop-flavored blues through a number of twelve-bar choruses, eventually (at 9:17) transforming the twelve-bar chorus into a stomping, boogie-woogie style figure along the lines of a Meade Lux Lewis or Jimmy Yancey number. This is carried through to the stock blues coda at 11:18 that brings the "Improvisations" to their conclusion.

Emerson's playing during the "Improvisations" is very impressive—his left hand technique really is daunting—and I'm glad that this recording was preserved for posterity. However, I must also admit this is not my favorite part of the show. Unlike ELP's large-scale works which rely on a masterfully paced ebb and flow towards and away from climactic points, Emerson's "Improvisations" are organized much like the music on Rick Wakeman's solo albums. A number of musical ideas are strung together, some original, some not, some cross-relating, some not: the overall effect is one of background music that one can either walk in on or walk out on at any given time without missing anything essential. Furthermore, the abundance of, and similarity of, the stride figures seems to guarantee a certain amount of redundancy: unless one is as big a fan of 1920s/30s stride piano as, say, Keith Emerson, it all tends to sound alike after awhile. I definitely don't think this section needed to be 11:53. Incidentally, it would have been wonderful—and still would be—if Emerson did undertake a solo tour in which he improvised a new piece every night á la Keith Jarrett.

---

[31] For instance, in 1986 Emerson ruefully commented about Lake, "I don't think he's got a jazz record anywhere in his collection." See Bob Doerschuk, "Keith Emerson: the Phoenix Rises from the Ashes of Progressive Rock," *Keyboard*, July 1986, 39.

After pausing briefly to acknowledge applause, the band launch into the closing verse of "Take a Pebble" (that is, the section following the last instrumental episode on the debut album). This wraps up the second third of the show, the "unplugged" segment, which has occupied 26:13 in all.

Jeremy Bender/The Sheriff. As a kind of interlude before the final third of the show the band play a medley of two of their "music hall" numbers, "Jeremy Bender"/"The Sheriff." Emerson plays both numbers on electric piano (or, according to Emerson, a de-tuned upright piano with a special pick-up). It's not particularly profound, but it is fun to try to identify all the brief musical quotes Emerson plays at the end of the much-extended coda of "The Sheriff."

Karn Evil 9. Finally, we reach the last third of the show, which is nothing less than an epic, thirty-five-minute performance of "Karn Evil 9" complete. Anyone with perfect pitch or a sensitivity to keys will notice the tonality of the 1st and 3rd Impressions is different here than on *Brain Salad Surgery*. This is because Greg Lake found that he was unable to sing the vocal parts in $A^\flat$ night after night, so the band was obliged to transpose the vocal sections down to F, much to Keith Emerson's chagrin.[32] I do miss the element of excitement that was created on *Brain Salad Surgery* when Lake was straining a bit in the upper reaches of his tessitura; on the other hand, Lake's voice seemed to record better here than on any of the previous numbers of *Welcome Back*, so the vocals are powerful, with a great deal of presence.

There are some other nice details as well. Lake's guitar solo on 1st Impression has a razor-sharp timbre that the studio version lacks, and contains some nice added ornaments. Some of Emerson's Moog settings are even more vibrant live than in the studio: check out the sample-and-hold of the 1st Impression (8:17), the steel drum setting of the 2nd Impression (18:53), and the mind-blowing sequencer part that ends 3rd Impression (from 33:20). Emerson changed the ending of 3rd Impression from a fade-out to a violent explosion for conceptual reasons, saying, "At first we ended the piece as it is on the record, but that confused everybody. It needed something more definite and the explosion adds emphasis to the question that the piece is supposed to pose."[33] (The question, of course, involving the possible ascent of the Computer to a position of godlike power.) Whether or not the fans at Anaheim understood the philosophical question being posed here, they reacted to the conclusion of 3rd Impression with unbridled enthusiasm: there is an immediate and pro-

---

[32] For just one expression of Emerson's chagrin see Milano, "Keith Emerson," *Contemporary Keyboard*, September 1980, 22–23.

[33] Keith Emerson, quoted by James Johnson, "Fingers' Cave," *New Musical Express*, January 19, 1974, 12.

longed roar of approval when the explosion shakes the arena at 34:30, a roar of approval that shows no sign of abating when it is faded out almost a minute later on the recording.

One final detail of the live version of "Karn Evil 9" worth commenting on is Carl Palmer's epic drum solo, which stretches from 11:15 to 15:15 of 1st Impression. I must admit that normally I am not a fan of drum solos, but this one is riveting; in comparing it to his solo on "Tank," recorded nearly four years earlier, one can see how Palmer has progressed not only technically but musically. Unlike the "Tank" solo, which has too many peaks and valleys, Palmer wisely presents fewer ideas but develops the ideas that are presented more exhaustively. As a result, although the *Welcome Back* solo is nearly twice as long as the "Tank" solo, it actually sounds shorter.

Basically, there are three main sections to the solo. In the first, from 11:15 to 12:54, Palmer moves a rapid-fire barrage of single-stroke rolls and other rudimental patterns around the kit while counterpointing with his bass drum pedal; the conclusion of this section, where he creates an imposing set of polyrhythms between hi-hat, drums, and cowbell, is especially interesting. This entire passage is almost along the lines of a theme with variations, since many of the rudimental patterns sound like variants of the same general rhythmic idea.

The second section, long a staple of a Palmer drum solo, features rapidly chugging bass drum eighth notes accompanying a halo of gong strikes and the ringing of a massive church bell suspended over Palmer's head, whose clapper he operated by pulling a string with his teeth. It was during this portion of the solo that Palmer's drum rostrum began to revolve, spraying the audience with laser lights. This section lasts until 13:58.

The final section begins with Palmer launching into another barrage of rudimental patterns across the kit. This time, however, he gradually slows down and quiets down until at 14:24 the solo is reduced to slow snare drum paradiddles. Then gradually he begins to build the solo back up; at 14:58 he seems to be fading out again, on a simple snare drum roll, but suddenly he launches into one final and incredible barrage, not unlike the multiple bursts of fireworks saved for the very end of a fireworks show. Is this solo flamboyant? Absolutely. But not only is it technically amazing, it's very musical, and the sense of drama Palmer brings to the decrescendo/unexpected crescendo at the end of the solo is genuine. In my opinion, it is one of a very few musically satisfying drum solos recorded during the 1970s.

Welcome Back captures just under an hour fifty minutes worth of music. Actually there was even more: after "Karn Evil 9" the band played the closing segments of *Pictures* as an encore. Including *Pictures*, however, would have required ELP to release *Welcome Back* as a four LP set, a move they felt could be risky. Eventually the band decided to release *Welcome Back* as a three-record set, without the encore, and to time the release to coincide with the end of their tour in late summer 1974.

1973-74 World Tour, Continued

The last date of the second leg of their tour, at Tulsa's Civic Center on March 7, was recorded for broadcast on the King Biscuit Flower Hour, a syndicated radio show that was heard on over three hundred radio stations at the peak of its popularity. A few of the Tulsa tracks appear on the *Emerson, Lake and Palmer* King Biscuit CD released in 1997: these are quite similar to the corresponding Anaheim tracks represented on *Welcome Back My Friends*, although the sonic quality of the Tulsa material may be marginally better. After the Tulsa show, ELP took a brief rest. They played just three shows later in the month: March 26 in Wichita, Kansas (included in *The Original Bootleg Series from the Manticore Vaults*, vol. 2), March 28 at the Los Angeles Coliseum, and March 30 in Memphis, Tennessee. Their sights were set on the event that was intended to be the crowning performance of their American tour and just may be the crowning performance of their career: the California Jam.

"Cal Jam," as it's often called, took place April 6, 1974, at the (no longer extant) Ontario Motor Speedway, Ontario, California, about forty miles east of Los Angeles. Attendance was, depending on whose numbers you choose to believe, somewhere between 175,000 and 350,000. While it has sometimes been called "the Woodstock of the West," Bruce Pilato is much more accurate in saying Cal Jam was "a corporate attempt to stage a West Coast sequel to Woodstock."[34] The sponsor was none other than ABC-TV. As Pilato notes, "The network had launched a successful late night rock concert TV series called *In Concert*, and was looking for a single event that could provide several weeks of programming. In addition to featuring big stars in a large concert setting, the network was also looking to streamline its weekly production costs."[35]

For anyone who views late-sixties/early-seventies rock from even a mildly idealistic perspective, there is something depressing in how convincingly Cal Jam demonstrates the takeover of "countercultural" music by the corporate Establishment. Nonetheless, Pilato is correct in saying, "The California Jam was a huge financial and artistic success."[36] Certainly,

---

[34] See Pilato's very comprehensive liner notes in ELP's *Then and Now* CD, Eagle Entertainment, CD 1001-2, 1998, 11.
[35] Pilato, *Then and Now* liner notes, 10.
[36] Ibid.

a number of the bands in the lineup (including ELP) put on electrifying shows. Furthermore, when it was over, ABC had grossed $5 million (£3 million), and Cal Jam had hosted the largest paying crowd ever west of the Mississippi.

I can think of no more eloquent testimony to how huge ELP had really become by this time—not just musically, or even financially, but as a cultural commodity—than the fact that although Cal Jam featured a number of the major acts of the seventies, including Deep Purple, Black Sabbath, the Eagles, Earth, Wind, and Fire, Black Oak Arkansas, Seals and Crofts, and Rare Earth, ELP out-heavied them all into the headliners' slot. To be more precise, officially ELP and Deep Purple were "co-head-liners," but in fact ELP occupied the closing position on the bill that a headlining band would occupy, forcing Deep Purple to take the stage before the sun set for the evening. This so enraged Deep Purple guitarist Ritchie Blackmore that he destroyed a $70,000 TV camera after his band's set. Perhaps Blackmore was somewhat pacified later on by the financial rewards: both ELP and Deep Purple were effectively paid twice, once for their performance and once for broadcast rights. The ELP segments of the show were broadcast on May 7 and June 10, 1974 (illogically in tandem with portions of the boorish Black Oak Arkansas' performance), introducing their music to an entirely new "mainstream" audience.

In 1998 Eagle Entertainment released a CD called *Then and Now* containing most of ELP's Cal Jam performance (the encore is not included), as well as material from their 1997 and 1998 tours. In 2005 Sanctuary released a two-DVD set, *Emerson, Lake and Palmer: Beyond the Beginning*, that includes ELP's entire Cal Jam performance, finally making ELP's most eagerly sought after bootleg video footage publicly available, as well as rendering the "Then" portion of *Then and Now* largely irrelevant. Not only is the sound quality of the CD problematic—it's even a bit lower grade than *Welcome Back*—the made-for-TV edits of the Cal Jam performance do not translate very smoothly to an audio-only format.

For instance, the TV broadcast of the ELP Cal Jam performance opened with "Karn Evil 9, 1st Impression, part 2" with Greg Lake singing "Welcome back my friends, to the show that never ends . . ." while physically motioning the audience to "come inside, come inside." This is a highly effective opening, and indeed, the logic of the TV edits of the performance rest largely on a number of visual cues that are lost on CD; in actual fact ELP played the 1st and 3rd Impressions of "Karn Evil 9" near the end of their set. The TV broadcast followed "1st Impression, part two," which features Palmer's revolving rostrum in full flight during his stupendous drum solo, with three segments that are meant to feature the three musicians. "Toccata" is badly butchered in order to feature Palmer's percussion movement—this makes absolutely no sense on the CD, but at least on the video version we hear the announcer's voice-over "Ladies and gentlemen, Mr. Carl Palmer," and we have some idea of what's going on. Next Greg Lake is featured in his vocal/acoustic guitar medley of "Still . . . You Turn Me On"/"Lucky Man." Finally Emerson is featured playing his "Piano Improvisations," which differ from the *Welcome Back* performance of two months before in just a few minor details; after a brief pause for applause, the band perform the closing segment of "Take a Pebble" together. This is followed by a riveting performance of "Karn Evil 9, 3rd Impression." Even the CD track of this performance is interesting—it contains some different Moog settings than Emerson had used in Anaheim two months earlier—but it's really on the video footage that it comes fully alive. Part of the pleasure of the video footage is simply being able to see Emerson, who has now abandoned his psychedelic silver lamé suits and space-age Elizabethan ruffs of the early seventies in favor of a more laid-back Doctor Kildare look, handle the difficult keyboard parts as he seems to effortlessly move from one side to the other of his U-shaped keyboard set up. Furthermore, the video footage of 3rd Impression is edited in such a way as to convey the music's concept as graphically as possible. We see ominous close-ups of the modular Moog's computer screen whenever the computer "speaks," for instance, and when Emerson's modular Moog belches smoke, sprouts wings, and turns to face the audience during the runaway sequencer climax, everybody understands the outcome of the Man vs. Machine struggle outlined in the lyrics. A fireworks display was timed to begin in exact unison with the closing explosion of 3rd Impression; this looks very flashy on a TV screen, but is scarcely audible on the CD.

For reasons that are unclear, ELP's Cal Jam performance of *Pictures*—they played the closing segment of "Baba Yaga" and "The Great Gates of Kiev" as an encore—is not included on the CD. Perhaps it's just as well: again, it's the visuals that dominate the performance. The piece proceeds as it traditionally had until the feedback episode near the end of "Gates." While the L-100 is still screeching in complaint from Emerson's manhandling, he jumps away from the instrument, literally bolts across the stage, and sits down at a nine-foot Steinway grand piano. This piano is suddenly lifted up several yards off the ground and begins spinning upside down; Emerson, who is secured to the bench by stirrups (the bench is in turn secured to the piano by steel rods), pounds out Sergei Rachmaninov's Prelude in C# minor, of all things. After approximately thirty seconds the piano is re-lowered, Emerson jumps off it, bolts back across the stage, and resumes "The Great Gates of Kiev" where he had left off. Obviously, this would not have worked very effectively on CD, where the sudden interruption of organ feedback by the Rachmaninov Prelude would have been nearly incomprehensible. It makes far more sense on the DVD, which indeed offers the best possible document of the band's idiosyncratic mixture of complex progressive rock and space-age vaudeville effects that characterized their 1973-74 World Tour.

After Cal Jam, ELP began preparation for their British mini-tour. To say that ELP returned to Britain as conquering heroes would be no exaggeration: unstoppable juggernauts might be more like it. By spring of 1974, ELP were huge: headlining Cal Jam was only the latest feather in their cap. In March they were featured on the cover of *Creem*, albeit in Lester Bangs's vituperative exposé (which we will revisit one last time at the end of this chapter). In April they were featured in the center spread of the *New Musical Express*, and given a very prominent feature in *Rolling Stone*, a surprisingly even-handed article by Judith Sims that may be one of the most penetrating articles on the band from that era. It is particularly interesting for its personality profiles of the musicians. Emerson is described as "slender and intense—a brooder, like [Marlon] Brando, but without Brando's overpowering physical presence." Lake "alternates between intensity and ironic cynicism, all the more ironic because of his angelic moon face." Palmer is "thin, intense, serious . . . an earnest young man, the easiest talker of the group." Sims added, "Emerson, Lake and Palmer are differentiated more by the instruments they play than by their offstage personalities. Their homogeneity is puzzling. They have the same purposeful dedication to the music and the same dynamic but humorless approach to their performances. They even look alike—blondish hair, medium height, furrow-browed intensity."[37] In May they were featured prominently in *Downbeat*, a jazz magazine that during the early seventies had increasingly focused on new electronic music—both progressive rock and jazz-rock fusion—that evinced a tilt towards instrumental virtuosity. And, of course, if you missed Cal Jam but lived somewhere in the U.S., you could catch ELP on ABC-TV when their performance segments were rebroadcast in May and June. ELP, it seemed, were everywhere.

ELP began their British mini-tour with shows on four consecutive nights, April 18–21, at London's Wembley Empire Pool. The quirky sax-bass-drums trio Backdoor opened for them each night.[38] Attendance for the four dates was in the vicinity of 36,000. Afterwards they played the Stoke Trenton Gardens on April 23, and Liverpool's Empire on four consecutive nights from April 29 through May 2. The British leg of their tour, then, consisted of nine shows in three cities.

By the beginning of the British mini-tour there was more than a little rumbling of discontent from the band's British fans; ELP hadn't played

---

[37] Sims, "ELP . . . What?" 18.
[38] For more on this interesting band see Martin, *Listening to the Future*, 217–18, and Forrester, Hanson, and Askew, *Emerson, Lake and Palmer*, 213.

in the U.K. since late 1972. In a *New Musical Express* feature in April, manager Stewart Young explained the band's absence:

> It's not the sound or the lighting, just that we can't physically get our stage equipment on the average British stage. Carl's drums weigh two and a half tons, and alone they'd simply smash through most stages. Also, we need a 60-foot area. On ticket prices we have no alternative because we have a very large production staff, most of whom have to be flown over from the States. As it is we'll be playing at a loss.[39]

In *The Music's All That Matters* Paul Stump suggests that the draconian tax laws enacted in Britain in 1974 forced British rock megastars out of the U.K., thus divorcing them from their root constituency: he sees this as a major factor in the decline of progressive rock between the middle and late 1970s.[40] At the risk of offending my British readers, I think this is an overly Anglo-centric view. If I get anything out of Young's remarks quoted above, it's that by early 1973 ELP planned their tours on the basis of American-sized stages and American-sized venues. Their stage show was designed to fit American-sized arenas, not British. Their budget was based on the premise of American-sized audiences, not British. Why? The answer is simple: the U.S. is where the money was. The fact that ELP could fill a 9,000-seat venue four nights in a row and lose money supports this view very eloquently, I think. To put the matter indelicately, by 1974 ELP had outgrown Britain. After their nine-show mini-tour of 1974, they did not perform in the U.K. again until 1992, a source of frustration—and even some bitterness—for many of ELP's British fans, who had been the band's earliest supporters in 1970 and 1971.

Just a few days after their final British gig, ELP were on the road again. Between May 6 and June 1 they played seventeen shows in eleven venues across Spain, Germany, Switzerland, Austria, the Netherlands, and France—the latter being the one European country that remained undeniably indifferent to ELP-mania throughout the band's career.

The final leg of ELP's World Tour commenced in late July after the band had taken the middle of the summer off, and found them back in the States. They played nineteen more dates between July 26 and August 24, all of them in progressive music's American bastion of the Northeast, the Mid-Atlantic states, and the eastern Midwest. A particularly memorable date was August 17, when a terrible rain storm shortly before show time seriously damaged much of ELP's equipment in Jersey City's open air Roosevelt Stadium, and nearly killed Emerson roadie Bobby Richardson when Emerson's keyboard stack—which Richardson was fran-

---

[39] Johnson, "Welcome Back My Friends."
[40] Stump, *The Music's All That Matters*, 183–84.

tically working to protect—came crashing down on him. Their final date of the tour—and last public performance for nearly three years, as it turned out—was an August 24 benefit show in New York City's Central Park, organized by ELP's old friend Scott Muni, who had broken *Pictures* in the U.S. some two and a half years earlier.

End of an Era

Just days after the World Tour had ended, in early September, 1974, the three-LP set *Welcome Back My Friends to the Show That Never Ends*, the live recording of the band's February Anaheim show, hit the streets, the second ELP release on the Manticore label. As I explained earlier, the band did not include the *Pictures* segment that had served as their encore because they did not want to turn *Welcome Back* into a four-LP set; normally a band could not even count on a three-record set to chart very highly.

But these were not normal times for ELP. The 1973-74 World Tour had brought them to the pinnacle of the rock world: in 1973-74 only the Rolling Stones, the Who, and Led Zeppelin grossed more from touring, and none of them were performing adaptations of Ginastera and Copland or thirty-five-minute rock suites of symphonic scope and complexity. ELP received the ultimate reward for their inveterate U.S. touring when *Welcome Back* hit number four in the Billboard charts on September 14— ELP's highest charting album of all in the U.S., their first album to chart higher in the U.S. than in the U.K. (where it charted out at a mere number five), and one of a very few three-record sets to break the American top ten during the vinyl era.

There was a general feeling that *Welcome Back* marked the end of an era for the band. Stewart Young remarked, "We've got over the hardest part now—the first few years when you learn to live with yourselves and your job. Now they can really branch out, and the stuff they're writing has never been stronger."[41] Keith Emerson also viewed *Welcome Back* as the capstone of an era for ELP, remarking, "We're putting out this triple live album, which in fact is a resumé of just about everything ELP has done since its inception, and what I feel we stand for."[42] Prophetically (although not necessarily in a positive sense), he added, "From now on, we can keep moving in the same direction or start the wheel turning all over again, which could be equally big and equally grotesque depending

---

[41] Stewart Young, quoted by Johnson, "Welcome Back My Friends."
[42] Keith Emerson, quoted by Roy Carr, "Loneliness of a Long-Distance Power Cell," *New Musical Express* July 27, 1974, 6.

on how you care to look at it."[43] We will pick up this particular strand of the plot in the subsequent chapters.

A Critique of the Blues Orthodoxy Ideology

ELP had reached the top, and presumably saw no reason that they would not remain there for years. They probably felt that the critics who had savaged them with such numbing regularity, the Lester Bangses and Robert Christgaus of the world, were fleas or mosquitoes, minor irritants, nothing more, whom could be safely ignored: after all, they had the support of the people who really counted, that is, their fans. However, before moving on to the next stage of our saga, I think it would be wise to turn our attention one more time to ELP's critics. Why? Because during the next two and a half years, ELP would be silent: their critics, however, would not, and would go on to forge a critical ideology that was quite different than the rock ideology that was current when Keith Emerson and Greg Lake first jammed backstage in San Francisco in December 1969. It was an ideology that would be hostile to progressive music generally, and to ELP in particular.

We have already examined the shift in that took place rock ideology between the early to mid-1970s, and given some consideration to how this shift impacted the reception of ELP's music. We have noted, specifically, how late-sixties belief that a utopian synthesis of musical styles might trigger (or at least mirror) a harmonious synthesis of divergent or antagonistic social and cultural systems gave way to a belief that such a synthesis was not only unachievable, but undesirable as well, because, the new argument ran, a synthesis of rock and classical styles was certain to drain the former's oppositional energy. Thus the "blues orthodoxy" of the rapidly rising *Rolling Stone* and *Creem* wing of critics. Running in tandem with this conviction was a belief that blues-based music was somehow automatically heartfelt, emotional, and "authentic," while progressive music was somehow automatically cold, heartless, and "sterile." While I have always found this a somewhat incredible argument, and remain astonished that it has been taken seriously for so long, I think that it is nevertheless needful to spend some time examining its manifestations as relates to ELP.

A basic tenet of the blues orthodoxy school of rock criticism is that progressive rock is, of necessity, cold, unemotional music. Dave Marsh: "Progressive rock sounds desiccated to me because it's so thoroughly divorced from the taproot of rock and roll: rhythm and blues."[44] Ethlie Ann

---

[43] Ibid.
[44] Dave Marsh, *The Heart of Rock and Soul* (New York: Plume Books, 1989), xv.

Vare on King Crimson: "The trouble with having four certified musical geniuses on the same stage at the same time is that if you aren't enjoying the show, you assume it's your fault . . . this is a concert, not an IQ test."[45] Lester Bangs on ELP: "Robot music mix-mastered by human modules who deserve purple hearts for managing to keep the gadgets reined at all."[46] In the previous three quotes we see the three principal reasons that orthodox rock critics see progressive rock as cold and unemotional, namely (1) it's too far removed from rock's "proper" R & B lineage; (2) it's too complex to be "felt" viscerally; and (3) it's too reliant on technology, which is seen to somehow interfere with the performer-audience interaction. It will be worth our while to examine each of these assertions in turn.

Evident in Marsh's statement is the blues orthodoxists' almost religious faith in the blues as a touchstone of musical "authenticity" and a taproot of all that is "natural" in music. Certainly there's the feeling that the blues and emotion in music are synonymous, that it's impossible to have one without the other. Popular music that has strayed too far from the blues is, by definition, music with little or no emotion.

But is this really a viable critical stance? I, for one, say it's not. The "blues centrism" of the blues orthodoxists is actually a contemporary manifestation of a Romantic primitivism that can be traced all the way back to the late eighteenth century and the "noble savage" of Jean-Jacques Rousseau.[47] The basic premise of all of the many manifestations of primitivism since Rousseau's time is that contemporary European (and from the later nineteenth century, white) society, with its overreliance on technology and complex bureaucracies, has entered a state of terminal spiritual and cultural sterility. However, the argument continues, non-European cultural sources that haven't been contaminated by European culture, technology, and social structures may serve as a conduit to a liberating primal energy that could, potentially, revitalize and revivify sterile and effete Western culture.

This kind of primitivism was, of course, important to nineteenth-century Romantic ideology, and was absolutely central to white critical approaches to twentieth-century African American musics of all kinds, especially jazz and rock.[48] One reason that the blues orthodox school of

---

[45] Quoted by Tamm, *Robert Fripp*, 136.

[46] Bangs, "Exposed!"

[47] Jacques Barzun sees the concept of the Noble Savage going back much further: to the ancient Roman historian Tacitus, who viewed the barbarian Germanic tribes as moral and free, the "civilized" Romans as decadent and slavish. The first Noble Savage was therefore blond haired and blue eyed! See Barzun's *From Dawn to Decadence*, 9, 107.

[48] The whole topic of the various manifestations of Romantic primitivism in twentieth-century jazz and rock criticism is too complex to go into here, but I highly recommend Robert Pattison's *The Triumph of Vulgarity: Rock Music in the Mirror of Romanticism* (New York: Oxford University Press, 1987) as a background to interested readers.

rock criticism defends rock so vehemently against nonblack (especially European classical) infusion is that these outside sources are seen as potentially corrupting sources of rock's primal, liberating energy. Of course, this is a very white view of what black music is all about: Bangs, Christgau, Marsh, and their cohorts have made black music serve white Romantic mythology.

As Allan Moore has demonstrated, the assumptions of the blues-orthodoxy wing of rock criticism concerning the blues tradition—and their attempts to measure the relative value of other musics based on criteria derived from that tradition—are not without serious difficulties. As I noted above, one of the major problems the Marsh/Bangs/Christgau school had with progressive rock was its relative lack of "black" influence. As Moore rightly points out, the basic premise behind this line of thought is the belief that black music is "authentic" and "natural" in a way that white music is not: "It [the critical stance of the blues orthodoxists] entails the assumption that blacks in the southern USA lived in a state of mindless primitivism, in which they expressed themselves through music 'naturally,' without the intervening of any musical 'theory'; hence the black sense of rhythm being 'natural' and 'unmediated.'" In fact, the blues are just as "theoretical" as any classical style one would care to mention, insomuch as the style is governed by a set of demonstrable, recurring principles. Furthermore, the insistence with which Bangs, Marsh, Christgau and company have imposed white Romantic primitivism on black American music shows little historical awareness of the degree to which earlier African American styles such as ragtime and jazz resulted from a black/white and a low-culture/high-culture fusion.[49] As Allan Moore goes on to note, the unreflective and extremely questionable critical stance of the blues orthodoxists has unfortunately taken root in academic writing on popular music as well:

> The "moldy fig" attitude is as alive as ever. [Christopher] Small (1987) considers the value of black music to lie in its subversive nature, which accrues to it because it is spontaneous, immediate, and "close to nature." [Simon] Frith talks dangerously of black music being "felt," perhaps implying that white music tends to be "thought," and therefore that blacks are incapable of

---

[49] Here are some questions for those of you who continue to buy into the blues-orthodoxy line of rock criticism. Was Charlie Parker's music "contaminated" after he became familiar with the music of Bartók and Stravinsky? Did Scott Joplin become a "race traitor" when he composed an opera? Is it okay for black musicians to draw on white musical forms and styles but not okay for white musicians working in a form that has its origins in black culture to draw on white musical forms and styles? Why are white rock bands that often mimicked black styles to the point of not giving proper credit to the original songwriter (i.e., the Stones and Zeppelin) celebrated, while white rock bands that drew equally on their own cultural heritage of European classical and folk styles (e.g., ELP and Yes) lambasted?

thought. Even more recently [Peter] Wicke has insisted that the blues were "a pure expression of genuine experience."[50]

Bill Martin, developing my assertion that the blues orthodoxists's notion of "authenticity" is simplistic and reductivist, notes,

> In their desire for "authenticity," these antiprogressive critics participate in not only a kind of essentialism, but even a kind of racism   and I do not mean so-called "antiwhite racism," but instead the kind that sees Black cultural achievements as flowing from some kind of racial essence rather than from the creative transmutation of cultural sources (i.e., hard work and hard thought, the source of great art, whatever its cultural background).[51]

Ironically, progressive rockers of the late sixties and seventies were working from the same general premise as the blues orthodoxists, that the white industrial society of their day was effete, alienating by its very nature, and spiritually sterile. The difference between Keith Emerson, Jon Anderson, and Robert Fripp on the one hand and Dave Marsh, Lester Bangs, and Robert Christgau on the other is that the progressive rockers' primitivism allows for appropriation not only of black blues forms, but of premodern European musics, Eastern musics, and dissident, subversive currents within European Romanticism and modernism. In other words, the primitivism of progressive rock allowed for a utopian eclecticism.[52] The blues orthodoxists would have none of it. Either music was blues-based, or it was unemotional. For a Dave Marsh, there was simply no other conduit to the liberating primal energy which alone could save contemporary industrial (or from today's vantage point, postindustrial) society.

If its lack of "black" influence was one perceived problem in progressive rock's alleged want of emotion, its supposed intellectualism and overcomplexity was another. Again, the driving impulse was a Romantic primitivism. According to the blues orthodoxists, rock's magic lay in its simplicity; there was no room for musical development beyond the modest expansion of harmonic, rhythmic, and structural resources achieved by late-sixties psychedelia.[53] Furthermore, any rock music that assayed to tackle philosophical or metaphysical subject matter was guilty

---

[50] Allan Moore, *Rock: The Primary Text; Developing a Musicology of Rock* (Buckingham, U.K.: Open University Press, 1993), 65.

[51] Martin, *Listening to the Future*, 140–41.

[52] As Bill Martin asked rhetorically, "Does this critical enforcement of what I've called 'blues orthodoxy' mean that there could not be a kind of rock music that took off from, for example, *Chinese* musical and cultural sources?" See ibid., 141.

[53] The major musical achievement of late-sixties psychedelic rock was its expansion of rock's timbral and textural resources.

of pretensions of the worst kind. As Dave Marsh said, listeners who wish to grapple with such topics are "better off listening to classical (or anyway, 'serious') music."[54] Rock should know its place, and aspire to functionality—in other words, rock as a consumable, as a background music for dancing, was to be commended over rock as Art (with its notion of transcendence), as a foreground music for listening.

The idea that rock music should not get too big for its britches, and should somehow be shielded from undergoing musical or topical development, would be almost laughable if it had not become so pervasive. However, maybe a bit of historical context might help here—if only the blues orthodoxists will avail themselves to it. In the 1930s, many Broadway critics saw works such as Jerome Kern's *Showboat* and George Gershwin's *Porgy and Bess*, with their obvious aspirations to European operatic conventions, as a threat to the "simplicity" and "purity" of the American musical theater tradition. Today historians recognize that a musical like *Porgy* didn't threaten the characteristically American nature of musical theater at all; what it did do was expose Broadway to a new range of expressive possibilities. Likewise, in the early phase of the bop revolution, bop's critics saw Charlie Parker, Dizzy Gillespie, and their peers as threatening the "simplicity" and "purity" of American jazz with their complex substitute chords of an obviously European classical provenance; today, however, they are credited with fundamentally expanding jazz's harmonic (and thus its expressive) vocabulary. One would have expected that after initially denouncing progressive rock for threatening to subvert the "purity" and "simplicity" of rock, critics would have acknowledged that it permanently expanded the harmonic, metric, structural, conceptual, timbral, and textural resources available to rock musicians—the timbral and textural expansions having come as a result of progressive musicians' interest in the possibilities inherent in recording studio technology, which the Beatles and their successors in the psychedelic rock movement had begun to exploit in the late sixties. However, the blues orthodoxists have been singularly unwilling to admit this painfully obvious fact, because it would expose the fundamental flaw of their notion that prog was an effete, evolutionary dead end, and would instead require that progressive be viewed as a mainstream (and watershed) style in the stylistic evolution of rock.

To be sure, I do understand the critics' complaints that progressive rock musicians sometimes (perhaps even frequently) drew on classical forms and techniques simply to impress their auditors, even when the musicians had no understanding of what such forms had meant to the musicians who originally created them, or how these forms might be used

---

[54] Marsh, *Heart of Rock and Soul*, xv.

to convey meaningful emotional or conceptual content. Indeed, critics who *like* progressive rock have often complained about these very faults.

I also understand the critics' gripe with progressive musicians for whom virtuosity became a fixation in itself, although, sad to say, the very fact of a progressive musician's virtuosity sometimes became a club with which a critic might beat him. Here's Lester Bangs on Keith Emerson: "Keith Emerson never played an interesting solo in his life. Hell, might as well admit it all the way, they're not even solos, they're just some guy racing all over a keyboard like Liberace trying to play Mozart behind a Dexamyl OD. To make the crucial distinction that trained fingers might as well be trained seals unless there's a mind flexing behind them."[55] It would be easy to be uncharitable here and simply say that Lester Bangs was not very bright: I'm not sure how anyone could listen to Emerson's playing on "Lachesis" or the 2nd Impression of "Karn Evil 9" and say it sounds like something a trained seal could accomplish. Indeed, it is tempting to see a Stalinist anti-intellectualism (or "anti-formalism") in the critics' insistence that rock should remain "simple" in order to retain its populist purity. It would certainly be easy to suggest that a critic like Bangs didn't like progressive rock because it was over his head: rather than make the effort to understand it, why not put a premium on musical simplicity?

However, I will take the high road and attempt to give a serious answer to the criticism implicit in Bangs's statement (more accurately, screed) quoted above. I hope that if I have demonstrated anything at all in this book, it is this: for the best progressive rock, classical forms and virtuoso chops are *not* ends in themselves—they are simply a means to an end, that end being the expression of feelings and ideas as emphatically as possible through music. At the risk of becoming wearisome, let me say it again—the importance of progressive rock's appropriation of classical forms is *not* that it automatically "elevates" rock by drawing on the trappings high culture, but rather that it gives progressive rock musicians a new and especially appropriate set of tools for expressing the visionary subject matter that was part and parcel of the late-sixties/early-seventies counterculture. Likewise, the importance of progressive rock's emphasis on virtuosity is *not* that so-and-so is a great musician because he can play so many thirty-second notes per second; rather, virtuosos (such as a Keith Emerson or a Carl Palmer) develop a very broad and deep vocabulary that, if appropriate used, allows them to express musical ideas and feelings in more and in different ways. I would not argue that Emerson or Palmer always used their virtuosity as wisely as they might have; young virtuosos in all styles of music tend to play a lot of notes just because they can, and

---

[55] Bangs, "Exposed!" 77.

only gradually realize the value of understatement. On the other hand, ELP did mature, and by their "golden age" (*Trilogy/Brain Salad Surgery*) they had made considerable strides in becoming a band that knew when to lay it on and when to hold back.

As for the accusation that ELP—or prog in general—was too "robotic" because of its perceived overreliance on technology, this seems an especially vacuous charge by the standards of the late 1990s and beyond, when the really cutting-edge styles (such as techno and rap) have tended to dispose of "musicians" altogether in favor of digital sampling and sequencing. True, by the standards of the early 1970s, prog seemed dauntingly technology-dependent: when Bangs said, "The sight of the massed ELP arsenal would chill the follicles off H. G. Wells,"[56] he probably was expressing a not uncommon opinion. On the other hand, when one thumbs through the most recent issue of *Rolling Stone, Spin, Option,* or *The Wire*, it's clear that at some point over the last twenty to twenty-five years critics overcame their aversion of music technology, based on the praise that is lavished on techno, rap, or related styles in which the music may be entirely electronically generated. So what happened?

In the early 1970s, the kind of state-of-the-art analog technology used with such virtuosity by ELP, Pink Floyd, et al. was unavailable to any but the wealthy, and therefore a stigma of elitism attached itself to the use of such equipment.[57] With the undeniable strain of primitivism inherent in the Bangs-Christgau-Marsh school of critics, it's easy enough to understand why the "hi-tech" music of prog could be lambasted for emotional frigidity, while the "low tech" music of soul, funk, and punk could be praised for its emotional immediacy.

What the critics didn't foresee, of course, was the digital revolution of the mid-1980s at the hands of rappers, ravers, and so on, gave music technology a new kind of street credibility, and logically enough critics abandoned their earlier linkages of hi-tech and emotional frigidity. By the time this shift in the critics' outlook took place during the 1980s, though, progressive rock had been so thoroughly discredited for so long that the critics felt absolutely no obligation to explain how music that relied completely on digital technology for its existence could be heartfelt and emotional, but music that relied on analog technology was of necessity cold, heartless, and sterile.

One issue that I have skirted a number of times in previous chapters is the pervasive feeling that ELP were controlled by their equipment. Was this a valid charge? On the whole, I would have to say no. Granted, some-

---

[56] Bangs, "Exposed!" 40.
[57] In the preprog era the availability of such equipment was even more circumscribed, being limited largely to composers and musicians who were on the faculties of major research universities.

times on the first three albums the synthesizer does sound like an exotic afterthought to the essential organ-piano-bass-drums instrumentation (*Tarkus* is almost certainly the worst offender in this regard). However, by the time of *Trilogy* and *Brain Salad Surgery* Emerson had made the Moog an integral part of the music. It is true that Emerson often did use the Moog as an orchestral substitute or as a more timbrally varied extension of the Hammond, but the fact is the Moog parts are not only crucial to the musical fabric, they are very distinctive: Emerson's Moog trumpet setting is every bit as individual as Jimi Hendrix's or Jimmy Page's guitar timbre. And the fact is that on some occasions Emerson was an extraordinarily imaginative synthesist, "Toccata," the 3rd Impression of "Karn Evil 9," and the live version of "Aquatarkus" being especially good examples.

Likewise, critics often cited the multiple keyboard set-up of the 1973-74 World Tour as a sign of Emerson's colossal vanity and addiction to new technology for its own sake. As I've already pointed out, though, due to the state of synthesizer technology of that era, Emerson needed that many to successfully reproduce the varied timbres required in ELP's two- to two-and-one-half hour live set. No one would have been happier than Emerson if one synthesizer could have negotiated all the timbral changes necessary for a live performance of ELP's repertoire. In short, there was little gimmickry involved in ELP's use of music technology, and such gimmicks as ELP did use (for example, Carl Palmer's synthesized percussion) can hardly be considered a central part of the band's sound.

So now we come to the central issue inherent in the preceding discussion of the blues orthodoxists and their primitivist ideology. Was ELP's music cold, heartless, unemotional, sterile, and lacking in feeling?

No. If anything, ELP's music in their first six albums takes in a surprisingly wide range of moods, feelings, and emotional landscapes. There's aggression ("Toccata," the instrumental sections of *Tarkus*), heroic striving ("Karn Evil 9"), and a pastoral tranquility that tends towards the slightly melancholy ("Take a Pebble" or any of Lake's best ballads). There's also romantic longing (the opening of "Trilogy"), macho rock-and-roll posturing ("Living Sin"), and a kind of transcendental space-age mystical rapture (the live version of "Aquatarkus"). And this is not a complete catalog of ELP's emotional repertoire—I don't know if one could compile such a thing, as it would be a bit different for each person—it's simply an example of the emotional range of the band's music.

ELP were keenly aware of the charges of "coldness" and "emotional sterility" that were often brought against their music. Unfortunately, on the whole they didn't answer these charges any more precisely than they answered the charges that they borrowed classical forms simply to make rock "respectable" and please the "elite." Sometimes Keith Emerson offered a wholesale rejection of any charges of unemotionalism:

How many different emotions are there? Like anger, hate, love. All these emotions are created from their opposite. Before they say we're being unemotional they'd better get to know us a lot better. They've got to get down to what created the emotion in the first place. The way we created a piece of music might come from a lot of different areas of emotion, but nobody has the right to criticize us and say it's unemotional until they really know exactly what it is that makes us create the music in the first place.[58]

At other times, however, he suggested that such charges could always be expected when virtuosity and structural complexity were an element in the music: "I know, it [the band's musical structure] has become extremely tight, I must admit. But we are striving for perfection and it's obvious that when you are, this feeling of discipline, lack of freedom if you like, is going to come about. But musicians like Oscar Peterson have been criticized for being so mechanical and it doesn't dispute the fact that he's an excellent musician."[59]

Part of the problem, which as far as I can see both ELP and their critics failed to grasp, is that by the 1973-74 period critics were tending to evaluate the emotional content of ELP's music and their stage show as if they were one and the same thing. They are not. There are simply no grounds for the charge that ELP's music is cold, sterile, and heartless. On the other hand, I'm afraid that some of the charges of unemotionalism that critics leveled against the band's monumental stage show may not have been without substance. Readers of *Rocking the Classics* may recall that I did not tend to see the monumental, extravagant stage productions that characterized the major rock bands of the 1970s in a terribly positive light. Allow me to quote myself:

The musical concert as a multimedia experience is a concept that has been pursued throughout much of the twentieth century—as early as 1911 the Russian composer Alexander Scriabin called for colored lights to flood the concert hall during the performance of his symphonic poem *Prometheus*—and is certainly a worthy goal. We have already seen that progressive rock was the first style of popular music to exploit synthesizers in a systematic way; the genre also must be given credit for developing psychedelic music's conception of the concert as a multimedia experience more thoroughly than any other contemporary genre of popular music. Yet there seems to be little doubt that the visual elements of these concerts became something of a two-edged sword for these bands . . . The problem with ELP's catapulting pianos and Pink Floyd's crashing airplanes is that the relationship between music and image became increasingly tenuous. As often as not, image was employed as a spectacle in and of

---

[58] Keith Emerson, quoted by Stein, "ELP," 9.
[59] Keith Emerson, quoted by Penny Valentine, "Keith Emerson in the Sounds Talk-In," *Sounds*, March 31, 1973, 26.

itself, as an attempt to make up for the loss of a meaningful symbiotic relationship between musicians and audiences that occurred when progressive rock bands made the move from clubs and small venues to arenas and stadiums.[60]

In closing this chapter, then, it is needful to consider the critical reception of ELP's stage show of the 73-74 era, with the goal of winnowing out which objections are justified and which are not.

It would appear that the shows ELP played in Japan during the summer of 1972 represented a kind of turning point. As personal interaction with the audience became increasingly impossible as the venues that they performed at became incrementally larger, they began to think in terms of a show that was specially designed for enormous venues and huge audiences. Said Barbara Graustark:

> A recent Japanese tour crystallized the idea in their minds to turn their concerts into travelling circus shows, presenting historic feats in rock entertainment as well as superb music. The Japanese concerts, they noted, were almost vaudevillian in appearance, with many people participating and each performer playing several instruments. Now, says Greg, ELP, too, are ready to change the structure of their new act . . . "I think the whole concert concept will become more showy to the point where it will almost become a gypsy caravan . . . It will give an aura like a circus trip."[61]

The 1973-74 World Tour marked the logical climax of this conception.

Of course, one could argue that to a point at least this concept of a rock concert was a logical outgrowth of the spectacularly increased size of rock audiences that bands like ELP played to. Simply standing on stage and playing works well enough for an audience of 500 or 1,000, but becomes problematic in front of an audience of 50,000 where audience members in the back of the stadium can barely see the performers. Thus there arose the staples of ELP's visual extravaganzas: laser lights, revolving drum rostrums, self-destructing modular synthesizers, catapulting pianos, a Moog ribbon controller that shot pyrotechnics over the audience's heads, and so on. One could argue that this kind of stage show is both peculiarly American (in that the parallels with Disneyland and the like are obvious) and very much a product of the early 1970s, when general economic prosperity made spectacle on this scale a viable proposition. If the following remark by Keith Emerson reveals mixed feelings about the band's reliance on visual spectacle for their live shows, it also shows his genuine perception of the psychology of his American audiences:

---

[60] Macan, *Rocking the Classics*, 63–64.
[61] Barbara Graustark, "ELP: Rock Kings Turn Gypsies For Pop Extravaganza," *Circus*, January 1973, 59.

All our visual effects are an external luxury as far as the audience is concerned, but I must stress that it doesn't affect my playing, so I go along with these things. I think audiences are like children. They've become overfed. If you give kids sweets they want more sweets until they become sick. The public has become used to mixed-media entertainment. Modern living today [1974] is programmed for a band like ELP—we write and perform music for today and that's precisely why Americans find our music easier to assimilate into their lifestyle than the British do. ELP hits them right between the teeth and they can't ignore us. We do invade their privacy. We do impose upon them, but the Americans love to be imposed on. [Were truer words ever spoken?] You can't ignore us . . . not in terms of volume but in terms of dynamics.[62]

Of course, the obvious, and not altogether unjustified conclusion one could draw here, is that ELP, instead of attempting to create a sort of symbiotic dialogue with their audience, simply aimed to bludgeon them into submission. This was a frequent charge from rock journalists of the time, who decried both the lack of spontaneity and the lack of opportunity for audience interaction in ELP's show.

As was too often the case, the band's defense of their stage show against charges of emotional sterility often weren't terribly eloquent. When Lester Bangs asked Greg Lake, "Don't you ever find that you reach a point where whatever emotional content the presentation might have is overrun and washed away by the force of sheer technology?" Lake answered, "Good question. No . . . no. Because we choose the places in which to express the emotions and the places in which to express the technique, hoping one doesn't interfere with the other."[63] Not exactly a rousing defense.

In many cases, attacks on ELP's stage show and attacks on ELP's music became confused. Peter Erskine's *New Musical Express* review of *Welcome Back My Friends* begins with the extremely unconvincing (and entirely unsupported) assertion that "reasonable scrutiny unearths the controversial suggestion that, when you come right close to it, the playing really ain't too bobby-dazzling—and that, after all, was always the traditional bolt-hole of the more 'reasonable' disbelievers."[64] However, Erskine quickly moves on to the issue that for him is the real crux of the matter, which is not the music at all, but rather the manner in which the music is presented in concert: "The thing about an ELP gig is that it does it all for you. Sit back, relax, turn off your mind and float off into the fog. There's no ques-

---

[62] Keith Emerson, quoted by Carr, "Loneliness of a Long-Distance Power Cell," 5.
[63] Bangs, "Exposed!" 77.
[64] Peter Erskine, "Pocket Calculator Rockers Wreak Digital Doze-Out" [review of *Welcome Back My Friends*], *New Musical Express*, August 3, 1974, 14. Notice how British reviewers like Erskine are beginning to adopt the cynical, pseudo-hip, slangy Brooklyn lingo of Lester Bangs and Robert Christgau by 1974.

tion of participation—not even a gently tapping foot, an occasional, nonchalant fingerpop; you're simply sat there like a bunch of dummies at a Cycling Proficiency lecture. It's humiliating."[65] A more levelheaded and responsible concert review by James Johnson of ELP live at Empire Pool, Wembley, on April 20, 1974, makes essentially the same point. Johnson acknowledges ELP's show was overpowering (unlike Erskine, Johnson doesn't deny the band's staggering musical execution), but at the expense of spontaneity or any real performer-audience interaction:

> Somehow as Keith and Carl positioned themselves among their equipment it was like the machinery was more immense than the man and had to be boarded carefully, in the fashion of astronauts placing themselves in a space capsule. Swiftly the spikey, leathered, buccaneer figure of Emerson struck the two opening chords of "Hoedown" and take-off was successfully completed.
>
> In execution the show was faultless. Somebody said later it might as well have been a film of the show, perfected some while back. At headlong speed, Emerson's manic, spiralling solos were note-for-note exact, mostly the slides were beautifully apt, and the spots pounded the stage with color. All was triumphal in the extreme.
>
> So much so everybody in the hall appeared glazed by it all. It was odd. Only when Emerson took a portable keyboard [the Moog ribbon controller], spurting blobs of fire into the front 30 rows, with a muscular roadie to help him on and off stage, did anybody edge forward in their seats . . .
>
> Certainly part of their attraction must lie in the show's grandiose nature. It's an epic. But then again, awe-struck wonder does not always endure for over two hours.[66]

Johnson clearly dislikes the generally serious nature of ELP's shows:

> An ELP concert is plainly a serious pilgrimage. The crowd who tramped the streets towards the Empire Pool on Saturday were uniform heavy-duty denim, unsmiling and dour, almost drab. I think few concerts in recent times have attracted a bunch of people less disposed towards frivolousness . . . At present the show is all rather humorless. One may be left open-mouthed at the size of it all, reeling at the sound and the complexity, reveling in the splendor, but it's so intense I wonder whether anybody, on either side of the stage, really had very much fun.[67]

Here I think Johnson falls victim to the prejudices of the then-rising blues orthodoxy school of rock criticism: rock shouldn't get too big for its britches and try to make a Statement, it should merely entertain, give the folks a pleasant bit of diversion, a nice escape from the pressures of the

---

[65] Ibid.
[66] Johnson, "Welcome Back My Friends."
[67] Ibid.

day. I believe that first of all, such a view sells rock far short of what it is (or at any rate was) capable of. Second, I believe that if we were to follow Johnson's criticism to its logical conclusion, there would be no room for Shakespeare's tragedies, Beethoven and Wagner (or much of any nineteenth-century German music), or movies like *Citizen Cain* or *Schindler's List*. This is not to say that entertainment can't sometimes also be art. Nor is it to say that humor never masks profundity. What I am saying, however, is that sometimes artists do not serve their public best by offering them "fun." Sometimes, if artists *do* have something serious to say (a possibility that the blues orthodoxists often seem to find almost incredible), it is best said seriously.

Therefore, I do not find Johnson's criticism of the lack of "fun" in ELP's music or stage show particularly damning. However, I do find that some of his other criticisms sink deeper. It cannot be denied that the lavish extravaganza that constituted ELP's stage show circa 1973-74 did indeed tend to eliminate opportunities for genuinely spontaneous audience-performer interaction. As I admitted in *Rocking the Classics,*

> There is no doubt that as these bands lost the opportunity to enjoy a symbiotic relationship with a distinct regional subculture, they increasingly called upon virtuosity, visual spectacle, and a certain sense of imperial remoteness to cement (and then hold) their large American fan base. To the degree that this is true, one could say progressive rock's love of spectacle was self-indulgent, its fondness for virtuosity and technical pyrotechnics exhibitionistic, and its penchant for fantasy a form of self-absorption.[68]

There is also no doubt that ELP were one of the earliest and most prominent practitioners of this new kind of stage show. However, let's put things in perspective. Even if we were to give ELP credit for "inventing" this kind of stage show—which I think may be giving ELP too much credit—the simple fact is that this new approach to the rock concert, as a multimedia special-effects extravaganza, would have happened whether there had been an ELP or not. No less a figure than Robert Fripp broke up King Crimson at the height of their powers in 1974 in part because he realized that most fans didn't *want* a more intimate and challenging performer-audience interaction; they *wanted* to be mute spectators at a multimedia extravaganza, something that Fripp (almost alone among major rock figures of his day) would have no part of.[69]

The fact is, ELP's stage show was no more bombastic or "unfeeling" than fellow progsters like Yes and Pink Floyd, and was in fact a model of good taste and concision compared to the ludicrous and vulgar concerts

---

[68] Macan, *Rocking the Classics,* 176–77.
[69] See Tamm, *Robert Fripp,* 75–76.

of many of the glam-rock acts of the seventies. Think Kiss, Queen, Alice Cooper, or perhaps more controversially (simply because their shows were more intelligent), Elton John or David Bowie: how much real performer-audience interaction was there at a seventies glam-rock show? And, if ELP's show was a model of taste compared to seventies glam rock, then it was a model of humility compared to some of the extravaganzas mounted by prominent acts of the eighties like U2, as Paul Stump has pointed out.[70]

In sum, it's not so much that I mind the critics ravaging ELP's stage show for its "sleek unfeeling lunar inhumaneness," as Lester Bangs put it.[71] What I *do* mind is how selectively and hypocritically the critics have targeted acts for this kind of show: when's the last time you heard a U2 (or even a David Bowie) show described in these terms? Just as the blues orthodoxists have vainly tried to isolate progressive rock from the mainstream of seventies rock, depicting it as an evolutionary dead end, they've tried to isolate ELP as practitioners of a "sterile" and "inhuman" type of multimedia rock show that was somehow a bizarre deviation from developments in mainstream rock of the seventies.

But it wasn't. ELP's stage show of the 73-74 World Tour was at the very cutting edge of what became the mainstream in seventies rock concerts. Keith Emerson was absolutely right when he said in 1974, "we write and perform music for today." We may rightly bewail that ELP, unlike Fripp, did not see the underlying dangers inherent in the conception of rock concert as multimedia spectacle, as three-ring circus, and that they did not see beyond the excesses of their times. However, we cannot reasonably say that ELP were some kind of bizarre deviation from the mainstream of their era: they exemplified the mainstream, and to some degree helped to create it. If any band perfectly encapsulated the confidence, idealism, and excesses of the 1970–75 post-countercultural era all at once, it was ELP.

---

[70] Stump, *The Music's All That Matters*, 346.
[71] Bangs, "Exposed!" 78.

11 Return of the Kings

Works, Volume I
(1975–1977)

Sabbatical: 1975-76

After their gigantic World Tour of 1973-74 finally ground to a halt, the trio scattered for a well-deserved respite from the public eye—a break that eventually extended to two and a half years. During that time, much changed. As I argued in *Rocking the Classics*, the optimistic, utopian spirit of the counterculture was made possible at least in part by the general economic prosperity of the 1960s, a prosperity that extended back to the post–World War II period. Paul Stump names a number of events he believes brought the optimistic "good vibes" mentality of the late-sixties/early-seventies counterculture to a screeching halt.[1] I would point particularly to the Yom Kippur War between Israel and its Arab neighbors of October 1973, and its aftermath, as watershed events. In an effort to punish Israel and its Western allies, the OPEC cartel, dominated by Arab oil-producing nations, raised its prices precipitously: between October 1973 and January 1974 the price of crude oil rose from $3.00 to $11.65 per barrel.[2] It did not take long for the results to be felt. Over the next two to three years, unemployment soared; as the cost of living began to rise much more quickly than wages, families saw their budgets strained, and standards of living began to fall for the first time in nearly two generations; inflation began to spiral out of control; and, as if in response, violent crime underwent a sudden and spectacular surge.[3] By the late 1970s, the optimism and utopianism of the counterculture seemed a distant memory, and the ambition of a countercultural musical style like progressive rock

---

[1] Stump, *The Music's All that Matters*, 261.
[2] David Hackett Fischer, *The Great Wave: Price Revolutions and the Rhythm of History* (New York: Oxford University Press, 1996), 208.
[3] Fischer, in his brilliant book, traces a convincing parallel between price surges and waves of violent crime from the fourteenth century to the present; see *The Great Wave*, 305–11.

351

seemed like empty bombast, all the more lamentable for its apparent inability to recognize its growing cultural irrelevance.

The year 1976 seems to have been an especially crucial demarcating point: disco and punk rock, two genres of music that seemed to be in opposition to every ideal that progressive music stood for, both emerged that year. Granted, punk rock, with its short, three-chord songs, nearly incomprehensible shouted lyrics, and its slam-dancing and body-pierced fans, was never more than a cult style in the U.S. during the 1970s: it was to be many years before its impact was fully felt. Likewise, disco, the most vapid and plastic transformation imaginable of sixties soul and seventies funk, only lasted a couple of years before it petered out.[4] Nonetheless, the impact of these two styles on popular culture of the time was huge. Disco returned dancing, which had been increasingly marginalized during the decade of rock's "golden age" (1965–75), to the forefront of popular music culture. Punk, with its self-consciously antivirtuoso and antiprofessional ethos, recovered rock as the "people's music": once again anybody who owned a guitar, an amplifier, and who knew a few chords could play rock and roll. Neither punk nor disco put any stock in the romantic transcendentalism and the modernist pretensions to cultural relevance that were so central to prog. By the late 1970s, New Wave, a style that united

---

[4] I am getting extremely tired of so-called scholars and critics who ought to know better labeling anybody who doesn't tow the orthodox rock historian's line that disco was "vital" and "important" as "racist" and "homophobic." Michael Campbell, in his frequently wrong-headed history of American popular music, *The Beat Goes On: An Introduction to Popular Music in America, 1840 to Today* (New York: Schirmer Books, 1996), is a particularly egregious offender. Campbell's claim that the remarkably unanimous opposition to disco among rock audiences of the later seventies evinces deep-seated racist and homophobic attitudes ("it is easy to infer sexual and racial prejudice in the virulent reaction against disco," 302; "homophobia was part of disco-bashing's hidden agenda," 303) is extremely problematic for two reasons. First, rock's white middle-class audience knew little of disco's origins among gays and blacks; much of their early knowledge of disco's cultural origins stems from the extremely popular movie starring John Travolta, *Saturday Night Fever* (1977), in which disco's tie to black culture is deemphasized and its tie to gay culture is entirely glossed over. Second, Campbell and his peers seem to find it incredible that rock audiences of the time could have been intelligent enough to intensely dislike disco because they understood it directly undermined every Romantic and modernist ideal that underpinned the "classic rock" era of 1965–75: music as prophetic utterance, the musician as prophet figure, instrumental virtuosity as symbol of transcendental experience. The fact is, while disco adheres to the repetitive structures and simple metric patterns of earlier African American forms (which made it seem intolerably simplistic to fans of ELP, Yes, Led Zeppelin, etc.), its practitioners usually show none of the subtlety in perpetually varying timbral and rhythmic parameters which made earlier styles of African American music that could have been equally simplistic (for instance, the blues) such musically rich forms. I would challenge a popular-music scholar who thinks I have disco "wrong" to demonstrate wherein its musical richness lies, rather than telling me I'm racist or homophobic because I'm dismissive of it.

disco's punchy bass lines and dance rhythms with punk's guitar riffs and fashion sense, was becoming all the rage on both sides of the Atlantic. I think it is possible to argue that by 1977, the year ELP launched their comeback, progressive rock was already as much a style of an earlier era as it is today.

Of course, the implications of this shift in zeitgeist were not immediately evident, and into the later 1970s the prog megabands retained their iconic, larger-than-life status. Certainly the ELP organization initially showed no signs of panic. To the contrary, its slow, methodical preparation for the band's reappearance showed a high level of confidence. The original plan of action had called for Emerson, Lake, and Palmer to each release a solo album at some point during the 1975-76 period. In the November 1974 issue of *Circus*, Manticore's Mario Medious is quoted as saying, "Right now Keith and Carl are both about fifty percent finished with theirs. Greg's written his whole album, but so far he's only recorded one track. It's called 'C'est la vie.'" Medious went on to say,

> Most of Greg's album will be acoustic, like this cut. [Here Medious played "C'est la vie" for the reporter.] On the other hand, Keith's and Carl's albums will both have a classical sound to them—a few cuts are going to have a big band feel. And Carl's has one out-and-out rocker. It's called "LA '74," because that's where and when it was recorded. Joe Walsh plays guitar on it, and Ian McDonald, who played sax for King Crimson, is on it.[5]

ELP fans will recognize both "C'est la vie" and "LA '74" from *Works, Volume I* (the latter had by its release been renamed "LA Nights"). In this interview Medious also mentions that the band's next single will be "Tiger in a Spotlight"—which, of course, was eventually released on *Works, Volume II*. In fact, a surprising amount of material that is associated with ELP's late-1970s output was recorded before 1975.

This is true, for instance, of Greg Lake's 1975 seasonal hit single "I Believe in Father Christmas," cowritten with Pete Sinfield. One of Lake's loveliest acoustic ballads, the single of "Father Christmas" features him accompanied by a hundred-piece orchestra and large choir. Originally, Manticore had planned to rush the record out in time for Christmas 1974, but, said *International Musician*, "it was felt that there was insufficient time for promotion, and in the way that only immensely secure and confident companies can do, Manticore planned for a 1975 Christmas season release. This time there was plenty of time for promotion."[6] A short promo film (a forerunner of the MTV music video) was shot in

---

[5] Jim O'Connor, "ELP Split for Solo Exploits," *Circus*, November 1974, 51.
[6] "Greg Lake," *International Musician*, January 1976, 15–16.

Israel in November 1975, and featured Lake playing his acoustic guitar in the cave where the Dead Sea Scrolls were found, interspersed with war footage and a clip of a soldier coming home and being greeted by his young daughter. The single was released shortly thereafter, and was a smash hit in the U.K., reaching number two on the British charts, although its impact in the U.S. was initially fairly marginal (it charted out at 95). Eventually, though, the single did become something of a perennial staple on FM rock radio in the U.S. Incidentally, the B-side of "Father Christmas" is "Humbug," an odd little ditty in which a male chorus repeats the title endlessly to a kind of gauzy, surreal ragtime accompaniment that sounds a bit like a musical excerpt from one of Woody Allen's absurdist comedies of the 1970s.

The year 1975 saw the trio slowly but methodically recording material for their solo albums. In April of that year, Emerson recorded some stride/boogie-oriented material with a small horn section in London's Advision Studios, including "Honky Tonk Train Blues" and "Barrelhouse Shakedown." In five sessions of November 18–19 and December 1–3, he recorded his Piano Concerto no. 1 with the London Philharmonic Orchestra, conducted by John Mayer, as well as orchestral arrangements of "Abaddon's Bolero" (from *Trilogy*) and Scott Joplin's "Maple Leaf Rag"; these sessions took place at De Lane Lea Studios, Wembley. Palmer's orchestral material was recorded at roughly the same time. His rocked-up arrangement of Sergei Prokofiev's "The Enemy God Dances with the Black Spirits" (second movement of the *Scythian Suite*), which features Palmer accompanying the London Philharmonic, was recorded at De Lane Lea in September. Joseph Horovitz's Percussion Concerto, with Palmer as soloist, was recorded in early 1976 (January 28 and February 1–2) at De Lane Lea, with Horovitz conducting the LPO.[7] Likewise, some of Greg Lake's acoustic ballads were recorded (or, in the case of "C'est la vie," partially re-recorded) at Advision during August 1975. Of the limited amount of material the band recorded together in 1975, just one short track has ever been released: the bluesy, hard-driving instrumental "Bo Diddley" which, as it turned out, was not released until 1993, when it appeared on the *Return of the Manticore* retrospective box set.

By early 1976, the musicians had enough material recorded for their solo albums, and began to debate the best strategy for releasing their solo work; they also began to work in earnest on generating material for a new group album. By then, however, another situation had reared its head. Since the draconian tax laws of 1974 had been passed by the British parliament, most British rock royalty had split the U.K.; they risked losing

---

[7] All these dates are taken from Philip Stuart's *London Philharmonic Discography* (Westport, CT: Greenwood Press, 1997).

too much of their income if they lived and worked in the U.K. more than a set number of days per year. ELP hung on longer than many of their peers; by early 1976, however, they too had enough.

While Keith Emerson was visiting the Montreux (Switzerland) Jazz Festival in July 1975, the founder of the festival, Claude Nobbs, informed him that a new state-of-the-art recording studio was being built in the city; would ELP be interested in residing in Montreux for a period of time? The suggestion was sympathetically received, and by February 1976 Emerson, his wife, Elinor, and five-year-old son, Aaron, Lake and his wife, Regina (neé Bottcher, a German model whom he had married in 1974), Carl Palmer, and a number of key members of the ELP organization had taken up residence on or near the shores of Lake Geneva: Emerson's second son, Damon, was in fact born in Montreux in April 1976. Emerson and Lake both owned large estates in southern England, Emerson's in Sussex, Lake's in Berkshire (although Emerson's house had burned down in 1975 and was being rebuilt at this time), but they were obliged to keep visits back to their British homes very short, stopping off just long enough not to be penalized by the stringent tax laws. Emerson, in particular, was to become a long-term exile from the U.K.: in December 1976, after the band's stay in Montreux had ended, he and his family moved to Nassau, Bahamas, where they soon afterward purchased a villa on a stretch of private beach. The Emersons did not permanently return to England until the early 1980s.

The band spent much of 1976 in Montreux working at Mountain Recording Studios: Greg Lake put finishing touches on a number of the acoustic ballads intended for his solo album, and the band as a unit recorded their epic arrangement of Aaron Copland's "Fanfare for the Common Man" in three separate sets of sessions in April, August, and September. The band's tracks for Keith Emerson's "Pirates"—arguably the last great ELP epic—were recorded in Montreux; in November, orchestral tracks were added in Paris at Pathé Marconi EMI Studios, with Godfrey Salmon conducting the Orchestra de l'Opera de Paris, and shortly thereafter, Greg Lake added his vocal part in London's Advision Studios.

By late 1976, with the exception of Greg Lake's single "I Believe in Father Christmas," ELP had been out of the public eye for over two years, an impossibly long time by 1970s standards. ELP realized that even for a band of their stature, it would be dangerous to stay out of sight much longer, especially since the pop music scene was beginning to change so rapidly. Faced with these changing circumstances, the band arrived at two fateful decisions, which, I think, marked the beginning of the end of the original incarnation of ELP. First, they decided to combine the best of the solo and group material on a two-LP set. The new ELP album was to be called *Works, Volume I*, a title chosen by Pete Sinfield, who remarked,

"The title was my idea. I suppose if you're going to be pretentious, you might as well do it big."[8] Carl Palmer attributes the idea of combining band and solo music to the band's manager, Stewart Young:

> Originally what happened is we all went off and recorded the pieces of music we each wanted to do. And after about six months, we got together and said we've got this and that of group material and this and that of individual stuff. So we played through the individual stuff, and suddenly it all clicked. Everybody had used an orchestra, had something with like brass and strings and woodwinds. And Stewart Young came up with the idea of packaging it this way . . . We also knew the problems about releasing individual albums. If you release them too close to each other, one takes the sales from the other. So when Stewart said how about doing it this way, we thought that would be interesting and went ahead and packaged it as you have it now.[9]

However, Emerson recalls Lake as having originated the idea of releasing the solo and group material in a single package: "The question was posed of what to do with all our material. Eventually, it was Greg's idea to record with a solo side apiece. It took me awhile to agree to that because I'd been wanting to do a total solo thing for a long time."[10]

Lake had privately expressed concern that the emphasis on the solo material was pulling the band apart, and the packaging idea for the new album (whether it was the idea of Lake, Young, or both) was a laudable attempt to demonstrate ELP's unity in diversity, to show the band could still function as a coherent unit while pursuing their individual interests. Unfortunately, I think the way *Works I* was packaged demonstrated precisely what ELP were trying to paper over: they were in fact pulling in very different directions, and finding any compelling strands of common interest was becoming increasingly difficult. The music of the three musicians was often so different that its proximity sounds rather arbitrary. Of course, this had always been the case to some degree: but one major factor behind the peculiar power of the first six albums is the tension generated by the musicians' attempts to resolve and reconcile their different interests. That tension is lost here. Furthermore, the group side of the album demonstrates one of the fundamental truths of all the great rock bands of the 1960s and 1970s: the

---

[8] Peter Sinfield, quoted by Stump, *The Music's All That Matters*, 218. Emerson, however, has said the idea for the title was his: see *Pictures of an Exhibitionist*, 306.

[9] Carl Palmer, quoted by Al Rudis, "Guess Who's Back With 35 Tons of Equipment," *Sounds*, May 21, 1977, 24.

[10] Keith Emerson, quoted by Jim Farber, "The Emerson, Lake and Palmer Tapes, Part 3: Keith Emerson," *Circus*, September 1977, 28. Incidentally, when Sonny Fox asked the band in a radio interview of May 14, 1977, whose idea the group-solo package was, Emerson replied it was Lake's; Lake, who was also present, made no protest or denial.

whole is inevitably greater than the sum of its parts. This demonstration, unfortunately, takes place at the expense of the individual members' solo material.

Even as the band was settling on the idea of releasing a two-LP set that would unite solo and group material, they also had to address how a tour to promote such an album would work. According to Emerson, Greg Lake had suggested that since the three had used orchestral accompaniment on their solo material, they ought to tour with an orchestra, and Emerson ought to write a large-scale piece for ELP with orchestral backing.[11] The more Emerson mulled over Lake's suggestion, the better he liked it. However, even for a band of ELP's stature, the idea of touring with a full orchestra posed huge obstacles. Taking a traditional symphony orchestra out on the road is, in and of itself, an enormously expensive proposition; ELP would be faced with the additional challenge of putting together a sound system sophisticated enough to create an acceptable mix of the orchestra's acoustic instruments and ELP's electronic gear. Based on later remarks, Lake and Palmer soon began to entertain grave doubts about the viability of the idea. However, Emerson became increasingly insistent on pursuing it, so the band began to address the issue of financing such an undertaking.

At one time ELP had entertained high hopes that their Manticore studio would become a cash cow, with other megabands regularly renting the facility and their equipment while they were off the road; these hopes never fully materialized, and by the end of 1976 the facility was sold. Likewise, the Manticore label was increasingly seen as expendable: by the end of 1976 ELP had helped such bands as remained on the label to find contracts elsewhere, the label was dissolved, and Manticore was reorganized as a publishing company (which it remained into the early 1980s). ELP renewed their relationship with their old label, Atlantic, signing a worldwide contract to handle future releases. These moves, which remind one a bit of the Roman Empire giving up its outlying provinces in order to more adequately defend its territorial heartland from the growing barbarian threat during the Empire's final days, generated some of the cash necessary to finance the orchestral undertaking. Emerson, Lake, Palmer, and Stewart Young put up huge sums of their own (one report had Emerson, Lake and Palmer putting up a million dollars each). By late 1976, Godfrey Salmon and his assistant Tony Harris had left for the U.S. in order to begin the process of auditioning young musicians in six different cities for positions in the ELP touring orchestra: by one report upwards of 5,000 prospective musicians requested an audition.[12]

---

[11] Emerson, *Pictures of an Exhibitionist*, 296.
[12] John Orme, "ELP: Blood, Sweat, and Real Tears as Money Turns U.S. Tour Sour," *Melody Maker*, July 9, 1977, 3.

By March 1977, ELP had set up camp in Montréal in preparation for a new North American tour. *Works I* was released to great music industry fanfare in late March. It charted at a respectable twelve in the U.S. charts, and remained in the top two-hundred for twenty-six weeks (the same length as *Tarkus*), demonstrating that interest in the band continued unabated despite the rapidly changing popular music scene. The album charted out slightly higher in the U.K., reaching number nine.

Works, Volume I
Side One: Keith Emerson

Side one of the LP format contained Keith Emerson's long-awaited Piano Concerto no. 1. Even before ELP's extended break, it was clear that Emerson wanted to move into the field of "serious" music. In fact, although the Concerto was recorded in 1975, he was sketching it by 1973, as is evidenced by the clip in the *Manticore Special* documentary that shows Emerson working through the cadenza of the first movement in the practice room of Stonehill, his Tudor manor house. Writing about Emerson's meeting with Alberto Ginastera in 1973, James Johnson remarked,

> Emerson seems quite impressed by the composer; the man's style and his general upright manner. Maybe he'd like to see himself in a similar position in years to come—as a respected musician and composer, and not just within rock circles. "I don't write for the music to be forgotten in six months. I like to think the music I've created is my own, that it hasn't come from anything else I've heard before, and it'd be nice for it to last."[13]

Clearly, a desire for respect among "serious" music circles and a concern that he no longer be regarded as a "mere" rock musician was beginning to gnaw at Emerson, and may explain his insistence that ELP only tour again if accompanied by an orchestra. Certainly, he was convinced by his experience with the London Philharmonic Orchestra that his rock background made him *persona non grata* in the rarified world of classical music. He has commented on the disrespect shown him by the LPO on a number of occasions:

> When I brought my piano concerto in to be recorded . . . I got the usual larking about. People would go to the back where the conductor couldn't see them and get the porny magazines out . . . This was the London Philharmonic. I took a ten-minute break that I didn't owe to them just so they could practice their

---

[13] Johnson, "Fingers' Cave," 11.

parts. In fact, it was the orchestra leader's decision that it might be a good idea. But they didn't practice one bit. They didn't even bother. They just sat there and smoked and talked.[14]

In fact, Emerson found the results of this initial session (October 16, 1975 at Kingsway Hall) unusable, and was obliged to schedule another round of sessions in late November/early December at Wembley's De Lane Lea Studios, this time with a hand-picked group of brass players, in order to achieve satisfactory results.

Emerson's Concerto is composed in the traditional three-movement format. While there is no extramusical program to the Concerto, he has suggested there were extramusical inspirations to the first and third movements:

> I wrote the first movement because I'd done the typical pop musician's thing and bought a house in the country; it was very nice and peaceful there, so it does reflect the countryside quite a lot. The last movement reflects how I felt at that time [1975] because the house I bought burned down, and there's a lot of anger and aggression in there, but leads in the end to a "we can get over this" sort of thing. It has a magnificent, triumphant sound at the end.[15]

Emerson added, "I could put the first movement into a sort of pastorale context, the second movement into a sort of baroque piece, and the last movement into a more modern way of writing; a very atonal sound."[16]

On separate occasions, Emerson told Dominic Milano and Blair Pethel that he sought John Mayer's advice about composing in sonata-allegro form.[17] I have always found this remark curious, because I am unable to hear any of the three movements in anything resembling sonata-allegro form. Concerning the first movement, *Allegro Giojoso*, Emerson remarked, "When I started I'd intended writing a series of variations for piano around one theme. I got through about four variations and it gradually got away from the original variation which I created, which gave me the clue that it would possibly be worked better into the concerto format."[18] This remark seems much truer to one's actual experience of listening to the first movement: I hear the movement as a kind of loose variation chain built around

---

[14] Keith Emerson, quoted by Milano, "Keith Emerson," *Contemporary Keyboard*, October 1977, 30.
[15] Keith Emerson, quoted by Dale Furnash, "Conversations: Emerson, Lake and Palmer," *Trouser Press*, May 1978, 28.
[16] Ibid., 27–28.
[17] Milano, "Keith Emerson," *Contemporary Keyboard*, October 1977, 30; Pethel, "Keith Emerson," 96.
[18] Keith Emerson, quoted by Dale Furnash, "Conversations," 27.

two distinct (although related) themes, falling into four sections; in the third section, a totally new theme is heard with its own variations.[19] My analysis of the movement follows.

Piano Concerto no. 1, First Movement: *Allegro Giojoso*

FIRST SECTION

Introduction (0:00–0:44). A single explosive orchestral chord is followed by the introductory theme, which creates an interesting union of opposites: its melodic outline is essentially atonal, but its rhythmic character is defined by a smooth outline of flowing sixteenth notes. It is treated fugally, with entrances of the theme in the low strings (0:11), woodwinds (0:21), and higher strings (0:31).

Transition (0:45–1:28). The busy, disinterested density of the opening introduction is suddenly swept away by a dreamy, lyrical, essentially ametric (never mind the 5/4 designation of the score) clarinet cantilena, supported by a cushion of gently swelling string chords.

Main Theme (1:29–2:04). The main theme is in fact a more tonally focused reworking of the largely atonal introductory theme, retaining that theme's overall melodic shape and flowing rhythmic character. It is initially heard in the high strings, supported by a triplet countermelody in the lower strings; the three against two rhythmic figure that results produces a languorous, gently swaying quality. At 1:48 the low brass and chimes enter with a solemn descending figure that prepares the way for the main body of the movement.

Main Theme, Variation One (2:05–2:24). Now the piano enters with the first variation of the main theme, basically at twice the speed of the orchestra's statement of it (the theme is now written in sixteenth notes rather than eighths), settling into the key of A♭ major, the closest key this movement has to a tonic. At first the piano is accompanied only by tuned percussion, but at 2:19 the flutes introduce a new figure that is answered by plunging piano arpeggios. This almost Mozartian question-answer phrase, quickly repeated, becomes the main theme's "tail," and is repeated in subsequent variations. The "tail" tends to be in a different key than the main theme, in this case, the dominant, E♭ major.

---

[19] For Pethel's analysis of the first movement, see "Keith Emerson," 99–104. Pethel and I agree on the four distinct sections; however, his analysis does not address the variationlike nature of the material. Incidentally, the atonal introductory theme (0:00–0:44) and its offshoots are based on a twelve-tone row; see Forrester, Hanson, and Askew, *Emerson, Lake and Palmer*, 202–5, for details. I do not dwell on the tone row in my analysis because I view it as a detail of (rather than the foundation of) the movement's structure.

Main Theme, Variation Two (2:24–2:43). Here the movement begins a lengthy crescendo. The main theme is again played by piano, this time with some string backing; the tail is played largely by piano now, with some quiet orchestral backing. Tonality shifts to F major.

Main Theme, Variation Three (2:43–3:10). The main theme is again taken by piano, but now with surging string accompaniment; at 2:55 the full orchestra presents the tail, including the plunging arpeggio figure, swinging it unexpectedly into G major, and bringing the movement to its first big climax.

Main Theme, Variation Four (3:11–3:35). As the tension dissipates somewhat, the piano pulls the theme back into its home key, A♭ major, and develops it over a rolling one-measure left hand ostinato, while a flute countermelody chatters away in the orchestral background.

SECOND SECTION

Introduction (3:36–3:56). A quietly pensive statement of the atonal introductory theme is presented by the piano and orchestra together; note the sudden agitation suggested by the swelling dissonant chord at 3:52–3:56.

Main Theme, "Jazz" Development (3:56–4:45). While the general melodic outline of the main theme is retained, the triplet rhythms that dominate this section are quite different from anything heard up to now and give this section a more swinging, jazzy character. Notice the reference to the main theme's "tail" at 4:19. This section climaxes from 4:25 to 4:34, when a four-bar piano figure is echoed by full orchestra. Throughout most of this section, the tonality is unstable, although it settles into E♭ major by the final cadence, which makes another reference to the main theme's tail.

THIRD SECTION

Chorale (4:48–5:08). An entirely new "chorale" theme is presented, largely by the brass, in the tonic, A♭ major.

Chorale, Variation One (5:08–5:29). The piano enters with a variation of the chorale theme in flowing eighth notes in the tonic, accompanied prominently by a flute countermelody; the interweaving of flute and piano in its upper register becomes something of an orchestration fingerprint in this movement.

Chorale, Variation Two (5:29–5:50). Strings take the chorale melody, supported by the winds and the piano's flowing sixteenth-note accompaniment, the latter creating a rhythmic link to the movement's main theme.

Chorale, Variation Three (5:50–6:18). Strings, brass, and the piano with its sixteenth-note obbligato accompaniment present a particularly grandiose statement of the chorale melody, bringing the movement to its second big climax.

FOURTH SECTION

Introduction (6:19–6:52). The atonal introductory theme returns in the orchestra, and rises to an agitated, almost agonized climax by 6:38. This is one of the most imaginative passages in the movement, both from a perspective of melodic development and orchestration.

Cadenza, part one (6:52–8:05). The first part of the huge piano cadenza consists of a finely handled development of the main theme, which begins in A♭ but soon moves to tonally remote areas. The manner in which the cadenza picks up the momentum from the previous orchestral statement of the introductory theme is particularly impressive.

Cadenza, part two (8:06–8:56). The second half of the cadenza returns securely to A♭ major, as the pianist's right hand part spins out triplet melodic figurines over a stride-like one measure bass ostinato in a manner reminiscent of George Gershwin's music. There is very little reference to any previous material here.

Main Theme Recapitulation (8:57–9:18). The movement ends with a final grandiose recapitulation of the main theme, presented by full orchestra and piano; unexpectedly, the main theme's tail, when it enters one last time at 9:14, does not reverse its tendency of modulating to a new key, so the movement ends in E♭ rather than A♭ major.

A few observations before moving on. The first movement contains some nice orchestral touches, interesting textures, pleasing lyricism, and, as one would expect, consistently interesting piano writing. Nevertheless, there are some undeniable weaknesses. The movement is pastoral, as Emerson suggests, but it's a bit on the emotionally superficial side, and could have used some of the intensely bittersweet emotional ambience that a master of the British pastoral school such as Ralph Vaughan Williams brought to his work; there's little real drama here, save perhaps in the first half of the movement's fourth section, which really is quite effective.

A second problem, as Emerson himself has alluded to, is that the movement doesn't hang together all that well structurally.[20] The entire third (chorale) section is essentially superfluous to the rest of the movement; little damage would be done to the movement's structural integrity if one were to excise the section and go directly from 4:45 to 6:19. (To the contrary, I believe this would serve to tighten the movement up a bit.) Likewise, the second half of the piano cadenza, while pleasant enough on

---

[20] See Furnash, "Conversations," 28.

its own, adds little to the overall trajectory of the movement, and could be eliminated without doing significant harm to the movement as a whole.

Piano Concerto no. 1, Second Movement: *Andante Molto Cantabile*

The short second movement, *Andante Molto Cantabile*, shares the first movement's pastoral character. Earlier I quoted Emerson's remark about this movement's "baroque" background, and there are some tendencies here that one might associate with the slow middle movement of a baroque concerto: the movement's overall A B A form, the circle-of-fifths chord movement in the middle section, and the irregular phrase lengths of the melodies, which suggest the baroque *fortspinnung* technique whereby a short thematic idea is continuously re-elaborated and "spun out."[21] Nonetheless, the biggest single influence I hear is of Mozart, and it's mainly the metrical waywardness of the melodic material that signals this isn't the slow movement of a Mozart piano concerto.

The first A section is occupied by a wayward fourteen-measure theme, solidly in C major, whose opening is loosely derived from the main theme of the first movement: the theme is stated by the orchestra, with the tone colors of violins, oboe, and clarinet predominating. Note the subtle reference to the "tail" of the first movement's main theme in this theme's "tail" at 0:29. The B section, which begins at 0:41, represents a development of A section material. The piano enters with a variant of the A section theme that passes sequentially through seven consecutive fifth-related chords before cadencing on the dominant, G major, at 0:53. The piano then introduces a new variant of the A section theme that is accompanied by ascending triads in parallel motion; this segment is brought to an end with a variant of the tail of the A section's theme, introduced at 1:01. The recapitulation (approximate, not identical) of the A section begins at 1:16; now the piano and orchestra present the movement's main theme together. At 1:56 there is a brief coda in which the final cadence (on a C major chord) sounds hollow and strangely barren.

The second movement is a study in musical mellowness. Its dynamics scarcely ever rise above *mezzo piano*, and despite the nice circle-of-fifths development in the B section and the interesting orchestration of the final cadence, there is no drama, or even tension, to speak of. The movement is only slightly more than two minutes long, and therefore the proportions of the Concerto as a whole (the first movement is over nine minutes long, the third, nearly seven) seem somewhat askew.

---

[21] Pethel is quite mistaken to call the form A B C (see Pethel, "Keith Emerson," 104–6).

Piano Concerto no. 1, Third Movement: *Toccata con fuoco*

If the first movement suggests Copland and Gershwin and the second, Mozart, the final movement, *Toccata con fuoco*, is a bit reminiscent of the music of Sergei Prokofiev in its fusion of percussive, dissonant chords with lyrical (albeit sometimes angular) melodies. The sudden violence of the third movement is somewhat jarring: here, for the first time in the Concerto, one hears traces of the composer of "Tarkus." The third movement falls into five distinct sections, of which the fourth and fifth transform thematic material from the first; the third section, meanwhile, refers back to the main theme of the first movement.

FIRST SECTION (0:00–1:16)

The movement opens with a driving one measure ostinato deep in the piano's bass that isn't dissimilar to the opening of "Eruption" (indeed, a 1989 rock arrangement of the movement included on Emerson's 2005 *Hammer It Out* anthology underlines the similarity). The ostinato's jagged melodic outline suggests a $B^\flat$ minor tonality, although $B^\flat$ is never firmly established as tonic. This ostinato is accompanied by brief, flickering orchestral melodic fragments—Blair Pethel aptly calls this "fire music"—which suddenly dissipate in the face of an agonized minor second dissonance ($B^\flat$ vs. A) at 0:12.[22] The ostinato resumes, and at 0:37 the piano presents the first substantial thematic material—chromatically rising parallel major triads that foreshadow the movement's main theme. The ostinato breaks off in favor of dissonant, percussive piano chords which alternate with jagged unison melodic runs; suddenly a plunging piano arpeggio shifts the music into a C tonality, and a new bass ostinato appears, accompanied first by urgently rising parallel fourths (0:59), then at 1:05 by the first statement of the movement's main theme, harmonized entirely by major triads.

SECOND SECTION (1:16–2:41)

The first statement of the theme is cut off very suddenly at 1:16 by uneasy iterations of the chimes over a low C. Suddenly the piano explodes into its most virtuosic statement of the Concerto, a series of neurotic, careening phrases that are periodically interrupted by equally agitated orchestral outbursts. Especially observant listeners will notice the use of some tricks first heard in "The Endless Enigma" and "Trilogy"—arpeggios outlining a series of triads a major third apart (1:34), arpeggiated "Enigma" chords

---

[22] Pethel, "Keith Emerson," 106.

(1:41), juxtapositions of triads a tritone apart (1:54). This section builds towards what one assumes will be a huge climax; unfortunately, the "climactic" point, reached at 2:05, involves a trite little tune in C major that's passed between piano and orchestra. The tune's banality and its tonal simplicity immediately dissipate the section's huge reservoir of built-up energy, and the final bit of keyboard pyrotechnics (plunging fourth chords at 2:21) seems like overkill given its context.

THIRD SECTION (2:42–3:32)

The second section comes to rest somewhat uneasily on a whole-tone sonority (2:34–2:41); what follows is a piano cadenza, a marvelously impressionistic recollection of the first movement's main theme, as if seen through haze or fog. For the most part the cadenza faithfully echoes that theme's flowing rhythmic motion, but near the end the rhythmic outline grows more jagged and uneasy (3:10) as the high strings reenter with a plaintive countermelody over the piano's whole-tone wash. At 3:23 the orchestra and piano suddenly recall some of the plunging bass figurations from the movement's opening, and this proves to be a transition to the next section.

FOURTH SECTION (3:32–4:53)

This section recapitulates much of the opening section's material, but in a more focused way. Over the familiar opening bass ostinato we hear the rising parallel fourths (3:32), then a much expanded statement of the first theme (beginning at 3:38), in which the piano's major triad reharmonization is effectively deployed among the high strings and brass. At 3:59 the statement of the main theme seamlessly moves into a new episode, a swinging piano figure (notated in 10/8, but with a 5/4 feel) over which the strings spin out an extension of the main theme. At 4:18 the piano renews the second section's nervous juxtaposition of triads a tritone apart underneath an increasingly impassioned orchestral counterpoint of strings, brass, and timpani, and orchestra and piano press on inexorably towards the movement's second big climax.

FIFTH SECTION (4:53–6:50)

The climactic passage (4:53) is a surprising transformation of the movement's main theme into a majestic, hymnlike melody. Blair Pethel criticizes this passage rather harshly for its sudden loss of rhythmic momentum.[23] He has a point, although Emerson could have corrected

---

[23] Blair Pethel, "Keith Emerson," 110.

this problem rather easily by having the piano play running eighth notes in the bass (a technique Franz Liszt and other nineteenth-century virtuosos often resorted to) rather than simply doubling the orchestra's dotted half-note chords. On the other hand, the ambiguous tonality of the "hymn" creates more tension than Pethel acknowledges; for instance, the first half of the hymn tune appears prepared to cadence on G major (5:03), when suddenly the second half of the hymn tune sets out from E major, heading towards a cadence on B major which is, again, evaded (5:13). A second repetition of the "hymn," from 5:14, features piano with flute obbligato, providing for a momentary winding down, as well as recalling a predominant instrumental combination of the first movement. At 5:34, the "hymn" breaks off momentarily in favor of an orchestral/piano episode that rebuilds tension, a particularly effective passage being the almost bluesy combination of duplet and triplet rhythms (recalling the very first orchestral statement of the first movement's main theme) at 5:44. A third and final statement of the "hymn" commences at 6:05, with the piano accompanying the full orchestra's statement of the tune with harplike ascending arpeggios. The movement closes with dramatic alternations between F major and D♭ major triads, and finally settles on the former as the pianist ends with an ascending glissando up the keyboard.

Emerson's Piano Concerto no. 1: An Assessment

By the 1970s, Keith Emerson was the latest in a line of musicians, stretching back into the early twentieth century, who had used their familiarity with the classical music tradition to enrich the popular music genre of which they were a master: one also thinks of George Gershwin, Duke Ellington, and Leonard Bernstein. Like these earlier figures, Emerson eventually found the pull of the concert hall irresistible, at least in part, presumably, because of the greater respect that high culture affords to practitioners of "serious" music.

As we are finally recognizing, however, the popular songs of Gershwin and Bernstein and the jazz compositions of Ellington are as important a contribution to the culture of their times as the great symphonic and operatic masterpieces of the nineteenth century were to theirs; on the other hand, the more ambitious (some might say "pretentious") "classical" works of these men, while interesting and accomplished, simply don't measure up to their nineteenth- and early-twentieth-century models. I would say the same is true of Emerson. "Tarkus" and "Karn Evil 9" stand as masterpieces of rock music in its most vital, "classic" era (1965–75); Emerson's Piano Concerto no. 1, on the other hand, while it contains some undeniably interesting moments, simply does not measure up to the piano concertos of Mozart, Beethoven, Brahms, and the other European Masters.

Part of the problem, I think, is Emerson worked too hard to compose a work he felt would be viewed as "respectable" by the classical music community, and in doing so submerged too much of his own musical personality. Emerson's most characteristic structures in his work with ELP circa 1970–74 showcase a loose conception of organicism wherein disparate musical blocks are tied together through a process of free but continuous variation: sometimes Emerson continuously transforms or varies his themes and motives ("The Three Fates," "Trilogy"), at other times the same theme or motive recurs in different textural contexts ("Tarkus"), and occasionally the two approaches are merged ("The Endless Enigma"). The 1st and 3rd Impressions of "Karn Evil 9" find Emerson working in a more tightly woven musical context than before, one in which sectional differences are deemphasized, and perhaps the Piano Concerto's more self-consciously developmental approach can be seen as a logical continuation of this trend. In his remarks about the Concerto, Emerson certainly seems at pains to point out the developmental aspect of the music:

> It surprised me that a lot of people who criticized the Concerto said that I'd scraped the surface. I think I would agree possibly as far as the first movement is concerned, but after I'd taken the set of variations and turned them around—reconstructing it to make a piano concerto—and continued on to write the second and third movements, those ideas really stretched out completely. The first subject in the third movement is stated right at the beginning and stretches through to the end.[24]

The fact is that there is no "right" way in which to compose a piano concerto; the only requirement for success in a piano concerto, symphony, or any other genre (classical or otherwise) is that the form grows naturally out of the implications of the material. The Concerto's cyclic form (where the main theme of the first movement reappears in new guises in later movements), and the attempt to more or less systematically develop the first movement's main theme, have the feel of concessions to conventions that Emerson apparently believed were hallmarks of a "proper" concerto. Of the three movements of the Concerto, the third, in my view, is the closest to being completely successful, because the structure by and large hangs together; it's also the one movement in which Emerson's stylistic voice is immediately recognizable. There's rather little in the first two movements that bears the unmistakable musical voice of Keith Emerson,

---

[24] Keith Emerson, quoted by Furnash, "Conversations," 28.

and one suspects that his attempts to grapple with "accepted" forms that were unfamiliar to him contributed to the lack of emotional immediacy and intensity in much of the musical material. It is ironic that tonality, which is a key factor in generating drama and tension in the late eighteenth- and nineteenth-century Germanic tradition that Emerson seems to aspire to in his Concerto, is used more effectively in a number of his "rock" pieces ("Karn Evil 9," "The Endless Enigma," "The Three Fates"), where tension is generated by two competing tonal centers vying for supremacy, than it is the Concerto.

Here the case of George Gershwin is instructive. His *Rhapsody in Blue*, a highly personal synthesis of Lisztian romanticism and 1920s jazz, is almost universally recognized as his most important symphonic work: yet, judged by the standards of nineteenth-century musical form, it has some undeniable structural weaknesses. Gershwin's later *Cuban Overture* shows a much more fluent grasp of academic structural models; nonetheless, hardly anybody claims *Cuban Overture* is a "better" piece than *Rhapsody in Blue*. Why? Whatever its structural faults, Gershwin's unique voice is immediately evident in *Rhapsody*; as Gershwin became more fluent in managing the "accepted" structural models, something was lost in the musical content, and *Cuban Overture* simply doesn't have the same sense of immediacy of vision, of "rightness," as *Rhapsody*. Therefore, I make the following claim, which will undoubtedly rankle some academics and purists: structurally speaking, "Tarkus" is a more successful work than Piano Concerto no. 1. Why? In "Tarkus," the form grows naturally out of the requirements of the material; in the Concerto, form and content never quite converge.

In the end, though, I don't want to be overly harsh on the Concerto. Back when Keith Emerson introduced his Concerto the public, the idea of a "rock" musician entering the world of classical music was unheard of: rock critics decried him as "pretentious," classical purists as a "barbarian." Today, over a quarter of a century later, much has changed: rock critics shrug, and the classical world welcomes "crossover" efforts by the likes of Paul McCartney, Eric Clapton, and Joe Jackson, not to mention the vapid symphonic arrangements of the rock songs of Pink Floyd, Yes, Kansas, et al. I am saddened by the fact that although Emerson opened the door first to these crossover efforts, the loss of ELP's iconic, larger than life status after 1980 made him *persona non grata* to classical record labels that otherwise might have been expected to subsidize him in the production of more classical music. Equally sad is this: recognizing that who's first at something isn't as important as who's best at it, the fact is Emerson's Concerto remains one of the most interesting and accomplished, but also one of the more thoroughly forgotten, classical works to emerge from the intersection of rock and classical music culture.

Side Two: Greg Lake

Like Emerson, who wished to use his solo side of the *Works* LP to establish his credentials as a "serious" composer, Greg Lake saw himself to
some degree redefining himself with his solo material. Even before their
long break, Lake had felt his bandmates never fully valued his contributions as a singer:

> Instrumentalists really don't respect singers. They live together with them,
> they need them, they enjoy them, but they do not respect them. So I get
> respect in the band as a bass player, and when I'm talking about music every-
> thing's great, but as a singer, you know, "Sing us a song, man. See you," and
> they're gone . . . Keith can relate to Carl musically but neither of them can
> relate to me musically. My art is as far away from what they do as a painter's
> . . . [but] I think if you can have any gift in music, the greatest gift is to be a
> singer.[25]

Clearly, by 1974 Lake was feeling a need to explore some facets of his
singing abilities and interests that he felt were being repressed in the
framework of ELP. In fact, after years of working overtime as an instrumentalist to match the virtuosity of Emerson and Palmer, it seems the layoff gave Lake an opportunity to reevaluate his musical priorities:

> My feeling [after the 1973–74 World Tour] was one of exhaustion and tired-
> ness. So there was a period where I had to sit and think about what I wanted
> to do. And I realized, when I stopped to think about it, that I am principally
> a singer. Up until that time, I'd given, I suppose, equal effort to playing the
> bass and to producing records and things like that. Having to reevaluate my
> future really made me think that my strength was in the fact that I was a singer
> first. And that thought, simple though it may be, took me ages to work out.
> Because all my life I've played in a group. It was a new thing to think of being
> only me as opposed to being part of a band. You aim to put the best foot for-
> ward, to do the thing you can do best. And the best thing I could do was sing
> songs, so sing I did.[26]

I think it's possible to argue that from the day Lake made the decision he
was primarily a singer, the end of ELP, at least in its original conception,
was in sight. Even if one doesn't agree with this assertion, it is undebat-
able that by the midseventies, Emerson and Lake were headed in very different musical directions. Certainly, there is no doubt that Lake never
aspired to the same level of bass or guitar virtuosity after the layoff as he

---

[25] Greg Lake, quoted by Rick Sanders and John Wells, "Greg Lake: Still He Turns Them
On," *Music Scene Top Ten Series: Emerson, Lake and Palmer*, May 1974.
[26] Greg Lake, quoted by Rudis, "Guess Who's Back," 24.

had before, some fine performances in the *Works*-era material (and even, to a lesser degree, on *Love Beach*) notwithstanding. In most rock bands this would be a minor detail, but to a band like ELP, founded as they were at least in part around the ideal of transcendental virtuosity, the whole chemistry of the band was changed, and the whole identity of the band altered, by one member's loss of faith, as it were, in the ideal that had once united them.

To be sure, the five songs that occupy Lake's portion of *Works I*, all cowritten by Lake and Pete Sinfield, were not sudden products of the 1975-76 period. At least two of the songs, "C'est la vie" and "Hallowed Be Thy Name," existed as early as 1973: the latter was, in fact, auditioned for *Brain Salad Surgery* (it lost out to "Still . . . You Turn Me On"). As I recounted at the beginning of this chapter, Mario Medious told a reporter as early as fall 1974 that Lake had an entire album worth of material written, although only "C'est la vie" was recorded at that time.

The songs that Lake used on *Works I* share a number of common features. All of the songs are solidly in the seventies folk-rock singer/songwriter vein. Lake's voice and acoustic guitar provide the song's backbone, sometimes (but not inevitably) accompanied by an understated rock rhythm section: if Emerson was rubbing shoulders with Copland and Gershwin, Lake was working in the territory of James Taylor and Harry Chapin. The songs are gorgeously arranged for orchestra and small choir by Godfrey Salmon and Tony Harris; it would be hard to overstate how masterfully the strings, in particular, are worked in, and how much atmosphere the orchestration imparts to the songs. The songs all showcase Lake's predilection for simple but effective modal chord progressions, Pete Sinfield's elaborate wordplay (although not nearly as overwrought as his final two albums with King Crimson), and some of Lake's finest performances as a singer.

The first song, "Lend Your Love To Me Tonight," is an abstrusely poetic ode to a one-night stand. The melody is one of Lake's most beautiful, and his plaintive vocal, backed by an exquisite chain of suspended acoustic guitar chords, recalls his finest work of the first two King Crimson albums in its poignance and almost painful sense of vulnerability—for one of the last times in his career. Unfortunately, the song has a major structural flaw: there is no contrasting material to the short verse. The arrangement works mightily to overcome this shortcoming in some fairly sophisticated ways: gradual layering in of instruments behind Lake's guitar, dramatic entrance of the rhythm section, a surprise modulation from the tonic, E major, to G major, signaled by the entrance of an overdubbed chorus of Greg Lakes (2:07), a momentary relaxation of tension when the song returns to E (3:04) followed by one final big crescendo (beginning at 3:30). Despite the beauty of the basic musical idea and the sophistication of the arrangement, though, there's simply not enough musical material here to justify a four-minute song, and "Lend Your Love To Me Tonight" seems to start losing steam shortly after the drum groove begins at 1:24, deflated by overrepetition. As with most of his other songs on *Works I*, Lake generates an effectively bitter-sweet ambience by mixing modes: in this case, Mixolydian and ordinary major.

Next comes "C'est la vie," which evokes Charles Aznavour and the French cabaret song in its instrumentation (guitar, accordion, strings, and woodwinds, no rhythm section), Lake's own "Still . . . You Turn Me On" in its D-tuning, and his "Take a Pebble" in its aura of melancholy and regret. Unlike "Lend Your Love," "C'est la vie" achieves a nice sense of variety through its use of four different chord cycles: one for the verse (0:07), one for the chorus (0:40), which features a "choral" overdub of Lake's voice reminiscent of "Lucky Man," and two during the lengthy accordion solo, the first beginning at 2:14 (this is repeated), the second from 2:37 (this is a variant of the chorus's chord cycle). Many have assumed Emerson was the accordion soloist on the studio recording of the song, but that is not the case. When asked if he played the solo, he said,

> No. I felt quite bewildered about that, because when Greg came into my house playing "C'est la vie," I got my accordion out and suggested that when he recorded it, it might be a good idea to put an accordion solo on it. I think it was at a time when we were being secretive about our solo projects. It was almost taboo for one of us to be in the studio when another of us was doing something for a solo album. I think that's why Greg brought in another accordion player. Anyway, onstage I copy that solo. I don't even know who the accordion player was on the album.[27]

The accordion solo adds a great deal of atmosphere to the song, and Lake's shift during the solo to triplet guitar arpeggios lends a pleasing Gallic touch. The final verse and chorus are augmented with a very opulent orchestral and choral accompaniment; it's hard to imagine the string section's soaring countermelodies being worked into the musical fabric any more perfectly. Nonetheless, while "C'est la vie" shows a good deal more compositional variety than "Lend Your Love," it lacks that song's passion and poignance, and has always left me somewhat cold, especially Lake's vocal (which, in my opinion, is bathed in entirely too much reverb—a production peculiarity that is evident in some of Lake's other *Works I* material as well). Nonetheless, "C'est la vie" became the best known of Lake's solo material off of *Works I*; it was released as a single and became a minor hit, reaching ninety-one on the American charts.

---

[27] Keith Emerson, quoted by Milano, "Keith Emerson," *Contemporary Keyboard*, October 1977, 52.

The third song, "Hallowed Be Thy Name," is the most ambitious of the set, and certainly the most unusual as well; there's nothing quite like it anywhere else in Lake's output. A number of lyrics by Lake and/or Sinfield use a "madman" as an iconic figure to convey alienation ("Knife-Edge," "The Miracle"), sometimes with intimations of hidden wisdom (something along the lines of the village idiot of Russian folklore, who is often a sage in disguise—the madman of King Crimson's "In the Wake of Poseidon" exemplifies this).[28] "Hallowed Be Thy Name," though, is the only Lake/Sinfield song premised on a conversation with a madman; furthermore, each of the song's four verses ends with a line from the Lord's Prayer, which is used to sum up the "teaching" that the madman gradually imparts to the protagonist. Musically, the song suggests a minor blues in E, although it doesn't adhere to the twelve-bar blues form. While one hears Lake strum his acoustic guitar a bit at the beginning, the real instrumental backbone of this song is provided by drums, bass, and an icy, abstracted blues-style piano part with evocations of free jazz that is reminiscent of the playing of former King Crimson pianist Keith Tippett. Godfrey Salmon's expertly scored orchestral arrangement, with its growling low brass and its strange, dissonant string glissandos, adds a great deal of film noir atmosphere to the song. Between the third and fourth verses an instrumental episode featuring increasingly agitated string figures begins to drive the song on to its climax, which is reached when Lake, in his final response to the madman, cries out, "Lead me into temptation"—a direct inversion of the Lord's Prayer.

Sinfield's baroque wordplay, the song's undertones of tortured self-exploration, and its embrace of a bleak existentialism tempered only by a romantic's longing to "break on through" social inhibitions in order to achieve new levels of sensation, reminds one of Peter Hammill, lead singer/lyricist of Van der Graaf Generator, and an artist that Greg Lake is seldom compared to. Nonetheless, this song never quite catches fire the way that the most compelling of Hammill's tortured soliloquies seem to, and while it's an interesting experiment, ultimately it doesn't feel like a totally successful one.

The next song, "Nobody Loves You Like I Do," is unusual for a different reason: it is the closest any member of ELP has come to doing a straight-ahead country and western song. Lake uses a heavily chorused twelve-string electric guitar to suggest a pedal steel guitar; "country" ref-

---

[28] As Jacques Barzun points out, the medieval court jester—another archetype that figures prominently in Sinfield's King Crimson lyrics—is also a sage in disguise. Says Barzun: "The post—the institution—of king's fool is a political device based on sound psychology, as well as on ancient religious belief . . . much of the time he is an entertainer, the jester in cap and bells; but at other times he says things nobody wants to hear and nobody dares to utter. The wise ruler listens and benefits." See Barzun, *From Dawn to Decadence*, 302.

erences are also supplied by the rollicking bass line (which sounds straight out of a Johnny Cash song), the prominent harmonica obbligato, a short Chet Atkins–like guitar solo, and some honky-tonk style piano by Keith Emerson in his only appearance on any of Lake's *Works I* songs. Emerson, incidentally, was not very happy about how his contribution to the song was treated, remarking, "I did a lot of ragtime piano in the middle, but it's mixed so far down that you can't hear it. It's not really worth mentioning."[29] During the final refrain, Lake is joined by the chorus, who evoke a down-home gospel choir; while the effect is somewhat undermined by the sawing violin lines (perhaps the only example of extraneous orchestration in any of Lake's songs on this album), it signaled the beginning of a fondness for gospel choir backing that Lake was to return to on a number of later recordings. While "Nobody Loves You Like I Do" is not a particularly profound song—it is probably the least substantive of his five songs on the album—it's good fun, and demonstrates yet again that despite their reputation as being overly dependent on European classical music, the members of ELP were familiar with a surprisingly broad range of American popular music styles.

The last song in Lake's set is the elegant "Closer to Believing." Set in the unusual key of C$\sharp$ major, "Closer to Believing" eschews the rock rhythm section entirely in favor of a lush backing of piano, orchestra, and chorus. It seems to evoke an earlier age of popular song—the thirties crooner repertoire, maybe (although there's no hint of jazz here), or perhaps even early twentieth-century operetta—although the modal mixing of ordinary major and Mixolydian, which Lake uses here to characteristically bittersweet effect, is not a part of either repertoire.

Of the five songs represented here, "Closer to Believing" is the most substantive both lyrically and musically. The lyrics are a particularly eloquent expression of the philosophical territory Lake had begun to stake out in "Still . . . You Turn Me On": in an era in which loss of religious faith and societal alienation is endemic, love and commitment between two individuals is the last sure anchor left. The structure of the song is such that the refrain ("I Need Me/You Need You/We Want Us") is only gradually revealed; it isn't heard at all until 1:29, and isn't fully heard until its second repetition at 2:38, when it's accompanied by a hazy, slightly out-of-focus cushion of strings. Thereafter, where one expects the verse to return (3:31), one hears instead an exceptionally pretty Swingle Singers type of wordless choral arrangement, accompanied by orchestra. Then the refrain returns, with Lake now accompanied by full chorus; when the verse finally does reappear, at 5:02, there is a feeling of growth, that the transformations of the refrain and the intervention of the choral episode

---

[29] Keith Emerson, quoted by Milano, "Keith Emerson," *Contemporary Keyboard*, October 1977, 52.

enable us to experience the verse differently, as if we're now surveying the same landscape from a higher mountaintop. Both Lake and Sinfield continue to hold "Closer to Believing" in high esteem. Sinfield has remarked, "One of my favorite, yet little known lyrics [is] on a very beautiful, if slightly flawed (like people really), song called 'Closer to Believing.' The lyric to this five and a half minute number took more than six months to write!"[30] Lake, for his part has remarked, "From a songwriter's point of view, this ["Closer to Believing"] is one of my favorites. I co-wrote it with Pete Sinfield, and we spent so long doing the lyrics; it was one of those things where we crafted and refined them forever. I used my Zemaitis twelve-string on that one."[31]

There is not a substandard song on Lake's side of *Works I*. The lyrics are thoughtful and well crafted; the vocals include some of the finest performances of Lake's career; and the orchestral/choral arrangements are—at the risk of beating this point into the ground—quite exceptional. Certainly, the material is never less than substantive. On the other hand, as a collection, the five songs are marred by a certain sameness, both of mood and of style. Specifically, "Lend Your Love To Me Tonight," "C'est la vie," and "Closer to Believing" are uncomfortably similar; even the "country" of "Nobody Loves You Like I Do" and the "blues" of "Hallowed Be Thy Name" seem more a function of the sophisticated arranging than any inherent quality of the songs themselves, which, one suspects, could have been just as easily arranged to sound like the other three. Lake admitted as much himself shortly after the album's release, saying, "I got into one frame of writing. And certainly 'C'est la vie' and 'Closer to Believing' are similar songs. They came from similar situations. So in a way, I didn't make it as varied as I'd hoped. But that's alright."[32] It is interesting to note that the two most successful songs, "C'est la vie" and "Closer to Believing," are the farthest removed from rock music in their nostalgic evocation of earlier twentieth-century popular styles. Based on the evidence of *Works I*, Lake, like Emerson, seemed poised to pursue a solo career that would cultivate different musical styles than his former group, and a more mature target audience.

Side Three: Carl Palmer

Carl Palmer's side of *Works I* is less unified than Emerson's or Lake's; rather than explore a single style, Palmer dabbles in several different

---

[30] Peter Sinfield, "Peter Sinfield and What He Did/Does," *ELP Digest* 9, no. 19 (23 October, 1994).

[31] Greg Lake, quoted by Andy Aledorf, "Lucky Man," *Guitar Legends*, no. 22 (1997): 10.

[32] Greg Lake, quoted by Rudis, "Guess Who's Back," 24.

idioms with the aid of a diverse slate of guest artists—not unlike solo albums by many other members of well-known seventies bands. Of the three, Palmer seemed to have the least trouble generating material: he would have had no problem filling an entire LP, had that been necessary. At the time when a solo LP by each band member was being contemplated, the pièce de résistance on Palmer's was to have been a Percussion Concerto, composed by Joseph Horovitz in collaboration with Palmer (who provided advice on the solo percussion parts), that he had recorded with the London Philharmonic Orchestra in early 1976. When the decision was made to limit each band member to one side of solo material on a two-LP set, the band decided that two concertos might push the patience of ELP's rock-oriented audience past the breaking point, and Palmer agreed to save his for a later release. Here's what he said at the time:

> I recorded a concerto with the London Philharmonic Orchestra. There's four movements and I play lots of xylophone, glockenspiel and crotales, which are like small tuned cymbals. I play lots of tuned percussion, because I'm really into that now, and timpani. That took me some time to record: learning it took about six months and I recorded it in bits and pieces because it was very difficult to get sounding right. I don't know when we're going to release it. Joseph Horovitz actually wrote the music and I designed what the percussion would play.[33]

Even after the first breakup of ELP, Palmer still harbored significant ambitions for this piece. In 1980, he remarked,

> I have a complete theatrical idea in my mind to incorporate myself playing all these instruments with the orchestra and using three females dancing in syncopation to what I'm playing. One of the things I would like to do is to make a film of my life story and I'd like to incorporate this particular Concerto into it. There are a lot of things in this Concerto that are fantastic. I've got this huge bucket full of chains that I pick up and throw at the gong which is suspended four inches above the ground. It makes a terrific sound. That's one of the things theatrically I would like to stage in such a way that it would be appealing to the audience. I'd like to do it at [New York's] Radio City.[34]

Incredibly, it took a quarter of a century after its recording—the occasion of the release of the Carl Palmer Anthology in 2001—for the Horovitz-Palmer Concerto for Percussion to enter the public domain. On the whole, it's a solid work, and I think it's truly unfortunate that it didn't get the hearing before a huge mass public that it would have in

---

[33] Carl Palmer, quoted by Furnash, "Conversations," 28–29.
[34] Carl Palmer, quoted by Iero, "Carl Palmer," 58, 60.

1977—but which it never will now. Cast in four movements, the Concerto opens with an ominous chromatic theme blared fortissimo by the wind section. The remainder of the first movement features driving, repetitive ostinato figures—reminiscent of Carl Orff or Stravinsky at his most accessible, perhaps—overlaid with urgent, heroic wind themes, with Palmer accompanying energetically on drumkit, timpani, and other percussion. The bittersweet, genuinely beautiful second movement evokes the slow movement of a Vaughan Williams symphony (the Second or Fifth especially): it's solidly in the English pastoralist style, which Palmer's very pretty tuned percussion obbligatos on glockenspiel, crotales and tubular bells embroider to unique effect. The short third movement is a fleet scherzo whose fugal passages evoke the taut interwar neoclassicism of Paul Hindemith or perhaps Walter Piston—here Palmer contributes motives on xylophone, temple blocks, cymbals, and drums. The fourth movement recalls the urgent character of the opening, and is a bit reminiscent of the frenetic, Stravinskian big-band jazz of Leonard Bernstein's *West Side Story* score. Towards the end of the movement the heroic wind theme of the first movement is recalled, after which Palmer launches into a long percussion cadenza; finally the ominous chromatic theme that had opened the Concerto returns to bring the work to a close.

The worst thing one could say about the Concerto for Percussion is that it does not reveal a particularly unique or distinctive compositional voice—the influences of Stravinsky, Orff, Vaughan Williams, Hindemith, and Bernstein are never subsumed into an individual vision, and it almost sounds as if the individual movements are studies in the style of composer X or Y. If Joseph Horovitz wasn't a particularly original composer, however, he was an excellent craftsman: the themes are substantive, the transitions fluently handled, the large-scale structures faultlessly paced, the orchestration well-conceived, and the percussion writing—which Palmer contributed a great deal of advice on—consistently interesting. My only complaint about the Concerto's structure involves the percussion cadenza of the last movement, which is too long, too unfocused, and which needlessly dissipates the energy that the movement had built up to that point; while the cadenza showcases Palmer's virtuosity well enough, it really doesn't serve the structural integrity of the work. On the whole, though, the Horovitz-Palmer Concerto compares favorably with Emerson's— while Emerson's reveals a more individual voice, the Horovitz Concerto reveals a surer grasp of large-scale symphonic structure. Both works are worthy of revival at some point by an enterprising symphony orchestra wishing to program something a bit off the beaten track.

It seems to me that of the three, Palmer was probably hurt the most by the decision not to release full solo LPs. There is no question that the release of a solo LP with the Concerto occupying one side would have cast the shorter pieces on the other side in a different light. As it is,

Palmer's side of *Works I* seems a shade unfocused, containing two classi-cally-oriented pieces, two funk numbers, and two tracks inspired by sev-enties big-band jazz-rock of the type plied by Maynard Ferguson and Palmer's own hero, Buddy Rich.

The first track on Palmer's side is an arrangement of the second move-ment of the *Scythian Suite*, "The Enemy God Dances with the Black Spirits," by Sergei Prokofiev (1891–1953). Prokofiev composed the *Scythian Suite* quite early in his career (1914–15), and its thick, dissonant chords, hypnotically repeated at a rapid tempo, suggest the influence of Stravinsky's *The Rite of Spring* (although even in this early piece Prokofiev's fondness for clear-cut, rather square melodies is self-evident). Palmer commented, "We were going to record 'The Enemy God' with the group originally but found it sounded better with an orchestra, so I immediately recorded it that way."[35]

I have the same philosophical disagreement with this track that I have with the entire *Works* orchestral tour. In my view, the orchestral rock of the late sixties was a phase that progressive rock had to go through in its earliest stage, as the musicians worked to understand classical structural and orchestral approaches from the inside out. Once the musicians had mastered these approaches, they were able to get on with the real goal of the genre—creating rock music that combined rock's rhythmic and tim-bral power with classical music's sense of scope and grandeur. Not one example of late-sixties orchestral rock was ever fully successful in coher-ently combining the rock and orchestral elements—invariably they are simply alternated—and the feeling of novelty is never far away. Likewise, here there is something very karaoke-like about Carl Palmer pounding out a rock backbeat while accompanying the London Philharmonic Orchestra as they blast away Prokofiev's early masterpiece. It may not sur-prise the reader to learn that I prefer the band's three-piece arrangement of this work, performances of which are available on *Works Live* and the King Biscuit *Emerson, Lake and Palmer* CD. Nonetheless, there is no question that Palmer's percussive orchestration here is masterful, similar to his accomplishment on "Jerusalem," and for this reason it is possible to enjoy the track even while disagreeing with its philosophical premise.

The next two tracks demonstrate Palmer's interest in seventies instru-mental funk. "L.A. Nights" features an all-star cast: Palmer, Keith Emerson on piano and Moog, Ian McDonald (the former King Crimson reedsman) on sax, and Joe Walsh (who was soon to join the Eagles), who provided guitar and scat vocal work. Palmer remarked, "I enjoy playing that kind of rock a lot, and I wanted to try and capture that energy if I could. The meeting with Joe Walsh was an accident; he was in the same

---

[35] Carl Palmer, quoted by Furnash, "Conversations," 27.

restaurant as I was, in L.A., and that was recorded in '74."[36] The track falls into two unequal halves. The first, in E minor, features a driving two-note bass riff over which McDonald lays out some fine frenetic sax leads; the second, featuring a lengthier bass riff in E major backed by a shuffle rhythm, showcases some nice interplay between Palmer, Emerson, Walsh, and McDonald, although it has gone on nearly sixty seconds too long by the end. Emerson, for his part, wasn't entirely happy with the mix: "I was also involved in the composition of 'L.A. Nights' [Emerson and Palmer cowrote the track], on which, again, I think the actual theme was too heavily mixed down. But that's Carl's side. It's his prerogative."[37]

Palmer initially composed the third track, "New Orleans," with New Orleans's premiere funk band, the Meters, in mind:

> "New Orleans" I initially wanted to record with the Meters, but they gave me so many hard times I decided I just wouldn't bother. They were so unprofessional about the approach that it was very difficult for me to get together with them. I just couldn't get into a situation where I was begging. I enjoyed the sound they made and it seemed to fit the music I'd written, so I figured I'd get them in. Anyway, that fell through so I hand-picked players. Colin Hodgkinson [bass] and Ron Aspery [woodwinds, keyboards] are from the group Backdoor [the sax-bass-drums trio that sometimes opened for ELP in 1974], for whom I'd produced their album *Activate*. I was friendly with them, personal, musical friends. The guitar player [Snuffy Walden] was from Stray Dog, which had been on our label, Manticore.[38]

The track is dominated by a hypnotically repeated blues riff in G, often doubled by what sounds like a voice run through a vocoder (a favorite effect of late-seventies funk); the only harmonic movement takes place underneath the bridge section's sax solo. Indeed, while "L.A. Nights" and "New Orleans" both feature some excellent playing by all involved, it's hard to avoid the impression that after a while the riffs are repeated longer than their harmonic interest warrants.

The fourth track is an arrangement of J. S. Bach's Two-Part Invention in D minor, featuring Palmer on vibes and the venerable James Blades on marimba. Blades (1901–1999), Palmer's teacher at London's Royal Academy of Music, was perhaps the most famous figure of Britain's small classical percussion establishment, having written an erudite, highly regarded book on classical percussion. I suspect the participation of Blades was the principal reason this track was included; musically, it's not

---

[36] Carl Palmer, quoted by Furnash, "Conversations," 28.
[37] Keith Emerson, quoted by Milano, "Keith Emerson," *Contemporary Keyboard*, October 1977, 52.
[38] Carl Palmer, quoted by Furnash, "Conversations," 28.

all that successful. At a time when mallet percussionists who played with four mallets like Brian Slawson and Leigh Howard Stevens were beginning to arrange four-part Bach fugues for solo marimba, there was nothing particularly galvanizing about having two players (especially two players of this caliber) each play a single melodic line with two mallets, and the overly slow tempo does nothing to add to the excitement. The real *coup de grace*, though, comes courtesy of Harry South's string arrangement. In the early part of the piece South simply adds a third melodic line for the strings, which works well enough, but approximately halfway through (0:45) the cushion of string chords become unbearably cloying. The result of the turgid tempo and saccharine strings is a dowdy track that does no credit to J. S. Bach's wiry little composition or the featured performers.

The last two tracks find Palmer taking on the legacy of his childhood idol, Buddy Rich. Of the fifth track, Palmer says, "I wrote 'Food For Your Soul' with a chap called Harry South, who's like England's Quincy Jones—he does a lot of music for detective television soundtracks. That was the jazz element I wanted to capture."[39] "Food For Your Soul" is an extremely credible big-band jazz-rock number that wouldn't have sounded out of place on one of Buddy Rich's or Maynard Ferguson's better albums of the seventies. South's arranging is terrific here (thankfully, there are no strings), Palmer's drumming is stunning yet fairly restrained (he wisely limits himself to two breaks, one fifteen and one about thirty-five seconds), and the chart is greatly helped by some hot Rhodes electric piano playing that reminds me of the work of the Ferguson band's Alan Zavod. "Food For Your Soul," which is the only one of Palmer's tracks coproduced by Greg Lake (Palmer produced the rest of his tracks himself), is arguably the highpoint of his *Works I* solo material.

The final track rearranges "Tank," from ELP's debut album, into the big-band idiom of "Food For Your Soul." The arrangement, by Palmer, Emerson, and Harry South, features Palmer and Emerson (on Moog, piano, and clavinet) accompanied by a big band and a string section. In an admirable show of self-discipline, Palmer cuts the two-minute drum solo that occupies the middle of the track on the debut LP down to a break that lasts just a few seconds; this greatly enhances the piece's structural integrity. Nonetheless, I've never totally been sold on the orchestrated "Tank." Lake's thundering bass part is missed—the bass is mixed far down here—and the contrapuntal intricacy of the criss-crossing clavinet lines of the original is lost, which saps the piece of some of its rhythmic edginess. The tradeoffs between the lightning fast clavinet/bass unison runs and the drum breaks at the end of the first

---

[39] Carl Palmer, quoted by Furnash, "Conversations," 27.

section are especially disappointing in their new guise; the clavinet/bass parts are rescored for strings, which sap the passage of much of its excitement and (again) lend it a somewhat dowdy character. The final section, in which the triumphal march's Moog parts are rescored for winds (except for Emerson's Moog solo, which appears very nearly in its original version), works better, without, however, lending anything vital or new to the piece. For me, the only "improvement" of the orchestrated "Tank" is the virtual removal of the drum solo. Nonetheless, "Tank" is a piece that lends itself fairly well to big-band jazz scoring, so interested listeners should compare the two versions and make up their own minds.

Side Four: Emerson, Lake and Palmer

Finally, we come to side four of the *Works I* two-LP set, where for the first time on the album we hear ELP featured as a group on two lengthy tracks that have become band classics: "Fanfare for the Common Man" and "Pirates." Greg Lake had this to say of "Fanfare for the Common Man," ELP's arrangement of Aaron Copland's brass-heavy orchestral favorite:

> We were recording in Montreux, Switzerland, in 1976, and Keith was playing it as a piece of classical music. I played this shuffle bass line behind him and all of a sudden it started to connect. Then Carl came in the studio and the three of us started to play it. Luckily enough, the engineer [John Timperly] had a two-track running, and that is what's on the record—the first time we played through the piece.[40]

While ELP's arrangement of "Fanfare for the Common Man" may well have had its genesis in a spur-of-the-moment jam, the final product heard on *Works I* appears not to have been put together as spontaneously as Lake suggests—according to the *Return of the Manticore* liner notes, it was recorded over a number of sessions during April, August, and September 1976. Emerson had this to say about the track:

> I sent the tape to [Copland's] publisher, because I knew that we had to have their permission to release the piece on our album. They initially told me that he didn't like it because it didn't have anything new or different on it. After that response I told them that I had only sent the parts of our version that were entirely Copland's, but that there was a long blues jam in the middle that I didn't think he would be too interested in. His agency told me that he was really a very open-minded man, and to send the whole tape for him to hear, which I did. It turned out that he loved it, and we became good friends after that. I love his music, and he seems to have taken quite an interest in mine.[41]

---

[40] Greg Lake, quoted by Aledorf, "Lucky Man," 10.
[41] Keith Emerson, quoted by Pethel, "Keith Emerson," 26.

Copland's own remarks suggest his enthusiasm may perhaps have been more apparent than real:

> Of course, I always prefer my own version, but what they do is really around the piece, I'd say, rather than a literal transposition [sic] of the piece. They're a gifted group. In that particular case I allowed it to go by because when they first play the "Fanfare," they play it fairly straight, and when they end the piece, they play it fairly straight. What they do in the middle—I'm not sure how they connect that to my music, but they do it somehow, I suppose.[42]

While the classical arrangement was nothing new for ELP's audience, "Fanfare" introduced some changes in the instruments played by both Emerson and Lake that surprised many ELP fans. Emerson's fans, in particular, were in for something of a shock when they played the group side of *Works I* for the first time. Emerson established his reputation playing Hammond organ, acoustic piano, and Moog synthesizers; none of these instruments are to be heard on the band side of *Works I*. Instead, "Fanfare for the Common Man" and "Pirates" feature only one keyboard: the Yamaha GX-1, the most advanced and expensive of the new generation of analog polyphonic synthesizers that were beginning to flood the market after 1975.[43]

Emerson purchased his GX-1 in early 1976 for the then-astronomical sum of $50,000. With its chrome pedestals and curved metallic body, it looked like a twenty-third-century Hammond organ.[44] The GX-1 had two five-octave polyphonic manuals, a third, smaller monophonic manual (all three manuals were touch sensitive, which at the time represented a revolution in electronic keyboard design), a twenty-five-note pedalboard, a ribbon controller, two swell pedals, and a springloaded knee controller. The different keyboards' voices could be coupled together so that sounds could be layered; timbres were controlled by rows of drawbar sliders and buttons above the middle manual, and the instrument could be programmed via miniature sets of controls hidden in drawers and panels on the instrument. This behemoth weighed in at approximately eight hundred pounds. Emerson owned one of the few specimens of this instrument that Yamaha actually sold; other GX-1 owners included Stevie Wonder, John Paul Jones (Led Zeppelin), and Jürgen Fritz (Triumvirat). Emerson's use of the Yamaha on "Fanfare" was not dissimilar to his use of his Moog arsenal as a kind of supersonic trumpet section on *Brain*

---

[42] Aaron Copland, quoted by Milano, "Keith Emerson," *Contemporary Keyboard*, October 1977, 30.

[43] A point of clarification: contrary to persistent rumors, the GX-1 is not the forerunner of Yamaha's highly successful digital synthesizers (e.g., the DX-7) of the 1980s. That distinction belongs to the Yamaha GS-1, a very different machine that was introduced in 1980.

[44] There is an excellent picture of it on p. 30 of the *Return of the Manticore* booklet.

Salad Surgery, although the instrument had its own distinctive sound. Furthermore, he developed some unique "gnarly" timbres on the Yamaha, produced by running the brass settings through heavy, high-speed vibrato, that are evocative of some of the overdriven, distorted Hammond organ timbres that characterized his work with the Nice during the late sixties.

Lake, for his part, replaced his Gibson Ripper with a custom-made Alembic Series II eight-string bass, with four sets of two strings that were tuned an octave apart.[45] This bass had a distinctive, highly unusual sound: the lower of each pair of strings rumbles with an almost subsonic frequency, while the higher of the pair jangles rhythmically, almost as if a tambourine were being struck as the lower string was plucked. The resulting sound, at once boomy and jangly, never struck me as being entirely ideal for ELP's music—I think it would have worked better in a setting where the rhythmic element of the bass line counted for more and the melodic element for less. Nonetheless, there's no doubt that Lake's Alembic, combined with Emerson's GX-1, gives ELP's late-seventies music a sonic sheen all its own.

ELP's "Fanfare for the Common Man" falls into three distinct sections. The opening section begins with a timpani overture by Carl Palmer; Emerson follows with a short snatch of the original "Fanfare" theme on an amazingly authentic GX-1 "trumpet" setting, after which the band launches into a full statement of Copland's fanfare theme. The arrangement is actually fairly straight, with two notable exceptions; the rhythm of the melody is somewhat altered to fit Lake and Palmer's backing shuffle groove, and Emerson interpolates what sounds like a funk guitar riff (it's actually played on the lower manual of the GX-1) in between the phrases of the "Fanfare" melody, which he plays on the middle manual using a trumpetlike setting. This "funk guitar" riff, which can be heard at 1:19, 2:01, and 2:43, sounds so realistic (the attack is very percussive in the manner of funk guitar technique) that for years I believed Lake had overdubbed the part on electric guitar; Emerson also does some highly authentic "funk guitar" comping underneath the "Fanfare" melody (2:33, 2:57). Another nice touch is the overdubbed timpani flourishes (2:10, 2:20, 2:28, and elsewhere). At 3:16 we hear the tail of Copland's "Fanfare," with its surprising modulation from C major to E major; while this passage ends Copland's "Fanfare," it is very nearly the beginning of ELP's, as the modulation to E major swings them into the heart of their arrangement, the legendary "blues jam."

---

[45] There is an excellent closeup of this bass on p. 6 of the *Return of the Manticore* booklet. Lake's bass was a Series II with Alembic's "Scorpion" body shape, walnut top, and many custom inlays.

This blues jam is the second and longest section of ELP's "Fanfare" arrangement. The heart of it is the exceedingly simple two-bar bass guitar ostinato (here one can hear the Alembic in all its booming/jangling glory), first heard at 3:23, and the accompanying shuffle groove on drums. For the next four and a half minutes, Lake only briefly abandons the ostinato, so Emerson is obliged to build up his solo over a totally static harmonic backdrop. He succeeds through a combination of gradually filling in the missing notes of the E-pentatonic scale until he's using an E-blues scale (thus increasingly melodic complexity), inexorably increasing the solo's rhythmic activity, slowly but surely guiding his improvised melodic line up to a registral high point, and gradually increasingly the melodic line's level of timbral distortion.

Emerson's solo begins at 3:30, as he spins out a simple blues melody on the GX-1's upper manual using a harmonicalike setting; what's most notable at this point is the simplicity of the melody and the amount of sonic space he leaves unfilled. Slowly, unobtrusively, rhythmic motion increases, new notes are added to the pentatonic melodic outline (B$\flat$, the flat fifth, at 4:05, C$\sharp$ at 4:19), and the overall register of the solo begins to rise, reaching e2 at 4:42, a2 at 4:46, b2 at 4:57 (here he begins introducing a small amount of vibrato), and finally e3 at 5:12: the flurry of notes beginning at 5:18 signals the solo's first climax. For me, this is the most impressive section of the entire solo: the buildup is gradual and inexorable, and my analysis here has had to ignore a number of other subtleties that also play a role in generating energy (for instance, how Emerson gradually begins to make his solo cut against the square rhythm of the Lake-Palmer groove in order to generate polyrhythmic tension— listen especially from 4:34 to 4:44).

The second phase of the solo begins at 5:25, as the "harmonica" begins to engage in a call-and-response with a "trumpet" section, which begins to regularly interrupt the "harmonica" solo with a short, ominous fanfare figure (Emerson used a similar technique in the organ solo of "Karn Evil 9, 3rd Impression"). By 5:52 this "trumpet" fanfare has become notably distorted as a result of a radical increase in vibrato speed, especially after it begins grinding the tritone E-B$\flat$ together (6:05). This phase of the solo climaxes as the "trumpet" and "harmonica" launch into a lengthy, complex jazz fusion–like melodic run beginning at 6:28.

The third phase of the solo is inaugurated by an obsessively repeated chromatic figure beginning at 6:45, which spills into the solo's most fantastical passage at 6:58, when Lake momentarily abandons his ostinato in favor of an agitated figure that cuts polyrhythmically against Palmer's shuffle rhythm, while Emerson distorts the "harmonica" and "trumpet" settings until one sounds like a bull elephant roaring and the other like a wailing siren. A morse-code-like iteration of the tritone E-B$\flat$ (7:15) leads to a final statement of the descending chromatic figure, accompanied by one of Palmer's patented frenzied snare-drum fills (7:30); thereafter an obsessively repeated and rhythmically off-balance melodic figure leads into the final segment of the solo, an impassioned development of the rising fifths from Copland's "Fanfare" theme. We hear this passage twice, first at 7:39, where it's extremely distorted and "gnarly," and once more at 7:50, where Emerson suddenly reduces the distortion, and cushions it with fuller backing harmonies, reducing the tension and preparing for a recapitulation of the opening section by smoothly transitioning the music back from E major to C major.

The recapitulation of the opening section, which begins at 8:00, is not exactly literal. The rhythmic values of the main theme are augmented, giving the "Fanfare" theme a greater expansiveness, and the "trumpet" timbre of the melody is more distorted now than it was in the exposition, reflecting the more experienced nature of the traveler who has passed through the blues jam. Only the close of the "Fanfare" theme is more or less literally recapitulated (from 8:34)—but even here there are some changes (i.e., the "funk guitar" breaks of the opening section are replaced by drum breaks). At 9:22, the tail of Copland's "Fanfare" again swings the music from C major to E major, and the entry of the blues bass riff suggests that yet another improvisational jam is in the offing; this time, however, the Lake-Palmer shuffle groove fades into the distance, one of a relatively few examples of a conventional pop music fadeout in the ELP canon.

"Fanfare for the Common Man" quickly became an ELP concert staple. Nonetheless, there is a certain segment of the ELP audience, especially those who preferred the fully composed epics like "Tarkus" and "Karn Evil 9," whom "Fanfare" always rubbed the wrong way. They found it too unfocused (almost like a more virtuosic Grateful Dead), a not particularly apt use of the band's compositional and orchestration talents, and, at worst, almost a self-parody of the self-indulgent aspect of the band that so grated ELP's critics. On the one hand, I see their point: the blues jam's shuffle groove does seem to go on forever, and I believe one could excise everything from 5:39 to 7:21, nearly two minutes of music, without doing any harm at all to the track's overall structural conception. On the other hand, self-indulgent as it is (especially the section from roughly 6:00 to 7:30), it still works as a *composition*, like all of Emerson's best solos ("Aquatarkus," or much earlier, the "Rondo" solo off the Nice's *Thoughts of Emerlist Davjack*): the mosaiclike linkage of motives, riffs, and tunes builds a powerful momentum, and one can only admire Emerson's ability to inexorably build up to huge climaxes over a static harmonic background.

In the U.K., a hugely compressed version of "Fanfare for the Common Man" was released as a single, and, shockingly, became a surprise number two hit during the summer of 1977. Moreover, the band shot a promo film of themselves doing a "live" performance of "Fanfare" (actually, they played along with the *Works I* recording) in an empty

Olympic Stadium, Montréal, in May 1977 after a freakish late spring snowstorm. The film is an interesting artifact in its own right: there's something surreal about their "performance," given while bundled up in heavy winter coats, in the cavernous, empty stadium filled with snow. The promo film shoot provided some of the more famous publicity photos of ELP from the late seventies—one such photo appeared on the back cover of *Works II*.[46]

Finally we come to the last track of *Works I*, and the pièce de résistance of the entire album, the Emerson, Lake and Sinfield collaboration, "Pirates." Emerson had this to say about the genesis of "Pirates":

> "Pirates" was going to go on my solo album. The story behind that is this: it had been suggested that I write the music to *The Dogs of War*, a novel by Frederic Forsyth. I started writing the music and Norman Jewison was producing the film. The next thing I know, he'd accepted the music but the idea of the film had been dropped. I don't know why. It was a good book and it would have made a damn good film. So here I was with no film but music that was still usable. I went to Greg and said, "Let's use this, and with the imagery I see behind this, you should write lyrics about mercenaries," and Greg said that he didn't like that and wanted to come up with something else.
>
> About a month later, Greg rang me up and he had Pete Sinfield with him, and he said "I just hit on a good subject, how about pirates?" I figured they do have a romantic imagery about them, like mercenaries, so I said okay. So then Greg and Pete worked like mad—the longest they've ever worked on one piece of music. They literally delved into the history of pirates and that's why the lyrics turned out so well.[47]

Lake recalls,

> In the case of "Pirates," Keith came up with this little bit of music. He thought, when he wrote it, of mercenary soldiers in South Africa. But it didn't sound like mercenary soldiers in South Africa . . . In the prelude to "Pirates," the music sounds like the sea. It didn't sound like the jungle. Then we thought "Who were the mercenaries of the sea? The pirates." We did a lot of research. Pete Sinfield and myself ordered all the books that had ever been written on pirates, and all the films on pirates, and we locked ourselves away for three weeks. We watched them all, and read all the books. We absorbed all this stuff. And then we got started, and the whole piece got written that way.[48]

---

[46] See also pp. 30–31 of the *Return of the Manticore* booklet. Greg Lake recalled it was so cold that the promo had to be shot in thirty-second segments. Lake: "We had to run into this trailer and dip our hands into hot water to stop them from freezing." See David Terralavoro, "Didja Know That . . . ," *Fanzine for the Common Man* no. 14 (July 1995): 24.
[47] Keith Emerson, quoted by Farber, "The Emerson, Lake and Palmer Tapes, part 3," 28.
[48] Greg Lake, quoted by Dave Gallant, "Greg Lake Tapes," *ELP Digest* 6, no. 17 (July 18, 1996).

The finished product, some 13:18 in length, features Emerson, Lake, Palmer, and the Orchestra de l'Opera de Paris, conducted by Godfrey Salmon: it is, quite simply, the most successful collaboration ever between a rock band and a symphony orchestra. It is also the most tightly woven ELP epic of the 1970s: I had more trouble formulating a convincing and coherent discussion of this piece's structure than I did any other ELP piece. The lyrics, unique for any ELP epic up to this time, present a coherent narrative. The story begins with a pirate captain recruiting his crew, who subsequently plunder a Spanish galleon, stop to hide part of their loot in an obscure bay, continue on to make a rowdy port-of-call in Portabello, and finally head back out to sea to do it all again. The storyline romanticizes pirate life in almost exactly the same way that gangster rap romanticizes the life of the modern black urban street gangster, and thus should be taken with a grain of salt. On the other hand, the lyrics do betray an attention to the historical details of a pirate's day-to-day life that lends "Pirates" an aura of authenticity.

When Emerson had composed his last rock-band/orchestral collaboration in 1969, the "Five Bridges Suite," he used the same approach that had been used by the Moody Blues, Pink Floyd, and Deep Purple in their rock/orchestral "collaborations": sections featuring rock band and sections featuring the orchestra are, for the most part, simply alternated. In "Pirates" his approach is subtler: to put it simply, he uses the orchestra as a particularly colorful and sumptuous extension of his synthesizer arsenal. At times orchestra and the rock trio do simply alternate: more often, though, the orchestra is gradually layered in until a huge climax is reached, often creating a vast web of orchestral counterpoint that Emerson could have only created through multiple studio overdubs. Because Emerson largely chooses timbres on his GX-1 that blend, rather than clash, with the orchestra, the transition from band to orchestra or the blending of band with orchestra is so subtle that it often takes concentrated listening to notice the shift from orchestral to band passages, or vice-versa. For the first, and perhaps last time in the rock era, in "Pirates" the orchestral and rock band writing is organically fused. "Pirates" is orchestrated rock in which the orchestrated passages actually rock.

The music of "Pirates" is so seamless, compared to previous ELP epics, that it is difficult to describe its distinct sections in terms that actually reflect one's listening experience. Nonetheless, I will attempt to do just that. At the very least, I believe one hears three distinct sections: an instrumental overture (0:00–3:35), the song proper (3:35–8:46), and a third section that is something of a microcosm of the entire piece, beginning with an instrumental passage (8:46–10:28), proceeding to a "new song" (10:29–11:40), and ending with a shortened recapitulation of the "main song" (11:40–12:18) and of the instrumental overture (12:19–13:18). Although there are none of the shifts between different musical "blocks" that are so characteristic of ELP's earlier epics—indeed, there are a number of motives, themes, and tunes that appear in all three sections—Emerson does make use of four dualities that lend "Pirates" a sense of progression and drama. First, there is the contrast between instrumental and vocal sections. Second, there is the contrast between sections featuring orchestra and band together and passages featuring the trio by itself. Third, there is the contrast between the stable tonality of the vocal sections and the far more nebulous tonality of the instrumental passages. Finally, there is the tug-of-war between two principal tonal centers a third apart—in this case, A major and C major/minor—that has characterized previous ELP epics such as "Karn Evil 9." Observing the use of these four dualities within the structure of "Pirates" will give us a much clearer sense of the track's trajectory.

Instrumental Overture (0:00–3:35). "Pirates" begins with a dissonant, icy synthesizer chord of indeterminate tonality that recalls the openings of "Tarkus" and "The Endless Enigma." The chord in question is a vintage Emersonian chord, bitonally voiced, something like a more dissonant diminished seventh (from the root, C–B♭–E–F♯–A). Note the dramatic use of increasingly fast vibrato at the final iteration of the chord from 0:41–0:48; a similar fast vibrato is used twice more during "Pirates" on important chords for dramatic purposes.

The main body of the overture begins with the orchestra's dramatic entrance with pounding string chords and offbeat percussion accents, first enunciated at 0:49. These insistent, pulsating string chords, vaguely reminiscent of the "Auguries of Spring" section of Stravinsky's *Rite of Spring* (although these chords are quartal, not bitonal like Stravinsky's), become one of the key thematic elements of "Pirates," and are stitched together with a number of other themes and motives to form a glowing, multihued mosaic during the remainder of the overture. Besides the string chords, which at first emphasize a C tonality but soon begin to drift, I would point to the martial brass motive (1:53), the longer and more fluid string theme (2:03, 3:21), the rocking GX-1 triads accompanied by a *molto perpetuo* bass guitar line (3:12), and the expansive, dramatic cadential figure which is heard twice, at 2:14 and again at 3:32. The orchestral textures are not particularly dissonant (although quartal harmonies are a basic factor whenever the pulsating string chords are heard); nonetheless, the sense of harmonic instability and the flux from one short theme to the next creates a sense of dynamic forward motion that inexorably pushes the overture on toward the main body of the song.

Song Proper (3:35–8:46). The song proper is, structurally speaking, the most complicated section of "Pirates"; the seamless effect of this section is rather amazing considering the abundance of material. The backbone of the entire section is the twenty-one-measure verse that commences at 3:35: a cheerful tune that never budges from A major, its hypnotically repetitive yet irregular phrase structure recalls the sea shanties of bygone days. It's repeated twice: while the orchestration is sumptuous both times, more orchestral counterpoint is worked in the second time, as an almost hornpipelike string/woodwind motive begins to assert itself as a countermelody.[49]

The two verses are followed by two repetitions of a sixteen-measure chorus, each with its own lyric. Again, Emerson creates a sense of growth by making an effective use of terraced dynamics. The first repetition of the chorus ("six days") is backed mostly by the trio, with short brass motives coloring key words ("spied," "roared"); the second repetition ("spare us") is far more sumptuously orchestrated, climaxing with the deliciously overblown D major triad at 5:23.

This chord begins the song proper's first instrumental section. Largely featuring the trio, it's more lyrical than virtuosic, with Emerson's harmonica-like GX-1 lead counterpointed by a surprisingly melodic Greg Lake bass line. The orchestra is worked in only towards the end, especially during the distinctive "wood block" section (5:58), where Carl Palmer's tasteful temple block theme, backed by *pizzicato* string chords, evokes Elmer Bernstein's "Magnificent Seven" theme and, more generally, Western movie scores, with its expansive and optimistic character.

The wood block section is followed by a third repetition of the verse ("the captain rose"), orchestrated much like the second verse, then, at 6:38, comes one of the most magical moments in the ELP canon: a quiet, reflective bridge section wherein all motion fades other than Emerson's softly lapping GX-1 arpeggios and Lake's quietly iterated A bass pedal points. As Lake begins singing of an indigo moonlit bay and pirates scattered around a fire, you can almost close your eyes and see the waves quietly rolling ashore: the musical and poetic imagery is that vivid. Structurally, the bridge serves as a halfway point, bringing the momentum of the first half of "Pirates" to a temporary halt, even as it dams up energy that will soon be released in the piece's latter half.

At 7:06, the bridge is followed by a fourth repetition of the verse ("our sails swell full"). This is the most richly orchestrated verse yet, with its heroic trumpet obbligato, jewel-like tuned percussion counterpoints, and velvet cushion of strings providing a vivid backdrop for Lake's voice—listen especially to the confluence of these elements under the words "buys any man a crown."

The second instrumental section of the song proper, beginning at 7:41, is both more sumptuously orchestrated and more rhythmically driving than the first, evoking the excitement of the band of pirates who have

---

[49] Compare especially the difference in orchestration between "I see your hunger for a fortune," first verse, and "The Turk, the Arab, and the Spaniard," second verse.

stripped a galleon of its loot and are now ready to make a port of call and live it up. The first half of this section transforms and develops the earlier wood block theme, first in C major (7:41), then E$^\flat$ major (7:50); this is the first time since the beginning of the song proper than the music has drifted from A major. Note the effective use of call-and-response between trio and orchestra here. The wood block theme is further transformed and developed at 8:05, once again alternating between C major (8:05) and E$^\flat$ major (8:14). Finally, a surging passage of three-part counterpoint (8:20) involving a chattering woodwind lead, a rising string line, and a melodic yet active bass guitar part settles the music more firmly into C major, and spills into a short vocal coda ("who'll drink a toast") at 8:30 which brings the song proper to an end. In this section, it is worth observing how effectively Emerson blends his orchestral and electronic resources; for instance, at 8:20 he doubles the woodwinds with his right hand and the strings with his left on the GX-1, producing a coloring that's a bit richer (and different) than the orchestra by itself would have been, while Lake plays a tubalike bass guitar line with more clarity than a tuba could have managed it. Notice the fast GX-1 vibrato on the B$^\flat$-major triad under "ours" (8:39–8:44), a subtle timbral link to the rapidly vibrated opening chord (0:41–0:48).

Development/"Second Song"/Recapitulation (8:46–13:18). The third and final section of "Pirates," beginning at 8:46 with a short drum break, once again flows remarkably well considering the variety of material that's passed through. Much of the third section of "Pirates" features the trio without the orchestra; not only does this tend to make the latter part of the section, when the orchestra reenters, sound more sumptuous, it also allows the band to rock out more convincingly without the excess ballast of the orchestral accompaniment.

The instrumental "development," from 9:09 to 10:28, offers a scintillating transformation and variation of the orchestral overture material, which is recast in a decidedly jazz-rock fusion vein. For instance, the pounding string chords of 0:49 return here in an entirely new context; beginning at 9:09 Emerson "comps" with the original chords in his left hand, while his right hand improvises a new melody that is divided between the two upper manuals of the GX-1 in a call-and-response format. At 9:52 we hear a more direct reference to the pounding string chords in their original guise, followed quickly at 9:54 by a reference to the martial brass motive first heard at 1:53. At 10:01, a frantically pressing passage of percolating GX-1 chords and a polyrhythmic, motoristic bass guitar line transforms a similar passage from the overture (from 3:12); then come more direct recollections of the familiar string theme (10:15—compare with 2:03 and 3:21) and the expansive cadence figure (10:26, recalling 2:14 and 3:32).

This cadence figure leads into what amounts to a second song, beginning at 10:29, which chronicles the pirates' debauches during their stay in Portabello. This "song" consists of two twenty-four-measure verses in C major ("landlord," "ten on the black"). Featuring only the trio, this section rocks harder than any of the previous vocal material, vividly evoking the excitement of the pirates on leave.

A short transition ("on the flood of the morning tide"), which serves to slow the music down, broaden it out, and swing it back to A major from C major, launches the recapitulation. First to be recapitulated, at 11:40, is the main verse of the song proper ("this company"). Again, the orchestration is very sumptuous; note especially the hornpipelike countermelody of the piccolo and the thrilling brass chord underlying "I" (12:07). At 12:19 the pounding string chords of the overture return, much closer to their original character than they were in the earlier development section, although the tonality now hovers around B major/minor. Finally, at 12:57 the vocal coda that originally had closed the song proper (8:30) is recalled; as Lake dramatically draws out "man" at 13:08, Emerson rapidly vibrates the underlying B$^\flat$ major chord on his GX-1, drawing a subtle link to the close of the first part of the overture (0:43) and to the close of the song proper (8:39). The B$^\flat$ triad moves on to a C major triad, ending "Pirates," and settling the tonal tug-of-war between A major and C major that has dominated the entire piece in favor of the latter.

"Pirates" is, by any standard one would care to use, one of ELP's great achievements. In fact, I would argue that it's "Pirates," not the Piano Concerto, that is the real tour de force of *Works I.* "Pirates" has come a long way from the bald juxtaposition of distinct musical blocks that characterizes "Tarkus," "The Endless Enigma," and other earlier ELP epics. While never abandoning the mosaiclike linking of themes, motives, and tunes that seems to underlie all his most representative works, here Emerson spontaneously creates the seamless, tightly woven large-scale epic he was unable to achieve with the more self-consciously "organic" Concerto: if there are any structural faults to "Pirates," I am hard-pressed to identify them. He uses tonality much more effectively in "Pirates," with its dynamic tug-of-war between two competing tonal centers, than he does in the Concerto. Furthermore, the variation of thematic material in the final section of "Pirates" achieves, seemingly without effort, the type of organic thematic transformation that he worked very hard (but failed) to achieve in the Concerto. Certainly the orchestration of "Pirates" (which Emerson completed in partnership with John Mayer) is colorful, vivid, and imaginative in its combination and contrasts of orchestral and electronic resources, and perfectly suited to the content of the music in a way that the Concerto's orchestration doesn't always seem to be. In short, "Pirates" comes off as a totally confident statement by a composer who knew what he wanted to say and said it with great fluency and panache; the Concerto, by comparison, sounds uncertain and overly self-conscious.

Of course, "Pirates" also benefits from the participation of one of the great rhythm sections of rock music. Then there is the matter of Greg Lake's vocals. In the album's liner notes, Lake is credited with "vocal interpretation," an indication of the unremitting seriousness with which the band now seemed to take themselves.[50] No matter. Lake's vocals on "Pirates" represent, in my view, his career performance: never before or again did he sing with the same combination of power and subtlety. There are, in fact, too many subtleties to his vocals to adequately cover here: I would simply suggest that the subtle continuum he creates between speech and song, his rasps and other vocal colorings of key words, and his phrasing and large-scale shaping of the lyrics' narrative, will repay multiple listenings.

Works I: An Assessment

Indeed, the critics who still took ELP seriously by 1977 (which, of course, no longer included anybody from *Creem*, *Rolling Stone*, *New Musical Express*, or *Melody Maker*) were quick to point to the almost magical synergy that still existed between the three musicians, a synergy that they found notable for its absence in the *Works* solo material. Bob Shaw of *Downbeat* put it particularly well:

> The main thing proven on *Works* is that in musical physics, the whole is often greater than the sum of its parts. Together, Emerson, Lake and Palmer have always made chartered, flowing sense; a strong concept of team play and tonal unity has aborted any pomposity. Their masterworks—"Take a Pebble," *Karn Evil 9*, and most of the *Tarkus* suite—have proven to be a capably representative easel for Emerson's bombastic figurines, Palmer's tympanic conceptions, and Lake's latent folkie yet exquisite chords and smooth voice.
>
> At their best, ELP's work has always had an onomatopoeic effect; the various war suites on *Brain Salad Surgery* were orchestrated with Moog-played bugle simulations and the military cadences of Palmer. Such close interrelationship between lyric and music persists here; the Emerson, Lake, and Pete Sinfield composition "Pirates" is backed up by the swirling tempos of the Orchestra de l'Opera de Paris, playing glissandos that are often used to portray the rolling waves of the ocean in seagoing classical works.
>
> Unfortunately though, ELP as a unit only occupies one-fourth of the disc space here. The other three sides are devoted to individual performances by the three band members. Here is where the boredom sets in, as the lone

---

[50] I remember, as a sixteen-year-old buying the album, looking at the "vocal interpretation" bit and thinking to myself, "Does that mean he sings it, too?"

musicians, for the most part free of customary accompaniment, all reveal serious technical deficiencies.[51]

Shaw goes on to catalog these "technical deficiencies": Emerson's unsure grasp of large-scale classical structure, Lake's inability to sing more than one type of song, Palmer's growing reliance on seventies funk clichés.

For some ELP fans, even "Pirates," for all its fluency and undoubted dexterity, was missing something. That something was aggression; many longtime fans found "Pirates" too smooth for its own good. They missed the timbral distortion, the nervous rhythmic energy, the harmonic dissonance, the jagged, muscular melodic lines that characterized "Tarkus," "Toccata," and earlier ELP epics. For me, it's "Pirates" rather than "Fanfare for the Common Man" or even the Concerto that most fully manifests the displacement of Alberto Ginastera by Aaron Copland as Emerson's primary influence. The result of this displacement is a pervasive mellowing out. "Pirates" has none of the strident timbres of earlier ELP epics; the shifting meters, while still present, are much more subtle now, almost hidden; rhythms and melodies, while retaining many Emersonian traits, are more fluid and less muscular than before; and Emerson's highly characteristic, biting bitonal chord voicings are greatly restricted here. In short, "Pirates," with its cheerful, major key vibe, lacks a certain fervor and urgency—criticisms sometimes leveled at Copland's music, which can be rather glib beneath its graceful, craftsmanlike exterior. Copland's influence, which on *Trilogy* brought some welcome restraint and subtlety to Emerson's compositional technique, here seems to sap it of some of its modernist fervor. If the metallic sheen of *Tarkus* evokes an out-of-control machine, the glittering luster of "Pirates" is reminiscent of a jewel-encrusted manuscript illumination. Both are valid; however, I can't help but feel that the former more honestly conveys the essence of the era that produced it.

Indeed, I'm not sure that "Fanfare" and "Pirates" are really "progressive" in the same way as the material on the band's first six albums. From 1970–74, ELP's music was always forward looking; "Fanfare" and "Pirates," on the other hand, seem to be more about finishing something old than beginning something new. Specifically, "Fanfare" seems to be one final expression of Emerson's late-sixties preoccupation with using a classical piece as a framework for exploring the possibilities of the psychedelic jam. I hear "Fanfare" as a modernization of "Rondo," and I'm not at all surprised that ELP's stage shows soon started fusing the two numbers together. "Pirates," meanwhile, seems to be a final manifestation of Emerson's preoccupation with creating a satisfactory fusion of rock and

---

[51] Bob Shaw, "*Works Volume I,*" *Downbeat,* October 6, 1977, 28.

orchestral elements that had first manifested itself nearly a decade earlier in the Nice's *Ars Longa Vita Brevis* and the "Five Bridges" suite. The fact that "Pirates" succeeds much better than either of the two works by the Nice does indicate Emerson's considerable growth as a composer between 1967 and 1977. However, I hear the group material of *Works I* as a final capstone to the band's six classic albums of 1970–74, rather than the harbinger of a new musical direction. As was to become painfully obvious all too soon, the band was, in fact, losing their struggle to establish a coherent new musical direction that could enable them to navigate the shifts in values and tastes that were shaping up as the seventies moved into the eighties.

One final note concerning "Pirates." *The Return of the Manticore* box set contains an entirely different mix of "Pirates" than that of *Works I;* the biggest difference involves the percussion accents during the orchestral overture, which on the box set's version are extremely vivid and at a couple of points (1:11, 1:23) actually sound like gunshots across the bow of a pirate ship. The band had hoped to use this mix on *Works,* but it contained a gap that could not be fixed with the analog splicing techniques of the 1970s; it turned out to be salvageable with the computerized digital splicing techniques of the nineties, though, and if you listen carefully you can hear (from 3:32–3:36) where the end of the overture and beginning of the song proper are digitally linked.

Works Live

The Show That Ended (April 1977 through March 1978)

Buoyed by the relative success of *Works I*, ELP pressed on with their preparations for a tour backed by a full orchestra and small choir. An article that ran in *Sounds* in May 1977 recounted:

In a basement rehearsal room in a seedy older area of Montréal, Emerson, Lake and Palmer began going through their parts for "Pirates" and other group-orchestra pieces alone in early April. The orchestra was rehearsing separately until a few weeks before the tour, when final dress rehearsals began. In all, the band spent eight weeks preparing before setting out, and it was taking the rehearsals seriously, going over and over both old and new material. Later it moved to the Expo Theater on the former site of Expo '67 and then to a hockey arena . . .

In addition to three busloads of orchestra musicians and choir, the ELP caravan will include seven 45-foot vans of equipment for the indoor dates, plus three more when the concert is open air. There will be about 10 outdoor stadium concerts on the American summer tour, with the first in Chicago's Soldier Field June 4.

In those equipment trucks will be the band's own indoor and outdoor stages, a 72,000-watt sound system similar to the one used last summer in the Montréal Olympic Stadium (only larger) and custom lighting designed by Nicholas Cernovitch, a ballet and opera lighting designer who's working on a new Martha Graham dance at the same time—in all about 25 tons of gear.[1]

Works Orchestral Tour

The scope of the planned orchestral *Works* tour made even the enormous 1973-74 World Tour seem modest by comparison. Besides the fifty-nine-member orchestra and six-member choir, there were to be nineteen tech-

---

[1] Rudis, "Guess Who's Back," 24.

nicians and twenty assistants, roadies, and production managers; the over-all tour entourage was estimated to contain between 115 and 120 people (the liner notes of the *In Concert* LP/*Works Live* CD lists 112 persons, including the band). The portable stage, custom designed by TFA/Electrasound in Boston, was sixty feet wide, forty-six feet deep, and was designed in such a way that only the musicians and their instruments were visible on stage; stage monitor speakers were sunk under the stage, with Emerson and Lake standing on grids so that monitor sound was pro-jected at them from below. Guitar patch cords and other cables were hid-den from view, while black carpeting and velour backdrops lent the portable stage a concert hall ambience. The stage included a hydraulic lift platform that rose fourteen feet above ground for conductor Godfrey Salmon.

As with earlier tours, ELP sought to create the illusion of a fully enclosed environment around them, and their portable stage came with its own portable "roof": thirteen pods suspended over the stage that cov-ered an eighty foot by eighty-foot area and extended partly over the audi-ence. This pod arrangement concealed tons of lighting grids and sound and light cables, and resulted in about four tons of equipment hanging from the stage ceiling.

The sound system was designed by Audio Analysts of Montréal, and was estimated in 1977 to be worth over a million dollars. The main PA system consisted of forty custom-built cabinets weighing 450 pounds each, and was driven by 72,000 watts of power. Three mixing boards were employed: one for the orchestra and choir, one for ELP alone, and one that mixed the total into the house mix heard by the audience. A special part of the sound system was the Frapp pickup:

> Made by an electronics genius in San Francisco, this little device has to be cus-tom-fitted to each instrument in the orchestra. In the mouthpieces of the trumpets, for instance, a little hole is drilled for the pickup to be inserted. What this Frapp pickup system will do is simply amplify the instruments to the high decibel level that the band plays. Other devices can do this, but the dif-ference is that most of them tend to "electrify" the sound of the instruments. With the Frapp, the sound will be true to life. All the subtleties and nuances of the violins will be heard, all the colors of the brass, all the shades of the woodwinds. At least that's what everybody hopes.[2]

The lighting system, designed by Nicholas Cernovitch and Rob Mitchell, used a computer-operated lighting board to achieve an array of dramatic effects with 311 separate spotlights and 60 different dimmer controls. Of course, the musicians' instrumental rigs were similarly elabo-

---

[2] Rudis, "Guess Who's Back," 24.

rate. Emerson's setup was centered around his new Yamaha GX-1, which he used for much of the *Works* material, but also included his Hammond C-3 and L-100 organs, the modular Moog, a Minimoog, a nine-foot Steinway grand piano, and an accordion; during the course of the tour, he added a Yamaha CP-70 electric grand piano, which he de-tuned for a "honky-tonk" effect on certain numbers ("Nutrocker," "Maple Leaf Rag"). Two technicians, Nick Rose and Chris Young, accompanied the tour to keep careful watch over the GX-1, which (like Emerson's old Moog setup) was notorious for tuning problems. Besides his Alembic Series II custom eight-string bass, Lake also toured with a Travis Bean electric guitar, a Zemaitis twelve-string acoustic, and three vintage Martin six-string acoustics. The linchpin of Palmer's rig was his stainless steel kit and revolving drum rostrum, both of which had seen action during the 1973-74 World Tour. He added some tuned percussion instruments he hadn't used before: besides timpani, gongs, and chimes, he now included xylophone, vibes, glockenspiel, and crotales in his setup.[3]

The *Works* tour was slated to begin May 24 in Louisville, Kentucky. In a radio interview with Sonny Fox held in Montréal on May 14, just a few days before the start of the tour, the band sounded oddly fatalistic, almost as if they were expecting disaster. When Fox asked the band if it was true there wasn't a great profit margin for the tour, Lake quickly answered, "No, there's a great loss margin, actually. I mean, it's so expensive that if we sell out every night and everybody comes to see the show, you know, we lose money at this point." He went on to try to put a brave face on the band's financial situation and depict the orchestral tour as the logical pinnacle ELP had always been evolving toward:

> You have to decide on priorities, you know. For us, it wouldn't have made it to have retired after that last tour and just vegetated somewhere in the country. We wanted to break new barriers and do new things, you know, so for us, we were compelled to do it, really . . .
>
> Incorporating our music into a symphonic and orchestral sense—that's the final extreme really you can go to musically . . . We became conscious that had we gone on repeating more and more electronic albums and gone further on that path we really wouldn't be achieving a lot and for us there had to be a change, you know, in what we did.[4]

---

[3] Much of this information was gleamed from "*Works* on the Road," Richard Robertson's 1977 article for *Hit Parader*; there is a reprint of this article in *ELP Digest* 3, no. 7 (April 12, 1993).

[4] Greg Lake, "Superstars Radio Network" interview with Sonny Fox, May 14, 1977. This interview was released in limited quantities in vinyl format as a promotional tool to be sent to radio stations. It is interesting for including the then-unreleased orchestral version of "Abaddon's Bolero" that is, in some details, different from the edited version that was finally released on Emerson's solo *Changing States* album of 1995.

Clearly, however, the band were bracing themselves for difficulties.

And unfortunately, problems were not long in coming. During the very first show, almost like an omen, a weld on a huge and complex lighting rig broke. Said Lake, "It cost us hundreds of thousands of dollars. The repercussions of it lasted for three or four days—we had to move Cincinnati back a day. And when you're carrying 120 people, you can't budget for expenses like that."[5] The broken light truss and its aftermath, however, were just the beginning of sorrows. In short order, three outdoor shows were cancelled: Tampa (after a riot that followed Led Zeppelin leaving a rain-soaked stage and not returning), Cleveland (after the promoter had a sudden attack of cold feet), and Pittsburgh (poor ticket sales). Tour coordinator Tom Mohler put it this way: "Three outdoor shows mean 70,000 people per show or 210,000 people at $10 per seat—which is over two million dollars. When the shows were pulled out from under us, it just couldn't be done. We had to start saving *now*."[6] Other unforeseen problems emerged as well, which, mixed with the issue of the cancelled shows, forced the band into jettisoning the orchestra. Emerson:

> There were a lot of things that were unforeseen that made us have to stop using the orchestra. There were many things, more than I can go into. One was a ruling by the union that musicians can't travel more than about 100 miles every day. But the thing is that people travel that far these days to see concerts. So we were packing places one night and then we'd travel 100 miles to the next place and we'd only have half the house filled. Of course, we were planning on having every place completely sold out so we could at least break even. And a lot of little things started piling up to put us behind. From then on it was impossible to catch up on the finances, so we just had to stop and go out as a three-piece.[7]

By mid-June, after fourteen shows, the orchestral tour had ground to a halt. The band decided to retain the orchestra for a few key dates, specifically three shows in New York's Madison Square Garden on July 7–9, and a show in Montréal's Olympic Stadium on August 26. This meant that the orchestra would have to be kept on salary through late August—at a cost of $40,000 per week. Nonetheless, the savings on indirect costs (setup, sound equipment, labor, trucks, etc.) came to $120,000 per week.

The sudden loss of the orchestra was traumatic on both an emotional and a practical basis. Lake recalls, "Their last date, they [the orchestra]

---

[5] Greg Lake, quoted by John Storm Roberts, "Progressive Rock's Classic Synthesizers," *Newsday*, July 3, 1977, 17.
[6] Tom Mohler, quoted by Roberts, "Progressive Rock's Classic Synthesizers," 17.
[7] Keith Emerson, quoted by Milano, "Keith Emerson," *Contemporary Keyboard*, October 1977, 30.

were crying whilst they played."[8] The biggest trauma, though, was experienced by Emerson:

> Now I've really got to work like hell with all those electronics to make up for what we lost. We practiced for a long time in Montréal [prior to the tour], just the three of us. Everything sounded very thin because I expected the orchestra to be in; I didn't play particular lines where the orchestra was going to be. Suddenly those lines were dropped, and we had two days to get it all together. It was easy for Greg and Carl because their parts were all the same. For me it was totally different, and now I have twice as much to do as I did before.[9]

The *Works* Orchestral Tour was only beginning to establish a distinctive identity along the lines of the 1973-74 World Tour when it ground to a halt. Nonetheless, based on the reviews of the time, reaction was mixed. By the 1990s, baby boomers had to some degree discovered symphonic music, and the idea of a rock band and orchestra performing an entire show together wasn't so novel anymore; in the late 1970s, however, a lot of ELP's young fans didn't know what to make of it, as demonstrated by a review of one of the band's two shows in Detroit's Cobo Arena on May 31 and June 1 that ran in *Time*:

> Conductor Godfrey Salmon rose 14 feet in the air atop a hydraulic podium. Silence reigned for a good second or two before the cries came from the audience: "Rock and roll!" "Get it on!" "It's boogie time!" Not quite boogie time . . . As Maestro Salmon gave the downbeat, 9,500 fans, many reared on the violent excesses of Alice Cooper and Iggy Pop, got the first sampling of what was in store for them. From 40 huge loudspeaker enclosures suspended from the ceiling came the mighty sounds of "Abaddon's Bolero" . . . The music built relentlessly, awesomely, powered by 72,000 watts worth of amplification, enough to start a medium-sized radio station . . .
>
> The Detroit fans warmed up slowly to ELP's new, sophisticated stylings. Jim Richter, 22, was overheard saying to his date, "You said I'd love these guys. This sounds like something on PBS!"

Tellingly, Emerson told the reviewer, "I listened to what I had been doing with all those synthesizers [on the first six ELP albums], and realized that I was hearing an orchestra in my head all along. And so I said, 'Don't kid yourself. If you want to hear it that way, hear it that way. Be happy.'"[10]

---

[8] Greg Lake, quoted by Roberts, "Rock's Classic Synthesizers," 18.

[9] Keith Emerson, quoted by Furnash, "Conversations," 29. As far as I can determine, Emerson had four days between his last orchestral show and first trio show to rearrange his parts.

[10] This review, "72,000 Watts in That Name," was reprinted in *ELP Digest* 9, no. 1 (January 26, 1999).

Nonetheless, as Emerson himself admitted on a different occasion, many ELP fans, who, of course, weren't privy to the idealized experience that only a composer can have of his own music, did not share his grief at the loss of the orchestra:

> Luckily, people have come expecting the orchestra and still haven't been too disappointed. In fact, a lot of people said we sound better without them. I'm inclined to disagree with that. They do get more of a chance to see ELP as a threesome, though. I think that some of them are under the impression that the orchestra is taking a lot of what we are meant to be doing away from us. It's really untrue. Actually, what the orchestra is enabling us to do is more of the ELP repertoire than we've ever done before. Like the "Bolero" from *Trilogy*. We tried doing that as a trio in all manner of ways. I even taught Greg to play keyboards on it.[11]

As my readers may have sussed, I, too, have some deep philosophical reservations with the whole premise of the *Works* Orchestral Tour. I will agree that selected numbers—"Abaddon," "Pirates," Emerson's Piano Concerto—work much better with, or even require, an orchestra. Where I really have a problem is the orchestration (or perhaps I should say re-orchestration) of ELP's rock arrangements of classical pieces. "Knife-Edge," *Pictures at an Exhibition*, and "Fanfare for the Common Man" were all successful translations of orchestral pieces to a rock idiom; a key part of the translation process were Emerson's keyboard arrangements, which, while replicating a symphonic spaciousness, also introduced a set of electronic timbres that were unmistakably "rock." With the *Works* tour, these pieces are rearranged for orchestra, with the trio simply playing and singing along in karaoke fashion: I see this not as "progressive," but as mere novelty. When Carl Palmer drummed along with the LPO for a mere one track on his side of *Works I*, it was possible to overlook the novelty aspect and simply enjoy Palmer's drumming; to listen to huge swaths of orchestral material which ELP dutifully accompanies, on the other hand, is not, for me, very enlightening. The music of ELP's first six albums is a true *fusion* of the band's classic, jazz, rock, and folk sources: the biggest problem with the *Works* Orchestral Tour is that it breaks the band's musical style back down into its individual components, so that the whole is no longer greater than the sum of its parts. To the contrary, the constituent elements of ELP's music now seem to coexist uneasily together.

John Rockwell, in his review of the band's July 7 show at New York's Madison Square Garden that was accompanied by orchestra, was quick to point out that the band's diverse stylistic offerings never quite cohered, and the result was like a somewhat ill-conceived musical variety show:

---

[11] Milano, "Keith Emerson," *Contemporary Keyboard*, October 1977, 32.

"The trouble with Emerson, Lake and Palmer, for all its talent and all its diversity, is that others—real classical performers, cabaret singers, and so on—can do what it does better, and the whole impact is disturbed by a pervasive, exploitative crudeness of taste."[12] Harsh? Perhaps. Accurate? I'm afraid, on the whole, the answer would have to be yes. Unfortunately, the *Works* Orchestral Tour became a convenient straw man for everything critics like Rockwell said was wrong with progressive rock—the haphazard mishmash of distinct musical styles, and so on—while at the same time doing little justice to the truly progressive pioneering work of the first six ELP albums.

After the last of the fourteen orchestral shows (June 16 in Evansville, Indiana), the band had a short break before they resumed as a three-piece in Philadelphia on June 20. They played eleven shows as a three-piece in June and early July before their three shows at Madison Square Garden on July 7–9 with orchestra and choir. During one of the Madison Square Garden shows, Lake ran into his old King Crimson cohort, Robert Fripp, who was now living in New York, where he was deeply involved in the local New Wave scene. Lake and Fripp, who had not seen each other for several years, agreed to go out for dinner after the final Madison Square Garden gig. What happened next isn't totally clear, as Lake and Fripp give divergent accounts, but both agree that they did go out to dinner, and that they had a conversation in Lake's limo after dinner that ended badly. Lake says he merely told Fripp he would like to jam with him sometime, and Fripp told him he wasn't interested; Fripp said Lake proposed reuniting the original King Crimson lineup, which Fripp refused to consider. At any rate, the two men would not meet again for several years, and this event seemed to mark the beginning of a slow but steady deterioration in their relationship.

The three Madison Square Garden dates were followed by a breakneck schedule of dates as a three-piece: fourteen more in July, sixteen in August. Finally, there came the climactic date of the first leg of the *Works* tour—indeed, it turned out to be ELP's last great moment of glory during the 1970s—their final show with the orchestra and choir, Montréal's Olympic Stadium on August 26. Attended by 78,000 fans (their biggest audience ever as a solo act, and one of the biggest audiences for a single band during the 1970s), parts of the Montréal show are captured on the *Emerson, Lake and Palmer Live in Concert* LP (1979, rereleased with a number of additional tracks on CD in 1993 as *Works Live*) and on the *Emerson, Lake and Palmer Works Orchestral Tour* video, released by Manticore Records in 1998. Neither the video nor the CD capture the

---

12 John Rockwell, "Emerson, Lake and Palmer + 60 = Rock," *New York Times*, Saturday, July 9, 1977, 8.

Montréal show in its entirety: the CD (but not the video) includes a number of tracks recorded in later 1977 and early 1978, when ELP were touring strictly as a three-piece and were including several tracks from *Works II* in their set. The entire Montréal set list, given below, is representative of their orchestral shows of May, June, and July.

1977:

1. Abbandon's Bolero (with orchestra) — On *Works Live*; a 1:11 excerpt used as background music at the opening of the video

2. Hoedown (as three-piece) — Not on *Works Live;* not on video

3. Karn Evil 9, 1st Impression, part 2 (as three-piece) — Not on *Works Live*; on video

4. The Enemy God (with orchestra) — Not on *Works Live*; on video

5. Tarkus (as three-piece) — Not on *Works Live*; not on video

6. C'est la vie (with orchestra) — On *Works Live*; on video

7. Lucky Man (Greg Lake solo) — Not on *Works Live*; on video

8. Pictures at an Exhibition (with orchestra) — On *Works Live*; on video

INTERMISSION (Featured promo film of "Fanfare for the Common Man" shot after freak May 1977 snowstorm at Montréal's Olympic Stadium)

9. Piano Concerto, 1st movement (Keith Emerson with orchestra) — Not on *Works Live*; not on video

10. Piano Concerto, 3rd movement (Keith Emerson with orchestra) — On *Works Live*; on video

11. Closer to Believing (Greg Lake with orchestra) — On *Works Live*; not on video

12. Knife-Edge (with orchestra) — On *Works Live*; not on video

13. Tank/drum solo (with orchestra) — On *Works Live*; on video

14. Nutrocker (as three-piece) — Not on *Works Live*; on video

15. Pirates (with orchestra) — Not on *Works Live*; on video

16. ENCORE: Fanfare for the Common Man/Rondo (with orchestra) — On *Works Live* (abridged); on video (complete)

As an event, the Montréal concert must have been quite an experience. Again, though, based on the evidence of the video and audio recordings, the verdict of the show's musical success is mixed. A few of the tracks—"Abaddon," "Pirates," the Piano Concerto—work far better with the orchestra than without, and are unqualified successes. Otherwise, the orchestral arrangements often seem superfluous (at best), and on numbers like *Pictures* and "Knife-Edge," the loss of rhythmic tightness and the occasional intonation problems create a plodding, elephantine feel that comes dangerously close to duplicating the image of ELP painted by Lester Bangs, Dave Marsh, and others as purveyors of turgid, middle-brow "classical rock." Personally, I feel the entire concept of the orchestral tour was misguided; however, the video and audio evidence is there for you, the reader, to listen to and judge for yourself.

In the three months between the first orchestral show on May 24 and the Montréal show on August 26, ELP played a grueling fifty-nine-show schedule, and they took a well-deserved break during September and the first half of October. During this period they did some retooling of their set list, both to reflect the permanent loss of the orchestra and to include several tracks from the soon-to-be-released *Works, Volume II*. The second leg of the *Works* tour was launched in Athens, Ohio, at the Ohio University Convocation Center on October 15, and comprised nine shows in October and twelve in November—all of them in the United States. Part of the November 25 show at Wheeling, West Virginia, is captured on the King Biscuit *Emerson, Lake and Palmer* CD. The last show of this leg of the tour, at the New Haven, Connecticut, Civic Center on November 30, is included in *The Original Bootleg Series from the Manticore Vaults*, vol. 2, and shows the band in especially fine form, offering a representative example of their set list for this leg of the tour. They opened with a rocked-up arrangement of Henry Mancini's "Peter Gunn" theme, followed by "Hoedown" and an abbreviated version of "Tarkus" ("Manticore," "Battlefield," and most of "Mass" are omitted). These latter two selections are taken at a somewhat more deliberate tempo than they were on the 1973-74 World Tour, which especially benefits the instrumental segments of "Tarkus"; otherwise, the arrangements are not terribly different, although Emerson now played some lines on the Yamaha GX-1 that he had formerly played on the Hammond. The next portion of the show featured several acoustic numbers: "Take a Pebble," solo piano versions of the first movement of Emerson's Piano Concerto (embroidered with some very nice glockenspiel work by Carl Palmer) and Scott Joplin's "Maple Leaf Rag," and an exceptionally nice "Take a Pebble" reprise. Greg Lake was featured in a solo role on two numbers, "C'est la vie" (joined by Emerson on accordion) and the familiar "Lucky Man."

The second half of the show opened with an arrangement of "Karn Evil 9, 1st Impression, part 2" that lacked the fire of the band's 1973-74 performances. Then came two numbers from *Works II*, "Tiger in a

Spotlight" and another Greg Lake ballad, "Watching Over You." The band reached way back into their repertoire by presenting "Nutrocker" in a revised and somewhat more sophisticated arrangement than before, featuring some nice bop-style soloing by Emerson. Next came a three-piece arrangement of "Pirates"; the band's playing was impressively tight, although the tempo seemed a bit rushed, and the loss of the orchestral lines are definitely noticeable at some points.[13]

The band played two encores. The first was a medley of "Fanfare for the Common Man" and "Rondo." Unlike the studio version of "Fanfare," in which the improvised GX-1 solo gradually builds to a shattering climax, generating a good deal of tension in the process, the live performance meanders through a long, unadventurous twelve-bar blues. The inclusion of "Rondo"—which by now had become little more than a vehicle for organ wrestling and long episodes of feedback—furthered the impression of an overly long jam in which moments of real musical substance were in critically short supply. The second and final encore was much more rewarding: a swinging version of Irving King's Tin Pan Alley–era classic "Show Me the Way to Go Home," another *Works II* selection featuring Emerson at his jazzy best and Palmer on some nicely understated vibes work. For some reason, "Show Me the Way to Go Home" isn't included on the *Manticore Vaults* release of this show.

As demonstrated by their magisterial performances of "Tarkus" and "Take a Pebble," ELP had suffered no decline in live performance skills. What did seem to have declined between 1974 and 1977 is the quality of their set list. The 1973-74 set list was one of the most challenging ever undertaken by any rock band, with Lake's solo ballads and the occasional throwaway song ("Jeremy Bender") more than balanced out by complete performances of "Tarkus" and "Karn Evil 9" and other substantial works like "Toccata" and "Take a Pebble." The 1977 set list, on the other hand, is lighter on the epics and rather heavier on frankly trivial numbers ("Peter Gunn," "Tiger in a Spotlight," "Nutrocker," "Maple Leaf Rag"), on long-winded jams of questionable musical substance (the "Fanfare"/"Rondo" medley), and on solo numbers that highlight the increasingly divergent musical interests of the trio. Newer fans seeing the band for the first time were still likely to be impressed, but many fans who had followed ELP through their seven-year career found the band to be coasting in autopilot.

Works II was released in late November 1977, roughly eight months after *Works I*. Many fans expected that ELP would follow up the unusual, semisolo format of *Works I* with a more conventional group album; such

---

[13] Some of Emerson's GX-1 settings are rather thin, especially during the instrumental overture; one can hear this in the performance of "Pirates" captured on the King Biscuit CD.

hopes were misplaced. *Works II* was an undisguised and unapologetic collection of musical odds and ends. It featured a roughly equal division between group numbers recorded in September 1973 during the *Brain Salad Surgery* sessions and solo numbers by the three musicians (three by Emerson, two each by Lake and Palmer) that hadn't been included on *Works I*. Several of the twelve tracks had been released as singles (including B-sides), although none had ever appeared on an ELP album.

Works II

The leadoff track of *Works II* is the Emerson, Lake, Palmer, and Sinfield collaboration "Tiger in a Spotlight," which then-Manticore president Mario Medious had touted as a future ELP single as early as 1974. "Tiger," recorded during the *Brain Salad Surgery* sessions, highlights Emerson's Moog Constellation setup (i.e., the Apollo and Lyra), although the promo film, shot in 1977, shows him playing his parts on the Yamaha GX-1. Cast in the form of a simple twelve-bar blues in F, "Tiger" features Emerson in his boogie-woogie mode; the semiautobiographical lyrics offer a meditation on the frantic pace of life on the road and the unfulfilled promises of fame. Many ELP fans dislike the song for its musical simplicity. Like any blues, though, musical interest lies not in large-scale structure but in the textural, rhythmic, and timbral details inserted within the confines of the twelve-bar structure, and on this level, I think "Tiger" succeeds reasonably well. Among the enjoyable details of the song are the interweaving of Lake's electric guitar obbligato with Emerson's boogie figures during the first two twelve-bar choruses (although Lake's guitar lines are farther down in the mix than I would like); Emerson's clever quotation of John "Dizzy" Gillespie's bebop standard "Salt Peanuts" from 1:57 to 2:06; the ominously falling Moog glissandos during the third chorus, beginning at 2:27; and the song's false ending on the Moog's "bull elephant" roar (beginning at 3:25), out of which a final verse dramatically reemerges at 3:52. Unfortunately, neither the Moog effects nor the electric guitar counterpoints were feasible in live performance, and as a result live renditions of "Tiger" have always struck me as rather bland.

The second track of *Works II* is one of the album's highlights, one of the band's least-known gems, and a rare Emerson-Lake-Palmer collaboration: "When the Apple Blossoms Bloom in the Windmills of Your Mind I'll Be Your Valentine." Both the whimsical title and the general musical content suggest the mid-1970s output of the so-called Canterbury bands; I especially hear some similarity between this track and parts of Soft Machine's *Bundles* (1975) and *Softs* (1976). "Apple Blossoms" is probably the closest ELP came to exploring the direction suggested by the opening section of "Tank," the main difference being that the latter is more rhythmically driving, while the space-funk/jazz-rock of "Apple Blossoms" is more laid back as it deliberately grooves its way through the cosmos. Both are fleet, airy, and far removed from the characteristically ponderous sound of ELP. The track is built on a short vamp figure of repetitive quartal harmonies that Emerson comps with his left hand; with his right hand he spins out long, spiraling lead lines that antiphonally alternate between his Moog Lyra and Apollo keyboards. Palmer's drums are recorded differently here than on any other ELP track; the closely miked hi-hat, rather than the bass drum, becomes the focal point, and the crisp, funky hi-hat and shimmering cymbals suggest the production approach of the ECM label's Manfred Eicher. Lake's bass lines also contribute much to the track. An interviewer once asked Emerson if he found Lake's bass parts too sparse; Emerson responded that he didn't think Lake's bass playing was "sparse" so much as it was often too reliant on repeating an ostinato figure over and over with little or no change (think "Stones of Years" or "Fanfare for the Common Man").[14] Here, though, Lake does a fine job moving the short, potentially boring bass ostinato around, molding it into a plethora of interesting melodic shapes; listen especially to his inspired run at 1:52. The track ends with a wonderfully impressionistic cascade of Moog notes that disappear into an atmospheric haze; one can only wish that ELP had spent more time exploring this tasteful, melodically inventive vein of spacey jazz-rock during the *Works* era.

The third track, Carl Palmer's "Bullfrog," shows a number of stylistic affinities to "Apple Blossoms," although the latter's air of timeless calm is replaced with an edgy, nervous energy. The track, cowritten with Backdoor's Ron Aspery and Colin Hodgkinson, features the same lineup as "New Orleans" from *Works I*. "Bullfrog" opens with a spasmodic, angular melodic head played in tight unison by a continuously shifting assortment of woodwinds, tuned percussion, and drums; we hear this theme at the beginning (with a distinct tail from 0:16–0:23), again at 0:27, incompletely at 1:36 (the tail), 1:45 (the head), and 2:40, and finally in its complete form from 3:14 to the end. Interspersed between repetitions of the main theme are a lengthy sax solo backed by drums and a temple block obbligato (0:43–1:35), a supremely strange episode from 1:48 to 2:39 featuring flute, gong, synthesizer, froglike aquatic bubbling

---

[14] Milano, "Keith Emerson," *Contemporary Keyboard*, September 1980, 22. Here one also notes Lake's frequent habit, on the first four ELP albums in particular, of simply doubling Emerson's left-hand figure. According to Emerson, Lake did not like to improvise, and tended to take the rough bass parts Emerson sketched out for him very literally, which would go a long way towards explaining his habit of repeating the same ostinato figure *ad infinitum*.

sounds, and some superb cymbal work, a funky bass solo (2:42), and a contrasting but equally jagged unison melody played by drums, bass, and sax (from 2:47).

I have always wondered why "Bullfrog" was not included on *Works I*; it is easily Palmer's most adventurous track, compositionally speaking, from the *Works* era, and features by far his most interesting exploration of tuned percussion. Indeed, I hear a number of striking similarities between "Bullfrog" and "Beelzebub," the first track of *Feels Good to Me*, the almost contemporaneous debut solo album of Palmer's great rival, Bill Bruford. Like "Bullfrog," Bruford's "Beelzebub" alternates between a jagged melodic head—played by Bruford on vibes in unison with the rest of the band—and several episodes that are equally brimming with nervous energy. Bruford, of course, went on to compose and perform some of the finest jazz-rock fusion of the late 1970s and 1980s, first with his eponymous band, then with Earthworks; based on the evidence of the much-underrated "Bullfrog," Palmer was poised to follow a similar direction. One can only wonder what might have happened if Palmer had organized a band to record an entire album of this kind of music after the breakup of ELP in 1980—rather than going on to the infinitely more pedestrian PM and Asia.[15]

The fourth track, "Brain Salad Surgery," has an interesting history. Like "Tiger in a Spotlight," "Brain Salad Surgery" was recorded during the September 1973 *Brain Salad Surgery* sessions; for a time Manticore considered releasing "Tiger" as a single with "Brain Salad Surgery" as a B-side. What eventually happened instead is that "Brain Salad Surgery" was released on a 7" flexi-disc given away in an early 1974 issue of *New Musical Express*; the flexi-disc also contained snippets of other tracks on the album, culminating with the final few seconds of "Benny the Bouncer." It was also released as a DJ copy with "Still . . . You Turn Me On."

Perhaps more than any other track, the Emerson-Lake-Sinfield song "Brain Salad Surgery" marks the apogee of a particular subgenre, what I've dubbed "progressive blues," that Emerson had been perfecting throughout his years in ELP. "Tiger in a Spotlight" had fused boogie piano lines and bluesy guitar leads with thoroughly modern analog synthesizer timbres; "Brain Salad Surgery" went a step further. Unlike "Tiger," it's not beholden to twelve-bar blues form (although the verses show traces of it), which frees the band up to be more structurally and metrically adventurous. Indeed, the extremely intricate metric shifts in the

---

[15] The Carl Palmer Anthology of 2001 includes another Palmer composition featuring the work of Aspery and Hodgkinson (along with guitarist Snuffy Walden), "The Pancha Suite"; this track, which was previously unreleased, is as inventive as "Bullfrog" (which was recorded at the same time), although it's not as polished.

opening instrumental episode are vintage ELP; so are the dynamics contrasts between the hard-rocking verses, which feature some of Lake's raspiest singing of the 1970s, and the quiet, yet intensely focused wah-wah electric guitar episode from 2:15 through 2:41. The Moog timbres are highly adventurous, featuring nearly subaudible synth bass glissandos that practically shake the walls; despite its ultramodern electronic sheen, though, "Brain Salad Surgery" drips with a blues sensibility, heard in Emerson's bluesy Moog filigrees, Lake's electric guitar counterpoints during the verses (which, even more than those of "Tiger," are buried too far down in the mix), and Palmer's funky cowbell parts. The lyrics also show a blues connection, with a series of sexually implicit double entendres otherwise unusual in the ELP canon. With nary a wasted note, "Brain Salad Surgery" captures both the intricacy and the energy of ELP in a bluesier-than-normal framework; clocking in at a concise 3:07, it would have been an excellent candidate for a hit single in late 1977 or early 1978 (I think it would have meshed well with late-seventies sensibilities) had it not been previously released. As it was, no other *Works II* track featured the same blend of concision, energy, accessibility, and musical substance.

When I played *Works II* for the first time in December 1977, I remember being impressed with the first four tracks, and thinking to myself that ELP had finally recaptured the magic of their first six albums. Unfortunately, after the fourth track, both the energy level and the level of creativity begin to wane. Track five, "Barrelhouse Shakedown," is a Keith Emerson tune that evokes the stride and boogie-woogie classics of the 1920s and 1930s that he had previously paid tribute to in the "Piano Improvisations" segments of his 1973-74 live shows. Recorded at London's Advision Sound Studios in April 1975, the tune features Emerson accompanied by a big band, whose parts were arranged by Emerson and Alan Cohen. As I've said, Emerson's straight-ahead stride playing isn't really my thing; however, anyone who enjoys that particular style will find much to admire in "Barrelhouse Shakedown."

Track six is a Greg Lake ballad, "Watching Over You." Written as a lullaby for his infant daughter, "Watching Over You" is a true solo track, with Lake handling vocals, guitars, bass, and the simple but tasteful harmonica solo in the middle of the song (although there are some gauzy male background vocal harmonies interspersed sporadically). It's a nice song, with some tasteful mandolinlike acoustic guitar parts (at 2:18, 3:31 and elsewhere), but its musical substance is fairly thin, it lacks the bittersweet modal mixings that give many of his songs an emotional bite, and becomes a bit syrupy by the end. Of Lake's *Works*-era ballads, "Watching Over You" is probably the least substantial, and I think he did well to include it on *Works II* rather than *Works I*. Nonetheless, it was a regular feature of the last two legs of the *Works* tour, from October 1977 through

March 1978; Emerson played Lake's harmonica solo on a harmonicalike GX-1 setting.

Another group track, the Emerson-Lake-Sinfield collaboration "So Far to Fall," kicks off side two of the LP format of *Works II*. Keeping in mind that during the *Brain Salad Surgery* rehearsals in early 1973 Greg Lake had described the new music as sounding like "a big band playing rock material—a fairly meaty thing,"[16] it's ironic that it's the outtakes from the *Brain Salad Surgery* sessions that eventually landed on *Works II*, rather than the material that was finally included on *Brain Salad Surgery*, that best fits this description. If there's any one song by ELP that sounds like a big band playing rock material, it's "So Far To Fall," which was recorded in September 1973, but which was released on *Works II* with horn parts that were added during the Advision sessions of April 1975 that had also produced "Barrelhouse Shakedown" and "Honky Tonk Train Blues."[17]

If "Tiger in a Spotlight" and "Brain Salad Surgery" attempt to create a kind of "space-age blues," "So Far to Fall" is an attempt to stake out an analogous subgenre of space-age big-band vocal jazz. The tempo of the song is rather slow; angular, syncopated melodic figures played in unison by electric guitar, bass, and Hammond organ (that instrument's only appearance on either *Works I* or *Works II*) alternates with furious outbursts of staccato horn chords and with Lake's icily declaimed vocal verses that wend their way through an imposing thicket of phrase extensions and metric shifts. The overall effect suggests a futuristic parody of big-band jazz.[18] The refrain (in two parts, at 1:33 and 1:51 and again at 2:58 and 3:15) "swings" a bit more, but "swing" is a relative term here: this is cold (not cool) jazz that deigns (rather than fails) to swing. In short, there's nothing quite like "So Far to Fall" in the ELP canon. I'm not certain that it's wholly successful. Other than the climactic bridge section at 3:34, which really does build up some passion, there's a sense of disconnect between the "earthy" big-band idiom and double entendres of the lyrics, on the one hand, and the icy intellectualism of the music on the other. Some bands might have generated a rich sense of ironic displacement from this sense of disconnect, but ELP were too earnest for that. Nonetheless, if "So Far to Fall" is a failure, it's certainly an interesting one.

The eighth track is an orchestrated version of the most famous ragtime number of all, "Maple Leaf Rag" (1899) by Scott Joplin (1868–1917),

---

[16] Johnson, "Lake the Strongman," 9.

[17] This from a phone conversation with Keith Emerson in late November 1999.

[18] I'm especially reminded of some of the arrangements by Bob Graettinger, best known for his "City of Glass," composed for the Stan Kenton band during the 1940s: Graettinger was able to take a simple Tin Pan Alley song like "Everything Happens to Me" and distort it into a dissonant, icily abstract credo to modernism.

featuring Keith Emerson and the London Philharmonic Orchestra. Given Emerson's interest in stride piano (of which ragtime was the closest ancestor) and the mid-1970s ragtime revival (spurred by the movie *The Sting*, which prominently featured Joplin's rag "The Entertainer"), the inclusion of "Maple Leaf Rag" is probably not all that surprising. Emerson's orchestration of the piece is competent, but the performance by the LPO does that organization no credit. The tempo is somewhat rushed, the intonation of the high woodwinds is frequently suspect, and the rhythmic phrasing of the melodic figures is often sloppy. Recorded under the baton of John Mayer as an afterthought at the same late November/early December 1975 sessions that produced the Piano Concerto no. 1 and the orchestral "Abaddon's Bolero," one can question whether it ought to have been released at all.[19]

The same, thankfully, is not true of the ninth track, the Greg Lake-Peter Sinfield ballad "I Believe in Father Christmas." Of the seven Lake acoustic ballads that came out of the *Works* era, "I Believe in Father Christmas" is the best; indeed, I rank it as one of his two or three finest songs of all. At first, the lyrics appear to merely address the loss of childhood innocence, as the protagonist sees Father Christmas "through his disguise"; as the song proceeds, though, Lake sings of his loss of faith in "the Israelite," and we realize that the song is mourning not only the loss of childhood innocence but the loss of religious faith and the sense of meaninglessness that results. In "Still . . . You Turn Me On" and "Closer to Believing," Lake held out hope that committed human relationships could replace the sense of meaning that had been lost with the decline of religious belief in a secular age; here he doesn't sound so sure, and when he sings at the close of the song "Hallelujah, Noel, be it heaven or hell / The Christmas we get, we deserve," the sense of bleak resignation is palpable. "Father Christmas" is the closest Lake comes to existentialism.[20]

Of course, the lyrics' lofty aspirations would fall flat without appropriate musical support; here, though, Lake comes through with music that is equal to the task of expressing the sentiments of the lyrics. The song's structure is fairly simple: a ten-bar instrumental introduction is followed by a sixteen-bar verse/ten-bar refrain pairing that's repeated three times. The chord structure is relatively simple, too, but Lake makes typically effective use of modal mixture to create a bittersweet ambience that meshes well with the lyrics: the prevailing D major ("Father Christmas" is yet another ballad utilizing Lake's favored open D guitar tuning) is displaced by D Mixolydian during part of the verse (0:37–0:44, 1:30–1:37,

---

[19] Emerson, *Pictures*, 285, explains the reasons for the LPO's sloppy performance. You might be surprised by the explanation.
[20] Although George Forrester may be correct to suggest that the sense of bleakness is more a contribution of Pete Sinfield than of Lake. See *Emerson, Lake and Palmer*, 99.

etc.). The melody of the verse is one of Lake's finest, with smooth, folk-songlike curves and a gradually rising contour (b1 on "they" at 0:20, c2 on "I" at 0:37, d2 on "peal" at 0:45); Lake sings it in his most fragile, painfully vulnerable voice grain. The melody of the entirely instrumental refrain is derived from the "Troika" of Sergei Prokofiev's *Lieutenant Kije* suite (1934), and fits Lake's verse melody like the proverbial glove. The gradual layering in of parts and the slow increase in dynamics is well done, and is a major aspect of the song's success: as with all of Lake's most successful ballads, small musical gestures often make a large impact. The layering of acoustic guitar parts during the introduction and first verse is exquisite; the song builds steadily with entries of the GX-1 (taking the Prokofiev melody) and sleigh bells during the first refrain, the entry of a pseudo-folky droning GX-1 bass part during the second verse, the more "orchestral" GX-1 harmonization of the final verse, and imposing yet tasteful acoustic piano coda. Other nice details include the delicate bouquet of acoustic guitar harmonics at 1:25 (highlighting "fairy story") and again at 2:04, and the melodic counterpoint between GX-1 and acoustic guitar during the second and third refrains.

Of all the major Lake ballads of the 1970s, I think "Father Christmas" is the most perfectly arranged, and I greatly prefer the delicate, tasteful arrangement of *Works II* to the single version of the song released in 1975. In the latter, the bombastic entry of orchestra and massed choir at the end of the song ruins its delicate beauty, and introduces a phony triumphalism that is totally at odds with the lyrics (but which is more in sync with the promo film, the imagery of which I happen to think is also at odds with the lyrics). After Rhino Records bought ELP's back catalog from Victory Records, they released a five-track EP that includes both mixes of "I Believe in Father Christmas" as well as "Humbug," the B-side of the single version, so it's now possible for an interested listener to quickly compare the two versions and arrive at his or her own preference.

"Close But Not Touching," cowritten by Carl Palmer and Harry South, features Palmer in a big-band jazz setting, and is a product of the sessions that produced "Food for Your Soul" and "Tank" from *Works I*. Of Palmer's three *Works*-era big-band jazz numbers, "Close But Not Touching" is probably the least substantive, and its inclusion on *Works II* makes sense. It starts rather curiously for a big-band jazz number: an almost John Philip Sousa–like march melody is played by flutes to the accompaniment of Palmer's military-style snare drumming. Eventually the full band takes up the flute theme and develops it in a more conventional big-band jazz-rock vein. It's not bad, but it never catches fire in the same way as "Food for Your Soul." The one genuinely interesting touch occurs near the end of the track, at 2:50, where, following a dissonant, screaming brass chord, a synthesizer drone and distant siren usher the return of the original flute theme, which Palmer now accompanies on full kit, until the procession fades into the distance.

The eleventh track is Meade Lux Lewis's 1927 boogie-woogie piano classic, "Honky Tonk Train Blues," a product of their April 1975 Advision sessions that also produced "Barrelhouse Shakedown." Emerson, playing a de-tuned piano, is accompanied by a small pickup band whose parts were orchestrated by Alan Cohen; the arrangement essentially copies Bob Crosby's arrangement of the tune from 1938. As with "Barrelhouse," fans who enjoy Emerson's straight stride/boogie-woogie playing are sure to enjoy this one. "Honky Tonk Train Blues" was released in Italy as a single with "Barrelhouse Shakedown" as the B-side, where it was a minor hit; a promo film was also shot for this track, featuring Emerson as a dapper pianist in a 1920s-like nightclub setting.

The final track of *Works II* is another 1920s classic, "Show Me the Way to Go Home" (1925), by Jimmy Campbell and Reginald Connelly, who wrote songs under the pseudonym "Irving King." The song begins with an unaccompanied swing-style jazz prelude by Emerson; the swing idiom allows Emerson to stretch out harmonically more than the stride or boogie numbers, and Emerson's jazz prelude highlights his genuine flair for swing rhythm and outside chord substitutions. The first verse features Lake's voice with sparse trio accompaniment; on the second verse, the trio is joined by orchestra, expertly arranged by Godfrey Salmon. The orchestra suddenly breaks off, as Emerson begins soloing over the chord changes with some fine support from Lake and Palmer. (Again, considering Lake's alleged lack of interest in jazz, he does an excellent job moving the bass line around the chord changes.) Emerson begins to furiously pound out big block chords at the end of the trio's second trip through the chord changes, and the solo segues directly into the refrain, with Lake singing "show me the way to go home" with the support of orchestra and a stomping black gospel-style choral backing. This proves to be the song's climax; the choir drops out, leaving Lake to sing the end of the verse with quiet support from piano and orchestra. Lake shows a fine command of the thirties crooner vocal style, although his vocals are drenched in too much reverb. Of the four tracks on this album that either cover or evoke early twentieth-century American popular music, "Show Me the Way to Go Home" is the most successful.

Works II: An Assessment

I feel that *Works I* has been consistently overrated by ELP fans; conversely, I believe *Works II* has been somewhat underrated. Despite its supposed disjointedness, much of *Works II* is united by a common theme: an exploration of, and tribute to, the earlier twentieth-century styles of American popular music from which rock sprang. This is evident in both Emerson's covers and evocations of prerock styles and in the group's *Brain Salad Surgery* outtakes, which are more blues based (or, in the case of "So Far to Fall," big-band jazz based) than anything from the first six ELP albums. In fact, I think that it's possible to argue that despite its obvious unevenness and the relative superficiality of a number of its tracks, *Works II* coheres a bit better than *Works I*. Interestingly, Robert Christgau—admittedly not the best judge of such matters, considering his self-admitted hatred of prog—rates *Works II* higher than any other ELP album he reviewed. In a cryptic little review that ran in *Creem* in early 1978, he gave the album a "C+," and said "When the world's most overweening 'progressive' group makes an album less pretentious than its title, galumphing respectfully through Scott Joplin and Meade Lux Lewis, that's news. But is it rock and roll?"[21]

Fans, however, who by and large didn't share Christgau's rigid blues orthodoxy that lends a semimagical virtue to any blues-based music, were underwhelmed. Having waded through the semisolo format of *Works I*, they looked to *Works II* to be the band's "real" group album. When they saw it was merely a collection of odds and ends, a good deal of it from the trio's solo projects, and that there would in fact be no "real" group album, they began deserting ELP in droves. *Works II* barely cracked the U.S. top forty, charting out at thirty-seven, and fell out of the top two hundred in fourteen weeks—the least successful ELP album up to that time in both categories. In the U.K. the album did somewhat better, charting out at number twenty.

Works Tour: Final Leg

Nonetheless, the relatively poor showing of *Works II* contributed to the growing impression that ELP were a band in decline, and cast something of a pall over the final leg of the *Works* tour, which, after taking a hiatus throughout December 1977, resumed with two dates in friendly territory at Montréal's Forum on January 16 and 17, 1978. The band played eleven more gigs (one more in Canada, the rest in the U.S.) during the remainder of January. A show they played on January 24 at Terre Haute, Indiana, is representative of their set list for the final leg of the *Works* tour; while it is not that different from their set list during the second leg of the tour, there were a few changes. Their shows now began with the Emerson/Palmer "Fanfare" theme immortalized at the beginning of the *In Concert* LP and *Works Live* CD: despite persistent rumors that the trio

---

[21] Reprinted in Christgau, *Rock Albums of the 70s*, 126.

numbers included on those recordings were recorded at Wheeling, West Virginia, in November 1977, in fact at least some of them must have been recorded in early 1978, since it was only during the final leg of the *Works* tour that their shows opened with the short "Fanfare." This moved directly into "Peter Gunn" (which now sometimes included a snippet of the "Mission Impossible" theme over the ostinato bass), "Hoedown," and the abbreviated "Tarkus" suite in which "Manticore" and "Battlefield" were excised ("Aquatarkus," rather different here from its 1973-74 incarnation, now regularly included a brief quote of John Williams's *Star Wars* theme). Then came the acoustic segment of the show: "Take a Pebble," solo piano renditions of the Piano Concerto's first movement and Joplin's "Maple Leaf Rag" by Emerson, the "Take a Pebble" reprise, and "C'est la vie" and "Lucky Man," featuring Lake in a solo role (Emerson contributing the accordion solo on "C'est la vie"). "Karn Evil 9, 1st Impression, part 2" was removed from the set list during the final leg of the *Works* tour; it was replaced by an abbreviated version of *Pictures at an Exhibition* (essentially, the Newcastle version of the piece without its middle segments—"The Sage," "The Old Castle/Blues Variation," and the third Promenade were removed). This was a good addition, adding some much-needed musical heft to the set list: although the arrangements were conservative (one wishes that Emerson might have used the GX-1 more in the piece's climactic sections), the band played it well. Then came "Tiger in a Spotlight," Lake's "Watching Over You," the Carl Palmer feature segment (the first section of "Tank," the drum solo, and "The Enemy God"), and the jazzed-up arrangement of "Nutrocker." The concert concluded with "Pirates" (which ended with the sound of two cannons being shot off together), "Fanfare for the Common Man" (now without "Rondo") as the first encore, and "Show Me the Way to Go Home" as the second and final encore. The addition of *Pictures* and subtraction of "Rondo" made for a somewhat more substantive use of their time, with the set list now including two hours of solid music.

February 1978 was a month of backbreaking touring, with twenty-four shows in twenty-eight days, including two shows at Toronto's Maple Leaf Garden (February 2–3), two at Nassau Coliseum (February 9–10), and two in Kansas City (February 27–28). The first half of March was just as intense, with nine shows between March 1 and March 13. I saw ELP live for the first time on March 4 at Detroit's now-defunct Olympia. They seemed tired and a bit dispirited, especially after a well-meaning moron tossed a "We Love ELP" banner onto Emerson's Moog during *Pictures*. (He somehow managed to toss it off without missing a note.) They played the same set list as the Terre Haute show of January 24, and I remember being particular wowed by Palmer's revolving drum rostrum with its flashing strobe lights, and by the band's commanding performance of "Pirates," with the cannon blasts on the final chord. The band did not return for an encore, despite several minutes of solid clapping, hooting, and hollering, so I never did get to hear their live "Fanfare for the Common Man" or "Show Me the Way to Go Home." After Detroit, ELP played just six more shows. The last, on March 13, was in Providence, Rhode Island's Civic Center, and was favorably reviewed in *Variety*, of all places. It was their forty-sixth show of 1978; since the beginning of the *Works* tour some ten months earlier, they had played over 120 concerts. What nobody suspected at the time is that the Providence show of March 13, 1978, marked the last time that Emerson, Lake and Palmer would play together in a live setting for over fourteen years.

13

Land's End on Love Beach

(Summer 1978 through December 1979)

The mood at the end of the *Works* tour was quite different than it had been at the end of any previous tour. Of course, the circumstances were quite different, too. Throughout their long history, ELP had always been a band on the way up, with each new tour carving out a bigger fan base and pushing album sales higher than the previous one. Now, ELP were beginning to see the same scenery coming down the hill of rock superstardom they had once seen going up. Their triumphant World Tour of 1973-74 had pushed *Welcome Back My Friends* to number four on the charts; six months of constant touring could push *Works, Volume II* no higher than thirty-seven. The 1973-74 World Tour had made ELP one of the highest-grossing bands of their era; after the spectacular debacle of the orchestral segment of the 1977-78 *Works* tour, it took months of touring for the band to simply recoup their losses and break even. Clearly, ELP had opened a new—and unwelcome—chapter of their saga.

For the first time since the turbulence that had accompanied the recording of *Tarkus* over seven years earlier, the band seriously considered calling it quits. In an open letter to the readers of *Contemporary Keyboard*, Emerson put it this way:

> At the end of the last American tour as a three-piece unit, we were considering a final separation. It was at the back of all our minds, but it was left unspoken. The orchestra tour plagued Greg and Carl as both a financial and artistic disaster, a view I totally disagreed with . . . The tour as a three-piece was long and very hard. We discussed during this last tour what would happen afterwards and what possibilities were open to us. One thing was certain: in order to continue, we would have to do a lot of cutting down. We even discussed a piano/bass/drums format.[1]

---

[1] Keith Emerson, "An Open Letter from Keith Emerson to the Readers of *Contemporary Keyboard*," *Contemporary Keyboard*, September 1980, 19.

The issue of a new album was also raised. Neither Emerson, Lake, nor Palmer evinced the slightest enthusiasm for such a project. However, according to Lake, ELP were contractually obligated to Atlantic Records for one more studio album.[2] Emerson has spoken of the matter more specifically: "After meeting with Atlantic Records we were finally persuaded to make one more album. Much to my reluctance, a commercial album was suggested, 'commercial' meaning we would compress all of the simpler ideas and make them into neat little radio-playable singles."[3] The die was thus cast for the most disastrous album of ELP's entire career.

ELP began recording the new album during the summer of 1978 at Compass Point Studios, near the Emerson family's home in Nassau, the Bahamas; Greg Lake and Stewart Young actually bought property nearby the studio, while Carl Palmer rented a hacienda. To say that the rehearsals didn't produce an explosive creative synergy would be an understatement: as Emerson recalls, "We'd go into the studio and just rap all day because we hadn't got any music down, and that was it."[4] Soon enough, though, a general direction to the sessions emerged. The band recorded several short, pop-oriented songs written by Greg Lake and Pete Sinfield; these were slated for the first side of the LP. Side two was to be devoted to a four-movement Keith Emerson epic. In a measure of how far Emerson and Lake had drifted apart both musically and personally, the concept and lyrics for this new epic were the result of a collaboration between Emerson and Pete Sinfield rather than Emerson and Lake; only with difficulty did Stewart Young persuade Sinfield to supply the lyrics for Emerson's composition, and Sinfield agreed to only if he didn't have to coauthor the lyrics with Lake, as he wished to finish the lyrics quickly and with a minimum of friction.[5] Emerson, for his part, was involved in cowriting just one of the five Greg Lake pop songs that ended up on side one of the LP; he has one (count 'em, one) lead keyboard line during the course of these five songs. Clearly the fissure in individual musical direction that had opened up during the *Works* era was quickly becoming an unbridgeable chasm.

Emerson recalls, "everybody but me wanted to get the hell out of Nassau."[6] Lake and Palmer left so expeditiously, in fact, that the album

---

[2] Hall, "Welcome to the Show," 48.

[3] Emerson, "An Open Letter," 19.

[4] Keith Emerson, quoted by Milano, "Keith Emerson," *Contemporary Keyboard*, September 1980, 17.

[5] See Forrester, Hanson, and Askew, *Emerson, Lake and Palmer*, 121, for details.

[6] Keith Emerson, quoted by Milano, "Keith Emerson," *Contemporary Keyboard*, September 1980, 17. Emerson recalls that immediately before Lake left Nassau, they had one final argument about the wisdom of the *Works* Orchestral Tour. See Emerson, *Pictures of an Exhibitionist*, 320.

was not fully produced in the sense of previous ELP albums, where all three members had reached a consensus on every detail of arrangements, the final mix, and packaging before the album was released. If you carefully read the liner notes of this particular album, you will notice that nobody is awarded the producer's title; Emerson was the de facto producer, although he saw his role more as a salvager, trying to make the best of the tracks as they existed at the point when Lake and Palmer left Nassau: "In the end I stuck the whole album together—nobody else showed up—and sent it off to Atlantic."[7] Lake's abandonment of his producer's role on this album set a new precedent—that he was no longer automatically entitled to produce a new ELP album—that was to perpetually destabilize the band during their periods of reformation during the 1980s and 1990s.

The packaging of the album soon became a point of contention between Emerson and Atlantic Records. Atlantic wanted to title the new album "Love Beach" (after one of the album's Lake/Sinfield pop songs, which in turn was named for a strip of beach on Nassau near Emerson's house), and feature a group photo of the three musicians on the beach of a small island off of Salt Cay, amidst the palm trees and sawgrass, decked out as bare-chested late-seventies disco stars. Neither idea sat well with Emerson:

> In the end I rang up Ahmet Ertegun [president of Atlantic Records] and said "Look, man, it makes us appear like a bunch of beach boys, which we're not." And he said "Oh, it doesn't really matter about album titles. What are titles, you know? Look at the name of the Beatles. What does that mean? It doesn't make any difference." So I said, "It makes a lot of difference to me because it doesn't fit the image of this band." But they went ahead anyhow. It's a complete letdown.[8]

In fact, while the title and album cover, which Emerson called "an embarrassment against everything I've worked for,"[9] may not conform to anything ELP had ever done before, they are inextricably intertwined with the new musical direction, such as it was, established on side one of the new album. *Love Beach* was released to an unsuspecting public in late November 1978, almost exactly one year after *Works II*. Before I launch into a detailed discussion of the album, it would be useful to momentarily consider the bigger picture, the changing musical currents of the late 1970s.

It is often said that punk and disco sank progressive rock and other ambitious late-sixties/early-seventies rock styles. This is not true, except

---

[7] Ibid.
[8] Ibid.
[9] Emerson, "Open Letter," 19.

perhaps in a very indirect way, especially in the North American market, which was the market ELP primarily concerned themselves with by the mid-1970s. The rock audience that bought ELP albums hated disco; it is simply untrue that rock consumers who had bought *Brain Salad Surgery* a few years back were now buying Sylvester and Donna Summers albums. It is true that in the hippest U.S. markets—New York City, the San Francisco Bay area, perhaps Los Angeles—the new punk music generated a loyal cult audience. However, punk was never more than a cult style in the U.S. during the seventies, and in most regions of the U.S.—the Midwest, the South, even much of the Northeast—it scarcely even attained cult status. Punk did exert an influence all out of proportion with its actual sales by powerfully influencing rock fashion, and thus highlighting the ties of ELP and their peers (Yes, Pink Floyd, Led Zeppelin, etc.) to an earlier era—that is to say, by making ELP and their peers seem old and unhip. However, it is simply not correct to say that fans deserted ELP in droves in order to purchase Sex Pistols and Dead Kennedys LPs. Even New Wave, the more commercially viable progeny of punk and disco, made headway fairly slowly amongst largely conservative U.S. audiences during the late 1970s, and while Devo, the Talking Heads, and Gary Numan may have won over some former ELP fans with their new style, they probably didn't win a lot. Most punk and New Wave fans were several years younger than ELP's fans, stood at the vanguard of a new generation (Generation X), and probably wouldn't have bought ELP albums anyway. So who *was* competing with ELP for album sales?

Starting around 1975 or 1976, during ELP's long (and ill-timed) hiatus, a number of slightly younger North American bands began to attain great popularity with American audiences. Bands like Boston, Kansas, Styx, Toto, and (from Canada) Rush and Heart had grown up listening both to British hard rock (above all Led Zeppelin) and progressive rock (ELP, Yes, Genesis, King Crimson, Jethro Tull, Pink Floyd). Their own music tends to fuse elements of these formerly separate styles, sometimes with a regional twist (such as Kansas's debt to the country-influenced southern rock of the Allman Brothers).

ELP and their British prog peers had come out of a late-1960s club scene where the target audience was eighteen- to twenty-five-year-olds of a decisively bohemian cast. As they began touring America and expanding their fan base, the core audience of the major British prog bands began to change, especially by becoming younger, more exclusively male, and more blue collar—thus, more culturally and politically conservative. It can be argued that through at least the mid-1970s the British prog bands continued to write with their original core audiences in mind—even if that original core audience was, by 1972, only a small fraction of the huge audience that made albums like *Trilogy, Dark Side of the Moon, Thick as a*

Brick, and *Close to the Edge* platinum sellers. However, bands like Kansas, Styx, Boston, and Rush appealed to this younger (and likely more blue-collar) audience from the beginning, and this was the audience that carried these bands to the top of the charts in the late 1970s.

But in order to appeal to this audience as directly as possible, these bands simplified British prog's musical syntax and its late-1960s utopian and apocalyptic themes. Even Kansas and Rush, the most musically sophisticated and "progressive" exponents of this new music (alternately called stadium rock, for the tremendous success experienced by these bands on the late-seventies stadium/arena circuit, and album-oriented rock, after the new style's increasing predominance of album-oriented radio format), never composed music of the harmonic or thematic complexity of ELP's *Tarkus* or King Crimson's *Lizard*. The phrase structures of the North American bands are far more predictably four-square and riff-oriented than the most representative British prog.

Not only was the music's syntax simplified; it was thematically and poetically simplified as well. This simplification is obvious if one chooses to compare the blank and free verse of a Jon Anderson (Yes), Peter Hammill (Van der Graaf Generator), Peter Gabriel (Genesis), or Peter Sinfield's King Crimson lyrics with the utterly predictable rhyme schemes of a Dennis DeYoung (Styx) or Kerry Livgren (Kansas). Even more tellingly, compare the ambiguous and doubled-edged readings one can impose on *Brain Salad Surgery* or Van der Graaf Generator's *Pawn Hearts* with the sophomoric "utopianism" of Styx's "Come Sail Away" or Kansas's "Point of Know Return," which essentially reduce sixties utopianism to teen escapism and wish fulfillment. The tendency of these newer bands to simplify the musical and lyrical substance of British prog tended to undermine many of progressive ideology's notions of authenticity, progress, originality, antiphilistinism, and transcendence that they ostensibly embraced.

In other words, by 1978 ELP were competing, not against punk or New Wave, but against a number of bands that had adopted and simplified key elements of the progressive rock style for an audience that ELP had largely lost touch with. This being said, this mainstream American rock audience of the late 1970s was essentially conservative, catholic in its tastes, and still accepted a number of key musical and ideological elements (i.e., notions of rock as art, artist as prophet figure, and increasingly watered down Romantic conceptions of idealism, authenticity, and transcendence) that had been introduced into rock by ELP and their late-sixties/early-seventies peers: there is therefore no reason that ELP could not have judiciously simplified their style to successfully compete against the Styxes, Totos, and Bostons of the world. The real problem, therefore, was not that the conception driving the five pop songs on side one of the *Love Beach* LP—to simplify key elements of the ELP approach for the late seventies—

was inherently misguided. The problem was simply that the execution of this conception was so badly done.

As fans and foes alike were quick to notice, on balance Kansas and even Toto circa 1978 sounded more like classic ELP than did side one of *Love Beach*.[10] It is hard to gauge exactly what audience ELP were trying to appeal to. A common feature of much of the music of Rush, Kansas, Styx, Toto, and so forth, were driving Led Zeppelin–like rhythm guitar parts, so, sensibly enough, Lake's electric guitar playing features prominently on the first five tracks of *Love Beach*. However, his rhythm guitar lines, with their jangly, only slightly distorted arpeggios, suggest midsixties surf music (or perhaps even the playing of his teenage idol, Hank Marvin) much more than Zeppelinesque power chords. While stadium rock was not about twenty-minute epics or twisted mazes of shifting meters, its fans still enjoyed (or at least tolerated) self-indulgent guitar and keyboard solos, and fairly intricate guitar and/or keyboard melodic figures (in between song verses, between verses and refrains, etc.) were de rigueur; the fact that rock's greatest keyboardist was allotted a grand total of one twelve-bar synthesizer lead during the first five songs of *Love Beach*, far from endearing the album to stadium rock fans, tended to turn them off. Indeed, on all of the Lake-penned songs of *Love Beach*, Emerson is essentially reduced to holding sustained background chords. There was simply nothing much about the "commercial" songs of *Love Beach* that stadium rock fans would particularly like, much less the thinning ranks of progressive rock diehards who were still praying for a new *Tarkus*. Musically, the songs are more in line with late-seventies soft rock; however, that was an audience that ELP had no previous interaction with, had never been marketed for, and had much less overlap with than the stadium rock fans that would have made a logical target audience. Furthermore, the frankly salacious nature of most of Lake's *Love Beach* lyrics, quite different from the pretty romanticism of his acoustic ballads, would not have been ingratiating to the average late-seventies soft-rock fan. It's hard to say what audience the "commercial" side of the *Love Beach* was intended to appeal to; by trying to please everybody, though, it pleased nobody.

Love Beach

Perhaps the first three songs on *Love Beach*—similar enough to sound like three variants of one song, and with similar subject matter—are best dis-

---

[10] Try this for yourself: listen to Toto's ELPish "I'll Supply the Love" or "Girl Goodbye" and then the *Love Beach* material. As formulaic as Toto were, they executed the formula effectively and sound a lot more like classic ELP than ELP does on "Love Beach" or the other songs on side one of the LP.

cussed together. "All I Want Is You," the first track, is the shortest and most innocuous of the three; in many ways it sets the tone for the entire first side of the LP. Based around a simple chord progression strummed by Lake on electric guitar, it is cheerful, pleasantly melodic, and utterly banal, with Emerson reduced to holding background chords and playing unobtrusive and unmemorable melodic filigrees. Much of Lake's *Love Beach* material features Emerson on GX-1 and two new additions to his setup, the Korg 3100 and 3300 polyphonic synthesizers; the Korgs' bright but very thin sound somehow perfectly suits the nature of the material. Carl Palmer, who had just retired his stainless steel kit to London's Royal Albert Museum (where it was stored for some years before being auctioned off, eventually becoming the property of Beatles drummer Ringo Starr), now drummed on a Gretch wooden drum kit; he alternates between a military drumming style that doesn't fit Lake's lovelorn lyrics (0:37) and virtuosic tom runs (1:34, 2:05) that represent a vain attempt to inject some badly needed excitement into the music, but which are pure overkill in this context. Lake, too, consistently overinterprets his vocals; the rasps, slides, and nasal colorings of key words that he had used to such brilliant effect in interpreting "Karn Evil 9" and "Pirates" sounds ludicrous here—a sudden injection of phony passion— as for instance the desperately rasped "S.O.S." of "You have sent your last S.O.S." at 0:48. Lake's bass lines are extremely minimal here, which, considering the long expanses of sustained keyboard chords, is no help to the arrangement. The one rather nice section to the song is the bridge (1:10), mostly because of some quietly effective hi-hat work by Palmer. Otherwise, it's easy to understand Emerson's and Palmer's bored demeanor as they dutifully perform their parts in a promo film of "All I Want Is You" shot for the British TV show *Top of the Pops* in 1978, which features Lake singing and playing electric six-string guitar.

The second song is the album's title track. "Love Beach" is built around a jangly electric guitar arpeggio that sounds more like sixties surf music than ELP. The song is longer and more structurally involved than "All I Want Is You," which doesn't necessarily serve it well, considering the thinness of its musical substance. The lyrics also wear thin very quickly. Sinfield's imagery about "pirate moons" and "silver spoons" comes off as rather pretentious in the context of a song about a one-night stand on Love Beach; once again Lake overinterprets key phrases (listen to the bridge at 1:18) in a misguided attempt to inject passion that instead merely calls attention to the banality of the lyrics.

If the first two songs are utterly banal, though, "Taste of My Love" is truly, spectacularly bad. It is, in fact, doubtless the most embarrassing song in the ELP canon, featuring a most unappetizing blend of lascivious, sexist lyrics, insipid music (once again a jangling electric guitar arpeggio is central to the song), and unbelievably ill-advised gestures of profundity.

In fact, some sections of it are so bad, they're almost funny. For instance, when Lake urges his lover to "get on my stallion and we'll ride" (2:00), Emerson responds with a GX-1 French horn hunting call. Blatantly calling attention to the banal, stereotypical nature of the lyrics' imagery by accompanying it with a musical gesture that evokes heroism and transcendence, one almost wonders if Emerson intended to ironically undermine the lyrics. (Knowing the earnest nature of this band, though, one doubts it.) Later on, when Lake sings (at 2:20), "Go down gently with your face to the East," and Emerson responds with a stereotypical Chinese pentatonic percussive theme, the song begins to take on the proportions of a bad joke. Unfortunately, it is like an unintentional joke the band members themselves don't seem to get, and we are left wincing, as at a comedian whose punch line fails but who goes right on with his monologue anyway, thinking he has said something else entirely.

The fourth track, "The Gambler," is the only Emerson-Lake-Sinfield collaboration on the album. A song about the joys of gambling, it is a bluesier number than the first three tracks, and it's fairly easy to discern Emerson's contribution to the song: the swinging shuffle blues refrain with its funky synth bass line, heard at 0:22, 1:14, and elsewhere, prefigures the interest in black gospel, funk, disco, and other African American styles he was soon to explore on his solo album, *Honky*. The arrangement here is a bit more interesting than on the first three tracks—the combination of jangling electric guitar arpeggios and harmonica in the verses is nice, and Emerson even gets to play a twelve-bar synthesizer solo from 1:44 (the "twiddly" timbre of the solo reminds me a lot of early-eighties dance music, and would sound at home on a Prince album). The song's bridge from 2:05 involves a nice call-and-response between Lake and what sounds like a small female black gospel choir, as he warns about the dangers of gambling on a woman. "The Gambler" is certainly no masterpiece—at best, it's roughly equal to such throwaway songs from previous albums as "Jeremy Bender" and "Benny the Bouncer"—but it's a cut or two above the first three tracks of this album.

The same can probably be said of the fifth track, the album's last Lake-Sinfield collaboration, "For You." The album's first minor key song, it's built around an obsessively repeated descending bass pattern that vaguely evokes Spanish flamenco music. The song begins with a rather imposing prelude featuring some bass-like electric guitar figures; the slow, mournful body of the song is built around Emerson's sparse piano accompaniment, Lake's equally sparse bass line, and, more surprisingly, his Roland guitar synthesizer arabesques, which embroider and comment upon his tale of woe and suffering at the hands of a selfish ex-lover. It's a pleasant enough song, although a bit repetitive. Also, like virtually everything else on *Love Beach*, the overall sound is thin and trebly, with the jangly guitar arpeggios and Korg chords predominating, and one wishes for the manfully dispatched bass lines (curiously, the bass lines are almost inaudible on side one of *Love Beach*) and muscular Hammond organ and Moog synthesizer timbres of days gone by. One also wonders why Emerson's GX-1 fanfare figure at the end of the song, which threatens to kick some life into it, is mixed so low, and is already nearly gone by the time it becomes audible at 4:17.

The one unqualified success on side one of the *Love Beach* LP is ELP's arrangement of "Canario," the final movement of *Fantasia para un gentilhombre* (1954) for guitar and orchestra by Spain's Joaquin Rodrigo (1901–1999). Rodrigo was something of a Spanish Aaron Copland (the two were almost exact contemporaries), writing gracefully crafted music with a strong bias towards folk idioms and with discreet modernist touches. ELP's arrangement is quite interesting, with the solo guitar parts being divided between Emerson's synthesizers and Lake's electric guitar, so that sometimes Emerson and Lake pass the melody back and forth between synthesizer and electric guitar, while at other times Lake's electric guitar line doubles the bass part, giving it a distinctive, diamond-hard timbral sheen. Lake's electric guitar playing, if not virtuosic in the manner of a John McLaughlin or a Steve Howe, is still quite agile—listen at 1:05, 1:28, 1:44, and elsewhere. Like many other ELP classical arrangements, this one includes a newly composed section, beginning at 2:36, in which a synthesizer lead line is spun out over a repetitive ostinato bass figure (here doubled by electric guitar). Indeed, this leads to one of the only two complaints I have concerning "Canario": both the structure and arrangement approaches feel a bit formulaic, as if ELP were self-consciously reworking the techniques that had made "Hoedown" such a successful number for them (not only is there the new solo section over an ostinato, but many of their arranging tricks, such as drums rhythmically doubling key thematic figures, sound very familiar). My second complaint I've already expressed: too little bass presence, and the overemphasis on the Korg synthesizers, results in a thin, trebly sound. Nonetheless, "Canario" proved ELP hadn't lost their ability to play an intricate, technically demanding arrangement, and one regrets the band never played this number live.

As readers may have sensed, I am not interested in propagating a revisionist interpretation of side one of *Love Beach*. Other than "Canario," which is quite nice (albeit not at all groundbreaking), it is really quite bad—spectacularly bad at times. What strikes one more forcefully than either the insipid music or the ridiculous lyrics is the colossal lapse of taste the three musicians must have experienced in order to agree to the release of such music.

Side two of the *Love Beach* LP is a different story. While "Memoirs of an Officer and a Gentleman," a four-movement suite by Keith Emerson and Pete Sinfield, is not above criticism—it certainly is not the new

"Tarkus" or "Karn Evil 9" many of ELP's long-time fans had been praying for—it is rather nice; in fact, revisiting it after many years, I was surprised at how well it had aged. Unlike the songs of side one, which showed the band aging most embarrassingly, side two suggested a more graceful way for the band to mature: while the music lacks the intensity and energy of their earlier epics, it evinces an agreeable calm and a new emotional subtlety that I can relate to better now, as a forty-some-year-old, than I could as a seventeen-year-old hearing the album for the first time. "Memoirs" proved that ELP could still write intelligent and intricate music, and the suite's more down-to-earth and human concerns do suggest both a new maturity and a dawning comprehension of the shifts in taste that were taking place. If ELP could have produced an entire album of music like this, and if Atlantic could have target-marketed the album to a slightly older, more mature audience, it's possible the subsequent history of ELP could have been rather different.

"Memoirs of an Officer and a Gentleman," like "Pirates," is a historical concept piece. The lyrics, set in the first person, tell the story of a young British officer who comes of age during the World War II era. In the Prologue, we encounter him—presumably as a much older man—walking the streets of London at night, and wistfully meditating on Britain's bygone days of military glory and imperial splendor. The first movement proper, "The Education of a Gentleman," takes us back in time and follows the young man's rise through the British public school system and into the armed forces. The second movement, "Love at First Sight," chronicles his courtship and marriage to the one true love of his life; in the third movement, "Letters from the Front," he has gone off to war, while his new wife has become a full-time nurse. Ironically, it is she, not he, that dies, killed during a German air raid, and the instrumental fourth movement, "Honorable Company," seems to take us back to where we first met our protagonist in the Prologue—as a much older man, looking back on the past, both his own and his country's, with a mixture of nostalgia and regret.

The "Prologue/Education of a Gentleman," which I'll henceforth refer to as the first movement (they're a single track on the LP, and move seamlessly from part to part), is my favorite track on the album; in fact, I think it's one of ELP's underrated gems. It is rather slow, does not rock out, and is not particularly virtuosic; on the other hand, it's one of Emerson's most beautifully lyrical compositions, with clean, uncluttered textures, rich, flowing chord progressions, and a fine sense of team play among the three musicians. The music is centered in C major, but a recurring melodic sequence serves to swing the music out of C major, often to E major (for instance at 0:44, 1:13, or at the end of the movement, at 5:21), or sometimes, to swing it back to C (1:46). The wonderfully impressionistic piano chords at the beginning set the stage for the rest of the movement, with rich chains of ninth chords (1:58, 2:08, 2:36 and elsewhere) and modal mixtures ($E^\flat$, $A^\flat$, and $B^\flat$ triads in the context of C major) smoothly slipping in and out of the home key. The texture here borrows the approach that had worked so well in the first and third movements of "Karn Evil 9": Emerson plays sustained chords with his left hand and melodic countermelodies with his right, allowing Lake's bass (which features prominently here for the first time on the album) to carry the low end unchallenged. Lake responds with some of the most lyrical, "singing" bass lines of his career: at 2:52, the beginning of "The Education of a Gentleman" part of the first movement, Lake's bass lines become something of a countermelody to his voice. His vocals, meanwhile, capture him in his most characteristic, clear-as-a-bell, heroic tenor, both poignant and passionate (listen to him sing at 3:11 or 4:18, for instance). There's some wonderfully tasteful interplay between Emerson's fanfarelike synth leads, Lake's lyrical bass lines, and Palmer's military-style snare figures during the instrumental episodes (2:36 or 4:41, for instance, where Lake smoothly doubles Emerson's synth lines on electric guitar) that hearken back to the sense of teamwork that guided the band during their heyday. The overall effect of the music is to blend the heroic aspect of "Karn Evil 9" with a new vein of nostalgia in a manner that perfectly conveys the conceit of the lyrics. Perhaps the only weakness is the ending; the sudden move into E major at 5:21, after so much emphasis on C, gives the ending a tentative, incomplete feeling, and prevents the movement from sounding completely self-contained.

The second movement, "Love at First Sight," seems to have two sources of inspiration. The first is "Trilogy," the opening section of which, like "Love at First Sight," is cast in the form of a nineteenth-century lied for voice with an active, very Romantic piano accompaniment. The second is the *Etudes*, opus 10 (1832) of Frederic Chopin (1810–1849). The first twelve seconds of the opening of "Love at First Sight" is, in fact, a direct quote of the opening section of Chopin's Etude in C major, opus 10, no. 1; thereafter, Chopin's presence bubbles just beneath the surface of Emerson's music, occasionally emerging openly.

After the quotation of Chopin's Etude in C major, Emerson plays a sixteen-bar passage (0:13–0:36) that introduces the chord progression of the vocal verse, woven into rippling piano figurations; the surging left hand part is based on the famous left-hand figure from measure nine of Chopin's "Revolutionary" Etude in C minor, opus 10, no. 12, altered here so it will work in a major key. The verse, although it begins in C major, is actually centered in G major, with Chopinesque circle-of-fifths chord movement, modal mixtures, and unresolved secondary dominants creating a colorful flow of major key harmony.

The second section of "Love at First Sight" consists of two verses, the "love at first sight" refrain, and a third verse. When Lake enters with the vocal verse (at 0:37), Emerson continues the surging left hand figures from the introduction, but replaces the intro's rippling right hand arpeggios with simple block chords in order to leave open space for Lake's vocal melody. "Love at First Sight" is probably one of the more difficult vocal lines Lake ever tackled—it ranges over an octave and a sixth, from b to g2—and it's a credit to Lake's vocal prowess that the intonation doesn't suffer and both the low and high notes are strong. The thirteen-bar refrain (from 1:30), based on an entirely different chord progression, is particularly pretty.

The long instrumental interlude, which begins after the third verse, mirrors the structure of the previous section. The first instrumental verse (2:17) features Emerson embroidering Lake's vocal melody; on his second time through the verse (2:42), his figurations become more fanciful, less linked to the vocal melody. When the refrain is reached at 3:06, Lake plays his vocal melody on acoustic guitar while Emerson weaves a new counterpoint of flowing eighth notes underneath; finally, at the third instrumental verse (3:27) Palmer enters with yet another counterpoint, a delicate glockenspiel line that interweaves in graceful arabesques with Emerson's flowing piano and Lake's acoustic guitar. In many ways, this section represents the first exploration of ELP's potential as an acoustic chamber group since "Take a Pebble," and one can only wonder why the band waited so long (essentially, until it was too late) to explore this once promising aspect of their output.

The final section recaps the verse-verse-refrain-verse structure of the previous two sections. When Lake's vocal verse reenters at 3:53, Emerson now accompanies with the heroic opening two-measure figure of Chopin's Etude in C major, which he transposes through a number of different keys in order to fit the chord changes; meanwhile, Palmer finally enters with an understated drum groove, which Lake supports with a sparse bass line. The second verse (4:20) represents the climax of the song, with Emerson layering in some discreet background GX-1 (or possibly Korg) chords. The refrain and final verse represent an "unwinding" of the song, as the rhythm section and synthesizer backing is withdrawn and the song is allowed to end quietly. On the whole, "Love at First Sight" is a very nice song, allowing ELP to explore a subtle, acoustically based facet of their musical personalities that they had mined too seldom over the previous eight years: the chamber-music-like interlude, with its fine sense of team play, is a particular highpoint. My one criticism of the song is that compared to its apparent influences ("Take a Pebble," the opening of "Trilogy," and, of course, the two Chopin Etudes), it comes off as a bit too sweet, almost a bit precious—a slight touch of angularity would have probably helped.

Of the four movements of "Memoirs," the third, "Letters from the Front," is probably the most original; rather than looking back to classic

the Thatcher and Reagan administrations in their respective countries during this period, and by the strong support of the British public for the Falklands War. It also was a poignant symbol of the beginning of the eventual (if incomplete) reabsorption of sixties hippies into the Establishment they had once despised and opposed.

Love Beach did not make the kind of impact that Atlantic had hoped for. The "pop songs" of side one of the LP received little radio airplay, so ELP won few if any new converts. The hip *Rolling Stone/New Musical Express* wing of rock critics were underwhelmed by *Love Beach*'s apparent attempts at accessibility: in a biting but wickedly funny review of the album for *New Musical Express*, Ian Penman reviews the short tracks of side one as if they cohere into a concept piece whose ultimate meaning is so deep that he, a mere rock reviewer, is unable to divine it. As one might expect, he dismisses "Memoirs" out of hand: "Side two is called 'Memoirs of an Officer and a Gentleman.' It is a concept. I think someone must have trodden on it. Will you sleep tonight, zombies?"[13]

While *Love Beach* did not convert the skeptics, it did appall a good number of long-time fans, many of who now began to turn on the band with a fury that suggested a sense of betrayal. With cries of "sellout" in the air, *Love Beach* proved to be a spectacular P.R. blunder. Hardly any new fans came on board, but a tidal wave of long-time fans deserted ship: I've always suspected that there were a good number of fans who didn't even make it through side one before throwing the LP down in disgust, and who therefore never checked out the more substantive "Memoirs" on side two. *Love Beach* did not even crack the American top forty, charting out at fifty-five, and fell out of the top two hundred in just nine weeks, both all-time lows for ELP. It did eventually go gold—the ninth and last ELP album to do so. In Britain, *Love Beach* topped out at an equally mediocre forty-eight.

By early 1979, the proverbial writing was on the wall, and *Circus* ran a short story to the effect that ELP planned to disband after a final farewell tour, to take place during the summer of 1979. That tour, however, never materialized. Carl Palmer later explained why:

At the beginning of '79 I tried to organize a farewell tour and spent two months working on it. You could truthfully say it was the last time I injected any energy in ELP. I used to act as organizer and tried to get the thing moving along. Not being a music writer I though I'd make up for it in other areas. So I tried to get this tour together and it was coming along well. Then there were internal problems, within the band! What we should play and how we should play it. Who should pick what tune, who should do what and in what

[13] Ian Penman, "The New Face of Techno Rock: On the Beach, Out to Lunch," *New Musical Express*, November 25, 1978.

ELP for inspiration, it anticipates some of Emerson's better work of the 1980s. The music is just as angular as "Tarkus"; however, the violence of "Tarkus" is smoothed out, replaced by a dry, understated coolness that is quite new. A point of reference for my classically informed readers is the shift in Stravinsky's output from the post-Romanticism of *The Rite of Spring* to the neoclassicism of *The Soldier's Tale*; while the rhythms, harmonies, and melodies of the two works are quite similar, the opulence, monumentality, and over-the-top violence of the former is quite different from the brittle austerity of the latter. In this sense, "Letters from the Front" may represent Emerson's highly personal response to late-seventies New Wave.

The lengthy instrumental introduction of "Letters" is based on a seventeen-bar segment that is repeated three times (0:06, 0:30, and 1:06), with extensions and variations, and is then developed at length (from 1:30). It's based around a passage of wiry two-part GX-1 counterpoint that alternates antiphonally with a series of short melodic riffs played in unison by electric guitar, bass, and Rhodes electric piano (the first and last time Emerson recorded with that instrument). The end of each repetition of this segment involves some knotty polyrhythms, such as the 6/8 against 4/4 effect of 0:20 and 1:09. After the third repetition of this segment, the contrapuntal GX-1 theme is extended and developed, while the tonality shifts from C to G major.

The thirty-two-bar vocal verse, repeated twice (2:17, 3:01) carries over many of the characteristics of the introduction. Dominated by the cool, bell-like timbre of the Rhodes electric piano, the verses continue to be defined by the vaguely jazzy feel of the 6/8 against 4/4 cross-rhythms (evident in the rhythm of the Rhodes accompaniment figure and especially in the rhythm of the verse's turnaround figure at 2:59), and by the colorful major key harmony in which seventh and ninth chords and chords borrowed from the parallel minor pull the music imperceptibly in and out of the home key. The verses vacillate between G Lydian and B major, although the latter is always implied, never explicitly sounded.

The moment when our protagonist receives the telegram saying that his wife has been killed in a German air raid is set in relief by a sudden cessation in musical motion, save for reverberating Moog arpeggios over a sustained G (3:34); he reacts in disbelief, accompanied by a progression of slowly unfolding, distantly related chords (G, F, A♭, E♭) that are punctuated by jagged melodic runs played in unison by Rhodes, bass, and drums (3:49, 3:55, 4:00, etc.). This bridge section is followed by one final statement of the verse (4:27), more passionate now than before, where our protagonist concludes that all he has been left is "what it means to be an Officer and a Gentleman"—the accompaniment figure is given a trumpetlike synth orchestration, and Emerson adds a heroic synth countermelody. The movement ends with the Moog arpeggios spilling across slowly vacillating G and A major chords that clinch the movement's G Lydian tonality. Musically, "Letters from the Front" may be the most interesting track on *Love Beach*: Carl Palmer felt strongly enough about his playing on the song to transcribe it and include it as one of just a few ELP pieces found in his *Applied Rhythms*. However, I've always wondered if the musical nature of the movement, with its cool, bell-like timbres, drifting major key harmony, geometrically intricate cross-rhythms, and angular melodic punctuations, was really suited to expressing the feelings of a man who had just lost his young wife.

The final movement is the instrumental march "Honorable Company." Starting quietly, it is built around a nine-bar march theme that is repeated a number of times, each repetition being a bit more fully orchestrated than before; as the march begins to pick up steam, the main theme begins to alternate with a secondary theme, first heard incompletely (0:32), then in complete form (at 0:53 and 1:23). From 1:36 to the end, the main theme is repeated eight times: all eight times it's accompanied by a synth trumpet countermelody, and the third (2:09) through eighth repetitions feature a second countermelody which changes each time. The gradual buildup of the movement, not to mention its march-like character, is reminiscent of "Abaddon's Bolero," but there are some differences. The rhythm is less driving, with the characteristic meter shift—two bars of three, a bar of four, a bar of three—recalling the loping feel of "Jerusalem." The tonal contour of the main theme, which moves from C major to E major back to C via G major, serves as a microcosm of the entire suite—the first movement also frequently moved from the tonic C major to E major, the second movement from G major to E minor, and the third movement from G major to B major (same tonal relationship as the first movement, but transposed up a fifth). The movement's major key harmony, lyricism, bright synthesizer orchestration, relaxed tempo, and loping metric feel unite to create a highly characteristic ambience of both heroism and nostalgia—much like the first movement. It's a nice ending to the suite, although it doesn't pack anywhere near the punch of "Abaddon," its putative model.

Love Beach: **An Assessment**

In many ways, "Memoirs" is a logical continuation of the musical direction established with "Pirates": the cheerful major key vibe, the bright, sparkling tone colors, the intricate but generally smooth rhythms, and the increasingly fluid, lyrical melodies. Only "Letters," with its dry, almost geometrical angularity, goes against the grain of these trends, and "Letters" has none of the rhythmic drive of "Pirates"—much less "Tarkus" or "Karn Evil 9." While I'm not bothered as much by the dis-

inclination of "Memoirs" to rock out as many ELP fans, I d[...] relative lack of bass presence (other than the first and, to a les[...] third movements), which, of course, mars all of *Love Beach*, [...] music sounding too thin. There are two other categorie[...] "Memoirs" doesn't compare that favorably to "Pirates." Whil[...] showcases a new sense of seamlessness, the four mov[...] "Memoirs" don't particularly cohere as a single piece—the shi[...] second to third movement is particularly jarring—and it's only [...] line and the tonal plan that tie them together. Second, and mc[...] ingly, unlike "Pirates," which really does sound like a departur[...] band's previous music, "Memoirs" wears its debt to previous [...] sics too openly—the first movement to "Jerusalem," the second [...] a Pebble" and "Trilogy," the last to "Abaddon."

The premise of the storyline merits consideration, too. [...] progressive rock, ELP's more epic pieces had always been [...] which in itself was cause for contempt on the part of blues ort[...] who argued all rock should always be strictly functional. Th[...] therefore totally missed the shift that took place in the nature [...] Romanticism between the early and late 1970s. "Tarkus" and "[...] 9" exemplify an oppositional Romanticism that confronts us with[...] ary, not-so-pretty picture of things as they will soon be, and chal[...] to take action now to prevent the hypothetical dystopia they pres[...] becoming reality. "Pirates" and "Memoirs," on the other hand, e[...] an escapist Romanticism that encourages us to shut out the pro[...] the here-and-now by daydreaming about exotic people, pla[...] times.[11] "Memoirs," in addition, evokes a very un-countercultu[...] of old-school patriotism that almost crosses the line into open [...] for the good old days of British imperial and colonial splendor[...] sense, I find Pete Sinfield's bashing of Margaret Thatcher in Paul [...] *The Music's All That Matters* disingenuous; there is nothing in [...] for "Memoirs" that Thatcher wouldn't have wholeheartedly a[...] of.[12] Indeed, "Memoirs" proved to be a very accurate mirror [...] increasingly conservative bent of both British and American cultu[...] ing the late seventies and early eighties, exemplified by the popul[...]

---

[11] I see a parallel to what took place in nineteenth-century British Romanticism as th[...] hewn, confrontational Romanticism of William Blake gradually gave way, as the Vict[...] progressed, to the gorgeous but essentially escapist work of the pre-Raphaelites.

[12] Stump, *The Music's All That Matters*, 234. Again, it seems like Stump was too o[...] by Sinfield to challenge some obvious inconsistencies in his remarks. To make my [...] clear: I have no problem with Sinfield choosing to write a patriotic lyric. I *do* have [...] lem with him writing a lyric that projects old-school British patriotism, and then [...] Margaret Thatcher for practicing the kind of conservative, nationalist politics that [...] appears to validate.

order. Although we were planning the end of Emerson, Lake and Palmer, it really wasn't being done as well as I thought it should. I realized, maybe I should just stop. You only have so much energy in life and then there's no more left. So that was it . . . Obviously the relationship between Greg and Keith is not so rosy, and that's one of the things that always disturbed me. I mean, we were intelligent people, sensitive and artistic, but not so well organized . . . I don't regret any of it and don't hold any grudges for it breaking up because it was inevitable. All I tried to do was guide it, so that at least it would have been methodical in the break up and give everybody a fresh start.[14]

Through much of the second half of 1979, the fate of ELP was in a kind of limbo; some fans hoped the failure of the farewell tour to materialize signaled a reconsideration of the decision to disband. Others suspected the farewell tour was merely being put on hold until it could be organized according to the band's exacting standards. Scarcely anyone thought the band was in the process of more or less dissolving without a trace.

In Concert

With the fate of the band still up in the air as far as the public was concerned, *Emerson, Lake and Palmer In Concert* was released in November 1979, almost precisely two years after *Works II* and one year after *Love Beach*. The cover showed ELP playing to 78,000 fans at Montréal's Olympic Stadium in August 1977 and the liner notes simply stated "Recorded at Olympic Stadium, Montréal": this wasn't entirely accurate, since four of the six tracks on side one of the LP were recorded elsewhere during the late 1977 and early 1978 legs of the *Works* tour, when ELP were touring as a three-piece. Although public interest in ELP had declined precipitously since August 1977, this live album at least afforded the opportunity for ELP—by any standards one of the great live bands of the seventies—to right their reputation a bit after the catastrophic blunder of *Love Beach*. Unfortunately, the almost uncanny intersection of bad luck and bad judgment that had plagued the band almost virtually every step of the way since their reappearance in early 1977 once again conspired to fatally compromise yet another potentially promising project.

The first problem was the sound quality. Considering the sophistication of the sound system ELP were touring with in 1977, *In Concert* should have been one of the most crystalline-sounding live albums of the late seventies. It didn't work out that way. As with *Love Beach*, the album

---

[14] Carl Palmer, quoted by Chris Welch, "Carl Palmer," *Musicians Only*, March 1980, 3.

had no credited producer, although Emerson was once again de facto producer. He did not have an easy time of it:

> There were a lot of problems getting the live album done. The 24-track broke down, and a lot of those mixes were done from two-track masters combined with the soundtrack from the video tape. It was a complicated process, but I got the best sound from it that I possibly could. It wasn't exactly state-of-the-art recording, but nevertheless I though it was important and that people needed to hear it.[15]

The chief result of these problems is that while the sound quality of the tracks the band recorded as a three-piece is fine (although not exceptional), the orchestral parts all sound very thin and one-dimensional. If the sound quality of *Welcome Back My Friends* is ultimately a cut below *Pictures at an Exhibition*, *In Concert* is easily a couple of cuts below *Welcome Back My Friends*.

If *In Concert* was marred by its poor sound quality, it was also marred by its highly peculiar selection of tracks. Granted, this was not all the band's fault. Emerson badly wanted to release *In Concert* as a two-LP set; however, Atlantic's executives, who realized that the end of ELP was at hand, insisted on one LP only, as they didn't wish to sink extra money into a band in the process of dissolution. Atlantic's decision left Emerson with a difficult decision concerning what to include and exclude: nonetheless, it's very easy to second-guess the album's track list. For instance, the two major group tracks of the *Works* era were "Fanfare for the Common Man" and "Pirates"; neither was included on *In Concert*. Instead, *In Concert* highlights two early ELP classical arrangements, "Knife-Edge" and "Pictures at an Exhibition," both of which appear here heavily orchestrated. The *Works* era is represented by four tracks, "Tiger in a Spotlight," "C'est la vie," "The Enemy God," and the third movement of Emerson's Piano Concerto. There is also the short opening fanfare and the arrangement of Henry Mancini's "Peter Gunn" theme, neither of which exist in a studio version. Unfortunately, the album's track selection gives a very spotty, uneven overview of what *Works*-era ELP were all about as a live band.

The album opens with "Introductory Fanfare," which segues into "Peter Gunn." Since the opening GX-1 fanfare theme (accompanied by Carl Palmer) was only added on the last leg of the *Works* tour, it's safe to say these two tracks were recorded in early 1978. The "Peter Gunn" arrangement, while pleasant enough, is pretty simplistic: Emerson plays the entire piece on GX-1, and doubles the famous bass line (also played

---

[15] Milano, "Keith Emerson," *Contemporary Keyboard*, September 1980, 22.

by Lake) throughout, thereby foregoing the opportunity to create textural variety (by playing two parts at once that are independent of the bass line) and coloristic variety in the keyboard orchestration. The structure, too, follows the "Rondo" and "Fanfare for the Common Man" blueprint (theme/solo over bass ostinato/theme) too closely for comfort, especially as neither the theme nor the solo of "Peter Gunn" is particularly substantive. "Peter Gunn" is, in short, pleasant but trivial. However, in a measure of the pervasive conservatism, timidity, and philistinism of Grammy award nominators (then as now), it was "Peter Gunn," rather than such ELP instrumental juggernauts of the past as "Toccata," "Hoedown," "The Barbarian," "Fanfare for the Common Man," or even "Canario," that was nominated for a Grammy award.

The third track, "Tiger in a Spotlight," was recorded during the latter portion of the *Works* Tour, sometime in late 1977 or early 1978. It lacks many of the details that gave the studio version a modicum of interest—the Moog glissandos, Lake's electric guitar counterpoints—and, like "Peter Gunn," is pleasant but trivial. The fourth track, the melancholy "C'est la vie," is the album's first track that was actually recorded at the August 26 Montréal show. It features Lake (joined by Emerson on accordion) backed by the ELP orchestra and choir. The thinness of the orchestral sound doesn't seem to hurt "C'est la vie" as much as the other orchestral tracks, and the live version of the song is very pretty, if somewhat lightweight. Prokofiev's "The Enemy God," the fifth track, was recorded by the trio during the latter portion of the *Works* tour. It's rather curious the band didn't include the orchestral version of "The Enemy God" which they did, after all, record at Montréal. On the other hand, their arrangement for three-piece really rocks and is, in my opinion, the highlight of side one of the *In Concert* LP. The arrangement is infinitely more intricate than "Peter Gunn," the music itself infinitely more substantive. The angular melodies, hairpin metric shifts, and carefully interlocking textures that characterize vintage ELP are well represented here, with the orchestral lines effectively divided between Emerson's keyboards and Lake's bass guitar (which plays independently of the keyboard parts throughout); there's also some nice call-and-response between Emerson's GX-1 and Hammond. The track showcases Carl Palmer's drumming at its best, very intricately worked out, with many ingenious rhythmic doublings of Emerson's and Lake's lines and no needless flash. Although not of the scope of "Toccata," "Enemy God" holds up well in comparison to ELP's better classical arrangements of the past. *This* is the track that should have received the Grammy nomination.

The last track on side one of the *In Concert* LP, recorded at the Montréal show, is "Knife-Edge," the urgent, hard-rocking classic from the band's debut album. "Knife-Edge" was, of course, an extremely successful arrangement of a classical work for the rock idiom—here, Emerson adds some of Janáček's original orchestration (especially for low brass) to the arrangement. In theory, this addition ought to work: in practice, it doesn't. Part of the problem I've already discussed—the presence of the orchestra reduces the song's rhythmic drive, which, combined with the not entirely secure intonation and the very one dimensional orchestral sound we hear on the record, creates an elephantine effect that comes dangerously close to duplicating the critical stereotype of ELP's music. Furthermore, there's something very superfluous about the orchestration: the orchestrated sections contribute little in the way of drama or climax, and by the end of the song, where ELP is dutifully accompanying the orchestra karaoke-like, one feels that one has been returned to the bad old days of late-sixties "orchestral rock," where the orchestral and rock sections alternate in a barely coherent mishmash.

Side two of the *In Concert* LP contains just two tracks, both recorded at Montréal: the third movement of Emerson's Piano Concerto, and an abridged arrangement of *Pictures at an Exhibition*. Unlike much of the rock material, the third movement of Emerson's Concerto is at least being heard here in its originally intended guise, and is comparable with its studio model. It is played slightly faster here, with more rhythmic drive, and actually feels tighter rhythmically than the LPO recording: were it not for the one-dimensional sound of the orchestra, I think this version would actually be preferable to the London Philharmonic's. As it is, Emerson enthusiasts can profitably compare and contrast the two.

Finally, we come to *Pictures*, which takes the Newcastle arrangement of the piece and eliminates "The Sage," "The Old Castle/Blues Variation," and the third Promenade. All of my criticisms of the orchestrated "Knife-Edge" apply here, only more so. When ELP dutifully accompanies the orchestra during "The Great Gates of Kiev," the central problem of the concept behind the *Works* Orchestral Tour comes into focus: rather than being fused together, the classical and rock aspects break back down into their constituent parts. Ravel's orchestration of *Pictures* had already solved all of the piece's coloristic and textural problems; so, in a very different way, had ELP's electronic arrangement. The "rock" passages add nothing essential to Ravel's orchestration, nor do the orchestral sections add anything to ELP's electronic arrangement, which had already achieved its own interior coherence. It is only with "Pirates," which was composed with interlocking blocks of orchestral and electronic tone colors as a central aspect of the work's structure, that the orchestral-rock confluence is truly beneficial or necessary. Why ELP didn't include "Pirates" on the LP—which would have made the strongest possible argument for the concept behind the *Works* Orchestral Tour—is anybody's guess.

In Concert: An Assessment

In sum, *In Concert* was a bona fide failure; ELP had followed up their worst studio album by far with their worst live album by far. Critical reaction was predictably negative; by now the only way one could distinguish a review by a former ELP supporter from a review by a longtime detractor is the amount of personal invective the review contained. Thus, *New Musical Express*'s Gavin Martin can't resist a swipe at ELP's fans:

> Yes it's another ELP live album, a 1977 recording made during their American/Canadian tour of that year as they presumably took refuge from the upswell of new wave iconoclasm and innovation going down in Blighty. [Anyone else detect some musical jingoism here?] Suitable then that our three heroes sound like desperate, aging musicians churning out their staid, lifeless formulas to a typically reactionary audience. [Ouch!] *In Concert* is a feebly flashy musical laboratory of clinical cynicism, serving up a soggy stew of ragged rock'n'roll remnants boiled with a crass classical flavoring.[16]

By the late seventies, this kind of smear tactic, implicating fans in the criminal unhipness of their favored bands, had become the standard tactic amongst the blues orthodoxist critics, who saw punk and new wave as the only legitimate future paths of rock, and who tried to shame fans away from such "evolutionary dead ends" as progressive rock. Unfortunately, by 1979 the output of most of the classic prog bands—certainly of ELP— was no longer making much of an argument for the continuing validity of the style. Reviews by former ELP supporters now evinced an outrage colored by a sense of betrayal. Jim Aikin of *Contemporary Keyboard*, a journal that had supported ELP into the late seventies, now turned both barrels on ELP:

> The demise of a once-proud band is documented in pitiless detail on this sloppily performed and badly mixed extravaganza, recorded in Montréal during ELP's abortive 1977 full-orchestra tour. As usual, Emerson's slashing, stabbing organ and synthesizer work are the only source of excitement or originality on the record. Titles include "Tiger in a Spotlight," "C'est la vie," the third movement of Emerson's Piano Concerto, Henry Mancini's "Peter Gunn" theme (?!), and a truly grotesque version of *Pictures at an Exhibition* featuring an entire violin section with all the tonal fidelity of a used Mellotron and the indigestible moaning of Greg Lake's vocal.[17]

In 1993, after having obtained rights to ELP's back catalog from Atlantic, Victory Records released *In Concert* with seven additional tracks

---

[16] Gavin Martin, "ELP in Concert," *New Musical Express*, December 1, 1979, 40.
[17] Jim Aikin, "Emerson, Lake and Palmer in Concert," *Contemporary Keyboard*, June 1980, 71.

that were not on the LP as a two-CD set retitled *Works Live*. The track listings of side one and side two of the *In Concert* LP become the starting point for the two respective CDs. The first CD adds "Watching Over You," "Maple Leaf Rag," "Fanfare for the Common Man," and "Show Me the Way to Go Home" to the six tracks of side one of the *In Concert* LP; "Fanfare" was recorded at Montréal, the other three during the last two legs of the *Works* tour in late 1977 and early 1978. The second CD adds "Abaddon's Bolero," "Closer to Believing," and "Tank" to the two tracks that had originally appeared on side two of the LP; all three of the additional tracks were recorded at the Montréal show. For reasons beyond my comprehension, "Pirates" was again excluded. The added tracks continue to highlight the central problems inherent to the *Works* Orchestral Tour, especially the sprawling and sloppily performed orchestrations of "Fanfare" and "Tank." On the other hand, the digitally remastered CDs do address some of the biggest sonic issues of the LP (the orchestra sounds bigger and fuller here), although by doing so it occasionally reveals intonation problems that were less apparent on the LP. The inclusion of the seven additional tracks also gives a much more balanced picture of what the ELP live show was all about during the *Works* era. Of course, by the time these improvements were made in 1993—some fourteen years after the fact—nobody, other than the most diehard ELP fans, knew or cared.

In Concert made almost no impact when it was released in late 1979; it charted out at number seventy-three, even lower than *Love Beach*, fell out of the top two hundred in ten weeks, and became the first ELP album not to be certified gold. Less than a month after its release, in late December 1979, the ELP organization, or what remained of it, finally released an announcement to the effect that the group had formally disbanded. Again, their timing couldn't have been worse. Even after the blunders of the orchestral tour and *Love Beach*, interest remained strong enough that had ELP announced their imminent breakup in early 1979 and followed the announcement with a well-executed farewell tour, they could have gone out of the seventies with some remnant of their iconic, larger-than-life status intact. As it was, the band went out with a whimper, not a bang: it was almost as if they had dissolved out of existence. Amongst the mainstream rock public, the band's demise was scarcely noticed.

The Best of Emerson, Lake and Palmer

Almost as a footnote to the ELP saga of 1970–79, *The Best of Emerson, Lake and Palmer* was released in November 1980—three years to the month after *Works II*, two years after *Love Beach*, and one year after *In*

Concert. There were few bands whose output was less suited to a single LP greatest hits package than ELP, in view of the fact that so much of their most representative tracks were at least ten minutes long: even so, the selection of tracks included on this LP are puzzling and hardly contribute to a representative overview of ELP during their golden age. Side one contained "Hoedown," "Lucky Man," "Karn Evil 9, 1st Impression, part two," "Jerusalem," and "Peter Gunn"; side two contained the single version of "Fanfare for the Common Man," "Still . . . You Turn Me On," "Tiger in a Spotlight," and "Trilogy." No "Knife-Edge," "Take a Pebble," "Tarkus," "Pictures," "Endless Enigma," "Toccata," or "Pirates." At the very least, dropping the essentially trivial "Tiger" and "Peter Gunn" in favor of "Knife-Edge" or an excerpt from "Tarkus" or "Pictures" would have given a slightly more well-rounded picture of ELP's full achievement during the seventies. As it was, it would not be until 1992, with the release of the two-CD set *The Atlantic Years*, that ELP would be served by a release that demonstrated the full scope of their achievement during the 1970s. *The Best of ELP* charted out at an anemic 108 on the U.S. charts and fell out of the top two hundred in seven weeks, even faster than *Love Beach*.

The Endless Enigma

In *Listening to the Future*, Bill Martin says,

> Critics and fans tend to focus on the actions of individual bands or musicians, asking questions of the "Why didn't they do . . . ?" variety. In my view, this approach is wrongheaded. The reason for this is not that hard to see. If art and thought are always a part of their time, then, if "their time" passes, there has to be a change. Everyone recognizes that there was a sea-change in music in the late seventies, and that the time of progressive rock—its "heyday," as I've been calling it—came to a close.[18]

On the one hand, it's hard to argue with this statement, because the evidence is there to support it: consider that 1978 and 1979 produced not only *Love Beach* and *In Concert*, but such lame albums as Yes's *Tormato*, Genesis's *Then There Were Three*, Jethro Tull's *Stormwatch*, and Gentle Giant's *Giant For A Day*. Even such an uncompromising band as Magma was reduced to proffering warmed-over Eurofunk on *Attahk*. About the only bright spot for progressive rock during this period were the two studio albums by U.K., *U.K.* (1978) and *Danger Money* (1979). U.K. started as a supergroup that featured John Wetton (bass and vocals) and Bill

---

[18] Martin, *Listening to the Future*, 254.

Bruford (drums), both recently out of King Crimson, as well as keyboard/violin prodigy Eddie Jobson (Curved Air, Roxy Music) and guitar virtuoso Allan Holdsworth (Soft Machine); by the second album, they had been reduced to an ELP-like keyboard trio featuring Jobson, Wetton, and drummer Terry Bozzio, who played the kind of music that many ELP fans desperately wished their heroes were still playing.[19] However, the musical climate was no longer right for even a group consisting of high-profile stars like U.K. to thrive, and by 1980, the band had dissolved. So, in light of what was happening in progressive rock circa 1978-79, I fully agree that ELP's gradual decline was nearly inevitable.

On the other hand, unlike the bands mentioned above, ELP did not gradually decline: in a relatively brief period (early 1977 to early 1979) they spectacularly self-destructed. In 1973-74, ELP were arguably the biggest band in rock: their only box office rivals during those two years, the Stones, the Who, and Led Zeppelin, are all in rock's Hall of Fame—both literally and figuratively speaking. Ask many teenagers today who the Stones, the Who, or Led Zeppelin are, and they'll know; ask them about ELP, though, and you're likely to evoke a blank stare or a shrug. No rock band has ever been so big for so long (seven years—from 1970 to 1977), crashed so suddenly, and fell into such perpetual obscurity ever since. For many ELP fans, then, the endless enigma has always been this: what, exactly, triggered ELP's spectacular self-destruction? And is there anything the band could have done to prevent it? In closing this chapter, I will attempt to answer both questions.

The first and biggest factor in the self-destruction of ELP was the loss of the interpersonal chemistry that had guided them through their six great albums of 1970–74. Like all the great bands of the seventies, ELP was greater than the sum of its parts. Emerson and Lake, for all their periodic acrimony and head butting, managed to compensate for each others' weaknesses and see each others' blind spots quite well. Emerson, left to his own devices, would have likely made a string of musically accomplished but uncommercial albums during the seventies: Lake showed a far better understanding of what was commercially viable, and what small compromises were necessary in order to make ELP albums gold and platinum sellers. Lake also understood—correctly, in my view—that Emerson's greatest gift was as a rock keyboardist and composer, not as a composer or pianist in the Great Tradition. Speaking many years after the heyday of ELP, Lake noted,

> If someone says to me, what is your vision of Keith Emerson, I would say "a great organ player." As a pianist, he is not one alone in the whole world, but

---

[19] See Appendix C for a detailed discussion of U.K.'s *Danger Money*.

as a Hammond organ player, he's extraordinary. He created an unbelievable energy and absolute magic with the instrument. So the music of Keith Emerson that means the most, to me anyway, is the Hammond organ and synthesizer side of what he does. But I'm not so sure that's true for him. I think maybe he likes the piano side of things more, and perhaps wants to be recognized for playing "real" music. And that's never the way I thought about it. I've always thought that the real respect for Emerson, Lake and Palmer came from the music we created ourselves and played ourselves, which was, in fact, our music.[20]

If Lake moderated Emerson's tendency towards self-indulgence, Emerson, for his part, challenged Lake, spurred him to try challenging ideas and develop talents that he otherwise probably wouldn't have. Lake has done his best work in tandem with a stronger musical personality than himself, a Robert Fripp or Keith Emerson; left to his own devices, he is too inclined to settle for frankly trivial musical ideas and to take the easy way out in matters of arranging and performance. Emerson spurred him on to become one of rock's more accomplished bassists of the seventies, to expand his already potent vocal abilities in areas he likely wouldn't have explored for himself, and to tackle "outside" musical ideas head on. The frankly pedestrian nature of much of Lake's solo music since 1980—both in its essence and in its realization—gives ample evidence of how much he benefited from association with two of rock's most imaginative figures, Fripp and Emerson, during the late sixties and seventies.

Before the band's long midseventies layoff, Emerson and Lake accepted each other's feedback, if not always graciously or gracefully. Afterwards, they didn't, with predictably disastrous results. During the late seventies, Emerson self-indulgently used ELP as a vehicle for aspiring to the Great Tradition; the result was the catastrophic *Works* Orchestral Tour and the third-rate *In Concert/Works Live* album. Lake, on the other hand, once he had decided he was principally a singer, never allowed himself to be challenged again: the result was ELP's increasingly pedestrian late-seventies set lists, with their overabundance of frankly trivial material, and Lake's refusal to apply himself to his bass playing with any of his former energy.[21] Although he seldom publicly alluded to it during the seventies, after ELP broke up Emerson was finally honest about the tension that had existed all along between he and Lake: "What can I say? We were two Scorpios, working on, at, or with each other all the time, regarding each other from a distance, each

---

[20] Greg Lake, quoted by Hall, "Welcome to the Show," 52.
[21] Just one example: when ELP played "Tank" in the late seventies, Lake no longer played the virtuosic unison runs with the keyboard part that had made the original version so electrifying.

one playing it very cautiously. Carl was always full of fun and games, and still is. He's great fun."[22]

If the loss of the band's formerly healthy interpersonal chemistry was a major factor in their demise, I think there is something to be said too for shifts in Emerson's compositional style. In a fascinating passage of his *Measure for Measure*, a parallel history of science and music, Thomas Levenson argues that of Antonio Stradavarius's many great instruments, none were greater than the violins and cellos he built between 1710 and 1720, after "he bought a particularly excellent and substantial log of maple in the Cremonese lumber mart early in the 1710s. That log lasted him until round 1720, and proved irreplaceable . . . After he had exhausted that one log he was never able to achieve that peak appearance again."[23] I think something similar could be said about Emerson's compositions. His work with the Nice, when he had first found his own voice, was based heavily on a happy fusion of the blues, forties and fifties jazz, and Bach. Around the time of the formation of ELP he had discovered Bartók, Janáček, and other Eastern European early modernists, and particularly Alberto Ginastera's music, and there was the sudden creative explosion evident in the first three ELP albums: the driving rhythms, hairpin metric shifts, and pungent bitonal chord voicings and quartal harmonies of early modernism were fused with elements already present in his writing to create the distinctive, immediately recognizable Emersonian style. Sometime in the midseventies the Bartók/Ginastera line of influence began to be exhausted, increasingly replaced by the graceful but often bland musical style of Aaron Copland. After *Brain Salad Surgery*, with a few notable exceptions, Emerson's music has never again evinced the same winning confluence of urgency, drive, swing, and sophistication.[24]

Perhaps there was nothing to be done about the deterioration of the band's interpersonal chemistry or the shift in Emerson's compositional style. However, ELP made three enormous blunders between 1977 and 1979 that were easily avoidable. First, in my view, the solo/band format of *Works I* was a catastrophic mistake: it undermined the very notion of diversity-in-unity that it was mean to convey, showed how far apart the musicians were drifting stylistically, and gave many people the impression

---

[22] Keith Emerson, quoted by Milano, "Keith Emerson," *Contemporary Keyboard*, September 1980, 23.

[23] Thomas Levenson, *Measure for Measure: A Musical History of Science* (New York: Touchstone Books, 1994), 222.

[24] Emerson's *Pictures of an Exhibitionist* suggests another plausible cause of Emerson's compositional decline of the late seventies, a matter that previously had been known of only through shadowy rumors among his fans: he had a serious problem with cocaine addiction between early 1975 and early 1977, which, he admits, sapped him of the desire to create new music. See *Pictures of an Exhibitionist*, 291–307, especially 292.

that ELP were using the ELP name to entice fans into buying music that wasn't in fact ELP—music they wouldn't have bought otherwise. What would I have suggested? In my view, ELP would have been far better off following their original game plan of 1974-75. They should have each released a solo album in 1976—this would have had the added benefit of getting them back into the public eye sooner—all three albums could have been released the same day, with great fanfare, by Manticore. (This is, incidentally, more or less what the five members of Yes did during 1976, a year in which that band neither toured nor released a new studio album.) In early 1977, they would have released a new studio album. Side one would have included "Tiger in a Spotlight," "When the Apple Blossoms Bloom in the Windmills of Your Mind," "Brain Salad Surgery," and "Pirates." Side two would have opened with "Bo Diddley," a hard-driving, all instrumental "progressive blues" number recorded in 1975 featuring Hammond, Moog bass, and some ferocious, almost punklike electric guitar playing by Greg Lake; filled with Bo Diddley-like guitar scratching, insane metrical shifts, and startling off-beat accents, this little gem went unreleased until it turned up on the *Return of the Manticore* box set in 1993.[25] "Bo Diddley" would have been followed by "So Far to Fall," "Fanfare for the Common Man," and "Show Me the Way to Go Home." It would have been a very strong album—at least as strong as *Trilogy*—with a great deal of coherence (via the "space-age blues" style of many of the tracks, and the debt to earlier American popular music evident in almost every track except for "Pirates"), and its own distinctive identity. The abundance of short but strong tracks, with their confluence of blues influence and vintage ELP musicianship and intricacy, would have set well with the rock public circa 1977. One thing I'm certain of: this hypothetical album would have cracked the top ten (which *Works I* didn't), and its successor, even if it was crummy as *Love Beach*, would have charted a lot higher than number thirty-seven (the highest chart position reached by *Works II*).

If the solo/band format of the two *Works* albums was ELP's biggest blunder of the late seventies, the orchestral tour was a close second. Keith Emerson continued to believe, even after the band's breakup in 1979, that the orchestral tour was the apex of ELP's career, the goal which everything they had done before had been leading toward, although he acknowledged Lake and Palmer didn't share his view. He saw *Works* occupying a similar place in ELP's trajectory as *Five Bridges* did in the Nice's:

---

[25] In a phone conversation in late November 1999, Emerson told me that he had wanted to include "Bo Diddley" on *Works II*, but was outvoted. Carl Palmer, in particular, was apparently unsatisfied with his playing on the track.

We [The Nice] broadened and expanded, and we reached the ultimate doing *The Five Bridges Suite*. But it left the other members of the band behind. They didn't feel completely involved. This is more or less what happened with ELP. The felt it was more my thing than theirs, but they went along with it because that was the only way we could stay together.[26]

In my view, the analogy between *Five Bridges* and *Works* is a false one. While I do believe that the symphonic-rock fusion of *Five Bridges* (and similar music of the late sixties) was a necessary stage that late-sixties psychedelic rock had to pass through on its way towards developing into a full-blown progressive rock style, the entire symphonic-rock premise of *Works I* feels more like history moving backwards than it does a logical outcome of what ELP had done circa 1970–74. Lake and Palmer apparently understood this from the beginning. Although the original idea for the orchestral tour may have been his, Lake appears to have never fully believed in it, although he had paid it lip service in the interviews he gave during the spring and early summer of 1977. Speaking many years later, he said,

The band sort of had to tag along with the orchestra, and in that way, it was a restriction. However well you do it, an orchestra is not that tight, not that together. Whenever you hear rock music done with an orchestra, almost invariably it hangs together very loosely. The bottom line was, I think the public preferred the three-piece band rather than the three-piece band with an orchestra. At least that's how it felt when we did live concerts.[27]

Characteristically, Carl Palmer had suggested a compromise solution that addressed both Emerson's intense longing for an orchestral component to the *Works* tour, Lake's justifiable objection (I quite agree with his comments above), and financial realities. The band would have done well to follow Palmer's advice:

The mistake was taking the orchestra on a night-by-night basis straightaway. What we should have done was make a film or series of television concerts, maybe five altogether, which was my suggestion at the beginning and one which we now [1978] all wish we had done. Of the five, three would have placed more emphasis on the individuals, but with the group playing. Maybe Keith would have done his concerto. For the second show Greg could have sung more of his songs, then I could have played more of my pieces. The other two shows would have been totally group oriented—past and present material. We had the facilities to get out the five shows in a period of three

---

[26] Keith Emerson, quoted by Milano, "Keith Emerson," *Contemporary Keyboard*, September 1980, 22.
[27] Greg Lake, quoted by Hall, "Welcome to the Show," 48.

months, possibly even two, and then to go out with an orchestra. I think it would have opened people's eyes a lot quicker to what we were about to present . . . Then again, it [the live orchestral shows] could only have been done in the major markets because the overhead of 120 people on the road is astronomical.[28]

If ELP had released solo albums in 1976, a top-notch, coherent group album in 1977, and had followed Palmer's advice in playing just a few major market orchestral shows, when 1978 rolled around both their reputation and their finances would have been fully intact. Then, even if *Love Beach* had been the next step of the ELP saga, it would have been a matter of a fluke bad album, rather than the culmination of a long downward spiral; a well-executed, highly publicized farewell tour in 1979 would have allowed them to exit the seventies with their iconic, larger-than-life status more or less fully intact, and would have likely made their revivals of the 1980s and 1990s subject to the same kind of interest that accompanied those of Pink Floyd or the members of Led Zeppelin. Finally, releasing a better greatest hits package, and not releasing *In Concert* at all, in light of the insurmountable sound quality problems it posed, could only have helped their reputation.

Of course, one can play "what if" forever. ELP's spectacular late-seventies self-destruction, unparalleled in rock history in its magnitude, will forever be part of the ELP annals. The fact is, though, ELP had already made an extremely powerful mark by 1977. In an eighteen-month period between mid 1970 and early 1972, ELP's first three albums were probably the single most influential factor in defining the emerging progressive rock style. Keith Emerson almost single-handedly raised the keyboardist to parity with the guitarist in rock music, and he, more than anyone else, was responsible for introducing the synthesizer into the mainstream of popular music: in late-seventies stadium rock, recycled Emerson Hammond and synth riffs were almost ubiquitous. The influence of Palmer's drumming was also notable, as can be heard by studying the work of Rush's Neil Peart or Kansas's Phil Ehart, while Greg Lake's vocal stylizations had a similarly wide impact. ELP were among the very first to view the rock concert as a multimedia extravaganza, and their 1973-74 shows, with their custom built, portable stages, elaborate light and sound systems, and spectacular visual effects—all designed with arena and stadium sized venues in mind—forever changed the face of live rock performance. Most importantly, there are the six great albums of 1970–74, including one of rock's great debut albums and 1973's *Brain Salad Surgery*, one of the great rock albums of the seventies. These six albums

---

[28] Carl Palmer, quoted by Furnash, "Conversations," 29.

do at times accurately mirror the self-indulgence, self-importance, and over-the-top earnestness that were an integral part of the late-sixties counterculture. Just as often, though, the first six ELP albums capture the countercultural perspective at its most ambitious, visionary, transcendental, and uncompromising.

After the Fall

First Sabbatical
(1980–1985)

During the early 1980s, no musical style was more desperately unfashionable than progressive rock; and no progressive rock band was more desperately unfashionable than Emerson, Lake and Palmer. ELP were not the only casualty, however. Yes appeared to dissolve after their substandard *Drama* LP of 1980, marred by its misguided attempt to achieve hip credibility by bringing two members of New Wave sensations the Buggles (keyboardist Geoff Downes and vocalist Trevor Horne) on board. Likewise, Pink Floyd appeared to be finished after the open acrimony that erupted between Roger Waters and the rest of the band over the making of the cinematic version of *The Wall*. Genesis, increasingly a vehicle for lead singer/drummer Phil Collins, had become a straight-ahead pop band with New Wave overtones by the time of *ABACAB* (1981). Jethro Tull seemed adrift during this period, releasing a series of albums that had increasingly little to do with their landmark progressive rock/folk-rock masterpieces of the 1970s. Gentle Giant disbanded after their miserable *Civilian* LP of 1980. Only King Crimson, who dramatically reemerged in 1981 after a seven-year hiatus, were making challenging music that could viably be called "progressive rock"; and Crimson's new music, while genuinely progressive in its ideology, featured a wiry, acerbic sound that was indebted just as much to early-eighties New Wave and the then-emerging "world beat" phenomenon as it was to their landmark recordings of 1972–74.

What was big in the early eighties? North American stadium rock, arguably the final playing out of sixties and seventies rock styles, remained enormously popular into the early eighties, although by the middle of the decade it was fading. New Wave gained a new level of mainstream acceptance in the early eighties; by the middle of the decade, it, too, began to fade. Heavy metal, which appeared to be dying a parallel death to prog during the late seventies, experienced a spectacular resurgence in the early eighties with the emergence of a new generation of bands spearheaded by

447

Iron Maiden and Judas Priest; before the middle of the decade two distinct wings of metal were emerging, one a pop-influenced glam-metal style (Mötley Crüe, Poison), the other the rabidly antipop, punk-tinged thrash style that eventually engendered speed metal and death metal. Prog's idealism and ambition (although not much of its actual stylistic practice) passed on to a group of "guitar bands" represented by U2, Big Country, and R.E.M. Outside of the confines of rock proper, the post-funk, postdisco, dance-based songs of Prince, Michael Jackson, and Madonna Ciccone were enormously popular among young black and white audiences alike during the 1980–85 period; and a new instrumental style called "New Age," a blend of ethnic, jazz, classical, and electronic elements began to make an impact amongst a segment of the aging baby boomer population who felt they had "outgrown" rock. This was the brave new world into which Emerson, Lake and Palmer launched out on their own during the early eighties.

Keith Emerson

Of the three, in my opinion it is Keith Emerson that created the most truly contemporary and ultimately the most substantive body of work circa 1980–85. Not coincidentally, Emerson was the only one of the three who removed himself entirely from the rock music scene of the time. From the time of *Trilogy* and *Brain Salad Surgery*, Emerson had been writing music of a distinctly cinematic character—the overture to "Endless Enigma" and "Karn Evil 9, 3rd Impression" come to mind—and by the midseventies he was openly expressing an interest in film scoring. Not surprisingly, then, the bulk of Emerson's energy from 1980–85 was directed towards writing movie scores.

His first movie score was for Dario Argento's *Inferno* (1980). Argento, an Italian film director who specialized in horror films, was a major figure in Italian popular culture of the seventies and eighties, and also commanded a cult following outside of Italy. Emerson described the genesis of his collaboration with Argento this way:

> My manager presented me with a script written by Italian film director Dario Argento, a particularly gory horror movie called *Inferno*. I flew to Italy, where in one afternoon I was shown Argento's past accomplishments, all horror movies, among them *Deep Red* and one of his more successful ones in America, *Suspiria*. I was a little apprehensive as to whether this was the right first movie for me to score, but Dario seemed so open to my musical ideas that I felt very free to try out anything. With that kind of working relationship, I felt it would be ideal for me to gain the experience I needed by working on *Inferno*.

I went back home and worked on composing the music. I got most of my ideas from reading film scores. I made some rough recordings and went back to Italy to be with Dario on the cutting and editing procedures and see if he liked my ideas. We ran my rough cassette against the movieola, after which I threw out some ideas and kept others. I was finally given a video cassette of the finished film minus sound, and I came back to Nassau with Godfrey Salmon, the conductor of the orchestra we had used on the ELP [*Works*] Tour, to work on the orchestration. Godfrey has had experience with putting music to movies, and he was invaluable throughout the whole business.[1]

Despite all its gore, the portentous plot of *Inferno* is rather silly; almost camp, in fact. A young lady named Rose rouses a vicious spirit, Mater Tenebrarum (Mother of Darkness) from its lair in her house—she loses her life, and it's left to her brother Mark (a musicology student!) to somehow halt Mater Tenebrarum's trail of destruction. Emerson entered the project with a very definite sense of where he wanted to go with the music:

I didn't want to make it sound like a Hammer Films horror movie score, like *Phantasm*, where you've got the usual rock and roll thing on the soundtrack. I wanted to make it more like the earlier Dracula movies, almost a romantic sort of scoring. It may have been a bit too romantic. It may have been more suited to a love story than a horror movie, but I got used to seeing it that way. It gave off a sort of sick feeling, and it worked.[2]

Inferno Soundtrack

In fact, Emerson gave the movie a better score than it deserved; the *Inferno* score is a major achievement, almost certainly the finest of his six movie scores, and probably his greatest solo album. As Emerson suggests, the rock aspect of his writing is much deemphasized here, with only three of the album's fifteen tracks being rock oriented. The other twelve tracks showcase Emerson's piano, with lush orchestral backing, in a context that almost suggests that the score cannibalized music intended for a second piano concerto. If so, this represents a great loss: the *Inferno* music is superior to Piano Concerto no. 1 in almost every area where one would care to compare the two. Part of the credit must go to Godfrey Salmon, who orchestrated *Inferno*: his orchestrations are more colorful, vivid, and idiomatic than Emerson's had been for the Piano Concerto. The bulk of the credit, however, must go to Emerson himself: the musical ideas of

---

[1] Emerson, "An Open Letter," 19.
[2] Milano, "Keith Emerson," *Contemporary Keyboard*, September 1980, 19.

Inferno are simply more substantive and compelling than those of the Concerto. The *Inferno* score features a return to the Bartók/Ginastera stylistic vein that had served him so well in his ELP days. In addition, *Inferno* served as a springboard for Emerson to explore a feverish, unsettling early twentieth-century expressionistic style along the lines of the earlier music of Arnold Schoenberg or Alban Berg. This was new territory for Emerson and his fans, and the results are never less than interesting and are, at their best, stunning.

The music of the opening track, "Inferno (Main Title Theme)" functions much like the overtures that open Richard Wagner's music dramas: several principal themes (or *leitmotifs*, to use the Wagnerian term) are stated, and then are continuously developed, transformed, and varied as the movie progresses and as the dramatic situation warrants. Because of the high quality of the music and the Wagnerian approach to thematic transformation, I will do something here I won't do in later discussions of the Emerson movie scores: give a brief track-by-track description. I hope this will prove helpful to anyone who wants to pursue a more detailed analysis of the relationship between the music and the movie's dramatic development.

Inferno (Main Title Theme). The "overture," so to speak, begins along the lines of a gently melancholy barcarolle, or Venetian gondola song, in 6/4 time, in C minor. Within the first minute or so, we hear the three *leitmotifs* that will dominate much of the rest of the score: the gently descending fourths and fifths at the very beginning; the melancholy main theme first heard at 0:11; and the passionate, fanfarelike figure first annunciated by piano and orchestra at 1:15. As the music builds in intensity and scope, the orchestra recalls the main theme at 1:37; soon thereafter piano and orchestra begin interweaving increasingly agitated and dissonant snippets of the descending fourths (1:45) and the fanfare (2:02), which lead into a final big climax. Afterwards the music tapers off and the quiet opening passage is recalled. The final chord (a D major seventh superimposed over a C minor triad) is quietly ominous, and sets the mood for much of what is to come.

Rose's Descent into the Cellar. At 4:56, this is the longest track, and one of the richest musically: it is, essentially, a gigantic variation and development of the opening overture. It opens with a quietly dissonant "corruption" of the overture's opening descending fourths, which here are stretched to tritones, and accompany a slithering chromatic flute line; as this passage peters out, it's followed at 0:56 by a sadly barren statement of the main theme, and then at 1:27 by a spectral, ghostly transformation of the fanfare figure. Several times the movement appears headed for shattering climaxes (2:20 and 3:27, for instance), which never quite materialize: as such, it's something of a study in frustrated yearning. The final section (from 3:32) is dominated by a darkly mysterious transformation of the falling fourths and fifths.

Taxi Ride (Rome). The first of the score's three rock numbers is a cheerful, energetic piece in 5/4 time, cast in a decidedly jazz-rock fusion vein. It features Emerson on Minimoog (the chattering, Jan Hammer–like lead line), piano, and Korg 3100 (the bell-like accompaniment), accompanied by his Nassau rhythm section of Kendal Stubbs (bass) and Frank Scully (drums), of whom more will be said in connection with Emerson's *Honky* album of 1981. Especially observant listeners may notice borrowed material from "Va pensiero" of Giuseppe Verdi's opera *Nabucco*—this is a quotation that the movie's Italian audience was probably more aware of than Emerson's fans elsewhere.

The Library. A short "pipe organ" solo that was actually realized by Emerson on the Korg 3100. It's atmospheric, but not particularly profound, with no thematic connection to the rest of the score.

Sarah in the Library Vaults. The first piece for orchestra alone, this is a quiet, flesh-crawling, wonderfully expressionistic number; the opening passage reminds me a bit of the beginning of Alban Berg's Piano Sonata, opus 1, with its spidery, chromatic voice leading.

Bookbinder's Delight. A short movement for piano and orchestra, based around a driving piano ostinato in the instrument's bass register and short bursts of agitated brass chords. The overall sound is similar in style and mood to the opening of the third movement of Emerson's Piano Concerto.

Rose Leaves the Apartment. For piano and orchestra. Begins similarly to "Rose's Descent," with a variation of the overture's descending fourths and fifths accompanied by a slithering, chromatic flute theme. This soon breaks off into more agitated, almost hallucinatory piano chords accompanied by bursts of orchestral sound. From 1:22, a crystalline, mystical transformation of the descending fourths and fifths, mostly for solo piano (there's some sparse orchestral accompaniment) evokes the music of Alexander Scriabin (1872–1915), a Russian composer whose music blends impressionistic and expressionistic elements. The Scriabin-like treatment of the descending fourths and fifths is developed at some length; at 2:48 it suddenly breaks off, as a driving piano ostinato (again in the bass register) and a kaleidoscope of dissonant string lines brings the movement to a most uneasy close.

Rose Gets It. The movement begins with a bone-chilling, atonal "melody" for solo soprano, joined at 0:29 by alto, and from 0:56 by tenor countermelodies; the "disembodied" effect of the wordless atonal choir is not dissimilar to the passages of György Ligeti's *Requiem* used by Kubrick in *2001*. Suddenly, at 1:22, in conjunction with Rose meeting her grisly fate at the hands of Mater Tenebrarum, the strings and piano explode with a driving, twisting chromatic theme, punctuated by screaming, dissonant brass chords. This huge climax rounds off the first half of the score (and the plot).

Elisa's Story. "Elisa's Story," which opened side two of the *Inferno* LP, is a shortened version of the opening overture, here played as a solo by Emerson on Yamaha CP-30 electric piano. Emerson de-tuned the CP-30 for this performance; the resulting ambience is of extreme age and decay.

A Cat Attic Attack. "Cat Attic Attack" begins with a recollection of the "corrupted," dissonant version of the descending fourths and the slithering chromatic flute theme that began "Rose's Descent" and "Rose Leaves the Apartment." The descending fourths begin to accelerate, and are soon swept away by driving piano chords and flickering, pointillistic orchestral textures that reach a mighty climax at 1:35. Thereafter a quiet, mystical piano theme appears to bring the movement to a close; at 2:14, however, orchestra and piano explode into a fury of renewed activity, with atonal, frantically racing motives that reach an even more immense climax on a series of tortured, dissonant chords from 2:48.

Kazanian's Tarantella. The beginning of "Tarantella" is similar to the end of "Cat Attic," with a call-and-response between a driving ostinato in the bass register of the piano and short, frantically iterated orchestral motives; the overall mood conveyed by the music is panic. From 1:14 on the music begins to acquire the character of a dissonant, frenzied dance in 12/8 time with frequent stop-time episodes; the piano ostinatos and chords are reminiscent of some of Alberto Ginastera's music. As with the previous movement, this one seems to end at 2:35, with the false ending followed by a series of massively dissonant chords and a mock-triumphal dance fanfare.

Mark's Discovery. Essentially a shortened recapitulation of the overture that eliminates the central development of the main themes and the reappearance of the quiet opening passage.

Mater Tenebrarum. The second of the track's three rock numbers. Ever wonder what ELP would have sounded like if Greg Lake had been relieved of his vocal duties and replaced by a large choir? "Mater Tenebrarum" supplies the answer. Emerson, mainly on Korg, and his "Nassau" rhythm section supply an aggressive, muscular instrumental backing that's rather reminiscent of "The Hut of Baba Yaga"; the choir, meanwhile, shrieks out baleful warnings, in Latin, concerning the evil intentions of Mater Tenebrarum in an idiom somewhere between Verdi's *Requiem* and Handel's *Messiah*. I've always felt the overall effect of this rather odd combination of styles is a bit camp; nonetheless, the track does show an aggression and drive that was all too absent in ELP's late seventies output. Emerson manages to slip in some wryly effective modulations, too (1:21, for instance).

Inferno Finale. The "Finale" begins with a driving, doom-laded piano ostinato deep in the instrument's bass registers, to which the orchestra adds a series of increasingly agitated and dissonant punctuations; at 1:36, this passage leads into a ponderous, tortured recapitulation and extension of the overture's main theme (i.e., from 0:11 of the opening track), and builds to a massive conclusion.

Cigarettes, Ices, etc. The score's third rock number, "Cigarettes" functions as a coda to the score as a whole. Based around a driving keyboard ostinato in 6/8, "Cigarettes" is rather like a cyborgian rearrangement of "America" kicked into overdrive, and is vintage Emerson—urgent, pressing, heroic. His "Nassau" rhythm section accompanies magnificently, with Kendal Stubbs' funky, Stanley Clarke–like bass lines being particularly impressive. The CD version fully restores the ponderous closing chord progression that was, for some reason, cut short on the LP.

Inferno: An Assessment

Inferno is a major achievement, and is one of the highlights of Emerson's career. Its classical tracks are characterized by a stylistic cohesion, emotional intensity, orchestral vividness, and brilliant sense of thematic transformation that, in my view, far surpasses the Piano Concerto no. 1. The three rock numbers, meanwhile, though shorter and much less imposing than the classical segments of the score, show a drive and sense of urgency that hearken back to the early days of ELP and represent a welcome change from much of the band's late seventies output. I've always thought that an orchestral suite for piano and orchestra could easily be assembled from *Inferno*, and would immediately displace the Concerto as Emerson's "legitimate" masterwork. Unfortunately, if *Inferno* is one of Emerson's great achievements, it is certainly not one of his better-known ones. The album was released in Europe in early 1980 on the German Ariola and the Italian Cinevox labels; while it was quite popular in Italy (where both Argento and Emerson were late-seventies pop culture icons), it made less of an impact elsewhere. In fact, in the U.S. it was available only as an import through Atlantic and was rather difficult to track down. Sadly, what should have been one of Emerson's greatest triumphs went largely unnoticed outside of Italy.

Incidentally, in 1997 *Inferno* was rereleased on CD by the Italian Cinevox label. The rerelease included, as a bonus track, a ten-minute "Inferno Outtakes Suite": music that accompanied the movie, but was not included on the original LP. Most of the sections of this suite are alternate takes of numbers already on the album (i.e., "Cigarettes, Ices, etc." and the overture) or atmospheric passages of sound effects. Some of the latter are quite bone chilling: for instance, the disembodied solo soprano line from 5:23 to 6:23, and the hallucinatory, sinister electronic passage from 6:23 to the end (with a particularly terrifying outburst at 8:03) that hearkens back to the *musique concrète* of the fifties. This is truly unnerving music that, I suspect, most people would not choose to listen to at night, alone, with the lights off.

While Emerson's *Inferno* score never garnered the popular acclaim it deserved, it did bring him to the attention of Hollywood. Emerson recalled many years later,

> It [*Inferno*] was an experience, and the success of that brought me to Hollywood where Martin Pohl was working on a Stallone film, *Nighthawks*. They sent me a script and photographs of some of the location shots. And just going by that, I sat down and came up with what I thought would represent a great theme. I was on the phone with Martin Pohl, and he said that "if you can bear in mind that what we want is something like *Naked City 2005*. Slight jazz overtones."
>
> So I made a tape, flew to L.A., and met with Martin. Stallone came in— he was much smaller than what I'd seen on *Rocky*—and I played him what I did on my eight-track tape recorder in the barn. I explained the direction that I saw the film going in. He didn't say much and walked out of the room. He took Martin Pohl, the producer, with him. Martin came back after about fifteen minutes rubbing his hands and said "We've got a deal—he loves it."[3]

Nighthawks features Stallone as a tough, blue-collar New York cop recruited to a small, elite task force charged with bringing in a notorious terrorist who has temporarily taken up residence in New York City. Like *Inferno*, the *Nighthawks* score opens with an easily recognized main theme that recurs a number of times during the course of the movie. Otherwise, though, the two scores are dissimilar—just as *Nighthawks'* plot of jet-setting intrigue is starkly different than *Inferno*'s plot of supernatural terror. The *Nighthawks* score shows little of *Inferno*'s classicism: instead, it is heavily electronic, and pervaded by a gritty, streetwise realism. The stylistic foundation of the score is early-eighties funk, with menacing, atmospheric electronic passages also prominently forefronted. Like *Inferno*, parts of *Nighthawks* were recorded in Nassau, with Emerson's Nassau rhythm section of Kendal Stubbs (bass), Neil Symonette (drums), and Frank Scully (percussion) playing prominent roles. The jazzy, brass-heavy orchestration was arranged by Harry Betts; Godfrey Salmon again conducted the orchestra, which was recorded in London's Advision Studios. Of course, a lot of the "orchestration" was provided by Emerson himself on Yamaha GX-1, Korg 3100 and 3300 polyphonic synthesizers, and the then-revolutionary Fairlight Computer Musical Instrument, which had pre-digital sampling capabilities that Emerson used with the aid of Kevin Crossley.

---

[3] Keith Emerson, quoted in *First Reflection*, reprinted in *ELP Digest* 5, no. 25 (October 11, 1995).

Nighthawks Soundtrack

On the whole, the *Nighthawks* score, while providing a fine musical back-drop for the movie, simply doesn't hold up as an independent musical experience in the way *Inferno* does. It needs the visual cues to justify the repetitive funk grooves, the lengthy passages of atmospheric keyboards, and the sudden juxtaposition of totally unrelated music. Indeed, beyond the main theme, the score seems somewhat lacking in memorable melodic material. There are a few tracks that stand out, though. "Nighthawking," the album's only track to feature Emerson on acoustic piano, is distinguished by a furious piano solo over a disco groove (this portion of the score accompanies a scene in which Stallone and a partner run into their terrorist nemesis in a discotheque); it is marred, though, by Paulette McWilliams's cheesy vocal. A superior version of this track, sans vocal, appeared later on *Honky*. "I'm a Man," the old Steve Winwood song from his days with the Spencer Davis Group, finds Emerson handling not only keyboards, but lead vocal: while not absolutely terrible, his airy, heavily processed tenor won't make anybody forget Greg Lake. The chief interest here is in the textural keyboard parts: the growling, guitarlike vamp figure and percussive "explosion" sounds blend with the bass and drums to create a gritty, polyrhythmic groove. "The Chopper," on the other hand, is the album's one track that hearkens back to classic ELP, with its pulsating, heroic 5/4 episodes. "Face to Face," meanwhile, recalls some of the menacing, bone-chilling string episodes from *Inferno*. The finale, "The Flight of a Hawk," after a quiet, almost sentimental opening, recaps the "Nighthawks" main title theme that opened the album.

Nighthawks: An Assessment

While it has some excellent moments and does manage to establish a unique identity—urban, funk-oriented, streetwise—the individual tracks of *Nighthawks* never cohere into a greater musical experience in the manner of *Inferno*. As such, *Nighthawks* is more an album for Emerson completists. The movie and soundtrack album were released in late April, 1981: *Nighthawks* became the only Emerson solo album to break the U.S. charts, topping out at 183 and remaining in the top two hundred for three weeks. It was not one of Sylvester Stallone's more popular movies: while many of Stallone's fans consider his work in *Nighthawks* to be one of his most subtle and understated performances, his Officer DaSilva character never really caught fire with the public in the manner of his Rocky persona. As a result, Emerson's career as a film composer didn't get the traction it certainly would have if the movie had been more popular. The album did attract a few positive reviews, including one in Emerson's old nemesis, *Creem*. After being out of print for many years, *Nighthawks* finally reappeared on CD as a limited edition private release, available on Keith Emerson's web site, in 2002.

In November 1981, Emerson's third post-ELP album and first "real" solo album, *Honky*, was released. Unlike *Inferno* and *Nighthawks*, which were fairly major productions, *Honky* has a spontaneous, off-the-cuff feel that suggests Emerson had grown tired of ELP's highly polished, tightly structured approach to recording. In an interview given during the summer of 1980, when the recording of *Honky* was in progress, Emerson said, "Currently I'm making another album here in Nassau. It's not a 'solo' album—they've all been solo albums as far as I'm concerned—but an album of styles and keyboard playing that I haven't been able to use in the past. I've found it a treat to play with funky players."[4] Later, he added, "I'm enjoying playing in a funky context, because it's such a change from the very technical approach ELP took . . . Quite honestly, I'm much happier now that I'm free of the pressure of going to the studio and arguing all the time, wasting all that money on studio time arguing instead of playing music."[5] About the title, Emerson said simply that the album was called *Honky* "'cos I'm the only white guy on the album."[6] *Honky* features a number of musicians that Emerson had met around Nassau; we have already encountered the *Honky* rhythm section on *Inferno* and *Nighthawks*. Emerson became acquainted with bassist Kendal Stubbs at Compass Point Studios, where he was a tape operator; Emerson remarked Stubbs "sounds like Stanley Clarke. He does all the bits."[7] Emerson alternated between two drummers, Neil Symonette (at that time a seventeen-year-old prodigy who had just been awarded a scholarship to Berklee School of Music) and Frank Scully.

African American music—stride, swing, bebop and cool jazz, boogie-woogie, rhythm and blues—had always been a profound influence on Emerson. It was a presence that was usually never too deeply below the surface in his ELP days, and one that occasionally surfaced as the primary influence on specific tracks. *Honky*, however, is almost unique in being a more or less explicit tribute to, and exploration of, his African-American musical roots; no Nice or ELP album, save perhaps *Works II*, downplays his debt to European classical music to the same degree. Thankfully, however, by and large Emerson avoids the slavish, quasi-historical adherence to particular styles (stride, boogie, and R & B, in particular) that, in my view, marred some of his ELP material in this vein. Here, the African

---

[4] Emerson, "An Open Letter," 21.
[5] Milano, "Keith Emerson," *Contemporary Keyboard*, September 1980, 17.
[6] Radio interview with Jim Ladd, late April, 1981.
[7] Milano, "Keith Emerson," *Contemporary Keyboard*, September 1980, 17.

American stylistic influences mix with Emerson's own distinctive progressive rock voice—adjusted in a way that befits the album's loose, funky approach. *Honky* also finds Emerson experimenting with Caribbean and Latin rhythms to interesting effect.

Honky

The first track, "Hello Sailor," is in many ways the best. Based on the famous "Sailor's Hornpipe" melody, it falls into three distinct movements. The opening movement is slow, dreamy, evocative. Emerson plays gentle, impressionistic chords on a de-tuned Yamaha CP-30 electric piano, while Kendal Stubbs slowly presents the "Sailor's Hornpipe" theme on bass; accompanied by the distant sound of surf, this section evokes a walk on a moonlit beach. As the music quietly trails off, Emerson suddenly launches into the second movement, which is actually George Malcolm's "Bach Before the Mast," a fugue for solo piano in the style of J. S. Bach that uses the "Sailor's Hornpipe" as its main subject. Emerson performs it with incredible drive and precision; you can almost imagine the pennants stiffly waving in the wind. The third and longest movement is a jazz fusion–tinged treatment of the "Sailor's Hornpipe" theme. It opens with Emerson playing a series of winding, intricate extensions of the Hornpipe theme on Hammond C3, accompanied in unison by Stubbs, guitarist Mott (chief engineer of Compass Point), and tenor saxophonist Andrew Brennan, who also contributes a nice solo. Emerson follows Brennan's solo with his finest Hammond solo since the *Brain Salad Surgery* period; the Hammond solo is periodically interrupted by unison statements of the Hornpipe theme in which Minimoog and the Korg synthesizers playing an increasingly prominent role. The music appears to quiet down; then a final development of the Hornpipe theme builds into a wonderful, heroic conclusion. "Hello Sailor" showcases many of the traits Emerson's fans most admired: the imaginative thematic transformations, the convincing interweaving of different musical styles, the faultless instinct for large-scale structure, and, of course, the superb playing. But while "Hello Sailor" is a mini-epic in the best ELP tradition, its looser feel and cheerful good humor is rather different than the standard ELP fare.

"Hello Sailor" segues into the second track, "Salt Cay." More loosely constructed, "Salt Cay" consists of three distinct sections: a Korg 3100 fanfare theme with some daunting syncopation (at the beginning and elsewhere), a funky Hammond organ episode (0:34), and a section based on Sonny Rollins's "Saint Thomas," where Emerson spins out twisting Minimoog leads over the cheerfully chirping Korg theme (1:12). The second half of "Salt Cay" mirrors the first, with the three sections being repeated in the same order; the only difference being that Emerson's Minimoog solo during the "Saint Thomas" section is greatly extended— too much, perhaps. Again, the prevailing mood is sunny and cheerful: a mood nicely conveyed in the "Salt Cay" promo film (played on the Italian *Variety TV* show in late 1980 and for years a mainstay on Emerson's web site), which, in one amusing segment, shows Emerson floating off to sea on an upright piano, which he pounds furiously all the while.

"Green Ice," the third and final track on side one of the LP format, is the album's first (and only) minor key number; its considerable rhythmic drive is generated by several distinctly Brazilian polyrhythms. Like "Salt Cay," this track is built around three discrete sections that are presented once, then repeated in a much expanded form. The first section features a one measure bass/piano ostinato, over which is layered offbeat, fanfare-like Korg chords (at 0:27), and then a brittle, edgy theme that passes back and forth between guitar and piano (0:33, repeated at 1:03). The second section features urgent, pounding piano chords in a call-and-response with bass figures (1:32); and the third section (1:45) is built around a bossa nova rhythm, over which a short, repetitive "Green Ice" vocal is declaimed by Emerson, Michael Hanna, and Shelly Lightbourn. During the second half of "Green Ice," it's mainly the first section that's extended, as Emerson and Mott spin out increasingly agitated piano and guitar solos, respectively, over the throbbing polyrhythms generated by the ostinato and offbeat Korg chords; an extra beat is always added near the end of the section, which heightens the off-balance, nervous energy. Like "Salt Cay," "Green Ice" may go on a bit too long; on the other hand, the exotic polyrhythms are quite different from standard ELP fare, and mark a new avenue of exploration for Emerson.

Side two of the LP format opens with "Intro Juicing," wherein a possibly inebriated Emerson, pretending to be a DJ for WAJR-Pittsburgh, sings short stanzas of "I'll See You In My Dreams" and "Shine On Harvest Moon," punctuated with uproarious laughter that segues directly into a cover of Billy Taylor's "Big Horn Breakdown." In this track, Emerson indulges his fondness for stride piano. However, his ingenious arrangement, wherein his Korg 3100 is run through a vocoder to create an extremely convincing simulation of a sax section that he uses to counterpoint his piano, prevents the tune from becoming a slavish tribute along the lines of some of his ELP material. Much the same can be said of the next track, a cover of Meade Lux Lewis's "Yancey Special." The arrangement here, by Emerson and Harry South, shows more imagination than the straight homage to Lewis's "Honky Tonk Train Blues" on *Works II*: Neil Symonette's drumming and percussion overlays on "Yancey Special" eschew the more predictable swing or shuffle rhythms in favor of a loping, calypsolike sway. Emerson, on piano, is joined by Pete King and If's Dick Morrissey on alto and tenor sax, respectively, with Morrissey contributing a fine solo. The third track, "Rum-a-Ting," features Emerson on Yamaha CP-30 electric piano and Minimoog. In 1980, Emerson related an interesting story concerning the genesis of the final track, "Jesus Loves Me":

> I've been going around to the gospel churches here in Nassau with a tape recorder. One Sunday night I'd finished in the studio, and I took Mott and his assistant Dennis Halliburton [engineers at Compass Point Studios] out, and we scouted around looking for a church. Down here they really get going on a Sunday night. So we were driving down the road, and we heard tambourines and shouting, so we stopped. I had my tape recorder, and I didn't want to disturb anyone, so I just stuck my microphone in the back window and sort of observed. But one of the preachers who was standing in the back invited us in, so we kind of dubiously sat in the back with all this raving going on and continued recording . . . [Then] the Reverend gets up and speaks to the congregation, and he says, "who are these visitors in the back of the church?" And I just said nothing. He said, "Do you have a spokesman?" I said, "Well, yeah, my name is Keith and this is my friend Mott and my friend Dennis." He said, "What is your purpose?" I said, "Well, I'm looking to record a gospel choir." He said, "What is your church?" I said "Church of England," I think, so he said "I'd like to see you often" and he hugged me hard.[8]

"Jesus Loves Me" opens with the sound of a Pentecostal preacher's thunderous exhortations, punctuated with the congregations equally fervent "amens"—probably a segment of the very service Emerson described taping above, at Nassau's Holiness Church of Deliverance. Emerson and his rhythm section (Kendal Stubbs, Neil Symonette) are joined by a gospel choir, the Kayla Lockhart Singers. For his first venture into this kind of music, Emerson shows a fine understanding of the black gospel idiom; he accompanies the choir on Hammond, but takes a solo on his Yamaha CP-30 electric piano, spinning out jazzy leads over his staccato, syncopated left hand chords and Stubbs's funky bass lines. Mott also takes a short guitar solo. The Kayla Lockhart Singers, meanwhile, contribute ecstatic melismas, rasps, and extemporized vocal counterpoints.

Honky: An Assessment

The cover of *Honky* is interesting and quite revealing, I suspect, of where Emerson found himself, emotionally and spiritually, at that particular juncture of his life. In the cover photo, Emerson is sitting on the front

---

[8] Keith Emerson, quoted by Milano, "Keith Emerson," *Contemporary Keyboard*, September 1980, 20.

patio of a small house. His black Bahamian friends, dressed informally, are all playing hand drums or dancing. But Emerson is dressed in a sharp white business suit, and he's on the phone. He looks as if he wishes he could hang it up. It would seem that on some level, Emerson desired to escape the pressures of superstardom, and beyond that, to escape the frantic Western pace of life and slavish devotion to career and economic advancement, to exchange it for the slower, less frantic, and less materialistic way of life of a third-world country like the Bahamas.

Honky reflects this shift in priorities. For those wanting profound and challenging music along the lines of *Tarkus*, *Brain Salad Surgery*, and *Inferno*, *Honky* is bound to be a disappointment. However, it has a different set of strengths. No other Emerson album (including his work with the Nice, ELP, and his two movie soundtracks) is less self-conscious, self-important, or pretentious. No other Emerson album is bathed with the same degree of sunny good cheer. And despite the fact there are no major masterpieces here (although I think "Hello Sailor" may fairly be called a minor one), there are no duds, either; the quality of the material, especially in terms of its performance, is uniformly high. *Honky* succeeds in creating the unique and distinctive tribute to African American music that Emerson had sought, but never quite managed, to create in his *Works*-era solo output. It also undertook some respectful and promising explorations of Caribbean musical idioms that nicely paralleled what fellow progsters Peter Gabriel and Patrick Moraz were contemporaneously doing with African and Brazilian styles, respectively: I always regretted that Emerson never pursued these explorations any further in later albums.

Honky was released by the Italian Bubble and German Ariola labels in November 1981. It was available in the U.S. only as an import, and unfortunately proved even harder to track down than *Inferno*. Once again, some fine music by Emerson never reached a larger public; I suspect a large majority of ELP's American fans not only never heard *Honky*, but never heard of it. In April 1985, the British Chord Records label, with whom Emerson had shortly before had an acrimonious falling out, rereleased *Honky* with a different track listing: "Rum-a-Ting" was excised and replaced by a new track, "Chic Charni," (which many Emerson fans recognized as "Nighthawking," from the *Nighthawks* soundtrack, without Paulette McWilliams's cheesy vocals—a welcome improvement). In the late 1990s, an authorized rerelease of *Honky* became available that included both "Rum-a-Ting" and "Chic Charni."

In 1982, Emerson was chosen to be music director for a Japanese animated film entitled *Harmagedon*. In line with the title, and with the Japanese animé genre generally, the plot of *Harmagedon* has portentous sci-fi overtones: a Transylvanian princess, a Japanese high school student, and a 2,000-year-old warrior are among a select cadre of psionic warriors who battle a gigantic alien entity who is bent on destroying the cosmos. Emerson composed roughly half of the soundtrack (twenty-two minutes worth, filling one side of an LP); the rest of the music was composed by Nozomu Aoki. Emerson's *Harmagedon* music was performed on his Korg 3100 and 3300 synths; on some tracks he is accompanied by drummer Jun Aoyama.

Harmagedon Soundtrack

Like his earlier soundtracks, Emerson's *Harmagedon* music manages to establish its own distinctive identity, evoking the impressionistic, richly layered, multihued electronic orchestrations of Jean-Michel Jarre or Vangelis. There are a couple of differences, though: Emerson eschews the throbbing bass sequences of these musicians in favor of real drums and electronically realized "bass guitar" parts, and much of his *Harmagedon* music is characterized by the clearly etched melodies and strongly marked rhythms that are Emerson characteristics. "Theme of Floi" is probably the most Jarre-like track of the set: drifting, impressionistic harmonies, occasionally punctuated by dissonant, vaguely ominous fanfares, are backed by sedate rock drumming and slowly treading chromatic bass lines. "Joe and Michiko," on the other hand, is more reminiscent of Vangelis: it's less rhythmic than "Floi," featuring a sentimental melody backed by bittersweet harmonies painted in electronic pastels, and occasionally interrupted by swirling, "cosmic" sequences. "Children of the Light," the soundtrack's only song, features vocalist Rosemary Butler; its bittersweet lyricism is reminiscent of Andrew Lloyd Webber ("Memories"), while its pulsating chromatic harmonies evoke Gustav Mahler, a composer Emerson was just beginning to discover at this time. While some of the song's fanfarelike interludes are truly gorgeous, I've always felt that drummer Jun Aoyama's shuffle rhythm didn't fit the song—a slow, understated straight 4/4 rock beat would have conveyed the song's sense of majesty more effectively. "Sonny's Skate State" is something of a "space-age stride" piece: the most prominent sonority is a brittle, clavinetlike synth part, with "squiggly" synth leads and a funky bass line also playing important roles.

The final two tracks of the soundtrack are the most reminiscent of ELP. "Zamedy Stomp" evokes "Aquatarkus" with its marchlike theme, treading bass lines, and increasingly dense textures; the main theme is periodically interrupted by a threatening fanfare, after which it reappears more richly orchestrated than before. The finale, "Challenge of the Psionic Fighters," is a heroic march in the tradition of the main theme of "Karn Evil 9, 3rd Impression." As with the previous track, the main theme is regularly interrupted by an ominous, agitated episode (eventually featuring Fujimaro Yoshino's electric guitar), after which it returns in progressively more massive orchestration.

Harmagedon: An Assessment

Emerson's music for *Harmagedon* is quite good, although there's not enough of it to build up a lot of intensity, and, unlike *Inferno* or *Nighthawks*, there are no thematic interconnections between the tracks. The soundtrack was released on Canyon Records in Japan in March 1983. Besides Emerson's six tracks, it includes five by Nozomu Aoki (these tend towards a lounge-jazz style), and an arrangement of J. S. Bach's Toccata and Fugue in D minor, BWV 565, that was used in the film. In April 1985 Chord Records released an album featuring Emerson's six *Harmagedon* tracks on side one and music from Derek Austin's *China Freefall* on side two. While it attracted a good deal of attention in Japan, where it hit number one in the charts, the *Harmagedon* soundtrack was very hard to find elsewhere, and went largely unnoticed: in the U.S., it was even more obscure than *Inferno* or *Honky*. In 1998, the original soundtrack—as opposed to the Chord Records release of 1985—was rereleased on the Japanese Volcano Records label.

Another project Emerson was deeply involved in during 1982 was scoring *Best Revenge*, a movie about drug smuggling that was director John Trent's last film. The movie itself is quite obscure, and such reviewers as deigned to notice it at all almost universally panned it. But if the movie is a failure, the same is not true of Emerson's score: it contains some terrific music, and in fact I would rank it his second best soundtrack after *Inferno*.

Best Revenge Soundtrack

Stylistically, *Best Revenge* is more eclectic and less single-minded in its exploration of a specific idiom than Emerson's previous four albums: rock and classical styles are sometimes alternated, and at other times fused, with great facility. The opening track, the delicate "Dream Runner" for solo piano (with some subtle synthetic string backing), is perhaps the most beautiful piece of music Emerson ever composed. Its aching, almost heartbreaking lyricism and bittersweet, painfully beautiful chord progressions (listen at 1:17, for instance) paint undertones of pensiveness, melancholy, and sadness that aren't normal Emerson fare, but which pervade much of the soundtrack to some degree. The following track, "The Runner," is a free rearrangement of "Dream Runner" for rock trio; the outstanding funk basslines and some excellent drumming by ex-Journey and Jefferson Starship drummer Aynsley Dunbar (who guests throughout the soundtrack) gives the composition a powerful rhythmic drive, and Emerson's Korg and Prophet-5 orchestrations transform the wistful melancholy of the opening track into an equally compelling sense of doomed heroism. More cheerful is "Wha'dya Mean," the third track, a late-seventies/early-eighties funk/fusion number along the lines of *Inferno*'s "Taxi Ride," albeit more conventional. Dunsbar's drumming is especially outstanding on this track, and Emerson contributes some very nice synth lines that evoke Jan Hammer's jazzy Rhodes electric piano work with the Mahavishnu Orchestra. "Wha'dya Mean" is followed by an awful, but mercifully short, song, "Straight Between the Eyes," featuring a lead vocal by Levon Helm. Characterized by its clichéd, gutterbucket blues guitar, it is notable chiefly for its uncanny resemblance to "The Breathalyzer," an equally bad song on Rick Wakeman's *Criminal Record* LP of 1977.[9]

The soundtrack's real center of gravity is the fifteen-and-a-half minute *Best Revenge* orchestral suite, which occupies most of side two of the soundtrack's LP format. In many ways it approaches the *Inferno* suites in quality, if not in scope. To be sure, it is more loosely constructed than *Inferno*—it does not develop its recurring motives with the same single-mindedness—and it is quite different stylistically. *Inferno* develops its early-twentieth-century expressionist idiom very exhaustively; the *Best Revenge* suite, on the other hand, draws together its rock, ethnic, and twentieth-century classical idioms more rhapsodically, almost in a stream-of-consciousness-like flow at times. Amazingly, though, the movement from one section of music to another section that is stylistically quite different feels natural, even inevitable, and the suite's overall structure is characterized by a nice ebb and flow towards and away from its major climaxes. The suite fuses its rock and orchestral components at least as convincingly as "Pirates"; Emerson's electronic keyboard orchestrations, backed by rock rhythm section, alternate with, or sometimes seamlessly blend with, the orchestral arrangement of John Coleman, who conducted the National Philharmonic Orchestra on the recording.

Like "Pirates," the *Best Revenge* orchestral suite is so tightly woven that it's hard to describe in terms of discrete sections: since it's (sadly) probable that relatively few of my readers have heard it (although it is included on Emerson's 2005 *Hammer It Out* anthology), I'll confine myself to a few broad observations. On the whole, the first half of the suite is more rock-oriented, the second more exclusively orchestral, although both halves interpenetrate rock and orchestral elements. The suite opens with a statement of the main title theme, "Playing for Keeps,"

---

[9] For more on Wakeman's *Criminal Record*, see appendix C.

by rock trio with orchestral backing (0:00–1:24); this theme is recapitulated at 4:14–4:57. Other notable passages include a flamencolike passage in 5/4 for rock trio (1:25–2:53); a heroic, ELP-like rock episode with shifting meters (2:54–3:34); a Middle Eastern development of the "Playing for Keeps" theme (3:35–4:13); an amazing, hallucinatory episode featuring polyrhythmic percussion, spacey keyboard ostinatos, and atonal orchestral fragments that cut against each other and the 4/4 drum groove (5:45–8:10); and a heartbreakingly beautiful flamenco guitar recollection of the "Dream Runner" theme (12:31–13:13). This is only a partial account of the suite's pleasures, however, which repay multiple listenings.

The *Best Revenge* soundtrack closes with its second song, "Playing for Keeps," the main melody of which has already been forecast in the orchestral suite. Thankfully, this song is far better than "Right Between the Eyes." It features Brad Delp on lead vocals: although he doesn't hit the stratospheric high notes that characterized his work with Boston, he sings with great verve nonetheless. "Playing for Keeps" is heroic, anthemic, with undertones of sadness that permeate much of the soundtrack; when Delp sings the line, "Each with his own serenade / making music that the world had refused to play," one wonders if this isn't a wry autobiographical comment by Emerson on his own post-ELP situation. The instrumental bridge (1:50) creates a nice sense of drama; note the ominous bass synth theme at 2:17, which is very reminiscent of the "Tramway" theme of *Nighthawks*. With some halfway decent exposure, it's not hard to imagine this song being a smash hit in the early eighties—stylistically, it's comparable to the better songs on the first Asia album—although its reflective, melancholy coda (3:07–4:20) might have been a turnoff for the A.O.R. listeners of the day, who would have expected a more obvious, clichéd ending.

The *Best Revenge* soundtrack was released in April 1985 by Chord Records. In the later eighties, it was rereleased by Chord on a two-for-one CD that also contained the *Murderock* soundtrack. It is currently out of print. One can only hope it will be reissued soon: other than *Inferno*, which is currently available, no other Emerson soundtrack is more deserving of a wider audience.

In 1983, Emerson was approached to score an Italian film, *Murderock*, directed by Lucio Fulci. Set in New York City, the plot involves a group of dancers trying out for a Broadway musical who are brutally murdered one by one, as a cop and a psychiatrist feverishly work together to track down the killer—something of a slasher *Chorus Line*. Like *Best Revenge*, it was a low-profile movie that was largely panned by such critics as noticed it, with one summary simply stating "sumptuous visuals lend weight to a thin story line." Emerson's soundtrack was released in May 1984 on the Italian Bubble label (which had released *Honky* two and a half years earlier), and was rereleased by Chord Records in April 1985 (coinciding with Chord's release of *Best Revenge* and its rereleases of *Honky* and Emerson's *Harmagedon* music). The movie itself appeared in 1984.

Murderock Soundtrack

Like *Best Revenge*, the *Murderock* LP is quite short; at not quite half an hour, it's even shorter, in fact, than *Best Revenge*. Unlike *Best Revenge*, a lot of the music here is rather pedestrian; while it serves the film well enough, it's probably the least substantive of Emerson's five film scores of the 1980–85 period. The problem is not that the music is bad (it isn't); it's that so much of it could have been written by anybody. The rhythm section, too (Tom Nicol and Derek Wilson on drums, Mike Sheppard on bass), while competent, doesn't bring the same level of intensity that Emerson's Nassau musicians brought to *Inferno* and *Nighthawks*, or that Aynsley Dunbar brought to *Best Revenge*. For instance, the instrumental "Murderock" theme sounds like it's from an early-eighties disco soundtrack, while "Tonight is Your Night" (featuring Doreen Chanter and Mike Sebbage on lead vocals) is a sentimental, almost syrupy soft-rock ballad that would have fit comfortably into an early-eighties top-forty radio rotation. Neither track shows any unique traits suggesting Emerson's authorship. "Streets to Blame," another song, is of marginal interest only because of the clever use Emerson makes of the transitional theme of the first movement of Ludwig van Beethoven's "Pathétique" Sonata, opus 13.

Granted, some of the material is of more substance. The soundtrack's third song, "Not So Innocent," begins with a quiet choralelike synth theme and a gentle, balladlike verse; the verse is suddenly interrupted, however, by the pounding 6/4 rhythms of the "Not So Innocent" refrain, replete with Emerson's unmistakable slashing fanfare figurines. All three of these sections are expanded and developed during subsequent appearances; as the song builds up to its climax during a final statement of the refrain and singers Chanter and Sebbage begin to ominously declaim "Not so . . . innocent," the listener hears unmistakably the roots of Emerson's finest song of the late eighties, "Desde la Vida."

The next track, "Prelude to Candice," is a solo piano piece based around the choralelike synth theme that opened "Not So Innocent"; it's an attractive, somewhat wistful piece, although it doesn't attain the sad beauty of "Dream Runner." "Don't Go in the Shower" is a short, ominous synth piece with rhythm section backing that's reminiscent of some of the *Nighthawks* material; had it been longer, it could have built up a great deal of intensity. "New York Dash" is a unique piece, rather unlike anything else in the Emerson canon: over an urgent, pressing rhythm section background, Emerson overlays spasmodic, disjointed, icily dissonant fanfare figures. The entire track is somewhat reminiscent of one of the climactic sections of Magma's *Köhntarkösz*. "New York Dash" segues directly into "Tonight Is Not Your Night": despite its title, this instrumental track has nothing to do with the song "Tonight Is Your Night," but rather varies and develops the material of "Don't Go in the Shower." The soundtrack's finale, "The Spillone," is a minor key instrumental funk track that lacks the intensity (and musical substance) of "New York Dash" or "Tonight Is Not Your Night." *Murderock*, although it contains some very interesting music, simply doesn't achieve the consistency of Emerson's previous soundtracks. A rerelease of the soundtrack by the Italian Cinevox label in 2001 adds four short, previously unreleased instrumental tracks of no major consequence.

Emerson's Solo Career, 1980–84: An Overview

In one sense, the 1980–84 period was a very productive one for Keith Emerson. His quantitative output is certainly impressive: three and one quarter hours of music, occupying five and one-half LP records. Qualitatively, his output is also impressive, considering the sheer volume of music he produced: among these six LPs is one truly great album, *Inferno*, a very good one (*Best Revenge*), and four other LPs that all have some very good material. The challenge of writing soundtracks pushed Emerson out of his comfort zone and forced him to grapple with many styles, some ultracontemporary, others traditional: from the gritty electronic funk of *Nighthawks* to the proto-electronic New Age of *Harmagedon* to *Honky's* exploration of Caribbean idioms to the majestic expressionistic fervor of *Inferno*, one is forcibly struck by how adventurous and musically expansive Emerson's output of the 1980–85 period was. The best of this music showed a musician who was still curious, still open, still learning, still experimenting: a far cry indeed from the "dinosaur" image of ELP that had developed during the late seventies.

Unfortunately, if the 1980–84 period was a productive and artistically successful period for Emerson, it was not a financially successful one: more pointedly put, Emerson did not "make it" as a film composer in the manner he had hoped to. To be sure, *Inferno* had been a promising start, and it produced the hoped for next step, a chance to score a major Hollywood film starring one of that period's most iconic screen personalities. While Stallone gave what many of his fans feel is one of his most deft and subtle performances in *Nighthawks*, the movie never caught fire with the public, and as a result the momentum of Emerson's film composing career began to wane. While *Harmagedon* did represent a high-profile assignment in the Japanese market, it wasn't what Emerson really needed, which was one more shot at a major Hollywood film score: that never came. Instead, he began scoring increasingly low-profile films, and even the release of the music from these films began to grow problematic; of the six Emerson LPs of the 1980–85 period, the one released solely on the Chord label, *Best Revenge*, is the most obscure of all (with *Murderock* a close second). By 1985, Emerson, who had by now returned to live in England, seems to have concluded his career as a film composer had stalled, and was preparing to return to the rock music scene he had left seven years earlier.

Greg Lake

In 1980, the same year Keith Emerson was working on *Inferno* and *Honky*, Greg Lake began to plot out his comeback to the rock scene, writing a series of songs, securing a recording deal from Chrysalis, and assembling a group of musicians to work with him. A number of these musicians were heavyweights: Toto's Steve Luthaker, David Hungate, and Jeff Porcaro, the E-Street Band's saxman Clarence Clemmons, and old friends Snuffy Walden (guitarist for the Manticore label's Stray Dog) and drummer Michael Giles, Lake's old mate from the original King Crimson. The most important presence in Lake's new project, however, other than Lake himself, was guitarist Gary Moore, who had achieved a certain amount of fame in the late seventies with Thin Lizzy and Jon Hiseman's Colosseum II, but who was to achieve his greatest acclaim as an important solo artist in the eighties metal scene.

Greg Lake

Lake's first post-ELP album, *Greg Lake*, was released in October 1981. The album contains a number of surprises. First, Greg Lake the instrumentalist is conspicuous by his absence: he plays no bass at all, and contents himself with sporadic rhythm guitar parts, allowing Gary Moore, Steve Luthaker, and Snuffy Walden to take the lead parts. Even in light of his rapidly declining interest in his bass and guitar work in ELP's late-seventies output, his single-minded concentration on vocals was a bit disconcerting to his fans. So was the radical stylistic break Lake made not only with the ELP sound, but also with his *Works*-era solo work: anyone who bought *Greg Lake* expecting a further exploration of the *Works* era's acoustically based singer-songwriter approach was bound to be gravely disappointed. So was anyone who bought the album expecting ELP-influenced progressive rock.

To be sure, it is totally understandable that Lake would want to make a clean break with the ELP legacy. It's also unsurprising he felt a need to step outside his acoustic ballad approach: as successfully as he had plied it in the past, by the late seventies he was beginning to exhaust that particular vein of writing, as was demonstrated by the sense of sameness that characterized much of his *Works*-era material. The problem with *Greg Lake* is not that the album explores new directions: rather, the problem is that the album fails to propound a coherent alternative to the old directions.

Lake said of the album, "It was a relief for me to play with a different sound in a different style of music. And I was doing things that were out of character. It's like trying on someone else's clothes, in a way. It's a strange experience, but it just felt right at the time."[10] Fair enough. When you're trying on someone else's clothes, though, you're exchanging your identity for theirs, and it's the lack of a distinctive, immediately recognizable identity that, in my opinion, sinks this album. The album drifts between heavy metal ("Nuclear Attack," "Retribution Drive"), Rolling Stones–influenced blues-rock ("Love You Too Much," featuring a Bob Dylan lyric edited by Lake with Dylan's permission), sentimental country-rock ("Let Me Love You Once Before I Go"), and conventional rock ballads ("It Hurts"). The album's most interesting song, "Someone" (featuring Clarence Clemmons on sax) hearkens back to "Hallowed Be Thy Name" with its exploration of spiritual malaise in the context of a surreal, icy blues idiom. About the only thing that ties these songs together is Greg Lake's voice.

If the lack of a unified creative vision is the album's biggest problem, though, it's not its only one. The album is characterized by a pervasive lack of memorable melodic material, all the more surprising considering Lake's track record during the seventies for creating simple but memorable (and often poignant) melodies. Also disappointing is the rather pedestrian arranging. To be sure, there is some dynamic soloing here and there on the album, and a few of the tracks are worth hearing simply for Gary Moore's powerful guitar work. When the soloist is "turned off," however, the arrangements are all too predictable, and one pines for some unexpected offbeat accents, some subtle instrumental counterpoint, some unexpected dissonant chords; all, of course, stock-in-trade of ELP's arrangements. Lake's lyrics are adequate—the only bona fide failure here is Gary Moore's lyric for "Nuclear Attack," with its not terribly profound observation, "You may never come back / from a nuclear attack"—but they're not particularly revelatory or thought provoking. In short, with its lack of a coherent stylistic direction, memorable melodic material, arrangement subtlety, or a compelling message, there was simply nothing

---

[10] Greg Lake, quoted by Bruce Pilato, *The Greg Lake Retrospective: From the Beginning*, liner notes, 23.

to distinguish *Greg Lake* from the many other pedestrian rock albums being churned out in the early 1980s.

Nonetheless, despite the rather nondescript nature of the material—and despite the precipitous decline of ELP's iconic status during the late seventies—Lake's name still commanded enough respect to allow the album to make a modest dent in the charts. *Greg Lake* hit number sixty-two in the American charts, and the country-flavored single "Let Me Love You Once Before You Go" (not even penned by Lake, but by Steve Dorff and Molly Ann Leiken, and dating back to 1975) hit number forty-eight in the single charts (ironically, the same position reached by "Lucky Man" some ten years before). Chrysalis agreed to finance a small tour to support the album, so out of the plethora of musicians Lake had worked with on the project, he put together a touring band consisting of himself (lead vocals and rhythm guitar), Gary Moore (lead guitar), Tristram Margetts (bass), Tommy Eyre (keyboards), and Ted McKenna (drums). The Greg Lake Band made a pre-album release appearance at the Reading Festival on August 30, 1981, and the actual tour commenced on October 9, at Aberystwyth University, Wales, and took in eighteen shows throughout the U.K., with the climactic show being November 5 at London's Hammersmith Odeon.

Greg Lake in Concert

This concert, recorded for the King Biscuit Flower Hour radio show, was released on the King Biscuit label in 1995 as *Greg Lake in Concert*. It spotlights a number of songs from *Greg Lake*, as well as a few carefully selected King Crimson and ELP warhorses. For me, the two highlights of the show are "21st Century Schizoid Man" and "Lucky Man." The former, while it lacks the subtlety of Crimson's studio performance from their debut album, is very powerful, and exceedingly tight—the fast unison passages of the middle section are very impressive. The Greg Lake Band's "Lucky Man," meanwhile, is notable for being the first arrangement of the song to take it totally seriously as a *rock* song. The short, rising sequential figure at the end of Lake's electric guitar solo, a mere detail in ELP's studio version, becomes a major structural element of the Greg Lake Band's arrangement, and Gary Moore's fiery solo, built around this figure, is revelatory, forcing many of us who though we knew this song to reassess it. After the Hammersmith Odeon show, the Greg Lake Band undertook a brief tour of the Eastern seaboard of the U.S. and Canada, playing eight shows in Toronto, Montréal, New York, New Jersey, and Pennsylvania. The band's North American tour, such as it was, did not ignite a groundswell of album sales for *Greg Lake*, and by mid-December, 1981, the tour had ended.

Manoeuvres

In 1983, Lake reconvened the lineup that had toured with him in late 1981 to record a second studio album. Once again recording for the Chrysalis label, Lake's second solo album, *Manoeuvres,* was released in July 1983. Looking back on the album many years later, Lake remarked, "It was a weird time for me, and for the music business. I was pressured into writing songs that the record company thought radio programmers wanted to hear. Hence, there was not the passion that the first album had. There were some nice ballads, but the record lacked the pure vision that a hit album needs to succeed."[11] Despite Lake's comments, though, I think it can be cogently argued that *Manoeuvres* improves on *Greg Lake* in at least two areas. First, the melodic material of *Manoeuvres* seems somewhat more memorable than the debut album's. Second, Lake seemed to be settling in on a couple of more or less coherent songwriting directions. Granted, there are a couple of songs that are obviously some record company executive's idea of what Lake ought to sing in order to generate a hit single. "A Woman Like You," from side one of the LP format, finds Lake working in an eighties R & B context (think of Lake singing a Lionel Richie song) to no great advantage. "I Don't Know Why I Still Love You," the album's final song, is a bathetic, kitschy, soft-rock ballad with the unforgettable lyric "Every time I see you my heart starts beating / boom-boom-boom." Ouch.

Other parts of the album, though, find Lake moving forward with a seemingly clearer sense of where he wanted to go. Other than his unfortunate venture into eighties R & B on "A Woman Like You," the other four songs of side one of the LP format (including the title track and the morally dubious "Too Young To Love") show a strong stylistic coherence. All are in the "pop metal" or "lite metal" vein pioneered by Van Halen in the late seventies and plied to huge commercial success in the early eighties by bands such as Bon Jovi and Def Leppard: heavy-metal rhythm guitar riffs and screaming guitar solos are seamlessly melded with snappy pop vocal hooks. It's not a very profound style and certainly isn't my thing, but Lake does it reasonably well; he also does a better job at throwing a bit of unpredictability into the arrangements (such as the displaced drum accents during the main riff of the title track) than he had on similar tracks of his debut album.

The material on side two of the LP format, on the other hand, entirely eschews the pop-metal approach of side one; the best of it looks back to Lake's work with ELP and his *Works*-era solo projects,

---

[11] Greg Lake, quoted by Pilato, *The Greg Lake Retrospective,* liner notes, 23.

something he had been disinclined to do on *Greg Lake*. "It's You, You've Gotta Believe," probably the album's best song (and its longest, at slightly over seven minutes), sounds as if it were cowritten by Keith Emerson. A hymnlike, inspirational rock song in the vein of Jeff Silbar's "Wind Beneath My Wings" (made famous by Bette Midler in 1982) and R. Kelly's "I Believe I Can Fly" (1996), "It's You, You've Gotta Believe" opens with an imposing and expansive Emerson-like keyboard fanfare theme, which recurs twice in its original form (1:52, 5:26) and is varied and developed on two other appearances (4:45 and 6:15, the latter a particularly impressive and majestic minor-key development). The verses feature one of Lake's exquisite arpeggiated acoustic guitar accompaniments, a facet of Lake's musicianship that was sadly repressed on *Greg Lake*. About the only thing missing here is one of Emerson's patented trumpetlike Moog solos during the final development of the keyboard intro. Otherwise, it's a fine song, and an important forerunner of similarly anthemic ELPowell and ELP songs such as "Lay Down Your Guns" and "Farewell to Arms." Another fine song from side two is "Haunted," a tasteful and unclassifiable track that hearkens back to Lake's explorations of prerock popular styles on *Works, Volume I*; I hear echoes of the country and western ballad, the jazz waltz, and the French cabaret song in "Haunted," although strictly speaking it's none of these. The highpoint of the song is undoubtedly the wonderful clarinet solo in the middle, by an (unfortunately) uncredited performer.

Although *Manoeuvres* seems a bit more focused than *Greg Lake*, there is still a noticeable disjunction, even to a casual listener, between the pop metal of side one and the adult-contemporary stylings of side two. Perhaps for this reason, Chrysalis seemed disinclined, or unsure of how, to market the record. It received no airplay, and did not crack the American top two hundred. It received virtually no promotion; not surprisingly, Chrysalis did not offer to fund a second tour by the Greg Lake Band.

By late 1983, Lake's solo career appeared to have fizzled out. But then he received an unexpected call. Asia's bassist and lead singer, John Wetton, had just had an acrimonious falling out with the band's record label. They needed someone with a similar voice, and with Wetton's bass guitar skills, to step in on short notice and learn Wetton's parts for several high-profile performances the band was to play in Japan in early December. Would Lake be interested? Since this call was made at the behest of Lake's former rhythm section mate in ELP, Carl Palmer, who was now Asia's drummer, we will pick up this particular strand of the storyline after reviewing what Palmer had been up to since the demise of his former band.

Carl Palmer

Like Emerson and Lake, Carl Palmer spent his first post-ELP year, 1979, out of the limelight: "I didn't work during all of 1979. I built a house that year in Spain. [More precisely, on Tenerife, one of Spain's Canary Islands, off of the northwestern coast of Africa.] I actually bought all the material, and stored it in an aircraft hangar, then built an hacienda-type house, which I had always wanted."[12] Another extramusical interest Palmer pursued at this time was karate. He first took up martial arts during ELP's 1975–76 sabbatical: when he returned for the *Works* tour in 1977, he was already noticeably more muscular than before. In October 1979, he went to Japan and took a test at Tokyo University, where he was certified a first-degree black belt.[13]

However, Palmer, always a somewhat driven man, was anxious to get back to work. During the summer of 1979, he found himself in Los Angeles, auditioning members for a new band he was putting together. In his first post-ELP interview, with Chris Welch, Palmer revealed he had formed a new band called PM. The band, he said, consisted of Americans he had met during his stay in Los Angeles: besides himself, Todd Cochran (keyboards), Barry Finnerty (lead guitar), John Nitzinger (rhythm guitar), and Eric Scott (bass). All four of Palmer's recruits sang; Cochran, Finnerty, and Nitzinger split lead vocalist and songwriting roles. After about two months of rehearsing, they recorded their first, and as it turned out, only, album, *1:PM*, in Munich during December 1979. Palmer told Welch that PM would be nothing like ELP:

> A lot of people will be surprised . . . I really didn't want to go into jazz-rock, fusion-rock, or classical music. Although I appreciated that with ELP and it was a unique situation, I really wanted something a little lighter musically, and heavier vocally. What I wanted was a vocal band. A big vocal band with great musicians. Mainly because I'd never done anything like that before . . . I play completely differently now—a lot more basic. That's due to the material. I'm playing for the songs. Before, my expertise would be used because of the arrangement. My technique and outlook on playing is pretty much the same as always, except I execute it differently. I didn't want to go for long, drawn-out arrangements.[14]

Palmer added that in order to best match the sound of his new band, he would no longer be using the wooden Gretch kit he played on *Love Beach*, but would be using a Premier kit with two bass drums: "I've been design-

---

[12] Carl Palmer, quoted by Hall, "Welcome to the Show," 48.
[13] Iero, "Carl Palmer," 14.
[14] Carl Palmer, quoted by Welch, "Carl Palmer," 3, 12.

ing this new group [PM], and trying to find out exactly which kind of sounds I need myself. And that's why I started playing with two bass drums. The last time I played two bass drums was when I was 18."[15] Palmer held no illusions that his connection to an iconic band of the seventies would guarantee the success of his new group: "I don't take anything for granted and expect people to buy the record, purely because of who I am. Any new situation you have to treat as back to square one. If you live on past merits, then you're fooling yourself . . . I didn't want to harp back on the past, so it's square one time and I've got to prove myself again."[16] Whatever one thinks of Palmer's musical projects of the early eighties, one can only admire his hustle, and his refusal to entertain a sense of entitlement—a weight that was to drag down not a few seventies rock superstars during the course of the new decade.

1:PM

1:PM was released by the German Ariola label in March 1980. It did not set the world on fire. Some comparisons might profitably be made between *1:PM* and *Greg Lake*, which was released about a year and a half later. I actually prefer the arrangements of *1:PM* to those of *Greg Lake*. The vocal harmonies of *1:PM* are fluent, if not downright slick, and the instrumental interplay is often quite accomplished and intricate, sometimes showing a New Wave linearity that is reminiscent of Joe Jackson, the Police, or the Cars. In fact, *1:PM* sounds more truly contemporary, more in tune with early-eighties currents, than *Greg Lake* does. Palmer's drumming is excellent: his intricate grooves, carefully arranged to interlock with bass and guitar rhythms, are never show-offy, and never overpower the song. If nothing else, *1:PM* allowed Palmer to retool his drumming approach, and provided him an excellent blueprint for his work in Asia.

In other areas, however, *1:PM* doesn't stack up so well in comparison with *Greg Lake*. Its melodic material is even more forgettable, and the lyrics of *1:PM* (by whichever songwriter) represent little more than the stringing together of the most banal clichés. Most importantly, *1:PM* lacks the voice of a Greg Lake or the guitar playing of a Gary Moore, which allowed at least some of the material on *Greg Lake* to work in spite of itself. PM attracted little attention in Europe, almost none in the U.S., and simply never quite happened. Sometime in late 1980 or early 1981, Palmer pulled the plug on the band. Looking back on the PM experience in 1983, Palmer showed no particular bitterness or regret:

---

[15] Carl Palmer, quoted by Iero, "Carl Palmer," 14.
[16] Carl Palmer, quoted by Welch, "Carl Palmer," 3.

We never played any concerts—we only did a couple of television shows. The record sales were very, very slow, but I didn't feel disheartened; I didn't feel it was actually necessary to take the band on the road and perform because the record sales didn't warrant it. In rock music, if you don't have the record sales, it's pointless to go out and perform . . . So that band never actually toured, and then I broke it up a year or 14 months later.[17]

To Asia

During 1981 Palmer did some work with Mike Oldfield, best known for his prog/minimalist hit of 1974, *Tubular Bells*. At the time, Palmer hoped he and Oldfield might end up with enough music to fill one side of an LP: Palmer's thinking was to release a solo album that included his collaborations with Oldfield (which he described as "electronic classical music") on one side, and his unreleased Percussion Concerto on the other. The project never generated the requisite amount of material, though, and eventually it was Oldfield who used one track of the Oldfield/Palmer collaboration, "Mount Teidi" (a real mountain, by the way, nearby Palmer's Canary Islands hacienda), on his album *Five Miles Out*, released in late 1981. By that time, the Oldfield/Palmer project, and the prospect of a Carl Palmer solo album, had petered out.

Palmer's post-ELP career was not finished, though; to the contrary, it had barely begun. In 1970, fame had found Carl Palmer for two reasons: because of the reputation he had garnered among fellow musicians, and because he had been in the right place in the right time. In 1982, history more or less repeated itself. Here's John Wetton:

> About three years ago [1980], Carl and I planned to have a band with Rick Wakeman, and this was to be done through Brian Lane, who managed Yes. Carl and I came to America and it just fell apart—thankfully. I'm sure if the band had actually come together, it never would have lasted any more than about three months. After U.K. [disbanded], I recorded a solo album, *Caught in the Crossfire* [1980], with E.G. Records, and I became very disenchanted with them. They told me, "If you were ten years younger, we'd put some commercial money into it." And I thought that it was definitely time to leave the company. So I went to Brian Lane. Overnight I changed my management, my record company, and my music publishing. Brian and I came to L.A. to see the same people we had talked to about the Palmer, Wetton, and Wakeman band [this would have been John Kalodner, who had just come to Geffen Records from Atlantic], and they said they were interested if we got something together. When we returned to London, Brian put me in contact with Steve [Howe]. He and I seemed to hit it off right away, and like U.K., we

---

[17]Carl Palmer, quoted by Mattingly, "Carl Palmer," 9.

formed it with the people we most wanted to work with. And they happened to be Geoff Downes and Carl Palmer. As soon as we got together, we knew it was a band.[18]

The band, of course, was Asia. Here's how Palmer, interviewed at about the same time, remembers things:

> It was during that period—that would be the beginning of '81—I took some time off, stayed at home, did a little bit of studying and what-have-you, and tidied up some of my personal business. It was around then that I got a phone call asking me if I would like to come and play in a band that had Steve Howe in it. Well, I'd known Steve for a long time, and I'd also known the manager for a long time. I came along and played; there was John Wetton, Steve Howe, and myself—there was no keyboard player. I wasn't too happy with that because I feel that with the amount of technology available today [1983], not to have a keyboard player is a bad idea. So I suggested that we have a keyboard player, and Steve Howe, having played with Geoff Downes in the last configuration of Yes, suggested that we try him. It seemed good to me, so the four of us played and we decided to be a band after about a week because it felt good.[19]

A lot of people, both critics and die-hard ELP, Yes, and King Crimson fans, have relentlessly savaged Asia over the years. I must admit some culpability here, as readers of *Rocking the Classics* are doubtless aware.[20] I still maintain my assertion that when one views Asia through the prism of progressive ideology, as many of us who were progressive music fans during the seventies did, the band doesn't look very good: the notions of transcendence, idealism, and authenticity that undergirded all the great progressive rock of the seventies are notable by their absence in Asia's output. Asia eschewed lengthy epics; "heavy" philosophical subject matter; long solos; shifting meters; or any of a range of other traits one associates with seventies prog. Unlike the great prog bands of the seventies, who were targeting young adults (i.e., ages eighteen to twenty-five) and who were addressing philosophical and cultural issues, Asia relentlessly targeted a teenage audience, with most songs playing off some variation of the "my girlfriend left me" angle. Anyone who approached Asia expecting the band to revive the glories of ELP, Yes, or King Crimson during their heydays were bound to be disappointed or disillusioned.

However, my views of Asia have mellowed somewhat over the years, and while I'm still keenly aware of what they're not, I'm also more will-

---

[18] John Wetton, quoted by Tom Mulhern, "John Wetton: Asia's Progressive Rock Bassist," *Guitar Player*, January 1983.

[19] Carl Palmer, quoted by Mattingly, "Carl Palmer," 10. In the quote cited above, Palmer actually said, "the beginning of '82," but this must be a mistake; Asia began rehearsing mid-1981.

[20] See *Rocking the Classics*, 189, for the relevant passage.

ing to acknowledge what they are. First, I now can look back and find some fairly delicious irony in the fact that at the time when the North American stadium-rock bands who had simplified the British progressive style to great commercial success during the late seventies were all beginning to fade out (Boston, Kansas, Styx, Heart, and more arguably, Rush had all done their best work by 1982), Asia appeared on the scene and beat them all—decisively—at their own game.

Asia

Furthermore, acknowledging there is nothing particularly challenging or adventurous about the material, one cannot deny that the first Asia album, in particular, contains an abundance of memorable melodies, some superb vocal and instrumental arrangements, and fine production. Wisely, in light of the sound the band sought, they brought in an outside producer, Mike Stone, who showed a clear understanding of what the band wanted: Carl Palmer's drums and John Wetton's bass had never sounded this full or massive before. Both pared down their style, creating a surprisingly spare but powerful sound featuring tightly interlocking bass/drum grooves.[21] Although Geoff Downes is absolutely not a soloist or a composer of the stature of Keith Emerson, Patrick Moraz, or Eddie Jobson—one reason I felt he was a poor match for Yes—he is a very effective pop keyboardist, demonstrating a formidable knowledge of the top-of-the-line keyboards at his disposal, and a flair for effective keyboard orchestrations.[22] Steve Howe is his normal brilliant self: Rick Wakeman once made a remark to the effect that Howe gives the album better performances than it deserves, but I think a more accurate observation would be that Howe brings a welcome angularity to Asia's arrangements, which otherwise could have grown too slick. Of the nine songs on Asia's eponymous debut album, six are quite strong, and the album's first three ("Heat of the Moment," "Only Time Will Tell," and "Sole Survivor") remain early-eighties pop-rock classics. Indeed, there is something about the first Asia album that hearkens back to the epic pop of the late sixties in its winsome mixture of lightweight subject matter, dependably tuneful melodies, and epic arrangements.

---

[21] In ELP, Palmer played off of Emerson's melodic figurines as often as he played off of the rhythmic patterns of Lake's bass guitar parts; in Asia, he usually plays off of Wetton's spare but effective bass lines.

[22] Part of the problem with Downes as a progressive rock keyboardist is that his harmonic vocabulary is so much more rudimentary (impoverished, some might say) than what one finds in Emerson, Moraz, Jobson, et al.

Asia: Sudden Success

When confronted by hostile interviewers who demanded to know why the members of Asia weren't fully employing their formidable instrumental abilities, the band were quite consistent in their response: they wanted to create a group sound in which the individuals were subsumed by the whole. Talking about the band's almost Wagnerian arrangements, Palmer said,

> There's a lot of orchestration. That's part of the thing about four musicians going for a collective sound, more than trying to project as great soloists all of the time. I think it pays off, myself. We do have a group identity, and I think that's important . . . I think of the days of Emerson, Lake and Palmer, the Mahavishnu Orchestra, and all these groups of great musicians . . . so what? There are lots of great musicians, but are there great bands?[23]

Wetton made a similar observation: "You see, what we tried to do was sacrifice the individual musicians for a group sound, and unfortunately, we can't have everything coming through 100%, except the group sound."[24]

The band had begun recording *Asia* in June 1981; they spent a full five months on the album, working with producer Mike Stone at Marcus Studios and Virgin Townhouse in London. *Asia* was released by Geffen Records in February, 1982: Roger Dean, Yes's long-time cover artist, was hired to produce one of his characteristic fantasy-tinged drawings that the band hoped would forge a link to the glory days of seventies prog. (Dean's cover for Asia featured a sea monster playing with a beach ball in the middle of the ocean; although it's hard to say how much Dean's cover had to do with the album's success, the band was to collaborate with him throughout the eighties.) It is probably fair to say its success took even the band members by surprise. By May, the album had hit number one on the U.S. charts, something that no Yes, ELP, or King Crimson album had ever done. The album remained at the number one position for an astonishing nine weeks, and spent thirty-five weeks in the top forty and sixty-four weeks in the top two hundred. "Heat of the Moment" hit number four on the singles charts in April, and "Only Time Will Tell" hit number seventeen on the single charts in July; "Sole Survivor," "Wildest Dreams," "Here Comes That Feeling," and "Time Again" also received substantial airplay.

But now there was a new medium to take account of, and the band had presciently prepared for it. By the time that MTV made its debut on

---

[23] Carl Palmer, quoted by Mattingly, "Carl Palmer," 13.
[24] John Wetton, quoted by Mulhern, "John Wetton." I must say that on their debut album, Asia did manage to create its own group vocal sound, as distinctive in its way as the group vocal sound of Yes or the Beatles.

cable television channels in August 1982, Asia had produced several videos featuring their hit songs from *Asia*; these were aired relentlessly during the early months of MTV. Asia were one of the most frequently aired acts during MTV's first year of existence: since there was less competition in the early days of MTV, when many major acts had yet to gear themselves to compete in the new medium, the impact of Asia's videos on viewership was proportionately greater. The music industry had been in a major slump during 1982, with less than fifteen percent of all releases making a profit: Asia bucked the trend in a major way. *Asia* was the best-selling album of 1982; by the time the band's second album appeared, in late 1983, *Asia* had sold approximately six million copies.

Asia toured the U.S. and Canada to support the album between mid-April and late June of 1982. I myself saw the band at Pine Knob, Clarkston, Michigan, on June 15. The haze of time has dimmed my memory somewhat; it had been over four years since I had seen ELP at Detroit's Olympia, and I had been to many shows in the interim, none of which impressed me quite as much. I do remember the band played virtually every track off of the album, something I had never seen a band do before, as well as a couple of tracks which John Wetton said would eventually be recorded for their next album (I believe one of these was "Midnight Sun," which immediately struck me as the best song of the show). Steve Howe played "Mood for a Day," and Palmer took his usual lengthy drum solo, which did not impress me as much as the one I had seen him take at the Olympia in 1978. Geoff Downes, dressed in a ridiculous jumpsuit, if I remember correctly, played a lengthy, and awful, keyboard solo that consisted of a number of short, unrelated, and uninteresting themes and sound effects strung together in the most perfunctory way imaginable. That solo confirmed me in my opinion that Downes, although a fine pop musician and songwriter, was simply not a progressive rock keyboardist in the same league with Emerson, Moraz, Wakeman, or Jobson.[25]

I remember also being disappointed with John Wetton's bass playing. I never had the privilege of seeing Wetton play with King Crimson circa 1972–74, and I hoped that in the looser context of a live performance he would cut loose with some of the razorlike, menacing bass lines that characterized his playing during that earlier period of his career. To the contrary, his playing was sparse and perfunctory—almost as sparse and perfunctory, in fact, as a lot of Greg Lake's bass playing was in the waning days of ELP. Wetton, like Lake, had apparently come to see himself almost exclusively in terms of a singer-songwriter, and had lost his inter-

---

[25] I must admit Downes's piano solo captured on *Live in Tokyo* represents a substantial improvement on what I heard at Pine Knob.

est in the instrumental side of what he did. In sum, my impression of Asia was that they were a typical pop band in that they came off better in the studio-controlled environment of their album than they did in a live setting—especially as their album relied so much on glossy vocal overdubs that simply weren't doable in a live environment. Asia toured about two more weeks after I saw them, took a vacation for the rest of the summer and early fall, and then undertook a shorter European tour that lasted through much of October 1982.

In early 1983, Asia reconvened to record their second studio album. Now recording in Quebec, they worked once again under the guidance of producer Mike Stone. The band were as meticulous as before, but the creative synergy that had marked the recording of their first album seemed to have dissipated. In August 1983, Geffen released the second Asia album, *Alpha*. With interest in the band still very high, *Alpha* shipped platinum; it did reach number six in the American charts, and spent eleven weeks in the top forty, eventually selling about three and a half million copies. With numbers like that, it would seem odd to consider the album a failure: nonetheless, both the band and many of its fans did, at least in relative terms.

Alpha

It's hard to say precisely what went wrong on *Alpha*. Probably the best explanation is that the band, having never had to go through an organic process of developing their sound as they slowly worked their way up the charts (as had Yes and, to some extent, ELP), simply peaked out too soon. While most of the material on *Alpha* certainly isn't bad, it doesn't sound particularly inspired, either, and there is evidence that the Asia sound established on the debut album was beginning to be used as a formula, to be repeated (with slight variations) as necessary. Probably the most noticeable difference between *Asia* and *Alpha* is that the melodies of the latter seem so much less inspired and memorable than those of the former; about half of the songs on *Alpha* are quite forgettable, even after one has heard them repeatedly. The two big hit singles of *Alpha*, "Don't Cry" (#10) and "The Smile Has Left Your Eyes" (#34) sound suspiciously like reworkings of, respectively, Phil Spector's 1963 hit for the Ronettes "Be My Baby" and Paul Simon's "American Tune" (although "Smile" mirrors only the melodic contour of "American Tune" and has none of its depth or substance).

There are other more subtle differences that also seem to contribute to the apparent decline of the second album. Wetton's bass playing seems to carry over its perfunctory quality from the '82 tour (see my observations above), and as a result the mix seems to be lacking a bit on the low end. Steve Howe's presence is not felt as strongly here as on the debut album (he receives no songwriting credits on *Alpha*), and one misses the sense of angularity his playing brought the first album: a lot of *Alpha* is too slick for its own good. Ominously for the band, the album's best song, "Midnight Sun," which hearkens back to Wetton's work with U.K. (note his flexible vocal line over the 7/8 pattern of the rhythm section), and is highlighted by a transcendent solo by Steve Howe, was among the first to be written, having been featured on the '82 tour. *Alpha* captures the work of a band that seemed to be running out of ideas.[26]

Asia launched a major North American tour in August 1983 to support their newly released hit album. The tour, which continued into the early fall, was not a happy experience for those involved. In October 1983, shortly after a high-profile MTV and Westwood One Radio Network simulcast of one of the band's sold-out shows for early December at Tokyo's Budokan Arena had been scheduled, John Wetton announced he was leaving Asia.

Enter Greg Lake. In 1992 he recalled, "I got a call from Carl one night. He said, 'But we've committed to do this show in Tokyo. Could you come along and help?' Then I learn it's a live satellite broadcast, you know, and I've got something like four or five weeks to prepare. And I just had to learn all new material. They were good songs and I slipped in quite comfortably. Not something I'd like to repeat, however."[27] Asia were scheduled for four dates in Japan: three (December 6–8) at the Budokan, Tokyo, and one (December 9) at Osaka Castle Hall, Osaka. One of the Budokan dates was aired on MTV as *Asia in Asia*; this show has long been available on videocassette, and was released on CD in 2001 as *Asia Enso Kai (Asia Live in Tokyo)*. Another of the Budokan dates was made into a radio station-only release record.

There was something deeply ironic about Lake taking over Wetton's vocalist-bassist role in Asia some eleven-plus years after Wetton had assumed Lake's former role as vocalist-bassist in King Crimson. During the seventies, Lake did not speak particularly kindly about the 1972–74 edition of King Crimson: "King Crimson was important, but only the first band; everything subsequent to that was just trash and a ripoff as far as I'm concerned. Imitation. It really wasn't very nice, and for me personally it was distasteful because I had put so much into that name. I'd rather it stopped and been respected for what it was."[28] Not particularly prudent

---

[26] "Midnight Sun" is somewhat reminiscent of U.K.'s "Rendezvous 6:02" in its subject matter—both feature a protagonist who is trying to convey an experience with the numinous that he only dimly comprehends.

[27] Greg Lake, quoted in *Creem*, reprinted in *Fanzine for the Common Man*, no. 12 (December 1992): 17.

[28] Greg Lake, quoted by Funtash, "Conversations," 28.

words. While one can perhaps understand Lake feeling this way about the *Lizards* or *Islands* lineup, it is beyond debate that the Fripp-Wetton-Cross-Bruford lineup of King Crimson is one of the great lineups of prog history, and their ferociously hard-edged, improvisational signature sound (which exerted more influence on prog bands of the nineties than any other "classic" prog band) was in no way an "imitation" of *In the Court of the Crimson King*. Of course, there is probably a deeper issue of rivalry here: Lake and Wetton both grew up in Bournemouth (although Wetton is a native of Derby, in the Midlands), have eerily similar voices (Lake's was more poignant, Wetton's more soulful when both were at their peak), and rather similar bass styles (during the seventies Wetton was a more authentic virtuoso, but by the eighties the playing of both had become quite sparse and rudimentary). So perhaps there was still some lingering resentment, some aspect of payback, when Lake took Wetton's Asia gig. The fact is, Lake did slip into Wetton's role very comfortably: Asia fans who were previously unaware of Lake's work were struck by the similarity of Lake's voice to Wetton's, and the fairly minimalistic bass style Wetton had developed in Asia suited Lake just fine. Based on the recorded evidence, the *Asia in Asia* experience created no sense of discontinuity with Asia's previous work: when listening to the *Live in Tokyo* CD, there are a few occasions (notably at the beginning of "Wildest Dreams") when one has to remind oneself that yes, it is Greg Lake, and not John Wetton, who is lead vocalist.

Naturally, the subject of Lake continuing his association with Asia was broached. However, in 1986 Lake told Teri Saccone of *Rock Scene*,

> It eventually got down to whether I would join the band as a permanent member, and my response was to tell them that I thought their musical direction was wrong. They were going in an extremely *overt* commercial path—a commercial rock-type direction, and I told them it would all end up in shreds unless they made a more progressive album. Since they disagreed with me and opted to go straight for the commercial vein, I didn't want to be a part of it.[29]

I always found this remark somewhat curious. I don't really see Lake's two solo albums, released almost contemporaneously with *Asia* and *Alpha*, as being any less "commercial" or more "progressive" than Asia's. Nonetheless, I acknowledge his integrity in declining to cash in on a potential financial windfall by becoming part of a band whose musical values he wasn't in alignment with. At any rate, by early 1984 Lake's brief association with Asia had ended, and the band were once again without a lead vocalist and bassist.

---

[29] Greg Lake, quoted by Teri Saccone, *Rock Scene*, December 1986. Reprinted in *Fanzine for the Common Man*, no. 5 (November 1990): 15.

During the course of 1984, Wetton rejoined Asia. In the meantime, however, Steve Howe left: perhaps not an entirely surprising move, considering his declining involvement on *Alpha*, as Asia became ever more dominated by Downes's keyboard orchestrations, Wetton's overdubbed vocal harmonies, and the Wetton-Downes songwriting team. Mandy Meyer, formerly of Krokus, a heavy-metal band in the Judas Priest mold that attained a middling level of popularity during the 1982–84 period, was brought in as his replacement. During 1985, the band returned to the studio in London with producer Mike Stone, and in November 1985 Geffen released *Astra*, the third Asia album.

Astra

Like *Alpha*, its predecessor, *Astra* lacks the abundance of memorable melodic hooks that made the debut album special. Mandy Meyer's guitar sound, although more massive than Howe's, is also more dependent on fat power chords; as a result, a lot of Meyer's parts tend to be absorbed into Downes's Wagnerian keyboard orchestrations, and one still misses the angular melodic guitar filigrees with which Howe brought an element of edginess to the first album. It must be said that the low end of *Astra* represents a big improvement on *Alpha*. Wetton's bass lines cut through more clearly, Palmer's bass drum sound is more massive than ever, and of the three Asia albums, this is the one where Wetton and Palmer totally jell as a rhythm section: some of their tightly interlocking rhythm patterns are really quite impressive, and in fact in a few tracks the Wetton-Palmer rhythm section manages to give a modicum of interest to otherwise tangentially viable songs. Carl Palmer was credited as cowriter (with Wetton/Downes) on two songs, one of which, "Too Late," is a catchy pop song that probably could have been a hit with some promotion. Although the album continues to dwell on the theme of teenage angst that pervaded the first two albums, it also contains two songs that warn of coming nuclear apocalypse, "Countdown to Zero" and "After the War"; the lyrics of the former are pompous and overwrought, but the latter is actually a pretty good song.

Astra produced just one hit single, "Go" (the album's only song, incidentally, with a hook that bears comparison to the hits from the first album): charting out at forty-six, "Go" fell far short of the success of the earlier singles. *Astra* itself only managed to hit sixty-seven; although it eventually reached gold status, it fell far short even of *Alpha*'s sales. Considering the fact that *Astra* is not a weaker album than *Alpha* (it may in fact be marginally stronger), perhaps this demands a brief explanation. I don't think the explanation is too difficult to understand.

The Digital Revolution

The period between the early and mid-1980s witnessed the digital revolution that touched every corner of the popular music industry. Perhaps the most obvious result of the digital revolution was the replacement, during the mideighties, of the vinyl 33 rpm 12" record with the compact disc (CD) as the primary medium of commercial music exchange. Recording was increasingly done in a completely digital context, eliminating the "dirtiness" or "warmth" of the analog recording process (depending on one's point of view), and the DAT (digital audio tape) replaced the old 1/8" analog reel-to-reel tape as the industry standard of recording preservation. There were many other equally far-reaching changes, though. The early 1980s witnessed the rise of sequencers, which enable a musician to program a part into a digital keyboard (perhaps a part that he or she cannot play in real time) and to re-create the part by merely activating a memory button. As I pointed out in *Rocking the Classics*,[30] this capability obsolesced, to a degree at least, the cult of instrumental virtuosity which had been such a hallmark of progressive rock, since it was now no longer a given, even in live performance, whether musicians were actually playing the parts they appeared to be playing. Also becoming common during this period were synthetic drum machines, which reproduced preprogrammed drum parts, and could be used to entirely replace a live drummer. This period also witnessed the rise of samplers, which allow one to prerecord a sound, store it in a digital keyboard's memory, and reproduce it at will: effects that were previously available only in the studio now became easy to re-create in live situations. Indeed, since the mid-1980s, the emphasis for aspiring electronic keyboard players has been on sampling rather than synthesis per se.

Above all, the early eighties were marked by the emergence of MIDI (Musical Instrument Digital Interface). Digital keyboards with MIDI capability can be linked together; one keyboard can be used to control an entire setup of digital keyboards, and more important, characteristic preset sounds from two or more digital keyboards can be mixed together to create yet different sounds. By the mideighties, many of these capabilities (sequencers, samplers, MIDI, etc.) could be used in conjunction, and specific sounds that on analog synthesizers had formerly been obtainable only through a painstaking manipulation of a whole series of knobs and/or patchcords could now be created, stored, and retrieved by simply pressing a button.

So what does this have to do with Asia and *Astra*? Plenty. When Yes, led by newcomer Trevor Rabin, launched their comeback in late 1983,

---

[30] Macan, *Rocking the Classics*, 191.

the music public was blown away with the very "contemporary" sound of the new Yes album, *90125,* which represented one of the first really comprehensive explorations of the potential of both digital keyboards and the digital recording process. The very hip, ultramodern sound of the new Yes album (which resulted not just from the extensive use of digital technology, but also from Rabin's deft incorporation of trappings of the lite metal style that was so popular in the early eighties), drove the album up to number five in the charts, the highest-charting Yes album since *Relayer* in early 1975.

Although *Astra* was released two years after *90125,* it sounds less "modern," much more a product of the early 1980s. In fact, I think the basic problem with *Astra* is not that it was a bad album per se, but simply that it attempted to perpetuate the original Asia sound at a time when that sound was becoming passé. While there are differences in sound quality between the three Asia albums (as I said, I think *Alpha* is the poorest sounding of the three), when played back to back, all three are shaped by the same basic sound, and indeed, acknowledging different mixes and mastering sessions, the music of all three could have come out of the same set of recording sessions. A cult band can get away with carrying on a given sound when the crest of its popularity has passed, but for a straight-ahead pop act like Asia, such a move is inevitably fatal. I suspect the relative commercial failure of *Astra* simply stems from the fact that by early 1986 (when "Go" was getting its most intensive airplay), the album sounded old-fashioned. The growing obsolescence of Asia's sound was especially problematic at a time when the "classic" A.O.R. radio format that had been a crucial component of the success of the first two Asia albums was on the wane. Even the *Emerson, Lake and Powell* album of 1986 sounds contemporary compared to *Astra*—but that's a story for the next chapter.

A tour had been planned in 1986 to support *Astra.* However, when Geffen saw that the album was going to reach no higher than sixty-seven in the American charts, and that their once-prized cash cow was going dry, the label quickly lost interest in the band, and declined to finance a tour. This decision, of course, was something akin to a death sentence for Asia. Although no formal announcement was ever made, Asia more or less dissolved, and by 1987, it was clear that the band had ceased to exist. But that, too, is a story for the next chapter.

Reformation, Part I

Emerson, Lake and Powell; 3 (1985–1988)

By 1984, the once-promising momentum of Keith Emerson's film-scoring career had waned, and he began to contemplate a return to the world of rock music. Initially, he conceived a solo project that would feature himself and a rotating cast of musicians—something along the lines of *Honky*, but focused on updating his epic, heroic seventies style for the eighties. Emerson told Russell Hall, "I had written about five tunes, and I took the demos to Polygram. I was approaching them for a solo deal. And a guy there, Jim Lewis, said, 'Well, look, I've been speaking with Greg. Why don't you do these with him?'"[1] Emerson wasn't entirely thrilled with the suggestion: he told Bob Doerschuk of *Keyboard*, "After I'd retrieved the phone from the pond, I agreed to meet Greg in London."[2] Emerson and Lake had not seen each other for some time, and apparently their relationship was still a bit raw. However, their meeting went smoothly enough for Emerson to agree to a one-off Emerson-Lake album. There was no talk of touring: Lake would sing over Emerson's demos, add bass lines, and session drummers would be brought in as needed.

However, once the project got rolling, around the middle of 1985, its scope began to expand. Jim Lewis and other Polygram execs were very impressed with the Emerson-Lake demos: they extended them a two-record deal, and offered to finance a tour to promote the first album. At this point, the question of the drummer's position became more crucial: using session drummers for the album was a workable proposition, but for the tour a permanent appointment would be necessary. Carl Palmer was not an option: he was under contract to Asia, and was working on the *Astra* album more or less concurrently with the

---

[1] Keith Emerson, quoted by Hall, "Welcome to the Show," 48, 50.
[2] Keith Emerson, quoted by Doerschuk, "The Phoenix Rises," 39.

Emerson-Lake sessions.[3] At first, Emerson and Lake tried working with several drummers in the Carl Palmer mold: technical, intricate, flashy (Simon Phillips was reportedly one such drummer). However, according to Emerson, "They were very proficient and very good in their own right, but a lot of what they did was a bit too flowery for us."[4] Emerson was beginning to yearn for a sparer, heavier drumming approach, so he invited Colin "Cozy" Powell, an old car-racing partner, to audition as permanent member. Powell (who in fact died in an auto accident in 1998) was a renowned drummer in his own right, best known for his work with Jeff Beck and Ritchie Blackmore's Rainbow: although he was no mere imitator of Led Zeppelin's John Bonham, he favored a similar style, featuring enormous, artillerylike snare drum hits and booming double bass drum parts. He was certainly a more conventional and less creative drummer than Palmer, but was also a heavier and a steadier one, and his style fit well with Emerson's more stripped down, austere eighties sound. From virtually the first rehearsal, Emerson, Lake and Powell clicked.

Now there was the question of what to call the band. Emerson, Lake and Powell, as it turns out, can also be called "ELP." The *Rolling Stone/Creem* wing of rock critics—who welcomed the return of the Emerson-Lake band with about as much enthusiasm as the residents of Washington, D.C., had welcomed the arrival of marauding British troops during the War of 1812—relentlessly bashed Emerson and Lake for choosing Powell just so they could still call themselves ELP, and cash in on the ELP name. (Interestingly, if Emerson and Lake had chosen Simon Phillips, they still would have been in the same situation!) Emerson made it clear that not only did they not choose Powell in order to be able to call themselves "ELP," they were actively seeking *not* to be called "ELP": "We were dubious about upsetting Carl, who greatly helped the sound of ELP in the seventies. For this reason, we do not refer to ourselves as ELP. We are Emerson, Lake and Powell."[5] The band was sometimes also referred to as ELPowell: as I will here, on occasion.

With Powell in place, during the latter half of 1985 the band went back and reworked the original Emerson-Lake demos, composing some new material as well. The final two tracks to be recorded for the band's debut album, *Emerson, Lake and Powell*, "Touch and Go" and "Mars, the Bringer of War," were completed in January 1986. Much of the album was recorded at Maison Rouge studios in London, with Tony Taverner

---

[3] Initially, Palmer was not thrilled about the Emerson-Lake reformation. When Bob Doerschuk asked Emerson if Palmer had expressed his feelings about the new project, Emerson hesitantly said: "Indirectly. He's probably had time to think about it by now." See Doerschuk, "The Phoenix Rises," 39.

[4] Keith Emerson, quoted by Doerschuk, "The Phoenix Rises," 40.

[5] Keith Emerson, quoted by Doerschuk, "The Phoenix Rises," 38.

engineering (he also coproduced the album with Lake). A substantial amount of recording was also done in Keith Emerson's barn studio on his Sussex property using the Fleetwood Mobile recording unit, in an attempt to better capture a drum sound that pleased all three band members; however, according to Emerson, Polygram found the results of Powell's drum sound in Emerson's home studio too "electronic," and those takes weren't used.[6]

Polydor had originally planned a February 1986 release of *Emerson, Lake and Powell*; however, a Keith Emerson ankle injury, which would have made the supporting tour impossible at that time, forced Polydor to postpone the album's release until May. The band had initially considered commissioning H. R. Giger to provide the album cover art. In the end, however, they decided a Giger album cover would create too strong of a link to their seventies work. Like many of their British rock peers (Yes, Genesis, Robert Plant and Jimmy Page of Led Zeppelin) they saw overreliance on their seventies heritage as a declaration of terminal unhipness that would greatly hinder them in their efforts to grow a younger fan base among listeners who had been toddlers during their glory years of 1970–74. They settled, therefore, on an abstract, severe, almost geometrical design of three interlocking side profiled heads against a plain beige background. This design, by Debra Bishop, does come off as very eighties-ish, and nicely reflects the retooling of the classic ELP undertaken on *Emerson, Lake and Powell*.

For despite the steady and achingly predictable barrage of attacks from hostile critics who said the new album represented "the same old ELP" (this from a review in *Musician Magazine*), in fact, it didn't. To be sure, a casual listener would notice continuity: epic tracks, massive keyboard orchestrations, and the more personalized ELP fingerprints such as Emerson's familiar bitonal chord voicings and trumpetlike fanfares, and Lake's golden tenor. Of course, this was enough for *Rolling Stone* to pass the death sentence:

> Art-rock bands ain't what they used to be. There was a time when such groups could be relied upon to come up with scores of horrendously hookless epics operating under brilliant titles like "The Curse of Baba Yaga." But these days Yes has gone high-tech, Robert Fripp thinks he's David Byrne, and the members of Genesis are hiding behind Phil Collins, hoping nobody asks too many questions about their past.
>
> If all this depresses you, then you're gonna *love* this comeback LP from Emerson, Lake and replacement *P* Cozy Powell. These guys are literally the only ones left in 1986 who still have the balls to serve up vintage crap like this. There are actually seven-, eight-, and nine-minute tracks here with titles and

---

[6] Doerschuk, "The Phoenix Rises," 40.

lyrics that would make the Moody Blues blush. Of course, the guys also include plenty of shorter songs, but pomp fans shouldn't worry; the short ones have just as much hot air as the long ones.[7]

And on it goes, thundering how little the new ELPowell differed from the old ELP. However, there are some important differences, and the single biggest difference involves the use of sonic space.

Whether or not one likes the seventies ELP style, there is no question that it's often busy, with Emerson's elaborate melodic figurines and Palmer's virtuosic rudimental fills leaving very little sonic space open. On *Emerson, Lake and Powell*, Emerson retools his own playing to parallel the shift from Palmer's complex rudimental parts to Powell's spare but enormous backbeats. The kind of busy, elaborate keyboard figurines that characterized the instrumental movements of "Tarkus," the "Endless Enigma" toccata, and large swaths of "Karn Evil 9" are almost completely absent on *Emerson, Lake and Powell*. Instead, the ELPowell sound is characterized by massively orchestrated keyboard chords that move in enormous homophonic blocks; trumpetlike fanfare figures, which often alternate antiphonally with Lake's vocal line, and sometimes cut dissonantly against the background chords; and harmonically sophisticated but melodically severe synth leads that show relatively few of the baroque curlicues that characterized Emerson's seventies work. Emerson's shift in style, combined with Powell's drumming approach, creates a new sound—massive, severe, austere—that is rather different from ELP's music of the seventies.

In some ways, I believe the ELPowell sound was foreshadowed by "Letters from the Front" on *Love Beach*. This song's bell-like tone-colors, simple chords that disguise a sophisticated tonality, geometrically intricate cross rhythms, irregular phrase structures, and angular melodic punctuations are all echoed in the most representative ELPowell material. The big difference is that the ELPowell sound is so much more gargantuan than the thin, over-trebly sound of "Letters."

Emerson, Lake and Powell also marks the first time that Emerson completely steps into the digital age. To be sure, the sound of the Yamaha GX-1 plays a major role on this album: in fact, it had never sounded this good before, emerging here with a fuller and more muscular sound than it had on any of ELP's recordings from the seventies. The Hammond C-3, too, makes a welcome reappearance, and its sound is often forefronted prominently. However, while we hear these two instruments a lot, we virtually never hear them in isolation: both were MIDIed, so their sounds are usually coupled with Emerson's state-of-the-art digital setup. Among other

---

[7] Jim Farber, "Emerson, Lake and Powell," *Rolling Stone*, June 28, 1986, 43.

keyboards, Emerson was using a Kurzweil 250, which was primarily responsible for the album's "choral" patches; an Oberheim Matrix-12; the Yamaha DX7 and KX88 keyboards and the QX1 (a digital sequencer); an Elka Synthex; the Korg DW-6000, DW0-8000, and Poly 800 keyboards; and the PPG Wave 2.3. Almost every keyboard part on the album couples sounds from two or more of these instruments; unlike the predigital era, where Emerson would have overdubbed an identical line on two different keyboards to get the blended sound he wanted, with MIDI different sounds from different keyboards could be "linked," so to speak, and then stored as a new patch, to be retrieved by the press of a button. Emerson admitted that a lot of the sophisticated digital programming skills necessary to quickly "link" sounds from different digital keyboards, and then store them as discrete patches, were beyond him, so he brought in two MIDI experts: Paul "Wix" Wickens, a top-flight Yamaha programmer in England, and American Will Alexander, technical manager at Fairlight with whom Emerson had first worked on the *Murderock* sessions. Although Emerson was not particularly fond of Fairlight's equipment, he and Alexander hit it off very well, and Alexander came to be a major presence in Emerson's career during the nineties.

Timbrally, then, the sound of *Emerson, Lake and Powell* is more complex than any of ELP's seventies music, even as it's melodically and rhythmically less cluttered. Producers Lake and Taverner, as well as Emerson and his techs, did a reasonably good job in avoiding the sterile, "dead" digital sound that plagued a lot of mideighties records at a time when digital recording was still in its infancy: listen, for comparison, to Yes's *90125* or Eddie Jobson's *Theme of Secrets*. Reverb, particularly, is used to good advantage. I must admit that occasionally I find the continuous complex mixture of electronic timbres a bit monotonous, and one of my few criticisms of this album is that some occasional unadorned Hammond C-3, Yamaha GX-1, or acoustic piano segments would have broken up the pervasively electronic tracks nicely, and created a better sense of timbral variety. A key element of seventies prog had, after all, been the systematic alternation of electronic and acoustic passages: that element is quite absent here. On the other hand, Emerson had wanted to create something different than the seventies ELP sound on *Emerson, Lake and Powell*, and he succeeds with the album's state-of-the-art digital electronics and spare, monolithic arrangements.

Lake's voice had matured a bit by the mideighties; while his upper range was still fully intact, his lower range was a bit fuller and richer than before. As Emerson said, "He's developed from a seven-foot Steinway to a nine-foot Bösendorfer Imperial, with the extra notes at the bottom."[8]

---

[8] Keith Emerson quoted by Bob Doerschuk, "The Phoenix Rises," 40.

Lake had by now abandoned his Alembic for a Spector bass; in my opinion, this was Lake's best-sounding bass since the Fender Jazz Bass of his early ELP days, and unlike either the Alembic or his Gibson Ripper, it recorded uniformly across both its upper and lower ranges. Lake shows a renewed interest in his bass playing here: while his bass lines are seldom virtuosic in the sense they sometimes were on the first six ELP albums, his parts aren't perfunctory either, and often create interesting interlocking cross-rhythms with Emerson's keyboard parts. One does wish that Lake's bass lines were pushed up a bit higher in the mix.

Emerson, Lake and Powell

Side one of the LP format (*Emerson, Lake and Powell* was the last ELP release for which vinyl was the primary medium) clocks in at twenty minutes, and features just three tracks: "The Score," "Learning to Fly," and "The Miracle." All three tracks are quite strong, and even though they're not conceptually related, they segue into each other so seamlessly than one inevitably hears the entire LP side as one long piece divided into three parts. It's certainly the strongest LP side Emerson and Lake had put out since side four of *Works I*: some might argue the strongest LP side since side two of *Brain Salad Surgery*.

"The Score," at 9:08 the album's longest track, is somewhat reminiscent of "Karn Evil 9, 3rd Impression" in mood with its major-key fanfares and march themes. "The Score" falls into four sections: an atmospheric overture (0:00–1:04), a triumphal march (1:05–3:45), the song proper (3:45–7:03), and a celebratory, toccatalike instrumental postlude (7:04–9:08). Like "Pirates," the discrete sections of "The Score" are quite tightly woven, linked by thematic and rhythmic similarities and by the actual recurrence of motives and themes. "The Score" is also given unity by its pervasive C tonality: as he often does, Emerson avoids potential boredom by perpetually mixing modes.

The "overture" section opens with a C 7 suspended fourth chord (C–F–G–B♭) that also plays an important part in "The Miracle" and "Touch and Go": the powerful ascending synth bass line (C–G–C) that rises out of the chord evokes the opening of Richard Strauss's *Also Sprach Zarathustra*. This ascending bass line leads into the main segment of the opening section, which is dominated by a fanfarelike GX-1 theme (first stated at 0:32) and a throbbing single-note synthesizer bass drone generated on the Yamaha QX1 digital sequencer.

The second sections of "The Score," heralded by the fiery GX-1 fanfare at 1:05, is dominated by the triumphal march theme annunciated at 1:20 and again at 1:43, 2:20, and 3:29. Each repetition of the march theme is interrupted by contrasting material: first by a repetition of the fiery GX-1 fanfare (1:36), next by a development of the main theme that momentarily wanders out of the pervasive C modal major (from 1:59), and finally by an ominous "choral" episode in C minor (from 2:37) that features the Kurzweil's choir patches and some nicely angular cross-rhythms doubled by Lake and Powell (2:42, 2:49, etc.).

The third section of "The Score" is the song proper. Lake's autobiographical lyrics, set to a simple vocal melody, use the imagery of a pick-up basketball game as an analogy for the resurrection of ELP (as ELPowell). The opening section's throbbing synthesizer bass drone returns here (3:45), as does the head of the opening section's fanfare theme, which now alternates with Lake's vocal (listen at 3:54, 4:07, and elsewhere); besides giving Lake's heroic vocal an appropriately stirring accompaniment, these two elements serve to unite the component sections of "The Score." Also contributing to the triumphal mood of this section is the pervasive "brighter than major" Lydian modality,[9] a product of the alternating C-major and D-major triads underlying the vocal line. The verse is followed by a refrain in C-minor that engages in some playful (or pompous, in the view of some critics) self-quotation: "it's been so long, you're welcome back my friends/to the show that never ends." The second verse (4:34) is accompanied by some assertive GX-1 "French horn" calls; after the refrain, an angular passage of offbeat chordal punctuations (5:10), doubled by keyboard, bass, and drums, lead into an all-instrumental third verse.

It's here (from 5:25) that we most clearly see the difference between ELPowell and seventies ELP. In the "old days," Emerson would have launched into a gonzo synth solo over the underlying chord progression of the verse. Here, though, he contents himself with holding sustained ninth chords, whose sounds shift kaleidoscopically through his use of changing vibrato and subtly shifting keyboard timbres; the lead line is Lake's spare but powerful throbbing bass theme. The result is a distinctive sound—massive, timbrally complex, almost severe in its lack of melodic or rhythmic ornamentation—that is rather different than seventies ELP.

Before the instrumental verse has been completed, the band suddenly break off into an ominous episode that brings "The Score" to its climax: at 5:48 a ponderous chromatic line, played in unison by Emerson and Lake and rhythmically doubled by Powell, builds up inexorably, seems to run out of steam as it slows to a near halt, and then snaps to life one final time as Emerson punctuates its conclusion with his patented "Enigma" chords, which here move in parallel motion (C♯–F♯–C to D♯–G♯–D, at

---

[9] The Lydian mode is a major scale with the fourth degree raised half a step (e.g. C–D–E–F♯–G–A–B–C).

6:22). This one serious challenge to the track's triumphal trajectory overcome, the song proper ends with the fourth and final verse (at 6:29), once
again accompanied by the throbbing C drone, and its refrain (6:54).

The final section of "The Score," a joyous toccatalike instrumental
postlude, is the only section that breaks off from the pervasive C-tonality:
it's almost entirely centered in F-major.[10] It's dominated by a cheerful
GX-1 theme, in a 12/8 shuffle rhythm, that we hear four times: at 7:04
(in incomplete form), at 7:29 (first complete statement), at 8:01 (second
complete statement), and finally, in incomplete form, at 8:32, after which
it breaks off at 8:45 into new material and eventually, at 9:00, spills into
a grand, Copland-like coda. Lake and Powell both contribute some nice
details to the arrangement during this section: listen to Lake's rapid fire
chromatically descending bass lines near the end of the theme's second
statement (7:52, 7:59), and to Powell's thundering double bass drum
work near the end of the theme's third statement (from 8:19). Although
I wouldn't label "The Score" as the album's very best track—I reserve
that honor for "The Miracle"—it does characterize the album's strengths:
its timbral subtlety, its admirable restraint and lack of clutter in matters of
arrangement, its unobtrusive but effective avoidance of four-square
phrases, and its evocative lyrics.

The final chord of "The Score" has scarcely stopped reverberating
before the band launches into the second track, "Learning to Fly." The
most conventional of the three songs on side one, the lyrics of "Learning
to Fly" address one of the favorite topics of rock mythology: a young man
goes to the big city to make a name for himself, and finds himself feeling
both threatened and exhilarated by the challenges of life in "the jungle."
The song's conventionality is more apparent than real, though: the chord
progressions and modulations are consistently interesting, and Emerson
slips in some dauntingly complex instrumental episodes. Like the best
material on the first Asia album, "Learning to Fly" strikes a nice balance
between pop accessibility and compositional sophistication.

"Learning to Fly" begins with a four-bar keyboard intro that forecasts
the verse's pulsing background synth chords and F♯ Lydian tonality.
Thereafter the song is rather reminiscent of some of the more successful
songs of the first Asia album in its structure and arrangement: a verse in
which vocals, pulsing keyboard chords, and bass line move in parallel
motion (beginning at 0:09) alternates with a chorus (from 0:27) wherein
vocals, keyboards, and the bass line are contrapuntally conceived. In addition to their textural differences, the Lydian modality of the verses alter-

---

[10] In Schenkerian terms, one could look at everything up to this section as a lengthy dominant preparation for this section's F tonality. It probably makes more sense, though, to hear
the F-tonality of this section as a transitional "stepping stone" towards the F♯-tonality of the
second track, "Learning to Fly."

nates with the more unstable (but Mixolydian-tinged) modality of the chorus, which tends to cadence uncertainly on an A$^\sharp$ minor triad (0:44). From 0:48, the four-bar intro, verse, and chorus are repeated a second time: notice how Emerson's antiphonal fanfare response to Lake's vocal (from 0:58) cuts dissonantly against the backing chords.

After the second chorus, Emerson eschews the expected vocal bridge in favor of a short but dauntingly complex instrumental fugato in C$^\sharp$ minor (first statement of the subject at 1:40, subsequent statements at 1:43, 1:46, and 1:50) that wends its way through a thicket of shifting meters; from 1:54, this is followed by a more conventional synth solo (featuring the GX-1). The synth lead serves as a modulatory bridge, so when the vocal verse returns at 2:08, it's now in G Lydian.[11] The verse isn't followed by the expected refrain: instead, from 2:25 there's another instrumental episode, in which Emerson further develops the earlier fugato subject against a daunting maze of offbeat bass and drums accents. This leads to a new chorus: from 2:34, Lake sings the "learning how to fly" refrain, in quasi-choral overdubbed vocal harmonies, to a variation of the verse's Lydian chord progression, with Emerson answering with increasingly ornate synth leads. A huge electric guitar power chord at 3:18 brings the song proper to a close. Thereafter, Emerson spins out a quiet, pipe organ–like codetta based on the vocal melody (listen especially at 3:28); from 3:37 the mood grows darker. A stock VI–VII–i (A$^\flat$ major–B$^\flat$ major–C minor) cadence is followed by the sound of synthesized wind (white noise) and the ominous tolling of a synthetic iron bell: suddenly we're swept into the turbulent third track, "The Miracle."

"The Miracle" has never received the attention lavished on "The Score." I don't know why: it's the best track on the *Emerson, Lake and Powell* album, and one of Emerson's greatest rock songs of all. Lake's lyrics are also worthy of commendation. Although prog rock has always been associated with sword-and-sorcery/quest-for-the-grail narratives, "The Miracle" is the first ELP song that actually falls into this particular genre of lyric. Lake's use of medieval imagery is particularly evocative here, and throughout this lyric the inspiration level of his imagery never flags.[12] The climax of the song, where Lake unexpectedly brings his narrative into the contemporary world—"lay your life upon the line / it's death for glory every time / you give up yours but I'll keep mine"—is especially powerful, because it invites us to reevaluate our nostalgic image of old-fashioned heroism in the context of modern-day notions of patriotism, nationalism, and imperialism.

---

[11] In Schenkerian terms, the G-tonality of the latter portion of "Learning to Fly" serves as a dominant preparation for the heavy emphasis on C minor during "The Miracle."

[12] Note his characteristic use of the "madman" character in his lyric.

Emerson's music achieves the same high level of inspiration as Lake's lyric. Even more than "The Score," Emerson's new manner of "monumental severity" comes to full fruition here. Isolated chord progressions are quite simple—often no more than two alternating triads, repeated at length—but the song's overall tonal movement is sophisticated and ambiguous in a way that nicely compliments Lake's lyrics. The textures of "The Miracle" are even more uncluttered than "The Score," and small melodic gestures (often used to musically "paint" key words) that would have gone unnoticed in ELP's seventies work make a big impact here.

"The Miracle" falls into three large sections: the main body of the song, a distinct section with a new verse (from 3:09), and a shortened recap of the main part of the song (from 5:32). It opens with a powerful, richly detailed ten-bar verse that introduces many of the conflicts that are played out through the remainder of the song. The verse's first six bars are based on the C7 suspended fourth chord (C–F–G–B♭) that opened "The Score," and feature an angular counterpoint between vocal melody, slashing keyboard countermelody, and syncopated bass line; its last four bars ("his talons shine like daggers," from 0:28) settle onto a D-minor ninth chord (D–F–A–C–E), and feature vocal line, keyboard accompaniment, and bass moving in parallel motion. The alternation between passages of angular counterpoint and massive homophonic chord blocks characterize the remainder of the track, and the conflict between C minor and D minor—which is never truly resolved—gives the song much of its restless, uneasy energy. The 10-bar verse is repeated from 0:40 ("another sword"), and is followed at 1:08 ("beyond the compass") by the song's first bridge section: set in E major, this section momentarily brightens the prevailing ominous mood. One notes and admires the simplicity of Emerson's chordal accompaniment throughout this section, which allows Lake's bass countermelody—simple in and of itself, but forming an angular counterpoint to his vocal line—to shine through. It also allows Emerson's occasional melodic countermelody (such as his ghostly melodic commentary on Lake's "the spectre begins to tremble" at 1:24) to emerge into much clearer relief than was possible in the busier arrangements of seventies ELP. This bridge is followed at 1:31 by the third statement of the verse: notice Emerson's shimmering synth arpeggios at 1:38 answering Lake's "On a sea of diamonds lies a ship of glass."

It's only at the song's two-minute mark that we hear the dramatic sixteen-bar refrain for the first time. The first half ("still the dragons") alternates ominously between a D♭ major triad and a tart B major triad with an added F; the second half ("it's going to take a miracle"), between A♭ and G♭ major triads. During the first half of the refrain, Emerson's chordal accompaniment moves in parallel motion with the vocal line, while Lake's angular, offbeat bass line cuts against it; during the second half of the refrain, Lake's bass line follows the vocal, while Emerson's keyboard supplies a countermelody. At the end of the refrain, the music's tonality is still far from stable: $A^\flat$ has not been securely established as tonic, but C minor no longer feels like the home key. Before the refrain's tonal orientation is settled, the music slips into a second bridge section ("stand clear," from 2:46), where the music again briefly brightens up into a C Mixolydian tonality.

This bridge, however, is but a momentary transition into the second main section of the song, which begins at 3:09. This section, which unfolds the battle sequence of Lake's lyrics, is dominated by a second verse—or antiverse, if you will—that for the first time during the song establishes a clear-cut tonic key: C minor. Against Emerson's simple, hypnotically repetitive backing chords and Lake's throbbing single-note bass line, little gestures make a big impression: for instance, the harplike synth line underlying "the tapestry is spun" (3:30), and the organ glissando highlighting "each one to its mark" (3:59). There's also a short but scorching Hammond C-3 solo (from 3:42) that recalls ELP's glory days. After the final repetition of this verse (from 3:55), a swelling passage dominated by the Kurzweil's choral setting (4:29) spills into the return of the first section's refrain, which proves to be the climax of the entire song: as Lake sings the "lay your life upon the line" segment, he accompanies his vocal with a thundering syncopated bass line in the deepest register of his instrument. This time, the second half of the refrain is allowed to cadence, on a series of sledgehammerlike iterations of the first verse's D minor ninth chord (at 5:26).

Even this doesn't bring a real sense of finality to the music, though, so the song moves on into an abbreviated recapitulation of the opening section. The original verse returns at 5:32, now more richly orchestrated (Kurzweil choral patches and doom-laden GX-1 fanfares have been added in the background), followed by the original refrain (6:01): the refrain is followed at 6:46 by a variation of the sledgehammer D-minor ninth chords that ended the second section. This time there's nowhere else for the music to go, and the final iteration of the chord echoes into oblivion: the effect is not unlike an enormous bomb blast that slowly reverberates into absolute silence. Lake's lyric suggests that short of a miracle, the quest he describes will not succeed; the tonality of Emerson's music, ambiguous to the end (it's very hard to accept D minor as a final resting point) suggests that no miracle is forthcoming. "The Miracle," like "Knife-Edge," is a masterpiece of controlled tension; it is a testament to Emerson's progress as a composer that "The Miracle" is both less flashy and far more sophisticated than its progenitor.

The first three tracks are so tightly woven that it's hard to imagine changing their order or removing one of them from the sequence: part of the power of "The Miracle," I think, stems from the fact that the previous two tracks have already built up a great deal of intensity, which "The

Miracle" pushes to yet a higher level. The tracks on side two of the LP format lack that level of coherence, and other than the final track, "Mars," they lack the epic intensity of the first three tracks. While they're nice enough in isolation, they don't really cohere into something bigger: one could easily change their order, or remove one or more of them entirely, without greatly altering the bigger picture. In sum, side two of *Emerson, Lake and Powell*, while eminently listenable, packs little of the punch of side one.

The first track of side two, "Touch and Go," is arguably the strongest of the lot, and the track closest in style and substance to the side one material: it was also a minor hit single for the band, charting out at number sixty in the American single charts. "Touch and Go" is the first "socially conscious" song in the ELP catalog, dealing with homelessness, an issue that was beginning to garner a great deal of attention in the U.S. during the mideighties, as well as the larger issue of rampant materialism of which homelessness was just one piece. Musically, "Touch and Go" is constructed from three building blocks. First, there is the C seventh suspended fourth chord (C–F–G–B♭, first heard at 0:13) that played an important role in "The Score" and "The Miracle" and which firmly anchors "Touch and Go" in C minor. Second, there is the two-bar electronic rhythm loop—a funklike pattern consisting mostly of metallic percussion hits but also including a "finger snap" and, every other bar, a "shaker." First heard at 0:13, in conjunction with the C7 suspended fourth chord, this pattern underlines the first set of verses (up through 1:03) and returns at 2:14 to accompany a dramatically quiet statement of the verse (here Lake and Powell subtly superimpose their own counter-rhythms against it) before the song's final climax. Finally, there is the English folksong "Lovely Joan," which Emerson expropriates as an instrumental refrain. Emerson probably encountered the "Lovely Joan" melody in Ralph Vaughan Williams's orchestral *Fantasia on Greensleeves* (1934), where the melody provides the basis of the B section in the Fantasia's overall A–B–A structure.[13] In "Touch and Go," a monophonic statement of "Lovely Joan" on the GX-1 is the first thing we hear in the song (through 0:12): thereafter we hear much-expanded statements of it at 1:03 (including a new extension at 1:15, where Emerson develops it for a moment in G Mixolydian), at 1:43, at 2:44, and richly orchestrated statements at 3:10 and 3:22 which bring the song to its climax, and include some agile descending chromatic bass lines by Lake (listen at 3:13 and 3:25). While "Touch and Go" does not attain the scope of the first three tracks, it does manage to distill many of their essences into a punchy, memorable three-and-a-half minute single.

---

[13] In fact, at the end of some 3 concerts in 1988 the band played a tape of *Fantasia on Greensleeves*.

Unfortunately, from this point the album's intensity and momentum begin to slacken. The fifth track, "Love Blind," is a pleasant, tuneful, but ultimately lightweight song. It's chiefly notable for Emerson's thoughtful orchestrations (listen for his effective use of the Kurzweil's choral patch at the beginning and his bell-like antiphonal responses to Lake's vocal at 1:29 and 2:20), and for a couple of nice synth solos, at 1:13 and 2:33, featuring the PPG Wave 2.3 (which was MIDIed to the GX-1 and an Elka Synthex). The sixth track, "Step Aside," is somewhat better; a straight-ahead swing jazz tune with some nice contemporary touches (Emerson's layered electronic orchestrations compliment his parts on Steinway grand piano very well), it probably would have been a hit on today's contemporary jazz radio format, had it existed in the mideighties. If nothing else, the song does a good job evoking fifties film noir (via Lake's Sam Spade–like persona) and is notable for its superb piano-bass-drums episode (1:55–2:37). Emerson's playing here evokes the Modern Jazz Quartet's John Lewis in its combination of swing and delicacy; Powell accompanies with surprising subtlety, considering his stylistic proclivities, and Lake, despite Emerson's perpetual grousing that he doesn't like or relate to jazz, moves the chord changes around with a good deal of finesse and a fine feeling for the swing walking bass style. I've always enjoyed "Step Aside" a lot; my only reservation is that it really has nothing to do with anything else on the album.

The seventh track, "Lay Down Your Guns," is an anthemic, somewhat sentimental track that uses the imagery of the title to develop the subject of a truce between quarrelling lovers. Like "Love Blind," it's tuneful, pleasant, and nicely orchestrated, and again features a tasteful synth lead by Emerson (the guitarlike Yamaha DX7 part at 3:00). On the other hand, I find it overly sentimental, with some overblown imagery in the lyrics ("and still our passion calls / and the juices fall like the rain from the sky"), and too many instances of Lake singing the lightweight lyrics with more passion than they deserve, especially in light of the blandly diatonic chord accompaniment (listen particularly to his overdone vocal delivery at 2:34). While "Lay Down Your Guns" certainly foreshadows "Farewell to Arms" from *Black Moon,* I think the latter, with its more universal message and more galvanizing melodic and harmonic ideas, is much superior.

Finally we come to the album's closing track: an arrangement of "Mars, the Bringer of War," the justly famous first movement of the orchestral suite *The Planets* (1917) by British composer Gustav Holst (1874–1934). Emerson has said that the track was recorded "almost as an afterthought" as the recording sessions were winding down, when Polydor specifically requested the band record one of their trademark rocked-up arrangements of an orchestral piece. They chose "Mars" because Cozy Powell had already worked up a percussion solo to the accompaniment of a tape of "Mars" with one of his former bands.[14]

Holst's "Mars" has provided the inspiration for countless war movie scores (just listen to the main theme of John Williams's *The Empire Strikes Back*, or the "Orc music" from Howard Shore's *Lord of the Rings* soundtracks). Perhaps the work's most distinctive feature is its one-bar rhythmic ostinato in 5/4; its blaring, brass-heavy orchestration and its ominous chains of chromatically rising and falling parallel major triads are also memorable. However, in "Mars" Holst creates a musical metaphor for war that goes much deeper than the surface rhythms and orchestrations. While "Mars" is cast in sonata-allegro form—an exposition with distinct first, second, and closing theme groups, a development, and a recapitulation in which the main themes return out of order—the tonal plan is all "wrong" for sonata-allegro form. In "Mars" there is a near-constant tonal conflict between the 5/4 rhythmic ostinato (sounded on C or its dominant, G) and the thematic material (centered in D♭ or its dominant, A♭), as the strands of music in C (or G) and D♭ (or A♭) grind against each other. As the piece reaches its climax, a series of apocalyptic, sledgehammerlike chords grate the two key centers together one last time (the voicing of the chord is C–A♭–D♭–G); at the end, only C and G are still sounding. Here Holst takes the war metaphor to its logical conclusion: since there is no possible resolution between the warring key centers, the C key center simply obliterates the D♭ key center, metaphorically speaking.[15]

"Mars"—urgent, driving, metallic, dissonant—would seem to be a tailor-made work for ELP. Nonetheless, I don't rank the ELPowell version of "Mars" as one of the great ELP classical arrangements. To be sure, Emerson's electronic orchestration is exceedingly rich in both its tone-colors and its kaleidoscopically shifting layerings: Emerson's orchestration of the opening synth theme at 0:10, with its sound somewhere between a foghorn and a four-story metal door scraping open, is particularly awe-inspiring. Likewise, he shows a good instinct for when to stick close to Holst's music (which he does for most of the track) and when to cut away into something different (the synth solo at 5:57, which replaces the recap of the parallel major triads in Holst's original music). However, there are three areas in which the ELPowell arrangement falls somewhat short.

---

[14] See Doerschuk, "The Phoenix Rises," 44. Lake, of course, had become familiar with "Mars" during his time in King Crimson.

[15] Anyone wanting a more thoroughgoing analysis of "Mars" may want to consult my "Holst's 'Mars': A Model of Goal-Oriented Bitonality," which gives the first comprehensive explanation of the piece's bitonal construction. See *Music in Performance and Society: Essays in Honor of Roland Jackson*, ed. Malcolm Cole and John Koegel (Warren, MI: Harmonie Park Press, 1997), 411–24.

First, like many too many orchestral conductors, ELPowell take "Mars" much too slow: in a two-piano arrangement of "Mars" Holst had suggested a tempo of 177 beats per minute, but ELPowell takes "Mars" at 128 beats per minute, and the piece feels like it's dragging at this tempo.[16] Second, the ELPowell arrangement shows insufficient attention to the rhythmic subtlety of Holst's score. Holst had wisely withdrawn the 5/4 ostinato at key junctures, both to highlight transitions and avoid monotony; the ELPowell arrangement often uses the ostinato where Holst didn't, blurring transitions and creating unnecessary rhythmic monotony (example: 2:19–2:39 of the ELPowell arrangement). More problematically, Powell's drumming during the closing theme of the exposition with its one-TWO-three-FOUR-five/ONE-two-THREE-four-FIVE backbeats, comes across as very ham-fisted and heavy-handed, much different than the fleet military-style drumming of the Holst score (here's where Carl Palmer's rudimental expertise on snare drum would have proved invaluable). Finally, while Emerson's orchestrations do get somewhat bigger as the track progresses, they don't necessarily get more strident, with the arguable exception of the synth solo (from 5:57), where the sudden thinning of the texture works against the climactic effect of the more strident tone colors. Otherwise, the arrangement's climactic section (from 6:43 on) lacks some of the punch that a simultaneous thickening of texture and increased distortion of tone colors would have provided. When my band Hermetic Science arranged "Mars" for our third album, *En Route* (2001), I knew I could not compete with the richness or complexity of Emerson's tone colors; I believed, however, that our adherence to Holst's suggested tempo, our attention to the rhythmic subtleties of Holst's orchestration, and the progressive increase in tone-color stridency would more than compensate.[17] Interested listeners can compare the two arrangements for themselves and decide which works best.

"Mars" is the end of the original *Emerson, Lake and Powell* album. When Polydor reprinted the CD in the early nineties, however, they added two bonus tracks. The ninth track, "The Loco-Motion," was the B-side of the "Touch and Go" single in the U.K. (but not in the U.S., where the B-side was "Learning to Fly"). Like "Mars," it's all instrumental, so we'll never know how Lake would have reinterpreted Little Evie's vocals on this early-sixties bubblegum-rock classic. Emerson's ponderous, intense introductory section, loosely based around Arthur Honegger's

---

[16] Holst practiced what he preached. A recording of the piece that he conducted, made in 1926 and available in recent years on the Koch International label, hews very close to his suggested 177 beats per minute.

[17] Maybe I should say our "near adherence" to Holst's suggested tempo! On the recording, we took the piece at 164 beats per minute. In live performance, we may have played it slightly faster sometimes—say 168–172 beats per minute.

symphonic poem *Pacific 231*, seems somewhat at odds with the light-weight melody of the verse (which finally enters at 0:44); indeed, in my opinion the arrangement goes on a bit longer than the rather thin substance of the original Carole King/Gerry Goffin song merits. On the whole, however, it's good fun, especially once one grows more acclimated to the jarring shifts between Emerson's urgent, driving interlude (from 2:07) and postlude (from 3:39) and the body of the song. The second bonus track, "Vacant Possession," is apparently a leftover song from the original sessions; it's in the same general vein as "Love Blind" and "Lay Down Your Guns," although not as polished in its arrangement. It's the closest track on *Emerson, Lake and Powell* in character to the material from Lake's *Manoeuvres*, and the only track to make substantial textural use of guitar. Perhaps the highpoint of the song is a lively instrumental interlude certainly penned by Emerson (3:01–3:22).

Emerson, Lake and Powell: An Assessment

In sum: *Emerson, Lake and Powell*, with its less-than-cohesive and uneven second side, doesn't quite measure up to the classic 1970–74 output. Nonetheless, the first side of the LP (that is to say, the first three tracks) are entirely successful, and represent an important addition to the ELP canon, as does (to a lesser extent) "Touch and Go." I've already pointed to the successful updating of the classic seventies ELP sound that was accomplished on *Emerson, Lake and Powell*: I'll close with two final observations. First, *Emerson, Lake and Powell* might represent Lake's most consistently successful achievement as a lyricist since the first ELP album (I'm not counting his 1973–78 collaborations with Pete Sinfield here): other than the lyrics of "Lay Down Your Guns," cowritten with Steve Gould, which are a bit overwrought, the imagery is evocative, and the narrative flow convincing. Finally, I can think of no other ELP album where the difference between Emerson's and Lake's contributions are so successfully minimized. While I'm assuming "Love Blind" and "Lay Down Your Guns" had some Lake involvement and the other six tracks were more strictly Emerson's (other than the lyrics, of course), the gaping stylistic chasm that often separated Emerson tracks and Lake tracks on their seventies albums is almost completely bridged here. It's ironic that on a project recorded more than a decade after their heyday, when they were hardly a band at all in the strictest sense of the word, Emerson, Lake and Powell manage in many ways to sound more like a true band than Emerson, Lake and Palmer had during their classic era.

Emerson, Lake and Powell was released in late May 1986. The initial results were encouraging. By July, the album had reached twenty-three in the U.S. charts, the highest-charting ELP album since *Works I*; in the

U.K. the album charted out a bit lower, at thirty-five. Meanwhile, "Touch and Go" hit number sixty in the singles charts: a video of the track directed by Jim Yukich that showed the band performing in the studio, with footage of steel workers spliced in, received a good deal of MTV airplay, and made MTV's Top 20 video list for 1986.

Emerson, Lake and Powell Tour

Ominously, however, while ELPowell generated genuine enthusiasm for a short time, by late summer interest in the Emerson-Lake comeback was beginning to wane. Considering how high *Emerson, Lake and Powell* charted, it dropped out of the U.S. charts disappointingly fast, in just twelve weeks: it did not achieve gold record status, having sold approximately 350,000 copies by the time the tour started, on August 15 in El Paso, Texas. By this time, the album was beginning to fall in the charts: this affected concert attendance, as did the fact that for some reason the first leg of the tour covered Texas, Oklahoma, and Louisiana, an area that had never been a hotbed of support for either ELP or progressive rock more generally. The attendance problem came to a head on August 23, when ELPowell played San Antonio. The night before, ZZ Top, the Lone Star State's homegrown rock heroes whose gutterbucket blues-rock reflected the prevailing tastes of many of Texas's rock music fans, had drawn 15,000; ELPowell drew around 3,000. Keith Emerson commented afterwards to German rock journalist Edgar Kluesener, "It's bordering on impudence that a simple band like that can draw so much more people than we can." While one suspects Emerson made this comment somewhat tongue-in-cheek—the fanaticism of ZZ Top's Texas fans during the eighties was well known—the sense of surprise and disappointment is real enough. After the San Antonio show, the band's management cancelled seven shows due to poor ticket sales, and ELPowell spent several days in San Antonio rehearsing and attempting to scale back the lighting show. Another casualty of the first leg of the tour was warm-up act Yngwie Malmsteen, the Swedish progressive metal guitar virtuoso, who had complained about shortage of room and had finally been thrown off the tour for refusing to play.

The Emerson, Lake and Powell Tour resumed September 1 in Cincinnati, Ohio. The band spent much of the next two months touring the Midwest, the Northeast, and the mid-Atlantic states—regions where interest in ELP, and prog generally, had always been high during the seventies—and generally attendance was somewhat better, especially in some of the major venues like New York's Madison Square Garden and the Meadowlands of New Jersey, where the band drew in the 13,000 to 14,000 range. However, the attendance issue never totally solved itself:

perhaps the nadir was September 30 in Lexington, Kentucky, where ELPowell played to roughly eight hundred people in a venue that seated close to 20,000. In late October, the tour shifted to the West Coast, with the band doing shows in Seattle, Portland, Oakland, Los Angeles, Orange County, and San Diego; the tour ended with a show in Phoenix on November 2. In all, the band played forty-one shows in two and a half months.

The open-air show the band played in San Diego on November 1 was representative of the Emerson, Lake and Powell tour set list. After a short snippet of "Fanfare for the Common Man," the band launched directly into "The Score" and "Learning to Fly"; both were very faithful to the studio versions, save only for the lack of vocal harmonies on "Learning to Fly." Disappointingly, the band didn't follow these two tracks up with "The Miracle," which I suspect would have been a magnificent live number; furthermore, the first three tracks of the *Emerson, Lake and Powell* album are so inextricably linked that removing "The Miracle," seemed to rob the first two of their inevitable climax. Nonetheless, the next song, "Pirates," came across very well, with Emerson's GX-1 sounding much fuller and more muscular here, MIDIed in with his digital keyboards, than it had in the seventies. The band then played a selection of numbers from the early days of ELP, including "Knife-Edge" and the first four movements of "Tarkus" ("Eruption," "Stones of Years," "Iconoclast," "Mass"), which moved seamlessly into two excerpts from *Pictures*, the final "Promenade" and "The Great Gates of Kiev." Lake then took a mini solo set, playing "Still . . . You Turn Me On" and "Watching Over You." Emerson, for his part, played two numbers the vast majority of the crowd had never heard before: "Dream Runner" (which he wryly introduced as "music from a movie called 'Debbie Does Dishes' . . . or something like that"), and "Creole Dance," a set of improvisations loosely based around the final movement of Alberto Ginastera's *Suite de Danzas Criollas* for piano.[18]

Lake then came back to play two more of his signature tunes, "From the Beginning" and "Lucky Man," with the band. The latter rocks out a bit more than it had in any of ELP's live arrangements of the seventies, probably reflecting the change it had undergone in the live shows of the Greg Lake Band. The band then launched into "Fanfare for the Common Man." Unlike ELP's late-seventies performances of "Fanfare," ELPowell's live version followed the premise of the *Works I* studio version: Emerson improvised a monophonic synthesizer solo over the bass-drums shuffle background, which started simply but eventually built up a good deal of

---

[18] In his "Creole Dance," Emerson quotes the beginning and a bit of the middle of the final movement of Alberto Ginastera's *Suite de Danzas Criollas*.

momentum, and spilled into a snippet of "Blues Variation" (from *Pictures*) as it reached its climax. The Emerson, Lake and Powell version of "Fanfare" is, in my opinion, the most successful live version of the piece, either before or since. The band then returned to the album material, playing "Touch and Go" and "Mars, the Bringer of War," which began with a NASA-like countdown sequence, and included a long electronic drum solo by Powell in the middle. This was the end of the show; the band returned for an encore, though, and did a medley of "Karn Evil 9, 1st Impression, part two," "America," and "Rondo."

Emerson, Lake and Powell were a very strong live band with a huge sound: certainly Emerson's Hammond organ and GX-1 parts sound much more powerful and muscular than they had during the *Works* tour. One gains a sense of the band's power from two Manticore Records releases of late 2003 that finally have made the live ELPowell experience available for commercial consumption. One of the two, *Emerson, Lake and Powell: The Sprocket Sessions*, documents a summer 1986 rehearsal for the band's upcoming tour: it's particularly noteworthy for including songs from the album that didn't make the tour's set list ("The Miracle" and "Love Blind"). The second, *Emerson, Lake and Powell Live in Concert*, documents a show played in Lakeland, Florida on October 4, 1986 (not, as the liner notes mistakenly say, November).[19] The band performs well enough, although there are some technical glitches, particularly keyboards being mixed too low or occasionally not coming through the mix at all (for instance, the Kurzweil during segments of "The Score"). My main criticism of this album is that a sizable portion of the band's set list is excluded: one really needs both albums together to get a panoramic view of Emerson, Lake and Powell's live repertoire. Incidentally, as good as ELPowell were live, I find it frustrating that they only played four tracks from their album: at the very least "The Miracle" and "Step Aside" should have been part of the set list.

While the tour was a musical success, it was not a financial one. The band found it necessary to change management midtour; finances never recovered, and Emerson later recalled, "I must have gotten back [from the tour] with less than $500 in my pocket."[20] Although there had been talk of a second Emerson, Lake and Powell album as late as December 1986, the tour had bled the band dry of the finances it would have needed for a new album. Emerson, Lake and Powell more or less dissolved, with

---

[19] Back in 1987, Cozy Powell presciently remarked about the Lakeland show, "It was recorded for Westwood One [Radio]. It was a disaster gig, we played really badly and I hope that tape never comes out though no doubt it will." See Cozy Powell and Frank Aiello, "Emerson, Lake and Powell USA Tour," *Fanzine for the Common Man*, no. 8 (June 1991): 9.

[20] Keith Emerson, quoted by Bob Doerschuk, "Keith Emerson," *Keyboard*, April 1988, 85.

Emerson and Lake on very uneasy terms due to the financial problems created by the tour; Cozy Powell moved on to other projects. Asked many years later about Powell's contributions, Carl Palmer said,

> I thought Cozy did a good job, I thought he was inexperienced with person-alities . . . with Keith and Greg you have to do it day by day, you just can't turn up and play. You make the phone calls, because they don't call each other, you have to call and do all that, which I've never minded doing, it's not a problem. I don't think Cozy, because he'd not been conditioned in that area, ever really got it. Bless his cotton socks, I think he did a good job but there's no way that he could come in and do what I did because Greg Lake trampled all over him, that's just Greg's personality, it's harder for Greg when I'm there, that's just the way it is.[21]

In early 1987, Brian Lane, longtime manager of Yes, succeeded in reuniting Emerson, Lake, and Carl Palmer, who was now free of any fur-ther obligations to the recently defunct Asia, and the original ELP spent two weeks in March 1987 rehearsing. The reformation attempt didn't click, though, and soon it blew up, with the Emerson-Lake relationship sinking into open acrimony and litigation over the financial aftermath of the Emerson, Lake and Powell tour. Emerson told *Detroit Free Press* critic Gary Graff in April 1988 that he and Lake "speak to each other through lawyers . . . I got fooled into it [the reunion], basically; he told me he had changed and blah, blah, blah. I can only take working with a prima donna for so long, and then it really upsets me."[22] So that was the end of Emerson, Lake and Palmer.

The Advent of 3

Well, sort of. Carl Palmer had stayed in touch with John Kalodner, Asia's point man at Geffen Records, and Kalodner, after the failed reformation of ELP, flagged Palmer's attention to a demo tape by a young musician named Robert Berry, a vocalist, bassist, guitarist, songwriter, and studio proprietor from the San Jose, California, area. Berry was amazed to receive a call from Palmer asking him to help form a new band, and he promptly moved to England to work with him. They couldn't find suit-able matches, though, so Berry joined GTR, a mideighties "supergroup" that had united former Yes and Genesis guitarists Steve Howe and Steve Hackett, after Hackett lost interest and abandoned ship. Even as Howe

---

[21] Carl Palmer, quoted by Frank Askew, "Interviews: Carl Palmer," *Impressions* 8 (October 2001): 8–9.

[22] Keith Emerson, quoted by Gary Graff, "Keith Emerson Seeks a Hit With His New Group, 3," *Detroit Free Press*, April 22, 1988, 8D.

and Berry began to work on material for a second GTR album, though, he received another call from Palmer, who explained he'd received a call from Keith Emerson asking him to do a session. As the two men talked, Palmer asked Emerson if he would be interested in forming a band with Berry and Palmer. Here's Emerson:

> I thought about it a bit and finally decided, "Hell, why not? Let's have a bit of fun now, and try to tap that market, which seemed to be wide open to us. So we got together, and we got a couple of girl singers as well, which Carl really enjoyed. He was running down to Frederick's of Hollywood to buy their outfits. And then someone with Geffen came over to England, and he saw the video we had made with these sexy girl singers, and we got a record deal. It became a really enjoyable experience.[23]

When Berry heard Emerson was interested, he informed GTR he was leaving—which, incidentally, proved to be that band's deathblow. Eschewing such excellent names as "Triton" and "Emerson, Berry and Palmer," the new band christened themselves "3."

Quickly 3 went to work, recording two demos ("Eight Miles High" and a second song that was never released) in June 1987. After three months of rehearsals, they recorded their first (and last, as it turned out) album, *To the Power of Three*, in September and October 1987 at London's E-Zee and West Side Studios. These sessions worked totally differently than any of ELP's. For the first time since his pre-Nice days, Emerson was not his band's primary writer; he contributed only two songs, "Desde la Vida" and "On My Way Home," while Berry contributed four (the band also recorded two cover songs). The band agreed that Berry and Palmer would produce the album; Emerson was given the final say in all arranging matters, not only of his own material, but of Berry's (and the cover tunes) as well.

Although typical Emersonian touches are apparent throughout *To the Power of Three*, the fact is that on all the tracks except the two Emerson originals the predominant musical personality is Berry, which gives the album a very different feel than ELP or ELPowell. While Berry was a progressive-rock enthusiast growing up—by his own admission he was a fan of both Emerson and Steve Howe—his real roots, as a singer, songwriter, and guitarist, are in West Coast stadium rock of the late seventies and early eighties: Journey and Toto will provide useful points of reference. Berry's voice is similar to Journey's Steve Perry—a soulful high tenor—and his guitar playing and songwriting also evoke early-eighties West Coast mainstream rock. Berry is a truly multitalented figure: not many musicians achieve his level of competence as a singer, instrumentalist, and song-

---

[23] Hall, "Welcome to the Show," 50.

writer. The main problem, given Berry's musical domination of the 3 album, is that neither his songwriting, singing, or guitar and bass work is particularly unique or immediately recognizable. As a result, large sections of the *To the Power of Three* album sound very much like the scores of other mainstream rock albums of the mideighties based in a style (late-seventies stadium rock) that was quickly fading: even Emerson's arrangements aren't able to impart a distinctive sound to very much of this material.

An additional factor in the lack of a distinctive 3 sound was the keyboard setup Emerson was now using. His original GX-1 was rendered unplayable by the Emerson, Lake and Powell tour. Soon after the tour ended he received a call from former Led Zeppelin bassist and keyboardist John Paul Jones: would Emerson like to buy Jones's GX-1? Emerson was delighted to, and soon after taking delivery of it, his techs transferred the custom electronics out of his original GX-1 into the new one. Emerson: "It worked for about a week. Then one day I left it switched on in my barn [studio], and went to make myself a sandwich or something in the house. When I came back, there's this pile of smoke hanging over it; I could smell it as I walked in. Burned transistors, or whatever. And that was that."[24] Besides his incredible technique, distinctive chord voicings and melodic figurines, and compositional mastery, Emerson had one other thing going for him throughout the seventies: his organ sound and his favorite Moog and GX-1 patches (especially the trumpetlike ones) were unique and immediately recognizable. As the Hammond became less important in his keyboard setup, he relied more than ever on the analog synthesizers to maintain that link with his past; the GX-1 played a particularly important role in the success of the Emerson, Lake and Powell album. The demise of the GX-1 broke a link, both symbolic and real, with the glory days of ELP. Emerson understood this: he told Bob Doerschuk, "I really need to get my own identifiable sounds again now that I've lost the GX-1. It's like Eric Clapton's guitar; nobody sounds like that."[25] Despite surrounding himself with a host of state-of-the-art digital keyboards—the Roland D-50, Kurzweil 250, Yamaha TX816 and KX88, Oberheim Matrix, and Korg DSS-1, among others—he did not manage to achieve a truly characteristic sound on 3; perhaps the closest he came is the breathy Roland D-50 patch (one can hear it at the beginning of "You Do Or You Don't," for instance) that recurs several times on the album. In balance, though, from the *To the Power of Three* album on, Emerson's digital synth patches have frequently tended to sound uncomfortably close to everybody else's.[26]

---

[24] Bob Doerschuk, "Keith Emerson," *Keyboard*, April 1988, 89.
[25] Ibid., 91
[26] As I point out in *Rocking the Classics*, this has become an issue for progressive rock of the nineties and beyond that uses digital synthesizers; see 192–95.

A similar remark could be made about Carl Palmer's drumming. Palmer was now using Dynacord electronic drums in addition to his Remo acoustic kit. Palmer's style had changed decisively during his time with Asia: by the time of 3, while he occasionally still deigned to demonstrate his staggering technique (on "Desde la Vida," for instance), by and large his drumming had become sparer, heavier, and more conventional than in the seventies. While some simplification of his style was to be expected even welcome during the eighties, by the time of 3 his more conventional approach to moving around the beat, combined with the very electronic sound of his drums (on both the acoustic and the electronic kits) robbed his drumming of much of that fleetness, characteristic lightness of touch, and rhythmic creativity and imagination that had been such a hallmark of his work with ELP. A good deal of the drumming on *To the Power of Three* could have been the work of any top-flight studio drummer.

To the Power of Three

Of the four songs on side one of the vinyl format of *To the Power of Three*—a format that was beginning to fade by the time the album was released in February 1988—two are by Berry, one by Sue Shifrin, a songwriting acquaintance of Emerson's, and one by Emerson, Berry, and Palmer. Berry's "Talkin' 'Bout," the album's opener, was featured in a video that received (very) modest MTV airplay in early 1988: it's memorable mainly for its inexorably rising keyboard riff, a C-pentatonic major scale harmonized in parallel fifths and octaves, that opens the song and subsequently accompanies the chorus. Some typically Emersonian touches can be found in the instrumental interlude, with its shifting metric accents, and in the rapid fire modulations of the chorus through D and E major at the end (the rest of the song was centered in C major). "Lover to Lover," another Robert Berry song (although Emerson and Palmer are also given writing credits) prominently features the band's three female backing singers (Suzie O'List, Kim Edwards, and Lana Williams) during the chorus. The metrically daunting instrumental interlude is very ELPish, but seems to sit rather uneasily in the fabric of the song at large; a short Hammond solo by Emerson prior to the last set of choruses fits far more naturally. The third song, "Chains," is by Sue Shifrin, although stylistically it's quite comparable to Berry's songs. Its catchy hook features a baroqueish sequence of chords centered in D minor; again there's an instrumental interlude (this one seems to fit the song better), with a nice digital pipe organ passage (at 2:38) that develops the short keyboard motif heard at the song's opening. Like "Talkin' 'Bout," this song modulates upwards (to E minor) after the instrumental bridge.

The real center of gravity on side one—indeed, the entire album—is "Desde la Vida," the only track that fully reveals what this band was capable of. Although credited to Emerson, Berry, and Palmer, it is clearly primarily by Emerson, and is of a piece with the first side of the *Emerson, Lake and Powell* LP. Epic in scope, the lyrics present a kind of mythic history (of California?) from its settlement to the present, at times alternating clauses in English and Spanish—not always, it must be admitted, to particularly good effect. The song (at 7:05 the album's longest) is broken into three short "movements." The first, "La Vista," begins by slowly unfolding its story of an epic past across a flamencolike descending fuzzed bass line and bell-like synth chords centered in D modal major. At 1:04 the tempo picks up and the meter shifts from 4/4 to 6/4; as Emerson spins out a lyrical synth lead over the increasingly active chord progressions, Palmer's drumming becomes more driving and virtuosic. Suddenly, at 2:00 the music pauses dramatically on an A major chord, with "industrial" gurgling sounds in the background: this signals the advent of the second movement, "Frontera."

"Frontera" opens with one of Emerson's greatest inspirations of the eighties: a driving, syncopated theme in 5/4 that, despite its textural complexity, is simply based around a D major suspended fourth chord that resolves. Notice the timpani-like synth bass theme (at 2:08), the heavily filtered synth lead (from 2:16), and Palmer's "industrial" offbeat Dynacord accents (2:09, 2:13, 2:17, 2:21, and elsewhere); like ELP's "Toccata" of fifteen years earlier, "Frontera" strikes a primitivist and industrial accent at the same time. The second main theme (2:32) is a heroically rising motive in 6/4 with offbeat hemiola accents that moves through B♭ and C major chords. Through the remainder of "Frontera," these two themes alternate.

The third and longest movement, "Sangre de Toro" (from 3:35), brings the historical narrative into the present. Berry's rhythmically flexible vocal, which spills across barlines, is accompanied by his pulsating bass line and punctuated by Emerson's heroic trumpetlike synth chords. After two verses that exemplify Emerson's penchant for irregular phrase lengths, the music is pared down to the pulsing bass line and drums; suddenly Emerson cuts loose with a ferocious ten-and-a-half-bar beboplike piano lead that's as galvanizing as anything he has ever recorded. This shifts to a progression of quartal chords (4:46) that transforms the heroically rising motive of "Frontera" (stretching its octave to a ninth and smoothing its original 6/4 contour to 4/4); Carl Palmer begins to counterpoint this motive with an increasingly frenzied drum part. From 5:05, Emerson accompanies Palmer's drumming with pounding quartal piano harmonies; the Emerson-Palmer exchange builds to a climax, then tapers off, with Berry's pulsing bass paving the way for the third and final verse ("again we awaken"). The verse segues directly into the two instrumental themes of "Frontera," first the heroically rising theme, now accompanied with new obbligato synth lines, and finally, at 6:13, the driving, syncopated 5/4 theme: as it begins to fade in the sonic distance, Berry and the female backup singers chant the "Desde la Vida" lyric.[27] "Desde la Vida" possesses many of the same characteristics as "The Score" or "The Miracle" from *Emerson, Lake and Powell*: in addition, although there's a nice sense of movement in the chord progressions, the tonality is almost entirely centered in one key, D (unlike the majority of Emerson's other epics), so the song's real interest lies in its timbres, textures, and rhythms. Berry, to his credit, sings it very well, and "Desde la Vida" represents an important addition to the ELP canon.

Side two opens with a 3 remake of the folk/psychedelic rock classic by the Byrds, "Eight Miles High." I don't like it. The original's tempo is slowed, its rock beat replaced with a funk rhythm that's marred by Carl Palmer's overly mechanical Dynacord accents (one and TWO and three AND four AND *ad infinitum*) and by an annoying Earth, Wind, and Fire–like synth "trumpet" riff. The original is urgent and exciting, with Roger McGuinn's frenzied, Coltrane-like guitar solo the highlight as it spills across barlines. The 3 version is turgid, almost parodistic (it sounds like a cheesy late-seventies funk band covering the song) and, unusually, even Emerson's synth solo at the end of the song (which MIDIed together the Oberheim Matrix, Yamaha TX816 and Korg DSS-1) fails to catch fire.

The next song, "Runaway," isn't much of an improvement: with its forgettable melodic material, it's the least interesting of the album's Robert Berry songs, and even the instrumental interlude, featuring a short guitar solo, doesn't perk the song up much. "You Do Or You Don't," the third song of side two, is quite a bit better, arguably Berry's best song on the album. Set in G major, it's a reflective song somewhat reminiscent of Procol Harum, although it doesn't attain the same sense of poignance and majesty as that band's best music. The instrumental interlude features some well-conceived modulations and a lyrical passage of Matthew Fisher–like Hammond work by Emerson; the instrumental coda features Berry's most exciting guitar work on the album.

The last song, "On My Way Home," was originally conceived by Keith Emerson as a solo piano ballad called "Lament for Tony Stratton-Smith," to be performed at the memorial service (held at London's Saint Martin's-in-the-Fields) of his old manager and mentor on May 6, 1987. Said Emerson, "I'd never played at a memorial service before. It's not an easy gig, quite honestly. You get up there and perform, and nobody claps.

---

[27] The song-speech technique used here is reminiscent of Emerson's "Not So Innocent" from *Murderock*.

Everybody cries."[28] The arrangement for full band on *To the Power of Three* shows Emerson developing a new ballad style: bittersweet, staunchly diatonic, containing some essences of earlier ELP "power hymns" like "Jerusalem," but more reflective. The song begins with a fluid, gentle statement of the verse on solo piano; this is followed at 0:30 by a second instrumental statement of the verse, this time by full band. (Here especially one hears the breathy synthesizer timbre that, in my opinion, is overused on this album.) Then comes an instrumental statement of the chorus (0:47), backed by Palmer's military-style drumming: the juxtaposition of the verse's C-minor tonality with its relative major, E♭, in the chorus gives the song much of its bittersweet quality. Another instrumental verse (1:13) is followed by the first vocal chorus (1:30); this is broken off suddenly at 1:54 by the instrumental interlude.

About this section, Emerson said, "When I wrote that piece, in the section where I go up to G, I incorporated a lot of themes from the Nice, because of the memories I associate with it . . . 'Rondo,' 'America,' the 'Five Bridges Suite.' I molded all these themes together."[29] To be honest, I'm unable to pick out these musical quotes in "On My Way Home" (although they're easily recognizable in "Lament for Tony Stratton-Smith"); I'm much more struck by this section's similarity to the overture of "Pirates," with its pulsing quartal harmonies (centered, as Emerson says, in G), supporting breathy lyrical synth leads, and punctuated by off-beat drum accents. A piano run leads back into an instrumental statement of the verse (2:47), and a final series of vocal statements of the chorus that take on a distinctly choral feel as the female back-up singers (from 3:29) are layered in behind Berry's hymnlike vocal. "On My Way Home" is a fine song: Berry sings it well, although a longtime ELP fan can't help thinking that the vocal melody was created with Greg Lake's voice in mind.

To the Power of Three: An Assessment

To the Power of Three isn't a bad album, per se; but it certainly isn't a memorable one, either, and if it wasn't for "Desde la Vida" (and, to a lesser extent, "On My Way Home") it would be thoroughly forgettable. I think the problem is, above all, that 3 were trying to mine a stadium-rock style that had reached its zenith a decade earlier, and hadn't produced a really

---

[28] Keith Emerson, quoted by Doerschuk, "Keith Emerson," 86. "Lament for Tony Stratton-Smith" is included on Emerson's 2005 *Hammer It Out* anthology. Incidentally, Stratton-Smith's memorial service was notable for reuniting the four members of the Nice for the first time since late 1968.

[29] Ibid.

vital album since Asia's debut LP of 1982; most of the music simply lacks any sense of a vital spark. A lot of rock journalists were puzzled by Emerson's about-face in musical direction from the *Emerson, Lake and Powell* LP. Gary Graff of the *Detroit Free Press* reminded Emerson that less than two years before the release of *To the Power of Three*, he had told Graff, "I'm not in this business to see how I can try to fit in. If the music I play happens to sell, then it's all well and good. But I'm certainly not going to adulterate my music and my art to fit in." When asked why the 3 album seemed to fly in the face of his earlier statement, Emerson replied, somewhat testily, "I think it's slightly obvious that the first 3 album is an outgoing attempt to have *the* hit single. The word is really accessible. I'm interested in getting a little more song-oriented, something I haven't been able to do before."[30] He told Bob Doerschuk, "This is the most commercial context I've been involved with in my career . . . I think it's now time to discover pop music, and treat it exactly as I treat the classics, jazz, and the blues—as the art form that it is."[31] Fair enough: but for his foray into this particular "art form" to succeed, he needed more memorable material, and less dependence on a highly commercial style that had peaked years earlier, and which offered no further opportunities for distinctive self-expression within its well-established parameters.

To the Power of Three did not set the world on fire. It received fairly minimal radio and MTV exposure, and barely cracked the American Billboard Top 100 albums (it peaked at 97). The 3 tour did at least manage to avoid the mistakes of the Emerson, Lake and Powell tour of 1986. Under the watchful eye of manager Brian Lane, shows were scheduled for much smaller venues than had been the case with the ELPowell tour: the payoff was that of thirty-five dates, only one was cancelled, and this was a voluntary cancellation, so the band could perform at Atlantic Records' 40th Anniversary celebration at Madison Square Garden on May 14.[32]

In order to reproduce the sound of the album as closely as possible, the band decided to tour with an electric guitarist, Paul Keller, and two female singers, Debby Parks and Jennifer Steele. (Parks was fired at the beginning of the tour; Steele, near its conclusion.) The 3 tour, which began on April 5 in New York, covered a lot of prime ELP territory of days gone by: the Northeast (including shows in Ottawa, Toronto, and Montréal, Canada), the Midwest, the West Coast, and the South (Texas, Georgia, and Florida). The last show was on May 21 in Fort Lauderdale, Florida. The entire 3 tour was done very inexpensively by bus.

---

[30] Keith Emerson, quoted by Graff, "Keith Emerson Seeks a Hit," 8D.
[31] Keith Emerson, quoted by Doerschuk, "Keith Emerson," 94.
[32] The band were billed as "Emerson and Palmer" for this event, although it was actually Emerson, Berry, Palmer, and guitarist Jim Keller. They played "Fanfare for the Common Man."

A show the band played at the Cabaret (seating capacity about five hundred) in Berry's stomping grounds of San Jose, California, on May 6 gives a representative sample of the 3 tour set list. Reflecting a more relaxed and less formal approach to presentation, the 3 shows were a departure from ELP's in that Emerson was no longer the band's primary MC; Emerson, Berry, and Palmer all took turns bantering with the crowd in between numbers. They opened with a version of "Fanfare for the Common Man" modeled closely on what Emerson had done with the number during the Emerson, Lake and Powell Tour: an improvised monophonic synthesizer solo over the shuffle bass in the middle, climaxing with the "Blues Variation" fragment. This led into "Desde la Vida," performed a bit too fast for comfort. (Shades of *Tarkus?*) Then came "Lover to Lover" and a four-piece arrangement of "Hoedown" in which Jim Keller's guitar plays a prominent role. Then two more songs from the album, "You Do Or You Don't" and "Talkin' 'Bout." Emerson's traditional solo piano spot featured him on "The Dream Runner" and "Creole Dance," the same two numbers he had played on the Emerson, Lake and Powell Tour. "On My Way Home" was next, then "Standing in the Shadows of Love," a new song slated for the (never-to-be-recorded) second 3 album. Finally, the show-ending medley: "America," "Rondo" (which interpolated a fragment of Rimsky-Korsakov's "Flight of the Bumblebee"), an epic (and overextended) Palmer drum solo, and a reprise of "Rondo." The encore was "Eight Miles High" which, interestingly, incorporated a bit of "Peter Gunn" into the synth solo. A live 3 album would be nice—3 were a strong live band—and would certainly be more welcome than yet another authorized live ELP recording from either the *Works* era or the nineties.

The band had hoped to add a short European leg to their tour, but it didn't pan out; Berry told David Terralavoro "We needed ten dates, and there were only five available, so we couldn't afford to do it."[33] After the tour, Emerson and Palmer returned to England, and Berry returned to San Jose, where he went back to working in his studio and writing songs for the next 3 album. In his interview with Bob Doerschuk in early 1988 Emerson had remarked,

> This band was brought together very quickly, so it's mainly been a question of me bringing in my songs and Robert bringing in his songs. I'm looking forward to developing this Anglo-American sound we're working on together . . . I think his compositions come off sounding very West Coast. Mine come off sounding very European. I'd like to try to hone off the edges, so to speak, or file away the differences.[34]

---

[33] Robert Berry, quoted by David Terralavoro, *Fanzine for the Common Man* no. 1 (August 1989): 4.
[34] Keith Emerson, quoted by Doerschuk, "Keith Emerson," 85.

Berry told me,

> At our last meeting in London I presented the song "The Last Ride into the Sun" to Keith. I had really tried to connect to what the 3 fans and the Keith fans would want. I had a demo done that sounded a bit like us playing the parts and Keith commented "That sounds like me playing." He didn't seem thrilled by the idea that I had tried to define more of an older ELP/Keith playing style in my newer presentations. That was the last time we talked about material for the next album. That also was our last official business meeting.[35]

Emerson had apparently begun to entertain doubts about the future of 3 well before this meeting: "The small clubs were a great experience, but I couldn't see myself doing another tour like that. And I couldn't see myself going back into the studio to make another album along those same lines. I didn't have any other ideas, and it all sort of fell through, but under great terms, really."[36]

In late 1988, 3's management announced to a largely indifferent world that the band had ceased to exist. Incidentally, interested fans may wish to check out Robert Berry's solo album *Pilgrimage to a Point* (1993), which contains several songs that were slated to be included on the never-to-be-recorded second albums of both 3 and GTR, including the above-mentioned "The Last Ride into the Sun."

---

[35] Robert Berry, e-mail to author, January 17, 2002.
[36] Keith Emerson, quoted by Hall, "Welcome to the Show," 50.

16 Second Sabbatical

(1988–1991)

Keith Emerson

As it turned out, the demise of 3 did not slow Keith Emerson down at all; he had other projects up his sleeve during the summer of 1988. For one, he had been approached to provide some music for an Italian film entitled *La Chiesa* (*The Church*) scripted by Dario Argento and directed by Michele Soavi. Despite the moral and aesthetic reservations Emerson had expressed on a number of occasions about Argento's films after working with him on *Inferno*, he agreed. The plot of the movie, which ends up being even grosser and more ridiculous than *Inferno*, is as follows. A church was built over the graves of a group of possessed souls during the Middle Ages, and when an ignorant librarian removes a stone from the catacombs, all hell breaks loose (no pun intended). Father Gus, a Catholic priest, struggles to find the ancient church's secret so it can crumble to dust, while in the meantime, people who have been trapped in the church either go insane or begin killing each other. Urgh.

La Chiesa Soundtrack

But if *La Chiesa*, the movie, released in 1988, is awful, the same can't be said of the soundtrack, to which Emerson contributed four tracks and which is, with a couple of glaring exceptions, very good. Emerson's first track, "The Church (Main Theme)," begins with rumbling melodic fragments played on a pipe organ's bass pedals, punctuated by menacing organ chords; eventually bass and drums enter, accompanying the lumbering chromatic main theme and an edgy, polyrhythmic subsidiary theme. These themes are repeated, then followed by a furious Hammond solo over a bass ostinato; a brief recap of the main themes brings the track to a close. "Prelude 24" is an arrangement of J. S. Bach's Prelude 24 in B minor from

515

Volume I of the *Well-Tempered Clavier*; Emerson's adaptation of the piece to pipe organ changes the wistful, melancholy ambience of the original (intended for harpsichord or clavichord) to something more lugubrious and bellicose. The third Emerson track, "The Possession," begins with an atmospheric passage featuring a wordless choral synth patch; thereafter, ponderous and atmospheric pipe organ themes, both accompanied by rhythm section, are alternated. His fourth track, "The Church Revisited," is essentially a varied recap of "The Church (Main Theme)"; the opening pipe organ solo segment is much longer here, and features some ingenious contrapuntal treatment of the main themes.

While Emerson's tracks are quite good, they only constitute about thirteen minutes of music. The bulk of the soundtrack was contributed by the Italian progressive rock band Goblin, long-time Argento collaborators, and this music is very good as well: stylistically, it falls somewhere between seventies Italian instrumental prog and eighties electronic ambient of a particularly dark hue. There are also two dreadful pop songs—one, by Zooming on the Zoo, in the manner of eighties Eurofunk (it even contains some rapping), the other by Definitive Gaze in a late-eighties alternative-rock style—but mercifully these only occupy seven minutes total. The soundtrack was released in LP format by the Italian Cinevox label in April 1989; a reissue on CD by Cinevox in 2001 added a bonus track by Emerson, a remix of "The Church (Main Theme)" that eliminates the pipe organ prelude but adds a longer recap of the main themes at the end of the track, and three substantial bonus tracks of previously unreleased music by Goblin.

The Christmas Album

Amazingly, at the same time Emerson was working on music for Argento's dark, twisted film, he was also recording music for a solo album featuring Christmas music. The resulting album, simply entitled *The Christmas Album*, was released in November 1988, and was dedicated to his deceased father, Noel Emerson, who died in 1981. Although it was a private release (Keith Records 1), Emerson secured U.K. distribution through Virgin Records; nonetheless, in the tradition of Emerson's other post-ELP solo albums and movie soundtracks, it was a low-profile affair. The album features a mix of traditional Christmas songs and Emerson originals (the former predominate) in a decisively electronic vein: in more than half the tracks even the bass and drums are programmed. Considering the traditional nature of the material, it's ironic that this is arguably Emerson's most thoroughgoing electronic album (only *Harmagedon* comes to mind as a rival), and no other Emerson album is so totally dominated by the sounds of digital synthesizers.

There are two originals. "Snowman's Land" features an attractive theme in 12/8 followed by a majestic, rousing marchlike middle section seasoned with some heroic synth leads and Carl Palmer–like electronic snare parts; the 12/8 theme is recalled at the end. "Captain Starship Christmas" is a fairly insubstantial song featuring the West End Children's Choir. Among the traditional numbers, "Variations on Little Town of Bethlehem" features some energetic, bebopish jazz piano variations; the melody is disguised throughout. "We Three Kings" kicks the original into a driving 12/8 overdrive; there's a nice blues piano/funk bass break towards the end (bass guitar courtesy of Les Moir), as well as an interpolation of J. S. Bach's D-minor Prelude from Volume I of the *Well-Tempered Clavier* (which Emerson had used many years earlier, in "The Only Way" from *Tarkus*). The Aria from J. S. Bach's *Christmas Oratorio* is nice, although it plods a bit, and is overreliant on breathy synthesizer timbres; it picks up a bit at the end, with highly electronic drum backbeats and some nice contrapuntal layering. "I Saw Three Ships" makes a very imaginative and effective use of synth timbres in the accompaniment figures, sounding "industrial" and bell-like at once; the reflective middle section is quite pretty. "Petites Liturgies of Jesus" is pretty, too, with its delicate bell-like synth sonorities, although it gets somewhat repetitive by the end. While the original melody of "It Came Upon a Midnight Clear" is not very recognizable, it's very beautiful, with some wonderful, almost stridelike digital harpsichord episodes; notice the clever contrapuntal interpolation of "It's Lovely Weather for a Sleigh Ride Together With You" against the main melody in the closing section. Finally, "Silent Night" takes Emerson back to the black gospel territory explored on *Honky*, and even reunites him with his old Nassau-era drummer, Frank Scully. The album's only track that eschews electronics, "Silent Night" features the London Community Choir, Scully, and Emerson, who provides some superb, exceedingly soulful blues piano accompaniment and solo breaks. "Silent Night" makes one wish Emerson had done more music in this vein.

The Christmas Album: An Assessment

One can make many of the same remarks about *The Christmas Album* as about *Honky*. If you're looking for challenging, epic material, look elsewhere. If you're looking for exceedingly well-crafted music that evinces very little pretension but loads of good cheer, *The Christmas Album* is a winner. In 1995, *The Christmas Album* was rereleased on CD with two newly recorded tracks. "Troika" is an arrangement of the famous melody from Sergei Prokofiev's *Lieutenant Kije Suite*, a portion of which Greg Lake had used in "I Believe in Father Christmas." This track is notable for some virtuoso electronic orchestration: the whistling chorus doubled by synthesized metallic percussion and punctuated by synthesized male "shouts" is particularly noteworthy. "Glorietta," dedicated to Emerson's mother, is something of an electronic orchestral suite in three semidiscrete movements. The first movement is majestic, almost Elgarish, with a plaintive, pastoral opening; the second, a 12/8 march reminiscent of Emerson's arrangement of "I Saw Three Ships" featuring military snare–style (electronic) drumming; the third is bittersweet and hymnlike, with a brief recap of the second movement's march theme towards the end. "Captain Starship Christmas" was expunged from the 1995 reissue of the album, but a 1999 reissue by the Gunslinger label restored the track, while retaining the two new tracks of the 1995 Sundown Records reissue.

Emerson's "Lost" Solo Album

Even as Emerson was giving interviews promoting the release of *The Christmas Album* and *La Chiesa* during the late-1988/early-1989 period, he revealed that he was about to embark on another solo project. He told a French journalist, "I'm working with a young genius named Kevin Gilbert. He just finished co-producing the new Madonna album. He is the leader of the group Giraffe, and he can play *Tarkus* as good as me. He will co-produce my new album."[1] He told another interviewer, "The reason I chose [to record] in California is that I have everything at my disposal out there. I have my programmers. I have a very good producer."[2] Over the week of July 4, 1989, Emerson went to work with Gilbert and Gilbert's frequent musical cohort Patrick Leonard in Leonard's Burbank studio, recording at least six tracks. Of the six that were eventually released, two were for piano solo, and four featured Emerson on piano, Hammond, and synths with drummer Mike Barsimanto, bassist Jerry Watts and (on some tracks) guitarist Tim Pierce. One of these six tracks was a remake of "The Church (Main Theme)"; three more were later to appear in substantially different arrangements as "Close to Home," "Romeo and Juliet," and "Changing States" on ELP's *Black Moon* album of 1992 (more on this later). During the same sessions, Gilbert took the master tape of the previously unreleased orchestral recording of "Abaddon's Bolero" (recorded by the London Philharmonic Orchestra in late 1975) and worked to improve its sonic quality and balance; Gilbert even added a tuba obbligato that he played himself.

---

[1] Keith Emerson, quoted by David Terralavoro, "Keith Emerson's Aborted 1989/90 Piano Solo Album," *Fanzine for the Common Man*, no. 14 (July 1995): 19.
[2] Ibid.

In August, Gilbert turned up on San Jose's KOME-FM in an interview with Greg Stone. Gilbert played two tracks from the sessions (the two which eventually became "Romeo and Juliet" and "Changing States"). He mentioned that he had shopped the recording around to several record labels; there had been some interest, he said, although the labels had suggested that any remaining tracks be song-oriented to allow for some radio airplay. Gilbert added that because of contractual obligations to his new project, Toy Matinee, he was unable to sing on the Emerson album himself; for this reason, he said, Emerson had returned to England to audition vocalists.

In October, Emerson was back in California: this time he was at Robert Berry's studio in Campbell (near San Jose) along with Gilbert (who was now playing bass and drums in the sessions), vocalist Gary Cirimelli, and guitarist Marc Bonilla. Berry has said that he contributed some lyrics to Emerson, who "chopped [them] up and used as he felt"; interestingly, Berry receives no writing, performing, or production credits on this album.[3] Emerson was in San Jose during the large earthquake of October 1989; Gilbert quipped, "It was brought to my attention that during the quake Mr. Emerson sought comfort, solace, and shelter from the falling debris under the same aforementioned organ he humiliates in his live performances—go figure. Such seeming inequities often accompany long-term relationships."[4] Only two finished tracks, both songs, came out of these sessions: "Shelter from the Rain" and "The Band Keeps Playing." At that point, Emerson had enough material for a viable solo album. He returned to Berry's studio for two weeks in mid-March 1990. It appears that nothing recorded at these sessions has survived, although it is possible that the *Tarkus*-like rock arrangement of the third movement of Emerson's Piano Concerto no. 1 that's included on his 2005 *Hammer It Out* anthology, featuring Emerson, Bonilla, Berry (bass), and Mickey Sorey (drums), was recorded at this time.

What happened to this album? Sometime during late spring or early summer 1990, Emerson was recruited to be part of the touring supergroup the Best, so the project was temporarily shelved. Within a few months of the conclusion of the Best tour, ELP had been reformed: as I said above, three of the tracks from this project appeared in different arrangement guises on ELP's *Black Moon* of 1992. As it turned out, this solo album was not to enter the public forum until early 1995, when a small U.K. label, AMP Records, released it under the title *Changing States*. I will discuss the album on a track-by-track basis when we reach the appropriate chronological juncture in our saga; it should be kept in

---

[3] Ibid.
[4] Kevin Gilbert, *Changing States* liner notes (AMP-CD026), 1995.

mind, though, that despite its chronological displacement, in fact *Changing States* is a product of the same era as *La Chiesa* and *The Christmas Album*.

The Best

So who were the Best? The Best were a supergroup uniting Emerson, guitarist Joe Walsh (The Eagles), bassist John Entwistle (the Who), guitarist Jeff "Skunk" Baxter (Steely Dan, the Doobie Brothers), drummer Simon Phillips, and lead singer Rick Livingston that was brought together to play some shows in Japan and Hawaii during autumn 1990. The idea behind the Best was not the creation of new material; rather, to see how the band members would interpret each others' well-known tunes (in fact, the set list was chosen by the band members nominating their favorite tunes of the other band members). A show played at Yokohama Arena in Japan on September 26, 1990, and broadcast on Japanese TV on New Years Eve gives a good idea of what the Best were all about. The set opened with "Life in the Fast Lane," from Walsh's Eagles days, and proceeded on to "My Wife," Entwistle's song from the Who; "Bodhisattva" from Baxter's tenure with Steely Dan; "Fanfare for the Common Man," Emerson's first feature, which spotlighted a towering bass solo by Entwistle; "Rikki Don't Lose That Number," another song from Baxter's Steely Dan days; a drum solo by Simon Phillips; "Rocky Mountain Way," another Joe Walsh tune; two Emerson features, "Creole Dance" and "America," his old showstopper with the Nice; "Boris the Spider," Entwistle's old feature number with the Who; "Reeling in the Years," a Steely Dan number famous for its scorching guitar solo by Baxter; and finally, "Taking it to the Streets," from Baxter's time with the Doobie Brothers, which began with a piano solo by Emerson.

After his short tenure with the Best, Emerson's busy solo career of the 1988–90 period trailed off. He talked of forming a band with some of his band mates from the Best, and also of touring with Ringo Starr's All Star Band. Before any of these plans could come to fruition, however, the opportunity came for ELP to reform: but that's a story for the next chapter.

Greg Lake

After the dissolution of Emerson, Lake and Powell in late 1986, Greg Lake disappeared from the public eye; he put his own home studio together and "just really got into programming and computerized music."[5] His first substantial post-ELPowell project came when he hooked up with his former mate from his short tenure in Asia, Geoff Downes: considering the pop/mainstream rock leanings of both, this is actually a logical fit. Downes told David Gallant, "Myself and Greg set up a studio for about a year, after I had been at Advision. Because it was two people coming together from very different directions Greg said it was like 'riding the tiger.' We wrote about eight songs altogether."[6]

Ride the Tiger, as the Lake-Downes project came to be known, lasted a bit less than a year, from fall 1989 to May 1990. Intriguingly, Lake and Downes brought in Michael Giles, Lake's old King Crimson cohort, to drum on several of the tracks: the nucleus of an actual performing band with an ELP-like keyboard trio lineup was thus in place. Of the approximately eight songs Lake and Downes wrote together, six were actually recorded at Lake's home studio in London as twelve-track demos. Even as Downes began to shop around the Ride the Tiger demo in spring 1990, however, he rejoined Asia, effectively stopping the project in its tracks.

The outcome was rather similar to that of Emerson's 1989-90 solo album: the material began to be cannibalized and used for different purposes than it was originally intended for. "Affairs of the Heart" was rerecorded by ELP with a different arrangement and made its way on to their *Black Moon* album; so did "Money Talks," although with a new chorus and a different arrangement under a different title ("Paper Blood"). "Street War" was later recorded by ELP with totally different music and included on *In the Hot Seat* (1994). "Love Under Fire," meanwhile, was recorded by Asia and included on the *Aqua* album of 1992. Two other songs, "Blue Light" and "Check it Out," were recorded by Ride the Tiger, but never reused in other contexts.

Two Ride the Tiger tracks, "Love Under Fire" and "Money Talks," are included on *From the Beginning: The Greg Lake Retrospective* (1997). "Love Under Fire," featuring Lake, Downes, and Giles, sounds very much like one of Asia's more poppish songs that happens to be missing a final layer of keyboard overdubs. "Money Talks," featuring just Lake and Downes (who handled drum programming) is a very stripped down, rhythmically oriented song that features Lake's declamatory vocal, electronic drums, bass, and sporadic keyboard punctuations—something of a precursor of ELP's "Black Moon" (the track, not the album) of 1992. The same could be said of "Check it Out," which, along with "Blue Light," appears on Lake's *From the Underground, Volume II: Deeper into the Mine* (2003).

[5] Greg Lake, quoted by David Terralavoro, "The Ride the Tiger Project," *Fanzine for the Common Man*, no. 16 (December 1996): 17.
[6] Ibid., 18.

After the Ride the Tiger project, Lake's solo career once again seemed to sputter out: it took the reformation of ELP, to be discussed shortly, to bring him back into the public forum.

Carl Palmer

Considering that he is normally the most musically active ELP member during the band's sometime lengthy sabbaticals, Carl Palmer was surprisingly low profile after the dissolution of 3; he remained out of the public eye for nearly two years, from mid-1988 to mid-1990. In May 1990, however, almost precisely two years after the end of the 3 tour, Palmer agreed to join a new edition of Asia with fellow founding members Geoff Downes and John Wetton. As Steve Howe was currently involved with the quasi-Yes band Anderson, Bruford, Wakeman, Howe—who were about to merge with Trevor Rabin's Yes and collectively make the catastrophic *Union* album of 1991—another guitarist was needed, so the band recruited guitarist/vocalist Pat Thrall. Deciding that the best way to reignite their careers would be a greatest hits package with a twist, Asia entered the studio in early summer 1990 to record four new tracks to be included on the upcoming greatest hits album. In an interview with Philadelphia's WMMR-FM's John Debella in late June 1990, Palmer said of the upcoming release, "It's an album we hope will launch our careers again in America. It shows people who we were and what we are now." He added that Asia hoped to tour the U.S. in September, possibly on a college tour: "We want to go out there with another band, because we need that support since we haven't been on the road for so long."[7]

The new album, *Then and Now*, didn't have the galvanizing effect the band had hoped for; released in the U.S. on September 1, it peaked at an anemic 114 in the charts. It did produce a minor hit single, "Days Like These," which peaked at number 64 on the U.S. single charts. Due to the lukewarm reaction to *Then and Now*, plans for a U.S. tour were scrapped. However, the band did undertake a short European tour during the summer (their June 23 gig at Nottingham is captured on *Now: Live in Nottingham*, released in 1997), a short Japanese tour in September and early October, and a second short European tour in late fall. Easily the most historic show of this tour is the one played live in Moscow's Red Square on November 9. A testament to the sudden and massive influx of Western cultural forms and values into the rapidly crumbling Soviet

---

[7] Carl Palmer, quoted by David Terralavoro, "Current News," *Fanzine for the Common Man*, no. 4 (July 1990): 3. Incidentally, while Thrall toured with this incarnation of the band, he didn't appear on *Then and Now*; the band used a succession of session guitarists in the studio.

empire, Asia were the first high-profile Western rock band to play at a highly publicized event in Russia (or in any of the other Soviet states): Palmer remarked in the late nineties, "What I remember about that show is that we had [Mikhail] Gorbachev's limo and we had to wait two hours for lunch from McDonald's."[8] The concert was filmed and recorded for video and CD release; a live album of the show, *Live Mockba 09-X1-90*, was released in November 1991.

In 1991, Asia returned to the studio to record a new album. Wetton had fallen out with the band and had left; his replacement was bassist/vocalist John Payne. Thrall, too, was gone, replaced by Al Pitrelli on guitar. Palmer recorded a number of songs with the new Asia lineup, seven of which made their way onto the resulting album, *Aqua*, released in June 1992.[9] However, by then, destiny had intervened. Palmer:

> While we [Asia] were doing a tour in Germany [later November, 1990], I got a call from a man named Phil Carson. He wanted to sign ELP, and he asked if I would record some film music with Greg and Keith. Well, there wasn't any film—he just said that—although he did have a script or something. Anyway, the three of us got together and talked, and we started playing together. We worked out some ideas, and in the end, Phil said, "Look, why don't I pay you to make an album."[10]

The album Palmer refers to, *Black Moon*, marked the reformation of the original ELP after a hiatus that dated back to 1978. Of course, the reemergence of ELP left Asia without a drummer; Geoff Downes, the last remaining original member and now the leader of Asia, used Nigel Glockner and Simon Phillips as sessions drummers during the recording, and brought in Michael Sturgis to drum on the *Aqua* tour. In all honesty, Palmer's drumming on *Aqua*, following the precedent he had set with 3, is neither attention-grabbing nor particularly distinctive; there isn't very much disjunction in drumming styles from track to track. Indeed, whatever magic Asia had managed to conjure on their first and, to a much lesser extent, second and third albums had vanished. So much as the album holds any interest at all, it is for Steve Howe's guest performances on several tracks. Howe stayed on with the band briefly, participating in their U.S. tour of early 1993.

---

[8] *The Official Original Asia Members Site*, "The History of Asia," http://www.originalasia .com/history.html.
[9] According to Palmer, seven of the tracks on *Aqua* feature his drumming: the credits and liner notes don't say which. See *Fanzine for the Common Man* no. 12 (December 1992): 16.
[10] Hall, "Welcome to the Show," 50.

Reformation, Part II

ELP Again
(1991–1993)

The world Emerson, Lake and Palmer reemerged into in 1992 was very different than it was in 1972, or even 1982. As different as the seventies and eighties were in tone and feel, they were united by the specter of nuclear annihilation. That threat was much reduced after the fall of the Soviet Union and breakup of the old Soviet empire into its component nation-states in 1991, which ushered in an "era of good feelings" in the Western world and a belief that somehow history in its linear and dialectic sense was finished—an era, and an illusion, that endured for an entire decade, until it was shattered by the atrocities of September 11, 2001.[1] The West of the Bill Clinton era was in many ways eerily like the Europe of the 1890s, another period that believed it had forever passed beyond the dangers of war and revolution—prosperous, complacent, hedonistic, fixated on the pursuit of meaning in momentary sensation (which in the 1990s had taken the form of cyberspace, recreational drugs, and casual sex).[2] The chief difference is that in the 1890s, such prosperity and hedonism was mainly the province of the upper classes and the intelligentsia, while in the 1990s, it had permeated every pore of Western culture.

While the nineties more or less institutionalized sixties hedonism (most obviously exemplified by Clinton's conduct in the White House, but also manifested in the movies, music, and television of the era), it had little use for sixties utopianism. Despite—or perhaps because of—its material prosperity, the nineties was a deeply cynical period. Its most important new musical form was rap, birthed in the ghettos of urban black America during the late seventies and early eighties, which rapidly displaced rock

---

[1] For the most famous exposition of this viewpoint, see Francis Fukuyama's *The End of History and the Last Man* (New York: Free Press, 1992).

[2] Those who feel that I have the nineties wrong here may wish to check out Haynes Johnson's *The Best of Times: The Boom and Bust Years of America Before and After Everything Changed* (New York: Harcourt, 2001).

as the principal musical genre of Western youth culture during the second half of the nineties. Gangsta rap, the commercial juggernaut of nineties hip-hop culture, offers a picture-perfect snapshot of the nineties aesthetic: nervous in its staccato delivery and its intricate, incessantly repeated rhythms, defiantly obscene, enshrining megavulgarity an overriding aesthetic principle, not so much anti- as a-musical (if punk had intentionally deemphasized musicianship, rap eliminated it entirely, relying instead on programming and sampling), sometimes darkly humorous, often deeply cynical. By and large, rap has not been an idealistic music in the sense of believing itself to be an agent of social and spiritual transformation; rather, it has sought to make the evil of its world bearable by dryly commenting on it, laughing about it, or glorifying it. Indeed, Hollywood and the major record labels romanticized the black street thug and made him at least as iconic to nineties popular culture as the white mobster had been to the popular culture of the thirties. Rap typifies postmodernism not only in its rejection of idealism, but also in its rejection of originality and "progress" as conditions of authenticity. Musical "invention" and "originality" in rap is confined to the reproduction, via sampling, and the re-presentation of a plethora of preexisting musical ideas in new configurations—somewhat like perpetually moving the items in a collage into different locations.[3]

The fact is, though, that the lack of originality that has typified the postmodern era of the eighties and beyond is endemic to virtually every style of music in the Western world—prog included. By the early 1990s, progressive rock had passed through three distinct stages, and was entering a fourth. The first phase of prog was the protoprogressive rock of the late sixties, when the style of rock plied by the Nice and others was developing out of, and away from, psychedelic rock; the second was the "classic" prog of the seventies, in which ELP, of course, played a major role. The third, the British neoprogressive movement of the eighties spearheaded by Marillion, IQ, Pendragon, and others, tended to simplify the "classic" prog sound (midseventies Genesis was a particularly influential model) and give it a harder edge.[4] By the early 1990s, "neoprog" had run

---

[3] Most of the generalities I have sketched out here concerning rap could be applied to techno, the other important genre of postrock popular music. While rap responds to social tension by romanticizing black urban street life (particularly by romanticizing the lifestyle of the black urban gang member), techno is more overtly escapist, shutting out the tensions of contemporary life by voyaging deep into inner space. In its emphasis on escape within, there is certainly a connection to be made between the some aspects of the ideologies of techno and late-sixties psychedelia. Like rap (and unlike late-sixties psychedelic rock), however, techno doesn't seem to embrace the notion of *progression*—in this sense both rap and techno are clearly the product of postmodern attitudes.

[4] See Moore's *Rock: The Primary Text* for an interesting discussion of how punk impacted eighties neoprogressive.

its course, and progressive rock was beginning to undergo the bewildering fragmentation that is indicative of the postmodern condition in general. No longer a commercially viable style and with little support from the major labels, progressive music of the nineties and beyond has become a geographically diffused fringe style with a thinly spread fan base in North and South America, the U.K. and continental Europe, and Japan, supported by a network of small, independent record labels, fanzines, mail-order catalogs, internet web sites, and progressive rock festivals. What has distinguished this fourth, "postmodern" phase of prog from its predecessors is that there has been no single overriding stylistic direction; nor has creative activity been centered in a particular geographic locale.

Above all, this fourth, postmodern phase of prog has not witnessed any real stylistic breakthrough. Many younger bands single-mindedly develop the sound of a particular band (or maybe two or three) from prog's "golden age": occasionally, the results can be stunning (for instance, the two albums released by the Swedish band Änglagård during the early nineties), but far more often the result is dreadfully boring, as hundreds of bands simply copy their favorite riffs and licks from classic ELP, Yes, Genesis, King Crimson, and so on. Other bands, especially in the U.K., have chosen to continue to work in the eighties neoprogressive style; usually this is even a less satisfactory choice, since the musical style is not as rich and not as open to development. Most of the more creative bands of the period have chosen to work in what I called, in *Rocking the Classics*,[5] a postprogressive idiom, blending aspects of progressive rock with other rock or nonrock styles, be it grunge (Sweden's Anekdoten), death metal (Sweden's Death Organ), rave and trance (Britain's Ozric Tentacles), electronic ambient (Djam Karet, from the U.S.), or ECM-style spatial jazz and twentieth-century classical chamber music (my own band, Hermetic Science). In each case, "originality" lies in creating a successful new hybrid from already existing stylistic formulas rather than the creation of a genuinely new style: such is the postmodern condition of prog.[6]

Another hallmark of prog in its postmodern stage is that since it is a fringe style,[7] most young bands will sell no more than a few thousand

---

[5] *Rocking the Classics*, 211.

[6] Of course, progressive rock itself is a hybrid style. But while prog and other late-sixties styles (fusion, for instance) merged formerly distinctive traditions (rock and jazz, rock and folk, rock and the classics), which involved bringing together elements of formerly separate musical cultures, the best that the most creative nineties prog bands can do is merge formerly distinct subgenres. Unfortunately, most contemporary prog does not even attain that level of originality.

[7] Prog is more properly called a "fringe" style than an "underground" style: there is, after all, an infrastructure (albeit a very small and very informal one) to support its continued existence and dissemination.

copies of their albums—at best—and will be obliged to keep their day jobs. On the other hand, younger prog bands are under no illusion they will receive radio exposure or MTV airplay. Therefore, they are free to release what they believe in, free of commercial strictures and the vagaries of the increasingly constrictive marketplace.

One might think that a band of ELP's status would be immune from both the stylistic vagaries and the commercial pressures of prog's postmodern phase; such an assumption would not be correct. Like other founding fathers of progressive rock that continued on into the nineties, ELP had to navigate between the Scylla of endless self-quotation (in order to maintain their "progressive" credentials, and some sense of continuity with their history), and the Charybdis of commercial sellout (in order to have some chance, however remote, at radio and/or MTV airplay, and thus, the coveted and increasingly mythic hit single). As we'll see, with their two studio albums of the nineties, ELP's success in navigating between these two dangerous rocks is at best middling; but then again, the same could be said about their seventies peers who remained active into the nineties (Yes, Genesis, Jethro Tull, Pink Floyd), excepting only (and arguably) King Crimson.

If there was any one person responsible for the reformation of ELP in the early nineties, it was Phil Carson, a former Atlantic Records executive. Carson had dreamed of reuniting ELP for years: in the early eighties, he had gone to Atlantic's chief, Ahmet Ertegun, and said, "We've got these two great bands on Atlantic who haven't made a record for years and yet have sold millions of albums. Emerson, Lake and Palmer and Yes . . . These bands should be out there working."[8] As it turned out, Carson did in fact play a major role in the resurgence of Yes under Trevor Rabin's leadership in 1983; he had less luck with ELP, although he did attempt, unsuccessfully, to sign ELPowell to Atlantic in 1985 (he was outbid by Polydor).[9]

However, Carson didn't relinquish his dream of a resurrected ELP. In 1990, with the financial backing of JVC (which brought with it an automatic presence in the Japanese market), Carson formed his own label, Victory Records. He immediately set his sights on ELP. Keith Emerson recalled that after the end of the Best tour in late fall of 1990, he ran into Carson in L.A.; Carson asked Emerson if he would consider making a film score with Greg Lake and Carl Palmer. Emerson:

> So I went on to England and met up with them. [This would have been early 1991.] We booked a rehearsal place for about two weeks. We went over all the

---

[8] Phil Carson, quoted by Chris Welch, *Close to the Edge: The Story of Yes* (London: Omnibus Press, 2000), 204.
[9] Ibid.

old material for the first couple of days, things like *Tarkus*, to get back into shape. I started coming up with some ideas for Greg to consider. Phil came over, and after hearing us, he said, "I have a proposition to make to you. I have this new record label. I love the material that you're doing. How do you feel about doing an album?"[10]

Emerson agreed, with one caveat: any new ELP studio album would have to be produced by an outside producer. Emerson remarked, "I didn't want to get into arguments with Greg or Carl, but it was very important that everybody's role should be clear . . . if we had a producer, we would leave it to him to produce and not interfere."[11] Emerson suggested Kevin Gilbert; Lake and Palmer, however, wanted a producer who had never worked with any of them, and who therefore could be trusted to be completely impartial. After interviewing several prospective candidates, the band chose an American producer, Mark Mancina, a longtime ELP fan. Mancina eventually earned the respect of all three musicians to the point that when the time for final mixdown came, he asked for suggestions, jotted down notes, and then did the mixing without the band being present. For Emerson, at least, Mancina's role as producer "made the process of doing an album much more pleasurable than it had been in the past."[12] Lake's feelings on the matter were more ambiguous; but that's a story for later on.

Much like the very first ELP album of more than two decades prior, most of the tracks of the new album, *Black Moon*, existed in other guises before rehearsals for the new album began. "Paper Blood" and "Affairs of the Heart" originated in the Lake-Downes Ride the Tiger Project; "Romeo and Juliet," "Close to Home," and "Changing States" were drawn from Emerson's unreleased 1989-90 solo album. As rehearsals progressed through a four-month period in early 1991, these five tracks were reworked, some more radically than others, to make them appropriate for ELP; the band also generated three new songs, "Black Moon," "Farewell to Arms," and "Better Days," and arranged a song by Mark Mancina, "Burning Bridges," and a new Greg Lake ballad, "Footprints in the Snow." Because of the relatively high proportion of preexisting material and the relatively simple, non-epic nature of much of the new music (at least by ELP standards), the band was able to begin recording during spring 1991, soon after rehearsals had begun, working both in London (Marcus Studios), where much of the initial recording was done, and in L.A. (SIR and Conway Studios), where finishing touches were added.

---

[10] Keith Emerson, quoted by Doerschuk, "Keith Emerson and ELP Again," 50.

[11] Ibid., 52.

[12] Ibid.

In early 1992, the band (which now included Stewart Young, who had been rehired to his old manager's position by ELP) began preparations for a world tour to support the release of the new album, *Black Moon*. Featuring a drawing of an eighteenth-century carousel on its cover, *Black Moon* was released on June 9 in the U.S.[13] In Japan, JVC released the album with a bonus track—a short, attractive Keith Emerson piece for solo piano entitled "A Blade of Grass."

As was now becoming usual with each release, the album featured some new hardware. Most radically, Carl Palmer, continuing a direction already becoming apparent on *To the Power of Three*, went over to a completely electronic drum sound:

> For the *Black Moon* album I struck a kit of Remo drums consisting of two 14" x 22" bass drums, 8" x 12" and 12" x 14" rack toms, 16" x 16" and 16" x 18" floor toms, and a 4" x 14" Noble and Cooley Zildjian Alloy snare drum. I say "struck" rather than "played," because when we recorded the album, all of my drums were filled with foam and then triggered with Simmons triggers. That's right, I had no acoustic drums at all—only sampled sounds. I had made all the samples myself over time, so it's hard to say where they all came from.[14]

To trigger the samples, Palmer used three Simmons and four Dauz pads. He continued to use Paiste cymbals. The elaborate menagerie of tuned and untuned percussion that had been integral to Palmer's work with ELP during the seventies was conspicuous by its absence during the *Black Moon* era.

Emerson's equipment changes were more modest in scope, and quite different in aim, than Palmer's. He had become concerned about how conventional his keyboards, with their typically late-eighties digital sonorities, had sounded on *To the Power of Three*, and he sought to reintegrate many of his old analog sounds—and in some cases, his old analog hardware—into his setup. Again working with Will Alexander (who by now had become not only his chief keyboard technician, but also his personal manager), Emerson concentrated especially on discreetly updating the sound of his Hammond C-3 by blending it, via MIDI, with the digital Hammond XB-2. As Emerson said, "In effect, we blended the analog Hammond to the digital one. I think I can honestly say that I've pretty much perfected that sound now."[15] While many of his long-term fans

---

[13] According to the *Return of the Manticore* box set, the *Black Moon* material was recorded in "Spring 1991." No one that I've asked has ever cogently explained why there was a lapse of several months between the completion of recording and the beginning of tour preparations. Was the *Black Moon* material recorded throughout 1991?

[14] Carl Palmer, quoted in "Ask a Pro," *Modern Drummer*, May 1995, 16.

[15] Keith Emerson, quoted by Doerschuk, "ELP Again," 52. Emerson's explanation of how the C-3 and XB-2 sounds are MIDIed is rather technical: interested readers can consult this article for details.

continue to prefer the "tacky" C-3 sound of the first four ELP albums—the Hammond sound on *Black Moon* is just a bit "clean" for my ears—it does have a lot of body, and it must be admitted the Hammond sounds better here than at any time since *Trilogy*. Emerson also MIDIed a Minimoog into his two main digital keyboards of choice on this album, a Roland JD-800 and a Korg 01/W, to recapture some of the heroic trumpet colors and searing pseudo-guitar timbres of days gone by. Will Alexander and Gene Stopp, an expert in analog synthesizer restoration, even restored Emerson's old modular Moog so that he could tour with it—although, as far as I can tell, it wasn't used on the *Black Moon* album itself.[16]

Black Moon

The first song on the album is the Emerson-Lake-Palmer penned title track, "Black Moon," at 6:56 the album's longest track. Depending on your point of view, "Black Moon" represents (a) the logical conclusion of the trend towards a massive, austere, stripped-down sound that began developing with ELPowell, or (b) the reduction *ad absurdum* of that sound. Certainly, it is one of the most harmonically static ELP tracks ever; not only is nearly all of the song centered in E minor, much of it is centered on a single open fifth, E–B, with any chord movement at all being the exception. Likewise, the vaunted ELP metric complexity is nowhere in evidence here; much of the music is organized around the ponderous, thumping two-bar bass/drums riff in 4/4 first annunciated at 0:49. Lake's lyric prophesies dire warnings of a coming environmental apocalypse. Much of the imagery comes from the Gulf War of early 1991: "I was watching the television one day, and I saw this report about all these oilfields being set alight, and this picture had the sun blacked out by all this smoke, but you could still see it and it looked like a moon, and then a black moon, and that started me thinking."[17]

Despite the strong continuity provided by the E minor tonality and the ponderous, ubiquitous two-bar riff, it's possible to hear "Black Moon" falling into six discrete sections. The song begins with a brooding, atmospheric "overture" that recalls the introductions of both "The

---

[16] Emerson brought the modular Moog with him on the Best tour; it was restored immediately thereafter. The restoration of Emerson's modular system, which had seen no use since the demise of ELP after the *Works* tour and had actually been left outside an entire winter in Buffalo, is a rather interesting story. See Mark Vail, "The World's Most Dangerous Synth," *Keyboard*, June 1992, 51.

[17] Greg Lake, quoted in the official press release for *Black Moon* (April 25, 1992), reprinted in *ELP Digest* 2, no. 10 (May 1, 1992).

Endless Enigma" and "Pirates": a drone on A, accompanying sparse, chromatic string synth lines, moves (at 0:28) into an ominous drone on E which serves as a backdrop for nervous atonal piano runs. At 0:42, a persistent rhythm featuring an odd electronic timbre—almost like an old-fashioned cash register—prefigures the rhythm of the bass/drums riff, which kicks in at 0:49, signaling the second section of the song. At 1:01 we hear the keyboard refrain—an elemental trumpetlike synth melody that overlays four repetitions of the bass/drums riff. Emerson recalls,

> Greg and Carl were hammering out this heavy, solid rock thing. Without saying a word, I went up to the keyboard and struck this chord. That prompted me to do the main figure of the song. Next thing I know is that Greg and Carl are going "That's great! Do that again!" I looked at them in disbelief and said "That? Is that all you want?" There were lots of times when I had to be held back from doing too much in the very early stages.[18]

At 1:26 Lake commences the first vocal verse; although the vocal melody is very elemental, the verse adds a tiny bit of harmonic variety to the song by ending on a C major synth chord in first inversion, thus momentarily breaking off the E drone of the bass/drums riff. After several more keyboard refrains and vocal verses, we reach the bridge at 2:51; the sudden shift to an F#-major chord ("in the night") after the long stretch of E-minor harmony is startling. The harmony slips back into E at 2:58 ("fire on the mountains"), while Emerson quietly introduces into the sonic background the two-bar "fugue subject" that is to become increasingly important throughout the remainder of the song.

The third section of the song is commenced at 3:23 with a quiet synth "accordion" break—a G-major arpeggio over a drone C—accompanied by some nice cymbal work by Palmer. At 3:34 the ubiquitous pounding riff returns, as does the "fugue subject" at 3:40. This flutelike theme doesn't behave like a real fugue subject; instead, it's simply repeated a number of times, with a new "countersubject" layered in every two bars. Before this "fugue" section can come to a climax, though, it's interrupted by a recapitulation of the vocal verse (4:11), then the keyboard refrain (4:35): this is the fourth section. At 4:59, a second "accordion" break—quietly alternating E-minor and A-major synth "accordion" chords, accompanied by some nice snare and electronic "timpani" fills—commences the song's fifth section. At 5:11 the "fugue subject" returns, this time accompanied by a series of four-bar countersubjects that are progressively layered in (5:24, 5:36, 5:48). The increasingly dense layer of counterpoint seems on the verge of petering out by 6:00, but at 6:07 the final section of the song

---

[18] Keith Emerson, quoted by Doerschuk, "ELP Again," 53.

begins when the band launch into a four-bar bass ostinato of ascending half notes (G–A–B–C♯, B–C♯–D–E), not dissimilar to the one that dominates "Aquatarkus," over which Emerson takes an increasingly frenzied Hammond solo, until the song grinds to a sudden halt at 6:56.

Almost immediately we're swept into the second track, another minimalistic, hard-rocking number, "Paper Blood." Again cowritten by Emerson, Lake and Palmer, "Paper Blood" provides the lyrics of the Lake-Downes song "Money Talks" (from the Ride the Tiger project) with a new chorus and totally different music. If "Black Moon" took on environmental apocalypse, "Paper Blood" addresses the follies of hypermaterialism. Lake:

> I was driving in London one day and I stopped at a traffic light and on the right side of me was a chauffeur-driven car with a dog in it on the front passenger seat and the man was driving with a chauffeur's hat on. On the left of me there was a tramp fishing for stuff out of the dustbin, looking for food. This ridiculous sight stuck with me for days: the dog being chauffeur-driven and the man looking in the dustbin for food. And I thought, what is that about? And the answer is money; the lack of it and too much of it, and then I thought, it's like blood, money is like blood, paper blood. That was the catalyst for the song.[19]

Although "Paper Blood" is similar to "Black Moon" in being harmonically static and metrically simple, the two songs draw on different sources: if "Black Moon" is ultramodern in its metal-like riff and almost raplike electronic back beat, "Paper Blood" mines the blues, even featuring a couple of short harmonica breaks by Lake. It's also structurally simpler than "Black Moon." Other than the five second Hammond intro, there's really only two musical ideas: the eight-bar Hammond/bass blues riff first heard at 0:05, which accompanies the vocal chorus, and the eight-bar vocal verse, first heard at 0:26, which is supported by alternating G-minor and C-major organ chords.

Lake's pithy lyrics are probably the best thing about "Paper Blood." The static G-minor harmony and the two eight-bar musical ideas that evoke pedestrian late-sixties blues-rock (think Deep Purple or Atomic Rooster) simply aren't up to successfully sustaining a song of 4:26. Even Emerson's frenzied Hammond solo over the riff at the end, which develops (or devolves, depending on your point of view) into "Rondo"-like aural assaults, isn't enough to fully kick the song into gear. I've lived with "Paper Blood" for over a decade now; my assessment of it has not substantially changed. While I initially took a similarly dim view of "Black

---

[19] Greg Lake, quoted in official press release for *Black Moon*, reprinted in *ELP Digest* 2, no. 10 (May 1, 1992).

Moon," my opinion of it has somewhat improved over time. Viewed strictly from a harmonic or metric perspective, "Black Moon" doesn't have a lot more going for it than "Paper Blood." In other ways, though, "Black Moon" is more musically rewarding. Certainly it has a greater variety of melodic material and textural and dynamics shifts. Furthermore, Palmer achieves some very interesting electronic timbres: the "cash register" sounds at 0:43, the odd "industrial" percussion fills at 3:41 and 4:54, the "backwards" drum sounds of 3:51, 3:57, 4:03 and elsewhere. Some of Emerson's digital synth effects are similarly interesting: the swirling chords at 2:56, the industrial roars at 3:03, 3:32, and 6:05. Lake ends nearly every iteration of the two-bar riff with a different E-minor pentatonic bass fill: some of these are quite creative (especially the one at 2:00), and nearly all of them are expertly doubled by Palmer. What "Black Moon" sacrifices in harmonic and metric subtlety (which is, admittedly, quite a lot), it regains—to some extent, at least—by attention to timbral, rhythmic, and textural detail.

The third track, "Affairs of the Heart," cowritten by Lake and Geoff Downes, marks a return to Lake's acoustic ballad style of the seventies. Indeed, Emerson remarked, "I suggested that this could be the new 'Lucky Man,' so we made a more acoustic arrangement of it than the one he had done with Geoff. Geoff's arrangement was great, but it was very horn-like, with a lot of synth padding."[20] Lake's lyrics, about a short-lived love affair, mark a return to the pretty romanticism that marked his earlier work:

> I was there [Venice] on a holiday and Venice is such a beautiful and romantic setting, a lovely place and full of art and a history of art, so it's just a great environment to write a song. There is a hotel there called the Danieli, and in the lobby is this huge and beautiful chandelier, and there was a beautiful girl sitting across the other side of the lobby and for some reason it all added up— Venice, the chandelier, the girl. The whole opening of the song just wrote itself, there and then.[21]

By 1991, Lake had lost some of the bell-like clarity of his upper vocal range that had made his singing of his acoustic ballads so compelling in his earlier days; this being said, "Affairs of the Heart" is a pretty song, and Lake turns in an admirably poignant performance. I'm reminded a bit of "Lend Your Love to Me Tonight"; while "Affairs" lacks that song's rich suspended chords, it does have something that "Lend Your Love" lacks— namely, a credible bridge section.

---

[20] Keith Emerson, quoted by Doerschuk, "ELP Again," 53.

[21] Greg Lake, quoted in *Black Moon* official press release, *ELP Digest* 2, no. 10 (May 1, 1992).

In fact, it is the bridge section that really makes "Affairs" work. The eight-bar verse (from 0:11) consists simply of strummed E major and A major chords; the first half of the eight-bar refrain (from 0:34), strummed B major and A major chords. (The second half of the refrain, reached at the "Affairs of the Heart" lyric, repeats the chords of the verse.) The bridge, however, reached at 1:45, relies on Lake's characteristic modal mixing, with its G major–D major–G major–A major progression, and summons that bittersweet tang and hint of sadness that had effectively raised lumps in so many throats in Lake's ballads of an earlier era.

The arrangement is effective, too. After a full verse and refrain in which Lake's voice and acoustic guitar are featured in a solo role, Emerson slowly begins to layer in subtle keyboard colorings: a flutelike arabesque (1:08) a wordless female synth vocalese (1:22), synth strings (1:44), beautiful piano backing during the bridge, and synth accordion during the re-transition to the verse (2:13). While some of these figures occur more than once, Emerson is careful not to overwhelm the song. In a testament to his growth in arrangement subtlety since the recording of "Still . . . You Turn Me On" some eighteen years earlier, he does not continually layer new parts in, but rather carefully withdraws some parts even as he adds others. Carl Palmer, too, exercises admirable restraint, even as he contributes to the song's sense of growth by adding some sedate and understated drumming when the verse returns after the bridge. For Lake's fans who had missed his acoustic ballad style throughout the eighties, "Affairs of the Heart" was a welcome return to form.

The fourth track is an arrangement of the "Dance of the Knights" section of Sergei Prokofiev's ballet score *Romeo and Juliet* (1936)—simply entitled "Romeo and Juliet" for purposes of the album. We have already encountered Prokofiev in our survey of the ELP oeuvre; while "Enemy God" is an early work, much influenced by Stravinsky's *Rite* and primitivism, *Romeo and Juliet* exemplifies his neoclassical phase, with its clearcut (albeit sometimes angular) melodies and simple but unexpectedly juxtaposed chords. While ELP's arrangement of "Enemy God" had worked quite well, their arrangement of "Romeo and Juliet" extends the streak of less-than-stellar arrangements—which began with ELPowell's "Mars" and was extended by 3's "Eight Miles High"—into the nineties. While part of the problem may be that "Dance of the Knights" is simply a weaker piece of music than "Enemy God," I think ELP's arrangement itself is also part of the problem: like "Eight Miles High," the track comes off as clinical and a bit turgid. To be sure, "Romeo and Juliet" is better than "Eight Miles High," and contributes some nice details: I like the synth pizzicato strings during the D minor episode at 0:55, the gloomy Hammond organ tremolo prior to the reentry of the main theme in E minor at 1:45, and the screaming finale of his synthesizer solo from 3:06 to 3:11.

I'm afraid the culprits here are Lake and Palmer. All of ELP's great classical arrangements of the seventies were driven by Palmer's nimble, melodically inventive drumming, with his clever rhythmic doublings of key thematic material; here he simply pounds out an obnoxiously heavy electronic backbeat, occasionally adding some simple fills, with predictably disastrous results. Lake's plodding and formulaic bass lines likewise add little to the arrangement. In my opinion, the version recorded by Emerson for his solo album in 1989 and released on *Changing States* in 1995 is superior. Although it's shorter and doesn't have all the orchestration subtleties made possible by his *Black Moon* studio set up, Emerson's rhythm section of anonymous session players provide the 1989 recording with an energy and sense of urgency that's lacking in the ELP arrangement. The use of electric guitar to subtly "heavy up" parts of the arrangement on the 1989 recording is another nice touch that the ELP arrangement unwisely eschews. Emerson has been quoted saying he was initially drawn to "Romeo and Juliet" because it reminded him of Jimi Hendrix's "Purple Haze."[22] While it's possible to hear the connection when listening to the Emerson recording of 1989, the ELP arrangement of "Romeo and Juliet" is simply too plodding to ever evoke Hendrix.

The album's fifth track, "Farewell to Arms," cowritten by Emerson and Lake, brings to a logical culmination a certain strand of songwriting—stately, hymnlike, inspirational—that was developing in both men's output during the eighties. Lake's "It's You, You've Got to Believe," Emerson's "On My Way Home," and especially ELPowell's "Lay Down Your Guns" are all obvious antecedents, as are Procol Harum's great rock anthems of the late sixties; unlike so many Emerson-Lake songs of the past, this represents such a thoroughgoing collaboration that it's hard to say who contributed what. Set in D major, the song clearly reveals the deepening and darkening of Lake's vocal tessitura: when he sang songs like this in the seventies (think "Jerusalem") he sang them in F, a minor third higher. Lake's wistful pro-peace lyrics ("antiwar" just isn't the right phrase)—so much more direct that his lyrics for *Tarkus* some twenty years earlier—may sound a bit naïve now in our post 9/11/01 world, but their sense of cautious hope prevent them from sounding too dated, and they definitely evoke the zeitgeist of Europe after the fall of the Berlin Wall in 1991.

Like the previous tracks of *Black Moon*, "Farewell to Arms" eschews the complex mazes of shifting meters and modulations that characterize vintage ELP: what enables it to work musically is its effective instrumental buildups, dramatic shifts of vocal tessitura at key moments, and discreet modal mixing that adds just enough harmonic variety to prevent bore-

---

[22] Doerschuk, "ELP Again," 60.

dom. It begins with a short pseudo-string orchestral introduction in A (modal major) that has virtually nothing to do with the rest of the song; indeed, the use of short "throwaway" intros becomes a somewhat annoying mannerism on *Black Moon*. Lake's first verse (0:25) is initially accompanied by quiet, hymnlike organ; a flowing piano accompaniment enters at 0:42, bass enters at the end of the verse (1:04), and a trademark pressed snare roll by Palmer initiates the "farewell to arms" refrain at 1:10. In an admirable show of restraint, Palmer sits out the remainder of the first refrain; a particularly nice touch is the conjunction of Lake's strummed guitar chords (which momentarily become the song's rhythmic backbone) and Emerson's melancholy, string orchestralike backing. A quasi-timpani flourish at the end of the refrain (1:45) ushers in the second verse, during which Palmer launches an understated rock groove and Emerson layers in piano and synth string backing.

It's the second refrain that drives the song to its climax. At 2:50 Lake suddenly shifts his vocal line up an octave. He now has to strain to hit these notes that were once a normal part of his range, and when he squarely hits the high notes of "we're all sharing this earth at the end of the day" the effect is galvanizing—somewhat like a singer successfully hitting "land of the free" at the end of the American national anthem. Immediately, before any energy is squandered, the band kicks into the "down this road" bridge, where borrowed (B♭ major and C major) chords lend some harmonic variety to the staunchly diatonic harmony of the verse and refrain; the bridge, in turn, is followed by a partly instrumental restatement of the refrain and, from 4:10, a lyrical, guitarlike Emerson synth solo (it's a Minimoog MIDIed to the Korg 01/W) over the chord changes of the verse. As the song begins to fade around 5:00, the synth solo is still unwinding; the last sounds we hear, as the song fades away, is the unmistakable whooshes of Emerson's trademark Hammond organ raking. "Farewell to Arms" may lack the energy and drive of "Jerusalem," but its stateliness and sense of agreeable calm bring the inspirational, anthemic vein evident in a segment of both Emerson's and Lake's music of the eighties to a new level of maturity.

Black Moon was the first ELP album not to be released in a vinyl LP format; it was available only as a CD or cassette. Not having a CD player at the time (I got my first one six months later, in December 1992), I purchased it on cassette: I therefore grew used to thinking about the album in terms of "side one" and "side two." The all-instrumental sixth track of the album, "Changing States," leads off side two of the cassette. It is, without question, the album's high point.

"Changing States" was first recorded by Emerson in 1989 for his solo album; you can hear this 1989 recording, retitled "Another Frontier," on his *Changing States* album of 1995. A triumphant piece in the spirit of the Moog-and-Hammond rock marches of "Karn Evil 9, 3rd Impression,"

"Changing States" was meant as a musical evocation of the fall of the Berlin Wall, thus continuing the thematic substance of "Farewell to Arms." Emerson composed the piece in a kind of rondo form, where statements of the main theme alternate with episodes of contrasting material; about halfway through the piece is a full-fledged fugue, with the fugue subject being based on the main theme. However, when he submitted this version of the piece to the band during the 1991 recording sessions, Lake and Palmer weren't enthused about the fugal episode:

> When I took it back to the band and played it with Greg and Carl, the fugal development didn't work out. There were lots of spaces in it that left Greg and, I guess, Carl feeling uncomfortable . . . there were a few gaps in the piece where there were no parts for them to play at all . . . I think they felt embarrassed at the thought that they'd be standing around on their own during some of those sections. Since it was important to project this as a piece for the whole band, I changed those parts.[23]

I know a number of ELP fans who feel that the 1989 version of the piece is superior to the *Black Moon* recording. From a purely formal compositional standpoint, their assertion may be arguable. From a standpoint of performance, however, the 1991 version of the piece blows away the 1989 recording. The reason? On this piece, unlike "Romeo and Juliet," Greg Lake and Carl Palmer fully apply themselves to the details of the arrangement and, above all, play like Greg Lake and Carl Palmer were once known to play. The results are breathtaking.

"Changing States" begins with a slow, dreamy, fantasialike Emerson solo that uses a pipe organ–like synth patch; the music drifts through a number of fragmentary themes and unfocused chord progressions that only gradually establish a C-major tonality. The music suddenly snaps into focus at 0:42, however, when Emerson sounds a dramatic synth trumpet fanfare in C minor; this leads to the first statement of the A section at 0:53. In the tradition of his work on *Brain Salad Surgery*, Emerson plays a melodically active left hand chord progression of straight quarter notes using a breathy synth patch (on the 1989 recording he played this part on Hammond); with his right hand he plays the complex trumpetlike main theme (first heard at 1:03) using a Minimoog MIDIed to a Roland JD-800. Emerson's unusually constructed main theme consists of four three-bar phrases of 4/4 followed by a four-bar phrase of 3/4; the juxtaposition of quadruple and triple meter generates the kind of polyrhythmic energy that had once been a hallmark of ELP. Harmonic interest is provided, meanwhile, by the modulation to E major from C major at the end of the

---

[23] Keith Emerson, quoted by Doerschuk, "ELP Again," 60.

third 4/4 phrase, and the return to C major during the 3/4 phrase. Palmer's well-conceived drum part marshals the polyrhythmic potential of this unusual phrase structure; note his characteristic one-TWO-three-four-ONE-two-three-FOUR-one-two-THREE-FOUR accents during the three-bar phrases in 4/4. While Lake's bass line is mostly rhythmic, contributing a great deal of forward push with its throbbing eighth-sixteenth-sixteenth-note motion, his thundering descending scalar riffs at the end of each statement of the main theme (listen at 1:43, for instance) add a lot of energy to the arrangement. The first statement of the main theme lasts from 1:03 to 1:36; the second, from 1:36 to 2:02.

The first contrasting theme (or B section) begins at 2:03; the texture thins a bit to feature Emerson's Hammond, Lake's offbeat bass accents, and Palmer's eighth-note ride cymbal part and excellent rhythmic doublings of Emerson's figurines. While the tonality shifts here to A^b major from the previous section's C major, Emerson retains the unusual phrase structure pattern—two three-bar phrases of 4/4 are followed by four bars of 3/4—as well as the edgy accents: the three-bar phrases of 4/4 sound like a bar of four, a bar of six, and a bar of two. The A section returns at 2:35; after Lake sounds another statement of the plunging bass riff at 2:43, Emerson again commences the main theme, but this time accompanies it with a reedy melodic counterpoint rather than the chordal accompaniment of its first two statements.

The C section begins at 3:13 with a rising sequential development of the main theme that passes through several keys and features some daunting offbeat accents; again we note some excellent melodic bass counterpoint by Lake at 3:19. The "fugue" of the original version would have begun at 3:29; here Emerson returns to the pipe organ patch of the track's opening, and instead of developing the main theme fugally, he develops it melodically and rhythmically, pulling it through a complex maze of shifting meters with the aid of Lake and Palmer. At 3:43 the main theme is heard yet again, and the music returns from the tonal uncertainty of the previous section into the glowing simplicity of C major.

The band commence the final contrasting section (that is, the D section) at 4:03. Featuring a more lyrical, less driving theme than the other episodes, the tonality now shifts to E^b major, although the theme's third phrase momentarily drifts back into C major (listen from 4:23 to 4:34). The unusual phrase structures continue: two five-bar phrases of 4/4 followed by two six-bar phrases of 4/4. This theme is repeated a second time beginning at 4:47 with some new Hammond organ figuration; it seems to be petering out by 5:25. Suddenly, at 5:38, ELP launch into one final statement of the A section. This time we don't hear the main theme—Emerson only plays the chordal left hand accompaniment figure—and we don't really need to, as Carl Palmer's ferocious double-time kit groove becomes the focus of attention and drives the piece to an almost delirious climax. When Emerson pauses on an A♭ major chord before sounding the final victorious C major triad at the end, it sounds like he's intentionally evoking the distinctive vibrato of the Yamaha GX-1.

"Changing States" is a *tour de force*. It is especially bracing when heard in its context on the album. The tempo of the entire first half of the album had been a bit too plodding for comfort, and "Changing States" brings a badly needed dose of high-octane energy; one notes, too, that there's as much tonal movement in "Changing States" as in the first five tracks combined. While Lake's and Palmer's very nonchalant and nondescript performance on "Romeo and Juliet" had raised some troubling questions, their playing on "Changing States" demonstrated to fans and critics alike that ELP were still capable of the effortless virtuosity that had defined their best music of the seventies. As detailed as I have been in my analysis of "Changing States," I've had to leave out a number of wonderful subtleties contributed by both Lake and Palmerto the arrangement: for instance, check out Palmer's virtuosic flourishes at 2:18, 3:22, 4:03, 4:17, and 5:00 and the tight bass/drums lick at 4:45–4:46. Compositionally, "Changing States" works very well, as Emerson single-mindedly develops the melodic, rhythmic, and harmonic potential of his main theme to excellent effect. "Changing States" is a track that will repay repeated listening.

The album's seventh track is a song written for the band by producer Mark Mancina called "Burning Bridges." Emerson recalls, "He wrote it with ELP in mind. Because Mark had played a lot of our music in his earlier days, he felt that this would be fitting for ELP today [1992]. When I heard it, it was uncanny because it felt like something I would have written myself. It fit the band totally."[24] I would have to ditto Emerson's assessment. Mancina was obviously a scholar of the ELP style: "Burning Bridges" contains several hallmarks of classic ELP, used with admirable subtlety, that were notably lacking in the album's previous songs.

"Burning Bridges" opens with a thirty second instrumental prelude which, like the opening of "Changing States," seems to gradually assemble itself out of discrete musical fragments: a quietly pulsing E♭ bass guitar note, a repeatedly strummed E♭ major acoustic guitar chord, a nervous, syncopated, percussive Hammond ostinato (from 0:08), and a pulsing string synth chord (foregrounded by 0:21). The quartal harmony that results from the confluence of the Hammond and synth string setting, E♭–F–B♭–E♭–A♭–D♭, is vintage Emerson.

Thereafter, the song is dominated by three musical ideas. The verse, first heard at 0:30, is almost folksonglike in its irregular phrase structure and alternating bars of 6/4 and 4/4; in fact, when Lake first sings the

---

[24] Keith Emerson, quoted by Doerschuk, "ELP Again," 64.

verse, Emerson doubles his melody in parallel fifths on the Hammond, further emphasizing its folklike character. After a second verse (at 0:50), the chorus is reached at 1:15. To the casual listener the chorus is especially memorable for Lake's angelic vocal harmonies on the "burn the bridges down" segment; on a more analytic level, I'm struck that Mancina creates a series of dichotomies between the verse and chorus that hearken back to the songwriting approach of classic ELP, especially to their *Trilogy* era. (Indeed, the stately pace of this song is a bit reminiscent of "The Endless Enigma.") For instance, the verse is modal (Mixolydian), while the chorus is diatonic major; the verse is centered in $E^\flat$, the chorus in $D^\flat$; the verse feels rough hewn with its irregular phrase structures and shifting meters, while the chorus conveys a feeling of elegance with its gorgeous vocal harmonies and smooth rhythms.

The third important musical idea is the instrumental ritornello that follows the chorus at 1:38. Dominated by Emerson's Hammond, this ritornello borrows another trick from *Trilogy* (specifically from "The Endless Enigma"): the $D^\flat$ major of the chorus is enharmonically reinterpreted as $C^\sharp$ major, which allows the music to explore keys that are far distant from the home key of $E^\flat$ major. In particular, the ritornello tends to pause dramatically on an E major triad ($^\flat$III of $C^\sharp$); one first hears this pause on an E major triad at 1:48, and, in the tradition of much of Emerson's best music, E ends up becoming a disruptive force, a rival tonic to the original tonic, $E^\flat$.

The second half of the song retraces the verse-chorus-ritornello construction of the first half with some variations and extensions. The verse (1:50) and chorus (2:15) are repeated—check out the cool effect that sounds like Lake singing the "burn the bridges down" segment through a transistor radio at 2:40. A longer statement of the ritornello commences at 2:43; it pauses on an E major chord at 3:00, and then swings directly into a heroic, Moog-like synth solo over the chord changes of the chorus, here transposed into E major. At 3:24 the chorus returns in its original key, now more richly orchestrated than ever. From 3:48 on we're treated to a number of statements of the instrumental ritornello, which deliver several more pleasant surprises: a series of angular drum breaks by Palmer from 3:48 to 3:58, the closest he comes to a "drum solo" anywhere on the album, a funky Hammond solo by Emerson featuring the stuttering repetitions of a single note that he had begun to favor in the late eighties (listen at 4:04, for instance), some heroic Moog-like synth leads, and finally, at 4:30, as the song grinds to a halt on an E major triad, the most deliciously grungy timbre that Emerson had wrung out of his Hammond since *Trilogy*.

Does "Burning Bridges" measure up to the *Trilogy* material it's obviously based on? Not quite. The transition from the verse to the chorus always struck me as a bit forced; after the synth solo, I find myself expecting an even more climactic passage featuring new material rather than a return of the same old chorus. Then there's Mark Mancina's lyric: despite some evocative imagery (I especially like the bit about rain scarring the mountainside), the images don't really add up to anything meaningful. Having said all this, "Burning Bridges" is an eminently listenable song, closer to classic ELP than any of the album's previous songs in its subtle use of shifting tonal centers and irregular phrase structures. If nothing else, the song is worth the price of admission simply for Emerson's gloriously grungy Hammond sound and Lake's angelic vocal harmonies.

The eighth track is a Keith Emerson solo piano composition, "Close to Home." Described by Emerson himself as "George Winston meets Rachmaninov,"[25] "Close to Home" went through three distinct incarnations: first as a synth piece, then as a piano piece with subtle string synth and acoustic guitar accompaniment (this is how Emerson recorded it for his 1989-90 solo project), and finally in the solo piano version recorded at Conway Studios in Los Angeles and released on *Black Moon*. What to say about the piece? Well, Emerson's description is actually rather apt. It's lyrical, featuring flexible, flowing rhythms, smooth melodies, and rather little dissonance; mostly quiet (although there's a couple of big climaxes featuring plunging scales); and romantic in sentiment. It is not modernist, nor is it a virtuoso showstopper.

Emerson casts the piece in a variation of rondo form known as sonata-rondo form: in this case, A–B–A–C–A′–B1–A–C–A.[26] Unlike Classic period composers such as Mozart and Beethoven whose movements in sonata-rondo form often tend to use contrasting themes for each section, Emerson's themes seem to naturally flow out of each other. The gentle, dreamy A theme is heard twice at the beginning (the second repetition begins at 0:25). The B section, which surges forward just a bit more, falls into two halves; the first at 0:46, the second (featuring flowing sixteenth notes in the left hand) at 1:07. The A theme returns at 1:20; an extension (from 1:44) flows into the C theme (at 1:57), with plunging scale figures that bring the piece to its first climax. As the climax ebbs away, Emerson launches into a variation of the A theme—the texture is thickened, the accompaniment made more active—at 2:12. This is followed by a development of the first half of the B theme (at 2:41), then its second half (at 2:58), climaxing with a jagged transformation of the tail of the A section at 3:10. The music soon grows calm; a more literal recapitulation of the A section commences at 3:27. Its extension is a bit different this time, leading into a final return of the C section and its plunging scale figures at 4:01, which bring the piece to its

---

[25] Keith Emerson, quoted by Doerschuk, "ELP Again," 62.
[26] In strict rondo form, only the A section returns.

third and final climax. "Close to Home" ends with a quiet statement of the A theme head at 4:18.

"Close to Home" is a tasteful, well-crafted piece, and a lot of Emerson's fans adore it. I wish I shared their enthusiasm: unfortunately, I don't. Unlike the sturdily diatonic harmony of the piano intro of "On My Way Home" or the modal harmony of "Dream Runner" (both pieces of which I'm very fond), "Close to Home" features a kind of chromatic harmony typical of nineteenth-century composers like Chopin or Rachmaninov—check out the frequent ♭II–V progressions (1:13–1:15 is the first) and the parallel ascending major triads (2:58-3:02), for instance. However, unlike Chopin or Rachmaninov, whose chromatic harmony results in frequent key changes and therefore generates a sense of dynamic tonal movement, the tonality of "Close to Home" is anchored in D♭ major almost all the way through—the only modulations involve two brief forays into B♭ major at the beginning of the B sections, at 0:46 and 2:41. For me, the combination of continuous chromatic harmony and static tonality becomes cloying after a while—it reminds me too much of the overly sentimental harmonies of the "sweet" dance bands (say Guy Lombardo's) of the thirties and forties. However, I do not dispute it is a lovely little piece for listeners who don't mind this particular aspect of it.

"Better Days," an Emerson-Lake collaboration, is the ninth track. It draws on two very different stylistic sources—the stately, somewhat melancholy rock hymns of Procol Harum (which seemed to exert a fairly pervasive influence on Emerson during the late eighties and early nineties) and Stevie Wonder–inspired seventies funk—and welds them into a surprisingly cohesive whole. Lake's lyrics are based on an event Emerson related to him about anonymously giving a homeless lady a large sum of money: they cover some of the same ground as "Touch and Go," but from a more optimistic (and personal) perspective.[27] Like too many other songs on *Black Moon*, "Better Days" begins with a largely irrelevant intro featuring "street noise" and soft synth string chords. Once the body of the song is reached at 0:18, though, it is characterized by the combination of rhythmic drive and structural intricacy that has characterized ELP's best work all the way through their career.

"Better Days" is built around four distinct sectional blocks: the verse, a transitional vocal episode, the chorus, and a lengthy, hymnlike Hammond organ theme. The verse, in turn, is based on the two-bar Stevie Wonder–like pseudo-Clavinet riff (it's actually played on a Roland JD-800) first annunciated at 0:18. At 0:27, Emerson layers in a bell-like pentatonic synth theme over the "Clavinet" riff; this pentatonic theme returns often in between the stanzas of the verses.

---

[27] For the full story on the lyrics, see Doerschuk, "ELP Again," 64.

The verses of "Better Days" are as harmonically static as those of "Black Moon"; there's no chord changes accompanying Lake's declamatory vocal, just the Clavinet riff, the sustained open fifths D–A (on synth), and the sporadically interspersed pentatonic synth theme. The band compensate for the lack of harmonic motion with a gradual buildup in textural background detail: when the second verse begins at 1:17, Palmer adds an effective "jungle" tom part, while Emerson layers in eight bars of a spitting, percussive Hammond obbligato (its sound here is even more gloriously grungy than on "Burning Bridges") followed by eight bars of a "Clavinet" obbligato. The transitional vocal episode, reached at 1:50, finally brings some tonal movement to the song, shifting the tonality down from D minor to C minor; it also introduces some angularity with its five-bar phrase structure and alternating measures of 6/4 and 4/4. The chorus, first reached at 2:02, mines a heroic vein with its modal borrowing (while the chords all pertain to D minor, the tonic chord itself is always D major), Emerson's fanfarelike open fifths on Hammond (enlivened by turning the Leslie vibrato on and off, something he had seldom done in the seventies), Palmer's military-style tom cadences, and Lake's plaintive, reverb-drenched vocals.[28]

Thereafter the structure repeats itself: a shortened third verse (2:36), the transitional vocal episode (2:52), and the chorus (3:05). At 3:39, the chord changes of the transitional vocal episode become the basis for an Emerson solo, as he creates a call-and-response between his Hammond and synth; this passage, in turn, serves as a transition into a new section, the lyrical, Procol Harum–like Hammond organ theme at 3:51. The sad majesty of this passage is similar to the mood of the chorus, but the chord progressions here are even richer, with Emerson mixing together chords drawn from D major and D Phrygian; the unpredictable shift between D major and D minor chords is especially affective. A final statement of the chorus (4:22) is followed by one more iteration of the Hammond organ theme (from 4:56); this final portion of the song is effectively driven by Palmer's double bass drum part, perhaps his most prominent use of his double bass drum setup on the album. "Better Days" has many of the same strengths as "Burning Bridges": structural interest, variety in its tonality, melodic styles, and phrase structures, and Emerson's colorfully distorted Hammond. Where it may have an edge over "Burning Bridges" is in its greater rhythmic energy.

Black Moon ends with a Greg Lake acoustic guitar ballad, "Footprints in the Snow." Set in D Mixolydian, it's similar in character to "Affairs of the

---

[28] In the seventies, Emerson used both hands to play the organ so frequently that he was seldom able to operate the Leslie vibrato on-off switch with his hands. By the early nineties, he had the Leslie vibrato output redesigned so that it could be controlled by a floor switch.

Heart," although perhaps not as distinctive. It begins with an incomplete statement of the chorus' chord changes, strummed on acoustic guitar. The first verse (0:22) features Lake's voice, strummed guitar chords, and sparse bass, as well as some equally spare keyboard padding by Emerson; it's followed by an incomplete statement of the chorus ("before you know") at 0:46, after which the verse and incomplete chorus are repeated. Perhaps the song's main novelty is that Lake doesn't give us a complete statement of the chorus until 1:25, by which time the song is nearly half over. (This is a technique Lake used before, for instance, in "Closer to Believing.") There's two more statements of the verse (1:53 and 2:45), and two more complete statements of the chorus (2:17 and 3:10); during the last verse, Lake layers in some nice acoustic guitar arpeggios underneath the strummed guitar chords in the foreground (from 3:00). Other than a couple of tambourine shakes and a bell tree hit at the end, there is no drumming and no percussion to speak of during "Footprints in the Snow."

Black Moon: An Assessment

In *The Music's All That Matters*, Paul Stump, in talking about Yes's ghastly 1991 album *Union*, said, "this horror made the reformation of ELP in 1992 seem a model of modesty by comparison . . . ELP's *Black Moon* did at least aspire to interest and excite the listener, and it would be a churlish mind that overlooked a vigor in the playing which had formerly been notable by its absence."[29] There is no question that *Black Moon* is the product of a band that is serious about *reforming* itself, revamping its approach for a new decade and a new aesthetic, moving forward into new and uncharted territory. I would have to say three positive things on behalf of this album. First, its terseness is admirable: of the ten tracks, only "Black Moon" and "Paper Blood" go on longer than their substance warrants. Second, one is impressed how much of a genuine collaboration the album is, especially considering how long it had been since Emerson, Lake and Palmer had worked together: one is unsure whether Emerson or Lake was the primary musical influence behind "Black Moon," "Paper Blood," or "Farewell to Arms," whereas one never entertained any such uncertainty about any of their seventies tracks. On songs like "Farewell to Arms" and "Burning Bridges," the use of Lake's acoustic guitar as an important textural component in songs dominated by Emerson's Hammond and synths is such a nice touch that one wonders why the band never thought to try it between 1970 and 1978. Third, the album *sounds* like a product of the nineties, which is what I'm sure the band wanted.

---

[29] Stump, *The Music's All That Matters*, 338–39.

While Mark Mancina's production is just a bit slick for my taste—some of the tracks may have profited from a leaner and meaner approach, as the sonic space is usually very full—he does succeed in translating the essence of their seventies sound into something valid for popular music audiences of the nineties. Specifically, Emerson's keyboard setup manages to sound simultaneously contemporary and individual in its blend of analog and digital sounds; likewise, while Palmer's drum sound is more electronic than I prefer, it certainly fit the parameters of nineties tastes, and some of his timbres are quite distinctive and interesting.

Having said all this, however, *Black Moon* does not make one forget the band's classic output of 1970–74. Why? First and foremost, the material simply doesn't measure up. I don't think most ELP fans expected a new "Tarkus" or "Karn Evil 9." What they did expect, however, was that besides updating their sound, ELP would distill the harmonic, metric, and structural subtlety of their classic era recordings into more concise packages. By and large, *Black Moon* doesn't deliver on that expectation. The harmonic and metric poverty of "Black Moon" and "Paper Blood" (by ELP standards, at least) is rather startling. While "Affairs of the Heart," "Farewell to Arms," and "Footprints in the Snow" are nice songs, they're rather predictable. "Burning Bridges" and "Better Days" do manage to deliver a few unexpected surprises through subtleties of tonality and phrase structure in the manner of ELP's classic ouput—perhaps not coincidentally, Palmer's drumming here is more in line with the intricacy of his seventies work than is his drumming on the album's first five tracks. However, of the ten tracks on *Black Moon*, only one, "Changing States," completely measures up to their past masterpieces. Certainly, *Black Moon* does not manage to put together an entire LP side's worth of very strong material in the manner of *Emerson, Lake and Powell*.

There's another problem with *Black Moon* that I've never heard anyone articulate before: by and large, it lacks the rhythmic energy and sense of momentum that characterizes ELP's output of the seventies. As I've already intimated, the first five tracks are rather plodding: while "Black Moon" and "Romeo and Juliet" assay to be ponderous, they skirt dangerously close to simply being turgid. The sixth track, "Changing States," finally jump starts the album with its driving tempo and polyrhythmic energy, and while "Burning Bridges" slows the tempo a bit, its metric and phrase structure irregularities and tonal uncertainties do manage to maintain the previous track's energy level. However, just when the album seems to finally be building up some momentum, "Close to Home" douses it; perhaps a major reason I never warmed to Emerson's attractive piano piece is what I've always perceived as its inopportune placement on the album. "Better Days" picks up the slack again; next to "Changing States," it's the album's most driving track. However, with Lake's pretty but lightweight "Footprints in the Snow," the album appears to simply peter out. If one thinks about ELP's great achievements—the debut album, *Trilogy*, *Brain Salad Surgery*, the first halves of *Tarkus* and *Emerson, Lake and Powell*, the fourth LP side of *Works I*—momentum is built and maintained over lengthy time spans. In comparison, *Black Moon* simply never builds up much sustained energy.

I've always felt that ELP recorded *Black Moon* with the time frame of the vinyl LP—forty to forty-five minutes—in mind; at the risk of offending Emerson and Lake fans, "Close to Home" and "Footprints in the Snow" sound like afterthoughts, or filler. In all honesty, I think *Black Moon* would have worked better as an LP-length album without those two tracks. Side one of the "LP" would consist of "Black Moon," "Paper Blood," "Affairs of the Heart," and "Romeo and Juliet"; side two, of "Changing States," "Burning Bridges," "Better Days," and "Farewell to Arms." While this solution would not have solved all the problems I enumerated above, the album would have cohered better, and the last four tracks would have been able to build up an uninterrupted momentum that would have raised the album's energy level a bit. At roughly forty-one minutes, my suggested eight track-version of *Black Moon* would clock in at approximately the same length as the first four ELP albums.

Black Moon didn't exactly skyrocket to the top of the charts. Receiving very little radio exposure, it peaked at seventy-eight—a bit better than *To The Power of Three*, but not nearly as good as *Emerson, Lake and Powell*—and stayed in the top two hundred for just four weeks. Victory Records had financed a rather extraordinary video, featuring a compressed version of "Black Moon," to publicize the album's release; filmed at a marble quarry on a mountain near Carrara, Italy, from a remote-controlled mini-chopper, it interspersed shots of Emerson, Lake and Palmer (each performing on top of his own sheer rock cliff), sequences of quarry workers pounding on marble boulders in rhythm with the bass/drums riff, and ominous close-ups of a blue (not black) moon. Directed by Bill Butt and produced by Audrey Powell of Hipgnosis fame, it was an imposing and unusual production that may well have won ELP some new converts from the MTV generation. However, when Victory saw the lackluster sales of *Black Moon*, they cancelled the release of the "Black Moon" single in the U.S., and the video was never shown on MTV or VH-1. Fortunately, the video has been preserved for posterity by being featured in its entirety on the ELP Video Biography, which had initially been planned for a summer 1992 release, but in fact was not available until early 1993.

The Atlantic Years

A positive development during the period leading up to the *Black Moon* World Tour was the release of *Emerson, Lake and Palmer: The Atlantic*

Years, a two-CD, two-and-a-half hour box set featuring digitally remastered excerpts, chronologically arranged, from the ten ELP albums of 1970 to 1979. The selections are exquisitely chosen—I agree with nearly everything that was included and/or excluded—and the digital remastering process gives the music a sense of clarity and spatial separation that Atlantic's CD reissues of the eighties (which sound no better than a clean vinyl LP) had lacked. Finally, nearly thirteen years after the announced dissolution of ELP, the band were represented by a *Best Of* package that did their legacy full justice. For me, *The Atlantic Years* remains the definitive ELP "greatest hits" package.

Black Moon Tour

On July 22, 1992, ELP played a special dress rehearsal for approximately three hundred fans at Tower Theater in Upper Darby, Pennsylvania, after which they mingled with the crowd and signed autographs. Two days later, on July 24, the band officially launched their *Black Moon* World Tour with a performance at Mann Music Center in Philadelphia; it was their first public performance in fourteen years, four months, and eleven days. (But who was counting?) Stewart Young and ELP's management team had studied the failures of the ELPowell tour carefully. The *Black Moon* tour hewed closely to the geographic areas where ELP were most popular during their glory years; the tour also targeted midsized venues (especially outdoor amphitheaters) that the band had a legitimate chance of filling, mostly avoiding the huge arena-sized venues whose frequent emptiness had caused so much grief for ELPowell. This strategy paid off handsomely. An individual with connections to the band's management told me that during the first half of the tour (which ended in early December) the venues the band played at were filled, on average, to 85 percent capacity; a very impressive figure for a band that had not toured for fourteen years, and whose new album had peaked at seventy-eight in the charts.

From Philadelphia, ELP moved across the northeast U.S. and eastern Canada (Quebec and Ontario) before moving through the Midwest. I myself saw ELP perform at the outdoor Pine Knob amphitheater, north of Detroit, on August 12; I was visiting my parents in Michigan at the time, and an old friend who had never seen the band live suggested that we catch their show. The first call to Ticketmaster produced abysmal seats. When I called back a day or two later, I was told I was in luck; two people with seats in the third row had cancelled, and we could have them if we wanted. As it ended up, we sat no more than twenty feet away from Keith Emerson. Unfortunately, we were also about twenty feet away from a massive row of speakers, and my ears rang for two days. It was certainly a different experience than when I saw the band at Detroit's Olympia in 1978, and practically needed binoculars to see the band members. Attendance seemed very good; I was, however, struck by the fact that while nobody seemed much younger than me (I was thirty at the time), a lot of the audience appeared ten or fifteen years older. While ELP clearly had retained a lot of their old fans, they did not appear to be gaining many new ones, based on the evidence of the faces I saw at their Pine Knob show.

The band began with a very short snippet of "Karn Evil 9, 1st Impression, part two" (the "welcome back my friends" bit), which moved without interruption into the first three movements of "Tarkus" ("Eruption," "Stones of Years," "Iconoclast"), then directly into "Knife-Edge." After pausing to greet the audience (Keith Emerson said "Hey Detroit, how are you," or something like that), they launched into two tracks from the new album, "Paper Blood" and "Black Moon." In the manner of the 1974 shows, this lengthy sequence of heavy electronic rock at the beginning of the show was followed by a more or less "unplugged" sequence. Emerson played "Close to Home" and an impressive rendition of "Creole Dance," after which Lake was featured on "From the Beginning," "Lucky Man," and "Affairs of the Heart," the latter two accompanied by Emerson and Palmer. Again in the manner of the 1974 shows, the third and final segment returned to electronic prog rock: they played "Pirates" and a compressed version of *Pictures* consisting of "Promenade," "The Gnome," "Promenade," "Baba Yaga" and "The Great Gates of Kiev," with Carl Palmer's drum solo incongruously inserted into "Baba Yaga."

After a boisterous round of applause when they left the stage, the band returned for an encore. They began with "Fanfare for the Common Man," which produced the first instance I had seen of fans dancing in the aisles at an ELP show (although it didn't last long—security chased the fans, all women, as I recall, back to their seats). This was followed by an abbreviated version of the Nice's "America"; after "America," the platform holding Emerson's keyboards suddenly turned in a 180-degree circle, revealing a phony-looking brick portico harboring Keith Emerson's Hammond L-100. After a moment of being too surprised to react, my friend Doug and I burst out laughing: within seconds, Emerson pulled the L-100 into center stage, and launched into the Nice's "Rondo" (Lake and Palmer had already commenced the throbbing bass/drums backing groove). After playing the main theme and the first section of his studio version solo, Emerson began to perpetrate the customary assault on the unfortunate instrument, including the mandatory quotation from Bach's Toccata and Fugue in D minor, which he played while lying underneath the Hammond. The band finished "Rondo" with a flourish, and then disappeared from the stage. This time no standing ovation of any length could coax them to return to the stage. As I recall, their entire show lasted just over ninety minutes. I was impressed with how well the band had played, but I wished that they had performed "Changing States" and one of the less obvious *Black Moon* songs (either "Burning Bridges" or "Better Days"). I also desperately hoped for something more from "Karn Evil 9"—in vain, as it turned out.[30]

After Detroit, the band played several more shows in the Midwest, after which the tour moved south (focusing on Texas) for a few selected shows, then west, concentrating mostly on the West Coast from San Diego north to Vancouver. A review of their August 26 show by the *San Diego Union* conveys the general critical consensus of the revamped ELP:

> The art rock of ELP, which seemed complex, massive, and weighty when they first began playing that sort of thing back in the early seventies, now just seems ponderous. It probably isn't the fault of Keith Emerson, Carl Palmer, or Greg Lake. Emerson wasn't his usual frenetic self, but his keyboard playing was classic (in each sense of the word). Palmer's drumming was crisp, controlled, and powerful, sometimes inventive. Lake's voice has gained a husky hue. He nearly lost it altogether at one point. [More on this shortly.] The elements combine, the sounds are all there, the stage effects are spectacular, the musicians give all, but they can't escape the inevitable: classical rock is a museum piece. The opening act was Bonham. Why, is beyond me.[31]

The American/Canadian segment of the first leg of the tour ended on September 6 in Vancouver. Between July 24 and September 6 they had played thirty-three shows.

Just four days later, on September 10, they arrived in Japan, playing eight shows over the next nine days. After a week off, they were in Europe, where they had not performed since 1974; the European segment of the *Black Moon* tour opened September 26 before an enthusiastic crowd of eighty-five hundred at Verona, Italy, a show that is featured on the *Emerson, Lake and Palmer: Welcome Back* Video Biography of 1993. Thereafter they played Budapest, Hungary, former Iron Curtain territory that had been inaccessible to them in the seventies. Then it was on to London's Royal Albert Hall, where the Nice were still under a lifetime ban for Keith Emerson's flag-burning behavior, but where, mysteriously, Emerson, Lake and Palmer had been sched-

---

[30] In fact, there were tunes in their repertoire they did not play that night. For instance, I was told that at the first few shows of the tour they played "Farewell to Arms"; when hitting the high notes on a nightly basis began to become problematic for Lake, the song was dropped from their set list. Lake refused to perform anything from "Karn Evil 9" other than the "Welcome Back My Friends" snippet, saying that the piece was too "dated" for the nineties.

[31] Reprinted in *Fanzine for the Common Man* no. 12 (December 1992): 11.

uled to play two sold-out gigs on October 2 and October 3, anxiously awaited by British fans who had not seen a live ELP show on their native soil in over eighteen years.

ELP's October 2 show is captured on *Emerson, Lake and Palmer Live at the Royal Albert Hall*, released on videotape in 1996; it is also the performance featured on the Japanese album of the same title (as we will see, the American and European audio release with this title features their October 26, not the October 2, Albert Hall performance). The videotape is an interesting document, with nice visuals and good (although not outstanding) sound. It features essentially the same set list I had seen them perform on August 12 Pine Knob, with a few substitutions. After being introduced by their long time supporter, DJ Alan Freeman, the band members emerge onto the stage: Palmer seemed to hardly have aged since his days with Asia, although both Emerson and Lake look a bit more mature (and, in Lake's case, a bit heavier) than during the ELP *Works* tour of 1977-78.

They begin with a longer snippet of "Karn Evil 9, 1st Impression, part two" than they had performed in their American and Canadian shows of the previous summer; as the band prepared to segue into the truncated "Tarkus" arrangement, the camera captures Emerson rubbing his right wrist with his left hand, as if he were in pain. It was a gesture that few audience members probably even noticed: as we'll see, however, it was an ominous portent of what was to come within a few short months. They play "Tarkus" well, and it's fun to see close-ups of all three members performing their intricate parts: watching Palmer lay out his part during "Eruption," with the intense concentration of a man defusing a bomb, is particularly fascinating. During "Iconoclast," Emerson grabs his ribbon controller and plunges into the audience, much to their delight. As in Detroit, the abbreviated "Tarkus" segues directly into "Knife's Edge." After pausing briefly to greet the audience and comment on how good it was to finally be home, they commence "Paper Blood," which Greg Lake (or "Muddy" Lake, as Emerson introduced him) inaugurates with a brief harmonica solo. Palmer performs this one with headphones on, so he can follow the click track that accompanies the sequenced backing female vocals.

Next comes "Creole Dance." The video features some nice close-ups of Emerson, who was clearly primed for this particular performance; his block chord right hand improvisation over the rolling left hand ostinato (from 24:58 to 25:49) is particularly amazing. Next, Lake plays a solo version of "From the Beginning," featuring some exquisite new acoustic guitar flourishes; his voice shows just the slightest trace of the hoarseness that was to increasingly plague him as the tour progressed. On "Lucky Man," Lake is joined by Emerson and Palmer; the arrangement was the closest the band had ever hewed to the studio version, including an almost note-for-note rendition of Emerson's famous modular Moog solo as the song reaches its denouement. Almost immediately, Emerson shouts "all aboard the honky tonk train," and plunges into "Honky Tonk Train Blues"; he's joined first by the crowd, who immediately begins clapping along, and momentarily by Lake's walking bass line and Palmer's swing drum groove. The ending—where Emerson repeats the final figure far more often that Lake or Palmer are expecting—is rather amusing.

They had not played "Honky Tonk Train Blues" in August; nor had they played the next number, "Romeo and Juliet." Although I'm not totally sold on the piece—Lake's and Palmer's accompaniment still seems very simplistic—it presses forward with more urgency than their studio performance, and Emerson's searing synth leads, without the studio version's overabundance of textural padding, are galvanizing. Even as the band strikes the final chords of "Romeo and Juliet," a skull-and-cross-bones is projected on the wall in back of the stage, and ELP tear into "Pirates." It's probably the high point of the show. Clearly Emerson had learned a lot about arranging his seventies repertoire for digital keyboards during the ELPowell tour, because his keyboard parts now sound far fuller and more orchestral than they had in the late seventies, when he played the piece exclusively on the Yamaha GX-1. The interplay between the three musicians is extremely tight, yet the performance almost swings, since the almost telepathic connection between them allows them to relax. On this number, Emerson indulges in his old seventies trick of playing keyboards on the opposite side of his U-shaped keyboard setup at the same time.

As "Pirates" ends, Doric columns and stained-glass windows are projected onto the back wall, and the band launches into their five-movement arrangement of *Pictures at an Exhibition*. Those who are familiar with the studio version of the piece that ELP recorded for the *Return of the Manticore* box set in 1993 will discern the outlines of that version clearly emerging in their live performances of 1992; the chief distinguishing characteristic of the band's new take on the piece, besides the paring away of the different movements to their essential passages, is how much Emerson's Hammond is deemphasized in favor of a mélange of massive digital synth timbres. Palmer's drum solo, inserted into "Baba Yaga," seems to me to have come full circle to the drum solo he played in "Tank" on their very first album; instead of developing one rhythmic and dynamic trajectory all the way through, as he had with tremendous success during his solos of the 1973-74 period, his solos now consists of a number of short episodes loosely pieced together. He even comes to a complete stop twice, which doesn't exactly do wonders for the solo's momentum: indeed, over the years, the musical considerations that had once played a role in his solos seemed to have been almost completely overridden by the "showbiz" aspects. Thankfully, Palmer's solo eventually leads back into the final segment of "Baba Yaga," and from thence into "The Great Gates of Kiev." While I'm not fond of all of the digital patches Emerson uses in the "new" *Pictures*—I would have liked more Hammond, personally—I must admit his piling on of digital timbres at the conclusion of "Gates" finally manages to give it the climactic feeling that ELP had never quite attained in the early seventies with Emerson's Hammond-and-Moog setup.

When the band reemerges for the encore, Palmer has changed into an ELP tee shirt, Emerson into a black leather motorcycle jacket and an ELP baseball cap that he wears backwards. They play "Fanfare for the Common Man," then "America." Suddenly, Emerson's keyboard platform begins to turn; before you know it, his keyboards are gone, replaced by an old battered Hammond L-100 sitting against a phony-looking brick wall. Emerson wrestles the instrument into center stage—at one point he's dangerously near Greg Lake's Persian rug, which had been brought out of retirement for the *Black Moon* tour; after playing the main theme of "Rondo," Emerson rides the instrument to center stage, knifes it, and while the instrument screeches in complaint, he pulls out a can of spray paint and spray paints the ELP logo on the phony brick wall. He then runs back to the organ, flips it down on top of him, and plays the Bach Toccata and Fugue in D minor quotation upside down and backwards. Even as he is doing this, another misdemeanor is committed; a man from the audience reaches to the edge of the stage and, in plain view of the camera, steals Emerson's baseball cap while he's still lying underneath the organ. (I wonder if the cops ever tracked him down?) Finally, Emerson jumps up, his keyboard setup reappears, he plays the final recap of the "Rondo" theme, and the show is over; the band takes their bows and leaves to thunderous applause from the audience. The video lasts ninety minutes; the concert itself was roughly fifteen minutes longer, since three numbers played at the concert ("Black Moon," "Close to Home," and "Still . . . You Turn Me On") were not included on the video. Those who did not experience ELP live during their 1992-93 *Black Moon* tour could do far worse than obtaining a copy of the *Live at the Royal Albert Hall* video.

Four days after the Royal Albert Hall gigs, ELP commenced a series of shows in German-speaking Europe, playing nine shows in Germany, one in Vienna, Austria, and one in Zurich, Switzerland, between October 7 and 20. October 23 found them in the Netherlands, October 25 in Manchester's Apollo, and on October 26 they were back at the Royal Albert Hall. It was this performance that is featured on the *Emerson, Lake and Palmer Live at the Royal Albert Hall* CD released in the U.S. and Europe by Victory Records. When John Collinge asked Keith Emerson why the Japanese release of *Live at the Royal Albert Hall* featured the October 2 performance instead of the October 26 performance, Emerson answered:

There was time limitation on it. The Japanese apparently wanted it in a big hurry, and we played three nights in all at the Albert Hall [October 2, 3, and 26]. I haven't actually heard the whole of the Japanese release so I don't know what that is, but it was pretty well mixed and released before we even knew anything about it. The one which is released now [in the U.S. and Europe] was engineered by the same engineer that did the *Black Moon* CD. I think they spent a little more time getting the stereo perspectives a lot better and all that sort of stuff.[32]

Live at the Royal Albert Hall

Alan Freeman again opens the show with the now traditional "Welcome back my friends to the show that never ends," after which ELP launch into the "Karn Evil 9, 1st Impression, part 2" excerpt, which now took in two full verses. As before, this snippet moved directly into the first three movements of "Tarkus," "Eruption," "Stones of Years," and "Iconoclast." It's a fairly conservative arrangement—the instrumental movements are quite similar to the studio version, while "Stones of Years" merely adds a few discreet digital synth patches and a short synth solo segment before the customary Hammond solo—but I like it. The tempo is a bit more deliberate than on *Welcome Back My Friends*, so it's now possible to hear every single note clearly in the instrumental movements, and Emerson's Hammond sounds much more full-bodied and nuanced here than it did on *Welcome Back My Friends*. It's an excellent performance, and my only complaint involves the totally extraneous episode of synth whooshes and whirrs added in "Iconoclast" between 7:38 and 8:54; this was the point in the show where Emerson did his routine with the Moog ribbon controller, but one wishes he had placed this episode somewhere where it wouldn't interrupt the surrounding musical fabric so glaringly. The "Tarkus" medley moves directly into "Knife's Edge." I miss some of the subtleties of the studio version—especially the spooky organ trill behind the second verse—but the driving Hammond organ ritornellos and solos still rock out. In fact, the Hammond sounds so good here I found myself wishing Emerson hadn't reorchestrated some parts (for instance, the Bach French Suite excerpt) with bell-like digital synth patches. The "Tarkus" medley and "Knife's Edge" are performed with ELP's characteristic precision, and also evince an energy that was sometimes absent in ELP's live performances of the late seventies.

The next two tracks are from *Black Moon*. "Paper Blood" opens with Greg Lake's harmonica solo, and thereafter is very faithful to the studio

---

[32] Keith Emerson quoted by John Collinge, reprinted in *Fanzine for the Common Man*, no. 13 (July 1993): 8.

version. I guess the one thing I would question is the necessity of sequencing the gospel-style backing female vocals: it sounds phony in this context, and the song would have worked just fine without the canned background chorus. Almost immediately the band launch into "Romeo and Juliet," a number they had not played when I saw them in Detroit in August. Again, while this performance isn't enough to totally convert me to the piece, it takes on a tauter, more muscular feel in its live incarnation than it had possessed in the studio version.

Now comes the "unplugged" and "semiplugged" sequence of the show. It commences with Emerson's "Creole Dance"; although Emerson had been playing this work live since 1986, this represented the first commercially available recording of the piece. He plays it with great aplomb and virtuosity; some of the single-line right hand sixteenth-note lines over the rolling left-hand ostinato (listen between 1:05 and 1:12 and 1:29 and 1:33) are quite amazing, showcasing Emerson at the height of his technical powers one final time before the onset of debilitating right arm problems in 1993. Emerson played the piece on MIDIed grand; I would have personally preferred it on straight acoustic piano, without the string padding that is sometimes layered in the background.

"Creole Dance" is followed by a solo performance of "Still . . . You Turn Me On," showcasing Greg Lake on vocals and acoustic guitar. If Emerson's right hand problem was still over the horizon at this point in time, Lake's vocal problems were becoming all too evident; his vocal condition had degenerated noticeably even since the Royal Albert Hall show of October 2, just three weeks earlier. Many years of smoking and an irregular practice schedule were beginning to rob one of rock's most distinctive vocal stylists of his (once) bell-like upper register; while the problem had remained latent on the studio album, it was now being painfully exposed after three months of continuous touring, which had pushed Lake's vocal stamina beyond the breaking point. It's rather painful to hear him sing the first chorus; one can almost hear his voice turn to ashes, somewhat ironically, when he sings "your flesh has crystallized" (1:13). The problem with hoarseness that Lake was starting to experience in his upper register was to grow even worse before it began to improve.

"Still . . . Your Turn Me On" is followed by "Lucky Man." Featuring Lake on acoustic guitar, Emerson on keyboards, and Palmer on full kit, it's easily the most faithful rendition of the studio version the band had ever undertaken: Emerson plays a MIDIed electric guitar solo in the middle of the song that's nearly a note-for-note copy of Lake's studio performance, and as the song approaches its denouement, he plays an almost note-perfect rendition of his famous modular Moog solo, including the shuddering low notes, on the original instrument, which was now used

exclusively for this purpose.[33] Emerson's textural string synth parts effectively fill at least some of the space that had been occupied by Lake's rich
vocal harmonies on the studio version. "Lucky Man," with its undemanding vocal line and relatively low tessitura, doesn't challenge Lake's voice
like "Still . . . You Turn Me On," and there's no sign of hoarseness here.

"Black Moon" is next. In live performance, the band has to forego
many of the textural subtleties of the studio version; some of Palmer's
sampled percussion parts, as well as some of Emerson's counterpoints
during the two "fugal" episodes, are lacking. On the other hand, the piece
is slightly faster here than on the studio album, and seems to press forward a bit more urgently; Lake's bass fills are both more intricate and
more spontaneous than in the studio version, lending the song some
added punch. Like the live performance of "Paper Blood," it represents
the song well, but probably won't convert anybody who didn't already
like the studio version.

"Pirates," the tenth and penultimate track, is arguably the album's
highpoint. At the time of the album's release, it was first live version of
"Pirates" available; it is superior to the three-piece version from the *Works*
tour that later appeared on the King Biscuit disc of 1997, and can profitably be compared and contrasted with the orchestral version of "Pirates"
on the *Works Orchestral Tour* video. As with this album's "Tarkus," one
appreciates the precision of the band's performance and the presence and
clarity of the recording. Although my general feeling is that analog keyboards have served ELP's music better than digital keyboards, I must
admit that Emerson's digital synth rig does "Pirates" far more justice than
the GX-1 did the piece when the band performed it as a trio in 1977-78;
the sounds are fuller, the timbres richer and much more diversified.
Emerson also introduces the Hammond into the arrangement, in conjunction with a searing digital synth timbre, not unlike that of "Romeo
and Juliet," during the latter portion of the song (from 8:50), to good
effect. Of course, one misses the fuller textures only possible with full
orchestra: on the other hand, the sound quality here is much better than
on the *Works Orchestral Tour* video. The biggest drawback, compared to
earlier versions, is probably Greg Lake's vocal. To his credit, Lake's voice
is quite strong here: only once (ironically during the quiet bridge section)
does his voice exhibit hoarseness. However, Lake is obliged to reshape his
vocal line throughout each verse in order to avoid most of the melodic
highpoints, which results in a certain loss of excitement—especially for
those who know the vocal part of the studio version. All in all, however,
"Pirates" reaffirms ELP's status as one of the great live rock bands of their
era.

---

[33] Although he didn't use the Moog's keyboard; it was accessed from a controller keyboard.

The next segment of their performance, comprising the truncated *Pictures at an Exhibition* and the Carl Palmer drum solo, was omitted from the album due to time constraints. This brings us to the final track, the encore medley of "Fanfare for the Common Man," "America," and "Rondo." "Fanfare" is not dissimilar to its incarnations during the ELPowell and 3 tours, although since it's not as long here, Emerson doesn't have time to develop his improvised solo over the shuffle drone bass on the same scale as he had in those earlier tours; the solo (which MIDIs together the Hammond and GX-1 harmonica timbres) still climaxes (at 4:22) on the "Blues Variation" theme from the original *Pictures at an Exhibition*. He ends the solo with the same development of the "Fanfare" theme as he had used in the studio version (from 5:12), then recaps the "Fanfare" theme proper.

A short drum flourish by Palmer swings the band into a truncated version of "America," which features Emerson's Hammond and the GX-1 lead trumpet timbres MIDIed together. There's no solo on this one; as soon as the band has finished playing the main theme, Lake and Palmer commence the throbbing bass/drum groove of "Rondo" as Emerson wrestles the Hammond L-100 into position. Eventually the band play the "Rondo" theme proper; this is followed by a short quote of Nicolai Rimsky-Korsakov's "Flight of the Bumblebee" (from 9:41) and a brief segment of Emerson's original solo from the studio version from the Nice's debut album (from 9:51) before there's a long segment of *musique concrète*-like electronic wailing, screeching, and groaning as Emerson leaps on top of the unfortunate instrument and begins to ride it across the stage. At 11:27 we are given the quotation from Bach's Toccata and Fugue in D minor that Emerson was wont to play backward and upside down, while lying underneath the instrument; finally, at 12:40 the "Rondo" theme is recapitulated, but now using the same Hammond/GX-1 trumpet patch that had been featured on "America." About a minute later "Rondo" comes to its grinding conclusion, and before the track fades on the album, we hear the snippet of the Respighi orchestral piece that played behind the band while they took their bows at the end of the show.

Live at the Royal Albert Hall: An Assessment

Live at the Royal Albert Hall, which was released three months later, in late January 1993, is a very credible live album. Of the four ELP live albums to that point, it has the best production values: in fact, in terms of clarity of sound, presence, and spatial separation, I would also rank it above the band's two live albums of the late nineties. It is certainly a big improvement over *Works Live*, not only in terms of sound quality, but also in terms of the higher energy level of the band's playing. Having said all this, I do have a major caveat, and it's not Greg Lake's voice, either, which one can live with. It's the set list. Much like the 1977-78 *Works* tour, the band plays too many short tunes, too many solo pieces, and spends too much time on flashy but musically negligible items such as Palmer's drum solo and Emerson's ribbon controller and Hammond-riding escapades. As a result, on too much of this album, it feels as if the band is just coasting along in second gear: only the truncated "Tarkus" and "Pirates" fully reveal what ELP were still capable of as a live band. I think it would have helped a bit if the entire show could have been included, as the presence of *Pictures* would have added a bit more musical heft. Unfortunately, the band was doing ninety to ninety-five minute shows now, not the two-and-a-quarter hour shows of the 1973-74 period, and releasing a set of two forty-five minute CDs didn't make much economic sense: especially when they could release one seventy-minute CD, as they in fact did.[34] Even the presence of *Pictures*, however, would not have disguised the fact that the set list of the 1992-93 World Tour did not compare very favorably to the set list of 1973-74. For that reason, the purchase of *Live at the Royal Albert Hall* didn't tempt me to get rid of my copy of *Welcome Back My Friends to the Show That Never Ends*. If only the latter had the sonic values of the former . . .

Five days after the final Royal Albert Hall show, ELP were at it again: between October 31 and November 23, they played shows in Spain, France, Belgium, Holland, Denmark, Norway, Sweden, Germany, and Italy. In late November they were back in the U.K. for three shows, all with nostalgic undertones: Bournemouth (Lake's home town) on November 25, Newcastle's City Hall (site of their live recording of *Pictures* in March 1971) on November 26, and Birmingham (Palmer's home town) on November 27. They played one more date in the U.K. (Bristol), then two shows in Germany; the final show of the first half of their *Black Moon* tour was in Hamburg on December 1, after which they took a forty-five-day break over the Christmas holidays. Between July 24 and December 1, ELP had played eighty-three shows in sixteen countries on three continents.

The second half of the *Black Moon* tour commenced in early 1993 with a series of twelve shows in Canada between January 13 and 26: not only did they play the predictable cities (Toronto, Montréal), but also smaller or more remote cities (Edmonton, Calgary, Regina, Winnipeg, Thunder Bay, etc.), some of which they hadn't visited before. Indeed, the

---

[34] In addition to *Pictures* and the Palmer drum solo, I believe Emerson's "Close to Home" and a Lake solo number—either "From the Beginning" or "Affairs of the Heart"—is also omitted. At most, thirty minutes of the show is missing—simply not enough to justify releasing it as a two-CD set.

second half of the tour was planned somewhat differently than the first: they covered smaller distances as they moved from one gig to the next, and, in order to not spread potential audiences too thin, they played at smaller venues than they had the previous summer, in some cases playing at smaller venues than they had played since the first year or so of their existence as a band. While this was perhaps cause for some melancholy reflection back on the good old days when they regularly packed out arenas and stadiums, it made sound financial sense: once again, planning was good, and the band frequently played to capacity or near-capacity crowds.

Welcome Back: The Video Biography

January 26, the day of their final Canadian show (in Sainte-Poi, Quebec) also marked two important ELP releases. One we have already discussed in depth: the *Emerson, Lake and Palmer Live at the Royal Albert Hall* CD, recorded the previous October 26. As I've said, it's a very credible live album and a worthy addition to the band's output. Unfortunately, it didn't crack the American top two hundred. The second release I have casually alluded to: *Emerson, Lake and Palmer: Welcome Back*, more frequently referred to as the ELP Video Biography. This eighty-minute video, eagerly anticipated by fans since the release of *Black Moon* the previous summer, originally had been slated for a Fall 1992 release, which seems rather fanciful, considering that the video contains footage from shows at Verona, Italy (September 26), and the Royal Albert Hall (October 2).

When *Welcome Back* finally was released, most fans found it to be a bit of a disappointment. Part of the problem is that neither the visual nor the sound quality is particularly sterling. An even bigger problem, though, is how the video is structured. I had hoped it would be a genuine biography that would give us a bit of insight into the musicians' early years, trace their rise through the British rock scene of the mid to late sixties, and give us a more or less coherent history of the rise and fall of ELP during the seventies and their reformation in the early nineties. If we were really fortunate, I thought, perhaps a few minutes would be spent on the band members' activities of the eighties.

Anyone who expects *Welcome Back* to be a real biography, however, is bound to be very disappointed. Instead, the video gives us bits and pieces of ELP performing excerpts from a number of their classics: in between each of the featured numbers is a short interview segment with one of the musicians, which sometimes does, and sometimes doesn't, cross-relate with the piece of music it is preceding or following. The performance spots come from all stages of their career, which is nice, but there's no clear coherence to what follows what, and it's not clear when or where some of the earlier spots were shot at. A lot of the material from the seventies is drawn from two other videos, *The Manticore Special* and *The Works Orchestral Tour*, which are both commercially available; also extensively featured is the October 2, 1992, Royal Albert Show (which has since become commercially available), and the September 26 show at Verona. There are a few excerpts from their legendary Cal Jam show of '74, including a shot of Emerson's grand piano catapulting off the ground and spinning upside down. Some of the video footage that accompanies the performance of given songs is, at best, extremely random: for instance, the video shows some footage of ELP performing "C'est la vie" in Montréal in August 1977, then, while the music is still playing in the background, suddenly switches to footage of a twentysomething Emerson zooming through the streets of Rome on his motorcycle. Funny, but I had never exactly heard "C'est la vie" as motorcycle riding music! Some of the footage is interesting—for instance, a scene inside the studio where the band are working with Mark Mancina on "Changing States," and another one where Emerson is playing "Eruption" on acoustic piano while talking about his compositional methods—and the video does do a service by preserving the lavish "Black Moon" video, which otherwise would have been lost to history, in its entirety. While *Welcome Back* may be of some interest, though, it's hard to avoid the impression that with a bit of forethought and effort, it could have been a lot better.

Late January found ELP performing a few dates in New England. A show the band played at Boston's Orpheum Theater on January 29 revealed the band's set list had undergone further minor mutations since late 1992. The snippet of "Karn Evil 9, 1st Impression, part 2" that had opened their 1992 shows was gone; the concert opened to the swelling introductory chord of "Tarkus," leading into the suite's first three movements, which as before, segued directly into "Knife's Edge." These "old tunes" were again followed by "Paper Blood" and "Black Moon," which ended the first third of the show. The "unplugged"/"semiplugged" segment again began with Emerson's "Close to Home" and "Creole Dance." Lake's segment consisted of "Still . . . You Turn Me On," which he performed as a solo, and a new addition to the set list, "C'est la vie," during which Lake was joined on stage by Emerson for the accordion solo. Then came "Lucky Man"—similar to the Albert Hall performances, except that Emerson's Moog solo was no longer so faithful to the studio version—followed by "Honky Tonk Train Blues." The final third of the show began with a second new addition to the set list, "Touch and Go," rather different than ELPowell's studio version but quite similar to what the band was to record later in 1993 for inclusion in the *Return of the Manticore* box set. Then came "Pirates," followed, surprisingly, by their old show-opener and another new addition to the set list, "Hoedown." Much like the "new" "Tarkus," this "Hoedown" is no longer blindingly fast in the manner of their 1973-74 performances; it's nice, though, to be able to hear every single sixteenth note, all of them cleanly played. Then came *Pictures*, with the Palmer drum solo, and finally, the familiar "Fanfare"/"America"/"Rondo" encore, complete with the requisite assaults on the Hammond L-100.

From New England the band moved down the East Coast, playing several dates in New York and Pennsylvania. Then there were fifteen shows in the Midwest, as ELP moved through Ohio, Michigan, Illinois, Wisconsin, Minnesota, Iowa, Nebraska, and Missouri. From there it was on to the Southwest and the West Coast for eight shows. Finally, in late March ELP launched their first-ever series of shows in Latin America, a barometer both of the increasing Westernization and growing prosperity of at least some segments of the population in those countries, and of the popularity of prog there: indeed, there was a thriving prog scene in South America (particularly in Argentina and Brazil) through much of the nineties. The Latin American segment of the tour began with two shows in Mexico City on March 19 and 20. From there it was on to Brazil, where the band played six shows between March 23 and 29, followed by a show in Santiago, Chile, on April 1, and finally two days in Buenos Aires, Argentina, on April 4 and 5, where they played two shows each day; the last Buenos Aires concert marked the conclusion of the *Black Moon* tour. ELP had played sixty shows in 1993; between July 24, 1992, and April 5, 1993, they had played 143 shows, meaning the *Black Moon* tour exceeded the scope of their world tour of 1973-74 (104 shows) and the *Works* tour of 1977-78 (123 shows). Certainly, from a perspective of geography the *Black Moon* tour exceeded all their previous tours, as ELP expanded their reach into new territory in Latin America and Eastern Europe. During the tour, ELP had played in twenty different countries on four continents.

Was ELP's *Black Moon*–era revival a success? It depends on one's definition of "success." If "success" means a monster hit single or a top ten album, then no, it wasn't. If "success" means aesthetic success—that is, the creation of an album that would take its place alongside their six classic albums of 1970–74—then no, it really wasn't a success; *Black Moon* is a decent album, but it's simply not in the same league as their earlier classics. Measured according to more modest and realistic parameters, however, the *Black Moon*–era revival clearly was successful. If the album itself was not a financial success, the accompanying tour clearly was, and ELP succeeded in the not-so-easy task of re-creating a sizable audience across a stunningly far-flung cross-section of the world's real estate who were henceforth willing to attend any performances that ELP were willing to give; perhaps this was the most eloquent proof of ELP's long-time contention that they were, above all, a great live band. While *Black Moon* was no masterpiece, it did manage to credibly retool the band's sound for the nineties, and it was coherent enough to lay a stylistic foundation that the band could proceed to build on and develop in future releases. In short, as the *Black Moon* tour wound down, the band had good reason to be optimistic about their future prospects: there were many reasons to believe that their next album, for which they were already beginning to generate new material during the latter segments of the tour, would be even better than its predecessor, building on its strengths while eschewing its weaknesses. Perhaps it would even generate the elusive hit single or MTV hit that would drive ELP back up to the top of the charts.

18

In the Hot Seat

(Summer 1993– December 1994)

The success of the *Black Moon* tour convinced Phil Carson and his cohorts at Victory Records that ELP's reformation had long-term potential, and therefore justified some long-term investment. Victory thus arranged to purchase the rights to the entire ELP back catalog from Atlantic, and hired Joseph Palmaccio of Polygram to digitally remaster all of ELP's albums of the seventies during the course of 1992; the result of Palmaccio's efforts was a sense of clarity, vividness, and spatial separation of parts that had been absent in the Atlantic ELP CDs of the eighties. Victory announced plans to release the first nine ELP albums (that is, through *Love Beach*) with their original track listings; fans particularly looked forward to the release of *Welcome Back My Friends* and *Love Beach*, neither of which had ever been released in CD format in the U.S. ELP's tenth album, *In Concert*, was to be rereleased with a number of additional tracks and retitled *Works Live*. In addition, Victory scrapped the original *Best of ELP* album of 1980 and put an entirely new *Best of* set together, correctly surmising that the seventy-minute CD format afforded a better opportunity to present a representative cross-section of ELP's output than the forty- to forty-five-minute format of the LP. The arrangement between Atlantic and Victory called for Atlantic to cease manufacturing and delivering ELP product during fall 1993; by the end of the year, Victory would begin shipping the newly remastered ELP CDs to fill any and all orders for ELP back stock.

Victory decided that the best way to publicize the appearance of the remastered ELP back catalog was to put together a new retrospective box set, which would be titled *The Return of the Manticore*, and released in November 1993. This was a sensible enough idea—other prog rock giants such as Yes and King Crimson had released lavish retrospective box sets shortly before—and noted British rock journalist Chris Welch was commissioned to write liner notes for the *Return of the Manticore* booklet. Initially, Victory hoped to include one pre-ELP song featuring Emerson and the Nice ("Hang on to a Dream"), Lake and King Crimson ("21st Century Schizoid Man"), Carl Palmer and the Crazy World of Arthur Brown ("Fire"), as well as an ELPowell song ("Touch and Go"). However, licensing difficulties proved insurmountable, so the label decided to simply have the band rerecord the four chosen songs. In addition, the band decided to record an abbreviated version of *Pictures*, since they had never rendered a studio recording of the piece, and a new arrangement of Lake's "I Believe in Father Christmas." Besides the six newly recorded tracks to be included on the first of the box set's four CDs, the band authorized the release of three previously unavailable tracks: a live recording of "Rondo" from ELP's show at the London Lyceum on December 9, 1970 (the show featured on *Rock and Roll Your Eyes*); a solo piano performance of Friedrich Gulda's jazzy Prelude and Fugue by Emerson, recorded surreptitiously at Advision in October 1971 (Emerson was supposedly surprised to learn that such a recording existed); and the *Works*-era gem "Bo Diddley," recorded at Manticore Studios in 1975, included after Emerson finally succeeded in getting Carl Palmer's assent.

During July and August 1993 Emerson, Lake and Palmer assembled themselves in Goodnight L.A. Studios (actually located in Van Nuys, adjacent to L.A.) to record the six new tracks. For reasons that are still not entirely clear, Mark Mancina did not return to fill the producer's role: his place was taken by Keith Olsen, a well-known figure in the L.A. rock scene who had worked with such successful corporate rock acts of the late seventies and early eighties as Fleetwood Mac, Foreigner, and Whitesnake. The plan was to record the six tracks for the box set first, then to immediately begin recording material for a new studio album that would be released in 1994.

Unfortunately, the six "box-set tracks" recorded during July and August of 1993 point up a fact that was to emerge with painful clarity on the studio album of the following year: Keith Olsen was not a good fit for ELP. While I did not agree with everything Mark Mancina did on *Black Moon*, there's no arguing that his production approach evinced an understanding of the factors that had given ELP their unique musical identity during the seventies. I think overall he did a good job updating their sound for the nineties without totally losing that singular musical identity that had once made them such a special band.

Olsen, however, seemed totally clueless as to what made ELP stylistically different than Foreigner or any other mainstream eighties rock act. As much flack as ELP had taken during the seventies about "overproduction," the beauty of ELP during that era, especially in their live performances, is that they were simply three musicians whose virtuosity and arranging resourcefulness allowed them to create a huge wall of sound in real time: as I convincingly demonstrated earlier in this book, their best work (think the debut album or *Brain Salad Surgery*) relies far less on overdubs than the music of many bands of similar stature who were supposedly less beholden to studio gimmickry (think Led Zeppelin). Now, under Olsen's "guidance," for the first time in their career their arrangements really do sound bloated. Furthermore, a good producer is acquainted with his musicians' strengths, which his production highlights; Olsen manages to make Emerson, Lake, and Palmer's playing sound pedestrian and, even worse, anonymous. Somehow, Olsen simultaneously over-produces and under-produces the band, with predictably devastating results, as I'll briefly demonstrate in my discussion of the six newly recorded "old songs."

Return of the Manticore: Newly Recorded Tracks

The first CD of the box set leads off with the newly recorded ELPowell anthem "Touch and Go." It's a big disappointment. The original had worked both because of its attention to sonic detail—Emerson's ominous choral synth patch and screaming synth trumpet, the ingenious rhythmic loop—and its well-planned and dramatic shifts in dynamics. This arrangement runs roughshod over both the song's particulars and its large-scale structural plan. Unlike Cozy Powell, who had shifted his drum part between verses and choruses and who had carefully interlocked his drum part with the rhythm loop when it was sounding, Carl Palmer simply bashes out the same simple groove all the way through. Emerson's keyboard timbres are far less vivid here than on *Emerson, Lake and Powell*; both the Kurzweil choral patch and the GX-1 supersonic trumpet are sorely missed. Since there are no shifts to speak of in the keyboard colors or the drumming, the original's rise and fall of dynamics, and the attendant sense of drama, is lost.

Next comes Emerson's feature, Tim Hardin's "Hang on to a Dream," which over time had become something of a signature song for the Nice. Emerson had personalized the song with his beautiful acoustic piano work, which, in both its folklike flourishes and modal jazz undertones, had provided an important precedent for ELP's "Take a Pebble." While I wouldn't have expected a regurgitation of Emerson's late-sixties piano licks on the rerecording, it is rather surprising to hear no acoustic piano whatsoever. Instead, after opening with a geometrical, abstract synth/bass counterpoint that seems to have nothing to do with the rest of the song, Emerson settles into a breathy synth accompaniment underneath Greg Lake's dirgelike rendition of the vocal. Most puzzling, perhaps, is the fact that the song's climax is marked off by an electric guitar solo—not by Lake, but by a semi-anonymous sessions player named Tim Pierce, who had worked with Emerson during the 1989 sessions for his solo album.

Now, I have nothing against using sessions musicians for specific parts on a studio album. However, for a band that always boasted that they play all their own music to prominently feature a little known musician, with no prior link at all with the band, on a recording that's meant to offer a historical retrospective, makes no sense to me at all. Perhaps it goes without saying that the pseudo-gospel choir backing at the end of the song seems utterly extraneous.

The third track is a rerecording of the King Crimson warhorse "21st Century Schizoid Man," of which Greg Lake was, of course, a coauthor. While it's better than the first two tracks, it is still something of a disappointment. I would have been curious to hear how ELP would have approached this number as a bona fide three piece: we don't find out here, because Tim Pierce's competent but not particularly distinctive guitar plays an important role in the arrangement, and Keith Olsen layers in (or, at least, tolerates) too many guitar and keyboard overdubs. Perhaps the biggest negative is that ELP only plays the beginning section of the song—the part dominated by the metalish guitar riff—so we never get the frantic, Mingus-like central instrumental rave-up that was at the heart of King Crimson's original recording. Certainly this cover does not hold the proverbial candle to the arrangement of the song that the Greg Lake Band played during their 1981 tour. At least we finally get to hear Emerson take a Hammond solo on this track.

It's ironic that the fourth track, a rerecording of the Crazy World of Arthur Brown's "Fire," although musically the least substantive of the set list here, is probably the most successful. Granted, it's embarrassing to hear a forty-five-year-old Greg Lake open the song by screaming Arthur Brown's famous line "I am the god of hell fire." If you can get past that, though, the rest of the track features a wiry, muscular arrangement that almost sounds as if it were recorded live; Emerson's fiery Hammond solo is a particular highpoint, but his trumpetlike synth comping during the choruses toward the end of the song is also nice, while the Lake-Palmer bass-drum groove generates a good deal of energy. This is the only one of the four rerecordings that made me want to hear ELP play the song in question live.

The fifth track is the studio recording of *Pictures at an Exhibition*. Those who are familiar with the arrangement of this piece that the band played on the *Black Moon* tour would not be surprised with this arrangement; it's essentially a more lavishly orchestrated version of the five movements they had been playing, minus the drum solo and with the addition of "The Sage" between the second Promenade and "Baba Yaga." Palmer commented,

> We've only ever recorded *Pictures* live and never had the opportunity to record it in a controlled situation. For this recording we added some new

music. [Although, apart from a few short transitions, it's hard to say what he means here.] There's been so much new technology since we recorded *Pictures*, the new version sounds a lot more dynamic. We've not only done justice to the piece, we've given it a new life.[1]

To which I would respond: ELP fans, don't throw out those old *Pictures at an Exhibition* albums! Granted, the '93 arrangement has some nice details, which I'll enumerate in a moment. However, it also has two fundamental flaws that prevent it from equaling the recordings done during the early seventies. The first involves structure. When ELP originally arranged the work in 1970, they reconfigured the Musorgsky piece in a way that allowed them to retain the work's scope, while at the same time making it work as a piece of rock music: the original ELP arrangement took on its own structural logic, with a series of peaks and valleys that build up to a satisfying final climax over the course of forty minutes. The '93 arrangement, on the other hand, is essentially an arrangement of an arrangement, with many of the original movements removed entirely, and several of the remaining ones pared down mercilessly: the transitions from one movement to the next now seem sudden and arbitrary rather than gradual and inevitable, and only the final movement, "The Great Gates of Kiev," lasts long enough to build up any real intensity. In other words, this arrangement lacks the satisfying structural logic of the original one.

Second, and more seriously, the marvelous sense of interplay between the three musicians that made the 1971 Newcastle recording so special is lost here, a victim of bloated overproduction. Sure, the synth patches are more variegated and vivid now, often sounding like real violins, real trumpets, and so on, but why bother with this kind of painstaking orchestral realism when we have so many recordings of Ravel's orchestration of the piece to choose from? I suspect I speak for many ELP fans in saying if I listen to ELP play *Pictures*, then I want to hear Emerson, Lake and Palmer project the piece as a band: as it is, Lake's bass lines are missing in action through large swaths of the piece, buried under the multiple synth overdubs, and even Palmer's drumming seems oddly extraneous and perfunctory through much of the arrangement. I don't think the loss of rhythmic energy that results from the absence of team interplay is adequately compensated for by the fuller, more vivid, and more realistic keyboard settings.

These two serious issues aside, the '93 arrangement of *Pictures* does have its moments. The opening "Promenade" is nice for the way that keyboard timbres are slowly layered in over the Hammond sound that had defined so much of the band's original arrangement. "The Gnome" also has some interesting keyboard timbres, although Lake's and Palmer's

---

[1] Carl Palmer, quoted by Chris Welch, *The Return of the Manticore* booklet, 21.

accompaniment is far more perfunctory now than their extraordinarily inventive parts of the early seventies. It's nice to hear "The Sage" again, and Emerson, using a bell-like synth patch, makes a series of increasingly explicit references to Musorgsky's "The Old Castle" as the piece progresses (listen at 6:24, 7:05, 7:48, and 8:32) that fit the arrangement nicely; however, one can't help missing Lake's marvelous acoustic guitar solo of the early seventies. Lake and Palmer pick up the rhythmic slack in "The Hut of Baba Yaga"; one wishes, though, that Emerson's Hammond wasn't swallowed under so many layers of digital keyboard patches. Of the six movements, "The Great Gates of Kiev" is probably the most successful in comparison to its early seventies model. Here Emerson's massive overdubs are justified as the work approaches its final climax, creating the kind of gigantic orchestral conclusion that Emerson's keyboard setup of 1971 simply wouldn't allow for, and some of the quiet chantlike episodes are nicely orchestrated as well.

The sixth and final new track recorded for the box set is Greg Lake's "I Believe in Father Christmas." It's hard to know why they chose it. Yes, it's one of Lake's finest songs—it's a personal favorite of mine—but there were already two distinct arrangements of the song available, the massive orchestral/choral arrangement of the 1975 single and the more modest and subtle trio arrangement of *Works II*. The 1993 arrangement simply splits the difference, as it were, without adding anything essentially new—unless one considers the black gospel choir–style finale an essential addition to the song, which I wouldn't.

Crisis

The six "box set tracks," then, are, at best, a mixed bag. The overall approach taken to production and arrangement did not seem to auger well for the upcoming studio release. Unfortunately, the uneasy fit between Keith Olsen and ELP was being eclipsed by still more serious problems. One was the condition of Greg Lake's voice. Everyone had hoped that the three month break after the end of the *Black Moon* tour would be sufficient for Lake's voice to recover; unfortunately, it wasn't, and in no time at all his voice was showing renewed signs of strain, with loss of upper register and pervasive hoarseness becoming an acute problem. One can hear this hoarseness particularly during *Pictures*, where Lake is challenged to pick off the higher notes he had once hit with ease, and where the loss of timbral clarity and resonance in his upper register is quite noticeable. The condition of Lake's voice was to become an issue throughout the remainder of the recording sessions for the new studio album—although, as we'll see, he had more room for flexibility and adjustment on the new material than he did on the box set's "old classics."

Even more serious was the condition of Keith Emerson's right hand. In early 1992, he began noticing problems in the fourth and fifth fingers of his right hand—he sometimes found they were curling up when he awoke at night, and he soon found that the accuracy and strength of his playing were affected. He consulted with Carola Grindea, a Romanian expatriate who had taught at London's Guildhall School of Music for many years and an expert in the Alexander technique, and studied with her for nearly a year, playing under her instruction throughout the duration of the *Black Moon* tour. Grindea quickly noticed what any of us who have watched Emerson played have observed—he plays with a tremendous amount of shoulder tension and forearm exertion—and coached him to play with less forearm weight and looser wrists.[2] Unfortunately, the weakness and curling in his fourth and fifth fingers grew worse, and after the *Black Moon* tour concluded he went to a surgeon in England, who put him through a series of nerve conduction tests. The tests revealed the possibility of a serious problem, but the surgeon recommended he wait several months before committing to surgery. Returning to the States, he commenced physical therapy, working under a therapist who performed muscular manipulation on his right shoulder. Therapy, too, proved ineffective, and finally the therapist recommended that Emerson consult Dr. Robert Bassett at Cedars-Sinai Hospital, Los Angeles. Emerson: "He advised me to have more nerve conduction tests done, which I did. They were very painful. Needles were actually put into the muscle in back of my arm and all the way through the shoulder. Then he checked out the left arm as well, in the same way. When Dr. Bassett saw the results, he said to his technician, 'There's definitely a problem here.'"[3] Emerson consulted another neurotherapist, this one in Santa Monica, who gave him a grim prognosis: therapy would not improve his situation,

---

[2] Although Emerson believes his problems stemmed from previous hand injuries (particularly when he punched a wall in anger in 1990), he acknowledges his technique may have been a factor. I believe that is likely. I have taught piano for over twenty years, and I have always coached my students to play with as little shoulder tension as possible, as excess shoulder tension over a period of years creates a likelihood of some type of hand problem. Such debilitating injuries are not as uncommon among great pianists as one might think. Glenn Gould, certainly the greatest concert pianist of his generation and arguably one of the greatest pianists of the twentieth century, attributed his decision to quit recording piano music (never realized, due to his sudden death from a stroke in 1982) to a desire to move on into other pursuits. In fact, Peter Ostwald, in his *Glenn Gould: The Ecstasy and Tragedy of Genius* (New York: W. W. Norton, 1997) makes a convincing case that Gould (whose technique, like Emerson's, was rather unconventional) was beginning to suffer a neurological disorder in his hand, not unlike Emerson's (but harder to pinpoint), that made it increasingly difficult for him to give performances of the caliber that he was accustomed to giving, probably contributing to his decision to abandon piano performance.

[3] Keith Emerson, quoted by Doerschuk, "Keith Emerson's Moment of Truth," *Keyboard*, April 1994, 88.

he needed surgery, and Dr. Bassett was the best surgeon he would find. So on October 5, 1993, midway through recording the new album, Emerson underwent an operation at Cedars-Sinai. Bob Doerschuk, interviewing Emerson about six weeks after the fact in late November 1993, gives a graphic description of how serious the surgery was: "There was a dramatic disparity in the size of his arms; they could have belonged to two separate people. Two long surgical scars, measuring ten and seven inches, sliced across the right elbow and forearm. At the time, maybe six weeks after his operation, he was unable to lift his arm above shoulder level."[4] Emerson explained, "I had the radial nerve operated on. As a result, I don't have a funny bone anymore; it's been shoved over to one side. If you bang my right elbow, I wouldn't feel it."[5]

After Emerson's operation, the inevitable question was: will it be possible to finish the studio album? Emerson told his band mates he was willing to attempt it, and they agreed the band should plow on. However, between Emerson's hand, Lake's voice, and growing divergence of viewpoint between the band (particularly Emerson) and Keith Olsen over the artistic direction of the new album—the Victory label was leaning on Olsen to shepherd the band along a more overtly commercial path than before—the recording experience was turning out to be anything but happy.

Return of the Manticore: An Assessment

Between early October and mid-November 1993, all work stopped to allow Emerson time to convalesce. In mid-November, however, it was back to work, since Victory had lined up some high-profile events to publicize the release of the new box set, *Return of the Manticore*, and the upcoming rerelease of the remastered ELP back catalog. *Return of the Manticore* hit the streets November 16. Since I've already shared my disappointment with its six new tracks in some detail, let me simply say that, in my view, the entire set is a bit of a letdown. Considering the four CDs contain a total of four and three quarters hours of music, it's rather incredible that there are only three previously unreleased tracks from the seventies, totaling twenty-two minutes; if one declines to count the live "Rondo" as previously unreleased (it was, after all, on the commercially available *Pictures at an Exhibition* video, which was simply the old *Rock and Roll Your Eyes* movie), there was really only two tracks totaling eight minutes of unreleased ELP from their classic period. The tracks of the box

----

[4] Ibid., 88.
[5] Ibid., 90.

set are not arranged chronologically, or with any other guiding principle that I can discern; while the booklet has some nice photographs, Chris Welch's liner notes are a bit of a disappointment, simply rehashing the basics of the band's history. The main problem with *Return of the Manticore*, however, is that serious ELP fans already had this music, except for the newly recorded material and the three previously unreleased tracks from the seventies, which most felt did not justify the considerable expense of the box set. For the casual fan, this was simply too much music, organized too incoherently; someone who wanted to be quickly and coherently walked through the essential ELP output was far better served by the chronologically arranged two-CD set *The Atlantic Years*, which unfortunately was withdrawn from the market to make room for *Return of the Manticore*. One of the few bright spots of the new box set was the alternate mix of "Pirates" included here, so different (and superior) to the mix of *Works I* that it could have been justifiably included under the "previously unreleased" rubric.

Towards a New Album

The day before *Return of the Manticore* was released, ELP appeared on the *Regis and Kathie Lee Show*, where they played an abbreviated version of "From the Beginning" for their somewhat clueless hosts. The same day they appeared at a listening party at New York City's The Hit Factory, where Carl Palmer revealed that ELP had completed four new songs for the upcoming album. On the day of the box set's release, November 16, they appeared on Howard Stern's radio show; Stern mercilessly needled Emerson, who did not seem to be in very good spirits. As the interview progressed, Emerson observed that he was still in a great deal of pain from his operation; he also revealed that his wife of twenty-three years, Elinor, was in the process of divorcing him. The band capped off the interview by playing "From the Beginning" and a parody of "Lucky Man." The next day, November 17, ELP headlined the Hungerthon benefit concert at New York's Beacon Theatre, which also featured Richie Havens, Southside Johnny, Roseanne Cash, Roger McGuinn, Janis Ian, and Buster Poindexter. ELP played a five-song, thirty-five-minute set consisting of "From the Beginning," "Still . . . You Turn Me On," "C'est la vie," "Lucky Man," and "I Believe in Father Christmas." Emerson walked on stage wearing a sling on his right arm, which he removed to play; he rubbed his arm throughout the set. Even though the keyboard parts to these songs—all Greg Lake ballads—were fairly undemanding, Emerson, given the condition of his arm, found it necessary to sequence some of the parts.

Over the next couple of days the band appeared at some surprisingly low-profile publicity events in the New York/Philadelphia area. For instance, one fan was astounded to arrive at a Circuit City in Montgomeryville, Pennsylvania, at 6 p.m. on a Thursday evening, and find Keith Emerson, Greg Lake, and Carl Palmer seated at a table in front of the store, autographing copies of the new box set. Then it was on to the West Coast; ELP appeared at a listening party at Sony Studios in San Francisco, played an informal in-house show at Los Angeles's Virgin Megastore, and, on November 23, were inducted into Los Angeles's Rock Walk of Fame on Sunset Boulevard. There were a few more publicity events in December; for instance, on December 17 ELP participated in the KLOS radio Christmas show at the Hollywood Palladium.

In early 1994 ELP returned to the studio to finish work on their album. The band and their producer were not congealing into one big, happy family. Emerson's right arm remained painful, and it remained necessary for him to sequence many of his parts. His ongoing divorce proceedings took a further emotional toll on him, as did the fact that he was now facing a £145,000 writ from Barclays Bank for unpaid debts stemming from a failed 1975 tax scheme. And there was beginning to be a great deal of friction both between Emerson and Keith Olsen, and between Emerson and Lake. Emerson had expressed a conviction that after the shorter, punchier songs of *Black Moon*, the new album ought to contain at least one longer concept piece. He was quite taken by a recent song by Bob Dylan, "Man in the Long Black Coat" (from Dylan's *Oh Mercy* album of 1989), whose dark, extraordinarily vivid storyline evokes a kind of gothic Western. Emerson remarked,

> Dylan tells a story in the song and I liked the vivid language he worked with. Originally I wanted to arrange the song so that it could fill an entire LP side. I wanted to tell Dylan's story again, but by musical means . . . I took the song into the studio and worked on it for quite a long time. In the end I had a musical concept, developed around "Man in the Long Black Coat" . . . a sort of Western, where the script is by Dylan and I'm the director, if you like. Unfortunately, Keith Olsen only wanted to have the script and not the film. He didn't want anything that looked even remotely like a concept on this album.[6]

As another interview with Emerson makes clear, Olsen's approach was—at the time, at least—supported by Lake and Palmer: "Keith Olsen and the band told me that I had added a different song to Dylan's when they listened to it. Then they suggested that I take out the part I wrote and make that into another song, because we had to pay a royalty to Dylan. I

---

[6] Keith Emerson, quoted by unknown author, "The Being Fifty Blues," *Keyboards*, November 1994, translated from German by Bill Wagner, translation reprinted in *ELP Digest* 5, no. 9 (April 4, 1995).

said I didn't care about that. I was inspired by Dylan's song, and as a result I arranged the song like this. So it shouldn't be separated."[7] In the end, Emerson's fifteen minutes of music was whittled down to two tracks: a four-minute arrangement of "Man in the Long Black Coat," and a four-minute song titled "One by One." Seven or eight minutes of Emerson's original conception simply vanished; when an interviewer asked him if he had written any music that didn't appear on the album, he responded "in my capacity as a songwriter, I've probably written a few thousand pieces for this album that didn't get used."[8]

Ominously, Olsen intentionally steered ELP in a direction they had only blindly stumbled into on *Love Beach*: an album chock full of radio-friendly singles. But the lack of creative unity went well beyond the "progressive versus pop" debate outlined above. As had happened on *Love Beach*, Emerson and Lake were again becoming increasingly disinclined to work together. For instance, when Emerson told the band that his hand would take a while to heal after the operation, Lake brought a keyboard player named Rick Barker into the studio and recorded at least one song, "Gone Too Soon," without any participation by Emerson. Emerson, for his part, grew disenchanted with Lake's lyrics for two of his songs, "Change" and "Thin Line," and ended up accepting lyrics from Bill Wray, a friend of Keith Olsen, instead. In fact, only three of the album's tracks were cowritten by Emerson and Lake. There were places in the arrangements where Emerson wanted electric guitar; since Lake was not interested in playing electric guitar on the album, Emerson was obliged to bring in Tim Pierce, who had helped out during the box set sessions. In fact, Lake was now even losing interest in playing bass. Emerson told a startled interviewer, "Greg didn't play guitar at all. Actually, he didn't even play bass a lot. I sampled Greg's bass sound and played keyboard with its sound."[9] Like *Love Beach*, the new album appeared to capture a band in the process of dissolution.

By March 1994, the band were in the overdubbing stage of the new album; there was talk of a late spring or early summer release, with a tour to begin in July, possibly featuring Steve Howe as the opening act. In May, the album was mastered, and was finally given a title: *The Best Seat in the House*. Now the release date was pushed back to August, and the tour to September. By June of 1994, the album had been retitled *In the Hot Seat*; a release date of August 3 was set for Japan, with release dates elsewhere to be determined. In the label's official press release announc-

---

[7] Keith Emerson, quoted by unknown author, "Keith Emerson," *Keyboard Magazine* [Japan] (October 1994), translated from Japanese by Atsuku Sasaki, translation reprinted in *ELP Digest* 5, no. 20 (August 12, 1995).

[8] Keith Emerson, quoted in "The Being Fifty Blues."

[9] Keith Emerson, quoted in Japanese *Keyboard Magazine* article of October 1994.

ing the imminent appearance of the new album, Greg Lake is quoted saying, "The title refers to the fact that we've come under a lot of pressure over the years, and I'm sure it will be the same this time around."[10] The album was to include the 1993 recording of *Pictures at an Exhibition* as a bonus track; the band said they wanted fans who may not have been able to afford the box set to hear the new *Pictures*. In addition, the Japanese release was to include a short solo piano piece by Emerson titled "Hammer it Out," a lively fusion of boogie-woogie and Ginastera, that he had recorded in 1992. Ominously, by June there was no more talk of a tour; Victory representatives, when pressed on the subject, cryptically remarked that the box set had not sold as well as they had hoped.

In the Hot Seat

In the Hot Seat was finally released in Europe on September 26, and in the U.S. on October 18. The first song, "Hand of Truth," gets the album off to a promising start: cowritten by Emerson and Lake, it may be ELP's finest song of the nineties. The success of the song is largely the result of the inspired forty-second instrumental ritornello that opens it; this ritornello, which contains three distinct musical ideas, encapsulates nearly all of the qualities that had made classic ELP so special. First, there's the driving opening theme, with its alternating bars of 5/4 and 4/4 and its right-hand keyboard figurines that interlock with the sharply etched left-hand chord progression; set in G minor, Emerson's contrapuntal keyboard part is ably backed by Lake's sparse but effective bass line, with Palmer's unobtrusive but intricate groove generating a good deal of polyrhythmic energy.[11] At 0:18 there's a new, darker theme: set in D minor, the keyboard melody (now in 4/4) is supported by Emerson's patented quartal harmonies, which gives it an urgent, pressing feel. The third theme, heard at 0:32, is a chain of fanfarelike major triads, related by fifths, that press inexorably back towards the G-minor tonic.

At 0:40 the entire ritornello is repeated; at 1:27 the band extend the third theme through a thicket of changing meters and shifting keys, which spills into a broad, triumphal bridge section whose heroic French horn

---

[10] Greg Lake, quoted in "Emerson, Lake and Palmer are Back in the Hot Seat with a Brand New Album," Polygram Press Release, reprinted in *ELP Digest* 4, no. 22 (November 10, 1994).

[11] Palmer's part, which contains none of the showiness of his seventies drumming, nevertheless repays close study. Note his placement of accents: ONE two three FOUR five ONE two THREE AND four in the bass drum, one two THREE four FIVE one TWO three FOUR in the snare, straight sixteenths on the hi-hat. It's the lack of any accent on beat two of the 5/4 measure that creates the "stutterstep" feeling.

calls and synth string arpeggios seem to push the music towards a climactic C major chord. The music never quite gets there, though, and instead Lake enters dramatically late with his vocal at 2:16. The vocal verse is built over the first two segments of the instrumental ritornello, with the third segment being replaced by a punchy vocal chorus ("we have the power," first reached at 2:48). After a second vocal verse, the song reaches its climax with a screaming Emerson synth solo, built over the chord changes of the chorus.[12] A final vocal chorus, followed by one last statement of the instrumental ritornello's opening theme, brings the song to a close.

I remember thinking, when I heard this anthemic, instantly memorable song for the first time, that perhaps ELP had finally recaptured the old magic; the sense of heroic striving, the irresistible polyrhythmic energy, were all in place. However, I also remember noticing that there seemed to be something "wrong" with the keyboard timbres; normally Emerson would have clothed his inspired thematic ideas in the vivid colors of a GX-1 or Moog-like synth trumpet patch, rather than the rather generic electric piano patch used here, while the Hammond is both buried in the mix and thin sounding. I also was struck by the fact that later repetitions of the ritornello contained none of the gradual contrapuntal layerings that Emerson often used to build climaxes. What I had noticed was in fact a problem that was indicative of the entire album: Keith Olsen simply didn't understand ELP's signature sound well enough to mix their music effectively. When an interviewer asked Emerson why the Hammond sound was so muted on "Hand of Truth," he responded "That was Keith Olsen's mistake. He was the producer. I didn't take part in the mixing."[13]

Emerson was also less than enthused about Greg Lake's lyric, an optimistic but vague call to social activism: "I don't think we should sing about changing society. If we do, we'll become like Bob Geldof."[14] In fact, Emerson was apoplectic when Lake said he wanted to title the song "We Have the Power"—"he must have read a book," Emerson snapped— and demanded the title be changed to "Hand of Truth," a snippet from the end of the chorus.

Despite its surprisingly monochrome keyboard timbres, "Hand of Truth" launches the album off to a very solid start, and leaves one excited to hear what the rest of the album will be all about. Unfortunately, "Hand of Truth" is the album's highpoint; nothing that follows it quite measures up. The next track, Greg Lake's "Daddy," begins to bring this reality home with painful clarity. Now, give Lake due credit for good intentions.

---

[12] This is Emerson's most impressive solo on the album. By his own admission, given the condition of his right hand, it took a number of attempts to get an acceptable take.
[13] Keith Emerson quoted in Japanese *Keyboard* article of October 1994.
[14] Ibid.

In 1993, while watching the TV show *America's Most Wanted*, he heard the story of Sara Anne Wood, a New York girl who was kidnapped and murdered; Lake's lyrics recount the experience of the girl's father in harrowing detail. Sara's father, Robert Wood, in fact founded a national non-profit center, the Sara Anne Wood Rescue Center, which funded the production and distribution of flyers, posters, and other information that was of help in locating missing children; a week after the release of *In the Hot Seat*, ELP donated $5,000 of the album's proceeds to the Rescue Center.

So what's the problem with "Daddy"? Simply this: while the song's sentiments are noble, it doesn't manage to rise beyond the realm of sentiment. It ranks with "Black Moon" as the most harmonically impoverished song in the ELP canon, but "Black Moon" has a range of textural, timbral, and rhythmic subtleties that "Daddy" lacks. "Daddy" is based on a two-bar progression that consists of a G minor electric guitar arpeggio alternating with a D minor arpeggio in first inversion. The ceaseless repetition of this two bar progression does produce a claustrophobic feeling of imprisonment that mirrors the father's hopelessness in the face of his daughter's disappearance. However, the repetition of such a doleful progression becomes, for me at least, almost unbearably cloying after a while; I think a contrasting bridge section would have strengthened the song, allowing for a sense of climax and release as the lyric reached its tragic conclusion when a man confesses to the girl's murder. As it is, the song reminds me a bit of a Greek tragedy that ends halfway through the storyline; the sense of gloom is pervasive, but one never experiences the emotional release that comes from following the plot to its inevitable outcome.

The third song, "One by One," is Keith Emerson's song (with lyrics by Greg Lake and Keith Olsen) that he had originally conceived as part of his epic arrangement of Bob Dylan's "Man in the Long Black Coat." Lyrically, it covers similar ground to earlier masterpieces like "Knife-Edge" and "The Miracle," mingling imagery of alienation ("still we all walk on / one by one"), supernatural terror, and urban violence. Musically, it's probably the densest song on the album, and it's the only song other than "Hand of Truth" that clocks in at over five minutes. It's constructed according to a familiar Emerson formula: instrumental prelude, song proper, and instrumental postlude. It begins with a dense, quasi-fugal section in a driving 4/4 that features both piano and synth patches: although the music seems to gravitate towards G♯ minor, its whole-tone flavoring gives it a harmonic vagueness that approaches atonality.

The song proper begins at 0:28; the meter shifts suddenly to 12/8, and the tonality slips more firmly into G♯ minor, anchored by a throbbing bass line. Emerson punctuates with sporadic offbeat bitonally voiced synth fanfares, rhythmically doubled by Palmer, who otherwise supplies a quiet backing groove on the hi-hat. After the first two verses (0:30 and 0:57), the chorus is reached at 1:25; the tonality shifts to the relative major, B, and Palmer commences a rock drum groove for the first time in the song, while Emerson's synth backing also becomes more rhythmically predictable. A third verse (1:57) and second statement of the chorus (2:25) is followed by a heroic, quasi-baroque pipe organ episode over a ground bass (2:58); after a last statement of the chorus (3:16), the band launch into a lengthy instrumental coda beginning at 3:58. Settling back into G♯ minor, it's based on a 12/8 variant of the two-bar "fugue subject" that opened the song; now, however, the development of the theme is rhythmic and melodic rather than textural and contrapuntal. Compared to many similar passages in the Emerson canon, it's a bit repetitive: often the two-bar theme is simply repeated again and again, with shifting offbeat accents courtesy of Emerson and Palmer. However, there's a nice momentary digression into G (4:16), and a marvelous stop-time extension of the main riff at 4:33.

"One by One" is a genuinely interesting song; however, in the incarnation of it set forth here, its component parts don't seem to cohere into a greater whole. The optimistic, major tonality of the chorus doesn't seem to fit the lyrics or the music of the rest of the song, and the shift from the dense 4/4 instrumental intro to the throbbing 12/8 verse sounds merely clever rather than organic and inevitable. Again, Keith Olsen's production seems to indicate a limited comprehension of the ELP corpus and progressive rock as a style; Emerson's synths sound thin and breathy (same problem as with "Hand of Truth"), and on a track where Lake is really working hard to interpret the lyrics through subtle vocal shading, Olsen ruins it all by running Lake's voice through a flangerlike effect. One wishes that one might someday hear this song as Emerson wished it to be heard.

The next song, the bathetic Greg Lake-Keith Olsen "Heart on Ice," is the first bona fide failure of the album. It seems to follow in the line of the saccharine soft-rock ballad that one finds scattered throughout Lake's solo career: "I Don't Know Why I Still Love You" from *Manoeuvres* (that's the one with the lyric "every time I see you my heart starts beating / boom-boom-boom") will serve as a useful point of reference. Indeed, some of the mixed metaphors here (for instance, "your love is a fire / a burning hurricane") are quite atrocious, and the unwholesome mixture of thin musical substance and overly serious, pompous vocal delivery is hard to take. Carl Palmer provides some sedate drumming that could have been by just about anybody; during a few passages Keith Emerson does his best Procol Harum organ imitation—listen especially at 2:40—in an effort to give the song a sense of majesty that it is simply incapable of assuming. (In this sense I'm also reminded of similar efforts Emerson made on some of Robert Berry's soft-rock strikeouts on the 3 album.) It is an unfortunate comment on Lake's overall artistic direction at this time that in the solo shows he did in late 1994, "Heart on Ice" figured prominently.

The fifth track, "Thin Line," written by Keith Emerson (music) with Bill Wray and Keith Olsen (lyrics), has two sources of inspiration, according to Emerson. The first was an intricate shuffle groove that he had heard Carl Palmer play on drums; Palmer's shuffle groove, in turn, suggested to Emerson a Neville Brothers, New Orleans funk–inspired song. Here Tim Pierce's stinging guitar licks are turned to good account, while the gospel choir–style background vocals that sounded so incongruous on *Pictures* '93 and "I Believe in Father Christmas" are perfectly idiomatic. Unlike "Hand of Truth" and "One by One," where Olsen seemed to have no idea how to mix Emerson's keyboards, Olsen seems to grasp what Emerson was up to here: Emerson's Hammond sounds gloriously tacky and percussive, and his synth trumpet section sounds much more vivid than the synth patches of his earlier tracks. Emerson turns in a terse but funky organ solo, and Greg Lake (or Emerson) contributes a funky slapped bass groove (from 3:56). Nonetheless, despite its strengths, the song seems a bit cold and somewhat stiff in the context of the funk idiom: I'm reminded a bit of "So Far to Fall" from *Works II* in this respect, although "So Far to Fall" is a more adventurous, less conventional take on big-band jazz than "Thin Line" is on New Orleans funk. Interestingly, the lyrics of the two songs cover fairly similar ground—the perpetual power struggle that goes on between men and women in a relationship.

Side two of the *In the Hot Seat* cassette (like *Black Moon*, the new album was released only in the CD and cassette mediums) opens with Bob Dylan's "Man in the Long Black Coat." After a long string of less-than-stellar covers—ELPowell's "Mars," 3's "Eight Miles High," ELP's "Romeo and Juliet"—fans were perhaps justified in entertaining low expectations: however, "Man in the Long Black Coat" turned out to be ELP's finest arrangement in many a year, and what's more, marks a genuinely new direction for the band. There's absolutely no attempt at instrumental virtuosity here: the arrangement is totally subservient to the dark imagery and mysterious narrative of Dylan's lyric. Besides its understatement, the overriding character of ELP's arrangement is its dark, brooding, mystery-laden atmosphere; I'm reminded of how Pink Floyd might have arranged this song during their classic *Wish You Were Here* period—that is, if either David Gilmour or Roger Waters could have rendered the vocal with sufficient intensity.

Emerson sets "Man in the Long Black Coat" in the darkly remote key of G$^\sharp$ minor, the only link it retains with the song that was to have been its continuation, "One by One." The last time Lake had sung in this key was on *Brain Salad Surgery*. Incredibly, throughout "Man in the Long Black Coat" he often sings an octave lower than he had then, fostering a growling baritone worthy of Johnny Cash. He uses this growl to dramatic effect several times during the course of the song: listen especially as he spits out "he had a face like a mask" (at 1:18). However, Lake also is able to push into the upper reaches of his tessitura when it's needed. His vocal interpretation is a major factor in the arrangement's success.

The song, as arranged by Emerson, consists of four sectional "cells." The first is the bleak, desolate ritornello that opens the song and occurs twice thereafter. Emerson's ritornello is a four-bar theme in 9/8 in which a high, thin, lonely keyboard line (imagine a doubled Rhodes electric piano and string patch) is answered by a deep, menacing, electric guitar–like riff, with bell-like, pointillistic flecks of sound quietly reverberating in the background. Lake and Palmer create a sense of edginess by accompanying Emerson's brooding 9/8 theme in 6/8, so that every three bars of their accompaniment coincide with two bars of Emerson's theme. The ritornello is presented twice at the beginning of the song (0:00–0:13, 0:14–0:27): Palmer accompanies during both statements, Lake during the second statement only.

The first verse (0:28) features Lake in his Johnny Cash–like baritone growl; Emerson provides only the sparsest accompaniment, largely doubling Lake's vocal with a synth bass line, so that Palmer's ingenious layering of sequenced percussion (the "conga" groove) and understated drum kit groove (played in real time) is foregrounded. The chorus (first reached at 0:49) is similar, but adds two more textural elements: a hard electronic snare hit, and a percussive electric guitar–like arpeggio. Throughout the song, it is the subtle layering in and withdrawal of small textural details like these that give the arrangement its brooding atmosphere. After the second verse (1:02) and chorus (1:24), we get the first statement of the bridge ("there are no mistakes in life") at 1:37. Here Lake suddenly pushes into the higher part of his tessitura, creating a dramatic climax, which is underscored by a sudden thickening of the accompaniment (greater bass presence, the first full-out drum groove, and suddenly luxuriant stringlike backing). Interestingly, the bridge emphasizes E major, VI in the key of G$^\sharp$ minor. In nineteenth-century music, the VI chord was often fraught with undertones of false or thwarted hope,[15] and it seems to have similar connotations here.

The bridge ends the first cycle of the song; we've now heard all four sectional cells, which the remainder of the song subtly varies and develops. A shortened version of Emerson's instrumental ritornello returns at 1:56; the third verse, from 2:10, features a fuller keyboard backing, as Emerson now begins to slowly reveal the melody's full harmonic poten-

---

[15] See Susan McClary, "Pitches, Expression, Ideology: An Exercise in Mediation," *Enclitic* 7, no. 1 (Spring 1983): 76–86.

tial, and introduces an ominous trebly dominant pedal point that hangs over the vocal melody like a dark cloud, reminiscent of his high, quiet Hammond trill during the second verse of "Knife-Edge." The chorus (2:32) is followed by the fourth and final verse, where Emerson's accompaniment now becomes more active, evoking a kind of gothic folk organum. The song climaxes with a second statement of the bridge (3:23), where Emerson's "synth organum" replaces his earlier stringlike backing, and finally, bookendlike, comes a full statement of the forlorn instrumental ritornello.

In my fairly skeletal account of the song given above, I have had to ignore all sorts of fascinating details. For instance, although the song is cast in 6/8 and conjures the faintest whiff of traditional honky-tonk rhythm (one-AND-AH two-AND-AH), the verse, chorus, and bridge all end with a bar of 9/8 followed by two bars of 6/8. Not only does this forge a link with the ritornello's cross rhythm; it also introduces an element of uncertainty and the unexpected that nicely complements Dylan's mysterious, ominous narrative. The textural layering, too, repays multiple listening; for instance, wisps of the ritornello's "distorted electric guitar" are recalled at key junctures during the verses. Because the arrangement's texture is kept lean, almost austere, small gestures like this make a big impression. Finally—and this is not meant to detract from ELP's totally successful arrangement—the fact is that Dylan gives them some awfully good material to work with, even by his sterling standards; these lyrics are extraordinarily vivid and multilayered.[16] By whatever standards one chooses to apply, ELP's "Man in the Long Black Coat" is a success, all the more because there's nothing else quite like it in the ELP canon; again, one can only wish that Emerson had been allowed to fully realize his original conception concerning the song's arrangement.

The seventh track, "Change," is, like "Thin Line," cowritten by Keith Emerson (music) with Bill Wray and Keith Olsen (words). When asked about this song, Emerson said, "That was another seed of disharmony. Greg thought it was like a sea shanty and a sailor's hornpipe. I thought it [the "sailor's hornpipe"] was a catchy riff. The problem was his lyrics . . . The song was rejected once because Greg couldn't write lyrics for it. In

---

[16] I can't resist one example: "Somebody said from the Bible he'd quote / there's dust on the man in the long black coat." Although he's familiar enough with the Bible to quote it, the "dust" evokes Jesus's charge to his apostles that if any town refused their message, they were to leave it, and, as a testimony against it, shake the dust from their shoes as they left; Jesus told them that on judgment day that it would be more tolerable for Sodom and Gomorrah than for the people of that town (Mark 6:11). Thus there is a suggestion that the man in the long black coat is a kind of Cain, a wanderer who is accursed of God. We also entertain the suspicion that the unnamed young woman who has left with the man in the long black coat will come to no good end.

the end, Bill Wray wrote good lyrics for this, too."[17] The "sailor's shanty" description is pretty accurate, with bubbling Hammond arpeggios further contributing to the "sea vibe"; I'm reminded a bit of some of the material from Emerson's *Honky* (especially that album's first two tracks). "Change" is based around a snappy, hornpipelike four-bar keyboard/bass riff in A Mixolydian, first heard at 0:28, that underlines each statement of the chorus. The song is also interesting for its use of two distinct sets of verses. There's an introductory verse in A major, heard at the song's beginning, that returns once towards its end (3:49); the main verse, which consists of alternating A minor and F$\sharp$ minor chords, is first heard at 0:45. As with many Emerson songs, there's an instrumental bridge, a colorful ten-bar chord progression that slides in and out of C major. It's repeated twice (2:03 and 2:31), the second time with a cheerful piano obbligato. Consistent with Emerson's other songs here ("Hand of Truth," "One by One"), the bridge's synth chords sound uncharacteristically thin and monochrome. This criticism aside, "Change" is a cheerful, lively song.

"Change" is followed by another bathetic soft-rock ballad, "Reason to Stay." Emerson explained,

> I didn't know about this until Keith Olsen told me there was a demo. Olsen though it suitable for Greg's voice. I listened . . . and thought it was terrible. The original arrangement, by Steve Diamond [who cowrote the song with Sam Lorber] was a typical California song with comfortable chords and modulations. I was allowed to do as I liked. First I cleared away all the keyboards and bass. I changed it totally and it became like a Randy Newman song. It's much better than the original.[18]

Emerson added that he had originally inserted a synth solo in the song, using his Korg Wavestation to evoke an electric guitar; when Keith Olsen told him a real electric guitar would sound better, Emerson replaced his solo with a solo by Tim Pierce.

Two comments here. First, while the arrangement may evoke Randy Newman, the song itself doesn't; Newman's most representative songs are witty and ironic, while this song is simply a saccharine soft-rock ballad. That being said, I must commend Greg Lake for his resourcefulness. Throughout the album, Lake does not fight his hoarseness and the loss of his higher register, but makes his vocal condition as it is at the moment work for him. On "Reason to Stay" he very nearly reinvents himself as a smoky-voiced, soulful R & B baritone; he sounds so comfortably at home in his "new" voice that it's startling to realize this is the same voice as the bell-like tenor that once upon a time interpreted "In the Wake of

---

[17] Keith Emerson, quoted in Japanese *Keyboard Magazine* article of October 1994.
[18] Ibid.

Poseidon," "The Only Way," and "I Believe in Father Christmas." While there are other places on the album where Lake's "new" voice serves him well (notably "Man in the Long Black Coat"), this is the song that most fully reveals how profoundly not only his range, but his vocal timbre, had changed.

The next track, penned by Greg Lake, Bill Wray, and Keith Wechsler, is "Gone too Soon." I suspect my assessment might be taken as a criticism, but it's not meant to be: "Gone too Soon" successfully realizes the formula that the band had aspired to, but miserably failed at, on side one of *Love Beach*. "Gone too Soon" is a cheerful, up-tempo rock song dominated by a tuneful, fanfarelike keyboard ritornello (heard first at 0:08, and a number of times thereafter) that sounds like it could have been Keith Emerson's, although all keyboards on this song are played by Rick Barker. While the main body of the song is cast in E Mixolydian, some smooth modulations (the bridge, at 1:42, is set in G Mixolydian, and the Tony Banks–like synth solo from 2:09, with its rapid-fire arpeggios, is in A) give a nice sense of tonal movement. Like all of the album's more pop-oriented material, it's well produced; clearly this is an idiom that Keith Olsen understood. If ELP had managed to make the "Gone too Soon" formula (cheerful up-tempo rock with a few unobtrusive prog rock trimmings) work across the entire first side of *Love Beach* back in 1978, it's possible that their subsequent history would have been much different. The problem is, by 1994 stadium rock hadn't been a popular style for at least a decade, and there was little chance of "Gone too Soon" getting any airplay—which, in fact, it didn't.

While the *In the Hot Seat* CD contains eleven tracks, ending with the 1993 recording of *Pictures at an Exhibition* (the Japanese CD ends with the short Keith Emerson piano piece "Hammer it Out," the twelfth track overall), the cassette ends with the tenth track, "Street War." Since it is the final studio cut of the ELP oeuvre, perhaps it is appropriate that it was cowritten by Keith Emerson and Greg Lake—just the third Emerson-Lake collaboration of the album. Perhaps it is also fitting that "Street War" evokes many of the hallmarks of early ELP. Musically, it's an urgent, almost frantic Hammond-and-synth dominated rock song characterized by edgy cross rhythms and complex instrumental episodes. The lyrics, too, hearken back to the themes of alienation and social unrest that the band had addressed as early as 1970. Now, however, the imagery is less symbolic and more straightforward: there seem to be references to the L.A. riots of 1992, the rise of the populist militia movements in the U.S. during the early nineties, and the public's fascination with blood-and-guts television programs such as "Rescue 911." Above all, there is an emphasis on the trends that tie these seemingly disparate events together; the loss of democracy to the forces of special interests that buy elections, and to a ruthless bureaucracy willing to "raise the sword of state" to keep the "peace."[19] "Street War," with its vision of creeping totalitarianism and rising social unrest, raises many of the same issues as "Tarkus," but in a more topical and straightforward way; it is certainly one of Greg Lake's finest lyrics.

"Street War" had its origin in the Lake-Downes Ride the Tiger project of the late eighties. When the song was resurrected for *In the Hot Seat*, Lake edited the lyric, and Emerson wrote completely new music. Although Lake has usually been taciturn about his songwriting collaborations with Emerson, "Street War" marks one of a very few songs about which he was openly critical of Emerson's contribution. In an interview with Dave Gallant, Lake remarked, "I used the lyric, and Keith wrote a whole new programming thing for it. I think Geoff's version was better. It had more sincerity. I thought the lyric was good, and that's why I wanted to use it. If you played the two versions, you wouldn't recognize them. Looking back on it, I prefer the version that Geoff and I did. It was highly impassioned."[20] One wishes that Lake had included the Lake-Downes "Street War" on the *Greg Lake Anthology* of 1997, so that ELP fans could compare the two versions and make up their own minds. Without that option, it's impossible for me to say whether Lake's assessment is sour grapes or dead-on accurate. I will say this, however: within the stylistic confines and track length constraints that Keith Olsen insisted Emerson work under, I think "Street War" works quite well: in fact, as an out-and-out rocker, I find it superior to both "Black Moon" and "Paper Blood" from their previous album.

The short instrumental intro to "Street War" is vintage Emerson: angular, edgy, geometric. The song begins with a two-bar motive consisting of two Bs, an octave apart, in 5/8; the 5/8 motive continues on when the introductory four-bar theme (from 0:04) that launches the song proper is stated in 4/4, generating a nervous, off-balance polyrhythm. At 0:09, the frantic, pile-driving one-bar keyboard/bass riff in B pentatonic enters that is to dominate the rest of the song; careful listening will reveal the entrance of a syncopated counter-riff at 0:15, which afterwards threads its way in and out of the mix. The sixteen-bar verse (from 0:19) is totally dominated by the ubiquitous riff; at 0:43, a sixteen-bar "anti-verse" (for want of a better term) swings the tonality from B minor to the relative, D major, with alternating D major and E♭ major triads, and is characterized by much richer keyboard accompaniment. At 1:05, the "Street War" chorus is reached, swinging the music back into B minor;

---

[19] Some of my readers may recall that the period between the release of *Black Moon* and *In the Hot Seat* witnessed not only the Rodney King beating and subsequent L.A. riots, but also Waco and Ruby Ridge.

[20] Greg Lake, quoted by Gallant, "Greg Lake Tapes."

note Lake's doubling of the words "Street War" an octave below his principal vocal line with a growling bass falsetto, which gives his call-and-response style chorus additional muscle. Emerson, for his part, demonstrates once more his ability to make an elemental Hammond part (he simply alternates between the open fifth-octave B–F♯–B and the quartal harmony B–E–A) sound imposing via the effective use of Leslie vibrato. From 1:28 the same four structural cells (intro, verse, antiverse, chorus) are repeated. At 2:47 there's a twelve-bar instrumental bridge that wends its way through a typically Emersonian thicket of modulating quartal harmonies and subtle melodic development. Then, from 3:04, a strident but hypnotically simple Emerson synth solo over the main riff brings the song to its climax, preparing the way for a final return of the chorus. The song ends with the same cadential formula (E major–D major–B major) used at the end of the intro theme.

In the Hot Seat: An Assessment

In the Hot Seat holds the dubious distinction of being the first, and only, studio album by ELP that did not break the American Top 200. Indeed, despite its overweening attempt to deliver the big hit single for the band, it got very little radio airplay—virtually none aside from "Daddy." To the contrary, the release of the album was one of the best-kept secrets of the music industry, ranking with Victory's more or less contemporaneous release of Yes's *Talk*. At least Yes toured to support their new album: in a dangerous repeat of the *Love Beach* precedent, ELP appeared to more or less dissolve after the album's release. Of course, the condition of Emerson's hand was a major factor in the cancellation of the proposed *In the Hot Seat* tour. But so were disappointing album sales and the increasingly dicey financial state of the Victory label itself.[21] Greg Lake assembled a band and did a few small-scale shows, mostly in the northeast U.S., in late October, early November, and then again mid-December 1994; his shows featured two songs from the new album ("Daddy" and "Heart on Ice"), as well as several classic Lake ballads such as "From the Beginning," "Lucky Man," and "I Believe in Father Christmas."[22] After the New Year, however, ELP became completely invisible, their future a question mark.

A somewhat perverse pastime of long-time ELP fans is debating whether *Love Beach* or *In the Hot Seat* is the band's biggest flop. I'm afraid that I'm unable to render a definitive verdict here. Let's start by judging

---

[21] Yes's *Talk* sold roughly 300,000 copies; *In the Hot Seat*, somewhat less.

[22] Lake's touring band of 1994 featured himself (lead vocals, rhythm guitar), Rob LaVaque (keyboards, vocals), Keith Wechsler (drums, programming), Robbie Robinson (bass and bass synth), and Alan Payette (lead guitars).

In the Hot Seat on its own merits. It contains three memorable songs: "Hand of Truth," "Man in the Long Black Coat," and "Street War." It contains another song, "One by One," that is ambitious, interesting, but flawed. It contains three songs—"Thin Line," "Change," and "Gone too Soon"—that are pleasant, well-crafted, but somewhat thin in terms of musical substance. And it contains three songs—"Daddy," "Heart on Ice," and "Give Me a Reason to Stay"—that are maudlin, bathetic, and best forgotten. If one were to take the best five songs and put them on one side of an LP or cassette, one would have half an album that is more or less comparable in quality to the *Black Moon* material. The songs on the second side of the LP or cassette, on the other hand, wouldn't compare to the *Black Moon* material nearly as favorably.

When comparing *In the Hot Seat* to *Black Moon*, several other comparisons spring to mind, and they inevitably favor the latter at the expense of the former. While the *Black Moon* material doesn't exactly cohere into a unified whole, it still coheres a lot better than *In the Hot Seat*, because it projects a sense of team play that *In the Hot Seat* utterly lacks. While I'm not bothered by the relative lack of keyboard virtuosity evident on *In the Hot Seat*, the thinness of a lot of its synth timbres, and especially the monochromatic colors of a lot of its synth arrangements, have always taken me by surprise; it's hard to know whether the ultimate responsibility lies with Keith Emerson, Keith Olsen, or both. Carl Palmer's drumming never sounded this anonymous on an ELP album before; other than "Hand of Truth" and "One by One," where Palmer's signature grooves are in evidence, a lot of the drumming here could have been contributed by any competent studio drummer. It seems as if the many years Palmer had spent with Asia had finally taken their toll—not so much on his technique, which was still formidable, but on his imagination and invention, which appeared to have atrophied under the weight of drumming to too much pedestrian material for too long. Finally, on *Black Moon* Mark Mancina, a deeply sympathetic producer, squeezed every ounce of potential out of the material. On *In the Hot Seat*, Keith Olsen, who seems to have never quite understood what ELP were all about, may have seriously hurt the final product through his incomprehension; it would certainly be a stretch to say his production was "sympathetic."

So was *In the Hot Seat* better or worse than *Love Beach*? In my view, it's an unanswerable question. There is nothing on *In the Hot Seat* anywhere near as embarrassing as the first few tracks of *Love Beach*, which remain the nadir of ELP's output. On the other hand, there is nothing on *In the Hot Seat* as ambitious as "Memoirs of an Officer and a Gentleman." If there is anything that would make one choose *Love Beach* as the worst ELP album, it's the impression that the band brought the whole disaster on themselves. On the other hand, it's not that hard to imagine that without Emerson's hand problem, without Lake's vocal difficulties (which he navigated with surprising success), and, above all, with a sympathetic producer, *In the Hot Seat* could have been a much better album. Perhaps that's what's so frustrating about it: listening to isolated bits and pieces of it (much of "Hand of Truth," parts of "One by One," "Street War," "Man in the Long Black Coat"), one can in fact hear the band continuing to explore and develop some of the ideas and directions posited on *Black Moon*.

Shortly after the release of *In the Hot Seat*, an interviewer asked Emerson if he was bitter about Keith Olsen's decision to nix his mini-epic arrangement of "Man in the Long Black Coat." Emerson was stoic about it: "I accepted his decision, and that was that."[23] He told another interviewer, "My opinions were mostly rejected by the majority. I didn't complain because I agreed that it [the album's content] should be a majority decision." He added, though, "In other cases I've refused to compromise to the end. I took an attitude like this in the seventies, because it's that attitude that made "Tarkus" and "Karn Evil 9." I may have to take an attitude like this now. I suppose I'll have to from now on, but I don't know what will happen after all this."[24] Clearly, Emerson had already decided that if there ever were to be another ELP studio album, it would only be under circumstances where his artistic vision could be fully realized.

In an interview conducted shortly after the release of *In the Hot Seat*, Carl Palmer appears solidly in the pro–Keith Olsen faction, saying, "When we first met we immediately liked his method of working . . . personally I'm very happy [with the new album]."[25] However, over time his opinion changed, and by the time of an interview with Aymeric Leroy in July 1997, he had clearly come over to Emerson's point of view, although he never acknowledges that he had formerly not shared it. His assessment below hits the proverbial nail squarely:

> [*In the Hot Seat*] was a disaster. All our fault. The problem was, we were in California, and we involved an outside producer called Keith Olsen. And Keith Olsen was the wrong person to work with us. Because he's into soft rock, Fleetwood Mac . . . If we made a mistake, we didn't make one, we made a hundred, all in a row! And at that time, Keith had his arm operation, he couldn't really play. But we had started, and we were trying to work out how could we go on, what we could do. And at the end of the day we ended up with lots of songs which didn't mean too much. That was the same feeling, the same problem that the group had when we made *Love Beach*, another disaster of ours.[26]

---

[23] Keith Emerson, quoted in "The Being Fifty Blues."
[24] Keith Emerson, quoted in Japanese *Keyboard* interview, October 1994.
[25] Carl Palmer, quoted by unknown interviewer, "Carl Palmer" *Percussioni* (November 1994), translated from Italian by Adriano Melis, reprinted in *ELP Digest* 6, no. 3.
[26] Carl Palmer, quoted by Leroy, "An Interview with Carl Palmer."

The cover of *In the Hot Seat* depicts an old coal-burning locomotive, emblazoned with the "ELP" logo, coming straight down the track towards the viewer, bearing down on a small wooden chair tied to the tracks (the proverbial hot seat). Scattered among the album credits are diagrams of the old ELP locomotive, complete with its measurements. Some fans saw some unintended symbolism in the album artwork. The band had all the diagrams: why didn't they use them to re-create the powerful old ELP of days gone by? If the band recognized something was in their way, blocking their progress, why didn't they plow on through it?

At any rate, after the end of the Greg Lake "mini-tour" in late 1994, ELP disappeared off the radar screen, and the future of the band was again in doubt. By mid-1995, the Victory label itself had evaporated, further complicating the band's future. History seemed poised to repeat itself all over again.

The End

(1995–1998)

When Chris Welch asked Phil Carson about the last days of Victory Records, especially as pertains to Yes's album *Talk*, Carson made an interesting observation:

> They [Yes] had been big from 1970 to 1990 so they'd had a good run. In the Billboard chart, even by the end of 1989 you would still see in the Top Twenty bands that had been around for 15 years or more. It was a unique period in the history of music when the parents and their teenage children were listening to the same groups. Led Zeppelin, Yes, Emerson, Lake and Palmer, Journey, and Boston were still being played on radio. That couldn't last forever and that's when the musical revolution of grunge came along. It broke so quickly the radio formats fragmented overnight and there was nowhere for Yes to get played. It has affected everyone of that generation since . . . That kind of music is over as far as kids are concerned.[1]

In hindsight, it would seem that Carson saw the symptoms clearly enough, but partly misdiagnosed the cause. By and large, grunge didn't finish seventies rock; rap did.[2] Grunge, after all, was connected to the Tradition—Kurt Cobain of Nirvana once cited King Crimson's *Red* as one of his favorite albums—and grunge's fans remained interested in the earlier rock music in which grunge's roots could be found.[3] The fact is, how-

---

[1] Phil Carson, quoted by Welch, *Close to the Edge*, 241.
[2] I would argue the most iconic seventies rockers—Pink Floyd, Led Zeppelin's Jimmy Page and Robert Plant—retained the interest of (and commanded the record-buying loyalty of) American youth culture into the midnineties, not the early nineties, as Carson suggests. Undoubtedly youth culture's interest in seventies rock was slowly fading during the first half of the nineties; perhaps Yes, not being quite as iconic as Pink Floyd or Zeppelin, faded as a commercial force a couple of years earlier than they did. Certainly ELP had faded as a commercial force during the eighties.
[3] On Cobain and King Crimson, see Welch, *Close to the Edge*, 130.

ever, that grunge represented the final playing out of rock as a culturally and musically vital force in popular culture—bands such as Nirvana, Pearl Jam, and Soundgarden crested between the early and midnineties, and rock has produced nothing of comparable culture impact or popularity since. By 1995, rock was forty years old, and had served as the *vox populi* for two generations; to the new generation that was beginning to come of age in the midnineties, rock was running out of things to say. The rap music that has increasingly displaced rock as the music of choice of the college-age (and younger) crowd since that time traces its roots back to sixties soul, seventies funk, and eighties dance music, not rock. Unlike fans of Pearl Jam or Primus, who would have heard echoes of earlier rock greats in the music of their favorite bands, fans of Tupac Shakur, Sean "Puffy" Combs, and the like have found the music of the Beatles, Led Zeppelin, or Yes nearly as foreign as the music of Duke Ellington or Glenn Miller. Although rap has never dominated popular culture as hegemonically as rock did during the seventies and eighties—through the present day (2006), rock retains a presence in the charts—I think it is fair to say that sometime between the early and midnineties, the Age of Rock ended.[4]

What this has meant is that from the midnineties on, rock icons of the sixties, seventies, and eighties who remain active in the music business are no longer seriously pursuing hit singles or platinum albums—Carlos Santana's hugely successful *Supernatural* (1999) being the one major exception that has proved the rule—nor are they trying to make serious inroads into a new generation of fans. Some periodically release new albums that are targeted to the over thirty-five demographic that listens to the "classic rock" format; others have ceased to worry about releasing new music, but simply tour—touring, unlike new album sales, remains a reliable source of income for sixties and seventies rockers even into the new millennium—playing hits of days gone by for their aging (and dwindling) fan base, who sometimes bring their curious (or not-so-curious) children to the shows. Seen against this backdrop, the final playing out of the ELP saga in the years following the Victory Records era of 1991–94 will hopefully make a bit more sense.

It was unclear in 1995 whether ELP still existed. In fact, by the latter part of 1994, when the *In the Hot Seat* fiasco was still playing itself out, Keith Emerson had agreed to embark on a major new solo project, which involved providing music for Marvel Comics' *Iron Man* television cartoon series. Emerson recalls,

---

[4] Undoubtedly, some will say that the sketch I've drawn here of the displacement of rock by rap as the primary music of youth culture between the early and midnineties is oversimplified. No doubt this is true, as I would have needed to devote pages to a nuanced description of this process. However, I believe that the overall trajectory of my account is correct.

A meeting was held in Marvel's California offices with Stan Lee, creator of action heroes, presiding. A discussion took place which revolved around making children's animated television more a family event by way of upgrading the music from its usual banality of cartoon music into film score extravaganza. That way, we rationalized, the kids would get to see their favorite characters and get a subliminal music appreciation course while at the same time watching with mum and dad. Well, that was the plan and I welcomed the challenge like any hopeful action hero, drawing the line at wearing my underpants over the top of my trousers.[5]

Emerson, who from 1994 lived more or less permanently in Santa Monica, on the west end of Los Angeles, composed and orchestrated the music for thirteen episodes of *Iron Man*, which aired weekly (with a number of the episodes being repeated) in U.S. markets between September 25, 1994, and April 2, 1995. As with his earlier film scores, it was exhausting work:

Every week I'd be presented a new challenging story, to compose the music and orchestrate, while Will Alexander would advise, sequence, and synchronize it all to a video . . . Will and I would often work way into the early hours of the morning. I'd sometimes fall asleep while Will adjusted something I'd played to fit a particular scene and then he'd wake me up to finish the last ten minutes. Then we'd have to get it all mixed and send it all to Marvel in time for them to put it to film.[6]

Emerson added that he had composed the music so quickly that when Will Alexander played him a passage of the score several years later, he didn't even recognize it: "Having written and played so much music over such a short period, I really didn't identify with it except that it did sound good."[7]

In the discographies that appeared on his web site during the nineties, Emerson listed the *Iron Man* music as part of his discography, which, to those of us who hadn't watched *Iron Man* and had no hope of ever hearing the music, seemed to be a bit of an affectation. But lo and behold, in spring of 2002 Emerson released a limited edition album, available only through his web site, containing seventy-three minutes of music from the *Iron Man* series entitled *Iron Man, Volume I*. The release of *Iron Man* is a milestone in Emerson's output, not only because it contains some excellent music, but also because it forced those of us who thought we understood the trajectory of Emerson's career after the eighties to reconsider our assessments. In other words, based on the evidence of *Black Moon* and

[5] Keith Emerson, liner notes to *Iron Man, Volume I*.
[6] Ibid.
[7] Ibid.

In the Hot Seat, I was comfortable in my view that Emerson's compositional powers had entered a state of terminal decline after the mideighties: the *Iron Man* music (which I never heard until the nineties were already history) has forced me to reconsider this view.

Iron Man, Volume I

Iron Man, Volume I consists of six tracks. The "Iron Man Main Title Theme" is followed by four lengthy (sixteen- to nineteen-minute) tracks, each comprising the music from a particular episode; the album ends with "Iron Man Alternate Theme." The short (roughly one minute) "Iron Man Main Title Theme" introduces the two main themes that will dominate, and unify, the remainder of the album, recurring, like Wagnerian *leitmotives*, in an almost endless array of variations. The first is Iron Man's theme, which Emerson aptly describes as "German steel foundry pulsation," a complex, heroic, trumpetlike theme that is accompanied by a pulsating, machinelike bass line and rhythmically vibrating flecks of background sound. At 0:31, the Iron Man theme is suddenly displaced by the theme depicting Mandarin, Iron Man's archenemy: Mandarin is represented by a menacing, chromatic neobaroque theme supported by enormous pipe organlike block chords.

The four tracks that dominate the remainder of the album show an inspiration and invention that was notable by its absence in a great deal of ELP's nineties output, indicating that Emerson's well of inspiration had in fact yet to run dry. The overall impression of Emerson's *Iron Man* music is of an electronic symphony which has seamlessly absorbed its rock influences—something of a nineties equivalent to "Abaddon's Bolero," although the music here is far more varied in mood and character. One hears echoes of all of Emerson's major film scores here, seamlessly brought together: the symphonic classicism of *Inferno*, the hi-tech urban funk of *Nighthawks*, the electronic New Age of *Harmagedon*, the gothic, neobaroque excesses of *La Chiesa*. Although all four of the lengthy tracks here contain common material, especially recurrences of the Iron Man and Mandarin themes, each manages to convey its own distinctive personality. The second track, "And the Sea Shall Give Up Its Dead," is something of a virtuoso variation chain of the Iron Man and Mandarin themes, which Emerson works and reworks into an amazing variety of musical characterizations and moods—high points include the reflective variant of Mandarin's theme at 3:20, the pastoral variant of Iron Man's theme from 4:20 through 4:58, and the mystical, pseudo-oriental development of Mandarin's theme from 11:44. Other highlights include the enormously powerful "electric guitar" riff at 0:57; the variation of the "Street War" ostinato at 2:07; and an agonized, angst-ridden battle theme (somewhat reminiscent of Prokofiev's "Romeo and Juliet," but even more ominous and urgent) at 14:35. It also contains the album's first statement of the floating, short wave radio–like sample-and-hold that depicts Mandarin's sidekick, Modoc, at 3:42.

If "And the Sea Shall Give Up Its Dead" is dominated by variations and developments of the Iron Man and Mandarin themes, the third track, "I Am Ultimo, Thy Deliverer" is characterized by an electronic symphonic expressionism that reminds one a bit of *Inferno*. One hears this link in the slow, quietly agonized quasi-symphonic opening, and in the booming, ominous Emersonian ostinato, evocative of "Eruption" or the opening of the Piano Concerto's third movement, that is stated at 2:08 and recurs with further development at 4:11 and again at 11:53. Of course, one also encounters some imaginative variants of the two primary *leitmotives*, including a beautiful "pizzicato string" statement of the Iron Man theme at 10:27 and a waltz-time statement of the Mandarin theme at 7:05 and again at 9:11. Other highlights include a cheerful, heroic rock march that evokes "Karn Evil 9, 3rd Impression" (6:41) and a seventies-ish jazz-rock episode that almost sounds like an unreleased ELP jam (at 14:04).

Parts of the fourth track, "Data In, Chaos Out" are evocative of the swirling electronic New Age stylizations of Emerson's *Harmagedon* music. One hears this vein of music most clearly in the drifting, atmospheric electronics of 5:18, 8:04, 12:01, and especially the "music of the spheres" episode at 14:12. Other passages of "Data In" are more forceful: the dramatic theme with offbeat, Stravinskian "horn" chords that opens the track, an electronic variant of the driving ostinato that opens the third movement of Emerson's Piano Concerto (first heard at 4:17, and then again at 13:46), and the heroic, "Karn Evil 9"-like rock march from "I Am Ultimo," which recurs here at 11:17. Again, there's some imaginative development of the Iron Man and Mandarin themes, especially the statement of the Iron Man theme accompanied by wisps of the second theme of Gustav Holst's "Mars" at 1:50, and the majestic "string orchestra" statement of Mandarin's theme at 14:32.

The fifth track, "Silence My Companion, Death My Destination" is both the longest (at 19:18) and stylistically the most varied. It shows a penchant for urban, funk-oriented material: the opening, as well as the minor-mode funk riff at 11:28, are reminiscent of some of the *Nighthawks* material, and there's an episode (6:35 to 7:48) featuring a kind of bizarre, psychedelic hip-hop: over a raplike bass and drums pattern, Emerson intersperses "jive" background jabber, atonal piano flourishes, and assorted spacey effects. There's also a number of quotes here; twice we hear excerpts of Sergei Rachmaninov's *Etudes-Tableaux*, op. 39, no. 5, in $E^\flat$ minor (at 5:06 and 15:47), which signal the appearance of classical piano virtuoso Van Cliburn on the screen, and Emerson also quotes his own music, with excerpts of "Tank" (16:20) and "Street War" (17:44). There's also a series of brooding, atmospheric passages dominated by a pulsating sequencer (8:37, 12:33, 13:34, 14:49). The album ends with the one-minute "Iron Man Theme Alternate," which begins with the ominous "battle theme" from 14:35 of "And the Sea Shall Give Up Its Dead," moves into a waltz-time presentation of the Mandarin theme (0:26), and ends (from 0:50) with a final presentation of the battle theme.

Iron Man: An Assessment

The *Iron Man* music is not structurally organic in the manner of the bulk of the *Inferno* score: there's a flow of recurring themes, to be sure, but episodes are seldom developed at length, and tend to move one into another in a stream-of-consciousness manner. Some Emerson fans might note a return here to the more mosaiclike structures of his earlier work, and perhaps it could be argued that this approach to structure has always suited Emerson better than his forays into "organic" classical forms. On the other hand, the sudden changes here, not only of musical mood and material, but of musical style, often seem arbitrary on purely musical grounds, and are supported primarily by the logic of the plot. Emerson fans are also likely to miss the presence of a real rhythm section, although Emerson and Will Alexander handle the drum programming fairly well.

These drawbacks aside, *Iron Man* is a major addition to the Emerson canon: some of the music here is among his most imaginative and ambitious in many years, the display of thematic transformation here is Emerson's most virtuosic since *Inferno*, and there is something magisterial in the synthesis of all his previous film score approaches into a musically coherent whole. Emerson fans who believe his compositional powers were steadily waning after the mideighties are urged to acquaint themselves with *Iron Man, Volume I*: hopefully the second volume implicitly promised by the album's title will sooner or later enter the public domain as well.

In February 1995, even as the new Iron Man installments with Emerson's music were being broadcast weekly, Emerson's long-lost solo album of 1989-90 was released. Six years earlier, in 1989, there was still an outside chance that an Emerson album might be released on a fairly substantial label and receive at least cursory airplay on "classic rock" stations; by 1995, it was clear those days were gone forever. Emerson's album, entitled *Changing States*, was released by a small British label, AMP Records, and was marketed primarily to the widely but thinly spread progressive rock taste public that was increasingly cohering around a series of fanzines, mail-order catalogs, internet sites, and progressive rock festivals. In discussing *Changing States* it's necessary to reiterate what I said earlier: unlike *Iron Man*, this album shouldn't be viewed as a snapshot of where Emerson was as a musician in the midnineties, but rather as a previously missing piece of his late-eighties solo career that also produced *La Chiesa* and *The Christmas Album*. *Changing States* contains nine different tracks, one of which is presented in a different mix as a kind of bonus track, for a total of ten tracks. Six tracks are from the July 1989 sessions at Patrick Leonard's Burbank studio; these are all instrumentals. Three tracks (two, actually, with one of the two tracks being presented here in two different mixes), both songs, are the product of the October 1989 sessions at Robert Berry's studio in Campbell; and finally, there's the 1975 orchestral recording of "Abaddon's Bolero," now remixed and remastered by Gilbert.

Changing States

Changing States opens with "Shelter from the Rain," a short, anthemic, riff-driven rock song featuring Gary Cirimelli (lead vocal), guitarist Marc Bonilla, producer Kevin Gilbert on drums and bass, and Emerson himself on Hammond and some discreet trumpetlike synth patches. It's reminiscent of some of the 3 material, but a bit heavier (due to Bonilla's rhythm guitar parts) and more melodically memorable. The lyrics, interestingly, offer the same call to a vague social activism that Emerson decried in "Hand of Truth." Emerson contributes a short Hammond solo, replete with organ raking, that prefigures his "Paper Blood" solo.

Next is "Another Frontier," the first of the album's three tracks that appear in different arrangements, and with different titles, on *Black Moon*. ELP fans already knew "Another Frontier" by its *Black Moon* title, "Changing States." As I said earlier, it is possible to argue that some of the changes ELP made to this number harmed its structural integrity, and some Emerson fans therefore prefer "Another Frontier"; personally, I prefer "Changing States," mainly because of the work of Lake and Palmer, who as a rhythm section put in their finest performance of the Victory Records era. (I also much prefer the dramatic double-time finish of "Changing States" to the less-than-dramatic fadeout of "Another Frontier.") One of the upshots of the release of the *Changing States* album is that ELP fans could now listen to both versions and make up their own minds; it's also interesting to be able to actually hear what was changed when a finished Emerson solo piece became an ELP number. On "Another Frontier," Emerson is accompanied by Jerry Watts (bass), Mike Barsimanto (drums), and Tim Pierce (guitar); Pierce, of course, was later to appear on the six tracks newly recorded for the 1993 box set, and again on *In The Hot Seat*.

The third track, "Ballade," was also a known commodity to ELP fans who were familiar with *Black Moon*, although they knew it as "Close to Home." In this arrangement, Emerson is accompanied by Gilbert on nylon guitar; Emerson also adds some discreet string synth patches, which alternately provide offbeat accents and a background sonic cushion in selected passages. Some may prefer the solo piano version on *Black Moon*; while I am usually of the "less-is-more" persuasion, I actually prefer "Ballade" to "Close to Home," not only because of the more variegated tone-colors, but because in key passages Emerson plays at a slightly more deliberate tempo that serves the music well.

The fourth track, "The Band Keeps Playing," features the Emerson-Gilbert-Bonilla-Cimirelli lineup of the opening track. This track is even more reminiscent of the 3 approach than "Shelter from the Rain," although here there's a noticeable tinge not only of funk (courtesy of Gilbert's bass-drums groove), but of R & B (courtesy of the unnamed female backing vocalist who increasingly dominates the choruses as the song progresses). Emerson contributes a short neobaroque synth episode in the middle of the song; otherwise, though, his Hammond playing is loose and funky. Marc Bonilla is able to make a bigger imprint here than on the opening track, although mainly in a rhythm guitar role. As the title implies, the lyrics address the determination of a large portion of the Western world to party on, oblivious to the many disasters and near-disasters that threaten our civilization.

The next track is something of a surprise: Emerson plays George Gershwin's "Summertime" in a piano trio format, accompanied by bassist Watts and drummer Barsimanto.[8] After two statements of the original tune (0:00–0:30, 0:31–1:00), Emerson begins to build the tension slowly and inexorably during a series of four solo choruses. His playing during the fourth and final chorus, from 2:29 to 2:57, is transcendental, with huge block chords, passed back and forth between the right and left hands in dauntingly syncopated exchanges, moving up and down the keyboard with a precision that's both startling and spontaneous. It's one of Emerson's greatest recorded moments in either a blues or jazz idiom. Unfortunately, Mr. Watts and Mr. Barsimanto, who appear to be rock musicians who know little about jazz, do not accompany with the appropriate degree of subtlety: Barsimanto's playing, in particular, is downright ham-fisted at times. Nonetheless, "Summertime" is a must-hear for Emerson's ferocious, Brubeck-like solo.

"Summertime" is followed by the title track of *La Chiesa*, which here is retitled "The Church," and features Emerson on Hammond and synths

---

[8] Some readers may recall the quotation of "Summertime" during the piano solo of the live "Hang on to a Dream" on the Nice's *Elegy*.

accompanied by Watts, Barsimanto, and guitarist Pierce. I prefer this performance to the title track of *La Chiesa*; it's less reliant on overdubs, and as a result it crackles with energy, for which the backing musicians deserve a lot of credit: listen, for instance, to the edgy, polyrhythmic organ/guitar episode at 0:50, and the daunting offbeat drums-bass accents at 1:11 and elsewhere. Emerson's bluesy Hammond solo is more forceful and pressing than its equivalent on the movie soundtrack, and is the finest example of the "stuttering," lightning-fast repetitions of a single note (listen especially at 2:28, and again at 3:04) that he became enamored with in his Hammond playing of the late eighties and early nineties. "The Church" is very nearly the equal of "Changing States"/"Another Frontier": one wishes that ELP had also tackled this one on *Black Moon*.

Next comes a short, wistful, and exceedingly attractive solo piano piece, "Interlude," which is one of my favorite Emerson solo piano pieces: it's poignant, but avoids the somewhat saccharine sticky-sweetness than in my view mars "Ballade"/"Close to Home." Cast in a simple AABA form, it's just over a minute and a half long, and is immediately followed by "Montagues and Capulets," which those familiar with *Black Moon* will recognize as Prokofiev's "Romeo and Juliet." As I said in an earlier chapter, I actually prefer this version, which features the Emerson-Pierce-Watts-Barsimanto lineup, to the one on *Black Moon*: it's shorter and lacks the lengthy concluding synthesizer solo of the *Black Moon* version, but it's more urgent and energized than "Romeo and Juliet," which suffers from the rather plodding and indifferent performance of the Lake-Palmer rhythm section. "Montagues and Capulets" also benefits from the subtle "heavying up" effect of Tim Pierce's rhythm guitar parts.

"Montagues and Capulets" is followed by the orchestral version of "Abaddon's Bolero," recorded by the London Philharmonic Orchestra under the direction of John Mayer way back in November-December 1975 and, some twenty years later, finally given its public release. As I have talked a good deal about the different versions of "Abaddon" on a number of occasions during the course of this book, let me simply summarize my main observations. For me, the definitive version will always be the electronic version captured on *Trilogy* in 1972. As I've said, while it's a fine piece that nicely displays Emerson's gift for complex, interesting thematic material, effective textural development, and energetic rhythmic counterpoint, in its orchestral guise it sounds a bit middlebrow. What really clinches the aesthetic success of the "Abaddon" of *Trilogy* is Emerson's virtuosic Moog orchestration, which defamiliarizes the familiar orchestral timbres just enough to give the piece an edge that the traditionally orchestrated version lacks. Furthermore, the LPO performance of 1975 is not entirely above criticism; producer Gilbert is, however, largely successful in minimizing, if not entirely eliminating, the most obvious glitches through his remixing and remastering efforts, and even adds a tuba obbligato of his own. The album ends with a second mix of "The Band Keeps Playing (Aftershock Mix)," which forefronts the rhythm section a bit more and therefore heightens the funk/R & B aspect of the song. Otherwise, it's not that different from track four, and one can legitimately ask if two mixes of this song were really necessary: the album clocks in at 46:23, counting the bonus track.

Changing States: An Assessment

There isn't a really weak track on the album, and some of this material (notably "Another Frontier," "The Church," and "Summertime") is more or less essential for Emerson fans. On the other hand, there's no denying that the impact of *Changing States* is much diminished by the simple fact that five of the ten tracks here had already been released in other guises. Furthermore, I can think of few, if any, of Emerson's other solo albums where it would be less accurate to say that the whole is greater than the sum of its parts: here the often-rewarding individual tracks never cohere into anything greater. Unlike his best soundtracks (including *Iron Man*) or even *Honky*, there is no unified, guiding vision at work here. I've often thought a better name for this album would have been *An Emerson Sketchbook*.

In September 1995, *The Illinois Entertainer*—not exactly the most obvious source of music industry information—ran an article reporting that Keith Emerson had just given his first public "performance" in nearly two years, at the Gand Musitech '95 in metro Chicago, where he lectured, played a boogie-woogie arrangement of "Flight of the Bumblebee," and supervised an all-kazoo performance of "Tarkus" in front of an audience of roughly two hundred. The article's author, Scott Carlin, interviewed Emerson briefly before the seminar. Emerson admitted that his recovery from the devastating surgery of November 1993 was far from complete: he still experienced some numbness in the fourth and fifth fingers of his right hand, and he had yet to regain his former stamina, speed, and precision. Emerson added that he was still optimistic that, given time, he would fully recover. Perhaps the most important question Carlin raised involved the status of ELP: would there be another studio album? "Emerson explained in detail why he thought not. Mainly because him and Lake don't see eye to eye on a lot of things. He doesn't need the aggravation of having to compromise his ideas. He did, however, say that he was going to be talking to Jon Anderson of Yes and possibly work something out concerning a joint project with ELP and Yes."[9] Emerson

---

[9] Scott Carlin, "The Gand Musictech Provides an Interesting Day With Keith Emerson," *Illinois Entertainer*, September 1995, 8.

also expressed frustration that Lake had refused to take vocal coaching, or otherwise seek help, when it became obvious during the *Black Moon* tour that the upper register of his voice was decimated. Will Alexander, who was also present, added that during the tour he had "tried to get Lake to take natural herbs for his voice but every time it was brought up, it only made Lake meaner and more obstinate."[10]

Clearly, even as late as fall 1995, the future of ELP remained questionable. When David Terralavoro contacted Bruce Pilato, Greg Lake's manager, in November 1995 to inquire about the status of ELP, Pilato would only say, "The official word, as I know it, is that ELP is still together, but there are no specific plans to work together at this time."[11] After his minitour of late 1994 to benefit the Sara Anne Wood Rescue Center, Lake dropped out of the public eye throughout 1995. Carl Palmer, meanwhile, explored forming a band with Midge Ure (ex-Ultravox), Mark King (ex–Level 42), and former Queen guitarist Brian May in late 1994 and early 1995; when Midge Ure pulled out, the project unraveled. Shortly thereafter, Palmer was faced with the unpleasant prospect of surgery for carpal tunnel syndrome in his right hand: in fact, it was necessary for him to have two surgeries, on both hands, in seven weeks. Many years earlier, in 1980, Palmer told an interviewer that karate hadn't damaged his hands or feet: in 1995, however, the verdict was that it was karate punches to wooden boards, not drumming, that had caused Palmer's carpal tunnel problems (Palmer has since abandoned karate in favor of fencing). Fortunately, Palmer's surgery wasn't as serious as Emerson's; later in the year he was able to return to drumming, and soon he had formed another band. Dubbed K-2, this band, which consisted of Palmer, John Wetton, and guitarist Mica Calvin, actually received some money from Sony to record an album, and appears to have recorded roughly a dozen songs. K-2 were a song-oriented band; Palmer told one interviewer that K-2's music recalled the Police, Rush, and ZZ Top (all famous guitar trios, one notes), while he told another interviewer that the band's music would be reminiscent of early Asia.[12] Apparently Sony lost interest in K-2 after they heard the demos, and other labels to whom the tapes were shopped were similarly disinterested; at any rate, the project dissolved without a record or tour. While it was rumored in the late nineties that one or more K-2 tracks would appear on Palmer's anthology, when the anthology finally appeared in 2001 the K-2 project was not represented.

---

[10] Ibid.

[11] Bruce Pilato, quoted by David Terralavoro, "Current News," *Fanzine for the Common Man*, no. 15 (January 1996): 4.

[12] See Terralavoro, "Current News," *Fanzine for the Common Man*, no. 15 (January 1996): 4; also David Terralavoro, "Carl Palmer's Recent Projects," *Fanzine for the Common Man* no. 17 (July 1997): 16.

Autumn of 1995 brought ELP the first really good news they had received in quite some time. The disintegration of Victory Records had left them without a label; now, however, Rhino Records, the most reputable archive label in the industry, stepped forward to acquire almost the entire ELP back catalog. To mark this event, in November 1995 Rhino released *I Believe in Father Christmas*, a five-track EP that includes the 1975 single "I Believe in Father Christmas" and its B-side, "Humbug," the *Works II* remix of "Father Christmas," "Troika" from Emerson's newly released reissue of *The Christmas Album*, and "Nutrocker" from *Pictures*. This EP, the cover of which shows the band in their winter coats in the now-familiar 1977 Montréal stadium photo shoot, was available on a seasonal basis for several subsequent years. In February 1996, Rhino reissued nine of the ten Atlantic-era albums, *Best Of*, *The Return of the Manticore* box set, as well as *Black Moon* and *Live at the Royal Albert Hall*; of the Victory Records–era releases, Rhino declined to acquire the rights to one album, *In the Hot Seat*, which ever since has been available only as a Japanese import. Later in 1996 Rhino reissued a deluxe edition of the one Atlantic-era album that had yet to be reissued, *Brain Salad Surgery*, which now included a bonus track consisting of interviews with the band members and a hologram version of Giger's famous cover. With this release, the ELP back catalog (barring only *In the Hot Seat*) was back in circulation. It's probably safe to say the Rhino reissues played a role in the revitalization of ELP during 1996.

1996 North American/Japanese Tour

For, in spite of the uncertainties of 1995, ELP came back from its near-death experience: in April 1996, the management of Jethro Tull announced that ELP would be participating in Jethro Tull's summer tour as special guest artists. Naturally, many ELP fans were horrified by the thought of their favorite band opening for anybody—even for a band of Tull's stature. Considering, though, that there was a certain stylistic overlap between Tull and ELP, and therefore some overlap of potential fans, and particularly considering that due to lingering concerns about Emerson's arm (and perhaps about Lake's voice), a two-hour headlining show was out of the question, the package tour made sense.

Tull's leader Ian Anderson, who himself was recovering from a serious knee injury when the tour commenced in August, was actually concerned about ELP's short set:

> I personally thought they should have played a bit longer, because they started out the tour doing just 50 minutes and no encore. It must have looked to their fans like Jethro Tull would not let them play any more than that, and it

didn't do us or them any favors. I managed to persuade their manager to get them to play an encore, even if it meant taking 15 minutes out of our set, but they still only played for barely an hour.[13]

Emerson and Palmer had made some equipment changes since the *Black Moon* era. Emerson now toured with an Alesis QS8 atop a GEM Realpiano Pro 2, two Korg Trinity Pros, Hammond C-3, modular Moog, a Kurzweil 2500, and a rack containing Alesis QS modules, a Korg Wavestation, a Realpiano module, a Voce V3, and a Roland GP100. Palmer, meanwhile, had dropped the electronics of the Victory Records era and was now touring with an essentially acoustic Premier kit.

Tull and ELP kicked off the '96 tour August 18 at Darien Center, Darien, New York. ELP opened with "Hoedown," returning the piece to its opening position it had last occupied in 1974. "Hoedown" was followed by "Touch and Go" and a particularly tasteful (and compressed) version of "Take a Pebble," which made a welcome reappearance in the ELP set list. Next came solo spots for Emerson ("Hammer it Out," from the Japanese *In the Hot Seat* release), and Lake ("Still . . . You Turn Me On"). By most accounts the highlight of the set was the "Tarkus"/*Pictures* medley (the first four movements of "Tarkus" followed without pause by "Baba Yaga" and "Great Gates of Kiev" from *Pictures*, with a brief drum solo by Palmer); this medley, which revived their ELPowell-era fusion of these two epics, was followed by "Lucky Man." Then came the set's biggest surprise: "Bitches Crystal," a song that ELP had not performed live even during the early seventies, because of the impossibility at that time of coordinating celesta, piano, and Moog parts in a live context. ELP wrapped up their set with a compressed "Fanfare"/"Rondo" (I think it's indisputable this medley was better for being compressed—it had become far too sprawling and unfocused in their early-nineties shows.)

Although Ian Anderson somewhat underestimated the length of their set (it lasted sixty-three minutes, not fifty), it is true that the band did not play an encore, nor did they join Tull onstage at any point. As the '96 tour progressed, ELP fans agreed that Emerson was playing well, although not always with the deadly accuracy of earlier days: his right-hand pinky finger sometimes let him down in rapid sixteenth-note melodic runs or in big block-chord progressions that moved in parallel motion. Most also felt that Lake was singing better than during most of the *Black Moon* tour: although the golden tenor of the seventies had settled into a dusky baritone, he was no longer plagued by persistent hoarseness.

---

[13] Ian Anderson, quoted by David Rees, *Minstrels in the Gallery: A History of Jethro Tull* (Wembley, U.K.: Firefly Publishing, 1998), 162.

In August, ELP and Tull played eleven shows in the northeast U.S. and Ontario; in September, the bands played twenty-three more shows, including a number in the Midwest and several on the West Coast. Many of the shows were in midsized amphitheaters, allowing ELP to play for bigger audiences than they had since the first segment of the *Black Moon* tour. In early October, ELP split from Tull and did a ten-show Japanese tour as headliners. Here they had to expand their set list somewhat. At their October 9 show, they opened with "Karn Evil 9, 1st Impression, part 2," followed in rapid succession by "Tiger in a Spotlight," "Hoedown," "Touch and Go," and "Bitches Crystal." Lake was spotlighted on "Still . . . You Turn Me On" and "From the Beginning," which were followed by "Knife-Edge." Emerson's solo spot now included two pieces: "Hammer It Out" and "For Kevin," a slow, sad ballad in memory of his recently deceased friend (and former producer) Kevin Gilbert. Then came "Take a Pebble," "Lucky Man," and the "Tarkus"/*Pictures* medley: the band now played "Fanfare"/ "Rondo" as an encore. Even with the added material, the show was only an hour thirty-five minutes. ELP ended the tour with a show at Bunka Center, Saitama Urawa-Shi, on October 19, having played forty-four shows in two months. Asked whether he thought the ELP component of the tour had been a success, Ian Anderson—who admitted to not having personally known any of the band members prior to the tour, but clearly aware of ELP history—said, "They got through the tour okay, and they were still talking to each other at the end, so it was a success in that respect!"[14] In fact, ELP were pleased enough with the outcome of their '96 tour to begin planning a more ambitious tour for the next summer.

In early 1997, even as they were planning the coming summer's tour, ELP resurrected the Manticore Records label. Administered by Lake's manager, Bruce Pilato, out of his Rochester, New York, headquarters, the Manticore label was no longer intended to function as a "real" record company—those days were gone—but as a private boutique label on which ELP could release previously unreleased live material, or could rerelease previously available material for which they were able to reclaim the copyright. The Official ELP Web Site was expanded to handle sales of Manticore label merchandise, which was not to be available through normal retail outlets. Despite the limited focus of the new Manticore label, ELP fans were heartened by its resurrection, both for its symbolic connection to the band's golden age, and because it suggested a real commitment on ELP's part to perpetuating their musical legacy.

---

[14] Ibid.

On March 15, 1997, Greg Lake attended a special event at London's Hotel Inter-Continental marking the release of the four-CD set *Epitaph*, which chronicled the best live performances of King Crimson's original lineup during 1969, and was released by Robert Fripp's new Discipline Global Mobile record company. All of the original lineup (including Pete Sinfield and road manager Dik Fraser) were in attendance, as were over a thousand fans. A slightly scaled-down version of the same event took place in New York a few weeks later (Pete Sinfield was unable to attend this one), but here the old tensions between Lake and Fripp resurfaced: Lake was infuriated that Fripp caused the rest of the band to wait on the rooftop of a building while he gave an interview inside, and then left while the band was being ushered in. There had been some talk of reviving the original lineup, which Fripp had been surprisingly supportive of, but after this event it was clear the Lake-Fripp relationship had deteriorated too much for such a plan to be practical: Fripp briefly considered offering Lake's position to John Wetton before the entire idea was dropped for good. Lake remains somewhat resentful about Fripp's habit of releasing archival King Crimson material on DGM without what he considers to be proper consultation of other ex-members.[15]

1997 World Tour

The 1997 ELP tour, which commenced in June, was more ambitious than its predecessor on two counts. First, ELP were now the headlining act; second, they were undertaking a world tour, with shows in North and South America as well as Europe. After two warm-up dates in the U.S., one in Las Vegas on June 12, the other in Atlanta on June 16 (where Kansas appeared as special guest artists), the 1997 World Tour started in earnest with seven dates, mostly in central Europe, between June 20 and June 29. Their show in Katowice, Poland, on June 22 was significant not only because it was ELP's first show in that country, but also because it was recorded and released later in 1997 as a live album, *Emerson, Lake and Palmer Live in Poland*. This album is unusual in that although it is an "official" ELP album, it was released only in Poland and Austria (by the Austrian label Metal Mind Records, who licensed the release through Manticore); it was available elsewhere as an import. *Live in Poland* is useful for providing a snapshot of the state of ELP's live shows during the 1996–98 period.

---

[15] For more on this and the Lake-Fripp relationship more generally, see Sid Smith, *In the Court of King Crimson* (London: Helter Skelter, 2001), especially 280–83.

Live in Poland

The album begins with "Karn Evil 9, 1st Impression, part 2." Even in 1977, when they had last played this number in its entirety, I felt it had lost some of its fire in comparison to the blistering performances of 1973-74, and I was relieved when it disappeared from their set in early 1978. This arrangement, however, is much worse than the late-seventies version. First off, since Lake now refused to play electric guitar, Emerson was obliged to play Lake's electric guitar solo (as well as the rhythm guitar part that had accompanied his Hammond solo) on synth: the breathy synth timbre he chooses for the solo line, as well as the somewhat "squishy" synth timbre he uses for Lake's former rhythm guitar figure, generate little of the power or excitement that the guitar had. Furthermore, Lake doesn't even bother to play his old rhythm guitar lines on bass, so that Emerson's Hammond solo has virtually no bass accompaniment: throughout the rest of the song, Lake's bass playing is extraordinarily sparse and perfunctory, which tends to rob the song of much of its rhythmic energy.[16] Palmer's peculiar tom part that accompanies Emerson's Hammond solo (from 1:45 to 2:19) doesn't seem to fit the arrangement, since it further emphasizes the lack of a firm bass line. While there is nothing wrong with the band's playing per se, the arrangement is so ill-conceived that it's hard to know why they bothered with it: compared to their great performances of this song circa 1973-74, it sounds eviscerated.

"Karn Evil 9, 1st Impression, part 2" was followed at the Katowice show by two short numbers, both staples of the '96 tour, that are not included on the album: "Tiger in a Spotlight" and "Hoedown." The fourth number of their set (and the album's second track), "Touch and Go," is actually a bit better than the band's studio recording on the *Return of the Manticore* box set, mainly because Emerson now uses a GX-1-like trumpet patch and a Kurzweil-like choral patch to better evoke the vivid orchestrations of the ELPowell arrangement, and therefore avoids the monochrome synth palette that had marred the '93 recording. Nonetheless, Carl Palmer's drumming is still a disappointment—as with the '93 studio recording, he uses the same drum groove all the way through the song, thus robbing it of the *chiaroscuro* effect Cozy Powell had achieved by changing his drumming between verses and choruses. As a result, ELP performances of this song have always lacked the dramatic contrasts of the ELPowell arrangement, and have tended to sound trivial by comparison.

---

[16] For instance, the funk bass guitar figure that one would expect to hear at 3:45 of the present arrangement is conspicuous by its absence.

The next track, "From the Beginning," is faithful to the *Trilogy* recording. There's no electric guitar solo in the middle of the song, of course, but Emerson's mellow Moog solo is faithfully rendered at the end of the song (Emerson also supplies bass lines throughout), and Palmer accompanies with an understated bossa nova groove, using his toms to evoke the studio version's conga parts. It's a bit lightweight, but tasteful.

"Knife-Edge," like "1st Impression," is a major disappointment, and for a similar reason. Few other ELP songs cry out for Emerson's over-driven and gritty Hammond sound as much as "Knife-Edge." During the *Black Moon* period, Emerson came closer to recapturing the classic early-seventies Hammond sound than he had at any time since 1974; it is for that reason that I find the performance of "Knife-Edge" captured on *Live at the Royal Albert Hall* compelling, even if I would have changed a few of the arrangement's details. During the 1996-97 tours, however, Emerson favored a Hammond timbre that was not just clean and glassy, but quite lacking in presence; it was in fact as if someone had castrated his Hammond, pardon the imagery.[17] For a song that depends as much on the overdriven Hammond sound as "Knife-Edge," the results are disas-trous: one almost cringes when one hears the first instrumental chorus (at 0:50) with its weak, colorless, flimsy Hammond timbre. It's a shame, too, because otherwise the band performs the song rather well.

The album's fifth track, "Bitches Crystal," is its first unqualified suc-cess. For some reason, the band excised the transitional passage that one expects to hear between the opening celesta solo (now played on a bell-like

---

[17] The difference in sound can be briefly explained as follows. Emerson's two Hammond C-3s, known as the *Pictures* C-3 (for its use on *Pictures at an Exhibition* and the debut album) and the *Tarkus* C-3 (used on the studio recording of *Tarkus*), were rebuilt in the 1990s along totally different lines. The *Pictures* C-3 was restored around 1990 by Hammond expert Al Goff, who rebuilt and recalibrated its tonewheel generator to recapture the origi-nal Hammond scream; Will Alexander subsequently wired the *Pictures* C-3 for MIDI. The remarkable Hammond sound of *Black Moon* is based on the original C-3 sound beefed up with sounds from the Hammond Suzuki XB-2 digital organ. The rebuild of the *Tarkus* C-3 took place later, and was done with the goal of retaining the instrument's original flavor: no MIDI, a tube pre-amp, the organ remaining a stand-alone component in Emerson's setup. It is the *Tarkus* C-3 that is heard on *Live in Poland*. Incidentally, the *Pictures* C-3 was Emerson's first C-3; it can be heard on the two ELP albums mentioned above. The *Tarkus* C-3, which Emerson purchased in late 1970 or early 1971, can be heard on *Tarkus* and sub-sequent ELP studio albums of the seventies that use Hammond organ; it is the C-3 he toured with between the summer of 1971 and 1978. Why the rebuilt *Tarkus* C-3 sounds so weak in comparison to the rebuilt *Pictures* C-3 I am unable to determine; the Hammond sound of *Live in Poland* certainly has none of the guts (and little of the color) of the Hammond sound of *Tarkus*, even though it's the same organ. Incidentally, contrary to pre-vailing wisdom, Emerson did not own a C-3 while in the Nice, although he occasionally rented one; his two Hammonds during his tenure with the Nice were an L-100 and an A-105.

synth setting) and the ferocious 3/4 boogie riff; this issue aside, the band plays this peculiar little song with real energy and panache. Although Lake couldn't scream like he did in the early seventies, and he was obliged to transpose the song down a step (here it's played in B♭ minor, not the original key of C minor), he picks off some surprisingly high notes that his fans had thought he'd lost forever. Meanwhile, while it was clear that Emerson's accuracy and precision were still not 100 percent, his boogie piano solo in the middle of the song has a ferocious, frenetic energy that rivals the studio version's, and his choice of patches for both the celesta and Moog "French horn" work quite well.

Track six on the album, titled "Piano Solo," is actually two distinct pieces. First is Emerson's now-familiar "Creole Dance," which benefits from not being played with the piano-strings patch which had marred the otherwise sterling performances of the *Black Moon* tour—Emerson now used a slightly electronic digital piano sound. From 5:05, the "piano solo" is in fact "Honky Tonk Train Blues," played by the full band in an arrangement that had changed little from the *Black Moon* period.

The album's seventh track (actually the set's tenth selection), "Take a Pebble," is its second unqualified success. During Lake's vocals, Emerson mixes some subtle string patches underneath the piano backing, which in this setting works very well; the instrumental section that immediately follows the vocals is exceptionally nice, with Lake turning in some of his finest bass work in many a year (listen particularly from 2:35 to 2:50). A short Emerson stride piano episode is followed by a beboplike section for full band that evokes the bop episodes of the 1973-74 "Piano Improvisations": this section climaxes with a brief quote of Miles Davis's "So What" at 3:49. Thereafter the improv winds down, and a hazy whole tone piano run (4:18) leads back to the final verse. The '97 "Take a Pebble" arrangement manages to compress virtually all the essential aspects of the original into a concise 6:36 presentation, while adding a couple of fresh and entirely appropriate details.

"Take a Pebble" is followed by the ubiquitous "Lucky Man." This arrangement is similar to the rather literal reading the band gave the song during the *Black Moon* tour, with Emerson's modular Moog solo at the end of the song retained by popular demand. The biggest change is that Lake's electric guitar solo in the middle of the song, which Emerson had played almost note-for-note on an electric guitarlike synth setting during the *Black Moon* tour, is here transformed into a Procol Harum–like episode on Hammond. As with "From the Beginning," it's a bit lightweight, but tastefully rendered.

The climax of the show is the "Tarkus"/*Pictures* medley familiar from the previous year's tour: the first four movements of "Tarkus" segue directly into the final two movements of *Pictures*. "Eruption" is well performed, but Emerson's Hammond is critically low in the mix until the movement is nearly done. "Stones of Years" is interesting in that the first half features the piano/string patch already familiar from "Take a Pebble" instead of the traditional Hammond accompaniment; Emerson even takes an extensive solo using the piano patch, before completing his solo on Hammond, which he then plays for the rest of the song. The performance of "Iconoclast" captured here is perhaps the best live recording of the movement, with the mixture of piano, Hammond, Lake's scratchy bass pedal point, and Palmer's "jungle" tom drumming being quite effective. The band also renders the fourth movement, "Mass," quite energetically, although I've never been enthused about some of the rather cheesy synth patches Emerson uses here. A similar problem mars "Baba Yaga" and "The Great Gates of Kiev": the pseudo-orchestral synth patches are too generic sounding, and one wishes that Emerson had retained the essence of his seventies Hammond-and-Moog orchestration and had saved the digital "orchestral" patches for the climaxes and other key episodes. However, while one can certainly question details of the arrangement, the band gives an energetic performance of the medley, and there's still a good deal of musical substance here.

The same is not true, alas, of the "Fanfare for the Common Man"/ "Rondo" encore medley, which, at nearly eighteen minutes, had become hopelessly sprawling and unfocused, and was going on far longer than its musical substance warranted. The structural plan was not too different from the *Black Moon* tour, although there were some new details. The synth patch Emerson uses for the opening of "Fanfare" lacks the timbral power or distinctiveness of his old GX-1 setting; obviously, a pervasive problem throughout *Live in Poland* is the overly generic synth patches and the weak, undistinguished Hammond sounds. After the "Fanfare" theme, Emerson improvises a solo on Hammond and then plays a spacey Moog solo that evokes the 1973-74 "Aquatarkus" solo.

At 4:11 the band segue into "Rondo," and it's here that sprawl really sets in. The opening theme is fine, although again, the nondescript Hammond sound doesn't serve the material very well. Perhaps the most bracing segment of the track is the modal synth "folk dance" (6:16), followed shortly by a snippet of the opening of Carl Orff's *Carmina Burana* (at 6:50). Palmer's drum solo extends from 7:35 to 11:45, far beyond reasonable limits, and now contains numerous short episodes and a couple of complete stops (7:45, 10:29) that rob the solo of the cumulative effect that had made his 1973/74 solos so compelling. While the 1997 solo is actually only slightly longer than the great solo captured on *Welcome Back My Friends*, it sounds twice as long.

From 11:45 Emerson treats the audience to the Hammond *musique concrète* sounds that had been bracing in the late sixties, but now sounded thoroughly dated; his *real* "Rondo" solo (i.e., notes instead of feedback) doesn't start until 13:19, and by 14:27 we're back to the feedback, now augmented by Moog blips and bleeps over the throbbing bass-drum groove. Eventually we get the familiar quotation of Bach's Toccata and Fugue in D minor, and finally, after yet more feedback, Emerson mercifully recapitulates the theme and brings the medley to its close. The "Fanfare"/"Rondo" medley goes on nearly ten minutes too long: my advice to the band would have been to drop the drum solo, drop the Hammond riding episode with its attendant sound effects (let's be honest—it was a bit embarrassing to watch a fifty-two-year-old man physically assault a Hammond), and try to wrap the medley up in eight minutes rather than eighteen. The total length of the Katowice show was about an hour twenty-five minutes: *Emerson, Lake and Palmer Live in Poland*, which excises two numbers, clocks in at seventy-seven minutes.

Live in Poland: An Assessment

As the reader has doubtless discerned, I have fairly serious reservations about *Live in Poland*; while the flimsy Hammond sound, generic synth patches, and less-than-bracing set list are my biggest concerns, the album's sonic values aren't that exceptional either. While some ELP fans preferred ELP's live shows of 1996-97 to those of the *Black Moon* tour, I happen to feel the sonic values of *Live at the Royal Albert Hall* are far better than *Live in Poland*, so much better that the latter's advantages (such as Lake's indisputably stronger voice) pale by comparison. When asked why the band allowed the album's release, Carl Palmer explained,

> We went to Poland and played . . . one of the places had very few people in it, it held about twelve, fifteen thousand, and I think there were three thousand . . . He's a very nice guy called Tommy, the promoter. He'd mortgaged houses and things, and we didn't want to see him go out of business [as a result of the poor ticket sales] . . . We were incredibly embarrassed, so we said "Look, we've recorded it . . . Why don't we mix you something up, we'll release it just in Poland" . . . I personally would have just given him the money back. It [the album] is not bad . . . [but] I can't say I'm going to play it tomorrow night when I get home, you know![18]

On June 28, a few days after the Katowice show, ELP startled fans in Kassel's Stadthalle by coming back on stage after "Rondo" was over—some fans were beginning to file out of the venue—and commencing a second encore, a medley of "21st Century Schizoid Man" (similar to their abbreviated version of the song on the *Return of the Manticore* box set), which segued into "America." Throughout much of the rest of the tour,

---

[18] Carl Palmer, quoted by Liv Whetmore, "Carl Palmer," *Impressions* 8 (October 2001): 8.

ELP retained the double encore format, which boosted the length of their shows to about an hour thirty-five minutes. Incidentally, when European fans asked the band's management about the reason for the relatively short shows, they were told that the condition of Emerson's hand and Lake's voice did not permit shows to be much over ninety minutes in length.

In July ELP played fourteen more European dates, mostly in Germany and Switzerland, but also with a few shows in Italy and one in Paris. Many of ELP's British fans—some of whom were still smarting over the band's eighteen-year absence between 1974 and 1992—were stunned that they were the only sizable Western European country left off the band's 1997 itinerary. While the band were in Paris, Carl Palmer, during an interview with Aymeric Leroy of the French prog rock journal *Big Bang*, intimated that a new studio album would soon be in the works:

> We have a brand new concept, which is fantastic. It's a global concept, that would mean as much to you as it would to a German, or an Englishman, or an American. I can't tell you what it is because we just . . . Well, it's the best idea we've had in a long time . . . We're looking at a concept [piece] that is probably forty minutes long. There will be other songs on the CD but this one body of work is about forty minutes.[19]

Palmer went on to say, "This tour is four months, and we have a great concept. And to be honest with you, the group only functions when it plays. When we play concerts, we get ideas. And when we don't play concerts, and we sit at home, it's rubbish. You know, a band is only a band if it plays together. It's the truest thing ever."[20] He added that the band hoped to have the new album ready for release sometime between mid and late 1998, and then tour throughout 1999 and possibly "into the new millennium."[21]

In August the band moved on to South America, where they played a series of twelve shows in Brazil, Argentina, and Chile. In September, the Show That Never Ends hit the U.S., kicking off a nineteen-show sequence on September 6 at Vienna, Virginia's Wolftrap, and by and large playing smaller venues than they had the previous year with Jethro Tull. As was customary, the tour began on the East Coast, proceeded through the Midwest, and ended with several West Coast dates; after a few days off, the band did six more Latin American shows, including shows in two countries—Peru and Costa Rica—that they had never visited before. They performed two shows at the Teatro National in San Jose, Costa Rica, on

---

19 Carl Palmer, quoted by Leroy, "An Interview with Carl Palmer."
20 Ibid.
21 Ibid.

October 8, both of which packed out the two-thousand-seat auditorium: the set list was identical to what they had been doing since late June, including the double encore. The final show of the 1997 World Tour was in Mexico City on October 11. The band had played sixty shows in four months.

In addition to the world tour, 1997 witnessed the release of three historically significant ELP and ELP-related albums. The revived Manticore label issued, as its very first release, *Emerson, Lake and Palmer Live at the Isle of Wight Festival*, the band's second performance, recorded live at the Isle of Wight Music Festival on August 29, 1970. This recording, which includes a bonus track consisting of the band members' recollections of the show, has already been discussed in detail in the context of ELP's debut album. King Biscuit Flower Hour Records (an imprint of BMG) released *Emerson, Lake and Palmer*. This two-CD album contains five tracks from their March 7, 1974, show at Tulsa's Civic Center (these are similar to the corresponding tracks on *Welcome Back My Friends*, which was recorded in Anaheim about a month earlier), as well as ten tracks recorded at Wheeling, West Virginia, on November 25, 1977, during the three-piece segment of their *Works* tour.[22] The bonus CD-ROM disk includes some short interview footage and concert footage of two songs, "Lucky Man" and "Paper Blood," recorded at the October 2, 1992, Royal Albert Hall show. Finally, Greg Lake became the first ELP member to release a career anthology. Entitled *The Greg Lake Retrospective: From the Beginning*, this two-CD retrospective, released on the Rhino label, contains two tracks featuring Lake with King Crimson; ten tracks recorded with ELP during the seventies; a track from Pete Sinfield's *Still* (1973) featuring Lake as lead vocalist; the 1975 single "I Believe in Father Christmas"; nine tracks from his early-eighties solo career; two tracks by ELPowell; two previously unreleased tracks from the Lake-Downes Ride the Tiger project; and five ELP tracks from the nineties. Incidentally, all three of the albums I've mentioned here include excellent liner notes by Bruce Pilato, as did a second Lake anthology released a year later, in 1998. Entitled *From the Underground: The Official Bootleg*, this was in some ways a more interesting release than *From the Beginning*, simply because of its less predictable track list. Besides long-unavailable singles from Lake's earliest bands, the Shame and the Shy Limbs, there are live Asia tracks with Lake and live ELPowell material that was unavailable on CD at the time of this album's release, as well as less obvious King Crimson

---

[22] The liner notes of the King Biscuit CD are incorrect to list the date of the Wheeling show as November 12: it was November 25. ELP did play a show on the campus of Kansas State University, Manhattan, Kansas, on November 12. Is *this* the show represented on the King Biscuit *Emerson, Lake and Palmer* album?

and ELP material. In 1998, Manticore released two full-length videos that the band had recently re-obtained rights to: *The Manticore Special* of 1973 and the famed Montréal orchestral show (titled *Emerson, Lake and Palmer: Works Orchestral Tour*) of August 26, 1977.

1998 North American Tour

In late March 1998 the management of Deep Purple announced that their band would be headlining a package tour in August that would also feature special guest artists Emerson, Lake and Palmer and progressive-metal virtuosos Dream Theater. Said tour, which was only to take in about twenty-five dates and was to be confined to the U.S. and south-eastern Canada, generated a series of rather pointed questions from ELP's increasingly restive fan base. First and foremost, why was ELP touring for a third consecutive summer without a new album to support? Were they becoming nothing more than an oldies act? Were there really plans for a studio album, or was talk of a new album just the proverbial pie in the sky? Would ELP be rehashing the same set lists as the past two years—which, in many essentials, had not fundamentally changed from the 1992-93 tour? Some fans also asked why the tours of 1996 and 1997 had expunged all references to ELP's output of the nineties. Granted, there were some sound reasons for doing so: most ELP fans, given their druthers, would prefer a given ten-minute segment of an ELP show to be occupied by "Hoedown" and "Karn Evil 9, 1st Impression, part 2" rather than "Black Moon" and "Paper Blood." On the other hand, as a number of fans pointed out, there was some decent material from both *Black Moon* and *In the Hot Seat* that had never been given the opportunity to come to life on stage; more importantly, ELP's single-minded emphasis on their seventies material during the 1996 and 1997 tours reinforced the impression that they were a band with a distinguished past, but without a real future.

In May, Keith Emerson played a couple of shows in the San Francisco Bay area with the band Dragon Choir, which was led by his late-eighties collaborator, guitarist Marc Bonilla. Soon thereafter ELP began rehearsals in Rochester, New York. The 1998 tour started with two ELP-only shows at very small venues in New Hampshire and Vermont on August 1 and 2; the first show featuring all three bands was August 3 at Poughkeepsie, New York. Thereafter the show moved from east to west, including three shows in southeastern Canada in the early segment of the tour; at the package shows Dream Theater performed first, then ELP, with Deep Purple headlining. (Maybe this was Deep Purple's revenge for ELP's appropriation of the headliner's position at Cal Jam some 24 years before?)

ELP's 1998 shows demonstrated to restive fans that the band still had a few surprises up their sleeve. First of all, Keith Emerson's Hammond C-3 sounded much better now than it had in '97; while it still didn't quite achieve the gloriously grungy timbre of the *Black Moon* era, its sound had a fullness of body and an edge that had been notable by its absence during the tours of the past two years. Even more important, ELP introduced some surprising changes into their set list.

A show the band played on August 28 at San Francisco's Warfield—almost their last show of the tour—is illustrative. They opened with a new instrumental piece, "Crossing the Rubicon," which they said represented a snippet of the music they were developing for their upcoming studio album. Roughly 1:40 in length, "Crossing the Rubicon" is based on a stately eight-bar march theme which is repeated a number of times with variation and minor development. While it's no masterpiece—it's simply too short to build up much momentum—it nevertheless offered an intriguing foretaste of what the new album might sound like. For, in spite of the lack of progress on a new album since the previous summer, the band assured interested parties that a new album was definitely still in the works. When Joe Lawlor, a reporter for the Warren *Tribune-Chronicle*, pumped Lake and Palmer for information after a show at Cuyahoga Falls' Blossom Music Center on August 21, they were reticent to share many details: Palmer reiterated that the album would be conceptual, and added it would probably have a more "orchestral" feel than their previous two albums. He thought that when they toured in support of the new album, they might find it necessary to bring along a horn section, a small string section, or some combination of the two.[23]

"Crossing the Rubicon" segued directly into "1st Impression, part 2," which was now shortened by the removal of the second vocal verse and the Hammond solo—just as well, probably, since otherwise it's similar to the lackluster '97 arrangement. The third number, "Hoedown," remained an evergreen—it was a bit more deliberate now than in the seventies, but remained an exhilarating little piece nonetheless, with just enough new touches (Greg Lake's harmonica solo at the beginning of the solo section, for instance) to keep it interesting for long-time fans. Next came "Knife-Edge": the arrangement was similar to that of the '97 tour, but it sounded much better now simply because Emerson's Hammond sounded so much more powerful than it had.

Emerson's solo segment was reduced to once piece, an arrangement for solo piano of the third movement of his Piano Concerto no. 1. Although it's painful to say this, in the interest of honesty, it's necessary:

---

[23] Joe Lawlor, "Interviews with Lake and Palmer," *ELP Digest* 8, no. 11 (September 27, 1998).

this was not a good choice. Why? Emerson's right hand was, at this point in time, simply not up to it. The movement's unforgiving plunges of parallel chords, not to mention its ruthlessly difficult jagged scalar runs, demand a high degree of strength, flexibility, and pinpoint accuracy from a pianist's fourth and fifth right fingers—in Emerson's 1998 performances, one hears smudged chord voicings (inevitably the top voice of the chord) and blurred scalar runs that one would have never heard in his pre-1993 performances. In addition, a quasi-boogie episode he inserted before the impressionistic middle section seemed out of context. On the other hand, the MIDI strings underlying the hymnlike final theme manage to evoke the orchestral accompaniment quite successfully.

Lake's solo segment was also reduced to a single song, "C'est la vie." A nice touch to this arrangement is that Emerson, after his accordion solo, no longer disappeared from the stage, as he had in performances of this song during the *Works* tour, but remained to supply an obbligato accordion part beneath Lake's final vocal verse. "C'est la vie" was followed by an arrangement of "Lucky Man" that was, in its essentials, very similar to the '97 tour's version of the song.

The real surprise of the set, indeed of the 1998 tour, came immediately after "Lucky Man," when ELP performed the complete "Tarkus" suite for the first time since 1974. At the San Francisco show, one could feel both the band's and the audience's energy ratchet up as soon as the swelling opening chords of "Eruption" became audible, and for the next nineteen and a half minutes, ELP miraculously managed to roll the clock back to the early seventies: Greg Lake effortlessly picked off the high notes of his vocal parts without even straining, while the instrumental interplay between the three musicians was impressively tight. This particular arrangement of "Tarkus" seemed to strip away all the interesting but inessential layers that had accrued during the years of arranging and rearranging the piece for live performance, revealing the essence of the original composition; yet it added just enough new detail to avoid sounding a note of slavish devotion to the 1971 studio recording.

Perhaps it would be worthwhile to briefly describe each movement. "Eruption" was powerful, precise, and largely faithful to the studio version. "Stones of Years" followed the model of the '97 arrangement: Emerson performed the first half on MIDI piano and then took a "double solo" during the lengthy instrumental middle section, first playing a hyperactive piano solo and then switching to Hammond, capping off the second half of his solo with an affective rising chord sequence unlike anything he had done in earlier tours. "Stones of Years" ended with a rich quasi-orchestral layering of Hammond and MIDI "French horns." "Iconoclast," again quite faithful to the original, was characterized by its marvelously tacky Hammond ostinato. "Mass" featured the metallic synth timbre of the 1973-74 arrangement: the instrumental middle section was now much compressed, although Emerson took a short solo using a MIDI stringlike synth setting. "Manticore" effectively contrasted two distinct Hammond timbres to set off its different sections: a glassy one was used for the opening and closing sections in C minor, while a tacky, percussive setting was used to set off the middle episode in A minor. Carl Palmer segued into "Battlefield" using the same quasi-melodic drum cadenza he had used in the studio version. Lake sang "Battlefield" in the original key, E minor, with no sense of vocal strain at all, and his electric guitar solo, while perhaps not quite as nimble as some of his solos of the 1973-74 tour, was characterized by what may have been the most massive electric guitar timbre he ever captured. Emerson backed Lake with a majestic pipe organ–like setting, eventually layering in some quasi-orchestral synth patches. After the beautiful closing guitar harmonics (unlike the '73/'74 version, "Epitaph" was not quoted), Emerson launched into "Aquatarkus," using a synth setting that fused the "quacking duck" sound of the studio version with the more liquid, metallic sheen of the '73/'74 arrangement. His synth solo was short and to the point; thanks to digital sequencing, he now kept the main march theme going underneath his solo, thus faithfully reproducing the full texture of the studio version for the first time in a live setting. Before one even had a chance to tire of his solo, the band launched into a pile-driving recapitulation of "Eruption" and brought "Tarkus" to a close as the crowd roared long and loud in approval. While I can think of previous live arrangements of "Tarkus" that are more interesting in terms of the detail brought to bear on individual movements (the '73/'74 "Aquatarkus" and the '97 "Iconoclast" come to mind), I can think of no previous arrangement of "Tarkus" that so concisely captures the piece's essence, projecting it as a tightly unified composition rather than as a series of fascinating but disparate movements strung together. In the twilight of their careers, ELP delivered a fitting capstone to their reputation as one of rock's greatest live bands ever. One can only hope that at some point the band will countenance the release of one of their August 1998 performances of "Tarkus," perhaps as part of the Manticore Vaults series of official bootlegs: if I were to point an uninitiated listener to the version of "Tarkus" that comes closest to capturing its essence, it would be this one.

Almost anything ELP (or anyone else) played after this would have been a letdown, and not surprisingly, their encore didn't sustain the same incredible level of intensity. Combining the best parts of their two '97 encores together into one longer encore, they began with the familiar solo synth trumpet theme that heralds "Fanfare for the Common Man." Instead of progressing directly into "Fanfare," though, they played "21st Century Schizoid Man," a much-abbreviated version of "Fanfare" (the long "blues jam" in the middle of the piece was reduced to a short Emerson Hammond solo), and "Rondo." The latter, after the opening theme, launched into a hyperkinetic rising and falling piano riff, and an intricate bass ostinato, doubled by the three musicians, which became the accompaniment figure for a snippet of "Flight of the Bumblebee"; then the opening "Fortuna imperatrix mundi" segment of Carl Orff's *Carmina Burana,* and a five-minute drum solo by Palmer. Next came the (overly) familiar organ-wrestling segment, with its quote of Bach's Toccata and Fugue in D minor, which led into the recap of the main Rondo theme. "Rondo" closed with a brief coda, highlighted by a new fanfarelike synth figure. The San Francisco show, as I said, came near the end of their brief 1998 tour; when they played their fateful final show of the 1998 tour in San Diego on August 31, they had played twenty-four shows in all.

American fans who had become suspicious that the band had entered a state of perpetual autopilot beginning with the 1996 tour were by and large deeply impressed with the intensity, precision, and élan of their "Tarkus" performances. Most agreed if the band could compose new music that demanded the same level of musicianship and involvement as "Tarkus" '98, the next ELP studio album would indeed be a special event.

Then and Now

In November 1998, while ELP fans were still waiting for further word on the new studio album, the Eagle Entertainment label released a two-CD set entitled *Emerson, Lake and Palmer: Then and Now.* The cover of the album featured an illustration by H. R. Giger depicting a mechanical-looking mouth with a wormlike tongue sticking out, the mouth being surrounded with Giger's characteristic spinelike cables; although there's no mention of it on the album, this was one of a series of illustrations that ELPowell had considered, but ultimately decided against using, for their 1986 album. Unlike a certain other ELP album of a quarter century earlier that also used a Giger album cover, the contents of this album do not measure up to the apocalyptic imagery of its cover. To the contrary, the biggest strength of *Then and Now* may be its lavish packaging: besides the uncredited Giger cover, there's eight pages chock full of color photos of the band members, both singly and together, at various stages of their careers, and another set of excellent liner notes by Bruce Pilato.[24] Otherwise, the recordings themselves are a mixed bag.

The "Then" segment consists of roughly forty minutes of music from Cal Jam '74. There's a butchered version of "Toccata"; some of the "Take

---

[24] One wishes ELP had hooked up with Pilato earlier, so he could have written the liner notes for the *Return of the Manticore* box set in 1993.

a Pebble" medley (Lake's solo "Still . . . You Turn Me On" and "Lucky Man" performances, Emerson's "Piano Improvisations" and the "Take a Pebble" reprise); "Karn Evil 9, 1st Impression, part 2," which includes a stupendous Carl Palmer drum solo; and an astounding performance of "Karn Evil 9, 3rd Impression." I discussed this recording some chapters ago in connection with Cal Jam '74; suffice it to say that while these performances are of staggeringly high quality, the arrangements are for the most part quite similar to those of *Welcome Back My Friends*, the sonic quality not as good, and what's presented here is not even ELP's entire Cal Jam set. Sanctuary's 2005 release of ELP's complete Cal Jam performance on DVD has both rendered the "Then" portion of *Then and Now* largely irrelevant, and filled in the last truly crucial gap in ELP's commercially available output.

The final thirteen minutes of the first CD, and the entirety of the second CD (approximately seventy-two minutes of music) comprise the "Now" segment of *Then and Now*. Described in the liner notes as "Now Tour '97/'98," in fact only two tracks, both on the first CD, are from 1998. Otherwise, the "Now" portion of *Then and Now* documents ELP's 1997 world tour, covering much of the same ground as *Live in Poland*.

The first of the three "Now" tracks on the first CD, "A Time and a Place," was a surprise addition to ELP's 1998 set list. It is startling to hear this song performed a fourth lower than it had been on *Tarkus* (B minor rather than E minor), which lends it a duskier hue than before, and the original's tempo is slowed down quite a bit: with Carl Palmer's drumming much heavier and more stripped down here (one is reminded of how Cozy Powell might have drummed on it), the song takes on a ponderous feel not unlike an early Deep Purple song. Once one gets used to the reinterpretation, though, "A Time and a Place" does work on its own terms. It's rather striking that among the many hits and misses of ELP's 1996–98 set lists, the *Tarkus* material (the "Tarkus" suite itself, "Bitches Crystal," and "A Time and a Place") was always rendered with authority: in the twilight of their career, ELP had somehow powerfully reconnected with their masterpiece of 1971.

"A Time and a Place" is followed by the third movement of Emerson's Piano Concerto, here arranged for solo piano, the album's second (and final) track drawn from the 1998 tour. Having already explained my concerns about this piece in connection with Emerson's San Francisco performance of August 28, I'll simply add that my concerns are borne out by this recording as well. The final track of the first CD is a performance of "From the Beginning" excerpted from their 1997 world tour.

The second CD more or less replicates the contents of *Live in Poland*, with a few additions and omissions. The CD begins with "Karn Evil 9, 1st Impression, part 2." This is followed by "Tiger in a Spotlight" and "Hoedown," the second and third tracks of the 1997 set list, both of which were omitted from *Live in Poland*. "Tiger in a Spotlight" is arguably the best live recording of this song available, with some energetic boogie-woogie piano courtesy of Emerson; this arrangement also manages to capture, to some degree at least, the studio version's dramatic false ending. "Hoedown" still crackles with energy, even if the sixteenth-note organ leads no longer always have the same breathtaking rhythmic precision as they had in the seventies. The synth solo in the middle is interesting for its presentation of the same quote of "Saint Thomas" that had appeared in "Aquartarkus" 1973/74; it was also during the middle of "Hoedown" that Emerson did his Moog ribbon controller routine. "Hoedown" is followed by "Touch and Go," "Knife-Edge" (the actual fifth track of the set list, "From the Beginning," having been displaced to the end of the first CD), and "Bitches Crystal." "Creole Dance," the eighth track of the '97 set list, is omitted from *Then and Now*, so on the CD "Bitches Crystal" is followed by "Honky Tonk Train Blues," "Take a Pebble," and "Lucky Man." The "Tarkus"/*Pictures* medley that was arguably the highpoint of the 1997 set list was excised from *Then and Now*, the biggest omission of the album, so "Lucky Man" is followed by the sprawling "Fanfare for the Common Man"/"Rondo" encore (similar to the version on *Live in Poland*, except that this performance includes a short snippet of "Abaddon's Bolero"). The album ends with the second encore of the '97 set list, the "21st Century Schizoid Man"/"America" medley, which wasn't on *Live in Poland*, since ELP added it to their set after the Katowice show. This medley is shorter and more focused than "Fanfare"/"Rondo"; "21st Century Schizoid Man" is similar to the band's arrangement on the 1993 box set, while this arrangement of "America" is reminiscent to that of the *Black Moon* tour.

Then and Now: An Assessment

As a package, how does *Then and Now* compare to *Live in Poland*? The biggest advantage of *Then and Now* is undoubtedly that it does not suffer from the indifferent sonic values of *Live in Poland*; the 1997-98 tracks all sound quite full and clear. Of course, this doesn't solve the other issues I noted in conjunction with *Live in Poland*, such as the spindly Hammond C-3 sound, the overabundance of generic-sounding synth patches, and the not-so-exciting 1997 set list (compounded here by the omission of the set list's most substantial number, the "Tarkus"/*Pictures* medley). One also misses the flow of a real show that *Live in Poland* captures; the selections of *Then and Now* were culled from a number of different shows. Since *Then and Now* made no effort to document a single show, one wonders why the band didn't choose to include a performance of the magisterial *Tarkus* 1998, which, I suspect, most ELP fans would have much preferred to yet another recording of the sprawling "Fanfare"/"Rondo" medley, with its endless segments of organ feedback, now shorn of the visual antics that gave at least minimal justification to the live presentation. In sum, from my perspective *Live in Poland* and *Then and Now* are more or less a tossup, which is a bit frustrating, since with better track selections the latter album could have clearly been the better of the two.

The End

Some ELP fans were becoming a bit concerned by the sheer quantity of live material the band was releasing: the period from 1993 to 1998 saw the release of three albums documenting the band's nineties shows (*Live at the Royal Albert Hall, Live in Poland, Then and Now*) and three more albums featuring previously unreleased recordings from the seventies (the King Biscuit *Emerson, Lake and Palmer, Live at the Isle of Wight Festival*, and, of course, the first forty minutes of *Then and Now*). However, fans remained hopeful that these releases were simply a strategy for keeping interest in the band alive while ELP completed their long-awaited and increasingly anticipated studio album. It was therefore with unexpected and startling suddenness that the ELP saga reached its final Wagnerian denouement. Fans who visited the Official ELP Web Site on December 1, 1998, were stunned to find, prominently posted, a "Special Announcement from Greg Lake." In the interest of accuracy and impartiality, I will here reproduce the announcement in its entirety:

> For some considerable time now, I have identified the need for ELP to move forward artistically, while at the same time, reestablishing the passion and innovative qualities that the band had so clearly demonstrated throughout the 1970s.
>
> During those years, the albums we made were driven by a unified desire to try and exceed the frontiers of modern contemporary music. We took the most cutting-edge technology of its time, along with sterling production values, and weaved it into the most compelling songs and music we could envision. Seven platinum albums later, I felt at least in some way, that we must have done something right.
>
> Unfortunately, in more recent times, ELP has failed to deliver the same vital and inventive music that had made it so endearing during its earlier years. I must accept my share of the responsibility for this, mainly because, for the sake of keeping harmony within the group, I compromised some of my essential beliefs, particularly in respect to the way the records were made in the studio.
>
> Although, as a result of these compromises, I was introduced to some of the world's very best producers—in particular, my good friend Mark Mancina, who has taught me so much and with whom I am currently working—I still

felt in my heart of hearts, among the most valuable contributions I could make to ELP was that of being its producer.

Sadly, in the case of this new record, it was not to be.

As we began planning and discussing the new album, increasingly, I did not feel comfortable with the artistic and musical directions that were being proposed.

I have therefore decided, it is in my own—and in the band's—best interest, that I depart at this time and pursue my solo career.

I am deeply grateful to all of the fans of ELP who have supported the band over the years, and it goes without saying, that I sincerely wish Keith and Carl the very best of luck in whatever future endeavors they may choose.

Kind Regards,

Greg Lake [25]

Within the week Keith Emerson and Carl Palmer had crafted their own response to Lake's announcement, which was also prominently featured on the Official ELP Web Site. Here is the text of the Emerson-Palmer response, once again unedited and in its entirety:

In light of Greg Lake's "tenure of resignation" announced to the media and public recently, Keith Emerson, Carl Palmer, and the management of ELP wish to jointly respond with the following statement:

It is with much regret that we have accepted the resignation of Greg Lake from the Emerson, Lake and Palmer organization. As we all know there are many sides to all stories and we wish to reply to Greg's statement.

In the course of the many years of the careers of the members of ELP, each has developed his own significant production skills to high degrees. It would seem that great developments should come from such a powerful collaboration, each member receiving his "fair share of credit where credit was due" based on his contribution(s) to the whole project. Unfortunately, Greg does not see it this way. He has rebuked all attempts to compromise from the "sole producer's credit" position to what is considered by all others to be the more reasonable shared "co-produced" or "in association with" credit where applicable; thereby removing any animosity that could be associated with "not receiving proper credit." This, along with his failure to present the other members of the band with any tangible new material for audition, leave us with no alternative other than to accept his resignation and likewise wish him luck in his future endeavors.

Both Keith Emerson and Carl Palmer will be announcing their future plans after the beginning of the New Year.[26]

---

[25] Although this announcement has long since been removed from *The Official ELP Global Web Site*, it is reproduced in *ELP Digest* 8, no. 15 (December 6, 1998).
[26] Ibid.

What exactly transpired in the weeks leading up to Lake's December 1 announcement? By drawing on a series of interviews and web site postings released in the weeks and months after the December 1 surprise, it is possible to piece together a fairly comprehensive account of each band member's viewpoint as to what went wrong. I will do my best to present the following accounts as impartially as possible; at any rate, one notes that by and large it is not the facts surrounding the split, but the interpretation of these facts, that are in dispute.

In early 1999, Keith Emerson agreed to give an exclusive interview to an ELP fan named Richard Stellar, to be posted on Stellar's "Close to Home" website, on the condition that Stellar make no further updates to his website after the interview was posted, and make no further claims that his was the official Emerson web site.[27] During the course of the interview, the issue of Lake's resignation inevitably was raised, and Emerson had plenty to say. One of several sore spots for Emerson involved his perception that Lake had let his vocal skills atrophy, which Emerson perceived as symptomatic of a lack of commitment to ELP:

> We got together for rehearsals, before the last tour with Deep Purple, in Rochester. I was a little saddened when Greg told me he hadn't sung in eight months. But, we persevered with going over all the bass notes and everything like that, key changes, etc. . . . At many points in our two-week rehearsal, if Greg didn't want to sing, we'd excuse him . . . The annoying thing is that both Carl Palmer and I have gone through grueling surgery. I can't tell you how traumatizing it is for a doctor to tell you that you may never be able to play again. I mean, I've gone through hell and back. But here's a guy who has a voice, and all he needs to do is train it, go to a voice coach—he's done nothing.[28]

The real crux of the dispute, however, once again revolved around the production question:

> Greg said "We've had Mark Mancina producing, we've had Keith Olsen producing, and none of these albums have done anything. We've had the greatest success when I was producing." Oooh, okay. Things have changed a little bit since then, Greg. These are different times. At first I went along with it, but then Carl said to me "no, no—we can't give him that credit automati-

---

[27] Will Alexander had at one time commissioned Stellar to create a semiofficial Emerson web site; later, when Emerson decided to launch an official web site under his own supervision, a dispute arose when Stellar declined to deconstruct his. The final compromise was that Emerson would give Stellar an exclusive interview to post on his web site; Stellar agreed to post no further material once the interview was posted, and to relinquish any further claims to being host of the official Emerson web site.

[28] This interview, which has been posted for several years on Stellar's website, is accessible at the time of this writing on http://www.interstellar9.com/emerson/interview.htm.

cally." Carl said to me, and the rest of the ELP management said to me, "if there is to be any production credit, it should be to you." So I said, I don't want to get into a battle over it, let's just get the album done. Carl said "why don't we just say produced by Greg Lake, in association with Keith Emerson." Greg was not willing to accept that.[29]

When Stellar asked him if he though production credit was the root issue of the conflict, Emerson made a surprising statement:

> Well, basically, I think that Greg was throwing out a decoy here. He was look-ing for an excuse not to do it. He knew that none of us would accept him pro-ducing the new album, and he stuck to his guns using that as an excuse to get out of the band. And I'd hazard a guess that he's probably secretly happy that he doesn't have to do this anymore.[30]

In February 2000, Frank Askew asked Carl Palmer to share his recol-lections surrounding the aborted ELP studio album:

> The music came around and I heard about four pieces, and I liked two and a half. They were Keith's; Greg doesn't write until the last minute. Keith asked me what I though about them, I told him what I thought was right or wrong. Greg asked me what I thought about them. I told him what I thought, he said we ought to call up Keith and tell him they're not good enough. I said, "I did-n't say that to you, I think this, this, this is good," and then it went from there. And so we said to Greg, "what have you got that you want to play?" And he had nothing. So that went round in a circle again, and then it came to the producer thing."[31]

Palmer's remark highlights the two issues that seemed to have been at the crux of every ELP crisis since the first one, in late 1970, that almost aborted *Tarkus*: stylistic direction and production credits. When asked how he would describe Emerson's new music, Palmer responded, "There was a sparkle there, but I can't describe it! There was part of it that we were playing on stage already . . . we just played a sixteen bar intro at the beginning of the set, that's how confident we were of it. Greg came up with the title ['Crossing the Rubicon']; that was his, he did do that!"[32]

For over two years, Lake made no further public statement about his decision to leave ELP, or the reasons behind it. However, it would appear at some point he felt a need to respond in greater detail to Emerson's and

---

[29] Ibid.
[30] Ibid.
[31] Carl Palmer, quoted in Frank Askew, Even Gaarder, and Liv Whetmore, "Carl Palmer: 4th February 2000," *Impressions*, no. 8 (October 2001): 6.
[32] Ibid., 7.

Palmer's public pronouncements. In response to a letter that appeared on his website from a fan identified only as "Colin," dated February 2001, Lake gave an extremely detailed apologia for his reasons for leaving ELP, which was particularly interesting in light of the fact that Colin had not asked him why he left the band, but had simply stated that he took the breakup of ELP as hard as some fans had taken the split of the Beatles some twenty-eight years earlier. Lake's response is so lengthy that I can't viably reproduce it all, only highlight key passages. Lake began by summarizing what he felt were his contributions, as producer, to the music of ELP during the band's golden age. He concluded by saying, "The fact that I produced the albums is perhaps less important than the effect it had on the band creatively. Because we did not use an independent or outside producer, the band was forced to take sole responsibility for all musical and artistic decisions itself. This internal interaction is what is often referred to as chemistry and it is this chemistry that is missing on some of the later recordings by ELP."[33] Talking of Mancina's and Olsen's work with the band, he said, "The problem was not with the quality or capability of the producers, it was, that by bringing a fourth member into the creative arena of the band, the chemistry had become completely altered."[34]

Finally, Lake directly addressed the issue of production as it pertained to the aborted ELP studio album:

> When it came to the subject of a new and possibly the last ELP studio album, I was clear in my own mind that it was only worth making if the original chemistry that made ELP so special could be recaptured. I did not want to make another album that felt in any way manufactured. I needed to get back to the real essence and the real spirit of ELP.
>
> I made it clear to everyone concerned that I felt strongly about recovering this chemistry and that I wanted to return to the formula of making albums which brought us so much success in the past. I also made it clear that I could only produce the album if there was agreement and goodwill amongst all the members of the band. Unfortunately this was not to be the case.
>
> At first Keith was totally against me producing the record but later agreed to go along with it, provided he was given a credit on the album as being Executive Producer. It was at this point I came to the realization that the whole focus about the future of ELP had shifted away from the artistic issues and had sunk into a personal conflict over credits. At this point there was nothing more I felt I had to contribute.

---

[33] At the time of this writing, the letter from Colin, and Lake's response to it, are still posted on *The Official Greg Lake Website*, as follows: http://www.greglake.com/newsite/feedback.asp?offset=15.
[34] Ibid.

Because there had been a lot of speculation about the upcoming new record, before making any public announcement regarding my intention to leave the band, I wrote Keith and Carl inviting them to make a joint statement in an amicable way on behalf of the three of us. They declined this offer.[35]

Some readers may look to me to judge this dispute, and perhaps assign culpability. After a good deal of consideration, I have decided to render no judgment. On the one hand, I feel a record producer is not unlike a baseball manager who receives too much credit when a team does well, and too much blame when a team does badly. There is no producer in the world that could have made *Black Moon* or *In the Hot Seat* into another *Trilogy* or *Brain Salad Surgery*, for the simple reason that *Black Moon* had relatively little material that was of *Trilogy*'s or *Brain Salad Surgery*'s caliber, *In the Hot Seat* even less. Therefore, I cannot really buy into Lake's argument if he means that his producing these albums would have somehow miraculously improved the quality of the material.

On the other hand, any thoughtful observer realizes there is something to Lake's argument that the interpersonal chemistry of ELP during the nineties was not what it had been during the seventies; indeed, as I've already pointed out, the interpersonal chemistry of ELP during the late seventies was not what it had been between 1970 and 1974. So the question becomes, could a situation where Greg Lake produced the albums of the nineties have yielded music that was more consistently the caliber of ELP's golden-age material, by forcing the three musicians to work directly *with* each other, rather than work indirectly with each other through the intermediary agency of an outside producer, which appears to have allowed them to forego the necessity of really *communicating* with each other? This is a question that I am not able to answer, and I'm not sure that anyone—even Emerson, Lake and Palmer—could answer with complete confidence. Suffice it to say that the events of late 1998 appear to have brought the band to an insurmountable impasse, forever ending the Show That Never Ends.

---

[35] Ibid.

After the End

(December 1998 through December 2004)

I can understand that some readers may be skeptical about my pronounce-ment that the Show That Never Ends has closed for the last time. "Wait a minute," I can imagine somebody saying. "They almost broke up in late 1970, but then they went on to do their best work between 1971 and 1974. They survived the break of 1975-76. And when they broke up in 1979, everybody was certain ELP were finished. Yet Emerson and Lake came back together in 1985. And when ELPowell folded in 1986, nobody ever thought that Emerson and Lake would work together again, but ELP reunited in 1991. And they survived the rough period of 1994-95, and recommenced working together in 1996." To which I would answer: yes, it is true that ELP have shown an elasticity and longevity that very few would have suspected them capable of in 1970, or even in 1980. However, I would argue that there are several factors at work, both internal and external to the band, that make it highly unlikely that ELP will ever work together again; and I think that as each year passes, the likelihood that they will never reform grows exponentially. Let me explain my reasoning.

First and foremost, as I said in the previous chapter, the Age of Rock is over; it ended sometime between the early and mid-1990s. When ELP reached their first crisis in late 1970, there was a powerful incentive for Emerson and Lake to resolve their differences; the band realized that not only were they hot commercial property, they were a hothouse of musical innovation at an exciting time when rock, as a musical style, was just reaching its artistic zenith. By the time of the 1975-76 "sabbatical," rock had already passed its creative high-water mark, but it was just reaching the point of its maximum confluence of cultural influence and enormous commercial profitability; there was huge pressure on the band to carry on. Even after their breakup in 1979, the ELP name carried a good deal of iconic power with it, and since rock remained the *vox populi* of youth cul-ture in the Western world throughout the eighties, the ELPowell and 3 projects had both aesthetic and commercial viability.

The ELP reformation of 1991-92 came at an opportune time for three reasons. First, while rap was beginning to move beyond its point of origin in America's black urban centers, rock was still the primary musical style of Western youth culture, and the rise of Nirvana and the Seattle grunge style signaled that rock still had some musical and cultural vitality left. Second, reflecting the twenty-year "nostalgia cycle" that seems to have been operative in the U.S. since at least the sixties, there was a large-scale revival of interest in seventies music and fashion underway in the early nineties; this benefited ELP both by renewing the interest of some of their lapsed fans of the seventies, and encouraging young people who were mere toddlers (or not yet born) when *Brain Salad Surgery* was released to check the band out. Finally, ELP were reuniting just as a small but fiercely loyal taste public was beginning to cohere around progressive music via a network of fanzines, mail-order catalogs, prog rock festivals, and web sites on a newly important medium, the internet. This newly coherent prog scene constituted an automatic, and loyal, audience for ELP.

Fast forward to the late nineties. Imagine, if you will, the three trends I just described—the continued vitality of rock into the 1990s, the rise of nostalgia for the seventies, and the progressive music revival of the early nineties—as waves: while the energy of the wave had dissipated somewhat by 1998 or 1999, it was not yet entirely spent. If ELP had released their studio album in 1998 or 1999 as planned, they could have used whatever energy remained in these waves to propel themselves forward.

In the years since ELP disbanded, however, all three of these trends have pretty much played out. By the midnineties, rap had largely succeeded in displacing rock as the primary music of youth culture; this is a process I already noted in the last chapter, and here I'll simply add that each year the displacement becomes just a bit broader and more permanent in scope.[1] Furthermore, within a year or two of the 1998 ELP breakup, seventies nostalgia began to be displaced by eighties nostalgia, as the oldest members of Generation X began to approach middle age, and the public's appetite for seventies music and fashion began to wane. Acknowledging these two trends, it seems highly unlikely that ELP will ever again have the opportunity to get the kind of record deal they could have as recently as 1998 or 1999.

The progressive music revival of the nineties, too, seems to be fading. Perhaps this is the time to pose the following rhetorical question: was there a progressive music revival during the nineties? In terms of absolute

---

[1] Reconsidering this statement at the time this book goes to press (early 2006), I must admit that rock has not faded as a commercial force as quickly as I had thought it might circa 2000-01. Nonetheless, it's hard to imagine it ever recapturing either its creative energy of 1965–75 or its commercial hegemony of 1970–90.

sales, no; the audience remained small, a tiny fraction of what it had been in the seventies, although it did grow modestly, and steadily, between the early and late nineties. In terms of an artistic revival, yes; I believe there was a window of time, between the very late eighties and the mid- to late nineties, when a body of music was produced that was comparable in quality to seventies prog. The best of this music, while firmly based around the basic elements of the seventies prog rock style, also acknowledged the passing of two decades by drawing inspiration from styles that had appeared (or had become prominent) since the seventies, and/or drawing on new mediums of music technology. Many of us had hoped that ELP might harness some of the creative energy of the nineties prog revival when they recorded their proposed studio album; unfortunately, it now appears there is little creative energy left in the movement itself.

Here I must interject a personal note. Even as I was working on my cultural and stylistic history of prog rock, *Rocking the Classics*, in the mid-1990s, I was composing music and putting together a band to record an album that I thought would posit one potentially promising avenue for contemporary progressive music. I continue to maintain that our first album, *Hermetic Science*, released in 1997, remains a unique, highly original, and stylistically cohesive milestone in the 1990s prog rock canon. The album is certainly unique in its instrumentation—featuring what amounts to a vibes (or occasionally marimba)-bass-drums power trio, with a number of other instruments used discreetly in textural roles. More importantly, the album is notable for its fusion of key elements of prog, ECM-style spatial jazz, twentieth-century classical modernism, and non-Western (particularly Asian) musical styles into a coherent and immediately recognizable sound. Under different circumstances, *Hermetic Science* could have given birth to a distinct subgenre of mostly acoustic progressive music.

Unfortunately, while this album received a good deal of critical acclaim, it did not sell particularly well, even by the modest standards of the nineties progressive rock community. We released two more albums, *Prophesies* (1999) and *En Route* (2001), which continued to explore the innovations of the first album, although the last (and to some degree the second) made a more explicit genuflection to the "canonic" seventies prog sound by somewhat deemphasizing the mallet instruments in favor of piano, Hammond, and analog synths. While our three albums of 1997–2001 certainly represent one of the most innovative and crucial bodies of progressive music produced by any one band during that four-year period, even our move towards greater conventionality in our second and third releases did not placate very many progressive music fans. As one critic put it in commenting on *Prophesies*: "Is this rather unusual music more progressive than that of most prog rock bands today? 'Yes,' I tend to say, but I doubt that many progheads will be seduced by Hermetic Science."[2]

It was at this point I recognized the Achilles' heel of the progressive music revival of the nineties: many of its fans were deeply conservative in their tastes, and would only brook minor departures from the "classic" progressive rock sound of the seventies.[3] This meant that once the initial wave of the nineties prog rock revival ended, bands were expected to recycle the same riffs over and over; additional stylistic shifts by and large were not welcome.[4] There was a period when I was galled by the fact that while Hermetic Science and a few other similarly adventurous bands were excluded from the progressive music festival scene, two particular bands that I won't name here, both of whom built their careers on recycling Yes, Genesis, ELP, King Crimson, and Pink Floyd riffs, were invited to play festival after festival. I have since come to accept the fact that the progressive music scene of the nineties has chosen to condemn itself to death by slow stagnation, unless there is a major change in its internal dynamic—which, unfortunately, I don't see on the horizon. I also came to realize that if a new and unknown band like us was expected to conform to the "classic" seventies prog sound, then the pressure on a band like ELP that helped forge that style would be enormous. If they had released an album during the high point of the nineties progressive revival, they might have been allowed some leeway, even while drawing energy from the genuinely adventurous work that was being done in some quarters; at this point, though, there appears to be relatively little artistic energy left in the contemporary prog scene, and still less tolerance for variance from the canonic style—even (perhaps especially) from a founding band of the genre.

For all of these reasons external to the band—the eclipse of rock by rap as the music of youth culture, the waning of nostalgia for the seventies, and the fading energy of the progressive music revival—the condi-

---

[2] Eric Neuteboom, "Hermetic Science: *Prophesies* [review]," *Background*, no. 70 (May 2000): 28.

[3] The inability of this music to "progress" is symptomatic of the postmodern condition, and is a result of forces that extend far beyond prog, or even rock itself. In *The Future of Jazz* (New York: A Cappella, 2002), edited by Yuval Taylor, a group of leading jazz critics bemoan the fact that jazz appears to be a music whose future—if it has one at all—involves endless self-repetition. The future of Western classical music has, of course, been in doubt for years. It is significant that the style of music in the Western world that presently shows the most creative vitality, rap, is based on an ideology to which the idea of "progression" is foreign.

[4] The fans do not necessarily deserve all the blame. The owners of most of the prog labels were similarly conservative in their tastes, as were the majority of prog music distributors. The fans who knew what they liked, and liked what they knew, by and large weren't given the chance to find if they might also like what they didn't yet know.

tions are less favorable than ever for the reformation of ELP. But there is a factor internal to the band that I think is an even stronger deterrent to the possibility of another ELP reformation: simply put, the relationship between Keith Emerson and Greg Lake has reached an impasse that would be exceptionally difficult to bridge. It seems clear that Emerson feels that he has inevitably found himself compromising his ideas to conform to Lake's production and stylistic point of view, and after the debacle of *In the Hot Seat*, sees no reason to make another ELP album under conditions where his ideas might again be fatally compromised. Lake, for his part, seems equally set in his belief that there is no reason to make another ELP album with an outside producer making decisions that Lake feels ought to be made by the band. Bridging this gap would take a tremendous emotional investment by both men, and in light of their shrinking fan base and the dwindling financial incentives for making another album, it seems unlikely this particular gap will ever be bridged. As our saga of ELP draws to its close, then, I will bring the reader up-to-date on the activities of Emerson, Lake and Palmer between the six-year period of December 1998 and December 2004, and finish with a few concluding observations.

Keith Emerson

Emerson's post-ELP career began slowly. One effort that began almost immediately, however, and has since been fruitful, was an attempt to return to circulation his back catalog of solo albums and soundtracks, most of which were out of print by 1999. In May 1999 he signed a distribution deal with a small Arizona-based label, Gunslinger Records, who agreed to rerelease *The Christmas Album* in late 1999 with all the original tracks of 1988, as well as the two tracks that were added on the Sundown Records reissue of 1995. In April 2000 Gunslinger rereleased *Honky*, again combining the original tracks of the 1981 LP release with the tracks added in the Chord Records rerelease of the mideighties. In 2001, the two Gunslinger reissues were made available in liquid audio format (which allows a person to download individual tracks directly from cyberspace to their computer hard drive for a set fee) via Emerson's web site, as was *Changing States*, one of the few Emerson albums that didn't go at least briefly out of print in the late nineties. Almost simultaneously with the *Honky* and *Christmas Album* reissues, Emerson's movie scores began to find their way back into print. The Japanese Volcano label rereleased the *Harmagedon* soundtrack on CD in May 1998. In 1997 the Italian Cinevox label reissued Emerson's *Inferno* as one of the first releases of their "The History of Soundtrack" series; in 2001, the label followed with reissues of his two other Italian film soundtracks, the long-out-of-print

Murderock and *La Chiesa.* As I've mentioned, early 2002 witnessed the rerelease of *Nighthawks,* as well as the release of the previously unavailable *Iron Man* music. By late 2002, of his ten commercially available solo albums and soundtracks of the 1980–95 period, only *Best Revenge* remains unavailable.

In the creative (as opposed to business) sphere, matters moved more slowly. From May 1999 there were rumors of a collaboration between Emerson and his longtime prog rock keyboard colleague (and rival) Rick Wakeman. As of April 15, 2000, when Emerson appeared at the Smithsonian Institute as part of their "The Keyboard Meets Modern Technology" program (other participants were Robert Moog and the late-sixties experimental rock band Mother Mallard), nothing had become of it, although there was now talk of a November 2000 Emerson-Wakeman album followed by a 2001 Emerson-Wakeman tour. As late as early summer 2001, Emerson was still saying he hoped to see the collaboration go forward. However, in August 2001 Wakeman announced that the Emerson-Wakeman project had been put on hold, and nothing further came of it.

Meanwhile, in early 2001 Emerson announced he had signed a contract with EMI to record a second piano concerto and an orchestral version of "'Tarkus" with piano obbligato. In July, he said that he was still working on the new piano concerto, and added that he was also in the process of recording a twenty-two-track album of solo piano pieces for EMI entitled *Emerson Plays Emerson.* As matters turned out, the concerto project was scrapped— EMI cancelled the sessions it had booked over the summer of 2001 with the London Symphony Orchestra when it was clear that Emerson would not have the new music completed in time, and Emerson, for his part, was not anxious to reschedule the sessions after learning that EMI expected him to reimburse the LSO for its rehearsal time. The *Emerson Plays Emerson* project, on the other hand, proceeded apace, even as Emerson spoke of his desire to reform the Nice: a rather astounding suggestion, considering that the band had broken up over thirty-one years earlier.

In early 2002, Emerson began to reemerge in the public limelight in England, where he had recently returned to live. On January 8, he recorded a big-band jazz version of "Tarkus" (with piano obbligato, of course) with the Johnny Dankworth Big Band—this aired on the BBC Radio 2 "Live from the Stables" series on March 25. On April 9, London's 100 Club hosted a special invitation-only event promoting the impending release of *Emerson Plays Emerson.* As expected, Emerson played several acoustic piano pieces from the upcoming album. He also read an excerpt from his autobiography, which he had been working on since the mid-1990s, about a not-so-pleasant encounter with Leonard Bernstein that he had experienced in the seventies; he added that he hoped the autobiography finally would be completed and published by

Christmas 2002. (He wasn't too far off: *Pictures of an Exhibitionist*, as he titled his autobiography, appeared during the summer of 2003.) The most dramatic event of the evening was undoubtedly the reunion of the Nice, which actually *did* take place: Emerson, his old mates Lee Jackson and Brian Davison, and guest guitarist Phil Hirbourne played a short set consisting of Meade Lux Lewis's "Honky Tonk Train Blues," George Gershwin's "Summertime," and the Nice's two signature instrumentals, "America" and "Rondo." Emerson told the delighted audience to expect to see more of the reunited Nice in coming months.

Emerson Plays Emerson

In May 2002 EMI released *Emerson Plays Emerson*, billing it as a collection of recently composed solo piano pieces by Emerson; this description, while not totally off the mark, wasn't totally accurate, either. Six of the album's twenty-two tracks had been released before: "The Dreamer" and "Prelude to Candice" were from the *Best Revenge* and *Murderock* soundtracks, respectively, "Interlude" and "Summertime" were from *Changing States*, and "A Blade of Grass" and "Hammer it Out" were bonus tracks from the Japanese releases of *Black Moon* and *In the Hot Seat*, respectively. In addition, the album contained two new studio recordings of previously available Emerson compositions ("Creole Dance" and "Barrelhouse Shakedown"), and two previously unreleased live recordings of already available tracks ("Close to Home" and "Honky Tonk Train Blues"). In sum, only twelve of the twenty-two tracks were previously unavailable in any guise. The album's title is also a bit misleading in that three of the twenty-two tracks ("Summertime," "Honky Tonk Train Blues," and the final "Medley") are covers, and on three of the twenty-two tracks ("Summertime," "B & W Blues," and "Honky-Tonk Train Blues"), Emerson is accompanied by a band.

Stylistically, the album focuses on two specific aspects of Emerson's musical personality. The majority of the tracks are short, limpid character pieces that mine the lyrical, diatonic vein of writing Emerson had begun to explore in the eighties; these pieces hearken back to the tradition of the lyric (as opposed to virtuosic) nineteenth-century character piece exemplified by Felix Mendelssohn's *Songs Without Words*, Frederic Chopin's Nocturnes, and Johannes Brahms's Intermezzos and Capriccios. Besides his eighties classic "The Dream Runner" (retitled "The Dreamer" for this collection), a particularly outstanding example of this kind of piece on *Emerson Plays Emerson* is "Outgoing Tide," whose impressionistic washes evoke the famous solo piano piece "Lotus Land" by English composer Cyril Scott (1879–1970), although the bittersweet poignancy of "Outgoing Tide" is characteristic of all of Emerson's best pieces in this genre. Only two of these pieces, "Creole Dance" and "Hammer It Out" (both previously available), evoke Emerson's virtuosic playing of the seventies: both are percussive and owe much to the music of Alberto Ginastera.

There are also seven or eight pieces that demonstrate Emerson's continuing engagement with his ragtime/blues/jazz roots. Noteworthy here are "Roll'n'Jelly," a short piece for solo piano in the style of Ferdinand "Jelly Roll" Morton, and "B & W Blues," a bop-style blues on which Emerson is reunited with drummer Frank Scully, a key figure in a number of Emerson's early-eighties projects (*Inferno, Nighthawks, Honky*).

Two of the jazz tracks, which happen to be the final two tracks of the album, are of special historical significance for Emerson archivists. The penultimate track is a recording of "Honky Tonk Train Blues" that was made when Emerson was a guest on Oscar Peterson's BBC television series *Piano Party* in 1976. Here Emerson is accompanied by Peterson's Big Band, and Peterson himself on a second piano, which even for a pianist of Emerson's stature must have been a daunting experience. Most interesting of all is the final track, "Medley," recorded by Emerson himself on reel-to-reel tape recorder in 1959 when he was fourteen. It features him playing segments of three Jazz Age classics, "Nicola," "Silver Shoes," and "I'll See You In My Dreams." Clearly, Emerson had yet to discover the music of Bud Powell or other pianists of the late forties bop revolution when he recorded these tunes; his playing here is solidly rooted in thirties stride piano techniques. If this recording does not reveal Emerson to have been a teenage prodigy, it certainly does show him to have possessed an unusually sophisticated understanding for a musician of his age of jazz syntax, with its subtle rhythmic and melodic inflections.

Despite its abundance of previously released tracks, new studio recordings of previously released tracks, and new live recordings of previously released studio tracks, most of Emerson's fans welcomed *Emerson Plays Emerson* as his most thoroughgoing exploration of one particular vein of his writing—the quasi-nineteenth-century piano miniature—that he had never systematically explored before. Even fans who deplored an almost complete lack of reference to his epic style of the seventies, and who criticized the album for a certain sameness of mood and uncharacteristically flat emotional trajectory, were impressed by the precision of his playing, which was cleaner and more authoritative than at any time since his ulnar nerve operation of 1993.

The Return of the Nice

As part of the reorganization of his personal and business affairs in the 2001-02 period that saw him return to Great Britain, Emerson hired

Stewart Young, ELP's longtime manager, as his personal manager (Will Alexander remains his keyboard technician). One immediate benefit of this management shift was that Emerson was invited to participate in Queen Elizabeth's Golden Jubilee festivities, playing in a concert attended by the Queen and the Duke of Edinburgh on Wednesday, May 22, 2002, at London's Royal Academy of Arts. Emerson, who admitted to being momentarily nonplussed when Prince Philip asked him prior to the concert whether he "banged or scraped," played "Creole Dance." Although a bit disappointed that the Queen did not remember his performance (with the Nice) at Princess Anne's "Coming Out" Ball in 1969, he was happy to see a number of fellow luminaries of the British rock scene of the seventies, including Jimmy Page, Brian May, and Kate Bush, in attendance, as well as former Prime Minister (now Lady) Margaret Thatcher; as Emerson put it, "it was almost like the whole cast of *Spitting Image* coming to life."[5]

In July 2002, it was announced that the Nice would undertake a (very) short British tour in early October, consisting of four dates: October 2 at Wolverhampton Civic Hall, October 3 at Newcastle, Lee Jackson's hometown, at the New Tyne Opera House, October 4 at Glasgow's Royal Concert Hall, and October 6 at London's Royal Festival Hall. These shows were divided into four segments. The opening segment featured the Nice (Emerson, Jackson, and Davison) with guest guitarist Dave Kilminister, whom Emerson had become acquainted with when he jammed one night in early 2000 with Carl Palmer's band Qango. After opening with a medley of "America" and "Rondo," the Nice reached far back into their repertoire, performing "The Cry of Eugene"—which Lee Jackson noted they had not performed live since David O'List left the band in 1968—"She Belongs To Me," "Little Arabella," "Hang on to a Dream," the Intermezzo of Jan Sibelius's *Karelia Suite*, and a second Dylan cover, "Country Pie." The short second segment of the concert featured Emerson playing three solo piano pieces from *Emerson Plays Emerson*: some combination of "Vagrant," "Outgoing Tide," "A Cajun Alley," "A Blade of Grass," and "Creole Dance" (the selections were different each night). The third segment offered the biggest surprise of the show—Emerson played "Hoedown" and a complete performance of "Tarkus" on his electronic keyboard rig, accompanied by Kilminister, bassist Phil Williams, and drummer Pete Riley. For the encore, Emerson was joined on stage by all the other musicians for stomping renditions of "Fanfare for the Common Man" and "Honky Tonk Train Blues."

Emerson played with a relatively small keyboard setup: grand piano, Hammond C-3, GEM ProMega 3, and a couple of other digital synths.

---

5 Keith Emerson, quoted on http://www.keithemerson.com/emo_meets.htm.

Unlike previous tours, some of the electronic keyboards were rack mounted, but Emerson was much more static in his stage presence than before: the days of Hammond wrestling appear, thankfully, to be over forever. Fans noted that while the precision and accuracy of *Emerson Plays Emerson* appears to have been no fluke—the quality of his playing was very high—there is no question that stamina remains an issue, and probably will for the remainder of his career. Almost everybody in attendance was impressed with Dave Kilminster's guitar work (his lead vocals on "Tarkus" were passable, if not memorable) as well as the workmanlike precision of the Williams-Riley rhythm section; the verdict on the Nice's performance was a bit more mixed. While retaining its characteristic rasp, Lee Jackson's voice has hardened since the late sixties—it has lost its former airiness—and, like Greg Lake, he has lost much of the upper portion of his range, rendering his vocals on certain songs ("Little Arabella," for instance) problematic. On the other hand, Jackson's bass playing was good, and Brian Davison's energetic drumming was a particularly nice surprise. Some attendees were put off by the loose, almost rough nature of the arrangements, but for me this had always been one of the hallmarks of the Nice, and one suspects that the dissatisfied audience members were probably ELP fans who were used to the extraordinary tightness—which on occasion could border on stiffness—of the Lake Palmer rhythm section. (It's also important to note that nearly everyone who attended one of these shows complained about the poor house mix.) After the shows, Emerson and his mates mingled with the audience—now more equally divided between men and women than in the heyday of the Nice and ELP, mostly over forty, in many cases over fifty, but including a surprising number of the young and curious—and suggested that future British dates were likely. Indeed, in October 2003 Emerson and his double band (the Nice and the Emerson-Kilminster-Williams-Riley lineup) undertook an eleven-show U.K. mini-tour, playing largely the same set list (with a few minor changes and emendations) as they had in 2002. By 2004, the revival of the Nice appeared to have run its course, and in late 2004, what was now being billed as the Keith Emerson Band (the Emerson-Kilminster-Williams-Riley lineup) toured the U.S. as opening act for the Scorpions, a German metal band popular in the U.S. between the early and mid-1980s.

Those who believe I have judged the Nice's 2002-03 reunion either too harshly or too leniently will be interested to learn that a three-CD set of the October 4, 2002, Glasgow show (two discs document the actual show, while a third is devoted to a 2001 interview of the Nice by Chris Welch), *Keith Emerson and the Nice Live Glasgow 2002: Vivacitas*, was released during the summer of 2003 by Sanctuary Records, so interested parties may judge the evidence for themselves. Perhaps the real questions raised by these shows—and it's the same questions raised by ELP's tours of 1996–98—should be posed to the fans. At this point in time, do fans want Emerson (and his peers) to simply re-create past glories (and memories)? Is there anything truly inspired, or creative, about playing a (nearly) thirty-five-year-old set list? Would fans support Emerson and his mates if they played new music? Or are they there simply for the warm nostalgia of hearing the hits from days gone by? (Here one notes the presence of ELP material in what was putatively a Nice concert.) Since the nineties, it has often been said that Emerson (and his peers among progressive rock's founding fathers) are no longer willing, or able, to create genuinely contemporary and adventurous music. Fair enough. If he did, though, would his fans give it a hearing? Or would they demand to hear another performance of "Fanfare" and "Rondo" instead?

In May 2005, Emerson became the final member of ELP to release a career anthology, *Hammer It Out: The Anthology*. One has to commend Emerson for resisting the temptation to simply deliver a Greatest Hits of ELP; if anything, his Hammond-and-Moog masterpieces may be somewhat underrepresented. Besides its highly idiosyncratic cross-section of Nice, ELP, ELPowell, and 3 material, *Hammer It Out* offers an excellent brief overview of his film scores of the eighties and his more recent piano music. I wish he had featured more of his work with the T-Bones (one track is included) and the VIPs (nothing included); the early 1966 through mid-1967 period remains something of a *tabula rasa* for those attempting to trace the development of the already highly individualistic vision that emerges on the first Nice LP. One also wishes for more unreleased material, although the previously unavailable 1966 cover of Brother Jack McDuff's "Rock Candy" with the T-Bones, the 1989 rock arrangement of the final movement of his Piano Concerto no. 1 (highlighting its stylistic similarities to the instrumental movements of "Tarkus"), and "Lament for Tony Stratton-Smith," the basis for 3's "On My Way Home," are all welcome additions to Emerson's commercially available output.

Greg Lake

Like Emerson, Lake's early post-ELP efforts were focused in the business rather than the creative sphere. One area of focus was his internet presence. Under the supervision of his manager, Bruce Pilato, Lake has always maintained the best website of the three band members—not only in terms of using the most-up-to-date visual and audio technology, but also in terms of content and opportunities for interaction between Lake and his fans. His web site contains, among other features, an "Ask Greg" column (this has been an important source of information for Lake's attitudes concerning the final ELP breakup), a complete listing of all gigs

Lake has played since 1969 with King Crimson, ELP, the Greg Lake Band, Asia, ELPowell, and others, an "I Was There" section (where fans can share their recollections of specific shows), as well as the more ordinary features—an extensive gallery, an online store, and so on. Of the three, Lake has also shown the greatest commitment to regularly updating the web site, which has even undergone two complete overhauls since the ELP breakup, first in January 2001, then again in December 2002. About the time of the January 2001 overhaul, Lake's two long-out-of-print studio albums of the early eighties, *Greg Lake* and *Manoeuvres*, became reavailable via his online gift shop.

Unfortunately, Lake's activities in the creative and musical spheres have been far more intermittent. In March 2001, it was announced that Lake would be part of Ringo Starr and his All Starrs Summer 2001 Tour. Fellow participants (besides Starr, of course) included seventies luminaries Roger Hodgson (ex-Supertramp, on keyboards, guitars, and vocals) and Ian Hunter (ex–Mott the Hoople, on guitars and vocals, and eighties stars Howard Jones (keyboards and vocals) and Sheila E (Prince's former drummer and backing vocalist). The tour commenced in Toronto on July 26, 2001, and took in twenty-nine dates in all, ending on September 2 with an open-air show at San Diego State University. Three songs written or cowritten by Lake featured in these shows: "In the Court of the Crimson King," "Karn Evil 9, 1st Impression, part 2," which forced Jones and Sheila E to do their best Keith Emerson and Carl Palmer imitations, respectively, and the ubiquitous "Lucky Man." An album commemorating this tour has since been released; its only Lake feature is "Lucky Man." As of early 2005, Lake has been involved in no other publicly active projects since his brief involvement with the All Starrs, and the solo album that was intimated at the time of ELP's demise in December 1998 has yet to appear, some six years later. While Lake has a history, dating back to the early eighties, of being the least prolific ELP member when in solo mode, his creative silence has grown so long at this point that one does wonder if his days as an active musical creator are over.

An announcement posted on his revamped web site in December 2002 promised a major announcement in 2003; while no new music was forthcoming during 2003, the year did mark the release of *From the Underground, Volume II: Deeper into the Mine*. The concept of this album is similar to that of *From the Underground*: rather than simply present a predictable best-of anthology, a number of rare, previously unavailable tracks are featured. On the whole, the tracks of *Volume II* are somewhat less interesting than those of the original 1998 release: there's a number of studio outtakes from *Greg Lake* and *Manoeuvres*, two previously unreleased tracks by Ride the Tiger (Lake and Geoff Downes), a live track each by King Crimson and the Greg Lake Band, and two live tracks by ELP. One of these, "Preacher Blues," was previously unavailable in any format:

recorded during a German show in 1971, it's a less-developed version of what eventually became "Tiger in a Spotlight."

Carl Palmer

As we have observed throughout the course of this book, Carl Palmer is a restless man who does not suffer musical inactivity gladly. Therefore it's probably no surprise that the corpse of ELP had scarcely grown cold (pardon the ghastly pun) when an announcement was made on April 1, 1999, that three quarters of the original Asia lineup—Palmer, John Wetton, and Geoff Downes—would reunite for a tour during the summer of 1999. Guitarist/vocalist Dave Kilminister, a member of Wetton's Band, was recruited to fill the position of Steve Howe, who had been a full-time member of Yes since 1996. However, on June 12, scarcely two months later, Downes pulled out of the project. This caused a good deal of acrimony; while Palmer has said (and continues to say) he will be happy to rejoin ELP if Emerson and Lake ever iron out their difference, he has ruled out ever working with Downes again.[6]

However, Wetton and Palmer decided to carry on with the project, even if on a smaller scale than what had been planned. They could not call the band "Asia"; John Payne now owns the rights to the name, and he and Downes continue to release new music with anonymous session players under the Asia moniker. During the fall of 1999, then, Palmer and Wetton dubbed the band "Qango," and recruited an unknown keyboards player named John Young to take Downes's place.

The Qango tour, which took place during the period of February through April 2000, was confined to the U.K. Although Qango generated very little original material, and hence no studio album, there is a limited edition release, by Manticore Records, that captures Qango as heard live at Birmingham's Robin Hood (February 3, 2000) and Southampton's The Brook (February 7). Unfortunately, there's nothing on the album from the band's gig at London's Astoria on February 4, when Keith Emerson joined them onstage for a performance of "Fanfare for the Common Man."

Qango: *Live in the Hood*

As one might expect, Qango's first order of business was Asia material: the live Qango album, entitled *Live in the Hood*, includes "Time Again,"

---

[6] Frank Askew, Even Gaarder, and Liv Whetmore, "Carl Palmer Interview," *Impressions*, no. 8 (October 2001): 5.

"Sole Survivor," and "Heat of the Moment." However, Qango also did a surprising amount of ELP material: "Bitches Crystal" (which gives ELP fans an opportunity to compare Wetton's vocal interpretation to Lake's), "Hoedown" (on which Young and Kilminster trade off the lead lines), and the ubiquitous "Fanfare for the Common Man," which includes the Palmer drum solo. The album also contains a not-so-obvious cover, Bob Dylan's "All Along the Watchtower," which Qango gives a hazy, surprisingly reflective reading of; a Qango original (by Wetton and Young), "The Last One Home," a quiet, lyrical ballad with some nice three-part vocal harmonies (but little of the fire of Asia's most representative material); and solo spots featuring Young and Kilminster. Although there was vague talk of more live dates—possibly even a studio album—after the end of the band's Spring 2000 U.K. tour, nothing further came of the project, and sometime during mid-2000 Qango quietly dissolved.

Do Ya Wanna Play, Carl?

Palmer, however, was not M.I.A. for long. In the fall of 2000, during a series of drum clinics he was giving in the U.S., he announced the formation of a new trio, the Carl Palmer Band, which he said would be touring the following summer. By early 2001, more details about the new band began to emerge. The Carl Palmer Band was to consist of Palmer, guitarist Shaun Baxter, who was affiliated with the Royal College of Music and Guildhall, and Dave Marks on six-string electric bass; both Baxter and Marks were only a few years older than Palmer's daughter Carissa, who turned eighteen during 2001. The trio's debut was slated for London's Royal Festival Hall on July 18. By March 2001, a modest U.K. tour had been sketched out, with the first leg of the tour commencing in July and a second leg beginning in October; in April, Palmer did a series of drum clinics in the U.K. In May, the long-awaited Carl Palmer anthology, entitled *Do Ya Wanna Play, Carl?*, was finally released by Sanctuary Records. The most important track of the anthology is undoubtedly the Horwitz-Palmer Concerto for Percussion—finally made available one-quarter century after it was recorded—but the anthology contains some other gems as well. There are a number of instrumental ELP tracks, including several less obvious selections, and a previously unreleased track, "Pancha Suite," recorded with Snuffy Walden and the members of Backdoor (the lineup that recorded "New Orleans"). There is the single "I Must Be Mad" and its B-side "Suspense," which Palmer recorded with the Midlands-based combo the Craig in 1966; besides demonstrating what a hugely accomplished rock drummer Palmer was by the age of sixteen, these recordings also reveal the degree to which his mature style was influenced not only by Buddy Rich (about whom more anon), but also by the Who's Keith

Moon. There's also an interesting 1966 single by the Chants, Britain's first all-black vocal group, "Love Light," in a kind of post-doo-wop vein, on which Palmer appears as a sessions drummer.

While there's nothing chronicling his work with Chris Farlowe and the Thunderbirds or the Crazy World of Arthur Brown (a live recording of "Fire" featuring Palmer would have been most welcome), there is a track, "Decline and Fall," from the first Atomic Rooster album, as well as some inter-ELP and post-ELP material highlighting Palmer's work with PM, Mike Oldfield, Asia, 3, and even Qango. Finally, there's a blistering live performance of "Shawnee" that features Palmer sitting in with the Big Band of his idol, Buddy Rich, at Soho's famous Ronnie Scott's jazz club in 1986. Indeed, the anthology's title comes from Rich's query "Do ya wanna play, Carl?" included at the beginning of the track, after Rich spotted Palmer in the audience; there's some genuinely funny dialogue included both before the band commences playing (Rich gruffly admonishes Palmer not to adjust the drums), and after the band finishes (the audience erupts in thunderous applause, which Rich encourages for a moment before abruptly commanding the audience to cool it and then ordering Palmer off the bandstand with mock severity). *Do Ya Wanna Play, Carl?* is what every anthology of this type ought to be, but few actually are: a representative cross-section of a long and distinguished career that deftly alternates well-known and long-available tracks with previously unavailable or hard-to-find ones.

Carl Palmer Band

The Carl Palmer Band commenced the first leg of their U.K. tour in July 2001. Their approximately two-hour set mostly featured instrumental ELP selections, ingeniously arranged so that Shaun Baxter took some of Emerson's keyboard parts on guitar, while Dave Marks took the rest of Emerson's keyboard parts, as well as Lake's bass lines, on six-string bass. ELP fans were delighted to find that the majority of the trio's ELP selections were pieces that the parent band had never played live at all, or had not played live for many years: the set list consisted of "Toccata," "Tank," "Hoedown," "The Barbarian," "The Enemy God Dances with the Black Spirits," "Fanfare for the Common Man," "Bullfrog," "Canario," and "L.A. Nights." The band also performed a couple of originals featuring Baxter and Marks. They retained the same general set list when they undertook the second leg of their U.K. tour, playing ten dates in October.

As the band began to gel into a cohesive unit, Carl Palmer decided to draw up a more ambitious schedule for 2002, in which gigs by the trio alternated with, or were tied to, the drum clinics that were becoming an increasingly important part of his professional life. The drummer's public

2002 schedule began with an appearance at a Frankfurt trade show on March 17, where he unveiled his new custom-made drum kit. Constructed out of Paiste cymbal alloy by Jeff Ocheltree, it was valued at $35,000; not cheap, but still far less pricey (relatively speaking) than the famous stainless steel kit of the seventies. Besides weighing less and sounding better (according to Palmer, at least), the design of the new kit also mirrored the fundamental shift in Palmer's drumming style between 1973 and 2002. The stainless steel kit, one might recall, was heavily biased towards the upper part of the kit, with just one bass drum and one floor tom but numerous mounted toms, and was perfectly suited for the intricate rudimental fills and elaborate rhythmic doubling of Keith Emerson's melodic figurines that were a hallmark of Palmer's drumming style during the seventies. The Ocheltree kit, on the other hand, is much more biased towards the lower end of the kit, consisting of two bass drums, two floor toms, two attached toms, and snare, mirroring the shift to the more stripped-down, groove-oriented approach, in which interlocking bass drum parts count for more and quasi-melodic tom and snare fills for less, that Palmer has developed since his time with Asia.

The unveiling of the new kit in Frankfurt was followed by a few drum clinics in Germany in late March, and several more in the U.K. in early April; the Carl Palmer Band kicked off their 2002 schedule with six U.K. dates between April 13 and 21. This was followed by seven dates in Italy between April 24 and 29, marking the trio's first appearance outside of the U.K., and several more shows in May—three in Germany, six in the U.K., and two more Italian shows with drum clinics. The trio took June off so that Palmer could do a series of drum clinics in the U.K. and Ireland, but the band hit the road again in July, playing several more gigs in Germany and Italy, as well as some sporadic dates in August and September. In October the band played two shows (one each in Switzerland and Germany), followed by twelve gigs in November that saw the trio conquer more new territory—besides playing the U.K., they also performed shows in the Netherlands, Belgium, and Spain.

A show they played at De Kade, Zaandam, Holland, on November 20 revealed a band that had gelled significantly since their debut some sixteen months earlier. Although the set list was still recognizable from the trio's earlier days, there had been some additions and emendations. After opening with "Hoedown," the band played three instrumental ELP chestnuts—"The Barbarian," "The Enemy God," and "L.A. Nights." The "solo segment" of the show began with a Shaun Baxter solo, passing into a jazzy jam by the entire trio, which in turn segued into Dave Marks's bass solo, in which references to Greg Lake's "From the Beginning" and the Police's "Message in a Bottle" were clearly discernible. A Marks-Baxter duet was followed by two more ELP numbers, "Trilogy" (a surprising and surprisingly successful selection, even without the opening acoustic piano/voice section) and "Canario." Then came an unnamed original by Shaun Baxter for full band, followed by "Bullfrog," "Toccata," a medley of "Eruption" and "Aquatarkus" from the "Tarkus" suite, and an arrangement of the opening of Carl Orff's *Carmina Burana*. For an encore, the trio played "Fanfare for the Common Man," including a drum solo by Palmer that was significantly more focused than his solos of the nineties. The length of the entire show was just a bit under two hours. By the time of the trio's final gig of the tour on November 30, they had played over sixty shows during 2002.

The band undertook an even more ambitious touring schedule in 2003, and a live album chronicling the trio's show of July 19, 2001, in Bilston, titled *Working Live: Volume 1*, was released in March 2003 by Sanctuary Records. The album contains most of the band's 2001 set list, namely "The Barbarian," "The Enemy God," "L.A. Nights," "Tank," "Bullfrog," "Toccata," "Canario," and Palmer's drum solo; the show's opener ("Hoedown") and closer ("Fanfare for the Common Man") were expunged, although Palmer's drum solo was excerpted from "Fanfare." In October 2004, Sanctuary released *Working Live: Volume 2*, which included six numbers culled from various U.K. shows of 2003: "Hoedown," "Trilogy," "J.Section," a band original, the "Eruption"/"Aquatarkus" medley, a six-minute jam based around the opening of Carl Orff's *Carmina Burana*, and an epic fifteen-minute arrangement of "Fanfare for the Common Man," including Palmer's drum solo.

My personal impression of the Carl Palmer Band is that it is potentially a very promising project. The two volumes of *Working Live* without doubt showcases Palmer's most energetic and fiery playing in many a year, and the trio has succeeded in forging a distinctive group personality not unlike ELP of the seventies: aggressive, brash, self-confident. As I can attest via my own work in Hermetic Science, a mutually beneficial situation arises when an older, more experienced (and developed) musician surrounds himself with younger musicians of possibly equal talent but less experience and knowledge. While the older musician supplies the guiding vision and (hopefully) an encyclopedic knowledge of past styles and techniques, and the sense of stability that comes with knowing what works and what doesn't in a professional context, younger musicians often supply a sense of energy that older musicians can't equal, and can pull the older musician out of his autopilot zone by introducing him to new styles and techniques or unorthodox ways of approaching a project that he would otherwise be oblivious to. I'm reminded especially of the success of Bill Bruford's Earthworks—since the late eighties Bruford has worked with a rotating cast of some of Britain's finest young fusion and jazz musicians who have spurred and challenged him, even as he has spurred and challenged them, producing some exciting and memorable music.

Which brings me back to the Carl Palmer Band. I have always felt there is one missing piece to Carl Palmer's long and distinguished career. In my view, in the late-seventies/early eighties period—about the time he was forming PM—he would have been far better served by recording an entire album of the quirky, edgy jazz-rock fusion style exemplified by his work with the members of Backdoor on "Bullfrog" and "The Pancha Suite"—an album that would have been something of an answer to Bruford's *Feels Good to Me* and *One of a Kind*, both of which are now acknowledged as highly personal classics of seventies jazz-rock fusion. What I would like to see the Carl Palmer Band do is deemphasize the ELP covers—though I commend them for their tasteful selection of appropriate and less obvious ELP pieces, I believe the covers have served their purpose in forging a recognizable group sound, and the trio has about passed through the phase when they can profitably remain something of a highly individual ELP cover band. Instead, I would like to see them record an album of originals that use Carl Palmer's quirky, highly individual seventies fusion style as a starting point, while also acknowledging his bandmates' obvious familiarity with eighties and nineties metal subgenres; indeed, "J.Section" from *Volume 2* gives a brief but compelling demonstration of the viability of a progressive-jazz-metal approach. Such a project might prove to be the best, and maybe last, hope that any ELP member has to create truly vital and meaningful rock music in the new millennium.

Sadly, in October of 2003, even as the trio was about to wrap up their schedule of live shows for the year (having again played a number of gigs in the U.K. and on the Continent), Shaun Baxter was involved in an auto accident that left him with a serious case of tinnitus, and was forced to retire from live performance. In November, Carl Palmer announced that the trio planned to recruit a new guitarist, and to return to live performance during the second half of 2004.

Emerson, Lake and Palmer

There is not much news to relate concerning ELP as a group since the self-implosion of December 1998. There was a persistent rumor throughout 1999 that ELP would regroup during 2000 in time to do a thirtieth anniversary tour in conjunction with Yes; nothing ever came of it. It was also rumored that BBC, as part of a series of broadcasts celebrating Aaron Copland's one hundredth birthday (also in 2000) extended ELP an opportunity to perform "Fanfare for the Common Man" live in the studio; again, nothing came of this invitation. Since mid-2000, even rumors of an ELP reformation have been few and far between. The most important post-1998 ELP development involves, sadly but predictably, the past instead of the future, specifically a series of authorized bootleg releases.

Some fans wondered about the validity of such a series of releases, pointing out—with a good deal of justification—that a disproportionate amount of ELP's authorized output already involves live recordings, all of which are of significantly higher sonic quality than standard bootleg level. While such concerns are not unjustified, the main problem with ELP's authorized live output is that certain periods of their performing history are overrepresented (above all the *Works* tour, but also the 1973-74 World Tour and the *Black Moon* period), while other periods (such as the 1972 *Trilogy* tour and the 1973 European tour, tours in which they played several works of which there were no authorized live recordings) have been completely unrepresented.

The authorized bootleg series sought to fill in the gaps, as it were. Entitled *The Original Bootleg Series from the Manticore Vaults*, the series, released by Castle Records, now numbers three volumes; the first two volumes appeared in October 2001, the third in July 2002. Volume one, which consists of seven CDs, contains music from Gaelic Park, New York City, September 1, 1971 (this is the famous gig where Emerson and Bob Moog met in person for the first time); Louisville Town Hall, Kentucky, April 21, 1972; Long Beach Arena, California, July 28, 1972; and Saratoga Performing Arts Center, Saratoga Springs, New York, August 13, 1972. These recordings are of typical bootleg quality—anybody expecting soundboard sonic quality will be quite disappointed—but are valuable for the performances of previously unavailable live material from *Trilogy* (for instance, we finally get a live "Endless Enigma"), as well as for chronicling the gradual development of "Tarkus" live. Volume two, consisting of eight CDs, contains music from London's Hammersmith Odeon, November 26, 1972 (this from a period when they were playing exceptionally well); the Henry Lewit Arena, Wichita, Kansas, March 26, 1974; Rich Stadium, Buffalo, July 26, 1974; and New Haven Civic Center, Connecticut, November 30, 1977 (this performance, of almost soundboard sonic quality, offers the most complete chronicle yet of ELP's work during the three-piece segment of the *Works* tour).

The third and most recent volume, containing five CDs, is a bit more unusual in that it features several famous (and already available) ELP shows. There's Anaheim Convention Center, California, February 10, 1974 (*Welcome Back My Friends to the Show That Never Ends*), now with the encore; Wheeling Coliseum, West Virginia, November 25, 1977, parts of which are included on King Biscuit's *Emerson, Lake and Palmer* album; Royal Albert Hall, London, October 2, 1992 (this is the performance captured on the *Live at the Royal Albert Hall* video); and Wiltern Theater, Los Angeles, March 16 (or 17) 1993, a soundboard-quality recording which many aficionados believe represents the finest account extant of ELP's live show during the 1992-93 *Black Moon* tour.

The 2004-05 period saw two new DVD releases, one of considerable importance, one of enormous importance. In late 2004, Eagle Rock Entertainment released *Emerson, Lake and Palmer: Live at Montreux 1997*, which chronicles ELP's complete performance at the Montreux Jazz Festival on July 7, 1997. I have already shared my concerns with ELP's 1997 shows: a spindly Hammond sound, generic synth patches, a set list too reliant on lightweight repertoire. All these concerns remain relevant here; however, *Live at Montreux* features a better combination of good sound quality and solid camera work than any other ELP shows currently available in visual format (London 12-9-70, Montréal 8-26-77, London 10-26-92), and that alone makes one more forgiving of some of the show's other shortcomings. During summer 2005, Sanctuary Records released the two-DVD set *Emerson, Lake and Palmer: Beyond the Beginning*. Far and away the most important segment of this DVD is the long-awaited footage of ELP's career-highlight Cal Jam set, finally made commercially available; *Beyond the Beginning* also contains a number of promo videos from the seventies, a sixty-minute documentary, previously unavailable private footage shot during 1973 of ELP rehearsing and attending a celebrity motor race, an interview with Bob Moog, and a segment on ELP's album covers. The Cal Jam performance alone makes *Beyond the Beginning* the essential ELP visual-medium document.

Other additions to ELP's recorded output since 1998 have been much more insignificant than the bootleg series or the two new DVDs. There have been an overabundance of greatest hits and best of packages, as well as an abridged version of *Then and Now* called *The Show That Never Ends*, and DVD releases of three of the ELP videos (*Live at the Royal Albert Hall, Welcome Back*, and the December 1970 Lyceum show). I might also note that *Brain Salad Surgery* was among an early batch of albums reissued in DVD audio format (using multichannel surround sound) by Warner Music/Rhino in November 2000, with "Lucky Man" included as a bonus track; longtime fans noted small but interesting differences in the mix.

The one new ELP album—or maybe I ought to say new "ELP" album—of the 1999–2004 period is *Emerson, Lake and Palmer: Re-Works*. Released in 2002 on the British Pilot label, the three-CD *Re-Works* set is the creation of British producer Mike Bennett. As its title suggests, *Re-Works* reworks characteristic passages lifted from ELP's seventies output in a techno context, specifically drum'n'bass and chill out. A lot of the most representative tracks (like "Re-Works One, Fanfare 2002 Golden Jubilation Mix," a reworking of "Fanfare for the Common Man" that won a good deal of acclaim in Britain's techno scene) involve short bits and pieces of representative ELP passages being sampled and manipulated, accompanied by swirling, liquid sound effects and a throbbing techno bass and drums background. Sometimes the given ELP sample is repeated ad infinitum until suddenly it's displaced by something totally different; at other times, one sample gradually morphs into another. My own personal favorite is "Digger's Mix," which, unlike most of the other tracks, doesn't manipulate bits and pieces of sampled material, but rather rearranges the totality of the opening section of ELP's "Fanfare" in a trance style, leisurely expanding ELP's three minutes of music into a nine-minute track.

I realize some of ELP's fans will find this music infuriatingly repetitive. I also suspect my readers recognize that I am not qualified to speak authoritatively on techno, as I lack the close familiarity with the genre to make fine distinctions as to a mix's relative aesthetic success; I am therefore unable to assay the success of this album relative to similar projects. I'll simply say I find this postmodern treatment of ELP considerably more bracing than the repetition of thirty-five-year-old set lists by aging musicians that seems to enthuse so many members of the contemporary progressive music scene. Incidentally, all three musicians gave their assent to this project; Emerson even contributed some keyboard parts, telling Bennett to use them as he wished.

After the End

We will end our saga by discussing the future of Emerson, Lake and Palmer. Let me clarify here: I am not talking about any future ELP albums that may ensue. Even if they do release another studio album—and I've already said why I don't think they will—the fact is, the vast majority, likely the entirety, of their creative work now lies behind them. I can't imagine anybody believing that the future of ELP holds six albums that will rival their output of 1970–74. Most of us would be astonished if their future held even one more album.

No, let's be honest: the future of Emerson, Lake and Palmer, for the most part, now lies in the hands of the historians and critics who will assess and evaluate the overall importance of their contribution to the rock music revolution of the late 1960s and 1970s. I have already enumerated the contributions of ELP to rock music history at a number of stages throughout this book; for the sake of clarity, let's summarize one last time. First, Keith Emerson totally revolutionized the role of keyboards in rock music, creating the role of the rock multikeyboardist, and almost single-handedly bringing the rock keyboardist to a level of parity with the guitarist. In his hands, the Hammond organ became a dynamic, expressive rock music instrument during the late sixties; his live work with the modular Moog during the early seventies, as well as his use of the instrument on the first three ELP albums, played a major role in the mainstreaming of the synthesizer, first in rock, soon in popular music more generally. He is arguably the greatest keyboard virtuoso in rock history. Among his possible rivals (Rick Wakeman and Patrick Moraz both come to mind) he is certainly the greatest composer: his mature style, which fuses elements of boogie-woogie, stride, fifties jazz, Bach, and the Bartók-Ginastera line of early-twentieth-century modernism with the rhythmic and timbral resources of rock, is distinctive and immediately recognizable. Indeed, as a composer of instrumental rock music (as opposed to a songwriter), he has few worthy rivals.

As a drummer, Carl Palmer took a style of rock drumming that was implicit in the work of the Who's Keith Moon, and began to become more explicit in the playing of the Hendrix Experience's Mitch Mitchell and King Crimson's Michael Giles, and pushed it to a new level. Like the drumming of Mitchell and Giles, Palmer's style was intricate, almost melodic, in its emphasis on the upper kit (and corresponding deemphasis of the lower part of the kit), which rhythmically doubled the melodic figurines of the lead instrument and supplied intricate fills. Like his predecessors, Palmer's style retained a link to jazz drumming that prevented the kind of stiffness and endless literal repetition of a groove that often has been the bane of rock drumming since the late seventies. What separated Palmer from predecessors like Mitchell and Giles was his staggering command of the rudiments and his close familiarity with the style of Buddy Rich, which gave him access to a seemingly endless variety of sophisticated fills and rhythmic doublings. The Lake-Palmer rhythm section completed the defining of a new approach to the rhythm section that had been begun by Noel Redding and Mitch Mitchell of the Hendrix Experience a few years earlier. In this new approach, the bass (which, in ELP, often doubled, or was doubled by, Emerson's left hand) became the real time keeper and the center of rhythmic gravity, while the drums became another melodic instrument, which rhythmically counterpointed the basic beat iterated by the bass. One can already hear this approach at work on "The Barbarian," "Knife-Edge," and the final section of "Tank" on ELP's first album.

As a vocalist, Greg Lake possessed one of the most beautiful natural voices in rock, a golden tenor that was much admired (and widely imitated) during the heyday of ELP. Lake was also a fine songwriter with a gift for writing simple but memorable tunes in a quiet, slightly melancholy folk-rock style. Nonetheless, it is their suitelike epics—above all "Tarkus" and "Karn Evil 9," but also some of their "shorter" epics and classical arrangements—that ELP principally will be remembered for. The scope of these pieces is not unrivalled—certainly the most representative works of Yes, Genesis, King Crimson, Jethro Tull, and Pink Floyd are comparable. However, the effortless virtuosity with which ELP rendered their epics, as well as the characteristic alternation between an almost inhuman, machinelike aggression (the instrumental sections of "Tarkus," "Toccata"), a hymnlike, religious solemnity ("The Only Way"/"Infinite Space," "The Endless Enigma," "Jerusalem"), and an optimistic, heroic striving ("Karn Evil 9, 3rd Impression"), are hallmarks of ELP.

Again, while the appropriation of elements of European classical music into rock was widespread during the late sixties and early seventies, no other rock band handled classical techniques and motifs with as much confidence and aplomb as ELP. Certainly no rock composer was more successful at blending classical structures with rock conventions at a deep (as opposed to surface) structural level than Keith Emerson— here his use of two opposing key centers to generate a sense of structural tension and drama in several major ELP works is particularly noteworthy—which is also why all ELP's best classical arrangements work as *rock* music. Emerson was probably the most important figure in making the vocabulary and structural approaches of classical music available to rock music at large. Having said this, it's important to also point up Emerson's command of both traditional and modern jazz styles, which enabled him to bring a sense of swing to ELP's music at appropriate moments—think of such disparate pieces as "Take a Pebble" and "Karn Evil 9, 1st Impression."

ELP created one of the great concept albums of the rock era in *Brain Salad Surgery*. Two of ELP's albums, *Brain Salad Surgery* and *Tarkus*, are notable not just for their music, but also for their cover art, and for the way that music, visual art, and words cohere into a kind of Wagnerian *Gesamtkunstwerk* that penetratingly comments on issues of technology, totalitarianism, and alienation endemic to the late twentieth century. They created one of the most accomplished debut albums in rock history with their eponymous release of 1970, and one of the great live albums of the first half of the seventies in *Pictures at an Exhibition*, notable both for its sonic clarity (remarkable at the time) and its staggeringly tight ensemble interplay. ELP also played a major role in redefining the nature of rock as a live music in the 1973-74 period. While one might decry the effects of their conception of live rock as a kind of space-age vaudeville where the music was tied to spectacular special effects—there's no doubt their conception tended to reduce opportunities for symbiotic performer-audience interaction by reducing the audience to mute spectators—there's no denying the influence of ELP's spectacular stage show of 1973-74 on rock during the remainder of the seventies—and beyond.

So will ELP be elected to the Rock and Roll Hall of Fame anytime soon? Don't hold your breath. As I pointed out earlier in this book, progressive rock at large—and ELP in particular—face an uphill struggle in gaining critical approbation (or even acknowledgement) from the contemporary rock music critical establishment. The blues orthodoxy (to borrow Bill Martin's apt term one final time) of Lester Bangs, Dave

Marsh, Robert Christgau, and a few other prominent American rock critics of the early seventies—with its dogma that the only popular music that possesses any genuine cultural vitality is music that demonstrates direct lineal descent from the blues—was a minority view until the 1973-74 period, at which point it conquered not only the major American rock journals (*Rolling Stone, Creem*) but the major British ones (*Melody Maker, NME*) as well. That a sudden shift in rock critical ideology took place during the 1973-74 period is not arguable: one need only read the reviews of ELP's first four albums from these journals (a number of which are quoted in this book) and then compare them with the reviews of ELP's albums that ran in these journals after 1973 (a number of which are also excerpted in this book) to see the fundamental shift in rock's critical ideology during this period. As I said in this book's introduction, why and how this shift took place during the 1973-74 period goes beyond the scope of this book to fully answer: I am hoping another writer will choose to write a book about it—or maybe I will someday.

What is inarguable is that between circa 1975 and 1980 blues orthodoxy became the institutionally accepted line of rock criticism—(the "institution" here being the major rock journals, which have exerted a profound influence over the thinking of record company executives, radio programmers, and eventually academic popular music historians)—and that since 1980 or so blues orthodoxy has exerted a hegemonic dominance over rock criticism and rock historiography. Today's younger rock critics are largely unaware that many rock critics circa 1968–72 hailed the progressive rock style when it first appeared: they have been taught via blues orthodoxy that intelligent rock critics have always scorned progressive rock, which, as I've demonstrated, is not true. They are also unfamiliar with an earlier rock critical ideology, which I here have called utopian synthesism, which actually viewed progressive rock not only as part of the mainstream of seventies rock (something the blues orthodoxists have vehemently opposed, arguing that prog was a bizarre evolutionary dead end), but possibly even the pinnacle towards which all earlier rock styles had been developing.

I believe that blues orthodoxy will eventually lose its hegemonic hold over rock historiography and the rock critical establishment. When it does, I hope that this book will have played a role in dislodging blues orthodoxy from the place of primacy it has occupied for thirty years. The end of the blues orthodoxists' monopoly over rock criticism and rock historiography will open the way for alternate interpretations of rock's history in which it will be possible to view progressive rock as occupying an important role in the mainstream of rock's development during the seventies. It will also allow for alternate interpretations of what made rock meaningful and gave it validity during its golden age, beyond some supposed spiritual connection with the blues, to which rock critics of the

Bangs-Marsh persuasion assigned an almost supernatural—one is tempted to say superstitious—virtue, largely as the result of a rather dubious primitivism that I analyzed earlier in this book. Then, and only then, will progressive rock in general, and the music of ELP in particular, receive a fair hearing, and be given the impartial assessment that it deserves.

The music of ELP faces an additional burden in getting a fair hearing, beyond the onus already faced by progressive rock at large. This burden involves the fact that due to the attempted scope, ambition, and transcendental virtuosity that marked the ELP project during its heyday, there's a certain strand of vulgarity that marks the band's most characteristic music—it's somewhat deemphasized in their most successful epics ("Tarkus," "Karn Evil 9"), to be sure, but it's never entirely absent. In a sense, I see ELP occupying a role in rock music analogous to that occupied by the music of Franz Liszt in nineteenth-century classical music, or the Stan Kenton Big Band during the golden age of jazz. Liszt, Kenton, and ELP were all concerned with writing epic, monumental pieces of music with intimations of the transcendental and sublime, both in terms of the virtuosity demanded and the "outside" musical vocabulary employed. At their best, all succeeded brilliantly—Liszt's Piano Sonata in B minor, the Kenton Band's *City of Glass*, ELP's "Karn Evil 9"—and the element of vulgarity, while never completely absent, is well in the background. At other times, at their less inspired moments, all three could write and perform music in which the element of vulgarity was uncomfortably foregrounded.[7]

I'm no aesthetician, but I suspect that anytime an artist takes a style that's already inclined towards the epic and monumental (be it seventeenth-century baroque, nineteenth-century Romanticism, bop-influenced big-band jazz, or progressive rock) and pushes the style in question towards its most ambitious reaches, a certain strain of vulgarity is unavoidable. Acceptance of late-sixteenth-century mannerism was a long time coming: it didn't come until the twentieth century, in fact. Full acceptance of the music of Franz Liszt had to wait until the 1960s and 1970s, when commentators were finally able to accept its inherent vulgarities as integral, even necessary (in light of the affect that Liszt wished to convey), and could therefore acknowledge the full scope of Liszt's originality and expressive achievement. Jazz critics are still not certain how to rank Kenton's achievement—his originality is obvious, the success of some of his most adventurous work (*City of Glass*) too clear to ignore, but the unselfconscious bombast of much of his most characteristic work still makes most jazz critics too uncomfortable to grant him full critical appro

---

[7] I should clarify here that I'm talking specifically about ELP's music. The element of vulgarity was *always* foregrounded in ELP's stage shows.

bation. Much of ELP's work, even much of their best work, is characterized by a certain bombast that does not sit well in the modern critical
environment, precisely because it is so unselfconscious, and lacks the whiff
of irony and self-parody that would make it more palatable to the postmodern critical taste. (Of course, postmodern critical taste has no patience
with any striving toward the transcendental or sublime—which are seen as
chimeras—hence the tags of "pretentiousness" and "pomposity" that are
regularly applied to progressive rock or any other style that actually seeks
to convey Meaning and Message.) This assessment raises issues that go
well beyond the confines of ELP's music, but I hope some scholar somewhere, well grounded in aesthetics, will carry this discussion further as
regards ELP's music.

There are two other matters that have prevented ELP's legacy from
being fully appreciated within today's progressive music community. First,
progressive music commentators have tended to undervalue the work of
trios in favor of five- or six-member bands since at least the early nineties,
when, at the dawn of the nineties prog rock "renaissance," quasi-symphonic fullness of texture and highly varied instrumentation came to be
viewed as essential aspects of the progressive rock style.[8] A second line of
thinking prevalent within the progressive music community that has
worked against a full appreciation of ELP's achievement is that the band
resorted to classical arrangements so often because they were low on creative inspiration. I understand this line of thinking springs directly from
progressive music's emphasis on originality as a key to progress. I would
merely point out that ELP's best arrangements do in fact manifest a high
level of originality.

Here it's worth pointing out that in the overall trajectory of Western
musical history, it's only since the early nineteenth century (since
Beethoven, specifically), that originality came to be gauged more or less
exclusively on the basis of the creation of completely original themes, new
and unusual chords and rhythmic figures, and unique structures. Earlier
eras saw originality less as the production of completely new material than
as the display of imagination in the treatment of previously existing music.
Throughout the sixteenth century, for example, most major composers
composed so-called parody Masses, that is, polyphonic vocal settings of

---

[8] I would direct interested parties to the "Gnosis" web site, where a large slate of reviewers
give rankings of zero to fifteen stars to literally thousands of progressive music albums
(http://www.gnosis2000.net), the average ranking of each album then being tabulated into
an overall ranking. I first noticed the prejudice against trios when I consulted the rankings
of the three albums by my own trio, Hermetic Science; I soon found that the best albums
of other major progressive rock keyboard and guitar trios (ELP, Rush, and Refugee spring
immediately to mind) had also been ranked lower than albums of roughly similar quality
released by bands with four, five, or six members (Yes, Gabriel-era Genesis, Gentle Giant).

the Mass Ordinary whose musical themes were mostly, or completely, drawn from previously composed Masses. The aesthetic success of these works was not judged on the creation of original melodic themes, or of startling new sonorities and rhythms, but rather on how successfully the material of the model was reworked and transformed into an essentially new composition, often by alternately referring to the model and filling intervening sections with new and original music. This is precisely the conception upon which ELP's best arrangements ("Pictures at an Exhibition," "Toccata," "Hoedown") are based.

The Endless Enigma Revisited

Finally, before ELP can receive their full due, the "endless enigma" for which this book has been titled must be fully addressed. As I said earlier in this book, no rock band has ever been so big for so long, crashed so suddenly, and disappeared with such finality from the landscape of mass popular culture, despite several attempts to reenter it. How could a band that was so successful, both artistically and commercially from 1970 to 1977—an enormous span of time by today's standards—self-destruct so spectacularly in such a relatively short period (between early 1977 and early 1979), then fail, with such numbing regularity, in attempt after attempt to put all the pieces back together? I believe I successfully solved this enigma in discussing the aftermath of *Love Beach*: let me summarize here. First and foremost was the loss of the interpersonal chemistry that guided ELP through their six great albums of 1970–74: it would seem that after the nontouring years of 1975-76 Emerson and Lake never really worked in tandem again in the sense of pursuing an artistic vision that they were both totally committed to. Second, I believe there is something to be said for my argument that Emerson's stylistic shift during the mid-seventies, as he fell more under the sway of Aaron Copland's smooth, graceful, but sometimes glib style and became less influenced by the muscular style of the Bartók-Ginastera line of musical modernism, was not necessarily in the best interest of his future rock music output: after the midseventies, only sporadically did Emerson's music evince the same winning confluence of urgency, drive, swing, and sophistication.

While it is possible the deterioration of the band's interpersonal chemistry or the shift in Emerson's compositional style during the mid 1970s were unavoidable, ELP made three enormous blunders between 1977 and 1979 that were completely unnecessary. The solo/band format of *Works I* was a catastrophic mistake, bringing the band short-term gain (by allowing them to peddle solo projects that many fans otherwise wouldn't have bought) at the price of permanently damaging their reputation. The orchestral tour was another huge blunder, squandering millions in revenue that was lost forever to ELP, further saddling them with the "dinosaur" image (somewhat deservedly, this time), and pleasing relatively few fans in the process. Finally, the band made a major error in allowing themselves to dissolve out of existence with scarcely a trace during 1979. Once they decided to call it quits, they should have undertaken a well-executed, highly publicized farewell tour in 1979, which would have allowed them to exit the seventies with their iconic, larger-than-life status more or less fully intact, and would have made later reformation attempts less of an uphill struggle.

Why didn't the various reformation attempts of the eighties and nineties ever fully succeed? First and foremost, such attempts are fraught with risk—if a band is getting back together simply to rekindle old memories, to provide their fans or themselves with a warm blanket of nostalgia, or to replenish bank accounts, then they are not going to produce any music—or even play a show—that's very compelling. The only way such a reformation will work is if the members come back together with an attitude of urgency; the band must believe they have something genuinely new to say, yet what they're saying must somehow be clearly connected with what they've said in the past. This is a tall order, more difficult than it sounds, and not many of the great bands of the seventies pulled it off with complete success during the eighties and nineties. (For instance, Yes pulled it off just once, with their *90125* album of 1983.)

Probably the best postseventies effort to come out of the ELP camp was the *Emerson, Lake and Powell* album of 1986: in some respects it struck a genuinely contemporary note, while in other ways it appeared to be a logical continuation of direction from their better music of the late seventies, and at its best it did convey a sense of urgency. It came off as a real collaboration between Emerson and Lake—ironically, *Emerson, Lake and Powell* sounds more like a group effort than any ELP album of the 1977–79 period. As we saw, incompetent management may have played at least some role in short-circuiting this first—and most promising—comeback attempt. But there is a pervasive problem with the *Emerson, Lake and Powell* album: there is too much obvious filler material occupying the second half of the album. This prefigured the main problem of the Victory Records–era releases, which saw the band intentionally simplifying their music and curbing their natural tendency towards the epic and monumental in a vain attempt to get radio airplay and get that one last hit single. The line of thinking prevailing among the band during the 1991–94 period appeared to be that a big hit single would propel them back to the top of the charts, and give them the clout to record the ambitious concept album they really wanted to write. Unfortunately, there was no big hit single, their radio-friendly approach of the *Black Moon/In the Hot Seat* era was not rewarded with substantial radio airplay, and they were left with two albums that had some fine moments, but in no way compared with their output of 1970–74.

By the time they were ready to buckle down and write that final epic concept album, all the old problems between Emerson and Lake—especially involving production, but also stylistic direction—had fully resurfaced, and the moment was lost forever. We'll never know if this album would have measured up to classic ELP; if Emerson had continued to develop the approach that characterized his *Iron Man* music (quasi-symphonic electronic music that sometimes was clearly "rock," and other times leaned more towards classical or ambient music), and if he had managed to secure full-fledged collaboration from Lake and Palmer, it might have been a very compelling effort indeed. But even if there's no more new music, and the Show That Never Ends is closed forever, we have the six great albums of 1970–74, and that music will live on as some of the most ambitious, exciting, imaginative, accomplished, and adventurous music of rock's golden age.

Appendix A:
A Critical Discography

The following constitutes a critical discography that is broken into three sections. The first section addresses the pre-ELP work of Emerson, Lake, and Palmer; the second, the recordings of ELP; the third, their solo albums, movie soundtracks, and recordings with other bands from 1980 on. Rankings range from zero to five stars, with half-star increments. Some ELP fans may feel I have ranked these albums somewhat harshly, to which I would respond: I am ranking ELP's work, as well as the solo albums of Emerson, Lake and Palmer and their work with other musicians, in the context of the very finest rock music of the late 1960s and 1970s; a five-star album therefore implies a classic of its time and genre. (Singles and EPs are not rated.)

All ELP studio albums and live albums (both those released during the lifetime of the band and posthumous live releases) are included. I have been more selective with "Best of"-type packages, of which there has been an unhealthy proliferation in recent years. Note that compositional credits are given on studio album tracks, but not for the tracks of the live albums, unless the tracks in question have not appeared on a previously released studio album. For Emerson's, Lake's, and Palmer's pre- and post-ELP bands (The Nice, King Crimson, Asia, and so forth) I've been even more selective about "best of" packages and live albums released long after the time of recording.

I make no effort to try to track either all mediums a given album was released in or all rereleases within a given medium. Through the late 1980s I chronicle the first LP issue of a given album, from 1990 on the first CD issue.

Emerson, Lake and Powell and 3 releases appear in the appropriate chronological locations among the ELP releases.

Singles by the Nice, ELP, and Asia are not represented here unless they are not currently available on an album.

Keith Emerson Pre-ELP Releases

WITH GARY FARR AND THE T-BONES

If I Had a Ticket (7" single)
CBS 202394 (U.K., summer 1966)
Recorded April 26, 1966, Marquee Studios, London, U.K.
Gary Farr, vocals; David Langston, guitar; Keith Emerson, organ; Lee Jackson, bass; Alan Turner, drums. With Kenneth Washington, guest lead vocalist, and Chris Barber, trombone
[No rating—B-side featured another group]

WITH THE VIPS

Stagger Lee/Rosemarie/Late Night Blues (7" EP)
Fontana 460 219 ME (France, March 1967)
Recorded early 1967, Marquee Studios, London, U.K. (?)
Mike Harrison, vocals and harmonica; Luther Grosvenor, guitars; Keith Emerson, organ; Greg Ridley, bass; Mike Kellie, drums
[No rating]
Although one is thankful for the inclusion of one previously unreleased T-Bones track on Emerson's 2005 *Hammer It Out* anthology, one wishes the anthology had put greater emphasis on Emerson's work with the T-Bones and the VIPs. This would have been especially valuable for attempting to chart Emerson's development as a rock organist, as his mature style is already well on its way to emerging by the advent of the Nice.

WITH THE NICE

The Thoughts of Emerlist Davjack
Immediate IMSP 016 (U.K., March 1968)
Immediate 52004 (U.S., 1968)
Recorded Autumn 1967, Olympic and Pye Studios, London, U.K.
Keith Emerson, piano, organ, harpsichord, occasional backing vocals; Lee Jackson, bass and lead vocals; David O'List, guitar and backing vocals; Brian Davison, drums and percussion

1. Flower King of Flies (Emerson-O'List-Jackson-Davison)
2. The Thoughts of Emerlist Davjack (O'List-Emerson)
   [released as U.K. single October 1967 with B-side "Azrial, The Angel of Death"]
3. Bonnie K (Emerson-O'List-Jackson-Davison)
4. Rondo (Emerson-O'List-Jackson-Davison)
   [arrangement of Dave Brubeck's "Blue Rondo á la Turk"]
5. War and Peace (Emerson-O'List-Jackson-Davison)
   [based on "Silver Meter," which was recorded, but never released, by the T-Bones]
6. Tantalizing Maggie (Emerson-O'List-Jackson-Davison)
7. Dawn (Emerson-O'List-Jackson-Davison)
   [Keith Emerson, lead whisper]
8. The Cry of Eugene (Jackson-O'List-Emerson)

★★★★1/2

Not only is this a seminal release in the progressive rock lineage, it is also one of the greatest psychedelic rock albums. The sound, which is raw, muddy, and exceedingly powerful, gives at least some sense of the experience the Nice's live shows conveyed at this time. Although David O'List was not a great guitarist, his presence brought a focus and discipline to Emerson's playing that one at times wishes for in his later work in trio settings; while Emerson's musical personality is already amply in evidence, it's impressive how well his parts serve the songs. (It can also be argued this is the last album Emerson played on for many years where his parts are consistently made to fit the songs, rather than the songs being chosen or developed to complement and highlight his extraordinary abilities.) Highlights include the ominous, dramatically building "Dawn," to which Emerson's "lead whisper" lends a suitably tense ambience; the melodic "Cry of Eugene," nicely colored by O'List's floating fuzzed guitar obbligato, whose linear, contrapuntal instrumental sections prefigure progressive rock; the bluesy psychedelia of "Tanatalizing Maggie"; and the powerhouse "Rondo," featuring an epic solo by Emerson that forever expanded the possibilities of the Hammond, and which is still extremely impressive for its gradual build-up, via slowly increasing rhythmic motion, textural activity, registral expansion, and timbral distortion, to an enormous, thrilling climax.

Ars Longa Vita Brevis
Immediate IMSP 020 (U.K., November 1968)
Immediate Z12 52020 (U.S., 1968)
Recorded Autumn 1968, Wessex Studios, London, U.K. ("America" recorded April 1968)
Keith Emerson, organ and piano; Lee Jackson, bass and vocals; Brian Davison, drums and percussion

1. America (Bernstein/Sondheim)/2nd Amendment (Davison-Jackson)
   [with David O'List, guitar; released as U.K. single with B-side "Diamond Hard Blue Apples of the Moon," June 1968; included on U.S., but not U.K., release of *Ars Longa Vita Brevis*]
2. Daddy Where Did I Come From (Emerson-Jackson)
3. Little Arabella (Emerson-Jackson)
4. Happy Freuds (Emerson-Jackson)
5. Intermezzo from Karelia Suite (Sibelius)/Don Edito el Gruva (Emerson-Jackson-Davison)
"Ars Long Vita Brevis" suite
6. Prelude (Emerson)
7. 1st movement-Awakening (Davison)
8. 2nd movement-Realization (Jackson-O'List-Emerson)
   [Malcolm Langstaff, guitar]
9. 3rd movement-Acceptance "Brandenburger" (Jackson-Emerson-Davison)
   [arrangement of J.S. Bach's Brandenburg Concerto no. 3, 1st movement]
10. 4th movement-Denial (Jackson-Emerson-Davison)
11. Coda-Extension to the Big Note (Emerson)

$\star\star^1/_2$

David O'List's departure from the band in October 1968 created a void that was not fully filled by the time this album was completed; in fact, much of this music had already been partially recorded as a quartet, and needed to be reworked for a keyboards trio before it was released. Beyond the fact that the band was obviously not yet comfortable with the trio format, there's also a certain lack of focus in sylistic direction. The first three tracks continue the first album's song-oriented approach; although they're quirky and charming, they lack the power and drive of the debut album's best songs. The Intermezzo of Jan Sibelius's *Karelia Suite* opens a new avenue that was to become of great importance to Emerson—the arrangement of orchestral works for rock trio—although this arrangement lacks the punch that characterized much of his later work in this genre. The entire second side of the LP format is occupied by a lengthy suite, "Ars Longa Vita Brevis," where the trio is joined in occasional passages by a sessions orchestra. The main problem here is that the suite is constructed by cobbling together shorter fragments that the band had been playing separately—some of which are quite strong in isolation—and unsuccessfully trying to make the fragments cohere into a meaningful whole. Perhaps the best thing that can be said about the album is that it opens up several new directions—orchestral rock, multimovement compositions, rocked-up arrangements of the classics—that proved to be of huge importance to Emerson's future output.

Nice [U.K.]
Everything as Nice as Mother Makes It [U.S.]
Immediate IMSP 026 (U.K., August 1969)
Immediate IMOCS 102 (U.S., November 1969)
Tracks 1–4 recorded early to mid-1969, Trident Studios, London; tracks 5 and 6 recorded live at the Fillmore East, New York, New York, April 9 and 10, 1969

#3 U.K.

1. Azrael Revisited (Emerson-Jackson)
2. Hang on to a Dream (Hardin)
3. Diary of an Empty Day (Emerson-Jackson)
   [Based on the fifth movement of Victor Lalo's *Symphonie espagnole*]
4. For Example (Emerson-Jackson)
   [Alan Skidmore, Joe Harriott, Chris Pyne, Kenny Wheeler, horns, first horn passage; Joe Newman, Pepper Adams, John Surman, horns, second horn passage]
5. Rondo '69 (Emerson-Jackson-Davison)
   [Arrangement of Dave Brubeck's "Blue Rondo á la Turk"]
6. She Belongs to Me (Dylan)

★★★¹/₂

The Nice's grueling touring schedule left little time for composing new material, and *Nice* is an example of a problem that to some extent dogged the band throughout their existence as a trio—an overreliance on cover songs and classical arrangements at the expense of original compositions. *Nice* also marks the beginning of an approach that characterized the rest of the band's authorized releases, whereby live and studio tracks are mixed—an approach that contributes to a certain loss of creative focus. Nonetheless, the band's third album shows them having taken significant steps toward reinventing themselves as a bona fide power trio, and O'List's absence is felt far less here than on *Ars Long Vita Brevis*. Highlights include "Azrael Revisited," a Nice classic, which somehow welds Rachmaninov, music hall, and faux doo-wop harmonies into a coherent whole through the agency of a driving 5/4 piano riff; the melancholy "Hang on to a Dream," whose folk-jazz arrangement prefigures ELP's "Take a Pebble"; and above all the epic arrangement of Bob Dylan's "She Belongs to Me," a *tour de force* of spontaneous composition by Emerson, Jackson and Davison that represents the band's finest recorded live performance. *Nice* is the jazziest of the band's albums, although the album's most jazz-oriented track, "For Example," is probably the weakest, with Jackson frequently being forced to sing out of his range.

Five Bridges

Charisma CAS 1014 (U.K., June 1970)
Mercury SR 61295 (U.S., 1970)
Recorded live at Fairfield Hall, Croydon, U.K., October 17, 1969 (tracks 1–7); recorded live at Fillmore East, New York, New York, April 9 and 10, 1969 (track 8); recorded at Trident Studios, London, U.K., Summer 1969 (track 9)
#2 U.K.

The Five Bridges Suite (Music Emerson, Words Jackson)
1. Fantasia. 1st Bridge
2. 2nd Bridge
3. Chorale. 3rd Bridge
4. High Level Fugue. 4th Bridge
5. Finale. 5th Bridge
   [Sinfonia of London, Joseph Eger, conductor; Jazz Ensemble (5th Bridge only) includes Alan Skidmore, Kenny Wheeler, John Warren, Pete King, Joe Harriott, and Chris Pyne]
6. Intermezzo from *Karelia Suite* (Sibelius)
   [Sinfonia of London, Joseph Eger, conductor]
7. *Pathètique* Symphony, no. 6, 3rd movement (Tchaikovsky)
   [Sinfonia of London, Joseph Eger, conductor]
8. Country Pie/Brandenberg Concerto no. 6 (Dylan-Bach, arr. Emerson)
9. One of Those People (Emerson-Jackson)

★★★★

For the first time since their debut album, the Nice deliver a focused, sustained exploration of a specific stylistic direction—in this case, the possibilities of symphonic rock. Although Emerson's "Five Bridges Suite" does not transcend the sixties tendency to simply alternate passages for orchestra and rock band, rather than subtly fuse them, it remains the most accomplished essay in sixties symphonic rock, and represents a huge advance over "Ars Long Vita Brevis"; each movement is interesting and substantive on its own terms, the alternation and pacing of different moods, tempos and tone colors from movement to movement is well-conceived, and the recap of the 2nd Bridges' thematic material in the Finale with different orchestration is effective. Emerson's Hammond work throughout the suite is astounding, and demonstrates an extremely subtle use of draw-bar coloring—more subtle, in fact, than he was ever to display with ELP, where he increasingly focused on achieving tone-color shading with the Moog instead. One does wish he had used the Jazz Ensemble (featured during the 5th Bridge) elsewhere during the Suite. The version of Sibelius's Intermezzo presented here actually rocks harder than the trio's version on *Ars Long Vita Brevis*, as Joseph Eger coaxes an energetic performance out of his orchestra, and the arrangement of the 3rd movement of Tchaikovsky's Symphony no. 6 makes surprisingly effective use of tone-color contrasts between orchestral and rock band episodes. The album's final track, "One of Those People," represents the perfection of the quirky strain of songwriting initiated on *Ars Long Vita Brevis*.

Elegy
Charisma CAS 1030 (U.K., April 1971)
Mercury SR 61324 (U.S., 1971)
Recorded live at the Fillmore East, New York, New York, April 9-10, 1969 (tracks 1, 4); at
    Trident Studios, London, U.K., Summer 1969 (tracks 2, 3)
#5 U.K.

1. Hang on to a Dream (Hardin)
2. My Back Pages (Dylan)
3. Pathètique (Tchaikovsky)
4. America (Bernstein-Sondheim)

★★★

Released posthumously (ELP were putting finishing touches on *Tarkus* at the time), *Elegy* makes available the Nice's final two previously unreleased studio tracks from the summer 1969 Trident sessions, as well as Fillmore East performances of two Nice favorites previously unrepresented by live recordings, "Hang on to a Dream" and "America." *Elegy* thus marks the third consecutive Nice album making use of both Fillmore East live material from April 1969 and Trident Studios recordings from the summer of 1969; one wonders if the group's discography wouldn't have conveyed a more coherent sense of their development if one album had been exclusively occupied by the Fillmore East performances, another by the Trident Studios material. At any rate, *Elegy* ends up being rather similar to *Nice* in its format, and, if not quite as strong, it still has its moments. While one misses the sense of coloristic variety the orchestra brought to the *Five Bridges* recording of Tchaikovsky's Pathètique, the trio version presented here is notable for the tight interaction between Emerson and his rhythm section, who turn in a superb performance. The cover of "My Back Pages" sounds a bit underdeveloped, but is notable for its driving instrumental middle section, the main theme of which ELP reused in the "Blues Variation" of *Pictures*. "Hang on to a Dream" and "America" may both be a bit overextended, although the former's interpolation of Gershwin's "Summertime" is a nice touch. *Elegy* forcefully illustrates a central facet of the Nice throughout much of their existence: a shortage of original material forced the band into an overreliance on cover songs and classical arrangements.

Keith Emerson With The Nice
Mercury 830457 (U.K., 1971)
Mercury SRM 2 6500 (U.S., 1971)
[No rating—reissue of *Five Bridges* and *Elegy*]
Repackaging *Five Bridges* and *Elegy* as a two-LP set, *Keith Emerson With The Nice* was an attempt to capitalize on Emerson's growing popularity during the early days of ELP, by making his late period work with the Nice available in a single LP package to an American audience that was largely ignorant of the band's existence during its lifetime. Has been rereleased on CD without three of the LP tracks.

Autumn to Spring
Charisma CS 1 (U.K., 1972)
Charisma CAS 1 0598 (U.S., 1973)
Collects tracks recorded between October 1967 and April 1968

1. The Thoughts of Emerlist Davjack
2. Flower King of Flies
3. Bonnie K
4. America/2nd Amendment
   [June 1968 single]
5. Diamond Hard Blue Apples of the Moon (Emerson-Jackson)
   [B-side of "America"]
6. Dawn
7. Tantalizing Maggie
8. The Cry of Eugene
9. Daddy Where Did I Come From
   [previously unreleased version with David O'List]

★★★½

Offers a smorgasbord of early Nice material. Important at the time of its release for making available "America" and its B-side "Diamond Hard Blue Apples of the Moon," neither of which appeared on any of the Nice's studio albums released in the U.K., as well as a previously unreleased studio version of "Daddy Where Did I Come From," recorded as a four-piece with David O'List.

The Swedish Radio Sessions
Sanctuary CMRCD 349 (U.K., 2001)
Recorded live for Swedish radio, December 1967 [exact date unconfirmable]

1. She Belongs to Me
2. Flower King of Flies
3. Sombrero Sam
4. You Keep Me Hanging On
5. The Thoughts of Emerlist Davjack
6. Rondo

★★★

This may possibly be the sharpest-sounding live release of the Nice to date—it is certainly better sounding than most of the BBC material. The playing is quite good, too, showing a band that has already become a tight performing unit. Unlike the 2002 BBC sessions release, though, which gives a broad overview of the Nice's overall career, this album's focus is much narrower—their early set list—and even then a lot of their most characteristic early material is missing. Highlights include "Sombrero Sam," which features some scorching organ work by Emerson, and "Rondo," which, although lacking the drama and inevitable build-up of the studio version, features interesting improvisations by both O'List and Emerson that are totally different than what's on the debut album. (Here one notes that with the Nice, "Rondo" was always a forum for improvisatory exploration—unlike ELP, on the other hand, where it became a vehicle for seemingly endless episodes of feedback and organ-wrestling.) [Two notes: Contrary to the liner notes, this session appears to have taken place in December 1967, not October. Also, Brian Davison was definitely the drummer, having replaced Ian Hague in late August.]

Here Come the Nice: The Immediate Anthology
Sanctuary CMETD 055 (U.K., 2001)

CD 1:
1. The Thoughts of Emerlist Davjack
2. Azrial (Angel of Death)
3. Sampler for *The Thoughts of Emerlist Davjack* LP
4. Flower King of Flies
5. Bonnie K
6. Rondo
7. War and Peace
8. Tantalizing Maggie
9. Dawn
10. The Cry of Eugene

11. America/2nd Amendment
12. Diamond Hard Blue Apples of the Moon
13. Daddy Where Did I Come From
14. Little Arabella
15. Happy Freuds
16. Intermezzo from Karella Suite/Don Edito el Gruva

CD 2:
1. Ars Longa Vita Brevis
2. Brandenburger
3. Azrael Revisited
4. Hang on to a Dream (long version)
5. Diary of an Empty Day
6. For Example
7. Rondo 69
8. She Belongs to Me

CD 3:
1. America (live)
2. Rondo (live)
3. The Thoughts of Emerlist Davjack (long version)
4. Flower King of Flies (alternative version)
5. Bonnie K (alternative version)
6. America (alternative version)
7. Dawn (alternative version)
8. Tantalizing Maggie (alternative version)
9. The Cry of Eugene (alternative version)
10. Daddy Where Did I Come From (alternative version)
11. Brandenburger (demo version)
12. Pathètique Symphony, 3rd movement (live)
13. Lt. Kije Suite, "Troika" (live)

[No rating]
For the aficionado of the Nice's Immediate-era output (that is to say, early and midpe-riod Nice), *Here Come the Nice* delivers everything one could want, including all tracks from their first three albums, *The Thoughts of Emerlist Davjack*, *Ars Longa Vita Brevis*, and *Nice*; all singles and B-sides; a number of outtakes, mostly alternative versions of material from the debut album; and a number of previously unreleased live tracks of Immediate-era material. It would be nice (sorry) if a similar set could be put together for the Charisma/Mercury material, or better yet, if a retrospective set of the Nice's entire career (both Immediate and Charisma) could be compiled.

The Nice: BBC Sessions
Sanctuary Records CMFCD 457 (U.K., 2002)
Contains recordings of six different BBC sessions, dating from October 22, 1967, to April 20, 1969. Tracks 1–11 are with David O'List; tracks 12–19, without.

10-22-67 TOP GEAR
1. Flower King of Flies
2. Sombrero Sam (Charles Lloyd)
3. Rondo (excerpt)

6-16-68 TOP GEAR
4. Get to You (Hillman/McGuinn)
5. Diamond Hard Blue Apples of the Moon
6. Brandenburger
7. Little Arabella (and Sorcery)

8-25-68 TOP GEAR
8. America/2nd Amendment
9. Lumpy Gravy (Frank Zappa)
10. Aries the Firefighter
11. Ars Longa Vita Brevis

8-29-68 POP NORTH
  12. Little Arabella
       [this is the studio version from *Ars Longa Vita Brevis*]

12-1-68 TOP GEAR
  13. Happy Freuds
       [this is the studio version from *Ars Longa Vita Brevis*]
  14. Brandenburger
       [this isn't "Brandenburger," rather, an odd, *musique concrète*-like free jam]
  15. Intermezzo from Karelia Suite

4-20-69 TOP GEAR
  16. I'm One of Those People
  17. Azrael Revisited
  18. Blues for the Prairies (Oscar Peterson)
  19. Diary of an Empty Day/Top Gear Signature

★★★★

It must be admitted that on a lot of this material—especially the material recorded during the David O'List days—the sonic values are somewhat wanting. That being said, none of the Nice's five authorized albums are exactly an audiophile's delight; even more than ELP, whose sound required a certain amount of polish and finesse to make its full impact, the Nice were at their best in a live setting, where their energy came through raw and undiluted. All this is to say that this may be the best introduction to the Nice for the uninitiated, even if there's no "Five Bridges" and only a snippet of "Rondo"; it features them in a live setting, it's streamlined (just one CD), and it gives an effective cross section of both the earlier Immediate and later Charisma/Mercury material, which other collections don't. At the same time, this isn't simply material the average fan is familiar with; there are performances of Frank Zappa's "Lumpy Gravy," Charles Lloyd's "Sombrero Sam," and the anonymously composed "Aries the Firefighter," all staples of the band's early live shows that went unrepresented on their five authorized albums of 1968–71. There are also performances by the four-piece lineup of material that was released by the trio: "Brandenburger," "Little Arabella," "Ars Longa Vita Brevis" (this being shorter, more focused, and much more effective than the later, overextended studio recording). Finally, there are some rarely performed numbers ("Diamond Hard Blue Apples of the Moon," which, along with "Flower King of Flies," features surprisingly effective vocal harmonies) and some scorching performances of their midperiod songs (I actually prefer the live performances of "Azrael Revisited" and "Diary of an Empty Day" to the studio versions on *Nice*). Keith Emerson apparently had some input in the track selection of this album, unlike the earlier BBC release for the Nice (1996), which should be avoided due to very poor sonic quality. [Note: contrary to the liner notes, Brian Davison drummed on all of this material, having replaced Ian Hague in late summer 1967.]

Vivicitas: Live at Glasgow 2002
Sanctuary Records SAN TD208 (U.K., 2003)
Recorded live at Glasgow, U.K., October 4, 2002
Keith Emerson, keyboards; Lee Jackson, vocals and bass (CD 1, tracks 5-6 of CD 2); Brian Davison, drums (CD 1, tracks 5-6 of CD 2); Dave Kilminster, guitar; Phil Williams, bass (CD 2); Pete Riley, drums (CD 2)

CD 1:
  1. America/Rondo
  2. Little Arabella
  3. She Belongs to Me
  4. The Cry of Eugene
  5. Hang on to a Dream
  6. Country Pie
  7. Karelia Suite

CD 2:
  1. A Blade of Grass
  2. A Cajun Alley

3. Tarkus
4. Hoedown
5. Fanfare for the Common Man
6. Honky Tonk Train Blues

CD 3 :
1. Keith Emerson and the Nice—Interview with Chris Welch 2001

★★¹/₂

What troubles me most about this package is the conception that underlies it. Above all, the billing—"Keith Emerson and the Nice"—is something of a misnomer: in my view, this album does not showcase a real reformation of a real band. The Nice are only part of the picture here, and what we really have is a traveling Keith Emerson revue: otherwise, I remain supremely unconvinced about the need to include nearly forty minutes of the ELP canon, including vastly overexposed warhorses like "Hoedown," "Fanfare for the Common Man," and "Honky Tonk Train Blues," in a program that claims to represent a resurrection of the Nice. "Tarkus," intended to be the set's pièce de résistance, suffers in comparison to ELP's magisterial 1998 reading, and the presence of the ELP material, in my view, under-mines the viability of the whole project: it's almost as if Emerson wasn't confident that the Nice could still deliver the goods over the length of a complete show, lacked confidence in the viability of the Nice's back catalog, and felt the need to prop the Nice and their music up with ELP material performed by a second band of younger musicians.

However, if one is willing to overlook the fact that this is more a celebration of Keith Emerson's past achievements than it is a document of a real reformation of a real band, there is some enjoyment to be had from *Vivicitas*. Lee Jackson's voice has hardened con-siderably since the seventies—its formerly airy quality is gone—and he has lost the upper part of his range, so the vocals are sometimes problematic (check out "Little Arabella," for instance). His bass playing is right on, however, and Brian Davison's energetic drum-ming is a pleasant surprise. The arrangements are loose—always a hallmark of the Nice—but show a nice blend of old and new touches. Other than the "Rondo/America" medley, which Emerson unfortunately beat to death during the nineties with ELP, the other Nice selections really do sound fresh, and Dave Kilminster does a fine job of delivering a stylis-tically appropriate late-sixties guitar sound that's similar to David O'List's, but somewhat more polished.

Unfortunately, the Nice only occupy CD 1. CD 2 is largely dedicated to ELP material, and while Kilminster and the Phil Williams-Pete Riley rhythm section do a fine job technically, the lineup never really gels into a band with a distinctive personality of its own that could *interpret* the material: the overall impression is of Emerson being accompanied by com-petent but anonymous sidemen.

In sum, I think the project would have been more successful had it remained what it was billed as—a reformation of the Nice. "Tarkus" could have been replaced by a three-piece version of "Five Bridges Suite" played by the Nice, and if the exclusion of the other ELP material had caused a shorter set list, oh well.

The third CD, a 2001 interview of the Nice by Chris Welch, largely covers ground already tilled by Martyn Hanson in his Nice biography *Hang on to a Dream* and by Emerson in his *Pictures of an Exhibitionist*, but may prove entertaining to those unfamiliar with either of these two books.

Greg Lake Pre-ELP Releases

WITH THE SHAME

Too Old to Go 'Way Little Girl/Dreams Don't Bother Me (7" single)
Poppy Records POP 501 1D3 593 (U.K., 1968)
Recorded late Summer/Autumn 1967, London, U.K.
Greg Lake, vocals and guitar; John Dickenson, keyboards, vocals; Malcolm Brasher, bass, vocals; Billy Nims, drums
[no rating; both A and B sides written by Janis Ian]

WITH THE SHY LIMBS

Love/Reputation (7" single)
Poppy Records 4190 (U.K., 1969)
Recorded latter part of 1968 (?), London, U.K.
Greg Lake, vocals and guitar; John Dickenson, keyboards, vocals; Malcolm Brasher, bass, vocals; Andy McCullough, drums. Possibly with Robert Fripp, guest guitarist on "Love."
[no rating; both A and B sides written by John Dickenson]
The Shame was Lake's band; the Shy Limbs were a Bournemouth band with whom Lake (and possibly Robert Fripp) guested for the purposes of recording a single. The Shame's "Too Old to Go 'Way Little Girl" and The Shy Limbs' "Love" are included on Lake's *Live from the Underground: The Official Bootleg* (1998).

WITH KING CRIMSON

In the Court of the Crimson King
Island ILPS 9111 (U.K., October 1969)
Atlantic SD 8245 (U.S., October 1969)
Recorded July–August 1969, Wessex Sound Studios, London, U.K.
#5 U.K., #28 U.S.
Robert Fripp, guitars; Greg Lake, vocals, bass guitar; Ian McDonald, woodwinds, keyboards, vibes, vocals; Michael Giles, drums, percussion, vocals; Peter Sinfield, words and illumination

1. 21st Century Schizoid Man including Mirrors (Fripp-McDonald-Lake-Giles-Sinfield)
2. I Talk to the Wind (McDonald-Sinfield)
3. Epitaph including March for no Reason and Tomorrow and Tomorrow (Fripp-McDonald-Lake-Giles-Sinfield)
4. Moonchild including The Dream and The Illusion (Fripp-McDonald-Lake-Giles-Sinfield)
5. The Court of the Crimson King including The Return of the Fire Witch and The Dance of the Puppets (McDonald-Sinfield)

★★★★★

At this late date, there is probably not a lot more to be said about this album, which, as Bill Martin, Paul Stump, and myself all concluded independently in our studies of progressive rock, is almost certainly the most influential album in prog rock history—it's impossible to imagine mature Yes or Genesis, Italian prog, and the prototypical prog rock "sound" without it. (Ironically, ELP were far less influenced by this album than most other prog rock bands just launching out in 1970-71.) As I point out in *Rocking the Classics*, the album's major songs each establish a specific genre of prog rock songwriting; as Bill Martin points out in *Listening to the Future*, while not a concept album *per se*, the songs cohere into an extremely powerful artistic statement that still resonates many years later, independent of the album's historical importance. All four musicians make crucial contributions. Fripp's mature approaches to both electric and acoustic guitar are already in evidence, and besides a commanding vocal performance throughout, Lake turns in some of his finest bass playing ever, especially during the instrumental section of "Schizoid Man." McDonald's multi-instrumental contributions constitute a *tour de force*, and in regard to the underrated Michael Giles, Carl Palmer has admitted that working out Giles's part to "21st Century Schizoid Man" note-for-note during early ELP rehearsals was an important learning experience as he solidified his concept of a drumming style that would be appropriate to ELP's music. The one track on the album that's open to criticism is "Moonchild," the improvised section of which goes on considerably longer than the musical substance warrants: however, the album earns its five star rating through a combination of artistic merit and historical importance.

In the Wake of Poseidon
Island ILPS 9127 (U.K., May 1970)
Atlantic SD 8266 (U.S., June 1970)
Recorded February–April 1970, Wessex Sound Studios, London, U.K.
#4 U.K., #31 U.S.

Robert Fripp, guitars, Mellotron, devices; Greg Lake, vocals; Michael Giles, drums and percussion; Peter Giles, bass; Keith Tippett, piano; Mel Collins, woodwinds; Peter Sinfield, words. With Gordon Haskell, vocal on "Cadence and Cascade."

1. Peace—A Beginning (Fripp-Sinfield)
2. Pictures of a City including 42nd at Treadmill (Fripp-Sinfield)
3. Cadence and Cascade (Fripp-Sinfield)
4. In the Wake of Poseidon including Libra's Theme (Fripp-Sinfield)
5. Peace—A Theme (Fripp)
6. Cat Food (Fripp-Sinfield-McDonald)
7. The Devil's Triangle
   a. Merday Morn (Fripp-McDonald)
   b. Hand of Sceiron (Fripp)
   c. Garden of Worm (Fripp)
   [based loosely on Gustav Holst's "Mars, the Bringer of War"]
8. Peace—An End (Fripp-Sinfield)

★★★½

Recorded early 1970, after the original lineup had collapsed, with Lake and Michael Giles appearing as sessions men, *In the Wake of Poseidon* comes across as an effort by Fripp to rework the contents of the first album according to his own tastes and preferences. It could be argued that technically it improves on the debut album, with more production and arrangement polish: what's missing, though, is far more important—the vital spark that animated the debut. *Poseidon* appears to rework not only the songs of *Crimson King* ("Pictures of a City" for "Schizoid Man," "Cadence and Cascade" for "I Talk to the Wind," "In the Wake of Poseidon" for "Epitaph") but even the order and flow of dynamics of the debut album, and as a result the debut's sense of inevitable progression is lost. Innovations include the insertion of a plainsonglike "Peace" theme at the beginning, middle, and end of the album to provide unity—the results are middling—and the reworking of Holst's "Mars" as an instrumental suite, "The Devil's Triangle." Again, the results are mixed—"Devil's Triangle" goes on too long and grows wearisome in sections—but does point forward to the thick, murky, intense instrumental textures that became a King Crimson trademark during the band's 1973-74 glory days. The album's highpoint is the title track: although dependent on "Epitaph," it's arguably even better, with a heartbreakingly poignant vocal by Lake (his overdubbed vocal "choir" at the end is particularly magnificent) that stands as a career highlight.

Epitaph—Live in 1969, Volumes One and Two
DGM DGM9607A/B (U.S. and U.K., April 1997)

CD 1:

BBC Radio Sessions
 1. 21st Century Schizoid Man
 2. In the Court of the Crimson King
 3. Get Thy Bearings (Donovan Leitch)
 4. Epitaph

Fillmore East, New York, November 21, 1969
 5. A Man, A City
    [An earlier version of "Pictures of a City" from *In the Wake of Poseidon*]
 6. Epitaph
 7. 21st Century Schizoid Man

Fillmore West, San Francisco, December 14, 1969
 8. Mantra (Fripp-Lake-McDonald-Giles-Sinfield)
 9. Travel Weary Capricorn (Fripp-Lake-McDonald-Giles-Sinfield)
10. Improv: Travel Bleary Capricorn (Fripp-Lake-McDonald-Giles)
11. Mars (Holst)
    [Eventually re-worked into "The Devil's Triangle" from *The Wake of Poseidon*]

CD 2:

Fillmore West, San Francisco, December 15, 1969
1. In the Court of the Crimson King
2. Drop In (Fripp-Lake-McDonald-Giles-Sinfield)
   [An earlier version of "The Letters" from *Islands*]
3. A Man, A City
4. Epitaph
5. 21st Century Schizoid Man
6. Mars

★★★★½

Twenty-seven years and a few months after the collapse of the original Crimson lineup, the release of *Epitaph* finally has made it possible for interested persons (some of whom hadn't been born yet when these shows were recorded) to experience—to some degree at least—what the original band were like as a live act. Considering that these recordings were never intended for release, but are either bootlegs or off-the-cuff recordings made directly from the mixing board for the band's private listening, the sonic quality is surprisingly good, and David Singleton is to be commended for his restoration of these tapes. The quality of playing is every bit what you would expect from this band, and it's interesting to note that at this point in time Ian McDonald is the band's dominant soloist, with Fripp usually playing the role of a quietly effective texturalist and ensemble player—the towering, angular solos for which he was to become famous were still, for the most part, a thing of the future. Although they don't stray too far from the "authorized" (i.e., studio) readings of their classics, there are enough shifts in detail from performance to performance to keep the listening experience continuously engaging. Especially interesting are the tracks that either were never recorded in the studio, or were later released in much different studio versions. For my money the most valuable component of this set is disc two, which chronicles the band's final show, at Fillmore West on December 15, 1969. (This according to the liner notes: the date of the show was almost certainly December 14.) While Fripp complains in the expansive liner notes (which are alternately enlightening and obfuscating, entertaining and infuriating) that this was one of the band's weakest performances, those of us who weren't there learn much from experiencing the entire performance from beginning to end, including the between-song patter, and Fripp's concerns aside, the dynamic ebb-and-flow of this show is certainly impressive. If there is a weakness to this box set, it's as follows: the repertoire of King Crimson '69 was rather small, and a more casual listener may find three versions each of "Epitaph" and "21st Century Schizoid Man" over the course of two CDs to be a bit much of a good thing.

Epitaph—Live in 1969, Volumes Three and Four
DGM DGM9607C/D (U.K. and U.S., April 1997)

CD 3:

Plumpton Festival, August 9, 1969
1. 21st Century Schizoid Man
2. Get Thy Bearings
3. In the Court of the Crimson King
4. Mantra
5. Travel Weary Capricorn
6. Improv
7. Mars

CD 4:

Chesterfield Jazz Club, September 7, 1969
1. 21st Century Schizoid Man
2. Drop In
3. Epitaph
4. Get Thy Bearings
5. Mantra
6. Travel Weary Capricorn

7. Improv
8. Mars
[No rating]
Currently available only as a Japanese import.

Epitaph—Live in 1969
Limited edition box set
DGMBOX2 (U.K. and U.S., April 1997)
Includes volumes 1–4 in a single box set
[No rating]
No longer available.

Live at the Marquee, 1969
DGM CD CLUB 1 (U.K., October 1998)
Recorded live July 6, 1969, The Marquee, London, U.K.

1. 21st Century Schizoid Man
2. Drop In
3. I Talk to the Wind
4. Epitaph
5. Travel Weary Capricorn
6. Improv (including "Nola" and "Etude no. 7")
7. Mars

Bonus track from October 17, 1969, Fairfield Hall, Croydon, U.K.
8. Trees
   [Note: This was the show at which the Nice's *Five Bridges* was recorded. King Crimson were the opening act.]
[No rating]
Outside of private subscription to King Crimson's collector's club, available only as part of a very expensive Japanese import set.

Carl Palmer Pre-ELP Releases

WITH THE CRAIG

I Must Be Mad/Suspense (7" single)
Fontana TF 715 (U.K., June 1966)
Recorded Spring 1966, Regent Sound Studios, London, U.K.
Geoff Brown, vocals; Richie Kingbee, guitar; Len Cox, bass; Carl Palmer, drums
[No rating; both songs by Geoff Brown]
"I Must Be Mad," in particular, is a much better than usual specimen of the midsixties "freakbeat" sound, and shows sixteen-year-old Carl Palmer quickly developing into an exception rock drummer; it also points up how much of an influence Keith Moon's drumming style was exerting on him at this point. Both the A and B sides are included in Palmer's 2001 anthology.

WITH CHRIS FARLOWE AND THE THUNDERBIRDS

Yesterday's Papers/Life is but Nothing (7" single)
Immediate IM 049 (U.K., May 1967)
Chris Farlowe, vocals; Albert Lee, guitar; Dave Greenslade, organ; Buggs Wadel, bass; Carl Palmer, drums
[No rating]
Palmer plays on the A side only.

Handbags and Gladrags/Everyone Makes a Mistake (7" single)
Immediate 065 (U.K., November 1967)
Same lineup as above
[No rating]

Palmer plays on the A side only. Unfortunately, none of Palmer's work with Farlowe is currently available.

WITH THE CRAZY WORLD OF ARTHUR BROWN

Nightmare/What's Happening (7" single)
Track 604 026 (U.K., November 1968)
Arthur Brown, vocals; Vincent Crane, organ; Nick Greenwood, bass; Carl Palmer, drums
[No rating]
Palmer plays on the B side only. Unfortunately, none of Palmer's work with Brown is available, either. There *must* be a bootleg of Palmer playing on a live performance of "Fire" somewhere!

WITH ATOMIC ROOSTER

Atomic Roooster
B & C Records CAS 101 (U.K., February 1970)
Elektra Records CAS 1010 (U.S., March 1970)
Recorded late 1969
Nick Graham, vocals, bass, flute; Vincent Crane, organ and piano; Carl Palmer, drums and percussion. With John DuCann, guitars, on "Friday the Thirteenth," "Before Tomorrow," and "S.L.Y."

1. Friday the Thirteenth (Crane)
2. And So To Bed (Crane)
3. Broken Wings (Grun-Jarome)
4. Before Tomorrow (Crane)
5. Banstead (Crane-Palmer-Graham)
6. S.L.Y. (Crane)
7. Winter (Crane)
8. Decline and Fall (Crane-Palmer-Graham)

★★★

Atomic Rooster were a "progressive" band at a time when the term meant something slightly different than it came to mean during the seventies: they were a band that experimented with melding the blues-rock and psychedelic rock styles of the late sixties with jazz, folk, and classical influences. Of course, the same could be said of the Nice and King Crimson: the crucial difference being that the characteristic sound of these latter two bands much more closely anticipates the progressive rock sound of the seventies in its narrower, more specific sense. Perhaps most characteristic of Atomic Rooster is a blues-based, proto-metal organ trio approach that anticipates Deep Purple's *Machine Head* of 1971; this vein of writing is especially evident on "Friday the Thirteenth," "Before Tomorrow," and "S.L.Y.," all of which use sessions guitarist John DuCann (who later became a full-time member of the band). However, the band also explores a melancholy, vaguely folk-rock vein that parallels early Caravan ("Banstead," the pretty "Winter") and a melodramatic big-band jazz-rock fusion that's reminiscent of early Blood, Sweat, and Tears ("Broken Wings"). There are also experiments in odd meters, interesting episodic shifts, and double-tracked piano and organ ("And So To Bed"). On this recording Carl Palmer's mature drumming style emerges fully blown: the lightning fast tom runs and rudimental fills are all here, as are the flamboyant drum solo ("Decline and Fall") and tuned percussion ornamentation ("Winter"). While *Atomic Roooster* is genuinely interesting and engaging in spots, it never rises above the level of experimentation with and dabbling in the various styles it engages; what it lacks that the debut Nice, Crimson, and ELP albums have in spades is a clear, focused sense of stylistic direction—that is to say, a sense of artistic vision. Certainly, Vincent Crane, while a competent organist, was no Keith Emerson, and Nick Graham was certainly no Greg Lake; it's hard to imagine Palmer would have remained musically satisfied in this lineup for very long.

Emerson, Lake and Palmer; Emerson, Lake and Powell; 3

Emerson, Lake and Palmer
Island ILPS 9132 (U.K., November 1970)
Cotilllon SD 9040 (U.S., February 1971)
Recorded July, September 1970 at Advision Studios, London, U.K.
#4 U.K., #18 U.S.

1. The Barbarian (Emerson-Lake-Palmer)
   [Arrangement of Béla Bartók's solo piano piece *Allegro barbaro*]
2. Take a Pebble (Lake)
3. Knife-Edge (Emerson-Lake-Fraser)
   [Based on the fifth movement of Leoš Janáček's *Sinfonietta*]
4. The Three Fates (Emerson)
   a. Clotho
   b. Lachesis
   c. Atropos
5. Tank (Emerson-Palmer)
6. Lucky Man (Lake)

★★★★½

One of the great debut albums in rock history. At its most conservative ("The Barbarian," "Knife-Edge"), it burnishes the organ trio conception of the Nice with a rhythmic precision, virtuosity, and polish the Nice had never been able to muster. The album's most visionary tracks ("The Three Fates," "Tank") still sound a contemporary note today. Its stylistic fusion of baroque and twentieth-century classical music, contemporary jazz, and folk elements in a rock matrix is so complete and assured that the impression is of a long-mature style, rather than an experimental mixture of disparate sources. The first of eight consecutive ELP albums produced by Greg Lake (and the first of four consecutive albums engineered by Eddy Offord), it was also a watershed at the time of its release for its sonic quality. Above all, it's consistent—every track on the album is strong, several are ELP classics—and it coheres very well, with well-conceived contrasts of mood, tempo, dynamics, and instrumentation from track to track.

Tarkus
Island ILPS 9155 (U.K., July 1971)
Cotillion SD 9900 (U.S., July 1971)
Recorded January, April 1971 at Advision Studios, London, U.K.
#1 U.K., #9 U.S.

1. Tarkus (Emerson-Lake)
   a. Eruption
   b. Stones of Years
   c. Iconoclast
   d. Mass
   e. Manticore
   f. The Battlefield
   g. Aquatarkus
2. Jeremy Bender (Emerson-Lake)
3. Bitches Crystal (Emerson-Lake)
4. The Only Way (Emerson-Lake)
5. Infinite Space (Emerson-Palmer)
6. A Time and a Place (Emerson-Lake-Palmer)
7. Are You Ready Eddy? (Emerson-Lake-Palmer)

★★★★

The "Tarkus" suite (which occupies all of side one of the LP format) is one of the watershed works in the development of the progressive rock style. Its complex, machinelike metrical episodes, metallic chords, strident electronic tone colors, and virtuosic ensemble interplay were revelatory at the time: the "Tarkus" suite is the taproot of much of the more challenging and experimental progressive music that followed, and may represent ELP's most visionary piece. Some thirty-five years later, it is still futuristic, still a challenging listen. Nonetheless, the *Tarkus* album is not above criticism. If it is an even more adventurous album than the band's debut, representing a genuine step forward, it's also more uneven (especially some of the material on side two of the LP format), doesn't cohere as well, and features the weakest production of the band's four studio albums of 1970–74, with a persistent muddiness in the lower registers.

Pictures at an Exhibition
Island HELP 1 (U.K., November 1971)
Cotillion ELP 66666 (U.S., January 1972)
Recorded live at Newcastle City Hall, U.K., March 26, 1971
#3 U.K., #10 U.S.

1. Promenade (Musorgsky)
2. The Gnome (Musorgsky-Palmer)
3. Promenade (Musorgsky-Lake)
4. The Sage (Lake)
5. The Old Castle (Musorgsky-Emerson)
6. Blues Variation (Emerson-Lake-Palmer)
7. Promenade (Musorgsky)
8. The Hut of Baba Yaga (Musorgsky)
9. The Curse of Baba Yaga (Emerson-Lake-Palmer)
10. The Hut of Baba Yaga (Musorgsky)
11. The Great Gates of Kiev (Musorgsky-Lake)
12. Nutrocker (Kim Fowley)

★★★★

It is *Pictures*, rather than the debut album, that shows most clearly the lingering traces of the psychedelic rock style that progressive rock developed out of (and away from). As such, it's something of a stylistic link between late-period Nice and ELP, and it must be admitted that some sections (such as the free-form jam at the beginning of "The Old Castle," the blues-rock jamming of "Blues Variation," the organ feedback episode near the end of "The Great Gates of Kiev," the entirety of "Nutrocker") don't totally cohere with the rest of the album, which shows the band reworking Musorgsky's masterpiece in a more recognizably progressive rock vein. Nonetheless, even a halfway impartial assessment of *Pictures* must acknowledge two major points in its favor. The tightness and discipline of the band's performance is astonishing: despite all the critical talk of "bloated egos," there's little overextension or solo indulgence here (save for "Old Castle"/"Blues Variation"). Furthermore, *Pictures* is probably the sharpest-sounding live rock album of the early 1970s: Emerson's Hammond never sounded this good in a live recording again, and Lake's vocals are livelier and more upfront than in ELP's two live albums recorded later in the decade.

Trilogy
Island ILPS 9186 (U.K., June 1972)
Cotillion SD 9903 (U.S., July 1972)
Recorded November 1971, January 1972 at Advision Studios, London, U.K.
#2 U.K., #5 U.S.

1. The Endless Enigma, part one (Emerson-Lake)
2. Fugue (Emerson)
3. The Endless Enigma, part two (Emerson-Lake)
4. From the Beginning (Lake)
5. The Sheriff (Emerson-Lake)
6. Hoedown (Aaron Copland)
7. Trilogy (Emerson-Lake)
8. Living Sin (Emerson-Lake-Palmer)
9. Abaddon's Bolero (Emerson)

★★★★$^{1}/_2$

There has long been a not insignificant minority of ELP fans who consider *Trilogy* to be ELP's finest achievement, and there's no question *Trilogy* marks a step forward for all three members. For Emerson, *Trilogy* signals a much more organic integration of Moog synthesizer into the arrangements than anything he'd achieved on the first three albums; Lake's singing becomes more assured and variegated, while Palmer's drumming shows growth in his understanding of band orchestration and above all, taste. *Trilogy* is the most good-humored and relaxed album of their classic period. In terms of concision, only the debut album suggests itself as a rival; in terms of consistency, only the debut album and *Brain Salad Surgery*. Unlike most other ELP albums, on *Trilogy* the short tracks reveal the same care and craftsmanship as the longer ones: *Trilogy* became the touchstone for the band's attempts of the late seventies and beyond to create music that was both accessible and multidimensional. It must be admitted that *Trilogy* finds the band polishing and perfecting existing approaches rather than exploring new territory: many fans missed the sense of intensity and urgency that characterized the most representative material of their first three albums.

Brain Salad Surgery
Manticore 87 302 IT (U.K., December 1973)
Manticore 66669 (U.S., December 1973)
Recorded June (Olympic Studios, London, U.K.), September (Advision Studios, London, U.K.), 1973
#5 U.K., #11 U.S.

1. Jerusalem (Parry-Blake)
2. Toccata (Ginastera)
   [Arrangement of Alberto Ginastera's Piano Concerto no. 1, fourth movement]
3. Still . . . You Turn Me On (Lake)
4. Benny the Bouncer (Emerson-Lake-Sinfield)
5. Karn Evil 9, 1st Impression, part one (Emerson-Lake)
6. Karn Evil 9, 1st Impression, part two (Emerson-Lake)
7. Karn Evil 9, 2nd Impression (Emerson)
8. Karn Evil 9, 3rd Impression (Emerson-Lake-Sinfield)

★★★★★

The zenith of ELP's output. Not only is it a prog rock classic, it's one of the great rock concept albums of the 1970s, with ELP's brilliant music, alternately heroic and ominous, Greg Lake's and Pete Sinfield's lyrics, and H. R. Giger's memorable cover art cohering into a *Gesamtkunstwerk* of Wagnerian scale. From a musical standpoint, ideas are expanded and developed more seamlessly and in larger paragraphs than before, and the tracks cohere magnificently. On no other ELP album is the sense of equality and teamwork as strong, with Lake's electric guitar work and Emerson's polyphonic Moog/Hammond arrangements opening a whole new sonic dimension for the band. No other ELP album is more effective in minimizing the differences in taste and interests between the three band members. The band's virtuosity reaches a new plateau here (as demonstrated in "Toccata" and "Karn Evil 9, 2nd Impression"), yet is more understated than before; no other ELP album is this consistent, with the arguable exception of their first. Production-wise, the band never sounded better: *Brain Salad Surgery* achieves a sense of clarity that was startling for its era.

Welcome Back My Friends to the Show that Never Ends—Ladies and Gentlemen, Emerson, Lake and Palmer
Manticore 88 147XT (U.K., September 1974)
Manticore MC3-200 (U.S., September 1974)
Recorded live at Anaheim, California, Convention Center, February 10, 1974
#5 U.K., #4 U.S.

1. Hoedown
2. Jerusalem
3. Toccata

4. Tarkus
   a. Eruption
   b. Stones of Years
   c. Iconoclast
   d. Mass
   e. Manticore
   f. The Battlefield (including "Epitaph")
   g. Aquatarkus
5. Take a Pebble, part I
6. Still . . . You Turn Me On/Lucky Man
7. Piano Improvisations (Emerson, including excerpts from Friedrich Gulda's "Prelude and Fugue" and Joe Sullivan's "Little Rock Getaway")
8. Take a Pebble, part II
9. Jeremy Bender/The Sheriff
10. Karn Evil 9, 1st Impression
11. Karn Evil 9, 2nd Impression
12. Karn Evil 9, 3rd Impression

★★★★

ELP were rewarded for their inveterate North American touring when *Welcome Back My Friends* charted out at #4, their highest-charting album of all in the U.S., and one of the few three-LP sets to break the top ten during the vinyl era. *Welcome Back* features one of the most challenging set lists undertaken by any rock band, ever—imagine complete performances of "Karn Evil 9" and "Tarkus" in one show, with "Toccata" and "Take a Pebble" thrown in for good measure—and the performances, which crackle with energy, are marked by a uniform level of virtuosity and panache. Unfortunately, *Welcome Back* does not measure up sonically to *Pictures*—the sound of Emerson's Hammond is often disappointingly thin, Lake's Gibson Ripper bass doesn't record uniformly across its range (too boomy in its low registers, too jangly in its high registers), and there's some bleed on Lake's vocal mikes—although Carl Palmer's drums never sounded better, and here one can here his famed stainless steel kit in all its glory. One can also wonder about the extremely fast tempos here, which at times (parts of "Tarkus," "Hoedown," "Piano Improvisations") border on overkill. Nonetheless, there are many highlights, including "Aquatarkus"—ELP's deepest foray into space rock, and Emerson's greatest achievement as an analog synthesist—and some magnificent performances of the *Brain Salad Surgery* material, especially the ferocious "Toccata" and "Karn Evil 9" (which includes the definitive Carl Palmer drum solo). *Welcome Back* provides a fine introduction to the world of ELP for the uninitiated.

Works, Volume I
Atlantic K80009 (U.K., March 1977)
Atlantic SD2-7000 (U.S., March 1977)
Recorded 1975-76
#9 U.K., #12 U.S.

Keith Emerson Tracks:
Piano Concerto no. 1 (Emerson; orchestration by Emerson and John Mayer) Keith Emerson, piano; London Philharmonic Orchestra, John Mayer, conductor

1. Allegro giojoso
2. Andante molto cantabile
3. Toccata con fuoco
Recorded De Lane Lea Studios, London, U.K., November-December 1975

Greg Lake Tracks:
4. Lend Your Love to Me Tonight (Lake-Sinfield)
5. C'est la vie (Lake-Sinfield)
6. Hallowed Be Thy Name (Lake-Sinfield)
7. Nobody Loves You Like I Do (Lake-Sinfield)
8. Closer to Believing (Lake-Sinfield)

Greg Lake, voice and acoustic guitar; various studio musicians (Keith Emerson, piano, track 7); Godfrey Salmon, string arrangements

Recorded Advision Studios, London, U.K. (1975), Mountain Recording Studios, Montreux, Switzerland (1976)

Carl Palmer Tracks:
9. The Scythian Suite, 2nd movement: The Enemy God Dances with the Black Spirits (Prokofiev)
10. L. A. Nights (Palmer-Emerson)
11. New Orleans (Palmer)
12. Two-Part Invention in D Minor (J. S. Bach; string arrangement Harry South)
13. Food for your Soul (Palmer-H. South)
14. Tank (Emerson-Palmer; arrangement Harry South)

Carl Palmer, drums and percussion; various studio musicians, including the London Philharmonic Orchestra (track 9), Keith Emerson (keyboards, tracks 10 and 14), Joe Walsh, guitar and scat vocal (track 10), Ian McDonald (saxophone, track 10), Snuffy Walden, guitar (track 11); James Blades, marimba (track 12); Harry South, arrangements, tracks 12-14

ELP Tracks:
15. Fanfare for the Common Man (Copland)
    Recorded at Mountain Recording Studios, Montreux, Switzerland, April, August, September 1976
16. Pirates (Emerson-Lake-Sinfield)
    Recorded at Pathé Marconi EMI Studios, Paris, France and Advision Studios, London, U.K., November 1976
    Orchestra de l'Opera de Paris, Godfrey Salmon, conductor

★★★

The turning point in ELP's fortunes. The packaging of the album (three solo LP sides and one group LP side) was a laudable attempt to demonstrate ELP's unity in diversity, to show the band could still function as a coherent unit while pursuing their individual interests. Unfortunately, the way *Works I* was packaged glaringly demonstrated what ELP were trying to paper over by showing how far apart the musicians were drifting from each other stylistically; many fans were also alienated by the apparent attempt to use the ELP name to entice fans into buying music that wasn't in fact ELP. While there are some real high points in the solo work of the three musicians, there are also some undeniable weaknesses: Emerson's Concerto at times demonstrates a less-than-sure grasp of large-scale symphonic structure, Lake's songs evince a sameness of mood and style, Palmer's material often highlights a triumph of drumming virtuosity over musical substance. The two ELP tracks, on the other hand, are both classics, although one notes that "Fanfare for the Common Man" and "Pirates" are more about finishing something old than beginning something new: "Fanfare" is one last expression of Emerson's late-sixties preoccupation with using a classical piece as a framework for exploring the possibilities of the psychedelic jam, and "Pirates" is a final manifestation of Emerson's interest in creating a satisfactory fusion of rock and orchestral elements that had first manifested itself nearly a decade earlier with the Nice's "Ars Longa Vita Brevis" and "Five Bridges Suite." The biggest failure of *Works I* was its inability to propound a coherent direction for the group to follow in the waning years of the seventies.

Works, Volume II

Atlantic K50422 (U.K., November 1977)
Atlantic SD19147 (U.S., November 1977)
Recorded September 1973 (group tracks), 1974–76 (solo tracks) at various locations
#20 U.K., #37 U.S.

1. Tiger in a Spotlight (Emerson-Lake-Palmer-Sinfield)
2. When the Apple Blossoms Bloom in the Windmills of Your Mind I'll Be Your Valentine (Emerson-Lake-Palmer)
3. Bullfrog (Palmer-Aspery-Hodgkinson)
   [Ron Aspery, woodwinds and keyboards; Colin Hodgkinson, bass]
4. Brain Salad Surgery (Emerson-Lake-Palmer)

 5. Barrelhouse Shake-Down (Emerson; horn arrangement Emerson-Alan Cohen)
 6. Watching Over You (Lake-Sinfield)
 7. So Far To Fall (Emerson-Lake-Sinfield; horn arrangement Emerson-Tony Harris)
 8. Maple Leaf Rag (Scott Joplin)
   [Keith Emerson, piano; London Philharmonic Orchestra, John Mayer, conductor]
 9. I Believe in Father Christmas (Lake-Sinfield)
10. Close But Not Touching (Palmer-South)
11. Honky Tonk Train Blues (Meade Lux Lewis, horn arrangement Alan Cohen)
12. Show Me the Way to Go Home (Irving King; arranged Keith Emerson-Godfrey Salmon)

★★¹/₂

After the peculiar solo/band mélange of *Works I*, many fans were under the impression that ELP's next album would be the "real" group album. When they found that *Works II* was another solo/band mélange, of outtakes, no less (the four group tracks were outtakes of the September 1973 *Brain Salad Surgery* sessions, the rest were outtakes of the band members' 1975-76 solo sessions or already-released singles and B-sides), they began to desert ELP in droves. Nonetheless, it's possible to argue that if ELP fans have tended to consistently overrate *Works I*, they've tended to somewhat underrate *Works II*. Despite its obvious unevenness and the relative superficiality of a number of its tracks, *Works II* coheres a bit better than *Works I*. Much of the album is united by a common theme: an exploration of, and tribute to, the earlier styles of twentieth-century American popular music from which rock sprang. Highlights include the first four tracks (which actually generate some energy and momentum) and the beautiful trio version of "I Believe in Father Christmas," much more tastefully arranged here than Lake's bombastic solo single of 1975.

Love Beach
Atlantic K 50552 (U.K., November 1978)
Atlantic SD 19211 (U.S., November 1978)
Recorded Summer 1978 at Compass Point Studios, Nassau, Bahamas
#48 U.K., #55 U.S.

 1. All I Want is You (Lake-Sinfield)
 2. Love Beach (Lake-Sinfield)
 3. Taste of Your Love (Lake-Sinfield)
 4. The Gambler (Emerson-Lake-Sinfield)
 5. For You (Lake-Sinfield)
 6. *Fantasia para un Gentilhombre,* final movement: Canario (Joaquin Rodrigo)

Memoirs of an Officer and a Gentleman
 7. Prologue/The Education of a Gentleman (Emerson-Sinfield)
 8. Love at First Sight (Emerson-Sinfield)
 9. Letters from the Front (Emerson-Sinfield)
10. Honourable Company (A March) (Emerson)

★★

The album that beached ELP (pardon the pun) for many years. Side one of the LP format (tracks one through six) is every bit as bad as the album's longtime reputation would suggest, excepting only the sprightly (if by no means groundbreaking) "Canario." What strikes one more forcefully than either the insipid music or ridiculous lyrics is the colossal lapse of taste the three musicians must have experienced in order to agree to the release of such music. The "Memoirs of an Officer and a Gentleman" suite that comprises side two of the LP format (tracks six through ten) is much better: while the music lacks the intensity and energy of their earlier epics, it evinces an agreeable calm and a new emotional subtlety in its storyline. "Memoirs" does wear its debt to previous ELP classics too openly—only "Letters from the Front," with its cool, almost geometric angularity, suggests a new direction, perhaps representing Keith Emerson's highly personal response to New Wave. The album has no credited producer (Emerson was de facto producer, though he saw his role more as a salvager), which set a precedent—namely, that Greg Lake was no longer automatically entitled to produce an ELP album—that was to perpetually destabilize ELP reformation attempts throughout the 1980s and 1990s. The overall sound is thin, over-trebly, and lacking in bass presence.

Emerson, Lake and Palmer In Concert
Atlantic K50652 (U.K., November 1979)
Atlantic SD19255 (U.S., November 1979)
Recorded live at Montreal's Olympic Stadium, August 26, 1977 (tracks 4, 6–8), elsewhere
during the *Works* tour late 1977/early 1978 (tracks 1, 2, 3, 5).
Godfrey Salmon, conductor
#73 U.S.

1. Introductory Fanfare (Emerson/Palmer)
2. Peter Gunn (Mancini)
3. Tiger in a Spotlight
4. C'est la vie
5. The Enemy God Dances with the Black Spirits
6. Knife-Edge
7. Piano Concerto no. 1, 3rd movement: Toccata con fuoco
8. Pictures at an Exhibition

★½

ELP followed up what was easily their worst studio album with what was easily their worst
live album. Again, there's no credited producer; again, Keith Emerson was de facto producer, although once more he saw his role more as salvager. The twenty-four-track mixer
on which this album was to have been recorded broke down, so the mixes had to be done
from two-track masters combined with the soundtrack from the videotape of the
Montreal performance: while the sound quality of the tracks the band recorded as a trio
are fine (although not exceptional), the orchestral parts sound very thin and one-dimensional. If *In Concert* was marred by poor sound quality, it was also marred by its highly
peculiar selection of tracks, which give a very spotty, uneven overview of what *Works*-era
ELP were all about as a live band. On "Knife-Edge" and "Pictures," there's something very
superfluous about the orchestration: the orchestrated sections contribute very little in the
way of drama or climax, and the presence of the orchestra reduces the music's rhythmic
drive. Indeed, in most of the orchestral segments the ragged rhythms, the orchestra's not
entirely secure intonation, and the record's one-dimensional orchestral sound combine to
create an elephantine effect that comes dangerously close to duplicating the critical
stereotype of ELP's music. The album's one gem is a trio version of "The Enemy God." A
month after this album was released, ELP officially announced their dissolution.

Works Live
Castle ESD CD 362 (U.K., November 1993)
Victory 828 477-2 (U.S., November 1993)
Recorded live at Montreal's Olympic Stadium, August 26, 1977 (3, 7, 8, 10–14); elsewhere
during *Works* tour of late 1977/early 1978 (1, 2, 4–6, 9)
Godfrey Salmon, conductor

1. Introductory Fanfare/Peter Gunn
2. Tiger in a Spotlight
3. C'est la vie
4. Watching Over You
5. Maple Leaf Rag
6. The Enemy God Dances with the Black Spirits
7. Fanfare for the Common Man
8. Knife-Edge
9. Show Me the Way to Go Home
10. Abaddon's Bolero
11. Pictures at an Exhibition
12. Closer to Believing
13. Piano Concerto no. 1, 3rd movement: Toccata con fuoco
14. Tank

★★½

In 1993, when Victory Records reissued remastered versions of ELP's back catalog, *In Concert* was rereleased with a number of previously unreleased tracks and retitled *Works Live*. While many of the black marks against *In Concert* remain a factor here (the sound quality of the orchestral material is marginally better now, but at the expense of occasionally exposing previously indiscernible intonation problems), in one respect *Works Live* significantly improves on *In Concert*: it gives a much more representative cross-section of ELP's live show during the *Works* era. Why there is still no group-orchestra performance of "Pirates," ELP's most significant new work of the *Works* era, on *Works Live* remains a mystery.

The Best of Emerson, Lake and Palmer
Atlantic SD 19283 (U.S., November 1980)
Atlantic K50757 (U.K., November 1980)
#108 U.S.

1. Hoedown
2. Lucky Man
3. Karn Evil 9, 1st Impression, part two
4. Jerusalem
5. Peter Gunn
6. Fanfare for the Common Man
7. Still . . . You Turn Me On
8. Tiger in a Spotlight
9. Trilogy

★★

Few rock bands of the sixties and seventies produced an output less suited to "best of" packaging than ELP. Even so, the motley assortment of tracks chosen for this album is incomprehensible. ("Tiger in a Spotlight"? "Peter Gunn"?!) It was to be another twelve years before ELP would finally be served by a set (*The Atlantic Years*) that adequately represented the full scope of their achievement during the 1970s.

The Best of Emerson, Lake and Palmer
Victory 383 480 036-2 (U.S., October 1994)

1. From the Beginning
2. Jerusalem
3. Still . . . You Turn Me On
4. Fanfare for the Common Man (single edit)
5. Knife-Edge
6. Tarkus
7. Karn Evil 9, 1st Impression, part 2
8. C'est la vie
9. Hoedown
10. Trilogy
11. Honky Tonk Train Blues
12. Black Moon (single edit)
13. Lucky Man
14. I Believe in Father Christmas

★★★½

It could be argued that ELP's output is not substantially better suited to a seventy-minute greatest hits package than a forty-minute one. That being said, this 1994 overhaul of the 1980 greatest hits package, which adds thirty more minutes of music, represents a substantial improvement. If nothing else, the inclusion of the complete "Tarkus" suite gives a better-rounded overview of ELP's output. (But why did they open the album with the mellow Greg Lake album "From the Beginning" instead of the uptempo "Hoedown"?) The album may still be weighted a bit too much towards Greg Lake ballads and short tracks; it could have been further improved (in terms of balance of styles and overall musical substance) by removing "C'est la vie" and "Honky Tonk Train Blues" in favor of "Toccata."

Emerson, Lake and Powell
Polydor POLD 5191 (U.K., May 1986)
Polydor 829 297-1 Y-1 (U.S., May 1986)
Recorded between mid-1985 and January 1986 at Maison Rouge, London, and Fleetwood Moblle, Sussex, U.K.
#35 U.K., #23 U.S.

1. The Score (Emerson-Lake)
2. Learning to Fly (Emerson-Lake)
3. The Mlracle (Emerson-Lake)
4. Touch and Go (Emerson-Lake)
5. Love Blind (Emerson-Lake)
6. Step Aside (Emerson-Lake)
7. Lay Down Your Guns (Emerson-Lake-Gould)
8. Mars, the Bringer of War (Holst)
9. The Loco-Motion (King-Goffin)*
10. Vacant Possession (Emerson-Lake)*
*Bonus tracks included on 1992 CD rerelease Polygram 829 297-2

★★★¹/₂

"Same old ELP" bellowed *Musician* when *Emerson, Lake and Powell* hit the streets, but, in fact, the album shows some significant departures from the signature sound of seventies ELP. The biggest shift involves the use of sonic space. On *Emerson, Lake and Powell* Emerson retools his own playing to parallel the shift from Carl Palmer's complex rudimental fills to Cozy Powell's spare but enormous backbeats, abandoning the baroque melodic filigrees of his seventies work in favor of massive blocks of chords punctuated on occasion by dissonant synth trumpet fanfares. The ELPowell sound—massive, severe, austere—is also differentiated from earlier ELP by its thoroughgoing exploration of electronic tone colors; this is the album where Emerson fully steps into the digital age. The first three tracks—"The Score," "Learning to Fly," and "The Miracle"—segue into each other so seamlessly that one inevitably hears the entire LP side as one long piece divided into three parts; it's the strongest LP side put out by Emerson and Lake since side four of *Works I*, if not side two of *Brain Salad Surgery*. Emerson, Lake and Powell even achieved a minor hit single with the short, punchy fourth track, "Touch and Go," but unfortunately the subsequent material, including an arrangement of Gustav Holst's "Mars, the Bringer of War," doesn't measure up to the high standard of the first four tracks. The album is commendable for its success in minimizing the difference between Emerson's and Lake's contributions; it's ironic that on a project recorded more than a decade after their heyday, Emerson, Lake and Powell often manage to sound more like a true band than Emerson, Lake and Palmer had during the late seventies.

3 . . . To The Power of Three
Geffen 924-181-1 (U.K., January 1988)
Geffen GHS 24181 (U.S., January 1988)
Recorded September-October 1987, E-Zee Studios and West Side Studios, U.K.
#97 U.S.

1. Talkin' 'Bout (Berry)
2. Lover to Lover (Emerson-Berry-Palmer)
3. Chains (Shifrin-Marlette)
4. Desde la Vida
   a. La Vista (Emerson-Berry-Palmer)
   b. Frontera (Emerson)
   c. Sangre de Toro (Emerson-Palmer)
5. Eight Miles High (Clark-McGuinn-Crosby)
6. Runaway (Berry)
7. You Do Or You Don't (Berry)
8. On My Way Home (Emerson)

★★

The band called 3, formed by Carl Palmer, Keith Emerson, and California singer-guitarist-bassist-songwriter Robert Berry after a brief (and unsuccessful) ELP reunion, was, in Emerson's words, "an outgoing attempt to have *the* hit single"; he said elsewhere it was an effort "to treat pop music as the art form that it is." The problem is that the material, much of it by Berry, mines an North American stadium rock style that had peaked out years before, and simply lacks any sense of a vital spark. Emerson's synth parts sound curiously anonymous, as does Palmer's drumming, which is additionally marred by its recourse to sterile electronics: listen especially to the turgid remake of the Byrds' "Eight Miles High." The one memorable track is Emerson's driving "Desde la Vida" suite, comparable in style and quality to the best material of *Emerson, Lake and Powell*.

[Note: from this point on in the ELP discography, the medium given is CD rather than LP]

The Atlantic Years
Atlantic CD 7567-82403-2 (U.S., May 1992)
Compilation of material recorded 1970–78

CD 1:
  1. Knife-Edge
  2. Take a Pebble
  3. Lucky Man
  4. Tank
  5. Tarkus
  6. Excerpts from *Pictures at an Exhibition* [Promenade/The Hut of Baba Yaga/The Curse of Baba Yaga/The Hut of Baba Yaga/The Great Gates of Kiev]
  7. The Endless Enigma, part one/Fugue/The Endless Enigma, part two

CD 2:
  8. From the Beginning
  9. Karn Evil 9 [1st, 2nd, and 3rd Impressions]
  10. Jerusalem
  11. Still . . . You Turn Me On
  12. Toccata
  13. Fanfare for the Common Man (special edit)
  14. Pirates
  15. I Believe in Father Christmas (original single version)
  16. Honky Tonk Train Blues
  17. Canario

★★★★¹/₂

The Atlantic Years, which unfortunately was only available for a year and a half (mid 1992 through late 1993), remains the definitive ELP collection; of all the box sets and "Best of" collections, it offers the most representative and tightly focused cross section of their best music of 1970–78. As one might expect, it's the 1970–74 period that's most fully represented, but their best music of the late seventies is here, too; indeed, if I was forced to pick the most vital two and a half hours of ELP's music of the seventies for a two-CD set, my track list would look a lot like this. This set was also important at the time of its release for being the first chance ELP fans had to hear digitally remastered versions of the band's seventies output.

Black Moon
Victory CD 828-318-2 (U.K., June 1992)
Victory CD 383-480-003 (U.S., June 1992)
Recorded 1991 at Marcus Studios, London, U.K. and Front Page Recorders, Redondo Beach, California
#78 U.S.

  1. Black Moon (Emerson-Lake-Palmer)
  2. Paper Blood (Emerson-Lake-Palmer)
  3. Affairs of the Heart (Lake)

 4. Romeo and Juliet (Prokofiev)
 5. Farewell to Arms (Emerson-Lake)
 6. Changing States (Emerson)
 7. Burning Bridges (Mancina)
 8. Close to Home (Emerson)
 9. Better Days (Emerson-Lake)
10. Footprints in the Snow (Lake)
11. A Blade of Grass (Emerson) [Japanese release bonus track]

★★★

There is no question that *Black Moon* is the product of a band that is serious about genuinely *reforming* itself, and there are three areas in which the album must be commended. First, its terseness is admirable: only "Black Moon" and "Paper Blood" go on longer than their substance warrants. Second, one is impressed how much of a genuine collaboration the album represents: for instance, one is unsure whether Emerson or Lake was the primary musical influence behind "Black Moon," "Paper Blood," or "Farewell to Arms." Third, while *Black Moon* sounds like an ELP album, it also sounds like a product of the nineties, thanks to the sympathetic production of Mark Mancina. Nonetheless, the material here seldom measures up to the cream of their seventies output, and it's not just because the band has simplified their harmonic, metric and structural approaches; by and large the *Black Moon* material lacks the rhythmic drive and sense of momentum that characterized their earlier work, with the tracks that assay to be ponderous ("Black Moon," "Paper Blood," "Romeo and Juliet") tending to come off as turgid. (Here "Changing States," which fully recaptures the driving polyrhyhmic energy of their earlier work, is a notable exception.) While *Black Moon* is no masterpiece, it did manage to credibly retool the band's sound for the nineties, and it was coherent enough to lay a stylistic foundation that the band could proceed to build on and develop in future releases.

Live at the Royal Albert Hall
Victory 828 393-2 (U.K., January 1993)
Victory 383-480-011-2 (U.S., January 1993)
Recorded live at the Royal Albert Hall, London, October 26, 1992

 1. Karn Evil 9, 1st Impression, part 2
 2. Tarkus (Eruption/Stones of Years/Iconoclast)
 3. Knife-Edge
 4. Paper Blood
 5. Romeo and Juliet
 6. Creole Dance
 7. Still . . . You Turn Me On
 8. Lucky Man
 9. Black Moon
10. Pirates
11. Medley: Fanfare for the Common Man/America/Rondo

★★★¹/₂

Sonically, this may be the best live ELP album ever, with superb clarity, presence, and spatial separation of parts; certainly Keith Emerson's Hammond hadn't sounded this good in a live setting since *Pictures*. It's certainly a big improvement over *Works Live*, not only in terms of sound quality, but in terms of the higher energy level of the band's playing. My main caveat, aside from the pervasive hoarseness of Greg Lake's voice (which one can live with) concerns the set list: there's too many short tunes, too many solo pieces, and too much time devoted to flashy but musically negligible items (particularly Emerson's ribbon controller and Hammond-riding escapades) As a result, on too much of this album it feels as if the band is just coasting along in second gear: only the truncated "Tarkus" and "Pirates" fully reveal what ELP were still capable of as a live band. (Here I would have suggested replacing the album's closing medley with the abbreviated *Pictures* arrangement the band played during this tour, which would have given the album added musical heft.) Set list aside, *Live at Royal Albert Hall* is a very credible live album.

The Return of the Manticore
Victory 828 459-2 (U.K., November 1993)
Victory 383 484 004-2 (U.S., November 1993)

CD 1:

1. Touch and Go
2. Hang on to a Dream
3. 21st Century Schizoid Man
4. Fire
5. Pictures at an Exhibition
   a. Promenade
   b. The Gnome
   c. Promenade
   d. The Sage
   e. The Hut of Baba Yaga
   f. The Great Gates of Kiev
6. I Believe in Father Christmas

[Tracks 1–6 recorded July and August, 1993 at Goodnight L.A. Studios, Van Nuys, California; Tim Pierce, additional guitars]

7. Introductory Fanfare/Peter Gunn
8. Tiger in a Spotlight
9. Toccata
10. Trilogy
11. Tank
12. Lucky Man

CD 2:

1. Tarkus
2. From the Beginning
3. Medley: Take a Pebble/Lucky Man/Piano Improvisations/Take a Pebble conclusion
4. Knife-Edge
5. Paper Blood
6. Hoedown
7. Rondo
   [previously unreleased; recorded live at the London Lyceum, December 9, 1970]

CD 3:

1. The Barbarian
2. Still . . . You Turn Me On
3. The Endless Enigma
4. C'est la vie
5. The Enemy God Dances with the Black Spirits
6. Bo Diddley (Emerson/Lake/Palmer)
   [previously unreleased; recorded at the Manticore Cinema, April 1975]
7. Bitches Crystal
8. A Time and a Place
9. Living Sin
10. Karn Evil 9 [1st, 2nd, and 3rd Impressions]
11. Honky Tonk Train Blues

CD 4:

1. Jerusalem
2. Fanfare for the Common Man
3. Black Moon
4. Watching Over You
5. Piano Concerto no. 1, 3rd movement
6. For You
7. Prelude and Fugue (Gulda)
   [previously unreleased; recorded October 1971]
8. Memoirs of an Officer and a Gentleman

9. Pirates
10. Affairs of the Heart

★★¹/₂

It should be understood that the relatively low rating of this retrospective box set does-n't reflect the quality of the music per se (after all, it does contain "Tarkus," "The Endless Enigma," "Karn Evil 9," "Toccata," and "Pirates"), but rather the package's conception and presentation. Simply put, this box set, which is supposed to make the strongest pos-sible argument for the centrality of ELP's output to rock music history by compellingly pre-senting a representative cross-section of the band's career, is a bit of a letdown. The six specially recorded tracks on disc one are certainly a disappointment; producer Keith Olsen shows a remarkably limited understanding of what made ELP such a distinctive and pow-erful band during their heyday, and the newly recorded tracks prefigure the disastrous misproduction that mars *In the Hot Seat*. Unfortunately, the set is a bit of a letdown in other areas as well. Considering the four CDs contain a total of four and three quarters hours of music, it's rather incredible that there are only three previously unreleased tracks from the seventies, totaling twenty-two minutes. The tracks of the box set are not arranged chronologically, or with any other discernible guiding principle; while the book-let has some nice photographs, Chris Welch's liner notes are somewhat perfunctory. It's a bit annoying that the individual sections of the long suites ("Karn Evil 9," "Memoirs of an Officer and a Gentleman," "The Endless Enigma") are not given individual tracks; if you want to go directly to the 2nd Impression of "Karn Evil 9," for instance, you're out of luck. The biggest problem with *The Return of the Manticore*, however, is that serious ELP fans already had this music, except for the newly recorded material and the three previously unreleased tracks, which most felt did not justify the considerable expense of the box set. For the casual fan, this was simply too much music, organized too incoherently; someone who wanted to be quickly and directly walked through the essential ELP output was far better served by the chronologically arranged two-CD set *The Atlantic Years*. One of the few bright spots of *ROTM* is the inclusion of an alternate mix of "Pirates" that is much more vivid than the long-familiar version from *Works I*.

In the Hot Seat
Victory 828 554-2 (U.K., September 1994)
Victory 383-480-034 (U.S., October 1994)
Recorded between Fall 1993 and Spring 1994 at Goodnight L.A. Studios, Van Nuys, California; Tim Pierce, additional guitars

1. Hand of Truth (Emerson-Lake)
2. Daddy (Lake)
3. One By One (Emerson-Lake-Olsen)
4. Heart On Ice (Lake-Olsen)
5. Thin Line (Wray-Olsen-Emerson)
6. Man in the Long Black Coat (Dylan)
7. Change (Wray-Emerson-Olsen)
8. Give Me a Reason to Stay (Diamond-Lorber)
9. Gone Too Soon (Lake-Wray-Wechsler)
10. Street War (Emerson-Lake)
11. Pictures at an Exhibition (Musorgsky-Emerson-Lake-Palmer)
    [1993 *Return of the Manticore* recording]
12. Hammer It Out (Emerson) [Japanese release bonus track]

★★

In the Hot Seat holds the dubious distinction of being the first, and only, studio album by ELP that did not break the American Top 200, and for years a somewhat perverse pastime of long-time ELP fans is debating whether *Love Beach* or *In the Hot Seat* is the band's biggest flop. There is nothing on *In the Hot Seat* anywhere near as embarrassing as the first few tracks of *Love Beach*, which remains the nadir of ELP's output; on the other hand, there's nothing on *In the Hot Seat* as ambitious as "Memoirs of an Officer and a Gentleman." *In the Hot Seat* contains three memorable songs ("Hand of Truth," "Man in the Long Black Coat," and "Street War") and one song ("One By One") that's ambitious, interesting, but flawed; the other songs are either pleasant, well-crafted, but thin in musical substance, or maudlin, bathetic, and best forgotten. In sum, the best songs of *In the Hot Seat* compare favorably enough with the *Black Moon* material, but the former album is far less consistent than the latter, and lacks its sense of team play. Carl Palmer's drumming never sounded this anonymous on an ELP album before, and while the relative lack of virtuoso keyboard parts is fully understandable, given the condition of Emerson's right hand at this time, the thin, monochrome synth patches are harder to explain: producer Keith Olsen, who seems to have never understood what ELP were all about, may have seriously hurt the final product through his incomprehension. What's most frustrating about *In the Hot Seat* is that it's not hard to imagine that without Emerson's hand problem, Lake's vocal difficulties (navigated surprisingly well here), and with sympathetic production, this could have been a much better album: in its best songs, one can hear the band continuing to explore and develop some of the ideas and directions posited on *Black Moon*.

I Believe in Father Christmas EP
Rhino R2 72242 (U.S., November 1995)
Compilation of ELP "Christmas" music

1. I Believe in Father Christmas
   [Greg Lake's November 1975 single version]
2. Troika from *Lieutenant Kije Suite* (Prokofiev)
   [from 1995 re-release of Keith Emerson's *Christmas Album*]
3. Humbug (Lake-Sinfield)
   [B side of Lake's 1975 single "I Believe in Father Christmas"]
4. I Believe in Father Christmas
   [ELP's *Works II* version]
5. Nutrocker
   [from *Pictures at an Exhibition*]
[no rating—specialty item]

To inaugurate their coming rerelease of ELP's back catalog, in November 1995 Rhino released this curious five-track EP containing Greg Lake's 1975 single "I Believe in Father Christmas" and its B side, "Humbug"; ELP's *Works II* version of "Father Christmas"; "Troika," from the 1995 Sundown Records rerelease of Keith Emerson's *Christmas Album*; and "Nutrocker" from *Pictures*. Although intended as a limited edition, the EP was successful enough that for a number of years after is original release date Rhino made the EP available during the Christmas season.

Live at the Isle of Wight Festival
Manticore M-CD101 (U.S., Fall 1997)
Recorded live at the Isle of Wight Festival, U.K., August 29, 1970

1. The Barbarian
2. Take a Pebble (includes "Tank")
3. Pictures at an Exhibition
4. Rondo
5. Nutrocker
6. Bonus Track (Emerson, Lake and Palmer discuss the 1970 Isle of Wight Festival)
★★

Many ELP fans were amazed when, in 1997, the premiere release of the revived Manticore Record label was *Emerson, Lake and Palmer Live at the Isle of Wight Festival*; few people were aware that ELP's segment had been taped, as Murray Lerner's sprawling documentary hardly features them at all. Recorded directly off the soundboard, it's an excruciatingly honest document that shows a young band in the midst of growing pains. The sound is raw, not the polished, sleek sound that ELP was to perfect in less than a year; not only does the playing lack the characteristic tightness that later characterized ELP, it occasionally crosses the line from loose to downright sloppy. Nonetheless, at some point one senses the crowd really getting caught up in the music, and by the end of the primitive arrangement of *Pictures* presented here, when Emerson and Lake detonate a pair of eight-hundred-pound antique cannons (the CD doesn't capture the sonic effect very well), the crowd roars in approval: clearly, even in this raw and primitive state the newness of ELP's sound strikes a chord for the hippies in attendance on that long-ago summer day. I suspect that for most of us, however, it will be impossible to hear this performance the way the audience heard it in 1970, and what one chiefly emerges with is a greater appreciation for what an amazingly tight, well-oiled machine the band had become a scant six months later when they recorded the Newcastle City Hall performance of *Pictures* that features on their third album. *Live at the Isle of Wight* is thus valuable chiefly as an important historical document.

King Biscuit Flower Hour: Emerson, Lake and Palmer
King Biscuit Flower Hour Records 70710-88025-2 (U.S., August 1997)
Tracks 1–10 (CD 1) recorded live at Wheeling, West Virginia, November 25, 1977; tracks 11–14 (CD 1) and 1 (CD 2) recorded live at Tulsa, Oklahoma, March 7, 1974

CD 1:
 1. Peter Gunn
 2. Tiger in a Spotlight
 3. C'est la vie
 4. Piano Improvisations [Piano Concerto no. 1, 1st movement, arranged for solo piano]
 5. Maple Leaf Rag
 6. Drum Solo
 7. The Enemy God Dances with the Black Spirits
 8. Watching Over You
 9. Pirates
10. Fanfare for the Common Man
11. Hoedown
12. Still . . . You Turn Me On
13. Lucky Man
14. Piano Improvisations

CD 2:
 1. Karn Evil 9 [1st, 2nd, and 3rd Impressions, complete]
 2. CD-ROM contains numerous still images, three interview clips [from *Video Biography*], and live performances of "From the Beginning," "Lucky Man," and "Paper Blood" [from *Live at the Royal Albert Hall* video, October 2, 1992, performance]

★★★¹/₂

For some years (until the release of *Manticore Vaults Volume 2*) the first ten tracks gave the clearest picture to date of what ELP's live show was all about during the trio segment of the *Works* tour. Previously unavailable live tracks include an arrangement of the first movement of Emerson's Piano Concerto for solo piano, and, finally, a *Works*-era performance of "Pirates"! While the keyboard parts of "Pirates," realized exclusively on the Yamaha GX-1, sound perilously thin in some places (this was a problem Emerson did not fix until the Emerson, Lake and Powell arrangement of 1986), it's nice to finally fully hear Lake's and Palmer's complex backing parts, which were always partly buried by the orchestra in the *Works*-era orchestral performances. Tracks 11–14 on disc one, and track 1 on disc two, capture a March 7, 1974, performance at Tulsa, Oklahoma. The arrangements are extremely similar to the February 10, 1974, Anaheim performance captured on *Welcome Back My Friends*, but the recording quality is actually marginally better; the high point is without a doubt the staggering performance of "Karn Evil 9" (here presented in its entirety), where Lake's intricate bass lines are finally completely audible. The rest of disc two is a CD-ROM containing numerous still images, three interview clips already available on the ELP Video Biography, and performances of "From the Beginning," "Lucky Man," and "Paper Blood" (from the *Live at the Royal Albert Hall* video). If I have a criticism of this package, it's that (a) the CD-ROM material seems largely redundant, and (b) the inclusion of material from '74, '77, and '92 causes a certain loss of focus. I would have suggested scotching the CD-ROM and either (a) including the complete Wheeling show or (b) including more of the Tulsa show.

Emerson, Lake and Palmer Live in Poland
Metal Mind Records PROG CD 0060 (Austria and Poland, Fall 1997)
Recorded live June 22, 1997, at Katowice, Poland

1. Welcome Back [Karn Evil 9, 1st Impression, part 2]
2. Touch and Go
3. From the Beginning
4. Knife-Edge
5. Bitches Crystal
6. Piano Solo [Creole Dance/Honky Tonk Train Blues]
7. Take a Pebble
8. Lucky Man
9. Tarkus [Eruption/Stones of Years/Iconoclas/Mass]/Pictures at an Exhibition [The Hut of Baba Yaga/The Great Gates of Kiev]
10. Fanfare for the Common Man/Rondo

★★¹/₂

Live in Poland was released (in Poland and Austria only) as a favor to a Polish promoter who lost a substantial sum of money promoting an ELP show in Poland. It was a noble gesture; unfortunately, one can entertain some fairly serious reservations about the album. Emerson's Hammond C-3 never sounded this thin and flimsy before, and too many of the synth patches are bland and generic sounding. The set list is often less than bracing, and the album's sonic values, while adequate, are by no means exceptional. Indeed, the sonic values of *Live at the Royal Albert Hall* are so much better that the advantages of *Live in Poland* (Lake's indisputably stronger voice) pale by comparison. High points of *Live in Poland* include superb performances of "Bitches Crystal" and "Take a Pebble" and some energetic playing during the *Tarkus-Pictures* medley. Low points include the ghastly arrangement of "Karn Evil 9, 1st Impression, part 2" and the epic sprawl of "Rondo."

Then and Now
Eagle Entertainment 1001-2 (U.S., November 1998)
Tracks 1–3 of disc 1 recorded live April 6, 1974, at Cal Jam, Ontario, California; tracks 4 and 5 of disc 1 recorded during ELP's 1998 tour; track 6 of disc 1 and all of disc 2 recorded live at various locations during ELP's 1997 tour

CD 1:

THEN—CAL JAM '74
1. Toccata
2. Take a Pebble Medley
   [Still . . . You Turn Me On/Lucky Man/Piano Improvisations/Take a Pebble]
3. Karn Evil 9, 1st Impression, part 2; Karn Evil 9, 3rd Impression

NOW—TOUR '97/'98
4. A Time and a Place
5. Piano Concerto no. 1, 3rd movement
6. From the Beginning

CD 2:

NOW—TOUR '97/'98 (continued)
1. Karn Evil 9, 1st Impression, part 2
2. Tiger in a Spotlight
3. Hoedown
4. Touch and Go
5. Knife-Edge
6. Bitches Crystal
7. Honky Tonk Train Blues
8. Take a Pebble
9. Lucky Man
10. Fanfare for the Common Man/Rondo
11. 21st Century Schizoid Man/America

★★★

Like a certain other ELP album of a quarter century earlier, this album uses an (uncredited) H. R. Giger cover illustration; unlike that album, however, the contents of this album do not measure up to the apocalyptic cover art. To the contrary, the biggest strength of *Then and Now* may be its lavish packaging: there's eight pages chock full of photos of the band members, both singly and together, at various stages of their careers, and some excellent liner notes by Bruce Pilato. The "Then" segment consists of roughly forty minutes of music from their legendary Cal Jam '74 performance: while the performances are of stunningly high quality, the arrangements are similar to those of *Welcome Back My Friends*, the sonic quality not as good, and what's presented here is not even ELP's entire Cal Jam set. The final thirteen minutes of the first CD, and the entirety of the second CD (about seventy-two minutes of music) comprise the "Now" section of *Then and Now*, and covers much of the same ground as *Live in Poland*. At least the "Now" material doesn't suffer from the indifferent sonic values of *Live in Poland*, featuring a full, vivid sound; of course, this doesn't solve the other problems that were noted in reference to the *Live in Poland* material. One also misses the flow of a real show that *Live in Poland* captures, as the "Now" selections of *Then and Now* were culled from a number of different shows. Since *Then and Now* makes no effort to document a single show, one wonders why the band didn't choose to include a performance of the magisterial "Tarkus" '98 instead of yet another live recording of the sprawling "Fanfare"/"Rondo" medley. In sum, *Then and Now* is only a marginally better investment than *Live in Poland*, which is frustrating, since with better track selections it could have clearly been the stronger of the two.

The Original Bootleg Series from the Manticore Vaults, Volume One
Sanctuary Records CMXBX309 (U.K., October 2001)

'Stomping Encore' Gaelic Park, New York, New York, September 1, 1971
The Stratasphere vs. The Spectre (CMDD311)

CD 1:
1. The Barbarian
2. Take a Pebble
3. Tarkus

CD 2:
1. Knife-Edge
2. Rondo [includes drum solo]
3. Piano Interlude [an early version of the "Endless Enigma" fugue for solo piano]
4. Hoedown

Louisville Town Hall, Louisville, Kentucky, April 1, 1972
The Iridescent Concubine (CMDD313)

CD 1:
1. Hoedown
2. Tarkus
3. Take a Pebble
4. Lucky Man
5. Piano Improvisations/Take a Pebble conclusion

CD 2:
1. Abaddon's Bolero
2. Pictures at an Exhibition
   (Promenade/The Gnome/Promenade/Hut of Baba Yaga/Curse of Baba Yaga/Hut of Baba Yaga/The Great Gates of Kiev)
3. Nutrocker
4. Rondo [includes drum solo]

Long Beach Arena, Long Beach, California, July 28, 1972
Celestial Doggie: The Lobster Quadrille

CD 1:
1. Tarkus
2. The Endless Enigma, part one/Fugue/The Endless Enigma, part two
3. The Sheriff

4.Take a Pebble/Lucky Man

CD 2:
1. Take a Pebble reprise [includes Piano Improvisations]
2. Pictures at an Exhibition
   (Promenade/The Hut of Baba Yaga/The Curse of Baba Yaga/The Great Gates of Kiev)
3. Hoedown
4. Grand Finale (Rondo/drum solo)

Saratoga Performing Arts Center, Saratoga Springs, New York, August 13, 1972
Iconoclastic Madness

CD 1:
1. Hoedown
2. Tarkus
3. The Endless Enigma, part one/Fugue/The Endless Enigma, part two
4. The Sheriff
5. Take a Pebble/Lucky Man/Piano Improvisations/Take a Pebble (conclusion)
6. Pictures at an Exhibition
   (Promenade/The Hut of Baba Yaga/The Curse of Baba Yaga/The Hut of Baba Yaga/The Great Gates of Kiev)

✶✶✶

Two general observations about the entire *Manticore Vaults* series. First, the sets consist of exactly what the titles suggest—bootlegs—that is, unauthorized recordings that were almost always made clandestinely, usually with inexpensive analog equipment under difficult conditions. Yes, it is true that occasionally an acoustically marvelous bootleg surfaces (usually one that was stolen from the soundboard by unauthorized persons)—but none of the four volume 1 shows are in that category, and audiophiles need not apply. (Of the four, the Saratoga Springs show is probably the best sonically: it's roughly equal to the sound quality of the Ontario Jam Show on *Now and Then*, which isn't saying very much.) Second, these recordings will for the most part not appeal to the casual listener: they will mostly be appreciated by longtime, hardcore ELP fans with a working knowledge of the band's repertoire who are interested in the development of the band's set lists—and changes in performances of individual pieces—over time. If one is willing to overlook these two limitations, there is much to enjoy here.

The earliest of the four shows represented here, *The Stratasphere vs. The Spectre*, is in some ways the most pleasant surprise, as of the four shows in volume 1 it's the most different from any of the band's authorized live recordings. Parts of it hearken back to the December 1970 Lyceum show immortalized on *Rock and Roll Your Eyes*, including "The Barbarian" and "Knife-Edge" (both of which were soon dropped from ELP's live show) and the "Rondo"/drum solo show-ender. Unlike the Lyceum show, however, there's a complete "Tarkus" that's the tersest and the closest to the studio version of the four performances in this volume—the instrumental movements aren't blindingly fast yet, and even given the relatively low-fi sound here, one can hear every note played by all three musicians. The encore is particularly interesting—Emerson plays a solo performance of the "Endless Enigma" fugue on piano, and then the band immediately launch into a rendition of "Hoedown" which differs in some interesting ways from the version they recorded two months later for *Trilogy*. For me, though, the highlight of this show is the "Take a Pebble" segment, which falls somewhere in between the more literal 12-9-70 Lyceum reading and the later, more "medleyized" version (where the beginning and end of "Take a Pebble" were separated by Lake's "Lucky Man" and Emerson's "Piano Improvisations"). Highlights include a beautiful acoustic guitar sequence by Lake (4:49–5:11) which can be heard on no other ELP recording and an amazing, almost Steve Howe–like series of acoustic guitar runs from 6:37 that make one desperately wish Lake had developed his acoustic guitar abilities more systematically; some stunning, boplike sixteenth-note runs over a rolling bass pattern by Emerson (from 9:20); and from 12:13 to 12:53, an inspired bop arrangement of part of the opening section of "Tank" for full band, including the only live performance I've ever heard of the daunting keyboard-bass call and response. The entire 19:10 "Take a Pebble" sequence, however, is full of wonderful little surprises, and demonstrates what a spontaneous (and subtle) band ELP could be. This show also captures a slice of Emerson's dry humor; he thanks the crowd for buying the *Tarkus* LP and making the band "a little bit richer," and then stops halfway through his dissertation on their new epic, the "Tarkus" suite, and, in his best imitation of a dour professor, asks "now are ya listenin' or not?"

The other three shows represented here, although they all have their moments, don't convey quite the same sense of excitement. I suspect the reason is that by 1972, the band's live classics ("Tarkus," the "Take a Pebble" medley) were beginning to develop into the versions that most ELP fans are familiar with from *Welcome Back My Friends*, and it's hard not to hear these early performances as simply "less developed" specimens of works that were definitively "perfected" during the 1973-74 world tour. Certainly the 1972 "Aquatarkus" bears no comparison to the magnificent space rock raga of the 2-10-74 *Welcome Back* show; it's little more than a string of synthesizer bleeps, buzzes, and whirrs, momentarily enlivened by a interpolation of Grieg's "Hall of the Mountain King" which Emerson plays simultaneously on modular Moog and Minimoog. The "Rondo"/drum solo encore had become little more than a vehicle for interminable aural assault; the band is to be commended for dropping the number from the 1973-74 set list, and one wonders why they insisted on reviving it nearly verbatim in the early nineties. The "Piano Improvisations," while undoubtedly more polished in '74 than '71, were also less spontaneous as they gradually ossified into tight compositions with relatively little space for real improvisation; this process is already in evidence in the 1972 shows. The *Pictures* excerpts are beginning to sound facile in comparison to the great Newcastle Hall recording of 1971. The material that comes off best in the 1972 shows is without a doubt the new music from *Trilogy*. ELP fans can finally enjoy an authorized live recording of "The Endless Enigma"; you'll wonder why this epic, which comes across very well live, graced their set list for less than six months. "The Sheriff" works better here as an organ trio piece than it did in its piano-bass-drums arrangement familiar from *Welcome Back*. The "Abaddon's Bolero" performance from the Louisville Show (which is certainly the weakest of the four shows represented here in terms of sound quality) is a surprisingly successful trio performance in which the band "cheats" by using some prerecorded tracks which Carl Palmer accompanies wearing headphones. Of the *Trilogy* material, only "Hoedown" was to be improved on later; Emerson's Moog solo had become more tightly focused and melodically substantive by 1974.

In sum: while I wouldn't rate volume 1 of the *Manticore Vaults Bootleg Series* as essential listening, a serious fan who wants a detailed sonic history of the band's development as a live act between early 1971 (*Pictures*) and early 1974 (*Welcome Back*) will find much to appreciate here.

The Original Bootleg Series from the Manticore Vaults, Volume Two
Sanctuary Records CMXDX330 (U.K., October 2001)

Hammersmith Odeon, London, U.K., November 26, 1972
A Right Cordial Shocker (CMDD310)

CD 1:
1. Hoedown (start missing)
2. Tarkus
3. The Endless Enigma, part one/Fugue/The Endless Enigma, part two
4. At the Sign of the Swinging Cymbal
5. The Sheriff
6. Take a Pebble
7. Lucky Man

CD 2:
1. Piano Variations/Take a Pebble reprise
2. Pictures at an Exhibition
   (Promenade/The Hut of Baba Yaga/The Curse of Baba Yaga/The Hut of Baba Yaga/The Great Gates of Kiev)
3. Nutrocker/Rondo/drum solo/Rondo reprise

Henry Lewit Arena, Wichita, Kansas, March 26, 1974
Waiting for the Corduroy Purpose (CMDD315)

CD 1:
1. Hoedown (start missing)
2. Jerusalem
3. Toccata
4. Tarkus
5. Benny the Bouncer
6. Jeremy Bender
7. Take a Pebble
8. Still . . . You Turn Me On
9. Lucky Man

CD 2:
1. Piano Improvisations
2. Take a Pebble (conclusion)
3. Karn Evil 9, 1st Impression [includes drum solo]
4. Karn Evil 9, 2nd Impression
5. Karn Evil 9, 3rd Impression

Rich Stadium, Buffalo, New York, July 26, 1974
My Darling Nemesis . . . The Illuminati (CMDD316)

CD 1:
1. Hoedown
2. Jerusalem
3. Toccata
4. Tarkus
5. Take a Pebble
6. Still . . . You Turn Me On
7. Lucky Man
8. Piano Improvisation

CD 2:
1. Take a Pebble (conclusion)
2. Karn Evil 9, 1st Impression [includes drum solo]
3. Karn Evil 9, 2nd Impression (opening sections missing)
4. Karn Evil 9, 3rd Impression
5. Pictures at an Exhibition
   (Promenade/The Hut of Baba Yaga/electronic improv/The Curse of Baba Yaga/The Hut
   of Baba Yaga/The Great Gates of Kiev)

New Haven Civic Center, New Haven, Connecticut, November 30, 1977
Strangely Beneficient (CMDD317)

CD 1:
1. Peter Gunn (start missing)
2. Hoedown
3. Tarkus
   (Eruption/Stones of Years/Iconoclast/Mass/Aquatarkus)
4. Take a Pebble
5. Piano Concerto, 1st movement
6. Maple Leaf Rag
7. Take a Pebble (conclusion)
8. C'est la vie
9. Lucky Man (end missing)

CD 2:
1. Karn Evil 9, 1st Impression, part two
2. Tiger in a Spotlight
3. Watching Over You
4. Nutrocker
5. Pirates
6. Fanfare for the Common Man/Rondo/Fanfare reprise

★★★$^{1}/_{2}$

The *Volume 2* bootlegs have two advantages over the *Volume 1* shows. First, the sound quality is, on the average, somewhat better, and second, the *Volume 2* shows capture ELP at the absolute height of their powers. On the other hand, unlike the *Volume 1* shows, the *Volume 2* material for the most part represents a segment of ELP's career that is already very well documented by a series of authorized live releases.

The one exception here is the November 26, 1972, show at London's Hammersmith Odeon. This recording was made near the end of ELP's British tour of late 1972, and indeed near the end of over eight months of touring promoting the *Trilogy* album: the band's performance of the 1972 set list peaked during the November-December British Tour, and therefore, of the four 1972 shows documented by the *Manticore Vaults* series, this one is the best. Since I discussed their Sheffield show of November 25 (a mere day earlier) in some detail in the text, I will not spend a lot of time here dissecting the particulars of this show, other than to note that at the Hammersmith they did not play *Pictures* in its entirety, as they had the night before, but merely a medley of the last five sections, probably because they played back-to-back shows this night. That small caveat aside, the British shows of November 1972 capture ELP's first career peak, which, in my view, they surpassed only once—during the world tour of 1973-74. The sound quality of the Hammersmith show is fair—that is, roughly equivalent to the better-sounding shows of *Manticore Vaults Volume 1*.

The 1973-74 world tour is represented by two shows in *Volume 2*: March 26, 1974, at Wichita, Kansas, and July 26, 1974 at Buffalo, New York. As one might expect, the level of musicianship is never less than superb in either. Nonetheless, in light of the fact that this phase of ELP's career, amazing as it is, is already represented by three authorized releases—*Welcome Back My Friends* (Anaheim, February 10), *King Biscuit* (Tulsa, March 7), and *Then and Now* (Cal Jam, April 6)—it can legitimately be argued that two more shows is overkill, especially given the fact that their sound quality isn't noticeably better than Hammersmith 11-26-72. Of the two shows, the Wichita performance of 3-26-74 seems the most unnecessary; the arrangements are very similar to those of the three authorized releases mentioned above, and about the only new element here is the first authorized release of a live "Benny the Bouncer" performance, which replaces "The Sheriff" in the set list.

The Buffalo performance of July 26 is more interesting for two reasons. First, this show was recorded towards the end of the 1973-74 world tour, so some of the arrangements had begun to change: one especially notes Emerson's liberal use of echoplex on some of his acoustic piano passages in "Take a Pebble" and "Piano Improvisations" to produce spacey reverberation of piano arpeggios that's somewhat reminiscent of Terry Riley's electronic organ work. Second, this show finally gives us an authorized release of the *Pictures* encore that ELP sometimes played during the 1973-74 World Tour. The biggest surprise is the lengthy electronic improv placed between "The Hut of Baba Yaga" and "The Curse of Baba Yaga," featuring Emerson's Moog (again liberally treated with echoplex), Palmer's synthesized percussion, and Lake's bass guitar; the resulting music parallels the shadowy, menacing atonal improvisations that King Crimson were making a specialty of in their contemporaneous live performances. (Unfortunately, during the segment of "The Great Gates of Kiev" that formerly had been devoted to Hammond feedback, Emerson repeats many of the Moog licks from the earlier band improv; as I've said many times, concision and self-discipline were never one of this band's strengths.) The Buffalo show is a valid inclusion, but I would have recommended replacing the Wichita show with a show from the band's early 1973 European tour, which featured earlier versions of tracks later recorded for *Brain Salad Surgery* that remain unavailable in any authorized release.

Finally, there's the New Haven performance of November 30, 1977. Unlike any of the other shows in either *Volume 1* or *Volume 2* of the *Manticore Vaults* series, this recording is very close to the sonic quality of the band's authorized live releases—I rate it at least as good as *In Concert/Works Live* on this count—and it's the best document to date of what ELP were about during the trio portion of the *Works* tour. (I've been told that the master tapes of this particular bootleg were stolen directly off the soundboard after the show, but I don't know if that's true or not.) I discuss this show at some length in the text, so I'll simply add that I consider "Tarkus" (especially the "Aquatarkus" segment), which isn't included in any of the previous authorized live releases of the *Works* era (*In*

Concert/Works Live, *King Biscuit*, the *Works Orchestral Tour* video) to be an especially valuable addendum to the ELP recorded oeuvre. For some reason, the band's second encore number of the show, "Show Me the Way to Go Home," isn't included here.

The Original Bootleg Series from the Manticore Vaults, Volume Three
Sanctuary Records CMYBX524 (U.K., May 2002)

Anaheim Convention Center, Anaheim, California, February 10, 1974; Wheeling Coliseum, Wheeling, West Virginia, November 25, 1977 (CMYBX524/1)

CD 1:
1. Hoedown (Anaheim)
2. Tiger in a Spotlight (Wheeling)
3. C'est la vie (Wheeling)
4. Still . . . You Turn Me On (Anaheim)
5. Lucky Man (source unknown)
6. drum solo/The Enemy God (end missing) (Wheeling)
7. Karn Evil 9, 1st Impression, part 1 (Anaheim)
8. Karn Evil 9, 1st Impression, part 2 (Anaheim)
9. Fanfare for the Common Man (Wheeling)
10. Take a Pebble (source unknown)
11. Pictures at an Exhibition (Anaheim?)
    (Promenade/The Hut of Baba Yaga/The Curse of Baba Yaga/The Hut of Baba Yaga/The Great Gates of Kiev [end missing])

Royal Albert Hall, London, U.K., October 2, 1992 (CMYBX524/2 & 3)

CD 1:
1. Tarkus
   (Eruption/Stones of Years/Iconoclast)
2. Knife-Edge
3. Paper Blood
4. Black Moon
5. Close to Home
6. Creole Dance
7. From the Beginning
8. Still . . . You Turn Me On
9. Lucky Man

CD 2:
1. Honky Tonk Train Blues
2. Romeo and Juliet
3. Pirates
4. Pictures at an Exhibition
   (Promenade/The Gnome/Promenade/The Hut of Baba Yaga/drum solo)
5. Fanfare for the Common Man/America/Rondo

Wiltern Theatre, Los Angeles, California, March 16 or 17, 1993

CD 1:
1. Karn Evil 9, 1st Impression, part 2
2. Eruption
3. Stones of Years
4. Iconoclast
5. Knife-Edge
6. Paper Blood
7. Black Moon
8. Close to Home
9. Creole Dance
10. Still . . . You Turn Me On
11. C'est la vie
12. Lucky Man
13. Honky Tonk Train Blues

14. Touch and Go
15. Pirates

CD 2:
 1. Hoedown
 2. Promenade
 3. The Gnome
 4. Promenade
 5. The Hut of Baba Yaga
 6. Drum Solo
 7. The Great Gates of Kiev
 8. Fanfare for the Common Man/America/Rondo

★★¹/₂

Compared to the first two volumes of *The Manticore Vaults* series, volume 3 is a bit of a cheat, costing more while delivering less, and less meaningful, music: in fact, it would be a downright swindle if it were not for one considerable saving grace, a complete March 16 or 17, 1993, show from LA's Wiltern Theatre. This show was from the final leg of the *Black Moon* tour, at which point the band's set list had expanded to just ten minutes shy of the two-hour mark, having added several items ("Touch and Go," "Hoedown," "C'est la vie") that weren't part of the 1992 shows. The sound quality, while not measuring up to *Live at the Royal Albert Hall*, is just as good as any of ELP's authorized live albums of the seventies, advances in digital technology having made the bootlegger's task much easier. The band performs very well: Lake's voice is actually stronger here than on the *Live at the Royal Hall* album, and for the most part Emerson's right hand affliction seems to be a thing of the future (although listen closely to "Hoedown" and see if you notice anything). The set list flows very nicely, and the show has a great energy: even the "Fanfare/America/Rondo" finale is tauter than usual, as Emerson fires off one clever quotation after another during "Rondo." Those in the know say that this is among the best shows ELP played during the entire *Black Moon* tour, and based on the recorded evidence here that's a plausible claim; this is certainly a worthy addition to ELP's live oeuvre.

Unfortunately, the two-CD Wiltern Theatre show is about the only worthwhile part of volume 3. The first set, one CD only, offers up a selection of bootlegs from Anaheim 2-10-74 (which most of us have known for decades as their authorized live album *Welcome Back My Friends*) and from Wheeling 11-25-77 (a show thoroughly chronicled on the *King Biscuit* album). In other words, it offers bootleg versions of material already available in sonically superior authorized releases. I suppose for extreme completists there might be some interest in comparing the house mix captured on the bootlegs with the board mix of the authorized releases, but that seems an extremely dubious reason to rerelease this material. The one consolation of the Anaheim/Wheeling CD is that we finally get the *Pictures* encore that was excluded from *Welcome Back My Friends*, albeit missing the final five minutes or so of "The Great Gates of Kiev."

The third proffering of *Volume 3*, a two-CD set of the band's Albert Hall show of October 2, 1992, is nearly as useless. Those familiar with the *Live at the Royal Albert Hall* video will realize that this is a bootleg of the same show the video chronicles, merely supplying the three tracks ("Black Moon," "Close to Home," "Still . . . You Turn Me On") excluded from the video. Those familiar with the authorized album *Live at the Royal Albert Hall* (recorded October 26, 1992) will find little difference in the details or quality of the 10-2 and 10-26 performances, other than the sonic quality of the authorized album is so glaringly superior.

While the liner notes of the first two volumes of the *Manticore Vaults* series, written by Martyn Hudson, are not bad, albeit not particularly revelatory, the liner notes of volume 3, by Paul Russell, are very amateurish. (Example: "*Tarkus* appears, all buzzing synths and squealing Hammond organ, this version shows that Emerson means business.") The track listings of volume 3 are a mess, containing numerous mistakes that I've done my best to correct above.

Emerson, Lake and Powell: The Sprocket Sessions
Manticore Records CD3008 (U.S., December 2003)
Recorded live in Sprocket Studio, London, U.K., Summer 1986

1. The Score
2. Learning to Fly
3. The Miracle
4. Knife-Edge
5. Tarkus [Eruption-Stones of Years-Iconoclast-Mass]
6. Pictures at an Exhibition [The Hut of Baba Yaga-The Great Gates of Kiev]
7. Lucky Man (excerpt)
8. Still . . . You Turn Me On
9. Love Blind
10. Mars, the Bringer of War
11. Touch and Go
12. Pirates

✷✷✷

Recorded live in London's Sprocket Studios during the summer of 1986 while the band were rehearsing for their upcoming North American tour, in many ways *The Sprocket Sessions* makes a more compelling case for Emerson, Lake and Powell's prowess as a live band than does *Live in Concert* (see below). Certainly the set list is more interesting: not only does this disc contain "Learning to Fly" and the "Tarkus"/"Pictures" medley, which were excluded from *Live in Concert*, it also includes a couple of tracks from *Emerson, Lake and Powell*, "The Miracle" and "Love Blind," that did not make the final set list. "The Miracle," which I believe is the finest track of *Emerson, Lake and Powell*, is particularly interesting: the track crackles with energy and Lake's performance is particularly riveting (he does an outstanding job handling the difficult voice/bass line rhythmic counterpoints), but Emerson's keyboard orchestrations are strangely monochrome, and one wonders if the song wasn't ultimately abandoned because Emerson was unable to arrive at a workable live keyboard orchestration that pleased him. The performances are better here than on *Live in Concert* and the overall mixes are better, although two weaknesses must be noted: the overall sound is not as spacious and open as on *Live in Concert*, and, as with that album, the bass lines are often mixed too loud relative to the keyboard parts. These weaknesses aside, if I were to choose just one of the two live Emerson, Lake and Powell albums, it would be this one, although the only way to get a fully rounded picture of what the band were like as a live performance entity is to get both.

Emerson, Lake and Powell Live in Concert
Manticore Records CD3009 (U.S., December 2003)
Recorded live in Lakeland, Florida, October 4, 1986

1. The Score
2. Touch and Go
3. Knife-Edge
4. Pirates
5. From the Beginning
6. Lucky Man
7. Fanfare for the Common Man
8. Mars, the Bringer of War
9. Karn Evil 9, 1st Impression, part two/America/Rondo

✷✷$\frac{1}{2}$

Emerson, Lake and Powell were an exceedingly strong live band. Their sound was enormous, a result of Cozy Powell's huge backbeats and Keith Emerson's MIDI'd Yamaha GX-1, which sounds much huger here than it did during his late-seventies work with ELP.

Unfortunately, this album does not make the strongest possible case for the band. The show was recorded for Westwood One radio on October 4, 1986 (not, as the liner notes incorrectly state, November 1986), and, as Cozy Powell later remarked, "It was a disaster gig, we played really badly and I hope that tape never comes out though no doubt it will." A lot of the problems involve the mix: important keyboard parts are radically under-mixed at key points (3:50 of "The Score," 1:55 of "Pirates"), and this is one of a very few ELP-related albums of which it can be said that the bass is consistently too loud relative to the keyboards. Part of the problem is that the album lacks several key numbers of ELP's typical set list, and therefore doesn't give a complete overview of what the band were about as a live act: there's no "Learning to Fly," no "Tarkus"/*Pictures* medley, and the solo piano set of Keith Emerson ("Dream Runner," "Creole Dance") as well as Greg Lake's solo set ("Watching Over You," "Still . . . You Turn Me On") are excised. Despite these not insubstantial weaknesses, the album is not without merit. Both "Fanfare for the Common Man" (here much more tightly focused and less sprawling than on any ELP live recording) and "Mars" (which is much more potent here than on the ELPowell studio album, where it is marred by too many keyboard overdubs) are extremely strong, and the playing is generally very good, even in the tracks like "The Score" and "Pirates" that are marred by some anomalies in the mix. In sum, *Emerson, Lake and Powell Live in Concert* has its moments; however, to get a totally rounded picture of the live ELPowell experience, one really needs *The Sprocket Sessions* in conjunction with this album.

Keith Emerson: Solo albums and movie soundtracks, 1980–

Inferno
Cinevox LP MDF 33/138 (Italy, February 1980)
Rerelease Cinevox CD MDF 306 (Italy, 1997)
Recorded in Nassau, Bahamas and Rome, Italy, 1979
Music by Keith Emerson; arranged by Keith Emerson and Godfrey Salmon; orchestrated and conducted by Godfrey Salmon. Keith Emerson, keyboards (all tracks); Frank Scully, drums, and Kendal Stubbs, bass, tracks 3, 13, and 15.

1. Inferno (Main Title Theme)
2. Rose's Descent into the Cellar
3. Taxi Ride (Rome)
4. The Library
5. Sarah in the Library Vaults
6. Bookbinder's Delight
7. Rose Leaves the Apartment
8. Rose Gets It
9. Elisa's Story
10. A Cat Attic Attack
11. Kazanian's Tarantella
12. Mark's Discovery
13. Mater Tenebrarum
14. Inferno Finale
15. Cigarettes, Ices, etc.
16. Inferno Outtakes Suite [1997 rerelease only]

★★★★½

Emerson's first movie score, a collaboration with Italian horrormeister Dario Argento, is a major achievement; it's the finest of his six movie scores, and probably his greatest solo album. *Inferno* served as a springboard for Emerson to explore a feverish, unsettling early-twentieth-century expressionistic style along the lines of the early music of Arnold Schoenberg or Alban Berg. This was new territory for Emerson and his fans: the results are never less than interesting, are often compelling, and are, at their best, stunning. Indeed, it can be argued that it is *Inferno*, not the Piano Concerto, that represents Emerson's greatest work in a straight "classical" idiom; the *Inferno* music is characterized by an emotional intensity, vividness of orchestration, brilliant sense of thematic transformation, and stylistic cohesion that far surpasses the Concerto. (Indeed, it was long rumored that *Inferno* cannibalized music intended for a second Piano Concerto; if so, this represents a regrettable loss.) The three rock numbers, though shorter and less imposing than the classical segments of the score, show a drive and sense of urgency that hearken back to early ELP. Essential, and one of the highlights of Emerson's career.

Nighthawks
Backstreet Records LP BSR 5196 (U.S., April 1981)
Rerelease Net Event CD A128022 (U.S., 2002)
Recorded in Nassau, Bahamas, and London, U.K., 1980
Music composed and performed by Keith Emerson; arrangements by Harry Betts; orchestra
on "Nighthawking" conducted by Godfrey Salmon. Keith Emerson, keyboards; Kendal
Stubbs, bass; Neil Symonette, drums; Frank Scully, percussion; Jerome Richardson, saxes;
Greg Bowen, lead trumpet; Tristan Fry, orchestral percussion.
#183 U.S.

1. Nighthawks (Main Title Theme)
2. Mean Stalkin'
3. The Bust
4. Nighthawking (Emerson/Mueller)
   [Paulette McWilliams, vocal]
5. The Chase
6. I'm a Man (Steve Winwood)
   [Keith Emerson, vocal]
7. The Chopper
8. Tramway
9. I'm Comin' In
10. Face to Face
11. The Flight of a Hawk

★★★

Perhaps Emerson's best shot at movie scoring stardom—*Nighthawks* starred Sylvester
Stallone, who was just reaching the zenith of his career in 1981—this score eschews
Inferno's classicism for a gritty, streetwise sound that draws heavily on early eighties funk,
and also forefronts menacing, atmospheric electronic passages. While the *Nighthawks*
score provides a fine musical backdrop for the movie, it doesn't hold up as an independent
musical experience the way *Inferno* does; it needs the visual cues to justify the repetitive
funk grooves, the lengthy, largely static passages of atmospheric keyboards, and the sudden juxtaposition of totally unrelated music. Indeed, beyond the rousing main title theme,
the score is somewhat lacking in memorable melodic material. Highlights include the ELPish
"The Chopper," with its heroic 5/4 episodes, "Nighthawking," with its furious piano solo
over a disco groove, and "I'm a Man," the old Steve Winwood song that features Emerson's
heavily processed vocals (which one can take or leave) and some fascinating textural keyboard parts which blend with bass and drums to create a throbbing polyrhythmic groove.

Honky
Bubble Records BLU 19608 (Italy, November 1981)
Rerelease Chord Records Chord 2 (U.K., April 1985)
Rerelease Gunslinger Records (U.S., 2000)
Recorded in Nassau, Bahamas, 1979-80
Keith Emerson, keyboards; Kendal Stubbs, bass; Neil Symonette, drums and percussion;
Frank Scully, drums and percussion (tracks 3 and 6 only); Dick Morrissey and Pete King,
saxes (track 7); Keith Emerson, Michael Hanna, Shelly Lightbourne, vocals (track 4); the
Kayla Lockhart Singers, vocals (track 10)

1. Hello Sailor Introduction (Emerson)/Bach Before the Mast (George Malcolm)
2. Hello Sailor (Emerson)
3. Salt Cay (Emerson)
4. Green Ice (Emerson)
5. Intro Juicing (Emerson)
6. Big Horn Breakdown (Billy Taylor)
7. Yancey Special (Meade Lux Lewis)
8. Rum-a-Ting (Emerson) [not on Chord rerelease]
9. Chic Charni (Emerson) [not on original Bubble Records release]
10. Jesus Loves Me (Emerson)

★★★¹⁄₂

For those wanting profound and challenging music along the lines of *Tarkus*, *Brain Salad Surgery*, and *Inferno*, *Honky* is bound to be a disappointment. However, it has a different set of strengths. No other Emerson album (including his work with the Nice and ELP) is less self-conscious or self-important. No other Emerson album is bathed with the same degree of sunny good cheer. And even if there are no major masterpieces here (although the "Bach Before the Mast"/"Hello Sailor" medley may fairly be called a minor one), there are no duds, either; the quality of the material, especially in terms of its performance, is uniformly high. *Honky* succeeds in creating the unique and distinctive tribute to African-American music that Emerson had sought, but never quite managed, to create in his *Works*-era solo output. It also undertook some respectful and promising explo rations of Caribbean musical idioms that nicely paralleled what fellow progsters Peter Gabriel and Patrick Moraz were contemporaneously doing with African and Brazilian styles, respectively.

Harmagedon
Canyon Records C28Y0044 (Japan, March 1983)
Rerelease Volcano Records CPC8-3003 (Japan 1998)
Recorded 1982 in Tokyo, Japan
#1 Japan
Keith Emerson, keyboards (tracks 2, 3, 4, 7, 9, 11, 12); Jun Aoyama, drums (2, 7, 12); Fujimaru Yoshino, guitar (12); Rosemary Butler, vocal (7)

1. Harmagedon Prelude (Nozomu Aoki)
2. Theme of Floi (Emerson)
3. Toccata and Fugue in D minor, BVW 565 (J. S. Bach, arrangement Emerson)
4. Psionic Princess (Aoki)
5. Joe and Michiko (Emerson)
6. Mission Revived (Aoki)
7. Children of the Light (Emerson/Tony Allen)
8. The Devil's Angry Growl (Aoki)
9. Sonny's Skate State (Emerson)
10. A Far Off Time (Aoki)
11. Zamedy Stomp (Emerson)
12. Challenge of the Psionic Fighters (Emerson)

★★★

Like his earlier soundtracks, Emerson's *Harmagedon* music manages to establish its own distinctive identity, evoking the impressionistic, richly layered, multihued electronic orchestrations of Jean-Michel Jarre or Vangelis; however, Emerson eschews the throbbing bass sequences of these musicians in favor of real drums and electronically realized "bass guitar" parts, and much of his *Harmagedon* music is characterized by the clearly etched melodies and strongly marked rhythms that are Emerson hallmarks. The final two tracks of the soundtrack, "Zamedy Stomp" and "Challenge of the Psionic Fighters," are driving rock marches that are more than casually reminiscent of ELP. Emerson's music for *Harmagedon* is quite good, although there's not enough of it to build up a lot of intensity, and, unlike *Inferno* or *Nighthawks*, there are no thematic interconnections between the tracks. Besides Emerson's six tracks, there's an arrangement of J. S. Bach's Toccata and Fugue in D minor, BVW 565, performed by Emerson, and five tracks by Nozomo Aoki— these tend toward a lounge jazz and/or kitschy electronic classical style. [Note: the rating given above applies to the entire album, not just Emerson's material.]

Best Revenge
Chord Records Chord 1 (U.K., April 1985)
Rerelease (with *Murderock*) on Chord Records Chord CD Coll 3 (U.K., 1989)
Currently out of print
Recorded 1982
Music by Keith Emerson. Keith Emerson, keyboards; Aynsley Dunbar, drums and percussion.

1. Dream Runner
2. The Runner
3. Wha'dya Mean

4. Straight Between the Eyes
   [Levon Helm, vocal]
5. Orchestral Suite to Best Revenge
   [Orchestrated by John Coleman; National Philharmonic Orchestra conducted by John Coleman]
6. Playing for Keeps
   [Brad Delp, vocal]

★★★★

After *Inferno*, this is probably Emerson's best movie soundtrack. Stylistically, *Best Revenge* is more eclectic and less single-minded in its exploration of a specific idiom than Emerson's previous four albums: rock and classical styles are sometimes alternated, and at other times fused with great facility. The opening track, the delicate "Dream Runner" for solo piano (with subtle string synth backing), is perhaps the most beautiful piece of music that Emerson ever composed. The soundtrack's real center of gravity is the fifteen-and-a-half-minute *Best Revenge* orchestral suite, which in many ways approaches the *Inferno* suites in quality, if not scope. Emerson is helped along the way by stand-out guest performances from drummer Aynsley Dunbar and by Boston's lead vocalist Brad Delp, who contributes a compelling vocal to the closing track, the movie's title track, "Playing for Keeps." Only one track, the ghastly "Straight Between the Eyes," is less than successful.

Murderock
Bubble Records BLULP 1819 (Italy, May 1984)
Chord Records Chord 4 (U.K., April 1985)
Rerelease Cinevox CD MDF 345 (Italy, 2001)
Recorded 1983 in London, U.K., and Rome, Italy
Music by Keith Emerson. Keith Emerson, keyboards; Mike Sheppard, bass and lead guitars; Tom Nichol, drums (1–4); Derek Wilson, drums (5–15); Doreen Chanter, lead vocal (2–4); Mike Sheppard, backing vocal (4).

1. Murderock
2. Tonight is Your Night
3. Streets to Blame
4. Not so Innocent
5. Prelude to Candice
6. Don't Go in the Shower
7. Coffee Time
8. Candice
9. New York Dash
10. Tonight is Not Your Night
11. The Spillone
12. Murderock, part 1*
13. Murderock, part 2*
14. Murderock, part 3*
15. Murderock, part 4*

[*Tracks 12–15 on 2001 Cinevox rerelease only]

★★½

Like *Best Revenge*, the *Murderock* LP is quite short; at not quite half an hour, it's even shorter, in fact, than *Best Revenge*. Unlike *Best Revenge*, a lot of the music here is rather pedestrian; while it serves the film well enough, it's probably the least substantive of Emerson's five film scores of the 1980–85 period. The problem is not that the music is bad—it isn't—it's that so much of it could have been composed by anybody. High points include the song "Not So Innocent," the pounding rhythms and slashing fanfare figurines of which anticipate "Desde la Vida"; the attractive solo piano piece "Prelude to Candice"; and the unique "New York Dash," whose urgently pressing rhythms and disjointed, icily dissonant fanfares recall French experimental progsters Magma. A 2001 rerelease adds four short, previously unreleased instrumental tracks of no major consequence.

The Christmas Album
Emerson Records/Virgin Music KEITH LP 1 (U.K., November 1988)
Rerelease Sundown Records BSM 1095D (U.S., 1995)
Rerelease Gunslinger Records (U.S., 1999)
Recorded in Sussex and London, U.K., 1988; additional tracks (1,7) recorded in Long Beach, California, 1995.
All arrangements by Keith Emerson. Keith Emerson, keyboards; Dudley Brooks, bass and lead guitars (1, 7); Greg Ellis, drums and percussion (1,7); Frank Scully, drums (11); Les Moir, bass (3); Mike Newborn, drum programming (7); Dave Bristow, drum programming (4); Mike Barnes, synth programming (4).

1. Troika [not on original 1988 release] (Prokofiev)
2. Variations on "O Little Town of Bethlehem" (Redner)
3. We Three Kings (Hopkins)
4. Snowman's Land (Emerson)
5. Aria from Bach's *Christmas Oratorio* (J. S. Bach)
6. Captain Starship Christmas [not on 1995 rerelease] (Emerson/Wright)
7. I Saw Three Ships (traditional)
8. Glorietta [not on original 1988 release] (Emerson)
9. Petite Litanies de Jesus (Groulez)
10. It Came Upon a Midnight Clear (Willis)
11. Silent Night (Gruber)

★★★½

One can make many of the same remarks about *The Christmas Album* as about *Honky*. If you're looking for challenging, epic material, look elsewhere. If you're looking for exceedingly well-crafted music that evinces very little pretension but loads of good cheer, *The Christmas Album* is a winner. The album features a mix of traditional Christmas songs and Emerson originals in a decisively electronic vein: in more than half the tracks the bass and drums are programmed. Considering the traditional nature of the source material, it's ironic that this is one of Emerson's most thoroughgoing electronic albums (only *Harmagedon* and *Iron Man* are rivals in this respect). Highlights include "Variations on 'Little Town of Bethlehem,'" which features some energetic boplike piano variations; "We Three Kings," which ends with a nice blues piano/funk bass break; and "It Came Upon a Midnight Clear," with its wonderful, stridelike digital harpsichord episodes. The final track, "Silent Night," the album's only nonelectronic track, revisits the black gospel territory of *Honky*'s "Jesus Loves Me" to excellent effect.

La Chiesa
Cinevox MD 33-192 (Italy, April 1989)
Rerelease Cinevox CD MDG 329 (Italy, 2001)
Recorded 1988 in Rome, Italy

1. Keith Emerson—The Church (Main Theme)
2. Goblin—La Chiesa
3. J. S. Bach—Prelude in B minor from *The Well-Tempered Clavier I*
   [Keith Emerson, synthesizers]
4. Goblin—Possessione
5. Keith Emerson—The Possession
6. Goblin—Lotte
7. Zooming on the Zoo—Go to Hell
8. Definitive Gaze—The Wire Blaze
9. Keith Emerson—The Church Revisited
10. Keith Emerson—The Church (single mix) [2001 rerelease only]
11. Goblin—La Chiesa (Suite) [2001 rerelease only]
12. Goblin—Suspence Chiesa 1 [2001 rerelease only]
13. Goblin—Suspence Chiesa 2 [2001 rerelease only]

★★★½

Another collaboration between Emerson and Dario Argento, the movie is awful, but the soundtrack, with a couple of glaring exceptions, is very good. Emerson contributes four tracks (five on the 2001 rerelease), all in a dark neobaroque idiom—the dominant timbre is that of a rumbling pipe organ—featuring lumbering chromatic themes and edgy cross-rhythms. While Emerson's tracks are quite good, they only constitute about thirteen minutes of music. The bulk of the soundtrack is contributed by the Italian progressive rock band Goblin, longtime Argento collaborators, and this music is very good as well: stylistically, it falls somewhere between seventies Italian instrumental prog and eighties electronic ambient of a particularly dark hue. There are also two dreadful pop songs—Zooming on the Zoo's evokes eighties Eurofunk (there's even some rapping), Definitive Gaze's eighties Seattle grunge—but these songs occupy seven minutes total, and can easily be skipped. [Note: the rating above applies to the entire album, not just Emerson's material.]

Changing States
AMP Records CD026 (U.K., February 1995)
Recorded 1989 in Burbank and Campbell, California
Keith Emerson, keyboards; Tim Pierce, guitars (2, 6, 8); Marc Bonilla, guitars (1, 4, 10); Jerry Watts, bass (2, 5, 6, 8); Mike Barsimanto, drums (2, 5, 6, 8); Kevin Gilbert, bass and drums (1, 4, 10), nylon guitar (3), tuba (9)

1. Shelter from the Rain (Emerson-Gilbert-Bonilla)
2. Another Frontier (Emerson)
3. Ballade (Emerson)
4. The Band Keeps Playing (Emerson-Gilbert-Bonilla)
5. Summertime (Gershwin)
6. The Church (Emerson)
7. Interlude (Emerson)
8. Montagues and Capulets (Prokofiev)
9. Abaddon's Bolero (orchestral version) (Emerson)
   [recorded in 1975; London Philharmonic Orchestra, John Mayer, conductor; Kevin Gilbert, tuba obbligato]
10. The Band Keeps Playing (Aftershock Mix) (Emerson)

★★★¹/₂

Although released in 1995, *Changing States* was recorded in 1989 and is of a piece with his work of the late eighties (*The Christmas Album, La Chiesa*). Six tracks are from July 1989 sessions at Patrick Leonard's Burbank studio (these are instrumental); three tracks (two, actually, with one of the tracks being presented in two different mixes), which are songs, are products of October 1989 sessions at Robert Berry's studios in Campbell; and there's the October 1975 orchestral recording of "Abaddon's Bolero" by the L.P.O., remixed and remastered by Kevin Gilbert. There isn't a really weak track on the album, and some of this material (notably "Another Frontier," "The Church," and "Summertime") is more or less essential for Emerson fans. On the other hand, there's no denying that the impact of *Changing States* is much diminished by the simple fact that five of the ten tracks here had already been released in other guises. Furthermore, I can think of few, if any, of Emerson's other solo albums where it would be less accurate to say that the whole is greater than the sum of its parts: here the often-rewarding individual tracks never cohere into anything greater, and unlike his most successful solo albums, there's no unified guiding vision at work here. A better name for this album would have been *An Emerson Sketchbook*.

Iron Man, Volume 1
Net Event A128021 (U.S., early 2002)
Recorded in Santa Monica, California, 1994-95
All music by Keith Emerson. Keith Emerson, keyboards; Will Alexander, sequencing and programming.

1. Iron Man Main Title Theme
2. And the Sea Shall Give Up Its Dead
3. I am Ultimo, Thy Deliverer
4. Data In Chaos Out
5. Silence My Companion, Death My Destination

6. Iron Man Theme Alternate

★★★★

The release of *Iron Man* is a milestone in Emerson's output, not only because it contains some excellent music, but also because it forced those who though they understood the trajectory of Emerson's career after the eighties to reconsider their assessment. In other words, based on the evidence of *Black Moon* and *In the Hot Seat*, it was easy to believe Emerson's compositional invention had entered a state of terminal decline: his *Iron Man* music forces one to reconsider this view. The *Iron Man* music is quasi-symphonic electronic music that sometimes is clearly "rock," and other times leans more towards classical or ambient music; some of the themes here are among his most vivid and imaginative in years, and the synthesis of all his previous film score manners into a musically coherent whole is magisterial. It must be admitted that the sudden changes, not only of mood but of musical style, can sometimes be jarring; on the other hand, one can argue that this mosaiclike approach to structure has always suited Emerson better than his forays into more "organic" forms, and at any rate, the different sections of the lengthy tracks here are held together by some of his most virtuosic displays of thematic transformation since *Inferno*. Some will miss the presence of real bass and drums, although the drum programming is handled reasonably well.

Emerson Plays Emerson
EMI 7243 5 57301 2 1 (U.K., May 2002)
Most tracks recorded 2001, except when noted.
All music by Keith Emerson, except when noted. Keith Emerson, piano.

1. Vagrant
2. Creole Dance
3. Solitudinous
4. Broken Bough
5. A Cajun Alley
6. Prelude to Candice
   [from *Murderock*]
7. A Blade of Grass
   [bonus track of Japanese pressing of *Black Moon*]
8. Outgoing Tide
9. Summertime (Gershwin)
   [from *Changing States*]
10. Interlude
    [from *Changing States*]
11. Roll'n Jelly
12. B & W Blues
    [Frank Scully, drums; Rob Statham, bass]
13. For Kevin (recorded live at The Gorge, Washington, September 27, 1996)
14. The Dreamer
    [from *Best Revenge*, where it's titled "Dream Runner"]
15. Hammer It Out
    [bonus track of Japanese pressing of *In the Hot Seat*]
16. Ballad for a Common Man
17. Barrelhouse Shakedown
18. Nilu's Dream
19. Soulscapes
20. Close to Home (recorded live at the Royal Albert Hall, October 2, 1992)
21. Honky Tonk Train Blues (recorded live with Oscar Peterson and his Big Band, 1976) (Meade Lux Lewis)
22. Medley: Nicola (Race)/Silver Shoes (Guarneri)/I'll See You in My Dreams (Jones/Khan) (recorded by Emerson at home on a reel-to-reel recorder, 1959)

★★★½

Prior to its release, *Emerson Plays Emerson* was billed as a collection of recently composed solo piano pieces by Emerson; this description is only partly correct. Six of the album's twenty-two tracks were previously released; the album also contains two new studio recordings of previously available Emerson compositions ("Creole Dance," "Barrelhouse Shakedown"), and two previously unreleased live recordings of already available tracks ("Close to Home," "Honky Tonk Train Blues"). The album's title is also a bit misleading in that three of the 22 tracks ("Summertime," "Honky Tonk Train Blues," and "Medley") are covers, and on three of the tracks ("Summertime," "B & W Blues," and "Honky Tonk Train Blues"), Emerson is accompanied by a band. Stylistically, the album focuses on specific aspects of Emerson's musical personality. The majority of the tracks are short, limpid character pieces that mine the lyrical, diatonic vein of writing Emerson had begun to explore in the eighties; among the newly composed pieces in this idiom, the poignant, impressionistic "Outgoing Tide" is particularly outstanding. There are also several pieces that demonstrate Emerson's continuing engagement with his ragtime/blues/jazz roots. The final track, a medley of three jazz-age classics recorded by Emerson when he was fourteen (the sound quality is surprisingly good), is historically important for underlining stride as an important taproot of his mature style. Even fans who missed references to his epic style of the seventies, and who criticized the album for a certain sameness of mood and uncharacteristically flat emotional trajectory, were impressed by the precision of his playing, cleaner and more authoritative than at any time since his ulnar nerve operation of 1993.

Hammer It Out: The Anthology
Sanctuary Records CMEDD1111 (U.K., May 2005)

CD 1:

1. Medley: Nicolette/Silver Shoes
   [Keith Emerson, solo piano; recorded 1959]

With the T-Bones
2. Rock Candy (McDuff)
   [previously unreleased 1966 recording]

With the Nice
3. Lumpy Gravy

Keith Emerson solo
4. Lament for Tony Stratton-Smith (Emerson)
   [previously unreleased 1987 recording]

With the Nice
5. America/2nd Amendment
6. High Level Fugue (fourth movement of "Five Bridges" suite)

With ELP
7. The Three Fates
8. The Old Castle/Blues Variation
9. Fugue (from *The Endless Enigma*)
10. Karn Evil 9, 2nd Impression
11. Piano Improvisations
12. Fanfare for the Common Man
13. Barrelhouse Shakedown
14. Honky Tonk Train Blues
15. Introductory Fanfare/Peter Gunn

Keith Emerson solo
16. Up the Elephant and Around the Castle
    [previously unreleased]

CD 2:

Excerpts from film scores and solo albums of the early 1980s
1. Inferno Main Title (from *Inferno*)
2. I'm a Man (from *Nighthawks*)
3. Hello Sailor/Bach Before the Mast (from *Honky*)
4. Orchestral Suite to Best Revenge (from *Best Revenge*)

WITH ELPOWELL
5. The Locomotion

WITH 3
6. Desde la vida

Excerpts from film scores and solo projects, late 1980s/early 1990s
7. The Church (from *Changing States*)
8. Hammer It Out (from Japanese release of *In the Hot Seat*)
9. Toccata con fuoco, rock version
   [previously unreleased 1989 arrangement]

WITH ELP
10. Changing States

From *Emerson Plays Emerson*
11. B & W Blues
12. Soulscapes
13. A Blade of Grass
14. Close to Home (live)

★★★¹/₂

To Keith Emerson's credit, *Hammer It Out* doesn't become a Greatest Hits of ELP; if any-thing, his Hammond-and-Moog masterpieces may be somewhat underrepresented. Besides the highly idiosyncratic selection of Nice, ELP, ELPowell, and 3 tracks, *Hammer It Out* offers a nice cross-section of his film score work of the 1980s and his more recent piano music. One does wish that the 1966-67 period of the T-Bones (one track) and the VIPs (no tracks) had received more emphasis, in order to listen for foreshadowing of the highly individual vision that suddenly emerges on the debut Nice album. One also wishes for a bit more unreleased material; contrary to the claims of the liner notes, neither "Lumpy Gravy" (*The Nice: BBC Sessions*, 2002) or "America/2nd Amendment" (*Autumn to Spring*, 1972 LP) are previously unavailable. Nonetheless, of the other four previously unreleased tracks, one is indeed thankful for the newfound availability of the T-Bones cover of Jack McDuff's "Rock Candy," "Lament for Tony Stratton-Smith" (precursor of 3's "On My Way Home"), and the 1989 or 1990 rock arrangement of the third movement of Emerson's Piano Concerto no. 1, which highlights its stylistic similarity to the instrumental movements of "Tarkus."

Keith Emerson: Selected Guest Appearances on Other Artists' Albums
(arranged chronologically)

- Rod Stewart—*An Old Raincoat Won't Ever Let You Down* (1969)
  (Emerson plays on "I Wouldn't Ever Change a Thing")
- Roy Harper—*Flat Baroque and Berserk* (1969)
  (The Nice play anonymously on "Hell's Angels")
- Various Artists—*Music from Free Creek* (recorded 1969, released 1973)
  (Emerson plays on "Freedom Jazz Dance," "Mother Nature's Son," and "On the Rebound")
- Peter Hammill—*And Close As This* (1986)
  (Emerson plays on, and co-authored, "Empire of Delight")
- Giovanni Jovanotti—*Jovanotti* (1990)
  (Emerson plays on "Giovane sempre," "Diritti e doveri," and "Sceriffo o bandito")
- Marc Bonilla—*E. E. Ticket* (1991)
  (Emerson plays on "White Noise")
- Tempest—*Turn of the Wheel* (1996)
  (Emerson plays on "The Barrow Man")
- Glenn Hughes—*The Way It Is* (1999)
  (Emerson plays on "Stoned in the Temple," "Don't Look Away")

Greg Lake: Singles, 1970–79

I Believe in Father Christmas/Humbug (7" single)
Manticore K13511 (U.K., November 1975)
Recorded 1974
#2 U.K.
[no rating: both songs cowritten by Lake-Sinfield]
Both the A side and B side are included on ELP's 1995 *I Believe in Father Christmas* EP.

Greg Lake: Solo Albums and Recordings with Other Bands, 1980–

Greg Lake
Chrysalis CHR 1357 (U.S., October 1981)
Chrysalis CHP 1357 (U.K., October 1981)
Recorded 1981
Greg Lake, vocals and rhythm guitar; Gary Moore, Steve Lukather, Dean Parks, and Snuffy
   Walden, guitars; Tristram Margetts, David Hungate, bass; Ted McKenna, Michael Giles,
   Jode Leigh, and Jeff Porcaro, drums; Clarence Clemmons, saxes; Tommy Eyre, Bill
   Cuomo, and Greg Mathieson, keyboards; Willie Cochrane and David Milner, backing
   vocals
#62 U.S.

 1. Nuclear Attack (Moore)
 2. Love You Too Much (Dylan-Springs-Lake)
 3. It Hurts (Lake)
 4. Black and Blue (Lake)
 5. Retribution Drive (Lake-Benyon-Eyre)
 6. Long Goodbye (Lake-Benyon-Eyre)
 7. The Lie (Lake-Eyre-Benyon)
 8. Someone (Eyre-Lake-Benyon)
 9. Let Me Love You Once Before You Go (Dorff-Leiken)
10. For Those Who Dare (Lake-Benyon)

★★

It's above all the lack of a coherent stylistic direction that sinks this album, which drifts
between heavy metal ("Nuclear Attack," "Retribution Drive"), blues rock ("Love You Too
Much," which features a Bob Dylan lyric edited by Lake with Dylan's permission), sentimental country rock ("Let Me Love You Once Before I Go"), and stereotypical early-eighties rock ballads ("It Hurts"). The album's most interesting song, "Someone" (featuring E
Street Band's Clarence Clemmons on sax) hearkens back to "Hallowed Be Thy Name"
(from *Works I*) in its exploration of spiritual malaise in the context of an icy, surreal blues
idiom. About the only thing that ties all these songs together is Lake's voice. The album
is also marred by a pervasive lack of memorable melodic material—all the more surprising considering Lake's track record during the seventies for creating simple but memorable melodies—and for its rather pedestrian arrangements. There is some dynamic
soloing here and there on the album, and a few of the tracks are worth hearing simply
for the powerful electric guitar leads of Gary Moore. On the whole, however, there's little here to distinguish *Greg Lake* from the many other pedestrian rock albums churned
out during the early eighties: the album was bound to be a disappointment both to those
expecting ELP-style prog rock and to those hoping for a further exploration of Lake's
acoustically based singer-songwriter approach of the *Works* era.

Manoeuvres
Chrysalis CHR 1392 (U.K., July 1983)
Chrysalis 41392 (U.S., July 1983)
Recorded 1983
Greg Lake, vocals and rhythm guitar; Gary Moore, lead guitar; Tristram Margetts, bass;
   Tommy Eyre, keyboards; Ted McKenna, drums

1. Manouevres
2. Too Young to Love
3. Paralyzed
4. A Woman Like You
5. I Don't Wanna Lose Your Love Tonight
6. It's You, You've Gotta Believe
7. Famous Last Words
8. Slave to Love
9. Haunted
10. I Don't Know Why I Still Love You

★★¹/₂

It can be cogently argued that *Manouevres* improves on *Greg Lake* in at least two areas: the melodic material of *Manouevres* is somewhat more memorable than the debut album's, and Lake settles on a couple of more or less coherent songwriting directions. Granted, there are a couple of songs that are obviously some record company executive's idea of what Lake ought to sing in order to generate a hit single: "A Woman Like You" finds Lake working in an eighties R & B context (think Lionel Richie) to no great advantage, and "I Don't Know Why I Still Love You" is one of the most bathetic, kitschy soft rock ballads imaginable. Other parts of the album, however, show Lake moving forward with a clearer idea of where he wanted to go. Most of side one of the LP medium finds Lake plying the (admittedly lightweight) lite metal style of contemporaneous bands like Bon Jovi with some success, the rousing "Paralyzed" being the most successful of these tracks. The album's second half, meanwhile, finds him reconnecting with some of the directions he had begun to stake out during the *Works* era. "It's You, You've Gotta Believe," the album's best song, is an anthemic, inspirational track that sounds as if it were cowritten by Keith Emerson; also notable is "Haunted," a tasteful and unclassifiable track that hearkens back to Lake's explorations of prerock popular styles on *Works 1*. Throughout the album the arrangements are more interesting than those of *Greg Lake*; Gary Moore again contributes a number of fine electric guitar solos.

King Biscuit Flower Hour: Greg Lake
King Biscuit Records 70710-88010-2 (U.S., July 1995)
Recorded live November 5, 1981, at Hammersmith Odeon, London, U.K.
Greg Lake, vocals and rhythm guitar; Gary Moore, lead guitar; Tristram Margetts, bass; Tommy Eyre, keyboards; Ted McKenna, drums

1. Medley: Fanfare for the Common Man/Karn Evil 9, 1st Impression, part 2
2. Nuclear Attack
3. The Lie
4. Retribution Drive
5. Lucky Man
6. Parisienne Walkways
7. You Really Got A Hold On Me
8. Love You Too Much
9. 21st Century Schizoid Man
10. In the Court of the Crimson King

★★★

Greg Lake in Concert makes the strongest possible argument for the material from his debut album: his band (which again features Gary Moore on lead guitar, and Lake himself on rhythm guitar) is exceedingly tight, and brings a fire to the debut album material that was lacking in the more clinical studio arrangements. Furthermore, here Lake is able to leaven the set list with a few carefully selected ELP and King Crimson warhorses, lending it a heft that the solo material by itself could not have provided. Highlights of the album include "21st Century Schizoid Man" which, while lacking the subtlety of King Crimson's performances, is very powerful, and amazingly tight; and "Lucky Man," which is notable for being the first arrangement of the song to take it totally seriously as a *rock* song, reinterpreting the song so radically (and successfully) that it forces those who know the song only via ELP to complete reassess it.

From the Beginning: The Greg Lake Retrospective
Rhino R2 72627 (U.S., 1997)

CD 1:

With King Crimson
  1. In the Court of the Crimson King
  2. Cat Food

With Emerson, Lake and Palmer
  3. Knife-Edge
  4. Lucky Man
  5. From the Beginning
  6. Take a Pebble (recorded live at Mar y Sol Festival, Puerto Rico, 1972)

With Peter Sinfield
  7. Still

With Emerson, Lake and Palmer
  8. Still . . . You Turn Me On
  9. Jerusalem
10. Karn Evil 9, 1st Impression, part 2

Works-era solo material
11. I Believe in Father Christmas
12. C'est la vie
13. Closer to Believing
14. Watching Over You

Greg Lake (post-ELP solo material)
15. 21st-Century Schizoid Man [from the *Greg Lake Live* King Biscuit album]

CD 2:

  1. Nuclear Attack
  2. Love You Too Much
  3. It Hurts
  4. Retribution Drive
  5. The Lie
  6. Let Me Love You Once
  7. Manouevres
  8. I Don't Know Why I Still Love You

Emerson, Lake and Powell
  9. Touch and Go
10. Lay Down Your Guns

Ride the Tiger (Greg Lake and Geoff Downes)
11. Love Under Fire (previously unreleased)
12. Money Talks (previously unreleased)

Emerson, Lake and Palmer
13. Black Moon
14. Paper Blood
15. Affairs of the Heart
16. Daddy
17. Heart on Ice

✯✯✯

The biggest strength of this anthology, aside from two discs featuring Greg Lake's voice, is the packaging, particularly the lavish (thirty-four-page) booklet featuring an introduction by Robert Fripp, superb liner notes by Bruce Pilato, and an outstanding discography. The biggest weakness involves track selection. The disc one material (i.e., through the end of the seventies) is outstanding, albeit somewhat predictable—it would have been nice to include Lake's pre-Crimson singles with the Shame and the Shy Limbs, as well as some live Crimson. Also, while Lake has come to view himself primarily as a singer, in his prime he was a much better than average bassist and guitarist, and at least one or two tracks highlighting his instrumental acumen ("The Sage" or "Canario," perhaps) would have been nice. This being said, it's mainly the disc two material that's problematic. It's nice to find two previously unreleased tracks from Lake's Ride the Tiger project with Geoff Downes, but do we really need *six* tracks from his first solo album? Also, the track selection here sometimes throws into question Lake's ability to accurately assess the strengths and weaknesses of his own material, as he excludes some of his better songs in favor of his most bathetic, kitschy songs of the eighties and nineties: why he includes the ghastly "I Don't Know Why I Still Love You" from *Manouevres* at the expense of "It's You, You've Gotta Believe" or "Haunted," or the awful "Heart On Ice" from *In the Hot Seat* at the expense of his commanding interpretation of "Man in the Long Black Coat," is anybody's guess. In sum, one wishes Lake had combined this collection's comprehensiveness with the more interesting and imaginative track selection of *Live from the Underground*.

From the Underground: The Official Bootleg
Greg Lake CD300 (U.S., 1998)
All tracks recorded live unless otherwise indicated

1. Touch and Go (Emerson, Lake and Palmer, 1993)
2. A Man, A City (King Crimson, 1969)
3. Don't Go Away Little Girl (1967 single with the Shame)
4. Medley: Still . . . You Turn Me On/Watching Over You (Emerson, Lake and Powell, 1986)
5. Daddy (The Greg Lake Band, 1994)
6. Retribution Drive (The Greg Lake Band, 1981)
7. Heat of the Moment (Asia, 1983)
8. The Score (Emerson, Lake and Powell, 1986)
9. Love (1968 single with The Shy Limbs)
10. Affairs of the Heart (Emerson, Lake and Palmer, 1992)
11. Learning to Fly (Emerson, Lake and Powell, 1986)
12. Lucky Man (Emerson, Lake and Palmer, 1974)
13. 21st Century Schizoid Man (The Greg Lake Band, 1981)

★★★¹/₂

The track selection here is far less comprehensive than that of Rhino's 1997 Anthology. That being said, it's also much more interesting. Eleven of the thirteen tracks were recorded live: the two exceptions are singles Lake recorded with the Shame and the Shy Limbs (released in 1968 and 1969, respectively), which finally makes Lake's pre–King Crimson work publicly available. While these two tracks are both musically thin, they're interesting for showing that Lake's early vocal style was already mature and fully recognizable. Wisely, Lake avoids loading the disc with too much live ELP—there's three tracks here with ELP, all fairly lightweight. The highpoints of the disc, rather, are a commanding performance, with King Crimson '69, of "A Man, A City" (retitled "Pictures of a City" for its studio release on 1970's *In the Wake of Poseidon*), and excellent performances of "The Score" and "Learning to Fly" with ELPowell (a band which at the time of this anthology's release was still unserved by an authorized live album). In sum, while *The Official Bootleg* offers a spottier overview of Lake's career than the *Anthology*, it fills in some vital missing gaps that the *Anthology* fails to, and in many ways offers a more interesting and idiosyncratic track selection.

WITH ASIA

Enso Kai: Live at the Budokan, Tokyo 1983
1804-Pilot 87 5231 (U.S., 2001)
see Carl Palmer section

From the Underground, Volume II: Deeper into the Mine
Creative Musical Arts GL-CD3004 (U.S., December 2003)

1. Black Moon (Emerson, Lake and Palmer live 1992)
2. Check It Out (Ride the Tiger)
3. Love Under Fire (Ride the Tiger)

4. Cold Side of a Woman (outtake from *Greg Lake*)
5. Step Aside (Emerson, Lake and Powell 1986 Sprocket sessions)
6. Preacher Blues (Emerson, Lake and Palmer live 1971)
7. Hold Me (outtake from *Manoeuvres*)
8. Heart On Ice (Greg Lake Band live 1994)
9. Blue Light (Ride the Tiger)
10. You're Good With Your Love (outtake from *Greg Lake*)
11. You've Really Got a Hold On Me (outtake from *Greg Lake*)
12. Epitaph (King Crimson live 1969)
13. Fanfare for the Common Man (Greg Lake Band live 1981)

★★¹/₂

From the Underground, Volume II: Deeper into the Mine is intended as a follow-up to Lake's *From the Underground: The Official Bootleg* of 1998. The concept, once again, is sound: make available previously unavailable (or not readily available) recordings that constitute a representative cross section of Lake's long career. The main problem with *Volume II* is that the material is, by and large, less interesting than the material featured on the 1998 release. Four of the thirteen tracks are outtakes from Lake's two studio albums, *Greg Lake* (1981) and *Manoeuvres* (1983): considering the spotty, highly uneven nature of those two albums, it is not surprising that these outtakes are not exactly "unreleased gems." Another three tracks are unreleased demos from Ride the Tiger, Lake's 1988-89 project with Geoff Downes: again, these aren't particularly compelling, since the best songs from the Lake-Downes partnership were cannibalized many years earlier, to be used on either ELP's *Black Moon* and *In the Hot Seat* or on Asia's *Aqua* album. (What *would* have been interesting is to include Ride the Tiger's recordings of one or more tracks—perhaps "Affairs of the Heart" or "Street War"—that were later reworked by ELP.) That leaves a series of previously unreleased live tracks: one by King Crimson, two by ELP, one by ELPowell ("Step Aside," which should have appeared on ELPowell's *The Sprocket Sessions*), and two by different incarnations of the Greg Lake Band. One of the ELP tracks, "Preacher Blues," is a previously unreleased live number from 1971 that is definitely of historical interest (it appears to have served as the prototype for the later "Tiger in a Spotlight"), although its musical substance is fairly slight; also of some historical interest is King Crimson's "Epitaph," recorded live at the July 5, 1969, free concert at London's Hyde Park that launched Crimson into immediate stardom. On the whole, though, *Deeper into the Mine* isn't as compelling as *The Official Bootleg*.

Greg Lake: Selected Guest Appearances on Other Artists' Albums

- Pete Sinfield—*Still* (1973)
  (Lake coproduced, plays electric guitar on "Hopes and Dreams," contributes backing vocal to "Wholefood," and joint lead vocal on "Still." The latter track is included on Lake's 1997 anthology.)
- Ringo Starr's All Starr Band—*Ringo and His New All-Starr Band* (2002)
  (Presents a cross-section of the repertoire of the 2001 All-Starr Band, for which Lake provided vocals and bass guitar. Only one of Lake's three feature tracks, "Lucky Man," is included on the album.)

Carl Palmer: Recordings with PM, Asia, the Carl Palmer Band, Etcetera, 1980–

WITH PM

1:PM
Ariola ARL 5048 A (U.S., March 1980)
Recorded December 1979
Carl Palmer, drums and percussion; Todd Cochran, keyboards and vocals; Barry Finnerty, lead guitar and vocals; John Nitzinger, rhythm guitar and vocals; Erlk Scott, bass and vocals

1. Dynamite (Nitzinger)
2. You've Got Me Rockin' (Cochran)
3. Green Velvet Splendor (Cochran)
4. Dreamers (Nitzinger)
5. Go On Carry On (Nitzinger)
6. Do You Go All the Way (Finnerty)
7. Go For It (Finnerty)
8. Madeline (Cochran)
9. You're Too Much (Cochran)
10. Children of the Air Age (Cochran)

★½

Give Carl Palmer credit where credit is due. Refusing to cash in on the ELP name or stylistic approach, his first post-ELP foray finds him working with a group of hand-picked session musicians from the U.S. that he attempted to forge into a top-flight song band. The vocal harmonies are fluent, if not downright slick. The instrumental interplay is often quite accomplished and intricate, at times showing a New Wave linearity reminiscent of the Police or the Cars: indeed, *1:PM* sounds more truly contemporary than the nearly contemporaneous *Greg Lake*. Palmer's drumming is excellent: he totally retools his drumming approach, and his intricate grooves, carefully arranged to interlock with the bass and guitar parts, are never show-offy, and never overpower the song. Unfortunately, the melodic content of the album is utterly forgettable, and the lyrics represent little more than a stringing together of the most banal clichés imaginable. Ultimately, *1:PM* demonstrates that even the most skillful arrangements cannot salvage negligible songwriting. For fans of Palmer, the album is important chiefly for serving as the "missing link" between his soloistic prog drumming with ELP and the sparer, more groove-oriented approach he adopted with Asia.

WITH ASIA

[Note: There has been a proliferation of live Asia product and "Best of" packages, some featuring Palmer, in recent years. I have included no "Best of" albums and only what I judge to be the three most important live Asia recordings that feature Palmer's drumming.]

Asia
Geffen Records GHS 2008 (U.S., February 1982)
Geffen Records 85577 (U.K., February 1982)
Recorded June–November 1981
John Wetton, bass and lead vocals; Steve Howe, guitars and backing vocals; Geoff Downes, keyboards and backing vocals; Carl Palmer, drums and percussion
#11 U.K., #1 U.S.

1. Heat of the Moment (Wetton-Downes)
2. Only Time Will Tell (Wetton-Downes)
3. Sole Survivor (Wetton-Downes)
4. One Step Closer (Wetton-Howe)
5. Time Again (Downes-Howe-Palmer-Wetton)
6. Wildest Dreams (Wetton-Downes)
7. Without You (Wetton-Howe)

8. Cutting It Fine (Wetton-Downes-Howe)
9. Here Comes The Feeling (Wetton-Howe)

★★★★

I'm sure many readers will be horrified by the rating I have given this album, so let me elaborate. If I were to judge this through the prism of progressive ideology, with its insistence on transcendence, idealism, and authenticity, *Asia* would fall very short indeed. However, Asia were not a progressive band: they were a pop-rock band, and on this one album, at least, an extremely good one. *Asia* contains an abundance of memorable melodies, some superb vocal and instrumental arrangements, and fine production: Carl Palmer's drums and John Wetton's bass never sounded this full and massive before. Asia manages to create its own group vocal sound, never an easy task, and Steve Howe's guitar playing brings a welcome angularity to the arrangements, which otherwise could have grown too slick. Of the nine songs here, six are quite strong, and the album's first three tracks are eighties pop-rock classics. Indeed, there is something about the first Asia album that hearkens back to the best late-sixties pop in its winsome mixture of lightweight subject matter, dependably tuneful melodies, and epic arrangements.

Alpha
Geffen Records GHS 4008 (U.S., August 1983)
Geffen Records 2 5508 (U.K., August 1983)
Recorded February through May 1983
Same lineup as *Asia*
#5 U.K., #6 U.S.

1. Don't Cry (Wetton-Downes)
2. The Smile Has Left Your Eyes (Wetton)
3. Never in a Million Years (Wetton-Downes)
4. My Own Time (I'll Do What I Want) (Wetton-Downes)
5. The Heat Goes On (Wetton-Downes)
6. Eye to Eye (Wetton-Downes)
7. The Last to Know (Wetton-Downes)
8. True Colors (Wetton-Downes)
9. Midnight Sun (Wetton-Downes)
10. Open Your Eyes (Wetton-Downes)

★★$^{1}/_{2}$

While most of the material on *Alpha* certainly isn't bad, it doesn't sound particularly inspired, either, and there's evidence that the Asia sound established on the debut album is beginning to be used as a formula, to be repeated with slight variations as necessary. Probably the most noticeable difference between *Asia* and *Alpha* is that the melodies of the latter are, for the most part, less inspired and memorable than those of the former. Steve Howe's presence is not felt as strongly here as on the debut album (he receives no songwriting credits on *Alpha*), and one misses the sense of angularity his playing brought to the debut. The production isn't as sharp, and the mix seems to be lacking a bit on the low end. The album's best song, "Midnight Sun," featuring a transcendent guitar solo by Howe, hearkens back to Wetton's work with U.K.

Astra
Geffen Records GHS 24072 (U.S., November 1985)
Geffen Records GEF 24072 (U.K., November 1985)
Recorded mid-1985
John Wetton, bass and lead vocals; Mandy Meyer, guitars and backing vocals; Geoff Downes, keyboards and backing vocals; Carl Palmer, drums and percussion
#68 U.K., #67 U.S.

1. Go (Wetton-Downes)
2. Voice of America (Wetton-Downes)
3. Hard On Me (Wetton-Downes-Palmer)
4. Wishing (Wetton-Downes)
5. Rock and Roll Dream (Wetton-Downes)

6. Countdown to Zero (Wetton-Downes)
7. Love Now Till Eternity (Wetton-Downes)
8. Too Late (Wetton-Downes-Palmer)
9. Suspicion (Wetton-Downes)
10. After the War (Wetton-Downes)

★★½

By the time *Astra* was recorded, Steve Howe was gone; not surprising, perhaps, considering that Asia had become ever more dominated by Geoff Downes's keyboard orchestrations, Wetton's overdubbed vocal harmonies, and the Wetton-Downes songwriting team. The guitar sound of Howe's replacement, Mandy Meyer, is heavier than Howe's, but also more dependent on fat power chords, which are often absorbed into Downes' massive keyboard orchestrations: one misses the angular melodic filigrees with which Howe brought an element of edginess to the first album. The low end of *Astra* represents an improvement on *Alpha*: Wetton's bass lines cut through more clearly, Palmer's bass drum sound is bigger than ever, and it's here that Palmer and Wetton totally gel as a rhythm section, with some of their tightly interlocking parts lending a modicum of interest to otherwise tangentially viable songs.

Aurora
Sony/Geffen ISAP 3155 (Japan, April 1986)

1. Too Late
2. Ride Easy
3. Daylight
4. Lying to Yourself
[no rating—specialty album]
A Japanese-only EP release. Palmer cowrote "Too Late."

Then and Now
Geffen Records 7599-24298-2 (U.S., September 1990)
The album's four new tracks recorded summer 1990 by Wetton, Palmer, Downes, and
    various session guitarists
#114 U.S.

1. Only Time Will Tell
2. Heat of the Moment
3. Wildest Dreams
4. Don't Cry
5. The Smile Has Left Your Eyes
6. Days Like These [new recording]
7. Voice of America
8. Prayin' for a Miracle [new recording]
9. Am I in Love? [new recording]
10. Summer (Can't Last Too Long) [new recording]

★★

Original members Downes, Wetton, and Palmer reunited in May 1990. Deciding that the best way to reignite their careers would be a greatest hits package with a twist, the band recorded four new tracks in early summer 1990 for inclusion on the album, using several session guitarists in the process, since Steve Howe was not available. One of the new songs, "Days Like These," was a minor hit single in the U.S., but the album didn't have the hoped-for galvanizing effect on the band's fortunes (there was no U.S. tour) and it came off as yet another attempt to capitalize on the success of their debut album, which remains the real "greatest hits" package.

Live Mockba 09-XI-90
Essential Records ESS CD 174 (U.S., June 1991)
Recorded live at the Olympijski Stadium, Moscow, Russia, November 9, 1990
John Wetton, bass and lead vocals; Geoff Downes, keyboards and backing vocals; Pat
    Thrall, guitars and backing vocals; Carl Palmer, drums and percussion

1. Time Again
2. Sole Survivor
3. Don't Cry
4. Keyboard solo
5. Only Time Will Tell
6. Rock and Roll Dream
7. Starless
8. Book of Saturday
9. The Smile Has Left Your Eyes (parts one and two)
10. The Heat Goes On
11. Go
12. Heat of the Moment
13. Open Your Eyes
14. Karianne

★★½

As a cultural artifact that points to the open conquest of the Soviet Union (soon to be the former Soviet Union) by Western pop culture, *Live Mockba* is important; its musical importance is much slighter. The boys' set list isn't all that different than it had been at their famous Budokan shows seven years before, although now John Wetton was back, Steve Howe was gone (replaced here by Pat Thrall), and a few songs from 1985's *Astra* were added to the set. Perhaps the most interesting aspect of the album is the two King Crimson classics ("Starless" and "Book of Saturday"), given new treatments here, although these performances won't make anyone forget Crimson circa 1973-74; additionally, these songs make the Asia fare sound awfully lightweight by comparison. The final number, "Karianne," was written during the *Then and Now* sessions.

Aqua
Musidisc 109284 (U.S., June 1992)
Recorded 1991
John Payne, bass and vocals; Geoff Downes, keyboards and vocals; Steve Howe and various studio guitarists; Carl Palmer (on seven tracks) and various studio drummers

1. Aqua, part one
2. Who Will Stop the Rain
3. Back in Town
4. Love Under Fire
   [written by Greg Lake and Geoff Downes for the Ride the Tiger project]
5. Someday
6. Little Rich Boy
7. The Voice of Reason
8. Lay Down Your Arms
9. Crime of the Heart
10. A Far Cry
11. Don't Call Me
12. Heaven and Earth
13. Aqua, part two

★½

Whatever magic Asia had managed to conjure on their first and, to a much lesser extent, second and third albums had vanished by the time *Aqua* was released. By this time, Asia was down to two original members, Downes and Palmer, Wetton having left and been replaced by John Payne. Palmer drummed on seven tracks (the credits don't say which seven) before abandoning the recording sessions in order to rejoin ELP for *Black Moon*; in all honesty, Palmer's drumming on *Aqua*, following the precedent set with 3, is neither attention-grabbing nor distinctive, and it's impossible to tell Palmer's work from that of the sessions drummers who were brought in to replace him. So much as the album holds any interest at all, it's for Steve Howe's guest performances on several tracks.

Live in Nottingham
Blueprint BP 253 CD (U.K., May 1997)
Recorded live in Nottingham, U.K., June 23, 1990
Same lineup as *Live Mockba 09-XI-90*

1. Wildest Dreams
2. Sole Survivor
3. Don't Cry
4. Voice of America
5. Time Again
6. Prayin' for a Miracle
7. The Smile Has Left Your Eyes
8. Only Time Will Tell
9. Days Like These
10. The Heat Goes On
11. Heat of the Moment
12. Open Your Eyes

★★

The comments made in regards to *Live Mockba 09-XI-90* are largely *apropos* here as well. On *Live at Nottingham*, one doesn't get the King Crimson material, but one does get two of the new songs from *Then and Now*, which this particular tour was promoting. The sound quality of this album is marginally lower than that of *Live Mockba*.

Enso Kai: Live at the Budokan, Tokyo, 1983
1804 Pilot 87 5231 (U.S., June 2001)
Recorded live at the Budokan, Tokyo, Japan, December 6–8, 1983
Greg Lake, bass and lead vocals; Steve Howe, guitars and backing vocals; Geoff Downes, keyboards and backing vocals; Carl Palmer, drums and percussion

1. The Heat Goes On
2. Here Comes the Feeling
3. Eye to Eye
4. Guitar solo
5. Only Time Will Tell
6. Open Your Eyes
7. Keyboard solo
8. The Smile Has Left Your Eyes
9. Wildest Dreams/Drum solo
10. Heat of the Moment
11. Sole Survivor

★★½

Because of the famed live telecast from Tokyo's Budokan and the resulting video, this album—which surprisingly was not released in audio-only format until 2001—captures Asia at the apex of their prominence, and is probably the one live Asia album to own, never mind the mediocre sound quality (it's mono). Greg Lake steps into John Wetton's role so comfortably that there are times ("Only Time Will Tell," "Wildest Dreams") that one has to remind oneself that yes, this is indeed Lake, not Wetton, providing lead vocals. The playing is tight; the major disappointment with Asia live is that the band simply is unable to fully reproduce the glossy, quasi-choral group vocals that are such an important part of the studio albums. While Howe, Downes, and Palmer all turn in nice solo spots, this material, as tightly arranged and relatively straightforward as it is, simply doesn't allow for the stretching out into transcendental spaces that characterized live ELP, Yes, and King Crimson at their peaks. Nonetheless, Steve Howe's guitar playing, in particular, provides just enough of an edge to keep the music from completely going into autopilot.

WITH QANGO

Live in the Hood
Manticore MANTVP-101CD (U.K., 2000)
Recorded live at the Robin Hood, Birmingham, U.K., and The Brook, Southampton, U.K.
February 3 and 7, 2000
John Wetton, bass and lead vocals; Dave Kilminster, guitars and backing vocals; John
   Young, keyboards and backing vocals; Carl Palmer, drums and percussion

1. Time Again
2. Sole Survivor
3. Bitches Crystal
4. Guitar solo
5. All Along the Watchtower (Bob Dylan)
6. The Last One Home (Wetton-Young)
7. Keyboard solo
8. Hoedown
9. Fanfare for the Common Man/Drum solo
10. Heat of the Moment

★★

After the breakup of ELP in December 1998, three of the four original members of Asia—
Wetton, Palmer, and Downes—agreed to a reunion tour in 1999. However, after Downes
backed out in order to continue working with John Payne—who now has rights to the
Asia moniker—Wetton and Palmer had to rename the band, as well as find a replacement
for Downes. After selecting John Young (Dave Kilminster had already been recruited for
the guitarist's position), the band was dubbed "Qango." As one might expect, the first
order of business was Asia songs, although Qango also did some ELP (John Wetton's interpretation of "Bitches Crystal" is particularly interesting), a hazily reflective read of the
Bob Dylan classic "All Along the Watchtower," and a Wetton-John Young original in the
vein of nineties Asia. It's all good fun but not particularly substantive, and the components of the set list (classic ELP and Asia, new songs, solos, the odd cover song) never gel
into a coherent musical vision.

Do You Wanna Play, Carl? Carl Palmer Anthology
Sanctuary Records CMEDD163 (U.K., May 2001)

CD 1:
1. Concerto for Percussion (Joseph Horovitz-Carl Palmer) [previously unreleased]
   [Recorded 1976; London Philharmonic Orchestra conducted by Joseph Horovitz; Carl
   Palmer, featured soloist, drums and percussion]
2. The Enemy God Dances with the Black Spirits
3. The Pancha Suite (Palmer) [previously unreleased]
   [Palmer, drums and percussion; Ron Aspery, woodwinds; Colin Hodgkinson, bass;
   Snuffy Walden, guitar; recorded during *Works* era]
4. Bullfrog
5. Toccata
6. Close But Not Touching
7. L.A. Nights
8. Canario
9. Tank
10. Two-part Invention in D minor
11. Fanfare for the Common Man
12. March Militaire (Schubert) [previously unreleased]
    [Outtake from Percussion Concerto sessions]

CD 2:
With the Craig

1. I Must Be Mad (Brown)
   [The Craig's 1966 single]

2. Suspense (Brown)
   [B-side of "I Must Be Mad"]

With the Chants
3. Love Light (Amoo)
   [1966 single by England's first all-black vocal group; Palmer was the sessions drummer]

With Atomic Rooster
4. Decline and Fall

With P.M.
5. You've Got Me Rockin'
6. Dynamite

With Mike Oldfield
7. Mount Teidi (Oldfield)
8. Ready Mix (Oldfield/Palmer)
   [7-8 recorded in 1981]

With Asia
9. Heat of the Moment
10. Wildest Dreams
11. Time Again

With 3
12. Desde la Vida
13. Eight Miles High

With Qango
14. Hoedown

With The Buddy Rich Orchestra
15. Shawnee (Barone) [previously unreleased]
    [Recorded live at Ronnie Scott's, London, U.K., 1986]

★★★★

Do Ya Wanna Play, Carl? is what every anthology of this type ought to be, but few actually are: a representative cross-section of a long and distinguished career that deftly alternates well-known and long-available tracks with previously unavailable or hard-to-find ones. The centerpiece is the Horovitz-Palmer Percussion Concerto, which finally entered the public realm a quarter of a century after it was recorded. Although the Concerto is not particularly original, it shows a sure grasp of large-scale structure, and the solo percussion writing is superb: one can only lament that it wasn't released in the late seventies, when in would have made a far bigger impact. The Concerto isn't the only newly available gem, however. "The Pancha Suite," which Palmer recorded with the same lineup that realized "New Orleans" from *Works I*, makes one wonder why Palmer didn't do an entire album of jazz-rock fusion after the dissolution of ELP in 1979; and there's a blistering live version of "Shawnee" recorded live (and off-the-cuff) by Palmer with Buddy Rich's Big Band in 1986. Palmer wisely includes his earliest recordings, with the Craig and the Chants, which show that at age sixteen he was already an accomplished rock drummer. About all that's missing is a recording with the Crazy World of Arthur Brown. (There has to be a bootleg recording somewhere of Palmer playing "Fire" with the band!) Although the layout of the liner notes and the order of the tracks is a bit confusing, this is an essential album for Palmer's fans and for historians of rock drumming more generally.

WITH CARL PALMER BAND

Working Live-Volume 1
Sanctuary 06076-86352-2 (U.K., March 2003)
Recorded live at Bilston (Birmingham), U.K., July 19, 2001
Carl Palmer, drums and percussion; Shaun Baxter, guitar; Dave Marks, six-string bass

1. The Barbarian
2. The Enemy God
3. L. A. Nights

4. Tank
5. Bullfrog
6. Toccata
7. Canario
8. Drum Solo

★★★

Working Live-Volume 2
Sanctuary 06076-86356-2 (U.K., October 2004)
Recorded live at various U.K. shows, 2003
Carl Palmer, drums and percussion; Shaun Baxter, guitar; Dave Marks, six-string bass

1. Hoedown
2. Trilogy
3. J.Section (Palmer/Baxter/Marks)
4. Medley: Eruption/Aquatarkus
5. Carmina Burana
6. Fanfare for the Common Man (includes drum solo)

★★★¹/₂

For those who believe Palmer's drumming has been in a state of decline for some time, the two volumes of *Working Live* have been a pleasant surprise, featuring Palmer's most commanding and energized drumming since the late seventies, and are especially important as the most complete fusion to date of his fleet, rudimentally intricate approach of the seventies with the heavier sound and greater bass drum emphasis of the eighties and nineties. Baxter and Marks are both bona fide virtuosos who capably keep up with Palmer; most importantly, the trio manages to forge a distinctive band personality that unites aspects of seventies progressive rock, eighties metal (one hears echoes of Eddie Van Halen, Gary Moore, and Joe Satriani in Baxter's playing), and nineties alternative (Marks is obviously familiar with the revolutionary bass guitar style of Primus's Les Claypool).

Volume 1, which showcases the band's 2001 set list (included here in its entirety excepting only "Hoedown" and "Fanfare for the Common Man") is imaginative and tastefully chosen, and the arrangements are ingenious to the extreme, especially Shaun Baxter's guitar orchestrations of Emerson's keyboard parts. While the performances of virtuosic and the arrangements are ingenious, though, there's a certain sameness of dynamics and a resulting lack of emotional depth: the music lacks the sense of *chiascurro*, the tints of light and shade, that ELP brought to "Toccata" or "The Barbarian."

The band apparently realized this; the six tracks of *Volume 2*, recorded during 2003, showed somewhat greater contrasts of dynamics and tone color, with Shaun Baxter's imaginative use of a battery of effects devices being especially impressive. While the ELP material provided an excellent forum for the band to forge a group sound, this music by and large is not ideally suited to a guitar power trio, and one hopes the band will use their imaginative arrangements of the ELP material as a springboard for creating original music more closely aligned with the idiomatic possibilities of their instrumentation and their brash, aggressive band personality. Indeed, *Volume 2*'s short but compelling "J.Section," which merges late-sixties electric bebop (think Larry Coryell or King Crimson's "Groon") with more contemporary jazz-funk (think Charlie Hunter) offers a tantalizing glimpse of what the Carl Palmer Band might achieve on an album of original compositions. Incidentally, *Volume 2* includes Palmer's most focused and musically compelling drum solo since the 1973-74 World Tour.

Carl Palmer: Selected Guest Appearances on Other Artist's Singles and Albums

- The Chants—"Love Light" (7" single, 1966)
  (This was Palmer's first paid session. The Chants have a minor footnote in the history of British pop by being the first British-based all-black vocal group. The single appears on Palmer's 2001 anthology.)
- Mike Oldfield—*Five Miles Out* (1982)
  (Palmer plays on Mount Teidi," which is included on his 2001 anthology, as is "Ready Mix," an outtake from the same sessions.)

Appendix B:
A Critical Videography

Pictures at an Exhibition
Classic Family Entertainment VHS G 153, 1984
ELP live at London's Lyceum Theater, December 9, 1970

SET LIST:
1. The Barbarian
2. Take a Pebble (including "Tank")
3. Pictures at an Exhibition
   a. Promenade
   b. The Gnome
   c. Promenade
   d. The Sage
   e. The Old Castle
   f. Blues Variation
   g. Promenade
   h. The Hut of Baba Yaga
   i. The Curse of Baba Yaga
   j. The Hut of Baba Yaga
   k. The Great Gates of Kiev
4. Knife-Edge
5. Rondo (including drum solo)

★★★½

A movie of the 12-9-70 Lyceum show, produced by Lindsey Clennel and directed by Nicholas Ferguson, was released in the U.K. in 1972 as *Pictures at an Exhibition* and in the U.S. in 1973 as *Rock and Roll Your Eyes*. When one considers that this was shot before similar productions featuring Yes (*Yessongs*), Pink Floyd *(Pink Floyd at Pompeii)*, and Led Zeppelin (*The Song Remains the Same*), one realizes how quickly ELP were acknowledged as one of the heavyweight acts of the British rock pantheon. There are two major caveats that must be expressed about this film: one, the sound quality is not particularly good (although digital remastering has helped to an extent), and two, the "psychedelic" visual effects that were all the rage in 1971 (swirling blobs of color that suddenly swallow up the musicians, the ridiculous Marvel Comics collage that interrupts the "Baba Yaga" sequence during *Pictures*) have aged spectacularly badly. One also wishes the film had been shot just a few months later—say March 26, 1971, when ELP recorded the version of *Pictures* that constitutes their third album—when the band were even better, and had *Tarkus* under their belts. Nonetheless, there is a lot to be said for this performance: the band are already becoming a well-oiled live ensemble—they've advanced light years from Isle of Wight—and the playing is never less than impressive, galvanizing at times. One is also struck by the band's spontaneity, unselfconsciousness, and obvious enjoyment of playing together—the gargantuan stage shows

717

and almost inhumanely perfected performances of the 1973-74 world tour were in the future—and it's impressive how much sound they get from their relatively small setup. The camera work (when one isn't being tormented by swirling blobs of color) is pretty good, with some nice close-ups. In sum, more than thirty-five years after the fact, the energy and enthusiasm conveyed by this performance still resonates.

Note: In 1984, this movie was released in VHS format in the U.K. and U.S. by Classic Family Entertainment containing only "Pictures at an Exhibition"; a Japanese import containing the entire show was released shortly thereafter. A DVD release in 2001 also features only "Pictures at an Exhibition."

The Manticore Special
Manticore VHS M-V1001, 1998

★★★¹/₂

A documentary shot during the final segment of ELP's Spring 1973 European tour, *The Manticore Special* (also known as *Brain Salad Days*) was originally broadcast on BBC2 on Boxer's Day, 1973. It was rather unique for its day: it's not a concert film, nor is it a biography of the band, although it does incorporate aspects of both. Mainly, it adopts a "day in the life of a band" approach, the "band" in this case being not just the musicians, but the entire ELP organization: manager, road crew, etc. It is genuinely enlightening in its depiction of life on the road for a seventies rock band from a more prosaic, less glamorized perspective than was the norm, highlighting the almost feudal social divisions that characterized the seventies megabands. Anyone hoping for either a conventional band biography or a really probing consideration of who ELP are as people and what their music is all about is bound to be disappointed; so will anybody who is looking for a straight concert film. However, anyone wanting to get a feel for the road life of one of the seventies' megabands will certainly find it of interest. There is some good concert footage: short segments of "Karn Evil 9, 1st Impression, part two" (with Lake playing a Zemaitis dual six-string guitar/four-string bass), "Still . . . You Turn Me On," and a complete performance of "Hoedown." An especially fascinating segment shows the band hashing out parts of the second and third Impressions of "Karn Evil 9" in the Manticore rehearsal facilities sometime in early 1973.

Note: Rereleased by Manticore Records in VHS format in 1998; released as a DVD in 2002 with *Works Orchestral Tour*.

Works Orchestral Tour
Manticore VHS M-V1002, 1998
ELP Live at Montreal's Olympic Stadium, August 26, 1977

SET LIST:
1. Abaddon's Bolero (partial)
2. Karn Evil 9, 1st Impression, part 2
3. The Enemy God Dances with the Black Spirits
4. C'est la vie
5. Lucky Man
6. Pictures at an Exhibition
7. Piano Concerto no. 1, 3rd movement
8. Tank/drum solo
9. Nutrocker
10. Pirates
11. Encore: Fanfare for the Common Man/Rondo

★★★

ELP taped their August 26, 1977, Montreal performance—a show that drew 78,000, and represented the band's final moment of glory during the seventies—with the intention of releasing it later (whether as a TV special or a movie is unknown). However, the financial crisis brought on by the tour's cost overruns, combined with the spectacular plunge in ELP's popularity during the 1978-79 period, caused the project to be indefinitely shelved, so it was not until 1998, when Manticore Records released the show in VHS format for the home video market, that it finally became available. While I continue to believe that the

Works Orchestral Tour remains a fatally flawed concept, the video makes a stronger argument for the concept than either the LP (*In Concert*) of 1979 or the CD rerelease (*Works Live*) of 1993. Partly this is because one can't help being impressed with the scope of the show when one actually sees the massed orchestra and choir. Partly it's a result of a better cross-section of the set list: for instance, here finally is an orchestral performance of "Pirates," the way it was meant to be heard. Be aware, however, that *Works Orchestral Tour* does not contain the complete Montreal show. The camera work is reasonably good, the sonic quality passable, although the problems with the original soundtrack are well known, and it's hard to hear evidence of extensive digital remastering here. Of course, the drawbacks of ELP's orchestral shows—occasionally ragged orchestral rhythms and intonations—remain. Above all, I'm still troubled by the impression that *Works Orchestral Tour* breaks the band's musical style back down into its individual components (classical music, prerock popular music genres, electronic rock) in such a manner that the constituent elements of ELP's music now seem to coexist uneasily together, as discrete parts of an ill-advised musical variety show.

Note: Released by Manticore Records in VHS format in 1998. Rereleased on DVD in 2002 with *The Manticore Special*.

Emerson, Lake and Palmer: Welcome Back
Strand Home Video VHS 8121, 1993

★★¹/₂

This eighty-minute "video biography" was eagerly anticipated by fans from the time *Black Moon* was released in summer 1992: when it finally appeared in January 1993, however, most fans found it to be a bit of a disappointment. Neither the visual nor the sound quality is particularly sterling. A bigger problem, however, is how the video is structured. Anyone who expects *Welcome Back* to be a real biography is bound to be disappointed. The video gives a number of snippets of ELP performing their classics, but no complete performances; in between each featured number is a short interview segment that sometimes does, and sometimes doesn't, cross-relate with the music that it precedes or follows. The performance spots come from all stages of the band's career, which is nice, but there's no real coherence to what follows what, and it's not clear when or where some of the earlier spots were taken from. A lot of the recognizable snippets are taken from three commercially available videos: *The Manticore Special, The Works Orchestral Tour,* and *Live at the Royal Albert Hall*. There's also extensive footage from the September 26, 1992, show at Verona, Italy, and a few excerpts from their legendary Cal Jam show of April 6, 1974. Some of the video footage that accompanies the performance of given songs is, at best, extremely random: for instance, we see a young Keith Emerson riding a motorcycle through Rome to the accompaniment of "C'est la vie," which I had never exactly heard as motorcycle riding music. There is some genuinely interesting footage throughout, and *Welcome Back* also does a service by preserving the lavish unreleased "Black Moon" video, which otherwise would have been lost to history. While *Welcome Back* is of some interest, though, it's hard to avoid the impression that with a bit more forethought and effort, it could have been much better.

Note: Released in VHS format by Strand Home Video in 1993. Released in DVD format in 2001.

Emerson, Lake and Palmer Live at the Royal Albert Hall
Image Entertainment VHS ID9697CL, 1996
ELP Live at London's Royal Albert Hall, October 2, 1992

SET LIST:
1. Karn Evil 9, 1st Impression, part 2
2. Tarkus (Eruption/Stones of Years/Iconoclast)
3. Knife-Edge
4. Paper Blood
5. Creole Dance
6. From the Beginning
7. Lucky Man
8. Honky Tonk Train Blues

9. Romeo and Juliet
10. Pirates
11. Pictures at an Exhibition (Promenade/The Gnome/Promenade/The Hut of Baba Yaga/ drum solo/The Great Gates of Kiev)
12. Encore Medley: Fanfare for the Common Man/America/Rondo

★★★^{1}/$_{2}$

Of the four full-length ELP live shows available on video, this one—which gives a near-complete account of the band's Royal Albert Hall show of October 2, 1992 ("Black Moon," "Close to Home," and "Still . . . You Turn Me On" are missing)—probably has the most winning combination of good visuals, good (albeit not outstanding) sonic values, and a good set list. Although this show doesn't evince the unbridled enthusiasm of the Lyceum 12-9-70 performance, coming across as more careful, and certainly much more prechore-ographed, ELP play with considerable energy and panache: the abbreviated *Tarkus* and "Pirates" are particularly outstanding. There is only a subtle hint of the pervasive hoarse-ness that was soon to become a major problem for Lake, while a very brief but ominous omen of Emerson's coming arm problem is captured when he's caught rubbing his right wrist with his left hand as *Tarkus* begins.

Note: Released in VHS format by Beckmann Communications in 1996. Released in DVD format in 2001.

Live at Montreux 1997
Eagle Rock Entertainment DVD EE 39040-9, 2004
ELP Live at Montreux Jazz Festival, July 7, 1997

SET LIST:
1. Introduction by Claude Nobs
2. Evil 9, 1st Impression, part 2
3. Tiger in a Spotlight
4. Hoedown
5. Touch and Go
6. From the Beginning
7. Knife-Edge
8. Bitches Crystal
9. Creole Dance
10. Honky Tonk Train Blues
11. Take a Pebble
12. Tarkus (Eruption/Stones of Years/Iconoclast/Mass)/Pictures at an Exhibition (The Hut of Baba Yaga/The Great Gates of Kiev)
13. Encore Medley (Fanfare for the Common Man/Rondo/Carmina Burana/drum solo/Rondo reprise)

★★★^{1}/$_{2}$

I have already pointed out the shortcomings of ELP's 1997 shows—the spindly Hammond sound, the generic synth patches, the less-than-bracing set list—and this DVD, which pres-ents the band's complete July 7, 1997, set at the Montreux Jazz Festival, illustrates all three tendencies. Nonetheless, this DVD does have one important factor in its favor: it features better camera work and better sonic values than any ELP show previously released in visual format. This factor alone may convince some who are inclined to view late-nineties ELP as little more than a glorified oldies band to check the DVD out. Even shorn of all the massed special effects of their heyday, ELP are a visually dynamic band, and this DVD therefore makes a stronger argument on behalf of ELP's late-nineties shows than the CDs *Live In Poland* or *Then and Now*.

Emerson, Lake and Palmer: Beyond the Beginning
Sanctuary Records DVD 06076-88418-9, 2005

DISC ONE:
Before the Beginning

1. Fire (The Crazy World of Arthur Brown)—1968 Beat Club
2. America (The Nice)—1968 Beat Club

3. 21st Century Schizoid Man excerpt (King Crimson)—1969 Hyde Park

ELP in Pictures

4. Take a Pebble—1970 Beat Club
5. Knife-Edge—1971 Brussels
6. Rondo/The Great Gates of Kiev—Montage from 1970 Isle of Wight performance
7. Rondo—1971 Brussels
8. Tarkus (Eruption)—1972 Tokyo
9. Hoedown—1973 Milan
10. Tank (drum solo only)—1973 Milan
11. Lucky Man—1974 Cal Jam
12. Karn Evil 9, 3rd Impression—1974 Cal Jam
13. Tocatta (percussion solo only)—1974 Aquarius
14. I Believe in Father Christmas—1975 original promo
15. Honky Tonk Train Blues—1976 Oscar Peterson TV Show
16. Fanfare for the Common Man—1977 Montreal promo
17. Pirates—1977 Montreal
18. Tiger in a Spotlight—1977 Pop Rock promo
19. Watching Over You—1978 Memphis
20. Tarkus (Eruption/Stones of Years/Iconoclast)—1992 Royal Albert Hall
21. Touch and Go—1997 Budapest

DISC ONE EXTRAS:
- Extended edit of unseen rehearsal film from 1973
- Sequence focusing on the history of ELP's album covers
- Extended edit of unseen Brands Hatch celebrity motor race featuring ELP
- Interview with Bob Moog

DISC TWO:
Cal Jam, April 6, 1974

1. Toccata
2. Still . . . You Turn Me On
3. Lucky Man
4. Piano Improvisations
5. Take a Pebble
6. Karn Evil 9, 1st Impression, part two (including drum solo)
7. Karn Evil 9, 3rd Impression
8. "Spinning Piano" sequence
9. The Great Gates of Kiev, conclusion

Beyond the Beginning documentary

★★★★

While preparing to submit the final copy of this manuscript for publication, I learned the rumors of the past few years were true: ELP had reobtained copyright clearance to their famed Cal Jam performance of April 6, 1974, and planned to release it on DVD as part of a lavish package that would attempt to forcefully convey, once and for all, what a truly great band they were at the height of their powers. The verdict? On the whole, I believe *Beyond the Beginning* goes a long way in capturing the magic of ELP in their prime. Nonetheless, I'm not convinced that the package couldn't have been even better.

The centerpiece of disc two is the Cal Jam show, arguably the climactic moment of ELP's career. The original two-inch master of the Cal Jam show was purged in the late seventies, so the footage on *Beyond the Beginning* derives from a first generation copy: while visually and sonically cleaner than the bootleg copies of the TV broadcast commonly in circulation (and improving on the Cal Jam portion of *Then and Now*), its sonic and visual values do not measure up to *Live at Montreux* or even *Live at the Royal Albert Hall*. Perhaps this is unavoidable: but one wonders why the complete encore, included on the original TV broadcast, doesn't appear here ("The Hut of Baba Yaga" and much of the "Great Gates of Kiev," up to the spinning piano sequence, are excised).

One can also question some of the tracks included in the centerpiece segment of disc one, *ELP in Pictures*. For instance, why do two tracks from the Cal Jam show appear in identical form here? Several of the tracks are mere snippets; for instance, "Tank" is simply a section of a Carl Palmer drum solo. The disc one extras, while interesting, are not indispensable (for instance, Bob Moog says nothing in the specially recorded interview that he hasn't said many times before), and the sixty-minute documentary on disc two, while promising an "honest" look at the band's history, virtually pretends ELP ceased to exist in 1979, thereby suggesting that the band members are still not prepared for a truly honest accounting of the events of the nineties. These flaws aside, *Beyond the Beginning* is probably the single most essential ELP visual document, and its modest price (in relation to its 250 minutes of content) does nothing to reduce its attractiveness.

Appendix C:
Recommended Further Listening:
A Critical Guide

Shortly after the Cream (featuring Eric Clapton) and the Jimi Hendrix Experience established the guitar power trio as a viable rock music configuration, Keith Emerson's two famous trios, the Nice and ELP, established a new rock music configuration: the multikeyboard power trio. This configuration is a development of the jazz piano trio—Emerson was familiar with the trio work of Art Tatum, Bud Powell, and Oscar Peterson in his formative years—and the jazz organ trio: Emerson's initial contribution was to combine the two lead instruments in a single lineup. However, if with the Nice, "multi-keyboard" simply meant Hammond organ and piano, by the time of ELP, it had come to also entail electric pianos (in Emerson's case, the Clavinet) and more importantly, analog synthesizers. For the most part, the multikeyboard trio configuration has remained closely linked to the stylistic boundaries of progressive rock—unlike the guitar power trio configuration, for instance, which was used by seventies bands as diverse as ZZ Top, Rush, and the Police. Nonetheless, the keyboard trio configuration has had an interesting history within the confines of prog and its close stylistic relatives, especially during the seventies, the golden age of such music, when it was used by several distinguished British and continental European bands: the trio format has provided the opportunity for some of rock's greatest keyboard virtuosos to display facets of their abilities that remained hidden (or underdeveloped) in their work in other configurations. The following mini-discography surveys thirteen albums that a fan of the Nice, ELP, and the keyboard trio format may wish to explore. A number of these albums date back to the seventies, an era when a keyboard trio could create commercially viable music, and highlight the work of several of Emerson's major colleagues (or, more accurately, perhaps, rivals); others are from the nineties prog rock revival, and show some different (and hopefully interesting) directions in which the keyboard trio format has been taken. The albums chosen for this critical discography were required to meet at least two of the following standards, namely (1) the album features a well-known rock keyboardist in a trio setting, (2) the album contains good (and in many cases, far better than merely "good") music, and (3) the album suggests an interesting and original solution to the challenge of working within the confines of a keyboard trio. Entries are arranged chronologically.

Egg
The Polite Force
Deram SML 1074 (U.K., 1970)
Recorded at Morgan Studios, Willesden, U.K.
Dave Stewart, organ, piano, tone generator; Mont Campbell, bass, vocals, piano ("Long Piece," part one), French horn ("Long Piece," part two); Clive Brooks, drums and percussion

1. A Visit to Newport Hospital (Campbell-Stewart-Brooks)
2. Contrasong (Campbell-Stewart-Brooks)

3. Boilk (Campbell-Stewart-Brooks)

Long Piece no. 3 (Campbell-Stewart-Brooks)

4. Part One
5. Part Two
6. Part Three
7. Part Four

★★★★

When one considers that this album came out roughly the same time as ELP's debut album and that the only successful rock keyboard trio available as a model to Egg were the Nice, one begins to understand what an innovative band this was. *Polite Force* wasn't even Egg's first album. Their eponymous debut appeared in 1969: although all the major hallmarks of the band's mature sound were already present, *The Polite Force* represents a more focused and accomplished exploration of the directions posited on the debut.

Dave Stewart, although a good pianist, is much more important as an organist: his unique style fuses the influence of Emerson with the fuzzed Coltrane-like lead lines of Soft Machine's Mike Ratledge and the analog delay techniques of American minimalist composer Terry Riley's electronic organ music (for instance, *A Rainbow in Curved Air*). Mont Campbell, the trio's vocalist, bassist, and principal composer, was deeply influenced by Stravinsky: his musical language is often similar to Emerson's on *Tarkus*—intricate metric shifts, quartal chord voicings, bitonal layers of ostinato patterns—but is less blues-based, less overtly dramatic, and less dependent on virtuoso display.

Egg's style is perhaps given its definitive expression in "Long Piece no. 3," where motoristic modal themes interlock in extraordinarily complex rhythmic configurations; a favored technique is to repeat a theme a number of times, while continuously shifting the accents, or constantly withdrawing and/or adding notes. The interaction between Stewart, Campbell, and drummer Clive Brooks is subtle and breathtakingly tight. The band is also capable of a somewhat melancholy lyricism, evident both in parts of "Long Piece" (especially part two) and in the autobiographical "A Visit to Newport Hospital," the closest they ever came to producing hit rock song material (predictably, it received no airplay). Of the album's diverse stylistic explorations, only the *musique concrète* passages that dominate the overly long "Boilk," as well as the close of parts one and three, have not aged well.

The band broke up in 1972, but regrouped to record one final album, *The Civil Surface*, in 1974. Although not as consistent as *Polite Force* (and much poorer sonically), it contains their two finest individual tracks, "Germ Patrol" and the amazing instrumental "Enneagram," a definitive expression of the fleet, intricately contrapuntal jazz-rock suggested by the opening section of ELP's "Tank." Egg left no musical heirs, which is regrettable, as the almost mystical Platonism of their geometric style—sometimes graceful, sometimes angular—remains unique. Stewart went on to experience some commercial success as a sideman in Bill Bruford's band in the late seventies, where he proved himself a deft synthesist, and as a U.K. singles act (with Barbara Gaskin) during the eighties.

Collegium Musicum
Live
Opus (Czechoslovakia, 1973)
Recorded live at the Concert Hall of Czechoslovak Radio, Bratislava, Czechoslovakia, July 22, 1973
Marián Varga, organ; Fedor Frešo, bass; Dušan Hájek, drums and percussion

1. Burleska/Burlesque (Varga-Frešo-Hájek)
2. Si nemožná/You Are Impossible, part I (Varga)
3. Si nemožná/You Are Impossible, part II (Varga)
4. Monumento/Monument (Varga-Frešo-Hájek)

★★★½

Like the other keyboardists mentioned in this section, Collegium Musicum's Marián Varga was deeply influenced by the work of Keith Emerson. However, unlike the other keyboardists discussed in this section, excepting only Dave Stewart of Egg, Varga's work shows little influence of—in fact, little acquaintance with—ELP. The Soviet invasion of Czechoslovakia in 1968 was followed by a period during which Western popular music was looked upon with deep suspicion by the authorities, and was unevenly disseminated. It's not surprising, therefore, that Varga's work with Collegium Musicum shows a certain unawareness of trends that came to dominate British progressive rock after 1970: well into the seventies, Collegium Musicum's music tended to sound like a product of the late sixties. However, if Collegium Musicum's isolation from mainstream currents in progressive rock's development tend to make their music sound somewhat dated in comparison to contemporaneous prog rock of Western Europe, it also gives Varga's work a certain sense of individuality and distinctiveness. If ELP's music shows one logical continuation of the Nice's musical legacy—a continuation that was largely in line with, and in fact deeply influenced, the development of the mature progressive rock style—Collegium Musicum's work suggests a parallel direction that ELP could have conceivably pursued.

Live, recorded in July 1973, is the band's third album, and features the same trio (Varga, bassist Fedor Frešo, and drummer Dušan Hájek) that recorded their first album, Collegium Musicum, in 1970; the second album, Konvergencie (1971) had added a guitarist, Frantisek Griglak, but the guitar parts were largely extraneous, and by 1973 Griglak was gone. Like nearly every other double LP set of the progressive rock era, Konvergencie suffers from long-windedness and overextension; it still contains some fine music, though, and it marks the emergence of Varga's mature organ style, which fuses Slovak folk motifs, musique concrète–like soundscapes, and a healthy dose of J. S. Bach. Live, which finds Varga further refining this stylistic formula, was the last album Hájek was to appear on, and most agree that Live captures Collegium Musicum at their peak.

There are several areas in which Live diverges quite decisively from what ELP were doing in 1973. While bassist Fedor Frešo had contributed vocals to the band's earlier recordings, Live is an entirely instrumental album—unusual in the context of progressive rock of the seventies. (The Dutch band Focus is the one band that conceivably could have served as a model, and indeed Varga's organ work suggests a familiarity with the playing of Focus's organist, Thijs Van Leer.) On Live, Marián Varga plays only one instrument, the organ—a limitation that Emerson had never imposed on himself even in his pre-Moog days. Varga's self-imposed limitation, while indisputably eliminating a number of potential stylistic directions, did allow him to develop Emerson's late-sixties experiments with electric organ timbres to their logical conclusion. I think it's possible to argue both that Varga is one of only a few rock organists to achieve a truly individual sound, and that he was the last to really expand the electric organ's timbral and textural vocabulary—I would argue that since Live, rock organists have simply been working with the sounds and playing techniques that Emerson and others like Varga forged circa 1967–72. (One possible exception may be Death Organ's Per "Wibärj" Wiberg: see below.) Even more than Emerson, Varga insists on exploding the illusion that the Hammond is a kind of substitute pipe organ, and forces us to acknowledge both its mechanical nature and the fact that it is an electric instrument. His ability to wring a seemingly neverending array of subtly shifting tone-color shadings out of his instrument remains impressive: I always thought the album's cover photo of the three musicians standing in front of an old piece of harvesting equipment is apropos, because there is something industrial about Varga's most characteristic organ sounds, rather like Russian composer Alexander Mosolov's use of the symphony orchestra to evoke the sound of heavy industry in orchestral pieces such as The Iron Foundry. However, Varga also excels at creating a set of cosmic, bell-like "celestial glockenspiel" sounds that are quite different from anything in Emerson's vocabulary, and suggest some acquaintance with either the music of Terry Riley or the music of organists like Soft Machine's Mike Ratledge and Egg's Dave Stewart, who were themselves influenced by Riley.

In short, Varga carried forth the psychedelic era's concern with discovering new electronic tone colors, and experimenting with the quality of the sounds themselves, well after progressive rock and other post-1970 styles had moved on to other areas of concern. Varga's attitude towards composition and improvisation also betrays a pre-1970 sensibility. The Nice's approach in pieces like "Rondo" or "America" was typical of psychedelic rock: a precomposed main theme, heard at the beginning and again at the end of the piece, was separated by long improvised solos over a repetitive bass/drum groove. By 1970, early British progressive rock bands (as opposed to the late-sixties psychedelic bands they had developed out of and away from), were coming to favor ever more elaborate and tightly arranged compositions, with many if not all details of the arrangements carefully worked out in advance, and improvised solos limited to specific sections of the piece; this is the reason that key changes, meter shifts, and instrumental counterpoint could be (and were) developed to much more elaborate levels in British progressive rock post-1970 than in British psychedelic rock of the late sixties. It would not be an exaggeration to say that in a ten-minute performance of the Nice's "Rondo," seventy to eighty percent of the piece's content was improvised, twenty to thirty percent of it was precomposed, whereas in a twenty-minute performance of ELP's "Tarkus," the ratio was reversed. (By the time ELP's own brand of progressive rock reached its high-water mark with "Karn Evil 9," the ratio was probably more along the lines of ninety percent composed, ten percent improvised.)

Structurally, the music on Collegium Musicum's Live has more in common with the Nice than with ELP. To be sure, at their best Collegium Musicum don't just play the theme, improvise a solo, and play the theme again at the end: their approach shows both more variety and more sophistication, and when the improvisations are really happening, the results are stunning. Perhaps the finest example of what the band could do within the compositional/improvisational framework they set for themselves is "Si nemožná, part one." This track opens with the piece's two main themes: a theme that sounds like a polka (or another two-step Slovak dance) kicked into overdrive is followed by a pile-driving J. S. Bach–like theme, replete with unexpected accent displacements. Each theme is repeated a second time; then the band explodes into a dynamic pseudo-baroque improvisation that seems to be a natural extension of the J. S. Bach–like theme. After this group improv winds down, Fedor Freso improvises a lengthy bass guitar cadenza, taking up both the polkalike theme (which he develops along quiet, reflective lines) and the Bach-like theme (which he turns into a driving, metallic sailor's hornpipe). Eventually the band reenters, launching into a psychedelic organ improv loosely based on the pseudo-Bach theme: this improv generates a new fanfare theme that the band will take up later.

But if part one of "Si nemožná" is a completely successful showcase of the rhythmic drive and sense of exhilarating spontaneity that could result from the band's fusion of improvisation and composition, part two shows some of the approach's pitfalls, especially the organ feedback episodes which, like Emerson's, often extend for much longer than necessary, and often seem totally arbitrary in context of the other musical material. The track does contain some musical substance, however, including some nice transformations of the new fanfare theme that emerged near the conclusion of part one, and the meditative section before the recap of the main themes from part one, when Varga uses his organ to evoke the peal of celestial bells, with the rhythm section providing some suitably dramatic punctuation.

It's the final track, "Monumento," however, which best illustrates why British progsters post-1970 became distrustful of psychedelia's extended jams. The main theme is based on the Finale of Igor Stravinsky's Firebird: the band repeat and vary the theme a number of times, after which Dušan Hájek launches into a seven-minute drum solo that has worn out its welcome long before it's done. Afterwards the main theme is dutifully recalled, and, some fourteen and a half minutes later, the piece ends. The main problem with "Monumento" is that no real sense of momentum is ever generated, since there's no sense of inevitability to the succession of musical ideas; a second problem is that when the band begins to rely on clichés (such as long drum solos) to extend the music, the substance of the music becomes very thin. (In this respect, it's no exaggeration to say there is as much richness of rhythmic, textural, and harmonic content in any two minutes of "Karn Evil 9" as there is in the entirety of "Monumento.") In short, if Collegium Musicum's music sometimes suffers in comparison to ELP's, it has nothing to do with the facility of the players: Varga, Frešo, and Hájek are all virtuosos. Rather, it has to do with the fact that ELP's composed music demonstrates more harmonic, metric, and textural substance than Collegium Musicum's music at any point that the latter's improvisational inspiration flags even slightly. At its best, however, Live is a marvelous testament to a band that succeeded in making accomplished, exhilarating and adventurous music despite the difficult conditions faced by rock musicians behind the Iron Curtain.

Le Orme
Felona e Sorona
Philips 6 323 023 (Italy, 1973)
Recorded at Studio Filorama, Milan, Italy, February 1973
Toni Pagliuca, organ, piano, string ensemble, analog synthesizers; Aldo Tagliapietra, vocals, bass, acoustic guitar; Michi Dei Rossi, drums and percussion

1. Sospesi nell'incredibile/Suspended in the Inconceivable (Pagliuca-Tagliapietra-Dei Rossi)
2. Felona (Pagliuca-Tagliapietra-Dei Rossi)
3. La Solitudine di chi protegge il mundo/The Solitude of He Who Protects the World (Pagliuca-Tagliapietra-Dei Rossi)
4. L'Equilibrio/Equilibrium (Pagliuca-Tagliapietra-Dei Rossi)
5. Sorona (Pagliuca-Tagliapietra-Dei Rossi)
6. Attesa Inerte/Lifeless Hope (Pagliuca-Tagliapietra-Dei Rossi)
7. Ritratto di un mattino/Portrait of a Dawn (Pagliuca-Tagliapietra-Dei Rossi)
8. All'infuori del tempo/To the Edge of Time (Pagliuca-Tagliapietra-Dei Rossi)
9. Ritorno al nulla/Return to Nothingness (Pagliuca-Tagliapietra-Dei Rossi)

★★★★

In a distant galaxy of a parallel universe, twin planets, Felona and Sorona, orbit a common sun, unaware of each other's existence. The people of Felona enjoy a happy, bountiful existence on their warm, sunny, beautiful planet; the people of Sorona, meanwhile, eke out a dreary, meager existence on their cold, gray world. The Supreme Being, upon seeing the overabundance of the one world and the want of the other, decides He will distribute all things equally between the two worlds. For a brief time, there is perfect equilibrium, and the people of Felona and Sorona enjoy equal happiness; then the equilibrium is shattered as the positive and negative energies that had animated the two planets are reversed, and both Felona and Sorona are destroyed. Such is the parable—equal parts fantasy and science fiction, and merging philosophical, religious, and political subtexts—upon which Le Orme's *Felona e Sorona* is based.

Le Orme formed in Marghera (near Venice) in 1966; by 1968 the band's three primary members, Toni Pagliuca (keyboards), Aldo Tagliapietra (vocals, guitar), and Michi Dei Rossi (drums) were present in the band, although Le Orme were a five piece at the time. After the bassist and the lead vocalist left the band in 1970, the three remaining members decided to remain a trio, based on the example of the Nice and ELP; instead of recruiting a new bassist, Tagliapietra switched from guitar to bass, and agreed to take on lead vocal responsibilities. It was this lineup that recorded the band's best albums: *Collage* (1971), *Uomo di pezza* (1972), *Felona e Sorona* (1973), *In Concerto* (1974), and *Contrappunti* (1974). Most fans believe that *Felona e Sorona* represents the band's high point.

Le Orme is often called the "Italian ELP," and since both bands are prog rock keyboard trios, there is some obvious stylistic overlap: certainly Le Orme, like nearly every other artistically ambitious rock band of the early seventies, were influenced to some extent by ELP's three groundbreaking albums of 1970-71. Nonetheless, Le Orme's music shows a somewhat different sensibility than ELP's. If one could imagine *Foxtrot*-era Genesis with much less guitar presence, one can get some idea of what Le Orme are about: early King Crimson, Van der Graaf Generator, and Italian prog rockers Banco and PFM offer other points of reference. While Le Orme's music is intricate, it usually eschews the muscular virtuosity of ELP in favor of a melancholy minor key lyricism; Le Orme's classicism is more romantic and less martial and heroic than ELP's, and while ELP tends to alternate classical and folk influences, Le Orme often fuses them.

Felona e Sorona is barely thirty-three minutes long—short even in the vinyl era. Other than the lengthy opening track (a bit over eight minutes in length), the eight subsequent tracks, each of which depicts a segment of the storyline, range from two to four minutes long. "Sospesi nell'incredible," the opening track, is easily the most diffuse: it opens with a mysterious chromatic theme that the band develops first melodically and rhythmically, then fugally; this episode serves as an overture to Tagliapietra's long vocal recitative, which is in turn followed by a number of discrete instrumental episodes. "Felona," launched by the ringing of "church bells" (chimes), is a cheerful, tarantella-like song extolling the joys of life on Felona. "La Solitudine di chi protegge il mondo," dominated by impressionistic washes of piano arpeggios, is a warm tone-painting of the Supreme Being in his exalted solitude as He contemplates the future of the two worlds. "L'Equilibrio," which depicts the moment where the Supreme Being makes His fateful decision concerning the future of Felona and Sorona, marks the first of the album's two big climaxes: Tagliapietra's passionate vocal is followed by a magical, almost incantational synth passage—the Supreme Being is preparing to cast the spell, if you will—and then a driving piano and Moog episode, in alternating bars of five and six beats (I believe I discern essences of the 5/4 riff of ELP's "Trilogy" here), evokes the dramatic moment where equilibrium is imposed upon the two planets.

"Sorona," which opens side two of the LP format, takes us back to pre-equilibrium Sorona, with its melancholy, minor key evocation of a cold, gray planet; there's virtually no percussion. "Attesa inerte," is a quiet yet disquieting song that's almost reminiscent of Pink Floyd: Tagliapietra's simple, almost sing-songish vocal line is accompanied by a plodding bass/drum groove in five, a high, slow-moving string ensemble line that shadows the vocal like a dark cloud, and a synth part that sounds like a car accelerating and de-accelerating in time with the music. The overall effect is one of alienation, powerfully depicting the hopelessness of Sorona's denizens. "Ritratto di un mattino" is a beautiful tone-painting that captures the transition from an eerie darkness to a beautiful sunrise, depicted by the displacement of ominous synth chords by a hymnlike electric guitar melody accompanied by swelling string ensemble chords. "All'infuori del tempo" is almost a kind of bookend to "Felona"; a cheerful, folklike vocal accompanied by acoustic guitar celebrates the arrival of light and joy to Sorona. It is interesting to note that the fanfarelike synth refrain between vocal verses is presciently similar to John Williams's famous main theme for *Star Wars*, although the movie appeared four years later. Suddenly, the music's mood turns from celebratory to pensive, preparing the way for "Ritorno al nulla," the album's second (and final) big climactic point: restlessly bubbling minor-key Hammond arpeggios, soon supported by a swelling Moog bass, augur the entrance of a driving bass/drums groove over which a screaming, doom-laden Moog soliloquy announces the destruction of the unfortunate planets. The track crescendos until the final explosive thunderclap of octaves deep in the bass register.

Like the best Italian prog of the seventies, *Felona e Sorona* is lyrical, dramatic, and nearly operatic at times, although Le Orme avoids both the vocal and instrumental histrionics that mars some Italian prog (think Il Balletto di Bronzo's vastly overrated *Ys*, for instance). Indeed, the band's fans have sometimes pointed to Le Orme's melodicism and restraint as proof of their "superiority" to ELP. Such comparisons are dangerous. Yes, Le Orme's music is generally more melodic, restrained, and tasteful than ELP's. On the other hand, it is useless to insist that Le Orme achieve the relentless rhythmic energy of ELP; for instance, tracks five through eight of *Felona e Sorona*, while very pretty, are more reminiscent of Pink Floyd than ELP in their slow, somewhat plodding tempos. Furthermore, *Felona e Sorona* showcases a band that are most effective as miniaturists writing short songs or instrumental movements that paint specific moods; the album's only lengthy track, the first, does not hang together particularly well, and shows little of the large-scale coherence of any number of ELP tracks of similar length. (One might note that the final two episodes of "Sospesi nell'incredibile," a passage of synth effects that already sounded dated in 1973 and a rather flaccid drum solo, are hardly bracing.)

Incidentally, during their first British tour of 1973, Le Orme agreed to release an English-language version of *Felona e Sorona* on Tony Stratton-Smith's Charisma label, with Peter Hammill translating the lyrics. While the merit of Hammill's highly individualistic translations remain a point of dispute to the present day, nearly everyone agrees that Hammill's translation changed the album into something rather different than the original recording; the original Italian version is therefore to be preferred. At any rate, the English-language version of the album has yet to be released on CD.

Refugee
Refugee
Charisma CAS 1087 (U.K., 1974)
Charisma FC 6066 (U.S., 1974)
Recorded February 1974, Island Studios, London, U.K.
Patrick Moraz, Hammond organ, Saint Albans' pipe organ, piano, electric piano, analog

synthesizers, marimba, Alpine horn; Lee Jackson, vocals, bass, electric cello; Brian Davison, drums and percussion

1. Papillon (Moraz)
2. Someday (Moraz/Jackson)
3. Grand Canyon Suite (Moraz/Jackson)
   1st movement: The Source
   2nd movement: Theme for the Canyon
   3rd movement: The Journey
   4th movement: The Rapids
   5th movement: The Mighty Colorado
4. Gatecrasher (Moraz)
5. Ritt Mickley (Moraz)
6. Credo (Moraz/Jackson)
   1st movement: Prelude
   2nd movement: I Believe
   3rd movement: Theme/4th movement: The Lost Cause
   5th movement: Agitato
   6th movement: I Believe, part II
   7th movement: Variation
   8th movement: Main Theme Finale

★★★★¹/₂

According to Martyn Hanson, after the Nice gigged in Basel, Switzerland, on October 29, 1969, Keith Emerson was holding court in the local hotel lobby, performing an improvised set for an awestruck crowd, when a sharply dressed young man walked up and asked it they could trade licks. The crowd's derisive laughter turned to astonishment when the young local matched Emerson virtually riff-for-riff. Enquiring about the young man's identity afterwards, Lee Jackson learned that his name was Patrick Moraz.

During the summer of 1973, Jackson ran into Moraz in London. Moraz's band Mainhorse had recently failed; Jackson's band Jackson Heights was in the process of disintegrating. Agreeing to try something together, they initially planned to work as a two-piece, but a few rehearsals suggested that a much more ambitious musical direction was emerging, and a full-time drummer was needed. Both Jackson and Moraz knew who they wanted, and in short order Jackson's old mate with the Nice, Brian Davison, had been brought on board. Signed by Tony Stratton Smith, the Nice's old manager, to his Charisma label, the band began composing and rehearsing during the fall of 1973, played their first gig in December of that year, and commenced recording an album in early 1974.

Released in mid-1974, *Refugee* remains a classic of keyboard-driven prog rock. Like virtually every other rock keyboardist, Moraz's Hammond playing can best be described as Emersonesque; in other areas, though, he shows a distinctive style. His piano work is more fluid and graceful, less muscular and percussive than Emerson's; if two of Emerson's chief influences are Oscar Peterson and Ginastera, Moraz's, by way of contrast, are Bill Evans and Ravel. Moraz was steeped in contemporary Eurofunk and was conversant with Jan Hammer's achievements with the Mahavishnu Orchestra, which colored his approach to the Moog and the Rhodes electric piano in a manner distinct from Emerson and other prog rockers. Of Emerson's prog-rock keyboard rivals, only Moraz had a similarly sophisticated grasp of jazz, meaning that Moraz was one of the few whose harmonic sophistication rivaled Emerson's. Based on his later work, I would say Moraz's supreme gift is as an improviser, not a composer—the reverse of Emerson. However, on *Refugee* he creates a series of totally convincing, tightly focused compositions, and Jackson and Davison, eschewing their looser approach with the Nice, show themselves equal to the tight rhythmic unisons and assorted textural details required by the elaborate arrangements.

The album's high point is probably the multimovement suite "The Grand Canyon." The piece opens with an atmospheric electronic keyboards overture, "The Source," which flows into a more clearly defined theme ("Theme for the Canyon"), first presented by Jackson on electric cello, then developed by full band; a beautiful piano interlude leads into Jackson's hymnlike paean to the beauty of the Canyon, "The Journey." This "hymn" builds to a majestic climax; a series of irregularly timed chords, played in tight rhythmic unison by keys, bass, and drums, spills into a frantic jazz-rock episode in seven ("The Rapids") featuring some amazing synth and electronic piano work by Moraz and the finest drumming of Davison's career, as he supplies a continuously shifting array of agile rhythmic doublings for Moraz's figurines. A barrage of drum fills lead into the final section, "The Mighty Colorado," which commences with a scorching Hammond solo by Moraz, followed by a recapitulation and further development of the main theme. Final statements of the theme, first by Moraz, then by Jackson on cello, brings the piece to a huge, crashing close. Each section of the piece moves into the next with a sense of inevitability; the development of the main theme is convincing, and the tight sense of ensemble interplay between the three musicians is extremely impressive. In short, "Grand Canyon" is a prog rock classic.

The album's other big multimovement piece "Credo," is conceptually different than "Grand Canyon"—Jackson expresses an agnostic, existentialist worldview that will be familiar to fans of Peter Hammill, Ian Anderson, Greg Lake, or Peter Sinfield—but is similar musically. If anything it's even more ambitious, although structurally it may not cohere quite as well, with the fascinating individual details of the arrangement occasionally subsuming the momentum of the piece as a whole. Noteworthy are the imposing opening "Prelude" featuring Moraz's Lisztian piano heroics, the sad majesty of the hymnlike "Lost Cause," which builds to a huge climax, and the frenetic "Agitato," another remarkable example of the band's ensemble virtuosity. The album's other three tracks are shorter and less ambitious: "Papillon" is a cheerful, major key pseudo-baroque (think Vivaldi, not Bach) organ raveup, "Ritt Mickley" (named for Moraz's pronunciation of "rhythmically") instrumental jazz-funk, and "Someday" a song in which Jackson comments on his recent divorce.

Throughout the album, Jackson and Davison play with more precision and virtuosity than they ever did with the Nice; for Davison, in particular, the album represents a career highpoint, although Jackson's electric cello work, as well as his rhythmic doublings of many of the Moraz-Davison unison passages on bass, is also impressive. While Jackson's voice retains its characteristic rasp—alas, he was never to be another Greg Lake—he sings the hymnal sections with a smoothness and fullness of voice he never attained with the Nice. Moraz's playing is astonishing throughout. If I have one criticism of this album, it's that there are persistently too many keyboard overdubs; while the problem isn't as bad here as it became on his solo albums of the late seventies (where keyboard overdubs sometimes swallow up excellent rhythm section work), there is on occasion a certain loss of rhythmic thrust under the layers of keyboards. Moraz would have benefited from a strong producer who took a "less is more" approach.

The album sold respectably enough that a U.S. tour supporting Eric Clapton was mooted, but then Rick Wakeman quit Yes, Moraz successfully auditioned, and Refugee were history. At the time Moraz's jump to Yes must have seemed to be a great career move, but considering his relatively brief tenure with Yes, and listening to this album, one can wonder in hindsight if perhaps Refugee would have been a better long-term choice. For years, *Refugee* was unavailable on CD; in 2004 it was finally re-released by Walhalla Records.

Triumvirat
Spartacus
Capitol ST 1-11392 (U.S., 1975)
Recorded at EMI Electrola Studio 1, Cologne, Germany, February–March 1975
Jürgen Fritz, organ, piano, string ensemble, analog synthesizers; Helmut Köllen, vocals, bass, acoustic guitar; Hans Bathelt, drums and percussion

1. The Capital of Power (Fritz)
2. The School of Instant Pain (Fritz-Bathelt)
   a. Proclamation
   b. The Gladiator's Song
   c. Roman Entertainment
   d. The Battle
3. The Walls of Doom (Fritz)
4. The Deadly Dream of Freedom (Köllen-Bathelt)
5. The Hazy Shades of Dawn (Fritz)

6. The Burning Sword of Capua (Fritz)
7. The Sweetest Sound of Liberty (Köllen-Bathelt)
8. The March to the Eternal City (Fritz-Bathelt)
   a. Dusty Road
   b. Italian Improvisation
   c. First Success
9. Spartacus (Fritz-Bathelt)
   a. The Superior Force of Rome
   b. A Broken Dream
   c. The Finale

★★★¹/₂

Founded in Cologne, Germany, in 1969, Triumvirat were a power trio modeled after the Nice, based around the multikeyboard work of Jürgen Fritz and the drumming of Hans Bathelt. The bass/vocalist position proved to be hard to fill on a long-term basis, and the frequent need to refill this position with a new person was to destabilize the band for much of its existence. Indeed, it was only in 1974, when Fritz's cousin Helmut Köllen joined as bassist-vocalist, that the "classic" lineup of Triumvirat was in place. It was this lineup that recorded what nearly everyone considers the band's two best albums, *Illusions on a Double Dimple* (1974) and *Spartacus* (1975).

Both are concept albums, the latter on a decisively more epic scale, dealing with the famous slave rebellion led by an escaped gladiator named Spartacus from Thrace (modern-day European Turkey). Beginning as a minor insurrection involving seventy or eighty gladiators who escaped from the gladiatorial school in Capua, the rebellion spread like a wildfire: at its peak in 72 BC, Spartacus, who was leading an army of 120,000 escaped slaves, won a series of brilliant victories against various Roman armies. The uprising was finally snuffed out in 71 BC by a huge force of six legions led by Marcus Licinius Crassus at a major battle near the headwaters of the Siler River in southern Italy; Spartacus was killed in this battle, and 6,000 of his followers who were captured were later crucified along the Appian Way from Capua to Rome. Although Spartacus probably had no thought of radically remaking Roman society along more egalitarian lines (as some modern Marxist historians have suggested), one can only admire the courage, organizational skills, and military brilliance of a lowly gladiator who held the world's mightiest army at bay for almost two years. One suspects that Triumvirat's *Spartacus* was probably influenced not only by historical accounts of the rebellion, but by Stanley Kubrick's epic movie of 1963.

Triumvirat have often been called "the German ELP"—although the vocals of their albums are in English, as the band was more interested in connecting with the huge U.S. audience of the time than with German-speaking audiences in central Europe—and this description is not inaccurate. Indeed, the central criticism brought to bear against Triumvirat is that not only is their music strongly influenced by the ELP model, it's often openly derivative. That is to say, as much as bands like Refugee and U.K. may sound like ELP on occasion, one is always aware that Patrick Moraz or Eddie Jobson, not Keith Emerson, are the keyboardists; to the contrary, Jürgen Fritz, accomplished keyboardist though he was, never really forged an individual sound, and frequently one can hear the debt to specific bits and pieces of the ELP canon a bit too easily for comfort.

While derivation on such a level does reduce a band's long-term importance, however, it does not necessarily prevent them from making good music. At their worst, Triumvirat link together a series of Fritz's ELP-derived musical themes (occasionally mixed, somewhat awkwardly, with Köllen's more pop-oriented offerings) that, while nice in isolation, don't manage to cohere into a greater whole. This is especially apparent on side one of the LP format, where new musical ideas are often introduced before the previous ones have been fully developed, thus stymieing the creation of any long-term momentum: listen particularly to the unfocused "The Walls of Doom." At their best, however, the band develop their ideas convincingly over time, generating a considerable sense of energy and momentum. In this regard, much of side two of the LP format is completely successful. "The March to the Eternal City," for instance, is based around a recurring episode of icy string ensemble chords accompanied by an ominously treading bass; it's interrupted several times, both by Köllen's vocal verses and by instrumental episodes, and seems to return more forcefully and ominously after each interruption. (One lengthy instrumental interruption, the "Italian Improvisation," creates an almost Tangerine Dream–like soundscape of throbbing bass, driving drum accompaniment, and soaring Moog arabesques, and is quite impressive.) The concluding "Spartacus" medley brings the album to a wholly convincing climax. It begins with a short, reflective, almost Elton John–like mini-song ("The Superior Force of Rome"), then erupts into the battle music of "A Broken Dream," where a driving Hammond/Moog-bass-drums riff, quite reminiscent of the verse music of "Karn Evil 9, 1st Impression, part two," alternates with Köllen's vocal bridges and virtuosic keyboard-bass-drum episodes that musically paint the progress of the battle between Spartacus's forces and the Roman legions—much like the instrumentals of "Karn Evil 9, 3rd Impression." Indeed, the Hammond-and-Moog dominated "Finale" is a driving "sad processional" that sounds as if it stepped directly out of the grooves of the 3rd Impression.

In sum, Triumvirat's best music works well on its own terms. Although the band seldom resorts to the odd or shifting meters effortlessly rendered by ELP, their use of displaced accents, unusual phrase extensions, and stop-time episodes create a similar polyrhythmic energy; the Köllen-Barthelt rhythm section is effective, at times generating the same sense of unstoppable rhythmic energy as Lake-Palmer. If Fritz's musical ideas are frequently derivative, they're still interesting, and he is particularly skillful at sequentially spinning out motives that drive towards a climax, or stitching together repetitions of a short theme with episodes of contrasting material to create an epic sonic tapestry. The album's production values are quite good: one wishes that Palmer's bass drum, in particular, had sounded as massive on ELP's 1970–74 material as Bathelt's does here. Vocally Köllen is no Greg Lake, but he has a pleasant voice, and at their best the lyrics (all by Bathelt) manage to evoke a sense of outrage at the cruelty that Spartacus and his compatriots faced, and sympathy for their cause.

Triumvirat peaked both artistically and commercially with *Spartacus*. They toured the U.S. backing Supertramp (and others) in 1975, and seemed poised to make further inroads into the U.S. market when Köllen suddenly left the band. Sadly, he died in 1977, a victim of accidental carbon monoxide poisoning. With *Pompeii* (1977), Triumvirat managed to make one more album that nearly attained the artistic level of *Spartacus*, but continuous personnel instability sapped the band of the energy it needed for further progression. Triumvirat dissolved, almost unnoticed, in the early 1980s.

In 2002 the band announced their reformation, and in 2003 *Spartacus* was finally rereleased on CD in a fully remastered version, with previously unreleased bonus tracks, by EMI.

Rick Wakeman

Rick Wakeman's Criminal Record
A & M Records SP-4660 (U.S., 1977)
Recorded at Mountain Studios, Montreux, Switzerland, April–June 1977
Rick Wakeman, pipe organ of Église Saint Martin, Vevey, Switzerland, Hammond organ, piano, Clavinet, Birotron, Minimoog, Polymoog, electric pianos; Chris Squire, bass (tracks 1–3); Alan White, drums (tracks 1–3); Frank Ricotti, percussion (tracks 1–3, 5–6); Bill Oddie, vocals (track 5); Ars Laeta Choir of Lausanne, Switzerland, Robert Mernoud, conductor (track 6)

1. Statue of Justice (Wakeman)
2. Crime of Passion (Wakeman)
3. Chamber of Horrors (Wakeman)
4. Birdman of Alcatraz (Wakeman)
5. The Breathalyzer (Wakeman)
6. Judas Iscariot (Wakeman)

★★★¹/₂

Of the thirteen albums in this discography, this is the one that I hesitated the most to include. Why? Simple: it's not the product of a real band. Nonetheless, having included the keyboard trios of Dave Stewart, Patrick Moraz, Eddie Jobson, and Tony Banks, I knew I would not be easily forgiven for neglecting Emerson's most famous rival, Rick Wakeman. There's one problem, though: Wakeman didn't play in a band that was a keyboard trio.

Even his solo albums (of which there are many) usually feature guitars prominently. *Criminal Record* has two advantages for the purposes of the present discussion. First, the first three tracks feature Wakeman accompanied by the formidable Yes rhythm section of Chris Squire (bass) and Alan White (drums), with incidental percussion by Frank Ricotti; these tracks are probably the closest we will ever come to knowing what a Wakeman-led multikeyboard trio would have sounded like. Second, I feel better about including *Criminal Record* in this discography because I happen to believe it is his finest solo album; his playing and arranging are as good here as on his earlier and more famous efforts (*The Six Wives of Henry the Eighth, Journey to the Center of the Earth, Myths and Legends of King Arthur and the Knights of the Round Table*), while his compositions are less piecemeal and more fully developed than before.

Let me begin with a comparison of Emerson and Wakeman. Musicologists who compare J. S. Bach and Handel, the two giants of the late baroque, often begin by noting that if the two composers had been called on to evoke, say, a lightning storm in their music, Handel would have made brilliant use of quasi-pictorial devices to depict flashes of lightning and crashes of thunder; Bach's evocation would have been subtler, since he would have been more concerned about evoking a person's emotional response to a lightning storm than in using music to depict its visual and auditory appearance. In other words, Handel tends to concentrate on evoking the outer appearance; Bach, the inner essence. (Incidentally, a similar comparison is often made between two giants of the late Romantic period, Richard Strauss and Gustav Mahler, with Strauss as Handel and Mahler as Bach.)

From my perspective, Wakeman plays Handel to Emerson's Bach. Wakeman is a virtuoso keyboard orchestrator in a sense that Emerson usually isn't, and is certainly Emerson's equal in terms of playing technique: as a result, he is often capable of creating a more brilliant surface to his music than Emerson. Wakeman is also extraordinarily fluent in creating modulations and smooth transitional passages, a talent that Yes benefited from enormously during Wakeman's tenure with them. In other areas, though, Wakeman suffers in comparison with his rival. His harmonic vocabulary is rather impoverished compared to Emerson's. Wakeman seldom uses either the rich jazz-based chords (ninths, elevenths, thirteenths) or the pungent bitonal chord voicings gleaned from twentieth-century modernists like Bartók and Ginastera that were the staple of Emerson's mature style, and as a result, Wakeman's harmonies tend to sound blandly diatonic by comparison. Wakeman's themes are usually less melodically and rhythmically sophisticated than Emerson's, and at times do not seem to deserve the glittering orchestrations and complex modulatory treatment they are given. Wakeman is the less fluent contrapuntalist of the two; not only does this make his textures less interesting than Emerson's, but his rhythms as well, since rhythmic independence of the melodic strands is one element Emerson uses to forge the polyrhythmic energy of ELP's best music. Finally, Wakeman usually has a less secure grasp of large-scale structure than Emerson, only occasionally showing Emerson's talent for continuously transforming and "growing" themes over lengthy spans of time, and for successfully building longer pieces around a series of increasingly big climaxes. At their worst, Wakeman's structures tend to consist of barely related episodes loosely strung together, unified only by his very real talent for creating smooth transitions; since the music doesn't build up energy over an extended time span, its expressive power is limited. As we'll see below, Wakeman does manage to transcend these limitations, to an extent at least, on *Criminal Record*; I continue to believe, however, that as a composer (as opposed to a keyboardist), Emerson is simply in a different league than Wakeman.

The first three tracks of *Criminal Record*, "Statue of Justice," "Crime of Passion," and "Chamber of Horrors," feature Wakeman accompanied by Squire, White, and percussionist Frank Ricotti. In interest of full disclosure, it should be noted that Squire and White did not record their parts at the same time as Wakeman, but overdubbed them later; this is an impressive achievement, especially given the intricacy of some of the music, but one wonders if the music wouldn't have rocked harder had the trio recorded together in real time. The work of both Squire and White (especially Squire) is immediately recognizable, although not as prominent as it would be on a Yes album: they play the role of a symphonic percussion section, highlighting key passages and reinforcing crucial rhythmic accents, nearly as much as the role of a rock rhythm section (i.e., keeping time and generating rhythmic energy via syncopation and rhythmic displacement). Wakeman's orchestrations are as brilliant as usual, and he deftly interlaces parts played on piano, Hammond, Birotron (a close relative to the Mellotron), Minimoog and Polymoog, and various electric pianos. All three tracks are somewhat episodic in their construction, but they cohere better than many of the tracks on previous Wakeman solo albums: the third track, "Chamber of Horrors," is particularly tightly constructed, with both the main theme and a subsidiary theme being convincingly transformed as the piece proceeds. One notes that the overall mood of these three tracks is cheerful, which is not exactly what you'd expect for music that is supposedly evoking crimes and criminals: this may lend weight to the oft-repeated charge that Wakeman's music is glib and seldom evinces deep feeling of any kind.

Side two of the LP format opens with "Birdman of Alcatraz," a solo piano piece. The most interesting section is the opening—a series of overdubbed trilled piano lines, reminiscent of Olivier Messiaen's stylized evocations of birdsong, flow into a pulsating, slow moving progression of pan-diatonic harmonies. Unfortunately, the rest of the piece is nowhere near this adventurous, but lapses into a somewhat sentimental "folk piano" vein, with slightly syrupy diatonic-modal colorations, that presages his "New Age" recordings for solo piano during the 1980s. At least his piano figurations are never less than interesting. "The Breathalyzer" is a somewhat ridiculous little piece that doesn't take itself too seriously: the first half is built around a cheerful calypsolike theme in five for an ensemble of overdubbed synths, periodically interrupted by pub piano episodes, while the second half of the song is a free blues in which vocalist Bill Oddie expounds on his night of drunken revelry and the ensuing consequences.

Now we come to the album's pièce de résistance, "Judas Iscariot." I pointed out in the main body of this book that I do not believe Emerson's stabs at Great Tradition respectability (for instance, his Piano Concerto) are likely to age as well as his prog rock epics, which I believe will ultimately be judged his "real" masterpieces. On the other hand, it's entirely possible to argue that Wakeman's finest moment as a composer is "Judas Iscariot," an epic cantata for wordless choir, pipe organ, piano, and Moog, wherein Wakeman is obviously working earnestly to create a Masterpiece. The biggest reason "Judas Iscariot" succeeds, in spite of its frequent lapses into four-square phrase structures, is because it's the most structurally cohesive long piece he ever composed; musical paragraphs are expanded to much greater length here than on his earlier albums without losing coherence, the main theme (and its three subsidiary themes) are convincingly transformed with an Emerson-like facility, and, for the first time in Wakeman's solo output, a long piece is successfully sculpted by gradual movement to and from a few big climaxes, giving the music a sense of dynamism that his earlier works lack.

"Judas Iscariot" could have profitably been retitled "Fantasia for Organ, Piano, Moog, and Wordless Choir," as this title gives a more precise sense of what the piece is about. Just over twelve minutes long, the piece falls into two roughly equal halves. It opens with a quiet episode for solo pipe organ that immediately introduces the main theme, a rising minor-key scalar figure; transitional passagework leads to the first variation of the main theme, a bigger pipe organ statement of the opening scalar figure accompanied by crashing piano chords in a triplet rhythm. The piece's first big climax is reached soon thereafter: a stern, declamatory theme on full organ counterpointed by Moog and piano figures. After this climactic passage trails off, Wakeman takes up the main theme on solo pipe organ and quietly develops it in inversion; at roughly 4:20 the wordless choir enters, leading the way to the piece's second big climax, on a new theme presented by choir with organ, Moog, and piano accompaniment. This climactic passage likewise trails off, and as the music grows calmer, the new choral theme undergoes two distinct transformations: first by organ and Moog, then by piano and choir.

At about 6:30 the solo pipe organ reenters and shortly thereafter presents a variation of the opening theme; this marks the beginning of the second half of the piece. This passage slowly builds into the work's third big climax, marked off by a huge passage for organ, Moog, choir, and tambourine; after this climax dissipates, there's a long organ trill, and then Wakeman launches into an extremely impressive pipe organ cadenza. The cadenza, in turn, flows smoothly into another new theme, a beautiful wordless chorale presented a cappella by the choir. The organ eventually reenters, first quietly commenting on the new chorale theme, then stitching in a beautiful variation of the opening theme in augmentation. Beginning quietly, almost mystically, this is one of Wakeman's most inspired passages ever; it evolves into a full-fledged development of the opening theme, and paves the way for the piece's fourth and final big climax, a variant of the stern declamatory theme which had marked the work's first climax but now grows even bigger with the presence of the choir. Besides the work's nearly faultless structural pacing, a big factor in its success is the orchestration: the Moog sounds like a totally natural extension of the pipe organ, and Wakeman is consistently imaginative in working his four primary "colors" (pipe organ, piano, Moog, choir) into ever-shifting combinations. Indeed, Wakeman used a similar arrangement approach on Yes's "Awaken," recorded almost simultaneously, which played an important role in making the piece one of the band's finest ever.

Surprisingly, at the time of this writing *Criminal Record* is available only as an expensive Japanese import. Hopefully this situation will be rectified; if there's any Wakeman solo album that deserves a wider audience, this is it.

U.K.
Danger Money
Polydor PD-1-6194 (U.S., 1979)
Recorded A.I.R. Studios, London, U.K., November 1978–January 1979
Eddie Jobson, organ, piano, analog synthesizers, electric violin, backing vocals; John Wetton, vocals, bass; Terry Bozzio, drums and percussion, backing vocals

1. Danger Money (Jobson-Wetton)
2. Rendezvous 6:02 (Jobson-Wetton)
3. The Only Things She Needs (Jobson-Wetton)
4. Caesar's Palace Blues (Jobson-Wetton)
5. Nothing to Lose (Jobson-Wetton)
6. Carrying No Cross (Jobson-Wetton)

★★★★

In 1977, bassist-vocalist John Wetton and drummer Bill Bruford, the famed rhythm section of King Crimson circa 1972–74, decided to form a band that would carry on the legacy of their former powerhouse group. Bruford brought along Allan Holdsworth, a virtuoso guitarist who had recently worked with the drummer on his first solo album; Wetton, for his part, recruited Eddie Jobson, a young keyboard and electric violin prodigy that he had met during a stint in Roxy Music. For all its talent, the problem with this lineup is that its members never agreed on the identity of King Crimson's legacy that they were ostensibly carrying forward. Bruford and Holdsworth saw it in terms of the inventive, quirky jazz-rock fusion that characterized Bruford's first solo album, *Feels Good to Me*; Wetton and Jobson, in terms of a more song-oriented, vocally based prog rock. Not surprisingly, this lineup did not much outlast the release of their eponymous debut album; Bruford and Holdsworth left (or were forced out, depending on the story), forming Bruford (the band), while Wetton and Jobson hired a young and then largely unknown drummer named Terry Bozzio, declining to replace Holdsworth, and went on to release their second album, *Danger Money*, in 1979.

Many fans prefer U.K.'s debut album; I am part of the minority that prefers *Danger Money*. Granted, the playing of the four principals on *U.K.* is never less than outstanding, but compositionally, only the multimovement suite "In the Dead of Night" emerges as a totally satisfactory achievement; much of the material on side two of the LP format, in particular, shows little compositional focus, often appearing to be little more than a series of improvisations over bass riffs or short chord progressions strung together with instrumental episodes and underdeveloped vocal verses. With *Danger Money*, the Wetton-Jobson songwriting team successfully implements their creative vision: song-oriented, vocally based prog rock with ample room provided for instrumental stretching out.

The model for *Danger Money*–era U.K. was obviously ELP, and the main achievement of U.K. here is not originality, but simply living up to the standard of the stylistic model so successfully, especially at a time when ELP themselves were faltering creatively (keep in mind that *Danger Money* appeared shortly after *Love Beach*). Eddie Jobson was a phenomenally talented multi-keyboardist who was just reaching his full potential when the classic rock era ended in the late seventies—he was only twenty-three when *Danger*

Money appeared. Jobson's approach to piano, Hammond, and analog synths (he especially favored the Yamaha CS-80) owes much to Emerson, but the gothic soundscapes he paints, with their evocations of impending doom, are a product both of his dark, massive synth orchestrations and minor key chromaticism, and are individual and distinctive. Jobson's playing is much less blues-based than Emerson's, but he does show ample acquaintance with seventies jazz-rock fusion, which prevents the kind of harmonic blandness that one often encounters in the work of British prog rock keyboardists (think Wakeman, Banks, or Downes). He also proves an imaginative and effective electric violinist, to the point where entire sections of songs could sometimes be carried with a violin-bass-drums lineup. Wetton has a similar voice to Lake's—a bit smokier and more soulful, perhaps—and by the time of this recording he was in the process of retooling the virtuosic bass approach of his King Crimson days into a sparer but more massive sound. Bozzio, while not yet fully demonstrating the polyrhythmic subtlety that was to mark his later work (or Bruford's work of this period), is already a daunting technician, and functions as a second solo voice at times, much as Palmer had in the confines of ELP.

"Danger Money," the title track, paints a kind of epic film-noir ambience to support Wetton's first-person tale of intrigue and brutal espionage: the song works largely on the strength of several alternately intense and mysterious instrumental episodes. "Rendezvous 6:02," one of the most beautiful prog rock songs of the seventies, supports Wetton's mysterious narrative of a dimly understood encounter with the numinous (a theme he returned to in Asia's "Midnight Sun") with a dramatically atmospheric instrumental arrangement. "Carrying No Cross" is the album's pièce de résistance: again, an ominously atmospheric keyboard arrangement is crucial in supporting Wetton's Dorian Gray–like tale of moral dissolution, but the real center of gravity is the epic instrumental middle section, brought to a frenzied climax by a icily forbidding piano episode that explodes into astoundingly virtuosic Hammond passagework. Among other songs, "The Only Thing She Needs" covers similar conceptual ground to ELP's "Bitches Crystal," and stylistically owes much to the jazz-rock fusion stylizations of the first U.K. album; "Caesar's Palace Blues" is notable for its see-sawing electric violin riff in five and its clever arrangement in which the violin takes both lead and textural roles; and "Nothing to Lose," a short, punchy, melodic song with a typically adolescent theme (running from responsibility); the song's music and lyrical content both anticipate the directions Wetton was soon to pursue with Asia.

Wetton and Jobson never got on particularly well, and U.K. split before the end of 1979. Interested persons may wish to check out *Night After Night: U.K. Live*, a posthumous live album of 1979, which is impressive for demonstrating how fluently the *Danger Money* lineup of U.K. brought off their elaborate arrangements on stage, including the three-part vocal harmonies.

Genesis
Duke
Atlantic SD 16014 (U.S., 1980)
Recorded at Polar Studios, Stockholm, Sweden
Tony Banks, keyboards, backing vocals; Michael Rutherford, basses, guitars, backing vocals; Phil Collins, lead vocals, drums, drum machine

1. Behind the Lines (Banks/Collins/Rutherford)
2. Duchess (Banks/Collins/Rutherford)
3. Guide Vocal (Banks)
4. Man of Our Times (Rutherford)
5. Misunderstanding (Collins)
6. Heathaze (Banks)
7. Turn It On Again (Banks/Collins/Rutherford)
8. Alone Tonight (Rutherford)
9. Cul-de-sac (Banks)
10. Please Don't Ask (Collins)
11. Duke's Travels (Banks/Collins/Rutherford)
12. Duke's End (Banks/Collins/Rutherford)

★★★

Although Genesis are easily the most famous band to appear in this appendix, I almost didn't include them. Why? Two reasons. First, in the eyes of the band's earlier fans, the *real* Genesis was the five-piece lineup of 1969–74—especially the famous one of 1971–74 (Peter Gabriel, lead vocals; Tony Banks, keyboards; Steve Hackett, guitars; Michael Rutherford, basses; and Phil Collins, drums)—or, maybe, the four-piece lineup of 1975–77 (the same lineup as above, but without Gabriel and with Collins assuming the lead vocal- ist's role). Of course, both the band and rock music historians tell us this is the snob's view: it is interesting to note, however, that the band's fans of the 1969–77 era have remained fiercely loyal to the band's legacy, whereas most of the "fans" of the band's pop era of the eighties and early nineties long ago abandoned ship. More to the point, after Hackett departed in 1977, the three remaining members agreed that it would not be feasible to perform live as a trio: for most of their subsequent career, Chester Thompson filled in for Collins behind the drum kit, and Daryl Stuermer filled Hackett's position, on the band's tours. Thus, it can be argued that although Genesis were a keyboard trio in their post- 1977 studio recordings, they never intended to work within the limitations of a keyboard trio in live performances, and therefore ought not to be included in an appendix that doc- uments keyboard trios. Nonetheless, I feel that they are too important a band to simply ignore here; furthermore, I think it is instructive to consider how they function as a key- board trio, even in the more artificial environment of a studio recording.

Duke, released in 1980, is Genesis's second album as a trio. It represents a much more successful adaptation to the trio format than *Then There Were Three* of 1978, Genesis's weakest album since their 1969 debut, which showed a band that sorely lacked the pres- ence of a full-time guitarist. Not only is the arranging better on *Duke*, but the songwrit- ing is stronger; it is also an important transitional album, simultaneously maintaining a link with their earlier progressive rock output (their work of the midseventies, in particu- lar) while anticipating many of their New Wave and pop tendencies of the eighties.

The twelve songs of *Duke* fall into two broad categories. Six of them ("Behind the Lines," "Duchess," "Guide Vocal," "Turn it on Again," "Duke's Travels," and "Duke's End") loosely cohere into what some fans call the "Duke Suite," chronicling the progress of an Everyman figure named Duke (represented on the cover by Lionel Koechlin's cartoon fig- ure), especially in regard to his seeming inability to establish meaningful relationships and his ensuing sense of alienation. Five of these six songs are group compositions. Of the other six songs, there are two each by Banks, Collins, and Rutherford: while these show little musical similarity (either to the "Duke" tracks or each other), they also tend to dwell on themes of loneliness, broken relationships, and social isolation, and thus tie in to the conceptual subject matter, if not the musical substance, of the so-called Duke Suite. It would be going much too far to claim, as some of the band's fans do, that *Duke* is a con- cept album per se; a hallmark of a genuine concept album is that the order of the tracks could not be changed without seriously damaging the album's musical flow and thematic coherence, whereas it's easy to imagine reordering these twelve tracks in any number of ways. (Indeed, I think the album could have been strengthened by putting the six "Duke" tracks together on one side of the LP format, rather than alternating them with the indi- vidually composed songs.)

Not surprisingly, perhaps, the group-composed "Duke" material is the strongest, and shows many of the qualities that marked the band's best material of the seventies. The justly famous "Turn it on Again" shows the band successfully melding the lean, lin- ear textures and motoristic polyrhythms of New Wave (think the Talking Heads) with their trademark shifting meters (13/4, in this case) to create a song that's tuneful, ener- getic, and filled with unexpected little twists and turns. "Behind the Lines" and the "Duke's Travels/Duke's End" medley that closes the album show the band had not lost their ability to generate considerable momentum via complex metric shifts, surprising chord changes and modulations, and imaginative riff development and thematic trans- formation. Furthermore, "Duchess" and "Guide Vocal" show that the band retain the reflective, lyrical, somewhat melancholy side of their muse. "Duchess," in particular, with its electronic "ethnic" drums (a then-new effect that was later to be grossly over- used, but which sounds fresh and appropriate here), its subdued but rich keyboard tap- estry, and its smoothly curving vocal melody, rendered with considerable passion by Collins, bears comparison with any number of Genesis's best songs of the seventies, in which the lyrics convey both an engrossing character study and a deeper philosophical preoccupation.

Unfortunately, the group-composed "Duke" material constitutes only half of the total album, and the songs written solely by Banks, Collins, and Rutherford are for the most part considerably weaker. Banks's "Heathaze" is probably the best of the lot; filled with surprising modulations and chord changes, its chorus, in particular, attains the sense of bittersweet poignance that marks his best work, although rhythmically the song plods a bit. His other contribution, "Cul-de-sac," shows more rhythmic energy, but seems unfinished; it contains isolated passages of snappy riffs and interesting chord progressions that never quite cohere into a larger whole. Of Rutherford's two songs, "Man of Our Times" is the best, with the strident guitar arpeggios of the verse generating some New Wave energy; its main fault is that it goes on two minutes longer than its substance warrants. "Alone Tonight" is, by comparison, maudlin and trivial. The same, alas, is true of Collins's two songs. "Misunderstanding" is easily the worst song on the album, utterly lacking in melodic, harmonic, and rhythmic interest, betrayed by its clichéd "you-done-me-wrong" lyrics, and unredeemed by its faux doo-wop piano chords and vocal harmonies—which, incidentally, lack any sense of the warmth essential to real doo-wop. Of course, the song was a smash hit in the U.S. (#14), which simply proves that audiences will buy anything if it's given sufficiently unremitting airplay. His other song, "Please Don't Ask," is quite a bit better, if for no other reason than the autobiographical lyrics come across as genuinely heartfelt, but the song's saccharine music prevents the lyrics (which are, at any rate, given an overly precious interpretation by Collins) from rising beyond the level of sentiment.

In sum, while *Duke* has its moments, it is no masterpiece. There are a couple of arrangement and production peculiarities that mar the album as a whole. At a point when the band had been pared down to a trio, one might have expected Tony Banks to step forward and fill more sonic space with a greater variety of tone-colors and textural configurations. *Au contraire.* Banks had, by this point, abandoned his four main keyboards of the seventies—Hammond organ, Mellotron, ARP Pro Soloist (ARP's answer to the Minimoog), and acoustic piano—entirely. Their place is not adequately filled by the Yamaha electric grand piano and the Polymoog which he relies on almost exclusively for *Duke*: these are used to produce a series of bell-like and stringlike washes of sound, the sonic equivalent of a landscape painter who refuses to paint with any colors other than pastel greens and earth tones. Furthermore, at a time when Steve Hackett's melodic electric guitar arabesques were no longer available to the band, it is odd that Banks's playing becomes more textural and less lead-oriented than before. I'm not saying that I wished *Duke* contained scads of two-minute keyboard solos, but one notes how little of Banks's playing here is melodically memorable: other than the sharply etched riffs he supplies behind some of the vocal hooks and his lead work on the overture to "Behind the Lines" and the closing medley, he's largely reduced to supplying sustained block chords and background arpeggios.

Indeed, Genesis's arrangement/production plan for *Duke* seems to have been to move the keyboards farther into the sonic background, and to project the drums and bass more aggressively. This was a sensible enough goal, given the trends in contemporary New Wave, but the production of the drums, in particular, is not very good, resulting in a flat, "dead" drum sound that impacts the entire lower end of the mix: the rather lifeless drum sound in the lower end of the mix, combined with the somewhat monochromatic keyboard timbres of the higher end, result in a thin, two-dimensional sound across the entire album. It is probably no coincidence that this was the last album that David Hentschel produced for Genesis. In some ways *Abacab*, the band's next album, represented a more successful realization of their musical vision: by then, however, they had become a straight-ahead pop band with some New Wave trimmings. One wishes a Banks-Rutherford-Collins album had been recorded when Genesis were still interested in projecting themselves as instrumentalists, as opposed to crafters of hit singles: of all of the band's trio albums, though, it is *Duke*, even with its undeniable flaws, that comes closest to suggesting what the Banks-Rutherford-Collins lineup was capable of as a rock multi-keyboard trio.

Death Organ
9 to 5
Ad Perpetuam Memoriam 9506 AT (Sweden, 1995)
Recorded at Abyss Studio, Nyhammar, Sweden, 1994
Per "Wibärj" Wiberg, (death) organ, backing vocals; Marcus Källström, drums, backing vocals; Klas Hägglund, bass; Patrik Schultz, lead vocals; Jocke Sjöström, lead vocals
All music by Death Organ/lyrics by Per Wiberg

1. Hate
2. Sane?
3. Workers
4. Abuser
5. Greed
6. Control
7. Miles Away

★★★

Okay, I cheated here: this band is a five-piece. However, two of the members are vocalists, so the instrumental lineup (frequently featured in this band's music without vocal decoration) is organ-bass-drums; incidentally, no other keyboard is ever used in Death Organ's music, making this album more dependent on the Hammond than any other album discussed in this section save Collegium Musicum's *Live*.

It must be admitted that this band's music will not be for everybody reading this book. Death Organ came together in the early nineties, and reflect the two major tendencies of the Swedish rock scene at that time: a strong interest in extreme styles of metal, and a rebirth of interest in prog rock of the seventies. Specifically, Death Organ is all about fusing late-sixties/early-seventies organ-driven hard rock with early nineties death metal, and undoubtedly there will be those who find the band's entire premise to be misguided. Perhaps the biggest single influence on Death Organ's music is Atomic Rooster's organist, Vincent Crane: like Crane, Death Organ's Wibärj excels at spinning out memorable four- or eight-bar riffs, and Death Organ songs are often sectional, with each section being built around a particular organ riff. Keith Emerson would seem to be a lesser influence: Death Organ's music displays none of Emerson's jazz or modernist influences, and Wibärj's playing showcases little of Emerson's soloistic virtuosity. Nonetheless, on occasion Death Organ is reminiscent of the Nice and ELP, especially their minor key, riff-driven, baroque-inflected numbers (think "Dawn," "Knife-Edge," "Time and a Place," and "Living Sin"). If Crane and Emerson represent one side of Death Organ's musical genealogy, late-eighties/early-nineties metal represents the other: one hears traces of Faith No More (an eighties Bay Area band that anticipated nineties rap-metal) and Fear Factory, a major player in the early nineties death metal scene. The lyrics, in English, are often somewhat bitter and angry in tone, and tend to deal with relationships that didn't pan out (the theme of betrayal frequently recurs), or else express disillusionment and existential angst with the course of the world. The cover art, an imaginative depiction of the Grim Reaper, captures the vibe of the album quite well.

The typical Death Organ song has several recurrent features. As stated above, many of the band's songs are sectional, with each section built around a particular organ riff. The verses are arranged in such a way that the two lead vocalists engage in a continuous call-and-response; one sings with a seventies blues-rock rasp, the other with a nineties death-metal growl, and, as more than one person has pointed out, the result is a bit like a constant call-and-response between Led Zeppelin's Robert Plant and the Cookie Monster from Sesame Street. Needless to say, it is this aspect of Death Organ's music that some listeners find most difficult to acclimate to. If the verses alternate the lead vocalists in call-and-response, the choruses bring them together in vocal harmonies: a number of Death Organ songs ("Hate," "Workers," "Abuser") feature somewhat bland, major-key vocal choruses that don't always seem to be an ideal fit with the dark, turbulent music that surrounds them.

Instrumentally, though, the band is very strong. Klas Hägglund is a formidable bassist, capable of accompanying Wibärj's organ riffs with either throbbing, sixteen-beat style funk bass lines or trebly, Chris Squire–like counter-leads; drummer Marcus Källström is also very good, and Death Organ is capable of creating a Magma-like rhythmic drive. Death Organ's songs frequently feature extended instrumental episodes or codas: at their best, as in their gripping development of a four-bar Bach-like ritornello during the long coda of "Abuser," a combination of sequential development of the melody, a gradual increase in volume, and imaginative transfers of the theme between bass and organ contribute to the creation of an enormous and exceedingly powerful climax.

Although he is not a virtuoso in the Keith Emerson mold, Wibärj is the first organ player in a generation to create an individual and personal sound; the menacing growl of his instrument in its lower registers, and its urgent peal in its higher registers—it often sounds no more than half a decibel away from feeding back—is distinctive and immediately recognizable. Wibärj uses organ feedback very musically. Unlike Emerson, who early on became far too dependent on creating feedback episodes that, while interesting in themselves, have little connection with the song of which they were nominally a part (e.g., the Nice's "Karelia," ELP's "The Great Gates of Kiev"), organ feedback becomes a key expressive feature of many Death Organ songs. For instance, feedback is used as an integral part of the song's texture during the opening riff of "Workers," the close of "Abuser," where it brings the development of the Bach-like theme to a fitting climax, the middle of "Greed," where it creates a sirenlike effect, and the end of the bass solo on "Control."

The pièce de résistance of 9 to 5 is the nine-minute-plus final track, "Miles Away," dedicated to the memory of the recently deceased giant of jazz trumpet and composition, Miles Davis (1926–1991). On the one hand, there is nothing remotely "jazz" about this hard-driving (and purely instrumental) rock epic. On the other hand, it is possible to hear the influence of Davis in the stark melodic simplicity and effective use of rests that characterize the track's eight-bar main theme, as well as in the theme's melancholy minor key lyricism and its use of open harmonies and modality to convey a sense of vast, limitless expanse. Like much of Death Organ's best music, "Miles Away" also displays considerable harmonic sophistication beneath its apparent simplicity. The composition consists of two main sections. The first is dominated by the main theme, in B minor, which is interrupted on one occasion by an episode featuring a complex, E minor bass riff that cuts polyrhythmically against the accompaniment. The second, longer section develops another of the quasi-baroque themes that Death Organ seem to excel in creating. The theme is repeated nine times in all; it's played on the bass throughout, and an important part of the development process involves the gradual addition of volume and distortion to both the bass line and the accompanying organ chords. These organ chords are all triads, which fosters the illusion of simplicity; however, the chord roots consistently move by whole tones, meaning that the theme is never in one key very long before sliding into a new one. It is the restless movement from one key to another, as the theme and its accompanying chords seem to seek out a home key that is never quite located, as much as the gradual but inexorable increase in volume, distortion, and register, that gives the piece's climax its shattering impact. Every three repetitions of the theme brings the overall chord cycle to a finish (at this point major triads have been sounded on eleven of the chromatic scale's twelve tones), and a new one is begun; the plan is very logical, mathematical even, yet it sounds very spontaneous, full of primitive energy, in performance. About the best compliment I can pay to "Miles Away" is this: it is the only piece of progressive music from the nineties that I ever gave serious consideration to covering with my band Hermetic Science.

In 1997, Death Organ released a second album, Universal Stripsearch, which represents a logical development of (and improvement on) many of the first album's main premises. The sound is fuller (in particular, there's a more clearly defined bass presence) and less murky. The vocal arrangements are more flexible and imaginative than before. The band relaxes the stereotypical call-and-response approach to the verses that had marked the first album; sometimes both of the vocalists actually sing at once (as opposed to the first album's predictable alternations between singing and monster growling), while at other times one sings and the other rhythmically declaims (here one perceives the influence of nineties rap metal). The vocal choruses become more sharply profiled melodically and better integrated into the rest of the song: in a couple of cases ("Done!" and "Satisfied"), the band even crafts memorable hooks. Again, the album's pièce de résistance is a nine-plus-minute closing track. Entitled "3D Days," it falls into two large sections: the first is built around an unusual three-bar riff (two bars of four plus a bar of five) that is imaginatively varied and developed, while the second shows the band moving away from the death metal influence in new and promising directions.

Dominated by a melancholy eight-bar progression of organ chords played with a kind of Infernal *voix celeste* setting and accompanied by stately drumming and a slowly treading bass line, this section opens into a kind of vast, limitless northern expanse of the imagination that reminds one of fellow Scandinavian rockers Sigur Rós, whose impressionistic, almost hallucinatory drone-rock may represent the most important contribution to rock during the late nineties. Eventually, the rhythm section drops out, leaving Wibärj spinning out a spooky, swelling organ fantasy. Before this dissipates into the æther, yet one last involuntary reference comes to mind: Hugh Banton's swirling organ soundscapes on Van der Graaf Generator's masterpiece, *Pawn Hearts*. It is possible that *Universal Stripsearch* is not so concise and tightly focuses as the first album: there's a bit more padding (the long, unnecessary instrumental codas of "Ahead," "Stripsearch," and "Repeat"). Furthermore, there is nothing on the second album to equal the achievement of "Miles Away."

Unfortunately, soon after the release of *Universal Stripsearch*, the band's small Swedish label, Ad Perpetuam Memoriam, folded, and soon thereafter, so did Death Organ. While the band's prog/death-metal fusion is undoubtedly not for everyone, it can be argued that Death Organ was one of a very few genuinely original bands to come out of the nineties prog revival: one can only wish they had the opportunity to record at least one more album on which they could have further developed and refined their approach.

Ars Nova
The Book of the Dead (Reu Pert Em Hru)
Musea FGBG 4255.AR (France, 1998)
Recorded at Studio Triade, Tokyo, Japan, August 1997 to August 1998
Keiko Kumagai, keyboards; Akiko Takahashi, drums; with guest musician Ken Ishita, bass
All music composed by Keiko Kumagai

1. Prologue: Re
2. Ankh
3. Interlude 1: Nut
4. The 42 Gods
5. Interlude 2: Anubis
6. Held of Iaru
7. Interlude 3: Sekhem
8. The Judgment of Osiris
9. Interlude 4: Nephthys
10. Ani's Heart and Maat's Feather
11. Epilogue: Hapi

★★★½

During the 1990s, Ars Nova achieved a certain level of fame in their home country of Japan, and among the worldwide progressive rock community, for two reasons: first, for their elaborate and virtuosic update of ELP's *Tarkus*-era soundscapes; and second, because they were, for much of their existence, at any rate, an all-female band working in a genre in which both musicians and fans were overwhelmingly male.

Ars Nova originally came together at a university in Tokyo in 1983; keyboardist Keiko Kumagai, who was to become the band's primary composer and moving force, joined in 1985. Shortly thereafter the band folded, and nothing more was heard of Ars Nova for several years. In 1992, as the worldwide prog rock revival began to pick up steam, Made in Japan Records convinced Kumagai to revive the band, and Kumagai, bassist Kyoko Saito, and drummer Yumiko Saito recorded *Fear and Anxiety*. Within a year, however, Kumagai's rhythm section deserted her, and during 1993 she recruited bassist Kyoko Kanazawa and drummer Akiko Takahashi. This lineup recorded *Transi* (1994) and *Goddess of Darkness* (1996); their performance at Progfest 1995 in Los Angeles brought them to prominence in the international prog rock community. *Goddess* and subsequent albums have been released in Japan by Made in Japan Records and in the rest of the world by the French Musea label, usually with slightly different track listings. In 1998 the band released

The Book of The Dead, a concept album based around the Egyptian Book of the Dead, with Ken Ishita (ex-Déjà Vu) filling in on bass for recently departed Kyoko Kanazawa. In 1999, the *Transi* lineup recorded some covers of classic keyboard-oriented seventies prog for an album called *Keyboards Triangle*, a joint project with another Japanese band, Gerard. The most recent Ars Nova album, *Android Domina*, was released in 2001: this album, which raised some eyebrows on account of the ladies' recently acquired bondage/S&M garb, also saw Kumagai give up on trying to fill the unstable bass guitarist's role, instead bringing in a second keyboardist, Mika Nakajima, to supply bass lines and background keyboard textures.

While many prog fans look on the *Transi/Goddess of Darkness* lineup as the "classic" Ars Nova configuration, it's possible to argue that *Book of the Dead* represents their zenith in terms of compositional maturity and consistency. The album is dominated by five substantial prog rock compositions that use the instrumental movements of ELP's *Tarkus* as their stylistic basis; these alternate with short, atmospheric keyboard interludes of no great consequence (although one of them, "Sekhem," is a fascinating experiment in polyrhythmically layered percussion, evoking a kind of postmodern belly dance). In the five prog rock tracks, textures are ordinarily very dense, dominated by angular ostinato patterns over which flicker an ever-shifting array of short motives, at times presented contrapuntally, and an occasional longer tune. Kumagai is a very effective keyboard orchestrator, favoring a mix of analog instruments (the Solina, a seventies-vintage string ensemble), analog-sounding instruments (digital piano, the Hammond XB-2, which she uses with considerable verve and imagination), and modern digital keyboards. She's an authentic virtuoso, and at times it's hard to believe one person can play in real time the dense web of keyboard counterpoint that often characterizes Ars Nova's music. She also possesses an apparently encyclopedic knowledge of keyboard-dominated prog of the seventies: at various times during *The Book of the Dead*, one can hear subtle references to ELP's "Baba Yaga" music (the opening of "Judgment of Osiris"), U.K.'s "Danger Money" (from around 5:00 of "Osiris"), Balletto di Bronzo's "Ys" (1:45 into "Ani's Heart and Maat's Feather"), and Rick Wakeman's "Judas Iscariot" (the first main theme of "Held of Iaru"). As the reader might guess, Kumagai's compositions are not particularly original in terms of their basic musical substance: what gives them distinction is her imaginative keyboard arrangements, which lend the almost unrelievedly dense textures a constantly shifting array of tone-colors. One might cite, to name just two examples, the interesting combination of Mellotron-like string melody with gamelan-like tuned percussion accompaniment in "Ani's Heart and Maat's Feather," or the oddly effective percolating filter sweep counterpoint to the heroic march theme at 3:00 of "The 42 Gods." However, the album contains a number of other interesting coloristic combinations along similar lines.

In another sense, though, the music of Ars Nova is very different from its stylistic sources: beneath the outward similarity of the driving ostinato patterns, the quartal harmonies and bitonal chord voicings, the odd meters, and the "symphonic" tone colors lurks a totally different structural dynamic. Indeed, like a lot of nineties prog both good and bad, listening to *The Book of the Dead* is rather like viewing seventies prog through a postmodern prism. The compositions of Ars Nova flash past in ever-mutating, flickering fragments rather than developing through gradual transformation and variation; despite the nervous (and often relentless) rhythmic energy, the compositions don't really "go anywhere," don't drive inexorably forwards towards a distant goal in the manner of "Supper's Ready," "Close to the Edge," or the "Karn Evil 9" Impressions. (Although one might conceivably point to a seventies precedent in the solo albums of Rick Wakeman.) To put it another way: Kumagai extends and elaborates her ideas totally convincingly within the sections of a composition, but one section moves to the next with a quick transition or with no transition at all, and the sections of an Ars Nova composition don't have the same dynamic interdependence as the sections of an ELP composition. One could switch the order of the sections, or eliminate some sections entirely, without doing drastic damage to the composition. Unlike the most characteristic seventies prog, it's not hard to imagine Ars Nova's music working in the MTV video format: nothing essential is lost if one tunes in after the beginning of the composition is done, or if one tunes out before the end of the composition is reached.

One example of Kumagai's approach to constructing lengthy pieces by linking more or less self-contained sections will need to suffice. "Held of Iaru," at 10:43 the album's longest track, begins with a pseudo-fugal "orchestral" prelude of approximately forty seconds—we'll call this section A. It's followed by a big Romantic theme reminiscent of part of Rick Wakeman's "Judas Iscariot," wherein a soaring Minimoog melody is accompanied by digital pipe organ and choral patches, this theme being interspersed with attractive bell-like passages and a Hammond episode. This whole theme complex can be labeled section B. A sentimental acoustic piano passage (section C) leads at 3:42 into an impressive piano cadenza with an overripe late-Romantic/early-modernist feel; in many ways this cadenza (section D) is the track's center of gravity, as it's the one section one couldn't imagine eliminating. The cadenza segues into a new section of music based around a throbbing rock rhythm and exemplified by a remarkable Hammond theme built around diminished seventh chords (at 5:44); this is the E section. A rare bit of keyboards-bass-drums interchange (more on this in a moment) leads into a return and expansion of the sentimental piano theme (C). The music eventually begins to rock out again at about 8:40, and at 9:19 the Hammond's diminished seventh theme, now diabolically distorted, is recalled. The finale (from 10:15) is very loosely based on the rock rhythm of 5:00. The overall structure, then, might be described as follows: A B C D E C E. It's interesting to note that within these loosely constructed episodic formats, the first themes are not necessarily the "main" ones, and it's often hard to determine which, if any, are a composition's "main themes." (In this track I hear the Hammond's diminished seventh theme as the "main" theme, simply because it's the only memorable theme heard more than once.) "Ani's Heart and Maat's Feather," the album's second-longest track, has a similar outline: A B C D E F D, with only one section (a Mellotron-like string theme with gamelan-like accompaniment) being recalled more than once. Even when an opening theme complex does recur at the end of a track ("Ankh," with its relatively simple A B C A outline), there's nothing inevitable about the opening section's return.

If one believes that progressive, goal-oriented structures are an essential part of progressive rock, then it's possible to argue that Ars Nova (and many other bands of the nineties prog revival) imbided the letter of seventies prog without ever really absorbing its spirit. Even if one doesn't see goal-orientation as essential to progressive rock, there is one area in which Ars Nova are weak in comparison to their putative models. To apply Bill Martin's useful concept, the center of rhythmic gravity is virtually always in the keyboard parts: even in ELP the three musicians play a more equal role in laying out the music's rhythmic backbone. Because in Ars Nova's music the rhythm section has such a strictly accompanying role (although Akiko Takahashi is technically a very adept drummer), and because the drums sound is so electronic and overproduced, the music often sounds as if Kumagai simply programmed the drum parts and recorded the bass parts on synth. In this respect, *Book of the Dead* reminds me less of ELP than of Keith Emerson's *Iron Man* soundtracks, with its programmed drums and its highly episodic structures in which musical logic is shaped by the plotlines of the cartoons that the music accompanies. Nevertheless, one can enjoy Ars Nova's music for Keiko Kumagai's outstanding musicianship and compositional fluency; Ars Nova certainly are an important and characteristic representative of many tendencies of the nineties prog rock revival.

Medeski, Martin and Wood
Combustication
Blue Note CDP 72434 93011 2 2 (U.S., 1998)
Recorded at The Magic Shop, New York, New York
John Medeski, keyboards; Billy Martin, drums and percussion; Chris Wood, basses and bass
   drum

1. Sugar Craft (Medeski-Martin-Wood)
2. Just Like I Pictured It (Medeski-Martin-Wood)
3. Start-Stop (Medeski-Martin-Wood)
4. Nocturne (Medeski-Martin-Wood)
5. Hey-Hee-Hi-Ho (Medeski-Martin-Wood)
6. Whatever Happened to Gus (Medeski-Martin-Wood-Steve Cannon)
7. Latin Shuffle (Medeski-Martin-Wood)

8. Everyday People (S. Stewart)
9. Coconut Boogaloo (Medeski-Martin-Wood)
10. Church of Logic (Medeski-Martin-Wood-Jason Kibler)
11. No Ke Ano Ahiahi (Traditional)
12. Hypnotized (Medeski-Martin-Wood)

★★★★

It has been said before, but it's worth repeating: since the late seventies, in virtually any musical genre you would care to mention, the most compelling innovation has taken place in the realms of tone-color and texture, and has usually been conducted by musicians whose imagination and invention supersedes their virtuosity. In both of these respects, Medeski, Martin and Wood—or, as they're often called, MMW—are wholly typical.

MMW, the most famous keyboard trio to emerge during the 1990s, came together in Brooklyn in 1991. They soon began playing clubs, and by early 1992 had released their first album, the self-produced *Notes from the Underground*. In 1993, they signed a deal with Gramavision, who released their second album, *It's a Jungle In Here*; in 1994 they undertook their first American/Canadian tour in an RV. They continued to tour incessantly in 1995 (now in a bus), and in 1996 they recorded *Shack Man*, the album on which a distinctive, immediately identifiable MMW sound emerges for the first time. *Shack Man* represented both an artistic and commercial breakthrough for the band, and when their contract with Gramavision expired the next year, there were seventeen labels interested in MMW. The band chose Blue Note records, the famous jazz label, and in 1998 recorded their first album for their new label, *Combustication*.

Like ELP, MMW are a very eclectic band, and as is the case with ELP's classical, jazz, folk, and rock sources, it's not always easy to explain how MMW's diverse influences—jazz, funk, hip-hop, trance—cohere. This is not to say ELP are a direct influence on MMW; indeed, I hear MMW having more in common with the Nice than with ELP. There's little prog rock influence discernible in MMW's music, but it is possible to hear some scattered similarities between some of the Nice's jazzier music (think "Little Arabella") and MMW: clearly there are some jazz and R & B roots shared by both bands.

On the other hand, MMW are much influenced by seventies funk and jazz-rock, and here's where I think it would be useful to compare MMW to a band that, to my knowledge, they've not been compared to before: the British jazz-rock band Soft Machine, especially that band's 1972-73 period (i.e., their albums *5*, *Six*, and *Seven*). The opening track of *Combustication*, "Sugar Craft," demonstrates this similarity especially clearly, paralleling the "stoner fusion" sound of midperiod Soft Machine to an almost uncanny degree. The tempo is slow and relaxed, almost narcotic. The backbone of the track is Chris Wood's short, syncopated bass ostinato, which is accompanied by a Billy Martin drum groove whose fusion of swing and march elements evokes the work of Soft Machine drummer John Marshall. John Medeski's Hammond organ floats over the top of the Wood-Martin groove, spinning out sparse, bluesy lead lines and vamp figures. Three times during the course of "Sugar Craft," the music is interrupted by a "cosmic" organ arpeggio that writhes about and overlaps itself in a sea of reverb: while I'm certain MMW's source for this type of episode is nineties trance, the resemblance to some of organist Mike Ratledge's work with Soft Machine (particularly the famous opening to "Out-Bloody-Rageous" from the Soft's *Three*) is striking. Like Soft Machine, MMW's keyboard-bass-drum arrangements leave a lot of open sonic space. Unlike Soft Machine, though, who use a horn player to fill in the open space, MMW use a DJ, DJ Logic, who guests on "Sugar Craft," "Start-Stop," and "Church of Logic": Logic's rhythmic scratches, pulsating buzzes and whooshes, and disjunct vocal fragments paint a kaleidoscopically shifting textural backdrop to MMW's music, and draws a subtle stylistic link between MMW and early hip hop.

Even the tracks that DJ Logic doesn't appear on show a careful attention to subtle textural detail. For instance, the outstanding "Nocturne," a slow, hazy, atmospheric track, is built over Chris Wood's perpetually repeated (but constantly varied) eight-bar bass line, and features a constantly shifting array of subtly varied percussive patterns and fragmentary keyboard melodies that sometimes alternate with, and other times are combined with, purely textural effects. In all, at least half of the tracks on *Combustication* sound like an update of midperiod Soft Machine for the nineties. The Soft Machine/MMW parallel is further reinforced by the fact that MMW's John Medeski favors the same three keyboards as Soft Machine's Mike Ratledge—Hammond, Rhodes electric piano, and acoustic piano, roughly in that order. (Medeski is also fond of the sound of the Hohner Clavinet, another classic seventies keyboard.)

However, *Combustication* is more than a mere update of midperiod Soft Machine. Two tracks, "Hey-Hee-Hi-Ho" and "Coconut Boogaloo," evoke Herbie Hancock's greasy jazz-funk of the seventies—indeed, both sound a bit like variants of Hancock's "Chameleon"—and feature a less atmospheric, grittier sound than the tracks discussed above. Both of these tracks contain interesting rhythmic elements. "Hey-Hee-Hi-Ho" features a unique episode of claps that cut polyrhythmically against a short, groove-oriented Billy Martin drum solo, while "Coconut Boogaloo" introduces a "stutter" rhythm that constantly varies the main theme, keeping both musicians and listeners on their toes. Both of these tracks also showcase Medeski's fondness for comping on the Clavinet with his left hand while spinning out a Hammond lead with his right.

Two other tracks, "Whatever Happened to Gus" and "Latin Shuffle," show MMW operating in a more or less straight-ahead modern jazz vein. "Whatever Happened to Gus" is built on a four-bar string bass riff with delicate bossa-nova-like drum accompaniment: this groove figure is overlaid with vaguely ominous, more or less atonal electronic keyboard figures that are largely textural in conception. The "lead" is Steve Cannon's spoken poetry, actually a stream-of-consciousness history of bop in which drummer Gus Johnson is hailed as the music's unsung key figure. The whole track evokes memories of live readings of Beat Poetry during the fifties. "Latin Shuffle" is the album's only track on which MMW evince an ELP-like flamboyance and virtuosity: over a rock solid, hypnotically repetitive two-bar bass ostinato, Billy Martin layers and intricate Afro-Cuban-style drum part, and Medeski spins out a virtuosic, boplike acoustic piano solo. At about the four-minute mark, Martin launches into a drum solo that evokes Max Roach's polyrhythmic soliloquies; eventually Wood reenters with his original ostinato, but now Martin launches into a swing pattern, and Medeski returns playing an extremely bluesy, funky Hammond organ vamp and solo that Jimmy Smith would have been proud of. While "Latin Shuffle" is not the most original or distinctive track on the album, it's one of the most important, because it's the album's one track that fully demonstrates what MMW are capable of as technicians.

Finally, on two tracks, "Everyday People" and "No Ke Ano Ahiahi," MMW mine an exceedingly soulful ballad style. The tempos are slow, but the feel is different than the Soft Machine–like tracks such as "Sugar Craft" and "Just Like I Pictured It": there's less emphasis on repetitive syncopated bass lines and textural experimentation, more emphasis on creating an almost bittersweet lyricism through Medeski's Hammond leads.

In sum: *Combustication* is the work of a band that have brought their stylistic sources into a nearly perfect balance: the band's two subsequent studio albums, *The Dropper* (2000) and *Uninvisible* (2002) have found them adjusting and refining certain elements of the *Combustication* sound without, however, introducing anything essentially new. (Even the horn arrangements of the two later albums hearken back to 1993's *It's a Jungle in Here*.) Some MMW fans have complained that Medeski's keyboard work is lower key, more textural, and farther in the background on *Combustication* than on some of the band's earlier albums, but that brings me back to my original premise: with a few notable and specific exceptions, in nearly all genres of contemporary music since the late seventies the most compelling innovations have taken place not in the areas of instrumental technique, compositional structure and elaboration, or harmonic and metric vocabulary, but in the realms of tone-color and texture. Heard from this perspective, *Combustication* is a significant achievement, and fans of ELP (or seventies prog more generally) who are willing to understand "progressive" as an aesthetic philosophy, an attitude of approaching music, rather than a fixed sound, will find much to appreciate here.

Hermetic Science
En Route
Magnetic Oblivion Records 3-MERM3-01 (U.S., 2001)
Recorded at Big Bang Studios, Loleta, California, June 2000 and July 2001

Ed Macan, tuned percussion (vibes, marimba, timpani), keyboards (acoustic piano, Hammond organ, ARP string ensemble, Micromoog, Rhodes electric piano, digital pipe organ, electronic harpsichord), 10-string lyre, soprano and tenor recorders; Jason Hoopes, bass guitar, electric six-string guitar, sitar, acoustic piano; Matt McClimon, drums and percussives, tracks 1–5; Joe Nagy, drums and percussives, dumbek, tracks 6–8

1. Mars, The Bringer of War [Doomsday Mix] (Holst)
2. Against the Grain, part one (Hoopes-Macan)
3. Against the Grain, part two (Macan)
4. Against the Grain, part three (Macan-Hoopes)
5. Against the Grain, part four (Macan)
6. Là-Bas (Macan)
7. Raga Hermeticum (Macan)
8. En Route (Macan)

[no rating]

I can imagine what some of you are thinking: shameless self-promotion! To which I say: if I didn't think Hermetic Science belonged here, I wouldn't have included us. The reasons I did are simple: I believe Hermetic Science contributed one of the most original and important bodies of music to the progressive rock canon between 1996 and 2001, and I believe we made one of the most imaginative uses of the trio format by any band, in any genre of music, during the same period.

Even as I was writing *Rocking the Classics* during the early to mid-1990s, I was planning the formation of a band whose music would address three areas of concern. First, as a mallet percussionist, I felt that the vibes and marimba had been much underused in progressive music, and, more generally, vibes technique had stagnated for a generation, with little progress having been made since the late sixties, when Gary Burton, Bobby Hutcherson, and a few others had developed the earlier hornlike conception of the vibes into a more texturally and harmonically sophisticated guitarlike approach. These musicians had generally used vibes and marimba in conjunction with another polyphonic instrument, and always with another lead instrument: I envisioned a power trio format in which the vibes (or marimba) would fulfill a polyphonic role, simultaneously supplying lead lines and accompanying chords—or, on occasion, lead lines, chords, and a bass line—much like a Hammond organ or piano, thus rendering the presence of other melodic instruments superfluous.

Second, I was becoming concerned about how musicians and fans of the nineties prog revival were becoming overly fixated on seventies prog to the exclusion of both the music that had influenced seventies progsters, and music that had been created since the seventies: the result was music that, at its best, expertly recreated the riffs, licks, and sounds of seventies prog, but lacked the dynamism, the spirit of adventure, that had marked the "classic" prog style. To put it another way: I believed (and still do) that if progressive music was and is to survive, its gene pool, which was becoming subject to an increasing level of interbreeding, needed to be opened back up to outside sources. I therefore decided that while I would make no effort to hide my debt to (and fondness for) ELP, Egg, or U.K.—music that, incidentally, provided me with very useful guidance for translating my musical vision to a trio format—I would also draw freely on a number of nonrock influences: the "spatial jazz" style associated with the ECM label, early modernist classical music (Holst and Vaughan Williams were especially potent influences), and various "ethnic" styles—particularly the North Indian raga, but also various types of Middle Eastern music. Finally, I was concerned with the "graying" of the progressive music culture, and had become convinced that its survival depended on passing a love for the music on to younger musicians. I therefore decided that Hermetic Science albums would be recorded with talented young bassists and drummers from the College of the Redwoods in Eureka, California (where I teach), and nearby Humboldt State University (in Arcata).

The first Hermetic Science lineup—myself, bassist Don Sweeney, and drummer Michael Morris—convened in January 1996, and during the course of the next fourteen months the music that would feature on the first Hermetic Science album was recorded: our eponymous debut album was released in November 1997. At a distance of over eight years, I continue to believe this is one of the relatively few really original and innovative albums to emerge from the nineties progressive music revival; while our later albums may be "better" in terms of arrangement savvy and instrumental and stylistic variety, our debut presents a totally organic and unified musical vision and may, ultimately, be our most important album. The characteristic Hermetic Science style emerges fully formed here, fusing the "floating" sound of the vibes with an intense yet agile rock rhythm section to create music that's alternately shadowy and luminous, mystically calm and restlessly striving, and that coheres through its tightly knit approach to structure that's based around subtle motivic and tonal cross relationships. I'm particularly proud of "Esau's Burden," "Fire Over Thule," and "Trisagion," although I believe nearly all of the album has aged well: only the quasi-gamelan arrangement of "Mars, The Bringer of War" now sounds like a failed experiment.

In 1998, we began work on our second album, *Prophesies*. I felt the first album had solved all the major challenges posed by the mallet percussion power trio formation: recording a second album with precisely the same instrumentation seemed both redundant and a bit dogmatic. At any rate, I wanted to somewhat deemphasize the debut's engagement with ECM-style jazz and Eastern music in order to explore of fusion of twentieth-century classical chamber music and rock, much like the Belgian band Univers Zero had done during the eighties. For that reason, keyboards (particularly acoustic piano, but also Hammond organ and ARP string ensemble) became as prominent in the arrangements as vibes and marimba. I also wanted to experiment with making the bass guitar parts of Andy Durham, who had joined the band as we were wrapping up recording sessions for the first album, a second lead line, which not only gave us more contrapuntal possibilities, but also allowed for a more equal distribution of the rhythmic center of gravity amongst the trio. The six-movement *Prophesies* suite, loosely based around the Old Testament Book of Jeremiah, reflects these new concerns; on the other hand, two additional tracks recorded in May 1999 (including a cover of Rush's "Jacob's Ladder") more closely reflect the approach of the first album. *Prophesies* was released in September 1999.

Almost immediately I set my sights on our next album, which I planned to base around a trilogy of novels by fin-de-siècle French author J. K. Huysmans, *À Rebours* (*Against the Grain*), *La-Bàs* (*Down There*), and *En Route*. I was aiming for a much bigger, more expressionistic sound, and realized this was the time to record "The Great Hermetic Science prog rock album." Therefore, the emphasis shifted to electronic keyboards—Hammond, Micromoog, ARP string ensemble, Rhodes electric piano, Roland EP9—with the vibes, marimba, and piano playing an increasingly textural (rather than lead) role in the arrangements. Since the sound coming from the lead instruments was so much bigger now, the bass guitar returned to its foundational/rhythmic role, driving the music aggressively forward in a way that was new for us; I was delighted to find that our new bassist, Jason Hoopes, could also play sitar, electric guitar, and piano, which gave us a host of new arrangement possibilities. Jason was also a composer, so for the first time, I could share compositional duties, and the synergy of our ideas gave the band a new creative energy.

The album opens with Gustav Holst's "Mars, The Bringer of War," which, of course, we had already done on the debut album, but which I intended to get "right" this time. I decided I wanted to create an inhuman, industrial feel to the piece that, given that "Mars" is Holst's comment on the mechanization of war and "mass production" of battlefield killing, seemed entirely appropriate. To this end, I ran the ARP through a fuzz box in various stages of distortion, and utilized the Moog to produce a series of strident, machinelike patches: the raspy, strident keyboards sounds, in conjunction with the driving tempo (unlike most, we actually took Holst's performance directive of 177 beats per minute seriously), contributed to what I believe is the most compelling rock arrangement of the piece, ever. The track is also important to the rest of the album for two reasons: it symbolizes unresolved conflicts (both musical and psychological) that the rest of the album must resolve, and it presents a soundscape dominated by distorted keyboards that the rest of the album must struggle to "purify"—to undistort, if you will.

Like "Mars," the four-part "Against the Grain" suite was recorded in June 2000 by myself, Jason Hoopes, and drummer Matt McClimon, a veteran of the *Prophesies* sessions. Part one slowly cross-stitches three ideas—a stern fanfare in five, a passionate, surging Hammond-and-ARP theme, and a quiet, pastoral piano and vibes episode—into a complex tapestry of sound that inexorably builds to a dramatic climax. Part two evokes early

Hermetic Science with its melancholy vibes theme, which swells and recedes several times before it grows into an increasingly agitated Moog-and-Hammond episode that's brought to a sudden halt by a ghostly transformation of the opening music. Part three is based around an eleven-bar bass guitar riff that ingeniously unites an edgy theme with a throbbing accompaniment figure: ARP and Hammond layer in an increasingly dense web of counterpoint, drawing the bass guitar theme and its ominous chromatic antitheme into a whirling, doom-laden dance-around-the-abyss. A darkly mysterious vibes cadenza leads into part four, a frantic piece dominated by the Hammond that evokes both Emerson and Alberto Ginastera in its driving ostinatos, metallic chord voicings, and intricate, machine-like cross rhythms.

The end of "Mars" brings the album to its first big climax; the end of "Against the Grain," to its second. It's only now that the album reaches its center of gravity, and the last three tracks, driven by the virtuosic drumming of Joe Nagy (who joined the band in time for the 2001 sessions) bring the album to a yet higher expressive level. "Là-Bas" is the only track in the Hermetic Science canon that indulges in the pseudo-baroque, Phantom of the Opera, gonzo keyboard histrionics so beloved to prog. However, given the subject matter of the novel that it's meant to evoke—a man who is slowly corrupted by his increasing involvement with Satanism, and who eventually participates in a Black Mass against his better judgment—the musical style is not only appropriate, but necessary. Furthermore, the piece also works on its own musical logic: the virtuosic, Widor-like pipe organ toccata, the belligerent, ponderous, dirge, and the spidery fugue, which eventually recalls both the toccata's booming pipe organ and the dirge's pounding rhythmic pattern, are all based around the same five-note motive. The close of the fugue, wherein shards of guitar feedback suddenly explode out of the final massive pipe organ chord, marks the album's biggest climax yet.

Initially I had planned to follow "Là-Bas" directly with "En Route," but I realized during the compositional process that a transitional—better yet, a transformational—track was needed between the two. Hence "Raga Hermeticum," in which an almost redemptive process of musical and psychological transformation unfolds. Besides its crucial conceptual role on the album, "Raga Hermeticum" also allowed me to revisit the slowing unfolding "Eastern" structures that I had initially grappled with in "Fire Over Thule" and "Trisagion" from the debut album. The scales and motivic ideas that will dominate the remainder of "Raga Hermeticum" are gradually revealed in the opening alap section, as sitar and ten-string lyre weave a mystical duet in which time hangs suspended. The next section represents one possible extension of the alap material, as a kind of Central Asian dance tune presented by ten-string lyre, recorder, and sitar over a throbbing bass guitar-dumbek accompaniment. Then comes a vibes-bass-drum episode in seven, where the alap material is expanded in a freer and more virtuosic direction—this would be what is known as the jhala of a traditional raga. Finally, the "Central Asian dance tune" is recapitulated in the manner of Western symphonic music, the theme now bigger, more lavishly orchestrated than in its original appearance, driving the track on to a huge climax.

"Raga Hermeticum" having cleansed the strident tone-colors, dissonance, and gloomy minor modalities that had previously dominated the album, the final track, "En Route," can now justifiably commence. En Route, the novel, chronicles the point at which Huysmans's protagonist, Durtal, returns to God and to the faith of his forefathers, extricates his life from the morass into which it had sunk, and in doing so, finds (or perhaps re-finds) himself. The musically and psychologically transformative effects of "Raga Hermeticum" accomplished, "En Route" is free to evoke the idea of spiritual ascension through two main themes—a stately, hymnlike piano introduction and a surging, inexorably ascending Rhodes electric piano theme—both of which are exhaustively developed and made to pass through one final "dark night" of the soul before they return, triumphantly, at the end, in reverse order, in their original, "innocent" state. It's a moving conclusion to what I believe is one of the finest progressive music albums of its era.

The recording of the final three tracks of En Route were a revelatory experience for me, giving me a much clearer insight into successful production techniques. Soon after the release of En Route in November 2001, I found myself wanting to remix and remaster the first two albums, and especially the first five tracks of En Route, to give them the same sense of vividness and depth, the same balance of fullness and clarity, as we had achieved in the final three tracks of *En Route*. The project of remixing and remastering the entire Hermetic Science output began in spring 2002, and was finished some three years later. On the first album, bass frequencies were subtly boosted in certain sections, vibes parts subtly thickened in a few climactic passages, and—best of all—Jason Hoopes contributed sitar drones to three tracks for which I had hoped, but failed, to locate a suitable sitar player back when they were originally recorded in 1996. On the second album and the first five tracks of *En Route*, the drums and bass guitar tracks were carefully remixed to give them a more consistent presence throughout, and to create a better, more even balance with each other and the lead instruments, while the mallet and keyboard orchestrations were subtly reworked in select passages to arrive at a better balance of parts. It is my hope that by the time you are reading this, *Crash Course: A Hermetic Science Primer*, a two-CD set containing the remixed and remastered original tracks from our three studio albums, will be available, as will *Delivering the Goods: Hermetic Science Live 2-4-2000*, which demonstrates what we were capable of in a live setting.

Niacin
Live! Blood, Sweat and Beers
Magna Carta CD MA-9063-2 (U.S., 2003)
Recorded live in Jakarta, Indonesia, and Tokyo, Japan, 2003
John Novello, Hammond organ, acoustic piano, Kurzweil 2600; Billy Sheehan, bass guitar; Dennis Chambers, drums and percussion

1. Clean Up Crew (Sheehan)
2. Do a Little Dirty Work (Novello-Sheehan)
3. Bullet Train Blues (Novello-Sheehan)
4. Hell to Pay (Novello-Sheehan)
5. Niacin (Novello-Sheehan)
6. One Less Worry (Novello-Sheehan)
7. I Miss You Like I Miss the Sun (Novello-Sheehan)
8. Klaghorn (Novello-Sheehan)
9. Three Feet Back (Novello-Sheehan)
10. Purple Rain (John L. Nelson)
11. No Man's Land (Novello-Sheehan)
12. You Keep Me Hangin' On (Dozier-Holland-Holland)
13. Front and Center (Novello-Sheehan)
14. Gelatin (Novello-Sheehan)

★★★

Typically, the music released on the Magna Carta label tends to fall somewhere between progressive rock and progressive metal, and tends to conform to a particular stereotype: very strong in terms of instrumental virtuosity, somewhat weaker in terms of originality, compositional sophistication, and variety of moods. Stylistically, Niacin is somewhat atypical of the Magna Carta roster in their emphasis on instrumental jazz-rock fusion with prog rock overtones; their musical values, on the other hand, conform fairly closely to other Magna Carta acts.

Niacin was formed in 1996 by keyboardist John Novello, bassist Billy Sheehan, and drummer Dennis Chambers. Novello, who primarily plays Hammond with Niacin, but occasionally doubles on piano for variety, is an experienced studio musician also known for having written an influential instructional method in contemporary keyboard styles. Sheehan came to prominence in the late eighties as bassist for David Lee Roth after the singer parted company with Van Halen and formed his own band; in recent years, besides his work with Niacin, he's also collaborated extensively with drummer Terry Bozzio (see the entry for U.K. above). Drummer Dennis Chambers has worked with a variety of musicians, from George Clinton's Parliament and Funkadelic to John Scofield to Santana. *Live! Blood, Sweat and Beers*, released in 2003, is Niacin's sixth album, and second live album: besides offering a representative cross-section of their career output, the album also documents the work of a band that over seven years has become a tight live unit, and, as Niacin are above all a live band, requiring little in the way of studio gimmickry to bring their music off, this album is probably the best introduction to their music.

There are two perspectives one can evaluate Niacin from: a prog rock perspective, or a postjazz perspective. Niacin's music does bear stylistic comparison to the more jazz-based instrumental prog rock, particularly instrumental ELP. John Novello is clearly familiar with Emerson's Hammond work circa 1970–74, and there are a couple of strands of Emerson's stylistic legacy that recur with some frequency in the Niacin repertoire. The main theme of a typical Niacin track is often based on a rapid-fire sixteenth-note Hammond line laced with blues inflections, of a type that those familiar with Keith Emerson's Hammond solos of the 1st and 3rd Impressions of "Karn Evil 9" will easily recognize: in the main themes of both "Bullet Train Blues" and "Front and Center," Novello also incorporates the type of spirally plunging arpeggios that were an Emerson stock-in-trade. In addition, Novello, like Emerson, is fond of harmonizing his themes with stacked fourths—one hears this technique in the coda of "Hell to Pay" and the main themes of "One Less Worry" and "Klaghorn": the quartally harmonized themes, combined with the driving rhythmic accompaniment of the Sheehan-Chambers rhythm section, lends the music the character- istic restless, pressing quality of classic ELP.

Indeed, Niacin calls to mind two post-ELP projects reviewed earlier: Keith Emerson's *Changing States* and the Carl Palmer Band's *Working Live*. In terms of virtuosity, Niacin equal the Palmer band, and surpass Emerson's studio lineups on *Changing States*: Billy Sheehan, in particular, is an authentic virtuoso, whose approach to bass guitar is some- what reminiscent of Jeff Berlin's. However, Sheehan and Chambers seldom engage in the polyrhythmic sparring that characterized Berlin's interaction with Bill Bruford in the Bruford band's work of the early eighties, and this points up where Niacin falls short of their prog rock counterparts: in matters of composition and arrangement. Compared to Emerson's compositions on *Changing States*, to which they are often stylistically similar, Niacin's are much less developed, with few modulations, little instrumental counterpoint, no thematic development to speak of, and relatively few intricate unison passages. The arrangements are often simpler as well: there's little thematic exchange between Hammond and bass, little movement of the rhythmic center of gravity amongst the trio. Niacin's approach to structure is pretty stereotypical: often a main theme is followed by a series of organ, piano, or bass solos around the main theme's chord changes, sometimes preceded by a slow intro, and occasionally interspersed with shorter subsidiary riffs— which, unfortunately, usually aren't developed. In terms of phrase structure and meter, Niacin's music is simpler than the standard fare of the Palmer band or Emerson's *Changing States* music. (One exception might be the 11/8 minor blues riff of "Hell to Pay," which may have been influenced by the famous 11/8 figure of the Allman Brothers' "Tied to the Whipping Post.")

Of course, it may be unfair to evaluate a band like Niacin, who bill themselves as a fusion band, according to the parameters of progressive rock, since fusion has always emphasized improvisation over composition. It might therefore be more useful to con- sider Niacin from a postjazz perspective by comparing them to MMW, discussed above, with whom Niacin share obvious jazz and R & B roots. Indeed, in some ways Niacin are closer stylistically to MMW than to ELP, as, like MMW, they share none of the latter's clas- sical or folk music trappings. One the one hand, Niacin are indisputably a more virtuosic band than MMW. On the other hand, they're a much less innovative one: MMW, as much as they may have grounded their project in seventies fusion, have forged ahead into new stylistic territory, both by drawing on new stylistic sources (trance, hip hop) and by deci- sively modifying the sensibility of seventies fusion, with its emphasis on virtuosity over atmosphere. There's little sonic exploration in Niacin's music, little of the filling in of sonic space with interesting textural details that gives MMW's music much of its distinctiveness.

For me, Niacin are at their best when they come closest to transcending these limita- tions. I especially like the album's closing track, "Gelatin." For the only time on the album, the bass (rather than the keys) presents the main theme, a sixteen-bar minor melody that, with the "clopping" drum accompaniment, sounds like the theme to a spaghetti Western; there are two subsidiary themes, which lend the composition some variety, and each time the main theme reappears in the bass, Novello's organ accompaniment becomes less chordal and more contrapuntal, giving the composition a sense of expansion and growth. "Niacin" is a short, anthemic composition featuring driving rhythm section accompani- ment and some intricate unison lines; it's more of a real composition and less of a continuous improv over recurring chord changes than most of the other tracks. However, there are many interesting passages, even in the tracks given over to lengthy improvisations over chord changes: for instance, the plunging quartal harmonies that enliven the end of "Hell to Pay," and the powerful bolero that opens the band's cover of "You Keep Me Hangin' On."

In sum: while Niacin are not a band that set a high standard in terms of innovation or compositional depth, they're terrific players, and ELP fans who enjoy that band's more R & B–tinged moments (think "Blues Variation" or the organ solos of "Karn Evil 9") will find much to enjoy in Niacin.

Appendix D:
A Complete List of Live Shows By Emerson, Lake And Palmer; Emerson Lake And Powell; and 3; A Statistical Summary And Analysis Of ELP's Tour Patterns

My two main sources in compiling this list of ELP's live shows are the Official Greg Lake Web Site, greglake.com, and the Forrester-Hanson-Askew tome *Welcome Back*. However, I have also done my own research, made a number of corrections and additions to the earlier lists, and compiled what I believe is the most accurate list yet of ELP/ELPowell/3 live shows. Notice I say "most accurate yet": this list still needs some revision and emendation to make it fully accurate, and I'm not confident of the complete accuracy of my list even as late in the band's career as the 1977-78 *Works* tour. I have put question marks by dates and/or locations I'm skeptical about; note that sometimes I may be skeptical of one or the other, at other times of both. There is still definitely some work to be done in this area. Anyone interested?

Shows featured on an authorized video or audio release are identified, as are shows featured in *The Original Bootleg Series from the Manticore Vaults*.

First Shows

August 23, 1970	Guildhall, Plymouth, England
August 29	Isle of Wight Festival, Isle of Wight, England
	[album *Live at the Isle of Wight Festival*]

Fall 1970 British/European Tour

September 19	Winter Gardens, Watford, England
September 24	Town Hall, Watford, England
September 25	City Hall, ?, England
September 26	Starlight Room, Boston, England
September 27	De Montfort Hall, Leicester, England
September 28	Guildhall, Portsmouth, England
October 1	City Hall, Leeds, England
October 4	City Hall, Newcastle, England
	[In all shows from Sept. 25–Oct. 4, Wishbone Ash and Farm open]
October 7	Dome, Brighton, England
October 9	Greens Playhouse, Glasgow, Scotland

October 11	Caird Hall, Dundee, Scotland
October 16	Technical College, Waltham, England
October 17	Brunel University, Uxbridge, England
	[with Opal Butterfly]
October 19	Colston Hall, Bristol, England
October 20	Winter Gardens, Bournemouth, England
October 21	Town Hall, Birmingham, England
October 24	Fairfield Hall, Croydon, England
October 25	Royal Festival Hall, London, England
October 27	City Hall, Sheffield, England
November 13	Kinetic Circus, Birmingham, England
November 22	Liverpool, England
November 26	Bremen, Germany
	[*Beat Club* TV performance]
November 28	Jahrhunderthalle, Frankfurt, Germany
November 29	Zirkus Krone, Munich, Germany
November 30	Nuremburg, Germany
December 1	Vienna, Austria
December 2	Stuttgart, Germany
December 4	Limathaus, Zürich, Switzerland
December 5	Stadthalle, Vienna, Austria
December 6	Festhalle, Böblingen, Germany
December 7	Manchester Free Trade Hall, Manchester, England
December 8	Saint George's Hall, Bradford, England
December 9	Lyceum, London, England
	[movie *Rock and Roll Your Eyes* (U.S.); *Pictures at an Exhibition* (U.K.)]
December 12	Leeds University, Leeds, England

Spring 1971 British Tour

March 4, 1971	ABC, Stockton, England
March 5	ABC, Hull, England
March 6	ABC, Lincoln (?), England
March 7	The Regal, Cambridge, England
March 10	Capitol, Cardiff, Wales
March 12	ABC, Plymouth, England
March 14	Civic Hall, Wolverhampton, England
March 17	Odeon, Cheltenham, England
March 18	Big Apple, Brighton, England
March 21	ABC, Blackpool, England
March 22	Free Trade Hall, Manchester, England
March 23	Saint George's Hall, Bradford, England
March 24	City Hall, Sheffield, England
March 26	City Hall, Newcastle, England
	[album *Pictures at an Exhibition*]
March 28	Odeon, Lewisham, England
March 29	Winter Gardens, Margate, England
March 30	Guildhall, Portsmouth, England
April 1	ABC, Wigan, England
April 2	Green's Playhouse, Glasgow, Scotland
April 3	Caird Hall, Dundee, Scotland
April 6	Winter Gardens, Bournemouth, England
April 7	De Montfort Hall, Leicester, England
April 9	Odeon, Birmingham, England

Spring 1971 American Tour

April 21	Theil College, Greenville, Pennsylvania
April 23/24	Eastown Theatre, Detroit, Michigan

April 25	Spectrum, Philadelphia, Pennsylvania
April 28	Sullivan County Community College, Loch Sheldrake, New York
April 30/May 1	Fillmore East, New York, New York
	[Edgar Winter and Curved Air open]
May 2	Shea Theatre, Buffalo, New York [I believe it probable there are missing dates between May 2 and 11]
May 11	Guthrie Theatre (?)
	[Note: there are Guthrie Theatres at Slippery Rock University, Grove City, Pennsylvania, and in Minneapolis, Minnesota. It is possible this one is neither of those.]
	[I believe it probable there are missing dates between May 11 and 19]
May 19	Kiel Opera House, Saint Louis, Missouri
	[May 11 and May 19 shows with Mott the Hoople]
May 26	Carnegie Hall, New York, New York
May 28	Upsala College, East Orange, New Jersey
May 29	Hatch Memorial Shell, Boston, Massachusetts
May 30	Bucknell University, Lewisberg, Pennsylvania

Summer 1971 European/British Tour

June 1	Stadthalle, Karlsruhe, Germany
June 2	Meistersingerhalle, Nuremberg, Germany
June 3	Konzerthaus, Vienna, Austria
June 4	Zirkus Krone, Munich, Germany
June 5/6(?)	Zoffingen, Zürich, Switzerland
June 10	Stadthalle, Offenbach, Germany
June 11	Meistersingerhalle, Nuremburg, Germany
June 12	Festhalle, Oldenburg, Germany
	[Greg Lake Web Site states Het Concertgebouw, Amsterdam]
June 13	Rheinhalle, Düsseldorf, Germany
June 14	Musikhalle, Hamburg, Germany
June 17	Philipshalle, Düsseldorf, Germany
June 20	Royal Theatre Drury Lane, London, England
	[I believe there are European shows missing between June 20 and July 17]

Summer 1971 North American Tour

July 17	Sports Arena, San Diego, California
July 18	Berkeley Community Center, Berkeley, California
July 19	Hollywood Bowl, Los Angeles, California
	[with Edgar Winter and Humble Pie]
July 23	Argodome, Vancouver, British Columbia, Canada
July 24	Paramount Theatre (?), Seattle, Washington
July 25	Paramount Theatre (?), Portland, Oregon
July 30	Music Hall, Houston, Texas
July 31	Municipal Auditorium, San Antonio, Texas
August 6/7	Pirates World, Dania, Florida
August 8/9	The Dome, Virginia Beach, Virginia
August 10	Hollywood Sportatorium, Miami, Florida
	[Forrester has this show on August 9]
August 12	Stanley Park Stadium, Toronto, Ontario, Canada
August 13	Place des Nations, Montréal, Quebec, Canada
August 14	New Jersey Convention Hall, Asbury Park, New Jersey
August 18	Syracuse Auditorium, Syracuse, New York
	[with Edgar Winter's White Trash]
August 20	Dayton, Ohio
August 21	Transit Auditorium, Chicago, Illinois
August 22(?)	Syria Mosque, Pittsburgh, Pennsylvania

August 28   Public Auditorium, Cleveland, Ohio
August 30   Bushnell Auditorium, Hartford, Connecticut
August 31   Alexandria, Virginia
September 1   Gaelic Park, Riverdale, New York
                     [*The Original Bootleg Series from the Manticore Vaults*, vol. 1]
                     [There may be one or more missing dates (Boston?) from early
                     September]
November 12   Music Hall, Boston, Massachusetts
November 13   Philadelphia Spectrum, Philadelphia, Pennsylvania
                     [with Yes]
November 14   Transit Auditorium, Chicago, Illinois
November 15   Eastown Theatre, Detroit, Michigan
November 25   Madison Square Garden, New York, New York
                     [with J Geils]
November 26   Shreveport, Louisiana (?)

Winter 1971 British Tour

December 8   City Hall, Newcastle, England
December 9   City Hall, Sheffield, England
December 10   Free Trade Hall, Manchester, England
December 11   Odeon, Birmingham, England
December 12   Capitol Theatre, Cardiff, Wales
December 13   London Pavilion, London, England (two shows)
December 14   London Pavilion, London, England (two shows)
December 15   London Pavilion, London, England (two shows)
December 17   Caird Hall, Dundee, Scotland
December 18   Edinburgh Empire, Edinburgh, Scotland
December 19   Greens Playhouse, Glasgow, Scotland
March 10, 1972   Capitol Theatre, Cardiff, Wales
                     [Not on Greg Lake Web Site]

Spring 1972 North American Tour

March 21   Denver Coliseum, Denver, Colorado
March 22   Long Beach Arena, Long Beach, California
March 23   Civic Auditorium, Santa Monica, California
March 24/25   Winterland, San Francisco, California
March 26   Arena, Saint Louis, Missouri
March 27   West Kentucky University, Louisville, Kentucky
March 28   Municipal Auditorium, Atlanta, Georgia
March 29   Orlando, Florida
March 30   Bay Front Center, Saint Petersburg, Florida
March 31   Miami Beach Convention Center, Miami Beach, Florida
April 1   Coliseum, Jacksonville, Florida
April 3   Mar y Sol Festival, Vega Baja, San Juan, Puerto Rico
April 4   New Haven Coliseum, New Haven, Connecticut
April 5   Music Hall, Boston, Massachusetts (two shows)
                     [with Dr. Hook]
April 7   Utica, New York
April 8   Shea Theatre, Buffalo, New York
April 9   Wooster College, Cleveland, Ohio
April 10/11   Academy of Music, New York, New York
April 12   Bucknell University, Lewisburg, Pennsylvania
April 13   F & M College, Lancaster, Pennsylvania
April 14   Sports Arena, Hershey, Pennsylvania
April 15   Spectrum, Philadelphia, Pennsylvania
April 17   Cobo Hall, Detroit, Michigan
April 18   Hara Arena, Dayton, Ohio
April 19   Arie Crown Theatre, Chicago, Illinois

April 20	Kent State University, Kent, Ohio
April 21	Town Hall, Louisville, Kentucky
	[*The Original Bootleg Series from the Manticore Vaults*, vol. 1]
April 22	Tarrant City Convention Center, Fort Worth, Texas
April 23	Muncipal Hall, Houston, Texas
April 25	University of Cincinnati, Cincinnati, Ohio
April 27	Thiel College, Greenville, Pennsylvania
April 28	Forum, Montréal, Quebec, Canada
April 29	Coliseum, Québec City, Quebec, Canada

Summer 1972 European Tour

June 4	Grugahalle, Essen, Germany
June 6	Deutschland Halle, Berlin, Germany
June 7	Musikhalle, Hamburg, Germany
June 8	Falkiner Center, Copenhagen, Denmark
June 10	Festhalle, Frankfurt, Germany
June 12	Meistersingerhalle, Nuremburg, Germany
June 15	Genoa, Italy
June 19	Olympia, Paris, France
June 24	Mehrzweckhalle, Wetzikon, Switzerland
June 25	Stadio, Bologna, Italy
June 26	Paleur, Rome, Italy
June 27	Stadthalle, Vienna, Austria
July 8	Concert 10 Festival, Pocono International Raceway, Pocono, Pennsylvania
	[also on bill: Three Dog Night, The Faces, Black Sabbath, Humble Pie, J Geils Band, Badfinger, Cactus, Edgar Winter]
July 12	Maple Leaf Gardens, Toronto, Ontario, Canada

Summer 1972 Japanese Tour

July 22	Kourakuen Stadium, Tokyo, Japan
July 24	Koshien Stadium, Osaka, Japan

Summer 1972 American Tour

July 27	Civic Auditorium, San Francisco, California
July 28	Long Beach Arena, Long Beach, California
	[*The Original Bootleg Series from the Manticore Vaults*, vol. 1]
July 29	Santa Monica, California
	[I believe there are shows missing between July 29 and August 9]
August 9	Southern Illinois University, Edwardsville, Illinois
	[Greg Lake Web Site incorrectly places August 9 in Asbury Park, New Jersey]
August 11	Mecca Arena, Milwaukee, Wisconsin
August 13	Saratoga Performing Arts Center, Saratoga Springs, New York
	[*The Original Bootleg Series from the Manticore Vaults*, vol. 1]
August 17	Arie Crown Theatre, Chicago, Illinois
August 19	New Jersey Convention Hall, Asbury Park, New Jersey
August 20	Convention Center, Asbury Park, New Jersey

Fall 1972 British Tour

September 30	Oval Cricket Ground, Kennington, South London, England
	[*Melody Maker*'s Poll Winner Concert]
November 10	Winter Gardens, Bournemouth, England
November 11	Gaumont Southampton, Southampton, England
November 12	Capitol Theatre, Cardiff, Wales (two shows)
November 13	Free Trade Hall, Manchester, England

November 15	Saint Georges Hall, Bradford, England
November 17	Greens Playhouse, Glasgow, Scotland (two shows)
November 18	Guildhall, Preston, England
November 19	Trenton Gardens, Stoke, England
November 21	Top Rank Suite, Liverpool, England
November 23	Capitol Theatre, Cardiff, Wales
November 24	Odeon, Birmingham, England (two shows)
November 25	City Hall, Sheffield, England
November 26	Hammersmith Odeon, London, England (two shows) [*The Original Bootleg Series from the Manticore Vaults*, vol. 2]
November 27	The Dome, Brighton, England
November 29	Odeon, Newcastle, England (two shows)
December 1	Caird Hall, Dundee, Scotland

Spring 1973 "Get Me a Ladder" European Tour

February 20, 1973	Kiel, Germany
February 25	Ludwigshafen, Germany
February 26	Freiburg, Germany
March 30	Ostseehalle, Kiel, Germany
March 31	Philipshalle, Düsseldorf, Germany
April 1	Forest National, Brussels, Belgium
April 3	Saint-Ouen, Paris, France
April 4	L'Arene, Poitiers, France
April 5	Palais des Sports, Caen, France
April 6	Palais des Sports, Lille, France
April 7	Palais des Expositions, Nancy, France
April 8	Palais des Sports, Lyon, France [April 5–8 French shows not noted by Greg Lake Web Site or Forrester]
April 10/11	Friedrich Eberthalle, Ludwigshafen, Germany
April 12	Stadthalle, Freiburg, Germany
April 13	Sporthalle, Cologne, Germany
April 15	Hallenstadion, Zürich, Switzerland
April 16	Ernst Merck Halle, Hamburg, Germany
April 17	Branby Hall, Copenhagen, Denmark
April 18	Scandinavum, Göteborg, Sweden
April 21	Oude Rai, Amsterdam, Netherlands
April 22	Grosse Westfallen Halle, Dortmund, Germany
April 23	Munsterland Halle, Münster, Germany
April 24	Olympiahalle, Munich, Germany
April 25/26	Konzerthaus, Vienna, Austria
April 28	Velodromo Vigorelli, Milan, Italy
May 2	Rome, Italy [Greg Lake Web Site and Forrester state Bologna]
May 3	Bologna Palasport, Bologna, Italy
May 4	Vigorelli, Milan, Italy
June 19	Olympiahalle, Munich, Germany
June 20	Oldenburg, Germany
June 23	Sadlers Wells Theatre, London, England

1973-74 North American Tour

November 14	Sportatorium, Hollywood, Florida
November 15	Civic Center, Tampa, Florida
November 17	Jai Alai Fronton, West Palm Beach, Florida
November 19	Municipal Auditorium, Atlanta, Georgia
November 20	Civic Center, Roanoke, Virginia

November 21	Convention Center, Louisville, Kentucky
November 22	Cincinnati Gardens, Cincinnati, Ohio
November 23	Civic Center, Charleston, West Virginia
November 24	Coliseum, Indianapolis, Indiana
November 25	Municipal Auditorium, Nashville, Tennessee
November 26	University of Illinois, Champaign, Illinois
November 28	State Fair Arena, Oklahoma City, Oklahoma
November 30	Memorial Auditorium, Des Moines, Iowa
December 1	Metropolitan Sports Arena, Minneapolis, Minnesota
December 2/3	Amplitheatre, Chicago, Illinois
December 4/5	Cobo Hall, Detroit, Michigan
December 7	Maple Leaf Gardens, Toronto, Ontario, Canada
December 8	Cornell University, Ithaca, New York
December 9	Montreal Forum, Montréal, Canada
December 10	Boston Gardens, Boston, Massachusetts
December 11	Spectrum, Philadelphia, Pennsylvania
December 13	Nassau Coliseum, Uniondale, New York
December 14	New Haven Coliseum, New Haven, Connecticut
December 15	Civic Center, Baltimore, Maryland
December 16(?)	Lyric Theatre, Baltimore, Maryland
December 17/18	Madison Square Garden, New York, New York
January 24, 1974	The Omni, Atlanta, Georgia
January 25	Memorial Coliseum, Tuscaloosa, Alabama
January 26	Barton Coliseum, Little Rock, Arkansas
January 28	Coliseum, Denver, Colorado
January 30	Salt Palace, Salt Lake City, Utah
February 1	Sacramento, California
February 2	Winterland, San Francisco, California
February 3	Long Beach Arena, Long Beach, California
February 9	Swing Auditorium, San Bernardino, California
February 10	Anaheim Convention Center, Anaheim, California
	[album *Welcome Back My Friends to the Show That Never Ends*; *The Original Bootleg Series from the Manticore Vaults*, vol. 3]
February 11	Coliseum (?), Seattle, Washington
February 12	Coliseum, Spokane, Washington
February 13	Coliseum (?), Portland, Oregon
February 14	Vancouver Gardens, Vancouver, British Columbia, Canada
February 15	Pullman, Washington
February 17/18	Cow Palace, San Francisco, California
February 20	Fresno, California
February 21	Sports Arena, San Diego, California
February 22	Activity Center, Tuscon, Arizona
February 23	University of New Mexico, Albuquerque, New Mexico
February 26	San Antonio, Texas (possibly Tulsa, Oklahoma)
February 27	Reunion Arena, Dallas, Texas
February 28	Astrodome, Houston, Texas
March 1	Louisiana State University, Baton Rouge, Louisiana
March 3	New Orleans, Louisiana
March 5	Saint Louis, Missouri
March 7	Civic Center, Tulsa Oklahoma
	[album *King Biscuit: Emerson, Lake and Palmer*]
March 26	Henry Lewit Arena, Wichita, Kansas
	[*The Original Bootleg Series from the Manticore Vaults*, vol. 2]
March 28	Los Angeles Coliseum, Los Angeles, California
March 30	Mid-South Coliseum, Memphis, Tennessee
April 6	Cal Jam, Ontario Motor Speedway, Ontario, California
	[album *Then and Now*]

Spring 1974 British/European Tour

April 18/19/20/21	Wembley Empire Pool, London, England [Back Door open]
April 23	Stoke Trentham Gardens, Stoke, England
April 29/30	Empire, Liverpool, England
May 1/2	Empire, Liverpool, England
May 6	Sporthalle, Munich, Germany
May 7/8	Palau d'Esports, Barcelona, Spain
May 13	Sindelfingen, Germany
May 16	Olympiastadium, Innsbruck, Austria
May 17	Stadthalle, Vienna, Austria
May 18/19	Olympiahalle, Munich, Germany
May 20/21	Wetzikon, Switzerland
May 23/24	Philipshalle, Düsseldorf, Germany
May 25	Ahoy Halle, Rotterdam, Netherlands
May 27/28	Palais des Sports, Paris, France
May 31/June 1	Festhalle, Frankfurt, Germany

Summer 1974 American Tour

July 26	Rich Stadium, Buffalo, New York [*The Original Bootleg Series from the Manticore Vaults*, vol. 2]
July 27	Performing Arts Center, Saratoga Springs, New York
July 28	New Haven Civic Center (or Yale Bowl?), New Haven, Connecticut
July 29	Providence Civic Center, Providence, Rhode Island
July 30	Cape Cod Coliseum, Yarmouth, Massachusetts
August 1	Capitol Center, Landover, Maryland
August 2	Civic Center, Pittsburgh, Pennsylvania
August 4	Municipal Stadium, Cleveland, Ohio
August 5	Hershey Park Arena, Hershey, Pennsylvania
August 7	Norfolk Scope, Norfolk, Virginia
August 10	August Jam, Charlotte Motor Speedway, Charlotte, North Carolina
August 13	Knoxville, Tennessee
August 14	Dayton, Ohio
August 15	Hershey Park Arena, Hershey, Pennsylvania
August 20	Roosevelt Stadium, Jersey City, New Jersey (reschedule of postponed August 17 show)
August 21	Spectrum, Philadelphia, Pennsylvania
August 24	Central Park, New York, New York (open air benefit show)

Spring/Summer 1977 North American Tour (*with orchestra)

May 24/25, 1977*	Freedom Hall, Louisville, Kentucky
May 26* (?)	Municipal Auditorium, Nashville, Tennessee (?)
May 29*	Riverfront Coliseum, Cincinnati, Ohio
May 31/June 1*	Cobo Hall, Detroit, Michigan
June 4*	Soldier Field, Chicago, Illinois
June 5*	County Stadium, Milwaukee, Wisconsin [J Geils, Foghat, Climax Blues Band open]
June 7*	Market Square Arena, Indianapolis, Indiana
June 9*	Dane County Coliseum, Madison, Wisconsin
June 11*	Saint Paul Arena, Minneapolis, Minnesota
June 12*	Memorial Auditorium, Des Moines, Iowa
June 14*	Terre Haute University, Terre Haute, Indiana
June 16*	Roberts Stadium, Evansville, Indiana [Forrester shows a June 18 show at Three Rivers Stadium, Pittsburgh, Pennsylvania; I believe this show was cancelled to

	give Emerson time to rearrange his parts to work in a trio format]
June 20/21	Spectrum, Philadelphia, Pennsylvania
June 23	The Omni, Atlanta, Georgia
June 25 (?)	Mobile, Alabama (?)
June 26	Jefferson Civic Center, Birmingham, Alabama
June 27	Civic Center, Knoxville, Tennessee
June 28	Greensboro Coliseum, Greensboro, North Carolina
June 29	Charlotte Coliseum, Charlotte, North Carolina
June 30	Coliseum, Columbia, South Carolina
July 3	Scope, Norfolk, Virginia
July 5	Jacksonville, Florida
July 7/8/9*	Madison Square Garden, New York, New York
July 10	Hartford Civic Center, Hartford, Connecticut
July 12/13	Boston Gardens, Boston, Massachusetts
July 14	Civic Center, Providence, Rhode Island
July 17	Municipal Stadium, Cleveland, Ohio
July 19	Brown Stadium, Cleveland, Ohio
July 20(?)/21	Civic Center, Baltimore, Maryland
July 22	Cobo Hall, Detroit, Michigan
July 23	War Memorial, Rochester, New York
July 24	CNE Stadium, Toronto, Ontario, Canada
July 27	The Corral, Calgary, Alberta, Canada
July 29	National Pacific University Center, Vancouver, British Columbia, Canada
July 31	Seattle Coliseum, Seattle, Washington
August 2	Memorial Coliseum, Portland, Oregon
August 5 (?)	Arena, Milwaukee, Wisconsin (?)
August 6/7	Alameda Coliseum, Oakland, California
August 9	Phoenix, Arizona
	[Journey open]
August 10	Sports Arena, San Diego, California
August 11/12	Long Beach Arena, Long Beach, California
August 13	Swing Auditorium, San Bernardino, California
August 14	Long Beach Arena, Long Beach, California
	[Forrester lists August 13-14 at Anaheim Stadium]
August 18	Arrowhead Stadium, Kansas City, Missouri
August 19	Civic Center, Tulsa, Oklahoma
August 20	Memorial Auditorium, Dallas, Texas
August 21	Sam Houston Coliseum, Houston, Texas
August 22 (?)	Anaheim Convention Center, Anaheim, California (?)
August 23	Kiel Auditorium, Saint Louis, Missouri
August 26*	Olympic Stadium, Montréal, Quebec, Canada
	[album *In Concert/Works Live*, video *Works Orchestral Tour*]
August 27*	Olympic Stadium, Montréal, Quebec, Canada
	[Forrester lists this date; Greg Lake Web Site doesn't]

Fall 1977 American Tour

October 15	Ohio University Convocation Center, Athens, Ohio
October 17	Madison Square Garden, New York, New York
October 18	Hershey Park Arena, Hershey, Pennsylvania
October 21	Eastern Michigan University, Ypsilanti, Michigan
October 22	University of Maryland, Columbia, Maryland
October 25	The Coliseum, Jackson, Mississippi
October 29	Baton Rouge, Louisiana
October 30 (?)	Mobile, Alabama (?)
October 31	Houston, Texas
November 8	Dane County Coliseum, Madison, Wisconsin

November 10   Hartford, Connecticut
November 12   Ahearn Playhouse, Kansas State University, Manhattan, Kansas
November 14   Illinois State University, Normal, Illinois
November 15   Michigan State University, Lansing, Michigan
November 20   Memphis, Tennessee
November 22   Von Braun Civic Center, Huntsville, Alabama
November 25   Coliseum, Wheeling, West Virginia
                       [album *King Biscuit: Emerson Lake and Palmer; The Original
                       Bootleg Series from the Manticore Vaults*, vol. 3]
November 26   Hollywood Sportatorium, Miami, Florida
November 27   Saint Petersburg, Florida
November 28   Tampa, Florida
November 30   New Haven Civic Center, New Haven, Connecticut
                       [*The Original Bootleg Series from the Manticore Vaults*, vol. 2]

Winter 1978 North American Tour

January 16/17, 1978   The Forum, Montréal, Canada
January 18   Kitchener Auditorium, Kitchener, Ontario, Canada
January 19   County Exposition Center, Columbus, Ohio
January 20/21/22   Universal Ampitheatre, Chicago, Illinois
January 24   I.S.U. Hulman Civic Center, Terre Haute, Indiana
January 25   Richfield Coliseum, Cleveland, Ohio
January 26   University of West Virginia, Morgantown, West Virginia
January 28   Capitol Center, Largo, Maryland
January 29   Civic Center, Springfield, Massachusetts
January 30   Cornell University, Ithaca, New York
February 1   Memorial Auditorium, Buffalo, New York
February 2/3   Maple Leaf Gardens, Toronto, Ontario, Canada
February 4   Boston Gardens, Boston, Massachusetts
February 5   Spectrum, Philadelphia, Pennsylvania
February 6   Rensselaer Polytechnic Institute, Troy, New York
February 8   Field House, Plattsburg, New York
February 9/10   Nassau Coliseum, Uniondale, New York
February 11   Princeton University, Princeton, New Jersey
February 12   Syracuse War Memorial Auditorium, Syracuse, New York
February 14   Southern Illinois University, Carbondale, Illinois
February 15   Assembly Hall, Champaign, Illinois
February 16   Western Illinois University, Macomb, Illinois
February 18   State University of New York, Plattsburg, New York
February 19   Lubbock Coliseum, Lubbock, Texas
February 20   Civic Center, San Antonio, Texas
February 21   Assembly Center, Tulsa, Oklahoma
February 22   Civic Center Coliseum, Amarillo, Texas
February 23   Civic Center, El Paso, Texas
February 24   Aladdin Hotel, Las Vegas, Nevada
                       [Greg Lake Web Site states Arizona State University, Tempe,
                       Arizona]
February 26   University of Colorado, Fort Collins, Colorado
February 27/28   Kansas City, Missouri
March 1   Checkerdome Arena, Saint Louis, Missouri
March 3   Boston Gardens, Boston, Massachusetts
March 4   Olympia Arena, Detroit, Michigan
March 6   New Haven Civic Center, New Haven, Connecticut
March 7   Riverfront Coliseum, Cincinnati, Ohio
March 8   The Omni, Atlanta, Georgia
March 10   Freedom Hall, Johnson City, Tennessee
March 12   Civic Center, Springfield, Massachusetts
March 13   Civic Center, Providence, Rhode Island

Emerson, Lake and Powell 1986 North American Tour

August 15, 1986	El Paso County Coliseum, El Paso, Texas
August 17	Lloyd Noble Center, Norman, Oklahoma
August 19	Lakefront Arena, New Orleans, Louisiana
August 20	Summitt Festival, Houston, Texas
August 21	Reunion Arena, Dallas, Texas
August 23	Municipal Auditorium, San Antonio, Texas
September 1	Riverbend Center, Cincinnati, Ohio
September 3	Massey Hall, Toronto, Ontario, Canada
September 5	Montréal, Quebec, Canada
September 8	Civic Center, Glen Falls, New York
September 12	Mann Center, Philadelphia, Pennsylvania
September 13	Meadowlands Arena, East Rutherford, New Jersey
September 15	Performing Arts Center, Providence, Rhode Island
September 16	Greatwoods Center, Mansfield, Massachusetts
September 19	Capitol Center, Landover, Maryland
September 20	Madison Square Garden, New York, New York
September 21	Syria Mosque, Pittsburgh, Pennsylvania
September 23	Richfield Coliseum, Cleveland, Ohio
September 25	Hershey Stadium, Hershey, Pennsylvania
September 27	Coliseum, Hampton, Virginia
September 28	Coliseum, Richmond, Virginia
September 30	Rupp Arena, Lexington, Kentucky
October 2	Fox Theatre, Atlanta, Georgia
October 4	Lakeland Arena, Lakeland, Florida
	[album *Emerson, Lake and Powell Live in Concert*]
October 5	Knight Center, Miami, Florida
October 12	Charlotte, North Carolina
October 14	Opera House, Boston, Massachusetts
October 16	Coliseum, Grand Rapids, Michigan (?)
October 17	Fox Theatre, Detroit, Michigan
October 18	Square Market Arena, Indianapolis, Indiana
October 19	Fox Theatre, Chicago, Illinois
	[Greg Lake Web Site states Rosemont Horizon, Rosemont, Illinois]
October 21	Saint Paul, Minnesota
October 22	Mecca, Milwaukee, Wisconsin
October 23	Stephens Auditorium, Ames, Iowa
October 26	Civic Auditorium, Portland, Oregon
October 27	Paramount, Seattle, Washington
October 29	Kaiser Pavilion, Oakland, California
October 30	Greek Theatre, Los Angeles, California
October 31	Pacifica Theatre, Costa Mesa, California
November 1	Open Air Festival, San Diego, California
November 2	Phoenix, Arizona

3 1988 North American Tour

April 6, 1988	The Chance, Poughkeepsie, New York
April 7	Chestnut Cabaret, Philadelphia, Pennsylvania
April 8	Sundance, Bay Shore, New York
April 10	Bayou, Washington, D.C.
April 11	Hammerjacks, Baltimore, Maryland
April 12	Toad's Place, New Haven, Connecticut
April 14	The Ritz, New York
	[Broadcast live on WNEW radio]
April 15	Paradise Theatre, Boston, Massachusetts
April 16	The Living Room, Providence, Rhode Island

April 18   Barrymore's, Ottawa, Ontario, Canada
April 19   Spectrum, Montréal, Quebec, Canada
April 20   Diamond Club, Toronto, Ontario, Canada
April 21   Syria Mosque, Pittsburgh, Pennsylvania
April 22   Agora, Cleveland, Ohio
April 23   Harpo's, Detroit, Michigan
April 25   Bogart's, Cincinnati, Ohio
April 26   Mississippi Nights, Saint Louis, Missouri
April 27   Vic Theatre, Chicago, Illinois
April 28   Billy's Old Mill, Milwaukee, Wisconsin
April 30   Uptown Theatre, Kansas City, Missouri
May 2   Boulder Crest, Boulder, Colorado
May 5   Fillmore, San Francisco, California
May 6/7   Cabaret, San Jose, California
May 8   The Palace, Los Angeles, California
May 9   Bacchanal, San Diego, California
May 10   After the Gold Rush, Phoenix, Arizona
May 12   San Antonio, Texas
May 14   Madison Square Gardens, New York, New York
                   [Atlantic Records 40th Anniversary Concert]
May 15   Xcess, Houston, Texas
May 17   Center Stage, Atlanta, Georgia
May 18   Jacksonville, Florida
May 19   Sweeney's Club, Orlando, Florida
May 20   ADV Island, Tampa, Florida
May 21   City Limits, Fort Lauderdale, Florida

Emerson, Lake and Palmer 1992 North American Tour

July 22, 1992   Tower Theatre, Philadelphia, Pennsylvania
                   [private show—press only]
July 24   Mann Music Center, Philadelphia, Pennsylvania
July 25   Jones Beach, Wantaugh, New York
July 26   Garden State Arts Center, Holmdel, New Jersey
July 28   Merriweather Post Pavilion, Columbia, Maryland
July 29   Great Woods, Mansfield, Massachusetts
July 31   Waterloo Village, Stanhope, New Jersey
August 1   Empire Center, Syracuse, New York
August 2   Palace Theatre, Albany, New York
August 4   Bushnell, Hartford, Connecticut
August 5   L'Agora, Québec City, Quebec, Canada
August 7   Montreal Forum, Montréal, Quebec, Canada
August 8   Finger Lakes P.A.C., Canandaigua, New York
August 9   Kingswood Amphitheatre, Toronto, Ontario, Canada
August 11   Nautica, Cleveland, Ohio
August 12   Pine Knob, Clarkston, Michigan
August 13   Riverbend Amphitheatre, Cincinnati, Ohio
August 15   Riverport, Saint Louis, Missouri
August 16   The World, Chicago, Illinois
August 17   Deer Creek, Indianapolis, Indiana
August 18   Chastain Park, Atlanta, Georgia
August 20   Starplex Amphitheatre, Dallas, Texas
August 21   Woodlands, Houston, Texas
August 22   Sunken Garden Theatre, San Antonio, Texas
August 24   Desert Sky Pavilion, Phoenix, Arizona
August 26   Open Air Theatre, San Diego, California
August 28   Universal Amphitheatre, Los Angeles, California
August 29   Bren Center, Irvine, California
August 30   Thomas Mack Center, Las Vegas, Nevada

September 1	Cal Expo Center, Sacramento, California
September 2	Concord Pavilion, Concord, California
September 4	Schnitzer Auditorium, Portland, Oregon
September 5	Summer Music Theatre, George, Washington
September 6	Orpheum Theatre, Vancouver, British Columbia, Canada

Fall 1992 Japanese Tour

September 10	Kyoikubunkakaikan, Kawasaki, Japan
September 11	Koseinenkinkaikan, Tokyo, Japan
September 12	Shi Kokaido, Nagoya, Japan
September 14	Koseinenkinkaikan, Osaka, Japan
September 16	Hitomikinekodo, Tokyo, Japan
September 17/18/19	Shibuya Kokaido, Tokyo, Japan

Fall 1992 European Tour

September 26	Arena di Verona, Verona, Italy
September 29	Sportshall, Budapest, Hungary
October 2	Royal Albert Hall, London, England
	[video *Live at the Royal Albert Hall*; *The Original Bootleg Series from the Manticore Vaults*, vol. 3]
October 3	Royal Albert Hall, London, England
October 7	Huxley's Neue Welt, Berlin, Germany
October 8	Kuppelsaal, Hanover, Germany
October 10	Stadthalle, Vienna, Austria
October 11	Stadthalle, Heidelberg, Germany
October 12	Winterhur, Zürich, Switzerland
October 13	Neu Siegerlandhalle, Siegen, Germany
October 15	Oberfrankenhalle, Bayreuth, Germany
October 16	Eissporthalle, Halle, Germany
October 17	E. Werk, Cologne, Germany
October 18	Grugahalle, Essen, Germany
October 20	Philharmonie, Munich, Germany
October 23	Congresgebouw, Hague, Netherlands
October 25	Apollo, Manchester, England
October 26	Royal Albert Hall, London, England
	[album *Live at the Royal Albert Hall*]
October 28	Kongresszentrum, Stuttgart, Germany
October 31	Cuartel Conde Duque, Madrid, Spain
November 2	Arena Auditorium, Valencia, Spain
November 3 (or 1?)	Sports Palace, Barcelona, Spain
November 5	Elysée Montmartre, Paris, France
November 6	Forest National, Brussels, Belgium
November 7	Congresgebouw, Hague, Netherlands
November 8	Falkoner Theatre, Copenhagen, Denmark
November 10	Centrum, Oslo, Norway
November 11	Konserthuset, Stockholm, Sweden
November 14	Donauhalle, Ulm, Germany
November 15	Kulturpalast, Dresden, Germany
November 16	Palasport, Turin, Italy
November 17	Palasport, Turin, Italy
November 19	Palasport, Modena, Italy
	[Greg Lake Web Site excludes Nov. 16, 17, 19 dates]
November 20	Palaghiaccio, Rome, Italy
November 21	Palatrussardi, Milan, Italy
November 23	Stadthalle, Freiburg, Germany
November 25	International Center, Bournemouth, England
November 26	City Hall, Newcastle, England
November 27	Symphony Hall, Birmingham, England

November 28   Colston Hall, Bristol, England
November 30   Kongresshalle, Frankfurt, Germany
December 1   Congress Centrum, Hamburg, Germany

Spring 1993 "Frozen North" North American Tour

January 13, 1993   North Alberta Jubilee Auditorium, Edmonton, Alberta, Canada
January 14   South Alberta Jubilee Auditorium, Calgary, Alberta, Canada
January 15   Center of the Arts, Regina, Saskatchewan, Canada
January 16   Walker Theatre, Winnipeg, Manitoba, Canada
January 18   Community Auditorium, Thunder Bay, Ontario, Canada
January 19   Sudbury Arena, Sudbury, Ontario, Canada
January 20   Centennial Hall, London, Ontario, Canada
January 21   Congress Center, Ottawa, Ontario, Canada
January 22/23   Massey Hall, Toronto, Ontario, Canada
January 25   Theatre Saint Denis, Montréal, Quebec, Canada
January 26   Salle Albert Rousseau, Sainte Poi, Quebec, Canada
January 28   Memorial Auditorium, Burlington, Vermont
January 29   Orpheum Theatre, Boston, Massachusetts
January 30   Providence Performing Arts Center, Providence, Rhode Island
February 1   Paramount Performing Arts Center, Springfield, Massachusetts
February 3/4   Radio Music Hall, New York, New York
February 5   Tower Theatre, Philadelphia, Pennsylvania
February 6   Symphony Hall, Allentown, Pennsylvania
February 8   Palumbo Center, Pittsburgh, Pennsylvania
February 9   Palace Performing Arts Center, New Haven, Connecticut
February 10   Mid Hudson Civic Center, Poughkeepsie, New York
February 12   Palace Theatre, Cleveland, Ohio
February 13   Veteran's Memorial Auditorium, Columbus, Ohio
February 15   DeVos Hall at Grand Center, Grand Rapids, Michigan
February 16   Ervin J. Nutter Center, Dayton, Ohio
February 17   Fox Theatre, Detroit, Michigan
February 19   Northrup, Minneapolis, Minnesota
February 20   Riverside Theatre, Milwaukee, Wisconsin
February 21   Chicago Theatre, Chicago, Illinois
February 23   Masonic Auditorium, Toledo, Ohio
February 24   Civic Center Theatre, Madison, Wisconsin
February 26   Adler Theatre, Davenport, Iowa
February 27   Stephens Auditorium, Iowa State University, Ames, Iowa
February 28   Peoria Civic Center, Peoria, Illinois
March 2   Music Hall, Omaha, Nebraska
March 3   Midland Theatre, Kansas City, Missouri
March 4   Brady Theatre, Tulsa, Oklahoma
March 6   Kiva Auditorium, Albuquerque, New Mexico
March 9   Boise State University Pavilion Arena, Boise, Idaho
March 11   Kingsbury Hall, University of Utah, Salt Lake City, Utah
March 12   Pioneer Theatre, Reno, Nevada
March 13   Wilson Theatre, Fresno, California
March 14   Warfield Theatre, San Francisco, California
March 16/17   Wiltern Theatre, Los Angeles, California
                     [One of these shows appears on *The Original Bootleg Series
                     from the Manticore Vaults*, vol. 3]

Spring 1993 Latin American Tour

March 19/20   Auditorio Nacional, Mexico City, Mexico
March 23/24   Rio de Janeiro, Brazil
March 25/26/27   São Paulo, Brazil
March 29   Porto Alegre, Brazil

April 1	Santiago, Chile
April 4/5	Estadio de Obras Sanitarias, Buenos Aires, Argentina (two shows both days)

Fall 1993 *Return of the Manticore* Promotional Mini-Tour

November 15	*Regis and Kathie Lee* television show (ELP play "From the Beginning")
November 16	Howard Stern radio show (ELP play "From the Beginning" and a parody of "Lucky Man")
November 17	Hungerthon Benefit Concert, Beacon Theatre, New York, New York (ELP headline)
November 23	Virgin Records Megastore, Los Angeles, California (ELP play short in-house set)
December 17	KLOS Live Christmas Broadcast, The Hollywood Palladium, Hollywood, California
	[Note: when compiling career concert statistics, the November 17 show was the only *Return of the Manticore* tour date counted]

Summer/Fall 1996 North American Tour
[Package tour; Jethro Tull headlines, ELP opens]

August 18, 1996	Darien Center, Darien, New York
August 19	Kingswood Music Theatre, Richmond Hills, Ontario, Canada
August 21	Montage Mountain, Scranton, Pennsylvania
August 22	Garden State Art Center, Holmdel, New Jersey
August 23	Merriweather Post Pavilion, Columbia, Maryland
August 25	Meadows Music Theatre, Hartford, Connecticut
August 26	Great Woods Center for the Performing Arts, Mansfield, Massachusetts
August 27	New York State Fair Grounds, Syracuse, New York
August 29	Hershey Park Amphitheatre, Hershey, Pennsylvania
August 30	Jones Beach Theatre, Wantaugh, New York
August 31	East Center, Camden, New Jersey
September 1	Riverplex Amphitheatre, Pittsburgh, Pennsylvania
September 3	Nautica Stage, Cleveland, Ohio
September 4	Polaris Amphitheatre, Columbus, Ohio
September 5	Pine Knob, Clarkston, Michigan
September 6	Riverbend Music Center, Cincinnati, Ohio
September 7	World Music Theatre, Tinley Park, Illinois
September 8	The Mark, Moline, Illinois
September 10	Northrup Auditorium, Target Center, Minneapolis, Minnesota
September 11	Marcus Amphitheatre, Milwaukee, Wisconsin
September 13	Riverport Theatre, Saint Louis, Missouri
September 14	Sandstone Amphitheatre, Bonner Springs, Kansas
September 15	Riverfest Amphitheatre, Little Rock, Arkansas
September 16	Fiddler's Green Amphitheatre, Englewood, Colorado
September 18	Desert Sky Pavilion, Phoenix, Arizona
September 19	Aladdin Hotel and Casino Theatre, Las Vegas, Nevada
September 20	Open Air Theatre, San Diego, California
September 21	Irvine Meadows, Irvine, California
September 22	Universal Amphitheatre, Los Angeles, California
September 24	Concord Pavilion, Concord, California
September 25	Reno Amphitheatre, Reno, Nevada
September 27	The Gorge Amphitheatre, George, Washington
September 28	Labor Day Amphitheatre, Salem, Oregon
September 29	Boise State University Pavilion, Boise, Idaho

Fall 1996 Japanese Tour
[ELP only; no Jethro Tull]

October 8	Sun Palace, Fukuoka, Japan
October 9	Festival Hall, Osaka, Japan
October 10	Shi Kokaido, Tokyo, Japan
October 12	Shibuya Kokaido, Tokyo, Japan
October 13	Kosei Nenkin Kaikan, Tokyo, Japan
October 14	Izumi T 21, Sendai, Japan
October 15/17/18	Nakano Sun Plaza, Tokyo, Japan
October 19	Bunka Ceter, Saitama Urawa Shi, Japan

Summer 1997 U.S. Appearances

June 12, 1997	The Joint, Hard Rock, Las Vegas, Nevada
June 16	Z-Ninety Free, Atlanta, Georgia

Summer 1997 European Tour

June 20	Kiss Station, Budapest, Hungary
June 22	Spodek, Katowice, Poland
	[album *Live in Poland*]
June 23	Palace of Culture, Prague, Czech Republic
June 24	Tollowood, Munich, Germany
June 26	Patinore de Kockelschuer, Luxembourg
June 28	Stadthalle, Kassel, Germany
June 29	The Paradiso, Amsterdam, Netherlands
July 1	Serandadenhof Atrium, Nuremburg, Germany
July 2	Elysée Montmartre, Paris, France
July 4	Peisenitzinsel, Halle, Germany
July 5	Westfallen Park, Dortmund, Germany
July 6	Daytona Festival, Lahr, Germany
July 7	Montreux Jazz Festival, Montreux, Switzerland
	[DVD *Emerson, Lake and Palmer Live at Montreux 1997*]
July 11	Museumshof, Fulda, Germany
July 12	Grosse Freiheit, Hamburg, Germany
July 13	Elbufer, Dresden, Germany
July 16	Cantania Jazz Festival, Sicily, Italy
July 18	Velodromo Quarto, Sardinia (Quartu), Italy
July 20	Piazza Olimpo, Mantova, Italy
July 21	Foro Italico, Rome, Italy
July 25	The Kingdom Festival, Bellinzona, Switzerland

Summer 1997 South American Tour

August 6	Teatro Guaira, Curitiba, Brazil
August 8/9	Gran Rex, Buenos Aires, Argentina
August 10	Avenida das Hortensias, Gramado, Brazil
August 12/13	Estadio, Santiago, Chile
August 15	Mineirinho Gymnasium, Belo Horizonte, Brazil
August 16	Metropolitan, Rio de Janeiro, Brazil
August 18/19/20	Olympia, São Paulo, Brazil
August 21	Gran Rex, Buenos Aires, Argentina

Summer/Fall 1997 American Tour

September 6	Wolf Trap Farm Park, Vienna, Virginia
September 7	Oakdale Theatre, Wallingford, Connecticut
September 9	State Theatre, New Brunswick, New Jersey
September 10	Beacon Theatre, New York, New York
September 11	Tower Theatre, Philadelphia, Pennsylvania

September 12	Harborlights, Boston, Massachusetts
September 13	Sands Hotel and Casino, Atlantic City, New Jersey
September 14	Westbury Music Fair, Westbury, New York
September 17	Nautica, Cleveland, Ohio
September 18	The Palace, Auburn Hills, Michigan
September 19	Rosemont Theatre, Chicago, Illinois
September 20	Riverside Theatre, Milwaukee, Wisconsin
September 21	Fox Theatre, Saint Louis, Missouri
September 23	Union Hall, Phoenix, Arizona
September 25	Universal Amphitheatre, Los Angeles, California
September 26	Concord Pavilion, Concord, California
September 27	Reno Amphitheatre, Reno, Nevada
September 28	Visalia Center, Visalia, California
September 30	Humphrey's, San Diego, California

Fall 1997 Latin American Tour

October 4	Muelle Uno, Lima, Peru
October 7/8	Costa Rica Teatro Nacional, San José, Costa Rica
October 10	Plaza de Toros, Monterrey, Mexico
October 11/12	Teatro Opera, Mexico City, Mexico

Summer 1998 North American Tour

[Package tour; Deep Purple headlines, Dream Theater and ELP open]

August 1, 1998	Hampton Beach Casino Ballroom, Hampton Beach, New Hampshire [ELP only]
August 2	Flynn Theatre, Burlington, Vermont [ELP only]
August 3	The Chance, Poughkeepsie, New York
August 4	Chamberland County Civic Center, Portland, Maine [not listed on Greg Lake Web Site]
August 6	P.N.C. Bank Arts Center, Holmdel, New Jersey
August 7	Meadow Music Theatre, Hartford, Connecticut
August 8	Great Woods, Mansfield, Massachusetts
August 9	Jones Beach Theatre, Wantaugh, New York
August 11	Bud Light Amphitheatre, Wilkes-Barre, Pennsylvania
August 12	E-Center, Camden, New Jersey
August 14	Finger Lakes Performing Arts Center, Canandaigua, New York
August 15	Pine Knob, Clarkston, Michigan
August 17	L'Agora, Québec City, Quebec, Canada
August 18	Molson Center, Montréal, Quebec, Canada
August 19	Molson Amphitheatre, Toronto, Ontario, Canada
August 21	Blossom Music Center, Cuyahoga Falls, Ohio
August 22	World Music Theatre, Tinley Park, Illinois
August 23	Grand Casino Amphitheatre, Hinkley, Minnesota
August 24	Marcus Amphitheatre, Milwaukee, Wisconsin
August 26	Fiddler's Green Amphitheatre, Englewood, Colorado
August 28/29 (?)	Warfield Theatre, San Francisco, California
August 30	Universal Amphitheatre, Universal City, California
August 31	4th and B, San Diego, California, open air show [ELP only]

STATISTICAL SUMMARY AND ANALYSIS OF ELP'S TOUR PATTERNS

(As stated at the beginning of this appendix, the final figures will doubtless be subject to some change; in particular, I'm certain there are more "lost" shows that will be uncovered. Nonetheless, I'm confident the overall trends I discuss below will not be changed by modifications to the number, or locations, of individual shows.)

NUMBER OF CAREER SHOWS: 736

By era: 463, 1970–78; 273, 1992–98
By year: 36 (1970), 90 (1971), 83 (1972), 57 (1973), 74 (1974), 77 (1977), 46 (1978), 84 (1992), 61 (1993), 44 (1996), 60 (1997), 24 (1998)
Continents performed on: Four (Asia, Europe, North America, South America)
Countries performed in: 25
The breakdownis shown on page 771.

COMMENTS ON FIGURE 1

When perusing the chart on page 771, one is struck by several salient issues.

1. First and most notable is the absolute dominance of the U.S., where some 56% of all ELP's shows were played. One notices this dominance already being asserted in the band's second year, 1971, and one sees it peaking in the years 1977-78, when 113 of ELP's 123 shows were played in the U.S. (the other 10 were played in Canada). The reason is not hard to establish. During the seventies, the U.S. contained approximately 50% of the world's record buying public, a powerful incentive for an English-lyric band to spend a lot of time touring the U.S. (indeed, this is the reason all the major British rock bands spent so much time in the States during the seventies). As ELP sold more albums, played before ever-bigger audiences, and reinvested more and more of their profit into growing their stage show, they reached the point in 1973 where it increasingly was not profitable—indeed, was often no longer feasible, due to the sheer size of their stage show—to play in any venue smaller than an arena (i.e., a 10,000- to 20,000-seat auditorium): the smaller venues of Europe therefore looked increasingly unprofitable compared to those of the U.S. and Canada. One notes that during the nineties, when ELP were no longer selling millions of albums and therefore had considerably scaled back the scope of their stage show, smaller venues again became a more feasible proposition—more profitable, as well, as the band realized it made more sense to sell out a 5,000-seat venue than to sell 5,000 tickets for a 20,000-seat venue—and therefore, while the U.S. remained a major factor in ELP's tour plans during the nineties, it did not regain its overwhelming dominance of the mid to late seventies.

2. It is interesting to note how important the German-speaking countries of central Europe were to ELP's tours—ELP played 65 shows in Germany, 9 in Austria, and 9 in Switzerland, for a total of 83. This is especially interesting in light of the fact that, Triumvirat aside, ELP's music appears to have made a far smaller impact on the rock music of Germany than of countries that the band visited far less (Italy, visited only seven times during the seventies and 17 times in all, comes to mind). This is a phenomenon that merits further consideration.

3. Note that during the seventies, ELP only toured the U.S. and Canada, Western Europe, and Japan. During the nineties they also visited three Eastern European countries (the Czech Republic, Hungary, and Poland) in the aftermath of the fall of the Iron Curtain, and six Latin American countries (Brazil, Argentina, Chile, Peru, Costa Rica, and Mexico), undertaking full-fledged mini-tours of Latin America in 1993 and 1997. Besides pointing up an explosion of interest in progressive rock in Brazil and Argentina, particularly, during the nineties—the sociological aspects of this phenomenon still call out for exploration—ELP's Latin American tours also point up the growing Westernization and affluence of at least some sectors of Latin America during this period. Could anyone have imagined ELP touring Brazil in 1971?

	1970	1971	1972	1973	1974	1977	1978	1992	1993	1996	1997	1998	Total
Argentina									4		3		7
Austria	2	1	1	2	2			1					9
Belgium			1					1					2
Brazil									6		7		13
Canada		3	2	2	1	5	5	4	12	1		3	38
Chile									1		2		3
Costa Rica											2		2
Czech Republic											1		1
Denmark			1	1				1					3
France			1	6	2			1			1		11
Germany	6	9	5	13	8			15			9		65
Great Britain	27	35	23		9			8					102
Hungary								1			1		2
Italy			3	4				6			4		17
Japan				2				8		10			20
Luxembourg											1		1
Mexico									2		3		5
Netherlands			1		1			2			1		5
Norway								1					1
Peru											1		1
Poland											1		1
Spain					2			3					5
Sweden				1				1					2
Switzerland	1	1	1	1	2			1			2		9
United States		41	44	25	47	72	41	30	36	33	21	21	411
TOTALS	36	90	83	57	74	77	46	84	61	44	60	24	736

FIGURE 1: CAREER SHOWS

4. It probably surprises nobody that next to the U.S., ELP played more shows (102) in their native land, Great Britain, than anywhere else. What might give room for pause, however, is that 85 of these 102 shows were played in the first two and a half years of the band's existence; between January 1973 and December 1998, ELP played all of 17 shows in Great Britain, a period during which they played 525 shows overall. Of course, there is some explanation in the fact that between the mid and late seventies, nearly all of ELP's energy was focused on the huge, and hugely profitable, U.S. market. How is it, though, that during the nineties ELP played more shows in Germany, Italy, Japan, Canada, and Brazil than in Great Britain? This is a question that has yet to receive a satisfactory answer.

NUMBER OF AMERICAN SHOWS: 411

By era: 270, 1970–78; 141, 1992–98
By year: 41 (1971), 44 (1972), 25 (1973), 47 (1974), 72 (1977), 41 (1978), 30 (1992), 36 (1993), 33 (1996), 21 (1997), 21 (1998)
States performed in: 43 (not counting Puerto Rico, where they played Mar y Sol Festival)
States never performed in: Alaska, Delaware, Hawaii, Montana, North Dakota, South Dakota, Wyoming
The breakdown is shown on pp. 773.

COMMENTS ON FIGURE 2

On the one hand, the results aren't terribly surprising. We are not startled to learn that the seven states ELP never visited are remote (Alaska and Hawaii), tiny (Delaware), or thinly populated (the Dakotas, Montana, Wyoming). Nor are we surprised that the two states ELP visited most are California and New York, the two most populous states during the 1970s.

If the results are studied more carefully, though, some interesting patterns emerge. One notes, for example, that ELP performed in Connecticut 13 times, nearly as often as they performed in Florida (14) and more often than they performed in Georgia or North Carolina, although all three of these states are much more populous than Connecticut. One also notes that just three adjacent states, New York, New Jersey, and Pennsylvania, account for 91 of ELP's 411 U.S. concerts (22% of the total); add the three southern New England states (Connecticut, Massachusetts, and Rhode Island) to this group, and the total is 125 shows, 30% of all shows ELP played in the U.S., although in 1980 these six states only accounted for 21% of the total U.S. population. Furthermore, the five Midwestern states surrounding the Great Lakes (Wisconsin, Illinois, Indiana, Ohio, Michigan) account for another 82 shows, 20% of the total. In other words, eleven states in the northeast and Midwest account for slightly over 50% of all ELP's American shows, with the northeastern states, in particular, being over represented relative to their proportion of the country's population. If we add the three Pacific coast states (California, Oregon, Washington), which account for another 61 shows, we've now accounted for 65% of all of ELP's U.S. concerts.

At this point I would like to revisit a topic I discussed in *Rocking the Classics*, now on a more detailed level than before. As readers of that book may recall, I argue that progressive rock was received especially favorably in three specific regions of the U.S.: the northeast (New England plus New York, Pennsylvania, and New Jersey), the eastern Midwest (that is, the five western Great Lakes states), and the Pacific coast states. With the statistical evidence of the ELP tour patterns correlating with the mass of anecdotal evidence I have continued to collect since the publication of *Rocking the Classics*, I am now prepared to accept my assertion as a more or less established fact, and advance an explanation.

In my view, there are two main factors driving the favorable reception of progressive rock in these three regions. First, these regions were settled by New England puritans or their descendents, and I believe a cultural memory of English folkways, social customs, and political attitudes has continued to linger not just in the northeast, but in the Midwest and in places like San Francisco, Portland (Oregon), Seattle, and their environs. As a result, I believe there was an openness among audiences in these areas to the deeply English elements of the progressive rock style: its musical debt to English folksong, Anglican choral music, and twentieth-century symphonic pastoralism, and its thematic debt to English folklore and medieval imagery, evident in its lyrics and cover art.

At this point some readers are probably saying, "In none of these regions are people of English descent any longer the majority of the white population, much less the population in general." True enough. However, as David Hackett Fischer convincingly demonstrates in *Albion's Seed: Four British Folkways in America*,[1] the folkways, social customs, and political attitudes of America's seventeenth- and eighteenth-century British settlers have lingered on in regions they settled long after their descendents no longer constituted a majority of the populace.

Indeed, this brings me to my second point. As I stated in *Rocking the Classics* (155), I believe that prog's appeal was in part that it offered a kind of mythical surrogate English ethnicity to its young white American audiences in regions where ethnic identity had become insecure and wobbly. Bill Martin takes up this point where I left off in *Listening to the Future* (138). Martin finds it troubling that "the interest that some Americans, mostly white, middle-class males, had in progressive rock is motivated by white identity formation," because "white identity formation, in the United States and in the West more generally, has always been a reaction formation. White means 'not-Black' (or 'not-Red,' '-

---

[1] David Hackett Fischer, *Albion's Seed: Four British Folkways in America* (New York: Oxford University Press, 1989).

	1971	1972	1973	1974	1977	1978	1992	1993	1996	1997	1998	Total
Alabama				1	4							5
Alaska												0
Arizona				1	1		1		1	1		5
Arkansas				1					1			2
California	3	7		10	8		5	4	4	4	4	49
Colorado		1		1		1			1		1	5
Connecticut	1	1	1	1	3	1	1	1	1	1	1	13
Delaware												0
Florida	3	4	3		4							14
Georgia		1	1	1	1	1	1			1		7
Hawaii												0
Idaho									1	1		2
Illinois	2	3	2		2	6	1	2	2	1	1	22
Indiana			1		3	1	1					6
Iowa			1		1			2				4
Kansas				1	1				1			3
Kentucky		2	1		2							5
Louisiana	1			2	1							4
Maine											1	1
Maryland		2		1	2	1	1		1			8
Massachusetts	2	2	1	1	1	4	1	2	1	1	1	17
Michigan	3	1	1		5	1	1	2	1	1	1	17
Minnesota			1		1			1	1		1	5
Mississippi					1							1
Missouri	1	1		1	2	3	1	1	1	1		12
Montana												0
Nebraska								1				1
Nevada						1	1	1	2	2		7
New Hampshire											1	1
New Jersey	2	2		1		1	2		2	2	2	14
New Mexico				1				1				2
New York	8	5	4	3	3	8	4	4	3	2	3	47
North Carolina				1	2							3
North Dakota												0
Ohio	2	4	1	2	4	3	2	4	3	1	1	27
Oklahoma			1	1	1	1		1				5
Oregon	1			1	1		1		1			5
Pennsylvania	5	6	1	4	3	1	2	3	3	1	1	30
Puerto Rico		1										1
Rhode Island				1	1	1		1				4
South Carolina					1							1
South Dakota												0
Tennessee			1	2	3	1						7
Texas	2	2		3	3	4	3					17
Utah				1				1				2
Vermont								1			1	2
Virginia	3		1	1	1					1		7
Washington	1			3	1	1		1				7
West Virginia			1		1	1						3
Wisconsin		1			4			2	1	1	1	10
Wyoming												0
(unknown)	1											1
TOTAL	41	44	25	47	72	41	30	36	33	21	21	411

FIGURE 2: AMERICAN SHOWS

Yellow,' etc.)" (138–39). I think Martin may have made a subtle but important misreading of what I said in *Rocking the Classics*, where, while I do speak of prog providing a surrogate ethnicity, I do not speak of "white identity formation" per se. I believe identity formation is *always* a reaction formation, among any group of people at any time. I do not believe that identity formation among whites always has an implicit racist component, as Martin's statement above seems to suggest. For instance, growing up in Michigan, near the Canadian border, during the sixties and seventies, I witnessed the coalescence of a particular identity formation amongst the French-speaking citizens of Quebec, who were reacting against what they perceived as cultural imperialism by English-speaking Canadians: this was identity formation, surely enough, but it was based around language, not racial, identity. Likewise, I would argue that during the late nineteenth and early twentieth century, the nationalist movements in the arts of Europe's more politically (and militarily) peripheral regions—Scandinavia, Eastern Europe—were part of a cultural identity formation that reacted to perceived cultural oppression by the great powers of the day, and that had both national and ethnic, but obviously not racial, dimensions.

In fairness to Martin, he acknowledges that identity formation, even as it is driven by a reaction against a perceived cultural threat, can also play a positive, as opposed to a negative, "I'm-not-such-and-such" role, by projecting a set of ideals that the group aspires towards. In the case of progressive rock in the U.S., Martin sees in its mythical Englishness (the term is mine, not his) a yearning for its "romantic, pastoral, and communitarian traditions—including a certain romance with the idea of the 'American farmer'" (139). I think Martin is essentially correct in his reading of which aspects of prog audiences (or at least, those most deeply engaged with the music) found especially meaningful: I would simply like to clarify why progressive rock seemed to have a special appeal for young whites in three specific regions: the Northeast, the Midwest, and the Pacific Coast.

In all three of these regions, the allegiance of young whites to "the old country" (wherever in Europe that was) was waning, without a distinctive new sense of white American ethnicity having arisen in its place, and prog's "mythical Englishness" assuaged an anxiety driven by feelings of ethnic and cultural rootlessness. I continue to believe, as I stated in *Rocking the Classics*, that in these regions allegiance to mainline Christian denominations was waning among the young, and prog, with its flights of fantasy and mysticism and its quasi-liturgical live shows, provided a kind of surrogate religion as well. My argument, in sum, is that the three regions where prog was especially popular share two features: a cultural link, direct or indirect, to America's seventeenth-century English settlers that made for a favorable reception of prog's deeply English elements, and a large white population that was not necessarily of English descent, but which sought in prog's idealized Englishness a surrogate ethnicity and religion to assuage anxiety over feelings of unrootedness that resulted from waning links to their actual ancestral ethnic identities.

One final issue: what of the regions where ELP (and prog more generally) wasn't as popular, the South and the West? These regions were settled extensively by Scots-Irish (rather than English) settlers, whose descendents would have felt little cultural affinity to the medievalism and musical Anglicanism of prog. The white population of these regions were (and are) much more religious than their compatriots of the Northeast and Pacific West, and by and large young whites in these regions didn't look to rock music as a surrogate religion during the seventies. Furthermore, I would argue the ethnic identities of white of the South and West were more secure than those of the Northeast, Midwest, or Pacific coast during the seventies: many southern whites can trace their lineage back ten to twelve generations in their region of birth, while relatively few whites in New England can trace their lineage in their region of birth much farther back than three. Whites of the South and West felt themselves possessors of a distinctive culture, which they celebrated in country-and-western music: young people of the southern and western states therefore were not in search of a surrogate ethnic or cultural identity and, so much as rock penetrated the South during the seventies, it was made to conform to southern political attitudes, cultural outlooks, and musical preferences (here one thinks of the Allman Brothers, Lynard Skynard, and ZZ Top).

In closing, it's worth noting two points. First, ELP's most intense touring activity in the South came in the mid to late seventies, their most intensive period of touring the U.S.; during the nineties, when they focused the geographical coverage of their tours more carefully to reflect areas where their fan base was most reliable, the South was very underrepresented. Second, regions where progressive rock and where country-and-western music were popular did not often overlap during the seventies, and with a few major exceptions, entirely in the Midwest, progressive rock was more popular in the "blue" states (to use parlance made popular by the 2000 presidential election) than in the "red" states.

Bibliography

Part 1: Books and Monographs

Adorno, Theodor. *Mahler: A Musical Physiognomy.* Translated from German by Edmund Jephcott. Chicago: University of Chicago Press, 1992.

Bacon, Tony, ed. *Rock Hardware: The Instruments, Equipment, and Technology of Rock.* New York: Harmony Books, 1981.

Barzun, Jacques. *From Dawn to Decadence: 1500 to the Present; 500 Years of Western Cultural Life.* New York: Harper-Collins, 2000.

Bowman, Durrell. "'Let Them All Make Their Own Music': Individualism, Rush, and the Progressive/Hard Rock Alloy." In Holm-Hudson, *Progressive Rock Reconsidered*, 183–217.

Bromell, Nick. *Tomorrow Never Knows: Rock and Psychedelics in the 1960s.* Chicago: University of Chicago Press, 2000.

Burnham, Scott. *Beethoven Hero.* Princeton, NJ: Princeton University Press, 1995.

Buskin, Richard. *Inside Tracks.* New York: Avon Books, 1999.

Campbell, Michael. *The Beat Goes On: An Introduction to Popular Music in America, 1840 to Today.* New York: Schirmer Books, 1996.

Cavallo, Dominick. *A Fiction of the Past: The Sixties in American History.* New York: Saint Martin's Press, 1999.

Chanan, Michael. *From Handel to Hendrix: The Composer in the Public Sphere.* London: Verso, 1999.

Christgau, Robert. *Rock Albums of the 70s: A Critical Guide.* New York: Da Capo Press, 1981.

Curtis, Jim. *Rock Eras: Interpretations of Music and Society 1954–84.* Bowling Green, OH: Bowling Green State University Popular Press, 1987.

David, Hans, and Arthur Mendel, eds. *The Bach Reader.* New York: W. W. Norton, 1966.

Davis, Stephen. *Hammer of the Gods: The Led Zeppelin Saga.* New York: Ballantine Books, 1985.

DeCurtis, Anthony, James Henke, and Holly George-Warren, eds. *The Rolling Stone History of Rock and Roll*, 3rd ed. New York: Summit Books, 1992.

DeRogatis, Jim. *Let It Blurt: The Life and Times of Lester Bangs, America's Greatest Rock Critic.* New York: Bantam Doubleday, 2000.

Eger, Joseph. *Einstein's Violin. A Conductor's Notes on Music, Physics, and Social Change*. New York: Tarcher/Penguin, 2005.

Emerson, Keith. *Pictures of an Exhibitionist*. London: John Blake Publishing, 2003.

Ernst, David. *The Evolution of Electronic Music*. New York: Schirmer Books, 1977.

Fischer, David Hackett. *Albion's Seed: Four British Folkways in America*. New York: Oxford University Press, 1989.

———. *The Great Wave: Price Revolutions and the Rhythm of History*. New York: Oxford University Press, 1996.

Forrester, George, Martyn Hanson, and Frank Askew. *Emerson, Lake and Palmer: The Show That Never Ends; A Musical Biography*. London: Helter Skelter, 2001.

Frith, Simon. *The Sociology of Rock*. London: Constable and Co., 1978.

Fukuyama, Francis. *The End of History and the Last Man*. New York: Free Press, 1992.

Gorman, Clem. *Back Stage Rock*. London: Pan Books, 1978.

Godwin, Joscelyn. *Harmonies of Heaven and Earth: Mysticism in Music from Antiquity to the Avant-Garde*. Rochester, VT: Inner Traditions International, 1995.

Hanson, Martyn. *Hang on to a Dream: The Story of the Nice*. London: Helter Skelter, 2002.

Hedges, Dan. *Yes: The Authorized Biography*. London: Sidgwick and Jackson, 1981.

Holm-Hudson, Kevin, ed. *Progressive Rock Reconsidered*. New York: Routledge, 2002.

———. "The 'American Metaphysical Circus' of Joseph Byrd's United States of America." In Holm-Hudson, *Progressive Rock Reconsidered*, 43–62.

———. "A Promise Deferred: Multiply Directed Time and Thematic Transformation in Emerson, Lake and Palmer's 'Trilogy.'" In Holm-Hudson, *Progressive Rock Reconsidered*, 111–20.

Johnson, Haynes. *The Best of Times: The Boom and Bust Years of America Before and After Everything Changed*. New York: Harcourt, 2001.

Jones, Landon. *Great Expectations: America and the Baby Boom Generation*. New York: Coward, McGann, and Geoghegan, 1980.

Kawamoto, Akitsugu. "'Can you Still Keep Your Balance?': Keith Emerson's Anxiety of Influence, Style Change, and the Road to Prog Superstardom." *Popular Music* 24, no. 2 (2005): 223–44.

Kravitt, Edward. "Romanticism Today." *Musical Quarterly* (Spring 1992): 93–109.

Lanza, Joseph. *Elevator Music*. New York: Saint Martin's Press, 1994.

Lendvai, Ernö. *Béla Bartók: An Analysis of His Music*. London: Kahn and Averill, 1971.

Levenson, Thomas. *Measure For Measure: A Musical History of Science*. New York: Touchstone Books, 1994.

Macan, Edward. "Concerning the Politics of Prog." *The Journal of Ayn Rand Studies* 5, no. 1 (Fall 2003): 173–88.

———. "Holst's 'Mars': A Model of Goal-Oriented Bitonality." In *Music in Performance and Society: Essays in Honor of Roland Jackson*, edited by Malcolm Cole and John Koegel. Warren, MI: Harmonie Park Press, 1997.

————. *Rocking the Classics: English Progressive Rock and the Counterculture*. New York: Oxford University Press, 1997.

Marsh, Dave. *The Heart of Rock and Soul*. New York: Plume Books, 1989.

Marsh, Dave, and John Swenson, eds. *The Rolling Stone Record Guide*. New York: Random House, 1979.

Martin, Bill. *Listening to the Future: The Time of Progressive Rock, 1968–1978*. Chicago: Open Court, 1998

————. *Music of Yes: Structure and Vision in Progressive Rock*. Chicago: Open Court, 1996.

McClary, Susan. "Pitches, Expression, Ideology: An Exercise in Mediation." *Enclitic 7*, no. 1 (Spring 1983): 76–86.

Montgomery, David. "The Myth of Organicism: From Bad Science to Great Art." *Musical Quarterly* (Spring 1992): 17–66.

Morgan, Robert. *Twentieth-Century Music*. New York: W. W. Norton, 1991.

Moore, Allan. *Rock: The Primary Text; Developing a Musicology of Rock*. Buckingham, U.K.: Open University Press, 1993.

Ostwald, Peter. *Glenn Gould: The Ecstasy and Tragedy of Genius*. New York: W. W. Norton, 1997.

Pareles, Jon, and Patricia Romanowski, eds. *The Rolling Stone Encyclopedia of Rock and Roll*. New York: Rolling Stone Press/Summit Books, 1983.

Pattison, Robert. *The Triumph of Vulgarity: Rock Music in the Mirror of Romanticism*. New York: Oxford University Press, 1987.

Pethel, Blair. "Keith Emerson: The Emergence and Growth of Style." D.M.A. Paper, John Hopkins University, 1987.

Pirenne, Christophe. "Le rock progressif anglais (1966–1977)." Ph.D. Dissertation, University of Liège, 2000.

————. *Le Rock Progressif Anglais (1967–1977)*. Paris: Honoré Champion, 2005.

Rees, David. *Minstrels in the Gallery: A History of Jethro Tull*. Wembley, U.K.: Firefly Publishing, 1998.

Robison, Brian. "Somebody is Digging My Bones: King Crimson's 'Dinosaur' as (Post) Progressive Historiography." In Holm-Hudson, *Progressive Rock Reconsidered*, 221–42.

Rockwell, John. "Art Rock." *The Rolling Stone Illustrated History of Rock and Roll*, 2nd ed., edited by Jim Miller. New York: Random House, 1980.

Schact, Janis. *Genesis*. London: Proteus Books, 1984.

Scheinbaum, John. "Progressive Rock and the Inversion of Musical Values." In Holm-Hudson, *Progressive Rock Reconsidered*, 21–42.

Sciabarra, Chris Matthew. "Rand, Rush and Rock." *The Journal of Ayn Rand Studies 4*, no. 1 (Fall 2002): 161–85.

Smith, Sid. *In the Court of King Crimson*. London: Helter Skelter, 2001.

Stradling, Robert, and Meirion Hughes. *The English Musical Renaissance 1960–1940: Construction and Deconstruction*. London: Routledge, 1993.

Street, John. *Rebel Rock: The Politics of Popular Music*. New York: Basil Blackwell, 1986.

Stuart, Philip. *London Philharmonic Discography*. Westport, CT/London: Greenwood Press, 1997.

Stump, Paul. *The Music's All That Matters: A History of Progressive Rock*. London: Quartet Books, 1997.

Tamm, Eric. *Robert Fripp: From King Crimson to Guitar Craft.* Boston: Faber and Faber, 1990.

Taylor, Yuval, ed. *The Future of Jazz.* New York: A Cappella, 2002.

Thompson, E. P. *Witness Against the Beast: William Blake and the Moral Law.* New York: The Free Press, 1993.

Vail, Mark. *The Hammond Organ: Beauty in the B.* San Francisco: Miller Freeman Books, 1997.

Volkov, Solomon. *Shostakovich and Stalin: The Extraordinary Relationship Between the Great Composer and the Brutal Dictator.* London: Little, Brown, 2004.

Von der Horst, Dirk. "Precarious Pleasures: Situating 'Close to the Edge' in Conflicting Male Desires." In Holm-Hudson, *Progressive Rock Reconsidered,* 167–82.

Weber, William. "Wagner, Wagnerism, and Musical Idealism." In *Wagnerism in European Culture and Politics,* edited by David Large and William Weber. Ithaca, NY: Cornell University Press, 1984.

Weinstein, Deena. "Progressive Rock as Text: The Lyrics of Roger Waters." In Holm-Hudson, *Progressive Rock Reconsidered,* 91–109.

Welch, Chris. *Close to the Edge: The Story of Yes.* London: Omnibus Press, 2000.

Part 2: Interviews, Features, Miscellaneous Articles

Aledorf, Andy. "Lucky Man." *Guitar Legends,* no. 22 (1997).

Altham, Keith. "Carl Palmer: Benny the Bouncers' Blues Variations." *Music Scene Top Ten Series: Emerson, Lake and Palmer,* May 1974.

———. "Greg Lake: Still He Turns Them On." *Music Scene Top Ten Series: Emerson, Lake and Palmer,* May 1974.

———. "Look, You Have to Join Us." *Music Scene Top Ten Series: Emerson, Lake and Palmer,* May 1974.

———. "The Manticore Tapes: The Last Reel—Greg Lake." *Music Scene,* ca. late 1973 or early 1974.

"Ask a Pro." *Modern Drummer,* May 1995.

Askew, Frank. "Carl Palmer's Drum Kits." *Fanzine for the Common Man,* no. 13 (July 1993).

———. "Interviews: Carl Palmer." *Impressions,* no. 8 (October 2001).

Askew, Frank, with Even Gaarder and Liv Whetmore. "Carl Palmer: 4th February 2000." *Impressions,* no. 8 (October 2001).

Bangs, Lester. "Exposed! The Brutal Energy Atrocities of Emerson, Lake and Palmer." *Creem,* March 1974.

Beardsley, Tim. "Decided by Limits Drawn." *ELP Digest* 6, no. 29 (December 13, 1996); *ELP Digest* is available online at www.brain-salad.com.

"The Being Fifty Blues." *Keyboards,* November 1994. Translated from the German by Bill Wagner. Translation reprinted in *ELP Digest* 5, no. 9 (April 4, 1995).

"Carl Palmer." *Percussioni,* November 1994. Translated from the Italian by Adriano Melis. Translation reprinted in *ELP Digest* 6, no. 3.

Carlin, Scott. "The Gand Musictech Provides an Interesting Day with Keith Emerson." *The Illinois Entertainer*, September 1995.

Carr, Roy. "Loneliness of a Long-Distance Power Cell." *New Musical Express*, July 27, 1974).

Crowe, Cameron. "Greg Lake Interview." *Hit Parader*, Winter 1974/75.

Dillingham, Mick. "Van der Graaf Generator: The David Jackson Interview, parts one and two." *Ptolemaic Terrascope*, May 1991 and Autumn 1991.

Doerschuk, Robert. "Keith Emerson." *Keyboard*, April 1988.

———. "Keith Emerson and ELP Again." *Keyboard*, June 1992.

———. "Keith Emerson: The Phoenix Rises from the Ashes of Progressive Rock." *Keyboard*, July 1986.

———. "Keith Emerson's Moment of Truth." *Keyboard*, April 1994.

Dove, Ian. "Greg Lake Interview." *Hit Parader*, Winter 74/75, 74.

"ELP Debut." *New Musical Express*. August 15, 1970.

Emerson, Keith. "An Open Letter from Keith Emerson to the Readers of *Contemporary Keyboard*." *Contemporary Keyboard*, September 1980.

"Emerson, Lake and Palmer are Back in the Hot Seat with a Brand New Album." Polygram Press Release. Reprinted in *ELP Digest* 4, no. 22 (November 10, 1994).

"Emerson, Lake and Palmer to Make 'Incognito' Debut." *New Musical Express*, May 30, 1970.

Farber, Jim. "The Emerson, Lake and Palmer Tapes, part 3: Keith Emerson." *Circus*, September 1977.

Furnash, Dale. "Conversations: Emerson, Lake and Palmer." *Trouser Press*, May 1978.

Gaer, Eric. "Emerson, Lake and Palmer: A Force to be Reckoned With." *Downbeat*, May 9, 1974.

Gallant, Dave. "Greg Lake Tapes." *ELP Digest* 6, no. 17 (July 18, 1996).

Graff, Gary. "Keith Emerson Seeks a Hit with His New Group, 3." *Detroit Free Press*, April 22, 1988.

Graustark, Barbara. "ELP: Rock Kings Turn Gypsies for Pop Extravaganza." *Circus*, January 1973.

"Greg Lake." *International Musician*, January 1976.

Hall, Russell. "Welcome to the Show! Emerson, Lake and Palmer in Their Own Words." *Goldmine*, December 6, 1996.

Iero, Cheech. "Carl Palmer." *Modern Drummer*, June/July 1980.

Johnson, James. "Fingers' Cave." *New Musical Express*, January 19, 1974.

———. "Lake the Strongman." *New Musical Express*, March 31, 1973.

———. "Under the Influence: Greg Lake." *New Musical Express*, June 9, 1973.

———. "Welcome Back My Friends to the Show That Never Ends." *New Musical Express*, April 27, 1974.

"Keith Emerson." *Keyboard Magazine* [Japan], October 1994. Translated from the Japanese by Atsuku Sasaki. Translation reprinted in *ELP Digest* 5, no. 20 (August 12, 1995).

Lawlor, Joe. "Interviews with Lake and Palmer." *ELP Digest* 8, no. 11 (September 27, 1998).

Leroy, Aymeric. "An Interview with Carl Palmer." *Big Bang*, August 1997. Reprinted in *ELP Digest* 7, no. 17 (September 8, 1997).

Mattingly, Rick. "Carl Palmer." *Modern Drummer*, December 1983.

Micallef, Ken. "Carl Palmer: From the Beginning." *Modern Drummer*, June 2005.

Milano, Dominic. "Keith Emerson." *Contemporary Keyboard*, October 1977.

———. "Keith Emerson." *Contemporary Keyboard*, September 1980.

Mulhern, Tom. "John Wetton: Asia's Progressive Rock Bassist." *Guitar Player*, January 1983.

O'Connor, Jim. "ELP Split for Solo Exploits." *Circus*, November 1974.

"One 2 One." The Official Greg Lake Web Site, http://www.greglake.com/newsite/feedback.asp?offset=30.

Orme, John. "ELP: Blood, Sweat, and Real Tears as Money Turns U.S. Tour Sour." *Melody Maker*, July 9, 1977.

Pekar, Harvey. "From Rock to ???" *Downbeat*, May 2, 1968.

Powell, Cozy, and Frank Aiello. "Emerson, Lake and Powell U.S. Tour." *Fanzine for the Common Man*, no. 8 (June 1991).

Roberts, John Storm. "Progressive Rock's Classic Synthesizers." *Newsday*, July 3, 1977.

Robertson, Richard. "*Works* on the Road." *Hit Parader*, 1977. Reprinted in *ELP Digest* 3, no. 7 (April 12, 1993).

Rosen, Steve. "Greg Lake of Emerson, Lake and Palmer." *Guitar Player*, September 1974.

Rudis, Al. "Guess Who's Back with 35 Tons of Equipment." *Sounds*, May 21, 1977.

Sanders, Rick, and John Wells. "Greg Lake: Still He Turns Them On." *Music Scene Top Ten Series: Emerson, Lake and Palmer*, May 1974.

Schact, Janis. "Emerson, Lake and Palmer: The Dagger Does More Than You Think." *Circus*, March 1972.

Sims, Judith. "ELP . . . What? ELP! . . . What? . . . ELP." *Rolling Stone*, April 25, 1974.

Sinfield, Peter. "Peter Sinfield and What He Did/Does." *ELP Digest* 4, no. 19 (October 23, 1994).

Stein, Kathi. "Emerson, Lake and Palmer Live." *Circus Raves*, August 1974.

Stellar, Richard. "The Closed to Home Interview: Raw Meat and Emerson," http://www.interstellar9.com/emerson/interview.htm.

Stewart, Tony. "*Emerson, Lake and Palmer*: 'Kill It' Says Greg." *Hit Parader*, December 1972.

Telford, Ray. "Eddy Offord." *Sounds*, January 12, 1974.

Terralavoro, David. "The Carl Palmer Story, Part 1: 1950–1971." *Fanzine for the Common Man*, no. 15 (January 1996).

———. "Carl Palmer's Recent Projects." *Fanzine for the Common Man*, no. 17 (July 1997).

———. "Current News." *Fanzine for the Common Man*, no. 4 (July 1990).

———. "Current News." *Fanzine for the Common Man*, no. 15 (January 1996).

———. "Didja Know That . . ." *Fanzine for the Common Man*, no. 14 (July 1995).

———. "Emerson and Lake." *Fanzine for the Common Man,* no. 15 (January 1996).

———. "Etc." *Fanzine for the Common Man,* no. 13 (July 1993).

———. "The Greg Lake Story, Part 1: 1947–1971." *Fanzine for the Common Man,* no. 15 (January 1996).

———. "The History of ELP: Part II." *Fanzine for the Common Man,* no. 4 (July 1990).

———. "Keith Emerson's Aborted 1989/90 Piano Solo Album." *Fanzine for the Common Man,* no. 14 (July 1995).

———. "The Keith Emerson Story, Part 1: 1944–1971," *Fanzine for the Common Man,* no. 14 (July 1995).

———. "The Ride the Tiger Project." *Fanzine for the Common Man,* no. 16 (December 1996).

Titus, Dale. "More than a Lucky Man." *Bass Frontiers,* September-October 1997.

Tyler, Tony. "The Master of Speed and Stagecraft." *New Musical Express,* October 12, 1972.

Vail, Mark. "The World's Most Dangerous Synth." *Keyboard,* June 1992.

Valentine, Penny. "Keith Emerson in the *Sounds* Talk-In." *Sounds,* March 31, 1973.

Welch, Chris. "Carl Palmer." *Musicians Only,* March 1980.

———. "The Heavy Metal Kid." *Melody Maker,* June 16, 1973.

Whetmore, Liv. "Carl Palmer." *Impressions,* no. 8 (October 2001).

Part 3: Liner Notes

Emerson, Keith. Liner notes, Keith Emerson, *Iron Man, Volume 1.* Net Event CD A128021, 2002.

Fripp, Robert. Liner notes, King Crimson, *Epitaph.* DGM CD 9607, 1997.

Gilbert, Kevin. Liner notes, Keith Emerson, *Changing States.* AMP-CD 026, 1995.

Pilato, Bruce. Liner notes, Emerson, Lake and Palmer, *Brain Salad Surgery* reissue. Rhino CD R2 72459, 1996.

———. Liner notes, Emerson, Lake and Palmer, *Emerson, Lake and Palmer.* King Biscuit Flower Hour Records CD 88025-2, 1997.

———. Liner notes, Emerson, Lake and Palmer, *Live at the Isle of Wight Festival.* Manticore M-CD101, 1997.

———. Liner notes, Emerson, Lake and Palmer, *Then and Now.* Eagle Entertainment CD 1001-2, 1998.

———. Liner notes, Greg Lake, *From the Beginning: The Greg Lake Retrospective.* Rhino CD R2 72627, 1997.

Robinson, Alan. Liner notes, Carl Palmer, *Do Ya Wanna Play, Carl? Carl Palmer Anthology.* Sanctuary Records CD CMEDD163, 2001.

Welch, Chris. Liner notes, Emerson, Lake and Palmer, *Emerson, Lake and Palmer: The Return of the Manticore.* Victory CD 383 484 004-2, 1993.

Musical Scores

Emerson, Lake and Palmer. Transcribed for keyboard by Keith Emerson and John Curtin. New York: Warner Brothers, 1977.

Emerson, Lake and Palmer: Anthology. New York: Warner Brothers, 1981.

Emerson, Lake and Palmer: Greatest Hits. New York: Amsco/Music Sales Corporation, 1996.

Emerson, Lake and Palmer: Tarkus. New York: Warner Brothers, 1980.

Palmer, Carl. *Applied Rhythms.* Cedar Grove, New Jersey: Modern Drummer Publications, 1987.

Reviews

Reviews are presented chronologically rather than alphabetically so that readers wanting to locate reviews of particular ELP albums can do so more readily. Be aware that this listing does not represent a complete listing of all reviews cited in this book, as a number of the reviews cited in the text (for instance, several of Robert Christgau's) are drawn from secondary sources.

Grossman, Lloyd. "Emerson, Lake and Palmer." *Rolling Stone*, April 15, 1971.

Neister, Alan. "Emerson, Lake and Palmer." *Creem*, February 1, 1971.

Brollick, Peter. "Emerson's Ride on the Organ." Concert review. *Dusseldorfer Nachrichten*, June 14, 1971.

Welch, Chris. "*Tarkus*—An Offer of 'ELP." *Melody Maker*, June 5, 1971.

Green, Richard. "'ELP Our Ear." Review of *Tarkus*. *New Musical Express*, June 12, 1971.

Welch, Chris. "ELP Exhibit Themselves." *Melody Maker*, November 27, 1971.

Carr, Roy. "Pictures at an Exhibition." *New Musical Express*, December 4, 1971.

Record Mirror. Unsigned review of *Pictures at an Exhibition.* December 18, 1971.

Stewart, Tony. "Trilogy." *New Musical Express*, July 1, 1972.

Welch, Chris. "The ELP Enigma." *Melody Maker*, June 24, 1972.

S. L. "Stale Salad: Emerson, Lake and Palmer's *Brain Salad Surgery*." *Melody Maker*, November 24, 1973.

Robbins, Wayne. "Brain Salad Surgery." *Creem*, January 1974.

Fletcher, Gordon. "Brain Salad Surgery." *Rolling Stone*, January 31, 1974.

Welch, Chris. "Welcome Back My Friends to the Show That Never Ends." *Melody Maker*, August 3, 1974.

Erskine, Peter. "Pocket Calculator Rockers Wreak Digital Doze Out." Review of *Welcome Back*. *New Musical Express*, August 3, 1974.

Shaw, Bob. "Works Volume I." *Downbeat*, October 6, 1977.

"72,000 Watts in That Name." Concert review. *Time*, 1977. Reprinted in *ELP Digest* 9, no. 1 (January 26, 1999).

Rockwell, John. "Emerson, Lake and Palmer + 60 = Rock." Concert review. *New York Times*, July 9, 1977.

Penman, Ian. "The New Face of Techno Rock: On the Beach, Out to Lunch." Review of *Love Beach*. *New Musical Express*, November 25, 1978.

Martin, Gavin. "ELP in Concert." Review of *In Concert*. *New Musical Express* (December 1, 1979).

Aikin, Jim. "Emerson, Lake and Palmer in Concert." Review of *In Concert*. *Contemporary Keyboard*, June 1980.

Farber, Jim. "Emerson, Lake and Powell." *Rolling Stone*, June 28, 1986.

Index

Index of Musical Works

Keith Emerson Solo Albums and Movie Soundtracks

Greg Lake Solo Albums